International Directory of
COMPANY
HISTORIES

International Directory of

COMPANY

HISTORIES

VOLUME 45

Editor

Jay P. Pederson

ST. JAMES PRESS

GALE GROUP
TM
THOMSON LEARNING

Detroit • New York • San Diego • San Francisco
Boston • New Haven, Conn. • Waterville, Maine
London • Munich

STAFF

Jay P. Pederson, *Editor*

Miranda H. Ferrara, *Project Manager*

Erin Bealmear, Joann Cerrito, James Craddock, Steve Cusack,
Kristin Hart, Melissa Hill, Margaret Mazurkiewicz, Carol Schwartz,
Christine Tomassini, Michael J. Tyrkus, *St. James Press Editorial Staff*

Peter M. Gareffa, *Managing Editor, St. James Press*

Library of Congress Catalog Number: 89-190943

British Library Cataloguing in Publication Data

International directory of company histories. Vol. 45
I. Jay P. Pederson
338.7409

ISBN 1-55862-463-5

Printed in the United States of America
Published simultaneously in the United Kingdom

.

St. James Press is an imprint of The Gale Group

Cover photograph: South entrance of Mall of America, Bloomington, Minnesota
(courtesy: Jay P. Pederson)

10 9 8 7 6 5 4 3 2 1

CONTENTS

Company Histories

PREFACE

The St. James Press series *The International Directory of Company Histories (IDCH)* is intended for reference use by students, business people, librarians, historians, economists, investors, job candidates, and others who seek to learn more about the historical development of the world's most important companies. To date, *IDCH* has covered over 5,400 companies in 45 volumes.

Inclusion Criteria

Most companies chosen for inclusion in *IDCH* have achieved a minimum of US$25 million in annual sales and are leading influences in their industries or geographical locations. Companies may be publicly held, private, or nonprofit. State-owned companies that are important in their industries and that may operate much like public or private companies also are included. Wholly owned subsidiaries and divisions are profiled if they meet the requirements for inclusion. Entries on companies that have had major changes since they were last profiled may be selected for updating.

The *IDCH* series highlights 10% private and nonprofit companies, and features updated entries on approximately 45 companies per volume.

Entry Format

Each entry begins with the company's legal name, the address of its headquarters, its telephone, toll-free, and fax numbers, and its web site. A statement of public, private, state, or parent ownership follows. A company with a legal name in both English and the language of its headquarters country is listed by the English name, with the native-language name in parentheses.

The company's founding or earliest incorporation date, the number of employees, and the most recent available sales figures follow. Sales figures are given in local currencies with equivalents in U.S. dollars. For some private companies, sales figures are estimates and indicated by the abbreviation *est.* The entry lists the exchanges on which a company's stock is traded and its ticker symbol, as well as the company's NAIC codes.

Entries generally contain a *Company Perspectives* box which provides a short summary of the company's mission, goals, and ideals, a *Key Dates* box highlighting milestones in the company's history, lists of *Principal Subsidiaries, Principal Divisions, Principal Operating Units, Principal Competitors,* and articles for *Further Reading.*

American spelling is used throughout *IDCH*, and the word "billion" is used in its U.S. sense of one thousand million.

Sources

Entries have been compiled from publicly accessible sources both in print and on the Internet such as general and academic periodicals, books, annual reports, and material supplied by the companies themselves.

Cumulative Indexes

IDCH contains three indexes: the **Index to Companies**, which provides an alphabetical index to companies discussed in the text as well as to companies profiled, the **Index to Industries**, which allows researchers to locate companies by their principal industry, and the **Geographic Index**, which lists companies alphabetically by the country of their headquarters. The indexes are cumulative and specific instructions for using them are found immediately preceding each index.

Suggestions Welcome

Comments and suggestions from users of *IDCH* on any aspect of the product as well as suggestions for companies to be included or updated are cordially invited. Please write:

The Editor
International Directory of Company Histories
St. James Press
27500 Drake Rd.
Farmington Hills, Michigan 48331-3535

ABBREVIATIONS FOR FORMS OF COMPANY INCORPORATION

A.B.	Aktiebolaget (Sweden)
A.G.	Aktiengesellschaft (Germany, Switzerland)
A.S.	Aksjeselskap (Denmark, Norway)
A.S.	Atieselskab (Denmark)
A.Ş.	Anomin Şirket (Turkey)
B.V.	Besloten Vennootschap met beperkte, Aansprakelijkheid (The Netherlands)
Co.	Company (United Kingdom, United States)
Corp.	Corporation (United States)
G.I.E.	Groupement d'Intérêt Economique (France)
GmbH	Gesellschaft mit beschränkter Haftung (Germany)
H.B.	Handelsbolaget (Sweden)
Inc.	Incorporated (United States)
KGaA	Kommanditgesellschaft auf Aktien (Germany)
K.K.	Kabushiki Kaisha (Japan)
LLC	Limited Liability Company (Middle East)
Ltd.	Limited (Canada, Japan, United Kingdom, United States)
N.V.	Naamloze Vennootschap (The Netherlands)
OY	Osakeyhtiöt (Finland)
PLC	Public Limited Company (United Kingdom)
PTY.	Proprietary (Australia, Hong Kong, South Africa)
S.A.	Société Anonyme (Belgium, France, Switzerland)
SpA	Società per Azioni (Italy)

ABBREVIATIONS FOR CURRENCY

$	United States dollar	KD	Kuwaiti dinar
£	United Kingdom pound	L	Italian lira
¥	Japanese yen	LuxFr	Luxembourgian franc
A$	Australian dollar	M$	Malaysian ringgit
AED	United Arab Emirates dirham	N	Nigerian naira
B	Thai baht	Nfl	Netherlands florin
B	Venezuelan bolivar	NIS	Israeli new shekel
BFr	Belgian franc	NKr	Norwegian krone
C$	Canadian dollar	NT$	Taiwanese dollar
CHF	Switzerland franc	NZ$	New Zealand dollar
COL	Colombian peso	P	Philippine peso
Cr	Brazilian cruzado	PLN	Polish zloty
CZK	Czech Republic koruny	Pta	Spanish peseta
DA	Algerian dinar	R	Brazilian real
Dfl	Netherlands florin	R	South African rand
DKr	Danish krone	RMB	Chinese renminbi
DM	German mark	RO	Omani rial
E£	Egyptian pound	Rp	Indonesian rupiah
Esc	Portuguese escudo	Rs	Indian rupee
EUR	Euro dollars	Ru	Russian ruble
FFr	French franc	S$	Singapore dollar
Fmk	Finnish markka	Sch	Austrian schilling
GRD	Greek drachma	SFr	Swiss franc
HK$	Hong Kong dollar	SKr	Swedish krona
HUF	Hungarian forint	SRls	Saudi Arabian riyal
IR£	Irish pound	W	Korean won
K	Zambian kwacha	W	South Korean won

International Directory of
COMPANY
HISTORIES

A. B. WATLEY, INC.

A.B. Watley Group Inc.

40 Wall Street
New York, New York 10005
U.S.A.
Telephone: (212) 422-1664
Toll Free: (888) 229-2853
Fax: (212) 634-9924
Web site: http://www.abwatley.com

Public Company
Incorporated: 1958 as A.B. Watley, Inc.
Employees: 144
Sales: $42.75 million (2000)
Stock Exchanges: NASDAQ
Ticker Symbol: ABWG
NAIC: 51121 Software Publishers; 52312 Securities
  Brokerage

A.B. Watley Group Inc. is a Wall Street securities brokerage firm that provides retail and corporate customers with direct-access electronic trading capabilities by means of its proprietary technology. As a direct-access broker, the company, instead of merely taking orders and executing them, offers its customers direct connections to the NASDAQ exchange by means of market makers or electronic communications networks. With the decline in business stemming from the end of the Wall Street bull market in 2000, A.B. Watley's losses mounted, and it began seeking to license its financial services technology as an added source of revenue.

Online Trading Pioneer: 1997–98

A.B. Watley, Inc. was founded in 1958 and functioned as a traditional brokerage firm until January 1997, when all the capital stock was purchased by Internet Financial Services, Inc. This company was founded in May 1996 by Steven and Robert Malin, primarily to serve the investors known as day traders: individuals or institutional clients such as professional money managers who sought to profit from small price movements in active stocks, making as many as 100 trades a day and usually

closing out their positions at day's end. The day-trading industry dates from 1988, when federally imposed rules were changed to allow individual investors to execute trades more easily on the NASDAQ exchange. The execution of such trades was enhanced in 1996, when new rules allowed the creation and operation of electronic communication networks, which permitted anyone with a connection to such a network to see all the bids and offers posted into the system for any NASDAQ-traded security. Internet Financial Services was one of many firms that sprang up in the mid-1990s with the intention of tapping this market by offering customers instant access to and information about stocks traded on the NASDAQ exchange.

The purchase of A.B. Watley gave Internet Financial Services a client list and a license to trade on the NASDAQ exchange since Watley, a registered broker-dealer, was a member of the National Association of Securities Dealers, Inc. Internet Financial Services began offering online trading to its customers over the Internet in March 1997. On its corporate web site it provided trading access and research and portfolio services. Its UltimateTrader proprietary software, according to Edward H. Baker of *Financial World,* turned "customers' computers into fullblown trading stations" at a cost of $300 a month plus per-trade charges. UltimateTrader was not intended for the occasional investor but for the hyperactive trader who might make ten or 20 trades a day, perhaps all on the same stock. "Its most revolutionary feature," Baker wrote, "is its ability to show traders exactly where the market is: who's bidding how much, who's asking how much, and at what prices trades are being made when. When you put in a bid on this system, you actually become part of that market." The system only reached its full potential, however, with securities listed on the NASDAQ exchange, since the New York and American exchanges still relied on floor trading.

UltimateTrader users were not actually buying and selling directly on the NASDAQ exchange, although what they saw was the same as the firm's own personnel were seeing on their own computers. The order appeared on the NASDAQ system as being placed by A.B. Watley, the subsidiary that functioned as Internet Financial Services' trading arm, or by a market maker of the customer's choosing. A confirmation of the trade appeared within one second, and the client's account was automatically deducted in the event of a purchase. The company's subsequent technology upgrades allowed customers direct access to exchanges and electronic communication networks.

Day-Trader's Mainstay: 1999–2000

Internet Financial Services accumulated $4.53 million in revenues in fiscal 1997 (the year ended September 30, 1997) and sustained a loss of $1.06 million. Its revenues doubled to $9.12 million in fiscal 1998, and its net loss dropped to $632,410. Among its 1998 expenses was the initiation of an advertising campaign expected to cost about $5 million. The following year Internet Financial Services became, in April, the first brokerage firm specializing in day trading to go public. It raised $12.7 million by selling about a quarter of its outstanding shares of common stock at $7 a share. The company changed its name to A.B. Watley Group Inc. in September 1999. Benefiting from the NASDAQ bull market, the stock quickly rose to $23 a share before retreating to about $11 a share. A.B. Watley's revenues more than doubled in fiscal 1999, rising to $20.99 million. It sustained a net loss of $801,602.

Theresa W. Carey of *Barron's* gave UltimateTrader high marks in March 1999, when the financial weekly rated A.B. Watley seventh among 22 online brokers for such qualities as trade execution, reliability, and range of services. "Ultimate Trader," she wrote, "was one of the first to exploit the Internet while avoiding the drag of the World Wide Web (a/k/a the World Wide Wait)." Watley Vice-President Anthony Huston told her that the firm was targeting the elite, high-end day trader. "We're going after the top 2 to 5 percent of the market," he said, "those with the time to learn and understand the software; above-average assets; above-average understanding of the markets; comfortable with new technologies; and a willingness to pay for data and trade-related services."

A.B. Watley also was offering client support between 8 a.m. and 8 p.m., with a staff that reached 45 in 2000. Its range of services through third-party relationships included unlimited check-writing, Visa credit cards, and access to more than 5,000 mutual funds. For institutional investors, a sales and trading desk facilitated and/or executed large-block transactions in about 500 thinly traded equity securities for clients who wanted such off-exchange transactions to remain anonymous. A.B. Watley earned about 22 percent of its fiscal 1999 revenue and 19 percent of its fiscal 2000 revenue from the activities of this desk.

In September 1999 A.B. Watley announced the creation of UltimateTrader Free. Available to clients who maintained an average cash balance with the firm of $20,000, it provided NASDAQ Level II real-time stock market quotes at no cost rather than the usual $20 to $50 a month, depending on the provider. It also included the usual extras, such as updated charts, positions, and buying power, and portfolio monitoring.

Without this plan, there was a monthly fee ranging up to $200, depending on the number of trades placed. The company's commission per trade varied from $12.95 to $23.95, depending on level of service and trade frequency. Some 71 percent of A.B. Watley's fiscal 1999 revenues came from UltimateTrader charges. Another 3 percent came from WatleyTrader, a recently introduced web-based rather than software-based version of the UltimateTrader platform. The introduction cut the firm's expenses because WatleyTrader was cheaper to operate than UltimateTrader, according to a company spokesman.

A.B. Watley more than doubled its revenues in fiscal 2000. Of total revenues of $42.75 million, commissions accounted for 77 percent; principal transactions for 13 percent; data service revenues for 5 percent; and interest and other income for 5 percent. Expenses rose even faster, however, and the company sustained a net loss of $9.85 million. It had about 11,000 retail customers at this time. In October 2000 A.B. Watley was replacing its Windows NT servers for its platform with Sun Microsystems servers, which the company said would be more scalable and reliable for users. Huston—now the company's president—said the firm had spent about $25 million since 1996 on technology developed in-house. This included the UltimateTrader II version of the company's platform, introduced in fiscal 2000. UltimateTrader II was said, by December 2000, to have already saved the firm $14.4 million per year because it was developed in-house and eliminated the need to pay fees to vendors.

A.B. Watley began marketing its direct-access technology in August 2000. Three months later, it licensed a service for active traders to E*Trade Group, Inc., with the potential, the company said, of reaping $3 million a month in revenue for the firm for three years. The bear market that began earlier in the year had seriously affected trading volume on Wall Street, but the number of full-time day traders was said to have held steady, at about 50,000, and they were said to have raised their activity by 55 percent, to an average 44 trades per day, according to a Bear Stearns & Co. Inc. analyst. Steven Malin maintained that A.B. Watley was the only firm able to provide a web-based system for active traders that could be scaled up for use by hundreds of thousands of traders. License fees were seen as a necessary means of raising revenue for Watley, which laid off 28 employees—20 percent of its workforce—in February 2001.

Coping with the Bear Market: 2000–01

Sagging revenues and higher operating losses took a heavy toll on the value of A.B. Watley's common stock, which reached a peak of $28.25 a share in March 2000. In an April 2001 private placement, the company sold more than two million shares at $5.50 a share for total net proceeds of $10 million. Earlier, in August 2000, an investment group had provided the company with an 18-month cash-for-shares credit line of $48 million, which A.B. Watley tapped to the extent of $2.85 million a month later. A.B. Watley purchased a struggling rival, On-Site Trading Inc., in November 2001 for about $5.6 million in stock, and it also assumed $1.8 million in On-Site's debts. Founded in 1994, On-Site Trading had 27 offices, primarily in the East, and was supporting about 1,300 active traders.

During the first nine months of fiscal 2001 ending at mid-year, A.B. Watley's revenues fell 37 percent compared with the

Key Dates:

1997: Steven and Robert Malin purchase securities broker A.B. Watley Inc. and begin offering online trading to its customers.
1999: The brokerage firm becomes the first day-trading specialist to offer shares to the public.
2000: A.B. Watley licenses direct-access technology to E*Trade Group, Inc.
2001: The bear market has seriously eroded A.B. Watley's revenues.

same period in 2000. Its net loss more than tripled during this period. The company had about 12,100 retail customers at midyear, but the number of UltimateTrader clients had fallen 36 percent from midyear 2000, to 2,036. Total billed transactions were also down by 36 percent, to 750,756. In July 2001 A.B. Watley lowered its monthly flat fee for active traders and reduced the minimum balance for this program to $5,000. It also cut its standard commission per trade by as much as 75 percent. The company, in late 2001, required a $10,000 deposit to open a flat-fee UltimateTrader II account; the minimum balance needed to maintain the account was now only $2,000. Transaction fees for this program ranged from $17.95 each for 1 to 49 trades per month to $8.95 each for 750 or more trades per month. There was no monthly maintenance fee for 20 or more trades per month; below this level, the fee was $50.

In December 2001 A.B. Watley's common stock was trading for only $2 to $3 a share. Steven Malin, the chairman and chief executive officer, owned 20 percent of the company's common stock in June 2001. Robert Malin owned 8 percent. Linda Malin, their sister and the firm's general counsel, owned 9 percent.

Principal Subsidiaries

A.B. Watley, Inc.

Principal Divisions

Electronic Products Division; Institutional Sales and Trading Division.

Principal Competitors

Charles Schwab & Co., Inc.; Datek Securities Corp.; E*Trade Group, Inc.; Fidelity Brokerage Services, Inc.; Quick & Reilly, Inc.; Waterhouse Securities, Inc.

Further Reading

"A.B. Watley Intros Flat Fee," *Financial Net News,* July 23, 2001, p. 3.
"A.B. Watley Preps Web-Based Direct Access Platform," *Financial Net News,* November 27, 2000, p. 6.
Baker, Edward H., "Video Games," *Financial World,* April 15, 1997, pp. 108, 110.
Basso, Peter, "A.B. Watley Improves Direct Access," *Wall Street & Technology,* October 2000, p. 28.
Carey, Theresa W., "Growing Pains," *Barron's,* March 15, 1999, pp. 30–31, 33.
——, "Online Ardor Cooling," *Barron's,* September 27, 1999, p. 66.
Gandel, Stephen, "On-line Broker Goes More B-to-B," *Crain's New York Business,* March 5, 2001, p. 42.
"Online Mergers: Yak Yak Yak," *IDD/Investment Dealers' Digest,* November 19, 2001, p. 48.
Schwartz, Nelson D., "Can't Keep a Good Day Trader Down," *Fortune,* February 19, 2001, pp. 148–50.
Smith, Geoffrey, "Day of Reckoning for Day-Trading Firms?," *Business Week,* January 19, 1999, p. 88.

—Robert Halasz

Abu Dhabi National Oil Company

Post Office Box 898
Abu Dhabi
United Arab Emirates
Telephone: 971-2-602-0000
Fax: 971-2-602-3389
Web site: http://www.adnoc.com

State-Owned Company
Incorporated: 1971
Employees: 19,300
NAIC: 211111 Crude Petroleum and Natural Gas
Extraction; 211112 Natural Gas Liquid Extraction;
213111 Drilling Oil and Gas Wells; 213112 Support
Activities for Oil and Gas Operations

Abu Dhabi National Oil Company (ADNOC) is one of the ten largest oil companies in the world. The state-owned enterprise is engaged in all phases of the oil industry. It has a complex and intricate holding company structure involving equity links with large Western oil enterprises. Abu Dhabi is the largest of the seven states that formed the United Arab Emirates (UAE) in 1971, and it is the heart of the UAE's oil industry. ADNOC accounts for at least 90 percent of the 100 billion barrels of oil reserves in the United Arab Emirates. The company operates two refineries; three oil production companies; the Abu Dhabi Marine Oil Operating Co. (Adma-Opco) for offshore exploration and production; Abu Dhabi Gas Industries Ltd. (Gasco), a natural gas production company; two maritime transport companies; and many other subsidiaries in the oil, gas, and petrochemical industries. ADNOC also provides gas and electrical power for local consumption as well as desalinized water. Its subsidiary Adnoc-Fod markets and distributes gas and fuel throughout the UAE and operates a network of 200 gas stations. The holding company is divided into 14 directorates, which comprise specific industry areas within the holding company. The holding company's management is itself answerable to the United Arab Emirate's Supreme Petroleum Council, which guides the Emirate's petroleum policy. The head of the Supreme Petroleum Council is Khalifa Bin Zayed Al Nahyan, who is also crown prince of Abu Dhabi.

Roots in Foreign Oil Interests

Although ADNOC dates only from 1971, it is necessary to understand the historical development of Abu Dhabi's oil industry in order to understand the present structure of ADNOC. Abu Dhabi was a latecomer to the Middle Eastern oil industry, only beginning production in 1962. The search for oil had begun nearly 30 years earlier, however. As elsewhere in the Middle East, this search was in the hands of foreign oil interests organized in a consortium. In 1928 a group of U.K., Anglo-Dutch, and U.S. international oil companies formed the Iraq Petroleum Company (IPC) with a concession that came to cover most of Iraq. Once the Iraq Petroleum Company was formed, each partner agreed that it would not hold concessions in any other part of the former territory of the Ottoman Empire except in association with all the other partners, and in the same proportions as the Iraq Petroleum Company. Most of the Persian Gulf states, including Abu Dhabi but excluding Kuwait, were included in this nebulous area. The oil companies involved marked in red on a map the boundary of the area to which they intended the agreement to apply, and it became known as the Red Line Agreement. Thus when attention turned to searching for oil in the Trucial States—as the UAE was known until 1971—a consortium with exactly the same ownership structure as IPC was formed. In 1935 a new U.K. company was formed, Petroleum Development (Trucial States) Ltd., commonly referred to as PDTC. PDTC's ownership was identical to that of IPC, with the Anglo-Persian Oil Company (later British Petroleum), Shell, Compagnie Française des Pétroles, and a group of two U.S. companies—Exxon and Mobil Oil—owning 23.75 percent each of the shares, and investor Calouste Gulbenkian's interests the remaining 5 percent. PDTC contacted all the sheikdoms offering arrangements for concession rights to explore for oil and to develop production should oil be found. In January 1939 Abu Dhabi granted PDTC such concessions for a period of 75 years.

Oil exploration in Abu Dhabi was slow to get started. It was delayed first by World War II. Thereafter, the IPC group focused on the search for oil in Qatar, where oil exports began in 1949.

Company Perspectives:

In cultivating customer relations we aim to be approachable, trustworthy and responsive to their needs and to pursue excellence in the quality of our products and the standards of our service.

Knowledge of the geology of the emirate was limited, and economic conditions there were very underdeveloped. The town of Abu Dhabi itself was no more than a tiny village, and there were no roads in the entire emirate in the 1950s. Drilling finally began in 1950, but the search for oil proved a prolonged one. In July 1953 a well was drilled in the Bab field in Murban, south of Tarif, but mechanical difficulties led to its being abandoned despite evidence of the presence of oil. Further drilling at Bab finally established the potential of the field by 1960. The Bu Hasa field was proved soon after when oil was discovered in commercial quantities, and exports started in 1963. In the following years, PDTC relinquished its concessions in the other Trucial States to concentrate its efforts on Abu Dhabi. In 1963, PDTC was renamed the Abu Dhabi Petroleum Company (ADPC).

Meanwhile, oil also had been discovered offshore by other companies. In 1951 Abu Dhabi had established that the concession granted to PDTC did not include the continental shelf belonging to the emirate. As a result, Abu Dhabi granted a concession to cover the offshore territory first to the International Marine Oil Company, which failed to achieve results, and then, in 1954, to Abu Dhabi Marine Areas Ltd. (ADMA), a new company two-thirds owned by British Petroleum (BP) and one-third by Compagnie Française des Pétroles. In 1959 ADMA's drilling barge struck oil at Umm Shaif, which is located 80 miles into the gulf near Das Island. In 1962 the first shipment of oil was loaded from Das Island. The onshore and offshore oil discoveries made Abu Dhabi a large-scale oil producer. Its oil production grew from zero in 1960 to 102.8 million barrels in 1965, and 253.7 million barrels in 1970. By that date its production was one of the largest in the Middle East, and about one-quarter of that of Kuwait.

State-Owned Company in the 1970s

During the late 1960s there was growing resentment in Abu Dhabi, as elsewhere in the Middle East, of foreign ownership of oil resources, and especially the consortium system. The government concluded a 50–50 profit-sharing agreement with ADPC and ADMA in 1965 and 1966, respectively. In 1971 the government established the Abu Dhabi National Oil Company (ADNOC) as a wholly state-owned company. Following the formation of the Organization of Petroleum Exporting Countries (OPEC), Abu Dhabi followed the general policy of requesting participation in the foreign oil companies active in its territory. ADNOC acquired, effective January 1, 1973, 25 percent of the assets of ADPC and ADMA. The finalization of the ADMA participation agreement was complicated by BP's announcement in December 1972 of the sale of a 30 percent interest in ADMA to the Japan Oil Development Co. (Jadco), formed by a consortium of Japanese companies. The government withheld its approval of this deal until March 1973, when

BP agreed to finance the construction of an ADNOC-owned refinery in Abu Dhabi. By a further agreement in December 1974, the ADNOC interest in the ADPC and ADMA concessions was raised to 60 percent. These two companies were reincorporated later as Abu Dhabi Company for Onshore Oil Operation and Abu Dhabi Marine Operating Company.

Abu Dhabi was distinctive among the OPEC members in the gulf in retaining the former concessionaire companies as equity holders in the operating enterprises. It did not, as elsewhere, seek to remove foreign ownership entirely. ADNOC, therefore, developed as a holding company with an intricate web of majority and minority equity stakes in other producing companies. The government was motivated in this strategy by a desire to pursue production and exploration as energetically as possible. As part of this aim, from the 1960s various new concessions were granted to mostly independent oil companies in areas relinquished by ADPC and ADMA, all of which included provisions for ADNOC to have the option to take up to 60 percent interest in successful ventures.

ADNOC established subsidiary companies specialized in the various sectors of the oil industry. In 1973 Abu Dhabi National Oil Company for Distribution was created to take over the marketing of oil products within Abu Dhabi, which was formerly in the hands of the Western oil companies. Abu Dhabi National Tankers was founded in 1975 to operate a tanker fleet. In 1973 the Abu Dhabi Gas Liquefaction Company was formed, owned 51 percent by ADNOC, 22 percent by Mitsui, around 16 percent by BP, around 8 percent by Compagnie Française des Pétroles, and 2 percent by Bridgestone Liquefied Gas. The gas liquefaction company opened a plant on Das Island in 1977 to process gas from the main offshore oilfields. ADNOC was also anxious that Abu Dhabi should have its own refinery capacity. ADNOC's first oil refinery—situated at Umm Al Nar—opened in 1976, and in 1981 the company opened a second refinery at Ruwais. These plants made the UAE self-sufficient in refined petroleum products, with a surplus to export. In 1990 the two refineries had a combined capacity of 180,000 barrels per day, while domestic UAE consumption was about 80,000 barrels per day of refined products.

New Ventures in the 1980s and 1990s

ADNOC also diversified overseas, again favoring joint venture and mixed ownership structures. Together with the Pakistani government, ADNOC formed Pak Arab Fertilizers Ltd., which started producing chemical fertilizers in Pakistan in 1978 and, by 1983, was producing 290,000 tons of calcium ammonia nitrate, 350,000 tons of nitrophosphate, and 50,000 tons of urea. The Pak Arab Refinery, another joint venture between ADNOC and the Pakistani government, started production in 1981. By 1990, however, ADNOC's foreign ventures remained much less substantial than those of the Kuwait Petroleum Corporation.

The 1980s was an unsettled period for the world oil industry, and Abu Dhabi could not isolate itself from the general problems. Demand for OPEC oil fell sharply by about 45 percent in the first half of the decade. Producer states such as Abu Dhabi found themselves—and their state oil companies—with large bureaucracies that were slow to respond to changing circumstances. In 1988 the UAE restructured its oil administration

Key Dates:
1962: Oil production begins in Abu Dhabi.
1971: Government establishes the Abu Dhabi National Oil Company.
1988: The company is restructured.
1998: The company is reorganized again; five new directorates are added.

with the aim of cutting out some of this bureaucracy. The department of petroleum was abolished, and a new higher council of petroleum was created. The organization of ADNOC was restructured as part of this process. ADNOC's board was replaced by an 11-member petroleum council, and Sohal Fares al-Mazrui was appointed as ADNOC general manager and secretary general to the higher council, chaired by UAE's president, Shaikh Zayed. The move was designed to improve relations between ADNOC and its foreign equity partners, as well as to bring the industry under closer government control. During 1989 Mazrui also was appointed head of the Abu Dhabi National Oil Company for Distribution. During 1987 and 1988 oil exploration and development were virtually halted, but in 1989 a series of new projects was given the go-ahead.

ADNOC proved itself one of the better managed state oil companies. The strategy of alliances with Western oil companies gave it access to skills and technologies that would have been hard to generate internally. Abu Dhabi's huge oil reserves also placed ADNOC in a powerful competitive position. In terms of sheer production capacity, ADNOC in 1990 had entered the ranks of the world's ten largest oil companies, with a sustainable output of around one million barrels per day, and sufficiently large oil reserves to enable it to keep operating for more than 100 years at 1990 production levels. The 1988 restructuring had enhanced the efficiency of the operating affiliates, and ADNOC was able to claim that its cost of producing a barrel of oil was one of the lowest in the world. The enormous damage done to neighboring Kuwait's oil production and refining facilities during the Iraqi invasion and occupation of that country between August 1990 and February 1991 enhanced the competitive advantages of the Abu Dhabi oil industry, at least in the short term, but it also served as a reminder of the political uncertainties of the gulf region.

ADNOC worked on expanding its oil production capacity after the Persian Gulf War. The company increased production at its Upper Zakum offshore oil field and at the onshore Bab field in the early 1990s. Some increased production went to foreign partners such as the Tokyo Electric Power Co., a large customer for the company's natural gas products. But demand also increased domestically. ADNOC spent between $5 and $6 billion in the early 1990s on several major projects. Aside from upgrading facilities at key oilfields, the company spent close to $2 billion to increase its production of electrical power and fresh water. ADNOC also expanded the capacity of its two refineries, Umm Al Nar and Ruwais, in the early 1990s.

Expansion of the Ruwais refinery continued in 1996. ADNOC formed a joint venture with the Finnish-Norwegian company

Borealis to put $1.1 billion toward development of a petrochemical plant at Ruwais. The plant was to produce high-density polyethylene and ethylene. In another joint venture, headed by the Japanese firm Sumitomo Trading, ADNOC also began building a $1 billion plant at Ruwais that would produce benzene and other so-called aromatic chemicals. ADNOC also laid more than a hundred miles of new pipeline in the mid-1990s.

In 1998, the company underwent a major reorganization. ADNOC aimed to continue its expansion, and it needed to revamp management to handle future growth. ADNOC's subsidiaries had been grouped into nine directorates. The company added five more directorates and around 200 management positions. The company formed some new subsidiaries at this time as well. The gas processing directorate was put in charge of a new subsidiary, Abu Dhabi Gas Processing & Pipelines (Gappco), and a new refining company, Abu Dhabi Refining Company (Refco), also launched that year. The next year the company created a new gas processing and pipeline company, Abu Dhabi Gas Co. (Atheer); the Abu Dhabi Oil Refining Company (Takreer); and, to operate its ethylene and polyethylene plants, Bourouge, or the Abu Dhabi Polymers Company Ltd.

Shortly after revamping the structure of the company, ADNOC focused on building the brand of its Adnoc-Fod subsidiary. Adnoc-Fod supplied fuel, gas, and lubricants to the UAE military and to commercial airlines, and ran more than 200 gas stations. The Adnoc-Fod gas stations had no competitors within Abu Dhabi, but the brand was not as strong in other parts of the Emirates. ADNOC developed a new logo for the stations, which was then applied throughout the company. The company also redesigned the stations themselves and began adding convenience stores.

ADNOC was still committed to major expansion by 2001. It planned to increase its oil capacity from 2.6–2.8 barrels a day in 2001 to 3.6 barrels a day by 2005. It continued to export heavily, particularly to Japan and Southeast Asia. The company also poured more money into developing its natural gas business. Worldwide demand for natural gas was increasing rapidly, and the company invested in exploration and development. Its two main natural gas companies were the Abu Dhabi Gas Liquefaction Company and the Abu Dhabi Gas Industries Company.

Principal Subsidiaries

Adco; Abu Dhabi Drilling Chemicals and Products; Abu Dhabi Gas; Abu Dhabi Gas Industries; Abu Dhabi Gas Liquefaction; Abu Dhabi Marine Operating Company; Abu Dhabi National Tankers; Abu Dhabi Oil Refining Company; Abu Dhabi Petroleum Ports Operating Company; Abu Dhabi Polymers Company Ltd.; Adnoc-Fod; National Drilling; National Gas Shipping; National Marine Services; National Petroleum Construction; Ruwais Fertilizer; Zakum Development.

Principal Competitors

BP p.l.c.; Royal Dutch/Shell Group; Exxon Mobil Corporation.

Further Reading

"Abu Dhabi Key to U.A.E. Growth Upstream and Downstream," *Oil & Gas Journal,* August 15, 1994, p. 27.

"Abu Dhabi National Oil Company and Its Group of Companies," *Institutional Investor*, August 1999, p. 17.

Acton, Maurice, "The Falcon Rising," *NPN International*, May 2000, p. 18.

Al-Otaiba, Mana Saeed, *Petroleum and the Economy of the United Arab Emirates*, London: Croom Helm, 1977.

Alperowicz, Natasha, "Borealis Discounts Adnoc Linkage," *Chemical Week*, August 7, 1996, p. 15.

——, "Japanese Consortium Plans Complex in Abu Dhabi," *Chemical Week*, January 31, 1996, p. 21.

Amir, Ghazail, "The Middle East Moves with Refining Deals," *Chemical Market Reporter*, March 17, 1997, pp. SR10–SR11.

"Big Spending to Expand Capacity," *Middle East Economic Digest*, December 4, 1998, p. 48.

Evans, John, *OPEC: Its Member States and the World Energy Markets*, London: Longmans, 1986.

Luciani, Giacomo, *The Oil Companies and the Arab World*, London: Croom Helm, 1984.

Mallakh, Ragaci El, *The Economic Development of the United Arab Emirates*, London: Croom Helm, 1981.

"The Role of State Oil Companies," *Oil & Gas Journal*, August 16, 1993, p. 62.

Siddiqui, Moin A., "The United Arab Emirates: Financial Report," *Middle East*, March 2001, p. 35.

Tippee, Bob, "Gas Receives New Priority in Abu Dhabi's Onshore Work," *Oil & Gas Journal*, August 11, 1997, pp. 51–54.

"UAE Operations Step Up Oil, Gas Production," *Oil & Gas Journal*, August 14, 1995, p. 18.

—Geoffrey Jones
—update: A. Woodward

Aggreko Plc

121 W. Regent Street
Glasgow G2 2SD
United Kingdom
Telephone: (+44) 141-225-5900
Fax: (+44) 141-225-5949
Web site: http://www.aggreko.com

Public Company
Incorporated: 1962
Employees: 1,800
Sales: £279 million ($417.2 million) (2000)
Stock Exchanges: London
Ticker Symbol: AGK
NAIC: 532490 Other Commercial and Industrial
   Machinery and Equipment Rental and Leasing

Aggreko Plc is the world's largest "temporary utility" company. The Glasgow, Scotland-based company specializes in the rental of power generators and other equipment, including air compressors, mobile air conditioning units, and other temperature control equipment chiefly to industry. The company's prestigious clients include the Super Bowl, the Olympic Games, and the movie industry (the company provided power generation for the production of the blockbuster film *Titanic*, among others). Aggreko also comes to the rescue of the world's utility companies, providing backup power generation for the city of New York and temporary utility services to the California market hard-hit by power shortages in the early 2000s. The North American market accounts for the largest share of Aggreko's revenues, at 50 percent of the company's £279 million ($417 million) in 2000. The United Kingdom and Europe contribute 28 percent of the company's annual sales; other markets, particularly among Asian countries, including China and India, add 22 percent of the company's sales, but also represent the fastest-growing markets for Aggreko. In all, the company operates more than 110 offices in over 20 countries. Spun off from Christian Salvesen Plc in 1997, as the company turned its concentration to logistics services, Aggreko is traded on the London stock exchange and is led by chairman Christopher

Masters and managing director Philip J. Harrower, who replaced one of the company's founders, David Yorke, in 2001.

Dutch Beginnings, Scottish Growth in the 1970s

Aggreko began as a small mobile generator rental business in the Netherlands in 1962 (Aggreko comes from the Dutch word for generator). Over the next decade, the company expanded its operations into other European market countries in continental Europe. At the beginning of the 1970s, Aggreko turned to the United Kingdom. In 1973, Aggreko opened an office in Glasgow, Scotland, headed by David Yorke and Gordon Tourlamain.

The Scottish office quickly outpaced its parent company, and Aggreko's headquarters—and market focus—eventually moved to the United Kingdom. Aggreko grew rapidly over the next decade, expanding notably into Norway to support the booming North Sea oil industry. Yet, lacking the funds for further expansion, Aggreko began to look for a larger partner.

In the early 1980s, British shipping to food processing conglomerate (and former leader of the worldwide whaling industry) Christian Salvesen had been looking for new business opportunities in order to shore up its operations damaged by the economic recession of the period. Already strongly present in Norway—the company's roots were historically Norwegian—Salvesen acquired Aggreko in 1984. The following year, Salvesen went public, and Aggreko became one of the company's key divisions.

Under Salvesen, Aggreko, which continued to be led by Tourlamain and Yorke, started to expand rapidly. By 1986, the subsidiary had increased its number of U.K. depots, while also boosting its presence on the European continent, adding depots in Paris and Marseilles to build on its existing French presence. In 1987, Aggreko added a new depot in Germany, two more in England, and then acquired rival Dutch company Van Rijn to reestablish itself as a major generator rental company to the Netherlands' market.

The year 1986 marked another turning point for Aggreko. In that year, the company made its first acquisition in the United

States, of Electric Rental Systems in Louisiana, marking Aggreko's entry into the North American markets. The company's new U.S. component, led by Gordon Tourlamain, began a rapid expansion drive, and, by the beginning of 1987, Aggreko had doubled its U.S. operations, with new facilities in Los Angeles, Texas, Alabama, Florida, and San Francisco.

Aggreko's North American presence took on still greater importance in 1988. In that year the company paid $4 million to acquire Mobil Air and Pierce Industrial Air. The purchase not only gave Aggreko a new business area—that of mobile air conditioning and other temperature control rental equipment—but also a position as leader of that market in the United States.

Part of Aggreko's success, both in the United States and in Europe, was its commitment to developing its own generator and equipment designs, allowing the company to adapt quickly to customers' needs. In 1986, the company introduced the first in a range of super-quiet generators. The following year, Aggreko began offering customized rental equipment.

At the end of the 1980s, Aggreko continued to explore new markets. In 1989, the company made its first move into the Asian Pacific markets with the acquisition of Singapore's Yeok Kong Electrical Company. The following year, the company expanded its position in that part of the world with the purchase of Generator Rentals Pty, based in Australia.

International Leader for the 21st Century

Changes at Salvesen had led that company to shed a large number of its operations to focus on a smaller core of logistics, food processing, and Aggreko. Aggreko itself represented the fastest-growing component of its parent company. While many other companies suffered through the economic recession at the end of the decade, Aggreko's business benefited from industry's increased interest in outsourcing for their generator and other climate control needs. After building up its temperature control wing in the United States, Aggreko introduced those operations to its European base in 1991. The company added temperature control rentals through an Antwerp, Belgium depot, and then introduced that operation to the United Kingdom, where it quickly became a segment leader.

Also in 1991, Aggreko acquired BDD, giving it another business component, that of industrial drying equipment rentals. Based in the United Kingdom, the new component also gave the company an entry into the Middle East markets. The company expanded elsewhere in that region, opening depots in Sharjah and Abu Dhabi in the United Arab Emirates. Meanwhile, in Asia, Aggreko set up facilities in Malaysia and Indonesia. Its Australian component was also growing, extending its network to six depots and 14 sales agencies. Aggreko then brought its new desiccant drying expertise to the United States, starting in 1992.

Back in Europe, Aggreko was eyeing a number of prestigious contracts. In 1992, the company won the contract to supply power to the 1992 Olympic Games in Barcelona, as well as the Winter Games in Albertville, France. Backing this effort was the opening of three new depots, in Barcelona, Seville, and Bilbao. The company received the power generation contract for the Lillehammer Winter Games of 1994, as well; yet the company's Spanish success proved short-lived and the company was forced to close its new Spanish depots by mid-decade. Around the same time, the company was exiting from another unsuccessful expansion move. In 1992, Aggreko had attempted to enter the lighting systems rental market in the United Kingdom, purchasing Light & Sound Design. Unable to find its place in that market, however, Aggreko sold off that operation in 1995.

Aggreko was restructured as part of an overall retooling of the Salvesen group, which decentralized its operations and placed responsibility more firmly in the hands of the management of the individual businesses. David Yorke had by then taken over day-to-day leadership of Aggreko, while Dr. Chris Masters had been named chief executive of Salvesen. Aggreko's operations were now organized along regional lines, rather than product segments, with divisions for North America, Europe, the United Kingdom, and the Pacific Rim. In the United States, the company set up its first national accounts program, appealing to the growing number of large corporate clients. That market had also grown to become the company's largest single market, building up to some 50 percent of Aggreko's total sales.

In 1995, Aggreko launched its own series of oil-free air compressors, particularly prized by the food processing and electronics industries, as these air compressors did not disperse the fine particles of oil thrown off by standard air compressors. The following year, Aggreko introduced its GreenPower series of environmentally friendly power generators. This new generation of generators was first used for the Olympic Games held that year in Atlanta.

A takeover attempt launched by rival logistics group Hays Plc for Christian Salvesen set in motion a chain of events that saw Aggreko become a separate company in 1997. While Salvesen had rejected the takeover offer, shareholder discontent forced Salvesen's board to restructure the company again, now tightening its focus to become a pure logistics player. Aggreko was spun off as a separate, publicly listed company headed by Chris Masters as chairman and David Yorke as managing director. The spinoff helped Salvesen raise funds to begin an aggressive acquisition program, while Aggreko became a more visible company in its own right.

The move was greeted warmly by the financial community and Aggreko Plc's initial public offering on the London Stock Exchange was a success. The company continued to build up its position as worldwide leader of the equipment rental market. While power generation remained the company's primary oper-

---

Key Dates:

1962: Aggreko is founded in the Netherlands as a power generator rental business.

1973: David Yorke and Gordon Tourlamain open Aggreko's U.K. subsidiary in Glasgow, Scotland.

1984: Christian Salvesen acquires Aggreko as part of a diversification program.

1986: Christian Salvesen goes public on the London Stock Exchange; Aggreko enters United States with acquisition of Electric Rental Systems Inc.

1987: Aggreko acquires Mobile Air and Pierce Industrial Air in the United States and becomes the leader in temperature control equipment rental market; company introduces customized rental equipment.

1989: Aggreko acquires Yeow Kong Electrical Company, based in Singapore, to begin expansion into Asia.

1990: The company acquires Generator Rentals Pty, in Australia.

1991: Aggreko launches temperature control rentals in Europe and the United Kingdom, acquires BDD, and adds desiccant dryer systems in the U.K. market before launching drying equipment in the United States the following year.

1995: The company launches oil-free air compressors in the North American market, later introducing these in Europe as well.

1997: Aggreko is spun off from Salvesen and becomes separate publicly listed company.

1998: The company acquires Tower Tech modular cooling tower rental business.

1999: Aggreko forms Aggreko International Power Projects (AIPP) to provide temporary multi-megawatt capacity on a global basis; the company also acquires U.S. sales agent L&S Industries.

2000: The company acquires air compressor rental fleet from Ingersoll Rand.

2001: Aggreko wins contract to provide power generation for 2002 Olympic Games in Salt Lake City.

---

ation, its temperature control and other equipment rentals were also becoming significant revenue generators. In 1998, Aggreko brought its oil-free compressor equipment to the United Kingdom and Europe. In the United States, the company bought Tower Tech, a provider of modular cooling towers and equipment for the chemicals, nuclear power, pharmaceutical, and other industries. That purchase cost the company $8.4 million.

Aggreko's power generation business had not only developed itself as a leading supplier of mobile power generation equipment and solutions, but also as a leading "temporary utility" company. Already by 1993, the company was completing projects developing as much as 100 MW of generating capacity. In 1999, the importance of this branch of operations was highlighted by the creation of a new division, Aggreko International Power Projects (AIPP). The new entity was formed in order to be able to provide multi-megawatt temporary power facilities around the world. The company quickly developed clients among many local and national governments. The

company's generator fleet found service in such far-flung locations as the war-torn Balkans, drought-crippled Africa, and in the United States, providing crucial supplementary power to such cities as New York. The state of California became another primary U.S. customer, as deregulation of the state's utility market had caused major power shortages in 2001. Many private companies turned to Aggreko at the same time, as the growing reliance on electronics and computers made continued, stable power source an absolute necessity.

Aggreko's focus in the United States had been primarily on generator rentals. In 1999, however, the company acquired L&S Industries Inc., based in Baltimore, Maryland. That company had been Aggreko's first sales agent in the United States in the late 1980s. Founded in 1983, L&S had initially targeted the engine repair and maintenance market, before changing its own focus to equipment rentals. The addition of L&S's strong service component helped expand Aggreko's service operations. It also marked the first time the company had acquired one of its sales agents.

In 2000, Aggreko, which was able to boast about its contribution to the blockbuster movie *Titanic*, added another worldwide operation, that of the air compressor rental fleet of Ingersoll-Rand. The two companies also announced a strategic alliance agreement as part of the acquisition. The company also secured a number of other prestige contracts that year, including power generation for Euro 2000 and the PGA Championships.

The announcement by General Electric that it was entering the power supply market at the beginning of the century—with the business expected to be online by 2002—sparked speculation that Aggreko might become GE's takeover target. Aggreko affirmed its intention to remain independent, while at the same time downplaying the coming competition from the global giant. Yet some observers cautioned that Aggreko's fleet of primarily diesel-based generators placed it at a disadvantage, as GE, capable of building its fleet from scratch, was able to choose among a number of new generator fuel technologies.

Nonetheless, Aggreko remained buoyant entering the new century. The company secured the contract to supply power to the 2002 Olympic Games to be held in Salt Lake City. Aggreko also received a new managing director, as David Yorke retired in April 2001, turning over the company's operational leadership to Philip J. Harrower. Aggreko meanwhile was riding high on a wave of power blackouts affecting California, which were expected to continue for some time as that market adjusted to the realities of deregulated utilities.

Principal Subsidiaries

Aggreko Holdings Limited; Aggreko UK Limited; Aggreko International Projects Limited; Aggreko Inc. (U.S.A.); Aggreko Holdings Inc. (U.S.A.); Aggreko Finance BV (Netherlands); Aggreko Investments BV (Netherlands); Aggreko Nederland BV (Netherlands); Aggreko Belgium BVBA; Aggreko Deutschland GmbH (Germany); Aggreko France SARL; Aggreko Norway A/S; Aggreko (Singapore) PTE Limited; Aggreko Generator Rentals Pty Limited (Australia); Aggreko (Malaysia) Sdn Bhd; Aggreko (Middle East) Limited (Cyprus); Aggreko Canada, Inc.; Aggreko SA de CV (Mexico).

Principal Competitors

Airlease Ltd.; Algeco SA; ATEL Capital Group; Caterpillar Inc.; Electro Rent Corporation; GATX Corporation; GE Power Systems Inc.; ICON Holdings Corp.; National Equipment Services, Inc.; PLM International, Inc.; Rental Service Corporation; TTX Company; United Rentals, Inc.; Willis Lease Finance Corporation.

Further Reading

Duckers, John, "Aggreko Surges Ahead by Plugging Power Gap," *Birmingham Post*, August 24, 2000, p. 27.

Hughes, Chris, "Aggreko Shows No Signs of Losing Power," *Independent*, August 24, 2001, p. 19.

Murry-West, Rosie, "Aggreko Proves a Cool Customer," *Daily Telegraph*, August 23, 2001, p. 58.

Potter, Mark, "Aggreko Profit Surges on US Power Shortages," *Reuters*, August 22, 2001.

—M.L. Cohen

Alexander's, Inc.

Park 80 West, Plaza II
Saddle Brook, New Jersey 07663
U.S.A.
Telephone: (201) 587-8541
Fax: (201) 587-0061

Public Company
Incorporated: 1955 as Farbro Corp.
Employees: 78
Sales: $63.97 million (2000)
Stock Exchanges: New York
Ticker Symbol: ALX
NAIC: 53112 Lessors of Nonresidential Buildings
(Except Miniwarehouses)

Alexander's, Inc. is a real estate investment trust (REIT) engaged in leasing, managing, developing, and redeveloping properties in the New York City metropolitan area. These properties were formerly units in a chain of Alexander's department stores. Its undeveloped block on Manhattan's East Side, formerly occupied by one of these stores, has been called the world's most valuable hole in the ground. Alexander's' activities are conducted through its manager, Vornado Realty Trust, which owns one-third of its common stock and leases its properties.

Thriving Retail Chain: 1928–70

George Farkas began working in his father's Brooklyn dress shop when he was eight. He opened his own store in New York's borough of the Bronx in 1924 and founded a much larger store—which he named Alexander's for his deceased father—in 1928, with an initial investment of $7,500. This store, located below the elevated tracks at 152nd Street and Third Avenue, was an immediate success, achieving sales of $500,000 in its first year. In the spring of 1929 the store was enlarged for the first of 30 times. Its founder later recalled to Leonard Sloane of the *New York Times,* "Fortunately, I had to sell all of my stock before the crash to pay for this expansion. We were also small enough and flexible enough to survive and grow during the Depression." Another Alexander's opened in

1933 at Fordham Road and Grand Concourse, also in the Bronx. This site became the company's headquarters and eventually expanded to ten times its original size.

Positioned somewhere between a full-service department store and a discount store, Alexander's specialized in low-priced clothing for its Depression-era customers who nevertheless had some pretensions to style. It kept its prices low by avoiding a downtown location, buying instead of renting its properties, investing heavily in labor-saving equipment, and not making alterations or deliveries or offering charge accounts or mail-order. Its buyers won a reputation for keen knowledge of the market and a nose for finding off-season bargain merchandise. Brand-name manufacturers selling to downtown stores did not want it known that Alexander's was hawking the same wares uptown for less, so the company did not display such lines in its windows or its advertisements, and it took out the labels if the manufacturer insisted.

Wartime and post-World War II prosperity brought Alexander's clients into the middle class but also dispersed them into the suburbs. Alexander's was quick to take advantage of the trend, opening, in 1951, a store in White Plains, the seat of Westchester County—the county directly north of the Bronx. Complete with a six-level garage, the new store was the first in Westchester to remain open evenings and brought the chain's annual sales in 1953—its 25th anniversary—to $47 million. By 1963 Alexander's had added outlets in Rego Park, Queens; Milford, Connecticut; and Paramus, New Jersey. In a quest for fashion leadership in the low-margin field and at the urging of Farkas's eldest son, it upgraded its merchandise by making exclusive arrangements with European manufacturers. (In 1965 Farkas admitted to *Business Week,* "We lost money on imports for years before we finally broke through.") Hard goods such as radio and television sets, artwork, and luggage were added. The company also redesigned and redecorated its stores; the Paramus outlet, for example, featured on its facade what was called the world's largest mural, a glass-and-steel abstract work that stretched the length of a city block. A subsidiary, Rent-A-Car Inc., became one of the largest rental car companies in the metropolitan area.

In 1963 Alexander's announced that it had acquired a T-shaped plot in the Manhattan block between East 58th and

59th streets and Lexington and Third avenues, just south of Bloomingdale's. Two additional purchases subsequently enlarged the property, and in 1965 Alexander's opened a seven-level flagship store on this site—the first new midtown Manhattan store built from the ground up since 1947.

Alexander's Department Stores, Inc. was a private corporation controlled, at this time, by Farbro Corp., a holding company owned by Farkas, his wife, and his four sons. In 1962 Louis Schwadron, a relative who had helped found Alexander's and owned, with his family, a large block of its stock, sold his 38 percent interest to E.J. Korvette, Inc., the largest discount store chain in the United States. The Farkas family, however, refused to sell Korvette the slightly more than 50 percent of the stock that it held. In 1967 Spartan Industries, Inc.—which had purchased Korvette—agreed to sell the Farkas family half these shares of Alexander's and to market the remainder in a public offering of stock. Alexander's, Inc., a publicly owned company, was established in 1968, with George Farkas's son Alexander as chief executive officer. An initial public offering of about 40 percent of the outstanding shares raised about $41 million.

Alexander's sales volume increased from $199.84 million in fiscal 1966 (the year ended in late July 1966) to $272.77 million in fiscal 1970. Net earnings rose from $2.19 million to $6.84 million during this period. A leased store opened along Sunrise Highway in Valley Stream, Long Island, in 1967. Three years later the company jointly established itself with R.H. Macy & Co. at Kings Plaza Shopping Center in Brooklyn.

Decline and Bankruptcy: 1970–92

Alexander's continued to add stores throughout the 1970s. It added an outlet at a shopping center in Garden City, Long Island, in 1971; two more at shopping centers in Edison and Eatontown, New Jersey, in 1972; a store in Flushing, Queens, in 1975; and stores in Yonkers and at Westchester Mall in Mohegan Lake, New York, in 1977. Another outlet opened in lower Manhattan's World Trade Center in 1980. Most sales continued to be by cash or check, but the company accepted its first credit card in 1972, subsequently increasing the total to four. About 75 percent of sales was apparel and accessories in the 1970s. The chain was not selling major furniture or appliances. Sales grew to $505.09 million in fiscal 1980, but net earnings peaked at $7.06 million in fiscal 1970 and totaled only $1.05 million in 1980. A serious misstep was the acquisition, in

1978, of Margo's La Mode, Inc., a women's apparel chain with 70 stores in five states. Alexander's shed this company in 1981 for about $7 million. That year Alexander's lost $9.57 million, more than half of which was attributed to Margo's losses and a write-off on its sale.

By this time Alexander's was ripe for acquisition by Steven Roth, an entrepreneur who had closed the Two Guys discount chain owned by Vornado Inc. and converted its properties into suburban shopping centers. Roth's Interstate Properties Inc. was Alexander's largest individual stockholder in late 1980, with 23.4 percent of the outstanding shares. Allied with two of George Farkas's sons, Interstate won five seats on the company board and effective control of the company. Robin Farkas, one of the insurgents, succeeded his brother as chief executive officer of Alexander's in 1984.

In 1987 Donald Trump, also interested in Alexander's real estate, purchased a big block of company stock. The following year both he and Roth purchased more stock, bringing their holdings to 27.2 percent each. The two agreed not to compete with each other for further control of the company. Alexander's revenues continued to hover around $500 million a year through fiscal 1987, but net earnings diminished, and in fiscal 1988 the company lost money. The Eatontown store closed in 1983 and the Westchester Mall store closed in 1986. During 1988–89 the company also closed the stores in White Plains, Milford, and Edison. "The eventuality is that Alexander's will disappear as a retailing chain," an investment analyst told Amy Feldman of *Crain's New York Business* in 1990.

In spite of these omens, Robin Farkas continued publicly to be upbeat about Alexander's future as a retailer, envisioning the opening of a new store every year. A new Bronx store did make its debut in 1990 and included an auto accessories department bounded by luggage on one side and housewares on the other. But Alexander's withdrew from an earlier foray into consumer electronics, because of its difficulty in competing with discounters, and it continued to concentrate on apparel.

The impasse between Roth and Trump ended in 1990, when Trump was forced to turn over his Alexander's stock to Citicorp as forfeited collateral for a loan guarantee that he could not meet. The company lost money again in fiscal 1990, 1991, and 1992—about $40 million in the last two years, Robin Farkas said in May 1992, when all remaining Alexander's stores closed. The company then filed for Chapter 11 bankruptcy protection. It sold its leases to the Valley Stream and Yonkers stores and the newest Bronx store to Caldor Corp., which also leased or subleased the Fordham Road and Flushing properties from Alexander's, plus part of the Rego Park location. The total price tag was $117 million. Conway Stores, Inc. leased the Bronx Third Avenue store.

Real Estate Investment Trust: 1995–2001

Alexander's emerged from bankruptcy in 1993. Vornado, now a REIT, purchased Citicorp's holdings in the company for $54.8 million in 1995 and agreed to provide it with up to $75 million of secured financing for a three-year term. The infusion of cash enabled Alexander's to meet a $28 million loan payment and avoid the alternative of having property auctioned. In return, Alexander's converted to a REIT, and Roth became its chief executive officer.

Alexander's, in 1998, purchased the half-share of Kings Plaza Regional Shopping Center occupied by R.H. Macy & Co. from Federated Department Stores, Inc. A $48 million renovation of the 1.1 million-square-foot property was scheduled for completion in 2001. The 303,000-square-foot Fordham Road location, vacated by Caldor's bankruptcy in 1995, was sold in early 2001 for $25.5 million. The Flushing property, including a 177,000-square-foot building, remained vacant. A 351,000-square-foot building on the Rego Park property was fully leased to retailers in 2000. Alexander's said in October 2001 that it had leased its choice Paramus property, located on 30 acres at the intersection of Routes 4 and 17, to a major retailer for $75 million in a 40-year deal, with an option to buy after 20 years. IKEA was reported to be the lessee.

The jewel in Alexander's crown was the two-acre East Side property, a city block now fully owned by the company. The empty six-story building on the site was razed in 1999, when New York City announced plans to overhaul its zoning code and limit new buildings to 495 feet in height. The site was excavated and a foundation for an 800-foot tower built before the site would be subject to the new code. Roth envisioned a 1.2 million-square-foot mixed-use project, including office and retail space, a hotel, and luxury condominiums. Prospective tenants, however, considered his demands out of line, and in 2001 the site was still vacant and its future unknown. Alexander's considered the capital required for the proposed building to be in excess of $650 million.

Alexander's revenues increased from $21.83 million in 1997 to $64.39 million in 1999 but declined slightly to $63.97 million in 2000. Its net income was $5.2 million in 2000. Total assets at the end of the year came to $403.31 million, and the debt was $367.79 million, of which the debt to Vornado Realty Trust was $115 million. Vornado owned 33 percent of Alexander's common stock. Roth was also chief executive of Vornado and managing general partner of Interstate Properties. Roth, Interstate, and the other two general partners of Interstate—David Mandelbaum and Russell B. Wight, Jr.—together owned 27.5 percent of Alexander's.

Principal Subsidiaries

ADMO Realty Corp.; Alexander's Department Stores of Brooklyn; Alexander's Department Stores of Lexington; Alexander's Department Stores of New Jersey; Alexander's Kings Plaza Center, Inc.; Alexander's of Brooklyn, Inc.; Alexander's of Flushing, Inc.; Alexander's of Rego Park, Inc.; Alexander's of Rego Park II, Inc.; Alexander's of Rego Park III, Inc.; Alexander's of Third Avenue, Inc.; Alexander's 175 Lexington Inc.; Alexander's Personnel Providers, Inc.; Alexander's Rego Shop-

ping Center Inc.; Alexander's Tower LLC; Alexander's Tower Operating LLC; 59th Street Corporation; 59th Street LLC; 59th Street Operating LLC; Kings Plaza Corp. N.Y.; 175 Lexington LLC; Ownreal Inc.; Sakraf Wine & Liquor Store, Inc.; Seven Thirty One Limited Partnership; U & F Realty Corp.

Principal Competitors

Acadia Realty Trust; Lefrak Organization Inc.; Simon Property Group, Inc.

Further Reading

Andelman, David A., "George Farkas, 78, Founder of Alexander's Store, Dies," *New York Times,* April 6, 1980, p. 26.

Bagli, Charles V., "Silk Stocking's Mystery Hole," *New York Times,* December 16, 1999, pp. B1, B8.

"Bargain Hunters Invade Silk-Stocking District," *Business Week,* August 7, 1965, pp. 112, 114.

Barmash, Isadore, "Alexander's New Focus: Retailing," September 4, 1990, pp. D1, D4.

——, "Stock Issue Set for Alexander's," September 15, 1967, pp. 69, 78.

Bartel, Benjamin, "Alexander's Inc.," *Wall Street Transcript,* March 21, 1977, pp. 56,540–56,541.

Birnbaum, Jeffrey H., "Dissident Holders of Alexander's Indicate They Have Won Control Without a Fight," *Wall Street Journal,* December 2, 1980, p. 2.

Feldman, Amy, "Roth Flashes Alexander's Trump Card," *Crain's New York Business,* August 20, 1990, pp. 3, 25.

"Furniture Retailer IKEA May Build Store in Paramus, N.J.," *Hackensack Record,* October 6, 2001.

"How to Cut Costs and Upgrade at Same Time," *Business Week,* December 8, 1956, pp. 72, 74, 76.

Kandel, Myron, "Personality: Promotion-Minded President," *New York Times,* May 27, 1962, Sec. 3, p. 3.

Metz, Robert, "Interest Grows in Alexander's," *New York Times,* April 1, 1982, p. D8.

Pacelle, Mitchell, "Control of Alexander's to Be Acquired by Real-Estate Developer Steven Roth," *Wall Street Journal,* February 7, 1995, p. A8.

Pellet, Jennifer, "Alexander's: Back on the Growth Track," *DM/Discount Merchandiser,* June 1990, pp. 88, 90–91.

Rudnitsky, Howard, "No More Mr. Nice Guy," *Forbes,* September 13, 1993, pp. 100, 102.

Sloane, Leonard, "Personality: From Small Merchant to Big," *New York Times,* October 20, 1963, Sec. 3, p. 3.

Valeriano, Lourdes Lee, "Alexander's Shuts Its 11 Stores, Files for Chapter 11 Shield from Creditors," *Wall Street Journal,* May 18, 1992, p. B7.

Zipser, Alfred R., Jr., "Alexander's, Begun with Capital of $7,500, After 25 Years Is a $47,000,000 Business," *New York Times,* October 4, 1953, Sec. 3, pp. 1, 5.

—Robert Halasz

American Electric Power Company, Inc.

1 Riverside Plaza
Columbus, Ohio 43215-2373
U.S.A.
Telephone: (614) 223-1000
Toll Free: (800) 672-1034
Fax: (614) 223-1823
Web site: http://www.aep.com

Public Company
Incorporated: 1906 as American Gas & Electric
   Company
Employees: 26,376
Sales: $13.69 billion (2000)
Stock Exchanges: New York
Ticker Symbol: AEP
NAIC: 551112 Public Utility Holding Companies

American Electric Power Company, Inc. (AEP) is a public utility holding company that generates, purchases, transmits, and distributes electric power. Nearly five million people in Michigan, Indiana, Ohio, Kentucky, Virginia, West Virginia, Arkansas, Louisiana, Oklahoma, Texas, and Tennessee are serviced by AEP's interconnected power grid delivering electricity from coal-fired, nuclear, and hydroelectric generating facilities. AEP also has two service subsidiaries: American Electric Power Service Corporation, a nonprofit organization providing management and technological services to affiliated companies, and AEP Energy Services, Inc., which provides the same services to nonaffiliated companies for profit. The company also serves 2.4 million customers outside the United States with its power holdings in Mexico, Brazil, Australia, China, the Philippines, and the United Kingdom. AEP has always served a multistate area, emphasizing consolidation of its subsidiaries, integration of its system, and technological leadership. It has become one of the largest electric utilities in the United States, with 38,000 megawatts of generating capacity and 224,000 miles of transmission and distribution lines.

Formation of the Company: 1906

The company was incorporated as American Gas & Electric Company in 1906, when the structure of the electric utility industry in the United States was changing from small, individually owned generator plants to consolidated single systems serving a large area. This change was seen in other industries as well. As president of the United States from 1901 to 1907, Theodore Roosevelt denounced such business combinations. By 1906, however, Roosevelt had come to believe that, with proper government regulation, the consolidation of businesses could be beneficial to the public interest. Thus when Richard E. Breed, Harrison Williams, and Sidney Z. Mitchell met in 1906 to consider forming a holding company to buy the 23 small companies held by Electric Company of America, they were in the right place at the right time.

Electric Company of America was itself a holding company founded in 1899 that, because of its directors' failure to grasp the economics of the newly developed industry, was in financial difficulty. Breed, a glass manufacturer in Marion, Indiana, was a major stockholder. Williams, Breed's brother-in-law, was a prominent financial entrepreneur. Mitchell was president of the utilities holding company, Electric Bond & Share Company, a subsidiary of General Electric Company. After some negotiation, Electric Company of America agreed to sell its assets for $6.28 million to American Gas & Electric Company (AG&E). The sale was completed in January 1907, with Breed and Williams as board directors of AG&E, Mitchell as chairman, and Henry L. Doherty—later to begin his own chain of electric companies—as president until 1910, when Breed stepped in.

The acquired companies were a varied lot, including nine utilities in Pennsylvania; four in New Jersey; and two each in New York, West Virginia, Illinois, Indiana, and Ohio. They supplied services that included electricity, gas, water, steam, and ice. For the most part, the companies' service was poor, their rates high, and their equipment faulty. Customers desiring new service often had to invest in the company since the operating company lacked financing to extend its lines.

Sidney Z. Mitchell had the experience and financial expertise to remedy this situation. An 1883 graduate of the U.S.

Company Perspectives:

In many ways, American Electric Power has been an industry powerhouse for decades. We pioneered many technologies and techniques that have become standard in the electric utility industry.

Thanks to the inventiveness, skill and drive of its people, AEP remains at the forefront of the restructured electric utility industry. Our achievements in 2000 provide a platform for even better performance in the years ahead.

Energy, information and people will be the primary ingredients for our future success. We are committed to being a powerhouse of energy and shareholder value.

Naval Academy, Mitchell had installed the first incandescent electric lighting system on a U.S. naval vessel. After leaving the navy in 1885, Mitchell met Thomas Edison and started working for him in New York City. That same year he left for the Pacific Northwest, where he ran Edison's operations for the next 20 years. He returned to New York in 1905 to help organize Electric Bond & Share Company (EB&S), of which he was soon president and chairman, with the responsibility of making the small operating companies turn a profit.

AG&E, while not owned by EB&S, did benefit from its financial services and was influenced by EB&S, because Mitchell simultaneously held the top positions in both companies. Mitchell's corporate strategy was guided by a few basic principles. First, sales were to increase by 6 percent to 8 percent each year. Second, small generating stations were to be replaced by larger, more efficient plants strategically located to allow for future growth and interconnection. Third, small operating companies located close together in one state were to be consolidated into one company. Fourth, the sales of preferred and common stock would provide for increased capital investment. Mitchell understood that utilities had inherent qualities that would force out competition and favor large holding companies. The cost of equipment was quite high and could be recouped only by companies with large customer bases. Quoted by his son, S.A. Mitchell, in *S.Z. Mitchell and the Electrical Industry*, Mitchell stated, "The only way that I know to make money in the public-utility business today, is by following the large volume of business, low cost of operation, low cost of money, low rates to the customers, and small margin of profit idea." In following this idea, AG&E had increased the number of kilowatt hours it provided from 53 million in 1907 to 427 million in 1917.

To increase consumption, the operating companies of AG&E established 24-hour service, gave away electric irons to new customers, and presented free toasters to households using the most electricity. In addition, the company rented vacuum cleaners to customers and ran cooking schools using electric ranges. As new plants came on line, rates were lowered and put on a sliding-scale basis, decreasing as consumption increased.

Mitchell also applied his principle of consolidation to AG&E. By 1910 Mitchell had sold all of the gas properties included in the original acquisitions, a policy the company

consistently followed in later years. He also sold some electric companies that could not be merged readily into a unified system. The largest of these isolated AG&E operations was in Rockford, Illinois. Retaining the companies in Marion and Muncie, Indiana; Bridgeport, Ohio; Atlantic City, New Jersey; and Scranton, Pennsylvania, Mitchell began acquiring smaller, adjoining companies, consolidating their operations and extending their lines into neighboring communities.

Having created several core markets in which to expand, AG&E began to construct long-range transmission lines to tie its properties together. An early step in consolidation was the construction of a 32-mile-long tie-line between Muncie and Marion. AG&E replaced existing equipment in this region with more powerful generators, and the Indiana properties became an interconnected system. This process was repeated in the area between Canton, Ohio, and Wheeling, West Virginia. George N. Tidd managed the ongoing consolidation and became president of AG&E in 1923 and chairman in 1924. By 1926 Mitchell had acquired additional properties in Virginia, West Virginia, and Kentucky.

The greatest cost of producing electricity was financing charges for new equipment. As cash flowed into AG&E from sales of unwanted properties, the company purchased more common stock in its partially owned subsidiaries. This in turn supported further issues of common stock and bonds to the public to raise more money for capital improvements.

The Golden Age of Growth: 1914–30

In 1914 the United States had opened to commercial shipping the Panama Canal, and World War I had begun in Europe. Following a period of strained neutrality, the United States entered the war in 1917, and the increased demands of wartime industries caused a 40 percent increase in the demand for electricity. At this time, Mitchell served on a committee of the War Industries Board overseeing electrical supply to defense plants. By interconnecting all generating plants, regardless of ownership, the committee achieved more balanced loads in order to meet war needs. This pooling system became popular in the postwar period. Implemented on a more limited basis than first conceived, it lowered production costs, created more reliable service, and contributed to company savings.

In the United States, the decade of the 1920s was characterized by a tremendous increase in industrial expansion and financial speculation. Mitchell was instrumental in establishing the principles upon which was based the first piece of federal legislation specifically aimed at regulating electric power, the Federal Power Act of 1920.

For power utilities, this was a golden age of growth, and AG&E flourished with the times. After reincorporating upon merging with Appalachian Securities Corporation, the company paid special stock dividends of 50 percent in 1925, 40 percent in 1927, and 50 percent in 1929. By 1926 AG&E had three primary electric power centers in place, one near Atlantic City, New Jersey; one in the Scranton area of Pennsylvania; and the third, known as the Central System, stretching from Virginia to Michigan. In building these systems, the company had constructed four "superplants," which went into operation from 1924 to 1930;

Key Dates:

1906: American Gas & Electric Company (AG&E) is incorporated.

1925: The company reincorporates after merging with Appalachian Securities Corporation.

1926: The company acquires additional properties in Virginia, West Virginia, and Kentucky.

1935: AG&E is forced to dispose of two noncontiguous companies—Atlantic City Electric and Scranton Electric.

1958: AG&E changes its name to American Electric Power Company (AEP).

1975: AEP opens its 2.13 million-kilowatt Cook nuclear plant in Michigan.

1980: AEP moves its headquarters to Columbus and acquires Columbus and Southern Ohio Electric Company.

1986: AEP's 2,022-mile-long, 765,000-volt transmission network stretching from Virginia to Michigan begins operation.

1996: Subsidiary AEP Communications is formed.

1997: The company acquires Yorkshire Electricity with New Century Energies for $2.8 billion.

2000: AEP acquires the utility holding company Central and South West Corp.

each was built outside the areas it would serve but near to fuel sources. This large-scale technology decreased unit costs.

Weathering the Depression

During the Great Depression with its monopoly shielded by regulation, AG&E and other utilities fared comparatively well. In 1933 revenues fell by 11 percent, the decline in industrial use being offset by residential customers, whose rate of use actually increased 20 percent between 1929 and 1933. U.S. President Herbert Hoover requested that electric utilities begin construction of facilities to meet future need to ease unemployment. Mitchell responded by directing companies controlled by Electric Bond & Share Company to spend $97 million on construction in 1930. Associated holding companies advanced more than $330 million to help the operating companies between 1930 and 1934. Mitchell retired in 1933, however. One of the last of the giants of the early era of electrical utilities, his greatest contribution was the financial management that had supported rapid growth.

The Public Utility Holding Company Act of 1935, which established the Securities and Exchange Commission to enforce its provisions, was designed to demolish pyramid holding companies such as AG&E, which had been built on a mountain of debt. The value of large interconnected systems serving a single area was widely accepted by this time, however, and while AG&E was forced to dispose of two noncontiguous companies—Atlantic City Electric and Scranton Electric—the Central System was left intact.

In 1939 the start of World War II in Europe led to increased production of war supplies, which lessened the effects of the

Depression. When the United States entered the war in 1941, there was a rise in power demand by wartime industries, which the utilities were able to meet. In addition, as construction priorities shifted to defense materiel, new generating equipment could not be built. After the war, demand dropped and industrial production returned to normal. While consumers rushed to buy the new appliances then available, the utility industry had to wait for the delivery of new equipment before it could resume growth.

Postwar Technological Advances

By 1949, Philip Sporn, a one-time assistant to Tidd who had become AG&E's president in 1947, announced that the worst of the power shortage was over. With comfortable margins of reserve, AG&E picked up 82,000 customers in 1948, representing 250,000 kilowatts of demand. Load expansion was bolstered by AG&E's sale of 45,000 electric ranges and 30,000 water heaters. To Sporn, the most significant problems of the decade ahead would be developing technology that could handle an expected doubling of demand and raising capital for new facilities costing an anticipated $500 million.

With Sporn in charge, AG&E increased the number of kilowatt hours provided to 23.3 billion in 1959, achieving growth through acquisitions, technological breakthroughs, and sales promotions. In 1948 the company bought Indiana Service Corporation in Fort Wayne and consolidated it with an AG&E subsidiary, Indiana & Michigan Electric Company. This was only one of six acquisitions during the years between 1945 and 1956.

Sporn had been an engineer with AG&E since 1920, and he was interested in the technical aspects of the power industry. As president of the company until 1961, Sporn's approach was to take risks with new, untested equipment in order to surpass competition. In the 1950s Sporn worked with General Electric Company on the design of a new 225-megawatt generator. After achieving favorable results with a prototype, he ordered another six units. AG&E became widely known for its technological leadership.

Sporn did not neglect the sales side of the business, however, and he structured it to mesh with the growth of the system. Sales of room air conditioners went up from 43,000 in 1947 to 1.67 million in 1958 and while this meant consumption, it also created a new problem: summer peaking of load demand. In 1955 Sporn began promoting heat pumps and home electrical heating as a way to achieve balanced seasonal loads. By creating demand, Sporn hoped to project future generating needs more accurately.

The development of nuclear power was also a major concern of the utility industry in the 1950s. To raise the enormous capital required for such development, Sporn urged that the Public Utility Holding Company Act be revised to allow private companies to develop facilities jointly. In 1954 U.S. President Dwight D. Eisenhower signed the Atomic Energy Act, making possible the private development of nuclear energy in the United States.

In 1958 AG&E changed its name to American Electric Power Company. During the 1960s the electric utility industry was a success story in which new equipment and business techniques encouraged growth and profits. This success was reflected in rising stock prices, with averages doubling between 1958 and 1965, and while the growth rate of demand advanced at an annual pace of 7 percent on average between 1920 and 1973, rates continued to drop.

The power failure in the northeast United States that prompted a power blackout in New York City in 1965 led to threats of federal intervention to guarantee reliability. Donald C. Cook, who had succeeded Sporn as president of AEP in 1961, argued that a proposed national power grid system was unworkable and that such federal intervention was not needed. As proof he pointed to the role of private industries in alleviating the blackout crisis by sending power to New York through their transmission lines. Nevertheless, regional power pool arrangements were worked out through the North American Electrical Reliability Council, a new industrial body.

Cook continued to address the problem of the national power supply when, in 1967, he told a National Power Conference in Washington, D.C., that most of the electrical systems in the United States were outmoded and inefficient. Cook called for their replacement. Within 25 years, he speculated, the country would be served by approximately 15 electric mega-systems. Indeed, in the late 1960s an industrywide trend toward corporate consolidation did emerge. As part of this, AEP absorbed Michigan Gas & Electric Company and proposed taking over Southern Ohio Electric.

Another trend in the late 1960s was a growth in the annual rate for electrical consumption to an unforeseen level. The need to increase capacity set off a race among utilities to buy new equipment, causing high prices and delays in delivery. To avoid these problems, AEP bought 2,200 megawatts of power equipment overseas in 1967, an unusual procedure for a U.S. utility.

Industry Decline and Recovery: 1970s–80s

The climate of expansion ended abruptly in the 1970s, in large part because of three factors: a general market decline set off by the OPEC oil embargo; rising costs that could not be offset; and a technological standstill, in which existing technologies could no longer provide higher levels of efficiency at lower costs. In 1973, the year the oil embargo began, 17 percent of power generation nationwide depended on oil. In the Northeast, the figure was 60 percent. As oil prices rose eightfold, the price of electricity shot up almost 50 percent. In 1974 power demand went down for the first time since 1970, in part due to exports to Japan; Cook suggested export restrictions.

Another problem for utilities in the 1970s was a series of federal regulatory acts spurred on by an increase in public awareness of the environmental movement. Jimmy Carter became U.S. president in 1977, and the National Energy Act of 1978 soon followed. For AEP, which used coal produced by subsidiary-controlled mines, the regulatory environment had become stifling. W.S. (Pete) White, who had become chairman of the board of AEP in 1976, predicted in 1979 that projected construction costs would be 40 percent higher for the company because of Clean Air Act amendments.

In the midst of declining demand and increased regulatory restrictions, AEP had opened its 2.13 million-kilowatt Cook nuclear plant in Michigan. For a time, the company was shel-

tered by its sales to other utilities, which could purchase electricity from AEP at a cost lower than they could produce it themselves. In 1980 AEP acquired Columbus and Southern Ohio Electric Company, located in the middle of its operating system, and moved its headquarters to Columbus, then the largest city it served. By 1982, however, a recession severely affecting industry in AEP's territories caused a drop in industrial sales of 18 percent. Sales to other utilities declined by 20 percent. In response, White cut salaries, froze wages, and laid off workers.

Recovery, however, came as early as 1984. In that year, increased auto sales led to the recovery of the aluminum and steel industries, which were AEP's largest industrial customers. As industrial sales rose 22 percent in the year's first quarter over the year before, sales to other utilities meeting the increased demand rose 40 percent. Residential and commercial demand rose 10 percent and 8 percent, respectively. For AEP, which had been granted a rate increase of $260 million in 1983, the corner had been turned. Although revenues would decline in both 1985 and 1990, AEP's financial situation generally improved from its 1983 low. In 1986 a project 19 years in duration, a 2,022-mile-long, 765,000-volt transmission network stretching from Virginia to Michigan, began operation. At a cost of $800 million, AEP established an electrical grid expected to serve into the 21st century.

AEP still faced three major problems in the late 1980s and early 1990s: completion of the Zimmer nuclear plant in Ohio, amendments to the Clean Air Act, and proposed deregulation of the utility industry. Begun in 1971 as a joint project of AEP and two other utilities, Zimmer was planned as an 810-megawatt nuclear facility, but the national controversy over the development of such plants, especially after the nuclear accident that occurred in 1979 at the Three Mile Island plant in Pennsylvania, helped to bring a halt to Zimmer in 1982. With the facility almost completed with an investment of $1.7 billion, the project was stalled. Then in 1984, despite industry skepticism, the company decided to convert Zimmer to a coal-fired plant. AEP's subsidiary, AEP Service Corporation, using modular construction methods, completed the conversion three months ahead of schedule and below budget by almost $300 million.

Expansion in the 1990s

With the completion of its Zimmer facility, AEP, for the first time since World War II, was not constructing any more generating capacity, but was planning carefully during a time when the very structure of the industry might change. Environmental concerns were affecting not only the choice of fuels, but also the structure of energy plants. To comply with the Clean Air Act, the company installed scrubbers designed to mitigate pollution on its coal-fired plants in 1992. In addition to modifying their plants, AEP began looking into the development of alternative energy sources. Later in the 1990s, this research led to the company's development of the Trent Mesa Project, a wind-power generation facility in Texas.

In the mid-1990s deregulation in several countries and industries affected AEP's business plan. Discussion in several states about opening up retail energy sales to competition encouraged AEP to begin advertising, both to protect its existing customer base and to introduce its name to potential customers in new areas. The telecommunications industry opened to new players with the passage of the Telecommunications Act of 1996; AEP jumped in with AEP Communications. Around the same time, the United Kingdom deregulated its electric market. In 1997 AEP formed AEP Resources to handle nonregulated corporate development and capital investment operations, and the new subsidiary went looking for British opportunities. Along with New Century Energies (later Xcel Energy), the company purchased Yorkshire Energies for $2.8 billion.

Several factors led to a drop in AEP's net income in 1997: The U.K. government decided the value of Yorkshire Energies had been misassessed and hit AEP with a windfall tax of $109 million. The Cook nuclear plant was shut down when the Nuclear Regulatory Commission expressed safety concerns. In addition, AEP faced increasing wholesale competition. Despite these setbacks, AEP announced a major expansion plan in December 1997—to buy the electric utility Central and South West Corp. in a stock swap valued at more than $6 billion. The deal immediately became mired in the regulatory approval process, which would end up lasting two and a half years.

Meanwhile, AEP Resources continued investing in foreign utilities. In 1998 it purchased 20 percent of the Australian power company Pacific Hydro; in 1999 the Pushan Power Plant, of which AEP owned 70 percent, came on line in China. AEP moved into natural gas in 1998 with the purchase of the natural gas midstream operations of Equitable Resources in Louisiana. The deal included natural gas storage and processing facilities and nearly 2,000 miles of intrastate pipelines. AEP expanded its reach in this industry when it bought the Houston Pipe Line Company from the ill-fated Enron Corporation in 2001. The $727 million purchase added 4,400 miles of natural gas pipelines to AEP's system and a 30-year prepaid lease on the operation of the Bammel Storage Facility. One of the largest natural gas storage facilities in North America, Bammel had a capacity of 118 billion cubic feet. In 2000, AEP returned its Cook Nuclear Plant to service.

Finally, in mid-2000, AEP completed its acquisition of Central and South West, yielding combined 1999 revenues of $12.5 billion and sales of nearly 200 million megawatt hours. Along with the addition of 1.8 million customers, AEP also gained another U.K. utility, SEEBOARD. Although the company considered combining SEEBOARD with Yorkshire Energies, it abandoned that plan later in the year. As a result of the acquisition, the company also anticipated $2 billion in savings over the next ten years from efficiencies resulting from the combination of the two companies' operations.

Later that year AEP announced a reorganization that would create two wholly owned corporations. One would handle AEP's nonregulated subsidiaries, both utility and non-utility. The other would hold AEP's regulated utility subsidiaries and its foreign utility subsidiaries that were subject to rates or tariff regulations. The plan would require Securities and Exchange Commission approval before it could be implemented.

AEP continued to expand on a smaller scale in 2001, with the takeover of the Quaker Coal Co. Quaker was in bankruptcy proceedings in Kentucky when the court approved AEP's plan to assume the company's assets and pay off its creditors.

Principal Subsidiaries

AEP Communications, Inc.; AEP Credit, Inc.; AEP Energy Services, Inc.; AEP Generating Company; AEP Pro Serv, Inc.; AEP Pushan Power LDC; AEP Resources, Inc.; Central and South West Corporation; Central Power and Light Company; CSW Energy, Inc.; Indiana Michigan Power Company; Kentucky Power Company; Ohio Power Company; Public Service Company of Oklahoma; Southwestern Electric Power Company; West Texas Utilities Company; Wheeling Power Company.

Principal Competitors

Cinergy Corp.; Entergy Corporation; Xcel Energy Inc.; UtiliCorp United Inc.

Further Reading

"AEP, CSW Garner Approval," *Electric Light & Power,* August 2000, p. 7.

Baird, Kristen, "American Electric Power Set to Turn on Ad Blitz," *Crain's Cleveland Business,* August 19, 1996.

Mitchell, Sidney Alexander, *S.Z. Mitchell and the Electrical Industry,* New York: Farrar, Straus & Cudahy, 1960.

Where the Future Is Now. . . ., Columbus, Ohio: American Electric Power Company, Inc., [n.d.].

White, W.S., Jr., *American Electric Power Company: 75 Years of Meeting the Challenge,* New York: The Newcomen Society in North America, 1982.

—Wilson B. Lindauer
—update: Susan Windisch Brown

American Golf Corporation

2951 26th Street
Santa Monica, California 90405
U.S.A.
Telephone: (310) 664-4000
Fax: (310) 664-6160
Web site: http://www.americangolf.com

Private Company
Incorporated: 1970
Employees: 22,000
Sales: $746 million (2000 est.)
NAIC: 71391 Golf Courses and Country Clubs; 71399
    All Other Amusement and Recreation Industries

American Golf Corporation is the world's largest golf course management company. The company runs over 300 golf courses across the United States and in Australia, Japan, and the United Kingdom. Its courses include municipal and public courses as well as private courses and country clubs. About half of American Golf's courses are owned by a sister company, National Golf Properties, Inc. National Golf Properties is a publicly traded real estate investment trust (REIT). Both companies are chaired by David G. Price. Price also owns a substantial stake in both companies. American Golf has a charitable arm as well, the American Golf Foundation. This nonprofit group endeavors to promote the game of golf particularly among women, young people, and poor or disadvantaged families. Increasing the popularity and accessibility of the sport is one of the goals of American Golf Corporation.

Seeing Golf from a Business Perspective: 1970s

American Golf Corporation (AGC) was founded by David G. Price, who purchased his first golf course in 1970. Price was the son of Welsh immigrants who moved to California during the Depression. Price studied economics at the University of Southern California, then joined the Navy and learned to fly fighter jets. During the Korean War, Price was a flight instructor. After his tour of duty was up, he returned to Los Angeles and earned a law degree at UCLA. His first job was with the leading entertainment law firm O'Melveny & Myers. Working at the firm brought Price into contact with such top stars as Marlon Brando and Bing Crosby. Hobnobbing with the illustrious was one form of compensation for young Price. But in terms of actual salary, the job paid very little. After two years with O'Melveny & Myers, Price only brought home $525 a month. Then Price's sister Joan introduced him to Joseph Drown, a well-known Los Angeles businessman and real estate magnate. Drown offered to double Price's salary if he would sign on as his personal attorney. Price left the law firm to work for Drown, and soon ran some of Drown's enterprises. Price became president of Getty Financial Corporation, Getty Resorts Corporation, and the Don the Beachcomber Restaurants, and was director and vice-president of the Hotel Bel Air in Los Angeles and of the U.S. Grant Hotel in San Diego.

Drown owned a lot of land in and around Los Angeles, including three golf courses. Price was not much of a golfer, but he was intrigued by the business possibilities of the courses. They were not doing well for Drown, and Price asked if he could buy them. He was sure he could manage them in a professional manner, applying sound business principles. As they were, golf pros managed them, and these people were more concerned with the game than with the finances. At first Drown resisted selling his courses. In 1970 he relented, stung by complaints about the golf course he had overheard while at the bar of his Yorba Linda Country Club. Price bought the Yorba Linda and two other courses from Drown, and then proceeded to run them as he thought they should be. This was the start of American Golf Corporation.

At first, Price's new business was a disaster. He knew the courses were not profitable, and not in good shape, but he was unprepared for the depth of their problems. In an interview with CNN (August 14, 2001), Price told the reporter that "everything that could go wrong went wrong." His friends reassured him that when he and American Golf went bankrupt, they would find him a new job. But Price persisted in spite of dreadful obstacles. All the grass on the fairways died at one course when a maintenance crew applied the wrong fertilizer. But Price solved the physical problems while going ahead with rearrangement of the management technique. He kicked out the golf pros and replaced them with people with a business background. He insisted on quick and accurate reporting of financial

Company Perspectives:

Our mission: To be the world leader in golf course management by providing first class facilities and services to the golfing community and operating with the highest standards of integrity and professionalism, while at the same time opening the game of golf to wider audiences.

statistics from each course. Within five years, the three courses were turning a profit.

Building a Network of Golf Courses: Mid-1970s–80s

Once the first small group of courses was running well, Price realized he had a model for turning around other troubled courses around the country—and there were thousands of them to choose from. AGC began buying up courses or taking over management contracts. When AGC started its acquisition program in the mid-1970s, there were over 8,000 public courses in the United States, including some 2,200 courses run by municipalities. The municipal courses made especially good targets for AGC. The municipalities for the most part managed their golf courses much as they would any other public park. Sometimes management decisions were captive to factions within a city bureaucracy. Often courses were in poor repair and losing money. Municipalities often resisted turning their courses over to private management, yet AGC was able to move in when the other option would have been the city closing the course down. AGC brought the courses back to profitability, and split the revenue with the city.

Through the 1970s and early 1980s, American Golf picked up management contracts for underperforming golf courses in many states. The company liked to take over a cluster of courses in one area, because it was actually easier and more cost efficient to run multiple courses than a single one. AGC could then offer golfers a centralized reservation system for the courses in the area, for example. The company liked to take over longstanding courses too, as opposed to newly built properties. In some cases, the problems of old golf courses seemed too much even for AGC's expertise. In the mid-1980s, the company snagged management contracts for five municipal courses in New York City. Some of these courses were dangerous—golfers had been mugged, and employees allegedly came to work only in order to play cards together, letting the grounds go to ruin. AGC pumped approximately a million dollars into the New York courses, hauling off the cars that had been left to rot on some, buying new golf carts, renovating the clubhouses, and repairing the irrigation systems. The company also did extensive marketing, to tell New Yorkers that the courses were now much improved. After two years, the courses began to be profitable. Eventually the city received between $150,000 and $500,000 per course annually. AGC did not disclose what its share of the revenue was. But overall, the company was quite profitable. By the end of the 1980s, its earnings were about 10 percent of its revenues, and total annual sales were around $300 million.

Moving More Upscale in the 1990s

American Golf had found success by leasing underperforming courses, such as those in New York City. The company was able to cut costs while improving the courses. The cleaned-up courses attracted more people to the game, and AGC usually managed to increase revenues substantially at properties it managed. By 1991, AGC managed about 80 public golf courses in 20 states, as well as a handful of private ones. The company was a solid earner, and it began to put some of its profits into purchasing more golf courses outright. In the early 1990s AGC spent some $500 million to buy 45 courses. At this point the company began to deviate from its earlier acquisition plan. Most of the courses it leased or owned had been public courses with a relatively low daily user fee. It ran courses near airports and ones that had been neglected city properties, not fancy country clubs. But the company realized that not all golfers were alike. Its customers included casual players as well as devoted amateurs, some who liked a no-nonsense course and others who preferred a touch of luxury. To diversify its properties, AGC began to buy up country clubs and private resort courses. By 1993, the company had 14 courses that were substantially more upscale than most of its others. It formed a separate management division, American Golf Country Clubs, to run these as a unit. Within a few years, the 14 country clubs had expanded to almost 70.

The company made another major move in 1993. As it began to own more courses, the company moved away from its original business plan of leasing and managing. Consequently, David Price formed a new company, National Golf Properties, Inc., in 1993. National Golf was a real estate investment trust (REIT), a publicly traded pool of real estate properties. REITs traded as stocks, but were required to pay out at least 95 percent of their income as dividends. National Golf Properties was the first golf REIT on the market. Its properties comprised about 50 golf courses when it debuted. It leased these to AGC, so that the original company now focused just on management. National Golf received a base rent for the courses it leased to its sister company, plus a percentage rent based on the course's revenue. The companies grew in tandem, though the REIT was public and AGC remained private, with most of the stock in the hands of Chairman David Price, family members, and other top management. Acquisitions were completed by National Golf, and the management contract in all but a few cases went to American Golf. By 1996, National Golf had spent more than $300 million to buy up some 70 more golf courses. A major transaction was the purchase in June 1996 of 43 golf courses from a Dallas-based competitor, Golf Enterprises Inc. This cost the company $160 million. By the end of 1996, American Golf operated over 250 golf courses, including a substantial number of private country clubs. Annual sales were around $490 million. National Golf Properties owned over 110 courses, and its stock was booming.

AGC managed a large number of courses nationwide, and it tended to own multiple courses in any one area. Its country club division began offering members special deals at other courses the company managed. It offered a Platinum Plus Golf & Travel Advantage program, which gave its members free access to over 200 courses across the United States. It ran a national reservation center, so members could book tee time at any AGC country club up to 60 days in advance. The reservation center also handled airline, hotel, and rental car reservations. The country club division also offered its members their own tournament, called the American Classic. Running tournaments became a very lucrative business for AGC.

Key Dates:

1970: David G. Price founds American Golf Corporation and buys first golf courses.

1980s: Company secures management contracts for five municipal golf courses in New York City.

1993: National Golf Properties is founded; company operates as a publicly traded REIT as well as sister company of American Golf.

1999: In a joint venture with ClubCorp, National Golf acquires 48 courses collectively known as the Cobblestone Golf Group from competitor Meditrust.

2001: American Golf signs first management contract for golf course in Japan.

While the company poured resources into its country club arm in the 1990s, it also moved to introduce more people to golf. AGC sponsored a Women in Golf Task Force, encouraging women to get out and play. It also gave free golf lessons to inner city kids and adults, to defuse the image of golf as an elite suburban pastime.

AGC and National Golf Properties continued to expand in the late 1990s, though the growing popularity of golf began to attract competition. National Golf Properties had been the only REIT of its kind when it went public in 1993. By 1998 it had several competitors, including Meditrust Inc. and Golf Trust of America. Among them all, they only owned several hundred of the 15,000 golf courses in the United States, and investors fueled their rising stock prices, expecting big expansion. But the price of golf course acquisitions went up, too. National Golf Properties moved more slowly in the late 1990s than it had earlier, waiting for good opportunities as the market as a whole overheated. In 1999 it acquired a group of 48 courses known as the Cobblestone Golf Group from its competitor Meditrust. It bought these in a joint venture with another company, ClubCorp. Meditrust had acquired the group for $540 million only a year earlier, then let them go for a deep discount. Another REIT competitor, Golf Trust of America, sprang up in 1997 but was in liquidation by 2001.

International Expansion in the 2000s

Golf grew more popular in the United States in the late 1990s, fueled by a variety of factors. These included the broad appeal of new golf superstar Tiger Woods, and Callaway Golf Company's "Big Bertha" club, which made the game easier for amateurs. Several golf company stocks and golf REITs hit Wall Street. Meanwhile, AGC began to expand overseas. It formed a new international subsidiary in the late 1990s, American Golf (UK), and began buying up courses in the United Kingdom. By 2000, the British subsidiary owned over 20 courses, and planned for a portfolio of 50 by 2003. Its courses ran the gamut from municipal courses to fancy private clubs. The subsidiary was said to be consistently profitable, bringing in annual revenue of £33 million by 2000. The U.K. subsidiary also followed its parent company plan, and worked to make golf accessible to

a broader swath of the population. The company held a special women's day at its courses in 2000, and drew thousands of eager beginners. Women made up only 7 percent of golfers in the United Kingdom, compared to 23 percent in the United States. The company believed it could increase its customer base in both countries by bringing more women into the game.

AGC also moved into Australia around the same time. By 2001 the firm owned two Australian courses. AGC's international division looked to Japan as another growing market. The company studied the Japanese golf scene for two years before closing on its first management contract there in 2001. This was to run the Aso Country Club, a famously picturesque club located in a northeastern suburb of Tokyo. AGC's subsidiary, American Golf Japan, took over the operation of the country club, and agreed to make extensive improvements to the grounds and facilities. This was the first time AGC-style professional management had been tried at a course in Japan. AGC hoped to grow its Japanese subsidiary to 30 to 50 clubs over the next five years, whether through acquiring managing contracts or through outright purchase. The firm continued to make acquisitions in the United States as well. In 2001 it bought two domestic courses, the Sierra Nevada Golf Park in Genoa, Nevada, and the Ko'olau Golf Club on the island of Oahu, Hawaii.

Principal Subsidiaries

American Golf (UK); American Golf Japan.

Principal Competitors

ClubCorp, Inc.

Further Reading

"American Golf Corp. Catches Its Breath and Speaks," *Business Wire*, May 14, 1997.

Capell, Kerry, "Golf Stocks: Sand Traps and Smooth Greens," *Business Week*, June 3, 1996, p. 126.

Carlson, Eugene, "Privatization Lets Small Firms Manage Everything from Libraries to Golf Courses," *Wall Street Journal*, April 2, 1991, pp. B1, B3.

Ciandella, Donald R., "Investors Take Swings at Unusual Property Niches and Expect Home Runs," *National Real Estate Investor*, July 1996, p. 83.

Egan, Jack, "Going After the REIT Stuff," *U.S. News & World Report*, July 19, 1993, p. 72.

Harverson, Patrick, "Golf Course Industry Hopes Tiger Opens a Fair Way," *Financial Times*, November 13, 2000, p. 28.

Kirkpatrick, David D., "American Golf Turns Away Suitors on Final Nine," *Wall Street Journal*, November 19, 1997, p. B14.

Lisovicz, Susan, and Gayla Hope, "Business Unusual," *CNN*, August 14, 2001.

Rudnitsky, Howard, "On the Green," *Institutional Investor*, August 2001, p. 95.

Samuelson, James, "Clubhouse King," *Forbes*, October 7, 1996, p. 14.

Slatin, Peter, "Buying a Course," *Barron's*, March 30, 1998, pp. G23–G24.

Taylor, John H., "Hole-in-One," *Forbes*, July 22, 1991, pp. 53–55.

—A. Woodward

Aon Corporation

123 North Wacker Drive
Chicago, Illinois 60606
U.S.A.
Telephone: (312) 701-3000
Toll Free: (888) 858-9587
Fax: (312) 701-3100
Web site: http://www.aon.com

Public Company
Incorporated: 1947 as Combined Insurance Company of
    America
Employees: 51,000
Sales: $7.38 billion (2000)
Stock Exchanges: New York Midwest London Toronto
Ticker Symbol: AOC
NAIC: 524128 Warranty Insurance Carriers, Direct;
    524130 Reinsurance Carriers; 524210 Insurance
    Brokerages; 541330 Administration Management
    Consulting Services; 541612 Human Resource
    Consulting Services

Chicago-based Aon Corporation is one of the largest insurance brokerage and consulting companies in the world. Through its subsidiaries in 2001, the Aon Corporation provided consumer insurance underwriting, human resources consulting and outsourcing, and commercial brokerage services. The company's brokerage business accounted for two-thirds of the company's sales and included reinsurance operations. The holding company grew rapidly through acquisitions during the 1980s and 1990s.

The corporate structure of Aon originated in 1980, when the Combined International Corporation was set up as a holding company for the acquisition-hungry Combined Insurance Company of America. The latter company had been formed in 1947 through the merger of the Combined Mutual Casualty Company of Chicago and Combined Insurance Company of America of Pennsylvania. Both companies belonged to self-made millionaire and self-help proponent W. Clement Stone. Stone controlled a number of insurance companies operating in various states at the time. He had begun his insurance career at the age of 16.

Company Origins in the Early 20th Century

W. Clement Stone was born on Chicago's south side in 1902. His father died when he was two years old, and by age six, Stone was earning money as a paperboy to help his dressmaker mother. At age 13 the entrepreneurial Stone had his own newsstand. At 16 he embarked on an insurance career, selling policies for an agency his mother had started in Detroit, Michigan.

In 1922, at the age of 20, W. Clement Stone set up a Chicago-based insurance agency with a $100 investment. During the 1920s the Combined Registry Company, which acted as agent for about six insurers, grew rapidly, employing 1,000 agents nationwide by 1930. The Depression hit the company hard, however, and Stone was forced to reduce the number of agents to 135. In 1939 Stone acquired his first insurance company, the American Casualty Company of Dallas, later known as the Combined American Insurance Company of Dallas. That same year he organized the Combined Mutual Casualty Company of Chicago, followed by the Combined Casualty Company of Philadelphia, renaming it the Combined Insurance Company of America, and paving the way for the 1947 merger.

When the Combined Insurance Company of America got its start just after World War II, the company wrote accident and health insurance, hospitalization, and non-cancelable accident and health insurance. An army of door-to-door salesmen carried Combined's policies directly to homes and businesses. At the end of 1947 Combined had assets of $2.2 million.

Expansion in the 1950s and 1960s

In December 1949 the company acquired the Boston Casualty Company, an accident and health insurer, and renamed it Hearthstone Insurance Company of Massachusetts. In 1954 Combined acquired the First National Casualty Company of Fond du Lac, Wisconsin. During the 1950s, Combined and its subsidiaries grew substantially. Between 1949 and 1959, premiums increased an average of 17 percent annually while assets jumped from $2.9 million to $20.3 million. The company relied on direct sales of low-cost accident and health policies, which were a good risk for Combined.

W. Clement Stone's personal philosophy—the "positive mental attitude," or PMA—was the cornerstone of the company's day-to-day operations. Stone, wearing a flamboyant bow-tie, was known to enter the boardroom shouting, "Is everybody happy?" Salespersons lived by slogans like "What the mind can conceive and believe, the mind can achieve" and "When you have nothing to lose and everything to gain by trying, by all means try." Employees were encouraged to greet each day with the upbeat maxim "I feel healthy. I feel happy. I feel terrific."

Sales pitches were memorized and repeated by the company's door-to-door representatives. W. Clement Stone remarked years later: "It's impossible to fail when you follow this step-by-step set-up." Indeed, Combined Insurance Company's sales continued to expand throughout the 1960s. By 1969 Combined's written premiums totaled $187 million, up from $27 million a decade earlier; assets were $225 million, up from $20.3 million.

In 1965 Combined began selling low-cost, low-benefit life insurance, which gradually became a significant segment of the company's business. In 1968 the company acquired the Commerce and Industry Insurance Company of New York, a fire and property insurer that sold to preferred commercial, institutional, and industrial clients. The Commerce and Industry shares were exchanged for 50,000 shares of the American Home Assurance Company of New York six months later.

Weathering Leadership Changes and Recession in the 1970s

In January 1970 Matthew T. Walsh, former executive vice-president and international sales manager, became president of Combined Insurance when the 67-year-old W. Clement Stone assumed the new offices of chairman and CEO. Walsh had been with the company since 1946. At the same time, Clement Stone, the 41-year-old son of the founder, became president of Combined's European operations. Although W. Clement Stone stepped down from the day-to-day running of the company, his influence directed the company.

Throughout the next decade, Combined pushed overseas. Having already penetrated English-speaking markets including Canada, Great Britain, Australia, and New Zealand in the 1960s, Combined entered West Germany in 1977, France in 1979, and Japan in 1980. Combined tailored its policies to fit conditions in these countries: in New Zealand, for example, where socialized medical programs cover virtually the entire

cost of hospitalization and doctors' bills, Combined sold supplemental policies that protected against loss of income in case of illness or accident. By 1980, 17 percent of the company's revenues came from outside the United States.

In December 1971, just two years after assuming the presidency of Combined Insurance, Matthew T. Walsh resigned. Walsh said he was leaving because his years at Combined had given him "sufficient means to do all the things I've always wanted to do while still young enough to enjoy them." W. Clement Stone resumed the president's chair until a replacement could be found. Clement Stone took the reins as president and chief operating officer in 1972 and became CEO in 1973.

The recession of 1973 sent stock prices plummeting. Between 1970 and 1977 Combined's price dropped about 66 percent. Nevertheless, growth continued at an impressive rate during the decade. Because Combined focused on the low end of the insurance market, the company did not suffer from problems that faced other insurers during the late 1970s. While those companies struggled with skyrocketing health costs and accident settlements, Combined prospered. Between 1969 and 1979 assets grew to $1.57 billion—about 16 percent annually.

New Holding Company and New Leadership: The Early 1980s

By the end of the 1970s, Combined Insurance Company was looking for acquisitions. In 1980 the company formed the publicly owned Combined International Corporation to act as a holding company, in order to avoid state-by-state regulation. The holding company was monitored by the Securities and Exchange Commission and was not subject to scrutiny by each state's insurance commission.

In 1981 the new Combined International Corporation made its first acquisition when it bought the Union Fidelity Corporation along with its Nashaming Valley Information Processing unit, for $105.5 million. Union Fidelity was an accident and health insurer, which excelled at direct-response marketing and sold 75 percent of its policies through direct-mail and newspaper campaigns. The unit was expected to give Combined's door-to-door marketers a needed boost. Combined suffered from the rising costs of recruiting and maintaining a large battalion of field representatives, and the company's domestic sales had been flat for the two years prior to the acquisition.

In March 1982 Clement Stone abruptly resigned as president and CEO of Combined, citing personal reasons. His father once again resumed control of the company. After his resignation, Clement Stone received a $3.4 million consulting contract.

At age 79, W. Clement Stone was once again caretaker of the company he had founded. At the same time, the company was troubled by stagnation in domestic premiums. Although the slump in growth was offset in the short term by excellent investment results, a plan to deal with rapidly changing markets was needed.

Combined solved its leadership problems with the acquisition of the Ryan Insurance Company in August 1982. Combined spent $133 million for the 18-year-old specialty insurer and brokerage, which had been a pioneer in credit life insurance for auto dealerships and extended mechanical warranty insurance agreements. Founder Patrick G. Ryan then became president and CEO of Combined. Stone remained chairman. Although W. Clement Stone had called an unexpected adjournment that lasted for five hours at the special shareholders meeting that had been called for the purpose of approving the acquisition, Stone finally approved the deal, and Combined at last had a new leader.

Pat Ryan's management style differed considerably from W. Clement Stone's. Ryan, while himself a good motivator, was generally described as less flamboyant and more diplomatic. The new CEO of Combined demonstrated his approach by announcing a major acquisition just two months after taking charge of the company's operations. Combined purchased the Chicago-based insurance brokerage Rollins Burdick Hunter Company for $109 million. Rollins Burdick, which was well known for its large corporate clients, absorbed Combined's other brokerage operations, making it the eighth largest insurance broker in the United States. The acquisition provided Combined with a source of fee income that was not readily susceptible to decline because of the less competitive nature of corporate insurance.

In 1982, although revenue rose 27 percent, net earnings dropped 19 percent. Ryan began to cut costs and integrate Combined's greatly diversified operations. In 1983 revenues grew 18 percent and operating earnings jumped 47 percent. The Ryan Insurance subsidiary stretched its extended warranty insurance to appliances, and Union Fidelity took advantage of the growing need for supplemental health insurance.

Acquisition Spree in the Late 1980s

In April 1986 Combined bought the Life Insurance Company of Virginia for $557 million. The acquisition further widened Combined's product line, notably adding an array of interest-sensitive universal life products for upscale markets.

In January 1987 the Rollins Burdick Hunter unit bought five regional operations: Allen, Hart, Franz and Zehnder of Los Angeles; Schroeter, White and Johnson of Oakland, California; Pilot Insurance Agency of Winston-Salem, North Carolina; Todorovich Agency of St. Louis, Missouri; and the agency operations of Springhouse Financial Corporation of Philadelphia, Pennsylvania.

In March 1987 Combined International Corporation's shareholders voted to change the name of the company to Aon Corporation. Patrick Ryan said the name change was necessary to eliminate confusion between the holding company and its subsidiary, Combined Insurance Company of America. Continuing its diversification, Aon bought the employee-benefits consulting firm Miller, Mason and Dickenson for $12 million in the summer of 1988, and in September bought the nation's ninth largest reinsurance agent, Reinsurance Agency. In January 1989 Aon restructured its subsidiary Rollins Burdick Hunter Company, setting up a holding company to oversee four units: Rollins Burdick Hunter Company, the brokerage; Rollins Specialty Group, a newly created unit concentrating on brokerage services for financial institutions, associations, and affinity groups; Miller, Mason and Dickenson, the newly acquired employee benefits consultant; and Aon Risk Services, a reinsurance brokerage operating through Aon Reinsurance Agency, formerly Reinsurance Agency.

Continuing Acquisitions Spree Through the 1990s

In 1990 Stone left the board of directors and the company he had founded. Ryan continued his growth-through-acquisitions strategy through the early 1990s, maintaining the company's focus on life and health insurance, life underwriting and specialty insurance, and insurance brokerage. In 1991, Aon acquired Hudig-Langeveldt, and the following year, Frank B. Hall.

By 1994, Aon had reached sales of more than $4 billion, almost twice the annual sales of the late 1980s. Net income also had doubled, to $360 million. Ryan, however, felt the company needed to shift its focus, eliminating its slow-growing life insurance and annuities business and beefing up its brokerage and specialty insurance businesses. Within a year, Aon had sold off all of its direct life insurance companies. It also added hostile takeover insurance for small and medium-sized businesses to its specialty insurance offerings.

Aon became the largest insurance brokerage in the world in 1996, primarily through its purchase of Alexander & Alexander Services Inc. Aon acquired the New York-based brokerage for

$1.23 billion. Aon's 1997 purchase of The Minet Group also helped pull the company into the lead. Its number one position was short-lived, however, as the rival brokerage Marsh & McLennan Cos. knocked them out with the purchase of Johnson & Higgins in 1997. Aon's size was still impressive: revenues of $5.8 billion in 1997 and 400 offices in 80 countries.

The company extended its global reach in 1998, with numerous overseas purchases. The most prominent acquisitions included Spain's Gil y Carvajal, France's Groupe Leblace de Nicolay, and Bain Hogg of Britain. Seven other purchases were made, primarily in Europe and Latin America. In addition to its purchases, Aon opened new offices and subsidiaries throughout the world, such as Aon Korea. The following year, Aon continued its international acquisitions, buying the Italian insurance firm Nikols Sedgwick Group, among others.

Expenses related to its acquisitions caught up with Aon in 1999. Although sales had exceeded $7 billion, net income fell to $352 million in 1999, down from $541 million in 1998. Integrating the new businesses and updating their technology were among the largest costs, although a restructuring of Aon's brokerage and consulting businesses added $120 million in costs. The collapse of the workers' compensation pool set up by the insurance firm Unicover Managers Inc. also led to $72 million in expenses for Aon, as the company settled litigation related to its underwriting of those pools.

Aon managed to boost income in 2000 to $474 million, despite a stagnant property and casualty insurance market. The integration of its acquisitions continued, as the company sought efficiencies through consolidation. In November 2000, Aon announced the layoff of 3,000 employees and a comprehensive business transformation plan for its brokerage unit, Aon Risk Services. Aon expected to spend $325 million on the restructuring plan, which would reorganize the subsidiary according to industry groups.

Aon continued to shift its brokerage and consulting businesses to more prominent positions within the corporation in 2001. That year, Aon announced plans to divest its underwriting unit, splitting it off to its shareholders. The spinoff would break Aon from the underwriting foundations established by W. Clement Stone in the years after World War II. Although Aon shied away from the voracious acquisitions of the 1990s, it did purchase ASI Solutions Incorporated in 2001. The Canadian company specialized in human resources outsourcing services and would be folded into Aon Consulting Worldwide.

Principal Subsidiaries

Aon Consulting Worldwide, Inc.; Aon Re Worldwide, Inc.; Aon Risk Services Companies, Inc.; Aon Services Group, Inc.; Aon Warranty Group, Inc.; Combined Insurance Company of America; Virginia Surety Company/London General Insurance.

Principal Competitors

American International Group, Inc.; Arthur J. Gallagher & Co.; Marsh & McLennan Cos.; Willis Group Holdings Limited.

Further Reading

"Aon's Game Plan for Future," *Business Insurance,* December 18, 2000, p. 2.

"Aon to Spin Off Underwriting Biz," *Crain's Chicago Business,* April 23, 2001, p. 38.

Arndorfer, James B., "Post-Acquisition Expenses Put Brakes on Aon," *Crain's Chicago Business,* April 24, 2000, p. 9.

Fritz, Michael, "The Man Who Made Aon a Global Power," *Crain's Chicago Business,* June 2, 1997, p. 1.

Garino, David, "Clem Stone Discovers That Positive Thinking Sells Insurance Policies," *Wall Street Journal,* February 27, 1969.

"Healthy Policy: Combined Insurance Thrives at Low End of Market," *Barron's,* February 4, 1980.

Johnsson, Julie, "Acquisitions Bolstering Insurer Aon's Bottom Line," *Crain's Chicago Business,* April 26, 1999, p. 28.

Machan, Dyan, "Devouring Risk," *Forbes,* August 23, 1999, p. 106.

—Thomas M. Tucker
—update: Susan Windisch Brown

Associated British Ports Holdings Plc

150 Holborn Street
London EC1N 2LR
United Kingdom
Telephone: (+44) 20-7430-1177
Fax: (+44) 20-7430-1384
Web site: http://www.abports.co.uk

Public Company
Incorporated: 1981
Employees: 3,088
Sales: £390.6 million ($583.0 million) (2000)
Stock Exchanges: London
Ticker Symbol: ABP
NAIC: 488310 Port and Harbor Operations

Associated British Ports Holdings Plc (ABPH) is the largest operator of seaports in the United Kingdom. The company also owns docks in the United States and provides port-related services, such as stevedoring and distribution. Created from the privatization of the former British Transport Docks Board in 1983, the company's core Associated British Ports subsidiary owns 23 ports covering much of the English and Welsh coastlines, including some of the country's most important ports, such as Southampton, Swansea, Grimsby, Cardiff, and Hull. Other docks held by the company include Barry, Ayr, Barrow, Immingham, Newport, Plymouth, Colchester, Talbot, and Whitby. Altogether, ABP's ports process more than 127 million tons of cargo per year. The company's purchase of American Port Services (Amports), a British-owned but U.S.-based business, gave it seaport operations in California, Delaware, Georgia, and Florida. ABPH also runs a property investment and development arm, Grosvenor Waterside Group, which focuses on redevelopment efforts of the company's unused port-side properties. Other companies under the ABPH umbrella include Northern Cargo Services, a stevedoring company operating in the Port of Hull, which was acquired in 2000; Exxtor Shipping Services, acquired in 1998, based in Immingham; and Amports UK, formed from the 2000 acquisition of the Berkeley Group. ABPH also owns shares in joint ventures, including Southamp-

ton Container Terminals (49 percent) with P&O Ports; and Tilbury Container Services, jointly owned by ABP, P&O Ports, and Forth Ports. The company, which trades on the London Stock Exchange, is led by CEO Bo Lerenius. ABPH has been restructuring in order to focus on its core ports and port services operations. This has led to the sell-off of a number of operations in 2000 and 2001, including its Red Funnel ferry service and the aviation management division of Amports, as well as plans to sell off a large part of its £650 million property portfolio.

Privatized Port Owner in the 1980s

British history is practically synonymous with the country's many seaports. Much of the country's political and economic power was derived from its fleet of vessels and the docks that served them. By the 20th century, however, as the country's power at sea was waning, and as it faced increasing competition from the United States and continental Europe, the country's docks began to slip into difficulties.

These troubles were compounded by the German air strikes of World War II, which razed many of the country's major ports. After the war, as the country faced the need to reconstruct much of its infrastructure, the government stepped in to take charge of the United Kingdom's most vital industries. Soon after the end of the war, the government, led by the Labour Party, voted to nationalize the country's transport-related industries under the British Transport Act of 1947. This legislation created the new British Transport Commission (BTC), itself attached to the Ministry of Transport. The BTC in turn operated through six executive branches, the Docks and Inland Waterways Executive; the London Transport Executive; the Railway Executive, which took over the struggling British Railways; the Road Hauler Executive, governing long-distance road freight transport; the Road Passenger Executive; and the Hotels Executive.

By the late 1950s, it had become clear that placing control of such diverse industries and operations under a single entity had been a mistake. Many of the executives, such as the Railway Executive, were operating under losses. The government sought means of restructuring the BTC, but finally, in 1960, published a White Paper that called for the abolition of the BTC alto-

Company Perspectives:

ABP is the UK's leading ports business, providing innovative and high-quality port facilities and services to shippers and cargo owners. We work in close partnership with our customers, responding quickly to meet their requirements and offering business solutions to their demands and problems.

gether. This move was carried out in 1962, when the BTC was broken up into five new authority bodies: the British Railways Board, the British Transports Docks Board, the British Waterways Board, the London Transport Board, and the Transport Holding Company.

The newly created British Transports Docks Board quickly ran into difficulties. Longstanding resentment among the nation's dock workers boiled into a six-week strike that crippled the industry in the 1960s. Dock workers were fighting against a number of traditional practices that many considered humiliating. Workers had, in fact, no guarantee of employment and port owners chose their laborers on a casual basis, grouping workers in pens each morning to choose the workforce for the day. These and other practices finally led to the dock workers' revolt in 1967.

The result of the strike was a victory for the nation's dock workers. In 1967, the British government passed a new British Dock Labour Scheme (replacing the one that had been instituted during the nationalization drive of 1947). Casual labor was abolished, and instead port owners were bound to employ only registered dock workers. This pool of workers then shared the available work; yet, when there was not enough work to go around, workers were still paid, albeit at a lower scale. Another important feature of the scheme was the lifetime guarantee of employment given to dock workers.

The dock workers' victory placed British docks under still greater pressure in the 1970s, as more modern—and government-subsidized—ports in Europe began to take business away from the United Kingdom's ports. At the same time, the growing size of many ships forced shippers to turn to larger ports, such as Rotterdam, Hamburg, and Antwerp, which were equipped to handle the larger payloads of the new generation of ships. The improvement of roads, train networks, and increased air traffic also provided direct competition to shipping and ports alike. By the late 1970s, the British government, under Labour leadership, was forced to consider privatizing a number of the government-controlled industries. The country's docks were among the first to be eyed for privatization. This process took on still greater steam with the arrival of the Conservative government, led by Margaret Thatcher, to power.

The privatization movement caught up with the British Transport Docks Board at the beginning of the 1980s. In 1982, the board was abolished, and a new body, Associated British Ports (ABP), was prepared for privatization. The newly created ABP was given control of 19 of the country's ports, including a number of its largest ports, such as Southampton and Cardiff. ABP was then taken public the following year as Associated British Ports Holding Plc (ABPH).

Port Services Leader for the 21st Century

ABPH, led by Sir Keith Stuart as chairman, started strongly and by 1986 was able to make the first of a series of one-for-one scrip issues. In 1987, ABPH branched out, purchasing Grosvenor Square Properties Group for £17 million in stock. The new subsidiary, renamed Grosvenor Waterside Group, gave ABPH an entry into the properties market, with a particular interest in the unused properties around the ports under the company's control.

ABPH added port services in 1988 with the acquisitions of Teignmouth Quay Company, for £3.4 million, and Essex's Colchester Dock Transport Company, for £4 million. That same year, ABPH formed a joint venture with Peninsular & Oriental Steam Navigation Company (otherwise known as P&O), called Southampton Container Terminals. ABPH's part of the joint-venture was 49 percent.

Despite such success during the 1980s, the company's profits remained under heavy pressure, particularly because of the payroll guarantees of the Dock Labour Scheme. At the same time, new vehicles, machinery, and other equipment were providing the company's European continent competitors with more efficient, less labor intensive operations, which enabled these ports to undercut ABPH's prices.

ABPH finally found relief in 1989, when the Thatcher-led government at last abolished the Dock Labour Scheme. As ABPH reduced its payroll and modernized its facilities, the company's profits began to grow again. In that year, ABPH acquired new port services operations with the acquisitions of Whitby Port Services and Slaters Transport, for £2.1 million. A more important acquisition came that same year, when the company paid £26.7 million in cash and shares for the Red Funnel Group, which added that company's tugboat services and car ferry operations.

ABPH now operated ports and provided ports services and had diversified into tugboat and car ferry services, as well as into property acquisition and development. This latter division was causing the company headaches, however, as the collapse of the British building market had left it with a large and underperforming portfolio. By 1992, the company was forced to write off some £62 million against its property portfolio, leading it to a net loss for the year of £36. 6 million.

Yet ABPH was back in the black a year later. The company had been able to expand its portfolio of ports, after the 1992 Ports Privatization Act enabled it to acquire the ports in Whitby, Teignmouth, and Colchester. The company also launched a number of new investment initiatives, including a five-year, £150 million revamp of its top port, Southampton. Meanwhile, ABPH continued to boost its port services operations, acquiring a 49 percent share of Tilbury Container Services.

In the mid-1990s, ABPH continued its drive to modernize its stable of 22 ports, spending more than £76 million in 1996 alone. The company was also redeveloping its property portfolio as the U.K. building market returned to health, and in the mid-1990s announced its intention to shed most of its non-port locations. Despite the return to health of the British economy, ABPH's own profits were lagging behind. In 1997, after ap-

Key Dates:

1947: The British Transport Act nationalizes ports and places them under the newly created British Transport Commission (BTC), attached to the Ministry of Transport.

1960: The British government publishes a White Paper recommending the breakup of the BTC.

1962: The BTC is dismantled and the British Transport Docks Board is created to control the nation's ports.

1967: Dock workers' strikes and other unrest lead to the passage of the National Docks Labour Scheme, which guaranteed lifelong employment to dock workers.

1982: The British government privatizes 19 ports as British Transport Docks Board is reformed into Associated British Ports.

1983: The Associated British Ports goes public as Associated British Ports Holding Plc.

1987: The company acquires Grosvenor Square Properties Group and begins property acquisition and development activities.

1988: The company acquires Teignmouth Quay Company and Colchester Dock Transport Company, forming the Southampton Container Terminals joint venture.

1989: The Dock Labour Scheme is abolished, and the company acquires the Red Funnel Group and Whitby Port Services and Slaters Transport.

1992: The company acquires ports in Whitby, Teignmouth, and Colchester.

1997: The Ipswich Port is acquired.

1998: The company acquires Exxtor Group Shipping Services and its roll-on, roll-off terminal at Immingham, and also enters U.S. market with £108 million purchase of American Port Services, a car terminal and aviation facilities management business based in England but operating in the United States.

1999: The company is forced to write down the value of Amports by £80 million as a result of a General Motors strike and other difficulties.

2000: ABPH sells Red Funnel for £71 million as part of a company refocus on core ports and ports services businesses.

2001: ABPH announces its intention to sell off Amports aviation operations.

pointing a new managing director, Andrew Smith, the company called in outside consultants for a strategic review. The result was a new strategy, based on organic growth, international acquisitions, and expansion of its services to existing customers, including the possibility of entering the distribution market.

Part of the company's expansion came in 1997, with the £12 million purchase of Ipswich Port. The following year, ABPH grew further, extending its services wing with the acquisition of Exxtor Group Shipping Services, for £15.6 million, adding that company's roll-on, roll-off terminal at Immingham Port. This purchase fit in with the company-announced intention to ac-

quire still more of the terminals, owned by shipping and other companies, operating at its ports.

In 1998, also, ABPH made a still more ambitious acquisition, paying more than £108 million to acquire American Port Services (Amports). That British company, which had been formed in 1988 to operate car terminals at the port of Benicia, California, had gone public with a listing on the London exchange in 1995, before adding new port terminals in Delaware, Georgia, and Florida. Amports then branched out into aviation facilities management, acquiring management contracts for a number of small airports in Teterboro, New Jersey; Gulfport, Mississippi; Farmingdale, New York; and a heliport in New York City.

The Amports purchase quickly turned sour. A strike at General Motors caused a huge drop in business, which was further hit by declining revenues from the hard-pressed Asian markets; before long, it had become apparent that ABPH had grossly overpaid for the acquisition. The misstep forced the resignation of Managing Director Smith in February. Keith Stuart too was to pay a price for the difficulties surrounding the Amports, which cost the company to write down the value of its U.S. subsidiary by some £80 million in 1999. The longtime chairman and guiding force of the company announced his intention to retire to the position of non-executive chairman in 2000. Instead of a direct replacement for either Smith or Stuart, the company opted instead to create the position of chief executive officer for Bo Lerenius.

Lerenius worked to streamline the company, returning its focus back to its core ports and port services operations. In 2000, the company announced the sale of its Red Funnel subsidiary to JP Morgan International Capital Corporation for £71 million. The company also announced its intention to sell off still more of its property portfolio. At the same time, ABPH moved to boost its port and cargo services holdings, buying Northern Cargo Services for £1.6 million and the Berkeley Group for £9.5 million. The latter company was then renamed Amports UK.

After fighting off a takeover attempt by Japanese group Nomura, which offered more than £1 billion for ABPH, the company continued its streamlining operation in 2001. In September of that year, the company announced its intention to sell off the aviation division of its still struggling U.S. subsidiary. This move prompted speculation that the company might sell off the rest of Amports and exit the United States altogether. The United Kingdom appeared a better target for ABPH's growth, although the company ran into a hurdle when its plans to expand the Southampton port ran into opposition from environmentalists at the end of 2001. Meanwhile, ABPH's revenues and profits were on the rise, topping £390 million and £135 million, respectively, in 2000. As the U.K. ports industry seemed to be preparing to enter a round of consolidation, ABPH, which continued to control more than 25 percent of the U.K.'s port activity, seemed likely to remain dominant in that market for the new century.

Principal Subsidiaries

ABP Research & Consultancy Limited; American Port Services PLC; American Port Services Inc. (USA); AMPORTS Cargo

Services Limited; AMPORTS Vehicle Terminals Limited; Associated British Ports; Exxtor Shipping Services Limited; Grosvenor Waterside Group PLC; Grosvenor Waterside (Holdings) Limited; Grosvenor Waterside Developments Limited; Grosvenor Waterside Investments Limited; Ipswich Port Limited; Northern Cargo Services Limited; Slaters Transport Limited; Southampton Container Terminals Limited (49%); Southampton Free Trade Zone Limited; The Cardiff Bay Partnership (45%); Teignmouth Quay Company Limited; Tilbury Container Services Limited (33%); Whitby Port Services Limited.

Principal Competitors

Forth Ports Plc; Hutchison Whampoa Limited; The Mersey Docks and Harbour Company; Powell Duffryn plc; Peninsular & Oriental Steam Navigation Company Plc; Stevedoring Services of America Inc.

Further Reading

"ABP Puts Ferries up for Sale at 80m," *Evening Standard*, June 14, 2000, p. 42

Carrell, Severin, "Objectors Set to Sink Super-Port," *Independent on Sunday*, November 25, 2001, p. 3.

Kar-Gupta, Sudip, "ABP Sees New Deals Boosting Future Growth," *Reuters*, February 22, 2000.

——, "AB Ports Takes Pounds 80m Hit from American Car Terminal Venture," *Daily Telegraph*, February 23, 2000.

Osborne, Alistair, "ABP Stung on Overseas Foray," *Daily Telegraph*, February 24, 1999, p. 1.

Shah, Saeed, "AB Ports to Sell Its U.S. Aviation Business," *Independent*, September 5, 2001, p. 21.

"Terrible Whiff on the Dockside," *Daily Telegraph*, February 23, 2000, p. 37.

—M.L. Cohen

Back Yard Burgers, Inc.

1657 N. Shelby Oaks Drive, Suite 105
Memphis, Tennessee 38134-7401
U.S.A.
Telephone: (901) 367-0888
Fax: (901) 367-0999
Web site: http://www.backyardburgers.com

Public Company
Incorporated: 1987
Employees: 1,000
Sales: $29.3 million (2000)
Stock Exchanges: NASDAQ
Ticker Symbol: BYBI
NAIC: 522110 Lessors of Nonfinancial Intangible Assets
(Except Copyrighted Works); 722211 Limited Service
Restaurants

Back Yard Burgers, Inc. offers a gourmet alternative to the traditional fast-food hamburger: a charbroiled, 100 percent Black Angus Beef burger dressed with fresh red onions, tomatoes, and green leaf lettuce. The company owns and franchises nearly 100 "fast-casual" restaurants in 17 states, primarily in the mid-south. In addition to a variety of burgers, the menu includes grilled chicken sandwiches; seasoned or waffle fries; milkshakes made from hand-dipped, premium ice cream; fresh-squeezed lemonade; and fresh-baked cobbler.

Out of Boredom, Back Yard Burgers in 1987

Lattimore "Lattie" Michael opened the first Back Yard Burgers drive-thru restaurant in 1987. Michael owned and managed the grocery store started by his father in Rosedale, Mississippi, but he wanted to start a business himself. He opened a discotheque in Jackson in 1979, but the Pearl River flood damaged the club and, after renovation, the melancholy mood of the town hampered business. He recovered from his losses and began to look for a new challenge. After reading an article about double drive-thru restaurants, Michael thought to open one himself. He considered a variety of foods—chicken, pizza, barbeque—and decided on hamburgers. To compete with the national fast-food hamburger chains, he decided to offer something different, a premium quality hamburger like those he made in his own backyard.

With a $124,000 bank loan and an investment from his two brothers, Michael opened the first Back Yard Burgers store in Cleveland, Mississippi, in March 1987. The small size of the store, at 525 square feet, on leased land allowed for a low start-up cost. For $1.69 Back Yard Burgers offered charbroiled, all beef hamburgers with fresh slices of red onion and tomato, pickles, green leaf lettuce, mustard, ketchup, and mayonnaise. With service at two drive-thru windows, the gourmet burger place filled an order in less than a minute, and each unit served 120 to 140 cars per hour, potentially generating up to $600 in sales per hour at peak business times. Although the store did not have indoor seating, Michael placed picnic tables outside, keeping with the backyard concept.

Within a few months Michael received inquiries about franchise opportunities. He had already considered the possibility that he might open another three or four stores if the first succeeded, so he had been careful in plotting the methods and procedures used at the original store. A year after Back Yard Burgers opened, a franchise store opened in Greenville, Mississippi. Soon more franchises opened, including two units in the Memphis area, three in Florida, and another in Mississippi. By the end of 1988, the company owned one unit and franchised 11 units; these garnered revenues and royalties of $561,000 that year. Back Yard Burgers' success attracted several private investors and, in January 1990, the company relocated to Memphis where it planned to develop into a major market area.

Franchisees found Back Yard Burgers an attractive investment, not only as a gourmet alternative niche, but also for its low cost. A franchise on leased land with a prefabricated building cost $260,000 to $400,000 to open compared with $1 million for national chain franchises. Costs included approximately $200,000 for the building and equipment, $35,000 for signs and canopies, a $16,000 franchise fee, which included four weeks of training for three managers, plus funds for site work and working capital. Franchisees paid a 1 percent advertising fee and 4 percent royalties to Back Yard Burgers. For each additional unit opened, a franchisee paid the company a $5,000 fee.

In 1990 Back Yard Burgers units opened in Tennessee, Alabama, Arkansas, Kansas, Texas, Georgia, Florida, Mississippi, and California. The San Diego store came into being after a Louisiana man stopped at the Greenville store. He was so impressed he called a friend in California to tell him about Back Yard Burgers. In addition to new franchises in North Carolina, Ohio, Missouri, Nevada, and South Carolina, several more stores opened in Tennessee and Arkansas.

Seeking to Build Critical Mass in Major Markets Following 1993 IPO

Back Yard Burgers prepared to take the company public in mid-1993. The company merged with Double S Development, the largest franchisee with five units, and American Back Yard Burgers, the Arkansas franchisee. With the merger the company owned and operated eight units, while franchisees operated 37 units, for a total of 45 stores in 13 states. The merger was designed to show higher operating income to potential investors by adding store revenues to income from royalties. The franchise fee increased to $25,000. To enhance the company's clout among investors, Back Yard Burgers hired veterans of the fast-food industry for executive positions: John Arnold from Wendy's for vice-president of franchise services; H. Ray Jones from Pizza Hut for vice-president of training; and Stephen Reid from Burger King for vice-president of research and development. Michael sold his supermarket to concentrate on his duties as chairman of the board and CEO of the company.

The initial stock offering took place in July. The company netted $9 million from a sale of 1.5 million shares at $6 per share. Back Yard Burgers applied the funds to pay $400,000 in debt, buy back the territory rights for Atlanta, fund a television advertising campaign, and open 14 company-owned restaurants in Memphis, Nashville, and central Arkansas. The company held commitments for 16 franchises as well.

With a critical mass of Back Yard Burgers stores in some markets, Back Yard Burgers began to advertise on television in the fall of 1993. Early commercials, titled "The Great Burger Wars," satirized the national competitors. In June, the company launched a series of commercials featuring Dennis R. Phillippi, a popular comedian in Memphis. In addition to regular performances at The Comedy Zone, Phillippi appeared on a children's television show and wrote a regular column for a local magazine.

As spokesperson for Back Yard Burgers, Phillippi brought his ability to develop a rapport with the public. Known as Dennis the Back Yard Burgers Guy, Phillippi obnoxiously asked questions of competitors' customers, then went on talking before they responded. The commercials advertised the company's burgers as bigger, at one-third pound compared with the one-quarter pound burgers at national fast-food chains. In addition, the angled grill made a healthier, tastier burger, as the fat rolled away from the patty during cooking. The commercials succeeded in increasing sales 10 to 15 percent over the previous year.

In September another commercial promoted the company's new bacon-cheddar and bacon-Swiss burgers. In these spots Phillippi encouraged patrons to attempt the tongue twister, "Back Yard Burgers' bigger, better, bacon burger." Phillippi introduced the new honey-mustard chicken sandwich in November. Franchisees in small markets used audio from the television commercials for less expensive radio advertising. Direct-mail advertising supplemented the television and radio commercials.

By the end of 1994, Back Yard Burgers owned and operated 26 units, while franchisees operated 39 units. The total of 65 units accounted for 12 store closures and 16 new store openings, and one store converted from a franchise to company owned. Sales from royalties and company-owned stores rose from $6 million in 1993 to $17.2 million in 1994. Same-store sales increased 6.4 percent on the strength of its television advertising. Net profit increased also, from $22,000 in 1993 to $682,000 in 1994. The company ended the year with commitments for seven single franchise units to open early the following year.

In 1995, Back Yard Burgers experienced a decrease in sales related to a lack of sustained interest on the part of its customers. Although sales from company-owned stores increased 35.8 percent to $21.2 million, with 14 new units opened in late 1994 and in 1995, same-store sales, from stores open more than one year, declined by 10.9 percent. The company attributed the decline to competitive discounting and promotions by the national chains as well as to a lack of indoor seating. Profits also declined as the costs of labor and of the company's own promotions increased. Back Yard Burgers changed its accounting system to better reflect the true valuation of impaired assets, resulting in a $2.56 million non-cash charge in 1995. Overall revenues of $22.7 million in 1995 garnered a net loss of $3 million.

The company addressed the concern with indoor seating as customers had often expressed a desire for a dine-in option. A store in Boone, North Carolina, added indoor seating in 1994, resulting in a 165 percent increase in sales. Research found that the public associated the double drive-thru restaurant with cheaper priced food. In converting double drive-thru units to a single drive-thru restaurant with indoor seating, the company created a new market niche between traditional fast food and casual dining, called fast-casual. The conversion to indoor dining cost $250,000 to $450,000 per unit, but most of these units experienced more than a 30 percent increase in revenues. By the end of 1996, 12 of 34 company-owned units and 25 of 47 franchise units had indoor seating.

Back Yard Burgers rebounded slightly in 1996 as the company increased menu prices 3.5 percent at the beginning of July, generating $22.3 million in sales from company-owned units

Key Dates:

1987: First Back Yard Burgers opens in Cleveland, Mississippi.
1988: First franchise opens in Greenville, Mississippi.
1993: Initial public offering funds expansion, television advertising.
1995: The company begins to add indoor seating at restaurants to improve revenues.
1999: After a period of stabilization, the company renews growth strategy.
2000: Back Yard Burgers introduces 100 percent Black Angus Beef burgers.

and $1 million in royalty fees. While same-store sales at company stores continued to stagnate, franchisees experienced a 3.7 percent increase. At the end of 1996, Back Yard Burgers counted 34 company-owned units, including ten in the Memphis area and 11 throughout Tennessee, and 11 in Arkansas, including five in Little Rock. Of 47 franchises, seven were located in both Tennessee and North Carolina, five each in Arkansas and Mississippi, and four each in Ohio and Florida. Other stores were located in Kansas, Alabama, Oklahoma, Nebraska, Kentucky, and South Carolina. In 1996 Back Yard Burgers recorded $24 million in revenues, including franchise fees for 11 new units, and $357,000 in net income.

Slowing Growth to Refocus for Late 1990s Expansion

Back Yard Burgers decided to slow development of new franchises and company stores to focus on improving operations and sales. The company increased its menu prices twice in 1997, by 4 percent in May and 3 percent in September. In January 1998 a new series of radio commercials featured the voice of John Hurley, who played J. Peterman on the popular television sitcom "Seinfeld." By November Back Yard Burgers had converted two-thirds of the company-owned and franchised stores. With 2,700 square feet of space, each dining room seated 84 people. In 1998 same-store sales increased 7 percent and 6.5 percent for company-owned units and franchises, respectively. The increases were attributed to the September price increase, the availability of indoor seating, and improvements in customer service. Increased sales at franchise units boosted royalty payments 11.5 percent to $1.3 million. Back Yard Burgers recorded systemwide operating revenues of $59.6 million, $25.1 million from 33 company-owned stores and $34.5 million from 48 franchises. Overall company revenues of $27.4 million garnered net income of $1.2 million.

By 1999 the company reinvigorated plans for franchise development agreements throughout the mid-south. In August the company signed an agreement to add five stores in the Kansas City area, in both Missouri and Kansas, where 13 units already existed. Another agreement committed to the addition of seven units in Louisville, Kentucky. New stores also were planned for markets in Texas, North Carolina, and Oklahoma.

To bring a new perspective into the business, the company hired Michael W. Myers as chief operating officer. Myers brought 14 years' experience with Whataburger, Inc., where he held the position of regional vice-president when he left for Back Yard Burgers. Myers initiated several new programs to improve operations, including implementation of incentive programs for unit managers. He eliminated coupons and discounting programs, a marketing approach that he viewed as sending a mixed message, given that the company was offering a premium product. The company also hired consultants to evaluate operations and facilities, including building design, signage, and site plans, to streamline the restaurant for a new prototype. In May 2000 Back Yard Burgers purchased franchise properties in Jackson, Tennessee; Tupelo, Mississippi; and Jonesboro, Arkansas—high-volume units that fit into the company's strategy to build critical mass for media advertising in the Memphis vicinity.

The most significant change Myers made sought to improve the Back Yard Burgers concept as an alternative, gourmet burger outlet through the introduction of a burger made with Black Angus Beef, the best quality beef available. After six months of testing 100 percent Black Angus Beef burgers in Memphis, the company instituted use of the branded beef at all company-owned stores in late 2000. The company rolled out Black Angus Beef at all franchises in early 2001.

Reestablishing Back Yard Burgers as a premium product resulted in a slight decline in sales during 2000. Michael and Myers attributed the decline to the loss of part of the customer base when the company cut its discount programs; the change, however, was intended to improve overall profitability and long-term growth. Company-owned stores generated $26.18 million in 2000 with 35 stores, down from $26.5 million in 1999. Same-store sales declined 5.6 percent at company-owned stores and 5 percent at franchises. Franchises paid $1.7 million in royalty fees on $42.3 million in revenues with ten new units opened in 2000. The company rebounded from a loss of $558,000 in 1999, due to an impairment charge of $1.4 million, to a net income of $466,000 on $29.3 million total revenue in 2000.

Back Yard Burgers continued with its growth strategy in 2001. The company logo was redesigned and a web site was launched that year. Back Yard Burgers opened small-sized outlets through co-branding with the convenience stores at gasoline filling stations. The fifth such unit opened in October 2001, with Back Yard Burgers being approached by the convenience stores in each instance.

Principal Competitors

Burger King Corporation; McDonald's Corporation; Wendy's International, Inc.

Further Reading

Allen, Robin Lee, "Back Yard Burgers Spots Use Comic As Front Man," *Nation's Restaurant News,* November 23, 1994, p. 12.
"Back Yard Burgers Ads Get a Helping of 'Seinfeld,'" *Memphis Business Journal,* January 12, 1998, p. 16.
"Back Yard Burgers Cooking Up 22 Franchises in Memphis in Next Three Years," *Memphis Business Journal,* July 29, 1988, p. 14.
"Back Yard Burgers Names COO Michael Myers President," *Memphis Business Journal,* April 6, 2001, p. 21.

''Back Yard Burgers Posts $2.95M Loss in FY 1995,'' *Nation's Restaurant News,* April 1, 1996, p. 12.

''Back Yard Burgers Profits Hit $682,000,'' *Nation's Restaurant News,* March 27, 1995, p. 14.

''Back Yard Burgers to Fuel Expansion with IPO Cash,'' *Nation's Restaurant News,* October 18, 1993, p. 13.

''Back Yard Burgers to Take Burger Battle to Air Waves,'' *Commercial Appeal,* May 18, 1994, p. B4.

Haman, John, ''Back Yard Burgers Soars in Central Arkansas,'' *Arkansas Business,* May 4, 1998, p. 23.

Hansen, Bruce, ''Businessman Bounces Back from Bankruptcy to Found Back Yard Burgers Empire,'' *Memphis Business Journal,* September 26, 1994, p. 46.

Lacy, Sarah, ''Back Yard Burgers Opens Seven New Stores in Expansion Blitz,'' *Memphis Business Journal,* August 20, 1999, p. 9.

Mason, Sonya, ''Low-Cost Concept Booming,'' *Mississippi Business Journal,* November 19, 1990, p. 10.

Milligan, Tara, ''Fast Food Joints, Gas Stations: Profitable Partnership,'' *Memphis Business Journal,* October 12, 2001, p. 3.

——, '' 'If You Serve a Better Product, You'll Come Out Ahead,' '' *Memphis Business Journal,* June 22, 2001, p. 13.

——, ''Myers' Changes Have Back Yard Burgers on More Stable Ground,'' *Memphis Business Journal,* September 28, 2001, p. 35.

——, ''Soft Economy Spurs Franchising Popularity Among Entrepreneurs,'' *Memphis Business Journal,* April 13, 2001, p. 1.

''New Burger Cooking in Charlotte,'' *Business Journal Serving Charlotte and the Metropolitan Area,* August 27, 1990, p. 14.

''New Outlet of Burgers Is Different,'' *Commercial Appeal,* December 3, 1989, p. C1.

Rengers, Carrie, ''Back Yard Business,'' *Arkansas Business,* May 24, 1993, p. 22.

Romine, Linda, ''Back Yard Offering Alternative to Fast-Food Burgers,'' *Memphis Business Journal,* July 1, 1991, p. 24.

Smyth, Whit, ''Back Yard Burgers Makes Future Bet on Dine-In,'' *Nation's Restaurant News,* November 16, 1998, p. 124.

—Mary Tradii

Bellway Plc

Seaton Burn House
Dudley Lane, Seaton Burn
Newcastle upon Tyne NE13 6BE
United Kingdom
Telephone: (+44) 191-217-0717
Fax: (+44) 191-236-6230
Web site: http://www.bellway.co.uk

Public Company
Incorporated: 1946 as John T. Bell & Sons
Employees: 1,806
Sales: £695.7 million ($1.1 billion) (2001)
Stock Exchanges: London
Ticker Symbol: BWY
NAIC: 233210 Single Family Housing Construction;
    233220 Multifamily Housing Construction

Bellway Plc is one of the top five home builders in the United Kingdom, selling more than 5,700 homes per year. The company, based in Newcastle, England, operates through a decentralized structure. Corporate headquarters provides financial and land management services, communications coordination, and management placement to a network of 14 more or less autonomous regional divisions. Each division is responsible for making its own decisions in such areas as housing types and design, materials and purchasing, construction methods, pricing, and sales, enabling divisions to tailor their business to the requirements of each local market. The approach, which backs Bellway's slogan as ''the local, national housebuilder,'' has enabled the company to post consistent turnover and profit increases. In 2001, the company's sales neared £700 million, while profits passed the £100 million mark. Bellway constructs exclusively for the residential market, with offerings ranging from apartments to high-end single-family homes and prices ranging from under £30,000 to more than £500,000. The company's average home selling price topped £119,000 in 2001. Bellway has been particularly active in exploiting British government legislation calling for so-called ''brownfield'' development—that is, building on derelict land plots in urban markets.

The company has consistently beat government-imposed quotas for brownfield development. In 2001, the company matched the 60 percent quota that builders are expected to meet before the year 2008. In all, Bellway owns or controls more than 16,700 land plots that have already received residential planning permission, and an equivalent number of land plots awaiting residential planning approval. The company is led by Chairman Howard Dawe and CEO John K. Watson, and is traded on the London Stock Exchange's 250 Index.

Postwar Construction Boom

The bombing of Britain during World War II reduced significant areas of the British residential housing to rubble. The postwar years presented new challenges and new opportunities for the country's construction industry. Much of the country's residential construction market had been placed under strict controls, and public sector building by the country's Housing Authority had grown to dominate residential housing to such an extent that private sector activity had been brought to a near standstill.

Building material shortages following the war and the slow progress of public sector reconstruction produced growing pressure for more private sector construction. A number of companies stepped in to fill the gap in new housing construction. One of these was the small family-owned firm led by John T. Bell, who was born in 1878. The company he began had long served its Newcastle-upon-Tyne community by the time that his sons, John and Russell, were decommissioned from the British Army in 1946. The younger Bells joined their father's business, which was then incorporated as John T. Bell & Sons.

The Bells rapidly sought to distinguish themselves from prevailing housing trends. The British residential landscape had long been marked by rather dreary designs, with housing laid out in straight lines, no front yards, and little landscaping in general. Residential communities rarely featured playgrounds, while few houses were large enough to include a garage. The Bell company brought its own designs to the market and began building a reputation for affordably priced housing. At the same time, the company launched a strong commercial development business as well.

During the 1950s, the Bell company began expanding throughout its northeastern England territory, offering a variety of home designs and layouts and other features. The company was joined by youngest Bell brother Kenneth Bell, who was later to lead the company as chairman for nearly 20 years.

In the 1960s, the Bell company spread to include much of the northern region of England. The company also entered Scotland during this decade. Supporting the company's growth was its decision to go public in 1963. John T. Bell died two years later. The economic boom years of the 1960s provided new demand for private housing, and the Bell company responded with a wide variety of home designs and an increasing number of features and options.

The decade saw dramatic changes in the construction industry itself, as new machinery and equipment and new building materials allowed houses to be built more quickly. Meanwhile, Bell maintained its commitment to innovative features, offering customers options such as central heating, insulation, and fully equipped kitchens, complete with washing machines.

Bell's housing activity increased rapidly during the 1960s, by the end of which the company boasted its participation in the building of Cramlington, in Northumberland, the first British town ever to be constructed by private companies. At the beginning of the 1970s, Bell began to eye its development as a nationally operating company, setting up its South East Division. The company's expansion plans were cut short, however, with the oil crisis of 1974, and the resulting recession that depressed the building market for much of the rest of the decade. Part of Bell's ability to survive the economic difficulties of the time was its policy of keeping all relevant operations in-house. This meant that the company controlled each step of the construction of a new house, acting as architect, engineer, estate planner, layout designer, and even landscaper.

National Expansion in the 1980s

Bell nonetheless managed continued growth for its residential housing business during this period, due to its careful financial policies and its continued focus on local markets. The company also continued to roll out new home features that attracted new home buyers. Such additions as central gas heating, improved insulation, heated bathrooms, and additional toilets became standard Bell home features. The company also began breaking away from the typical row house design to begin developing houses, which by then usually featured larger gardens and garages, around cul-de-sacs.

By the end of the decade, the company's private homes business had grown to represent a strong percentage of the company's overall operations. In 1979, the residential homes business was split off from the parent company's commercial properties wing, and renamed as Bellway. In 1981, the newly independent house building company went public, as Bellway Ltd.

Over the next decade, Bellway expanded throughout the United Kingdom, becoming a nationally operating home builder. Corporate headquarters remained in Newcastle; yet instead of centralizing all of the company's operations at its headquarters, Bellway, now led by Kenneth Bell, preferred a decentralized approach that allowed its regional divisions a great deal of autonomy in order to respond more appropriately to their local markets.

Bellway received a boost during the 1980s with the deregulation of the British banking industry. Home loans now became much easier to achieve, and a whole new class of buyer turned to Bellway for its homes. The company name became an important brand among new home purchasers during the decade. The Bellway brand was aided by the company's success at gaining industry approval, including winning a number of "What House? Best Innovation" awards.

By the end of the 1980s, Bellway was selling some 1,700 homes per year. The crash of the British housing market, and the international recession that followed, put a crimp in the company's growth, however. The building crisis was to last well into the 1990s, shaking up the British construction industry. Nonetheless, Bellway was able to continue to post sales gains, raising the number of homes sold per year to more than 2,000 by 1993, while clinging to profitability. The company, however, was forced to reduce its level of property acquisitions, as land prices began once again to climb.

Top Five Home Builder for the 21st Century

The British housing market emerged from its slump toward the middle of the 1990s. By then Bellway had held on to become one of the country's largest-volume home builders, planning to raise its sales to more than 4,000 homes per year by mid-decade. Aiding the construction market in general was new British legislation governing the implementation of so-called "brownfield" sites. Conceived as an urban renewal initiative, the new legislation, which also served to protect against overdevelopment of the British countryside, called for home builders to devote a percentage of their activities to the development of derelict urban sites. Initially set at 50 percent, and then raised to 60 percent of new homes by 2008, the initiative encouraged home construction companies to return to the United Kingdom's cities.

Bellway became an active proponent of the brownfield initiative, buying up a number of urban properties, launching a number of new divisions focused on urban development projects, and outpacing the government's own timetable—in 1997, Bellway had already matched the initial 50 percent mark, and by the end of the decade had surpassed the 60 percent level as well. Examples of the company's brownfield projects included the conversion of a shuttered hospital complex into apartment units, and the building of a 5,000-home community on a 500-acre site in London. The latter project was also part of a change in the company's strategy, adopted in 1994, to focus its expansion efforts on the London and southeast market.

Key Dates:

1946: John T. Bell is joined by sons John and Russell to form the John T. Bell & Sons home building company in Newcastle.

1950s: Kenneth Bell joins the company; Bell begins expansion beyond Newcastle.

1960s: The company begins to expand throughout northern and northeastern regions of England and into Scotland.

1963: The company goes public on London stock exchange.

1970s: The company launches its southeast division to enter London and outlying regions.

1979: John T. Bell spins off its home building business as Bellway, with Kenneth Bell as chairman.

1980s: Bellway expands throughout United Kingdom, establishing autonomously operating regional divisions.

1981: Bellway Plc takes listing on London stock exchange.

1993: The company's home sales top 2,000.

1994: British government launches ''brownfield'' initiatives; Bellway adopts new strategy to focus on London and southeastern region.

1997: Kenneth Bell dies and is replaced by Howard Dawe as chairman; company sells more than 5,000 homes.

2001: Company's average per-home sales price reaches £119,000.

Kenneth Bell died in 1997 and was replaced by managing director Howard Dawe as acting chairman (Dawe was formally appointed chairman in 1999). By then, the company—along with the U.K. building sector—was back on track, posting revenue topping £398 million and unit sales reaching more than 5,000 homes in 1997. The company's profits were also strong, at £50 million on the year. The company was also benefiting from price increases, particularly in the booming southern region around London, helping the company's average total per-unit sale price to reach £77,200. Yet the company was reaping the rewards of its earlier decision to focus on the London and southern markets, where average home prices topped £93,000, compared to an average £64,000 in the north.

At the end of the 1990s, as the national housing market fully recovered, Bellway began to target especially high-end locations, enabling it to push its turnover and profits still higher. Difficulties in obtaining planning permission, as new home construction was subjected to stricter rules, made it more complicated for the company to achieve its expansion objectives, yet by 1999 the company had topped the 5,000-homes-per-year mark. In 2000, that figure had passed 5,700 homes, while for the first time, the company's average home selling price reached more than £100,000. At the same time, Bellway had been steadily increasing its land bank, with more than 15,000 properties already granted building permission, and an equal number of properties in the pipeline.

The year 2000 saw the beginning of a consolidation drive among the United Kingdom's home building industry. A number of the company's competitors were entering into a round of mergers and takeovers. Yet Bellway remained out of this competition, setting its sights on building up its own market share instead. As Alan Robson, the company's finance director, explained to the *Financial Times:* ''We have been focusing on organic growth, but the recent consolidation has created opportunities for us to acquire land and staff, as companies reorganize themselves.''

Poor weather and planning delays hampered Bellway's growth in 2001, however, and at 5,725 homes sold the company just barely topped its unit sales of the previous year. Yet the company's focus on higher-end properties, as well as its national position, enabled it to post a strong increase in per-unit sales, which topped an average of £119,000 in that year. Meanwhile, Bellway reported its sixth consecutive profit increase, and at the end of fiscal 2001, Bellway revealed profits topping £100 million for the first time in its history. With a land bank featuring nearly 17,000 plots with planning permission, and an equal number of plots awaiting permission—nearly a third of which were expected to receive planning permission in the coming fiscal year—Bellway seemed certain to remain one of the United Kingdom's top volume home builders.

Principal Subsidiaries

Bellway Homes Limited; Bellway Properties Limited; Bellway (Services) Limited; Bulldog Premium Growth I Limited; Bulldog Premium Growth II Limited; Litrose Investments Limited; The Victoria Dock Company Limited (60%).

Principal Competitors

Barratt Developments plc; George Wimpey PLC; Taylor Woodrow plc; Wilson Bowden plc.

Further Reading

Ahmad, Sameena, ''Bellway Builds on Housing Recovery,'' *Independent*, October 29, 1997, p. 24.

Gimbel, Florian, ''Bellway Sees Rise As House Prices Increase,'' *Financial Times*, August 11, 2001.

Griffin, Jon, ''Bellway Homes in on a Record,'' *Evening Mail*, April 4, 2001, p. 21.

O'Connor, Brian, ''Bellway's Broader Base Brings in 100 Mil,'' *Daily Mail*, October 17, 2001, p. 65.

—M.L. Cohen

Big Dog Holdings, Inc.

121 Gray Avenue
Santa Barbara, California 93101
U.S.A.
Telephone: (805) 963-8727
Fax: (805) 962-9460
Web site: http://www.bigdogs.com

Public Company
Incorporated: 1992
Employees: 1,300
Sales: $115.2 million (2000)
Stock Exchanges: NASDAQ
Ticker Symbol: BDOG
NAIC: 44814 Family Clothing Store

Big Dog Holdings, Inc. is one of the fastest growing retailers in the United States. The company manufactures and sells sportswear accessories and licenses its name and logo to other products such as backpacks and hot sauces. All Big Dog products feature one of three distinct trademarks: ''Big Dogs,'' ''Big Dog Sportswear,'' or ''Logo Dog.'' The Big Dog logo—an oversized, panting Saint Bernard, projects the image of ''leader of the pack.'' The company is known for its catchy slogans, such as ''If you can't run with the big dogs, stay on the porch.'' Most of the company's sales stem from its oversized, brightly colored sportswear, which presents an image of ''quality, fun, and a sense of humor.'' Big Dog clothing appeals to people of all ages and demographics, but its sportswear is particularly appealing to baby boomers and their children, pet lovers, and people who love the outdoors.

Big Dog markets its products through retail, wholesale, Internet, and mail-order channels, but the bulk of its sales are from its retail stores. Big Dog owns 200 stores across the United States and one in Puerto Rico, and the company's retail sales account for more than 90 percent of total revenues. The company also has a line of children's apparel stores called Little Big Dogs and markets a line of Big Big Dogs sportswear, designed for big and tall customers. Its wholesale division sells Big Dog sportswear to specialty stores and upper-scale department stores

such as Dillard's and Nordstrom. The company has a Big Dog Club with more than 30,000 members and operates the Big Dog Foundation, which donates funds to charities. Big Dog had sales of more than $115 million in 2000.

''Big Puppies'' in 1983

The concept for Big Dog Holdings, Inc. was conceived on a rafting expedition in 1983. Before venturing out onto the water, a group of river-rafters was given a pair of oversized, brightly colored shorts. The gang loved the shorts, and one enthusiastic river-rafter replied, ''Man, these puppies are BIG!'' The phrase ''big dogs'' caught on and became the inspiration for Big Dog sportswear, which became known among river-rafters and beach-goers as ''big puppies.'' The company first operated under the name Sierra West Manufacturing and was a wholesale sportswear dealer that sold its products to retail stores. It had only ''limited sales'' until it was acquired by its present management in 1992. The company considered 1992 the year that Big Dog Holdings, Inc. was founded.

Expansion in the 1990s

Big Dog's new owners included fashion-industry veteran Andrew D. Feshbach. Feshbach served as the chief executive officer, president, and director of Big Dog. He also served as the chief financial officer of the company from 1992 until 1997.

Feshbach assembled an aggressive management team that focused on rolling out Big Dog stores nationwide. The new management team also expanded the company's product line to include shorts, casual shirts, fleece tops and bottoms, loungewear, boxer shorts, swimwear, and sleepwear.

The company grew quickly. When Big Dog was acquired in 1992, it had only five stores. By 1997, it had 134 stores from Hawaii to Maine. Sales likewise improved. Sales in 1992 were about $11.4 million. By 1997, they had risen to $68.7 million. In 1997, Big Dog launched an initial public offering to pay off debt and raise money for further expansion.

Under Feshbach's guidance, the company was split into several divisions. Its retail division was the fastest growing and most successful. Big Dog had an advantage over many other sportswear retailers in that its clothes were not seasonal and dependent on the fashions and colors of a particular season. Most Big Dog fashions could be marketed year-round.

The company set ambitious goals to open new Big Dog stores each month. The stores were decorated with amusing local themes. Big Dog advertising showed celebrities such as actor Arnold Schwarzenegger and NFL player Reggie White wearing Big Dog sportswear.

The company opened Little Big Dogs stores at some locations as well. Little Big Dogs stores sold infants and children's sportswear and were adjacent to Big Dog stores. The company also sold a popular line of clothing called Big Big Dogs to fit large and tall customers.

The company's mail-order division distributed high-quality color catalogs designed with jaunty graphics. The company mailed out millions of catalogs each year. Big Dog also introduced its *Magalog*, a catalog that combined fun photos and stories from its *Spots Illustrated* newsletter.

Big Dog's wholesale division was its original division. The company sold its products to specialty shops and department stores such as Dillard's, Casual Male, Nordstrom, Belk Stores, Phoenix Big and Tall, the Brass Buckle, F.A.O. Schwarz, and Parisiah.

In addition to its traditional wholesale division, the company marketed its products through a corporate, wholesale division. Its corporate division sold Big Dog products to companies to give to their employees as gifts and incentives. Big Dog also made special-order shirts for companies with their logo on them. Big Dog also sold other products in its corporate division, such as coffee mugs, pens, and mouse pads.

In addition, the company marketed its products through its Internet division, BIGDOGS.com. Customers could order Big Dog products through the web site and also learn about the company. The company used the slogan "Surf with the Big Dogs" to market its online store.

Feshbach and his associates also formed the Big Dog Club, which had more than 30,000 members in 2001. The club was for people "who enjoy pets, leisure, sports and, of course, Big Dogs." Members received a special ID card, a newsletter, and enjoyed special discounts on Big Dog products.

Big Dog formed the Big Dog Foundation to raise money for charities such as the SPCA, Special Olympics, and DAWG (Dog Adoption and Welfare). The company held an annual parade to raise money for the Big Dog Foundation.

Brand Licensing and Leveraging in 1999

In 1999 the company began licensing its name and imaging to products other than clothing. Big Dog formed partnerships with other companies to use its name and logos on plush backpacks, hot sauces, and toys. Under the terms of its licensing agreements, Big Dog marketed the products along with the other company in the agreement. The products were sold in Big Dog stores. Some of the companies with which Big Dog entered into licensing agreements were Nabisco, Kellogg's, Hill's, Science Diet, MGM/VA, Coca-Cola, Andersen Consulting, Dollywood, Busch Gardens, Yamaha Motor Corporation, Toyota, and AT&T. Big Dog believed that licensing agreements were an economical, safe way to expand its business. According to Feshbach, they allowed the company to "leverage its brand further without adding significantly to its expenses."

In 1999, Big Dog entered into a licensing agreement with Golden West Specialty Foods, a $2.7 million manufacturer and distributor of spices and condiments sold to gourmet food shops. Golden West introduced Big Dog food "waker-upper" sauces such as Doggone Hot Sauce and Hot Dog Pupper Sauce.

Big Dog also formed other licensing partnerships. Under its agreement with Mango Teddy Bear Company, headquartered in Anchorage, Alaska, Big Dog logos appeared on Mango's backpacks, shoulder purses, key chains, and "Baby's First Big Dog" velour toys.

Big Dog entered into another agreement in which it co-branded a credit card with MBNA and formed a partnership with Fox-Interactive to help promote Fox's new CD-ROM, Aliens vs. Predator. Under the terms of this agreement, the first 10,000 customers to purchase the CD would receive a free pair of Big Dog boxer shorts. Both Fox and Big Dog promoted the offer.

Big Dog hoped to form licensing partnerships with companies outside of the United States. To help it reach this goal, in 2000 the company signed an agreement with BHPC Marketing, Inc. The following year Big Dog signed its first substantial international license to use its trademark in South Korea.

Licensing agent Jacki Blum said that Big Dog hoped to discover additional licensing opportunities in the pet industry. "The pet area is hugely significant for the future of the company. Dog food seems like a possibility, at least more so than puppy Prozac, but you never know what's going to happen when you're inside the Big Dog house," Blum explained.

PETsMART in 2000

In 2000, Big Dog and PETsMART joined forces. With more than 530 stores in North America and Canada, PETsMART was the number one U.S. specialty retailer of pet supplies. PETsMART was also a leading Internet pet supply retailer. As part of the agreement, PETsMART.com marketed Big Dog's merchandise through its online and offline advertising. In turn, Big Dog promoted PETsMART in its retail stores, catalogs, and throughout its web site. "PETsMART.com clearly has the brand, assets, management team and customer franchise to win in the highly competitive Internet pet space. Aligning with PETsMART.com not only provides our customers with the Internet's best retail solution for service, selection, and care, but also establishes Big Dog as a meaningful hand in the pet world," explained Feschbach.

A "Crazy" Deal in 2001

In the beginning of September 2001 Big Dog signed a deal to purchase Honolulu, Hawaii-based Crazy Shirts, Inc. Crazy Shirts was a private, casual sportswear manufacturer. Big Dog agreed to pay $10 million for the company, which had filed for Chapter 11 bankruptcy. Crazy Shirts sold its high-end T-shirts, knit tops, and accessories in its stores and through its web site, crazyshirts.com. It had sales of almost $50 million. Industry analysts thought the move was a good one.

By the end of September, however, Big Dog had backed out of the deal. The company expressed concern over the drop in retail sales following the September 11 terrorist attacks on the United States. Big Dog unveiled a line of stars-and-stripes shirts that boosted its own sales, but it was concerned that Crazy Shirts' sales were significantly hurt by a weakening economy and the sharp decline in Hawaiian tourism after September 11. "We simply did not see the value at the levels the bidding eventually reached for a company that was already in bankruptcy and under tremendous pressure as a result of the events of September 11," said Feshbach in the *Knight Ridder/Times Tribune Business News*. Feshbach added that Big Dog might still be interested in the acquisition later on, but at a reduced price. The Crazy Shirts purchase would have been Big Dog's first acquisition. The company obtained a $30 million line of credit from Wells Fargo to fund future acquisitions and expansions.

A Big Big Future

At the beginning of the 21st century, Big Dog's future looked bright. In the third quarter of 2001, the company posted a net income of $1.9 million on revenue of $30.2 million. In the future the company planned to expand its Little Big Dogs and Big Big Dogs sportswear lines, which accounted for 42 percent of its total retail sales in 2000, up from 39 percent in 1999. The company was conducting an ongoing search to land a "doggie prime-time animated series," according to Blum. With its new partnership with BHPC Marketing, it hoped to further license its products overseas.

Principal Subsidiaries

Big Dog USA, Inc.

Principal Competitors

The Gap, Inc.; The Disney Stores; Eddie Bauer, Inc.

Further Reading

Andreoli, Teresa, "Playing with the Big Dog," *License!*, February 1999.
"Big Dog to Continue Expansion with $30 Million from Wells Fargo Retail Finance: Casual and Active Wear Retailer to Grow Operations in Select U.S. Markets with New Financing," *Business Wire*, November 7, 2001.
Ginsberg, Steve, "Big Dog, Tired of Barking, Sinks Teeth into the Wharf," *San Francisco Business Times*, April 10, 1998.
"PETsMART Gets Hooked with Big Dog," *Advertising & Marketing*, September 2, 1999.
Rubel, Tim, "California Company to Buy Crazy Shirts," *Honolulu Star-Bulletin*, September 11, 2001.
"Santa Barbara, California-Based Clothing Retailer Sues General Motors Over Ads," *Santa Barbara News-Press*, March 20, 2001.
"Santa Barbara, California, Retail-Based Casual Clothing Retailer Won't Buy Bankrupt Chain," *Knight Ridder/Tribune Business News*, November 1, 2001.
Stanley, T.L., "Fox Interactive Plays with Big Dogs," *Brandweek*, March 1, 1999.
Vrana, Debora, "Big Dog Chases IPO, Hoping to Fetch $49 Million; Apparel: Casual Firm Files to Join a Market That's Keen on New Public Stocks in Fashion But That Has Seen Young Shares Dip in Last Year," *Los Angeles Times*, August 9, 1997.

—Tracey Vasil Biscontini

BLP Group Companies

Boron, LePore & Associates, Inc.

1800 Valley Road
Wayne, New Jersey 07470
U.S.A.
Telephone: (973) 709-3000
Fax: (201) 791-1121
Web site: http://www.blpgroup.com

Public Company
Incorporated: 1981
Employees: 536
Sales: $167.9 million (2000)
Stock Exchanges: NASDAQ
Ticker Symbol: BLPG
NAIC: 561499 All Other Business Support Services

Boron, LePore & Associates, Inc., now doing business as BLP Group Companies (BLP), is a Wayne, New Jersey, medical education communications agency that offers a broad range of services to more than 50 clients, including such major pharmaceutical firms as Bristol-Myers Squibb, Bayer, Merck, and Roche, as well as biotech firms, managed care organizations, medical societies, and trade associations. With its net work of wholly owned communications companies, BLP organizes peer-to-peer meetings and symposia, creates continuing medical education programs and distance learning programs, and offers speaker training, advocate development, publication planning, and editorial services. BLP maintains a large database of people who attend its hosted events in order to provide follow-up and to generate audiences for future events. Although in recent years it has expanded to offer product marketing, contract sales, and sales force logistics, the company is deemphasizing these areas in order to position itself as the country's only publicly traded, pure play medical education company.

Company Origins to 1981

BLP was founded and incorporated in New Jersey in 1981 by Thomas S. Boron as a boutique marketing research firm for pharmaceuticals in Bergen County, New Jersey. The company organized focus groups of doctors in order to provide feedback on clients' products. Out of this work grew peer-to-peer dinner meetings that became the backbone of the company's business. At these dinners, ten to 12 doctors or other healthcare personnel discussed a client's drug, with BLP personnel acting as moderators. The company would then codify the responses for the client. In the process, BLP began to build up a database of participants to these dinners. This information allowed for follow-up and helped in generating lists of future peer-to-peer dinners. As business increased, Boron added staff, including Thomas Boron's brother, Gregory, who joined the company in 1985 after serving as a major in the U.S. Army. Also joining BLP in that year was Patrick G. LePore, who had been employed the previous six years at the pharmaceutical firm of Hoffman-LaRoche, serving as a product manager for two years before becoming a product director.

Gregory Boron became BLP's chief financial officer in January 1991. A year later, Thomas Boron stepped down as the company's chief executive officer in favor of LePore. The peer-to-peer business grew modestly, topping $20 million in annual revenues in 1994, resulting in a $1.6 million net profit, generated by almost 4,000 peer-to-peer meetings. The landscape in the healthcare industry, in the meantime, was undergoing some significant changes, with the growing influence of health maintenance organizations leading to increasing emphasis on cost containment. BLP's pharmaceutical customers now began to look for ways to reduce operating costs and elected to outsource such functions as research and development, as well as marketing and sales. To take advantage of these new opportunities, BLP began to position itself to offer more services to a wider customer base.

In 1995, BLP hosted more than 4,300 meetings and introduced educational conferencing services geared toward physicians and other healthcare professionals who were required to complete a minimum number of hours in continuing education in order to maintain certification in their professions. For the 50 to 350 participants that attended these conferences it was a way to fulfill requirements at no cost. For the pharmaceuticals that funded the conferences it was essentially a marketing expense. In fact, some of the conferences were not intended to satisfy continuing education requirements. Because BLP was not an

Company Perspectives:

Boron LePore fills a specific need for our clients—helping them communicate with, educate, and influence their audience and giving them the resources and expertise they need for greater impact.

accredited organization, it worked in conjunction with universities and other educational organizations that were responsible for producing the program curriculum and educational materials. BLP also taped the conferences and provided them to professionals who were unable to attend. Revenues for this new business were $1.2 million in 1995.

Introducing New Services in 1996

In 1996, BLP significantly increased the number of peer-to-peer meetings it hosted to more than 7,700 and introduced more new services, resulting in $40 million in revenues, almost double the total from the previous year. Not only did BLP also increase the number of educational conferences it hosted, it offered other conferencing services that were more clearly marketing oriented. Pharmaceutical companies sponsored the events with the help of BLP, retaining medical experts to discuss a client's new drug or some other pertinent medical topic. BLP took advantage of new technologies to televise the conferences via satellite to a number of U.S. locations. Audience participation at remote locations was achieved by the use of two-way audio as well as special keypads. These capabilities formed the basis of BLP's new teleservices business, which offered an inexpensive alternative to in-person sales calls in order to promote, market, and sell drugs or other products to a wide variety of physicians, pharmacists, and other healthcare personnel. BLP was especially optimistic about making these services available to smaller pharmaceutical companies that wanted to promote a product without incurring the expense of purchasing their own telecommunications equipment. For the year, the new teleservices business generated nearly $1.4 million, and the company initiated plans to open a teleservices center in Norfolk, Virginia. Also in 1996, BLP introduced product marketing services, providing pharmaceutical companies with the opportunity to increase sales on products that they might not have enough resources to promote. Furthermore, BLP looked to obtain the rights to market certain products, thereby increasing potential rewards, although the company assumed greater risks if it failed to reach sales levels commensurate with promotional expenses. In the fourth quarter of 1996, BLP augmented its peer-to-peer meeting business by organizing symposia that were similar to its educational conferences but conducted on an in-person basis only. A typical symposium was staged over a weekend, attended by 50 to 300 physicians and focused on a particular drug or treatment protocol. Paid experts in the field made presentations to the attendees, who in turn were being groomed to serve as consultants or spokespersons for the sponsoring pharmaceutical company. BLP helped in all phases of planning a symposium, from choosing locations and arranging travel for participants, to identifying likely speakers. The company also had to be vigilant about making sure that symposia followed the guidelines set down by industry and professional associations regarding travel and lodging expenses and other payments to physicians, which had been instituted in order to prevent conflicts of interest. Because the profit margin was lower than that of its other services, however, BLP elected to pursue slower growth in this area.

In light of its rapidly evolving business, BLP began to reorganize late in 1996. The company was reincorporated in Delaware and LePore became chairman of the company in addition to his chief executive responsibilities. Gregory Boron was named chief operating officer and an executive vice-president. In 1997, BLP began to offer contract sales services, essentially creating a boutique sales operation to fill in the gaps created by staff cuts in large pharmaceuticals. In addition, BLP hoped to target emerging pharmaceuticals needing help in launching their first products. BLP's database of physicians who had attended its peer-to-peer dinners and conferences over the past decade proved to be an important asset in this regard. According to Boron in press remarks, "As a result of our invitations to all of these dinner meetings that we do, we call 6,000–8,000 doctors a day; that database is updated daily. We know when a doctor opens his office, who his receptionist is. We know who stocks his closet. We know who invites the doctor to the meeting. We know what meetings the doctor attended, when he attended them and what he reacts to."

Going Public: 1997

To fuel its ambitious program, BLP went public in September 1997, selling more than 3.7 million shares at $17.50 each to raise $65.4 million. BLP stock, trading on the NASDAQ, would subsequently increase in value by some 20 percent after the company announced its results for 1997. Revenues increased by 81 percent over the previous year, approaching $73 million, while net income totaled more than $6.1 million. Not only did the new services contribute to the bottom line, BLP core business grew as well. The Norfolk, Virginia, teleservices facility opened in 1997. Furthermore, in late 1997, BLP began to offer sales force logistics services to pharmaceuticals.

In January 1998, the company gained a sales office in Chicago by acquiring assets from Decision Point, Inc. for $800,000. This purchase not only expanded the firm's geographic reach but added sales and marketing talent. BLP made additional acquisitions in 1998. It acquired privately held Strategic Implications International, Inc. to bolster its continuing medical education business, paying $9 million in cash and stock. Unlike BLP, Strategic Implications was accredited by a number of medical associations. Two months later, BLP acquired Medical Education Systems, Inc. To pay for these purchases and fund further growth, the company made a secondary offering of stock, selling 2.9 million shares at $30 each.

Although BLP made great strides in diversifying its business, it remained highly dependent on a single customer, Glaxo Wellcome Plc, which accounted for almost $40 million of BLP's 1997 revenues of $72.9 million. In October 1998, Glaxo announced that it would not use BLP for any further symposia or advisory panels in 1999. Although BLP management maintained that in fact the company had been lessening its dependence on Glaxo and that it would continue to do significant business with the giant pharmaceuticals, investor reaction was quick and harsh, as BLP shares lost a third of their value.

Without the impending loss of Glaxo's business, BLP should have received an enthusiastic response from investors after it announced its 1998 results. The company more than doubled revenues over the previous year to nearly $165 million, and net income followed suit, topping $10 million. Gregory Boron then announced that he was leaving the company to "pursue personal interests." Clearly, however, the company would not be able to keep pace in 1999, a fact confirmed when BLP reported a first quarter loss, while BLP stock, which had been trading over $43 just before the Glaxo announcement, fell to the $9 level. In April 1999, BLP hired Bear, Stearns & Company to consider strategic alternatives, including the possibility of selling the company. Following more disappointing results during the second quarter, BLP instituted cost-cutting measures, including the reduction of the workforce by 10 percent across all divisions. Although it did not close any offices, the company did give up space in both its New Jersey and Virginia operations. By the fall of 1999, the situation appeared to stabilize, and BLP announced it was no longer looking to sell the company. In fact, it began to buy back stock at its depressed value. For the year, revenues fell below $150 million, and the company posted a loss of $583,000.

In 2000, BLP began to de-emphasize contract sales service, offering it merely as a complementary service. The company opted instead to focus on its medical education business. In May 2000, it paid $2 million to acquire North Carolina-based Consumer2Patient, Inc., which included Physician to Physician, LLC and Alternative Media Solutions, LLC. The companies provided educational services for both physicians and patients. In June 2000, BLP paid $9 million in cash and stock to acquire Armand Scott, a New Jersey-based business with operations in New Jersey, Illinois, Tennessee, and California. Armand Scott created and implemented education programs, as well as pro-

vided other services for pharmaceutical, medical device, and biotechnology companies. Not only did the company's business complement BLP, it added geographic reach. BLP returned to profitability in 2000, increasing its revenues beyond 1998 levels, to nearly $168 million, while posting net profits of $5.4 million. Optimism also returned to the company. Medical education spending by pharmaceuticals appeared to be growing 15 percent to 20 percent a year, and the medical education market overall now totaled $3 billion a year. More narrowly focused on medical education, and moving away from contract sales and marketing services, BLP looked well positioned to carve out a significant share of the medical education field, which was made up of a large number of small privately held companies as well as some larger companies that offered medical education only as a secondary effort. Controlling just 10 percent of the market, BLP had plenty of room for continued growth. Moreover, the price of its stock had recovered and the company had no debt. Over the next several years, BLP was likely to selectively pick up acquisitions that would expand on its base of clients, services, and geographic reach. In particular, the company was interested in establishing a presence in the potentially lucrative Midwest and California markets.

Principal Subsidiaries

Armand Scott, Inc.; Boron LePore, Inc.; Consumer2Patient, Inc.; Medical Education Systems, Inc.; Medical Media Communications, Inc.; Strategem Plus, Inc.; Strategic Implications International, Inc.

Principal Competitors

Quintiles Transnational Corp.; Nelson Communications Inc.; IMS Health Incorporated; PDI, Inc.; Ventiv Health, Inc.

Further Reading

"Boron, LePore, & Associates, Inc.," *Pharmaceutical Executive,* December 1998, p. 12.

"Glucophage Peer-to-Peer Meetings Increase Physician Scripts 20%," *Pink Sheet,* February 2, 1998.

Goldblatt, S. Dan, "Stock to Watch: Boron, Lepore & Associates," *Business News New Jersey,* September 13, 1999, p. 18.

"Patrick LePore," *Wall Street Transcript,* September 14, 2001.

Shook, David, "Drug Marketer Exceeds Forecast," *Record* (Bergen County, N.Y.), November 5, 1998, p. B01.

——, "Fair Lawn Firm's Stock Falls 32%," *Record* (Bergen County, N.Y.), October 24, 1998, p. A14.

—Ed Dinger

BP p.l.c.

Britannic House
1 Finsbury Circus
London EC2M 7BA
United Kingdom
Telephone: (207) 496-4000
Fax: (207) 496-4630
Web site: http://www.bp.com

Public Company
Incorporated: 1998 as BP Amoco PLC
Employees: 107,000
Sales: $148.06 billion (2000)
Stock Exchanges: London New York Chicago Pacific
   Toronto Tokyo Paris Zurich Frankfurt
Ticker Symbol: BP
NAIC: 32411 Petroleum Refineries; 211111 Crude
   Petroleum and Natural Gas Extraction; 211112
   Natural Gas Liquid Extraction (pt); 48621 Pipeline
   Transportation of Natural Gas (pt); 48611 Pipeline
   Transportation of Crude Oil; 48691 Pipeline
   Transportation of Refined Petroleum Products; 42271
   Petroleum Bulk Stations and Terminals; 42272
   Petroleum and Petroleum Products Wholesalers
   (Except Bulk Stations and Terminals); 324191
   Petroleum Lubricating Oil and Grease Manufacturing;
   42269 Other Chemical and Allied Products
   Wholesalers

Formed by the 1998 merger of British Petroleum Company and Amoco Corporation, BP p.l.c. is the third largest oil company in the world. The company is integrated, with operations in three main segments. The first, exploration and production, operates in 29 countries and produces 1.93 million barrels of crude oil and 7.6 billion cubic feet of natural gas each day. BP's second segment consists of ''downstream'' businesses such as refining, marketing, supply, and transportation. In this segment, the company operates 23 oil refineries, with total daily throughput of 3.2 million barrels, and 29,000 service stations around the world.

BP's third major segment is the production of petrochemicals—substances obtained from petroleum. BP's petrochemicals are used in a wide range of applications, including packaging, fuel additives, synthetic rubber, detergents, cosmetics, and pharmaceuticals. The company is the world's largest maker of purified terephthalic acid, a substance used to manufacture polyester and fibers and resins used in bottles and containers. The company also has growing operations in solar power.

British Petroleum: Early 20th-Century Origins

BP originated in the activities of William Knox D'Arcy, an adventurer who had made a fortune in Australian mining. In 1901 D'Arcy secured a concession from the Grand Vizier of Persia (now known as Iran) to explore for petroleum throughout most of his empire. The search for oil proved extremely costly and difficult, since Persia was devoid of infrastructure and politically unstable. Within a few years D'Arcy was in need of capital. Eventually, after intercession by members of the British Admiralty, the Burmah Oil Company joined D'Arcy in a Concessionary Oil Syndicate in 1905 and supplied further funds in return for operational control. In May 1908 oil was discovered in the southwest of Persia at Masjid-i-Suleiman, the first oil discovery in the Middle East. The following April the Anglo-Persian Oil Company was formed, with the Burmah Oil Company holding most of the shares.

The dominant figure in the early years of the Anglo-Persian Oil Company was Charles Greenway. Greenway began his career in the firm of managing agents who handled the marketing of Burmah Oil's products in India. Invited by Burmah Oil to help in the formation of Anglo-Persian Oil, he became a founding director, was appointed managing director in 1910, and took the position of chairman in 1914. The first few years of the company's existence were extremely difficult, and it survived as an independent entity in large part through Greenway's skill. Although Anglo-Persian Oil had located a prolific oil field, it encountered major problems in refining the crude oil. The company also lacked a tanker fleet and a distribution network to sell its products.

For a time Anglo-Persian Oil risked being absorbed by one of the larger oil companies, such as the Royal Dutch/Shell

Company Perspectives:

Energy and materials, used safely and efficiently, are essential to the prosperity and growth of the world. Sustaining and enhancing our quality of life ultimately depends on energy. Demand for energy continues to rise by 2–3% a year.

BP's goal is to play a leading role in meeting these growing needs, and so aiding global development, without damaging the natural environment.

We believe our involvement in the global economy is a positive and progressive one. Innovation is the hallmark of how we work with people, technology, assets and relationships. Our objective is always to be constructive and to use our expertise to produce creative solutions to every challenge.

Our success depends on our making, and being seen to make, a distinctive contribution to every activity in which we are involved.

Group, with whom it signed a ten-year marketing agreement in 1912. But in 1914 Greenway preserved the independence of Anglo-Persian Oil by a unique agreement with the British government. Under the terms of this agreement, negotiated with Winston Churchill, then first lord of the Admiralty, Greenway signed a long-term contract with the British Admiralty for the supply of fuel oil, which the Royal Navy wished to use as a replacement for coal.

At the same time, in an unusual departure from the United Kingdom's laissez-faire traditions, the British government invested £2 million in Anglo-Persian Oil, receiving in return a majority shareholding that it would retain for many years. The transaction provided the company with funds for further investment in refining equipment and an initial investment in transport and marketing in fulfillment of Greenway's ambition to create an independent, integrated oil business. In return for its investment, the British government was allowed to appoint two directors to the company's board with powers of veto, which could not, however, be exercised over commercial affairs. In fact, the government directors never used their veto throughout the period of state shareholding in the company. On paper Anglo-Persian Oil was state controlled until the 1980s; in practice it functioned as a purely commercial company.

Growth to Global Prominence During World War I

World War I created considerable opportunities for the fledgling enterprise. Although within Persia the authority of the shah had almost disintegrated, and in 1915 Anglo-Persian Oil's pipeline to the coast was cut by dissident tribesmen and German troops, demand for oil products was soaring. Between 1912 and 1918 there was a tenfold increase in oil production in Iran. The war also created opportunities for Greenway to further his ambition of establishing an integrated oil business. In 1915 Greenway founded a wholly owned oil tanker subsidiary, and within five years Anglo-Persian Oil had more than 30 oil tankers. In 1917, in his biggest coup, Greenway acquired British Petroleum Company, the British marketing subsidiary of the European Petroleum Union. The European Petroleum Union, a Continental alliance with significant Deutsche Bank participation, had been expropria-

ted by the British government as an enemy property. In 1917 Greenway also decided to establish a refinery at Swansea, Wales, with improved refining technology that could produce petroleum products for British and European markets.

World War I, coupled with Greenway's skill, led to Anglo Persian Oil's emergence by the late 1920s as one of the world's largest oil companies, matching Royal Dutch/Shell and Standard Oil of New Jersey in stature. During the 1920s the company made a major expansion in marketing, establishing subsidiaries in many European countries and, after the expiration of the agreement with Shell in 1922, in Africa and Asia. New refineries were established in Scotland and France, and a research laboratory erected in Sunbury, Great Britain, in 1917 greatly expanded the company's activities. In the early 1920s there were some criticisms of the management of Anglo-Persian Oil within the British government and some suggestions that the state shareholding be privatized, but in November 1924 a decision was made to retain the government's equity stake.

Greenway's successor was John Cadman, a former mining engineer who had been a professor of mining at Birmingham University before World War I and who had become a major figure in official British oil policy during the war. In 1923 he became a managing director of Anglo-Persian Oil, and in 1927, chairman. He introduced major administrative reforms and, in the words of business historian Alfred Chandler, as quoted in *Scale and Scope: The Dynamics of Industrial Capitalism,* "was one of the few effective British organizational builders." Cadman was successful in overcoming the excessive departmentalism and lack of coordination that had formerly characterized the company. In 1928, he also joined forces with other leading oil companies in a clandestine price-fixing agreement among the world's largest oil companies.

Depression and the Threat of Iranian Nationalism in the 1930s

In the 1930s one of Cadman's greatest challenges came from the growth of Persian nationalism. Previously, in 1921, the old dynasty of shahs had been overthrown by an army colonel, Reza Khan, who made himself shah in 1925. Reza Khan was determined to reverse the foreign political and economic domination of his country. Anglo-Persian Oil had a symbolic role as a bastion of British imperialism, and, following growing resentment of declining royalty payments from the company due to its falling profits during the Great Depression, the government of Persia canceled its concession in November 1932. The dispute eventually went to the League of Nations, and in 1933 Persia signed a new 60-year concession agreement with Anglo-Persian Oil that reduced the area of the concession to about a quarter of the original and introduced a new tonnage basis of assessment for royalty payments. Anglo-Persian Oil had the formidable backing of the British government, and Persia gained little out of the dispute.

The oil company, which was renamed Anglo-Iranian Oil in 1935—the year Persia became Iran—became a renewed target of nationalist discontent after World War II. The Iranians complained that their dividends were too small, and the signing of 50–50 profit-sharing agreements between governments and oil companies elsewhere—in Venezuela in 1948 and Saudi Arabia

Key Dates:

1889: Rockefeller's Standard Oil Trust establishes the Standard Oil Company (Indiana).

1892: The Standard Oil Trust is liquidated; Standard Oil (Indiana) becomes a subsidiary of Standard Oil Company (New Jersey).

1901: William Knox D'Arcy obtains a concession from Persia to explore for petroleum there.

1908: D'Arcy's company becomes the first to strike oil in the Middle East.

1909: D'Arcy and Burmah Oil form the Anglo-Persian Oil Company.

1911: The government orders Standard Oil Company (New Jersey) to relinquish control of its subsidiaries; Standard Oil (Indiana) becomes an independent company.

1914: The British government acquires a controlling interest in the Anglo-Persian Oil Company.

1915: Anglo-Persian forms an oil tanker subsidiary.

1917: Anglo-Persian acquires British Petroleum Company.

1923: Standard (Indiana) acquires 50 percent of the American Oil Company, which marketed an antiknock gasoline under the brand name "Amoco."

1925: Standard (Indiana) buys an interest in the Pan American Petroleum & Transport Company in the largest oil industry consolidation to date, giving Standard entry into oil fields in Mexico, Venezuela, and Iraq.

1929: Standard (Indiana) and five other Standard companies organize the Atlas Supply Company to sell automobile tires and other accessories.

1932: Standard (Indiana) sells Pan American's foreign interests.

1933: Persia signs a new 60-year concession with Anglo-Persian Oil.

1935: Anglo-Persian is renamed Anglo-Iranian Oil when Persia becomes Iran.

1945: Amoco Chemicals is formed.

1948: Standard (Indiana) forms a foreign exploration department to spearhead exploration efforts in Canada and other countries.

1951: The Iranian oil industry is nationalized, ousting Anglo-Iranian Oil.

1952: Standard Oil (Indiana) is the nation's largest domestic oil company.

1954: Anglo-Iranian Oil is renamed the British Petroleum Company, returns to Iran.

1957: Standard (Indiana) reorganizes, consolidating nine subsidiaries into four larger companies.

1961: Standard (Indiana) begins to use the brand name Amoco heavily in its advertising and subsidiary names.

1967: British Petroleum becomes the second largest chemicals company in the United Kingdom.

1969: BP makes a major oil find at Prudhoe Bay in Alaska, partners with Standard Oil Company of Ohio (SOHIO) to develop the property.

1970: BP discovers the Forties field, the first major commercial oil find in British waters.

1978: Standard Oil (Indiana)'s tanker Amoco Cadiz runs aground, dumping thousands of tons of oil off the French coast.

1985: Standard Oil (Indiana) changes its name to Amoco Corporation.

1987: BP acquires SOHIO, forms BP America; the British government sells its shares of BP.

1988: Amoco buys Dome Petroleum, Ltd., of Canada.

1992: Amoco becomes the first foreign oil company to explore the Chinese mainland.

1994: Amoco restructures, replacing its three major subsidiaries with a network of 17 business groups.

1996: BP merges its European refining and marketing operations with Mobil Corporation.

1997: Amoco begins a divestiture program designed to shed noncore properties.

1998: British Petroleum acquires Amoco Corporation, forming BP Amoco PLC.

2000: BP Amoco acquires Atlantic Richfield Co. and Burmah Castrol, changes its name to BP p.l.c.

---

in 1950—fueled criticism of Anglo-Iranian Oil within Iran. Extensive negotiations ensued between the company and the Iranian government. Anglo-Iranian Oil eventually offered substantial concessions, but they came too late and were repudiated by the nationalist government of Muhammad Mussadegh.

On May 1, 1951, the Iranian oil industry was formally nationalized. Several years of complex negotiations followed, and eventually, a 1953 coup—in which the British government and the United States Central Intelligence Agency (CIA) were implicated—resulted in the overthrow of Mussadegh. After his removal from power, an agreement was reached that allowed the return to Iran of Anglo-Iranian Oil—renamed the British Petroleum Company in 1954—but not on such favorable terms as the company had secured after the early 1930s dispute. Under the accord, which was reached in August 1954, British Petroleum held a 40 percent interest in a newly created consortium of Western oil companies, formed to undertake oil exploration, production, and refining in Iran.

Diversification: 1950s–60s

The events of 1951–54 had encouraged BP to diversify away from its overdependence on a single source of crude oil. The Iranian nationalization deprived the company of two-thirds of its production. The company responded by increasing output in Iraq and Kuwait and by building new refineries in Europe, Australia, and Aden (now part of Yemen). Oil exploration activities were launched in the Arabian Gulf, Canada, Europe, north Africa, east Africa, and Australia. Meanwhile, BP, which had moved first into petrochemicals in the late 1940s, became the second largest chemicals company in the United Kingdom in 1967.

The company's future was secured at the end of the 1960s by major oil discoveries in Alaska and the North Sea. In 1965 BP found gas in British waters of the North Sea. In October 1970 it discovered the Forties field, the first major commercial oil find in British waters. Throughout the 1960s BP also had been looking for oil in Alaska, and in 1969 this effort was rewarded by a major discovery at Prudhoe Bay on the North Slope. In the previous year BP had acquired the U.S. East Coast refining and marketing operations from Atlantic Richfield Company, and the stage was now set for a surge of expansion in the United States. Through its large share in Prudhoe Bay, BP owned more than 50 percent of the biggest oil field in the United States, and it needed outlets for this oil.

The solution was a 1969 agreement with the Standard Oil Company of Ohio (SOHIO), the market leader in Ohio and several neighboring states. Under the agreement, SOHIO took over BP's Prudhoe Bay leases as well as the downstream facilities acquired from Atlantic Richfield. In return, BP acquired 25 percent of SOHIO's equity. In 1970 BP and SOHIO engaged in a seven-year struggle to develop the Prudhoe Bay oil field and construct the 800-mile Trans-Alaska Pipeline system, which was finally completed in 1977. By the following year BP had taken a majority holding in SOHIO. Later, in 1987, BP would acquire SOHIO outright and merge it with BP's other interests in the United States to form a new company: BP America.

Oil Crisis of the 1970s

The oil price shocks and the transformation of the balance of power between oil companies and host governments that occurred in the 1970s caused many problems for BP, as for other Western oil companies. BP lost most of its direct access to crude oil supplies produced in countries that belonged to the Organization of Petroleum Exporting Countries (OPEC). The company's oil assets were nationalized in Libya in 1971 and Nigeria in 1979. BP and Shell clashed with the British government in 1973 over the allocation of scarce oil supplies. BP's chairman, Sir Eric Drake, refused to give priority to supplying the United Kingdom, despite forceful reminders from Prime Minister Edward Heath that the government owned half of the company.

Problems in the oil industry prompted BP to diversify away from its traditional role as an integrated oil company heavily dependent on Middle Eastern oil production. Beginning in the mid-1970s, BP built up a large coal business, especially in the United States, Australia, and South Africa. BP's chemical interests also expanded during this period, especially after 1978, when it acquired major European assets from Union Carbide and Monsanto. Also in the mid-1970s, BP became active in mineral mining, acquiring Selection Trust, a mining finance house based in Great Britain, in what was then the London stock market's largest ever takeover bid.

CEO Sir Peter Walters, who took BP's helm in 1981, guided a five-year acquisitions binge costing approximately £10 billion. It included the purchase of the Purina Mills animal feed company in 1986 as well as the purchase of the remaining shares in SOHIO. In 1981 SOHIO acquired Keiecott, the largest U.S. copper producer.

Seen retrospectively, this diversification strategy was not always a wise one. A major world recession after 1979 led to considerable overcapacity, forcing BP to close down or sell off parts of its chemicals business in the early 1980s. Late in the decade, the energy conglomerate sold off its coal and minerals interests in the United States, Canada, Indonesia, Australia, and South Africa, netting £428 million in the process. BP started to consolidate its upstream business through divestment in the late 1980s. Another sale of selected worldwide oil and gas interests and assets brought in $1.3 billion. In 1990 and 1991 sales of exploration interests and assets in New Zealand, France, The Netherlands, and from the BP Exploration division in particular totaled £830 million.

One notably successful acquisition was Britoil, a company established by the British government in the 1970s to participate in North Sea oil exploration. Britoil had become one of the largest independent oil exploration and production companies, and in acquiring it, BP almost doubled its exploration acreage in the North Sea.

The late 1980s saw considerable changes at BP. In October 1987 the government under Prime Minister Margaret Thatcher sold its remaining shares in the company as part of a privatization program. The timing of the share issue was particularly unfortunate, as the world's stock markets collapsed between the opening and closing of the offer. One result of the sale was that by March 1988 the Kuwait Investment Office had built up a 21.6 percent stake in the company; government regulatory authorities subsequently reported that this share was reduced to less than 10 percent.

In the early 1990s British Petroleum sought to consolidate its activities to focus on its traditional areas of strength in "upstream" areas—oil and gas exploration, field development, production, pipeline transportation, and gas marketing—and "downstream" areas—oil supply trading, refining, and marketing—as well as in chemicals manufacturing. As a result of its corporate shuffling, BP now focused on its three core businesses: oil exploration and production, oil refining and marketing, and chemicals.

Project 1990 Under CEO Horton

In 1990 BP announced Project 1990, a fundamental change of its corporate structure. The primary aims were to reduce organizational complexity, reshape the central organization and reduce its cost, and reposition BP for the 1990s. Project 1990 was the brainchild of BP's chairman, Robert Horton. Horton earned a reputation for saving money and rose to prominence at BP by cutting costs first at the company's tanker division, then progressing to BP's chemicals subsidiary. Eventually becoming chairman and chief executive officer of BP Oil in 1990, he set out to cut $750 million from BP's annual bottom line by revamping the corporate culture.

At the heart of the scheme was a conviction that BP had become overly bureaucratic and that strategic flexibility was handicapped as a result. In 1990, Horton said, "What I'm trying to do is simply, refocus, and make it clear we don't need to have hierarchies. We don't need to have baronial head office departments. This is a fundamentally different way of looking at the way you run the center of the corporation." Under Project 1990, nearly 90 percent of corporate center committees were abolished, with individuals taking responsibility instead. Hierarchically structured departments were to be replaced by small flexible teams with more open and less formal lines of communication.

Unfortunately, Project 1990 quickly came to represent wholesale job cuts and low morale. Between 1990 and 1992, more than 19,000 positions—more than 16 percent of the total workforce—were cut. The intended result of the job cuts was to shorten the lines of command and promote individual responsibility, but workloads were not redistributed in the process. Project 1990 earned a poor reputation among employees, because some of the most basic measures to promote good communication and efficiency were eschewed for job elimination. Horton also insisted on maintaining BP's dividend—despite cuts in other vital areas.

As a result of Project 1990's shortcomings, many employees lost faith in it, according to a 1991 internal survey. Horton's personal abrasiveness and tendency to dictate, rather than cultivate, change earned him an unflattering nickname: "The Hatchet." He was forced to resign on June 25, 1992, after BP sustained its first ever quarterly losses. Sales had slid from $66.4 billion in 1990 to $51.9 billion in 1992, and profits declined from $3.2 billion to an annual loss of £458 million ($811 million).

Restructuring Under New Management Team in the Mid-1990s

Horton's role was split between Lord Ashburton, the nonexecutive director who had led the mutiny, and Sir David Simon, who advanced from chief operating officer to chief executive officer. Ironically, however, Simon and Ashburton soon found that they needed to accelerate, not reverse, Horton's plan. First, they organized the company's interests into three primary divisions: BP Exploration, BP Oil, and BP Chemicals. The new organizational scheme allowed the parent to better analyze and pinpoint underperforming and noncore assets with a view to improvement or elimination. Of the $4 billion in assets targeted for divestment were BP Nutrition and the company's controlling stake in BP Canada. The company also planned to reduce debt by $1 billion annually and invest $5 billion per year on capital projects.

From 1993 to 1995, BP cut another 9,000 people from the payroll, reducing employment to less than 54,000 by the end of 1996. Reorganization efforts also focused on the troubled American subsidiary, BP Oil, which contributed more than $20 million of the parent company's 1992 loss. Cost-cutting measures at the subsidiary ran the gamut, from selling 300 California and Florida gas stations, to employee buyouts eliminating 600 to 700 jobs, to the close scrutinization of travel vouchers.

The ongoing cuts (which were expected to bring employment down to 50,000) brought home a stern reality; as an unnamed source told *Oil & Gas Journal* in 1996, "There is no doubt among staff that BP is a lean and mean machine these days, and not the Rolls-Royce among oil companies it once thought itself." Ashburton and Simon also halved BP's "fat-cat" dividend, a measure Horton had been reluctant to take. In 1995, Sir John Browne, former chief of Exploration, took over as BP's chief executive. The change in leadership was to bring about even greater shifts in the company's focus, direction, and size.

Under Browne's guidance, BP accelerated its use of strategic partnerships to cut the cost of doing business around the world. In 1996, for example, the company merged its European fuel and lubricants business—including pipelines, terminals, road tanker fleets, refineries, depots, and retail sites—with Mobil Corporation. The joint venture operated in 43 countries and held a 12 percent share for fuels and an 18 percent share for lubricants in the European market. A joint venture with China's Shanghai Petrochemical Company expanded BP's chemical interests in Asia while limiting the company's liabilities. The company hoped to target Southeast Asia and Eastern Europe for new downstream operations. In 1997, BP announced that it would build its first service stations in Japan. Also in 1997, BP acquired a 10 percent equity stake in AO Sidanco, a major Russian oil and gas company, as well as 45 percent of Sidanco's majority interest in a separate Russian company with major oil and gas properties in east Siberia.

The partnerships and acquisitions of the mid-1990s were mere foreshadowings of much bigger deals to come. In 1998, BP made history by acquiring Amoco Corporation, the fifth largest oil company in the United States and the largest producer of natural gas in North America. The $50 billion deal was both the first megamerger in the oil industry and largest industrial merger ever made. It was a highly significant move for BP; not only did it add substantially to the company's oil operations, but more important, it gave the company a leadership position in natural gas. With demand for gas expected to grow much faster than demand for oil in the coming years, it was critical for BP to move in that direction.

Early Days at Amoco: The Late 1800s

Amoco had been in business since 1889, although it had been known as Standard Oil Company (Indiana) until its name was changed in 1985. The company was formed outside Whiting, Indiana, a location chosen by John Rockefeller's Standard Oil Trust as a refinery site close enough to sites in the growing midwestern market to keep freight costs low, yet far enough away to avoid disturbing residents.

From the beginning, the Whiting facility was organized as a self-supporting entity, planning for long-term expansion. Although refining was its main activity, it also constructed oil barrels for transportation and manufactured an oil-based product line consisting of axle grease, harness oil, paraffin wax for candles, and kerosene produced from the crude oil. The oil itself flowed to Chicago and other midwestern cities via two pipes originating in Lima, Ohio. Land transportation began on the refinery's grounds, at a railroad terminal belonging to the Chicago & Calumet Terminal Railroad, a company over which a Standard Oil interest had gained control. This terminal's placement gave the company exclusive use of the tracks, access to the West and the Southwest, and a direct route that eliminated the expense of switching tolls.

Standard (Indiana) had no direct marketing organization of its own. After the Standard Oil Trust was liquidated in 1892 by order of the Ohio Supreme Court, the 20 companies under its jurisdiction reverted to their former status and became subsidiaries of Standard Oil Company (New Jersey). The functions of Standard Oil (Indiana) were then expanded to include marketing.

The company's capitalization was increased from $500,000 to $1 million, which was divided into $100 shares. Standard Oil still owned about 54 percent of Standard (Indiana). Standard (Indiana) used the extra cash to buy Standard Oil Company (Minnesota) and Standard Oil Company (Illinois), formerly P.C. Hanford Oil Company, an oil marketing organization in Chicago. The extra capital expanded Standard's sales territory, which was broadened even further when the property of Chester Oil Company of Minnesota was bought. Other acquisitions followed, and by 1901 the company was marketing through its own organization in 11 states.

At first, Standard (Indiana) had few competitors in the petroleum-product market. It enjoyed about 88 percent of the business in kerosene and heavy fuel oil. After competition began to grow, Standard (Indiana) fought back with strategically placed bulk storage stations and subsidiary companies in competitive areas that cut prices and drove competitors out. Earnings rose from $605,781 in 1896 to a high of almost $4.2 million in 1899, but the company's competitive practices and its growing market share made it the target of government agencies.

Independence and Growth Through Acquisition: The Early 1900s

In 1911, after a court battle lasting almost three years, Standard Oil Company (New Jersey)—the parent company to Standard (Indiana) and other Standard companies—was ordered to relinquish supervision of its subsidiaries. Gasoline sales had risen from 31.6 million gallons to 1.57 billion between 1897 and 1911. Once independent, Standard (Indiana) began to cater to the burgeoning automobile market, opening a Minneapolis, Minnesota, service station in 1912. Chicago's first service station opened in 1913, and by 1918, there were 451 altogether. Together with growing sales of road oil, asphalt, and other supporting products, the automotive industry provided one-third of all Standard (Indiana) business.

To get as much gasoline out of each barrel of crude as possible, Standard formulated the cracking process, which doubled the yield by separating the oil's molecules, by means of heat and pressure, into a dense liquid plus a lighter product that would boil in gasoline's range. The possibility of cheaper gasoline and a new line of petroleum-based products made the method attractive to other refiners, who licensed it, accounting for 34 percent of the company's total profits between 1913 and 1922.

With the end of World War I, company Chairman Colonel Robert Stewart's top priority was to find a secure source of crude oil, to meet the rapidly expanding demand for gasoline and kerosene. Before the war, Standard had depended on the Prairie Oil and Gas Company for its supply, but military needs diverted Prairie's crude to the refineries along the Atlantic seaboard. To obtain a reliable source of crude oil, Stewart acquired 33 percent of Midwest Refining Company of Wyoming, in 1920. A half interest in the Sinclair Pipe Company was purchased in 1921, for $16.4 million in cash, improving transportation capacity. Sinclair's 2,900 miles of pipeline ran from north Texas to Chicago, encompassed almost 6,000 wells, and ran through oil-rich Wyoming.

Standard bought an interest in the Pan American Petroleum & Transport Company in 1925. The interest, costing $37.6 million, was the largest oil consolidation in the history of the industry, giving Standard (Indiana) access to one of the world's largest tanker fleets and entry into oil fields in Mexico, Venezuela, and Iraq. In 1929 Standard (Indiana) acquired another chunk of Pan American stock through a stock swap, bringing its total ownership of Pan American to 81 percent.

Pan American also introduced Standard to the American Oil Company, of Baltimore, Maryland. Started by the Blaustein family, American Oil marketed most of Pan American's oil in the eastern United States and was 50 percent owned by Pan American and 50 percent owned by the Blausteins. The Blausteins were initiators of the first measuring gasoline pump and inventors of the high-octane Amoco-Gas that reduced engine knocking.

Though expensive, these investments proved to be sound; by 1929, the Depression notwithstanding, Standard Oil (Indiana) was second only to Standard Oil (New Jersey) as a buyer of crude oil. Equally profitable as a supplier, the company's net earnings for 1929 were $78.5 million after taxes.

In 1929 Stewart was followed as CEO by Edward G. Seubert, who continued to strengthen Standard's crude oil supply. With an eye to future supply security, Seubert shifted the emphasis to buying and developing crude oil-producing properties like McMan Oil and Gas Company, a 1930 purchase that provided 10,000 barrels daily. Also in 1930, Standard acquired both the remaining 50 percent interest in the Sinclair Pipe Line Company and the Sinclair Crude Oil Purchasing Company for $72.5 million, giving it control over one of the country's largest pipeline systems and crude oil buying agencies. These subsidiaries now became the Stanolind Pipe Line Company and the Stanolind Crude Oil Purchasing Company; they were joined in 1931 by the Stanolind Oil & Gas Company, a newly organized subsidiary absorbing several smaller ones.

In 1929 a retail venture called the Atlas Supply Company, which was co-organized with five other Standard firms, had been organized to sell automobile tires and other accessories nationwide. The Great Depression, however, made competition fierce by the end of 1930. Even worse conditions threatened after the largest oil field in history was found in east Texas in late 1930. The new field caused production to rise quickly to a daily average of 300,000 barrels in 1931, glutting the market. Ruthless price-cutting followed. Standard (Indiana) did not engage in this practice, preferring instead to curtail exploration and drilling activities. As a result, only 49.9 billion barrels were produced in 1931, as against 55.1 billion the year before, and the company's 13 domestic facilities operated well below capacity. The 45,073 employees worked on construction projects, and accepted wage cuts and part-time employment to minimize layoffs. The flow of cheap crude oil continued, often in excess of limits set by state regulatory bodies; gas sales were accompanied by premiums like candy, ash trays, and cigarette lighters. Track-side stations, where gasoline was pumped from the tank car into the customer's automobile, posed another price-cutting threat. Also prevalent were cooperatives organized by farmers, who would buy tank cars of gasoline for distribution among members to save money. These conditions caused 1932 earnings to reach only $16.5 million—down from $17.5 million in 1931.

In 1932 Standard decided to sell Pan American's foreign interests to Standard Oil (New Jersey). These properties cost Standard Oil (New Jersey) slightly less than $48 million cash plus about 1.8 million shares of Standard Oil (New Jersey) stock.

By 1934 the worst of the Depression was over. Activities in Texas led the Stanolind Oil & Gas Company to the Hastings field, which held 43 producing wells by the end of 1935. Also in 1935, more oil-producing acreage in east Texas came with Stanolind Oil & Gas Company's $42 million purchase of the properties of Beaumont-based Yount-Lee Oil Company, an acquisition that helped Stanolind Oil & Gas to increase its daily average production to 68,965 barrels.

During the 1930s overproduction began to threaten, and federal and state governments tried to curb oil production with heavy taxes. Standard felt the bite in Iowa's 1935 chain-store tax, which could not be justified by its service stations' profit margin. Therefore, the company turned back leased stations to their owners, and leased company-owned stations to independent operators, to be operated as separate outlets. By the following July, all 11,685 Standard (Indiana) service stations were independently operated and the company was once more primarily a producer distributing oil at wholesale prices. This move spurred the newly independent entrepreneurs, whose increased sales helped to achieve a net profit for Standard of $30.2 million for 1935.

Foreign Exploration, Domestic Reorganization at Mid-Century

When Standard reached its 50th year in 1939, during World War II, its research chemists were working to improve the high-octane fuels needed for military and transport planes. Standard's engineers cooperated with other companies to build the pipelines necessary for oil transportation. By 1942, the ''Big Inch'' pipeline carried a daily load of 300,000 barrels of crude from Texas to the East Coast, where most of it was used to support the war effort. Loss of manpower and government steel restrictions curbed operations, yet the company produced 47 million barrels of crude and purchased about 102 million barrels from outside sources. Other wartime products from Standard plants included paraffin wax coatings for military food rations, toluene (the main ingredient for TNT), butane, and butylene for aviation gasoline and synthetic rubber.

On January 1, 1945, Seubert retired as president and chief executive officer of the company. He left behind him 33,244 employees, sales of crude oil topping the 1944 figure by 37.1 percent, and a gross income of $618.9 million. Seubert was succeeded as chairman and CEO by Robert E. Wilson, formerly president of Pan American Petroleum & Transport Company, and Alonzo W. Peake became president. Peake had been vice-president of production.

The management style instituted by Wilson and Peake differed from the centralized, solo authority Seubert preferred. The two men split the supervisory authority, with no overlap of direct authority. Wilson was responsible for finance, research and development, law, and industrial relations, while Peake's commitments included refining, production, supply and trans-

portation, and sales and long-range planning. Responsibility for operating subsidiaries was split between the two. The result was a decentralized organization, making for swifter, more cooperative decision-making at all levels.

In 1948 Stanolind Oil & Gas formed a foreign exploration department to head exploration attempts in Canada and other countries. The new team spent more than $98 million by 1950, with Canada and the Gulf of Mexico its prime targets.

By 1952 Standard Oil (Indiana) was acknowledged as the nation's largest domestic oil company. It possessed 12 refineries able to market products in 41 states, plus almost 5,000 miles of crude oil gathering lines, 10,000 miles of trunk lines, and 1,700 miles of refined product pipelines. By 1951, gross income had reached $1.54 billion.

In 1955 Peake retired as president, to be succeeded by former Executive Vice-President Frank Prior, who inherited the problem of a decrease in allowable production days in the state of Texas, as a result of additions to oil reserves in the state. The rising amount of imported oil was another problem that surfaced during Peake's tenure. The total had swelled from 490,000 barrels per day in 1951 to 660,000 barrels in 1954.

Nevertheless, cheaper international exploration costs spurred Standard (Indiana) to again become active in the growing foreign oil arena that it had all but left in 1932 when it sold Pan American's foreign interests. To handle international land leasing and joint ventures, the company organized Pan American International Oil Corporation in New York, as a subsidiary of Pan American Petroleum. Foreign operations included exploration rights for 13 million acres in Cuba, obtained in 1955; a subsidiary company formed in Venezuela in 1958, for joint exploration of 180,000 acres together with other companies; and 23 million acres obtained for exploration in Libya.

The traditional oil industry profit arrangement for international activities had been an even split between the company and the host government, although several firms had quietly bent the guidelines. Standard (Indiana) broke openly with this custom in a 1958 deal with the National Iranian Oil Company (NIOC), in which Standard (Indiana) split the profits evenly, then gave NIOC half of its own share, to which it added a $25 million bonus.

The late 1950s also saw domestic reorganization. In 1957 the company consolidated nine subsidiaries into four larger companies. Stanolind Oil & Gas Company became Pan American Petroleum Corporation, consolidating all Standard Oil (Indiana) crude oil and natural gas exploration and production. American Oil Pipe Line Company, a former subsidiary of American Oil, was merged into Service Pipe Line Company— which had been known as Stanolind Pipe Line Company until 1950—focused on oil transport. Crude oil and natural gas purchasing operations were combined to form the Indiana Oil Purchasing Company; and Amoco Chemicals Corporation consolidated all chemical activities into a single organization. Total income for 1957 was about $2 billion.

Changes Under CEO Swearingen: The 1960s–70s

In 1960 company President John Swearingen succeeded Prior as chief executive officer, the chairmanship being left vacant. Swearingen turned both domestic and foreign operations over to subsidiaries, making Standard Oil (Indiana) entirely a holding company. Operating assets were transferred to the American Oil Company, into which the Utah Oil Refining Company also was merged. American Oil's responsibilities now included the manufacture, transport, and sale of all company petroleum products in 45 states, although limited marketing operations in three other states also were maintained. This consolidation allowed the company to develop a national image and provided more efficiency in staff use and storage and transport flexibility. Coverage being national, the company was able to advertise nationally and demand better rates from ground and air transporters.

Standard (Indiana) also became concerned with product trade names. The 1911 breakup had left several former Standard (New Jersey) subsidiaries in different areas of the country with the Standard Oil name and rights to the associated trademarks. American Oil thus had the right to use the Standard name only in the 15 midwestern states that had been the company's original territory. Thus, in 1957, the word "American," together with the Standard Oil (Indiana) logo, was used in all other states. Since a five-letter name was easier for motorists to note, in 1961 the company began to replace the brand name American with Amoco, the name first coined by American Oil's original owners for the high-octane, anti-knock gasoline that had powered the Charles Lindbergh trans-Atlantic flight. Familiar within the company since the 1945 organization of the Amoco Chemicals Corporation, "Amoco" was used increasingly on products and by subsidiaries, until, by 1971, major subsidiaries everywhere had "Amoco" in their names.

In 1961 Standard's total income reached almost $2.1 billion, yielding net earnings of $153.9 million. Continuing with methodical reorganization, Swearingen oversaw the expansion and modernization of the company's domestic refining capacity as well as 11 of its 14 catalytic cracking units. An aggressive marketing program featured large, strategically placed retail outlets, plus the addition of Avis car rental privileges to the credit card services that had been in operation since the early 1930s. By the end of 1966 there were 5.5 million card holders, encouraging American Oil to go national with its motor club.

Because only 8 percent of its assets was located overseas, Standard (Indiana) still lacked a large foreign market for crude oil. Swearingen moved swiftly to close the gap. By 1964 foreign explorations were taking place in Mozambique, Indonesia, Venezuela, Argentina, Colombia, and Iran. Refining and marketing also were flourishing, through the acquisition of a 25,000-barrel-per-day refinery near Cremona, Italy, and about 700 Italian service stations. About 250 service stations also were opened in Australia in 1961, along with a 25,000-barrel-per-day refinery. Other foreign refineries were to be found in West Germany, England, Pakistan, and the West Indies. In 1967 Standard began production in the Persian Gulf Cyrus field, by which time the huge El Morgan field in the Gulf of Suez was producing 45,000 barrels daily.

The market for Standard's chemical products also increased during the mid-1960s. To keep pace with demand for the raw materials used in polyester fiber and film, the company built a new facility at Decatur, Alabama, in 1965, adding another in Texas

City, Texas, a year later. There were also 641 retail chemical fertilizer outlets in the Midwest and the South. The popularity of polystyrene for packaging also grew. All of these advances ensured profitability; overall chemical sales rose to $158 million by the end of 1967, on total revenues of almost $3.6 billion.

Fuel shortages and the wave of OPEC price rises, nationalizations, and takeovers of the early 1970s underlined the importance of oil exploration. Swearingen's strategy was to accumulate as much domestic exploration acreage as possible before other companies acted, while organizing production in developing foreign markets that were not too competitive.

To capitalize on concern about air pollution, the company introduced a 91-octane lead-free gasoline in 1970 at a cost in excess of $100 million. Although motorists were initially reluctant to accept the 2 cent-per-gallon price rise, the 1973 appearance of catalytic converters on new cars assured the success of the fuel.

Environmental matters came to the fore again in 1978, when an Amoco International Oil Company tanker, the Amoco *Cadiz,* suffered steering failure during a storm and ran aground off the French coast, leaking about 730,000 gallons of oil into the sea. The huge oil spill cost $75 million to clean up and left its mark on the area's tourist trade as well as its ecosystem. The French government brought a $300 million lawsuit against Amoco that eventually led to a $128 million judgment against Amoco. Amoco appealed the ruling, but the U.S. Circuit Court of Appeals in Chicago not only upheld the judgment but increased it to $281 million. Amoco chose not to appeal this ruling and paid the French government $243 million and the affected Brittany communities $38 million.

In late December 1978 the Shah of Iran was overthrown, and Standard (Indiana) hurriedly closed its Iranian facility and evacuated American staff members after all American employees of Amoco Iran Oil Company received death threats. The year 1978 had seen record-breaking production in Iran, and its loss resulted in a 35 percent production decrease in the company's overseas operations. Despite these turbulent events, net income was $1.5 billion in 1971, on total revenues of $20.197 billion.

By the end of the 1970s, chemical production accounted for about 7 percent of company earnings. To gain more visibility with consumers, Standard (Indiana) began to stress end-product manufacture as well as the production of ingredients used in manufacturing processes. The trend had begun in 1968, when polypropylene manufacturer Avisun Corporation was purchased by Amoco Chemicals Corporation from Sun Oil Company. The $80 million price tag included Patchoque-Plymouth Company, maker of polypropylene carpet backing. By 1986 a 100-color line plus improved stain resistance made Amoco Fabrics & Fibers Company's petrochemical-based Genesis carpeting a serious competitor of the stain-resistant carpeting offered by du Pont. Other strategies focused on market stimulation for basic industrial products. Since this required specialized marketing skills, the company divided its chemical operations among four subsidiaries.

Name Change and Reorganization: 1980s–90s

In 1983 John Swearingen retired as chairman of the board. In his stead came Richard W. Morrow, who had been president of the Amoco Chemicals Corporation from 1974 until 1978, before assuming the Standard (Indiana) presidency in 1978. In 1985 Standard Oil Company (Indiana) changed its name to Amoco Corporation. Morrow also presided over the 1988 acquisition of Dome Petroleum, Ltd. of Canada, which was later merged into Amoco Canada. Dome, owning 28.7 million acres of undeveloped, arctic region land, improved Amoco's oil and gas reserves. The Dome purchase was hard-won, costing Amoco $4.2 billion. Other chances to expand oil and gas exploration in 1988 came with the acquisition of Tenneco Oil Company's Rocky Mountain properties, for approximately $900 million.

Amoco Corporation began the 1990s with record revenues of $31.58 billion and net income of $1.91 billion. By 1990, the need for raw materials had expanded internationally, moving strongly toward Europe and the Far East. Joint ventures in Brazil, Mexico, South Korea, and Taiwan met the growing demand for polyester fibers, helping to generate about 35 percent of business overseas.

H. Laurence Fuller took over as chairman in 1991 amidst a downturn in Amoco profits owing to weakening demand for petroleum products and reduced prices caused by the recession. Revenues fell to $28.3 billion in 1991 and to $26.22 billion in 1992, while net income declined to $1.17 billion and $850 million, respectively. Fuller aimed not only to turn around the company's fortunes but also to overtake Exxon, the top U.S. oil company, in profitability. Fuller began this effort with a 1992 restructuring intended to reduce costs and improve efficiency. Approximately 8,500 employees were axed—16 percent of Amoco's workforce—contributing to $600 million in savings. Exploration operations were cut back from a wildcatting strategy spread out over more than 100 countries to a targeted search for oil and gas in 20 countries with proven reserves. China became a prime target area; after establishing an offshore drilling operation in 1987, Amoco signed a deal in 1992 to become the first foreign company to explore the Chinese mainland, thought to hold more than 20 billion barrels of oil.

This restructuring served as prelude to an even larger reorganization effort initiated in 1994. A total of 4,500 more jobs would be cut over the next two years, with projected savings of $1.2 billion each year. Amoco's organizational structure was completely overhauled. The three major subsidiaries—Amoco Production Company, Amoco Oil Company, and Amoco Chemical Company—that had been responsible for the three major areas of operation were replaced by a decentralized structure with 17 business groups divided into three sectors: exploration and production, petroleum products, and chemicals. A Shared Services organization was created to share the resources of Amoco's support operations.

Amoco's chemical operations were overhauled during these restructurings by shedding such weak areas as oil well chemicals and by increasing expenditures in fast-growing areas such as polyester. One result was that profits from Amoco's chemical sector increased from $68 million in 1991 to $574 million in 1994 thanks in large part to its 40 percent share of the world market in paraxylene and purified terephthalic acid, both used to make polyester, the demand for which grew dramatically, especially in Asia.

New product expenditures also were bolstered during this period. With demand for alternative and cleaner-burning fuels on the rise, Amoco introduced Crystal Clear Ultimate, a cleaner-burning premium gasoline, and test-marketed compressed natural gas for use by fleet operators. Also tested were shared service stations that offered Amoco gas and fast food (from McDonald's and Burger King), or such services as dry cleaning (DryClean U.S.A.). These tests were so successful that Amoco planned to roll out 100 such units in 1995 at a cost of $100 million.

In 1994, Amoco made one of its largest natural gas finds off Trinidad and Tobago. The company embarked on a drive to become a leader in natural gas-powered electricity generation, creating Amoco Power Resources Corporation to pursue this venture and purchasing a 10 percent interest in electricity facilities in Trinidad and Tobago.

With the cost of oil and gas exploration soaring and lean operations not able to withstand the failure of a risky venture, more and more oil companies turned to joint ventures in the early and mid-1990s to spread the risk. Amoco was a member of a ten-company consortium that signed an agreement in 1994 with the Republic of Azerbaijan to develop oil fields in the Caspian Sea. Also in 1994 Amoco joined with rivals Shell Oil and Exxon to finance a $1 billion offshore oil platform in the Gulf of Mexico, to be the world's deepest. In 1995, Shell and Amoco created a limited partnership to develop oil fields in the Permian Basin area of west Texas and southeast New Mexico. In 1997, Amoco partnered with the Argentina oil company Bridas Corp. to form Pan American Energy—an exploration and production company that planned to conduct operations in Argentina, Brazil, Paraguay, and Uruguay.

The middle and late 1990s also were marked by continued divestitures. In 1995, the company sold its motor club business to a subsidiary of Montgomery Ward and its credit card operations to Associates First Capital Corporation, a Ford subsidiary. Two years later, it announced a major divestiture program, designed to shed nonfundamental properties and allow a tighter focus on core assets. The company sold off Amoco Gas Co., a gas pipeline and processing unit in Texas, to Tejas Gas Corp. The same year, the company sold a large portion of its domestic exploration and production assets—including oil and gas properties in Oklahoma; upstream oil and gas operations in Colorado; production properties in Wyoming, Montana, Colorado, and North Dakota; and coalbed-methane reserves in Alabama's Black Warrior Basin.

BP Amoco: An Energy Powerhouse in the Late 20th Century

The British Petroleum-Amoco merger was finalized at the end of 1998. The new company—named BP Amoco p.l.c.— was 60 percent owned by BP shareholders and was headed by BP's CEO Sir John Browne. Amoco's former CEO, Laurance Fuller, was co-chairman of the board, an office he shared with BP Chairman Peter Sutherland. BP shareholders owned 60 percent of the company. The merger served a dual purpose for both BP and Amoco. In the short term, it reduced costs by eliminating areas of overlap between the two organizations— most notably, in the reduction of approximately 10,000 jobs. In the long term, the pooling of BP's and Amoco's assets and revenues allowed the company to finance more development and take on larger projects.

But the oil giant's frenetic growth did not stop with the merger. Just a few months after closing the Amoco deal, the company announced yet another major acquisition: Atlantic Richfield Co. (Arco). Arco, which was based in Los Angeles, had been in the oil business since 1866—longer than either British Petroleum or Amoco. The company operated refineries and a 1,700-unit chain of gas stations in the western United States. It also held major oil and gas reserves, most of which were in Alaska. Together, in fact, BP Amoco and Arco would have controlled almost 70 percent of the oil production in Alaska—a degree of control that made the Federal Trade Commission (FTC) uncomfortable. The FTC refused to approve the merger until the company agreed to sell off Arco's Alaskan holdings, and the deal was delayed for months before finally closing in the spring of 2000.

Meanwhile, BP Amoco was pursuing still another acquisition. In March 2000, the company agreed to purchase Burmah Castrol, a U.K. lubricants group. Burmah Castrol was the maker of Castrol brand motor oil, one of the world's best-selling car motor oils. The company also manufactured chemicals used in the foundry, steel, and construction industries. The acquisition, which was finalized in mid-2000, gave BP Amoco the second largest market share in lubricants in Europe. In addition, like Amoco and Arco, it allowed the company to reduce costs by eliminating redundant jobs.

The year 2000 also marked a major change in corporate identity. Known in the two years since the merger as BP Amoco—a marriage of two strong trade names—the company shed "Amoco" from its name, becoming simply "BP p.l.c." The well-known Amoco name and logo were replaced with a new BP logo and color scheme—a green and yellow sunburst. Industry analysts speculated that the changes were intended to help the company move away from its longstanding identity as an "oil company" and reposition itself as an "energy company"—one with operations in oil, natural gas, and solar power.

Browne's aggressive acquisition strategy proved to be both well timed and well executed. The last years of the 20th century were marked by rapidly increasing prices in both crude oil and natural gas—hikes that paid off handsomely for BP. At the same time, the company began to realize the large cost reductions promised by its acquisitions. In 2000, the company made $12 billion in pretax profits—a record for a U.K. company.

Looking Ahead

Unsurprisingly, it appeared that natural gas would play an important role in BP's future. The company planned to increase its gas marketing and trading business by 9 to 11 percent annually over the first three years of the 21st century. In comparison, the company expected its retail petroleum business to grow by only 3 to 4 percent annually. By 2003, BP estimated gas to account for more than 40 percent of its daily hydrocarbon production.

BP also planned to increase its operations in solar power. In 2001, the company signed a deal with the Spanish and Philip-

pine governments to bring solar power to 150 Philippine villages—the largest solar energy project ever undertaken. BP also planned a fivefold expansion of its solar photovoltaic cell manufacturing operation in Spain. When complete, the Spanish operation would be one of the largest solar facilities in the world. The company planned to have a solar business worth $1 billion by 2007.

Principal Subsidiaries

Amoco Egypt Gas (U.S.A.); Amoco Egypt Oil (U.S.A.); Amoco Energy Company of Trinidad and Tobago (U.S.A.); Amoco Trinidad (LNG) B.V. (Netherlands); Atlantic Richfield Company; Atlantic Richfield Bali North (Indonesia); BP America (U.S.A.); BP Amoco Capital; BP Amoco Company (U.S.A.); BP Amoco Corporation (U.S.A.); BP Amoco Norway; BP Australia; BP Canada Energy; BP Capital BV (Netherlands); BP Chemicals; BP Chemicals Investments; BP Developments Australia; BP Espana; BP Exploration Co.; BP Finance Australia; BP France; BP International; BP Nederland; BP Oil International; BP Oil New Zealand; BP Oil UK; BP Shipping; BP Singapore Pte; BP Solar; BP Southern Africa; Britoil; Burmah Castrol; Deutsche BP; Standard Oil Co. (U.S.A.); Vastar Resources Inc. (U.S.A.); Abu Dhabi Marine Areas (33%); Abu Dhabi Petroleum Co. (24%); China American Petrochemical Co. (Taiwan; 50%); CoTo Finance Partnership (50%); Empresa Petrolera Chaco (Bolivia; 30%); Erdolchemie (Germany; 50%); Lukarco (Kazakhstan; 46%); Malaysia-Thailand Joint Development Agency (Thailand; 25%); Pan American Energy (Argentina; 60%); Ruhrgas AG (Germany; 25%); Rusia (Russia; 25%); AO Sidanco (Russia; 10%); Unimar Company Texas (Indonesia; 50%).

Principal Competitors

ChevronTexaco Corporation; Exxon Mobil Corporation; Royal Dutch/Shell Group.

Further Reading

Bahree, Bhushan, Christopher Cooper, and Steve Liesman, "Bigger Oil: BP to Acquire Amoco in Huge Deal Spurred by Low Energy Prices," *Wall Street Journal,* August 12, 1998, p. A1.

Beck, Robert J., "State Companies Lead OGJ 100 World Reserves, Production List," *Oil and Gas Journal,* September 28, 1992.

"Big Problems: British Petroleum," *Economist,* February 8, 1992. "BP After Horton," *Economist,* July 4, 1992.

Chelminski, Rudolph, *Superwreck: Amoco, The Shipwreck That Had to Happen,* New York: Morrow, 1987.

Cook, James, "First-Rate Company," *Forbes,* May 1, 1989, pp. 84–85.

Dedmon, Emmett, *Challenge and Response: A Modern History of Standard Oil Company (Indiana),* Chicago: Mobium Press, 1984.

Fairhall, David, *The Wreck of the Amoco Cadiz,* New York: Stein and Day, 1980.

Ferrier, R.W., *The History of the British Petroleum Company* (Vol. 1), Cambridge: Cambridge University Press, 1982.

Giddens, Paul Henry, *Standard Oil Company (Indiana): Oil Pioneer of the Middle West,* New York: Arno Press, 1976.

Guyon, Janet, "When John Browne Talks, Big Oil Listens," *Fortune,* July 5, 1999, p. 116.

Jones, Geoffrey, *The State and the Emergence of the British Oil Industry,* London: Macmillan, 1981.

Knott, David, "BP Sharpening Focus on Improved Shareholder Value, Efficiency," *Oil and Gas Journal,* July 8, 1996, pp. 22–26.

——, ''British Petroleum Maps Strategy for Continued Gains,'' *Oil and Gas Journal,* March 22, 1993, pp. 25–29.

Mack, Toni, ''Catching Up to Exxon,'' *Forbes,* March 13, 1995, pp. 64, 66.

Melcher, Richard A., Peter Burrows, and Tim Smart, ''Remaking Big Oil: The Desperate Rush to Slash Costs,'' *Business Week,* August 8, 1994, pp. 20–21.

O'Connor, Brian, ''Dealmaker Browne May Dazzle with Another Lightning Strike,'' *Daily Mail,* November 22, 2001, p. 77.

''An Oil Major Redefines Its Role,'' *Petroleum Economist,* February 1, 2001, p. 3.

Palmeri, Christopher, ''A Good Match in the Oil Patch,'' *Forbes,* September 21, 1998, p. 88.

Strauss, Gary, and Thor Valdmanis, ''BP, Amoco Nozzle Up: Oil Companies Pump Out $50 Billion Merger Deal,'' *USA Today,* August 12, 1998, p. 1B.

Therrien, Lois, ''Amoco: Running Smoother on Less Gas,'' *Business Week,* February 15, 1993, pp. 110–12.

''Whittle-Down Economics,'' *Oil and Gas Investor,* November 1992, pp. 43–46.

Yerak, Rebecca, ''Plugging the Drain at BP Oil,'' *Plain Dealer* (Cleveland), January 26, 1993.

—Geoffrey Jones and Gillian Wolf
—updates: April Dougal Gasbarre,
Shawna Brynildssen

Brake Bros plc

Enterprise House
Eureka Science & Business Park
Ashford, Kent TN25 4AG
United Kingdom
Telephone: (+44) 123-320-6000
Fax: (+44) 123-320-6006
Web site: http://www.brake.co.uk

Public Company
Incorporated: 1961
Employees: 7,454
Sales: $1.69 billion (2000)
Stock Exchanges: London
Ticker Symbol: BKB
NAIC: 422420 Packaged Frozen Food Wholesalers

Brake Bros plc is one of Britain's leading food suppliers to caterers in the United Kingdom and France, with designs on future European expansion. Members of the founding Brake family continue to own a major stake in the business, approximately 43 percent. The company, selling most of its products under its own label, operates through eight divisions, created in large part by an aggressive acquisition program that followed the company's initial public offering in 1986. Brake Bros Foodservice, the core of the business, is the top provider of frozen foods to U.K. caterers, offering more than 1,000 products. Larderfresh supplies fine foods, including fresh fish and seafood, to chefs. Country Choice supplies frozen products to bakers. Twin Chef prepares specialty dishes for the catering industry and also provides bacon and cooked hams, frozen vegetables, and desserts. Offering a variety of chilled and frozen foods, Puritan Maid targets major catering operations with multiple locations that require consistent quality. Watson & Philip is a wholesaler of chilled grocery products to chefs and caterers and also distributes non-food and cleaning products. With its own fish processing and smoking capabilities, M&J Seafood is a supplier of high quality fish and seafood to caterers. Brake France offers chilled and frozen products that are appropriate to French caterers.

The Start of a Brotherly Business: 1958

The three Brake brothers—William, Frank, and Peter—were brought up and trained in the catering industry. In 1958, they struck out on their own, starting a business to supply poultry to caterers, at first working out of a pub kitchen. Taking advantage of their contacts with caterers they expanded their business in 1963 by beginning to distribute frozen foods, which until then had not been generally well regarded by the foodservice industry. By bringing an improved quality to frozen foods, Brake Bros was instrumental in raising overall standards in the United Kingdom. The company again showed forward thinking in 1969 when it opened a cooked food factory to prepare frozen meals, positioning Brake Bros to take advantage of a growing pub food market. Frozen foods proved to be so successful that the company eliminated its original poultry processing business in 1974. Over the next dozen years Brake Bros continued to grow its business, in large part through a number of acquisitions.

By 1986, Brake Bros operated 16 cold storage depots located throughout the United Kingdom in order to service more than 35,000 customers, which included pubs, restaurants, hotels, hospitals, schools, and factories. In the years 1984 and 1985, the company increased its number of depots from eight to 15. As a result, revenues and pretax profits soared, more than doubling from 1982 to 1986. To fuel continued growth, in particular the opening of more depots, Brake Bros elected to make an initial public offering of stock in October 1986. Each brother retained a 25 percent stake, while the remaining 25 percent was sold at 125 pence a share. Each brother would realize about £3 million, and after expenses the company netted approximately £4.3 million. In an interview with the trade publication *Quick Frozen Foods International,* Frank Brake explained, ''Although the flotation gave us the financing to expand more quickly, we still applied the same financial and management controls right across the business and ensured that borrowing was kept to a minimum. The stability this gave the company allowed our planned progression, first to a national frozen food distributor and then into chilled and multi-temperature, all within foodservice.''

Brake Bros took a major step in national expansion in 1987 when it established an operation in Scotland. Over the next few

---

Company Perspectives:

Our shared objective is to be the leading food service supplier to the catering industry, providing profit opportunities for our customers, developing employees to their full potential, and generating profit for re-investment in the business to the benefit of our shareholders, customers, and employees.

---

years, the company also grew externally through a series of acquisitions, including S.H. Wickett & Sons in 1989, Elmdale Foods in 1990, and Midfish and Everfresh Frozen Foods in 1991. The company also acquired London Larder and created a fine foods division, Larderfresh, moving beyond frozen foods to chilled food distribution in order to service the quality hotel and restaurant market, which chose fresh foods over frozen. Earnings were depressed somewhat in 1991, due to the unexpected expense of establishing the fine food business, as well as a fire that destroyed a cold storage facility in West Yorkshire. Nevertheless, revenues increased by 14 percent over the previous year, reaching £223 million.

France Expansion: 1992

Brake Bros looked to grow overseas and through niche U.K. markets. It turned to France in 1992, acquiring frozen food suppliers Anjou Surgelation and Cogehalles to form the basis of its Brake France division, to which it added further French purchases. In May 1993, Brake Bros completed its largest acquisition to date when it bought Country Choice Foods for £14 million in stock, a move that allowed the company to enter a new market sector, supplying frozen bakery products. Country Choice was a well established and profitable national distributor with eight depots. While this acquisition immediately added to Brake Bros' earnings, the new fine foods business lost money as it established itself. Moreover, the U.K. catering market suffered through a period of stagnant growth. The French operation, in the meantime, appeared at least able to reach a break-even level. Despite these difficulties, Brake Bros increased revenues to almost £354 million in 1993, and pretax profits exceeded £19 million.

Larderfresh and Brake France continued to produce a drag on earnings in 1994, although management remained committed to both businesses, believing they would be instrumental to the future growth of Brake Bros. These difficulties, however, were more than offset by the improving U.K. catering market that benefited Country Choice and the company's frozen food business overall. The result was a significant increase in sales, which topped £400 million, and pretax profits, which improved to £23.5 million. Brake Bros also bolstered its fresh and frozen fish business in 1994 by acquiring Jesse Robinson, a Nottingham distributor.

In 1995, Larderfresh increased its sales by nearly 70 percent, thereby dramatically cutting into its losses. Brake French, on the other hand, posted a modest profit, helped in large measure by the mid-year acquisition of Frigosud SA. Overall, Brake Bros improved its earnings by 15 percent, a pace the company

had maintained since going public ten years earlier. A November 1995 acquisition, however, would hamper that impressive string of results. Brake Bros acquired Puritan Maid and its multi-temperature food distribution business from the Forte hotel chain at a cost of £7.4 million. It promised to be a pivotal addition to Brake Bros, which would now be able to tap into the growing market of large catering chains that preferred a single vendor for foods at all temperatures: ambient, chilled, and frozen. The company also signed a valuable three-year deal to supply Forte hotels and restaurants. Taking over Puritan Maid, however, proved to be problematic. To avoid relying on Forte, the company took on too many additional customers, but business quickly outstripped capacity, leading to many dissatisfied customers. Additional staff had to be hired and facilities contracted, which resulted in a spike in operational costs that could not be offset by contracted prices with customers. At one point, Puritan Maid was losing £1 million each month. Although in 1996 the company continued to improve on its earnings over the previous year, its impressive decade-long growth rate was curtailed, and investors responded by bidding down the company's stock. Larderfresh finally turned the corner, and after five years the French operations also appeared ready to make significant contributions. Brake Bros would have to depend on both divisions coming through in order to offset Puritan Maid, which was likely to require a lengthy period of time before it would be able to turn around.

Brake Family Control Easing in 1997

The Puritan Maid difficulties led CEO Frank Brake to announce that the company had to abandon a £20 million multi-temperature national food distribution center that had been in the works. Cost-cutting measures were implemented, including the elimination of 200 jobs. Moreover, the Forte distribution deal was also renegotiated and customers unwilling to agree to new contract terms were terminated. It was also becoming clear that the company was facing a transition period in which the founding fathers of the business would have to turn over operational control to executives outside the Brake family. William Brake, after 40 years with the company, stepped down as executive chairman. Frank Brake, at 63 years old, then assumed the position, and 52-year-old Ian Player, chief executive of the seafood division at Albert Fisher, was hired as the new group chief executive, taking over on July 1, 1997. In addition, a new finance director was hired. Despite problems in 1997, Brake Bros was still able to bolster its dessert business by acquiring Dairyfresh Desserts, supplier of spongecakes and puddings.

Under Player's leadership, Brake Bros made inroads in restoring Puritan Maid to health, cutting losses significantly. In October 1998, the company acquired the food distribution business of Watson & Philip to combine with Puritan Maid in order to broaden offerings to major catering clients, in particular room temperature products such as pastas and tea, as well as non-food products. Brake Bros, however, suffered some setbacks in 1998. Brake French again lost money after finally breaking even, and U.K. sales were depressed as people chose to eat out less, a change attributed to fears about the economy as well as the month-long World Cup soccer tournament that many stayed home to watch on television. Brake Bros was further troubled by the installation of a new IT system that resulted in £3 million

Key Dates:

1958: Brothers William, Frank, and Peter Brake establish the company, supplying poultry to caterers.
1963: The company begins to distribute frozen foods.
1969: The company opens first cooked food factory.
1974: The company abandons the poultry business in favor of frozen foods.
1986: The company goes public.
1992: Brake Bros enters the French market.
1995: Puritan Maid is acquired.
2000: M&J Seafoods is acquired.

in unexpected costs. Nevertheless, the company grew revenues to nearly £760 million in 1998 and posted a pretax profit of more than £30 million.

Brake Bros continued to address its problems with Puritan Maid and Brake France in 1999, as revenues showed dramatic improvement, increasing to £967 million, while pretax profits topped $36.1 million. The company was now positioned to renew its efforts at expansion, earmarking £100 million for acquisitions, with an emphasis on improving its fresh fish business. In March 2000, Brake Bros acquired M&J Seafoods, the U.K.'s largest independent distributor of fish and seafood, at a cost of £44 million. Already strong in the pub business, Brake Bros now gained an increased presence with some major restaurant groups through the M&J addition, as well as a large airline catering business. The M&J operation included ten depots, two processing plants, and a fish-smoking facility. Brake Bros made another major acquisition in July 2000, picking up the 100-year-old family-run Cearns & Brown, a major U.K. food wholesaler, at a cost of £23.7 million in cash and the assumption of £8.3 million in debt. While traditionally selling such groceries as pasta and canned food, in the previous ten years Cearns & Brown had branched into chilled and frozen foods. After opening a major London depot, however, the company began to struggle. For Brake Bros the acquisition was a good fit on a number of levels. Not only did Cearns & Brown add 12 more depots spread across the United Kingdom, its business complemented the earlier addition of Watson & Philip, the two having been active competitors. By merging Cearns & Brown into Watson and Philip, Brake Bros gained both sets of customers. Moreover, Cearns & Brown's strong position in ambient products helped moved Brake Bros closer to achieving its goal of attaining the same kind of market leadership it held in frozen foods with ambient and chilled foods. The company also bolstered its position in France by acquiring three frozen and chilled food companies in southeast France at a cost of £16 million. Then in May 2001, Brake Bros paid £17 million to acquire Szymczak Nadreau SA and Valette SA, in the process gaining a controlling stake in Carigel S.A., a major French

supplier of frozen and chilled products to caterers. Because of these additions, Brake France now covered 65 percent of the French catering market, making it the country's second largest chilled and frozen food distributor.

As a result of 18 months of aggressive expansion, Brake Bros saw its earnings fall off in 2000, but once the company fully digested its new holdings it appeared well positioned to continue its steady rate of growth. Major opportunities in the United Kingdom were limited, however, with consolidation of the larger players all but completed and smaller, family-owned businesses less likely to come up for sale. Brake Bros began to look to Continental Europe, hoping to take advantage of a strong base in France to gain inroads in new markets. With major countries including Germany, Italy, and Spain presenting few ready opportunities, Brake Bros considered establishing a presence in the Benelux countries, either through partnerships or outright acquisitions. What was not in question, however, was the desire of the company, even with decreasing participation of the founding Brake brothers, to continue its efforts to keep growing even larger.

Principal Divisions

Brake Bros Foodservice; Larderfresh; Country Choice; Twin Chef Foods; Puritan Maid; Watson & Philip; M&J Seafoods; Brake France.

Principal Competitors

Booker Cash and Carry; Diageo plc; Hillsdown Holdings, PLC; Kraft Foods, Inc.; Northern Foods PLC; Perkins Foods; Unilever; Uniq plc.

Further Reading

Abrahams, Ray, "Frank Brake Celebrates Frozen Foods As British FF Federation Turns 50," *Quick Frozen Foods International,* July 1998, p. 114.

Blackwell, David, "Puritan Maid Unsettles Brake Bros," *Financial Times,* March 27, 1997, p. 32.

Harvey, Amanda, "Brake Bros Adds Foods Wholesaler Cearns & Brown to Its Shopping Cart," *Scotsman,* July 15, 2000.

Kemp, Graham, "Another Acquisition by Brake Bros. Turns the Focus on to UK Merger Scene," *Quick Frozen Foods International,* October 1, 1993, p. 72.

Milton, Catherine, "Expansion Costs Hold Back Brake," *Financial Times,* September 22, 1993, p. 31.

Smith, Alison, "Brake Bros Upbeat on Year Despite Drop in Profits," *Financial Times,* September 10, 2001.

Tomkins, Richard, "Brake Brother's Market Debut," *Financial Times,* October 31, 1986, p. 26.

Wray, Richard, "Brake Bros' Player Says Looking at Expansion into Benelux Countries, *AFP-Extel News,* March 24, 1999.

—Ed Dinger

Bremer Financial Corp.

445 Minnesota Street, Suite 2000
St. Paul, Minnesota 55101
U.S.A.
Telephone: (651) 227-7621
Toll Free: (800) 908-BANK; (800) 908-2265
Fax: (651) 312-3550
Web site: http://www.bremer.com

Private Company
Incorporated: 1943 as Otto Bremer Company
Employees: 1,700
Total Assets: $5 billion (2001 est.)
NAIC: 551111 Offices of Bank Holding Companies

Bremer Financial Corp., a bank holding company, operates under a unique ownership structure. Owned by its employees and a nonprofit foundation, it is the only entity of its type in the United States. Founder Otto Bremer, a German immigrant, was at one time the largest investor of bank stocks in the Midwest. By returning much of the holding company's profits to the communities it serves, the Otto Bremer Foundation perpetuates the vision established by its namesake. Bremer Financial offers banking, investment, trust, and insurance services to customers in a three-state area.

Building Business Relationships: 1880s–1940s

Otto Bremer and his younger brother Adolph immigrated to the United States from Germany in 1886. The Midwest, where the young men settled, had experienced a period of rapid growth: the population had exploded and business opportunities were abundant. Otto Bremer's first job was as a stock clerk for a wholesale hardware business in St. Paul, Minnesota. In 1887, he took a bookkeeping position with the National German-American Bank—he had three years of elementary banking training in Germany, according to a *Ramsey County History* article by Thomas J. Kelley. Bremer eventually became chief clerk.

The boom days of the 1880s were followed by a bust in the early 1890s. Banks in St. Paul's sister city of Minneapolis went under. The National German-American Bank had to suspend operations for a time. By the end of the decade, the nation was in a deep economic depression.

Otto Bremer left the National German-American Bank at the turn of the century to make a run for the office of city treasurer. A well established and respected member of the community by this time, he won the election and served for five terms. (He had an unsuccessful but closely contested race for mayor in 1912.) Meanwhile, his brother Adolph was making his own headway in St. Paul's business community. One connection led to a romance as well. Adolph married Marie Schmidt, the daughter of North Star Brewery owner Jacob Schmidt, in 1896.

While serving as city treasurer, Otto Bremer became a charter member of the board of directors for the American National Bank. The bank was formed in 1903 through the merging of two St. Paul banks. Bremer held 50 of the 2,000 shares of capital stock. The charter members of the board of directors, well aware of potential pitfalls, operated a conservative banking business, unlike the days of wild growth when banks and customers were extended beyond their means.

Brother Adolph's responsibilities also continued to grow. When the brewery was reorganized as the Jacob Schmidt Brewing Company in 1899, he was named president. Adolph Bremer took over operating control when Schmidt died in 1910. He brought Otto in as secretary and treasurer shortly thereafter.

As Adolph gained ownership in the brewery, Otto Bremer increased his holdings in the bank, becoming a major shareholder by 1916. Adolph joined his brother on the American National Bank board of directors that year.

In 1921, Benjamin Baer, the bank's second president and an original board member, died. Otto Bremer was named chairman. He also bought much of Baer's stock and by 1924 gained controlling interest in the bank.

The brewery and its sales agencies in rural Minnesota, North Dakota, and Wisconsin provided a direct link to the Bremers and American National Bank in St. Paul. The brewery or the Bremers owned the land or buildings the sales agencies occupied, creating a starting point for further business relationships in the communities.

Otto Bremer became an advisor to local bankers, who often formed corresponding partnerships with American National. Dependent on the cyclical agricultural economy, country banks needed loans from city banks with a more diverse and therefore a more stable of base of business. Otto Bremer formed a deep commitment to the rural communities, and when economic disaster struck he was there to help.

Trouble began with a ramp-up of farm production in response to the needs created by the United States' entry into World War I. Farmers began planting more acres and buying expensive machinery. Agricultural land increased in value. Farmers took out larger loans to drive the expansion. Demand collapsed following the war. Harsh weather conditions in the Midwest further hampered farmers. Loans went unpaid. A recession hit the nation in 1920, taxing city banks supporting the stressed country banks.

"Bent on maintaining the public trust in the country banks, Otto Bremer loaned them his good name and his money. Throughout the 1920s banks came into the fold of the American National Bank or the Bremer group," wrote Kelley. Eventually, Bremer had to begin borrowing against his assets to keep country banks afloat.

By 1933, he held large or controlling interests in 55 banks in Minnesota, North Dakota, Wisconsin, and Montana, apart from his holdings in American National. However, he was $8 million in debt. The backing of Adolph Bremer's shares in the Jacob Schmidt Brewing Company and a loan from the Federal Reconstruction Finance Corporation helped Otto Bremer keep his stock in American National and the country banks in the family.

Despite the one-two punch delivered by the farm recession and Great Depression, the Bremer brothers had kept control of both the brewery and the bank. When Adolph Bremer died in 1939, Otto Bremer succeed him as president of the Jacob Schmidt Brewing Company.

In 1943, he created the Otto Bremer Company. The bank holding company consolidated his holdings in the country banks and would protect them from being sold to settle his estate, according to the Kelley article.

The Otto Bremer Foundation was formed the next year to make charitable grants in the communities served by the country banks. The ownership of the Otto Bremer Company was transferred to the foundation in 1949. After Bremer's death in 1951, the banking chain entered an extended period of consolidation. The brewery was sold in 1954, but descendants of

Adolph Bremer held stock in American National until it was sold to Milwaukee-based Firstar Corp. in 1996.

Legacy and Tradition Threatened: 1960s–80s

Robert J. Reardon, who joined the holding company in 1961, was named president in 1967, and the next year became a trustee of the Otto Bremer Foundation. He was dedicated to upholding Otto Bremer's tradition of commitment to the rural communities in which the banks were located. But, a year after Reardon took over leadership of the Foundation, a federal tax law was passed that threatened to dismantle the Bremer legacy.

The 1969 tax law required charitable foundations to cut their ownership in for-profit enterprises to 50 percent by May 26, 1989. The law had been enacted to weed out charitable trusts being used as tax shelters for corporate profits.

"In its original form, the law presented something of a Catch-22 to the Bremer Foundation," a 1984 *American Banker* article posited. Local banks with enough capital to buy the bank holding company could not do so due to antitrust regulations. Interstate banking laws of the time blocked the sale of the company to banks outside Minnesota. Non-banking organizations were eliminated from the pool of potential buyers by federal bank holding company law. In addition, the Internal Revenue Service's interpretation of the holding company's status further complicated matters: Reardon was able to circumvent that roadblock with the help of local congressmen. He had met with less success when he went to Congress to seek exemption from the tax law itself.

Bremer Financial Corp. began coordinating the activities among its banks beginning in 1983. A number of factors prompted the move. To begin with, the Bremer Foundation had been unable to find a solution to the 1969 tax law dilemma, and the deadline was looming. The banking industry itself was in a period of change, thanks to deregulation. Moreover, the agricultural economy, with which the company's rural and small town banks were still closely tied, was in deep trouble once again.

To strengthen the operation, the holding company reorganized into five regional groups. One bank president within each region was designated to lead the drive for more coordination and cooperation among the member banks.

To increase diversification, Bremer Financial Services Inc. added discount brokerage and trust services. Established in 1973, the enterprise at first performed audits and credit reviews of the banks. Later bond purchasing and other financial services were introduced. The company also upped its marketing activities and established a common name: First American.

By 1985, First American banks were writing off bad loans to the tune of $21.5 million, up from $4.6 million in 1983. The severe downturn in the rural economy had also made the prospects for selling off the banks in order to comply with the 1969 tax law more difficult. Banks located in agriculture-dependent regions were struggling across the nation: potential buyers would be looking for bargains.

Meanwhile, Bremer Financial Corp. continued to strengthen itself internally. Data processing was centralized and standard-

Key Dates:

1886: Bremer brothers arrive in the United States.
1933: Otto Bremer holds interest in 55 banks in Minnesota, Wisconsin, North Dakota, and Montana.
1943: Otto Bremer Company is created.
1944: Otto Bremer Foundation is established.
1951: Otto Bremer dies.
1969: Tax law threatens Bremer legacy.
1983: Holding company reorganizes, and the independent banks take a common name, First American.
1989: Foundation sells part of holding company to employees.
1998: Banks take on Bremer name for the first time.
2001: Bremer Financial purchases 11 branches from Firstar Bank, its first significant purchase in Twin Cities metropolitan area.

ized lending procedures were developed. Loan managers were trained to spot potential problems and intervene early.

All in all, despite challenges, Bremer Financial Corp. stayed the course. David Shern, former state banking commissioner, said in a 1987 *Star Tribune* article by Joe Blade, "That is one of the best-run bank holding companies in Minnesota." As it had been in Otto Bremer's day, the corporation stepped in to strengthen its banks when they encountered trouble. "That is a very clean operation. They are solid people. They run good banks," he said. Total assets were $1.6 billion, according to the Blade article.

In 1989, Bremer Foundation solved its tax law problem by selling 8 percent of the holding company to its employees and giving them majority voting rights. The foundation retained 92 percent of the economic value of the holding company.

Eye Toward Big City Growth: 1990s–2001

Beginning in the early 1990s, Bremer Financial set its sights on modernization. A big investment in technology improved efficiency and cut costs. The company also upgraded banking services and moved into new business areas. Although it was late in the game, Bremer Financial Corp. began offering proprietary mutual funds in 1997.

The entry of banks into the investment management business had peaked in 1992 and declined to a trickle since then. Bremer planned to target the retirement market. The bank holding company had been selling mutual funds since the mid-1980s through a partnership with Invest Financial Corp., but established its own equity growth fund and an intermediate bond fund using $60 million of corporate trust assets.

First American opened its first Twin Cities grocery store branches in mid-1997. The bank had operated in grocery stores in other areas since 1990. The move was part of an effort to expand its presence in the metropolitan area. The company had already increased its commercial business by adding international business services.

Also in 1997, the Otto Bremer Foundation, Bremer Financial Corp., and Bremer employees pitched in $1.5 million to help with disaster relief in the Red River Valley. The area bordering eastern North Dakota and northwestern Minnesota was devastated by flooding in the spring of that year. Tim Huber, reporting for *CityBusiness* in August, noted that the founder "would have appreciated the relief effort." Catastrophic aid was one of the foundation's original purposes.

Reminiscent of earlier days, Bremer Financial found when it entered the Fargo, North Dakota market that the foundation's support of the region's nonprofit organizations had already prepared the ground for business relationships with many in the community.

The Bremer Foundation received the profits of the individual banks through dividends from the holding company and in turn distributed them back into the communities through charitable grants. According to the Huber article, the Foundation and Bremer employees received $12.5 million in dividends in 1996.

Even though Bremer Financial had no Wall Street investors to satisfy, the corporation needed to perform well to maintain its independence. The company strived to sustain annual earnings growth of 10 percent. In 1996, it exceeded the mark. Earnings were $31.8 million, up from $27.1 million the previous year.

The seven First American banks located in the Twin Cities underwent a name change in July 1998. The holding company's remaining banks and the trust and insurance operations would take on the Bremer name toward year-end. The move marked the first time the banks themselves would wear the founder's name. The company also planned to open its first bank location in downtown St. Paul, longtime home of its corporate and foundation headquarters.

Bremer Financial projected the costs related to the name change would exceed $1 million. The company planned to emphasize Bremer's historical commitment to community in its marketing. At the time, mergers were eliminating some well-known names in Twin Cities banking. Minneapolis-based Norwest would take the name of California-based Wells Fargo, and First Bank System opted for U.S. Bank, following its purchase of Portland's U.S. Bancorp.

Norwest's assets were $96.1 billion. U.S. Bancorp's were $71 billion. Another large Minnesota-based banking concern, TCF Financial, followed well behind with $9.7 billion. Acquisitions helped Bremer Financial grow from $1.4 million in assets in 1984 to $3.2 billion in 1997.

Bremer could put its name back on a building in downtown St. Paul following the purchase of Dean Financial (a building bearing the Bremer name had been razed in the late 1990s). In addition to gaining a significant physical presence, Bremer added $312 million in assets, 11 offices, and four bank charters to its holdings in the 1999 deal. Overall, Bremer would hold 50 banking offices in Minnesota, 31 in North Dakota, and 16 in Wisconsin.

The holding company finally attained a long-sought goal when it purchased 11 branches from Firstar Bank. In addition to boosting its visibility in the metro area, the deal also eased

Bremer Financial's reliance on the farm economy. The acquisition was made possible, according to a February 2001 *American Banker* article, when federal regulators told Firstar, which was about to buy U.S. Bancorp, to divest some of its Twin Cities branches in order to preserve competition. Gaining $769 million in deposits, Bremer Financial climbed a notch in the Twin Cities market, moving from sixth to fifth, and became the third largest holder of deposits in the state, up from fifth. The Firstar purchase was the company's ninth acquisition since 1993.

However, the deal took an unusual turn when the Department of Justice required some commercial accounts, the chairman of Firstar Bank Minnesota, and five commercial managers to be moved to Bremer. In general, deposits and branches were involved in divestitures, not specific accounts and personnel, according to a February 2001 *Star Tribune* article.

Keeping with the tradition of building community connections, Bremer Financial Corp. formed a partnership with the Minnesota Council of Nonprofits in 2001. The council's 1,110 members, both large and small organizations, would be offered a variety of special services, including favorable interest rates on deposit accounts and certificates of deposit. About 25 percent of the state's financially active nonprofits were members of the council, according to a June 2001 *Star Tribune* article. Minnesota's nonprofit community held about $24 billion in total assets.

Principal Competitors

Wells Fargo & Company; U.S. Bank; TCF Financial Corp.

Further Reading

Blade, Joe, "Bremer Foundation Caught in a Bind," *Star Tribune (Minneapolis)*, April 5, 1987, p. 1D.

Chin, Richard, "R.J. Reardon, Social Services Booster, Dies," *St. Paul Pioneer Press*, January 24, 1995, p. 5C.

DePass, Dee, "Bremer Agrees to Buy Banks of Dean Financial," *Star Tribune (Minneapolis)*, January 27, 1999. p. 3D.

——, "Bremer, Nonprofit Council Form Banking Partnership," *Star Tribune (Minneapolis)*, June 9, 2001, p. 1D.

——, "Firstar Managers Joining Bremer," *Star Tribune (Minneapolis)*, February 22, 2001, p. 1D.

"A Dilemma for Minnesota's Bremer," *American Banker*, June 8, 1984, pp. 16+.

Hage, Dave, "Another Union Battle Puts Willmar in Spotlight," *Star Tribune (Minneapolis)*, May 3, 1987, 1D.

Huber, Tim, "First American Shops for Growth," *CityBusiness*, June 6, 1997.

——, "Foundation Fosters Bremer Legacy," *CityBusiness*, August 8, 1997.

Hughlett, Mike, "At Last: A Bremer Bank," *St. Paul Pioneer Press*, June 25, 1998, p. 1D.

Jackson, Ben, "Bremer Making Twin Kill in Twin Cities Branch Deal," *American Banker*, February 5, 2001, p. 6.

Kelly, Thomas J., "The American National Bank and the Bremer Brothers," *Ramsey County History*, 1988, pp. 3–13.

Lutton, Laura Pavlenko, "Small Banks Taking Name of Philanthropic Founder," *American Banker*, July 13, 1998, p. 7.

——, "U.S. Says Profit-Sharing Plan Short Changed Workers," *American Banker*, January 6, 1999.

Talley, Karen, "Fewer Banks Trying Their Luck with Proprietary Mutual Funds," *American Banker*, April 28, 1997, p. 1+.

—Kathleen Peippo

BROWN ≡ BROTHERS HARRIMAN

Brown Brothers Harriman & Co.

59 Wall Street
New York, New York 10005
U.S.A.
Telephone: (212) 483-1818
Fax: (212) 493-7287
Web site: http://www.bbh.com

Private Company
Incorporated: 1931
Total Assets: $2.8 billion (2000)
NAIC: 522110 Commercial Banking

Brown Brothers Harriman & Co. is America's oldest, largest, and most prestigious private bank. Because its 40 partners share unlimited liability, the bank's deposits are not insured by the Federal Deposit Insurance Corporation (FDIC). The resulting need for consensus among the partners has played a large part in the bank's conservative approach to doing business and led to a perception of Brown Brothers as a stuffy institution. Through the course of the 1990s, however, it has taken steps to dispel that notion. Brown is especially known for its personal banking services for wealthy customers, in particular ''old money,'' from which many of the bank's partners also hail. In reality, this business represents just a third of the bank's money management activities, and more recently Brown Brothers has made efforts to attract the newly affluent, generally targeting individuals with at least $5 million in investable assets. It provides similar investment management services for private companies. Brown Brothers also engages in merger advisory activities as well as general commercial lending, a third of which is made to importers of such commodities as coffee, cocoa, sugar, textiles, precious metals, petroleum, and seafood. A major source of the bank's profits is derived from doing custodial work for foreign firms that need to maintain a large U.S. cash balance in order to buy and sell stocks on Wall Street. In addition to its longtime headquarters at 59 Wall Street and a site across the Hudson River in Jersey City, Brown Brothers maintains domestic offices in Boston, Charlotte, Chicago, Dallas, Los Angeles, Palm Beach, and Philadelphia, as well as overseas branches in London, Dublin, Naples, the Cayman Islands, Luxembourg, Zurich, Hong Kong, and Tokyo. Brown Brothers has nearly $1 trillion under management and boasts assets of $2.8 billion.

Brown Brothers Harriman & Co. Dating to 1800 Baltimore

The forefather of Brown Brothers was Alexander Brown, a linen merchant from Belfast, Ireland, born in 1764, who immigrated to the United States in 1800 and settled in Baltimore, where his younger brother was already engaged in business. With its location on the Chesapeake Bay, Baltimore was a thriving port as well as distribution center for goods destined for the interior of Maryland and Virginia and points west. Brown opened an ''Irish Linen Warehouse'' and was so successful that he soon enjoyed a veritable monopoly on Baltimore's linen trade. He then began to export tobacco, wheat, and other produce, and deal in foreign exchange. In 1805 his eldest son William entered the business as a partner, and by the next year William set up a business in Philadelphia that failed, as did another attempt in 1809. A second son, George, became a partner in 1808, followed in 1810 by Alexander Brown's third son, John, resulting in the business being renamed Alexander Brown & Sons. It was John who in 1818 finally established a Philadelphia branch (John A. Brown & Co.), which would become the direct ancestor of today's Brown Brothers Harriman. William, in the meantime, established an English branch of the family business in Liverpool. Although the headquarters of the family firm remained in Baltimore, the bulk of business was now conducted between the Philadelphia and Liverpool houses. As the United States grew, however, New York began to replace Philadelphia as the nation's commercial center, especially after the completion of the Erie Canal in 1825, which linked New York to commerce with the West. It was in October of that year that Alexander Brown's youngest of four sons, James, established Brown Brothers & Co. near the wharves of Manhattan's South Street, an area devoted to the dry goods trade. Rather than a branch of his father's house, however, it was created to support the business of William & James Brown & Co. of Liverpool, in particular the reshipment of Southern cotton.

James focused on the banking aspects of the business, working in concert with a dry goods merchant named Samuel Nicholson. He also took in as a partner a Baltimore cousin named

Stewart Brown. After Alexander Brown died in 1834, James Brown sold the dry goods business, apparently realizing that more money could be made from financing the trade than in actually importing the goods. Brown Brothers, already established as one of Manhattan's major international merchant banks, moved its offices to Wall Street in 1835, across the street from the Merchant Exchange, where more than half of U.S. imports and a third of exports were handled. When Alexander Brown's estate was settled in 1836, both Stewart Brown and Nicholson became general partners in all of the Brown businesses. Following an economic downturn in 1837, Liverpool-based Joseph Shipley became a partner of the English branch, resulting in a name change to Brown Shipley & Co. In 1838 Nicholson established a New Orleans agency that greatly expanded the company's foreign exchange and credit operations and firmly positioned Brown Brothers in the banking arena.

John A. Brown and George Brown left the business in 1840, selling their shares to William and James, leaving James the head of American operations, which also expanded to Boston during this period. More economic troubles in 1857 caused the firm to increasingly focus on banking operations and to ease out of importing and exporting completely. The two brothers shared power until William's death in 1864, and control passed entirely to James. In 1868 new articles of partnership were drawn up. By this time, William's sons had died, his grandsons were too young, and only two of James's sons had enough experience to run the business, making it necessary to bring in outside partners and thus jeopardizing the Brown family's control of the firm. Reorganized, however, Brown Brothers was now better suited to a changing world. Its credit business became so lucrative that the partners contributed outside money to maintain sufficient working capital. When William's grandson, Alexander Hargreaves Brown, became a partner in 1875, not only was family control restored, but a major portion of William's estate returned to the firm, helping Brown Brothers to prosper in the final decades of the 19th century.

By the 1890s Brown Brothers faced new competition from life insurance companies and the trust companies in which they invested in order to engage in industrial financing and speculation. For many years Brown Brothers had invested in securities on behalf of valued customers, but instead of an accommodation, by the end of the century the purchase of securities on commission was a major part of the firm's business. In 1892 the bank introduced travelers credits for use in the United States, Canada, and Latin America. Four years later the American Express Company simplified the concept with its travelers checks, and Brown Brothers in 1900 introduced foreign travelers checks. During this period the financing of reorganizing railroads, as well as railroad construction, became a major part of the firm's business. Brown Brothers also became involved in the consolidation of electric trolley car lines.

At the start of the 20th century the firm was a transatlantic partnership still very much dominated by the Brown family. In early 1907, for instance, both the London and New York heads were Browns, as were seven of the 14 partners. Once again, however, Brown Brothers faced the problem of passing control to a younger generation, which had become increasingly critical of older management, charging that the firm was falling behind the competition. Articles to renew the partnership, drawn up in 1907, granted greater authority to junior partners. Moreover, there were now tensions between the New York and London sides of the partnership, prompting serious consideration of the possibility of splitting into two firms. It was World War I, and the taxes levied to finance the conflict in both the United States and England finally made the old relationship untenable. On January 1, 1918, the two Brown partnerships became independent of one another. In 1946 the London partnership would incorporate, becoming Brown, Shipley & Co., Limited.

Brown Brothers Merging with Harriman in 1931

Like the rest of the United States, which prospered during the postwar economic boom of the 1920s, Brown Brothers was caught short by the stock market crash of 1929. The firm had underwritten a large number of corporate stocks and government bonds, and with the collapse in the market was unable to sell these securities without incurring ruinous losses. Moreover, the firm had lost a number of older and wealthier partners, through retirement or death, and had to honor the prearranged withdrawal of their funds. As a result, Brown Brothers was severely overextended and by 1930 had no recourse but to seek new capital. Refinancing came from the merging of Brown Brothers with the banking firms established by the sons of the late railroad magnate Edward Herman Harriman: William Averell Harriman and E. Roland Harriman. According to company lore the idea of joining the businesses was first broached during a card game on a train that was bound for a reunion at Yale University. There is no doubt, however, that Yale ties between the principals were instrumental in the merger. Numerous men from both firms graduated from Yale, including Harriman's vice-president and director Prescott Bush, grandfather of President George W. Bush.

The Harriman brothers inherited wealth from both sides of their family. By contrast, their father, better known as E.H. Harriman, worked his way up, starting out on Wall Street as an office boy. Although his grandfather had been a successful businessmen, as were his uncles, Harriman's father was a clergyman. At the age of 21 in 1869, Harriman borrowed $3,000 from an uncle to buy a seat on the stock exchange. He first became involved in transportation when he bought a boat that traveled the Hudson River between New York and Newburgh. He became interested in railroads after marrying Mary Williamson Averell, the daughter of an upstate New York banker and railroad president. Harriman rebuilt a small line that he resold for a healthy profit to the Pennsylvania Railroad. He then became vice-president of the Illinois Central Railroad, which served as a stepping stone to his assuming control of the Union Pacific Railroad, famed as one of the two railroads that completed the first transcontinental line but was now long neglected

Key Dates:

1800: Alexander Brown immigrates to the United States, establishing a linen import business in Baltimore.
1810: Branch opens in Liverpool (U.K. business eventually shifts headquarters to London).
1818: Branch opens in Philadelphia.
1825: Branch opens in New York.
1834: Alexander Brown dies.
1843: The New York office moves to Wall Street.
1918: The New York and London partnerships begin to operate separately.
1931: Harriman family firms merge with the firm to create Brown Brothers Harriman.
1978: Roland Harriman dies.
1998: The firm names its first two female partners.

and in poor financial condition. He assumed the chairmanship in 1898, and bought stock in the company, which would form the basis of his great fortune as he revitalized the business. In addition, Harriman became involved in a steamship line to the Orient, as well as interests in banks and insurance companies.

Harriman died in 1909, shortly before his eldest son, Averell, began his college studies at Yale. Roland was just 14 at the time of his father's death. As soon as he graduated from Yale, Averell went to work for the Union Pacific, becoming vice-president for purchasing within two years. During World War I, rather than serve in the military, he turned to shipbuilding. In addition, his banking firm, W.A. Harriman and Company, became involved in a wide range of American and European businesses, including mining, steel mills, motion pictures, and aviation. Roland, who also graduated from Yale, joined W.A. Harriman and Company in 1922, becoming vice-president the following year. In 1927 the brothers formed Harriman Brothers and Company, which along with W.A. Harriman and Company would finally merge with Brown Brothers in 1931, with Roland serving as a vice-president.

Aside from abundant Yale loyalties, the two firms were a good fit: Brown Brothers needed an infusion of cash and the Harriman brothers gained access to long-cultivated business relationships. It was a mixing of the old with the new, and it was generally conceded that Brown Brothers was in need of change. Not only did the atmosphere ease, with the partners becoming more accessible to both staff and clients, the firm placed a new emphasis on its domestic banking business. Following the change of banking laws with the Glass-Steagall Act in 1933, which forced banks to choose between the commercial banking business and the investment banking business, Brown Brothers opted to stay in domestic banking, where already two-thirds of its business was conducted. Its investment banking business was spun off, one day becoming part of Drexel Burnham Lambert. Brown Brothers was allowed, however, to retain a seat on the New York Stock Exchange without registering as a broker, an advantage that would prove lucrative over the years.

Although Roland Harriman would be far more involved with Brown Brothers than his brother, Averell's career in public service would add greatly to the luster of the firm. Averell—unlike Roland, who was a staunch Republican—became a leading Democrat, initially serving with President Roosevelt's National Recovery Administration before starting a career as a diplomat during the early days of World War II. He took part in all of the major Allied summits, becoming a close personal friend of Britain's Prime Minister Winston Churchill. From 1943 to 1946 he served as the U.S. ambassador to the Soviet Union, then became ambassador to England for a short time before becoming President Truman's secretary of commerce. After failing in a bid to become the Democratic candidate for the presidency in 1952, he successfully ran for governor of New York. When John F. Kennedy won the presidency in 1960, Averell became an ambassador at large, then returned to private life after Richard Nixon assumed the presidency in 1969.

Changes and Improvements in the Late 20th Century

Brown Brothers thrived for decades, opening offices around the world, and developing relationships with foreign institutions that helped it build a lucrative cross-border custody business. The youth and vitality that the Harriman brothers brought to Brown Brothers in 1931, however, eventually waned, and by the mid-1970s the firm was once again seen as old and out of touch, an enclave of elitist Ivy Leaguers. A number of staff members, unwilling to wait at least 15 years before becoming partners, left to start their own firms. Prescott Bush died in 1972. Roland Harriman retired in 1978 at the age of 83 and died later that year. Averell Harriman would die in 1986. The firm made some inroads in reversing its country club image in 1983 when it named Terrence M. Farley as its managing partner. Farley was a graduate of City College of New York's Baruch School of Business, who started out as one of the bank's tellers, attended night school, and worked his way up in the firm. Soon after he took charge, some of the elder partners were eased out. Despite these changes, Brown Brothers continued to receive criticism about its lackluster financial performance, especially compared with the spectacular returns realized by the likes of junk bond king Michael Milken.

In light of the indictment of Milken and the savings and loan scandal of the 1980s, the conservative approach of Brown Brothers regained some credibility in the early 1990s. Nevertheless, the firm took steps to improve its business. It was particularly aggressive in upgrading its information technology, which would provide an important competitive edge in its custodial services. In 1991 it created a pilot project, the 1818 Fund, which raised $325 million from institutional partners to fund medium-sized companies. It was so successful that additional 1818 Funds would be offered over the ensuing decade, as well as other investment funds, including one geared toward Europe. In 1998 Brown Brothers admitted its first two women partners, Kristen F. Giarrusso and Susan C. Livingston. In 2000 the firm opted to quit the brokerage business to focus on money management for its patrons. It also continued to invest in information technology to support its global custodian business, with a special interest in the increasingly important funded retirement savings plans in Japan and Europe, similar to 401(k) plans. As it had for close to 200 years, Brown Brothers continued to blend tradition with forward thinking, albeit at times with seeming reluctance.

Principal Competitors

The Bank of New York Company, Inc.; The Goldman Sachs Group, Inc.; Northern Trust Corporation.

Further Reading

Delamaide, Darrell, ''How to Make Money with Style,'' *Euromoney,* January 1991, p. 16.

Groenfeldt, Tom, ''The Road Less Traveled,'' *Institutional Investor International Edition,* March 2001, p. 91.

Kouwenhove, John A., *Partners In Banking: An Historical Portrait of a Great Private Bank, Brown Brothers Harriman & Co. 1818–1968,* New York: Doubleday & Company, 1968.

''Partners in Profit: Brown Brothers Harriman,'' *Economist,* April 9, 1994, p. 87.

Stock, Helen, ''Brown Brothers Relishes Unique Role,'' *American Banker,* August 4, 2000, p. 1.

Willoughby, Jack, ''Living in the Past,'' *Forbes,* July 11, 1988, p. 64.

—Ed Dinger

BTG, Inc.

3877 Fairfax Ridge Road
Fairfax, Virginia 22030
U.S.A.
Telephone: (703) 383-8000
Toll Free: (800) 432-4284
Fax: (703) 556-9290
Web site: http://www.btg.com

Wholly Owned Subsidiary of The Titan Corporation
Incorporated: 1982
Employees: 1,800
Sales: $224.8 million (2001)
NAIC: 541512 Computer Systems Design Services

BTG, Inc. provides information technology (IT) expertise to government and commercial enterprises. The U.S. Department of Defense accounts for 60 percent of sales. A variety of federal and state agencies avail themselves of BTG's services. The company has facilities in 11 states and Washington, D.C.; its employees also work at customer sites. IT giant Titan Corporation acquired BTG in late 2001.

Origins

Edward Bersoff founded BTG, Inc. in 1982. (The initials stood for Bersoff Technology Group, not Bill The Government, reported the *Washington Post.*) Before founding BTG, Bersoff had been an executive at CTEC Inc., a systems integration firm in Wilkes-Barre, Pennsylvania, for several years, and before that he worked for Logicon, Inc. He had begun his career in the Army, which assigned him to a NASA facility in Cambridge, Massachusetts, in the 1960s.

BTG was headquartered in Falls Church, Virginia, a suburb of Washington, D.C. The company was dedicated to systems development, including requirements analyses, design, development, product assurance, maintenance, and training. The company's original four employees worked out of a basement at first.

A 1987 plan for Logicon Inc., a publicly traded electronic systems and high-tech services company, to acquire BTG was canceled due to falling stock prices. Bersoff felt that BTG, then billing $25 million a year, was too small to survive on its own in the era of post-Glasnost defense cuts. He sought to double the firm's size in 1990 by buying Systems Exploration International (SEI), a computer engineering support company based in San Diego. Before BTG could acquire it, though, SEI had to settle an $875,000 claim from Olin Corp., a huge conglomerate, which had sold SEI its Martin & Stern subsidiary two years earlier. The bizarre episode resulted in Martin & Stern employees being evicted from their offices after the company missed a rent payment to Olin.

In spite of the defense slowdown, BTG's revenues grew 15 percent to about $30 million in 1991, though profits were static. BTG's specialty, software for intelligence analysts and commanders in the field, was in high demand following the Persian Gulf War, noted the *Washington Post.* The company had 300 employees, its most to date. Still, like most other defense firms, BTG found capital increasingly harder to obtain.

In April 1992 BTG and Hughes Aircraft Co. won a contract to supply the Navy with up to 4,300 computer workstations. The deal was potentially worth $100 million over eight years.

By this time, BTG had begun to look for work outside the defense sector. It installed an electronic security system at George Washington University. The company collaborated with the National Institutes of Health to develop a system to produce 3-D X-rays. The Federal Aviation Administration tapped BTG for a ten-year program to overhaul the country's air traffic control system.

A New Business in 1992

In 1992, BTG merged with BDS Inc., a Sterling, Virginia, computer reseller valued at $27 million. BDS's vending capabilities complemented BTG's software systems business nicely. After the merger, BTG was organized into two operating units: BTG Systems and BDS Technologies. Entering the reselling and systems integration business would help BTG boost reve-

Company Perspectives:

Our Goal: Ensure our client's success. At BTG, we believe that technology must help clients accomplish their missions and business goals. Whether your business is government or commercial, our job is to understand your needs and apply the right level of technology to satisfy them. Technology is not leading-edge—unless it gives you the edge over your competitors.

nues by 800 percent in the next four years. The company was eventually reorganized into three units: engineering for defense agencies; engineering for civilian and commercial markets; and reselling.

BTG logged revenues of $103.6 million in fiscal 1994. Profits were $1.8 million. Defense work still accounted for three-quarters of business. The company won a $160 million contract to provide defense and intelligence agencies with off-the-shelf software and services.

In July 1994 BTG paid $2 million for ACTech, a company that customized computers for the Department of Defense and had annual revenues of $15 million. Arlington's Delta Research Corp., which specialized in environmental management for military bases, was acquired later in the year for $3 million.

Public in 1995

Around 1992, venture capitalists that had invested in BTG were pressuring Bersoff for a quick development of one of the company's product lines, and the subsequent opportunity to exit the venture within a year via an initial public offering. Bersoff negotiated for a less accelerated approach; BTG went public in December 1995. The offering netted $9 million and Bersoff retained 20 percent ownership in the company. By this time BTG had more than 600 employees. Revenues for fiscal 1995 were $156 million.

Spencer Gifts, operator of mall novelty stores, hired the firm to develop an encryption system for handling customers' credit card information over the telephone. Then, in September 1995, BTG bought Concept Automation Inc. (CAI), another Washington-area systems firm, hoping to reduce dependence on defense work. CAI boasted contracts with several non-defense federal agencies and had annual revenues of about $84 million.

In December 1995, two partnerships, led by BTG and Cordant Inc., together won a $929 million Air Force contract to allow defense and intelligence agencies to order computers and software via the telephone and the Internet. BTG won a similar, $1.1 billion contract from the Department of Transportation in May 1996. This merely set up BTG as one approved vendor among several, however—part of a new government procurement policy designed to allow agencies to order equipment and services more quickly than the traditional, cumbersome "winner takes all" approach of awarding large contracts to a single vendor.

The company moved to a new headquarters in Fairfax, Virginia, around 1996. Annual revenues jumped from $214 million to $156 million in that fiscal year. Net income, down slightly to $3 million, was affected by federal government shutdowns.

The company was expecting 1997 revenues to exceed $400 million. This proved nearly accurate and soon BTG was aiming for revenues of $1 billion by fiscal 2000. This would not happen, in part because of the sale of the company's product reselling unit in February 1998, which cut product sales 84 percent.

In spite of BTG's considerable success in the government sector, margins were shrinking there and the company's management felt a need to diversify into the faster-growing commercial sector. In mid-1996, BTG formed a subsidiary, Community Networks Inc. (CNI), to provide high-speed cable modem internet service. Loudoun County, Virginia, was its first test market. The commercial market proved difficult to enter, and CNI was a case in point. BTG invested more than $5 million in CNI while failing to sign up enough customers. Bersoff announced plans to fold CNI, which was costing BTG $400,000 a quarter, into BTG's other operations in 1997, ending its existence as an independent subsidiary. Commercial ventures accounted for only 11 percent of BTG's business in 1997, hurting both its bottom line and share price, reported the *Washington Post*.

Buying and Selling in the Late 1990s

In late 1997, BTG announced plans to buy New York-based Micros-to-Mainframes Inc., a commercial sector network integration specialist, for $25 million. A few months later, BTG sold its reseller division, which had 320 employees, to rival Government Technology Services Inc. (GTSI) for $23 million in cash and stock. A group of five BTG vice-presidents made a competing offer for the unit; the division's employees were not happy about GTSI's plans for job cuts or the prospect of working for their archrival, whom Bersoff himself had once compared to *Star Wars* villain Darth Vader. Ultimately, GTSI prevailed over the management group. The deal left BTG with a 30 percent holding in GTSI, although it began selling those shares back to GTSI in February 1999. The divestiture marked BTG's return to being a pure services company, noted one analyst in the *Washington Times*.

BTG reported a $35.2 million net loss for the fiscal year ending March 31, 1998, mostly due to the sale of the reselling division and the discontinuance of the CNI cable internet venture. Revenue was $588.9 million.

BTG bought STAC Inc. of Fairfax, Virginia, for $5 million in January 1999. The $14 million purchase of SSDS Inc., a Denver-based network security firm, followed in the spring of 2000. BTG then bought Research Planning Inc., a local provider of high-level support services, for $9 million in April 2001. The fact that 90 percent of Research Planning's 450 employees held security clearances made it an attractive buy, according to Bersoff.

Key Dates:

1982: BTG is founded by Edward Bersoff.
1992: BTG enters product reselling business via acquisition of BDM, Inc.
1995: BTG goes public on the NASDAQ stock exchange.
1996: Short-lived CNI cable internet venture is launched.
1997: BTG sells reseller business to rival GTSI.
2001: The Titan Corporation completes purchase of BTG.

Annual revenues slipped to $225 million in fiscal 2001 from $249 million the year before. Titan Corporation, a $1 billion San Diego defense technology firm, announced in September 2001 that it was acquiring BTG for $174 million in stock and cash, including the assumption of $32 million in debt. BTG became a wholly owned subsidiary of Titan after the merger.

Principal Subsidiaries

BTG Systems Engineering, Inc.; BTG Technology Resources, Inc.; Delta Research Corporation; Nations, Inc.; STAC, Inc.

Principal Divisions

Analysis and Consulting; Solutions Development; Systems Integration; Operations and Support.

Principal Competitors

CACI International Inc.; Dynamics Research Corporation; Emergent Information Technologies, Inc.; PRC Inc.; Science Applications International Corporation; SM&A Inc.

Further Reading

Behr, Peter, "The High Price of Money: Giving Up Some Control," *Washington Post,* July 17, 1995, p. F15.

Bhambhani, Dipka, "Stock Price No Concern to Fairfax, Va.-Based Information Technology Firm," *Washington Times,* March 27, 2000.

Cassidy, Padraic, "Acquisitive Titan Grabs BTG in $174 Million Deal," *Daily Deal,* September 20, 2001.

Chandrasekaran, Rajiv, "BTG to Offer Internet Link Via Cable; Loudoun County to Be Test Market," *Washington Post,* August 7, 1996, p. F1.

Day, Kathleen, "Two Va. Companies Make Acquisition Bids," *Washington Post,* September 22, 1995, p. C3.

"800 Percent Growth; BTG's Venture into Reselling and Systems Integration Has Boosted Sales from $50 Million in 1992 to $213 Million in 1996," *VAR Business,* August 15, 1997, p. S144.

Estrada, Louie, "Unfazed by Defense Cuts, Contractor Extends Its Reach," *Washington Post,* August 22, 1994, p. F11.

Haggerty, Maryann, "BTG's Stock Wounded by High Expectations," *Washington Post,* January 30, 1995, p. F25.

Hinden, Stan, "BTG Studies the ABCs of Going Public," *Washington Post,* November 7, 1994, p. F29.

Kopecki, Dawn, "Growth for Growth's Sake at BTG Inc. Worries Analysts," *Washington Times,* November 24, 1997.

Leibovich, Mark, BTG's Commercial Sector Struggle; Government Contractor Finds Rough Sailing As It Charts a Course in Unfamiliar Waters," *Washington Post,* November 3, 1997, p. F5.

——, "BTG Vice Presidents Bid for Unit Sought by GTSI," *Washington Post,* January 23, 1998, p. G1.

Lipton, Eric, "Two Fairfax Firms Win $929 Million Contract," *Washington Post,* December 2, 1995, p. F1.

Pearlstein, Steven, "The Big Squeeze; Pentagon Cuts Bring a New Era for Area Defense Firms," *Washington Post,* January 13, 1992, p. F1.

Richman, Tom, "Beyond the Start-Up Team," *Inc.,* December 1987, p. 53.

Schatz, Willie, "Dispute Put the Brakes on BTG Takeover Plans; Apparent Settlement Reached to Acquire SEI," *Washington Post,* May 7, 1990, p. F5.

Schrage, Michael, "Software Research Group Set; 11 Major Contractors to Combine Efforts," *Washington Post,* October 10, 1984.

Sugawara, Sandra, "Vienna Firm, Hughes Win Computer Contract," *Washington Post,* April 2, 1992, p. B10.

Swisher, Kara, "Government Contractors See Changes in Competition," *Washington Post,* May 25, 1996, p. F1.

—Frederick C. Ingram

Bush Brothers & Company

1016 East Weisgarber Road
Knoxville, Tennessee
U.S.A.
Telephone: (865) 588-7685
Fax: (865) 584-9337
Web site: http://www.bushbeans.com

Private Company
Incorporated: 1922
Employees: 540
Sales: $240 million (2001 est.)
NAIC: 311423 Dried and Dehydrated Food Manufacturing

Bush Brothers & Company, family owned and operated, is the nation's leading producer and marketer of baked beans. Bush Brothers produces nine varieties of baked beans, marketing the product line under the Bush's Best brand name. The company also processes and markets a variety of other food products, including Chili Magic Chili Starter, hominy, sauerkraut, spinach, turnip greens, collard greens, and roughly a dozen varieties of beans and peas. Bush Brothers' products are processed at three plants located in Augusta, Wisconsin; Shiocton, Wisconsin; and Chestnut Hill, Tennessee, where the company was founded in 1908. Condon Bush, grandson of founder A.J. Bush, serves as chairman and chief executive officer.

Founded As a Tomato Cannery

Bush Brothers originated as an enterprising solution to keep a family together. In Jefferson County, near the Smoky Mountains of Tennessee, A.J. (Andrew Jackson) Bush worked as a school teacher during the early years of the 20th century. His time outside the classroom was spent operating a two-room country store he owned in Chestnut Hill, the small town where he and his family resided. Although A.J. Bush enjoyed the financial security of two jobs, he realized his sons and daughters would be forced to leave Chestnut Hill to find employment unless he provided the means to keep the Bush family in Chestnut Hill. Toward this end, A.J. Bush scored resounding success. A century later, the family had a succession plan in place to confer company leadership to the fifth generation of the Bush family.

A.J. Bush enlisted the help of his two eldest sons, Fred and Claude, to start Bush Brothers in 1908. The trio opened a tomato cannery in Chestnut Hill, which served as Bush Brothers' sole focus during the company's first decades of business. Staffed by A.J. Bush's sons and daughters, the tomato cannery fared well, becoming a fixture in Jefferson County. By the beginning of World War I, Bush Brothers' plant was canning at capacity, the federal government ranking as the company's most important customer. Out of every ten cans of tomatoes produced by Bush Brothers, nearly nine were earmarked for the war effort, providing the company with a steady flow of business that enabled it to take root in Chestnut Hill.

After the war, Bush Brothers continued to prosper. In 1922, the company was incorporated, and five years later, during its 20th anniversary, Bush Brothers expanded for the first time. A second food processing plant, located in Oak Grove, Tennessee, was acquired. A third facility, located in Clinton, Tennessee, joined the fold three years later, in 1931. The year also marked the ascension of the second generation of the Bush family to a leadership position. Fred Bush, A.J. Bush's oldest son, was named president in 1931, inheriting the difficult task of shepherding Bush Brothers through the Great Depression.

Post-World War II Diversification

Bush Brothers escaped the economic ruin surrounding the company during the devastating 1930s. World War II and the great postwar economic expansion that followed fueled Bush Brothers' transformation from a tomato cannery into a diversified food processor. In 1944, the company ventured outside its native state for the first time, acquiring the Blytheville Canning Company in Blytheville, Arkansas. In 1948, the company developed the Bush's Best brand, a label that would soon appear on a variety of Bush Brothers' products. The foray into other product lines began in 1952, when the company introduced canned dry beans. Bush Brothers canned dry beans found a receptive audience on the market, encouraging the family to diversify further. One year later, the company introduced Show-

71

Company Perspectives:

Founded in 1908 by A.J. Bush, Bush Brothers & Company is based in Knoxville, Tennessee. The food company began with canned tomatoes and has grown to include great tasting, high quality products that your family loves. Three generations later, Bush Brothers & Company is still family owned and operated, working for the same ideals that were set forth by A.J. Bush more than 90 years ago. When it comes to giving your family the best, you can trust Bush to give its best.

---

boat Pork & Beans, followed by the development of canned southern peas in 1955.

Bush Brothers was a more than 60-year-old company before it introduced the signature product that defined its success at the start of the 21st century. The product was baked beans, which first emerged after a change in the company's senior management had occurred. In 1965, Fred Bush's younger brother Claude was named chairman. C.J. Ethier, the husband of A.J. Bush's daughter Lena Maye, was appointed president and chief executive officer concurrently. Fred Bush and Ethier, with the help of A.J. Bush's grandson, a young Condon Bush, put the Bush family recipe for baked beans on the market in 1969. Baked beans debuted under the Bush's Best Original label, a new brand name for a new product that would serve as the foundation of Bush Brothers in later years.

Ethier was named chairman in 1978, the same year Condon Bush was elected president of the company. Under their stewardship, two new varieties of baked beans were introduced, Baked Beans Onion, in 1981, and Vegetarian Baked Beans, in 1984. Steadily, Bush Brothers climbed to the number three position in the baked beans market, trailing only corporate giants ConAgra Foods and Campbell Soup Company by the end of the 1980s. It was an impressive rise, but Bush Brothers' greatest gains were yet to come. The company's aggressive and ambitious attack on the baked beans market in the 1990s transformed the Bush family enterprise and created a new market champion.

Focus on Baked Beans Beginning in the Early 1990s

The decade of historic change began in 1991, when Bush Brothers' board of directors, for the first time, included a majority of directors outside the Bush family. That same year, Condon Bush was named chairman and C.J. Ethier's son, Jim Ethier, was selected as president and chief operating officer. The two cousins resolved to embark on a marketing campaign of unprecedented scale in support of the company's baked beans brand. Their decision made Bush's Best Baked Beans the company's core product, signaling a new era in which marketing prowess would determine success. Historically, baked beans had received little advertising support from producers, ConAgra Foods and Campbell Soup included. The market category was deemed "undermarketed" by industry observers, presenting an ideal opportunity for an aggressive marketer to exploit. Bush Brothers sought to be such a marketer, taking on an unfamiliar role that required a number of substantial changes to its operations.

To spearhead the company's marketing assault, Bush Brothers hired Ron Dix, a veteran in the packaged goods industry. Dix became Bush Brothers' first ever director of marketing. His first major task was to assemble a brand management team, something that Bush Brothers had never had before. Dix wanted to hire talented, experienced food marketers from the industry's stalwart participants, but Bush Brothers' management believed the location of the company's executive offices weakened its ability to attract the industry's most talented marketers. After spending 84 years based in Chestnut Hill, the company decided to relocate to the larger metropolitan area of Knoxville, Tennessee, completing the move in 1992.

The marketing campaign that began to take shape in Knoxville revolved around a television commercial that would feature a company spokesperson. The search to find the star for the proposed series of commercials included auditions of Condon Bush and Jim Ethier, but the two senior executives lost out to the younger generation. Jay Bush, the 29-year-old son of Condon Bush and the plant manager at the company's Shiocton, Wisconsin, facility, won the role. The advertising campaign featured Jay Bush explaining why Bush's Best Baked Beans "taste so darned good." The commercials aired regionally in 1993, the same year the company launched a "Homestyle" version of baked beans and expanded distribution of baked beans into the Northeast. In 1994, the advertising campaign expanded nationwide, as did the distribution of Bush's Best Baked Beans, which began appearing on supermarket shelves in the Pacific Northwest.

The advertising campaign was a quick and stunning success. Within a year of its launch, the campaign vaulted Bush Brothers into the lead in the under-marketed baked beans category, ahead of ConAgra Foods' Van Camp's brand and Campbell Soup Company's Campbell's brand. According to Bush Brothers' estimates, the company nearly tripled its market share in the baked beans category by 1994, taking command of a market that generated an estimated $400 million in sales annually. Ecstatic about the progress, the Bush Brothers management team pressed ahead, both with new product introductions and with the highly successful series of television commercials. In 1995, the company introduced Bush's Boston Baked Beans in the New England market, the same year Duke, a golden retriever, first appeared as Jay Bush's on-air sidekick. Duke served as the less-than-trustworthy guardian of the secret family recipe, persistently threatening to divulge the ingredients to Bush Brothers' competitors.

On the heels of the company's rousing success with baked beans, Bush Brothers took another ambitious leap, introducing a new brand in 1996. Bush's Chili Magic Chili Starter, the first canned chili to contain all the seasonings needed to make homemade chili, pushed Bush Brothers into a new market category. The product, a concentrate that only required the consumer to add meat and tomatoes, was available in four regional styles, traditional, Mexican, Texas, and Louisiana Hot. Chili Magic represented the largest product launch since the company introduced Bush's Baked Beans, its release supported by a national advertising campaign that began in October 1996. Although the company refrained from releasing financial figures, industry observers estimated that Bush Brothers had set aside more than $10 million for the marketing campaign, a total

Key Dates:

1908: A.J. Bush and his two sons start Bush Brothers & Company as a tomato cannery.
1922: Bush Brothers is incorporated.
1928: A second plant, located in Oak Grove, Tennessee, is acquired.
1944: The Blytheville Canning Company is acquired.
1948: Bush's Best Brand first appears.
1969: Bush's Best Original Baked Beans debuts.
1992: Company headquarters are moved from Chestnut Hill to Knoxville.
1993: Highly effective baked beans marketing campaign begins.
1996: A new brand, Bush's Chili Magic Chili Starter, is introduced.
2001: Expansion of the company's Chestnut Hill plant begins.

that was roughly equivalent to the amount spent in support of Bush's Baked Beans.

During the late 1990s, Bush Brothers introduced several new baked beans products, fleshing out a product line that was recording consistent and robust growth. Bold & Spicy Baked Beans debuted in 1997 and Barbecue Baked Beans followed in 1999. Bush Brothers ended the decade occupying a dominant position in the baked beans category. The company's nearest rivals, ConAgra Foods and Campbell Soup, never effectively countered Bush Brothers' assault on the market. Neither company had responded to the marketing campaign launched by Bush Brothers in 1993, at least in terms of advertising spending. By 1999, Bush Brothers was spending an estimated $14 million on marketing its baked beans products. Together, ConAgra Foods and Campbell Soup spent less than $1 million on baked beans advertising. In 1999, in fact, Campbell Soup chose not to advertise its baked beans at all.

With baked beans sales rising, Bush Brothers pressed ahead to widen its lead further. In 1999, the company began planning for an expansion to its production capacity. After two years of preliminary planning, the project began to take shape in early 2001, when site preparation began at the company's processing plant in Chestnut Hill. Bush Brothers earmarked more than $100 million for the expansion and renovation project, which promised to give the company a new, 220,000-square-foot facility. The expansion, to be completed by mid-2003, was expected to triple the company's production capacity.

As Bush Brothers prepared to complete its first century of business, spirits ran high at the company's Knoxville headquarters. Bush Brothers was recording double-digit increases in sales on an annual basis, registering consistent, strident growth as the company's competitors watched their sales totals shrink. The company controlled 50 percent of the $470-million-in-sales baked beans market in 2001. Its closest rival, ConAgra, held a 24 percent share, while the number three company, Campbell Soup, controlled 7.5 percent of the market. Based on these figures, coupled with a succession plan in place for the fifth-generation of Bush leadership, Bush Brothers promised to figure as a dominant food processor in the years ahead.

Principal Subsidiaries

Blytheville Canning Co.

Principal Competitors

B&G Foods, Inc.; Campbell Soup Company; ConAgra Foods, Inc.

Further Reading

DeLozier, Stan, "High Demand for Baked Beans Pushing Move," *Knoxville News/Sentinel,* February 16, 2001, p. B1.
Flaum, David, "Chestnut Hill, Tenn.-Based Tomato Cannery Keeps Leadership Close to Home," *Commercial Appeal,* May 6, 2000, p. 32.
Matzer, Marla, "Bush Bros. Spices Up Mix Market," *Brandweek,* October 7, 1996, p. 14.
Thompson, Stephanie, "Ads Boost Bean Business, Folksy Spots, Big Budget Drive Bush's Beans to Top," *Advertising Age,* February 26, 2001, p. 3.

—Jeffrey L. Covell

Callaway Golf Company

**2180 Rutherford Road
Carlsbad, California 92008
U.S.A.
Telephone: (760) 931-1771
Fax: (760) 930-5015
Web site: http://www.callawaygolf.com**

Public Company
Incorporated: 1982
Employees: 2,600
Sales: $837.6 million (2000)
Stock Exchanges: New York
Ticker Symbol: ELY
NAIC: 33992 Sporting and Athletic Goods Manufacturing

Callaway Golf Company is the premier manufacturer of golf clubs in the United States. The company sells more golf clubs than any other firm, and has the lion's share of the $3 billion golf equipment industry, eclipsing the higher-profile brand names such as Wilson, Spalding, and MacGregor. Callaway's most famous club, the ''Big Bertha'' Driver, is the most popular piece of equipment sold to golfers. Callaway has about a third of the U.S. golf equipment market, and its annual sales dwarf its nearest several competitors. Besides its line of drivers, Callaway also makes putters and golf balls, and licenses Callaway golf wear through apparel maker Ashworth Inc. The company began a meteoric rise to fame and fortune with the introduction of Big Bertha in 1991. The success of Callaway Golf Company is attributed to Ely Callaway, who transformed a modest company into a worldwide powerhouse. Callaway led the company until his death in 2001, at the age of 82, from pancreatic cancer.

Early Career in Textiles and Wine

Ely Reeves Callaway, Jr., was born in La Grange, Georgia, a small town about 60 miles southwest of Atlanta. Ely's grandfather, a Baptist preacher, owned and operated a plantation with approximately 20 slaves. When the Union forces defeated the Confederacy in the U.S. Civil War during the 1860s, the Callaways lost their entire fortune. Ely's uncle, Fuller Callaway, was the primary force behind the family's resurgence. He first went into farming, then into dry goods, later into banking, and finally into the cotton mill trade. Ely's father worked for his uncle, but when the young Ely Reeves, Jr., graduated from Emory University, his father advised him not to work for the family.

In June 1940 Ely was working as a runner in the factoring department of the Trust Company of Georgia, and decided to take an army reserve correspondence course. Commissioned six weeks later, Ely went to Philadelphia and began working in the apparel-procurement division of the quartermaster's depot. Callaway was soon promoted to major, a significant achievement for a young man of 24, and was in charge of 70 civilians and two lawyers. During this time, he was buying approximately 70 percent of the total wartime production of the U.S. cotton apparel industry, and was dealing with such companies as Levi Strauss, Hart, Schaffner & Marx, and Arrow Shirt on a daily basis. When the war ended, Callaway decided to go to work for Deering, Milliken & Company in order to continue a career in the textile and apparel industry.

Callaway rose quickly in his chosen profession. In 1954, after he became involved in a disagreement with Roger Milliken's brother-in-law, however, Milliken fired him unceremoniously. Undismayed, Callaway found a job at Textron Industries and, under the supervision of Royal Little, oversaw the merger of Robbins Mills and American Woolen, two large textile mills. When Textron sold Callaway's division to Burlington Industries, Callaway was part of the package deal. By 1968, Callaway was appointed president of Burlington Industries.

Callaway's new post as president of the largest and most influential textile company in the world merely fueled his ambition. When he was passed over for the position of chairman in 1973, Callaway quit abruptly. Picking up his family, he moved from the East Coast to California in order to start a wine making company in the tiny town of Temecula. Although the land that Callaway had purchased was not prime grape growing country, nonetheless he persevered until his venture began to pay off. Callaway Vineyard & Winery was soon supplying its products to well-known restaurants such as the Four Seasons in New York City. He sold the operation to Hiram Walker in 1981 at a price of $14 million. In just a few short years, Callaway had garnered a profit of over $9 million.

Starting Over with Golf

At the age of 60, Callaway thought it was time to relax, and, hearkening back to his youth and the years when he was a tournament champion, he began in earnest to resume his game of golf. One day on the golf course, he became acquainted with a hickory-shaft club that had a steel core. The club was made by Hickory Stick, a tiny California company run by two entrepreneurs, Richard Parente and Dick De La Cruz. Callaway liked the golf club so much that he called up its manufacturers to tell them so. Parente and De La Cruz, short of money and looking for someone to invest in their company, asked Callaway for help. In 1984 Callaway purchased the small enterprise at the bargain basement price of $400,000, and pinned his own name to the company.

Callaway Golf Company, under the direction of Callaway himself, immediately began to conceive of strategies to increase both its profile and its revenues in the highly competitive sports equipment market. Callaway decided the best way to achieve the above goals was to introduce new products, and within four years of acquiring the company he had his design staff come up with a new premium-priced item that did away with a large amount of the neck of the club, while extending the shaft through the clubhead. This club was called the S2H2, short for Short Straight Hollow Hosel. Callaway funded development of the new club by signing up investors, including the General Electric Pension Fund. The pension fund invested $10 million in Callaway Golf in 1988. The response to Callaway's new design was nothing less than phenomenal. Golfers responded to the heavier-weighted clubheads that included a lower center of gravity, and sales shot up dramatically, as did the profile and reputation of Callaway's company. By the end of 1988, company sales amounted to approximately $5 million. One year later, sales had doubled to $10.5 million. In 1990 sales doubled again, and by 1991, revenues skyrocketed to $54.7 million, an increase of nearly 150 percent.

Ruling the 1990s with Big Bertha

In 1991 Callaway created the "Big Bertha" Driver, an oversized driver named for the huge gun used by the Germans during World War I to drop shells on Paris from six miles away. The principle behind Callaway's creation of the metal wood driver was that it put more weight around the perimeter of the head of the club, resulting in a thinner face. According to Callaway, this gave the golfer a greater "feel" at the time of impact with the ball. Moreover, the golfer did not have to hit the ball precisely on the button to obtain directional control and good distance. Soon golfers were swearing by them, and sales surpassed all the other brands of golf clubs made in America.

With the company growing rapidly, Callaway decided to take it public in February 1992. With 2.6 million shares of stock offered on the New York Exchange at $20 per share, the stock had jumped to $36 per share by the end of the day. The capital provided by the stock offering enabled Callaway to expand his manufacturing capacity. The demand for the company's golf club was rising at unexpected rates, and management at the firm needed more cash to take advantage of what has always been regarded as a notoriously faddish market in the golf equipment industry. By the end of 1992, sales had reached $132 million. At the end of April 1993, the price per share of Callaway Golf Company stock had increased to an impressive $54. In 1993, when sales were reported at $255 million, the company had surpassed the better known names in the sporting goods industry such as Wilson, Spalding, and MacGregor to become the revenue leader in the field. As sales and stock price continued to climb, Ely Callaway's personal share rose to a hefty $86 million.

In 1994 Callaway Golf Company introduced an innovative design for irons that would accompany the highly successful "Big Bertha" Metal Wood Drivers. The new irons, created with the same principles in mind as Callaway's "Big Berthas," were an immediate hit on the golf course. Priced at $125, the steel-shafted irons were approximately 20 percent more costly than conventional premium clubs. For $175, a golfer could purchase the new design with a graphite shaft. Since nearly all the company's clubs relied on a new development in casting technology, supplies of the new clubs were limited and helped keep the price per iron high. A total set of nine irons and three woods purchased from Callaway Golf Company at the suggested retail price amounted to the small fortune of $2,325. Yet golfing enthusiasts, both amateur and professional, happily bought the company's wares. By the end of fiscal 1994, sales had risen to $449 million.

At the beginning of 1995, there were only three major companies in the golf equipment industry, including Callaway Golf, Cobra Golf, and Taylor Made, a division of Salomon, which was a prominent manufacturer of skis in France. These three firms were clobbering the remaining competition. Revenues at Callaway Golf in 1994 had increased substantially over the previous year, while revenues at Cobra Golf shot up an astounding 121 percent during the same period. There seemed to be no end to the prospects for these three companies. Nearly 400 golf courses were opened in the United States in 1994, with approximately 800 more under construction. The baby-boomer generation was approaching its golfing years, and the sport was gaining in popularity all over the world, especially in the countries of the Pacific Rim.

Yet trouble loomed on the horizon as increased competition among the three major companies and a gathering group of both new and old golf equipment firms threatened to cut into profit margins. Wilson, Spalding, and other companies saw an opportunity to secure a share of the market with new products made from aerospace-grade materials and composites. When a golfer

Key Dates:

1984: Ely Callaway buys Hickory Stick, which becomes Callaway Golf.
1991: Company launches Big Bertha driver.
1998: Company claims approximately 70 percent of pro golfers worldwide use Callaway clubs.
2000: Callaway golf balls debut.
2001: Founder Ely Callaway dies.

swings a club, the wrists rotate, and the head and shaft of the club twist, creating a centrifugal force that tends to pull the club from the golfer's hands. When the golfer then hits the ball, for every millimeter the ball is hit off the center of the club's head, there is a corresponding penalty in distance. When Callaway's designers created "Big Bertha," they revolutionized the industry by taking advantage of a major technological innovation, namely, investment casting. This process was an improved technique for making metal club heads and enabled designers to shift the weight of the club around with greater precision than ever before. With other innovations, Callaway's people designed a club that allowed a golfer to actually control more of the centrifugal force of a swing directly onto the ball.

One company, Goldwin Golf, began to use 7075-T6 aluminum, an aerospace-grade material, in its manufacture of golf clubs. Management at Goldwin guarded their production process as carefully as a national secret. Another development by the same company resulted in the design of a club head that weighed a mere 140 grams, approximately 30 percent less than the average weight. GolfGear, yet another firm on the cutting edge of golfing technology, began using an aluminum-vanadium alloy. Only three firms in the industry could forge the new metal. Some companies also began using titanium, which is lighter and denser than steel, resulting in a longer driving range. Titanium drivers were particularly popular in Japan, where they made up over 60 percent of all drivers used. In that market, the seemingly prohibitive cost of approximately $700 for a club was not an insurmountable deterrent.

In spite of the competition, however, Callaway Golf Company continued as the leader in the golf equipment industry. In the mid-1990s the company built a $9 million research, development, and test facility for the purpose of staying ahead of the game. The facility was a state-of-the-art complex, including a 260-yard driving range, which was peppered with hundreds of testing sensors, four kinds of bunkers, and three types of grass in order to simulate the golfing conditions at any course around the world. Callaway expected the highly sophisticated setup to yield even more innovative golf club designs. Since the development of new technologies for designing and new material for manufacturing golf clubs had become so essential to keeping abreast of the industry, the inability to introduce a new product for even two or three years could spell disaster for any golf equipment company.

Keeping Afloat in the Late 1990s

By the late 1990s, Callaway's sales had risen to over $800 million, up from only $5 million a decade earlier. The company's production facility churned out expensive clubs, running three shifts six days a week. Every golfer knew the Big Bertha, and a score of famous amateurs accepted Callaway stock as recompense for appearing in advertisements for the club. Entertainers including rock star Alice Cooper and Canadian singer Celine Dion endorsed the Big Bertha. Even computer mogul Bill Gates took time off from running Microsoft to appear in a Big Bertha commercial. By 1998, Callaway claimed that almost 70 percent of all professional golfers worldwide used a Callaway driver. The company held about a third of the U.S. driver market, and a company spokesperson told *Golf Magazine* (May 1998) that Callaway wanted 100 percent. Callaway's annual sales were double that of its nearest competitor, and the company hoped to break the billion-dollar mark soon.

Yet conditions were not absolutely favorable to Callaway's continued advance. Wet weather brought on by El Niño in 1998 kept sales flat, and the crash in the Asian financial market also dampened things. Over 16 percent of Callaway's total sales came from Asia, and the weakened economy there had a direct effect on the company. The firm began to diversify. Callaway acquired a putter manufacturer, Odyssey Golf, in 1997, and revamped a small publishing company run by Ely Callaway's son into Callaway Golf Media, which put out coffee table books on golf. Callaway also launched Callaway Golf Experience in the late 1990s, a computer- and video-aided fitting center designed to align customers with the right clubs. Callaway also introduced new clubs, bringing out the Big Bertha Steelhead metalwood line in mid-1998, and following with the Great Big Bertha Hawk Eye Woods the next year. But Callaway's most dramatic move was into the golf ball market. By 1998, Callaway let it be known that it had invested at least $100 million in developing a new golf ball. The ball market ran a high profit margin, and sales industry-wide were growing at a steady pace. With its excellent brand name recognition, the move into balls seemed appropriate for Callaway.

These new strategies may have meant long-term gains, but in the short term, the company was not doing well. Imitators with cheaper drivers had snatched market share from Callaway. Two upstart companies, Orlimar Golf Equipment Co. and Adams Golf Inc., together took over 20 percent of the U.S. driver market by the fall of 1998, sending Callaway's share down. By the end of 1998, Callaway stock had crashed, sales were down 17 percent, and profits had dropped 80 percent. Ely Callaway, who had stepped away from the day-to-day running of the company in 1996, agreed to come back full time as chief executive and try to turn things around. Callaway promptly axed 700 employees, divested unprofitable lines, and trimmed costs all around. Golf equipment sales across the industry began to rebound somewhat. The company brought out its pricey, high-tech Rule 35 golf ball in 2000. But the long-anticipated product launch did not prove as beneficial to the company as it had hoped. Nike Golf, a division of the well-known shoe company, also brought out a golf ball that year, and convinced golf superstar Tiger Woods to use it. Woods won three championships in 2000 using the Nike balls. Callaway expected ball sales of about $70 million for 2000, but brought in less than half that.

With conditions still rocky at the company he brought to prominence, 81-year-old Ely Callaway announced in the fall of 2000 that he would continue to run the firm "indefinitely." The company restructured, folding its previously separate ball unit into the parent company. Mr. Callaway continued to fight for the company's reputation and market share. The firm surpassed even the Biggest Bertha with the ERC II in 2000, a new driver with the largest ''sweet spot'' yet. Unfortunately, the U.S. Golf Association banned the ERC II from its competitions. Callaway appealed the USGA's decision, and filed suit against the Royal Canadian Golf Association over the same issue. Ely Callaway was diagnosed with pancreatic cancer in the spring of 2001, and died in July that year. The company carried on under the direction of Ron Drapeau. Though sales recovered somewhat in the first half of 2001, with the whole economy evidently slowing, the company did not predict a return to its former growth rate. Yet the company appeared to be in sound shape on some fronts. It had no debt and a sizeable cash reserve. Drapeau expected to lead the company much as Ely Callaway had done, concentrating on innovative product introductions aimed at the average golfer.

Principal Competitors

Orlimar Golf Equipment Co.; Fortune Brands Inc.; Nike Golf.

Further Reading

Barkow, Al, ''A Controversy Going Longer Than the Drives,'' *New York Times*, July 15, 2001, p. SP11.

Brull, Steven V., ''Can Callaway Find the Green?,'' *Business Week*, November 30, 1998, pp. 83–84.

''Callaway on Callaway,'' *Daily News Record*, June 22, 1995, p. 8.

''Ely Callaway: He Did It His Way,'' *Business Week*, July 23, 2001, p. 44.

Gallagher, Leigh, ''Fore!,'' *Forbes*, December 13, 1999, p. 382.

''Heavy Artillery,'' *Fortune*, May 30, 1994, p. 167.

Impoco, Jim, ''Ely Callaway Hits the Green,'' *U.S. News & World Report*, April 11, 1994, p. 47.

Jaffe, Thomas, ''Big Bertha's Big Bucks,'' *Forbes*, December 21, 1992, p. 344.

Leavens, Sydney, ''Callaway's New CEO Plans to Keep Grip on Old Strategy,'' *Wall Street Journal*, August 8, 2001, p. B4.

Marcial, Gene G., ''Jazzy Picks from the Common Fund's Motley Crew,'' *Business Week*, April 5, 1993, p. 78.

Perry, Nancy J., ''How Golf's Big Bertha Grew,'' *Fortune*, May 18, 1992, p. 113.

Phalon, Richard, ''Big Bertha's Sweet Spot,'' *Forbes*, May 11, 1992, p. 130.

Pittman, Alan P., ''Sales of Callaway Balls, Clubs Robust, Reports Say,'' *Golf World*, March 31, 2000, p. S1.

Purkey, Mike, Tara Gravel, and Scott Kramer, ''Great Big Empire,'' *Golf Magazine*, May 1998, p. 102.

Saporito, Bill, ''Can Big Bertha Stay in the Driver's Seat?,'' *Fortune*, June 12, 1995, pp. 110–16.

Sirak, Ron, ''At Your Service,'' *Golf World*, January 26, 2001, p. 36.

Stogel, Chuck, ''Callaway Drives Toward the High End Again,'' *Brandweek*, January 18, 1999, p. 12.

Strege, John, ''Callaway Combines Club, Ball Divisions to Bolster Efficiency,'' *Golf World*, August 18, 2000, p. S1.

——, ''Callaway's Ball Business Enters New Phase Without Yash at Helm,'' *Golf World*, November 24, 2000, p. S1.

Witford, David, ''Opposite Attractions,'' *Inc.*, December 1994, pp. 60–68.

—Thomas Derdak
—update: A. Woodward

CANADIAN PACIFIC RAILWAY

www.cpr.ca

Canadian Pacific Railway Limited

Gulf Canada Square
401 - 9th Avenue SW, Suite 500
Calgary, Alberta T2P 4Z4
Canada
Telephone: (403) 319-7000
Fax: (403) 319-7567
Web site: http://www.cpr.ca

Public Company
Incorporated: 1881 as Canadian Pacific Railway
   Company
Employees: 17,519
Sales: C$3.66 billion (US$2.44 billion) (2000)
Stock Exchanges: Toronto New York
Ticker Symbol: CP
NAIC: 482111 Line-Haul Railroads; 485112 Commuter
   Rail Systems; 487110 Scenic and Sightseeing
   Transportation, Land; 488210 Support Activities for
   Rail Transportation

Canadian Pacific Railway Limited is the smallest of the six major North American railways, known as Class 1 railways. Its 14,000-mile network includes a transcontinental main line in Canada extending from Vancouver to Montreal, as well as a number of collector and feeder lines; the Canadian network extends for about 9,300 miles. In the United States, the company's rail lines consist of 3,200 miles in the Midwest operated by Soo Line Corporation, a subsidiary; and 1,500 miles in the Northeast operated by another subsidiary, Delaware and Hudson Railway Company, Inc. Alliances with Union Pacific Corporation and other rail firms extends Canadian Pacific's rail services throughout the other areas of the United States and into Mexico as well. While its core business is the transport of bulk cargo, containers, and automobiles, Canadian Pacific also runs commuter rail services in Vancouver, Toronto, and Montreal and a tourist train located in the Canadian Rockies. The company also offers intermodal services through a network of 23 intermodal terminals and nine major rail yards as well as supply chain management services through subsidiary Tronicus Inc.

Canadian Pacific Railway Company was formed in 1881, and four years later it completed construction of the first transcontinental railway in Canada. Over the succeeding decades, the company expanded into a number of other industries, including hotels, steamships, oil and gas, mining, airlines, telecommunications, and shipping services. In 1971 a new holding company was formed called Canadian Pacific Limited, with Canadian Pacific Railway and the other businesses becoming subsidiaries of the new parent. On October 1, 2001, Canadian Pacific Limited was broken up into five separate publicly traded companies, one of which was called Canadian Pacific Railway Limited and consisted of the original railway and related operations.

Late 19th Century: Founding of CPR and Completion of Transcontinental Railway

The building of the Canadian Pacific Railway was a demanding battle, both physically and politically. After negative reports from both explorers and surveyors, a long and sometimes bitter parliamentary dispute, and threats of refusal by British Columbia to become part of the Canadian Dominion, a contract to build the rail line was finally approved by royal assent on February 15, 1881. The following day, the Canadian Pacific Railway Company (CPR) was incorporated. The company established its headquarters in Montreal. A group of railroad professionals, known as The Syndicate, who had come to Canada from Scotland as fur traders, headed up the railroad's first management team. The Syndicate chose George Stephen, a former president of the Bank of Montreal and one of the principals involved in the organization of the St. Paul, Minneapolis and Manitoba Railway as CPR's first president. Stephen was assisted by CPR Vice-President Duncan McIntyre, who left his post as president of the Canada Central Railway to help build the country's first and only transcontinental railroad.

Under the terms of the government contract, CPR received $25 million in investor-subscribed funds and 25 million acres of timberland, which eventually included the land's subsurface resources. These important assets provided the basis for the company to raise more capital. Several stock issues were floated, and large loans were made to further finance the project. In 1882 the company issued $30 million worth of CPR stock to various New York investment syndicates, followed by the sale of 200,000 shares of common stock on the New York Stock Exchange (NYSE) the following year—becoming in the process the first non-American firm to be listed on the NYSE (CPR shares were first listed on the Toronto Stock Exchange in 1892). To complete the project, CPR floated a $15 million bond issue through a London-based investment house. Although the company's contract allowed CPR ten years to complete the railroad's construction, the project took less than half that time. Construction of the main line was completed on November 7, 1885. At the time the Canadian Pacific Railway was the longest and costliest railroad line ever built. The first regular passenger train to use the new line, the "Pacific Express," departed from Montreal on June 28, 1886, arriving in Port Moody, British Columbia, on July 4.

The completion of the line had many effects on both the company and the Canadian economy. The subsurface resources acquired in the land deal with the Canadian Parliament put the company into the coal, zinc, lead, gold, silver, and—later—gas businesses. The railway opened the prairies for settlement, and CPR was involved in agricultural development, including irrigation and wheat farming. A rail connection from the more industrialized eastern regions to the Pacific Coast enabled the company to expand into the export shipping business and opened up many opportunities in the Far East. It was also believed that the railway's consolidating effect on the Canadian provinces stifled further northern expansion by the United States. The company, then known to most Canadians as the CPR, continued its steady growth well into the mid-1900s.

Early Development of Related Activities

Moves into related activities began as early as 1886 when the company chartered seven ships to carry tea and silk from Asia to the West Coast of Canada, thereby providing eastbound freight for the railway. This marked the beginning of CPR's steamship services—later known as CP Ships. In 1903 CP Ships began serving the trans-Atlantic market. CP Ships became renowned in the early decades of the 20th century for its luxury passenger liners—the famous Canadian Pacific Empress class ships. These boats sailed the world's oceans from 1891 to 1970. The speed and reliability of the CP Ships fleet led to lucrative mail contracts on both trans-Pacific and trans-Atlantic routes. In 1922 CP Ships entered the cruise market.

CPR also began building hotels and dining rooms along the railway in order to provide passengers with food and shelter. The architect of this strategy was American railroader William Cornelius Van Horne, who had joined the company as general manager at the beginning of 1882. Van Horne had previously served as general manager of the Chicago, Milwaukee & Saint Paul Railroad. He would succeed Stephen as second president of CPR in 1888. Envisioning a string of grand hotels along the railway, Van Horne built the company's first hotel, Mount Stephen House, high in the Canadian Rockies in 1886. Two years later came the opening of the famed Banff Springs hotel, located in the Canadian Rockies of Alberta. Next came Chateau Lake Louise, completed in 1890, and Le Chateau Frontenac, which opened its doors in 1893. Most of the hotels were modeled on French chateaus and eventually achieved landmark status. These operations formed the basis for Canadian Pacific Hotels, which eventually was running hotels and resorts in every major city serviced by the railway.

CPR's involvement in the oil and gas industry also had an early start, although it would be many more years before energy became a significant part of the company operations. In 1883 a CPR crew drilling for water near Medicine Hat made the first natural gas discovery in Alberta. This was the Milk River formation, which remains one of the largest discoveries in western Canada. Initially, when CPR sold parts of its vast land holdings it would sell the mining and mineral rights as well. By 1912, however, this policy was reversed and CPR began reserving rights to "all mines and minerals under the lands" for property that it sold. This made possible the company's later activities in both mining and energy.

The company in its early years added to its already rich natural resource holdings. In 1898 it acquired British Columbia Smelting and Refining Company, and in 1906 merged this and other properties into the Consolidated Mining and Smelting Company of Canada Limited, later known as Cominco Limited. In 1905 CPR purchased the Esquimalt and Namaimo Railway and 1.5 million acres of timber on Vancouver Island.

Yet another nonrailroad activity was undertaken in 1942 when CPR merged ten local airlines to form Canadian Pacific Air Lines (CP Air). In 1955 this airline pioneered the polar route when it began flying from Vancouver to Amsterdam over the North Pole. It would eventually become—for a time—Canada's second largest airline.

As early as 1920 CPR began using all-steel railroad cars. In many instances these units weighed nearly 60 tons, which limited the number of cars that could be pulled by a steam-powered locomotive. The Great Depression and then World War II slowed the introduction of diesel-powered engines to the railroad industry. By 1954, however, CPR completed the conversion of its locomotives to diesel power. Because of the ruggedness of much of the terrain over which CPR operated, the company used some of the largest diesel-powered trains in the world. Eventually, these units were capable of hauling 10,000 tons of cargo and were powered by as many as 11 diesel engines.

1950s Through 1970s: Organizing and Further Exploiting Nonrailroad Assets

Throughout its first 75 years in business, CPR's explosive growth resulted in poor record-keeping, and only in 1956 did the company institute a comprehensive inventory of its assets. The inventory took seven years. It quickly became apparent that

Key Dates:

1881: Canadian Pacific Railway Company (CPR) is formed to build a transcontinental railway; headquarters are established in Montreal.

1883: CPR stock is listed on the New York Stock Exchange.

1885: The company completes construction of Canada's first transcontinental railway.

1886: CPR charters seven ships to carry tea and silk from Asia to Canada, marking the beginning of steamship operations, later known as CP Ships; the company's first hotel, Mount Stephen House, is completed, initiating what will later be called Canadian Pacific Hotels.

1958: Canadian Pacific Oil and Gas Limited is formed as a subsidiary.

1971: A new parent company, Canadian Pacific Limited (CPL), is formed, with CPR and the company's other operations becoming subsidiaries; CP Oil and Gas merges with Central Del Rio Oils to form PanCanadian Petroleum Limited.

1990: CPL takes full control of Soo Line Corporation.

1991: Delaware and Hudson Railway Company, Inc. is acquired.

1995: Company headquarters are moved to Calgary.

1999: CP Hotels acquires Fairmont Hotels, leading to the creation of Fairmont Hotels and Resorts Inc.

2001: CPL demerges into five separate publicly traded companies: Canadian Pacific Railway Limited, PanCanadian Petroleum, CP Ships, Fording Inc., and Fairmont Hotels.

the CPR's vast holdings warranted further exploitation and development. CPR formed a wholly owned subsidiary, Canadian Pacific Oil and Gas Limited, in 1958 to develop and explore its mineral rights on more than 11 million acres of company-held western Canada land. With the completion of the CPR's forest and real estate surveys, two more subsidiaries were formed. Marathon Realty Company Limited was incorporated to manage and develop the company's vast, nationwide real estate holdings. Pacific Logging Company Limited was to be responsible for reforestation and the development of tree farming on CPR's timberlands.

As the survey of company holdings reached completion, it became clear that the development of the CPR's nonrailroad assets needed to be centralized under a separate holding company. CPR formed Canadian Pacific Investments Limited in 1962 to administer the development of CPR's natural resources and real estate holdings and to operate as an investment holding company.

During most of CPR's first 80 years, the company was owned by foreign interests, primarily English, French, and American. The transition to a majority of Canadian ownership began after the end of World War II and was completed in 1965. In that year, Ian Sinclair, CPR's chairman, assumed control of the company's burgeoning enterprises. Sinclair brought to bear his influence and power to finally reverse the flow of foreign investment into the company.

In November 1967 the company offered to the public $100 million in convertible preferred shares of CPR stock. At the time, it was the largest single stock issue in Canadian history and provided an opportunity for Canadians to share more directly in the resource development of their country. In a major reorganization in 1971, a new parent company was formed called Canadian Pacific Limited (CPL), with Canadian Pacific Railway becoming a subsidiary of the new company, as did the various other operations. In 1980 Canadian Pacific Investments Limited changed its name to Canadian Pacific Enterprises Limited (CP Enterprises).

There were also significant changes at Canadian Pacific Oil and Gas. In 1964 CP Oil and Gas purchased a stake in Central Del Rio Oils, based in Alberta. Central Del Rio had a large production base stemming from its discovery of the 1.5-billion-barrel Weyburn oil pool in southeast Saskatchewan. In 1969 CP Oil and Gas became a wholly owned subsidiary of Central Del Rio, giving CPR a stake in the publicly traded Central Del Rio. Two years later CP Oil and Gas and Central Del Rio were merged to form PanCanadian Petroleum Limited, one of Canada's largest gas and oil companies. The publicly traded PanCanadian was now majority owned by Canadian Pacific Limited.

Sinclair took the company into the hotel business in the United States and to locations as distant as Jerusalem. An airline catering business in Mexico City was also purchased. Sinclair's railroading focused on the transportation of goods and raw materials rather than people. In 1976 the Canadian government formed Via Rail Canada Inc. as a nationwide passenger rail service. Via Rail gradually began taking over responsibility for passenger train operation from both CPL and archrival Canadian National Railway Company (which had been formed by the Canadian government in 1917), a process largely complete by 1979. At the close of Sinclair's tenure in 1981, CPL's railroad inventory comprised 69,000 freight cars, 1,300 locomotives, 3,600 maintenance and equipment cars, and only 57 passenger cars.

Deep Difficulties in the 1980s

Sinclair was succeeded by Frederic Burbidge in 1981. Burbidge acquired leadership of a company that was about to have the worst decade in its history. A worldwide recession coupled with extremely poor crop years in the early 1980s in both Canada and the midwestern United States resulted in thousands of empty Canadian Pacific and Soo Line boxcars. Many of CPL's nonrailroad businesses were highly cyclical. PanCanadian Petroleum helped compensate for the rail operations' poor performance for a time, but with the collapse of oil prices in 1986, the company was faced with profound difficulties.

William Stinson replaced Burbidge as CPL's chairman in 1985. Stinson, who had been with the company for 30 years, starting as a management trainee in 1955, was the youngest chairman in the company's history. He set out to streamline the company's operations.

Stinson oversaw the sale of CPL's 52 percent interest in Cominco Limited, which had become one of the world's largest zinc producers. By selling off what had been a money-loser since 1981, Stinson raised $472 million and removed an expensive liability. On the heels of the Cominco sell-off, the company divested itself of CP Air in a $300 million deal with Pacific Western Airlines in 1987. CP Air had not shown any profits since 1980; the sale also eliminated nearly $600 million in long-term debt. On December 6, 1985, with the consent of both companies' stockholders, CPL and CP Enterprises merged into one company. Under the terms of the merger, CP Enterprises became a wholly owned subsidiary of CPL.

After the sale of Cominco and CP Air, Stinson worked to turn around three of CPL's other subsidiaries: AMCA International Limited, a producer of structural steel, the Soo Line, and Algoma Steel Corporation, an Ontario-based steel manufacturer. Stinson's plan was to focus CPL in four major core businesses: freight transportation, natural resources, real estate, and manufacturing. Stinson's cutbacks, sales, and restructuring had a positive effect, and the company showed a profit of a little more than $58 million in 1987. One project that Stinson did not attempt to curtail was the construction of the longest railway tunnel in North America. The Macdonald Tunnel, located in British Columbia's Selkirk Mountains and more than nine miles in length, was completed in 1988. That same year, CP Hotels bought the hotel chain of Canadian National Railway, gaining such properties as the Chateau Laurier in Ottawa and Jasper Park Lodge in Alberta and becoming the largest hotel operator in Canada. CPL also purchased a 47.2 percent voting interest in Laidlaw Inc., a waste management company, for C$499.3 million. There was one further divestment in the late 1990s, however, that of the company's steel production operations, including Algoma Steel and AMCA International.

The years 1988 and 1989 showed little improvement for CPL's financial outlook. The Canadian economy was in a weakened condition. The company's forest products division reported a net operating loss of more than $190 million in 1989 because of the depressed market for paper products. Marathon Realty showed a net operating loss that same year of more than $17 million. The company's rail division held its own in 1989, however, and Laidlaw had a record-breaking year.

Early 1990s: Restructuring and Recovery

As CPL entered the 1990s, the company's restructuring efforts suffered a major setback in a ruling by the Supreme Court of Ontario. Under the court's decision, CPL was prohibited from spinning off Marathon Realty as a separate public company. CPL had planned to distribute 80 percent of the shares of Marathon Realty to its common stockholders while retaining a 20 percent interest itself. The court ruled that the transaction would penalize CPL's preferred stockholders. At the same time, it appeared that CPL's performance would be further hindered by the lingering weakness in the company's forest products division.

The company's rail business increased in 1990, largely because of a resurgence in grain shipments. That year CPL acquired the 44 percent of Soo Line that it did not already own. CPL officials expected the transaction to make possible greater integration of the rail systems. Early in 1991 CPL bought another rail company, the Delaware and Hudson Railway, oper-

ating in the northeastern United States. This bolstering of the U.S. rail operations was an important development given the increased U.S.-Canada trade that was already occurring as a result of the Canada-U.S. Free Trade Agreement of 1989.

CPL suffered during the economic downturn of the early 1990s. After posting a net income of $744 million in 1989 and $354 million in 1990, the company began to lose money. Part of the problem was a decline in rail traffic. But that lull was augmented by weak prices for oil and gas and a major slump in real estate markets, among other problems. Furthermore, the CPL organization was relatively bloated and inefficient, despite recent attempts to boost productivity. CPL executives responded to mounting losses by intensifying efforts to reorganize and increase efficiency. To that end, CPL jettisoned several poorly performing operations, including several lackluster rail lines. The company also sold its troubled forest products division, consisting of a 60.7 percent stake in Canadian Pacific Forest Products Limited, to a group of underwriters for C$697.8 million in 1993. At the same time, it beefed up its investments in its more successful divisions, particularly its shipping group.

Despite gains in its shipping division and a few other segments, CPL suffered losses totaling more than $1.5 million between 1991 and 1993, which was partly the result of restructuring write-offs and accounting changes. By 1994, though, restructuring initiatives were beginning to bear fruit. Indeed, CPL had slashed its workforce from more than 75,000 in the late 1980s to less than 40,000 by 1994, reflecting a significant liquidation of assets. Meanwhile, company sales plunged from more than $10 billion in 1990 to roughly $6.5 billion in 1993. Finally, in 1994, CPL returned to profitability with a net income of nearly $400 million.

In September 1994 CPL offered to pay C$1.4 billion (US$1.04 billion) for the Canadian National Railway's rail operations in eastern Canada and the United States. CPL believed that the deal would benefit both companies, each of which had been racking up heavy losses in eastern Canada. The combination would eliminate excess rail capacity in eastern Canada. Canadian National opposed the unsolicited proposal, and in December 1994 the Canadian government blocked the deal.

By 1995, CPL had reorganized all of its operations into eight different companies. Transportation-related businesses, including rail (CPR) and container-shipping (CP Ships) operations, accounted for about 57 percent of total company revenues. Energy related businesses, which included oil and gas (PanCanadian Petroleum) and coal (Fording Coal) segments, made up about 29 percent. Finally, hotel (CP Hotels) and real estate (Marathon Realty) businesses accounted for 14 percent of CPL's sales. CPL also continued to hold a 47.2 percent interest in Laidlaw and a 48 percent stake in Unitel Communications Holdings Inc.

Unitel was a new name for CPL's telecommunications arm, which had been known as CNCP Telecommunications Limited. Rogers Communications Inc. had acquired a 40 percent stake in CNCP in 1989. In June 1992 Unitel received permission from the Canadian Radio-Television and Telecommunications Commission to provide public long-distance telephone service. The following year, AT&T Corp. purchased a 20 percent stake in

Unitel, reducing CPL's stake to 48 percent and Rogers' stake to 32 percent.

1996–2001: Deconglomerating Under O'Brien

David O'Brien became president of CPL in 1995 and then chairman and CEO, succeeding Stinson, the following year. Dramatic changes would take place under what would turn out to be his short tenure of leadership. O'Brien had begun his career as a trial lawyer in Montreal, before moving into the oil and gas industry in western Canada, eventually becoming executive vice-president of Petro-Canada Limited. In 1990 he became head of PanCanadian Petroleum. As president of CPL, O'Brien began shaking things up by moving the company's headquarters from Montreal to Calgary in 1995. As Chairman and CEO O'Brien quickly jettisoned the firm's three main noncore assets: the stakes in Unitel and Laidlaw were sold off in 1996 and 1997, respectively, and in 1996 CPL sold Marathon Realty for C$952 million (US$693.2 million) to a partnership formed by Oxford Properties Group Inc. and General Electric Capital Corporation. At this point, CPL consisted of five wholly or majority owned subsidiaries: Canadian Pacific Railway, CP Ships, PanCanadian Petroleum, Fording, and CP Hotels.

O'Brien believed that in the new era of free trade and globalization, CPL's structure—a holding company for several companies that were major players in the Canadian market—no longer made sense. Increasingly powerful shareholders were demanding ''pure plays'' that could compete on an international basis. Thus, O'Brien reasoned that eventually CPL would need to be broken up. The separate operating companies, however, would need to be strengthened first before being left to fend for themselves.

The last years of the 20th century were therefore spent expanding and improving the profitability of the five businesses. CPR, for example, embarked on a multiyear program of jettisoning about 5,400 miles of underperforming track, aided by changes in Canadian regulations that made it easier to dispose of rail lines. At the same time it launched a massive capital improvement program to bring the railroad up to international standards. A number of new locomotives were purchased, bringing the average age down to 18 years, from 22. An impetus behind the increased investment in the railroad was the 1995 privatization of Canadian National Railway, which meant that CPR would no longer have to compete with a government-owned company that did not have shareholders clamoring for profits.

From 1997 to 2000 CP Ships completed several acquisitions, including Lykes Lines, Contship Containerlines, Ivaran Lines, and CCAL. Revenues during this period increased from US$1.6 billion to US$2.6 billion. Already the second largest energy producer in Canada, PanCanadian Petroleum completed the largest acquisition in its history in 2000, the oil and gas division of Montana Power Company.

A number of developments were also occurring at CP Hotels, the largest hotel operator in Canada. In 1997 CP Hotels spun off 11 of its hotels, mainly those located in large cities, into a real estate investment trust called Legacy Hotels. The company continued to run the hotels and kept a one-third interest in the REIT. CP Hotels maintained ownership of 16 hotels, particularly its historic resort properties. The Legacy deal raised almost C$600 million in capital for expansion. In early 1998 CP Hotels bought Delta Hotels Limited, a Canadian chain, for about C$94 million. This doubled the number of rooms under management and gave the company a moderately priced chain to go along with its traditional high-end properties. CP Hotels also gained its first properties outside of Canada in 1998 by paying US$540 million for Princess Hotels International Inc., an operator of seven resorts in sunny destinations in Barbados, Bermuda, Mexico, and Arizona. Continuing to seek international growth, CP Hotels in October 1999 acquired Fairmont Hotels, owner of seven high-end properties in the United States, including the Fairmont San Francisco (the first Fairmont hotel, having opened in 1907) and the Plaza in New York. This acquisition led to the creation of Fairmont Hotels and Resorts Inc. and the addition of the Fairmont name to the CP Hotels (e.g., the Fairmont Banff Springs).

Early 21st Century: A New Era of Independence

By late 2000, strong performances by all five of the CPL subsidiaries led O'Brien to conclude that the time had come to act. In February 2001 the company announced that it would split itself into five publicly traded independent companies— CPR, CP Ships, PanCanadian Petroleum, Fording Inc., and Fairmont Hotels and Resorts. The demerger was completed on October 3, 2001, with holders of CPL stock receiving various amounts of stock in the five companies, which, with the exception of the already public PanCanadian, each gained listings on both the Toronto and New York Stock Exchanges. Canadian Pacific Limited ceased to exist, and O'Brien became chairman of PanCanadian.

The railroad unit, through which the PCL conglomerate had been built, returned to its roots as a standalone publicly traded company under the slightly revised name Canadian Pacific Railway Limited. Robert J. Ritchie was president and CEO of the company, a position he had held since 1995. Although clearly a much stronger company than just a few years previous, thanks to the heavy capital investments and the efficiency initiatives of the 1990s, CPR faced a somewhat uncertain future given that its 14,000 miles of track made it the smallest of the six major North American rail systems. There was much speculation regarding the possibility of a merger with Union Pacific or with archrival Canadian National.

Principal Subsidiaries

Soo Line Corporation (U.S.A.); Delaware and Hudson Railway Company, Inc. (U.S.A.); Tronicus Inc.

Principal Competitors

Canadian National Railway Company; Burlington Northern Santa Fe Corporation; Union Pacific Corporation; CSX Corporation.

Further Reading

''Another Rail Way,'' *Forbes,* March 1, 1972, p. 28.
Barker, Robert, ''Green Light for Canadian Pacific,'' *Barron's,* May 26, 1986, pp. 13+.

Bary, Andrew, "From Sleepy to Sleeper: Canadian Pacific's Revival Is Apparent Everywhere but in Its Stock Price," *Barron's,* May 18, 1998, pp. 30, 32–33.

Berton, Pierre, *The Last Spike: The Great Railway, 1881–1885,* Toronto: McClelland and Stewart, 1971, 478 p.

Binkley, Alex, "In Canada: Shrinking for Growth," *Railway Age,* February 1998, pp. 47–48.

Blaszak, Michael W., "Canadian Pacific Railway on Its Own," *Trains,* May 2001, pp. 18–19.

"Canadian Pacific Runs Off the Rails—and into Prosperity," *Financial Times of London World Business Weekly,* July 21, 1980, p. 10.

Bliss, Michael, "The Company That Built a Country: Canada's Most Storied Company Is About to Be Broken Up," *Globe and Mail,* August 31, 2001, p. 46.

Byrne, Harlan S., "Parting Ways: Canadian Pacific Units Seek Fulfillment on Their Own," *Barron's,* October 29, 2001, pp. 17–18, 21.

Clark, Marc, "The Remaking of a Household Name," *Maclean's,* January 20, 1986, p. 39.

Eagle, John A., *The Canadian Pacific Railway and the Development of Western Canada, 1896–1914,* Kingston, Ont.: McGill-Queen's University Press, 1989, 325 p.

Eliot, Jane, *The History of the Western Railroads,* New York: Bison Books, 1985.

Freeman, Alan, "Canadian Pacific Overhaul Boosts Profits," *Wall Street Journal,* October 12, 1988.

——, "Canadian Pacific Plans a Merger with Subsidiary," *Wall Street Journal,* September 9, 1985.

Freeman, Kenneth D., et al., *The Growth and Performance of the Canadian Transcontinental Railways, 1956–1981,* Vancouver, B.C.: Center for Transportation Studies, University of British Columbia, 1987, 345 p.

Gormick, Greg, "Canada's Troubled Railroads," *Railway Age,* February 1991, pp. 62–68.

——, "For CP, a Long, Long Trail," *Railway Age,* November 1994, pp. 35–37.

Hallman, Mark. "CP President Calls It Quits," *Financial Post,* December 14, 1994, sec. 1, p. 3.

——, "CP Surges Back to $393M Profit from $191 M Loss," *Financial Post,* February 7, 1995, sec. 1, p. 9.

——, "New CP Executives Face Difficult Times As Strike Looms," *Financial Post,* February 14, 1995, sec. 1, p. 3.

"How—and Why—CP Rail Is Reorganizing," *Railway Age,* December 1995, p. 20.

Kimelman, John, "O Canada!: How Long Will We Have to Wait for Things to Improve at Canadian Pacific?," *Financial World,* January 19, 1993, pp. 22+.

Koch, George, "Full Throttle: Canada's Railroads—and Their Profits—Come Steaming Back," *Barron's,* September 13, 1999, p. 24.

Kozma, Leslie S., and Charles W. Bohi, "Canada's New Rail Barons: Shortline Pioneers Have Expanded Nationwide," *Trains,* February 1999, pp. 38–44.

Masters, John, "Time Passages: The CPR and the Future," *Canadian Business,* November 1985, pp. 10+.

McMurdy, Deirdre, "Breaking Up Is Good to Do," *Canadian Business,* October 15, 2001, p. 15.

——, "Canada Inc.: Canadian Pacific's Struggle to Reinvent Itself Mirrors That of the Entire Canadian Economy," *Maclean's,* May 17, 1993, pp. 30–32.

McMurdy, Deirdre, and Barbara Wickens, "A Corporate Diet: CP Slims Down by Selling Off the Forests," *Maclean's,* August 23, 1993, pp. 36–37.

Meyer, Richard, "Blurred Image," *Financial World,* February 7, 1989, pp. 22+.

Nemeth, Mary, and Liz Warwick, "Down the Line: CP Rail Announces a Move to Calgary—and Another Wave of Layoffs," *Maclean's,* December 4, 1995, pp. 52–53.

Newman, Peter C., "CP Ltd.: Betting on the West's Dominance," *Maclean's,* May 20, 1996, p. 44.

Ryans, Leo, "CP Undergoing Major Restructuring," *Journal of Commerce,* February 27, 1987.

Sheppard, Robert, "The Very Last Spike," *Maclean's,* February 26, 2001, pp. 48+.

Simon, Bernard, "Canadian Pacific Plots Its Demise," *New York Times,* September 26, 2001, p. W1.

Verburg, Peter, "New Kid on the Beach," *Canadian Business,* February 12, 1999, pp. 52–54, 56.

Wilson-Smith, Anthony, "Putting CP on a Different Track: A Tough Competitor Reshapes His Company," *Maclean's,* November 16, 1998, pp. 46–47.

—William R. Grossman
—updates: Dave Mote, David E. Salamie

C A P E L.
I N C O R P O R A T E D ®

Capel Incorporated

P.O. Box 826
831 North Main Street
Troy, North Carolina 27371
U.S.A.
Telephone: (910) 572-7000
Toll Free: (800) 334-3711
Fax: (910) 572-7198
Web site: http://www.capel-rugs.com

Private Company
Incorporated: 1957 as A. Leon Capel and Sons, Inc.
Employees: 450
Sales: $50 million (2000 est.)
NAIC: 314110 Carpet and Rug Mills; 421220 Rugs
    Wholesaling

Capel Incorporated is the oldest and one of the largest manufacturers of rugs in the United States. Located in the textile and furniture producing region of North Carolina, Capel produces thousands of rug designs each year at its Troy headquarters and its manufacturing facilities worldwide. The company has captured an annual average of 7 percent of the $1 billion area rug market. Capel distributes its wares through a vast network of retailers throughout the United States and the world. Contracts for proprietary lines of merchandise with Pottery Barn, L.L. Bean, and other retailers have contributed to Capel's stellar reputation as a purveyor of fine floor coverings.

The Early Years: A New Departure

In 1917, A. Leon Capel, an industrious 17-year-old North Carolinian, began a manufacturing company dedicated to the production of mule harnesses and ropes. His father, William Elijah Capel, was a prominent citizen in Montgomery County, North Carolina. Among the senior Capel's many enterprises was the buying of faltering textile mills which he then restored to workable condition and sold for profit. It was one of these businesses that his son A. Leon Capel took over and named Gee Haw Plowlines.

However, A. Leon's entrepreneurial enterprise was destined to be short-lived when, according to family lore, Capel traveled to Atlanta searching for distributors eager to sell his products. It was during that trip that Capel took notice of a newspaper article announcing the unveiling of Henry Ford's new invention, the mechanical tractor.

A future dedicated to the production of mule ropes and harnesses for plowing fields appeared to be anachronistic overnight. Capel's Gee Haw Plowlines, like many other businesses of the era, was faced with industrial and technological advances at a revolutionary rate. Capel, though challenged, was not defeated. Economy and thrift were strong traditional values in the early 20th century and Capel sought out another manner in which to use his inventory of rope products and the machinery and knowledge he had acquired. Capel gambled on a future in mechanical rug production, and created a family company that would produce quality goods for decades to come.

For centuries, cultures had produced hand-tied, hand-knotted rugs all over the world. Early American pioneers had decorated their homes with handmade rag rugs and animal skins. Capel found that by using his machines to braid rope and yarn, and completing the process by sewing the braids into concentric circles of ever increasing size he could produce beautiful area rugs that were useful, durable, fashionable, and affordable. It was the first time braided rugs were manufactured on a mass scale outside the home. A. Leon Capel aptly renamed his new business New Departure.

In order to grow his business, Capel bought his own loom in 1926. He began producing chenille yarn for rug use. Capel found chenille to be durable enough to hold up to foot traffic yet able to provide the comfort and warmth that customers desired. Capel found a market for his rugs and production continued to grow throughout the decades.

The Next Generation

In the 1930s Capel's wife, Clara, gave birth to three sons and a daughter—A. Leon, Jr., Jesse, Arron, and Blanche. All three sons entered the family business in their 20s. In 1957, A. Leon Capel renamed his company A. Capel and Sons, Inc. to include the second generation owners. Jesse took over the business in 1957 until Leon was discharged from the Army and Arron finished school. All three owned an equal share of the company and served as its co-directors. Jesse Capel served the company as executive director in charge of manufacturing, and as the company's treasurer, Arron Capel managed Capel's retail operations and domestic spinning facilities as executive director, and A. Leon Capel was executive director of sales and marketing for the company.

The company bought its first spinning mill in 1936 when it took over an operation that had closed during the Great Depression. Ironically the mill had been rebuilt by A. Leon Capel under his father's direction years before. Capel purchased another mill in 1960 to enlarge its operations, and in the process founded Capelsie Mills, Inc. The following year the Capels founded another corporation to manage the company's real estate holdings, and Capel Real Estate was established.

Capel was involved in every step of its production from the time wool or synthetic materials arrived at its plants. Spinning, dyeing, braiding, knotting, weaving, sewing, packaging, distribution, and marketing were all done under the supervision of Capel family members. Capel expanded to include imported rugs in 1963. It began growing its foreign inventory with Spanish needlepoint rugs, and wool specialty rugs from Belgium and Holland. Area rugs from the Near and Far East also were included in the company's stock. Domestic products in Capel's line came from North Carolina and Dalton, Georgia looms, while imports originated from China, Belgium, and Egypt, with the company maintaining its status as one of the largest importers of rugs from India.

In 1972 the company's founder, A. Leon Capel, passed away, leaving his sons equal ownership of the family business. The legacy of fine rug-making continued. In 1978, one of Capel's early original designs, known as "Old Homestead," was inducted into the Chicago-based Floor Covering Hall of Fame. Braided rugs, more so than any other area rugs, were identified with Americana and the colonial and pioneer lifestyle, and Capel had a lot to do with the association.

By the late 1990s, according to an article in *Business North Carolina,* the rug manufacturer was selling its products through 10,000 retail stores in all 50 states. The company also had vendors in Canada, Australia, Japan, Europe, and South America, and processed over 500 orders a day.

The company remained family owned and operated, with third generation Capels, known as G3, taking over more and more of the corporate leadership. Kea Capel Meacham, Jesse Capel's daughter, acted as marketing and creative services director; her siblings J. Smith and Mary Clara were the imports manager and administrative services coordinator, respectively; Ron, Arron's son, worked as general manager of retail; his other son, Richard, was manufacturing manager; and Leon's daughter Cameron controlled human resources for the retail division.

The family did not always agree on the direction the company should take. Consolidation in the rug industry during this time had many businesses clamoring for their share of the retail market. In 1998, Capel brought on board a family-business facilitator to assist in defining the company's future leadership and direction.

According to home furnishing analysts in 2000, area rugs was the fastest growing segment of the $11 billion floor covering industry. As within many other home industry segments, innovations in rug design and materials were leading to a wide selection of rug styles, from traditional to very contemporary. Capel, known for its high quality colonial style braided rugs, grew its operation to include over 100 different rug styles. Prices for the company's products ranged from $10 to close to $12,000, depending on the size and type of rug.

High Fashion Floor Coverings: 1990s–2000s

In an October 25, 2001 *Washington Post* article, Kea Capel announced, "We're not just about colonial anymore, and all those braided rugs aren't just oval anymore either. While still a core product for the company, they're looking considerably snappier these days. One pattern called Sunnyside Up is woven in alternating rows of chenille and cotton in pinks and other candy colors . . . it's one of the hottest patterns in our line." Braided rugs in differing shapes, animal prints, flat weave, even camouflage fabric had all made there way into Capel's contemporary lines.

In 1998, when aromatherapy was a growing market in home products, Capel developed a scented braided rug by placing scent pellets within the fabric core. In the bold departure, Capel manufactured two rug prototypes, in cedar pine and floral fragrances.

In June 2001, Capel reopened a showroom on Fifth Avenue in the Home Textiles Building after moving its New York base of operations 23 years earlier. The company had moved its showroom to Third Avenue in 1978 to be included in the New York center of the floor covering market, but found its market increasing in textiles and so wanted to be back on Fifth Avenue. Capel began to cater to customers at the Home Textiles Show, where bed and bath buyers attended in great number. The company's imported Indian and Chinese cotton rugs, competitively priced from $9.99 to $29.99, were well received by specialty stores and catalog merchants, making a presence on Fifth Avenue a strategic investment. In April 2000 Capel secured a large booth at the Home Textiles Show in Manhattan and, as a result, signed a significant number of partnerships with top retailers.

The company had attempted to use resources wisely through its years of rug production. Capel manufacturing facilities recycled over 10,000 pounds of yarn a day, either converting it into reusable yarn or selling it to converters. The company made

Key Dates:

1917: A. Leon Capel begins Gee Haw Plowlines.
1918: A. Leon Capel begins manufacturing braided rope rugs, names his business New Departure.
1926: Capel buys local North Carolina loom to produce chenille yarn for rugs.
1936: Capel buys a small spinning loom in Capelsie, North Carolina.
1957: The company is renamed A. Capel and Sons, Inc. as Capel's sons enter the family business.
1960: The family founds Capelsie Mills, Inc.; during the decade, Capel begins selling its goods in the international marketplace.
1961: Capel Real Estate Corporation is formed.
1963: Capel begins importing rugs.
1972: A. Leon Capel dies.
1978: Capel's rug design "Old Homestead" is inducted into the Floor Covering Hall of Fame.
1980: A. Leon Capel and Sons, Inc. changes its name to Capel Incorporated.

chenille yarn out of odds and ends of fiber threads that were hand color-matched and plied back into yarn. Through the Bob Timberlake collection Capel participated in the Keep America Beautiful Program, a national nonprofit public education program emphasizing responsible reuse and waste conservation practices in U.S. communities.

Capel began focusing a good part of its distribution through other name brand retailers in the 1990s. The company entered agreements with large volume well-known companies partially in response to the consolidation of the retail sector, which Capel had sold to throughout its years. According to an article in *Business North Carolina,* Leon Capel opined, "The biggest challenge most manufactures, and certainly Capel, are facing is the changing format of retail." Capel explained that 80 percent of the market was moving to large discount chains such as Home Depot, Sears, Target, Wal-Mart, and Kmart.

The company had considered opening its own line of retail storefronts. It had maintained six showrooms around the country, as well as eight separate outlet stores for a number of years, but its retail/outlet facilities had been within North Carolina and Virginia.

In the 1990s, Capel secured merchandise deals with L.L. Bean and Pottery Barn Kids. Other companies with product ties to Capel included Linens 'n Things, La-Z-Boy Furniture Galleries, and ABC Carpet and Home.

In August 2001 *Home Textiles Today* announced that Capel had signed a licensing agreement with wildlife artist Dick Idol to manufacture rugs depicting outdoors motifs from the artist's work. The company had not had any such agreements since 1997 but saw the trend towards wildlife themes as a significant enough market to justify pursuing the license.

Capel sold directly in a limited way through its eight retail sites in North Carolina and Virginia but Internet sales growth was expected to be a substantial piece of the company's direct sales in the future. The company redesigned its web site in 2001. The web site showcased 150 standard designs, styles, and colors utilizing an easy format to search through company inventory. The site made it easy for consumers to view and select products. The redesigned site also increased the number of visitors to www.capel.com from roughly 12,000 per month to nearly one million. The web site offered promotional enticements including a monthly rug giveaway to one lucky winner.

At the end of 2001, Capel Incorporated stood as a successful family-owned and operated business that had endured for almost a century. The company was responsive to industry changes, determined to construct good products within a broad price range, and working tirelessly to maintain its market share in a competitive industry. Leon Capel, Jr., explained the company's direction in the Home Furnishing Network's trade publication *HFN* when he said, "creativity, foresight and financing are key to Capel's growth and its ability to avoid major problems." As to the future, Capel mused, "It is unknown, but Capel Inc., will continue to be an aggressive leader in rug manufacturing—both domestic and import."

Principal Divisions

Capelsie Mills, Inc; Capel Real Estate and Development.

Principal Operating Units

Manufacturing; Retail Operations; Domestic Spinning; Sales and Marketing.

Principal Competitors

Colonial Mills Carpet, Inc.; Robin Industries, Inc.; Oriental Weavers USA Incorporated; Shaw Industries, Inc.; Mohawk Industries, Inc.; Orian Rugs Inc.; Costikyan Ltd.; Harounian Rugs International; 828 International Trading Co. Inc.; Aladdin Manufacturing Corp.; Nourison Rug Corp.

Further Reading

"Area Rug," *Home Accents Today,* January 2001, p. 64.
"A Braid Apart," *HFN,* November 20, 2000, p. 21.
"Capel Sets Splash on Imports," *HFN,* October 21, 1996, p. 35.
Garau, Rebecca, "Capel's Scent Sensibility," *HFN,* January 12, 1998, p. 20.
"Gray Dawn: Textile Makers Search for Answers in 2nd Half," *Home Textiles Today,* August 20, 2001, p. 12.
Herlihy, Janet, "Financial Facts of Licensing Ring True," *HFN,* April 12, 1999, p 56.
——, "Handmade Vendors Choose Paths at Market; Some Focus on Specialty Niches; Others Go For Broader Appeal," *HFN,* August 2, 1999, p. 13.
Rogers, Patricia Dane, "One Firm That Puts on Quite a Floor Show," *Washington Post,* October 25, 2001.
Schuka, Terrilynn, "Plowlines to Area Rugs," *HFN,* June 14, 1999, p. 18.
Switzer, Liz, "Pile Drivers," *Business North Carolina,* July 1999, p. 42.
Wyman, Lissa, "Rug Makers Proudly Recycle," *HFN,* October 9, 1995, p. 18.
——, "Taking the Floor; Large Rugs Supplant the 6-by-9," *HFN,* December 16, 1996, p. 11.

—Susan B. Culligan

Career Education Corporation

2895 Greenspoint Parkway, Suite 600
Hoffman Estates, Illinois 60195
U.S.A.
Telephone: (847) 781-3600
Fax: (847) 781-3610
Web site: http://www.careered.com

Public Company
Incorporated: 1994
Employees: 4,900
Sales: $325.29 million (2000)
Stock Exchanges: NASDAQ
Ticker Symbol: CECO
NAIC: 611310 Colleges, Universities, and Professional
   Schools

Career Education Corporation (CEC) operates a string of for-profit professional schools and colleges on about 40 campuses that grant associate's, bachelor's, and master's degrees in the fields of visual communication and design technologies, information technology, business studies, and culinary arts. In the latter category, CEC institutions offer training certified by prestigious French cooking school Le Cordon Bleu. The company's schools are located around the United States and in Canada, England, and the United Arab Emirates. The publicly traded firm is one of the largest for-profit educational concerns in the United States, having grown rapidly since its 1994 founding through an aggressive acquisition strategy.

Beginnings

Career Education Corporation was founded in January 1994 by John M. Larson to take advantage of the consolidation opportunities afforded by the fragmented post-secondary education industry. Larson, a graduate of Stanford and the University of California at Berkeley, had nearly 20 years' experience in the field of education, having worked for Phillips Colleges, Inc. and National Education Centers, Inc., among others. The new company's strategy was to grow by acquiring established

schools which it would then make more profitable. Its initial focus was institutions offering business studies, visual design, and information technology programs. The first purchase made by CEC was the Al Collins Graphic Design School in Tempe, Arizona, which had been founded in 1978. In mid-1994 a second institution, Brooks College of Long Beach, California, was also acquired. Revenues for the company's first year were $7.5 million.

CEC's business strategy was to purchase promising schools and then upgrade them. This typically involved improving their facilities and adding new course offerings. The company limited its acquisitions to schools that offered training in fields in which there was a strong continuing demand for workers, and which attracted motivated students. A major goal of CEC was improvement of student retention and graduation rates, and high job placement percentages. The company also sought to emphasize programs that would serve people throughout a lifetime of learning, with degree offerings that ranged from the associate's up to the master's level.

In July 1995 CEC added Brown Institute of Mendota Heights, Minnesota, and Allentown Business School of Allentown, Pennsylvania. Brown had been founded in 1946, while Allentown's history went back to 1869. Both offered training in computer technology and visual design.

In October 1996 CEC entered the field of culinary arts when it acquired the Western Culinary Institute of Portland, Oregon. The restaurant and food service field was expected to have a shortage of workers for some time to come, giving education providers in that area a solid opportunity for growth. The following spring the School of Computer Technology of Pittsburgh, Pennsylvania, and Fairmont, West Virginia, was acquired for approximately $5 million. Some $1.8 million more was paid to the institution's former owners as part of a non-competition agreement. Another multi-campus operation, the Katharine Gibbs Schools, was bought in the summer from K-III Communications Corp. The 85-year-old Gibbs Schools, with a half-dozen locations in the middle Atlantic and New England states, offered business training. K-III received $19 million, as well as $7 million in non-compete payments. At about the same time an agreement was reached for the acquisition of the International Academy of Merchandising and Design, which had locations in Chicago and Florida. The price tag was $6.5 million plus $2 million in non-compete money.

Initial Public Offering

In the fall of 1997 CEC announced plans to issue 2.85 million shares of stock on the NASDAQ exchange for the purpose of repaying debt. The IPO was launched in early 1998, and raised more than $45 million for the company. In March CEC purchased the Southern California School of Culinary Arts, located in Pasadena, California, for $1 million. Another cooking school was acquired in July when the Scottsdale Culinary Institute of Scottsdale, Arizona, was bought for $10 million.

At the end of the year plans were made to acquire the Harrington Institute of Interior Design, a 400-student school located in Chicago. The $3.5 million deal was finalized in January 1999, and boosted CEC's totals to nearly 16,000 students at 21 campuses in 13 states and two Canadian provinces. Revenues stood at $144.2 million, with net income of $4.3 million, almost 20 times the amount of four years earlier.

In December 1998 the company formed the CEC Educational Foundation to fund scholarships for students enrolled in CEC schools. With many pursuing an education while working part or full-time, and with educational costs constantly rising, the foundation was intended to make it easier for CEC students to finish school. Much of its funding came from alumni and from firms that routinely recruited CEC graduates. The company also formed a Professional Education Loan program in partnership with the Student Loan Marketing Association (Sallie Mae).

Scoring a Coup with Le Cordon Bleu: 1998

A major agreement was reached in late 1998 with the French culinary arts school Le Cordon Bleu to offer its first sanctioned programs in the United States through CEC schools. Le Cordon Bleu had been founded in Paris in 1895 and was renowned as one of the finest institutions of its type in the world. The Cordon Bleu training program emphasized classic French cooking techniques which could be applied to any type of cuisine. Le Cordon Bleu had schools in Paris, London, Tokyo, Australia, and Ottawa, Canada. The first U.S. programs would be offered at CEC's Brown Institute campus in Minnesota, where the new Midwest Culinary Academy was set to open in January 1999, and later at other locations.

The company's acquisitions continued in the spring of 1999 when McIntosh College of New Hampshire was bought for $5 million and Briarcliffe College of New York was purchased for $20.6 million. The latter had 1,300 students at two campuses in Bethpage and Patchogue, New York. In June Brooks Institute of

Photography of Santa Barbara, California, was bought. Brooks, acquired for $6.6 million, had some 300 students enrolled in photography and filmmaking courses.

In August an agreement to purchase another cooking school was reached. The California Culinary Academy, a publicly traded company, would be acquired for approximately $22 million when the deal was finalized the following spring. The school, like most acquired by CEC, had a relatively long history, having been founded some 20 years earlier. California Culinary, CEC's sixth culinary arts acquisition, was headquartered in San Francisco and operated satellite campuses in Salinas and San Diego.

In December Washington Business School was purchased. The 49-year-old school operated out of Tysons Center, Virginia, near Washington, D.C. CEC would update its programs to offer associate's degrees and add new classes that would complement the school's business-oriented curriculum. The deal cost the firm $3 million.

Early 2000 saw the purchase of the Culinary and Hospitality Institute of Chicago for approximately $5.5 million. Known as CHIC, the school had approximately 700 students. CEC committed $10 million to doubling its size to 40,000 square feet. During CHIC's first year in operation as a CEC unit the school's income more than doubled, increasing from $5 million to $11 million.

CEC's Le Cordon Bleu agreement was expanded during 2000 to include restaurant management training, which would be taught at the Western Culinary Institute in Portland, Oregon, beginning in January 2001. By this time six of CEC's eight culinary arts schools were offering Le Cordon Bleu-authorized training. To prepare for the management program, CEC spent $2 million on new facilities at Western, which included computer labs, a charcuterie, and a restaurant dubbed the International Bistro, which students would operate as part of their training. The program included special attention to point-of-service technology that would record seating arrangements, process orders, track cash flow, and provide reports on labor costs and expenditures.

In July 2000 CEC purchased SoftTrain Institute of Toronto, Canada, which offered information technology training, for $500,000. The school had been founded in 1988, and plans were soon afoot to offer some of its programs at other CEC schools. Another small Canadian acquisition followed in the fall when Retter Business College of Ottawa was purchased for $400,000. Retter offered training in multimedia web development, software engineering, and computer network engineering. Its name was subsequently changed to the International Academy of Design and Technology at Ottawa.

Purchase of EduTrek: 2000

In October 2000 CEC announced its largest purchase to date with the acquisition of EduTrek International, Inc. Georgia-based EduTrek owned and operated American InterContinental University (AIU), which had some 4,700 students at campuses in Atlanta, Los Angeles, Ft. Lauderdale, Washington, D.C., London, and Dubai, United Arab Emirates. AIU, founded in 1970, granted bachelor's and master's degrees in visual com-

Key Dates:

1994: John M. Larson founds Career Education Corporation, begins acquisitions.
1996: CEC enters field of culinary arts with purchase of Western Culinary Institute.
1998: Company completes its IPO on the NASDAQ.
1999: Company begins to offer Le Cordon Bleu-certified culinary arts programs.
2000: Purchase of EduTrek International, Inc. brings 4,700 students, six U.S. and foreign campuses.

munication and design, business studies, and information technology. The deal involved the exchange of 1.2 million shares of CEC stock as well as assumption of debt, for a total price of approximately $70 million. The company's plan for AIU was to cut costs by restructuring operations and to increase advertising to attract more students. For fiscal 2000 CEC's income hit a record $325.3 million, with profits of $21.4 million.

The company was now employing a number of methods for recruiting students, including web sites, direct mail, television and print media, and high school visits. CEC targeted a mix of people that included recent high school graduates, older students, and international students. The company's marketing efforts were boosted by partnerships with college guide publisher Peterson's and online college application service Embark. In addition to classroom training, CEC also offered distance learning over the Internet in some disciplines. The firm's focus on raising student retention rates was showing strong results, with an average of 76 percent remaining enrolled year-to-year in 2000. A new program, "Save Our Students" (S.O.S.), was launched in 2001 to further increase this figure. The company's job placement record was one factor that brought its students back, with 94 percent of CEC graduates gainfully employed within six months of graduation. The rate was an even better 98 percent for the culinary arts programs.

The year 2001 also saw CEC open a new branch of the Katharine Gibbs Schools in Philadelphia. The new campus was the ninth unit for Gibbs, which had more than 8,000 students enrolled at this time. Two programs in information technology and two in business studies would be offered. Others in visual communication and design technologies were to be added later. The main campus offered a wireless multimedia learning resource center, classrooms, a bookstore, and a student lounge. Students could buy a wireless laptop computer that would connect them with faculty, educational resources, and the Inter-

net. During the year CEC also opened a new campus of the International Academy of Design and Technology in Orlando, Florida. In August, Texas Culinary Academy was bought for $1.1 million, followed in December by the acquisition of the Pennsylvania Culinary Academy of Pittsburgh for $44 million, further solidifying the company's offerings in this category.

After only eight years in business, Career Education Corporation was proving phenomenally successful, its revenues having grown more than 40-fold. The company was also scoring with its customers, boasting high student retention and job placement rates. With a large number of independent postsecondary schools still potentially available for purchase, CEC looked to be on track for continuing growth and profitability.

Principal Subsidiaries

Al Collins Graphic Design School, Ltd.; Allentown Business School, Ltd.; Brooks College, Ltd.; Brown Institute, Ltd.; CEC Educated Staffing, Inc.; CEC e-Learning, Inc.; CEC Holdings I, Inc.; CEC Management, Inc.; The Cooking and Hospitality Institute of Chicago, Inc.; EduTrek International, Inc.; Harrington Institute of Interior Design, Inc.; IAMD, Limited; International Academy of Merchandising and Design (Canada) Ltd.; Market Direct, Inc.; Retter Business College Corp. (Canada); School of Computer Technology, Inc.; Scottsdale Culinary Institute, Ltd.; SoftTrain Institute, Inc. (Canada); Southern California School of Culinary Arts, Ltd.; Western Culinary Institute, Ltd.

Principal Competitors

DeVry, Inc.; Apollo Group, Inc.; ITT Educational Services, Inc.; Education Management Corp.

Further Reading

"Chicago-Area Education Company Buys California Culinary School," *Monterey County Herald*, August 6, 1999.
Knowles, Francine, "Career Education," *Chicago Sun-Times*, November 20, 2000.
Marshall, Jon, "Growing Career Ed Ready to Go Public: School Firm Wins As Post-Secondary Market Blossoms," *Crain's Chicago Business*, November 17, 1997.
McCormick, Brian, "Expansion on Menu for Cooking School; New Parent Adds to CHIC's Space, Refines Program," *Crain's Chicago Business*, March 26, 2001.
Obra, Joan, "Restaurant Training Ground Makes Quiet Debut in Portland, Ore.," *Oregonian*, July 6, 2001.
Smith, Geoffrey, "Career Education Thrives Amid Slowdown," *Chicago Sun-Times*, July 5, 2001.

—Frank Uhle

Carter Lumber Company

601 Tallmadge Road
Kent, Ohio 44240
U.S.A.
Telephone: (330) 673-6100
Fax: (330) 678-6134
Web site: http://www.carterlumber.com

Private Company
Founded: 1932 as Carter-Jones Lumber
Employees: 4,300
Sales: $570 million (2000 est.)
NAIC: 421300 Lumber and Other Construction Materials
   Wholesalers

Family owned and operated for three generations, Carter Lumber Company is a regional lumberyard chain based in Kent, Ohio. The company owns approximately 250 stores in nine states, and is growing by ten to 15 units per year by focusing mostly on smaller towns in Ohio, Illinois, Indiana, Michigan, North Carolina, South Carolina, Kentucky, and Virginia. Serving smaller markets has helped the much smaller stores of Carter Lumber to thrive in a business generally dominated by such home improvement giants as Lowe's and Home Depot. While the latter may feature stores of 100,000 square feet, a typical Carter Lumber store is just 6,000 square feet. The company positions itself as a true lumberyard, devoted to both contractors, who account for almost 70 percent of its business, as well as do-it-yourself customers. Although it features plumbing, electric, and heating departments, Carter Lumber does not sell appliances and other home improvement merchandise. Because of the size of its chain, however, Carter Lumber does enjoy the benefits of volume purchasing in order to discount prices. In addition to stocking building materials, Carter Lumber also sells kits which include all the necessary materials for building projects that range from full-size houses and garages (its most popular kits) to smaller projects such as decks, swing sets, and kitchen designs. In addition to its stores, Carter Lumber owns two lumber and supply distribution centers, a 2,000-acre horse and cattle farm, and approximately 60,000 acres of timberland in Arkansas.

Company's Founder Born in 1898

The life of Warren E. Carter, the founder of Carter Lumber, is the quintessential American success story. He was born in Arkansas in 1898 in former slave quarters, then his family moved to a heavily wooded area in Arkansas in 1904 to raise hogs. To help clear the land, Carter became handy with an ax and also gained skills sawing logs and making barrel staves. He received an elementary school education, then dropped out of school after the eighth grade, a choice typically made by rural youth at the time. He went to work transporting logs with teams of horses through the Arkansas woodlands to the sawmills. In the 1920s he became the white foreman of a team primarily comprised of black workers who loaded lumber for a sawmill onto railroad cars ten hours a day, six days a week. He quickly displayed traits that were a harbinger of his personal ethic and future business career. Within months, his team became productive enough to reduce the cost of loading a railroad car from 84 cents to 76 cents. To reward his men, he requested and received a two and one-half cent raise, despite complaints from other teams. He continued to improve the productivity of his men, so that within a year the cost per carload had been reduced to 64 cents, and by the time he left the job, his men had seen their pay increased by a nickel to 50 cents a day. Carter would become known for his habits of hard work and honesty, as well as showing a compassion for other people. He became a civic leader, actively involved in politics and charitable endeavors such as Goodwill Industries and the Salvation Army.

Carter gained some additional education, attending business school in Tyler, Texas. In 1927 he traveled to Akron, Ohio, to visit his brother Frank, who worked at the Goodyear Tire plant. After dropping his brother off at work one day he visited a lumberyard to talk to the owner, Clyde Gough, who immediately hired Carter as his general foreman at $22 a month. With the advent of the Depression, business suffered and by 1932 Gough lost the lumberyard in a bank foreclosure. Carter teamed with coworker T. Neil Jones to buy the Gough assets from the bank, creating Carter-Jones Lumber. It was an austere operation at first, with Carter paying himself just $12 a week to support his wife and three children while living in quarters at the yard. Despite difficult business conditions, Carter-Jones Lumber turned a $1,600 profit in its first year.

Company Perspectives:

In 1932 Warren E. Carter opened a lumberyard in Akron, Ohio: The Carter-Jones Lumber Company. His idea was to operate a lumberyard based on the simple principle of providing the greatest customer service while offering quality products at a fair price. Through the years this idea has helped the Carter Lumber Company grow to one of the top building material retailers in the country.

By today's standards Carter might be considered a workaholic, a trait that became a source of friction between the two partners. Jones sold out in 1937, although according to Carter they remained the best of friends the rest of their lives. Aside from working hard, Carter also displayed a sense of honesty that was apparently rare in the lumberyards of the day, when it was common practice for an estimate for the amount of wood required in a building project to be an elastic number. Extra charges always emerged, so that a developer was never certain of his costs until the final bill came in. After loading lumber onto train cars and being held accountable for every piece, Carter ran his lumberyard the same way, estimating and delivering to contractors exactly what was needed and ordered. Despite being informed by fellow lumberyard owners about the proper way to run such a business, Carter ignored their advice, and in short order contractors were giving him their business, because they knew they could count on his honesty. Carter also drew another lesson from his days loading railcars. Knowing the value of a strong bond between workers and a leader, he delegated hiring to his managers, insisting that each department head should hire his own people.

Carter's business grew to the point where he was soon able to open lumberyards in the Ohio towns of Wooster and Fairlawn. (His brother Louis entered the lumberyard business as well, establishing the Wooster Lumber chain, which would eventually be absorbed by Carter Lumber in 1972.) Carter also became involved in the construction of tract housing in a number of small Ohio towns. A respected business leader, he served in major positions with the Akron Builders Exchange, the Ohio Association of Retail Lumber Dealers, the Akron Chamber of Commerce, and the Better Business Bureau of Akron. He even ran for mayor of Akron in 1955. Although defeated, he was glad in retrospect that he had not been distracted from his thriving business. To supply his growing operations, he bought thousands of acres of timberland in Arkansas, including the house and land where he grew up.

Changes Following 1964 Heart Attack

The energetic Carter suffered a heart attack in 1964, but it would prove to be far from debilitating. Nevertheless, in 1966 he took steps to protect his wealth and assets for his children by creating Building Services Co., a partnership designed to own the assets of Carter Lumber and pass the benefits onto his heirs. Although Carter would step back from the business, allowing his son, Van Dale Carter, to succeed him as chief executive officer, he would continue to come into the office a few days a week for many years to come, insuring that his influence on the company would endure.

In the mid-1960s Carter Lumber owned 12 yards. By the end of the decade the company expanded beyond lumber, adding plumbing, electric, and heating departments to better serve contractors as well as the growing do-it-yourself market. Under Van Carter the company began to grow at a steady clip. By the mid-1980s Carter Lumber boasted more than 150 stores. To support such a large-scale operation, a management training program was instituted. In keeping with the principles of Warren Carter, each management trainee started out in the warehouse and manually unloaded boxcars to become familiar with what the stores sold, piece by piece.

The company ran into some problems making the transition to a second generation of management. In 1985 the Carter family experienced a public rift when four members filed a suit against the company and some of its officers, in particular Van Carter, alleging that the Building Services partnership had been deliberately drained of assets in order to deprive them of their rightful share of the family's wealth. All of the plaintiffs had been formerly employed by Carter Lumber, but according to the suit had been afraid to question Van Carter's operation of the business, concerned that he would retaliate by firing them. Now that they no longer worked for the company, they lodged a number of charges in their suit, which requested an audit and $1 million in punitive damages. Warren Carter was not named in the suit and the matter was eventually resolved outside of the public spotlight, but it was a nasty open spat for an extremely private family.

Third Generation Taking the Helm: 1988

Van Carter died in 1988 and leadership of the company passed to a third generation, his son Bryan Carter. Other grandchildren also assumed prominent roles in the organization. As the company continued to add stores to its lumberyard chain in the 1990s, it faced a new challenge from the rise of Home Depot and Lowe's. Although Carter Lumber was well established and believed that its reputation for providing quality service and products with a personal touch would keep it competitive in a changing retail world, it had never promoted itself much beyond the publication of a monthly Sunday flier. While modesty was an admirable trait in the company's founder, which led Carter Lumber to favor service over promotional efforts, it was apparent to the new generation of management that Carter Lumber had to improve its marketing. Before it could even consider an advertising campaign, however, it needed to know what consumers thought about the company, rather than what the company thought about itself. A study by an Ohio advertising and public relations firm revealed that contractors now viewed Carter Lumber as a store for the do-it-yourself market, while general consumers thought of it as catering to contractors. The contractors were turning to small yards, which they saw as specialists in their particular fields. Consumers, meanwhile, were shopping at big box stores, not realizing that Carter Lumber was selling higher quality goods at cheaper prices and offering more knowledgeable advice for the do-it-yourselfer. To educate the contractor market, Carter Lumber developed a newsletter, ''Plane & Simple,'' to announce new programs. Each store added a contractor sales representative who traveled to sites to not only provide complete lists of supplies offered by Carter Lumber, but to also take orders and offer advice. The stores made a point of staying current on area building codes to

Key Dates:

1927: Warren E. Carter moves to Akron, Ohio.
1932: Carter and T. Neil Jones start Carter-Jones Lumber.
1937: Jones leaves the business.
1988: Van Carter dies, leaving third generation in charge.
2000: Warren Carter dies at age 101.

make sure that they stocked approved products, an important benefit for both contractors and do-it-yourselfers. Carter Lumber also initiated a customer loyalty rewards program for contractors, giving away televisions, stereos, gas grills, and weeklong trips to Hawaii. On the consumer side, the company introduced a similar incentive program, and to increase brand recognition launched a marketing campaign that featured radio and television advertising. It even spent money on signage behind homeplate at Jacobs' Field, home of the Cleveland Indians baseball team.

With a thriving economy that stimulated the building of new homes, along with improved marketing, Carter Lumber flourished in the late 1990s, continuing to add stores at the rate of around ten a year, with the emphasis remaining on the smaller towns often overlooked by big box rivals. To take advantage of the rise in building starts, the company again engaged in some contracting. Not only did this stimulate lumber sales but served as another way to form bonds with the commercial customers they engaged on the projects.

In 1999 Carter Lumber was rocked by scandal when it fired, then sued, its chief financial officer of ten years, Kenneth J. Azar, Jr., accusing him of fraudulently appropriating more than $6 million, which he transferred to a number of financial companies he controlled, and used to purchase real estate, including an $815,000 home. He also faced criminal charges, which he would eventually settle by pleading guilty in a settlement with state prosecutors.

In June 2000 Warren E. Carter died at the age of 101. The company he founded continued to grow under the leadership of his grandchildren, despite a flagging economy that severely crippled the number of housing starts and depressed lumber prices that adversely affected the bottom line. For a privately run company that was born out of the Depression and did not have to answer to shareholders, however, a downturn in the economy was not cause for panic. Carter Lumber was well positioned to continue its long-term pattern of steady growth.

Principal Competitors

84 Lumber Company; The Home Depot, Inc.; Lowe's Companies, Inc.

Further Reading

Benton, Theresa M., "Not Ready to Retire at Age 65," *Toledo Business Journal,* March 1, 1997, p. 44.

Ethridge, Mary, "Portage, County, Ohio-Based Lumber Company Refashions Its Image," *Akron Beacon Journal,* March 22, 2001.

Flint, Troy, "Lumber Company Abuzz," *Cleveland Plain Dealer,* September 24, 1998, p. 1C.

Geiger, Peter, "Carter-Jones Relatives Sue Firm, Family," *Akron Beacon Journal,* August 29, 1985, p. C1.

Gleisser, Marcus, "Carter-Jones Lumber Accuses Ex-CFO of Taking $6.2 Million," *Cleveland Plain Dealer,* November 23, 1999.

McGonigal, Diana, "A Lumbering Giant Wakes Up," *Small Business News-Cleveland,* October 1, 1998, p. 22.

Scott, Dave, "Former Lumber Company Owner in Akron, Ohio, Turns 101," *Akron Beacon Journal,* August 13, 1999.

Vanac, Mary, "Lumber Business a Family Affair," *Akron Beacon Journal,* August 12, 1994, p. B10.

—Ed Dinger

Cephalon, Inc.

145 Brandywine Parkway
West Chester, Pennsylvania 19380
U.S.A.
Telephone: (610) 344-0200
Fax: (610) 738-6590
Web site: http://www.cephalon.com

Public Company
Incorporated: 1987
Employees: 650
Sales: $111.79 million (2000)
Stock Exchanges: NASDAQ
Ticker Symbol: CEPH
NAIC: 54171 Research and Development in the Physical, Engineering and Life Sciences

Cephalon, Inc. is an international biopharmaceutical company that specializes in drugs to treat neurological and sleep disorders. The company's activities encompass the discovery, research, and development of new treatments as well as the sales and marketing of finished products.

Cephalon has three proprietary products that account for almost all of its sales revenue in the United States. The drug Provigil promotes daytime wakefulness and is used to treat narcolepsy, a disease characterized by a propensity to fall asleep during the day. Provigil is also used to combat fatigue associated with other disorders, such as depression and multiple sclerosis. A second product, Gabitril, treats partial seizures associated with epilepsy. Finally, the drug Actiq is prescribed to manage pain in cancer patients. Cephalon's European headquarters in Guildford, England, manages the sale of eight products in the United Kingdom, France, Germany, Switzerland, and Austria. Branch offices are located in France and Germany. The company has also expanded its international reach through marketing collaboration agreements with pharmaceutical companies in Asia, Mexico, and Europe. Under the agreements, Cephalon is able to sell its products through a third party without having to maintain its own sales force abroad.

True to its roots as a small research house, Cephalon continues working to develop new treatments. Products currently under development include therapies for prostate and pancreatic cancer as well as Parkinson's disease. The company is also working on finding new applications for its three centerpiece products. Meanwhile, sales and marketing has become an ever more prominent sector of the company's operations. Of Cephalon's 650 worldwide employees, about 250 work in the sales and marketing organizations.

A Small Research House: 1987–91

Cephalon was founded in 1987 by two venture capital firms, Burr, Egan, Deleage & Co. and Hambrecht & Quist Life Science Partners. The firms recruited Frank Baldino, Jr., a senior biologist who was conducting neuroscience research for DuPont, to head the company. In the early years, Baldino kept Cephalon focused on research. About 30 scientists worked in a 10,000-square-foot laboratory, specializing in the discovery of neurological growth factors that could be used to treat diseases such as multiple sclerosis, strokes, and amyotrophic lateral sclerosis (ALS, or Lou Gehrig's disease). The chemicals under development were intended to prevent the brain cell death associated with the diseases.

As a small research house, Cephalon initially avoided involving itself in activities that would require maintaining a sales staff, managing clinical trials, and shepherding new drugs through the Food and Drug Administration (FDA) approval process. With no product to sell, Cephalon's only asset was its scientific expertise. That expertise proved sufficient to attract investors, and the company managed to fund its operations through research grants and contracts with larger pharmaceutical firms. The 1990 discovery of an enzyme, Clipsin, that plays a major role in Alzheimer's disease, for example, led to an agreement with Schering-Plough. Under the agreement, Schering-Plough provided Cephalon with $20 million to continue its Alzheimer's research in exchange for exclusive worldwide rights to any technologies developed.

By the end of 1990, Cephalon had accumulated a deficit of $7.26 million since it began operating in November 1987. However, the company continued on a path of confident expansion. In March 1991 the staff had grown to 49 employees, who worked in an enlarged 31,000-square-foot lab. That April Cephalon completed its initial public offering, raising $59.4 million at a price of $18 a share. However, the share price dipped to $14.75 several weeks later amid general concern that biotechnology stocks were overvalued. The company would have to produce tangible results to retain investor confidence.

Banking on Myotrophin in the Mid-1990s

In late 1991 Cephalon received orphan drug approval for its product Myotrophin. Orphan drug status gives a company the right to market a product exclusively for seven years, and is granted for drugs not considered profitable enough to justify development without such a guarantee. Thus Cephalon began an eight-year, ultimately unsuccessful, occupation with Myotrophin. The drug, known as a neurotrophic factor, promoted the survival of neurons and was being developed as a treatment for ALS. Cephalon subsequently bought a plant in Maryland to manufacture Myotrophin for research purposes, and entered into an agreement with Chiron Corporation to manufacture the drug on a larger scale if it should be approved by the FDA.

Meanwhile, a successful $23 million equity offering in April 1993 showed that investors retained confidence in Cephalon. The company received $17 million in revenues that year from contracts with large pharmaceutical firms, and grew to 222 employees by year's end. Besides Schering-Plough and Chiron, Cephalon worked with two other firms. In a collaboration with SmithKline Beecham, Cephalon was researching the use of protease inhibitors, chemicals that impede the process of cell death, to aid in the treatment of Alzheimer's. It was also working with SmithKline Beecham on a line of drugs that had potential for stopping abnormal cell growth in cancer patients. With the Japanese firm Kyowa Hakko Kogyo Co. Ltd., Cephalon was developing chemicals to inhibit the action of kinases, a type of protein that causes cell death in Alzheimer's and Parkinson's patients. In addition, the first step toward the development of the narcolepsy treatment Provigil was taken in February 1993, when Cephalon bought from the French company Laboratoire L. Lafon all rights to develop, market, and sell Provigil's main ingredient, modafinil. Such wide-ranging research efforts caused the accumulation of a $35.6 million deficit between 1987 and the end of 1993.

In 1994 failures at other clinics made Wall Street wary of biotechnology stocks, and Cephalon's share price fell from a high of $19.50 in the first quarter of 1994 to $5.75 in mid-1995. But the company trusted in the potential of its own technologies. On June 12, Cephalon announced positive results of clinical tests of Myotrophin. The tests showed that Myotrophin appeared to slow the progression of ALS. Cephalon's shares rose 400 percent on the news. Although European tests, announced in the fall, showed less conclusive results, the company's stock continued to climb.

In 1995 Cephalon took a decisive step away from its research-only roots by establishing a sales force. Because Cephalon did not yet have a product to sell, the sales force sold other companies' drugs. In an arrangement with Bristol-Myers Squibb, Cephalon sold the company's drugs to neurologists, thus giving its own sales force the opportunity to establish the connections and experience that would pay off once Cephalon was marketing its own products.

The first major stumbling block for Myotrophin came at the beginning of 1996, when the FDA refused to allow Cephalon to expand tests of the drug. On January 19, shares fell 34 percent to $23.37 in reaction to the news. The FDA pointed to conflicting results between European and American tests as the basis for its decision. Critics of the tests also charged that the clinical trials of Myotrophin were poorly designed. The test groups were too small, they said, and records were kept in such a way that many patient deaths were not counted. Because the trials were testing disease progression, not mortality rates, patients who were taking Myotrophin were sometimes removed from the study before they died and hence were not included in the final statistics. The confusion over clinical trial results led a group of investors to file a suit against Cephalon charging that the company was misleading in its reporting of Myotrophin test results. The suit was eventually settled in August 1999 for $17 million, although Cephalon denied any wrongdoing.

In 1996 Cephalon sold the plant that it had been using to manufacture Myotrophin. However, Cephalon and its partner Chiron still hoped that the drug would gain final approval. In June 1996 the FDA made Myotrophin available to some ALS patients, but strongly urged the company to conduct a third study of the drug. Cephalon was reluctant to do so, however, since it had already invested $180 million in a drug with a fairly small potential market. More bad news came in May 1997, when an FDA advisory panel rejected Myotrophin as an ALS treatment. Once again Cephalon stock plummeted 35 percent to $13. Nevertheless, both Chiron and Cephalon planned to continue to pursue approval for Myotrophin, pointing out that the panel's recommendation did not amount to a final decision by the FDA.

In May 1998 the FDA ruled that Myotrophin was potentially approvable, contingent on additional clinical studies. However, Cephalon had already poured too many resources into Myotrophin to embark on another multi-year study. The company finally gave up on the drug in 1999, disappointing both the National ALS Association, which had hoped the drug could become an effective treatment, and ALS patients who had been given special access to Myotrophin. CEO Frank Baldino expressed regret that a potentially useful drug failed to gain FDA approval. He said additional tests would be justified for a drug designed to treat a disease that affected five or six million people, but only 25,000 to 30,000 people nationwide had ALS.

Developing a Solid Product Line: 1998–2001

Fortunately, Cephalon's other drug development projects had been proceeding more successfully. The narcolepsy drug Provigil received preliminary approval from the FDA in December 1997 and final approval in December 1998. Company stock rose 12 percent as investors hoped the new product would make up for the Myotrophin fiasco. In February 1999 Provigil was launched in the United States. Sales of the drug exceeded expectations, reaching $25 million by the end of the year. Sales in 2000 were $72.1 million and 2001 sales were expected to reach $130 million.

Cephalon hoped to expand the applications for Provigil beyond narcolepsy. In January 2000 test results were announced showing that the drug was effective in warding off fatigue in multiple sclerosis patients and shift workers. According to test results released in October 2001, Provigil also increased daytime wakefulness in patients suffering from obstructive sleep apnea, a disorder causing a person to wake frequently throughout the night because of obstructed breathing passages. Tests in 2000, however, failed to demonstrate that the drug was effective in treating attention deficit hyperactivity disorder (ADHD). Use of Provigil also expanded geographically through marketing collaborations with foreign companies, including an October 1998 agreement with Mercke GmbH to market Provigil in Austria and Switzerland and a November 2000 agreement with Choongwae Pharma Corporation in Korea.

Actiq, Cephalon's second major proprietary drug, received FDA approval in November 1998 and was launched in the United States in March 1999. At the time, the drug was manufactured and marketed by Abbott Laboratories. Cephalon acquired worldwide product rights to the drug in October 2000 through its merger with Anesta Corporation of Salt Lake City.

Actiq is prescribed to treat pain in cancer patients. Specifically, the drug targets sporadic flare-ups, known as breakthrough cancer pain, that overcome the medication already being used to treat chronic pain. Actiq provides fast-acting, short-term relief from breakthrough pain, which can last from 30 minutes to several hours.

Besides the acquisition of a new product, Cephalon's merger with Anesta gave the company access to a new drug-delivery technology, the Oral Transmucosal System. Using the OTS system, Actiq is absorbed through the mucous membranes of the cheek and passes directly into circulation without having to go through the liver. As a result, a flare-up of pain can be eased within 15 minutes. Sales of Actiq in 2000 were $15 million, and 2001 sales were expected to reach $45 or $50 million as Cephalon worked to establish the product as the medication of choice for breakthrough cancer pain.

Like Provigil, Actiq developed a worldwide reach. In October 2000 the drug was approved for sale in the United Kingdom, and in June 2001 the drug was granted marketing authorization in 16 other European counties. Through marketing collaborations with companies such as Swedish Orphan AB, Elan Pharmaceuticals Ltd. in the United Kingdom, and Grupo Ferrer Internacional SA in Spain, Cephalon planned to launch Actiq commercially throughout Europe. Cephalon also granted rights to Orphan Australia to market and distribute Actiq in Australia and New Zealand.

Cephalon acquired a third major product in January 2001. All rights to Gabitril, a treatment for partial seizures related to epilepsy, were bought from Abbott Laboratories for $100 million. The drug had been approved by the FDA in September 1997 and was launched in the United States in 1998. Numerous epilepsy drugs already on the market competed with Gabitril, but the drug nevertheless garnered $23 million in sales in 2000. In order to widen the market for the drug, Cephalon began investigating the use of Gabitril as a mood stabilizer for various psychiatric disorders.

Besides its three main products in the United States, Cephalon marketed seven products through its European subsidiary. In the United Kingdom, those products included Anafranil, a treatment for depression and obsessive compulsive disorder; Lioresal and ITB Therapy, treatments for spasticity; Ritalin, an ADHD drug; and Tegretol, for epilepsy. The company also marketed two Parkinson's medications in Europe: Xilopar in Germany and Apokinon in France. A 30-person sales team in Europe supported Cephalon's activities there.

Research and development remained central to ensuring Cephalon's long-term profitability. In collaborations with such international partners as TAP Holdings, Kyowa Hakko Kogyo, H Lundbeck, and, as of December 2000, the R.W. Johnson Pharmaceutical Research Institute, the company was researching kinase inhibitors, compounds that either enhance cell survival or cause cell death. The compounds had potential for treating neurological and oncological diseases.

Cephalon's extensive library of proprietary compounds provided ample fodder for research. Products under development in 2001 included CEP-701, a compound that had been shown to cause the death of cancer cells by inhibiting the activity of a certain kinase, or protein. The compound was being developed to treat prostate and pancreatic cancer. Phase one testing was also just beginning on a second compound, CEP-7055, which was found in preclinical studies to prevent the development of the blood supply required for tumors to grow. Cephalon hoped that the experience with Actiq would pave the way for success with these further cancer drugs. The company was also working on a compound, CEP-1347, that could inhibit the progression of Parkinson's and Alzheimer's.

The deals leading to the acquisition of Actiq and Gabitril, as well as the resources invested in continued research, contributed to Cephalon's growing net loss. The company reported losses of $55.4 million for 1998, $70 million for 1999, and $101.1 million for 2000. But the establishment of three successful proprietary drugs finally gave Cephalon the prospect of stable sales revenue, while the products under development gave the company growth potential. CEO and founder Frank Baldino believed that the company was laying a solid foundation for profitability in the near future.

Principal Subsidiaries

Anesta Corporation; Cephalon (UK) Limited.

Principal Competitors

American Biogenetic; Amgen, Inc.; Athena Neurosciences; Cell Pathways; Cortex Pharmaceuticals; Draxis Health Inc.; Genset; GlaxoSmithKline; Builford Pharmaceuticals; NeoTherapeutics; Neurocrine; Orphan Medical; Sanofi-Sunthélabo.

Further Reading

Armstrong, Michael W., "Cephalon Inks $20 Million Deal, *Philadelphia Business Journal,* June 4, 1990, p. 13.
——, "Cephalon Is Headed Public with $37.8 Million Offering," *Philadelphia Business Journal,* March 25, 1991, pp. 1–3.
——, "Cephalon's Find May Lead to Alzheimer's Test," *Philadelphia Business Journal,* March 12, 1990, pp. 3–4.

"A Bright-Eyed and Bushy-Tailed Drug," *Business Week,* January 11, 1999, p. 50.
Brooke, Bob, "Cephalon Waits for Green Light from FDA," *Philadelphia Business Journal,* December 13, 1996, p. 34.
"Cephalon's Stock Plunges on ADHD Results for Provigil," *BioWorld Week,* August 7, 2000, p. 2.
"Company Acquires Rights on Drug to Treat Narcolepsy," *Wall Street Journal,* February 2, 1993.
George, John, "Another Step Closer," *Philadelphia Business Journal,* August 24, 2001, p. B6.
——, "Cephalon Buys Rights to Anti-Epileptic Drug," *Philadelphia Business Journal,* November 3, 2000, p. 4.
——, "Cephalon Expands into Cancer Treatment," *Philadelphia Business Journal,* July 24, 1998, pp. 5–6.
——, "Cephalon May Pull Plug on Its ALS Drug," *Philadelphia Business Journal,* November 27, 1998, pp. 4–5.
——, "Cephalon Partnership Could Bring in $40 M," *Philadelphia Business Journal,* June 4, 1999, p. 6.
——, "Cephalon's Provigil May Have Wider Uses," *Philadelphia Business Journal,,* January 28, 2000, p. 9.
——, "Despite Loss, Cephalon Says It's on Right Road," *Philadelphia Business Journal,* March 2, 2001, p. 9.
——, "New Drug's Sales Beat Forecasts," *Philadelphia Business Journal,* May 14, 1999, pp. 3–4.
——, "Result of Tests Are Critical for Future of Drug Company," *Philadelphia Business Journal,* June 9, 1995, p. 8.
Hower, Wendy, "New Issues Suffer As Wary Investors Cool to Biotech," *Boston Business Journal,* May 6, 1991, pp. 1–2.
Shaw, Donna, "Pennsylvania Biotech Company Cephalon's Research Continues to Boost Revenues," *Knight-Ridder/Tribune Business News,* May 17, 1994.
Tanouye, Elyse, "Cephalon Shares Sink on FDA Setback; Firm and Partner Chiron to Push Ahead," *Wall Street Journal,* May 12, 1997.
——, and Ralph T. King, Jr., "Critics Question Drug Testing by Cephalon," *Wall Street Journal,* January 22, 1996.

—Sarah Ruth Lorenz

CHICO'S®

Chico's FAS, Inc.

11215 Metro Parkway
Fort Myers, Florida 33912
U.S.A.
Telephone: (941) 277-6200
Fax: (941) 277-5237
Web site: http://www.chicos.com

Public Company
Incorporated: 1983 as Chico's Folk Art Specialties
Employees: 3,500
Sales: $259.4 million (2001)
Stock Exchanges: New York
Ticker Symbol: CHS
NAIC: 44812 Women's Clothing Stores

Chico's FAS, Inc. is a prominent chain of women's clothing and accessories stores. The company began with one modest shop, but grew quickly in the 1990s. As of 2001, the chain had nearly 300 stores in 40 states. Most are directly owned and operated by Chico's, while about a dozen are franchised. Chico's targets women of relatively high income and over 35 years of age. The growing demographic of the aging baby boomer has been a goldmine for the chain, which designs its clothes to suit plumper figures and relaxed but not flamboyant tastes. The company designs and sells its own lines exclusively. Chico's saw double-digit growth in the late 1990s, even at a time when the retail environment as a whole was flat or shrinking. Founders Helene and Marvin Gralnick continue to run the chain.

Drifting Around Mexico in the 1970s

Chico's FAS was founded by the husband-and-wife team of Helene and Marvin Gralnick. Marvin Gralnick was born in 1935 and grew up in a suburb of St. Louis, Missouri. After dropping out of college, he moved to Mexico in 1964. In 1971, he met Helene, a Florida native who was vacationing in Guadalajara. They married there and went into business together designing fringed leather vests for export to the United States. The couple loved Mexico, and their business at the time seemed more of a way to get by than the start of a multimillion-dollar

retail empire. In fact the Gralnicks lost what money they had a few years later, when the value of the peso tumbled during the Mexican economic crisis of 1976. They moved back to the United States, settling in a Florida resort spot, Sanibel Island. They continued to support themselves by selling Mexican imports, going down to Mexico four times a year to buy art work and clothing. In 1983, the couple opened their first store, an 800-square-foot space that had formerly housed a tobacco shop. This was Chico's Folk Art Specialties. Chico was a bilingual parrot owned by a friend. The emphasis of the shop was on Mexican arts and crafts, though the Gralnicks also sold clothing, such as hand-knitted Mexican fishermen's sweaters. Soon it became clear that the clothing was the biggest draw, and the couple repositioned the store as a funky boutique selling its own Chico's brand apparel. In 1985, the Gralnicks opened a second store, on Captiva Island, Florida. Chico's opened its first franchise two years later. This came about because one customer, a Minnesota woman, had fallen in love with Chico's style while vacationing in Florida, and she convinced the Gralnicks to let her become a franchisee.

Struggling for a Niche in the Early 1990s

Chico's became a quiet hit, and the Gralnick's franchised more stores. It seemed a reasonable way to expand the company, because the founders did not have enough capital of their own to set up in new markets. The Gralnicks both worked to design the clothes, which they then had made for them in Mexico. Marvin Gralnick also designed and built distinctive display crates, and the stores were decorated with idiosyncratic Mexican furnishings. Overall, the Chico's look was relaxed, offering casually romantic clothes that spoke of vacation and ease. The pieces fit loosely, and were mostly made of natural fabrics such as cotton and linen. Some items were printed by hand, so that each garment was unique. Separates could be mixed and matched easily, and prices were relatively modest. Chico's franchises opened in shopping centers in other resort communities and in some suburban locations.

In 1990, the company shortened its name to Chico's FAS, Inc. Marvin Gralnick became CEO, and a former franchisee, Jeff Zwick, became president. By 1992, the chain had expanded

Company Perspectives:

Established in 1983, Chico's began in a small store on Sanibel Island, Florida, with Marvin and Helene Gralnick selling Mexican folk art and cotton sweaters. Now, 18 years later, we have grown to over 280 stores in 40 states. From our exclusive, private-label designs to our most amazing personal service, Chico's is truly a unique retail environment. When you walk into any Chico's store, you can depend upon the sales staff to coordinate, accessorize, and help you build a wardrobe to suit your needs. All of our products are designed and developed by our Product Development Team in our headquarters in Fort Myers, Florida, which enables us to provide you with new styles every week. We're moving fast, but not without you. Get yourself to Chico's!

to 60 stores, with a mix of franchised shops and company-owned units. Chico's was thriving, and the Gralnicks thought about retiring. They took the chain public in 1993, selling stock on the NASDAQ. The initial public offering went well, and the Gralnicks themselves made a reputed $40 million. With that sizeable nest egg, the Gralnicks left the company, giving Zwick the leadership position. But without the founders' vision, the company quickly reached a crisis. Under Zwick, the Chico's look metamorphosed from relaxed to oversized. New designs came out in loud colors. The stores carried more stock, and new stores opened in regional malls, which the company had previously avoided. The eclectic look that had set Chico's apart was lost, and customers fell away. Within a year under the new management, net income had fallen by half.

Jeff Zwick resigned in 1994, with the chain clearly failing. The Gralnicks returned, with Marvin Gralnick reclaiming the CEO position. The senior vice-president of operations became interim president, until the company hired Melissa Payner to take the job. Payner had been a merchandiser at the jeans company Guess and at the upscale department store chain Henri Bendel. She was in her mid-30s when she took over the presidency of Chico's. She worked closely with Marvin Gralnick, traveling to Guadalajara with him to see the source and inspiration of the Chico's look. Under Payner's direction, the clothes came back to their original palette, mostly earth tones, black, and red, forgoing the bright prints Zwick had brought in. The clothes also became more tailored, losing the oversized look that had not sold well. In addition, the company bought back most of its franchises, so it had more control over each retail outlet.

Same-store sales began to inch up in 1996, even though the specialty apparel niche as a whole was shrinking at the time. (Same-store sales is a key economic indicator for retailers, comparing sales growth at stores that have been open for at least a year.) Nevertheless, Chico's' troubles were not behind it. Where Zwick had moved the Chico's look to bigger and looser, Payner went in the other direction. The clothes she emphasized seemed designed for a younger figure. The stores began stocking short skirts and cropped tops, and this look was equally out of sync with Chico's' ideal customer. The Chico's woman was from 35 to 65, had a household income of around $75,000, and liked to be comfortable but well-dressed. The tight, short look

of 1996 proved as unappealing as the loud, baggy look of 1994 had been. Payner resigned in February 1997, and Marvin Gralnick became both CEO and president.

Focusing on the Aging Baby Boomer in the Late 1990s

Sales had begun to slump again at the end of Payner's tenure. Almost as soon as Marvin Gralnick took over the presidency, same-store sales went up. By the end of the year, the chain was seeing double-digit same-store sales growth. Chico's had grown to over 130 stores in 32 states. The company seemed to have found its niche again, and was determined to keep it. Chico's' core consumer base was the aging baby boomer. These women had come of age in the 1960s and were now in their prime. They had money to spend and appreciated comfort, style, natural fibers, and a certain lack of stodginess. Chico's had been enormously appealing to this class of customer when it first opened, and it pursued the market now almost unopposed. Other successful chain apparel retailers such as The Gap and The Limited were aimed at younger women. Talbots, Inc, a longtime merchandiser of resort wear and other apparel, projected a more conservative image.

Chico's applied innovative tactics to get and keep customers. It lavished attention on shoppers. Chico's sales clerks received many more hours of training than at comparable chains, and they were taught to build personal relationships with customers. One unique thing about Chico's stores was that the dressing rooms lacked mirrors. The customer then had to emerge from the dressing room to see how she looked. Sales clerks were to make astute judgments about fit and style and also offer accessories or additional pieces of an ensemble. Another ploy Chico's adopted was nonjudgmental sizing. Chico's clothes came in size 0, 1, 2, or 3. A woman who in another store would be wearing a size 16 might be flattered to fit into a 3 at Chico's. Chico's also offered a lifetime discount program to shoppers who had spent at least $500. This Passport Club program was initiated in 1994, temporarily withdrawn, then revived again in the late 1990s. Chico's strove to make its customers feel valued, and apparently many older women felt other stores did not treat them as well. Helene Gralnick, who remained vice-president of design and concept, felt she knew what the Chico's woman appreciated. She told *Women's Wear Daily*, in a June 13, 2001 interview, that the typical Chico's woman "likes to have a little dessert, and may not be too thrilled with her butt." So clothes were not only loose, but styled to make women look slimmer. They washed easily. Some product lines emphasized that they could be jammed in a suitcase and then worn without ironing. Chico's also kept the price of its clothes down. Most of the designing was done in-house, overseen by Helene Gralnick. This gave the company greater control over its merchandise costs. Most items retailed between $20 and $150.

By 1998, Chico's was one of the brightest lights in retailing. The company opened more stores, carefully picking likely spots. Chico's worked with a consulting firm that compiled a complex database of consumer characteristics to find good locations for new stores. Though the chain saw potential to grow to perhaps 700 stores, it only opened about 30 to 50 stores a year in the late 1990s, aiming for controlled growth rather than blanketing the country. Chico's began advertising in national magazines for the first time in 1998. By 1999, the stores began

Key Dates:

1983: The Gralnicks open their first store on Sanibel Island.
1987: The first Chico's franchise is opened
1990: The company name is shortened to Chico's FAS.
1993: The company goes public on NASDAQ; Gralnicks retire.
1994: Gralnicks come out of retirement to direct company.
2001: Chico's stock is listed on New York Stock Exchange.

stocking some different types of items, such as soaps and aromatic oils, candles, watches, and shoes. New stores moved to a larger format, of about 1,800 square feet, to accommodate the growing product mix and to make room for a special section to house sale items. Chico's also reinstated its Passport Club program in 1999, which gave a lifetime 5 percent discount to shoppers who had accumulated $500 in sales. This was a nice reward program for frequent shoppers, but it also provided Chico's with a wealth of information about its most dedicated customers. In 1999, the Passport Club had some 300,000 members. This grew to 900,000 two years later. The company also put out a catalog and began selling through a Chico's web site.

Chico's stock did well as the company continued to roll out impressive sales statistics. Sales for 1999 were over 40 percent higher than 1998 figures, and nothing seemed to hold the company back. It still had room for geographic expansion, and its customer base seemed to be growing. An industry analyst quoted in the *Wall Street Journal* (February 22, 1999) stated that Chico's' core demographic of women aged 45 to 65 would grow by at least 24 percent a year until 2005. Chico's just needed to keep serving this market well, and success seemed inevitable. The company brought in a new executive vice-president in 2000, Tedford Marlow. Marlow had previously worked at Saks Fifth Avenue, The Limited, Marshall Fields, and Neiman Marcus. Marlow instituted some more formal management procedures, such as weekly meetings and additional layers of mid-level executives. With his long career in retail, he also appeared to be a possible successor to Marvin Gralnick, who had already retired once in 1993 and was nearing 70.

In April 2001, Chico's moved its stock from the NASDAQ to the more prestigious New York Stock Exchange. The chain planned to add another 60 stores that year, bringing its total up over 300. It brought out television ads and renewed its print ad campaign with a marketing budget of $10 million. Chico's had posted double-digit sales gains every month since June 1997, and the chain showed no signs of slowing. Its Passport Club for preferred shoppers had grown to over a million members, and the company also sold its clothes and accessories through its catalog and web site. Passport Club transactions and catalog and online sales all gave the company the added bonus of supplying data about its customers. Catalogs, for example, arrived in mail boxes with a discount coupon. By tracking sales made with the coupon, the company had a finely focused tool for identifying who bought what.

Customers continued to buy. By mid-2001, the overall retail environment had slumped to what looked to be its worst state in over ten years. Yet Chico's continued to boom. Despite a major stock market slow-down and grim news of recession, Chico's customers kept spending. Chico's Chief Financial Officer Charles Kleman said in an interview with *Women's Wear Daily* (August 9, 2001) that the Chico's customer was "going to spend on apparel whether the stocks are up or down, since the last thing she will give up is her looks." Overall sales for the three quarters ending in November 2001 were up almost 50 percent over the same period a year earlier. Same store sales for the third quarter grew 7 percent. Though this was less than the double-digit gains of previous quarters, Chico's' strong performance stood out in a retail environment that was clearly in trouble. Chico's named a new president and chief operating officer, Scott Edmonds, in the fall of 2001, and Helene and Marvin Gralnick also affirmed their commitment to stay on at Chico's until at least 2004.

Principal Competitors

Talbots, Inc.; The J. Jill Group, Inc.; Coldwater Creek Inc.

Further Reading

Berry, Kate, "Chico's Expects to Meet Estimates for Quarter, Year," *Wall Street Journal*, February 22, 1999, p. B17B.
"Chico's Loss Widens," *WWD*, March 12, 1997, p. 12.
Clark, Evan, and Jennifer Weitzman, "Righting Retail's Ship," *WWD*, October 2, 2001, p. 1.
Clark, Julie, "Chico's Gives Women What They Want," *Display & Design Ideas*, September 2001, p. 6.
Cuneo, Alice Z., "Chico's: Jim Frain," *Advertising Age*, October 8, 2001, p. S19.
"Easy Does It," *People Weekly*, November 12, 2001, p. 119.
Hanover, Dan, "Return Engagement," *Chain Store Age Executive*, July 1999, p. 45.
Henderson, Timothy P., "Chico's Locates Growth Opportunities with Lifestyle and Demographic Database," *Stores*, July 2000, pp. 66–68.
Lee, Georgia, "Making the Big Time," *WWD*, April 11, 2001, p. 1.
Moin, David, "Chico's Fast Track," *WWD*, June 13, 2001, p. 13.
Moukheiber, Zina, "The Un-Gap," *Forbes*, September 9, 1996, pp. 44–45.
Pascual, Aixa M., "How Chico's Got Its Groove Back," *Business Week*, June 11, 2001, p. 111.
Ridge, Pamela Sebastian, "Chico's Scores Big with Its Nonjudgmental Sizes," *Wall Street Journal*, March 8, 2001, pp. B1, B4.
"Still Looking Chic at Chico's," *Business Week*, October 15, 2001, p. 135.
Tosh, Mark, "Dissatisfied Marvin Gralnick Returns to Run Chico's," *WWD*, November 14, 1994, p. 10.
Weitzman, Jennifer, "Chico's Continues to Surge," *WWD*, August 9, 2001, p. 3.

—A. Woodward

Christian Salvesen Plc

500 Pavilion Drive
Northampton NN4 7YJ
United Kingdom
Telephone: (+44) 1604 662 600
Fax: (+44) 1604 662 605
Web site: http://www.salvesen.com

Public Company
Incorporated: 1872 as Christian Salvesen & Co.
Employees: 13,630
Sales: 737.8 million ($1.18 billion) (2001)
Stock Exchanges: London
Ticker Symbol: SVC
NAIC: 541614 Process, Physical Distribution, and
    Logistics Consulting Services

Once known for its whaling fleet, Christian Salvesen Plc has recreated itself as a major European logistics company for the 21st century. Based in Northampton, England, the company offers warehouse design, fleet management, packaging, processing, and other distribution support services for customers ranging from supermarket leaders Safeway and Tesco, to retailers such as Ikea, to food producers including Danone and Chiquita Brands. About half of Salvesen's £738 million turnover comes from its Food and Consumer division, with operations primarily in the United Kingdom. The company's Industrial Division works under contract with such clients as General Motors, Texaco, Agfa, and Exxon Mobil. Salvesen, which split off its former Aggreko generator rental business in 1997, has been focusing increasingly on the European continent. Already by 2001, the company's European sales had grown to 45 percent of total revenues, with plans to raise that percentage to 50 percent. The company's expansion has come not only through internal growth but through an ambitious acquisition program as well, with purchases in France, Germany, and Spain that have strengthened the company's operations. In 2001, Salvesen has moved to bring all of its business under the single Salvesen brand name. Some 35 percent of the company, traded on the London Stock Exchange, remains in the hands of the founding Salvesen family. Operations are guided, however, by Chairman Jonathan Fry and CEO Edward Roderick.

Whaling Leader in the 20th Century

Theodore Salvesen, a native of Norway, had set up a shipping and forwarding agency with a partner in Leith, Scotland, in 1846. Theodore Salvesen was joined by younger brother Christian Salvesen, then 24 years old, in 1851. The younger Salvesen proved an ambitious businessman, and in 1853, Theodore turned over his share of the partnership Turnbull & Salvesen & Co.

The company's chief activity was in shipbroking, but it also established an import-export business, notably shipping Scottish coal and Norwegian timber. Ship management became another important part of the business in the middle of the 1850s. A Glasgow office was opened in 1869.

Christian Salvesen left the partnership in 1872 and set up his own business, based in Leith. The new company took the Norwegian flag as its symbol and continued to base its operations on trade between Scotland and Norway. Shipping began to play a larger role in the company's operations toward the end of the century, particularly with the involvement of Salvesen's sons, Theodore, Tom, and Fred. The company acquired its own fleet of cargo vessels—the company's coal exports were its chief source of income—and also began operating a cargo liner route between Scotland and Norway, before extending its cargo operations to the Mediterranean, and particularly the ports of Malta and Alexandria.

Salvesen turned over the business to his sons in the 1890s; Theodore Salvesen proved the most aggressive businessman of the three and launched the company into a new area of business. At the time, the company had begun importing and marketing whale oil and other whale-based products. In 1891, determined to compete against the Norwegian whaling industry, the company purchased a stake in its own whaling vessel. The company began to build up a fleet of whaling vessels around the close of the century. A purchase of a majority stake in an Icelandic whaling company in 1902 turned out to be unprofitable for the company. Yet by 1905, Salvesen itself had built up a fleet of ten whale catchers and owned and operated a number of whaling stations. As the Atlantic whale population dwindled in the early years of the century, Salvesen turned south, opening in 1907 a base in the West Falklands from which to hunt the Antarctic whale populations. In 1909, the company opened a second, more profitable base in southern Georgia.

By 1912, Christian Salvesen was the leading whaling company in the world, with bases in Iceland; the Faroe, Shetland, and Falkland Islands; and southern Georgia. Despite losing one of its ships at the start of World War I, Salvesen's whaling operations continued throughout the war, when demand for whale oil was heightened by the war effort. Following the war, the company took advantage of the increased demand—and high prices—for ships and sold off a large part of its fleet. This move, and the company's longheld policy of retaining a large proportion of its profits, helped keep the company afloat during the economic crisis years of the late 1920s and 1930s. Nonetheless, the company was forced to close a number of its whaling stations.

The company was less fortunate during World War II, which saw a good portion of its fleet destroyed or requisitioned for the war effort. At the end of the war, the company began to rebuild its fleet, boosting not only its whaling operations but its overall cargo shipping lines as well. Taking the company's lead was Harold Salvesen, son of Theodore, who in turn began hiring management from outside the family. While Salvesen remained a family-owned and controlled firm for a good time to come, the company's new management helped it to transform itself from a traditional family-owned company to a modern business.

With the development of new types of oils and other products from fossil fuels, demand for whale oil dropped in the 1950s. The company was also faced with tightening quotas—first introduced in the 1920s—and rapidly declining whale populations. Salvesen began to transition away from whaling in the late 1950s and by 1963 had exited the industry altogether. A year later, Harold Salvesen retired, replaced by nephew Max Harper Gow, himself a great-grandson of Christian Salvesen.

Diversification in the 1970s

Gow remained as company chairman until 1981 and led Salvesen into a new era of diversified operations. An early addition to the company's activity stemmed from an experiment Salvesen had carried out in the 1950s, in which the company had fitted out a new type of deep-sea fishing trawler that was capable not only of catching fish and loading the catch up a whaler-like stern ramp, but also processing and freezing the fish. The experiment led the company to acquire a cold store facility in Grimsby in 1958 to store its catches. At the time, frozen foods were just beginning to be embraced by consumers, and Salvesen quickly found a market for its surplus cold storage space among neighboring food processing companies. By the

early 1960s, the company had branched out to offer freezing facilities as well.

In 1965, Salvesen's food processing business took on a greater scale when the company acquired the cold storage facilities of Frigoscandia. In 1967, Salvesen pushed further into the food processing industry, acquiring vegetable processing operations. At the same time, the company abandoned its deep-sea fishing experiment in the face of stiff international competition. Rising demand for Salvesen's products also led to a new demand for transport services as well. In 1969, the company bought up trucking company Daniel Stewart and began building a nationally operating fleet of vehicles. By 1973, about 25 percent of the company's sales came from its food processing operations and transportation operations.

At the same time, Gerard Elliot, another Salvesen family member—and future company chairman—had been developing another diversified business, replacing whaling with fishmeal production and processing. The company boosted its fish-related activities during the 1960s and 1970s. The company's overseas shipping operations were winding down as the industry turned toward large bulk carriers. At the beginning of the 1970s, Salvesen began selling off some of its ships; meanwhile the company's fish operations turned away from fishing and more toward fish selling. The company also ended one of its original operations, shutting down its ship's agent business that had been part of the company since its founding in 1846.

However, the company had not yet abandoned shipping. During the 1960s, the company had developed a successful business in another shipping line, that of coastal coal shipments. This wing, developed by another Salvesen family member, was started up in 1962 when the company acquired Henry & MacGregor, based in Leith. The company built up a larger fleet of coal carriers, most of which were operated under contract with the Central Electricity Generating Board. Meanwhile, Salvesen remained committed to maritime operations, finding a new opportunity with the development of the North Sea oil fields in the early 1970s. The company began operating drill ships in 1973, then shifted its concentration to the operation of safety ships and other services for offshore oil platforms.

Another area of diversification was in home building and property management, begun in 1964. Operating under the Whelmar name since the acquisition of that company in 1969, Salvesen's home building division grew to become the fourth largest homebuilder in the United Kingdom during the 1970s. Supporting this business was the addition of brickmakers J&A Jackson in 1973. By the time of the economic crisis of that decade, home building and related operations were the company's largest revenue generator and accounted for more than half of Salvesen's profits. The collapse of the building market in the second half of the decade led the company to rationalize its homebuilding operations, reducing its sphere of activity before exiting the market altogether in the mid-1980s.

Refocusing in the 1980s

The arrival of Gerald Elliot as chairman ushered in a new area of streamlined operations for the company. Salvesen now moved to restrict its expansion focus on a more narrow range of

Key Dates:

1846: Theodore Salvesen founds Turnbull & Salvesen partnership as shipping agents in Leith, Scotland.

1851: Christian Salvesen joins brother's company, then takes over Theodore's share of the partnership in 1853.

1872: Christian Salvesen leaves partnership and sets up his own shipping company, Christian Salvesen & Co.

1891: The company purchases its first whaling vessel, later becoming the world's largest whaling company.

1958: Salvesen acquires its first cold storage facility in Grimsby.

1962: Company reduces its deep-sea shipping activity and launches coast coal shipments.

1963: Salvesen exits whaling industry.

1964: Salvesen begins its involvement in home building.

1969: The company acquires Whelmar home builders and becomes fourth largest private U.K. home builder.

1973: The company Acquires J&A Jackson bricklayers.

1982: Salserve is formed and dedicated to frozen and chilled food logistics business for Marks & Spencer.

1984: Salvesen acquires Aggreko and enters generator rental market.

1985: Company goes public on London stock exchange.

1990: Salvesen exits shipping after nearly 150 years.

1993: The company acquires Swift Transport Services and enters industrial logistics market.

1995: Salvesen acquires 40 percent of Germany's Wohlfarth.

1997: The company demerges from Aggreko, which is spun off as separate publicly listed company.

1999: Salvesen acquires Transportes Gerposa in Spain.

2000: Salvesen acquires full control of Wohlfarth.

2001: The company acquires France's Darfeuille and wins record ten-year £260 million contract with Tesco.

operations. Among these was the company's rapidly growing Food Services division, which had been developing rapidly in the late 1970s. The company had expanded beyond simple transportation services to offer a wider range of distribution services; its frozen food distribution contract with Marks & Spencer was illustrative of this. Food Services also brought Salvesen onto the European mainland, with the opening of a first cold storage facility in France in 1977, followed by new facilities in both France and Belgium. Marks & Spencer prompted the company to expand its services through the opening of a series of dedicated frozen and chilled foods storage facilities, beginning in 1982. These formed the basis of the company's Salserve subsidiary.

In 1981, the company approached the U.S. market, acquiring Merchants Refrigerating Co., giving Salvesen nine cold storage facilities throughout that country. Three years later, the company took on a new wing, acquiring Aggreko, a fast-growing specialist in the rental of power generators.

Salvesen went public in 1985. Its new status prompted the company to streamline its operations, shedding its seafood and home building divisions in 1986. The company also sold off parts of its offshore oil activities, such as Salvesen Offshore Services. The company's remaining offshore oil divisions, including Salvesen Oilfield Technology, as well as a number of other industrial-focus businesses, were regrouped under a new Industrial division.

Throughout the late 1980s and into the 1990s, Aggreko continued to grow quickly, expanding throughout much of its western European base, before entering the U.S. market in 1986 with the acquisition of Electric Rental Systems, based in Louisiana. In 1968, the company paid $4 million to acquire two mobile air conditioning specialists, Mobilair amd Pierce Industrial Air, becoming a leader in that market. Aggreko moved farther afield, adding acquisitions in Singapore and Australia.

Until the mid-1980s, Salvesen had concentrated on food distribution services. In 1986, the company responded to a new request from Marks & Spencer to develop distribution facilities for hanging garments and other household items. By 1988, the company's distribution business had grown sufficiently to allow the company to separate it from its Food Services division. In that year, Gerald Elliot retired, replaced by John West. For the first time, the company's chairmanship was given to someone from outside the Salvesen family.

Major Logistics Player for the 21st Century

West continued the company's concentration on its core elements, notably Food Services, Distribution, and Aggreko. The company exited shipping altogether in 1990. In 1992, Salvesen Oilfield Technology was sold off as well. Then in 1995, the company sold its Salvesen Brick operation for £63.5 million. Meanwhile, a restructuring of management had moved much of the company's administrations to its three remaining divisions.

After shrugging off a takeover offer from rival Hays Plc in 1996, Salvesen continued its restructuring drive. In 1997, the company slimmed down further with the spinoff of Aggreko as a separate, publicly listed company. At the same time, Salvesen began looking for buyers for its food processing division. Unable to find a buyer, the company proceeded in restructuring the division, eliminating a number of its vegetable processing and packing plants. These moves fit in nonetheless with the company determination to refocus itself yet again, now as a dedicated logistics company with a focus on food and consumer goods transport on the one hand, and industrial logistics services on the other, a business first entered into with the £84 million acquisition of Swift Transport Services in 1993. Another important addition was a 40 percent stake in Germany's Wohlfarth, acquired in 1995.

Salvesen continued boosting its logistics operations through acquisitions in the late 1990s, beginning with the purchase of Spain's Transportes Gerposa for £66.6 million in 1999. The company's new management team, composed of Chairman Jonathan Fry and CEO Edward Roderick, continued to focus on building the company into a major player in the European logistics market. Toward achieving this goal, the company now began to unify its operations under the single Christian Salvesen brand name. The company also stepped up its international operations at the end of 2000 with the acquisition of full control of Wohlfarth. Two months later, the company's industrial distribution wing grew through the purchase of France's Darfeuille, based outside of Lyon.

By mid-2001, Salvesen appeared to have successfully completed its transition to a dedicated logistics group, particularly after winning a record ten-year, £260 million contract with British supermarket giant Tesco. With sales of more than £730 million at the end of its 2001 fiscal year—and more than £830 million when including annualized contributions from its most recent acquisitions—Salvesen had taken a place among the top players in the rapidly consolidating European logistics market.

Principal Subsidiaries

Salvesen Logistics Ltd; Christian Salvesen SA (France); Christian Salvesen (Belgium) NV; Christian Salvesen Nederland BV (Netherlands); Agro Handelsgesellscaft mbH (Germany); Christian Salvesen Gerposa SA (Spain); Tendafrost Frozen Foods Ltd; Inverleith Insurance Co. Ltd.; Wohlfarth GmbH & Co. Spedition (Germany); Darfeuille Associes SA (France).

Principal Competitors

DHL Worldwide Inc.; Exel SA; Hays Plc; Tibbett & Britten Group Plc; Wincanton Plc.

Further Reading

Benedich, Mark, "Logistics Firm Salvesen Sees Rapid Growth," *Reuters*, June 6, 2000.

Murray-Watson, Andrew, "Salvesen Blames Fuel Price for Profits Drop," *Scotsman*, June 6, 2001, p. 3.

"Salvesen Sales Get Big Tesco Boost," *Evening Telegraph*, June 5, 2001, p. 3.

Tyler, Richard, "Salvesen Turns Other Cheek to 2.4pc Loss," *Birmingham Post*, November 29, 2000, p. 19.

Watson, Nigel, *The Story of Christian Salvesen*, London: James & James Ltd., 1996.

—M.L. Cohen

CIGNA Corporation

One Liberty Place
Philadelphia, Pennsylvania 19192-1550
U.S.A.
Telephone: (215) 761-1000
Fax: (215) 761-5515
Web site: http://www.cigna.com

Public Company
Incorporated: 1981
Employees: 43,200
Total Assets: $95.09 billion (2000)
Stock Exchanges: New York Pacific Philadelphia
Ticker Symbol: CI
NAIC: 524113 Direct Life Insurance Carriers; 524114
Direct Health and Medical Insurance Carriers; 524292
Third Party Administration of Insurance and Pension
Funds; 523920 Portfolio Management; 525110
Pension Funds; 525120 Health and Welfare Funds;
525930 Real Estate Investment Trusts; 525990 Other
Financial Vehicles; 551112 Offices of Other Holding
Companies

CIGNA Corporation is an insurance and financial services organization focusing on employee benefits, with its healthcare operations being the largest of its units. In addition to healthcare, CIGNA offers the following products to its U.S. customers: group life, accident, disability, and dental insurance; pension, profit-sharing, and retirement plans; and investment management. Outside the United States, the company offers, through CIGNA International, individual and group life, accident, and health insurance and pension products. CIGNA developed its focus on employee benefits during the 1990s, when it beefed up its healthcare operations and divested its personal property/casualty insurance operations and its U.S. individual life insurance and annuities activities.

CIGNA Corporation was formed in 1982, when INA Corporation, with its strong position in property and casualty insurance, and Connecticut General Corporation, with its strength in life insurance and employee benefits, merged. The resulting corporation immediately became one of the largest international, publicly owned insurance and financial services companies based in the United States. CIGNA gained its preeminent position by combining some of the oldest and most important companies in the insurance marketplace. The oldest of its predecessor companies was Insurance Company of North America (INA), a company rich with tradition. INA was formed by a group of prominent Philadelphians in November 1792, in Pennsylvania's State House, where the Declaration of Independence had been signed just 16 years earlier. Connecticut General Life Insurance Company was incorporated in 1865. That company began to expand from its focus on life insurance and employee benefits almost a century later, when it acquired another company with a long history of its own, Aetna Insurance Company, in 1962. Significant acquisitions since the formation of CIGNA include the American Foreign Insurance Association (AFIA), acquired in 1984 to expand the international operations; EQUICOR-Equitable HCA Corporation, a major employee benefits provider, purchased in 1990; and Healthsource, Inc., a managed-care firm based in New Hampshire, acquired in 1997.

Founding of INA in Philadelphia in 1792

Insurance Company of North America was organized in Philadelphia, then the financial center of the United States and its busiest port, when the country was just beginning to develop economically. With only 32 corporations and few native manufacturing concerns in the country, all marine insurance was written in London or in the United States by private individuals or partnerships that could afford to underwrite coverage.

In November and December 1792 a group of businessmen—including a carpenter, a cobbler, and a stationer, as well as bankers, lawyers, and merchants—met to set up a general insurance company. These businessmen had their own concerns at heart: they felt that their businesses could not grow unless reliable insurance was made available close to home. Only two small fire insurance companies had been formed in the new nation so far, and Philadelphia businessmen sought greater protection.

Insurance Company of North America wrote several policies on December 19, 1792, its first day in business. John M. Nesbitt, a Philadelphia merchant, was elected president of the company

Company Perspectives:

At CIGNA, we intend to be the best at helping our customers enhance and extend their lives and protect their financial security. Satisfying customers is the key to meeting employee needs and shareholder expectations, and will enable CIGNA to build on our reputation as a financially strong and highly respected company. We believe: Providing the customer with products and services they value more than those of our competitors is critical to our success. Talented, well-trained, committed and mutually supportive people working to the highest standards of performance and integrity are what make success possible. The profitable growth of our businesses makes career opportunities and personal growth possible. Profitability is the ultimate measure of our success.

and Ebenezer Hazard, secretary. Hazard, a businessman, scholar, and historian, was responsible for the daily conduct of business. He kept the office open under sometimes less than ideal conditions, remaining in Philadelphia during the yellow fever epidemic of 1793. The Insurance Company of North America was incorporated by the Pennsylvania state legislature in 1794 and authorized to write marine, fire, and life insurance.

The company initially insured only ship hulls and cargoes in local and international commerce. In late 1794, however, INA's directors and officers agreed to insure buildings and their contents against fire, becoming the first U.S. company to offer insurance on personal possessions and on business inventories.

In the early 19th century, INA followed the pioneers west. In 1807 INA set up its first agency, in Lexington, Kentucky, establishing the American agency system. The company appointed independent agents as far as the frontiers of Pennsylvania, Kentucky, Ohio, and Tennessee. Banking on westward expansion, INA invested in toll bridges and toll roads and bought bonds of the just purchased Louisiana Territory.

INA's westward expansion helped the company stay afloat when its marine insurance business lost money. Problems began in 1799 when Great Britain began to seize U.S. ships at sea. The maritime embargo of 1808, the War of 1812, and the depression of 1813 all had detrimental effects on the company's marine profits.

After the War of 1812 ended in 1815, the insurance environment became more competitive. As rates fell, INA faced a different kind of threat. John Inskeep, who became INA president in 1806, had the company invest profits instead of paying dividends. This conservative investment and reserve policy, coupled with its expanding fire insurance business, kept the company profitable.

In the mid-19th century, INA played a major role in forming the Philadelphia Board of Marine Underwriters, an organization that standardized premium rates and policy formats, gathered statistics, reported on insurance fraud, and kept up with commercial regulations and maritime law. A committee of the board reported on the seaworthiness of all vessels that entered the Port of Philadelphia. The board helped reduce operating expenses for the companies involved.

The formation of the Philadelphia Board of Marine Underwriters coincided with the high point for marine insurance in the 19th century. Between 1840 and 1861 U.S. foreign-trade tonnage quadrupled. The increase was due partially to the new clipper ships. Clipper ships were well built and had excellent safety records; in short, they were good insurance risks.

By 1859 INA had entered another lucrative area: the company insured gold shipments from the California gold fields, discovered a decade earlier. Its agent in California, Joshua P. Havens, sent premiums to INA's Philadelphia office in gold dust, which the secretary exchanged for currency.

From 1861 to 1865, when the Civil War disrupted many of INA's traditional markets, the company compensated by placing even more emphasis on the potential in the West. In 1861, as secession spread, the directors stopped accepting business or renewing policies in the South. In 1863 they organized offices in the West into a separate department. From 40 appointed local agents in the territory in 1860, the western business department grew to 1,300 agents by 1876. In 1875, a decade after the Civil War, a southern department was also added.

INA's Survival of a Series of Disasters: 1835–1906

Expansion in the West increased business but also posed a new risk. Rapidly growing cities were not well-built cities, and INA suffered losses in a series of major fires: 700 buildings burned in New York City in 1835; 1,000 buildings were lost in Pittsburgh, Pennsylvania, in 1845; most of St. Louis, Missouri, was lost in 1851; and Portland, Maine, was destroyed almost totally by fire in 1866.

The Great Chicago Fire, which started on October 8, 1871, burned about 17,450 buildings valued at $200 million. Claims for that fire left many insurance companies bankrupt. A total of 83 other companies could settle their claims only in part. INA was one of the 51 companies that did pay in full, settling legitimate claims totaling $650,000. Its reliability brought in new business.

INA, however, faced an even heavier loss a year later. The Boston Fire of November 9, 1872, gutted 600 buildings at a cost of $75 million, causing the collapse of 25 more insurance companies. INA faced the heaviest claim total—$988,530— but again paid in full.

On April 18, 1906, a 48-second earthquake shook San Francisco, California. Earthquake damage was slight, but the resulting fires were uncontrollable because water mains had ruptured. INA sent special agent Sheldon Catlin to the city to settle claims. Catlin found that most of the damage to property came from the fires, which had burned out of control for three days, not from the earthquake itself. Since INA was liable for fire damage but not earthquake damage, his determination was not a popular one within INA. Under pressure from other insurance companies, the home office decided to settle all claims at two-thirds value. On Catlin's recommendation, however, INA reversed its own decision, and agreed to pay all claims in full. That amounted to a liability of $3.7 million, plus $1.3 million in claims due from INA's affiliate, Alliance Insurance Company. INA was one of the 27 companies that paid claims from the San Francisco earthquake and fire in full.

Key Dates:

1792: Insurance Company of North America (INA) is formed in Philadelphia as a marine insurer.

1794: INA is incorporated and is authorized to write marine, fire, and life insurance.

1819: Aetna Insurance Company is founded to sell casualty insurance.

1865: Connecticut General Life Insurance Company (CG) is founded.

1913: CG begins offering group life insurance.

1918: A group of U.S. insurance executives form the American Foreign Insurance Association (AFIA) to offer insurance written by its members overseas.

1962: CG acquires Aetna as its property and casualty arm.

1967: To diversify its activities, INA creates a holding company, INA Corporation, with Insurance Company of North America becoming its main subsidiary; in a similar move, CG creates its own holding company, Connecticut General Insurance Corporation.

1978: INA diversifies into health insurance.

1981: Connecticut General Insurance Corporation is renamed Connecticut General Corporation.

1982: INA and CG merge to form CIGNA Corporation.

1984: CIGNA acquires AFIA and merges it into its existing international operations.

1987: The Aetna Insurance subsidiary is renamed CIGNA Property and Casualty Insurance Company.

1990: CIGNA acquires EQUICOR, the sixth largest provider of employee benefits in the United States.

1996: Regulators approve CIGNA's plan for a split in its domestic property and casualty operations, between ongoing policies and previous policies related to asbestos and environmental liabilities.

1997: Healthsource, a New Hampshire-based managed-care firm, is acquired.

1998: The company's U.S. individual life insurance and annuity operations are sold to Lincoln National Corporation.

1999: CIGNA sells its domestic and international property and casualty operations to ACE Limited of Bermuda.

As the company was expanding its fire insurance coverage, it also expanded its marine coverage inland. In 1890 INA established a lake-marine department in Chicago to cover risks during transit on rivers, lakes, and canals. The company originally refused to insure steamboats, an important part of the movement to settle the Mississippi River Valley, because steamboat captains were considered too reckless. At the end of the century George W. Neare & Company, a steamboat operator, persuaded INA President Charles Platt that insurance coverage was necessary to revitalize river transport. The company selected its risks carefully and eventually prospered in the field.

INA faced losses in its regular marine division in the last decade of the 19th century because such risks were hard to classify. During the mid-1890s Benjamin Rush, a conservative, old-line Philadelphian who came to work at INA as assistant to President Platt in 1894, worked nights and weekends with two young clerks to compile profit-and-loss statements for 198 route and cargo categories over a five-year period. His statistical analysis allowed the company to select risks more carefully. In 1900 INA posted the first profit in its marine line for many years, and the line remained profitable until World War I. Rush's work earned him the title ''father of modern marine underwriting.''

Expanding industry before World War I meant growth in the fire insurance business. John O. Platt, a nephew of Charles Platt and head of INA's fire branch, set up the improved-risk-engineering department to devise ways to make industry safer and thereby lower insurance risks. The department eventually offered three services: property valuation, fire prevention, and rate analysis.

Rush succeeded Eugene Ellison as president in 1916, in time to face claims due to attacks by German U-boats—INA paid $21,740 as its share of the coverage for the *Lusitania*, for example—and fires caused by sabotage in U.S. munitions plants. Nevertheless, World War I did not seriously threaten profits.

INA's Addition of Automobile Insurance in the Early 20th Century

Despite a generally conservative outlook, INA often insured unusual risks. Hence, in 1905, the company began to insure automobiles against fire and theft and added collision coverage in 1907. By the end of World War I, demand for this type of coverage had grown so much that INA organized a casualty affiliate, Indemnity Insurance Company, in 1920. The Great Depression hit Indemnity hard, but in 1932 INA brought in John A. Diemand, who had extensive experience in casualty insurance, to improve the company's performance.

With the approach of World War II, INA faced new problems. Male employees enlisted, and the company was not fully staffed. Cities were unable to replace outdated firefighting equipment, increasing risks. Auto insurance fell off because of gas rationing, and the lack of new-home construction affected property insurance lines. Ships unused to taking wartime security measures were lost to the Germans.

INA again found new and unusual risks to insure. The company wrote policies covering the accidental death of war correspondents and photographers, expanded its aviation coverage, covered test pilots, and insured 30 scientists working on the development of the atomic bomb at the Manhattan Project. ''We were pulling rates out of the air,'' Edwin H. Marshall, underwriter for these unusual coverages, told William H.A. Carr in *Perils, Named and Unnamed*.

INA Chief's Promotion of Multiple-Line Underwriting in Postwar Period

In the postwar years INA boomed along with the economy. During the 1940s, Diemand, by now president of the company, tackled a longstanding issue. INA had organized a casualty affiliate in 1920 because INA itself was forbidden by law to offer a full line of insurance. Diemand's advocacy of multiple-line underwriting authority, earlier promoted by Rush, now became a crusade. "Every company should have the privilege of meeting the requirements of any policyholder at any time as long as there is no law or ruling of an insurance department to prevent it," Diemand said in his address on INA's 150th anniversary. Diemand felt that multiple-line underwriting would provide broader and more convenient coverage for policyholders, who would have access to insurance packages from one agent, and at the same time would enable companies to cut processing and marketing costs.

Diemand's major opposition came from insurance cartels and conservative insurance associations that regulated insurance sales. In 1945 Public Law 15 left regulation of the insurance industry to the states, and slowly states extended the right to sell multiple-line insurance. By 1955 the right had been granted in all states. This victory allowed Diemand to pioneer the company's comprehensive homeowners policy, offering fire, theft, personal liability, medical payment, and extended coverages.

In 1964 Bradford Smith, Jr., succeeded Diemand as chairman of the board and chief executive officer. Smith automated operations, reorganized the company along functional lines, and emphasized participative management, which he defined as taking individual responsibility and cooperating with all company branches.

Changes in the U.S. business environment as well as changes within the company prompted another reorganization in 1967. Insurance Company of North America became the major subsidiary of INA Corporation, which added diversified services through other subsidiaries and extended its regional and international network of offices. As part of its expansion, INA Corporation organized or acquired several life insurance subsidiaries, which remained relatively small compared with its major interests in property and casualty insurance. In 1978 the company diversified into a related area when it began acquiring hospital management companies and health maintenance organizations (HMOs).

All of these moves reflected INA's desire to become a major financial organization offering a broad range of services. In 1981 the company saw a merger with Connecticut General Corporation (CG) as a way to achieve that goal. CG offered a major presence in employee benefits and life insurance to complement INA's activities in property and casualty insurance, and a combination was a way to operate more efficiently through economies of scale.

Founding CG in 1865 to Sell Life Insurance

Connecticut General dates back to 1865, when Guy R. Phelps, one of the founders of Connecticut Mutual Company, saw a need for "substandard" insurance, or life insurance for poor risks. Originally the new firm was to be called Connecticut Invalid, but because of concern that the word "invalid" could be read in two ways, it became Connecticut General Life Insurance Company and began to insure healthy lives along with substandard risks. Two years later the company withdrew completely from insuring higher risks and, through conservative management, survived a period when many other life insurance companies failed.

Under President Thomas W. Russell, the company prospered from post-Civil War growth in life insurance sales. Within a few years, CG had agents in more than 25 states, but increasing competition, rate cutting, and poor public perception of a company that had insured the disabled caused the sales force to shrink as quickly as it had grown. By the 1870s CG concentrated on New England and a few surrounding states.

The company's early policies, handwritten by clerks who had to demonstrate good penmanship to get the job, reflected the society they served. Death from drinking, hanging, or dueling canceled a policy. Travel was also restricted: a policyholder could not travel south of Virginia or Kentucky from June to November because of additional risk of illness due to heat. Late premium payments led to the automatic cancellation of a policy, with no grace period. Policies had no cash value, and benefits were paid in a lump sum, 90 days after proof of death, signed by five witnesses, was received.

Under Russell, CG weathered the depression following the panic of 1873 and a takeover attempt by Continental Life Insurance Company of Hartford, Connecticut. By 1880 the firm was again stable and began to grow.

Russell died in 1901 and was succeeded by Robert W. Huntington, who had joined the company as a clerk 11 years before. CG had only 12 home-office employees and was licensed to do business in four New England states, as well as New York, Pennsylvania, and Ohio. Huntington emphasized good investments, especially in farm mortgages, railroads, and utilities. He also cut operating expenses and used the savings to enter new areas.

CG First Offering Group Insurance in 1910s

In 1912 CG created an accident department. The next year CG began to offer group insurance, insuring the 100 employees of the *Hartford Courant*. Group insurance developed slowly for CG until 1917, when changes in corporate taxes made it a deductible expense. CG established its group department in 1918 and got its first big contract—covering the 5,400 employees of Gulf Oil—that year. Business picked up again in 1919, when contributory plans were developed. Previously, employers had paid the total cost of coverage.

World War I meant a growing economy and more group insurance coverage, but when an influenza epidemic struck in the autumn of 1918, CG was hit particularly hard because it had a high proportion of very young policyholders. Although claims were high, the epidemic eventually encouraged more life insurance business.

During the 1920s Frazar Bullard Wilde, head of the company's Accident Division, brought CG into another new area, aviation insurance. Wilde had served in the field artillery in France during World War I, where the use of airplanes captured his imagination. In 1926, when other insurance companies were not yet convinced of the validity of insuring flight, Wilde began writing policies that covered aircraft passengers. In 1930 the company wrote a group life insurance policy for Western Air Express, which included 46 pilots, and in 1932 CG insured 1,000 employees of United Airlines as well.

When the stock market crashed in 1929, CG's diversified investments kept the company going, but within two years new business had decreased sharply and business cancellations mounted. In addition, the company's heavy investment in farm mortgages meant that, with increasing foreclosures and the inability to lease farms, CG became a farm owner. In most cases, the company retained the former owners as managers and encouraged them to save their pay to buy back the property.

Estate Planning and Employee Benefits in the 1940s and 1950s

In 1936 Wilde succeeded Huntington as president. The new leader emphasized high-quality products and a good sales force. Ten years later he supported a new approach to marketing life insurance that would have a major impact on the company: estate planning. Stuart Smith, who had joined the company during the Great Depression, brought the estate planning concept to CG. He emphasized the sale of life insurance as part of complete estate planning. When Smith was promoted to the home office in 1946, CG made estate planning the company's only approach to selling insurance. Smith taught the technique to Connecticut General agents, which enabled them to plan insurance coverage by taking into consideration a client's total assets, family circumstances, and plans for the future.

Another focal point after the war was the development of group hospital and surgical benefits to compete with the Blue Cross and Blue Shield plans that had just been created. Just as CG had supported emerging technology after World War I by insuring airline pilots and passengers, after World War II the company began insuring atomic energy workers, covering employees of the Brookhaven and Argonne laboratories.

CG had established a group pension service as early as 1929 to serve its group insurance policyholders. The introduction of a number of government policies encouraged growth in this arena. The Social Security Act, passed in 1935, stimulated private savings for pensions to supplement the government program; the Revenue Act of 1942 provided some tax incentives for employers to establish pension programs; and, after 1960, changes in Connecticut state law led to significant growth in CG's pension business.

Also in the postwar years, CG pioneered the financing of shopping centers, and company investment became a major factor in the development of the modern suburban shopping mall. In addition, CG financed commercial agricultural enterprises and provided loans on urban residential and business properties.

CG's Acquisition of Aetna in 1962

In 1962 CG purchased Aetna Insurance Company (Aetna), a major firm in fire and casualty insurance, in order to broaden its position in insurance. Aetna brought a history even longer than its new parent's to the acquisition. The company was established in 1819 to sell casualty insurance, and two years later it became the first U.S. company to sell insurance in Canada. In 1851 the company began to sell life insurance too, but just two years later this part of its operations was spun off into a separate company, which became known as the Aetna Life and Casualty Company (known later as Aetna Inc.). The Aetna Insurance Company faced the same marine insurance risks as did INA, and it also was hit by massive claims due to urban fires in the late 19th century. Aetna's directors acted on a policy they voiced frequently after the Chicago Fire in 1871: "Every dollar must be paid." And pay they did. The company paid $3.78 million after the Chicago Fire, $1.6 million a year later in Boston, and almost $3 million following the San Francisco Earthquake and Fire. Aetna's ability to cover fully all of its losses enhanced its reputation as a major fire insurance company.

By the 1960s the acquisition of Aetna, with its sound fiscal management and preeminent position in fire and casualty insurance, was attractive to CG, which aimed to gain market position in property and casualty insurance, where it had virtually no operations at all. The acquisition was part of a trend in the industry toward larger companies that could offer full lines of insurance. To support its own diversification, CG created a holding company, Connecticut General Insurance Corporation, with Connecticut General Life Insurance Company becoming a subsidiary; this occurred in 1967, the same year that INA made a similar move.

After acquiring Aetna as its property and casualty arm, CG began dramatic expansion of employee benefits programs, such as group health insurance and pensions. CG was most successful in life, health, and pensions, with its property and casualty operations remaining small. By 1981 group life and health benefits accounted for 33 percent of the company's operating income; individual life, health, and annuities for 28 percent; and property and casualty business for only 18 percent—down from almost 35 percent a decade earlier. In 1981, prior to the merger with INA, Connecticut General Insurance Corporation was renamed Connecticut General Corporation.

Formation of CIGNA Through 1982 Merger of INA and CG

As the trend toward larger multiline insurers accelerated, in 1981 INA and CG announced that they would bring their complementary interests together by forming CIGNA Corporation ("CIGNA" being a combination of the two company's initials). INA's strengths were the mirror image of CG's, with an extensive presence in the property and casualty fields, where it had operated the longest, and relatively small operations in group insurance. INA also had a strong international presence, while CG had focused primarily on U.S. markets. By March 31, 1982, all necessary approvals had been secured, and CIGNA was formed. Robert D. Kilpatrick of Connecticut General and Ralph Saul of INA became joint CEOs, and the board of directors was drawn equally from both predecessor organizations. In 1983 Philadelphia was selected as the headquarters for CIGNA.

The new company got off to a difficult start because of a declining economy in the early 1980s, but the anticipated economies of scale did materialize, and the company continued to expand. In 1984 CIGNA acquired AFIA, formerly the American Foreign Insurance Association, to strengthen its position abroad (and also to resolve the conflict between INA's independent international operations and Aetna's membership in AFIA).

AFIA had been formed in 1918 by a group of insurance executives to offer insurance written by its members overseas.

After exploring conditions for insurance sales in Australia, New Zealand, Japan, Hong Kong, India, and Singapore, the board of AFIA established agencies in South America, Asia, and the Far East. AFIA weathered the Great Depression, but World War II, which engulfed many of the areas where the company was most profitable, slowed growth and cut profits. By 1949, however, AFIA was back on its feet and ready to expand along with the booming postwar economy. In 1984 the company had contacts in more than 100 countries and offered CIGNA a good way to expand its international market. Merged into CIGNA's own substantial international operations, AFIA Worldwide became part of CIGNA International, which was renamed CIGNA WorldWide.

In 1987 the Aetna Insurance Company subsidiary was renamed CIGNA Property and Casualty Insurance Company. Two years later, CIGNA gave up the use of the Aetna name altogether when it transferred its rights to this trade name to Aetna Life and Casualty Company. In November 1989 William H. Taylor was named chairman of CIGNA, replacing the retiring Kilpatrick; Taylor had joined Connecticut General in 1964, was named chief financial officer upon the formation of CIGNA in 1982, and had become CEO in November 1988. Also in 1989, the company formed CIGNA International Financial Services to provide individual and group life and health insurance outside the United States. In 1993 CIGNA WorldWide and CIGNA International Financial Services were merged under the recycled name, CIGNA International.

1990s and Beyond: Focusing Increasingly on Healthcare and Employee Benefits

By 1990 CIGNA was operating effectively in an insurance marketplace noteworthy for ever larger competitors, and the company continued the trend when it acquired EQUICOR-Equitable HCA Corporation, a large group insurance and managed healthcare company and the nation's sixth largest provider of employee benefits, for $777 million. The acquisition accelerated the growth of CIGNA's managed healthcare programs. From 1985 through 1993, the company invested a total of $1.5 billion to build a major managed-care business, just as the managed-care industry was beginning to explode. The newly renamed CIGNA HealthCare was by the early 1990s the company's largest and most profitable unit. By 1997 CIGNA HealthCare offered a full range of group medical, dental, disability, and life insurance products, with traditional fee-for-service plans marketed in all 50 states. The unit operated managed-care networks in 43 states, the District of Columbia, and Puerto Rico.

CIGNA HealthCare grew even larger in 1997 when it acquired Healthsource, Inc.—a managed-care company with about 1.1 million members in HMOs operating in 15 states—for $1.4 billion, plus the assumption of $250 million in debt. Healthsource had been founded in 1985 by a group of doctors in Hooksett, New Hampshire, as an HMO serving rural areas and smaller cities. The company grew quickly through acquisitions but was experiencing some growing pains by the time of its acquisition by CIGNA. With the addition of Healthsource, CIGNA's medical HMOs had a total membership of 5.3 million, and the company's fee-for-service medical plans counted seven million members.

CIGNA added to its employee benefits offerings in October 1997 with the formation of CIGNA IntegratedCare. This unit—a joint initiative of CIGNA HealthCare, CIGNA Group Insurance, and CIGNA Property & Casualty—was formed to offer employers fully integrated worker's compensation, disability, and medical-management services. This integrated approach was intended to lower employer's costs and improve care by eliminating gaps and redundancies.

At the same time that it was bolstering its employee life and health benefits operations, CIGNA was exiting from various noncore businesses and attempting to stem chronic losses incurred by CIGNA Property & Casualty. Generally, the company was looking to eliminate those business lines that were not strategically connected to other CIGNA businesses. For example, in the early 1990s the company's international operation dropped residential, auto, and travel insurance, while residential insurance also was dropped domestically. In July 1997 CIGNA announced that it would sell CIGNA Individual Insurance, which included individual life insurance and annuity operations in the United States, to Lincoln National Corporation for about $1.4 billion in cash; the deal was completed in January 1998.

CIGNA's property and casualty business, meanwhile, was continuing to lose money at an alarming rate because of weak underwriting standards and poor relations between the unit and its agents. Furthermore, a potential time bomb hung over it in the form of a large number of asbestos and environmental liabilities—potentially more than $4.5 billion worth—which was depressing the unit's financial-strength rating. These ratings are crucial to insurers in winning new business. CIGNA decided to create a "fire wall" between its problematic and standard liabilities by separating its domestic property and casualty operations into two units: one—called INA Holdings—to handle all ongoing business, and another—called Brandywine Holdings Ltd.—to handle the asbestos and environmental liabilities. With this division in place, INA Holdings' ratings were expected to improve, and it was hoped that CIGNA's property and casualty business might return to the black.

By early 1996, regulatory approval for the split had been received, despite opposition from industry competitors who were concerned that Brandywine might eventually run short of funds and have to be bailed out by a state guaranty fund—financed by the insurance companies themselves. In March 1997, a Pennsylvania appeals court vacated the plan's approval by the state of Pennsylvania and ordered new hearings. In 1999, however, the Pennsylvania Supreme Court upheld the reorganization. In July 1999 CIGNA sold both INA Holdings and Brandywine Holdings, as well as its international property and casualty business, to ACE Limited, an insurer based in Bermuda, for $3.45 billion. For CIGNA, exiting from the property and casualty sector meant that CIGNA could focus even more strongly on its health, life, and pension operations. Despite the divestiture, CIGNA still had to contend with litigation arising from the 1996 reorganization. The plaintiffs—which included units of two U.S. insurers, American International Group, Inc. and Chubb Corporation—had continued their legal battle by taking their case to California state court. There, they were initially rebuffed by a California Superior Court judge but then won an appeal in July 2001 from a higher court, which ruled that a trial could proceed on the matter of whether CIGNA's reorganization had violated the state's unfair competition law. CIGNA seemed likely to appeal the case to the California Supreme Court.

In January 1999 H. Edward Hanway was named president and COO of CIGNA, having previously served as head of the company's healthcare unit. During 2000 Hanway became chairman and CEO, succeeding the retiring Taylor, who during his 12 years at the helm had transformed CIGNA from a multiline insurer to a firm focused on employee benefits—health insurance, group life insurance, retirement plans, and the like. Continuing to narrow the company's focus, Hanway exited from the reinsurance business during 2000. Part of the reinsurance operations—the domestic individual life, group life, and accidental death portions—were sold to a subsidiary of Swiss Reinsurance Company in July 2000 for $170 million. The remainder were placed into a run-off business, and CIGNA stopped underwriting new reinsurance business. During 2001, CIGNA sold its majority-owned Japanese life insurance operation to Yasuda Fire and Marine Insurance Company, Limited.

With its string of strategic divestments, CIGNA had committed itself to a future focused on the employee benefits portion of the insurance and financial services industries. This appeared to be a prudent strategy, although managed care was a particularly volatile sector of the insurance market, and CIGNA saw its net income fall during 2001 as a result of double-digit increases in medical costs. The faltering economy and stock market of 2001 also were having negative effects on CIGNA's retirement and investment services operations.

Principal Subsidiaries

CIGNA Holdings, Inc.; Connecticut General Corporation; CG Trust Company; CIGNA Dental Health, Inc.; CIGNA Financial Services, Inc.; CIGNA Health Corporation; Connecticut General Life Insurance Company; CIGNA Global Holdings, Inc.; CIGNA Investment Group, Inc.; CIGNA Intellectual Property, Inc.

Principal Divisions

CIGNA Healthcare; CIGNA Group Insurance; CIGNA Retirement & Investment Services; CIGNA International.

Principal Competitors

Blue Cross and Blue Shield Association; Aetna Inc.; UnitedHealth Group Incorporated; Kaiser Foundation Health Plan, Inc.; PacifiCare Health Systems, Inc.; Humana Inc.

Further Reading

Bennett, Johanna, and Laurie McGinley, "Cigna Medicare-HMO Retreat May Signal Trend," *Wall Street Journal,* June 5, 2000, p. B2.

Burton, Thomas M., "Lincoln Agrees to Buy Units from Cigna," *Wall Street Journal,* July 29, 1997, pp. A3, A8.

Byrne, John A., and Richard Morais, "Cignoids Versus Afians," *Forbes,* September 24, 1984, p. 218.

Carr, William H.A., *Perils, Named and Unnamed: The Story of the Insurance Company of North America,* New York: McGraw-Hill, 1967.

Connecticut General Life Insurance Company, 1865–1965, Hartford, Conn.: Connecticut General Life Insurance Company, 1965.

"Could Cigna Be a Merger Casualty?," *Financial World,* September 19, 1984, p. 86.

David, Gregory E., "Beauty and the Beast," *Financial World,* November 9, 1993, pp. 79–81.

Hals, Tom, "The Cigna Split: What Will Be the Fallout?," *Philadelphia Business Journal,* February 16, 1996, p. 1.

James, Marquis, *Biography of a Business, 1792–1942: Insurance Company of North America,* Indianapolis, Ind.: Bobbs-Merrill, 1942, reprint, New York: Arno Press, 1976.

Jebsen, Per H., "Cigna Forms Unit to Offer New Services," *Wall Street Journal,* October 6, 1997, p. A11.

Kertesz, Louise, "Quiet Giant: Among Managed-Care Plans, Cigna HealthCare Is the Biggest and Most-Often Overlooked," *Modern Healthcare,* March 10, 1997, pp. 90+.

Lenckus, Dave, "CIGNA Reorganization Plan Unleashes Criticism," *Business Insurance,* December 23, 1996, p. 19.

Lohse, Deborah, "Cigna's Finalizing of Restructuring Is Dealt a Blow," *Wall Street Journal,* June 11, 1998, p. A6.

Lohse, Deborah, and Nancy Ann Jeffrey, "Cigna Is in Talks to Sell Operations to Ace," *Wall Street Journal,* December 23, 1998, p. A3.

Loomis, Carol J., and Margaret A. Elliott, "How Cigna Took a $1.2-Billion Bath," *Fortune,* March 17, 1986, p. 46.

Lublin, Joann S., "Cigna Director's Diversity Challenge Hits a Dead End," *Wall Street Journal,* June 15, 1998, p. B1.

Milligan, John W., "Robert Kilpatrick Hangs Tough," *Institutional Investor,* September 1987, p. 257.

O'Donnell, Thomas, and Laura Rohman, "The Honeymooners," *Forbes,* May 10, 1982, p. 124.

Ruwell, Mary Elizabeth, *Eighteenth Century Capitalism: The Formation of American Marine Insurance Companies,* New York: Garland, 1993.

Scism, Leslie, "Cigna Restructuring Plan Is Set Back," *Wall Street Journal,* March 6, 1997, p. A4.

——, "Cigna's Pact to Buy Healthsource Inc. to Boost Firm's Managed-Care Business," *Wall Street Journal,* March 3, 1997, p. A4.

——, "For Cigna, Property-Casualty Line Still Proves Tricky," *Wall Street Journal,* August 21, 1995, p. B4.

Souter, Gavin, "ACE Suing CIGNA over Terms of Sale," *Business Insurance,* December 18, 2000, pp. 1, 34.

——, "ACE to Buy CIGNA's P/C Units," *Business Insurance,* January 18, 1999, pp. 1, 22.

Weber, Joseph, "Is CIGNA's Asbestos Plan Fireproof?," *Business Week,* December 16, 1996, p. 118.

Weber, Joseph, William Glasgall, and Richard A. Melcher, "Is Cigna Creating a Time Bomb?," *Business Week,* November 6, 1995, p. 158.

—Ginger G. Rodriguez
—update: David E. Salamie

EST. 1941

Coach, Inc.

516 West 34th Street
New York, New York 10001
U.S.A.
Telephone: (212) 594-1850
Fax: (212) 594-1682
Web site: http://www.coach.com

Public Company
Incorporated: 1941
Employees: 2,700
Sales: $616.1 million (2001)
Stock Exchanges: New York
Ticker Symbol: COH
NAIC: 448320 Luggage and Leather Goods Stores;
    448150 Clothing Accessories Stores; 454110
    Electronic Shopping and Mail-Order Houses; 316990
    Other Leather and Allied Product Manufacturing

Coach, Inc. is a designer, producer, and marketer of a prestige line of handbags, briefcases, luggage, and accessories. The company made its reputation selling sturdy leather purses in unchanging, traditional, classic styles, and it remains one of the best-known leather brands in the United States and has a growing reputation overseas. In addition to its main product line, the company offers Coach brand watches, footwear, and home and office furniture through agreements with licensing partners. Nearly two-thirds of company sales are derived from direct-to-consumer channels. These include about 190 Coach stores in the United States—of these, approximately 120 are retail stores and the remainder are factory outlets—direct mail catalogs, and an online store. There are also 175 Coach locations outside the United States, in 18 countries. The company's indirect channels include the wholesaling of Coach brand products to approximately 1,400 department and specialty store locations in the United States. Formed in 1941, Coach was family owned and operated until 1985, when Sara Lee Corporation purchased the firm. Coach remained a subsidiary of Sara Lee until 2001, when the firm regained its independence via a spinoff.

Era As a Family-Run Business Beginning in the 1940s

Coach was founded in 1941 as a family-run workshop based in a loft on the edge of Manhattan's garment district. The company started with just six leather workers who made small leather goods, primarily wallets and billfolds, by hand. In 1946, Miles Cahn, a lifelong New Yorker, came to work for the company. By 1950, he was running the factory for its owners. The company's employees, members of Local 1 of the Pocketbook and Novelty Workers Union, continued to manufacture billfolds throughout the 1950s, producing small profits for the small concern.

By 1960, Cahn had taken notice of the distinctive properties of the leather used to make baseball gloves. With wear and abrasion, the leather in a glove became soft and supple. Following this model, Cahn devised a way of processing leather to make it strong, soft, flexible, and deep-toned in color, as it absorbed dye well. At his wife Lillian's suggestion, a number of women's handbags were designed to supplement the factory's low-margin wallet production. The purses, given the brand name Coach, were made of sturdy cowhide, in which the grain of the leather could still be seen, instead of the thin leather pasted over cardboard that was used for most women's handbags at the time. This innovation marked the company's entry into the field of classic, long-lasting, luxury women's handbags that Coach would come to define.

In 1961, after more than a decade of running the leather workshop, the Cahns borrowed money to buy out the factory's owners and take possession of Coach. Throughout the next decades, Coach produced solid handbags in an assortment of basic styles. For the most part, the company steered clear of fast-moving trends, opting instead for traditional, conservative elegance and quality. Gradually, high-priced Coach products developed a reputation and a certain cachet. In the late 1960s, as fashion changed radically, Coach deviated somewhat from its traditional product line, introducing additional models that were designed to complement trendier styles in clothing. In 1969, the company began to market items such as a structured bucket bag, which was produced for only one season, and a fringe "shimmy" bag.

By the early 1980s, the Coach plant occupied four floors of a building on West 34th Street. The company was manufacturing purses, briefcases, billfolds, and belts, using skilled laborers, many of whom had emigrated from Argentina. Paying their workers wages that were a dollar or more higher than rates in other factories, the Cahns enjoyed good labor relations with their employees, which allowed them to produce a steady flow of Coach products.

In the late 1970s and early 1980s, Coach took two steps to diversify its channels of distribution. Under a new vice-president for special products, the company began a mail-order business, and also began to open its own specialty stores, to sell Coach products outside a department store setting. Sales of Coach products grew steadily throughout this period, until demand began to outstrip supply. Department stores were selling all the Coach bags that the company could produce, and by the early 1980s it had become necessary to ration the products to various vendors. Despite the potential for vast expansion of their market share, the Cahns continued to run their business in the same way that they always had. They had little desire to move their factory out of its urban Manhattan setting, to a place where rents and taxes might be lower, space more readily available, and wages cheaper. In addition, they did not want to change their methods of production so that goods could be made more quickly, at the expense of quality or workmanship. Instead, they continued to run their business on a personal level, maintaining first-name relationships with many of their workers, and inviting department store buyers from New York to tour their factory, to observe the craftsmanship that went into each Coach bag.

In 1983 the Cahns purchased a 300-acre dairy farm in Vermont as a weekend diversion from their business in New York. Although the property was intended to provide a vacation home and retirement destination, the Cahns began to raise goats and market goat cheese under the brand name ''Coach Farms'' shortly after buying the farm. By 1985, they were commuting twice a week between Vermont and New York. In the summer of that year, after determining that none of their three children had any desire to take over the family leatherware business, the Cahns decided to sell Coach.

Expanding Under Sara Lee in the Late 1980s

In July 1985, the Cahns cemented an agreement with the Sara Lee Corporation, which also sold foodstuffs and hosiery. In return for a sum reported to be around $30 million, the conglomerate took control of the company's factory, its six boutiques, and its flagship store on Madison Avenue in New York. Sara Lee promised that it would continue to operate Coach in the way in which it had always been run. At the time of the sale, the Cahns split $1 million of the proceeds with 200 longtime employees, on the basis of their seniority. Taking over leadership of Coach as president was Lew Frankfort, who had joined the company in 1979 as vice-president of business development.

Under its new owners and new president, the company prepared for a rapid expansion. The basic strategy for this expansion was to add to the number of products that bore the Coach name, and to increase the number of customers buying these goods. Accordingly, the company added several new styles of handbag in an updated classics line, and also began a major expansion of its channels of distribution. In early 1986, new boutiques were opened in Macy's stores in New York and San Francisco, and in two Bamberger's stores. Additional Coach outlets were under construction in stores in Denver and Seattle, and agreements had been reached to open similar boutiques within other major department stores later in the year. In addition, Coach opened its own stores in malls in New York, New Jersey, Texas, and California. By November, the company was operating 12 stores, along with nearly 50 boutiques within larger department stores. The company projected that the expansion would boost sales for 1986 to $25 million, a gain of 45 percent over the previous year.

A significant part of sales was expected to come from the newly introduced Coach Lightweights line of products, which featured lighter weight leather and bags with new shapes. This line was intended to broaden the company's customer base by appealing to women who lived in the South and West, where warmer weather made lightweight handbags more desirable. The Lightweights line featured handbags in smaller sizes, for ease of access, and lighter spring colors, such as taupe, light brown, and navy. This line quickly came to comprise 15 percent of the company's overall sales.

To keep up with growing demand for Coach products, the company doubled its workforce, leased additional space for factory operations, and expanded the work week to six days. Despite these measures, however, by the fall of 1987, Coach was again unable to meet all orders for its goods, and the company began to seek additional room for expansion. In addition, to better control the circumstances under which its products were sold, Coach slashed the number of department stores retailing its goods by 50 percent. Despite continued strong demand, the company did not increase its prices to keep pace with a sharp rise in the cost of leather. By the end of 1987, Coach had nearly doubled its revenues, despite its reduction of retailers and the increase in the price of leather.

In December 1987, Coach opened a new flagship store on Madison Avenue, in New York. The two-story store, with a

Key Dates:

1941: The company is founded as a family-run workshop, making small leather goods in Manhattan.
1946: Miles Cahn joins the company.
1950: Cahn begins running the factory for its owners.
1960: The Coach brand of sturdy cowhide purses is introduced and becomes the company's signature, luxury, trademark.
1961: Cahn and his wife, Lillian, buy out the factory's owners.
Late 1970s/Early 1980s: Company begins a mail-order business and opens its first specialty stores.
1985: The Cahns sell Coach to Sara Lee Corporation for about $30 million; Sara Lee begins expanding Coach's product line and its channels of distribution.
1988: The company begins international push, opening boutiques in England and Japan.
1989: Sales reach $100 million, five times the level of 1985.
1992: The product line is expanded to include outerwear and luggage.
1997: The company enters into its first licensing agreement, a deal with Movado Group for a line of Coach watches.
1999: The company enters the e-commerce realm with the launch of coach.com.
2000: Sara Lee sells 17 percent of the newly named Coach, Inc. to the public through an IPO.
2001: Sara Lee spins off its remaining interest in Coach to Sara Lee shareholders.

marble and mahogany interior, featured an atrium and a gallery of leather art, as well as the full range of Coach products. The company expected to sell $5 million worth of handbags in the store's first year.

Coach solved its production problem by opening a plant near Miami, Florida, where its Lightweights collection was manufactured, in 1988. The plant's production supplied 22 freestanding stores and 300 different retailers, making Coach products available in more than 1,000 locations. Although the traditional line and the Lightweights products were emphasized, Coach further expanded its offerings to include more business items for men and women. Among the new products were briefcases, wallets, and diaries.

Coach's first nonleather product was introduced in 1988. Silk scarves, sold in four designs that related to leather goods, were planned to complement the other Coach products. Each of the 36-inch silk squares was manufactured in Italy and priced at $60. Although the company estimated that first-year sales of this line, which also grew to include men's ties and suspenders, would reach $2 million, the products were eventually discontinued, after it was determined that their equestrian designs, featuring bridles and stirrups, made them look too much like products from a Coach competitor, Hermès.

Coach took its first steps overseas in 1988. The company had long noted that many of the customers in its New York store were foreign tourists, and Coach executives believed that this indicated that demand abroad justified international expansion. The company began by opening Coach boutiques in England and Japan, setting up one outlet in Harrod's department store in London, and five in Mitsukoshi stores in Tokyo and other Japanese locations. These stores carried a full line of Coach products, and mimicked the look of Coach stores in the United States, with mahogany and brass fixtures and marble floors. The company planned to train foreign sales staff and hoped to take advantage of the low international value of the dollar to boost sales through lower prices.

As Coach continued its international push in 1989, opening a freestanding store on Sloane Street in London, company sales had quintupled to $100 million in a period of four years and the number of company stores had grown to 40. Coach established its first store in Continental Europe, with a 500-square-foot outlet in Stuttgart, Germany. By 1990, the Coach push to enter international markets had created 19 in-store shops in Japanese Mitsukoshi department stores, with six more slated to open in 1991. Coach solidified its position in the Japanese market by renewing its agreement with Mitsukoshi, making it the exclusive distributor of Coach products in Japan. In addition, Coach joined with another company to open a boutique in a Singapore shopping area, and Coach opened a store in Taipei, Taiwan. With international sales making up 10 percent of the company's revenues, Coach saw the Pacific basin as a key area for further growth.

The company's Far East push was driven by the popularity of Coach goods with Asian tourists in New York, and also by the belief that the company's understated style, lacking in logos or obvious status symbols, was beginning to supplant the vogue for flashy designer goods. To support sales of its products in the Far East, Coach began an advertising campaign to stress the ways in which Coach expressed the American spirit.

Coach's expansion overseas was coupled with domestic expansion, and production again was increased. In addition to its new facility in Florida, the company moved its New York area operations from Manhattan to Carlstadt, New Jersey.

Continuing to Expand the Product Line: Early 1990s

Coach's success in expanding its brand awareness had caused other manufacturers to imitate the company's trademark styles and shapes in their own products. To prevent this infringement of the company's unique designs, Coach sued a number of other manufacturers to stop them from imitating Coach styles. In 1990, the company won a suit in federal court against several other companies, including Ann Taylor and Laura Leather Goods. The ruling awarded the company damages for trade dress infringement.

Coach sales continued to grow in the early 1990s. By May 1991, revenues had increased by more than a fifth over the previous year, and annual sales had reached $150 million. The company continued to broaden its product line, while retaining the qualities identified with its prestigious brand name. Overall, Coach planned a dramatic shift in its identity in the 1990s. "We're going for positioning as Coach the brand, as opposed to Coach the leather company," the company's president told

Crain's New York Business. ''I can't see a limit to Coach's growth in the foreseeable future.''

To bolster that growth, Coach hired a designer to lead a 16-person product development department, to create new objects that could be marketed under the Coach name. In its women's line, the company sought to introduce products in more fashionable colors, without watering down the Coach reputation. In this way, the company hoped to overcome the built-in drawback to high quality and timeless styling, which was that customers rarely needed to replace a product. It launched a line of desk accessories, and an all-leather travel collection was introduced.

In addition, the company began to sell a line of goods for men that included suspenders and socks. This fast-moving category had grown to provide 40 percent of the company's sales. Coach capped off its recent growth in products for men by opening two Coach for Business stores, which were devoted specifically to products for men, on Madison Avenue in Manhattan and in Boston. With these stores, the company hoped to shift its image, repositioning itself as a full-range accessory maker, rather than merely a handbag manufacturer.

Coach announced that it would move more aggressively into the leather accessories market and also try to market its products to younger customers in 1991. To do so, the company hired a new, young advertising agency, which designed a campaign featuring descendants of famous Americans using Coach products, with the theme, ''An American Legacy.''

By early 1992, Coach had expanded its number of stores worldwide to 53 and had enhanced its line of men's and women's socks, to further exploit the appeal of the Coach brand name. Later that year, the company added gift items, including picture frames and belts. In the fall, Coach increased the scope of its handbag line, introducing the Sheridan collection, which featured textured, treated leather that would not burnish like other Coach items but was also more scratch resistant; and the Camden collection, which was styled with brass accents.

Coach stepped up its catalog sales effort in the fall of 1992, mailing ten million mail-order brochures to former customers and likely prospects. The company's catalog operations, though small, were the most profitable of its branches. Coach turned to its mail-order operations to test market its latest innovation in November 1992, when the company began to offer leather outerwear. Providing five styles for men and women, made of soft, waterproof leather, the outerwear was joined by fabric luggage, another departure from Coach tradition, as the company tried to push the boundaries of its identity even further.

As Coach broadened its product offerings, it also broadened the variety of its handbags. Coach moved away from dark, staid colors to brightly hued bags, introducing the Manhattan collection in the spring of 1993. To keep up with demand for this wide variety of new products, Coach expanded its manufacturing activities to Puerto Rico. In late 1994 Coach opened a new flagship store in New York City, its first two-level unit and its largest store yet. The following year Frankfort was named chairman and CEO of Coach. Around this time, Coach expanded its product line yet again with the launch of the Sonoma collection, which included handbags, backpacks, wallets, and belts featuring relaxed styling and suede and textured leathers. The firm also opened the first freestanding Coach store in Japan.

Late 1990s and Beyond: Licensing and Going Solo

During the fiscal year ending in June 1996, Coach opened what it called its Pacific Rim flagship store in Waikiki, Hawaii, as a way to promote the brand to Asian tourists. In addition to continued international growth, the licensing of the prestigious Coach brand also came to the fore in the late 1990s. In 1997 the company entered into its first licensing agreement. It agreed to allow its name to be used on a line of watches to be developed by Movado Group. During fiscal 1998 a Coach leather phone case was introduced through a licensing deal with Motorola, Inc. The following year, a line of premium furniture bearing the Coach name was launched through a licensing deal with Baker Furniture Company.

Sales and profits at Coach suffered from 1997 to 1999 as a result of the combination of the economic difficulties in Asia and changes in consumer tastes, particularly a shift away from leather and toward mixed material and nonleather products. A revamp of the product line in 1999 aimed at reversing the sales slowdown, with an emphasis on attracting younger customers. The core handbag line began to feature more colorful cotton twill and other lightweight fabrics, and while the company maintained its classic leather offerings, a number of slow-moving colors were phased out. Still more license agreements led to the introduction of Coach picture frames, eyewear, and footwear. Coach increasingly offered in its shops, stores, and catalogs lower-priced accessory items whose affordability enabled younger consumers to buy a Coach product. The company also began remodeling its major retail stores in late 1999, seeking to better showcase its new assortment of products. Another important development was the launch of coach.com in October 1999, which marked Coach's entrance into e-commerce. On the manufacturing side, Coach looked to increase operating margins by turning increasingly to outsourcing and shifting from domestic production to production in lower cost markets. Whereas only about 25 percent of Coach products were produced by independent manufacturers in 1998, around 80 percent of the products were made by outsourcers just two years later. Coach was clearly making a rapid shift from manufacturer to designer and marketer while making sure that its manufacturing partners maintained the level of quality for which the brand was known.

While Frankfort was leading this revitalization effort, Sara Lee came to the decision to spin off Coach as part of its own reorganization. As part of the much larger Sara Lee, Coach had seen its revenues increase from about $19 million in 1985 to $540.4 million in 1997, before declining to $507.8 million in 1999. By mid-2000 there were 106 Coach retail outlets in the United States and 63 outlet stores. Prior to the IPO, the improved financial condition of Coach was already evident, as revenues for fiscal 2000 climbed 8.1 percent to $548.9 million and net income surged 130.9 percent, jumping from $16.7 million to $38.6 million. In early October 2000, Sara Lee sold off 17 percent of the newly named Coach, Inc. to the public. Through the IPO, 7.38 million shares of Coach stock were sold at $16 per share, raising $118 million on the New York Stock Exchange. Frankfort remained Coach's chairman and CEO. In April 2001 Sara Lee fully divested itself of its Coach holdings by spinning off the remaining interest to Sara Lee shareholders. Sara Lee netted $1.1 billion in the process. For the fiscal year ending in June 2001, Coach had very encouraging news in its first annual report: net income had jumped 65.9 percent, to $64 million, and net sales had surged 12.2 percent, to $616.1 million.

In addition to accelerating the development of new products and new product categories, modernizing its store designs, and improving its margins through outsourcing, the newly independent Coach also sought to further expand its channels of distribution both at home and abroad in the early 21st century. After opening 15 new retail stores in the United States during fiscal 2001, Coach aimed to open 20 more new stores for each of the next two years. Overseas, Coach continued to concentrate on the Japanese market, mainly because Japanese consumers spend a great deal more on a per capita basis on handbags than American consumers. Already boasting 76 outlets in Japan—62 department store boutiques and 14 retail stores—Coach sought to increase its presence in this important market by forming Coach Japan, Inc., a 50–50 joint venture with Japan's Sumitomo Corporation, in June 2001. Through Coach Japan, the company aimed to add another 25–30 Coach locations in Japan within two or three years. Another of the firm's growth strategies for the early 21st century was to promote the purchase of Coach products as gifts. It was already clear that a substantial amount of the company's sales were gift purchases, but the company felt it could take greater advantage of this fact by developing new products tailored to gift giving and by improving advertising and promotion. One clear example of a product line perfectly suited to the gift-giving niche was jewelry, and in November 2001 Coach introduced its first jewelry collection in a joint effort with Carolee Designs, Inc. The silver jewelry line featured some items that combined silver and leather. It seemed clear that Coach was well positioned to leverage its strong reputation for prestige and quality and its tradition of producing classic, and classy, products into a successful era of independence.

Principal Subsidiaries

Coach Services, Inc. (Maryland); Coach Leatherware International, Inc.; Coach Stores Puerto Rico, Inc.; Coach Japan Holdings, Inc.; Coach Japan Investments, Inc.; Coach (UK) Limited; Coach Europe Services S.r.l. (Italy).

Principal Competitors

Dooney and Bourke PR Inc.; Kate Spade L.L.C.; Gucci Group N.V.; I Pellettieri d'Italia S.p.A. (Prada); Wilsons The Leather Experts Inc.; Kenneth Cole Productions, Inc.; Hermès International; Jones Apparel Group, Inc.; Liz Claiborne, Inc.; Polo Ralph Lauren Corporation.

Further Reading

Barker, Robert, "Coach May Carry Too Much Baggage," *Business Week,* September 11, 2000, p. 173.

Berman, Phyllis, "Goat Cheese, Anyone?," *Forbes,* September 18, 1989.

Berry, Kate, "The Pocketbook Issues in the Future of Coach," *New York Times,* August 20, 2000, Sec. 3, p. 8.

Fallon, James, "Coach Opens First Overseas Store in London," *Women's Wear Daily,* May 19, 1989.

Feitelberg, Rosemary, et al., "Sara Lee to Sell Non-Core Units," *Women's Wear Daily,* May 31, 2000, p. 2.

Gault, Ylonda, "Buyers Riding Coach; Leather Maker Growing," *Crain's New York Business,* May 6, 1991.

Gordon, Joanne, "Serial Tinkerer," *Forbes,* September 3, 2001, p. 86.

Grant, Lorrie, "Coach Bags Old Ideas: Classy Pursemaker Branches Out," *USA Today,* April 24, 2001, p. B3.

Karimzadeh, Marc, "Coach Inc. Expanding in Jewelry," *Women's Wear Daily,* June 26, 2001, p. 2.

Karr, Arnold J., "Coach Files for IPO in First Move to Part Company with Sara Lee," *Women's Wear Daily,* June 20, 2000, p. 2.

Much, Marilyn, "Japan's Handbag Hunger Feeds Designer's Growth," *Investor's Business Daily,* August 17, 2001.

Newman, Jill, "Coach Hits New Heights," *Women's Wear Daily,* January 8, 1988.

——, "Coach's International Approach," *Women's Wear Daily,* September 21, 1990.

Rewick, C.J., "Trying New Accessories: Coach Builds on Handbag Success with Furniture, Towels, Other Items," *Crain's New York Business,* June 21, 1999, p. 25.

Ryan, Thomas J., "Coach IPO Heralds New Era," *Women's Wear Daily,* June 26, 2000, p. 10.

Ryan, Thomas J., and Brian Scott Lipton, "Coach Hopes to Raise $99 Million in IPO," *Daily News Record,* August 30, 2000, p. 13.

Strom, Stephanie, "A Women's Chain Beckons to Men," *New York Times,* July 24, 1991.

—Elizabeth Rourke
—update: David E. Salamie

Consolidated Edison, Inc.

4 Irving Place
New York, New York 10003
U.S.A.
Telephone: (212) 460-4600
Fax: (212) 982-7816
Web site: http://www.conedison.com

Public Company
Incorporated: 1936 as Consolidated Edison Company of
   New York
Employees: 13,464
Sales: $9.43 billion (2000)
Stock Exchanges: New York Midwest Pacific Amsterdam
Ticker Symbol: ED
NAIC: 551112 Public Utility Holding Companies

Consolidated Edison, Inc. (Con Ed) is one of the largest publicly owned utility holding companies in the United States. The company boasted $16 billion in assets and more than $8 billion in revenues in 2000. Its largest business in 2001, the transmission and distribution of electricity, gas, and steam, was handled by two regulated subsidiaries: Consolidated Edison Company of New York, Inc., which served New York City and Westchester County, New York; and Orange and Rockland Utilities, Inc., which served an area covering parts of New York, New Jersey, and Pennsylvania. The company's unregulated subsidiaries included Consolidated Edison Solutions, Inc., a retail energy services company; Consolidated Edison Energy, Inc., a supplier of wholesale energy; Consolidated Edison Development, Inc., an energy infrastructure developer; and Consolidated Edison Communications, Inc., a telecommunications infrastructure company.

Lighting New York: 1823–80

Con Ed began as New York Gas Light Company, founded in 1823 to provide gas for New York's street lamps and homes. Gas illumination had been introduced only recently in the United States and, at first, met widespread resistance due to concerns about safety, but its economy and efficiency soon made gas the standard light source for much of the 19th century. By the last quarter of the century, New York Gas Light and five rival companies supplied gas to the great majority of New York's already vast population, much of which could not imagine a time when the city had been without gas light.

An alternative source of illumination was under intense scrutiny by the 1870s, however; this was electricity. After years of experimentation, the first electric arc lights began appearing in U.S. cities in that decade, and it was soon obvious that electricity would one day become the standard illuminant. The arc light was, nevertheless, a crude and dangerous innovation, suitable only for outdoor lighting of public space, and a host of inventors around the world continued searching for an acceptable alternative.

Among the men who became interested in the future of electric light was Thomas Alva Edison, already famous for his invention of the phonograph and a series of improvements in telegraphy. It was clear to Edison that electricity was destined to light the world, and in 1878 he focused his energies on solving the problems remaining in its development. To make electric light truly universal, two things were needed: a sturdy and economical form of incandescent illumination; and a power grid able to distribute safe, reliable electric current from its source of generation into distant apartments and homes, something that had not yet been attempted on a large scale. Incandescence was a well-known method of illumination, but no one had yet found a material able to withstand long hours of operation without burning up. The inventor shelved his other projects and devoted himself and his considerable staff to experiments in electric light.

The scope of Edison's ambition in these ventures can hardly be overestimated. In essence, he was proposing to design and build the system of electric power distribution upon which the entire world remains dependent. Literally everything had to be created—generators, transmission lines, switching equipment, and protective devices; and, within the home or office, internal wiring, outlets, lamps, meters, and even the light source, the bulb, itself. Such an immense project naturally would require capital, and in October 1878 Edison's group joined forces with Wall Street financiers in forming the Edison Electric Light

Company. Edison's backers included J.P. Morgan and the Vanderbilt interests, both of whom saw the potential of the new system. With his financing in place, Edison redoubled his experiments, and by the end of 1879, working furiously to best the efforts of Joseph Swan in England, he had devised a workable incandescent light using a filament of high-heat-and-electric-resistant ''thread'' in an evacuated glass globe.

Edison simultaneously had solved most of the generation and transmission problems, and by 1880 was ready to apply to the city of New York for permission to build the nation's first commercial electric power station. At that point a legal technicality forced the creation of a subsidiary corporation, Edison Electric Illuminating Company, to act as an operating company on behalf of Edison Electric Light, which would remain only a holding company and in control of all patents. The newly formed Edison Electric Illuminating applied for and received its license—apparently with the help of liberal payments to New York's open-handed city government—and at 3 p.m. on September 4, 1881, current began to flow from the generators at 255-57 Pearl Street in lower Manhattan. London's Holborn Viaduct Station had gone on-line nine months earlier; it too was an Edison project. The Pearl Street Station, like all of Edison's later generating plants, could supply power only a mile or two in any direction from the plant before its direct-current electricity began to lose voltage, but for several years its design was unchallenged and imitations sprang up everywhere. By the spring of 1883 there were some 334 Edison plants in operation, most of them considerably smaller than the one at Pearl Street.

The success of Edison's power system was an event of the first order; the advent of electricity changed every aspect of modern life. Locally, Edison found himself quickly enmeshed in the struggles and strategies generated by any such leap in technology. The inventor and his associates incorporated many subsidiary manufacturing companies in order to build power stations wherever they were wanted, and by 1884, greatly assisted by a young financial wizard, Samuel Insull, Edison had even gained control of Edison Light as well as Edison Illuminating. As an innovator in electricity, however, Edison's day was past; in the great debate that shortly arose as to the relative merits of alternating current (AC) and direct current (DC), Edison stuck with his original conception of DC generators long after the rest of the industry had recognized AC as the wave of the future. By the late 1880s George Westinghouse had won the battle of the currents, and Edison had long since dropped active participation in his electrical holdings.

Consolidation of the Gas and Electric Companies: 1880–1900

Given this situation, Edison was more than happy to listen when a group of German financiers led by Henry Villard proposed the formation of a new electrical combination, to include all of Edison's manufacturing companies and the valuable stock of Edison Electric Light, the holding company. Although the latter had come under the managing direction of Edison's group in an 1884 proxy fight, its largest block was controlled by the interests of J.P. Morgan. In the complex negotiations leading to the creation of Villard's new company—later to be known as General Electric—Morgan used his stock position and financial muscle to demand and win 40 percent of General Electric's stock, while Edison settled for 10 percent and enough cash to make his fortune. Meanwhile, the creation of General Electric led to Edison Illuminating being spun off on its own in a utility market increasingly crowded with efficient AC competitors and the newly roused gas companies.

New York's gas companies were hardly pleased by the success of electric lighting. Edison's earliest announcements on the subject had sent gas stocks reeling, and in 1884 the city's six largest gas concerns joined forces in a new utility giant called Consolidated Gas Company of New York. This merger initiated a long process whereby the scores of small electricity, gas, and steam companies operating in the greater New York area would be melded into the single and far more efficient entity known since 1936 as Consolidated Edison Company of New York. At first, the electric and gas concerns faced each other as rivals, each side augmenting its forces by annexation or combination with neighboring firms.

The gas companies, including New York Gas Light Company, united in Consolidated Gas, while the bulk of Manhattan's electricity supply was collected in 1898 under the umbrella of The New York Gas & Electric Light, Heat & Power Company (NYG&ELH&P). NYG&ELH&P also gained a controlling share of Edison Electric Illuminating. Consolidated Gas bought NYG&ELH&P in 1899, when Consolidated Gas decided to use its superior financial might to overcome a growing technological gap by buying up as many electricity companies as it could. In 1901 Consolidated Gas merged the electric companies it controlled, including Edison Electric Illuminating, NYG&ELH&P, and others into a single subsidiary known as The New York Edison Company. Thus the gas companies themselves became providers of electricity, and by 1910 controlled, under the name of New York Edison, most of the electricity generated in Manhattan and the western portion of the Bronx.

By that time, of course, electricity had become the standard source of power not only for illumination but for a widening variety of household gadgets and industrial tools. Alternating current had won the day, allowing the construction of very large central generators capable of serving vast numbers of customers at long distances. New York Edison gradually replaced its last few small DC-generating stations, and the city's power network began to assume its modern structure. In particular, as it became apparent that large-scale power distribution was by nature a type of monopoly, utility companies came under the regulatory control of the state legislature in Albany, New York. The power

Key Dates:

1823: New York Gas Light Company is founded.
1884: New York Gas Light Company merges with five other gas companies to form the Consolidated Gas Company of New York.
1899: The company buys the New York Gas & Electric Light, Heat & Power Company.
1901: The company merges with Edison's Illuminating Company to create the New York Edison Company.
1936: Consolidated Edison Company of New York is created from the combined holdings of New York Edison.
1962: Con Ed begins operation of a private atomic power plant.
1967: Charles F. Luce is appointed chairman and begins a turnaround of the ailing company.
1974: State government buys two of Con Ed's generating plants for $612 million.
1999: Con Ed sells its generating plants for $1.65 billion and buys Orange & Rockland Utilities, Inc., for $790 million.
2001: Terrorist attack on World Trade Center destroys two Con Ed substations and interrupts power to 12,000 customers.

of the legislature to fix rates of return for utilities was tested in a landmark court case arising out of its 1906 attempt to limit Consolidated Gas's price for its gas to 80 cents per 1,000 cubic feet. The United States Supreme Court eventually ruled that while governmental bodies had a clear right to oversee the operation of utilities, they could not set rates so low as to prevent the utilities from earning a reasonable rate of return on investment; in the case of Consolidated Gas, however, the rate of 80 cents was not found to be excessively low. In the course of its analysis, the Court estimated Consolidated Gas's asset value at $56 million.

For many years Consolidated Gas and its subsidiary New York Edison grew quietly. The long process of unifying New York's various power companies continued, and by 1932 Consolidated Gas was the largest company in the world providing electrical service. The final step occurred in 1936 when Consolidated Gas became Consolidated Edison Company of New York. Under the direction of Hudson R. Searing, the previously cool relations between Edison's gas and electric divisions were quietly improved, and the gigantic combine took on its present configuration as New York City's sole power company.

Con Ed Monopoly Developing
a Bad Reputation: Mid-20th Century

As the single purveyor of light and electricity to New York's millions of inhabitants and workers, Con Ed attracted the suspicions and criticism that accompany a monopoly. When Mayor Fiorello La Guardia threatened to create a municipal power utility to compete with Con Ed during the Great Depression, company executives worked to develop closer relationships with other members of the city's government. Con Ed was the city's largest employer of construction workers and paid more taxes than any other single organization in the city, and, in large part through the efforts of Charles Eble—later Con Ed's chief executive—was able to stave off La Guardia's threat. The interests of New York City and Con Ed meshed from the mid-1930s on.

In 1955 Con Ed was among the first utilities to apply for permission from the Atomic Energy Commission to build and operate a private atomic power plant. Permission granted, Con Ed built its reactor at Indian Point, New York, some miles up the Hudson River from New York City, inaugurating what it hoped would be a new era of clean, cheap power for New York. Con Ed's path-breaking project took far longer and much more money to build than anyone had expected. When it was completed in the early 1960s, Indian Point's cost per kilowatt of capacity was 2.5 times that of a conventional generator, adding to a general growing perception among New Yorkers that Con Ed was an inefficient utility. The origins of this reputation seem to be split between the unavoidable difficulties of supplying power in so complex an environment as New York City and Con Ed's failure to meet that challenge.

The burdens of a New York City utility are severe. Since the 19th century, most utility lines and pipes have been required by law to be laid underground, vastly increasing Con Ed's expense for upkeep and expansion of its system. Con Ed has more miles of underground wire than the rest of the nation's utilities combined. New York's extremely dense population creates additional problems, and the high percentage of residential users necessitates the metering, billing, and servicing of thousands of relatively small accounts, in contrast to a utility with a higher proportion of industrial customers. The preponderance of office workers in Manhattan means that Con Ed must be prepared to supply a midday peak of electricity far greater than its 24-hour average, forcing the construction and maintenance of a generating capacity larger than would otherwise be needed. Such underutilized capacity is highly inefficient for power companies, whose single greatest burden is the cost of construction and upkeep. Con Ed also pays extremely high taxes, which it passes on to customers through its rates. Thus Con Ed, in effect, collects taxes on behalf of the various city, state, and federal agencies, taxes that have helped make Con Ed the nation's most expensive utility for many years. Finally, space restrictions in New York made it much easier for Con Ed to repair old power stations than to build new ones, which meant that by the 1950s much of its physical plant was antiquated and inefficient. Despite that handicap, Con Ed was the subject of some of the earliest restrictions on air pollution adopted in the United States, further increasing its already excessive costs.

The upshot of these unique drawbacks was to make Con Ed an expensive and erratic provider of gas, electricity, and steam; but some of its problems lay with management as well. By the 1960s, Chairman Charles Eble and his team of top advisors had all been with the company for a number of years, and many felt that they had developed an aloof, isolated mentality that angered New Yorkers, irate over poor service, high bills, and a series of famous blackouts beginning in 1959. Typical of the company's poor handling of public relations was its 1962 effort to build a second atomic power plant in the middle of the borough of Queens; such judgment helped make Con Ed notorious. Equally damaging was Con Ed's poor financial performance. While 1965 revenues of $840 million made Con Ed the nation's largest utility, its revenue growth was very slow, net earnings were low, and earnings per share were moving up at only 4 percent per year, or half the pace of a typical competitor such as Commonwealth Edison in Chicago.

Luce Turnaround: 1967–82

The man chosen to lead Con Ed out of this trough was Charles F. Luce. Appointed chairman in mid-1967, Luce was formerly an under-secretary with the Department of the Interior. He was chosen both for his abilities and because he was an outsider to New York power politics. The new chief executive took a number of decisive steps toward the renewal of Con Ed: a virtual makeover of top management; division of the company into six operating divisions, one for each city borough plus one for suburban Westchester County; the addition of several new plants; plans to replace aging equipment; and a new emphasis on customer service.

Con Ed's stock price continued to drop, however, and the company soon found itself in the worst crisis of its history. After agreeing in 1972 to halt the use of coal for environmental reasons, Con Ed was dependent on oil for 85 percent of its generating capacity when the OPEC oil embargo doubled the price of crude in the fall of 1973. As fuel price increases could not be passed along to customers for about four months, and Con Ed was in the midst of yet more construction projects to increase capacity, the company was suddenly faced with a critical shortage of cash. Luce took the unprecedented step of withholding dividends in the first quarter of 1974, unleashing an avalanche of criticism from stockholders, Wall Street, and other utilities, who watched their own stocks follow Con Ed on a sharp decline.

Luce had a second, far more important strategy. Knowing that the state government had no interest in seeing New York's power supply disrupted by financial collapse, Luce persuaded it to buy two of Con Ed's generating plants that were still under construction. At one stroke, Con Ed received $612 million in cash and was relieved of the heavy cost burden associated with new plant construction. What additional power Con Ed required was bought back from the state; but 1973 and 1974 also marked the beginning of a long decline in the expansion rate of New York's energy usage, partially in response to the high price of oil and partially as a result of vigorous conservation campaigns promoted by Con Ed, which realized that nothing could be better from a financial perspective than an end to the cycle of borrowing required for new generating equipment and plants.

Stable Operations in the 1980s and 1990s

By 1978 Con Ed was regarded as one of the most efficient and profitable utilities in the country, and Chairman Luce was credited with a remarkable turnaround of the once-hated institution. Customer complaints dropped off dramatically, earnings per share and the stock price rose, and Con Ed gradually eased itself back into a more balanced pattern of fuel usage, much of it natural gas and nuclear. In the 1980s Con Ed operated smoothly and quietly. The generally conservative pattern of energy usage in New York allowed Con Ed to avoid the costly construction projects that once threatened to sink it, keeping earnings high.

During the late 1980s, Con Ed even began posting the lowest rates of customer interruption for any utility in the country, which, in light of its long tradition of sub-par performance, may be its most impressive achievement. Charles Luce's decision to sell off two of the company's plants in 1974 made possible a renaissance at Con Ed.

Luce retired in September 1982 and was succeeded by Arthur Haupsburg. By this time Con Ed had begun an era of stability in its electric rates. A rate increase requested in April 1982 and granted the following year was its last for a decade; in April 1990 the utility extended its current electric rates until 1992. Haupsburg retired in September 1990 without having had to request a single electric rate increase. During his tenure, electric sales rose, fuel prices generally declined, and dividends were increased annually. Con Ed had ample capacity to meet the demand generated by the healthy local economy.

Eugene R. McGrath became chairman, president, and chief executive officer upon Haupsburg's retirement. He faced a somewhat different situation than did his predecessor. Con Ed remained financially strong, but the New York City area's economy had weakened. Con Ed launched a major energy conservation program in 1990, with the goal of reducing customers' electric energy usage by 15 percent by 2008, as compared to expected consumption without the program. Con Ed planned to spend about $4.2 billion on the program during that period. To maintain its power supply, Con Ed continued modernizing its existing plants and signed contracts with several prospective independent power producers.

In 1992 Con Ed requested, and received, a rate hike, the first in almost ten years. Despite the long-term rate stability, Con Ed still had extremely high rates; its 12-cents-a-kilowatt-hour charge doubled the national average. With its aging plants and the city's stringent environmental controls, Con Ed could only generate power at 7 cents a kilowatt hour, compared to independent power producers, who could manage at 5 cents a kilowatt hour. In addition, taxes accounted for 25 percent of Con Ed's revenues in 1993, by far the highest in the country.

Cost-cutting and more efficient operations were high priorities for Chairman McGrath in the 1990s, as the company prepared for the deregulation of the electric generating market. Between 1990 and 1993 the company laid off 3,000 workers, and by 2000 it had reduced its workforce by another 3,000.

McGrath's plans called for Con Ed to minimize its power generation and maximize its power distribution after deregulation. The company's greatest assets in the mid-1990s were its transmission and distribution systems, whereas the generating plants accounted for only 20 percent of company assets. McGrath refused to upgrade or build new plants in anticipation of selling them off and buying power from independent producers after deregulation.

Deregulation in the Late 1990s

In 1997 the first phase of a five-year process of deregulation began, allowing some commercial and residential customers to choose their power supplier. Although only 10,000 commercial customers and 50,000 residential customers in New York could purchase electricity on the open market by 1998, by 2002 all of

Con Ed's three million customers would have that freedom. Con Ed, however, continued to distribute the power, regardless of who generated it.

Deregulation required Con Ed to develop a plan with government agencies and consumer groups for its organization and operation. As part of that plan, Con Ed reorganized under a new holding company, Consolidated Edison, Inc., in 1998, with different subsidiaries handling its regulated and nonregulated businesses, including a new power marketing group. The same year, Con Ed announced plans to buy Orange and Rockland Utilities, Inc., which operated in New York state, New Jersey, and Pennsylvania. The $790 million deal was completed in 1999 and helped protect Con Ed from acquisition by a large national power company.

McGrath's long-held plan to sell off the company's generating plants came to fruition in 1999, when Northern States Power, KeySpan, and Orion Power paid a total of $1.65 billion for the facilities. Con Ed used the money to finance its Orange and Rockland acquisition, to buy back some of its stock, and to entice other possible merger partners.

The company found such a partner quickly, arranging to purchase Northeast Utilities for $3.5 billion in cash and stock and the assumption of $3.9 billion of Northeast's debt. After numerous talks with regulators and consumer groups on how to divide the savings generated by the merger, the deal fell through in 2001.

Enthusiasm for deregulation waned in 2000 when a summer power shortage caused blackouts in New York City. Although Con Ed received the brunt of consumers' criticism, it had little actual power to control the situation, having in large part exited the power generation business. In addition, Con Ed had been required by deregulation to reduce its long-term contracts with energy suppliers, forcing the company to pay high spot prices during peak demand.

The September 11, 2001, terrorist attack on the World Trade Center severely damaged Con Ed's infrastructure in lower Manhattan. Two substations adjacent to the twin Trade Center towers were destroyed, and major transmission cables were significantly damaged, leaving 12,000 customers without electricity. The company moved quickly to bring generators, new cables, and around 2,000 repair workers into the area to restore service. Insurance was expected to cover the replacement of the substations, and federal aid was expected to cover the $400 million in Con Ed expenses related to the attack.

Principal Subsidiaries

Consolidated Edison Communications, Inc.; Consolidated Edison Company of New York, Inc.; Consolidated Edison Development, Inc.; Consolidated Edison Energy, Inc.; Consolidated Edison Solutions, Inc.; Orange and Rockland Utilities, Inc.

Principal Competitors

American Electric Power Company, Inc.; Energy East Corporation; Keyspan Corporation; Niagara Mohawk Holdings, Inc.

Further Reading

"Government Alert: Con Ed Won't Charge More," *Crain's New York Business,* October 15, 2001, p. 12.

Keenan, Charles, "Businesses Jolted; Deregulation Spurs Megabills for Megawatts," *Crain's New York Business,* August 7, 2000, p. 1.

Lentz, Philip, "Con Ed Fighting to Keep Savings in Big Merger," *Crain's New York Business,* October 18, 1999, p. 1.

——, "Con Ed Makes Switch to Competition," *Crain's New York Business,* May 5, 1997, p. 26.

——, "Utility Mergers Could Leave State with 2 Behemoths," *Crain's New York Business,* May 18, 1998, p. 3.

Norman, James R., "A Beleaguered Tax Collector," *Forbes,* December 20, 1993, pp. 47–48.

O'Hanlon, Thomas, "Con Edison: The Company You Love to Hate," *Fortune,* March 1966.

"The Real Story on Power Woes," *Crain's New York Business,* July 3, 2000, p. 8.

Silverberg, Robert, *Light for the World: Edison and the Power Industry,* Princeton, N.J.: Van Nostrand, 1967.

—Jonathan Martin
—update: Susan Windisch Brown

Courts Plc

The Grange, 1 Central Road
Morden, Surrey SM4 5PQ
United Kingdom
Telephone: (+44) 20 8640 3322
Fax: (+44) 20 8410 9400
Web site: http://www.courts.plc.uk

Public Company
Incorporated: 1933 as Courts Ltd.
Employees: 9,709
Sales: £732 million ($1.17 billion) (2001)
Stock Exchanges: London
Ticker Symbol: CRTO
NAIC: 44211 Furniture Stores; 44312 Computer and
    Software Stores- Retail

Courts Plc is one of the United Kingdom's leading retail furniture and home appliance companies. Yet, with more than 300 stores operating in 20 countries worldwide, Courts is also a globally operating company that can boast that the sun never sets on its retail empire. Based in Surrey, Courts operates more than 100 stores in the United Kingdom, including England, Wales, and Guernsey. The company's U.K. network of High Street shops and larger edge-of-town superstores contribute 40 percent of Courts' annual sales, which topped £732 million in 2001. The bulk of the company's retail network operates from Antigua and Barbuda, Barbados, Belize, Dominica, Fiji, Grenada, Guyana, Indonesia, Jamaica, Malaysia, Mauritius, Papua New Guinea, St. Kitts and Nevis, St. Lucia, St. Vincent and the Grenadines, Singapore, Trinidad and Tobago, and Bermuda. In these markets, the company is generally the domestic market leader; the majority of the company's overseas revenues come from its home appliance and electronics sales. The Caribbean and southeast Asian markets each generate more than 25 percent of Courts annual sales. Courts Plc is listed on the London Stock Exchange. A number of its subsidiaries, including those in Jamaica, Malaysia, Barbados, and Mauritius, have been listed on their local stock exchanges as well. While the company's overseas expansion has thrived, its attempt to move into more

markets nearby has proven more difficult. In 2001, Courts was forced to exit Ireland after several years of losses there. Led by Chairman Paul Cohen and Managing Director Bruce Cohen—the Cohen family, which built the chain from a single store in 1946, holds a 40 percent interest in the company—Courts has been shifting its emphasis on development of its superstore concept for the new century. The new concept broadens the company's retail mix beyond furniture and appliances to include "everything for the home under one roof."

19th-Century Furniture Retailer

The first of what was to become the Courts furniture retail chain was opened in Canterbury, England, in 1850. William Henry Court inherited the store in 1860. Under Court's ownership, the store, originally a small one-man shop operating in the shadows of the Canterbury cathedral, grew into a thriving retailer and furniture maker. In order to supply his store, Court began producing his own furniture, opening a number of workshops. Courts furniture became known for its quality, and the store soon attracted a growing clientele from beyond Canterbury itself. Nonetheless, Courts remained a single-store operation throughout its first century of business. William Court's son Percy took over the store in the early 1930s, registering it as a limited company in 1933. Under Percy Court, the store expanded, adding garden displays to its furniture displays. The company also capitalized on the fame of *The Canterbury Tales*, adding Chaucer to its logo and encouraging customers to "make a happy pilgrimage" to the store.

World War II nearly ended the Courts retailing name, however. In 1942, the German air raids over England had caused widespread devastation, including the Courts store, which suffered a direct hit during a bombing raid.

At the end of the war, Percy Court sold his family's store to three brothers, Albert, Edwin, and Henry Cohen. The Cohen brothers had come from the family that had built up the British and Colonial Stores Group, which operated furniture stores in England, Scotland, Wales, Ireland, and Canada chiefly under the brand name Cavendish & Woodhouse. British and Colonial at one point counted among the world's largest furniture retail

---

Company Perspectives:

Courts is a truly global company specializing in the retailing of home furnishing and electrical products with stores trading somewhere in the world at every hour of the day and night, 365 days a year, producing sales of over £2 million a day and profits of over £1 million a week. We are proud to have outstanding international management in all our centers of operation, who will help the Group to achieve increasing success in the future.

---

chains. Percy Court sold the company to the Cohen brothers in 1946, but remained with the company as a director—he was responsible for store displays—until his death.

The Cohen brothers sought to build on Courts' reputation for quality furniture in the region and began to plan the first phase of the Courts company's expansion. By 1949, the family had added five more stores to the Courts network. In order to encourage consumers, who had been hard hit by the economic hardships of the postwar era, to buy at its stores, Courts began offering credit. Customers came, and the company began a steady expansion drive through the 1950s, adding two or three new stores each year.

Courts' expansion remained limited to its southern and eastern England base, and by 1959, the company's chain had swelled to 35 stores, including its first store in Cardiff, Wales. That same year, Courts went public on the London Stock Exchange. The public offering was to enable the company to continue to develop its U.K. business over the next decades.

Yet, the end of the 1950s also saw the company turn to the overseas market for expansion. Rather than developing an export business, however, Courts determined to bring only its brand name and retailing expertise to its new markets. Products for its new stores were to be furnished from their local markets, and the company also adopted a policy of hiring practically all of its overseas employees locally.

Jamaica became Courts' first foreign market when the company opened a store in Kingston in 1959. Less than a year later, the success of the first Courts store led the company to open a second Jamaican store in Mandeville. Meanwhile, the first of a new generation of the Cohen family were joining the company, starting with future Chairman Paul Cohen in 1956, who was joined by Bruce Cohen in 1964.

International Expansion in the 1970s

By the mid-1960s, Courts' overseas success encouraged the company to pursue a wider international expansion plan. Yet, Courts specifically sought smaller overseas markets, many of which had roots in the British colonial era, in which the company was able to achieve market dominance. This "big fish in a small pond" formula brought the company to Barbados in 1965.

Despite Courts' success in that market, the small size of Barbados meant that the company would not be able to expand its operations there beyond a few stores. Instead, Courts responded

to the market's geographical limitation by expanding its product offerings. Barbados became the first of the Courts stores to offer a wider range of products than just furniture, as the company introduced home appliances and other household equipment, such as sewing machines and bicycles. This product mix was to become adopted by all of the company's foreign stores—and quickly became the largest source of store sales—before being introduced to the company's growing U.K. operations as well.

Courts' Jamaican operations had continued successfully throughout the 1960s. In 1969, the company decided to place its Courts Jamaica subsidiary's shares on the Jamaican Stock Market. In this way, the company continued its original policy of building a strong local base for its international subsidiaries. The public listing helped the company's Jamaican operations expand to become one of the largest of the foreign Courts subsidiaries. The company's retail network on the island was eventually to grow to more than 30 stores. Courts began to expand throughout the Caribbean region, opening subsidiaries and stores in Antigua and Barbuda, Belize, Grenada, Guyana, Dominica, St. Kitts and Nevis, St. Lucia, Trinidad and Tobago, St. Vincent, and the Grenadines. In all, the company's operations in the region consisted of some 120 stores and provided 27 percent of the company's total sales at the turn of the 21st century.

Courts turned from the Caribbean to the Asian Pacific at the start of the 1970s. In 1971, Courts entered Singapore, which was to provide a springboard for the company's expansion throughout the region. In that same year, Courts also opened a store in Suva, the capital of the Fiji Islands. That store was to be only the first of a chain of more than 20 stores operating in the Fiji island chain under both the Courts and the new Homecentres store names. In 1978, the company's Barbados operations became the next Courts subsidiary to go public on its local stock exchange.

Other markets followed in the early 1980s, including the Channel Islands, which saw the first of its Courts stores in 1980; St. Lucia, where the company opened the first of six stores in 1981 (a seventh store was announced for 2002); and, with the first of nine stores opening in 1983, in Papua New Guinea. As with the company's other overseas stores, stores in the new market featured a diversified mix of products ranging from furniture to home appliances.

Meanwhile, back in the United Kingdom, Courts had continued its steady expansion, and by the mid-1980s the company's retail network there neared 100 stores throughout the south and east of England and in Wales. In 1985, Courts began to adapt the diversified product mix of its international operations to its domestic stores. With the addition of home appliances and electronics goods, Courts began to develop a new "superstore" retail concept. Rather than take up residence in the company's traditional High Street locations, the new superstores were located on the outskirts of town. These locations provided the opportunity for larger floor space as well as a widened customer base than its center-of-town stores.

A Mammoth Retailer for the 21st Century

In the mid-1980s Courts continued to enter new markets, now using a new store name, Courts Mammoth, reflecting the

Key Dates:

1850: Courts furniture opens in Canterbury, England.

1860: William Henry Court inherits the store and opens workshops to begin producing his own furniture.

1932: Percy Court takes over operation of the Courts store.

1933: The company is incorporated as Courts Ltd.

1942: Courts store takes a direct hit during German bombing raids.

1946: Percy Court sells the store to the Cohen family, who begin expansion of the company.

1950: Courts opens sixth store.

1959: Courts goes public on London Stock Exchange, opens its first store in Jamaica.

1965: The company opens a store in Barbados, which becomes first store to feature diversified home furnishings product mix.

1969: The company floats Jamaican subsidiary on the local stock exchange.

1971: The first Courts store opens in Singapore.

1978: The company's Barbados store goes public on the local stock exchange.

1985: Courts launches the Mammoth superstore concept, opens first Courts Mammouth (the variant spelling designed to appeal to a French-speaking clientele) store in Mauritius.

1987: The company enters Malaysia with Courts Mammoth superstore concept.

1990: The company lists Courts Mauritius store on the local stock exchange.

1992: Courts Singapore store goes public on local stock exchange.

1996: Courts opens its first store in Dublin, Ireland.

2001: Courts Malaysia goes public on the Malaysia stock market; the company also pulls out of Ireland and forms joint venture to enter South African market.

Grant to enter Guyana in 1993. The company later added operations in Central America as well, in Belize.

Back at home, Courts began preparing an assault into other U.K. regions. In 1996, the company began opening stores in the north of England. The company also opened its first branch—a superstore in Dublin—to take it into Ireland, followed by a second store in Blanchardstown. Yet, while the company's foreign operations remained dynamic through the end of the decade, the company's U.K. branch was starting to struggle, with profits brought down by its difficulties in penetrating the north of England and steady losses at its Irish location. By 2000, the company's U.K. operations were in a slump—despite contributing 40 percent of the company's revenues, profits amounted to just £1.5 million. In comparison, the company's southeast Asian branches added £24 million in operating profits, and its Caribbean network generated nearly £40 million in profits.

By the end of its 2001 fiscal year, the company's inability to penetrate the Irish market forced it to close its stores there. The company had also placed its U.K. operations under review and put into place a restructuring plan designed not only to shave off some £20 million per year in costs, but also to rejuvenate the Courts brand image and to recast the company as an upmarket retailer. The company continued its shift toward an emphasis on superstores, boosting that concept with the introduction of new textile and curtain boutiques. The company now sought to redefine its store concept as "everything for the home under one roof."

If the company's U.K. operations were falling behind a bit, its overseas network continued to flourish at the start of the new century. One of the most dynamic of the company's markets was Malaysia, where the company had rapidly built a network of more than 50 Courts Mammoth stores. In the fall of 2001, the company continued its policy of floating its subsidiaries, taking a listing on the Malaysian stock market for that subsidiary, while announcing plans to increase its store network in that country to nearly 70 by the end of 2002.

The Cohen family, which still held 45 percent of the parent company Courts Plc, began preparing to turn over the company's operations to a new generation at the turn of the century, particularly with the naming of Stephen Cohen to take over as managing director of the company's U.K. division in 2000. The company also began making plans to expand into a new market, that of South Africa, forming a joint venture with the Profurn Group, while also targeting entry into Madagascar. Courts Plc had successfully negotiated more than 150 years of history and had built its network into one of the most international of furniture retailers.

stores' large size and diversified product mix. In 1985, the company opened its first store in Mauritius, in the Indian Ocean, where the store name became Courts Mammouth to appeal to the market's French-speaking population. Two years later, Courts Mammoth opened in Malaysia, which became one of Courts' single most important foreign markets. The company also continued its expansion in the Caribbean, opening up stores in Antigua and Grenada. By then, the company had seen a changing of the guard, as former Managing Directors Paul and Bruce Cohen took up the chairman and chief executive seats, respectively.

Courts' foreign expansion continued into the 1990s. At the beginning of the decade, the company's Mauritius operations became the next subsidiary to be listed on the local stock exchange. Two years later, Courts Singapore also became a public company, listing on that country's stock exchange. Meanwhile, Courts added operations in Trinidad and Tobago, forming a partnership with local company Huggins Retail in 1991; the company also ventured onto the South American continent for the first time, through a partnership with Geddes

Principal Subsidiaries

Courts (Antigua and Barbuda) Ltd.; Courts (Barbados) Ltd.; Courts (Belize) Ltd.; Courts (Dominica) Ltd.; Courts (Fiji) Ltd.; Homecentres (Fiji) Ltd.; Courts (Grenada) Ltd.; Courts (Guyana) Inc.; Courts (Ireland) Ltd.; Courts (Jamaica) Ltd.; Courts Mammoth (Berhad, Malaysia); Courts (Mauritius) Ltd.; Courts (PNG) Ltd. (Papua New Guinea); Courts (St. Kitts-Nevis) Ltd.; Courts (St. Lucia) Ltd.; Courts (St. Vincent) Ltd.; Courts (Singapore) Ltd.; Courts (Trinidad) Ltd.; Courts (UK)

Ltd.; Courts Worldwide Purchases Ltd.; Canterbury Investments Ltd. (Bermuda); Courts (Overseas) Ltd.; CFGB Ltd.

Principal Competitors

Dixons Group plc; Harrods Plc; House of Frazier Plc; James Beattie Plc; Marks & Spencer Plc; MFI Furniture Plc.

Further Reading

"At This Price? Courts," *Guardian*, June 15, 2001.
"Courts, Pressac, Country Gardens Midas," *Mail on Sunday*, August 15, 2000.
Richards, Amanda, "Good Reception for Leap in Courts Profits," *Daily Express*, February 8, 2000.
Sefton, Caroline, "Courts," *Hemscott Invest*, June 14, 2001.

—M.L. Cohen

Croda International Plc

Cowick Hall, Snaith, Goole
East Yorkshire DN14 9AA
United Kingdom
Telephone: (+44) 1405-860-551
Fax: (+44) 1405-861-767
Web site: http://www.croda.co.uk

Public Company
Incorporated: 1925
Employees: 4,000
Sales: £365.9 million ($546.2 million) (2000)
Stock Exchanges: London
Ticker Symbol: CRDA
NAIC: 32519 Other Basic Organic Chemical
   Manufacturing

Croda International Plc is the world's leading specialist manufacturer of oleo-chemical ingredients and products for the beauty, hair care, healthcare, and household products industries. The company's oil-based products, developed for the most part from natural sources, are used in a variety of applications, ranging from shampoos and cosmetics to treatments for asthma and varicose veins. The company remains largely unknown by consumers who nonetheless most likely use Croda's products on a daily basis—yet the company has also gained some fame as the maker of "Lorenzo's Oil," as the company's synthesized rapeseed extract was called in a major motion picture. Croda has decided to focus entirely on its core specialty products and therefore eliminate its industrial chemicals and coatings divisions. In 2000, the company sold off its adhesives business, and in early 2001, Croda sold off its resins operations. Croda's focus on its core oleo-chemical products reflects the strong demand and high margin for these products, which are essential to such globally operating businesses as Unilever, Procter & Gamble, Avon, and Revlon. Croda itself is a multinational corporation, with headquarters in East Yorkshire, England, guiding the operations of its production facilities in Europe, North and South America, Asia, Africa, and Australia. One of the last of the United Kingdom's independent publicly listed chemicals com-

panies, Croda has joined in the worldwide chemicals industry consolidation, while remaining itself a potential takeover target by one of its far larger competitors.

Manufacturer of Grease in the 1920s

George Crowe launched Croda as a maker of lanolin—a grease derived from sheep's wool—at a former waterworks near Rawcliffe Bridge, England. George Crowe, who had previously operated as a shipper, was pursuing an idea for producing lanolin introduced to him by an acquaintance, one Mr. Dawe. At the time, lanolin was becoming an important product for its many applications, which ranged from serving as a base for cosmetics to functioning as a waterproofing agent for rope and textiles, and as a dressing for leather goods. A number of extraction processes had been developed on the European continent for producing lanolin, but the United Kingdom, with no domestic lanolin production, was forced to rely on imports of lanolin.

Crowe purchased the Rawcliffe Bridge site in 1925 for £7 and installed his nephew, Philip Wood, then 22 years old, as manager of the new business. Crowe's optimism was reflected in the choice of the company's name—combining "Cro" from Crowe and "da" from Dawe—yet Dawe's process quickly proved flawed. Dawe disappeared, having at least given Croda part of its name. Wood did not give up, however. With the help of a chemist brought over from Belgium, Wood went to work developing a new extraction process. By the end of the year, Croda had succeeded in producing its first lot of lanolin—three barrels' worth.

Despite this success, the company barely kept afloat through the end of the decade. If lanolin had found a variety of uses, the company was unable to profit from the as yet small market, and its losses began to mount. By 1930, the company had gone through all of its funds. Croda might have gone under, if not for the release of a report from the National Physical Laboratory that revealed another attribute of lanolin, that of its ability to prevent the formation of rust. This newly discovered property gave the lanolin market a boost and before long Croda had recovered financially.

Croda continued to grow through the 1930s, despite the worldwide depression, and by the end of the decade had gained a foothold not only in its domestic market, but also in the export market. Yet the outbreak of World War II forced the company to turn its production to the manufacture of camouflage paints, gun cleaning oils, insect repellents, and other products needed for the British war effort. The company's government contracts, however, provided no profits.

Following the war, Croda converted its production back to its original interests. In 1949, the company met with a new setback when Philip Wood died at the age of 46. With no ready successor—Wood's son, Frederick, was only 23 at the time—the company restructured its direction into a management committee. Frederick was given the job of sales director. Then, in 1950, the younger Wood was sent to the United States to establish a new subsidiary operation there. The company's presence in the United States was to prove a key component to its later success. The timing was certainly right, as the cosmetics and personal care market was just beginning to grow into one of the world's most lucrative markets.

International Chemicals Group in the 1960s

Wood opened an office in New York City and hired his first employee, Kurt Neulinger, who had formerly worked for the company's U.K. office. Wood and Neulinger began touting Croda Inc.'s first products, lanolin oil and lanolin alcohol, to the companies in the emerging personal care sector. When Wood was called back to head the parent company in England in 1953, he was replaced as president by Michael Cannon, who was the son of a former assistant to Philip Wood. Cannon, with Neulinger as vice-president, began to expand Croda Inc.'s customer base, built around three of its parent company's core products—Lanolin, Hartolan, and Polawax. All three were to help Croda build a leading position for itself in the burgeoning cosmetics and personal care products industries. But it was especially Polawax, a nonionic self-emulsifying wax particularly used for hair care products, that helped Croda's early U.S. sales. A large-scale order for Polawax from one of the largest American cosmetics companies helped establish Croda as a major ingredients supplier to that market.

In the United Kingdom, under Frederick Wood, Croda was enjoying a period of rapid growth as the company expanded into the production of a variety of oleo-chemical products (i.e., oil-based), while also developing an international presence. By the early 1960s, the company had launched subsidiaries in Italy and Germany, and then, farther abroad, in Japan. Each of these ventures proved successful as the company's fortunes rose on the booming cosmetics and hair care industries. By then, too, Croda had outgrown its original facilities—while production continued at Rawcliffe Bridge, the company's headquarters had moved to Snaith and then, in 1956, to Cowick Hall.

The following year, Croda, which had been growing organically by extending its product range and its sales both at home and overseas, made an important acquisition. In 1957, the company purchased, through its Croda Inc. subsidiary, the lanolin business from Hummel Chemical Company, based in Brooklyn, New York. That acquisition gave Croda the financial backing to build its first production facilities in the United States. The following year, the company's new subsidiary, called Hummel Lanolin Corporation, began production from its own facility in Newark, New Jersey.

The 1960s saw the company undergo a dramatic expansion beyond its lanolin and personal care products base to become a diversified specialty chemicals business with interests in a variety of industries. After going public in 1964, Croda went on an acquisition spree, launching a series of takeovers—not all of which were welcomed—and adding such large-scale competitors as United Premier and Midland Yorkshire Holdings. In 1968, Croda acquired British Glues & Chemicals, giving Croda that company's Toronto, Canada-based WH Harris & Co., which became a key component of Croda's specialty chemicals production. Meanwhile, in the United States, the company's Croda Inc. subsidiary continued to boost the parent company's fortunes with its own successes. One of these was the launch of a men's hair dressing called Score, which helped establish the company as a leading provider of ingredients and products for the rapidly growing ethnic hair care sector.

Croda International lived up to its name as the company expanded worldwide, establishing subsidiaries and partnerships in Spain, Austria, Australia, Canada, South Africa, Mexico, New Zealand, and Zimbabwe. The company was also expanding in the United States, with the acquisition of the Bald Eagle Corporation, based in Pennsylvania, in 1965. In 1976, the company formed a joint venture, Croda-Carson, with the Carson Chemicals division of Quad Chemical Corp. and began producing ingredients for the laundry products market. After acquiring full control of the partnership in 1981, Croda changed that subsidiary's name to Croda Surfactants. In 1987, the company merged its four U.S. subsidiaries—Hummel Lanolin, Bald Eagle, Croda Surfactants, and Croda Inc.—into a single unit, Croda Inc. The company then shut down its Newark plant and moved much of its operations to a new site in Edison, New Jersey.

Croda remained largely unknown to the consumer market, despite its position as a leading supplier of ingredients to many of the world's largest cosmetics and other personal care and household products groups. In the mid-1980s, the company nonetheless achieved a degree of recognition as the developer of a fatty acid derived from rapeseed oil that proved successful in treating a rare disease, adrenoleukodystrophy. That product helped save the life of a young Italian boy. The story was turned into a successful film, and the Croda oil became known as "Lorenzo's Oil," after the name of the film. The company had also gained the attention of a competitor, which had launched a takeover attempt of Croda in the early 1980s. Yet Croda clung to its independence.

Key Dates:

Key Dates:

1925: George Crowe buys abandoned waterworks at Rawcliffe Bridge, creates Croda, and places nephew Philip Wood in charge of producing lanolin.

1930: National Physical Laboratory attributes rust-prevention properties to lanolin, opening new markets for Croda and rescuing the company from bankruptcy.

1949: Philip Wood dies; Croda's management is reformed under a management committee.

1950: Frederick Wood, son of Philip, is sent to New York to found company's U.S. subsidiary, Croda Inc.

1953: Wood is called back to United Kingdom to take over leadership of company.

1957: Croda Inc. acquires Hummel Lanolin and begins manufacturing in newly built Newark facility.

1964: Croda goes public on the London Stock Exchange and begins aggressive expansion drive.

1965: Croda Inc. acquires Bald Eagle Corporation in Pennsylvania.

1968: Croda acquires British Glues & Chemicals, which also gives it operations in Canada.

1976: Croda Inc. begins Croda-Carson joint venture with Carson Chemicals.

1981: Croda takes over full control of Croda-Carson, which is renamed Croda Surfactants.

1987: Croda Surfactants, Hummel Lanolin, and Bald Eagle are merged into Croda Inc.

1988: Croda acquires John Kerr & Co. and enters production of fire extinguisher chemicals.

1997: Croda acquires Sederma of France, a maker of ceramides for cosmetics and skincare applications.

1998: The company begins restructuring to focus on core oleo-chemicals market; sells off its paints, dyes, and soap operations; and acquires Westbrook Lanolin, a maker of medical-grade lanolin-based products.

2000: Croda continues its reorientation with the sale of adhesives business to Sovereign Specialty Chemicals Inc.

2001: Croda sells off its resins operations to Cray Valley Ltd. and plans a full exit from its industrial chemicals business.

Oleo-Chemicals Specialist in the 21st Century

Despite its brief bout of consumer popularity, Croda remained focused on serving its corporate customers. Croda also retained an interest in new product categories. In 1988, the company added a new line of products when it acquired John Kerr & Co. Based in Manchester, England, the Kerr company was founded in 1905 as a supplier of fire extinguisher products before becoming, in the 1930s, a producer of fire extinguishing foams and liquids.

In the 1990s, the company's business was organized into three primary divisions, those of Oleo-chemicals, Industrial Chemicals, and Coatings. During the early 1990s, the company focused on expanding its coatings business, making a number of acquisitions that also brought it into the manufacture of ingredients for paints. Yet by the late 1990s, Croda decided to streamline its business. The rapid consolidation of the worldwide chemicals industry—which saw the creation of a number of massive, globally operating companies—was making it more and more difficult for the company to compete in a number of its markets.

At the end of the decade, Croda restructured its operations to focus on two core components, Oleo-Chemicals and Industrial Chemicals. The company moved to sell off much of its newly non-core operations, including its soap manufacturing wing and its paints and dyes operations. By the year 2000, Croda was prepared to go still further in its restructuring. The company now decided to concentrate entirely on its high-margin oleo-chemicals division and begin exiting from its industrial chemicals production. This process was begun with the sale of its entire adhesives business to Sovereign Specialty Chemicals Inc., based in the United States. In February 2001, the company unloaded its resins operations to Cray Valley Ltd. The company expected to sell off its remaining industrial holdings in the early years of the new century.

The company's focus on oleo-chemicals was at the same time strengthened by a number of acquisitions, including the 1998 purchase of Westbrook Lanolin, based in the United Kingdom, which specialized in developing lanolin-based products for the medical market. Croda's presence in the healthcare market was further enhanced by the development of natural oil-based treatments for such conditions as varicose veins and asthma. Meanwhile, Croda's beauty products and cosmetics activities were given a boost by its 1997 purchase of France's Sederma. That company had become an important ingredients supplier through its development of ceramides—complex lipid molecules designed to adhere to the skin and provide waterproofing and moisture-loss protection. Croda also entered the fast-growing dietary supplements field, using its capacity to produce highly purified ingredients. Croda had successfully made the transition to the world's leading independent specialty oleo-chemicals group. Yet, as the company competed in a market increasingly dominated by global mega-corporations, some observers began to question just how long into the new century Croda will be able to maintain its independence.

Principal Subsidiaries

Croda Chemicals Ltd; Croda Colloids Ltd; Croda Food Services Ltd; Croda Universal Ltd; Westbrook Lanolin Company; Croda Argentina SA; Croda Surfactants (Australia); Croda do Brasil Ltda (Brazil); Croda Canada Ltd; Croda spol s.r.o. (Czech Republic); Croda Food Services Ltd (Ireland); Croda France SA; Sederma SA (France); Crodarom SA; Croda GmbH (Germany); Croda Hong Kong; Croda Magyaroszág Kft (Hungary); Croda Chemicals (Pvt) Ltd (India); Croda Italiana SpA (Italy); Croda Japan KK; Croda Mexico SA de CV; Croda Poland Sp z o o; Croda Singapore Pte Ltd; Croda Chemicals (SA) Pty Ltd (South Africa); Croda Korea (South Korea); Croda Oleochemicals Ibérica SA (Spain); Croda Nordica AB (Sweden); Croda Inc (U.S.A.); Croda Universal Inc (U.S.A.); Croda Zimbabwe (Pvt) Ltd; Croda Chemicals International Ltd; Croda Cosmetics & Toiletries Ltd; Croda Overseas Holdings Ltd; Croda World Traders Ltd; Croda Investments BV Industrial Chemicals (Netherlands); Croda Application Chemicals Ltd;

Baxenden Chemicals Ltd; Croda Distillates Ltd; Croda Fire Fighting Chemicals Ltd; John L Seaton & Co Ltd; Celtite Pty Ltd (Australia); Croda Uniser SA (France).

Principal Competitors

ATOFINA; BASF Aktiengesellschaft; Ciba Specialty Chemicals Holding Inc.; Clariant Ltd; The Dow Chemical Company; E.I. du Pont de Nemours and Company; Henkel KGaA; Hercules Incorporated; Imperial Chemical Industries PLC; Mitsubishi Chemical Corporation; Rhodia SA; Sumitomo Chemical Company, Limited; Union Carbide Corporation.

Further Reading

Brown, Jessica, "Croda Gears up in Oleo-Chemicals," *Chemical Week*, September 6, 2000, p. 34.
"Croda's Core Will Oil Wheels of Success," *Birmingham Post*, August 3, 2001, p. 21.
Firn, David, "Croda Manages to Cushion Fall in Tough Market," *Financial Times*, August 2, 2001.
——, "Croda May Herald Consumer Slowing," *Financial Times*, October 31, 2001.
Guerrera, Francesco, "Croda to Cut Costs As Profits Fall," *Independent*, March 24, 1999, p. 21.

—M.L. Cohen

Crown Media Holdings, Inc.

6430 S. Fiddlers Green Circle, Suite 500
Greenwood Village, Colorado 80111
U.S.A.
Telephone: (303) 220-7990
Toll Free: (800) 820-7990
Fax: (303) 220-7660
Web site: http://www.crownmedia.net

Public Subsidiary of Hallmark Entertainment, Inc.
Incorporated: 1991 as Crown Media Inc.
Employees: 420
Sales: $66.8 million (2000)
Stock Exchanges: NASDAQ
Ticker Symbol: CRWN
NAIC: 512120 Motion Picture and Video Distribution;
   513210 Cable Networks; 513220 Cable and Other
   Program Distribution

Crown Media Holdings, Inc. operates the Hallmark Channel, a pay television network available over cable or satellite in the United States and more than 100 international markets. The company is a public subsidiary of Hallmark Entertainment, Inc., which in turn is a subsidiary of Hallmark Cards, Inc. Internationally, the Hallmark brand has been associated with pay television services since 1995. In the United States, the Hallmark Channel was launched in 2001.

1991–94: Acquiring and Operating Cable TV Systems

Crown Media Inc. was established in 1991 by Hallmark Cards Inc. to acquire cable television systems and programming ventures. The company was 98 percent owned by Hallmark, with Crown Chairman and CEO James Hoak owning the remaining 2 percent. Hoak was a veteran of the cable TV industry and the former chairman of MSO Heritage Communications.

Crown's initial objective was to establish three geographic cable system clusters with a total of 500,000 subscribers by the end of 1994. The Dallas-based company's first purchase involved ten cable systems owned by Jones Crown Partners, a partnership between Jones Intercable and Hallmark Cards that was established in 1989. Also included in the acquisition was one system owned by Jones Intercable. Altogether, the newly acquired cable systems had about 140,000 subscribers and were small-market systems located in Wisconsin.

Before the end of 1991, Crown Media acquired St. Louis-based Cencom Cable Associates Inc. Cencom controlled cable systems serving about 550,000 subscribers. Cencom managed systems serving 390,000 of those subscribers and owned and operated systems serving 160,000 of those subscribers. Following the acquisition of Cencom, Crown Media was one of the top 20 multi-system operators (MSO) in the United States.

When Crown Media planned to move Cencom's headquarters from St. Louis to Dallas, Cencom's top executives—including president and CEO Howard Woods, COO Barry Babcock, and CFO Jerry Kent—broke away to form a new cable company, Charter Communications, Inc., in January 1993. In 1998, Charter Communications was acquired by Microsoft co-founder Paul Allen for $4.5 billion.

Toward the end of 1993, Hallmark Cards hired investment banker Goldman, Sachs to evaluate Crown Media, which had grown to 800,000 subscribers. In June 1994, Hallmark Cards broke up Crown Media and sold its cable systems to Charter Communications and Marcus Cable for $900 million.

1994–2000: Hallmark's Pay Television Channels Evolving into Crown Media Holdings

The sale of Crown Media's cable systems marked a change in direction for Hallmark Cards' cable strategy from a multi-system operator to a content provider and developer of pay television channels. In 1994, Hallmark Cards acquired RHI Entertainment, Inc., for $365 million. RHI was a leading producer of long-form television programming, including made-for-television movies and miniseries. RHI and Hallmark had been frequent television production partners in the past, and together they had co-produced five Hallmark Hall of Fame television specials. Other well-known RHI productions included *Lonesome Dove, Scarlett,* and *Gypsy.* In addition, RHI owned a film library of more than 1,800 hours of programming, including *Laurel & Hardy* and *The Little Rascals.*

Company Perspectives:

Crown Media Holdings, Inc. owns and operates pay television channels dedicated to high quality, broad appeal, entertainment programming. The company currently operates and distributes the Hallmark Channel in the U.S. and the Hallmark Channel in more than 100 international markets. The combined channels have more than 73 million subscribers worldwide.

Our channels benefit from a long-term program agreement with a subsidiary of Hallmark Entertainment, Inc., our parent company. These program agreements generally provide exclusive pay television access to Hallmark Entertainment, Inc.'s first-run presentations and extensive library of original made-for-television movies and miniseries. Hallmark Entertainment, Inc.'s library consists of more than 4,000 hours of programming, including eight of the 10 most highly rated made-for-television movies for the 1993 through 1999 television seasons, based on A.C. Nielsen ratings. Programs contained in the library have won more than 110 Emmy Awards, Golden Globe Awards, and Peabody Awards.

Following the acquisition of RHI Entertainment, Hallmark Cards formed Hallmark Entertainment, Inc. in 1994 as a private subsidiary and parent company of RHI Entertainment. In mid-1995 Hallmark Entertainment expanded its business into pay television by forming Hallmark Entertainment Network, Inc. and launching its first pay television channel, the Hallmark Entertainment Network, in Belgium, the Netherlands, and Luxembourg. The Hallmark Entertainment Network held off from launching a domestic pay channel because of a lack of carriage space and because the domestic rights for much of its programming was held by others.

In May 1998, Hallmark Entertainment and The Jim Henson Company formed a partnership for the purpose of launching The Kermit Channel in Asia and Latin America in September 1998. Distribution for the 24-hour pay television channel would be handled by the Hallmark Entertainment Network, which had about six million subscribers worldwide. Programming on Kermit consisted of *The Muppet Show* and other children's programs.

In November 1998, Hallmark Entertainment expanded its family entertainment business when it acquired a 22.5 percent interest in Odyssey Holdings, operator of the Odyssey Network. The Odyssey Network was established as the Vision Interfaith Satellite Network in 1988 by the National Interfaith Cable Coalition, a consortium of religious groups. Margaret Loesch, former worldwide vice-chairman of Fox Kids Network, was hired in 1998 to transform Odyssey into a family-oriented network. In April 1999, Hallmark Entertainment relaunched the Odyssey Network as ''the first network for today's family.''

2000: Crown Media Holdings Created

Crown Media Holdings was created in 2000 by Hallmark Entertainment for the purpose of going public and reorganizing the company's ownership structure. Crown Media Holdings was created as a subsidiary of Hallmark Entertainment. As part of the reorganization and Crown Media's initial public offering (IPO), Crown Media became the parent company of the Hallmark Entertainment Network and gained a 77.5 percent interest in the Odyssey Network. It did so when Hallmark Entertainment, Chase Equity Associates, Liberty Media, and the National Interfaith Cable Coalition transferred their interests in entities that owned and operated the Hallmark Entertainment Network and the Odyssey Network to Crown Media Holdings in exchange for its shares.

At the time of its IPO, Crown Media had more than 50 million subscribers worldwide. It operated two international networks: the international Hallmark Entertainment Network and The Kermit Channel, and it was part owner of the Odyssey Network. Due to conditions in the U.S. stock market, Crown Media delayed its IPO from April to May 2000 and reduced the number of shares offered from 12.5 million to ten million. The offering price was $14 a share, and the IPO raised about $140 million.

Following Crown Media's IPO, Hallmark Entertainment retained control of the company through its ownership of all of Crown Media's Class B shares, which were worth ten votes each. Robert Halmi, Jr., the president and CEO of Hallmark Entertainment, became chairman of Crown Media. He joined Hallmark Entertainment when it acquired RHI Entertainment, where he was the president and CEO. David Evans, who joined Hallmark Entertainment in 1999 to help take what became Crown Media Holdings public, was named president and CEO of Crown Media Holdings.

At the time of its IPO, Crown Media had yet to turn a profit, and its prospectus warned that there were no guarantees that Crown Media would achieve or sustain profitability. Crown Media (as Hallmark Entertainment Network, Inc.) lost $35.5 million in 1998 on revenue of $23.7 million, and in 1999 it lost $56.7 million on revenue of $31.9 million.

As part of Crown Media's reorganization of the Hallmark Entertainment Network, programming on The Kermit Channel in Asia was transferred in November 2000 to the Hallmark Network, where it would air for six hours a day. Most of The Kermit Channel's Asian audience lived in the Philippines. In addition, The Kermit Channel would continue to air in India, where it was distributed by Modi Entertainment Network.

2001: New Ventures and Acquisitions

At the beginning of 2001, Crown Media formed a new company, Crown Interactive, to make programming from its affiliated companies available to interactive television viewers. Crown Interactive's first test involved a video-on-demand service in Singapore, where customers could view movies from the Hallmark Entertainment library. The company planned to add an e-commerce site in the future.

In March 2001, Crown Media assumed full ownership of the Odyssey Network. It acquired the remaining 22.5 percent interest in Odyssey from German media company EM.TV & Merchandising, which gained the interest when it acquired The Jim Henson Company in February 2000. Crown Media exchanged 5.4 million shares, which represented an 8.2 percent interest in Crown Media, for the German firm's interest in the Odyssey Network.

Once Crown Media gained full control of the Odyssey Network, the company announced that the network would be renamed the Hallmark Channel in August 2001. At the time of the announcement in April, Odyssey reached 29.5 million homes. While Odyssey had gained virtually no recognition among consumers, Hallmark was a well-known brand. To facilitate the rebirth of Odyssey as the Hallmark Network, Crown Media had to renegotiate its agreement with the National Interfaith Cable Coalition, which still retained the right to run 40 hours of weekly programming on Odyssey. As part of its new agreement with the religious consortium, Crown agreed to help the coalition create and distribute a religious digital cable network. In addition, the religious group agreed to cut back its programming to 14 hours a week—including a seven-hour block on Sunday morning—and make it less overtly church-related and more broadly spiritual. Later in the year Crown Media entered into a relationship with satellite TV operator DirecTV that expanded the Hallmark Channel's distribution to some 40 million subscribers.

Crown Media also planned other original programming for the Hallmark Channel. Projects announced for 2001–02 included two miniseries: *Johnson County War,* written by *Lonesome Dove* author Larry McMurtry, and *Stranded,* a four-hour family adventure inspired by the classic novel *Swiss Family Robinson. Scandal in Bohemia,* the third movie in a series of films based on the Sherlock Holmes short stories, was scheduled to be shown on the Hallmark Network. In addition, three series were in the works, including *Telling Stories with Tomie dePaola* from The Jim Henson Co., *The Neverending Story* based on Michael Ende's bestselling novel, and a high school drama.

In April 2001, Crown Media acquired 700 titles from the film library of Hallmark Entertainment Distribution, a wholly owned subsidiary of Hallmark Entertainment, Inc. The films would be shown on Crown Media's cable networks and could also be licensed to other distributors. In addition, Crown Media planned to use the titles as part of Crown Interactive. As a result of the transaction, which involved Crown Media assuming $220 million in debt and issuing more than 30 million shares of stock,

Hallmark Cards and Hallmark Entertainment would own about 65 percent of the outstanding common stock of Crown Media. The transaction, which required stockholder approval, was completed on October 1, 2001.

After reporting quarterly losses in the first half of 2001, Crown Media announced a new initiative and reorganization of its domestic and international operations in October. The company planned to capitalize on opportunities for operating efficiencies and to realize economies of scale with its global brand. The plan called for more regional input throughout the world, with greater sensitivity to regional and local distribution and programming issues. The company planned to further strengthen the global Hallmark Channel brand. Overall, Crown Media anticipated a 15 percent reduction in its global workforce as it sought to achieve greater efficiencies in its operations.

Principal Subsidiaries

Crown Media Distribution; Crown Media International; Crown Media United States; Crown Entertainment; H&H Programming—Asia.

Principal Competitors

A&E Television Networks; AOL Time Warner Inc.; Discovery Communications Inc.; Fox Entertainment Group, Inc.; USA Networks Inc.; Walt Disney Company; Viacom Inc.

Further Reading

Brown, Rich, "$900m for Hallmark Cable," *Broadcasting & Cable,* June 27, 1994, p. 7.

Butcher, Lola, "Crown Media's Plan to Be Big-Time in Communications Hits Full Swing," *Kansas City Business Journal,* September 27, 1991, p. 14.

——, "Crown Media Will Operate Just-Purchased TV Systems," *Kansas City Business Journal,* August 9, 1991, p. 10.

"Colorado Television Network Operator Buys 700 Film Titles," *Knight-Ridder/Tribune Business News,* April 14, 2001.

"Crown Media Forms Unit," *Denver Business Journal,* January 26, 2001, p. 6A.

"Crown Media Gains Control of Odyssey," *Multichannel News,* March 19, 2001, p. 2.

"Crown Media IPO Goes off at $14 Per," *Multichannel News,* May 8, 2000.

"Crown Media to Gain TV Shows, Movies from Hallmark Division," *Knight-Ridder/Tribune Business News,* July 20, 2001.

"DirecTV Will Carry Hallmark Channel," *Knight-Ridder/Tribune Business News,* August 22, 2001.

Farrell, Mike, "Odyssey Parent Heads Down IPO Path," *Multichannel News,* February 7, 2000, p. 40.

Galetto, Mike, "Henson, Hallmark Team up to Launch 'Kermit,'" *Multichannel News,* May 18, 1998, p. 40.

"Hallmark Cards Inc.," *Kansas City Business Journal,* July 5, 1991, p. 22.

"Hallmark Swallows Kermit in Crown Media Reshuffle," *Television Asia,* November 2000, p. 6.

Hicks, L. Wayne, "Pay-TV Company Expands, Plans IPO," *Denver Business Journal,* February 4, 2000, p. 12A.

Higgins, John, "Hoak Hot to Trot," *Multichannel News,* May 6, 1991, p. 36.

Higgins, John M., "Can Odyssey Inspire Cash?" *Broadcasting & Cable,* April 10, 2000, p. 116.

——, "Hallmark to Buy Cencom," *Multichannel News,* September 23, 1991, p. 1.

——, "Odyssey to Hallmark," *Broadcasting & Cable,* April 2, 2001, p. 16.

Hogan, Monica, "Hallmark Crowns Channel's Rebranding Plan," *Multichannel News,* July 16, 2001, p. 48.

——, "Hallmark Ponies up for DirecTV Carriage," *Multichannel News,* August 27, 2001, p. 3.

Reynolds, Mike, "Hallmark's Odyssey Takes New Tack," *Multichannel News,* April 2, 2001, p. 8.

Tobenkin, David, "Hallmark Buys RHI for $365 Million," *Broadcasting & Cable,* May 2, 1994, p. 30.

—David P. Bianco

CVS/pharmacy

CVS Corporation

One CVS Drive
Woonsocket, Rhode Island 02895
U.S.A.
Telephone: (401) 765-1500
Fax: (401) 766-2917
Web site: http://www.cvs.com

Public Company
Incorporated: 1922 as Melville Shoe Corporation
Employees: 99,000
Sales: $20.09 billion (2000)
Stock Exchanges: New York
Ticker Symbol: CVS
NAIC: 446110 Pharmacies and Drug Stores; 454110
    Electronic Shopping and Mail-Order Houses

Although it trails arch-rival Walgreen Co. in terms of overall revenues, CVS Corporation is the largest drugstore chain in the United States in terms of number of stores and number of prescriptions filled. CVS operates more than 4,100 stores in 27 states in the northeastern, mid-Atlantic, southeastern, and midwestern regions of the country and in the District of Columbia. These outlets carry either the CVS or CVS/pharmacy names and range in size from about 8,000 to 12,000 square feet; many of the newer freestanding locations include a drive-through pharmacy. Nearly 10 percent of all prescriptions filled in the United States are handled by CVS pharmacies. Supplementing the core retail pharmacy business of CVS are several other operations: a pharmacy benefit management business that provides services to managed care and other organizations; a specialty pharmacy unit that includes a mail-order pharmacy and a small chain of about 40 CVS ProCare retail pharmacies, which offer special services for patients with long-term health conditions, such as HIV/AIDS and multiple sclerosis, that require complex and expensive drug regimens; and an Internet pharmacy located on the Web at CVS.com.

The history of CVS is intertwined with that of Melville Corporation, whose own history dates back to the late 19th century but ends in 1996 when it changed its name to CVS

Corporation. For much of its life, Melville was known chiefly for its chain of discount footwear stores, Thom McAn. During the late 20th century, however, Melville acquired more than a dozen other retailing operations. Among these was the Consumer Value Stores (CVS) retail drug chain, which Melville acquired in 1969, six years after that chain was founded. Melville continued as a retailing conglomerate into the mid-1990s, when the company then decided to concentrate on its best-performing chain, CVS. The company divested the last of its non-drugstore chains in 1997.

Concentrating on Shoes from the Late 19th Century to the Early 1960s

Melville Corporation traces its roots back to 1892, when Frank Melville, a shoe jobber, took over the three stores owned by his employer, who had left town under a cloud of debt. Melville parlayed the three New York shops into a small but thriving chain. In 1909 he brought his son, John Ward Melville, into the family business. The younger Melville, who dropped the "John" and was known by "Ward," was named vice-president in 1916 and became the driving force behind much of the company's growth. He ran the corporation for nearly half a century and served as chairman of the board until the day he died in 1977 at the age of 90.

While serving in the army during World War I, Ward Melville struck up a profitable friendship with J. Franklin McElwain, a New Hampshire shoe manufacturer. Together they devised a method to mass-produce shoes and distribute them at low prices through a chain of stores, which they decided to name after a Scottish golfer, Thomas McCann, shortened to Thom McAn. They opened the first Thom McAn store in New York in 1922, offering a few simple styles of men's shoes at the fixed price of $3.99. That same year, Melville Shoe Corporation was incorporated.

Despite the lack of variety, the discounting scheme was an immediate success, and new stores were opened all over the Northeast. By 1927 when the Thom McAn chain had grown to more than 300 stores, demand outstripped the capacity of McElwain's Nashua, New Hampshire plant, which produced

20,000 pairs a day. Consequently, McElwain acquired a new plant in Worcester, Massachusetts.

Melville Shoe, like other businesses, suffered during the Great Depression. In 1932, for example, sales dropped more than 21 percent from 1931 levels, from $26.2 million to $20.5 million. Despite rumors of bankruptcy that circulated in 1933, Melville Shoe weathered the storm with careful management, prudent expansion, and financial innovation. Melville made a public stock offering in 1936, taking its place on the New York Stock Exchange. Throughout the 1930s, Melville continued to open more outlets. By 1939 Melville operated 650 Thom McAn stores and also marketed its products through its smaller John Ward and Frank Tod shoe store chains.

In 1939 Ward Melville moved to centralize and unify the entire production and marketing operation under one corporate head. He proposed that Melville merge with McElwain's manufacturing company, J.F. McElwain Company, which then produced about 11 million shoes annually for Melville. The stockholders of both companies approved the merger in December 1939. The following year, J. Franklin McElwain and Ward Melville participated in a ceremony to commemorate the production of their 100 millionth pair of shoes.

In 1940 as the economy started climbing out of the Depression, Melville posted sales topping $40 million for the first time. Sales continued to climb through the war years. The growth continued unabated until 1952, when total sales actually fell for the first time since the Depression. The decline from $92 million to $90 million signified the first inkling of a weakness in Melville's time-tested strategy of producing a few styles of relatively cheap shoes. In an expanding and competitive economy, diversity and specialization became increasingly necessary. Accordingly, Melville began to add more women's and children's shoes in an effort to diversify.

In 1952 Melville acquired Miles Shoes, a chain of 151 stores. With this acquisition, better results were realized immediately: sales for 1953 increased about 20 percent, topping $108 million. By 1955 Melville had grown to include 12 factories and 850 stores. The following year, Ward Melville, then 69, was named chairman of the board, although he retained his post of chief executive officer. Robert C. Erb assumed the post of president, which Melville had vacated.

As part of a sustained effort to increase market penetration, Melville created a new division in 1960. The new unit, Meldisco, was dedicated to leasing and supplying family shoe departments in self-service discount department stores. That

year, however, earnings declined slightly from the 1959 totals—to $6 million in profit on sales of $151 million. The trend continued in 1962, as sales climbed to $176 million while net income dropped to about $5 million.

In 1964 Francis C. Rooney, a vice-president, succeeded Robert Erb as president. Over the next two decades, Rooney oversaw tremendous growth at Melville that transformed the nature, breadth, and scope of Melville's operations. Between 1962 and 1967, sales jumped 50 percent and net profits tripled. By 1967 sales topped $260 million. At the end of the 1960s, Melville was the nation's largest shoe retailer, operating 1,400 Thom McAn, Miles, and Meldisco outlets. The growth also brought increasing differentiation and specialization, as Thom McAn turned into a suburban-based family chain, whereas Miles specialized in women's and girls' shoes.

Diversification of Melville in the Late 1960s and 1970s

In 1968 Melville made one of its most important moves of the decade, opening the first of its Chess King stores, a clothing chain geared toward fashion-conscious teens and youth. This was Melville's first venture into the fashion industry, but it was not to be its last. In 1968 Melville also acquired Foxwood, renamed Foxmoor, a 16-store apparel chain that catered to young women.

The following year brought even more expansion. Melville bought three companies: the Consumer Value Stores (CVS) chain of drug retail outlets; Mark Steven, Inc., a firm that distributed products to CVS; and Retail Store Management, Inc. The first Consumer Value Store opened in Lowell, Massachusetts, in 1963 as a discount health and beauty aid store in which customers bagged their own merchandise. It was founded by brothers Sid and Stanley Goldstein and Ralph Hoagland. The CVS name was first used in 1964, by which time the founders were running a 17-store chain. A key development came in 1968 when pharmacy departments began to be added to the CVS outlets, prompting the company's eventual emergence as a leading drugstore chain. At the time of its acquisition by Melville, the CVS chain consisted of 40 stores.

Buoyed by these acquisitions, Rooney boldly predicted in 1969 that Melville would attain total sales of $1 billion by 1975. By 1970 Melville, the fifth largest and most profitable U.S. shoemaker, operated 1,644 total retail outlets. In 1972 Melville was ranked as the 43rd largest retailing company in the United States, with sales of $512 million, and more than 15,000 employees.

Not satisfied with this accretion, Melville continued to expand. In 1972 Melville acquired Clinton Merchandising, Inc., which operated 80 Clinton Drug and Discount stores in the Midwest and Northeast, as well as Metro Pants Co. and Spotwood Apparel, Inc., both manufacturers of men's and boys' clothing. The Clinton stores were merged into the CVS chain. That year Melville left its longtime midtown Manhattan headquarters for a larger building in Westchester County, New York.

Melville's expansion took on an international character in the 1970s as well. In 1971 Melville entered into a joint venture with C.F. Bally of Switzerland, contracting to sell the upscale Bally shoe line in the United States. The same year, Melville

Key Dates:

1892: Frank Melville, a shoe jobber, takes over three stores owned by his employer.

1909: Melville's son, Ward Melville, joins the company and will eventually become the driving force behind much of the company's growth.

1922: Company opens the first Thom McAn shoe store; Melville Shoe Corporation, which will later be renamed Melville Corporation, is incorporated.

1936: Melville goes public, gaining a listing on the New York Stock Exchange.

1963: The first Consumer Value Store (CVS) opens in Lowell, Massachusetts, as a discount health and beauty aid store in which customers bag their own merchandise; founders are brothers Sid and Stanley Goldstein and Ralph Hoagland.

1964: The CVS name is used for the first time.

1968: Melville begins diversifying outside of shoes with the opening of the first Chess King clothing store; CVS outlets begin to add pharmacy departments, prompting CVS's development into a leading drugstore chain.

1969: Melville acquires the CVS chain.

1975: Melville acquires the Marshalls apparel store chain.

1981: Kay-Bee Toys chain is acquired by Melville.

1982: Linens 'n Things is added to the Melville roster.

1985: Stanley Goldstein is named president of Melville, becoming CEO and chairman the following year.

1990: Peoples Drug Stores, a 490-store chain, is acquired by Melville and is merged into the CVS chain during the early to mid-1990s.

1992: Restructuring of Melville, involving the closure of as many as 800 stores, is launched.

1993: The Chess King and Accessory Lady chains are sold off.

1994: CVS enters the pharmacy benefits management field with the creation of PharmaCare Management Services.

1995: Melville announces a sweeping overhaul, aimed at concentrating on the CVS chain; Marshalls is sold to TJX Co.

1996: Kay-Bee Toys, the Wilsons leather goods chain, and the This End Up furniture chain are sold off; FootAction and Meldisco are spun off into a new public company called Footstar, Inc.; the Thom McAn chain is folded; Melville moves its headquarters to that of CVS, in Woonsocket, Rhode Island; Melville Corporation changes its name to CVS Corporation; CVS completes an IPO of 67.5 percent of Linens 'n Things.

1997: The company acquires Revco D.S., Inc. and its more than 2,500 drugstores; CVS divests its remaining interest in Linens 'n Things and sells Bob's Stores to a management-led group, thereby jettisoning its last non-drugstore operations.

1998: CVS pays $1.48 billion for Arbor Drugs, Inc., a chain with more than 200 stores mainly in southeastern Michigan.

1999: Goldstein retires as chairman of CVS; Thomas M. Ryan succeeds him as chairman and CEO; Soma.com, the first major online pharmacy, is acquired and is rebranded CVS.com; CVS ProCare, a chain of specialty pharmacies, is launched to serve patients with chronic diseases and conditions.

2000: Stadtlander Pharmacy, a mail-order specialty pharmacy serving patients with chronic diseases, is acquired.

---

formed a European buying company. In 1973 Melville initiated a venture to market Thom McAn shoes in Japan.

Despite the diversification, shoes still accounted for 71 percent of Melville's $765 million in sales in 1974. That year, the CVS chain generated sales in excess of $100 million and had grown to include 232 units, although only 45 of the locations had pharmacies. In 1975 Melville branched out further into nonshoe retailing when it bought Marshalls Inc., then a chain of 32 retail apparel stores. Expansion continued apace in 1977, when Melville bought the 36-unit Mack Drug Co. chain and merged it into the CVS unit.

In 1976 Melville, then the nation's 32nd largest retailing company, belatedly reached Rooney's vaunted goal of $1 billion in sales, due to the combination of acquiring new chains and expanding existing units. In 1976 total receipts from the firm's 3,300 outlets totaled $1.2 billion. As part of a continuing trend, the footwear sales portion declined to 60 percent.

Upon Ward Melville's death in June 1977, Francis Rooney, who already held the posts of president and chief executive officer, was named chairman of the board. The transition marked the end of an era and the beginning of a new one in which shoes would play an increasingly smaller role in the Melville scheme.

By 1978 Melville operated 3,812 stores and had sales of $1.75 billion. Shoes accounted for about 53 percent of the total.

Accelerating Diversification in the 1980s and Early 1990s

As the 1970s came to a close, Melville continued to boom. In 1980, Melville, with 48,000 employees and more than 4,500 stores, saw its 26th straight year of increased sales. CVS had grown to 408 locations, with sales totaling $414 million, making the chain one of the top ten drugstore chains in the United States. That year, Kenneth Berland was named to the post of president.

The following year, in which sales soared to $2.8 billion, Melville acquired Kay-Bee Toy and Hobby Shops Inc. By 1982 Melville, the largest U.S. shoe retailer, operated nearly 5,200 total stores. These included 470 Chess King, 588 Foxmoor, 433 CVS, and 1,200 Thom McAn outlets. In 1982 Melville added leather retailer Wilsons to its roster, and the following year it acquired home furnishings specialist Linens 'n Things, which had been founded in 1975.

Despite the recession of the early 1980s, sales rose to $3.3 billion in 1983; nevertheless, Melville suffered some retrenchment during the 1980s. The firm began to phase out six of its seven shoe factories in late 1983, eventually terminating about 2,000 jobs. In 1985 Melville sold the 614-store Foxmoor chain, whose sales were declining. The same year, Melville shut down 72 Thom McAn outlets. Despite the closures or sales of various stores, 1985 receipts rose to $4.7 billion, and profits surged to $219 million. CVS sales surpassed the $1 billion mark for the first time.

In 1985 Stanley Goldstein, the CVS cofounder who joined Melville when his corporation was acquired by the shoe giant, succeeded Berland as president and took his place as heir apparent. The following year, Goldstein was named chairman and chief executive officer, replacing the retiring Rooney. To Goldstein fell the task of building on Rooney's phenomenal record. Rooney had transformed the firm from a successful shoe company into a diversified retailing giant.

Melville's expansion continued under Goldstein. In 1987, while amassing $5.9 billion in sales, Melville acquired 25 Heartland and Pharmacity drugstores and 36 Leather Loft stores. In 1988 Melville bought athletic footwear retailer Finish Line as well as Bermans Specialty Stores.

In 1989 Melville underwent some structural renovation. The firm created a profit-sharing plan and an employee stock ownership plan, under which about 6 percent of the company's common stock was distributed among its employees.

The year 1989 brought to a close a remarkably successful decade, one in which sales and earnings both increased more than threefold. The Melville that left the 1980s was vastly different from the one that entered that decade. In 1989 shoes, once the firm's mainstay, accounted for only 22.5 percent of total sales; the apparel sections accounted for 36 percent; and the drugstore business accounted for 28 percent. The toys and household furnishing division accounted for the remainder of sales.

This trend continued in 1990, as Melville acquired more non-footwear retail outlets. Melville bought both Circus World Toy Stores Inc., which it folded into the Kay-Bee division, and Peoples Drug Stores, a 490-store chain. By the end of 1990, Melville operated 7,754 stores and listed 119,000 employees on its payroll. Sales for 1990 totaled $8.68 billion. Further expansion came in 1991, when Melville acquired FootAction Inc., a Dallas-based chain of 128 athletic footwear stores, for $46 million.

Mid-1990s: Retrenchment, Restructuring, Emergence of CVS Corporation

Retrenchment came to the fore in 1992 and 1993, however, as Melville struggled in a more difficult environment for retailers. In early 1992 CVS exited from the California market when it sold all 85 of its stores in that state to American Drug Stores Inc., a unit of American Stores Company, for $60 million. In December of that same year Melville announced a major restructuring involving the closure of up to 800 stores and a pretax charge of $347 million. About 390 of the 730 Thom McAn locations were subsequently shuttered, as were 240 of its 1,250 Kay-Bee stores and 75 smaller Linens 'n Things outlets. In addition, the 500-plus-unit Chess King chain was sold off in the spring of 1993 to Merry-Go-Round Enterprises Inc. and the 114-store Accessory Lady chain was sold to Woolworth Corporation in November 1993. Of the closed units, about 100 of

them were converted to faster growing formats, most notably, FootAction. With these series of moves, Melville was focusing more strongly on CVS and Marshalls, which together accounted for more than 60 percent of the company's sales and operating profit, as well as Kay-Bee Toys and the up-and-comers FootAction and Linens 'n Things.

Another development in the early to mid-1990s was the merger of Peoples Drug Stores into CVS, which thereby gained locations in Maryland, Pennsylvania, Virginia, West Virginia, and the District of Columbia. In 1994 Thomas M. Ryan, a pharmacist, was named CEO of CVS, which now had more than 1,350 locations. CVS was by far the largest of Melville's chains, with 1994 revenues of $4.3 billion, or 38 percent of Melville's overall revenues of $11.3 billion. During 1994 CVS entered the burgeoning market for pharmacy benefit management services by forming PharmaCare Management Services to serve managed care and other organizations.

With its financial performance faltering and shareholders increasingly agitating for change, Melville in October 1995 announced a sweeping restructuring through which it planned to spin or sell off several of its businesses to focus primarily on its most profitable unit, the CVS drugstore chain. Melville had already agreed to sell Marshalls, its second largest chain, to arch-rival TJX Cos., in a $600 million deal that closed in November 1995. Next to go, during the first half of 1996, were Kay-Bee Toys, which was sold to Consolidated Stores Corp. for about $315 million, and the Wilsons leather goods chain and the This End Up chain of furniture stores, both of which were sold off through management-led buyouts. Later in 1996, Melville spun off two of its footwear operations, the 444-unit FootAction chain and Meldisco, operator of leased shoe departments in nearly 2,200 Kmarts and almost 400 Payless Drug Stores, into a new public company called Footstar, Incorporated. The Thom McAn chain was closed down, after the conversion of about 100 of the stores to FootAction outlets.

In addition to CVS, Melville also had planned initially to retain the Linens 'n Things chain and Bob's Stores, a 34-unit chain selling off-price active apparel. In mid-1996, however, the company announced that it would shed those operations as well by the end of 1997. In September 1996 Melville moved its corporate headquarters from Rye, New York, to the headquarters of CVS in Woonsocket, Rhode Island. Two months later, Melville changed its name to CVS Corporation. Goldstein continued to serve as chairman and CEO, and Ryan was named vice-chairman and chief operating officer. Shortly after becoming CVS Corporation, the company completed an IPO in which it sold a 67.5 percent interest in Linens 'n Things to the public. CVS sold its remaining interest in Linens 'n Things during 1997.

Late 1990s and Beyond: Reaching for the Top Through Major Acquisitions

The newly focused CVS moved quickly to become one of the top players in the rapidly consolidating U.S. drugstore industry. In May 1997 CVS acquired Twinsburg, Ohio-based Revco D.S., Inc. for $2.8 billion in stock plus the assumption of $900 million of Revco debt. Revco had about 2,600 drugstores located in 17 midwestern, southeastern, and eastern states. To gain regulatory approval, CVS had to sell 120 Revco drugstores, mainly located in Virginia. As a result, CVS emerged from the deal with nearly 4,000 drugstores in 24 states and the District of Columbia, giving it the largest store count in the industry. In terms of revenues, however, it ranked number two behind Walgreen Co. CVS, in the meantime, sold the last of its non-drugstore units in November 1997 when it sold Bob's Stores to a management-led group.

In early 1998 Ryan was named president and CEO of CVS, with Goldstein remaining chairman. The company completed yet another significant—albeit much smaller—acquisition in March 1998, a $1.48 billion deal for Troy, Michigan-based Arbor Drugs, Inc. Operating primarily in southeastern Michigan, Arbor had more than 200 stores and nearly $1 billion in revenue during fiscal 1997. The addition of Arbor increased CVS's store count to nearly 4,100 and also made CVS the country's largest dispenser of prescription drugs as it now filled more than 11 percent of all prescriptions. CVS still trailed Walgreen in revenue, but its 1998 sales of $15.27 billion were nearly three times the level of 1996.

In addition to pursuing acquisitions, CVS also was growing organically by aggressively opening new locations. In 1998, for example, the company announced plans to open as many as 200 stores in New York City over a three-year period. At the same time, some of the older locations, particularly those in strip malls, were being closed down in favor of freestanding sites, some of which began featuring drive-through pharmacies.

An end of another era occurred in April 1999 when Goldstein retired as chairman of CVS, 36 years after cofounding the first Consumer Value Store. Ryan was named chairman and CEO. Later in 1999 CVS acquired Soma.com, the first major online pharmacy, for $30 million in stock. The web site, soon rebranded CVS.com, enabled customers to order prescriptions and general merchandise for either in-store pickup or mail delivery. Another initiative in 1999 was the launching of CVS ProCare, a chain of specialty pharmacies, about 1,500 square feet in size, serving patients with chronic diseases and conditions that require complex and expensive drug regimens. The market for specialty pharmaceuticals, estimated at about $16 billion in 1999, was a particularly fast-growing segment of the drug industry, but it was highly fragmented, consisting mostly of mom-and-pop operations. CVS clearly saw the potential for being a consolidator in this segment of the market. Its first such acquisition came in September 2000 with the purchase of Stadtlander Pharmacy, a Pittsburgh-based subsidiary of Bergen Brunswig Corporation, for $124 million. Stadtlander generated annual revenues of $500 million by selling drugs by mail-order to patients with chronic conditions. By the end of 2000, CVS's specialty pharmacy business consisted of mail-order operations and 46 CVS ProCare pharmacies located in 17 states and the District of Columbia. Overall, CVS saw its revenues surpass the $20 billion mark for the first time in 2000, while net income reached a record $746 million.

After entering four new markets in 2000—Chicago; Tampa and Orlando, Florida; and Grand Rapids, Michigan—CVS continued to enter new territories in 2001, expanding into Fort Lauderdale, Florida, and Las Vegas, Nevada. The latter would represent the chain's first presence west of the Mississippi since selling its California stores in 1992. CVS also announced in 2001 plans to expand into Phoenix, Arizona; Miami Beach, Florida; and three new markets in Texas: Dallas, Houston, and Fort Worth. In February 2001 CVS launched a chainwide loyalty card program called ExtraCare that would offer cardholders exclusive savings, mailings, and health information. The company's fortunes turned south later in the year, however, as profits began to decline. Management cited a lack of new prescription drug introductions, the growth of mail-order prescription services, and increasing competition. CVS had also had difficulty filling positions for pharmacists and been forced to shut down some pharmacy counters as a result. Furthermore, the general economic slowdown had taken a toll on sales of general merchandise. In October a major restructuring was launched, involving the elimination of 300 jobs, the closure of 200 underperforming stores (including ten CVS ProCare units), and a $350 million charge. It was difficult to foresee whether these events were a momentary blip in a record of consistently positive performance for CVS since its emergence out of Melville in 1996 or the beginning of a deeper crisis.

Principal Subsidiaries

CVS Rhode Island, Inc.; CVS Center, Inc.; CVS Foreign, Inc.; CVS Pharmacy, Inc.; Nashua Hollis CVS, Inc.; CVS Vanguard, Inc.; CVS Meridian, Inc.; CVS New York, Inc.; CVS Revco D.S., Inc.; Revco Discount Drug Centers, Inc.; Hook-SupeRx, Inc.; Big B, Inc.; Arbor Drugs, Inc.; PharmaCare Management Services, Inc.; ProCare Pharmacy, Inc. (95%); CVS Washington, Inc.; CVS Rx Services, Inc.

Principal Competitors

Walgreen Co.; Wal-Mart Stores, Inc.; Rite Aid Corporation; Eckerd Corporation; The Kroger Co.; Albertson's, Inc.

Further Reading

Arditi, Lynn, "CVS Prescribes $30-Million Internet Dosage," *Providence Journal,* May 18, 1999, p. E1.

——, "CVS to Take Over Midwestern Chain," *Providence Journal-Bulletin,* February 10, 1998, p. A1.

Auerbach, Jon G., "CVS Unit Chief Ryan Says Purchase of Revco Enhances Managed-Care Ties," *Wall Street Journal,* February 10, 1997, p. B8.

Barmash, Isadore, "Retailing: The Special Case of Melville Corp.," *New York Times,* April 4, 1982.

Berner, Robert, "CVS: Will Its Growth Elixir Work?," *Business Week,* July 9, 2001, pp. 50, 53.

——, "Merck, CVS Agree to Link Internet Sites," *Wall Street Journal,* October 6, 1999, p. A3.

Bird, Laura, "Melville Is Jarred by Shot Across the Bow from Calpers," *Wall Street Journal,* February 16, 1995, p. B4.

——, "Melville Plans Spinoffs, Sales of Businesses: Firm, Pressed by Holders, to Focus on Drugstores After Split into Three," *Wall Street Journal,* October 25, 1995, p. A3.

——, "Melville to Close Thom McAn Shoe Chain in Effort to Focus on CVS Drugstores," *Wall Street Journal,* June 4, 1996, p. B9.

Bulkeley, William M., "CVS to Buy Arbor Drugs for $1.48 Billion," *Wall Street Journal,* February 10, 1998, p. A3.

Chakravarty, Subrata N., "Reshaping the Last," *Forbes,* September 17, 1990.

Fasig, Lisa Biank, "CVS: Falling Profits Lead Drugstore Chain to Close 200 Stores," *Providence Journal,* October 31, 2001, p. E1.

Fleming, Harris, Jr., "For Better," *Drug Topics,* March 2, 1998, pp. 104, 106.

"Grooving Shoe Sales to a Young Market," *Business Week,* April 27, 1968.

Hackney, Holt, "Melville Corp.: Portrait of a False Bargain," *Financial World,* November 23, 1993, p. 21.

Hechinger, John, "CVS to Shut 200 Stores, Trim 300 Jobs," *Wall Street Journal,* October 31, 2001, p. B9.

Henderson, Barry, "Drugstore Cowboys?: Riding the Accounting Bronco at CVS," *Barron's,* June 5, 2000, pp. 19, 21.

Johannes, Laura, "CVS Pushes Online Plans with Purchase of Soma.com for $30 Million in Stock," *Wall Street Journal,* May 18, 1999, p. B8.

Mammarella, James, "Melville De-Diversifies," *Discount Store News,* November 6, 1995, p. 1.

"Melville Steps into the Billion-Dollar Class," *Business Week,* April 11, 1977.

Muirhead, Greg, "CVS-Revco Merger Will Create $13 Billion Chain," *Drug Topics,* February 17, 1997, p. 19.

Nelson, Emily, "Consolidated Stores to Buy KayBee Toys from Melville Corp. for $315 Million," *Wall Street Journal,* March 26, 1996, p. A4.

Philippidis, Alex, "Melville Looks to Improve Performance," *Westchester County Business Journal,* April 17, 1995, p. 1.

——, "Splits-ville for Melville and City It Called Home," *Westchester County Business Journal,* April 29, 1996, p. 1.

Pressler, Margaret Webb, "Chain's Expansion Gives Headaches to Rivals, Critics," *Washington Post,* February 3, 1998, p. D1.

Rooney, Francis C., *Creative Merchandising in an Era of Change,* New York: Newcomen Society in North America, 1970.

Rudnitsky, Howard, "Fancy Footwork," *Forbes,* March 29, 1982.

Rundle, Rhonda L., "CVS to Buy Most of Bergen Unit for $124 Million," *Wall Street Journal,* July 6, 2000, p. B12.

Sloane, Leonard, "Ward Melville, 90s Shoe Magnate, Dies," *New York Times,* June 6, 1977.

Tooher, Nora Lockwood, "CVS: On Its Own Again," *Providence Sunday Journal,* June 23, 1996, p. F1.

——, "New Boy on the Big Board," *Providence Journal-Bulletin,* October 16, 1996, p. F1.

——, "New Prescription for Leadership at CVS Corp.," *Providence Journal,* April 15, 1999, p. F1.

Trachtenberg, Jeffrey A., "Melville Corp. Plans to Close Up to 800 Stores," *Wall Street Journal,* December 22, 1992, p. A2.

—Daniel Gross
—update: David E. Salamie

Davis Service Group PLC

4 Grosvenor Place
London SW1X 7DL
United Kingdom
Telephone: (+44) 20-7259-6663
Fax: (+44) 20-7259-6948
Web site: http://www.dsgplc.co.uk

Public Company
Incorporated: 1987
Employees: 12,063
Sales: £470.94 million ($703.3 million) (2000)
Stock Exchanges: London
Ticker Symbol: DVSG
NAIC: 812320 Drycleaning and Laundry Services
(Except Coin-Operated); 812332 Industrial
Launderers; 812331 Linen Supply; 332311
Prefabricated Metal Building and Component
Manufacturing

London-based Davis Service Group PLC operates in three primary areas: Textile Maintenance, Tool Hire, and Building Systems. Each division is operated as a more or less autonomous business, with its own board of directors and management, while Davis Service Group, led by Chairman Neil Benson and CEO John Ivey, provides overall direction. Textile Maintenance is the company's largest division, generating half of the company's £470 million in 2000 sales. The division is primarily active in the United Kingdom under operating company Sunlight Services Group, but also has operations in Ireland, Germany (Spring Grove Services), and in France (Modeluxe Linge Services). Sunlight Services is the United Kingdom's leading provider of textile and uniform rental and cleaning services and is also the historical core of Davis Service Group. The company's fast-growing Tool Hire business, HSS Hire Service Group PLC, operates a string of some 400 tool hire shops across the United Kingdom. The company is also active in the United States, with a chain of HSS stores in Florida. In 2001, HSS acquired Denver-based RentX, giving it 74 new stores in 13 states. Davis's Tool Hire division, which also operates hire services for catering and event equipment and materials handling equipment, contributes 29 percent of the com-

pany's annual sales. Davis's third division, Building Systems, is active under the name Elliot Group and specializes in prefabricated and modular temporary building rentals and sales for the construction and other industries. This division is also in the process of developing prefabricated housing products for the residential market. Davis Service Group has grown strongly through both organic growth and a series of targeted acquisitions.

Reversing into Services in 1987

Davis Service Group traces its origins through its primary operating companies. The company's textile maintenance division stemmed from Sunlight Services, itself founded in 1900 as a laundry service. Over the course of the century, Sunlight Services developed into a leading provider of textile maintenance and rental services, with an emphasis on uniforms for the hospitality, medical, police and fire services, and other industries. John Ivey was appointed as company CEO and executive deputy chairman in 1973 and began plotting to build Sunlight into one of the United Kingdom's leading services companies. The company expanded beyond cleaning services, adding security services under subsidiary Security Arrangements Group and commercial cleaning services under the Pall Mall Group.

In 1987, Sunlight Services agreed to be acquired for £8 million by publicly listed automobile dealership and rental group Godfrey Davis (Holdings) PLC. That company had been formed in 1920 and had built up a small but highly successful network of luxury automobile dealerships. After going public in 1959, Davis rose to become one of the United Kingdom's leading car dealership and rentals groups. The company also entered into the property market, specializing in the ownership and management of residential park homes under its Godfrey Davis Park Homes subsidiary. Related to this business was the company's Godfrey Davis Portable Buildings subsidiary, which specialized in the rental and sale of portable building structures. In 1981, Davis sold off its automotive rental operations to Europcar, leaving it with its four car dealerships, vehicle leasing business, portable buildings group, and property management activity.

The merger with Sunlight in 1987 turned out to be more of a reverse takeover—Ivey took over the role of CEO and most of the new Godfrey Davis company's executive management and

---

Company Perspectives:

The Future: The Davis Service Group seeks to develop and expand the range of products and services provided through a combination of organic and acquisitive growth. This strategy has resulted in the individual group companies having leading positions in their individual markets—primarily in the UK but with an expanding international presence.

---

board came from Sunlight. Yet Godfrey Davis provided its name as well as its listing on the London stock exchange, enabling Ivey to raise funds to begin building his services empire.

The Godfrey Davis Park Homes subsidiary was sold off a year after the merger. At the same time, the company made the first of a series of carefully targeted acquisitions, buying up Newbury Laundry Company Limited and expanding its textile maintenance business into the Thames Valley region.

Godfrey Davis, as the company continued to be called, next sold off Sunlight's security subsidiary, exiting that highly competitive market. Instead, the company acquired Falcon Industries, paying £44 million in September 1998. That company was itself composed of three separate businesses, Plantpak and Glenco, both of which were plastics manufacturers, and the Elliot Group. The latter company, originally founded in 1963, had grown into an important designer, manufacturer, and provider of portable and modular building systems. Elliot then absorbed Godfrey Davis Portable Buildings and became the umbrella company for all of the parent company's building systems operations.

In April 1989, Davis sold off the plastics division of the former Falcon Industries as the company narrowed its focus to the services sector. At the same time, the company, through its Pall Mall subsidiary, acquired Tappe Catering Limited. That company was a catering specialist for the Ministry of Defence.

Sunlight Services was boosted in 1989 with the £5.6 million acquisition of Practical Uniform Company, which designed and manufactured uniforms and industrial and protective clothing and equipment. Several months later, the division was boosted again with the purchase of Co-operative Laundry Society. At a price of £11.35 million, the acquisition extended the company's textile maintenance operations into the northeast of England.

In 1991, Godfrey Davis sold off three of its car dealerships (it disposed of the last of its dealerships two years later) in order to concentrate entirely on its growing operations in the services sector. The sale of this business prompted the company to take on a new name, The Davis Service Group. The following year, Davis Service sold off its Godfrey Davis vehicle leasing operation, to the Bank of Scotland, which kept the Godfrey Davis name.

By then, the company had made a new acquisition, of Presco (Holdings) Ltd, which specialized in the manufacture, sale, and rental of portable steel-clad and modular building structures. Presco's operations were added to the Elliot Group in 1991.

A larger acquisition came in May 1993, when Davis acquired the tool hire business of John Mowlem for a price of £53

million. This purchase brought the company into a new area of operation, that of tool hire and equipment rentals, which was renamed as HSS Hire Service Group PLC. HSS, founded in 1957, had been the originator of the tool rental shop in England and, through the end of the century, established a network of more than 400 shops across England featuring a growing array of tools and small plant equipment. HSS began renting catering equipment in 1968, which led the company to form a separate subsidiary for its event hire business in 1980. A more recent addition had been the launch of another subsidiary, dubbed Lift & Shift, which was formed in 1989 to specialize in materials handling equipment rentals.

Focus on Services Group: The New Millennium

Although HSS's growth was in large part organic through the 1990s, its textile maintenance counterpart began the subject of a strong acquisition program. In 1994, Davis acquired Lakeland Pennine Group, primarily active in the northwest of England. The company then moved to focus its textiles business entirely on the cleaning and maintenance site, selling off Practical Uniform Company in 1995.

Less than a year later, Davis became the undisputed leader in the United Kingdom's textile services sector when it paid £136 million to acquire Granada subsidiary Spring Grove Services Limited. That company, which specialized in work clothes for the food and pharmaceuticals industries, but also contained a component for renting washroom towels and doormats, had been founded at the end of World War II and had grown to become one of the top companies in the United Kingdom, with operations in Ireland and Germany as well. Spring Grove had seen a succession of owners at the end of the 1980s and beginning of the 1990s before being acquired by Granada in 1993.

In 1997, Davis narrowed its focus to just three core divisions: Textile Maintenance, Tool Hire, and Building Systems. As part of this restructuring, the company sold off its Pall Mall subsidiary. That company was split into two halves, with the first half, containing its public sector catering and cleaning services, sold in June 1997 to Granada's Sutcliffe for £8.4 million. At the end of that year, the second half of the company was taken over in a management buyout worth more than £8.3 million.

Davis continued to add to its textile services wing as the decade neared an end. In 1998 it acquired Laundrycraft Ltd., which operated primarily in the midlands region of England. The following year, the company paid £30 million to acquire Midland Laundry Group. A specialist provider of linen rentals and laundry services to the healthcare sector, Midland brought Davis five new laundry facilities in the United Kingdom. At the end of the decade, the company made a new move to expand beyond its domestic market. In April 2000, the company acquired Blanchisserie Teinturerie de la Bièvre, which provided textile maintenance services in the Paris area and became part of the company's French subsidiary, Modeluxe Linge Services.

Elliot Group also had been showing strong growth. In 1999, the division added Strumech Engineering Ltd., which gave the company a range of products to support the telecommunications industry, particularly the mobile telephone market. The acquisi-

Key Dates:

1900: Laundry company Sunlight Services is founded.
1920: Godfrey Davis begins car dealership; becomes a prominent automotive rental and leasing company.
1957: A tool hire shop is launched, which later becomes HSS Tool Hire.
1959: Godfrey Davis lists on the London stock exchange, then enters portable building sales and rentals.
1963: Elliot Group is founded, which later becomes part of Falcon Industries.
1968: HSS begins catering equipment rentals.
1973: John Ivey is named CEO of Sunlight.
1981: Godfrey Davis sells off automotive rental business.
1987: Godfrey Davis acquires Sunlight Services for £8 million.
1988: The company acquires Newbury Laundry Company; sells off Sunlight's security services division; acquires Falcon Industries, including Elliot Group.
1989: The company acquires Practical Uniform Company and Cooperative Laundries Society Ltd.
1991: Three of four Godfrey Davis car dealerships are sold off; the company is renamed as Davis Service Group; acquires Presco (Holdings) Ltd.
1992: The company sells off Godfrey Davis Contract Hire to Bank of Scotland.
1993: The company acquires HSS Hire Service Group PLC and enters tool hire market.
1994: The company acquires Lakeland Pennine Group Ltd.
1995: The sale of Practical Uniform Company is completed.
1996: The company acquires Spring Grove Services from Granada, which also includes operations in Ireland and Germany; HSS launches first test store in Florida, HSS Rental Stores.
1998: The company acquires Laundrycraft Limited.
1999: The company acquires Strumech Engineering Holding and Midland Laundry Group.
2000: The company establishes operations in France with the acquisition of Blanchisserie Teinturerie de la Bièvres; acquires Redispace & Johnson from Initial Plant Services Ltd.
2001: The company pays $46 million for 74-store chain RentX Industries, based in the United States.

tion the following year of Redispace & Johnson, which had been the portable building division of Initial Plant Services, cost the company £21 million and doubled the size of Elliot's build-ing hire operations. At the same time, Elliot was preparing to branch out into the residential market, designing its own range of prefabricated homes.

HSS, meanwhile, had begun testing the waters of the huge and as yet highly fragmented U.S. market, opening its first U.S. shop, called HSS Rental Stores, in Florida in 1996. After testing the viability of its HSS Tool Hire concept, the company began a rollout of the network across the state of Florida. The company then began looking for opportunities to expand further in the United States and, in July 2001, acquired Denver-based RentX Industries Inc. That company had built up a network of 74 tool rental stores operating in 13 states. For a price of $46 million, the RentX acquisition gave the company an instant position as a major player in the U.S. tool rental market. The company then began adapting its new store network to its HSS concept, while launching a $25 million investment program for its new subsidiary.

In little more than a decade, John Ivey had guided Davis Service into the top ranks of the United Kingdom's services sector. The company also had made the beginnings of a possible international expansion—prompting some analysts to propose that the company might narrow its focus still further, possibly jettisoning its Elliot Group component, in order to concentrate on the international development of its fast-growing textile maintenance and tool hire businesses.

Principal Subsidiaries

HSS Hire Service Group PLC; The Sunlight Services Group Limited; Spring Grove Services (Ireland) Limited; Spring Grove Services GmbH (Germany); Modeluxe Linge Services SA (France); Elliott Group Limited.

Principal Competitors

Algeco SA; ARAMARK Corporation; ATCO Structures Ltd.; Ecolab Inc.; Hewden Stuart Plc; ISS-International Service System A/S; Rentokil Initial plc; The ServiceMaster Company; Steiner Corporation.

Further Reading

Cave, Andrew, "Davis to Buy Granada Workwear Business," *Telegraph,* September 6, 1996.
"Davis Cleans Up," *Daily Telegraph,* September 12, 1997.
"Davis Service Buys RentX Industries," *Industry News,* August 2001.
Foley, Stephen, ed., "Davis Service," *Independent,* September 6, 2001, p. 21.

—M.L. Cohen

Delphi Automotive Systems Corporation

5725 Delphi Drive
Troy, Michigan 48098-2815
U.S.A.
Telephone: (248) 813-2000
Fax: (248) 813-2670
Web site: http://www.delphiauto.com

Public Company
Incorporated: 1998
Employees: 211,000
Sales: $29.14 billion (2000)
Stock Exchanges: New York
Ticker Symbol: DPH
NAIC: 336312 Gasoline Engine and Engine Parts
   Manufacturing; 336322 Other Motor Vehicle
   Electrical and Electronic Equipment; 33633 Motor
   Vehicle Steering and Suspension Components (Except
   Spring) Manufacturing; 33634 Motor Vehicle Brake
   System Manufacturing; 33635 Motor Vehicle
   Transmission and Power Train Parts; 336399 All
   Other Motor Vehicle Parts Manufacturing; 54171
   Research and Development in the Physical,
   Engineering, and Life Sciences

Delphi Automotive Systems Corporation is the world's largest and most diversified manufacturer of automobile components. It was spun off in the mid-1990s from the world's largest manufacturer of automobiles, General Motors (GM), which still accounted for 70 percent of its business in 2000, although it counts all of the world's manufacturers of light vehicles among its clients. The vast enterprise, occupying 190 factories in 31 countries, claims an invention a day, a new product or process every week. Sixty percent of the company's workforce is based outside North America.

Origins

Delphi Automotive traces as its earliest antecedent the New Departure Bell Company, founded in Bristol, Connecticut, in 1888 to manufacture the earliest known doorbell-ringing device. The company's talent for innovation soon extended to transportation, with the 1897 introduction of the first bicycle coaster brake.

Other Delphi predecessors have been involved in automobile lighting since 1906 and manufacturing wooden auto bodies beginning in 1908. In 1908, Albert Champion, who had been making spark plugs in America since 1899, joined Buick Motor Co. to make spark plugs in the AC Spark Plug Division, which was acquired by General Motors founder Billy Durant in 1909. Durant acquired Dayton Engineering Laboratories, which would become Delco, in 1914.

The self-starting engine, introduced in 1912 by Charles F. (''Boss'') Kettering and first installed on Cadillac cars, freed motorists from having to hand crank their engines. Frank and Perry Remy (dynamos and magnetos), Packard, Harrison, and Alfred P. Sloan (GM president) are other automotive pioneers whose stories form part of Delphi's earliest beginnings.

Other pre-Delphi innovations included the Ring Terminal, developed in 1930; the first car radio (1936); the first radio with mechanical push-button presets (1939); and safety power steering (1951). Delphi's predecessors revolutionized auto air conditioning in 1954 by collecting all components under the hood for the first time. The first production airbag system debuted in 1973. Rack and pinion steering followed the next year.

Grouping Operations in 1991

In 1991, General Motors organized its many separate parts operations—spread across some 200 plants—into its Automotive Components Group (ACG). Sales were $19.3 billion in 1991, but the unit posted significant losses. GM officials decided to sell off noncore businesses, a process that would take three years to complete. Operations that were sold were those that made vacuum pumps, radiator caps, small motors and actuators, starter motors, generators, wiring, rear axles, and magnets—these together accounted for about $3.5 billion in sales. Lighting, chassis, environmental systems, batteries, engine management, and seating operations were retained.

Company Perspectives:

Achieving optimum performance requires system expertise.

An automotive vehicle, in its most basic form, is a group of interacting systems. That's why we believe it's critical to design, test and manufacture each component and module as part of the integrated system in which it operates. We call it the Delphi Automotive Systems approach.

After ensuring that each system is integrated with other related systems, we use our extensive experience in the automotive industry to meet your vehicle's space/weight restrictions, mechanical interfaces, assembly processes, human ergonomics requirements, environmental exposure parameters and service procedures. As a result, the benefits you will gain from partnering with Delphi Automotive Systems are: fully integrated technology; quality components, systems and modules; faster, lower-cost assembly; better inventory control.

When you put it all together, the Delphi Automotive Systems approach ensures a perfect match between components, systems and the vehicles in which they are used.

Key Dates:

1888: Delphi Auto's earliest predecessor is founded.
1991: GM organizes parts holdings into Automotive Components Group.
1992: J.T. Battenberg, III, takes the helm at ACG.
1995: ACG is renamed Delphi Automotive.
1996: Delphi institutes lean manufacturing practices.
1997: GM's Delco Electronics is transferred to Delphi.
1999: Delphi is spun off from GM.
2001: Delphi plans to cut 5.5 percent of workforce (11,500 jobs).

These divestments were the first stage of an historic shift away from vertical integration at General Motors, a company that had once produced even the smallest parts for its cars. GM lagged rivals Ford and Chrysler in making the change to lower cost, outside suppliers, which typically were not unionized.

A new group of managers was placed in charge of ACG in 1992. The new CEO, J.T. Battenberg, III, had risen through a number of engineering positions at GM. Battenberg led the restructuring, persuaded his superiors to create a new headquarters building in the Detroit suburbs, and came up with the group's new name. ACG was renamed Delphi Automotive in January 1995 to help establish its independent identity in the industry. Delphi had six divisions at the time. Sales approached $27 billion for the year.

Delphi began implementing a Japanese-style lean manufacturing system in 1996. The company also began to transform itself into a global supplier. Asia and the Pacific Rim were seen as a critical region for the company's planned growth. China was planning to double its market, requiring up to three million vehicles per year. Manufacturers such as Daewoo Group of South Korea also were expanding capacity. Delphi had several major joint ventures in the region. By the end of 1997, Delphi had invested $300 million on plants in the People's Republic of China, where GM had a major automaking venture (as did Volkswagen). The company's technology, such as that in airbags, was increasingly in demand. Almost 85 percent of Delphi's Asian sales were coming from clients other than GM. Delphi would be hit hard by the currency devaluations that attended the 1998 Asian financial crisis, but would remain committed to its investment in the region. Delphi also had four wholly owned plants in India.

On the other side of the world, Delphi Europe also was able to win a large proportion of business—47 percent—from clients other than GM and its subsidiaries. The unit had 38,000 employees in 63 plants. GM was then accounting for 80 percent of Delphi's global revenues.

GM's Delco Electronics Corporation was transferred to Delphi in late 1997 as part of a transaction in which GM spun off its defense electronics business, Hughes Electronics Corporation, which had operated Delco for the previous 11 years.

Going Public in 1999

GM conducted an initial public offering (IPO) of 17.7 percent of Delphi's shares in February 1999, which raised $1.7 billion. The IPO had been delayed about a year while Delco was being combined with Delphi. By this time, Delphi had spent six years preparing for its independence, selling off 14 lines of business with sales of $6 billion a year, and closing or selling 62 unprofitable plants.

When GM completed Delphi's spinoff in May 1999, the newly independent company was twice as large as Visteon Corporation, the parts maker that was being spun off from Ford. Revenues were about $28.5 billion in 1998, when the company posted a net loss of $93 million.

Delphi, which had 200,000 employees, had its share of strikes. Union workers protested the loss of jobs and benefits likely to come from outsourcing and globalization; the United Auto Workers had always opposed Delphi's separation from GM, believing this would lead to wage concessions.

Delphi was focusing its research on products that were capital-intensive, rather than labor-intensive. This included electric power steering and a "PC Car" project to bring multimedia services into vehicles. High-tech products accounted for a third of company revenues in 2000.

Delphi sought to expand its core businesses via acquisition soon after its spinoff. Several companies were acquired in the first year, including TRW Inc.'s Lucas Diesel parts unit, bought for $871 million in November 1999. Delphi also bought a wiring harness plant in Asia and entered a number of joint ventures. A joint venture with Palm Inc. was creating a way for drivers to control their Palm Pilots via voice recognition systems.

In July 2000, Delphi announced plans to dismiss 900 manufacturing workers in Europe as part of a restructuring there. The cuts amounted to about 2 percent of its European workforce. The next March, the company announced plans to reduce its worldwide workforce by 11,500 jobs, or 5.5 percent, mostly through attrition. The automobile industry as a whole was experiencing a slowdown. Sales slipped a bit to $29.1 billion in 2000. Slowing auto sales in the fall of 2001 resulted in Delphi's customers making fewer cars and ordering fewer parts.

While looking to expand its business apart from its old parent, Delphi also risked having GM assign its business elsewhere. DENSO Corporation, Toyota's parts spinoff firm, quadrupled its business with GM in four years, attaining sales of $1 billion with the automaker by 2001. Delphi was scheduled to lose its right of last refusal for replacement business in North America with GM on January 1, 2002.

Delphi was aiming to grow its nonautomotive revenues to $700 million by 2005. Sales to the communications, military, aerospace, agriculture, and construction markets stood at $422 million in 1999.

Principal Subsidiaries

Delco Electronics Corporation; Delphi Automotive Systems (Holding), Inc.; Delphi Automotive Systems LLC.

Principal Divisions

Dynamics & Propulsion; Safety, Thermal & Electrical Architecture; Electronics & Mobile Communication.

Principal Operating Units

Delphi Automotive Systems; Aftermarket Operations; Audio and Mobile MultiMedia Systems; Electrical/Electronic Systems; Energy Systems; Engine Management Systems; Intellek Sensors and Actuators; Interior and Occupant Protection Systems; Microelectronics; Ride and Handling Systems; Thermal Systems.

Principal Competitors

DENSO Corporation; Johnson Controls, Inc.; Magna International; Robert Bosch GmbH; Siemens AG; TRW Inc.; Valeo S.A.; Visteon Corporation.

Further Reading

"ACG Ready to Transfer Technology to Korea," *Business Korea,* January 1995, p. 39.

Blumenstein, Rebecca, "GM Is Moving Its Delphi IPO to Slow Lane," *Wall Street Journal,* October 2, 1997, p. C16.

——, "GM Seems Likely to Shut or Sell Parts of Delphi, Delco While Merging Them," *Wall Street Journal,* January 20, 1997, p. A4.

Blumenstein, Rebecca, and Fara Warner, "GM to Make Delphi Unit Independent," *Wall Street Journal,* August 4, 1998, p. A3.

Bradsher, Keith, "11,500 Jobs Are Being Cut at Big Maker of Auto Parts," *New York Times,* March 30, 2001, p. C1.

Brown, Andrew, Jr., "Learning to Think Lean: Delphi Lean Engineering Initiatives," *Automotive Manufacturing & Production,* May 2000, pp. 76–77.

Byrne, Harlan S., "Oracle of Delphi," *Barron's,* October 4, 1999, pp. 22–24.

Content, Thomas, "Delphi Sets Stage for Parts Business; Future Holds Consolidation, Globalization," *USA Today,* November 2, 1999, p. B3.

Creswell, Julie, "America's Elite Factories," *Fortune,* September 3, 2001, pp. 206A–206L.

"Delphi Orders Zero Defects," *Purchasing,* April 5, 2001, pp. 23–24.

Eisenstein, Paul, "Components of Success Come Together," *Professional Engineering,* February 24, 1999, pp. 23–24.

Flaherty, Julie, "Creative Renewal at Delphi," *New York Times,* June 11, 2000.

Gardner, Greg, "Asian Flu Hits Delphi," *Ward's Auto World,* July 1998, p. 81.

——, "In for the Long Haul," *Ward's Auto World,* December 1997, pp. 69–71.

Keenan, Tim, "The Delphi Diet," *Ward's Auto World,* August 1995, p. 34.

McClellan, Barbara, "Delphi's Passage to India Perfects Process," *Ward's Auto World,* December 1999, pp. 68–70.

Meredith, Robyn, "Reading the Speedometer of G.M.'s Spinoff," *New York Times,* May 30, 1999.

Murphy, Tom, "Delphi Loses Its Appendix," *Ward's Auto World,* October 2001, p. 61.

——, "Life After Spin-Off," *Ward's Auto World,* August 2001, pp. 34–36.

Nauss, Donald W., "GM Plans to Spin Off Delphi Car Parts Unit," *Los Angeles Times,* August 4, 1998, p. D1.

Pullin, John, "Leaner, Meaner, Cleaner," *Professional Engineering,* July 25, 2001, p. 26.

Royal, Weld, "Spotlight Shines on Maquiladora," *Industry Week,* October 16, 2000, pp. 91–92.

Shah, Jennifer Baljko, "Staying Efficient Despite Tough Market Dynamics," *EBN,* August 27, 2001, p. 33.

Stevens, Tim, "A Perfect Union," *Industry Week,* October 18, 1999, pp. 52–54.

Taylor, Alex, III, "Stepping on the Gas," *Fortune,* May 15, 2000, pp. 265–74.

Verespej, Michael A., "$29 Billion Baby," *Industry Week,* June 12, 2000, pp. 61–62.

White, Gregory, "Delphi, Palm to Supply Cars with Web Link," *Wall Street Journal,* October 12, 2000, p. B10.

Winter, Drew, "Outside the U.S., Delphi Gets Leaner," *Ward's Auto World,* August 1998, p. 43.

Zoia, David E., "No Sleeping Giant," *Ward's Auto World,* January 1995, p. 24.

—Frederick C. Ingram

DynCorp

DynCorp

11710 Plaza America Drive
Reston, Virginia 20190
U.S.A.
Telephone: (703) 261-5000
Fax: (703) 261-4800
Web site: http://www.dyncorp.com

Private Company
Incorporated: 1946 as California Eastern Aviation Inc.
Employees: 23,000
Sales: $1.81 billion (2000)
NAIC: 541513 Computer Facilities Management
    Services; 54169 Other Scientific and Technical
    Consulting Services; 56121 Facilities Support Services

DynCorp, one of the largest employee-owned firms in the United States, has not been a very high-profile company, yet its behind-the-scenes logistics support operations for the Defense Department are extensive. The company provides ground support for Air Force One, maintains the State Department's telephones, and contracts coca (cocaine) eradication missions in Colombia. The U.S. Department of Defense accounts for a little less than half of DynCorp's total revenues. Some of DynCorp's earliest customers, such as the White Sands Missile Range in New Mexico, have remained loyal to the company for more than 50 years. CEO Paul Lombardi expects continued growth, most especially in providing services to state and local governments, due to the lack of a dominant player in that highly fragmented market.

War Surplus Origins

California Eastern Airways, Inc. (CEA) was not the only air cargo line started by military pilots returning to the United States after World War II. Nor was it the most enduring, as a purely civil transport enterprise. CEA would diversify, however, into one of the country's most important defense contractors. Within a year of its founding in 1946, California Eastern was serving both coasts. The company participated in the U.S. military airlift during the Korean War.

The purchase of Land-Air, Inc. in the early 1950s brought CEA into a new field of technical services. Land-Air operated missile ranges and modified aircraft for government agencies. In 1951, CEA's total revenues exceeded $6 million. The next year, the company merged with Air Carrier Service Corporation (AIRCAR), which sold commercial aircraft and spare parts to foreign airlines and governments. AIRCAR left the civil aviation business in 1957, focusing instead on defense and aerospace engineering, commercial electronics, and data management.

Dynalectron in 1961

By 1961, CEA needed a new name to more accurately reflect its diversified empire. The name Dynalectron Corporation was culled from 5,000 employee suggestions.

Dynalectron diversified into the energy services business via the 1964 acquisition of Hydrocarbon Research, Inc. At the end of the decade, the company instituted a plan to expand the commercial aviation services business while entering the specialty construction contracting field.

In 1976, Dynalectron established a headquarters in McLean, Virginia. The company restructured into four main operating groups: Specialty Contracting, Energy, Government Services, and Aviation Services. Dynalectron had made 19 acquisitions in its 30 years.

CEO Charles G. Gulledge reported that Dynalectron ended 1976 with stockholders' equity of $30 million, assets of $88 million, and a backlog of $250 million, all record numbers. Annual sales were a bit less than $300 million in the mid-1970s. The company posted a $1.5 million loss in 1978 due to write-downs on wastewater treatment plants being built by a subsidiary, AFB Contractors Inc. After this loss, the company ended its diversification program, focusing instead on cost-cutting to reduce debt.

One of the company's smaller subsidiaries provided the prospect of continued growth. Since 1963, the company's Hydrocarbon Research (HRI) unit had been developing a process to liquefy coal to produce a fuel for boilers. This work attracted national attention due to the Arab oil embargos of the 1970s and the public debate over energy policy. By the early 1980s, Texaco Inc., Ruhrkohle of West Germany, and C. Itoh & Co. of Japan had agreed to market Dynalectron's proprietary H-Oil process.

Other projects in which Dynalectron was involved included training helicopter pilots and technicians in Saudi Arabia. By 1981, Dynalectron had acquired another 14 companies, mostly in the aviation services field, which now encompassed cargo handling and aviation fueling. The company also had established a computer component repair business. Two public offerings of stock helped provide the capital for the purchases.

Revenues were $640 million in 1985; a third of the company's business was coming from the Defense Department. Revenues grew to $749 million in 1986.

In April 1987, Dynalectron agreed to pay $1.5 million to settle two bid-rigging cases related to its largest subsidiary, Dynalectric Co. A spokesman maintained the settlement was more a matter of financial expediency than an admission of any wrongdoing.

New Name, New Owners in the Late 1980s

Dynalectron adopted the DynCorp name in 1987. The company had become North America's fourth largest electrical contractor; its defense contracting and aviation services businesses were also considerable.

In early 1988, a management buyout took DynCorp private again and established an Employee Stock Ownership Plan (ESOP) following a hostile takeover attempt from Miami financier Victor Posner. An investment group led by DynCorp Chairman Jorge E. Carnicero paid $246 million for the company.

A restructuring grouped the company, which had 16,000 employees, into Government Services and Commercial Aviation Services divisions. DynCorp instituted a strategy to make it less dependent on defense work: by 1995, according to the plan, 40 percent of its contracts would not be defense-related, the professional services business would grow, and the company would achieve annual sales of $1.2 billion.

DynCorp aggressively pursued the emerging information technology (IT) business in the early 1990s, buying ten companies between 1990 and 1993 (Bell Technical Operations; Program Resources, Inc.; Meridian Corporation; Viar & Company; Aerotherm Corporation; Becon Services; B-K Dynamics; Science Management Corporation's Information Systems Division; Technology Applications, Inc.; and Network Management Inc.). A new group, Applied Sciences, was formed to encompass them in 1990.

Another business unit, Information & Engineering Technology (I&ET), was formed in 1994, charged with capturing large IT service contracts. In October of that year, DynCorp bought CBIS Federal Inc., renaming it DynTel Corporation.

DynCorp revenues reached the $1 billion mark in 1994. The company had posted losses, however, for the previous five years. Profits returned as revenues slipped to $909 million in 1995; new contacts worth $1.7 billion pushed the company's backlog toward the $3 billion mark. DynCorp reported receiving six merger proposals after posting the results.

In August 1995, DynAir, the commercial aviation unit, was sold in two pieces to Sabreliner Corp. of St. Louis and London's Alpha Airports Group PLC. DynAir had accounted for 5,000 of DynCorp's 23,000 employees.

Focus on IT in the 1990s

Under CEO Dan Bannister, DynCorp was dedicating itself to its role as one of the fastest growing providers of IT services in the Washington, D.C. area. Still, these services were accounting for less than 20 percent of the company's total revenues. Most of the company's work came from the low-tech "roads and commodes" end of the business.

Dyncorp posted record revenue and backlog figures in 1996, giving ample reason to celebrate during the company's 50th anniversary year. At the beginning of 1997, another banner year, Dan R. Bannister became company chairman while Paul V. Lombardi assumed the titles of president and CEO. Lombardi had joined the firm five years earlier as head of its Governmental Services Group.

Some new businesses were added during the mid-1990s. Data Management Design, Inc., a provider of workflow solutions, was acquired in 1996. DynSolutions, added in 1997, developed information management systems for commercial users. DynCorp Management Resources, also added in 1997, focused on state and local government services.

In February 1998, DynCorp bought FMAS, a health information systems provider. Later in the year, DynCorp entered a unique public-private partnership to operate the Virginia Space Flight Center.

GTE Information Systems was acquired in late 1999 and renamed DynCorp Information Systems. It would soon install a unique, completely wireless computing infrastructure at Virginia Union University. The acquisition was one of DynCorp's more troublesome; the company eventually sued GTE for misinformation regarding the profitability of a phone system for prisoners.

During 1999, DynCorp moved to a new headquarters building in Reston, Virginia. The company's impressive financials continued to grow throughout the late 1990s and into 2000, in large part due to an industry-leading 66 percent contract win rate. Backlog was $6 billion in the spring of 2001.

DynCorp organized its healthcare services business under the new AdvanceMed LLC subsidiary in January 2001. Reve-

Key Dates:

1946: Pilots returning from World War II form CEA air cargo business.
1951: CEA merges with AIRCAR civil aviation services company.
1961: CEA is renamed Dynalectron Corporation.
1964: Hydrocarbon Research, Inc. is acquired.
1976: Dynalectron restructures and relocates to McLean, Virginia.
1987: Dynalectron becomes DynCorp.
1988: Management buyout takes DynCorp private following a hostile takeover attempt from Miami financier Victor Posner.
1994: Annual revenues reach $1 billion as company focuses on IT.
2001: Growth in local and state government services helps push backlog to $6 billion.

nues were about $75 million a year; the unit specialized in predictive outcome analysis for large insurers and hospitals.

Lombardi was bullish on the prospect of future growth in services for state and local governments, due to its huge size and lack of dominant players. DynCorp's Management Resources unit had grown 40 percent in 1998 alone. In late 2001, DynCorp planned to merge this business with TekInsight, a public IT company, holding a 40 percent ownership in the new company to be called DynTech.

The September 11 terrorist attacks on the World Trade Center and the Pentagon had implications for a variety of DynCorp's lines of business. The company operated INS stations along the Mexican border. According to the *Washington Business Journal*, many defense agencies consulted with the firm regarding contingency plans and the government asked DynCorp to make its emergency telephone system completely wireless. DynPort Vaccines, a joint venture with Porton International Ltd., researched biological weapons.

Principal Subsidiaries

AdvanceMed LLC; Dyn Marine Services, Inc.; DynCorp Information Systems LLC; DynCorp Management Resources, Inc.; DynCorp Systems & Solutions, Inc.; DynCorp Technical Services; DynCorp TechServ; DynSpace Corporation; DynTel Corporation.

Principal Divisions

DynCorp Information and Enterprise Technology; DynCorp Information Systems; DynCorp Technical Services.

Principal Competitors

Electronic Data Systems Corporation; Lockheed Martin Corporation; PRC Inc.; Raytheon Company; Science Applications International Corporation; TRW Inc.

Further Reading

Celarier, Michelle, "Catch-23: Private Industries Bidding Against Government Entities for Pentagon Contracts Often Face Obstacles and Lose Money," *CFO: The Magazine for Senior Financial Executives,* June 1998, pp. 50–58.

Chandrasekaran, Rajiv, "The Bloom Is on DynCorp," *Washington Post,* August 5, 1996, p. F9.

Day, Kathleen, "DynCorp Discussing the Sale of a Division; Reston Firm's Aviation Services Unit on Block," *Washington Post,* August 8, 1995, p. D1.

——, "DynCorp Retools with a Focus on Information Technology," *Washington Post,* August 14, 1995, p. F8.

——, "A Welcome from the Music Man," *Washington Post,* August 14, 1995, p. F8.

"Dynalectron: Determined That Synfuels Will Fuel the Company's Growth," *Business Week,* June 28, 1982, p. 130.

Haggerty, Maryann, "Engineering a Career in Energy Programs at DynCorp," *Washington Post,* June 14, 1993, p. F11.

Isikoff, Michael, "Dynalectric Indicted on Bid Rigging Charge; McLean Firm, Former President Agree to Plead Guilty, Forgo Appeal of Earlier Conviction," *Washington Post,* April 24, 1987, p. F1.

——, "Dynalectron Officer Indicted for Bid Rigging," *Washington Post,* September 20, 1986, p. D1.

——, "Dynalectron Puts Official on Paid Leave," *Washington Post,* October 30, 1986, p. E1.

Jones, William H., "Dynalectron Corp. Posts 'Large, Unexpected Losses,'" *Washington Post,* March 13, 1979, p. D10.

——, "Dynalectron Has an Oil Answer," *Washington Post,* July 12, 1978, p. E1.

——, "Dynalectron May Be Part of Coal Conversion Plan," *Washington Post,* May 17, 1979, p. C1.

Kady, Martin, II, "DynCorp Rallies the Troops to Keep Up with the Demand," *Washington Business Journal,* October 26, 2001.

Koklanaris, Maria, "DynCorp Acquires Local Firm in Bid to Diversify; Company Seeks to Cut Pentagon Dependence," *Washington Post,* May 6, 1991, p. F6.

Lemke, Tim, "DynCorp Could Gain More Business from Defense," *Washington Times,* September 24, 2001, p. D5.

McCance, McGregor, "Initiative Helps Keep Computing Systems Updated in Virginia," *Richmond Times-Dispatch,* July 21, 2001.

McCarthy, Ellen, "Calif. Firm Confirms Plan to Buy DynCorp Unit," *Washington Post,* October 5, 2001.

Mintz, John, "FBI Probes DynCorp on Fort Belvoir Work," *Washington Post,* January 11, 1994, p. D2.

"A New Push for Coal-to-Oil Technology," *Business Week,* November 7, 1977.

Southerland, Daniel, "DynCorp Unit Picked to Run U.S. Oil Reserve," *Washington Post,* November 24, 1992, p. D1.

Sugawara, Sandra, "DynCorp Wins Big Energy Job," *Washington Post,* April 23, 1994, p. C1.

Wakeman, Nick, "DynCorp Revs Up 'Horsepower' in Gov't Market," *Washington Technology,* April 2, 2001, p. 1.

Wreden, Nick, "Unblinking Customer Focus," *VAR Business,* July 6, 1998, p. 69.

—Frederick C. Ingram

Entergy Corporation

639 Loyola Avenue
New Orleans, Louisiana 70113
U.S.A.
Telephone: (504) 576-4000
Fax: (504) 576-4428
Web site: http://www.entergy.com

Public Company
Incorporated: 1949 as Middle South Utilities
Employees: 14,100
Sales: $10.01 billion (2000)
Stock Exchanges: New York Midwest Pacific
Ticker Symbol: ETR
NAIC: 221122 Electric Power Distribution; 22121
 Natural Gas Distribution; 221112 Fossil Fuel Electric
 Power Generation; 221113 Nuclear Electric Power
 Generation; 551112 Offices of Other Holding
 Companies

Entergy Corporation is a holding company for utilities that supply electrical energy to over 2.5 million customers in the middle south of the United States, including Arkansas, Louisiana, Mississippi, and Texas. The nation's second largest owner of nuclear power plants, the company also owns plants run on coal, natural gas, oil, and hydroelectric power. Its subsidiaries also provide natural gas service in New Orleans and parts of Arkansas and Missouri. Another Entergy subsidiary buys and sells energy on a wholesale basis. Other services include nuclear plant decommissioning and license renewal, power plant construction, and energy distribution. A $10 billion energy powerhouse, Entergy faces controversial issues such as energy shortages, disposal of radioactive wastes, emission of air pollutants, and global warming.

Origins and Early History

Although Entergy was incorporated as a public company called Middle South Utilities (MSU) in 1949, its four constituent power companies had operated as an interdependent system for 25 years. These companies were Arkansas Power & Light, Louisiana Power & Light, Mississippi Power & Light, and New Orleans Public Service, Inc. In 1981 Arkansas-Missouri Power was merged into Arkansas Power & Light after having been owned by MSU since the early 1970s.

During the 1950s, the company was one of the fastest-growing utility systems in the United States, largely because of the industrialization of its territory and the ensuing rise in the standard of living. Much of this expansion sprung from industrial development programs initiated by MSU-supplied companies. Among the more significant and economically resilient industries founded were oil, natural gas, and chemicals. Large manufacturers, including General Motors, built plants in the region. Reynolds Metals brought the area the electricity-intensive aluminum industry. In addition, from 1945 to 1955, use of electricity per residential customer in the middle South rose faster than the national average. Three of the four constituent companies did not have a rate increase from the end of World War II until the early 1960s. From 1947 through 1951, MSU and its predecessor companies spent $236 million on plant expansions, financed by common stock sales in 1950, 1951, and 1952.

In 1953 MSU became involved in a dispute with the U.S. government. Edgar H. Dixon, head of MSU, and Eugene A. Yates, head of the Southern Company, proposed a plant to supply power to the Tennessee Valley Authority (TVA), which would make this power available to the Atomic Energy Commission. The plan stirred up a battle in Congress between those favoring government ownership of utilities and those favoring investor ownership, eventually causing U.S. President Dwight Eisenhower to void the contract. Although the government claimed that the contract's cancellation was based on a conflict of interest by an investment banker, Adolphe Wenzell, who was advising both the utilities and the government, the utilities sued the government in 1955. The U.S. Court of Claims found no conflict of interest and granted the utilities $1.8 million in damages in 1959.

1960s–80s: Nuclear Energy and Other Developments

Despite the legal battle, the 1950s were prosperous for Middle South, as the next decade would also prove to be. In

Company Perspectives:

Entergy's long-term strategy is to leverage our scale and industry expertise to establish Entergy as a premier integrated wholesale energy company. Our defined strategic initiatives are to expand our nuclear generation portfolio, develop power projects in selected growth markets, build our commodity marketing and trading capabilities, and strengthen our core utility franchise. Our expertise in nuclear power operations, our unparalleled scale in natural gas-fired generation, and our strong commitment to customer service are the foundation for successful execution of our wholesale energy strategy.

1961 MSU was one of 11 private power firms, headed by Robert Welch of Southwestern Electric Power Company, to offer to exchange energy with the TVA, whose surplus summer power would be exchanged for the companies' surplus power in the winter, effecting considerable savings for both parties.

In a similar agreement in October 1967, Middle South united with Southern Company to coordinate planning and operation of their facilities for ten years. Such partnerships were part of a general trend among utilities to foster joint ventures and cooperation. The plan included mutual assistance in case of emergencies that would reduce probability of large-scale power failures. The firms also planned to coordinate building of plants and long-distance power lines. The two systems were already directly connected with each other through transmission facilities in Mississippi and Louisiana and indirectly connected through neighboring systems.

The increasing need for electricity in MSU's region called for $1.12 billion worth of construction during the 1960s, or about $118 million per year during the decade. During the 1960s, total electric energy sales almost tripled, going from 10.4 billion kilowatt-hours in 1959 to 31 billion kilowatt-hours in 1969. Although annual electricity use per household increased more than two and a half times, and revenue per customer nearly doubled, increased efficiency meant that the average cost to the customer per kilowatt-hour decreased 28.6 percent during the decade.

When founded, MSU assumed unlimited availability of natural gas as its major fuel source. During the 1960s, however, gas became increasingly scarce, and MSU had to consider other fuel options. In 1967 the company began construction of its first nuclear plant, built by its Arkansas Power & Light subsidiary. The $140 million plant was erected in Russellville, Arkansas, at the Dardanelle Reservoir on a 1,110-acre parcel of land. It began producing energy in 1974. Beginning in 1969, due to the Federal Power Commission's heightened restriction of interstate natural gas delivery, MSU founded its System Fuels, Inc. subsidiary to provide fuel for utility operations. By 1974 the subsidiary had located six natural gas wells. It also purchased fuel oil. By 1974 MSU was building four 700-megawatt coal-fired units, the first to go into operation in 1978. MSU bought the coal for these units from Kerr-McGee Oil Company and Peabody Coal Company.

MSU was a leader in the trend toward nuclear energy. In the 1970s it planned to derive 43 percent of its new capacity—2,965 megawatts—from nuclear power plants. Among the company's most significant research projects were those underway at the Southwest Nuclear Research Center near Fayetteville, Arkansas. Installed there was the Southwest Experimental Fast Oxide Reactor, which at the time was the only reactor in the United States fueled with plutonium oxide. Its purpose was to verify the safety and desirability of breeder reactors. To back the project MSU joined with 13 other investor-owned companies, called Southwest Atomic Energy Associates, as well as General Electric, the U.S. Atomic Energy Commission, and the Karlsruhe Nuclear Research Center of Germany.

In 1974, with the company's Arkansas nuclear plant in operation, two MSU subsidiaries, Mississippi Power & Light and Middle South Energy, Inc., began construction of two more nuclear plants at the Grand Gulf station in Mississippi. During the early 1970s, however, the system continued to rely on natural gas. In 1974 oil provided 27 percent of total fuel requirements, gas 68 percent, and nuclear and hydroelectric production about 5 percent.

In 1975, to secure a steady fuel supply until its nuclear and coal-based facilities would be in full operation in the 1980s, MSU entered a joint project with Northeast Petroleum and Ingram Corp. The companies founded Energy Corporation of Louisiana to build a $300 million refinery in Garyville, Louisiana, producing low-sulfur fuel oil. Floyd Lewis, who began as a lawyer with New Orleans Public Service, became president of MSU in 1970. He led the company through a decade of growth despite mounting economic stress. Debilitating outside factors included the Middle East oil embargo and the attendant rise in fuel costs; environmental and other controls on construction; inflation and interest rates that increased building costs; and the nuclear accident at Three Mile Island that strengthened the resolve of the U.S. antinuclear movement. In 1977 sales topped $1 billion, a 23 percent increase from 1976.

By 1977 MSU was involved in its most ambitious construction program ever. From 1970 through 1976, it had spent $2.67 billion on plant expansion. Expenditures of $2.37 billion were anticipated for 1977 through 1979. However, while new production sites formerly lowered utility rates, the opposite became true: new plants, whether coal or nuclear, were time-consuming and expensive to build—six to eight years for a coal-run facility and ten to 14 years for a nuclear plant, with a cost of $1,000 to $2,000 per kilowatt. MSU sought numerous rate increases to cover its costs, but regulators would not allow the construction costs to be reflected in rates until the plants were operational. MSU continued to build, tying up capital in plants under construction that it was unable to invest to generate income for most of the decade. From 1974 through 1985, MSU sank $6.1 billion into construction of its Grand Gulf and Waterford nuclear plants. During construction, MSU was able to disguise its financial weakness through the allowance for funds used during construction, which allowed it to register the profits it would make on its construction assets if the plants were in fact producing. In 1985 such noncash credit constituted 91 percent of MSU's earnings.

Reality set in, however, after production began at Grand Gulf in mid-1985. The facility, owned by MSU subsidiary Sys-

Key Dates:

1949: Middle South Utilities (MSU) is incorporated.
1961: MSU begins a power exchanging contract with the Tennessee Valley Authority (TVA).
1967: MSU begins a cooperative agreement with Southern Company; construction begins on Russellville, Arkansas nuclear plant.
1969: Subsidiary System Fuels, Inc. is founded.
1974: Construction begins on two Grand Gulf, Mississippi nuclear plants.
1975: MSU begins a joint project to build the Garyville, Louisiana refinery.
1981: MSU's Arkansas-Missouri Power is merged into Arkansas Power & Light.
1988: Company consolidates management of its four nuclear plants.
1989: Middle South Utilities is renamed Entergy Corporation.
1996: CitiPower is acquired in January.
1997: London Electricity is acquired in February.
1998: Company sells London Electricity and CitiPower.
1999: Pilgrim Nuclear Station is purchased.
2000: Entergy acquires TLG Services and Indian Point 3 nuclear plant and signs agreements with The Shaw Group, Koch Industries, and Framatome Technologies.
2001: Merger fails between Entergy and FPL Group Inc.

tem Energy Resources, Inc., sold power wholesale to MSU's four operating companies according to an allocation established by the Federal Energy Regulatory Commission. The commission also set the wholesale cost of Grand Gulf's power. The rate increases needed to cover these costs were so high—up to 20 percent—that state regulatory commissions initially refused any increase at all.

The company absorbed more than $330 million in Grand Gulf construction costs, planning to recover the rest through gradual rate increases over the next decade. It also took a substantial loss on its $950 million investment in the rudiments of the second Grand Gulf plant, whose construction was halted by the Mississippi Public Service Commission (MPSC). MSU stopped paying its common stock dividends in order to save money. Mississippi regulators finally granted a $326 million interstate wholesale rate increase to Mississippi Power & Light in September 1985.

In 1986 President and Chairman Floyd Lewis was hospitalized, and Edwin Lupberger assumed Lewis's duties as MSU's difficulties continued. The interest rate the company had to pay on its debt rose, and common stock sold for 50 percent to 75 percent of book value, as contrasted with the 110 percent to 120 percent typical of a healthy utility stock. Lupberger, in an interview with *Forbes,* July 28, 1986, characterized the company's situation as "more uncertain than it's been since the Depression."

In 1987 the Mississippi Supreme Court rescinded the MPSC's 1985 rate increase. Mississippi Power & Light ap-

pealed to the U.S. Supreme Court, saying that cancellation of the increase would bankrupt it. At the same time, Louisiana regulators reduced by $28 million a $76 million increase granted to another subsidiary. Standard & Poor's lowered its ratings on $7 billion worth of MSU debt and preferred stock. On June 28, 1988, the U.S. Supreme Court ruled that the 1985 Mississippi rate increase was valid, and as a result MSU's security ratings were upgraded. More than $200 million that had been collected, but held in escrow pending the court's decision, was released on August 11, 1988. Although earnings continued to be lower than the previous year, overall financial stability of the organization was on the upswing, as evidenced by the reinstatement on September 10 of its quarterly common stock dividend for the first time since its 1985 suspension. By the end of 1988, the company's financial recovery was basically complete, although its stock continued to sell at 75 percent of book value, nearly 39 percent less than the industry average. In late 1988, MSU consolidated the management of all four of its nuclear plants at System Energy Resources, a move expected to lower costs by $23 million.

Lawsuits questioning other nuclear investments continued to plague MSU. Lupberger, fearing the uncertainty and strain of more drawn-out litigation, negotiated a compromise agreement called Project Olive Branch, settling the suits out of court. This hoisted the company's return on capital nearer to the industry average of 8.6 percent. Its stock price rebounded as well.

Developments in the 1990s and Beyond

At the annual meeting on May 19, 1989, shareholders approved changing MSU's name to Entergy Corporation. Heading into the 1990s, the company had largely regained financial stability. In 1991 its New Orleans Public Service subsidiary reached an agreement with the New Orleans City Council that let the utility recover a portion of its investment in the Grand Gulf nuclear plant. Late in 1991 Entergy increased its common stock dividend.

One of the biggest changes in the nuclear power industry came with federal deregulation that began in the early 1990s. Public entities sold their nuclear plants for very low bids. Most private companies did not want such risky ventures, but Entergy decided to expand its nuclear power operations. In 1999 it purchased the Pilgrim Nuclear Power Station in Plymouth, Massachusetts. The following year it acquired two more facilities: the Indian Point 3 plant in Westchester County, New York, and the James A. Fitzpatrick plant in Oswego County, New York. In 2001 it expected to close its purchase from Con Edison of Indian Point 1 and 2 plants.

Thus Entergy played a key role in the resurgence of the nuclear power industry. Entergy and Exelon, the industry leader, spent almost $4 billion to buy 15 nuclear plants. The private owners of such plants by the late 1990s had "reversed years of mismanagement and cost overruns to turn the plants into the reliable, profitable atomic engines they were meant to be," said *Time*'s Daniel Eisenberg. Of course, the storage of radioactive waste remained a challenge for the nation's 103 operating nuclear plants that produced about 20 percent of the country's electricity.

Meanwhile, Entergy owned, managed, or invested in many fossil-fuel and hydroelectric generating plants that in 2001 generated over 30,000 megawatts of electricity in the United States and other nations. Only five of its generating units used hydroelectric power. Seven units used coal. According to its web site, Entergy had 58 units that used oil, natural gas, or a combination of the two energy sources.

Entergy Corporation's operating revenues went from $7.16 billion in 1996 to $9.53 billion in 1997, $11.49 billion in 1998, and $8.77 billion in 1999. Its consolidated net income in 1996 was $490.6 million. That went to $300.9 million in 1997, $785.6 million in 1998, and then $595 million in 1999.

The firm's 2000 annual report described a good year for Entergy. It had four quarters of record earnings, and its stock price at the end of the year was at a record level. Entergy ranked first among surveyed American utilities for its one-year progress in customer satisfaction, according to a study published in April 2000. Other 2000 highlights included forming a joint venture called Entergy-Koch, L.P. with Koch Industries, a major energy trading and marketing firm, and cooperating with The Shaw Group to create EntergyShaw, L.L.C., a power plant construction firm. Entergy in 2000 also acquired TLG Services, a nuclear decommissioning company, and signed a contract with Framatome Technologies to help nuclear plants renew their licenses.

In 2001 Entergy and other power companies continued to deal with divisive issues such as global warming and climate change. Since some blamed carbon dioxide emissions from fossil fuel plants for the so-called greenhouse effect, Entergy and some other energy companies committed themselves to the reduction of such emissions.

Another power controversy in 2001 was electrical transmission. Entergy proposed a privately funded expansion of the grid system that was disputed by municipal power agencies and other critics. Such public policy disputes kept Entergy's leaders busy as they dealt with state regulatory bodies and the Federal Energy Regulatory Commission (FERC).

The good news for the power industry was the growing population's increased demand for electrical energy. That helped fuel Entergy's rising stock prices. Its shares increased 63 percent over one year to about $41 per share at the end of April 2001. If Entergy continued to meet the needs of the American people during what some called an energy crisis, its future looked promising.

Principal Subsidiaries

Entergy Arkansas, Inc.; Entergy Gulf States, Inc.; Entergy Louisiana, Inc.; Entergy Mississippi, Inc.; Entergy New Orleans, Inc.; Entergy Operations, Inc.; System Energy Resources, Inc.; Entergy Nuclear Generation Company; Entergy Nuclear Operations, Inc.; Entergy Thermal.

Principal Competitors

AEP Industries, Inc.; Reliant Energy; Southern Company.

Further Reading

Blankinship, Steve, "Mergers and Acquisitions," *Power Engineering*, May 2001, p. 21.

Brull, Steven, "Mushrooming Profits," *Institutional Investor*, May 2001, pp. 38–45.

Cook, James, "A Nuclear Survivor," *Forbes*, July 28, 1986.

Eisenberg, Daniel, "Nuclear Summer," *Time*, May 28, 2001, pp. 58–60.

Gray, Robert T., "The Timeless Skills of a Modern Manager," *Nation's Business*, December 1983.

Lorenzetti, Maureen, "CO(2) Battles Just Beginning," *Oil & Gas Journal*, March 26, 2001, p. 25.

Radford, Bruce W., "Entergy's Grid Grab," *Public Utilities Fortnightly*, March 1, 2001, p. 4.

Sidel, Robin, "FPL, Entergy Blame Each Other As They Call off $8 Billion Merger," *Wall Street Journal*, April 3, 2001, p. A4.

Wald, Matthew L., "Countdown at Indian Point 3: An Early Test of Nuclear Plant's New Private Ownership," *New York Times*, May 13, 2001, p. 13.

—Elaine Belsito
—update: David M. Walden

experian®

Experian Information Solutions Inc.

505 City Parkway West
Orange, California 92868
U.S.A.
Telephone: (714) 385-7000
Fax: (714) 385-7349
Web site: http://www.experian.com

Wholly Owned Subsidiary of Great Universal Stores PLC
Incorporated: 1996 as Experian Corporation
Employees: 12,000
Sales: $1.44 billion (2001)
NAIC: 56145 Credit Bureaus; 514191 On-Line
    Information Services

Experian Information Solutions Inc. is an international leader in information services. Formerly a division of automotive and electronics giant TRW, the company is one of the big three consumer credit reporting services in the United States, along with TransUnion Corp. and Equifax Inc. The company is also the market leader in consumer credit reporting in Great Britain, and it does business in about 50 countries worldwide. Experian maintains exhaustive databases on consumer credit and business credit, and tailors these in various ways for direct marketers, magazine publishers, lenders, collection agencies, and others. The company also runs a National Fraud Database, which offers consumer identification and authentication for companies that use on-line credit card transactions. And Experian's National Business Database keeps tabs on roughly 14 million small and mid-sized businesses in North America. In 1996 Experian merged with CCN, the credit reporting unit of the British company Great Universal Stores.

Growth Out of Automotive Electronics: 1960s

The company that became Experian Information Solutions began as a unit of TRW. TRW was founded in 1901 as the Cleveland Cap Screw Co. It began by making cap screws, bolts, and studs, but soon its main product was welded valves for cars made by automotive pioneer Alexander Winton. The company went through several owners and name changes early in the

20th century until in 1926 it took the name Thompson Products Inc. At that time it made a variety of parts for both the automotive and aviation industries. In 1958, Thompson Products merged with Ramo-Wooldridge Corp. and took the name Thompson-Ramo-Wooldridge. Ramo-Wooldridge was a leading company in the defense electronics industry. The merged company became a giant in defense and in automotive parts. It invented many key automotive components such as the permanently lubricated steering linkage and the seat-belt pretensioning device. By the mid-1960s, the company shortened its name to TRW and began a global expansion, acquiring plants in Germany, Brazil, and the United Kingdom.

While TRW was developing rack-and-pinion power steering and seat belt technology, it also launched a consumer credit information bureau. The company began compiling a consumer database in the mid-1960s. Starting in the mid-1970s, TRW also operated a small-business database. TRW's information division grew by both internal expansion and acquisition. By the mid-1980s, TRW Information Services, as the consumer credit unit was called, had credit histories on file of approximately 90 million Americans. At that time, TRW Information Services was the largest U.S. credit reporting agency.

Making a Name in the 1980s

Information services was apparently a profitable business, yet it had little to do with the main products of the rest of TRW. ''TRW brass had never been comfortable with the information business,'' claimed *Direct* in a March 1, 1999 interview with Experian CEO D. Van Skilling. Though TRW hung on to the unit for a long time, there were indications by the 1980s that the information services division was not as well run as it might have been. In 1984, someone stole an account password from the consumer credit division and posted it on an electronic bulletin board. The company moved quickly to change the password and halt any leaks of private credit information, but the event did little for TRW's reputation. TRW also seemed uncertain how to present itself to consumers. Consumers did not come up against their credit reports in most cases unless there was a problem. In 1986, TRW launched a new consumer-oriented business, TRW Credentials Service, which let subscribers access their credit histories once a year for a $30 fee. Years later, TRW was forced to allow consumers a free annual look at their credit reports. In 1989, the company finished a study of consumer attitudes toward credit reporting. It found a wealth of problems and complaints. Even if consumers had bad experiences with another credit reporting bureau, TRW seemed to take the heat, as it was so large and well known.

That year, D. Van Skilling took over as chief executive of TRW's Information Systems and Services division. Skilling's career path was somewhat indicative of TRW's discomfiture with the division. He had a bachelor's degree in chemistry, and worked in naval intelligence during the Korean War. Skilling then worked in various areas, including marketing, of TRW's oil field equipment group, and also in the industrial products group. Nothing in his background directly prepared him for working in information services, yet he became the head man of the division. Skilling quickly realized that the company's computer systems were outdated and insufficient. (Perhaps he had help with this. Skilling claimed that he had given Bill Gates the only job he ever held before he went on to found Microsoft.) In addition, the information from the consumer study also showed that much could be improved. The company began investing in upgrades, spending some $30 million between 1989 and 1991. But Skilling was apparently not able to make changes quickly or thoroughly enough to forestall a public relations disaster.

Two years into Skilling's term, in 1991, a story of egregious credit reporting errors at TRW received wide press. TRW used subcontractors to gather information for the millions of credit reports it had on file. Apparently because of the errors of one part-time worker hired by a subcontractor, thousands of people in New England found themselves with bad credit reports. In the town of Norwich, Vermont, the worker had gone into the town hall and asked for the names of people with liens against their property because of unpaid local taxes. But what actually went into the worker's report were the names of the people who *had* paid their taxes—all 1,400 of them. Some of these people found themselves denied credit, and the problem was revealed. TRW at first claimed the Norwich case was an isolated incident. But as more similar cases cropped up across New England, the company eventually was forced to delete all local tax data from consumer files for people in Vermont, Rhode Island, Maine, and New Hampshire. The *Wall Street Journal* (October 14, 1991) relayed the case of a small-town funeral home director who claimed to have been switched to five different numbers when he called TRW to complain about an erroneous credit report. It took the company a week to respond to him. The New England

autumn proved a picturesque background for television and magazine stories about the mammoth, unresponsive company and the beleaguered little guy. Things could hardly have looked worse for TRW. Months before the New England story broke, more than a dozen states had filed suit against the company. The suits alleged that TRW used sloppy procedures to create credit files on consumers, that the company did not adequately respond to consumer complaints, and that in some instances, after errors were corrected at consumer insistence, the company reinserted the faulty data into the consumers' files. The suits also alleged that TRW illegally sold consumer data to direct marketers.

TRW settled all the cases quickly, signing a consent decree in December 1991 promising to give credit rating information to consumers promptly and clearly. Consumers could order one free copy of their credit report each year. Despite the obvious problems in the information services division, TRW made it plain that it was hanging on to the unit. TRW's overall earnings were slowing, and it had to put several operations on the auction block. But even as it was trimming costs elsewhere, TRW invested more in Information Systems and Services. After spending $30 million between 1989 and 1991, the company budgeted another $26 million for upgrades in the division for 1992.

A Spinoff and a Sale: Mid-1990s

There was no doubt that the Information Systems and Services division was valuable to TRW. It did not break out financial figures for the unit except to say that it contributed less than 10 percent of the company's revenues. But the division had about a 35 percent share of the U.S. credit reporting market, and the industry seemed poised for growth. As data management became more sophisticated, the credit reporting industry looked forward to being able to sell precisely targeted lists of consumers to marketers and lenders. TRW used its database expertise in the mid-1990s to help in its own political lobbying efforts. It created a database called Constituent Relations Information Systems (CRIS) in 1994 which in part kept track of over 8,000 government officials and their stance on issues that might affect TRW. Keeping records of a couple thousand legislators and their aides was small potatoes to a company that now had 180 million individual credit histories on file. It took in some 33 million new pieces of information every single day, and growth potential seemed strong, as long as it could come up with more ways to organize and market its data.

Nevertheless, information services remained a strange fit with the rest of TRW. D. Van Skilling had overseen great changes in the division since taking over in 1989. But he believed the division could do more as an independent company. Constrained by top management at TRW, he told them "Play me or trade me," according to the *Direct* article quoted above. Skilling and more than 60 other top executives at the unit went in with two leading buyout firms and raised cash to take the Information Systems and Services division private in 1996. The buyout firms were Bain Capital and Thomas H. Lee Co. Both these firms had been involved in high-profile transactions in the early 1990s. Thomas H. Lee had earned $900 million for itself and its investors when it sold Snapple Beverages to Quaker Oats in 1994, and Bain Capital had managed to acquire the clinical diagnostics unit of chemical giant Du Pont in 1995, just months before the TRW deal. The investment group gave TRW $1.01 billion in cash for the credit reporting unit, along with stock adding up to a 16 percent share in the new company. At the time of the sale, the unit was bringing in about $540 million in annual revenue. TRW was pleased, claiming the cash would allow the company to make investments in its remaining automotive and aerospace businesses.

The newly independent company took the name Experian. It planned to increase its business in target marketing, that is, the tailoring of its databases to suit specific customer needs; it also wanted to expand into overseas markets. So Experian made an offer to the British conglomerate Great Universal Stores to buy its credit reporting unit, CCN Group Ltd Great Universal Stores was perhaps best known for its steadfast outerwear unit, Burberrys. CCN was the largest credit reporting company in the United Kingdom, and it was responsible for some 5 percent of Great Universal Stores' profits. CCN had apparently been interested in buying the information services unit from TRW for years, but talks had gone nowhere. When Great Universal Stores received the offer from Experian, it responded by asking to buy Experian for $1.7 billion. Experian's spinoff from TRW had not been finalized until September 1996, and the offer from Great Universal Stores came in November. The price was right, as it gave the investment group some $500 million over what they had just paid to TRW. Thomas Lee and Bain Capital each tripled the $100 million they had put into the deal, and several millionaires were minted from the group of TRW executives involved in the spinoff.

CCN changed its name to Experian, and the company operated from two headquarters, one in Nottingham, England, and the other in Orange, California. The newly merged company quickly made acquisitions of its own. It bought two direct marketing firms, Metromail and Direct Marketing Technology. The company touted itself as much more than a credit reporting agency. It had vast files on both consumers and small businesses, and it found more ways to use these resources. In 1998 Experian debuted a so-called publisher co-op database, called CircBase. This database combined lists of magazine subscribers with catalog ordering information. It covered over 70 million households, and gave magazine publishers more specific data about their customers. Older databases on this model had only been able to generate lists of consumers sorted by more general factors such as age, sex, income, and ZIP code. But CircBase was able to identify consumers who had actually bought certain items, such as cookware or fishing gear. This gave subscribers a clearer idea of who might be interested in a cooking or fishing magazine, for example.

By 2000, Experian was strongly interested in building business on the Internet. Moving beyond direct mail marketing, the company looked into targeted e-mail marketing, forming a joint venture with a volume e-mail company called FloNetwork Inc. FloNetwork used what was called permission-based marketing, where consumers were in a more interactive relationship with the marketer, asking for information. FloNetwork offered Experian its expertise in online communication, and Experian gave the marketer more access to European and U.K. markets. Experian also acquired an e-mail marketing firm, Exactis.com, in 2000, spending $13.5 million for it. Another key piece of online business Experian developed was fraud prevention. It had developed its own consumer identification technology when it began offering credit reports online, so that only the appropriate person could access the report. Experian then offered this technology to other businesses selling merchandise or services online.

In other new businesses, Experian began offering a risk-assessment tool called Cross View Solutions, which helped lenders assess potential customers who had little or no credit history. The company also began pursuing the collections market, selling its database services to companies searching for people who had fallen behind on bills or loan payments. Experian spent millions of dollars in the early 2000s improving its small business database. It collected information on some ten million businesses, combing through thousands of phone directories and following up with telephone interviews. In mid-2000 its business database contained files on about 15 million businesses, and the company aimed to add another nine million.

By 2001, Experian had focused its growth plans on four main areas: risk management, fraud prevention, collections, and authentication and marketing. It planned to expand its international business, too. International business accounted for about 35 percent of the company's revenue, with the rest from North America. In the United Kingdom, the company had about a two-thirds share of the consumer credit reporting market. In business credit reporting, the company was locked in a tie with Dun & Bradstreet for first place in the U.K. market. Experian laid off some workers in the United States in 2001, in a move geared to increase efficiency. The company announced it would drop some unprofitable product lines, and try to move more of its services to the Internet.

Principal Subsidiaries

Experian Direct Technology.

Principal Divisions

Experian North America; Experian International.

Principal Competitors

TransUnion Corp.; Equifax Inc.; The Dun & Bradstreet Corporation.

Further Reading

Beeler, Amanda, "Experian Touts Service via Webcast," *Advertising Age*, February 14, 2000, p. 26.

"Case of the Missing Password," *Time*, July 2, 1984, p. 53.

"CCN Group Adopts Experian Name," *American Banker*, June 20, 1997, p. 12.

Daley, James, "TRW Goes to Washington," *Forbes ASAP*, June 6, 1994, pp. 127–28.

Ennis, Teresa, "New Life for Database Co-Opetition," *Folio*, December 15, 1999, p. 19.

"Experian and FloNetwork Form Alliance to Deliver Powerful Email Marketing Solutions to UK and Europe," *Canadian Corporate News*, September 12, 2000.

Hayes, Thomas C., "A New Start at a TRW Hot Spot," *New York Times*, December 15, 1991, p. F12.

Hirsch, James S., "Buyout Group Hits $500 Million Jackpot," *Wall Street Journal*, November 15, 1996, p. A5.

"Keeping an Eye on Your Credit Profile," *Business Week*, January 20, 1986, p. 82.

Ladwig, Kit, "Global Credit Risk Signal Changes," *Collections and Credit Risk*, July 2001, p. 43.

"Large British Retailer to Buy U.S. Credit-Data Company," *New York Times*, November 15, 1996, p. D2.

Lucas, Peter, "Think Global, Act Local," *Collections and Credit Risk*, July 2001, p. 26.

McGeer, Bonnie, "Vendor Eyes the Future with Revamped Database and New Pricing Structure," *Small Business Banker*, May 2000, p. 8.

Miller, Michael W., "Rash of Errors Blemishes TRW Credit Reports," *Wall Street Journal*, October 14, 1991, pp. B1–B2.

"The Noise Was Great; the Result Was TRW," *Automotive News*, April 29, 1996, p. S104.

"Orange, Calif.-Based Credit Reporting Firm Experian Lays Off 150," *Knight-Ridder/Tribune Business News*, July 14, 2001, p. ITEM01195040.

"The Right Relationship," *Folio*, November 2000, p. S3.

Schultz, Ray, "Skilling's Laws," *Direct*, March 1, 1999, p. 9.

"TRW Credit Reporting Unit to Be Sold for $1 Billion," *New York Times*, February 10, 1996, p. 38.

"TRW Promises to Change Its Ways," *Business Week*, December 23, 1991, p. 38.

"TRW's Credit-Data Unit Nears Accord with States," *Wall Street Journal*, December 6, 1991, p. A7.

—A. Woodward

Fannie Mae

3900 Wisconsin Avenue, NW
Washington, D.C. 20016
U.S.A.
Telephone: (202) 752-7000
Toll Free: (800) 732-6643
Fax: (202)-752-4934
Web site: http://www.fanniemae.com

Publicly Owned Government Corporation
Incorporated: 1938 as National Mortgage Association of
   Washington
Employees: 4,200
Total Assets: $675.07 billion (2000)
Stock Exchanges: New York
Ticker Symbol: FNM
NAIC: 522298 All Other Non-Depository Credit
   Intermediation

Fannie Mae, also known as Federal National Mortgage Association, is the largest nonbank financial services company in the world. A shareholder-owned company, Fannie Mae is one of the largest corporations in America. It operates exclusively in the secondary mortgage markets, serving the single-family and multifamily housing markets. Fannie Mae also works to stimulate housing and community development across the nation. While holding $675 billion in assets, Fannie Mae also guarantees in excess of $700 billion in Mortgage-Backed Securities (MBS). The one-time government agency has made a tremendous impact on the home finance industry since it was chartered by Congress in 1938. Regulated by the federal government, Fannie Mae is an unusual instrument in the American economy.

Federal Support of National Housing Market: 1930s–40s

Fannie Mae was originally designed to help relieve the nation's housing problems during the Depression. Title III of the Federal Housing Act of 1934 provided for the incorporation of private national mortgage associations to create a national secon-dary mortgage market. But in February 1938, since no private associations had yet formed, the Federal Housing Administration chartered the National Mortgage Association of Washington to buy and sell mortgages. Its name was changed three months later to the Federal National Mortgage Association, or FNMA, and it has been known as Fannie Mae ever since.

The federal government took an interest in facilitating home mortgages as a way to invigorate the residential construction industry as well as to provide adequate housing for its citizens. The Depression had taken a heavy toll on private lending institutions. Fannie Mae's primary purpose was to establish a secondary mortgage market to rejuvenate original lenders such as mortgage banks, savings and loan associations, and commercial banks by stimulating enough cash flow to allow them to make new loans. Fannie Mae bought mortgages insured by the Federal Housing Administration (FHA) from these private lenders, and either kept them for its own portfolio or sold them to private investors.

The secondary market Fannie Mae created also made private lenders confident about making FHA-insured mortgages, which some had been reluctant to do. Once assured that they could easily turn these mortgages into cash if they needed to, lenders were more inclined to extend mortgage credit. In addition, the secondary mortgage market helped smooth out discrepancies between capital-rich and capital-poor regions of the country. Fannie Mae could buy mortgages from the South or West and sell them to investors in the capital-rich East. In this way a Boston banker could invest in Arizona mortgages while a local lender in Arizona was no longer limited in the number of loans he could make by the cash deposits of his customers. Under Sam Husbands, who presided over the association from 1938 to 1948, Fannie Mae bought 66,947 FHA-insured mortgages and sold 49,048.

In 1949, Fannie Mae expanded its activities to include buying and selling loans guaranteed by the Veterans Administration (VA). As veterans returned from the war and the great American baby boom got underway, Fannie Mae was busier than ever. The association bought 133,032 mortgages in 1950 compared with 6,734 in 1948. Some critics viewed Fannie Mae's growth with alarm, however, charging that the company had brought government too far into the private sector.

Transforming Fannie Mae: 1950s–60s

In 1954, Congress responded with the Federal National Mortgage Association Charter Act, which turned Fannie Mae into a mixed ownership corporation. The Treasury of the United States was issued nonvoting preferred stock, and nonvoting common stock was sold to mortgage lenders, who were now required to own stock in order to sell mortgages to Fannie Mae. Fannie Mae was made responsible for special assistance for certain mortgages when the president or Congress requested, and also for the management of mortgages acquired before 1954.

Throughout the 1950s and early 1960s Fannie Mae continued to buy and sell FHA and VA mortgages. But in 1966, primary mortgage lenders found themselves temporarily without the liquid resources to make new mortgages. Fannie Mae, until then a relatively minor player in the secondary market because it was restricted to government-insured (FHA and VA) mortgages, became the largest buyer in the market. The cost of borrowing enough money to purchase all the mortgages was high enough that Fannie Mae's profits dropped significantly that year. Lending eased at the end of 1966, relieving the pressure on Fannie Mae. But when mortgage funds became scarce again a year later, it became clear that major changes were necessary to ensure Fannie Mae's continued prosperity.

In 1968, Fannie Mae began the transition from mixed ownership to a private corporation. The Housing and Urban Development Act of 1968 split the old Fannie Mae into two separate corporations: the new Fannie Mae conducted secondary mortgage market activities just as the old one had done, while a new company called the Government National Mortgage Association (GNMA), or Ginnie Mae, assumed the ''special assistance'' and ''management'' functions of the old Fannie Mae, guaranteeing FHA and VA mortgages. The Treasury Department's preferred stock was retired and a schedule was set for nonvoting common shares to become voting ones. The Department of Housing and Urban Development (HUD) maintained ''regulatory power'' over the new Fannie Mae. Any stock, obligation, or other security had to be approved by the Secretary of HUD. The secretary could also require that a reasonable number of Fannie Mae purchases were in step with HUD's goal of assuring quality housing for moderate and low-income families.

On December 2, 1969, President Richard Nixon dismissed Raymond H. Lapin as chief of Fannie Mae. A Democrat, Lapin had been appointed president of the association by President Lyndon Johnson in July 1967 and had overseen Fannie Mae's transitional period. The ousted chief filed suit in federal court claiming that his removal was politically motivated and that Nixon had failed to show ''good cause,'' but the courts twice refused to reinstate Lapin. In January 1970, Oakley Hunter took over as president; Fannie Mae's transition to private control was completed on May 21, 1970. The new board of directors had 15 members, ten elected by the stockholders and five appointed by the president.

Sailing into Choppy Economic Waters: 1970s–80s

As a private corporation, Fannie Mae had to adjust to the growing complexity of the secondary mortgage market. In 1972, the company bought its first conventional mortgages— mortgages not insured by the FHA or guaranteed by the VA— and in 1974, Fannie Mae began buying condominium and planned unit development mortgages. This flexibility kept the company profitable through the first half of the 1970s.

As interest rates began to rise in 1979, Fannie Mae faced the most critical period in its history. Because the company borrows the money it uses to purchase mortgages through debentures and short-term notes, it is especially vulnerable to rising interest rates. The skyrocketing rates of the early 1980s put Fannie Mae's new chairman, David O. Maxwell, to the test. Maxwell replaced Hunter in 1981, a time when Fannie Mae was losing millions of dollars by borrowing at high interest rates to carry mortgages at lower ones. Maxwell initiated several programs to transfer some of the interest-rate risk to someone else. One of these was to begin buying adjustable-rate mortgages (ARMs), especially since many primary lending institutions were shifting to ARMs. The interest rate on ARMs varies: if interest rates go up, the homeowner pays more per month; if they go down he or she pays less.

Fannie Mae also began selling mortgage-backed securities (MBS) in 1981 to help finance its mortgage purchases and to generate fee income. These securities were attractive investments because they were more liquid than the usual packaged mortgage pools. Fannie Mae's MBS ''Swap Program'' allowed lending institutions to trade loans directly for the more liquid securities. Fannie Mae guaranteed the timely payment of interest and principal on the securities. By 1988, Fannie Mae had issued more than $140 billion in mortgage-backed securities.

By 1985, Fannie Mae was profitable again. The company had survived the interest-rate nightmares of the early 1980s and had positioned itself against future interest-rate risk through ARMs and MBSs. That year, Fannie Mae began borrowing money from abroad to finance its purchases, since the 30 percent withholding tax on foreign investment had been abolished. Continuing to respond to changes in the home finance market, Fannie Mae began marketing real estate mortgage investment conduits (REMICs) in 1987. These securities could be specifically tailored to an investor's needs in terms of maturity dates, allowing Fannie Mae to attract investors not traditionally interested in mortgage-related investment products.

In 1988 Fannie Mae celebrated 50 years of service to the home finance industry with record earnings of $345 million in the first three quarters alone. Of the $400 billion Fannie Mae had pumped into the nation's mortgage industry in the past half century, $300 billion of it came after 1980. Under Chairman David Maxwell's aggressive leadership, Fannie Mae had be-

Key Dates:

1938: The National Mortgage Association of Washington is chartered to boost nation's depressed housing market.

1949: The Association is authorized to begin buying and selling loans guaranteed by the Veterans Administration.

1954: The Association is rechartered as a mixed ownership corporation.

1968: The Association is divided in two: Fannie Mae continues in the secondary market sector as a private, shareholder-owned entity, while the newly created Government National Mortgage Association, or Ginnie Mae, guarantees FHA and VA mortgages.

1972: Fannie Mae buys its first conventional mortgage—those not backed by FHA or VA.

1983: Fannie Mae begins purchasing conventional multifamily housing loans.

1988: Fannie Mae stock is added to the S&P 500.

1996: Fannie Mae marks its tenth consecutive year of record earnings.

1999: Franklin D. Raines takes over the leadership of Fannie Mae; the mission statement is changed.

come more profitable than ever. Tellingly, in 1988, Fannie Mae was added to the Standard and Poor's 500 stock index.

The secondary mortgage market had changed dramatically since 1938, but Fannie Mae had shown remarkable agility in adapting to those changes. As large corporations such as Sears and Citicorp became more active in the secondary mortgage market, Fannie Mae would have to continue its innovative ways in order to remain competitive.

Steady Growth: 1990s

Fannie Mae's total income in 1990 was $1.9 billion with 34 percent coming from fees and other service income and 66 percent from investment income. A portion of the company's money went toward the Fannie Mae Foundation (FMF), founded in 1979 for the purpose of making charitable contributions. In 1991 FMF earmarked more than 50 percent of its grants for programs supporting housing, community development, and social concerns. In 1992, FMF made its largest grant to date, $5.5 million to help establish the National Center for Lead-Safe Housing.

Fannie Mae launched the "Opening Doors to Affordable Housing" initiative in 1991. In a little under two years, the corporation produced $10 billion in purchases for low- and moderate-income and special needs housing. In 1994, Fannie Mae expanded the initiative by way of the "Trillion Dollar Commitment." Also that year Fannie Mae instituted its Partnership Office initiative, a program designed to bring together major players, including lenders, local governments and nonprofit groups, builders, and developers, to work toward expanding affordable rental and homeownership opportunities in their areas.

The mid-1990s was marked by a spike in Congressional interest in the activities and regulation of Fannie Mae and Freddie Mac, and in 1995 the Department of Housing and Urban Development (HUD) established new goals for Fannie Mae's low- and moderate-income housing financing. In 1996, Fannie Mae marked its tenth consecutive year of record earnings.

In 1998, Fannie Mae passed the halfway point toward fulfilling its Trillion Dollar Commitment. "Mortgage lending is big business, with big money and big numbers bandied about daily. Still, the entire industry paid attention in March 1994 when Fannie Mae announced its $1 trillion initiative, vowing to provide home mortgages to ten million families, focusing primarily on low-income and traditionally underserved borrowers," wrote Blaise Zerga for *InfoWorld* in May.

Technological improvements such as automated mortgage financing with new underwriting applications allowed Fannie Mae to make rapid progress toward its goal, according to the article. Fannie Mae provided software and training to loan officers of lending institutions: the result was a dramatically shortened mortgage application process.

James A. Johnson, who had guided Fannie Mae through the decade of growth, was succeeded as chairman and CEO by Franklin D. Raines in 1999. Fannie Mae—now officially operating under that name—also changed its mission statement that year, placing an emphasis on affordable rental housing as well as home ownership.

Facing a Fractious Future: 2000 and Beyond

Bankers and trade groups meanwhile had become more vocal regarding government-sponsored enterprises (GSEs) such as Fannie Mae, saying income tax breaks, exemption from Securities and Exchange Commission filing fees, and the perception of government backing, gave the GSEs a competitive advantage.

"With their leverage ratios and cost of capital, you're not on a level playing field with them," the chief executive officer of Wells Fargo Home Mortgage told *American Banker* in 2001. "They have a charter to help foster homeownership in America, but when they expand into other products and other issues, you have to ask, 'Why should they continue to leverage those government benefits, because they're really outside that mission.' "

The organization's traditional role in the industry had been to provide a source of liquidity for the fixed rate conforming mortgage market, but Fannie Mae had begun playing a larger role in the subprime lending, multifamily, and adjustable rate markets. Competitors feared erosion of business in those key areas.

According to a May 2001 *Birmingham Business Journal* article, Fannie Mae and Freddie Mac controlled about 43 percent of the U.S. mortgage market. That percentage was expected to exceed 90 percent by 2003.

The article also asserted that the realities of Wall Street pushed Fannie Mae to pursue growth. To do so the GSEs entered riskier areas such as subprime lending and home-equity lending, thereby drifting further from their mission.

Detractors also pointed with concern to the enterprise's level of reserves. Members of Congress pushed for higher reserve amounts and increased regulation of the GSEs as the new century began.

The increasing involvement of the GSEs in multi-unit housing also drew ire. HUD had pushed Fannie Mae to increase its efforts in creating affordable housing, and the company upped its activity in the multifamily area to meet its goals. Competitors balked at the move and contended the GSEs' automatic underwriting networks had become so integral to the multifamily lending industry, they had to work hand-in-hand with them or risk being pushed out of the market.

Washington, D.C.-based FM Watch, a coalition of organizations monitoring the activities of the GSEs, fought to keep them within the boundaries of their missions. In particular, FM Watch viewed the underwriting network as a threat to competition and a vehicle by which Fannie Mae could encroach on the primary mortgage market. Moreover, the group asserted that the GSEs actually did little to ease the need for low- and moderate-income housing given HUD's broad definition of what was considered affordable. GE Capital Services, Chase Manhattan Corporation, and Wells Fargo & Company were among the members of FM Watch.

Supporters of the GSEs said the agencies historically stayed in the mortgage market when others were driven out by tough times. During the early 1990s, while S&Ls were going belly up and banks were edgy, Fannie Mae stayed in the commercial housing market. In addition, they said because GSEs could borrow money more cheaply, this translated into lower rents for tenants. Finally, the GSEs had programs targeting rural areas and small properties, situations other large players in the mortgage industry were unlikely to touch.

Franklin Raines predicted continued growth for Fannie Mae based on ongoing desire for homeownership and increased willingness to borrow, according to a November 2001 *American Banker* article. He nixed the idea of going into new areas of business, such as credit card debt, to drive growth, a move that would surely be opposed by critics and would require Congressional approval.

As the year drew to a close Fannie Mae continued to thrive, despite economic recession and war in Afghanistan. "People will give up a lot of other things before they give up their homes," Raines told *Money* magazine in December. "That is what makes this such a good business to be in." Fannie Mae was on track to mark its 15th consecutive year of double-digit earnings growth, a feat expected to be matched by only two other S&P companies, Home Depot and Automatic Data Processing.

Still, the future was not certain; if Congress withdrew its charter, Fannie Mae would lose its competitive advantage. In addition, there was a limit to the percentage of the mortgage market Fannie Mae could swallow up, which limited growth in that area. Plus, concerns about the GSEs' influence on the marketplace were being expressed by powerful figures in government, including Federal Reserve Chairman Alan Greenspan.

Yet, Fannie Mae had many allies in Washington, as some of its former executives were among Democratic and Republican insiders. Fannie Mae also was no shrinking violet about touting its own cause. According to *Money* magazine, Fannie Mae and FMF had spent about $75 million in advertising since 2000 to position itself in the public consciousness as a purveyor of the American Dream of homeownership.

Principal Competitors

Freddie Mac; General Electric Capital Services.

Further Reading

Bergsman, Steve, "BIG Competition," *Mortgage Banking,* May 2001, p. 35.

Birger, Jon, "The Rock: Under CEO Franklin Raines, Mortgage Financier Fannie Mae Is As Close As You'll Get to Owning an Invincible Earnings Machine," *Money,* December 1, 2001, pp. 37 + .

Federal National Mortgage Association: Background and History, Washington, D.C.: FNMA, 1975.

"GSEs Dominate Earnings Among Giants," *National Mortgage News,* July 19, 1999, p. 3.

Housing America: An Overview of Fannie Mae's Past, Present and Future, Washington, D.C.: FNMA, 1986.

Mandaro, Laura, "Behind Anti-GSE Sentiment, Some Simple Math," *American Banker,* March 30, 2001, p. 1.

Rieker, Matthias, "Fannie Chairman Predicts Continued Profit Growth," *American Banker,* November 14, 2001, p. 20.

"Think Private for Housing," *Birmingham Business Journal,* May 4, 2001, p. 30.

Zerega, Blaise, "Desktop App Reduces Loan Approval Time to Minutes," *InfoWorld,* May 25, 1998, p. 128.

—Tom Tucker
—update: Kathleen Peippo

Florida's Natural Growers

---

650 Highway 27
Lake Wales, Florida 33853
U.S.A.
Telephone: (863) 676-1411
Fax: (863) 676-0114
Web site: http://www.floridanatural.com

Cooperative
Founded: 1933 as Florida Citrus Canners Cooperative
Employees: 880
Sales: $605 million (2001 est.)
NAIC: 311411 Frozen Fruit, Juice, and Vegetable
    Manufacturing

Florida's Natural Growers is the largest citrus cooperative in the state of Florida and the second largest orange juice producer in the country, behind Tropicana. Headquartered in sunny Lake Wales, Florida, the company was founded by a group of Florida citrus growers in 1933. The cooperative comprises 13 grower organizations that represent more than 1,000 farmers. The company credits its not-from-concentrate (NFC) juice for much of its $605 million in annual sales and says the juice has that "right-from-the grove, fresh-squeezed taste." Florida's Natural Growers markets its NFC juice under the brand name Florida's Natural. Varieties include Original Orange, Home-Squeezed-Style Orange, Growers Style Orange, and Orange Juice Plus Calcium with Added Vitamin C, Ruby Red Grapefruit, Ruby Red Grapefruit Plus Calcium with Added Vitamin C, Lemonade, Apple Juice, Orange-Pineapple Juice, Cranberry Apple Juice Cocktail, and Raspberry Lemonade. The company also manufactures other brands of juice including Donald Duck (its original brand), Bluebird, Adams, and Texsun. Its products are sold to the foodservice industry, retailers, and vendors. The company exports to 40 countries primarily in Europe, Japan, and the Caribbean. Florida's Natural Growers is known for its national advertising campaigns that use real employees rather than actors and show footage from orange groves in its hometown of Lake Wales, Florida.

Florida Citrus Canners Cooperative in 1933

Florida's Natural Growers began in 1933 when a group of citrus growers decided to work together to process grapefruit and grapefruit sections. They formed a cooperative in which they owned the land, the company, and shared the company's profits. They called themselves the Florida Citrus Canners Cooperative. A year after it began, the company packed 422,000 cases of grapefruit sections and juice and processed 3,000 boxes of fruit a day. By 1940, the growers decided to invest in expensive equipment so they could begin producing frozen concentrated orange juice. This decision was a good one. The company's sales soared. Juice drinkers nationwide sipped the company's Donald Duck canned orange juice on a regular basis. In 1969, the company changed its name to Citrus World.

Not-From-Concentrate Juice in 1987

Citrus World enjoyed modest but steady sales until the late 1980s. In 1987 Citrus World introduced its Florida's Natural brand in a variety of flavors. Florida's Natural was a not-from-concentrate (NFC) juice. Like fresh-squeezed juice, NFC juice was 100 percent premium juice containing no added water, sugar, or preservatives. The company believed that NFC juice tasted better than concentrated juice, which has the water extracted and then added again before it is served.

Florida's Natural hit the market at just the right time. Minute Maid was exiting the NFC juice market because it believed that concentrated juice tasted better than NFC. Procter & Gamble also was pulling out of the orange juice market. Florida's Natural took the place of these juices. People tried Florida's Natural and liked the juice and its brightly colored cartons with a ready-to-drink pour spout that was easy to open and helped keep the juice fresh.

National Advertising in 1991

Citrus World invested heavily in advertising in 1991. Its national television and magazine ads emphasized the company's local origins. Its television ads reached 93 percent of all U.S. households and were seen by 2.5 billion people. Two of its television spots, "Rush Hour" and "Truck," showed an 18-

Company Perspectives:

Florida's Natural Growers is a cooperative of citrus growers located in Lake Wales, Florida. First founded in 1933, our cooperative has always had a clear focus on what we do best . . . producing premium quality orange juice from the tree to your glass.

People often recognize Florida's Natural Growers' slogan: "We own the land, we own the trees, we own the company." This consistent message of our growers owning the land, the trees, and the company has helped to establish the coop's commitment to quality and a difference you can taste.

wheeler on its way to the Lake Wales citrus groves. While traveling through town, the truck passed local landmarks that highlighted the leisurely, small-town nature of Lake Wales. Viewers saw a sleeping cat in a storefront window with an American flag. The commercials sent the message that Florida's Natural "takes all the time we need to make our juice just right."

Industry experts pointed out that while Citrus World's $13 million advertising campaign was large, it paled in comparison with the $40 million Tropicana spent on media ads. They referred to Citrus World and Tropicana as a "David vs. Goliath" scenario. Still, Citrus World's advertising worked and it helped propel the company to become the number two orange producer in the country. "We have been patient," said the company's CEO Steve Caruso in the *Tampa Tribune*. "It has been an orderly growth."

In 1997, Citrus World welcomed a new member to its coop for the first time in 20 years—the Orange Growers Marketing Association. Orange Growers added a million boxes of citrus a year to Citrus World's production.

A Name Change in 1998

The year 1998 was a great one for Citrus World. As it celebrated its 65th anniversary, the company enjoyed record sales. At this time, Citrus World decided to change its name to Florida's Natural Growers to reflect its best-selling product, Florida's Natural. "Although Citrus World appears in much local literature and rolls off many local lips, Florida's Natural is how the company is known at national and worldwide levels," explained Production Manager Mandy Hancock. The company felt in the past it was best known for brands such as Donald Duck, but that the brand name Florida's Natural would eventually become synonymous with their company.

The company originally had marketed Florida's Natural as "Fresh 'n Natural," but the Food and Drug Administration did not want the company using the word "fresh" in the name because the juice is pasteurized. Pasteurized juice is heated to kill bacteria and molds.

Florida's Natural Growers published a cookbook to mark their anniversary and new name. *Florida's Natural Favorite Recipes from Our Groves* was a hardbound, 112-page volume that included recipes for appetizers, soups, main dishes, salads, breads, desserts, and drinks.

Also in 1998, the company profited from troubles in Brazil, the largest exporter of orange juice in the world. Tree diseases that affected citrus trees in Brazil hurt a significant portion of that country's crop in 1998. Brazil's citrus shortage increased the price of orange juice in the United States and spiked citrus sales in Florida.

Florida citrus growers had been affected by Brazil's citrus production in the past: first in 1962 when a freeze in the United States caused tremendous citrus losses. The United States turned to Brazil to fulfill its demands for citrus. Freezes hurt Florida a second time in the 1980s. Brazil produced so many oranges this time that Florida citrus growers had to lower their prices to compete, and Brazilian citrus growers purchased several orange juice processing plants from bankrupt citrus growers in Florida. Florida's Natural Growers helped plant 15,000 additional trees in south Florida to protect citrus growers against freezes and lessen dependence on Brazil.

Sun Pac Foods and China in 2000

In 2000, Florida's Natural purchased Sun Pac Foods' processing plant in Bartow. The facility was renamed Florida's Natural Bartow and added 175 acres to the cooperative. "Sun Pac's processing plant is ideally suited to support the expansion of our brand," explained Caruso in a company press release. Caruso added that Florida's Natural had a strong need for additional processing facilities and had been using Sun Pac's processing lines for about six years. "We have run quite a bit of fruit through their lines to meet the demands of our sales growth," he said. "We hope to grow that facility to handle our processors' and our market's needs."

Sun Pac processed primarily specialty citrus, such as tangerines and tangelos, which took more time and effort than common citrus. Industry analysts said the purchase reflected a trend toward consolidation in the citrus industry. Sun Pac processed about 5.5 million boxes of specialty citrus a year and employed about 80 people.

During the same year, the company received the "okay" to begin exporting its juice to the 1.25 billion people in China. Prior to 2001, Beijing had import restrictions that prohibited Florida from selling oranges to China. Citrus growers had high hopes for the market in China, which had welcomed McDonald's and Kentucky Fried Chicken (KFC).

Florida Agriculture Commissioner Bob Crawford traveled to China with the first shipment of oranges, which were autographed by Florida's Governor Jeb Bush. "We hope to sell a lot of citrus here," Crawford said. "The United States has a tremendous food production capability. China needs food, and we think we have a good partnership."

Record Sales and a Grove House in 2001

In 2001 the company posted record sales for the tenth consecutive year. Sales jumped 10 percent from 1999 to 2000. The record $605 million in sales included an average of one million cases of juice or about three million gallons boxed and shipped per week and 23 million cases of citrus processed that year.

Key Dates:

1933: Florida Citrus Canners Cooperative is formed.
1940: Coop begins producing frozen concentrated orange juice.
1969: Coop changes its name to Citrus World.
1987: Citrus World introduces Florida's Natural not-from-concentrate juice in ready-to-pour containers.
1991: National advertising campaign is undertaken.
1997: Coop welcomes a new member for the first time in 20 years.
1998: Coop changes its name to Florida's Natural Growers.
2000: Coop purchases Sun Pac Foods, begins exporting to China.
2001: Florida's Natural opens Grove House, a new visitor center.

During the same year, Florida's Natural opened a visitor center called the Grove House. The Grove House replaced a hospitality center that the company closed 15 years earlier. Visitors touring Florida's Natural missed the center and frequently asked management why it was shut down. The company thought a new center would better please its customers.

Local architect Ed Pilkington designed the new Grove House to resemble an old Florida "cracker" house with a tin roof. The Grove House was built on a nine-acre parcel. Visitors viewed many exhibits that taught them about the citrus business. They also learned about horticulture and the way weather affected citrus crops. "We are very excited about this project as it will provide an excellent opportunity for consumers to learn more about our cooperative and the products that we grow and process," said Caruso.

A Sunny Future

Although the citrus industry would always be vulnerable to weather conditions, as of early 2002, industry experts predicted that Florida's Natural Growers would continue to grow. Even with its rapid gain in market share, however, most analysts believed that the company had little chance of overtaking mammoth Tropicana to become the number one orange juice company in the country. Said Caruso in the *Tampa Tribune:* "They could squash us if they wanted to, and if we had something to sling at them, we would have already done it by

now." Yet, surpassing Tropicana was not necessarily key to the company's success. In 2001 Florida's Natural Growers' NFC juice was extremely popular and the company's sales were growing. The company continued to invest millions in technology at its processing plants to maximize space and minimize waste and the time it took to process citrus. The work ethic of its coop members also played a significant role in the quality of the company's juice. The Florida farmers vowed to never let their company's success go to their heads. They still kept an image of Donald Duck on one of their water towers to remind them of the cooperative's humble beginnings.

Principal Competitors

Tropicana Products, Inc.; Louis Dreyfus Citrus; PepsiCo, Inc.

Further Reading

Brown, Susan, "Global Juice Strategy," *Florida Trend,* May 1997.

Bygrave, William, "Citrus World Name Changed to Match Major Juice Brand," *Associated Press,* November 20, 1998, http://www.polkonline.com/stories/112098/bus_citrus.shtml.

——, "Florida's Natural Offers Cookbook," *News Chief,* November 22, 1998, http://www.polkonline.com/stories/112298/lak_cookbook.shtml.

——, " 'Grove House': A Fruitful Escape for Tourists," *News Chief,* March 29, 2001, http://www.polkonline.com/stories/032901/bus_grove.shtml.

——, "2.5 Billion People to See New Florida's Natural Ads," *News Chief,* October 10, 1999, http://polkonline.com/stories/100599/lak_naturalads.shtml.

"Citrus World Renames Cooperative," *Supermarket News,* December 28, 1998.

"Citrus World to Buy Sun Pac Foods Plant," *News Chief,* April 21, 2000, http://www.polkonline.com/stories/042100/bus_citrus-world-sun-pac.shtml.

"Florida's Natural Growers Choose Intermec's Rugged Computer for Wireless Solution," September 2001, http://www.mobileinfo.com/news_2001/Issue36/Intermec_Florida.htm.

Kurtenbach, Elaine, "Florida Fetes Start of Citrus Shipments to China," *Associated Press,* March 28, 2000, http://www.polkonline.com/stories/032800/sta_china-citrus.shtml.

Merlo, Catherine, "A Star Is Born," *Rural Cooperatives,* July/August 1998.

Power, Paul, "Pulp Friction," *Tampa Tribune,* December 22, 1997.

Schneider, Mike, "Florida Citrus Benefits from Brazil Woes," *Associated Press,* November 29, 1998, http://www.polkonline.com/stories/112998/sta_juice.shtml.

—Tracey Vasil Biscontini

FRONTLINE

Frontline Ltd.

Mercury House, 101 Front St.
Hamilton HM12
Bermuda
Telephone: (441) 295-6935
Fax: (441) 295-3494
Web site: http://www.frontline.bm

Public Company
Incorporated: 1948 as London & Overseas Freighters plc
Employees: 29
Sales: $599.9 million (2000)
Stock Exchanges: New York
Ticker Symbol: FRO
NAIC: 483211 Inland Water Freight

Legally a Bermuda corporation, Frontline Ltd. is a shipping company operated out of Oslo, Norway, by dynamic Chairman and CEO John Fredriksen. In a series of moves since the mid-1990s, Fredriksen has assembled the world's largest oil tanker fleet, totaling more than 80 vessels, primarily in the Suezmax and VLCC sizes. Suezmax tankers have capacities between 120,000 and 170,000 in deadweight tons, while VLCCs (very large crude carriers) are between 200,000 and 320,000 in deadweight tons. Major oil companies are Frontline's main customers, followed by petroleum products traders and government agencies. Despite Frontline's large fleet and robust revenues, it is run by a staff of just 30 people, the company relying heavily on the outsourcing of its operations. Vessels are either owned by or chartered to subsidiaries or affiliated companies. Those owned directly by Frontline are registered and fly under the flags of a variety of countries, including the Bahamas, Liberia, Singapore, Norway, and Panama. Furthermore, costs are kept low because independent ship management companies vie for the company's business. They provide an array of services, from maintenance and shipyard supervision to accounting and crewing. Most of Frontline's vessels are crewed by Russians, Indians, or Filipinos.

Corporate Lineage Dating Back to 1948

Technically, the corporate history of Frontline can be traced back to the formation of London & Overseas Freighters plc in 1948 in the United Kingdom, but in reality the story of Frontline is that of Norwegian John Fredriksen, who rose from working class origins to become a shipping magnet with a personal worth of some $600 million. For centuries, shipping has been an important industry in Norway, which boasts of a number of great families involved in the business: the Bergesens, the Mosvolds, the Uglands, and the Wilhemsens. Fredriksen, in contrast, was the son of a welder, born at the close of World War II. He became involved in shipping at an early age, acting as an errand boy before becoming a shipbroker when he was just 16. Although others owned the ships, Fredriksen was soon investing his own money on ventures. Still quite young, he moved to New York and quietly added to his wealth in the shipping business. Operating in what was traditionally a secretive business, Fredriksen was able for many years to hide the fact that he owned ships by posing as a front man. Much of his success, according to colleagues, was the result of detachment. Unlike others in the business, he did not love ships and was rarely seen on one. He was able to dispassionately buy and sell vessels, with more of a soul of a dealmaker than a traditional Norwegian shipping magnate. Also unlike his Norwegian counterparts born into wealth, Fredriksen had a reputation as a rough character who indulged in drinking binges. He was described by many as a modern-day Viking. Overall, he was considered aggressive, ambitious, and coarse, less concerned with scruples than in achieving success.

In the early 1970s, shipowners went deep into debt to expand their tanker fleets, emboldened by inflation that increased rates and ship values and the belief that the Mideast oil trade would continue to flourish. Ships, as a result, became the object of capital speculation, as investors bought and sold them with little regard for their actual use. Subsequent oil discoveries in Alaska, Mexico, and the North Sea, however, brought petroleum products closer to consuming centers and hurt the Mideast trade. Moreover, consumers cut back on oil consumption. The Suez Canal, which had been closed since 1967, reopened in

Company Perspectives:

The Company's vision is to provide the customers with a flexible and reliable transportation service, and use this flexibility to develop unique industrial relations that will give material benefits to the customers as well as the Company.

1975, further curbing the demand for large tankers. Dry-cargo vessels then underwent a shipbuilding craze, based on a projected increase in coal and grain shipments that failed to be sustainable. The result by the early 1980s was a glut in ships of all kinds and shipping rates so low that many vessels were seized by banks and their owners forced out of business.

Fredriksen, still operating in the shadows, assembled a tanker fleet at the estimated cost of $1.5 billion during the boom period, and while others failed during the bust cycle, he was not only able to survive, but positioned himself as an important figure in the shipping industry. This transformation was not accomplished, however, without doing business with some dubious customers, as Fredriksen shipped crude to and from Lebanon and Syria. He was especially successful in running crude for Iran during its long war with Iraq, described by his Norwegian biographer as "the lifeline to the Ayatollah." He also gained some notoriety when he was jailed in Norway for a few weeks while authorities investigated allegations that his ships burned cargo oil as fuel. In the end, he was released and never charged, and although he maintained his innocence he admitted to the unusual practice of his ships burning "slops."

The Rise of Fredriksen As a Major Shipowner: 1980s–90s

It was in 1986 that Fredriksen first came into the open as a shipowner. When the depression in the shipping industry showed signs of easing in 1988, he was recognized as one of a new breed of international shipowners. In the mid-1990s he would begin to emerge as a major player, accomplished in large part by his recognition that the tankers constructed in the 1970s were now aging and would have to be replaced. Instead of commissioning new tankers, he decided to build his fleet through acquisitions. His first major purchase came in 1996 when he paid $55 million in cash to acquire Frontline AB, a shipping company that had been incorporated in Sweden in 1985 and was listed on the Stockholm Stock Exchange. He kept the tankers and sold off the bulk cargo ships. In 1996 Frontline AB generated revenues of $110.5 million, while posting a loss of $14 million.

In 1997 Fredriksen acquired London & Overseas Freighters (LOF) for $132 million. LOF had suffered through the shipping depression of the early 1980s, which forced it to cut its fleet of ten tankers to just three. In 1992 the company was reincorporated in Bermuda. Once the property passed into his hands, Fredriksen then created a new Bermuda corporation, Frontline Ltd., into which he merged the assets gained from Frontline AB and then merged with LOF. The process was completed in May 1998, with LOF emerging as the surviving corporate entity. It

subsequently assumed the Frontline Ltd. name. Aside from the ships that came with the Frontline AB and LOF acquisitions, Fredriksen garnered greater access to investors, particularly in New York.

Also in 1997 Fredriksen made a play for the Swedish tanker company ICB Shipping, which owned a fleet of six Suezmaxes and six VLCCs. Although he was able to acquire 51 percent of its shares, he was only able to amass 31 percent of the votes. What ensued was a contentious two-year hostile takeover fight. ICB enlisted the help of a white knight, selling a controlling interest to Greek shipowner John Angelicoussis. True to form, Fredriksen employed hardball tactics, threatening the board and running advertisements in the Swedish press. It was not until he succeeded in buying out another shareholder that Fredriksen gained the upper hand and was finally able to secure control of ICB.

In 1997 demand increased for the kind of large tankers that Fredriksen owned. Day rates, which were only $8,000 per day just three years earlier, now reached $60,000, a level not seen in some 20 years. For the year, Frontline saw its revenues increase to $197.2 million and profits soar to $22.8 million. A downturn in the Asian economy, however, would begin to have an adverse effect on the tanker business. Although Frontline added to the size of its fleet in 1998, lower shipping rates produced a negligible gain in revenues over the previous year at $203.9 million. Nevertheless, income improved significantly, to $31.9 million. Shipping rates continued to erode in 1999, when high world oil inventories caused by the soft Asian economy prompted the OPEC oil cartel to cut production in order to maintain prices. Decreased demand for large tankers also caused postponement in the delivery of new tankers as well as the scrapping of many ships. Moreover, an old tanker that sank off the coast of Brittany and spilled some 70,000 barrels of oil, caused oil companies to eschew aging tankers over the more expensive and safer tankers that generally comprised Frontline's fleet. While Frontline saw revenues for 1999 grow to $253.2 million, it nevertheless lost $86.9 million.

Acquisition of Golden Ocean Group: 2000

As OPEC increased production in 2000 and, because there was less available tankers, shipping rates improved. Fredriksen was once again better positioned than his competitors. He looked to take advantage of the misfortunes of Golden Ocean Group, a tanker company that was unable to weather the Asian recession. Based in the Channel Islands and incorporated in Liberia, the Golden Ocean fleet consisted of 17 VLCCs, five of which were under construction, and 11 modern dry bulk ships. It had been assembled by shipping veterans Robert Knutzen and Fred Cheng, who relied on $296 million worth of New York junk bonds. After the company was forced to file for Chapter 11 protection in January 2000, bondholders jockeyed for the assets.

Frontline paid 11 cents on the dollar to acquire $46.75 million of the bonds in order to enter the bankruptcy proceedings as a creditor interested in restructuring the business. A plan to make Golden Ocean a wholly owned subsidiary of Frontline was agreed upon when a second group appeared: Bentley, an alliance of two Greek shipping families, Restis and Kollakis. Bentley had quietly bought up stock in some of the debtors, in the process acquiring an equity position in Golden Ocean and gaining four directors on the board. The restructuring processwas now thrown open by the bankruptcy judge. With control of Golden Ocean's board, Bentley was able to obstruct Frontline's bid, which would pay up to 27 cents on every dollar invested and considered a better offer than Bentley's. According to the *Times* account of the proceeding, "The Bentley appointees' reluctance to sign led to rising tensions around the table. In the event, the appointees abstained, assuming that the board had locked Frontline into 22 to 27 cents on the dollar for the creditors. It was only later that they realized that, under Liberian law, abstention counts as a no-vote, and the board had accidentally kicked out the Frontline offer." Frontline returned with a lower bid of 17 cents on the dollar, reportedly prompting shareholders to consider suing the Bentley-controlled board for failing in their fiduciary responsibilities. With the pressure mounting on Bentley, one of its representatives ran into a Frontline executive in New York. Together they worked out a compromise in a hotel bar. In the end, Fredriksen got the 24 ships and Bentley took a quick profit on its investment in the Golden Ocean bonds.

Aside from adding the tankers of Golden Ocean, as well as its dry bulk fleet, Frontline acquired several other new and used tankers in 2000. The extra capacity was welcomed, as shipping rates soared, nearing 30-year highs. Frontline's revenues more than doubled, reaching $600 million, while the company earned an incredible $313.9 million. With the largest tanker fleet in the world, Frontline entered 2001 looking to continue its pattern of growth. It announced a "newbuilding" program that would begin with the construction of two Suezmaxes and three VLCCs. In the summer of 2001 it acquired Mosvold Shipping Ltd., in the process acquiring three contracts for new VLCCs as well as two VLCCs built in the mid-1970s. Frontline also gained interests in two other VLCC newbuildings with partners Euronax Luxembourgh S.A. and Overseas Shipholding Group.

Altogether Frontline would either own or have significant interests in ten new vessels worth almost $700 million. At the same time, the company was selling ships, thereby lowering the age of its tanker fleet to just under six years of age, with two-thirds of the vessels boasting environmentally safe double hulls.

In August 2001 Frontline shares were listed and began trading on the New York Stock Exchange, giving the company a greater access to the capital markets for continued growth. With size came competitive advantages. According to a 2001 *Forbes* profile of Fredriksen, "For the past three decades ship owners willingly gave brokers information about the availability and position of their ships. But the two Fredriksen-dominated tanker pools now can afford to be coy about their fleets' whereabouts, making it tougher for oil companies to drive a bargain. The Fredriksen supertanker pool also threatens to blacklist brokers who cut it out of large contracts." Frontline was situated to further its consolidation of the VLCC segment, which remained very much fragmented. With the phasing out of single hull tankers, Frontline's modern fleet also looked to take advantage of an increasing demand for safer ships. Despite a downturn in the world economy, the near-term outlook for shipping appeared promising, as did the prospects for Frontline. The terrorist attacks on the United States on September 11, 2001, however, did hold the potential for the disruption of oil shipments from the Middle East. Nevertheless, such turmoil could actually favor Frontline and Fredriksen, who in earlier years grew wealthy from a heated conflict between Iran and Iraq. He was unlikely to shy away from any future challenges.

Principal Subsidiaries

CIB Shipping AB; Floating Storage, S.A.; Alliance Chartering LLC.

Principal Competitors

Knightsbridge Tankers; Neptune Orient; OMI Corporation.

Further Reading

Buckingham, Lisa, and Mark Milner, "Volatile Viking of Shipping Tycoon John Fredriksen Is Riding High," *Guardian,* October 25, 1997, p. 024.

Crisione, Valeria, "Merchant Fleets on the Brink of a Sea Change," *Financial Times,* October 26, 2001.

Gorham, John, "Viking Raider," *Forbes,* April 30, 2001, p. 76.

Harrison, Pete, "Sunk in the Battle for a Supertanker Fleet," *Times,* September 1, 2000, p. 27.

Machalaba, Daniel, "Nautical Upheaval: Shipping Firms Suffer As Boat Values Decline and Freight Rates Fall," *Wall Street Journal,* November 5, 1985, p. 1.

Stickel, Amy L., "Foreign Companies Wind Up in U.S. Bankruptcy Court," *Corporate Legal Times,* May 2001.

—Ed Dinger

Geerlings & Wade, Inc.

960 Turnpike St.
Canton, Massachusetts 02021
U.S.A.
Telephone: (781) 821-4152
Fax: (781) 821-4152
Web site: http://www.geerwade.com

Public Company
Incorporated: 1986
Employees: 79
Sales: $37.2 million (2000)
Stock Exchanges: NASDAQ SmallCap
Ticker Symbol: GEER
NAIC: 445310 Beer, Wine, and Liquor Stores; 45439
  Other Direct Selling Establishments

For choosy wine connoisseurs and novices alike, Geerlings & Wade, Inc. offers premium wines and accessories through direct mail and on its web site as well as in retail stores. The company is required to obtain liquor licenses in each state in which it operates. Despite being active in only half of the continental United States, Geerlings & Wade is still the nation's leading direct marketer of wine and wine accessories. It sells premium as well as lower-priced wines in the half case or case and also provides consumers with information on wine choice and storage.

1986–90: A Company Founded by Wine Connoisseurs

Huib Geerlings and Phillip Wade were friends and wine connoisseurs who found themselves frustrated by the lack of information provided to wine buyers by American retailers. They believed that wine should be rated and purchased based on taste; however, they found that most American consumers were making their wine-buying choices based on price or reputation.

Then came the slow-arriving case of Bordeaux Grand Cru that Huib Geerlings ordered for a Thanksgiving dinner. Ordered from France, he received the wine long after Thanksgiving, but in time for New Year's. That experience, combined with a love of wine,

was the spark that began the development of a business plan—for a U.S. direct marketing company to sell and ship wine.

The entrepreneurs joined together to form a new company—Geerlings & Wade, to not only succeed in the business arena of profitability but also to educate the public and take away the intimidating factors that often accompany wine selection. Huib Geerlings, age 33, and Phillip Wade, age 29, were trained accountants, but they left their jobs as auditors at Coopers & Lybrand in Boston to turn their passion for wine into a new venture.

Geerlings and Wade decided that the best way to select the wines they would sell was exactly the same way they had always selected wines themselves—by actually tasting them. Hence, they went to the source, in France, Italy, Australia, Chile, and California, and selected the wines personally based on a combination of quality and price. Through the relationships they developed at hundreds of wineries, the new company obtained wine at lower prices and then marketed those to the consumer.

As their marketing vehicle, Geerlings and Wade selected direct mail as a non-threatening and most affordable way to get both the wine and the consumer information into the hands of its customers. The wine would then arrive on the customer's doorstep, as promised.

Founded in Canton, Massachusetts, Geerlings & Wade could at first only sell its products in Massachusetts. However, it soon expanded to Connecticut, New York, Illinois, Florida, California, and New Jersey. While some types of direct marketers can expand in regional chunks of customers, liquor laws require that Geerlings & Wade must have a licensed sales facility in each state in which it operates. By 1989, the company had sales of $479,000.

1990–94: Success Highlighted by Initial Public Offering

Seven years of success led Geerlings & Wade to the NASDAQ, with an initial public offering (IPO) in 1994. The previous year, 1993, had been extremely successful for the company—with net income rising 105 percent and sales rising 93

Company Perspectives:

We will establish and maintain a personal and lasting relationship with our customers who appreciate fine wine. We will provide unparalleled service and quality, value-oriented products, as well as informative education to enhance our customers' total wine experience.

percent to $12.4 million. The company offered 1.4 million shares of stock in its IPO, raising approximately $10 million.

In the first half of 1994, sales growth continued to rise through the company's direct mail efforts. In August of that year, the company hired Robert L. Cosinuke as director of marketing, a newly created position. "Mr. Cosinuke is our first executive manager with a professional direct marketing background. His experience establishing direct marketing programs for some of the leading companies in the industry will allow us to take advantage of more sophisticated techniques and elevate our direct marketing efforts to an entirely new level," said company President Phillip Wade.

The company's philosophy remained the same—quality wines at good prices. The wine list was intentionally short. In direct opposition to the "mega-store" concept, Geerlings & Wade offered a limited selection so as not to overwhelm and intimidate the wine buyer, especially some of those new customers who might not be comfortable with deciding between hundreds of wines.

In October 1994, the company expanded to the state of Washington, bringing the total states served to eight. Washington was the eighth largest market for table wine in 1993, and Geerlings & Wade was then able to market to the state before the holiday shopping season in 1994.

In early 1995, Geerlings & Wade announced record growth of 233 percent in fourth-quarter 1994 earnings. Orders climbed to 1,000 cases a day and brought a 63 percent increase in sales.

Facing New Challenges: 1995–99

Direct marketing had its cost, and in 1995 Geerlings & Wade was caught off-guard with rising packaging and mailing expenses as well as higher wine prices and a weaker U.S. dollar. "We had some unsuccessful wine offerings in 1995," said Chief Financial Officer Peter McAree in an interview with the *Boston Globe* in May 1996. "At times we did not have the proper level of planning, and we could not take the time needed to find a quality product and pull together the mailing with the planning and foresight to market it. We also found that, in prospecting for new customers, we did not achieve the rates of repeat business that we had in the past."

Profits were flat in the first quarter of 1995, causing the stock price to drop from $17.25 in March 1995 to $4 a share in October. By May 1996, the company was struggling with stock price and internal issues, and cofounder and President Phillip Wade announced his resignation, effective as soon as a successor could be named.

Jay Essa, a former Gallo executive, was named president and CEO in September 1996, bringing over 20 years of wine industry experience to the position. "Jay Essa brings to Geerlings & Wade an in-depth understanding of the wine industry and, equally as important, considerable expertise in understanding consumer demand for select, table wines," said Huib Geerlings, in a company press release. Cofounders Huib Geerlings and Phillip Wade remained as directors of the company with Geerlings serving as chairman of the board.

In 1997, the company made its first entry in Internet e-business with the signing of a marketing agreement with Peapod, Inc., an online grocery and delivery service. Geerlings & Wade's wines would now be a part of an online ordering service with customers accessing products through the Internet as well as the traditional direct marketing methods.

Also in 1997, Geerlings & Wade announced its intent to acquire Passport Wine Club, an Internet company with sales of $1 million. "We plan to operate Passport Wine as an independent entity and use it as a springboard to further develop our continuity business. Passport Wine will contribute to our growth in several ways. It will strengthen our Internet presence by adding a second web site from which wine buyers can purchase wine online," said Jay Essa, president and CEO. In May 1998, Geerlings & Wade launched its own web site at www.geerwade.com to market wines as well as provide online information for customers about wine selection. In July, the purchase of Passport Wine Club was finalized.

In 1998, the growth was back for Geerlings & Wade with a 3.2 percent jump in sales and a net income of over $1 million, compared to 1997 income of $823,000. "Customers have responded well to our house mailings and the fall catalog, and we acquired many new accounts from our focused acquisition mailings," said Jay Essa, president and CEO.

In 1999, the company expanded to Texas, New Hampshire, and Rhode Island. With the new expansion, the company could sell its products, through the mail and the Internet, to more than 81 percent of the wine-consuming American public. That same year, the company announced a series of initiatives to lead it to its next level of growth. Those initiatives included developing a new and better web site, implementing new computer hardware including addressing Y2K compliance issues, expanding the marketing department, and developing a creative advertising campaign.

In March 1999, Geerlings & Wade announced its support of the "Hatch Bill," legislation which would give states the power to enforce federal laws against illegal direct shipping of alcoholic beverages. "First, we want to let our customers and shareholders know that the Hatch Bill does not pose a threat to our business because we have always operated within those state laws that others have tried so hard to circumvent. The advent of new technologies like the Internet has made illegal cross-border shipping more prevalent. Many of our competitors ship across state lines with little or no regard for the law. There is a right way to operate this kind of business, and states have every right to insist that their laws be obeyed in this way," said Jay Essa, president and CEO.

By September 1999, it seemed a sellout was imminent. Geerlings & Wade had agreed to be purchased by Liquid

Key Dates:

1986: Company is founded by Huib Geerlings and Phillip Wade.
1989: Company expands beyond Massachusetts.
1994: Geerlings & Wade makes initial public offering.
1996: Phillip Wade resigns as CEO; Jay Essa is named as replacement.
1997: Geerlings & Wade launches web site and Internet purchasing.
1998: Geerlings & Wade purchases Passport Wine Club.
1999: Liquid Holdings, Inc. agrees to purchase Geerlings & Wade.
2000: Liquid Holdings purchase falls through; Jay Essa resigns as president and CEO, and is replaced by David Pearce.
2001: Geerlings & Wade is downgraded to the NASDAQ SmallCap Market.

Holdings Inc. for $40 million in cash. The company said that the 105 employees would not be affected. However, in February 2000 the agreement automatically terminated due to Liquid Holdings not obtaining financing from sources acceptable to Geerlings & Wade. ''This has been a long process for everyone involved in the transaction,'' said Essa. ''We think it's appropriate to take some time to assess the direction the company will head from this point on.''

2000 and Beyond: New Strategies for Growth

The failed deal, coupled with a $1.5 million loss for 1999, may have been reasons prompting Jay Essa to resign in April 2000 as CEO and president, in a move characterized by the *Boston Globe* as ''abrupt.'' Chief Financial Officer David Pearce was named as Essa's replacement.

In 2000, the company's net income was still negative, albeit a gain over 1999 with a loss per share of 12 cents compared to 1999's 39 cents. Net sales were lower, however. Fourth quarter 2000 sales were encouraging, as was the net income figure of

$509,000. Total Internet sales increased 180 percent from 1999 to 2000, although CEO David Pearce cautioned that the growth in Internet sales could not be expected to maintain at that rate each year. Besides the failed merger and CEO Essa's departure, 2000 was also plagued with an inventory that was too high.

In April 2001, Geerlings & Wade was transferred from the NASDAQ to the NASDAQ SmallCap Market because the company failed to comply with the exchange's minimum market value requirements. The decision was made after a hearing before the qualifications panel. In response, Pearce said, ''We do not believe that being listed on The Nasdaq SmallCap Market will materially affect the Company or our stockholders.''

Embracing the new technology of the Internet and continuing its expansion within the United States, Geerlings & Wade was on the road to further success in the 21st century after some tumultuous changes between 1999 and 2001. Huib Geerlings and Phillip Wade's original vision, however tenuous, had become a reality—quality wine, lower prices, and timely delivery to a broad population.

Principal Competitors

eVineyard.

Further Reading

''Company News: Geerlings & Wade Agrees to a Deal with Liquid Holdings,'' *New York Times*, September 29, 1999, p. C4.

''Geerlings & Wade Enhances Web Site,'' *Boston Globe*, January 1, 1999, p. C5.

Mencke, Claire, ''Geerlings & Wade Inc.,'' *Investor's Business Daily*, October 27, 1994, p. A6.

''Pipeline: Geerlings & Wade Inc.,'' *Investor's Business Daily*, May 10, 1994, p. A6.

Rosenberg, Ronald, ''Geerlings & Wade Inc.,'' *Boston Globe*, May 21, 1996, p. 50.

Shao, Maria, ''The Wine Is in the Mail,'' *Boston Globe*, September 25, 1994, p. 81.

Treiser, C. Kinou, ''Geerlings & Wade Inc.,'' *Investor's Business Daily*, March 23, 1995, p. A6.

—Melissa Rigney Baxter

General Bearing Corporation

44 High Street
West Nyack, New York 10994
U.S.A.
Telephone: (845) 358-6000
Toll Free: (800) 431-1766
Fax: (845) 358-7414
Web site: http://www.generalbearing.com

Public Company
Incorporated: 1958
Employees: 727
Sales: $59.39 million (2000)
Stock Exchanges: NASDAQ
Ticker Symbol: GNRL
NAIC: 332991 Ball and Roller Bearing Manufacturing;
  333513 Machine Tools, Metal Forming Type

General Bearing Corporation manufactures, sources, assembles, and distributes a variety of bearing components and bearing products, supplying original equipment manufacturers and the industrial aftermarket, principally in North America, under the Hyatt and General trademarks. Chinese joint ventures manufacture some of these components and products. A Romanian joint venture produces a variety of machine tools for boring, turning, milling, and grinding metalwork pieces.

Growing Manufacturer: 1958–85

Seymour Gussack worked for Grant Pulley and Hardware, his father's hardware manufacturing business, until 1958, when he and his brother Milton each invested $2,500 to found General Bearing Corporation in Mineola, New York. The company began as an engineering-oriented supplier designing bearings for a variety of special industrial applications. Its clients included Chrysler and AMF. General Bearing's search for supplies led to profitable overseas alliances with Japanese and Polish firms. The company began marketing standard precision bearings to original equipment manufacturers in 1965 and added miniature unground bearings to its product line the

following year. These miniature bearings were being made for rotary solenoids, tuning controls for high-fidelity record player systems, potentiometers, and business machines, in quantities of 10,000 to 100,000 per order. The company's costs for making bearings were reduced by foregoing the grinding step. General Bearing also was producing ball transfers. In Mineola, Swiss-made machines, engaged in the fine-blanking process, were press-forming steel parts such as levers and cams, producing close tolerances and relatively smooth edges. Company headquarters were in West Nyack, New York, which was also the site of the bearing plant.

General Bearing's sales came to more than $8 million in 1967, up from about $4 million in 1962. More than half of the company's bearings were being made in the United States, with the rest imported chiefly from Japan and England. Its four divisions were Genbearco International, which was marketing the unground miniature bearings, standard precision bearings, and pillow block; Global Ball & Bearing, which handled sales of balls made overseas; BMB, the exclusive U.S. distributor of English-made BMB miniature and instrument bearings; and Monarch Die, where the Mineola plant was press-forming steel parts.

General Bearing moved its domestic manufacturing operations to a new, company-built facility in Wilson, North Carolina, in 1969. Bearings and bearing components produced at this plant were sold primarily to the automotive market. The company, in 1975, formed a distribution division that sold General Bearing's line of products, both manufactured and imported, to industrial distributors throughout the United States, thereby supplementing its marketing to original equipment manufacturers. A Mexican subsidiary was established in 1977.

In 1979 General Bearing completed a new one-story, $2.6 million, 100,000-square-foot factory in Wilson that replaced the older five-story facility. The new plant had the capability to increase bearings output by 50 percent and included automatic assembly equipment, an automatic scrap-processing system, and an automated energy control system. Also installed was a totally integrated online business information control system at the West Nyack headquarters. In 1983 the company moved its distribution center and bearing assembly operations to Blauvelt, about five miles south of West Nyack.

Turning to China for Manufacturing: 1986–2000

General Bearing sold its Wilson plant to Nucor Corporation in 1986. It was replaced by an 80,000-square-foot leased facility in Union, New Jersey. In 1987 the company expanded its field of operations by purchasing Hyatt-Clark Industries Inc. Formerly a division of General Motors Corporation, Hyatt-Clark, before its recent liquidation, had been primarily a manufacturer of tapered roller bearings for the automotive and railroad industries. This purchase allowed General Bearing to acquire a large amount of equipment to establish new domestic manufacturing capabilities, utilize the well-known Hyatt trademark, and gain entry into the tapered roller bearing market and the railroad market.

The Hyatt-Clark acquisition also became the foundation of a multinational manufacturing organization producing ball and roller bearing components in China for finishing and distribution by the Union plant and an Israeli joint venture. Using most of the equipment obtained from acquisition of the million-square-foot Hyatt-Clark factory in Hyatt, New Jersey, Shanghai General Bearing Co., Ltd. was established as a joint venture in 1987 to serve automotive original equipment manufacturers in the United States, Europe, and Asia. One Shanghai installation was a 72,000-square-foot plant utilizing about $10 million in Hyatt-Clark manufacturing equipment. The other was a 55,000-square-foot complex performing assembly and secondary operations on components made at the first plant. General Bearing's Chinese partner provided the workforce and facilities.

The output from the Chinese plants was sent mainly to General Bearing's Union facility, where the company installed new computer numerical-control machining centers, grinders, and turning machines, as well as assorted machining, heat-treating, grinding, and assembly equipment from Hyatt-Clark. In addition to upgrading its finishing and assembly capabilities for automotive bearing lines, the Union plant reestablished production of Hyatt-Clark's railroad products, including journal boxes and traction motor bearings. The Israeli operation was established as a joint venture with Delek Investment & Properties Ltd., a unit of a major oil firm. This unit was charged with finishing bearing products for North American and European customers.

General Bearing's expansion was the result of antidumping rulings and a Department of Defense directive requiring U.S.-made bearings in military-related products. These developments combined to create a greater need for bearings and other industrial parts production for the automotive industry. By 1990 the company had experienced an increase in production volume of 150 percent. Its operations were enhanced by the implementation of a cost-effective materials-handling system for distribution operations in its 35,000-square-foot warehouse. This sys-tem allowed order pickers to pick, sort, and pack orders in one step. Travel time to deliver completed orders to the packing station was virtually eliminated.

All was not well at General Bearing, however. The company had borrowed $12 million for the Hyatt-Clark purchase and, before establishing its Union plant, had attempted to reopen the massive Hyatt-Clark factory—with the staff maintained for this purpose—but had been unable to do so because of potentially incurring liability under applicable environmental laws. A subsequent attempt to establish a plant next to a company warehouse in Orangetown, New York, was blocked by local opposition.

With General Bearing unable to fulfill orders for Hyatt-Clark's output, the company incurred a combined net loss of $5.5 million in 1991 and 1992. World Machinery Company, a private firm controlled by the Gussack family that held 77 percent of General Bearing's shares of stock, filed for chapter 11 bankruptcy reorganization of General Bearing in 1991. The company reemerged from bankruptcy in 1993 after World Machinery paid off the loan, receiving in return General Bearing notes and the remainder of the company's shares. Seymour Gussack's son, David, became president of the company in that year.

In 1994 Shanghai General Bearing was certified as a supplier of wheel bearings to Shanghai Volkswagen, but in 1995, despite an operating profit, the parent company incurred a net loss because of recalls of 10,000 bearings to the railroad industry due to defects. General Bearing fared better in 1996, when it recorded a net profit of $1.36 million. That year the company returned to West Nyack, locating on an 18-acre site with a 155,000-square-foot industrial area—chiefly for assembly rather than production—and 35,000 square feet of office space.

General Bearing became a public company in 1997, when it raised $5.3 million from its initial public offering of common stock. That year the company opened its third joint venture for the production of bearings in China, the Ningbo General Bearing Co., Ltd. Also in 1997, General Bearing won a $54 million contract to supply wheel and axle bearings to General Motors over the next three years. General Bearing allowed its union lease to expire in 1998. That year Chinese joint ventures provided 72 percent of the company's bearings and 82 unaffiliated manufacturers provided the remainder. The year 2000 began with the acquisition of a controlling interest in Jiangsu General Ball & Roller Co., Ltd., a leading Chinese ball bearing manufacturer, to manufacture high-precision steel balls and rollers in Rugao City, Jiangsu Province.

General Bearing, according to a company executive interviewed in 2000, reduced its cost structure by 25 percent by transferring the majority of its operations to China while maintaining—and even improving—the quality of its products. Every lot received in West Nyack was being inspected prior to acceptance, using, with few exceptions, a zero-defect acceptance plan that required the entire lot to be placed on hold if any part failed to meet specifications. A new inspection center had been established in China, and General Bearing planned to gradually shift most inspection from West Nyack to Yuyao City, China, so that shipments would ultimately go directly from "dock to stock" when arriving in the United States. According to a *Tooling & Production* article in 2000, "A visit

Key Dates:

1958: General Bearing is founded by Seymour Gussack.
1967: The company's annual sales pass $8 million.
1987: General Bearing purchases Hyatt-Clark Industries Inc.; the company founds the first of several Chinese manufacturing joint ventures.
1991–93: General Bearing is operating under Chapter 11 bankruptcy protection.
1997: General Bearing becomes a public company with its initial stock offering.
2000: The company acquires World Machinery Co., a machine tool manufacturer.

to any of the factories reveals modern production equipment and management systems equal to those in Japan, Europe, or the U.S. All will be soon ISO 9002 certified.''

General Bearing, in July 2000, acquired World Machinery Company, which just prior to the acquisition owned 75 percent of the outstanding common stock of General Bearing. Principally owned by members of General Bearing's board of directors and senior management, World Machinery was mainly involved with the manufacture and sale of machine tools. A 60 percent owned subsidiary had, in 1998, purchased 51 percent of a privatized factory in Bacau, Romania, and had, with minor exceptions, the exclusive right to market its products. World Machinery lost money in 1998 and 2000.

General Bearing in 2000

General Bearing's sales (including World Machinery) came to $64.34 million in 1999 and $59.39 million in 2000. The company attributed the 2000 drop in revenue mainly to a decrease in orders for railroad bearings due to the slowing U.S. economy and to a slump in its machine tool business. Its net income for the two years was $2.24 million and $1.88 million, respectively. The OEM Division accounted for 63 percent of sales in 2000, the Distribution Division for 22 percent, and the Machine Tool Division—that is, World Machinery—for 15 percent. The former two were profitable, but the Machine Tool Division sustained an operating loss of $2.7 million. Sales outside the United States accounted for 11 percent of the total. General Bearing's long-term debt was $16.45 million at the end of 2000. Members of the Gussack family owned about half of the company's common stock in June 2001.

General Bearing's products included ball bearings, tapered roller bearings, spherical roller bearings, and cylindrical roller bearings, both to the industrial aftermarket and, under the Hyatt and General trademarks, to original equipment manufacturers. These products were being used in a broad range of applications, including automobiles, railroad cars, locomotives, trucks, heavy-duty trailers, office equipment, machinery, and appliances. Original equipment customers included 8 of the top 12 U.S. manufacturers of heavy-duty trailers, Visteon Corp., Burlington Northern/Santa Fe Railroad Co., Pitney Bowes Inc., and Eastman Kodak Co. Industrial aftermarket customers included the two largest industrial distributors in the United States, each of which had more than 400 outlets. General Bearing was obtaining 76 percent of its bearings and components from various Chinese joint ventures and the remainder from about 50 unaffiliated manufacturers working under short-term contracts.

General Bearing's machine tools included horizontal boring mills, bridge and gantry mills, vertical turning lathes, heavy-duty lathes, roll grinders, belt grinders, and vertical grinders. These were being produced by W.M. Works, formerly known as Masini Unelte, Becau, S.A. A subsidiary of the works was selling most of these products in the United States and also marketing its own product lines of WMW HECKERT production milling machines and WMW Radial Drills, manufactured by independent suppliers abroad. This subsidiary also was importing and distributing CETOS grinding machines from the Czech Republic. Machine tool customers included Boeing and Chrysler.

Principal Subsidiaries

World Machinery Company; World Machinery Group, BV (60%); WMW Machinery Company, Inc.

Principal Operating Units

Distribution Division; Machine Tool Division; OEM Division.

Principal Competitors

American Koyo Corp.; FAG Holding Corporation; NSK Corporation; NTN Bearing Corporation of America; SKF USA Inc.; Timken Corporation; Torrington Company.

Further Reading

Auguston, Karen A., ''A Back-to-Basics Approach Doubled Our Productivity!,'' *Modern Materials Handling,* February 1990, pp. 52–53.

Gabriele, Michael C., ''General Bearing Goes Multinational,'' *Metalworking News,* July 4, 1988, pp. 5, 26.

''Gen'l Bearing Building New Plant in N.C.,'' *American Metal Market,* October 23, 1978, p. 14.

''Quality Commitment Ensures Off-Shore Production Success,'' *Tooling & Production,* July 2000, pp. 37–38.

Storey, Warren, ''Hustling, Ambitious Genbearco,'' *Metalworking News,* April 1, 1968, p. 18.

—Robert Halasz

Genmar Holdings, Inc.

100 S. 5th St., Ste. 2400
Minneapolis, Minnesota 55402
U.S.A.
Telephone: (612) 339-7600
Fax: (612) 337-1930
Web site: http://www.genmar.com

Private Company
Incorporated: 1986 as Genmar Industries, Inc.
Employees: 6,500
Sales: $858 million (2000 est.)
NAIC: 336612 Boat Building

Genmar Holdings, Inc. is the largest manufacturer of recreational boats in the United States. Comprised of 12 different companies, Genmar builds over 300 models of boats at nine manufacturing locations in the United States and Canada. Genmar's product line runs the gamut from small fishing skiffs to luxury yachts. The company's boats are sold by 1,300 dealers in all 50 states and more than 30 foreign countries. Minneapolis-based businessman Irwin Jacobs assembled Genmar over the course of 24 years as he gradually bought small or bankrupt boat manufacturers. Larson Boats, the oldest of the companies owned by Genmar, dates back to 1913, and many of the other companies were founded in the 1950s or 1960s. In a series of often complicated transactions in the 1980s, the components of Jacobs's boat-building empire emerged from their parent company Minstar and coalesced into a single boat-manufacturing company under the name Genmar. Genmar is focused on increasing its market share through technological innovation and exceptional customer service. New manufacturing methods such as VEC and Roplene have allowed the company to improve the strength of its products and develop cleaner manufacturing processes. The company's brand names include Aquasport, Carver, Crestliner, Glastron, Larson, Logic Marine, Lund, Ranger, Trojan, Wellcraft, Four Winns, Hydra-Sports, Javelin, Lowe, Seaswirl, and Stratos.

Piecing Together a Boating Empire: 1978–89

Irwin Jacobs earned the nickname "Irv the Liquidator" for his aggressive business practices in the 1970s and early 1980s. In takeover attempts, both successful and unsuccessful, of major corporations such as Pabst Brewing Co. and Kaiser Steel Corp., he earned the reputation of a corporate raider who preferred to dismantle failing enterprises rather than operate a business.

Jacobs had honed his business skills from an early age. He obtained his first business experience selling used feed bags for the Minneapolis-based family business Northwestern Bag. Later, after a two-day stint at college, he developed a knack for liquidating the merchandise of defunct retail stores. Jacobs's first major profits came when he negotiated loans for deals with Grain Belt Breweries and the bankrupt W.T. Grant & Co. Soon Jacobs was a familiar figure on the Minneapolis business scene, known for his opulent lifestyle that included a silver Rolls Royce and a mansion with two-inch thick marble floors.

Jacobs acquired the first component of what was to become Genmar in 1978, when he bought a 25 percent controlling stake in Arctic Enterprises, Inc., a Minnesota snowmobile company that also happened to make Larson and Lund boats. Larson, located in Little Falls, Minnesota, made small fiberglass fishing boats. Lund was located in New York Mills, Minnesota, and had been making aluminum fishing boats since 1948.

Arctic went downhill after Jacobs's acquisition. Two years with little snow, a resulting decline in sales, and high interest rates pushed the company to bankruptcy by 1981. Jacobs subsequently sold the snowmobile business, built a profitable company around the boating divisions, and renamed the company Minstar. He also began playing a more active role in the company's management. Revenues for the boating division in 1982 were $25.3 million.

Minstar's focus on powerboat manufacturing was soon diluted as Jacobs used the company as a general investment vehicle. In the spring of 1983 Minstar bought a moving and storage business known as Bekins Co. The following year Jacobs acquired the Florida-based holding company Aegis Corp., whose businesses included ship repair, natural-gas compressors, and tread rubber. The company also owned Wellcraft Boats of Sarasota, Florida, a manufacturer of fiberglass fishing boats, sport cruisers, and the high-performance Scarab line.

A few months later Jacobs expanded Minstar's operations to include a stake in an oil and gas exploration company. Nevertheless, the company's boating sector continued to grow. New York-based AMF Inc. became a part of Minstar in 1985. The company manufactured sport and leisure products, but also marketed the Hatteras line of boats. Hatteras specialized in luxury yachts, most of them over 50 feet in length and with prices of over $1 million. Soon after the acquisition Jacobs fired the company's management, sold about a dozen of its peripheral business units, and kept only the sports products and Hatteras businesses. By now Minstar was manufacturing Larson, Lund, Wellcraft, and Hatteras boats. Revenues for the four brands reached $242.6 million in 1985.

In mid-1986 the four boat manufacturers were consolidated and spun off as a new company, Genmar Industries Inc., 82 percent of which was still owned by Minstar. Eighteen percent, or five million shares, of the new firm's stock was sold to the public in a July initial public offering, raising $57.5 million. The boat manufacturing business was prospering, and Genmar planned an expansion at four plants to increase production by about 40 percent. The company also bought Glastron, a manufacturer of entry-level and mid-range sport boats, in mid-1987. The acquisition of Henry Boats Inc. of Ohio was considered, but a negotiations impasse scuttled the deal.

Genmar attained record profits for 1987. Operating income reached $35.9 million, up 70 percent from the year before, on revenues of $448 million. Minstar as a whole, however, was not performing as well. Multiple acquisitions had caused the accumulation of considerable debt and, with operations in such disparate areas as oil-drilling services and sports equipment, investors were unsure just what Minstar's business focus was.

In response, in 1987 Jacobs considered having Genmar buy Minstar and spin off the non-boatmaking operations of its former parent company. A decline in the stock market, however, made the deal unworkable. As an alternate strategy for increasing the value of company stock, Minstar began buying back some of its shares. The company also went ahead with plans to

trim its peripheral operations and focus on Genmar's boat industry. In 1988 Minstar went completely private, bought out by Jacobs's IJ Holdings Corp. Jacobs and Carl Pohlad, a Minneapolis investor, paid shareholders about $400 million in cash and notes, which meant that Jacobs, the largest shareholder, received $105 million, a considerable profit over his original investment in the company.

Growth During Hard Times: 1989–94

The late 1980s were a turning point for the boat building industry. Throughout the prosperous mid-1980s, banks had been willing to provide loans for up to 80 percent of the cost of a million-dollar yacht. The high-end Hatteras boats were one of the most profitable divisions of Genmar's operations. Revenues rose yearly, reaching a peak of $518.2 million in 1988. The following year, however, marked the onset of leaner times. Banks tightened up credit and in 1990 Congress imposed a luxury tax on any boat whose cost exceeded $100,000. Between 1988 and 1991, sales of powerboats in the United States declined from 524,000 to 278,000 units. At Genmar, revenues fell for the first time in 1989 and in 1990 the company recorded a net loss of $11.7 million.

The slump continued into 1991, forcing many smaller boat manufacturers out of business. Jacobs took advantage of his competitors' troubles to increase his own holdings. He bought Miramar Marine Corp., based in Pulaski, Wisconsin, by purchasing the company's junk bonds and becoming its largest creditor. After the company went bankrupt, Jacobs held a 94 percent stake. The acquisition added the Carver and Ranger brand names to Genmar's lineup. Carver boats, manufactured in Pulaski, were a family of value-priced luxury yachts ranging in length from 32 to 53 feet. Ranger manufactured fiberglass freshwater fishing boats at a plant in Flippin, Arkansas.

Genmar's sales suffered as dealers began to shrink their inventories. Jacobs refrained from pressuring dealers to buy, since a smaller inventory put the dealers in a good position to eventually take over business from competitors that went under. In the short-term, however, Genmar had to close two plants. Its workforce declined to 2,900 from a maximum of 5,500 in 1988. The company's main competitors, Brunswick and Outboard Marine, were likewise having to trim their operations. During the rough years of the recession, Jacobs showed his faith in Genmar by turning over some of the profit from his personal dealings to the parent company Minstar.

By 1993 Minstar's boat-building operations had lost over $100 million and the company had been forced to restructure its debt twice. Adding to the debt, Aquasport Marine Industries was acquired. The company was known for fiberglass fishing boats with such innovations as a center console and a walkaround cubby cabin design. The boats ranged in size from 16 to 27 feet.

Prosperity in the Mid-1990s

Genmar's aggressive acquisition strategy paid off when the boat market improved around 1994. The company recorded its first operating profit in five years, although the company's net loss was still $21.9 million after factoring in taxes, investment losses, and interest expense. In a confirmation of the potential of the boat manufacturing business, Genmar's boat-building operations finally took decisive precedence over the remnants of Minstar in 1994. A new private company, Genmar Holdings, Inc., absorbed Minstar and became the parent company for 11 different boat manufacturers. Investors such as the Orlando Magic basketball team and the State of Wisconsin Investment Board contributed $165 million in new equity to finance the enterprise.

Positive developments followed the restructuring. The yacht-builder Hatteras announced plans to hire between 500 and 700 people for its North Carolina plant; and the Miramar plant in Wisconsin, which three years earlier had been bankrupt with zero employees, had boosted its employment to 700 and was still hiring. The luxury tax on high-end boats was also repealed that year. In addition, Genmar struck a deal with Sam's Club to have the warehouse retailer display Genmar boats and sales brochures and offer special deals to its members.

In 1996 Genmar achieved its first net profit since 1989, earning $275,000 on revenues of $618.1 million. Revenues were up 13 percent from the previous year. The bottom line was helped by lower administrative and manufacturing expenses—Genmar's workforce had declined from 5,200 in 1995 to 4,900 in 1996. Sales were strongest in the areas of recreational powerboats and yachts.

The following year brought a dispute with the National Marine Manufacturers Association, a group that Jacobs had helped found in the 1970s. Jacobs had watched with displeasure as more and more manufacturers of personal watercraft, such as Jet-Skis, joined the association in the 1980s. Jacobs finally withdrew his companies and his financial support from the organization in 1997, protesting that the group supported the rights of personal watercraft over boats. He announced plans to fight the growth of the personal watercraft sector, saying that the new industry stole customers of traditional boats and that the smaller, louder watercraft disturbed those who wanted to fish or ski on a serene lake.

In December 1998 Genmar acquired Horizon Marine of Junction City, Kansas, makers of Nova boats. Jacobs planned to

take advantage of the acquisition of a new factory to boost production of aluminum boats. The plants in Little Falls and New York Mills, Minnesota, and the facility in Ontario, Canada, where Lund, Crestliner, and Ranger boats were being manufactured, were operating at full capacity. The acquisition allowed Genmar to free up production potential by transferring the manufacture of Ranger boats to the Kansas facility.

New Technology for the New Millennium

Another acquisition followed in 1999. Logic Marine Inc., based in North Carolina, was bought from Pacific Resources Group (PRG), an Indonesian conglomerate that had started the firm five years previously. The Indonesian recession had pressured PRG into downsizing Logic, despite the fact that the manufacturer produced a quality line of mid-level fishing and skiing boats using a clean, strong new technology. Genmar now acquired this new manufacturing technique, known as Roplene. The Roplene method involved injecting a polyethylene resin, which was naturally buoyant and had five times the strength of fiberglass, into a mold and then rocking the mold during the hardening process to produce an even, seamless hull. Now that Logic was part of the Genmar domain, the company planned to add 20 employees and triple its output to about 220 boats per year.

Jacobs considered an initial public offering for Genmar in August 1999, but formally withdrew the idea in December in light of the possibilities offered by a second new manufacturing technique. The technology was known as VEC, short for virtual engineered composites. The process had been developed in Pennsylvania by Gene Kirila and Bob McCollum under the name Pyramid Operating Systems Inc. VEC was an automated fiberglass molding process that could be remotely controlled via the Internet. Each VEC cell was a portable mini-factory that used a chemical molding process to create a shape predetermined by computer input.

Jacobs recognized the potential for such a flexible and efficient manufacturing process in 1998, when he began to provide Kirila with financial backing to develop the VEC technology. An experimental plant began producing boats with VEC in Little Falls, where the great advantages of the new method were evident. Instead of a plant filled with the stench of styrene, where workers in protective gear swabbed sheets of fiberglass inside molds and used hand-held power tools to sand the hulls into shape, computer-controlled machines handled most aspects of production. The new method took up less space, required considerably less hardening and curing time, and injected less pollution into the air. Because hulls produced with the VEC technology were higher quality than those produced using the traditional method, Genmar was able to offer a lifetime warranty on newly purchased boats and a one-year, rather than 90-day, cosmetic warranty on cracks and bubbles. In 2000 a 100,000-square-foot VEC production facility was unveiled in Little Falls, with the potential for producing 10,000 boats a year.

Genmar was in a position to expand further in 2000, as sales revenue hit a record high of $858 million with an operating profit of $61 million. An opportunity presented itself when Genmar's longtime competitor, Outboard Marine Corporation, went bankrupt. In 2001 Genmar purchased Outboard Marine's boat-making division. The acquisition brought in the Javelin, Four Winns, Stratos, Hydra-Sports, Seaswirl, and Lowe boat lines. Outboard Marine's Evinrude and Johnson engine brands, which Genmar used on many of its own boats, were bought by the Canadian manufacturer Bombardier Inc. Jacobs announced plans to restart Outboard's manufacturing operations and recall many laid-off workers. With 18 boat brands and an estimated 20 percent market share, Genmar overtook Brunswick Corporation to become the country's leading boatmaker.

A minor scandal hit the company in March 2001 when Gary Schultz, the former chief financial officer of the Lund Boat Co., was charged with the theft of $1.8 million from the boat manufacturer. He was suspected of having embezzled as much as $12 million over the course of 16 years. Federal investigators took over the case.

In October 2001 Genmar made its first downsizing move in several years. The company agreed to sell Hatteras Yachts Inc. to Brunswick for $80 million. Brunswick also announced plans to trim some jobs. The deal left Genmar with 17 brands of boats. With a broad product line and control over the promising Roplene and VEC production methods, the company expected to continue in its position as a leader in the boat manufacturing industry.

Principal Subsidiaries

Genmar Canada; Genmar International.

Principal Divisions

Aquasport; Carver; Crestliner; Glastron; Larson; Logic Marine; Lund; Nova; Ranger; Trojan; Wellcraft; Four Winns; Hydra-Sports; Javelin; Lowe; Seaswirl; Stratos.

Principal Competitors

Brunswick Corporation; Fountain Powerboats Industries, Inc.; Yamaha Motor Corporation.

Further Reading

Blade, Joe, "Minstar-Genmar Merger Is Off," *Minneapolis Star Tribune*, October 28, 1987.
"Brunswick to Buy Hatteras for $80 Million in Cash," *New York Times*, October 25, 2001, p. 4.
Burns, Matthew, "Minnesota Firm Sees Logic in Its Future," *Triangle Business Journal*, July 23, 1999, p. 5.
Button, Graham, "Irwin Jacobs' Golden Shoestring," *Forbes*, April 27, 1992, p. 58.
Carideo, Anthony, "Jacobs Collects Bonds of Miramar," *Minneapolis Star Tribune*, February 24, 1990, p. 1D.
"City Boat Builder Plans to Expand," *Minneapolis Star and Tribune*, February 19, 1987, p. 5M.
Feyder, Susan, "Boat Builder Genmar Holdings Earns Its First Operating Profit in Five Years," *Minneapolis Star Tribune*, May 3, 1995, p. 1D.
——, "Economy an Ill Wind for Boatmakers," *Minneapolis Star Tribune*, August 26, 1991, p. 1D.
——, "Genmar Buys Boat Company in an Effort to Boost Production," *Minneapolis Star Tribune*, December 5, 1998, p. 4D.
——, "Genmar Holdings Posts First Net Profit Since 1989," *Minneapolis Star Tribune*, April 4, 1997, p. 1D.
——, "Genmar Sales Up; Operating Profits Fall," *Minneapolis Star Tribune*, April 4, 1996, p. 3D.
——, "Genmar Withdraws IPO Plan amid Talks," *Minneapolis Star Tribune*, December 10, 1999, p. 1D.
——, "Irwin Jacobs' Minstar Has Bleak Year; Auditors Ponder Its Future," *Minneapolis Star Tribune*, April 18, 1992, p. 1D.
——, "Minstar to Spin Off Boats into New Firm," *Minneapolis Star and Tribune*, May 24, 1986, p. 5B.
"Genmar Completes Its Initial Offering," *Wall Street Journal*, July 10, 1986, p. 1.
"Genmar Has Record Profits, Revenues," *Minneapolis Star Tribune*, February 6, 1988.
"Genmar Has Record Revenue, Profit," *Minneapolis Star Tribune*, August 12, 2000, p. 2D.
Gibson, Richard, "Minstar's Jacobs to Sell AMF Businesses," *Wall Street Journal*, August 30, 1985, p. 1.
——, "Smaller Boat Sales Are Hitting Rocky Patch," *Wall Street Journal*, April 23, 2001, p. B4C.
"Judge Backs Sale of Some Outboard Assets," *Wall Street Journal*, February 12, 2001, p. B9.
Kotlowitz, Alex, "Minstar to Be Bought by Unit, but Move Isn't Expected to Affect Jacobs's Plans," *Wall Street Journal*, August 3, 1987, p. 1.
Levy, Melissa, "Jacobs Pulls Companies out of Boat-Builder Association," *Minneapolis Star Tribune*, November 20, 1997.
Marcotty, Josephine, "Volvo Will Buy Stake in Jacobs Firm," *Minneapolis Star Tribune*, February 7, 1990, p. 1D.
Miller, James P., "Boat Maker Genmar Holdings Inc. Plans Initial Public Offering of $100 Million," *Wall Street Journal*, August 20, 1999, p. B10.
Mills, Karren, "The Future of Boatbuilding?," *Minneapolis Star Tribune*, August 26, 2000, p. 1D.
Peterson, Susan E., "Jacobs Forms a Team to Restructure Boat Firms," *Minneapolis Star Tribune*, February 11, 1994, p. 3D.
Phelps, David, "Federal Investigators Take Over Embezzlement Case of Ex-Lund CFO," *Minneapolis Star Tribune*, April 28, 2001, p. 3D.
Rudnitsky, Howard, "Any Offers?," *Forbes*, October 15, 1990, pp. 48–49.
Schuster, Lynda, "Aegis's Board Urges Holders to Accept Jacobs Firm's Sweetened $59 Million Bid," *Wall Street Journal*, May 8, 1984.
Sheehan, Dennis P., and Clifford G. Holderness, "Raiders or Saviours? The Evidence on Six Controversial Investors," *Fortune*, September 19, 1983, pp. 150–55.
Sloan, Allan, and Mary Kuntz, "The Hunt Is Better Than the Catch," *Forbes*, December 2, 1985, pp. 38–40.

—Sarah Ruth Lorenz

Genuine Parts Company

2999 Circle 75 Parkway
Atlanta, Georgia 30339
U.S.A.
Telephone: (770) 953-1700
Fax: (770) 956-2211
Web site: http://www.genpt.com

Public Company
Incorporated: 1928
Employees: 33,000
Sales: $8.37 billion (2000)
Stock Exchanges: New York
Ticker Symbol: GPC
NAIC: 421120 Motor Vehicle Supplies and New Part
Wholesalers; 441310 Automotive Parts and
Accessories Stores; 421830 Industrial Machinery and
Equipment Wholesalers; 422120 Stationery and Office
Supplies Wholesalers; 421210 Furniture Wholesalers;
421610 Electrical Apparatus and Equipment, Wiring
Supplies, and Construction Materials Wholesalers

Genuine Parts Company is one of the largest automobile parts suppliers in the United States, providing parts to about 5,800 NAPA Auto Parts stores across the United States and Canada, 800 of which are owned by the company. The company maintains close ties with the National Auto Parts Association (NAPA), owning approximately 90 percent of the trade association's member distribution centers. After selling only auto parts for almost 50 years, Genuine diversified into industrial replacement parts and office supplies in the mid-1970s. Then in the late 1990s Genuine moved into the wholesaling of electrical and electronic materials with the acquisition of EIS, Inc. About half of the company's revenues are generated by its automotive group, with about 28 percent coming from the industrial group, 16 percent from office products, and about 7 percent from the electrical/electronic materials group.

1920s–60s: From One Store to Nationwide Distributor

Genuine Parts Company was founded by Carlyle Fraser in 1928 when Fraser bought a small auto parts store in Atlanta. The store had six employees and capital of $40,000 when he acquired it. Sales reached $75,000 the first year, although the store lost about $2,500. Independent garages for car repair were spreading with incredible rapidity, providing Genuine with a swiftly growing market for its parts. Genuine bought auto parts from manufacturers such as Tenneco and sold them to parts stores, called jobbing houses, which sold them to the independent garages. From the beginning, Genuine pushed swift, reliable service as a way to outflank the competition. The firm also used its relationship with NAPA, the trade association cofounded by Fraser in 1925. NAPA set standards and sold parts to jobbers.

Genuine's business was in some respects helped by the Great Depression. Many people could not afford to buy new cars, so they held onto aging automobiles and bought the replacement parts needed to repair them when they broke down. In 1936, about $2 was spent on parts for the average one-year-old car, whereas a three-year-old car required $10 in parts. During the 1930s, company sales went from $339,000 to $3.18 million.

Genuine continued to grow during World War II. Consumers again held onto their older cars, sometimes having little choice because automakers were devoting much of their capacity to the war effort. By the same token, the War Production Board only allocated resources to parts manufacturers to build ''functional'' parts for cars. This restriction meant, for instance, no fenders or door hardware were available to sell to those needing them. With auto sales slacking, the average vehicle was 7.28 years old in 1946, compared with 4.77 years old in 1941 before the United States entered the war. As a result, $19 in parts were bought for the average car in 1945. In the year of its 20th anniversary in 1948, the company had $20 million in sales. That same year the company went public, selling 150,000 shares of common stock at $11 per share (thanks to a series of stock splits, an investor who had bought one share in 1948 would have had 205.04 shares by April 1997).

Company Perspectives:

With over 73 years of distribution expertise, our well positioned, regionally located distribution centers provide us with the unique ability to adapt our product and service lines to better suit our customers' needs. GPC's commitment and reputation for just-in-time service positions us as a critical partner in our customers' success.

GPC began to diversify its product lines over 27 years ago into several end-markets with strong growth opportunities. Although each product is unique, we have leveraged 73 years of distribution know-how to manage these businesses the GPC way—continually improving operating and distribution efficiencies. The self-contained synergies of distribution in our combined end-markets provide a solid platform of growth for the Company.

With the prosperity of the 1950s and the increasing number of families with two cars, Genuine expanded at a tremendous pace. It opened NAPA operations in Boston in 1950, Omaha in 1955, Jacksonville and Miami in 1956, Denver in 1957, and Minneapolis in 1959. By 1962 the firm owned 97 retail stores and 12 warehouses along the East Coast and in the South and had annual sales of about $80 million. Rebuilt parts accounted for 15 percent of sales. Although it still bought parts from manufacturers, Genuine did some parts rebuilding itself, including clutches, brake shoes, and pumps. To increase its slice of that business, in 1968 the firm acquired Atlanta-based John Rogers Co., a rebuilder of auto engines. In 1969 Genuine diversified out of the auto business for the first time, buying Beck & Gregg Hardware Co., a 103-year-old distributor of home appliances, building goods, and sports products (this business was sold in 1985).

By the late 1960s, Genuine was a nationwide distributor, supplying 2,500 independent jobbers and owning 33 of the 55 NAPA distribution centers, which then served 4,000 jobbers throughout the United States. The first NAPA brand parts were introduced in 1966. Genuine also supplied parts for trucks, tractors, power boats, and power tools.

Diversifying in the 1970s

Expansion outside the United States began in 1972, when Genuine acquired auto parts distributor Corbetts, Ltd., which was based in Calgary, Alberta. Corbetts served more than 100 jobbing stores. Genuine also began an expansion into Europe in 1973, but this proved to be a short-lived endeavor as the European operations were sold off in 1978.

The OPEC oil embargo in 1973 played havoc with the auto parts market. With the rise in gasoline prices, consumers drove less and needed fewer auto parts in the short term. The oil shortage, however, also led to recession in 1973 and 1974. Car owners held onto their older cars, driving up sales and prices of auto parts in the longer term. Nearly 90 million cars were being driven in the United States, and approximately 60 percent of them were over three years old, making them likely candidates for car parts. An increasing number of these vehicles were small cars, whose parts tended to wear out faster than those of bigger cars. Although cars were being driven for fewer total miles than ever before, more of those miles were in urban areas, resulting in greater wear on the parts. Do-it-yourself sales soared, and mass marketers such as Sears Roebuck and J.C. Penney began increasing parts orders from distributors. Genuine's sales reached $500 million in 1973, twice as much as its nearest competitor, APS; that figure, however, represented just 2 percent of the fragmented auto parts market.

Auto parts were becoming more elaborate and expensive as a result of technology advances and stricter pollution standards. In 1975, attempting to diversify, Genuine picked up a wholesale office supplies firm, S.P. Richards Co. In 1976, under the leadership of CEO Wilton Looney, Genuine also expanded into the industrial parts business with the acquisition of Motion Industries, Inc. Looney believed that industrial parts would be recession-proof in the same way that auto parts were: during recessions industrial firms would buy replacement parts for existing machinery rather than purchasing new equipment. In 1979 the firm bought a Michigan-based industrial parts distributor, Michigan Bearing Company, to expand that segment of its business.

In 1978 Genuine installed a computerized point-of-sale system for billing customers, tracking inventories, and automatically ordering replacements for parts that were sold. The system, developed with Data General Corp., cost $24,000 to $30,000 per complete system, and grew to include 900 jobbers by 1982. This system gave Genuine an important advantage over competitors, because no other independent distributor could match the services Genuine could offer.

Staying Ahead Through Acquisitions and Retooling in the 1980s

Genuine's sales reached $1.6 billion in 1981, of which 63 percent came from the distribution of parts, 22 percent came from industrial replacement parts, and 8 percent from office-supply products. The firm had 55 U.S. distribution centers for auto parts and four in western Canada, selling to about 5,200 jobbers, of which it owned about 350. Genuine ran six distribution centers and 160 branches for industrial parts, selling to 50,000 customers. Office supplies were being sold to more than 5,000 retailers in 15 states. Genuine's leading item overall was spray paint used for touch-ups, which accounted for 8 percent of sales. Exhaust products, filters, hoses and belts, and batteries accounted for between 3 and 6 percent of sales each.

The number of vehicles in the United States continued to rise, reaching 160 million by the end of 1981, with an average age of 6.5 years. Parts for imported cars accounted for only about 10 percent of inventory, despite rapidly growing import sales in the United States. Since the imported parts broadened inventory, the trend to buy imports was seen as increasing Genuine's advantage against smaller, less well-financed competitors.

In 1982 Genuine bought General Automotive Parts Corp. of Dallas in a stock swap valued at about $250 million. General Auto had stores in 12 states in the southwest, north, and central regions of the United States. Genuine also was opening about

Key Dates:

1925: Carlyle Fraser is one of the cofounders of the National Auto Parts Association (NAPA).

1928: Fraser founds Genuine Parts Company after buying a small auto parts store in Atlanta.

1948: The company goes public.

1966: The first NAPA brand parts are introduced.

1972: The company expands into Canada with the purchase of auto parts distributor Corbetts, Ltd.

1975: Genuine diversifies through the purchase of S.P. Richards, an office supplies wholesaler.

1976: The company expands into industrial parts with the acquisition of Motion Industries.

1982: The firm acquires Dallas-based General Automotive Parts Corp.

1998: Atlanta-based EIS, Inc., a distributor of electrical and electronic materials, is acquired; Genuine acquires the 80 percent of Montreal-based UAP Inc. that it does not already own.

1999: The company acquires Johnson Industries, Inc., an Atlanta-based auto parts distributor.

five outlets a year, most in major cities. To better supply them, it opened NAPA distribution centers in Dallas, Houston, and San Antonio in 1983, and Portland, Maine, in 1984.

A recession hit the United States in 1982 and hurt Genuine's supposedly recession-proof industrial parts business. The recession was severe enough to temporarily shut down some factories, and closed factories do not buy parts. As a result of its diversification, about 35 percent of Genuine's sales came from operations other than auto parts, up from 10 percent ten years earlier.

NAPA was an increasingly important part of Genuine's business. NAPA's 72 distribution centers sold parts to 5,200 NAPA jobbers, who sold parts to local mechanics. Genuine owned 55 of the distribution centers, and 350 of the 5,200 jobbing sites. Genuine thus had 85 percent of NAPA's sales, although that accounted for only 5 percent of the nationwide market for replacement parts. About 85 percent of Genuine's 100,000 auto and truck parts bore the NAPA brand name. Genuine used its NAPA connection to give it leverage over the 5,200 NAPA jobbers. If a jobber began buying less than 85 percent or so of its parts from Genuine, the firm might open another NAPA shop in the same area. If jobbers kept Genuine happy, they would find little direct competition and excellent service. Genuine delivered parts overnight to most of its customers, enabling them to keep their inventories, and thus costs, low. Genuine began refurbishing its image in the mid-1980s, raising awareness of the NAPA brand name and redesigning its stores. Most of the firm's nearly 500 stores installed brighter lighting, updated the layout of sales floors, and added a blue and yellow color scheme that drew attention to the NAPA logo.

Replacement part sales sagged in the mid-1980s, barely keeping pace with inflation. Car and truck sales had slumped in 1982 and 1983, meaning fewer cars needed parts several years later. Cars were being built better and generally started to need replacement parts after four years rather than three. Customers increasingly brought their cars back to their dealers for repairs, and the dealers got parts directly from the manufacturers. As Japanese cars steadily acquired U.S. market share, parts suppliers were slow to begin carrying them in sufficient numbers. Warm winters in 1988 and 1989 were partly to blame for the drop in sales as well because alternators, batteries, and other parts tended to fail during very cold weather. At the same time, Genuine's competition was heating up. Specialty shops such as Midas and Jiffy Lube were expanding rapidly, and retail chains were increasing their automotive operations.

To help compensate, Genuine tried to increase its efficiency and started a new marketing campaign. Genuine signed agreements with Midas, Montgomery Ward, and others to supply some of their auto parts. To make jobbers aware that it carried foreign parts, Genuine put out a catalogue focusing on imported car parts. By 1990 most of the 6,000 retailers who bought parts from Genuine were connected by computer to one of the firm's 64 NAPA distribution warehouses. In addition to getting parts to jobbers quickly, Genuine used the computer system to keep track of who was selling how many parts and why.

Changes in the auto industry did have some benefits: if cars needed parts less often, the parts continued to increase in cost, with some costing twice what they had 20 years earlier. At the same time, Genuine's other businesses continued to grow at higher rates. Sales for the industrial group were $547 million in 1988, with profits of $35.7 million. Office product sales came to $450 million, with profits of $36.7 million.

1990s and Beyond: Continued Growth, Major Acquisitions

In late 1993 Genuine strengthened its industrial parts business by acquiring Berry Bearing Company for about $300 million worth of stock. Bearings were seen as a stable seller in a recessionary economy as firms delayed purchases of new equipment. Expansion into Mexico began in 1994 when Genuine formed a joint venture with Auto Todo, based in Puebla, Mexico, to distribute automotive replacement parts in that country. In 1995 NAPA entered into an agreement with Penske Corporation to become the exclusive parts supplier for more than 850 Penske Auto Centers. That same year, S.P. Richards bolstered its operations through the acquisition of Horizon USA Data Supplies, Inc., a Reno, Nevada-based wholesaler of computer supplies. Another development in the mid-1990s was the revamping of hundreds of NAPA stores, including the creation of superstores with about 8,000 square feet of space, in an effort to attract more do-it-yourselfers. Coinciding with this remodeling program, which continued into the late 1990s, was an advertising campaign emphasizing the same theme—that NAPA stores served more than just auto repair shops. By year-end 1996, there were 5,700 NAPA stores, 750 of which were owned by Genuine Parts. Revenues surpassed the $6 billion mark for the first time in 1997, the company's 70th year in operation.

The late 1990s featured a series of acquisitions as Genuine sought to increase its pace of growth and return to the double-digit annual increases in sales and earnings the company had enjoyed in earlier years. Perhaps most significantly, Genuine entered a new, and potentially higher growth, line of business through the July 1998 acquisition of EIS, Inc., a distributor of electrical and electronic materials, in a deal valued at about $180 million. Also based in Atlanta, EIS achieved $522.4 million in sales in 1999, its first full year as a subsidiary of Genuine. In December 1998 Genuine spent about $231 million to buy the 80 percent of Montreal-based UAP Inc. that it did not already own. Since 1989 Genuine had held a minority stake in UAP, a distributor of auto and industrial parts with annual sales of $555 million. In January 1999 Genuine further expanded its auto parts group by acquiring yet another Atlanta-based firm, Johnson Industries, Inc. With annual revenues of $120 million, Johnson served new-car dealers and owners of large vehicle fleets, such as Federal Express. Also in 1999, Genuine acquired Brittain Brothers, Inc., a NAPA distributor based in Oklahoma City that served more than 190 stores in Oklahoma, Missouri, Arkansas, and Texas. Meantime, S.P. Richards gained its first presence in Canada through the 1998 purchase of Norwestra Sales, Inc., which was based in Vancouver, British Columbia, and was expected to serve as a base for a Canada-wide operation. This spate of major deals enabled Genuine to post a 21 percent increase in net sales for 1999, to $7.98 billion. The late 1990s also saw Genuine Parts develop e-commerce capabilities in each of its four product groups.

Despite continued softness in the automotive aftermarket, Genuine managed to post net sales of $8.37 billion for 2000, marking 51 straight years of sales gains. Profits edged up as well, hitting $385.3 million, giving the company 40 consecutive years of profit improvement. Dividends also rose that year, the 45th consecutive year of dividend increases. With one of the best track records in American business, an increasingly diversified range of operations, and a more aggressive approach to growth, there seemed to be no reason to suspect that Genuine Parts' remarkable history of success would not continue.

Principal Subsidiaries

Balkamp (89.6%); EIS, Inc.; L.O.C.O.A. Laminating Company of America; Scottsdale Tool & Supply de Mexico, S.A. de C.V.; Genuine Parts Holdings, Ltd. (Canada); Genuine Parts Company, Ltd. (Canada); GPC Mexico, S.A. de C.V.; GPC Trading Corporation (Virgin Islands); Johnson Industries; Motion Industries; Motion Industries (Canada), Inc.; S.P. Richards; Hori-zon USA Data Supply, Inc.; Norwestra Holdings (Canada); MJDH Holdings Ltd. (Canada); Norwestra Sales (1992), Inc. (Canada); UAP Inc. (Canada); Garanat Inc. (Canada); UAPRO Inc. (Canada); United Auto Parts (Eastern) Ltd. (Canada); Services Financiers UAP Inc. (Canada); Automoteur Terrebonne Ltee (Canada); Centre di Culasses du Quebec Inc. (Canada); Reusinage Knight Inc. (Canada); Manco Trucking.

Principal Operating Units

Automotive Parts Group; Office Products Group; Electrical/Electronic Materials Group; Industrial Parts Group.

Principal Competitors

General Motors Corporation; Ford Motor Company; AutoZone, Inc.; Advance Holding Corporation; The Pep Boys—Manny, Moe & Jack; CARQUEST Corporation; General Parts, Inc.; CSK Auto Corporation.

Further Reading

"As Good As New," *Barron's,* November 3, 1969.
"Auto Par Puzzle," *Business Week,* February 7, 1942.
Bond, Patti, "Genuine Parts to Diversify by Acquiring EIS in a $200 Million Deal," *Atlanta Journal,* May 22, 1998, p. F1.
Byrne, Harlan S., "Genuine Parts Co.," *Barron's,* November 20, 1989.
——, "More Than Autos," *Barron's,* December 18, 2000, p. 34.
Byrne, Jon A., "A Nasty Little Shock," *Forbes,* October 25, 1982.
Cronkleton, Robert A., "New Concept Unveiled in NAPA Store," *Kansas City Star,* February 8, 1995, p. B3.
"Genuine Parts," *Business Week,* August 25, 1934.
Gordon, Mitchell, "In High Gear," *Barron's,* March 22, 1982.
Judge, Paul C., "Thrives on Breakdowns," *New York Times,* September 20, 1990.
Luke, Robert, "Genuine Parts Growth Lag an Incentive for Changes," *Atlanta Constitution,* January 19, 1999, p. E1.
——, "Genuine Parts Makes Still Another Acquisition," *Atlanta Journal/Constitution,* October 31, 1998, p. H1.
——, "Genuine Parts Shops for Growth, Acquisition," *Atlanta Constitution,* October 30, 1998, p. E2.
Pacey, Margaret D., "Nearly Recession-Proof," *Barron's,* April 11, 1974.

—Scott M. Lewis
—update: David E. Salamie

Giorgio Armani S.p.A.

Via Borgonuovo 11
20121 Milano
Italy
Telephone: 39-02-723-18-1
Fax: 39-02-723-18-452
Web site: http://www.giorgioarmani.com

Private Company
Incorporated: 1975
Employees: 3,900
Sales: L 2.0 trillion (EUR 1.03 billion) ($972.6 million)
(2000)
NAIC: 53311 Lessors of Nonfinancial Intangible Assets
(Except Copyrighted Works); 54149 Other Specialized
Design Services; 315221 Men's and Boys' Cut and
Sew Underwear and Nightwear Manufacturing;
315222 Men's and Boys' Cut and Sew Suit, Coat,
and Overcoat Manufacturing; 315223 Men's and
Boys' Cut and Sew Shirt (Except Work Shirt)
Manufacturing; 315224 Men's and Boys' Cut and
Sew Trouser, Slack, and Jean Manufacturing; 315228
Men's and Boys' Cut and Sew Other Outerwear
Manufacturing; 315231 Women's and Girls' Cut and
Sew Lingerie, Loungewear, and Nightwear
Manufacturing; 315232 Women's and Girls' Cut and
Sew Blouse and Shirt Manufacturing; 315233
Women's and Girls' Cut and Sew Dress
Manufacturing; 315234 Women's and Girls' Cut and
Sew Suit, Coat, Tailored Jacket, and Skirt
Manufacturing; 315239 Women's and Girls' Cut and
Sew Other Outerwear Manufacturing; 315993 Men's
and Boys' Neckwear Manufacturing; 315999 Other
Apparel Accessories and Other Apparel
Manufacturing

Giorgio Armani S.p.A. is one of the world's leading fashion houses. Few designers are credited with changing fashion to the same extent as its namesake, Giorgio Armani, who is the firm's sole shareholder, managing director, and chairman of the board. The group is unique in remaining aloof from waves of consolidation in the luxury goods industry. Armani has invested instead in extending control over manufacturing and distribution of its products. The group has about 250 outlets in 34 countries and also markets its wares in exclusive department stores.

Origins

Giorgio Armani was born on July 11, 1934 and, along with his brother and sister, grew up in the industrial town of Piacenza in northern Italy, which was bombed repeatedly during World War II. His sister Rosanna told *Newsweek*'s Christopher Dickey that Armani spent 40 days in the hospital when he was burned by a flare a classmate had found on the street.

The Armanis moved to Milan in 1949. Armani went to medical school for two years but dropped out in 1957 to take a job as a buyer for the La Rinascente department store, a job he held for about seven years. He then worked as a fashion designer for Hitman, Nino Cerruti's men's clothing company, before establishing himself as a freelance designer in 1970.

Armani formed his own company, Giorgio Armani S.p.A., on July 24, 1975, at the suggestion of his enthusiastic partner, Sergio Galeotti. One story, retold in *Forbes,* has the pair selling their used Volkswagen for startup capital. Another version, in a later edition of *Forbes,* puts the startup figure at $100,000.

The first products were ready-to-wear clothes for men and women. The company was successful from the beginning; first year sales were $1 million. In 1978, a licensing agreement with GFT (Gruppo Finanziario Tessile) allowed Armani to invest in a new headquarters building. The building, a 17th-century palazzo at 21 Via Borgonuovo, Milan, would house not only offices but a theater for fashion shows as well as Armani's personal residence. Armani would be credited for inventing the Italian fashion industry, particularly in Milan.

The next year, 1979, saw the establishment of the Giorgio Armani Corporation in the United States. Giorgio Armani would be counted among the world's leading fashion houses by the end of the decade.

Part of the success was due to Armani's bold design gambles, which developed a more casual chic by such touches as removing padding from the traditional men's suit jacket. Women's clothes were made more comfortable and less showy. Other designers and knock-off artists would copy the look, but the original retained a dedicated following.

Owning the 1980s

The collection, by this time, had already been expanded to include several new lines, such as Mani, Armani Junior, and underwear and swimsuits. Armani and Emporio Armani brands of jeans were launched in the early 1980s, a decade known for its designer jeans. Emporio Armani was a lower-priced version of the flagship line; Emporio Armani and Giorgio Armani boutiques were both soon opened in Milan.

Giorgio Armani was one of the first designers to exploit the marketing power of media stars. He began a long relationship with Hollywood when he designed Richard Gere's wardrobe for the 1980 film *American Gigolo*. A string of other movie credits would accumulate throughout the next two decades, including *Batman* (1989) and *Pulp Fiction* (Emporio Armani) and, appropriately, *Ready to Wear* (both 1994). Armani was also responsible for much of the pastel wardrobe for the stars of *Miami Vice*, the hit TV series of the late 1980s.

Armani sponsored or provided wardrobes for the musical tours of several pop musicians, including Paul Simon, Billy Joel, David Bowie, and Eric Clapton. In 1999, Emporio Armani Fragrances, which was promoting the new perfume "G," sponsored world tours for Ricky Martin and Lauryn Hill.

The early 1980s also saw an extension of the Giorgio Armani name to fragrances, licensed by L'Oréal (formerly H. Rubinstein). Eyewear was licensed to Luxottica S.p.A. in 1988.

Galeotti, Armani's partner and the one who had handled the day-to-day management, died of AIDS in 1985 and left Armani his 50 percent interest in the firm. Armani subsequently surprised some observers with his business sense. He immediately set out to expand the Emporio Armani line beyond jeans. In the next six years Emporio sales increased from $75 million to $209 million.

A variety of new enterprises proliferated in the last half of the 1980s. The first Armani Junior store opened in Milan in 1986. Giorgio Armani Japan, a joint venture with Japanese Itochu Corporation, was created in 1987. The first Emporio Armani Express restaurant opened in London as the 1980s drew to their inevitable cross-branding conclusion. Giorgio Armani also opened the restored Doney bistro in Florence in 1989. On another front, *Emporio Armani* magazine had begun publishing in January of the same year.

Armani turned down a 1989 takeover offer by the Jeanne Lanvin design house. Luxury conglomerates Gucci and LVMH would also offer to buy out Armani. While competitors Prada and Gucci expanded through expensive acquisitions of other luxury brands, Armani preferred to tighten its control on the production and marketing of its products. The company began buying shares in its manufacturers, including Antinea S.r.l. and Intai S.p.A., in 1989 and 1990. Antinea had gross sales of $25 million and made women's clothes for the Emporio Armani brand. Intai, maker of Armani ties, grossed $16 million a year.

New Ventures in the 1990s

The firm's revenues were $306 million in 1990; retail stores provided $160 million; royalties and fees accounted for $130 million; and Armani's own manufacturing operations added another $16 million. Net income after taxes was an impressive $54.2 million. Total retail sales, including those of licensed products, amounted to $1.6 billion. The company carried no debt. Although many high fashion boutiques were suffering as the 1980s economy began to sputter, Giorgio Armani Boutiques were still able to command stellar prices for their high-end threads.

A *Forbes* cover story in October 1991 noted Giorgio Armani's meticulous attention to detail throughout his fashion empire. Armani's small group of intensely loyal advisors—including his sister, Rosanna, head of the in-house advertising agency—held board meetings with the passion of an Italian family argument.

The first Armani Exchange (A/X) store opened in New York's Soho district in 1991. The Exchange sold $90 jeans and $75 T-shirts—costly enough for weekend clothes, but much less pricey than the Armani Boutique's dress clothes. The clothes and stores were licensed to the U.S. division of Simint S.p.A., a publicly traded company based in Modena, Italy, in which Armani held a 20 percent interest (later increased).

Bloomingdale's, Saks Fifth Avenue, Neiman Marcus, and other U.S. department store chains together opened another two dozen or so A/X sections within their stores in 1992. Despite initial projections of opening up to 150 free-standing A/X stores, the venture had begun to falter by 1994, when the chain had 41 outlets, resulting in a huge loss for Simint. The *Economist* blamed the large royalty, usually 10 percent, which went to the designer from each garment sold. Simint sold the A/X chain to Ong Beng Seng, a Singapore-based company, for L 20 billion ($12.5 million) in June 1994.

Armani later pursued the strategy of maintaining a very small number of these lower-priced outlets to maintain the brand's allure, as well as the profit margins he expected. In fact,

Key Dates:

1970: Giorgio Armani establishes himself as a freelance designer.
1975: Armani and Sergio Galeotti establish Giorgio Armani, S.p.A.
1978: Armani enters licensing agreement with GFT.
1979: Giorgio Armani Corp. is established in the United States.
1980: *American Gigolo* brings Armani fashions to the big screen.
1985: Giorgio Armani becomes sole owner of firm after Galeotti's death.
1989: Armani begins acquiring control of its factories.
1991: A/X store opens in New York.
1997: Collezioni Giorgio Armani stores open in Milan, London, and Tokyo.
2000: Armani opens $73 million Milan megastore during 25th anniversary year.

Armani was unique among brands in limiting the maximum amount of business its licensees could each generate.

Alitalia hired Armani to design new outfits for its flight attendants and the interiors of its MD-11 airliners in the early 1990s. The firm also designed the uniforms for Italy's 1994 World Cup soccer team, and those for Britain's Newcastle United team in 1999.

In 1996, Armani opened two stores in Manhattan, one an Emporio Armani store, and the other, the four-story flagship of the chain. The first Collezioni Giorgio Armani stores opened in Milan, London, and Tokyo in 1997. The same year, the first Armani Jeans store opened in Rome and Armani watches were introduced.

July 1997 was marked by the murder in Miami of Armani's fiercest rival in Milan, the flamboyant Gianni Versace. The next month, Armani was reported to be considering either taking his company public or taking in a partner, and the Armani Group underwent a reorganization.

Police canceled an Emporio Armani fashion show in Paris on March 12, 1998, citing security concerns. To some, this affront seemed rather to be a sign of the longstanding rivalry between the French and Italian fashion industries.

The Armani Group continued to roll out new categories of products. An accessories division was created in 1999; the first accessories store would open in Milan two years later. Also in 1999, Armani entered e-commerce with armaniexchange.com, and bought two menswear factories from its longtime licensee GFT for L 55 billion. Consolidated revenue rose 12 percent in 1999, though net income fell 12 percent, largely due to taxes on a sale of shares held in Luxottica.

25th Anniversary in 2000

In 2000, Armani posted operating profits of L 374 billion (EUR 193 million) on consolidated net revenues of L 2 trillion (EUR 1.03 billion), which were up 20 percent for the year. Global retail sales exceeded L 7 trillion (EUR 3.6 billion).

During 2000, the company launched a joint venture with the Zegna Group, called Trimil, to produce and distribute the Armani Collezioni line of men's clothing. Giorgio Armani Cosmetics debuted. Armani Casa, a home fashion store, opened after years of planning. A series of Armani-related web sites were launched and plans for a new headquarters office were underway. (Armani was, though, unable to acquire the armani.com name, which was held by a Canadian artist named Anand Ramnath Mani.)

During the year, Armani was honored with an exhibit at New York's Guggenheim Museum for changing the way people dressed in the previous quarter century. At this stage in his career, Armani was finding inspiration in the marriage of Eastern minimalism and Western luxury.

The billionaire designer also honored himself in 2000 by opening a three-level, $73 million megastore in Milan called Armani/Via Manzoni 31. "I just wanted to give a present to myself on my twenty-fifth anniversary," he said at the opening. The store carried not just clothes, but flowers, books, food (sushi), and home furnishings.

The company was hit by the departure of several key executives, including Managing Director Giuseppe Brusone, who had been with Armani for 15 years. He was later appointed to the CEO spot at Donna Karan International, a unit of LVMH.

In 2001, Giorgio Armani announced plans for a joint venture with Vestimenta S.p.A., one of its earliest licensees, to produce and distribute its top line of men's and women's clothes. Armani was also acquiring control of its Hong Kong retail network from Joyce Boutique Holdings Ltd. Armani continued to resist the trend towards consolidation in the luxury goods industry.

Principal Subsidiaries

Antinea S.r.l.; Giorgio Armani Corporation (U.S.A.); Giorgio Armani Asia Pacific Limited (Hong Kong); Giorgio Armani Japan (85%); Intai S.p.A.; Simint S.p.A. (53.24%); Trimil (51%).

Principal Competitors

Gianni Versace, S.p.A.; Gruppo Ermenegildo Zegna; Gucci Group N.V.; I Pellettieri d'Italia S.p.A. (Prada).

Further Reading

"A R Mani Beats Armani," *Managing Intellectual Property,* September 2001, p. 16.
Agins, Teri, "Who Loves Armani? Actors, Car Washers and Senior V.P.s," *Wall Street Journal,* October 31, 1990, p. A1.
Ball, Deborah, "Armani Looks Sharp As Sales Climb 20 Percent," *Wall Street Journal,* January 17, 2001, p. B5.
——, "Armani's Net Profit Fell 12 Percent for 1999 and Analysts Say Expansion Is Needed," *Wall Street Journal,* June 16, 2000, p. B8.
——, "Armani Stands at Crossroads amid Consolidation," *Wall Street Journal,* October 24, 2000, p. B17.
Blonsky, Marshall, and Edmundo Desnoes, "Fashion As the High Art of Fantasy," *Christian Science Monitor,* October 26, 2000, p. 9.

Cardona, Mercedes M., "Giorgio Spritzes Up G to Help Revitalize Image," *Advertising Age,* August 16, 1999, p. 12.

Celant, Germano, and Harold Koda, *Giorgio Armani,* New York: Abrams, 2000.

Dickey, Christopher, and Dana Thomas, "Armani After All," *Newsweek,* September 3, 2001, pp. 34+.

Ebenkamp, Becky, and Sloane Lucas, "Armani Goes Smalltown for A/X Chain Campaign," *Brandweek,* July 27, 1998, p. 5.

"Fashion Victimhood: Et tu, Giorgio," *Economist,* May 21, 1994, p. 74.

Fiori, Pamela, and Oberto Gili, "The Quiet Man," *Town & Country,* January 1998, pp. 70+.

Ginsberg, Steve, *Reeking Havoc,* New York: Warner, 1989.

"Giorgio Armani May Look for Business Partner," *Wall Street Journal,* August 21, 1997, p. B6.

Givhan, Robin, "Pulled Out from Under Armani; Police Cite Concerns Over Security and Halt Designer's First Paris Show," *Washington Post,* March 12, 1998, p. C1.

Goldstein, Lauren, "Armani Looks Ahead," *Time,* June 19, 2000, p. B25.

Green, Laurence, "Emporio Armani Logo," *Marketing,* April 29, 1999, p. 10.

Heller, Richard, "Armani the Indispensable," *Forbes Global,* November 12, 2001.

——, "Last Man Standing," *Forbes,* November 12, 2001, pp. 70–72.

Herman-Cohen, Valli, "An Appreciation," *Los Angeles Times,* October 20, 2000.

Hirschberg, Lynn, "Giorgio on My Mind," *Harper's Bazaar,* October 2000, pp. 188+.

Levine, J., "Dare e togliere (Give and Take Away)," *Forbes,* October 28, 1991, pp. 115+.

McNatt, Robert, and Monica Larner, "Armani's Monument to Armani," *Business Week,* October 23, 2000, p. 14.

Rossant, John, "Will A/X Get Ax?," *Business Week,* May 30, 1994, p. 48.

Trachtenberg, Jeffrey A., "Armani Gamble Wins Support of Big Stores," *Wall Street Journal,* February 21, 1992, p. B1.

Yaeger, Lynn, "Pantsuits at an Exhibition," *Village Voice,* November 14, 2000, p. 20.

—Frederick C. Ingram

Harry Winston Inc.

718 Fifth Avenue
New York, New York 10010
U.S.A.
Telephone: (212) 245-2000
Fax: (212) 489-6715
Web site: http://www.harrywinston.com

Private Company
Incorporated: 1932
Employees: 200
Sales: $85 million (2001)
NAIC: 448300 Jewelry, Luggage, and Leather Goods
   Stores

Harry Winston Inc. is the corporate name of The House of Harry Winston, one of the world's most prestigious luxury jewelers. The worldwide operation is run from a Fifth Avenue location in New York City, where the company not only maintains a salon open to a select clientele, but also operates workshops that design jewelry and cut, polish, and set gems. Harry Winston also owns a salon in Los Angeles, where it tends close ties to Hollywood and is spotlighted during each year's Academy Awards, when famous actresses borrow multimillion-dollar jewelry for the evening. In addition, Harry Winston salons are found in Paris, Geneva, Tokyo, and Osaka. Approximately one-fifth of the company's income is generated by less expensive jewelry manufactured in Rhode Island and Hong Kong and sold to mass-market retailers, who are forbidden to reveal the source of the merchandise in order to preserve Harry Winston's reputation for exclusivity.

Harry Winston and the Birth of His Company: 1890s–1930s

When Harry Winston established his business in 1932, he already had many years of experience in the jewelry business. His father, a Ukrainian immigrant named Jacob Winston, had opened a jewelry retail and repair shop in Manhattan's upper west side in 1890. His mother died when Harry was seven, and a year later he and his father, who suffered from asthma, moved to the West Coast for health reasons and opened a jewelry store in the center of the Los Angeles business district at a time when the film industry was just beginning to establish itself in the area.

According to lore, Harry early on demonstrated an ability to recognize valuable stones when at the age of 12 he noticed a two-carat emerald ring on a tray of junk jewelry in a pawnshop window. He bought the ring for 25 cents and resold it two days later for $800. He dropped out of high school at the age of 15 and went to work for his father to devote himself full-time to the store as well as to visit boomtown saloons, where he sold gems to oil prospectors who struck it rich.

At the age of 18, Harry moved back to New York with his father, who opened another Manhattan jewelry store, which he would operate until just before his death in 1929. With $2,000 saved from his California enterprises, Harry began to operate entirely on his own, buying and selling in the New York Diamond Exchange, which required sound, quick decisions and the boldness of a gambler. In 1916, at the age of 19, he started his own company, The Premier Diamond Company, located at 535 Fifth Avenue. In a matter of just two years, Winston was able to parlay his limited capital into a stake of $10,000 in cash and jewelry worth another $20,000. Unfortunately, an employee ran off with all of his money and inventory. With the help of bank financing, Winston was able to maintain his independence and rebuild his business. Because at his first appointment bank management mistook him for a messenger, he subsequently hired a distinguished looking gentlemen to serve as a front. He soon turned to the estate sales of the wealthy to buy jewelry that had gone out of fashion. He removed the stones and, to prepare them for resale, had them recut and reset to offer greater brilliance in a modern setting. His first major estate sale occurred in 1925, after which his activities gained notice in newspaper society columns. Winston achieved a national reputation in December 1930 when he bought the famous jewelry collection of mining tycoon B.J. "Lucky" Baldwin, which included the largest diamond ever sold in a U.S. public auction, a 39-carat-emerald-cut diamond. Although the collection also included a 26-carat ruby that was one of the largest rubies in the world, Harry Winston became linked to diamonds, especially large ones.

In 1932, Winston closed down Premier Diamond and established Harry Winston, Inc. in order to begin producing his own line of jewelry. He sought to highlight the jewels' own shapes by minimizing the setting. He was supposedly inspired one Christmas season when he observed how a holly wreath was shaped by its leaves, then applied the concept to jewelry design, relying on light platinum settings that allowed for the three-dimensional arrangement of stones, so that they, rather than the metal, dictated the design. He had a particular dislike for the yellow-gold used in older settings, which he felt distorted the color of the gems. His flair for new designs and penchant for publicity allowed Winston to flourish during the Depression years, when he became a major figure in the New York diamond business who in many ways was personally responsible for keeping the industry afloat in the city. He boosted New York while at the same time he gained an international reputation when in 1935 he paid $700,000 to De Beers Company for the 726-carat Jonker diamond, named after a South African man, Jacobus Jonker, who found the stone on a farm. Winston's plan to split the diamond into smaller stones for reselling was so fraught with peril that even Lloyd's of London would not insure the company for damage. He essentially risked his entire investment, which only added greater emphasis on his decision to have the work done in New York rather than Europe. It was the first major stone, in fact, to be cut in the United States. After a number of European experts examined the diamond and indicated precisely where it should be divided, Winston turned to Lazare Kaplan, a Russian-born immigrant, to do the work, paying what was an incredible sum of $30,000. After nearly a year of study, Kaplan concluded that if he followed the advice of the European experts he would destroy the Jonker diamond. He determined his own plan and successfully split the giant stone into 12 diamonds, the largest at 126.65 carats. Winston was then able to sell the results for a total of $2 million, realizing a hefty profit on his investment.

Acquiring the Hope Diamond: 1949

Over the ensuing decade Winston acquired other large, uncut diamonds, including the 726.6-carat Vargas, discovered in Brazil in 1938, and the 155-carat Liberator, discovered in Venezuela in 1943. Winston also continued to purchase cut stones through estate sales. In 1949, Winston paid $1 million for the world's most famous diamond, the sapphire-blue Hope Diamond, notorious because of a curse supposedly attached to it. According to the myth, the Hope Diamond was originally part of a 112.5-carat diamond stolen from the statue of a Hindu goddess in India in 1642 and smuggled out of the country by Jean-Baptist Tavernier, a French gem merchant. He sold it to the King of France, Louis XIV, who had the stone cut down to 67 carats. He subsequently died of smallpox and Tavernier at the age of 80 was attacked and devoured by wild dogs. Louis XIV and his wife Marie Antoinette then inherited the throne and the diamond and were ultimately beheaded during the French Revolution. These deaths established a foundation for a later belief that the Hope Diamond was cursed and anyone who touched it would come to a disastrous end. A recut 44.5-carat stone surfaced in London some 30 years after the death of Louis XIV and Marie Antoinette. It was purchased by merchant Henry Thomas Hope, whose name has been attached to the diamond ever since. He gave it to his wife, who ran off with another man, and eventually was forced to sell it to fend off bankruptcy. A succession of ill-fated owners of the Hope Diamond followed. In 1911, the famous Paris jeweler Pierre Cartier sold the stone to Washington socialite Evalyn Walsh McLean and, according to some, essentially used the "curse" as a marketing ploy, going so far as to insert a clause in the sales contract stating if any fatality occurred in the family within six months, the Hope Diamond could be exchanged for jewelry equal to the $180,000 McLean paid for the stone. She certainly had her share of family troubles over the next 46 years, and in fact died of pneumonia wearing the Hope Diamond, but the curse did not scare off Harry Winston. He acquired it as part of McLean's jewelry collection for an estimated $1.5 million.

Winston then combined the Hope Diamond with a number of other jewels to create a touring exhibit called the Court of Jewels, which traveled around the country for the next four years. Although it was good showmanship and garnered excellent publicity, the tour, and others that followed, were very much an expression of Winston's deep love of gems. Because so many of the finest examples were in private hands, he simply wanted the public to have a chance to share his joy in appreciating beautiful stones. In 1958, he donated the Hope Diamond to the Smithsonian Institution's Hall of Gems and Minerals, sending it by registered mail in a plain wrapped package. Over the years, he donated more gems to the Smithsonian, gems which one day would be housed in the Winston Gallery that now serves as an entrance to the Janet Annenberg Hooker Hall of Geology, Gems, and Minerals.

For uncut stones, Winston, like other diamond dealers, was reliant on "The Syndicate," De Beers Consolidated Mines, Ltd., which had so much control of diamond production, around 85 percent, that it could essentially determine who could buy diamonds and name the price. In the 1940s, Winston sought an independent source of uncut stones by funding a South American jewel-hunting expedition. Other attempts followed, including one in Sierre Leone that almost resulted in the severing of his relationship with De Beers. The parties settled their differences and Winston was able to negotiate a better deal with De Beers. He would become the Syndicate's largest customer.

Winston opened a Geneva salon in 1955, followed two years later by a Paris salon. His reputation as the King of Diamonds during this period was reflected in the song "Diamonds are a Girl's Best Friend," made famous by Marilyn Monroe, who uttered the tag line, "Talk to me, Harry Winston." He was friends with Hollywood royalty as well as actual royalty and was a frequent guest for tea with the Queen of England. Although known for big diamonds and showrooms with drawn shades where salespeople often outnumbered the few customers permitted to enter, Winston had other operations that contributed to his business. He sold industrial diamonds, as well as less

Key Dates:

1896: Harry Winston is born in New York City.
1916: Winston establishes his first company, The Premier Diamond Company.
1930: Winston buys the B.J. ''Lucky'' Baldwin collection of jewels, which includes largest diamond ever sold in a U.S. public auction.
1932: Harry Winston Inc. is formed.
1935: Winston acquires the 726-carat Jonker diamond.
1949: Winston acquires the Hope Diamond.
1957: Paris Salon opens.
1958: Hope Diamond is donated to Smithsonian Institution.
1978: Harry Winston dies.
1980: Tradition begins of lending jewels to be worn at the Academy Awards.
1986: Beverly Hills salon opens.
2000: Harry Winston's son Ronald buys out his brother Bruce Winston's share of business.

expensive engagement rings that could be purchased through such pedestrian channels as Montgomery Ward mail-order catalogs. By the early 1960s, Winston was estimated to generate as much as $50 million in annual revenues. Because he was such a private man, the accuracy of this amount could not be verified. Winston was so private that he refused to allow his photograph to be taken, claiming that this decision was at the behest of his insurer, Lloyd's of London.

As Harry Winston aged, he faced the question of passing on the business to his two sons, who proved to have divergent personalities. He was prompted to utter an oft repeated statement: ''I have two sons, one a genius, one a moron.'' The eldest, Ronald, eagerly learned about the jewelry business from his father. He graduated from Harvard University with majors in both chemistry and English, then studied rocket propulsion at New York University before honoring his father's request that he help him run the family business. Younger brother Bruce, on the other hand, showed little inclination for academics and was far less ambitious than his brother. After spending only a few months at American International College in Springfield, Massachusetts, he dropped out to travel around Europe. At the age of 18 he married a dancer, and they divorced three years later. Concerned that Bruce might squander his inheritance, Winston wrote a will that split the business between his sons, but Ronald was to be awarded his stake outright, while Bruce would have his shares held in trust. Every five years, 20 percent would be turned over to Bruce, who would also receive a living from a trust run by his brother and two trustees.

Death, Succession, and the Future: 1970s–2000s

Harry Winston died at the age of 84, and Ronald took over the family jewelry business. He talked about the need to make the salons more accessible to a younger clientele, a theme that he would repeat periodically but never actually act upon. Ronald was credited with starting the practice of lending jewelry to actresses for the Academy Awards, which served as the firm's

most overt effort at publicity. He also oversaw the opening of a new salon in Beverly Hills in 1986 and Tokyo in 1988. He also launched Winston's Ultimate Timepiece Collection, which created and sold watches in the $100,000 price range.

When Harry Winston's wife died in 1986, Ronald attempted to get his brother more involved in the business, naming him to the board of directors. For the most part, however, Bruce remained uninterested, reportedly signing whatever documents that required his signature without even reading them and generally preferring to spend his time sailing and driving his collection of sports cars. According to his attorney, Edward Wohl, Bruce in 1989 began to question Ronald's running of the company, especially in light of several years of reported losses. Moreover, during this period Ronald increased his salary from $350,000 a year, the same amount Bruce drew, to $1.13 million. Ronald claimed he was entitled to the money because he actually ran the company. Bruce went to court in 1990, seeking a full accounting of Harry Winston, Inc., and Ronald responded in January 1991 by calling a special meeting of the board of directors in order to claim the 50 percent of company stock promised to him by his father's will, then promptly dismissed his brother from the board. This act set off a bitter, decade-long legal battle.

The Winston brothers wasted few opportunities to castigate one another in the press, creating a public relations nightmare for a company that traded on decorum and taste. Ronald accused Bruce of being under the control of his attorney, Wohl, whom he claimed would realize more money in legal fees than Bruce if he simply sold his share of the business in a reasonable settlement. Bruce, on the other hand, accused Ronald of using company assets for his personal benefit. He pointed to Ronald's charging of expenses incurred in Beverly Hills during a bizarre effort to train for the 1988 Olympics. Ronald hoped to represent the Marshall Islands in the 100-meter sprint at the age of 47, but the country failed to qualify for the games. He insisted that the expenses charged to Harry Winston Inc. were related to the opening of the company's salon on Beverly Hill's Rodeo Drive. Nevertheless, Ronald further revealed an eccentric nature during legal proceedings. Like his father, he was reluctant to be photographed and insisted that a Lloyd's of London policy forbade pictures for security reasons. During one videotape deposition he wore a plastic pig mask, and in another he donned a Lone Ranger costume.

To settle the suit Ronald offered his brother $4.5 million, which he subsequently increased to $17 million, and finally $28 million in September 1997. Bruce refused these offers and eventually the court forced Ronald to return his stock to trustees and abide by their decision on the selling of the company. In the end, Ronald acquired complete control of Harry Winston Inc., buying out his brother for $54.1 million in the summer of 2000. In order to finance the deal Ronald took on a partner, the private equity investment firm Fenway Partners.

With the squabble with his brother finally ended, Ronald planned to take Harry Winston into a new era. He hired a new marketing firm to create an ad campaign to position the company as a lifestyle brand. Looking to bring in executive talent that had shied away from the company in recent years, he then hired Patricia Hambrecht, formerly with Christie's, to serve as president. He also hoped to attract new customers by offering more jewelry that cost less than $100,000, lowering the minimum price from $6,000 to $4,000. Even perfume, handbags, and eyeglasses under the Harry Winston label were entertained. The company looked to open as many as 15 salons in such major cities as Chicago, Las Vegas, London, and Hong Kong, as well as to renovate the older Fifth Avenue and Paris locations. Overall, Ronald hoped to soften the image of Harry Winston, a task that would entail a wholesale change in attitude for its sales personnel. Even at this late date, one media account of the changes at the company told of a woman at the Fifth Avenue salon who was shopping for earrings in the $35,000 price range. She was advised to try Tiffany's.

Principal Competitors

Bulgari S.p.A.; Cartier S.A.; Compagnie Financière Richemont A.G.; Montres Rolex S.A.; Tiffany & Co.

Further Reading

Burleigh, Nina, "The Trouble with Harry Winston," *New York,* January 18, 1999, pp. 46–53.

Conroy, Sarah Booth, "Hope & Despair: The 'Curse' of the Diamond," *Washington Post,* September 29, 1997, p. D2.

Parr, Karen, "Harry Winston Buffs Its Image," *Women's Wear Daily,* July 13, 1998, p. 8.

Shor, Russell, "New York Judge Orders Sale of Harry Winston," *Jewelers Circular Keystone,* March 1998, p. 78.

Wade, Lambert, "Gems in the Rough: Sibling Feud Tarnishes the Diamond Empire Built by Harry Winston," *Wall Street Journal,* February 14, 1996, p. A1.

Wadler, Joyce, "Tranquility Elusive for Famed Jeweler's Heir," *New York Times,* October 17, 2000, p. B2.

Well, Melanie, "Reconstructing Harry," *Forbes,* October 1, 2001, p. 93.

—Ed Dinger

House of Fraser PLC

1 Howick Place
London SW1P 1BH
United Kingdom
Telephone: (+44) 20-7963-2000
Fax: (+44) 20-7828-8885
Web site: http://www.houseoffraser.co.uk

Public Company
Incorporated: 1849 as Arthur & Fraser
Employees: 6,784
Sales: £847.3 million ($1.24 billion) (2001)
Stock Exchanges: London
Ticker Symbol: HOF
NAIC: 452110 Department Stores

House of Fraser PLC bills itself as the United Kingdom's leading retailer of designer brands—the department store chain boasts nearly 2,000 of them, including a number of popular in-house brands featuring the company's own designs. House of Fraser operates 52 department stores throughout the United Kingdom under a variety of signages, including 15 House of Fraser and six Rackhams stores, but also including Army & Navy Stores, Arnotts, Barkers of Kensington, Binns, Cavendish House of Cheltenham, Dickins & Jones, Dingles, DH Evans, David Evans, Frasers, Hammonds, Howells, Jollys, Kendals, and Schofields. Many of these store names operate as a strictly local or regional business, and often represent a single store. Yet the company's past attempts at rebranding its stores under a common name has usually met with strong local resistance. House of Fraser's average store size stands at around 100,000 square feet, although its largest stores reach more than 300,000 square feet. The company sells a full range of home furnishings in most of its stores (its smaller stores have fewer departments), including furniture, appliances, housewares, and linens, but clothing—and especially women's clothing—makes up the bulk of its sales. The company has performed a turnaround in the new millennium, reorienting its image as an up-market, fashion house; the company also has been pursuing an ambitious refurbishing program as it revamps many of its aging stores. Meanwhile, House of Fraser has embarked on a new expansion drive at the beginning of the century, calling for the addition of five new stores by 2003—and acknowledging its interest in acquiring some of its smaller competitors.

Founding a Department Store Empire in the 19th Century

The House of Fraser started out as a small draper's shop in Glasgow, Scotland. In 1849, Hugh Fraser, who had completed his draper's apprenticeship, joined with partner James Arthur to open their own store, called Arthur & Fraser, in Glasgow's Buchanan Street. After Fraser died, his sons took over the business, changing the store's name to Fraser, Sons & Co. in 1873. Over the decades, the store began adding more items, then new departments, eventually becoming a full-fledged department store.

The future Lord Hugh Fraser, representing a new generation of Frasers, was born in 1903 and left school to join the family business. In 1941, Hugh Fraser was named chairman and managing director, which at the time still consisted of the single Buchanan Street store. Yet under its new chairman, the store—and the company—was to undergo substantial growth, and by the early 1960s was to become the preeminent department store group in the United Kingdom.

Fraser began adding new stores in the years following the war, and by 1948, the year the company went public, Fraser had already built up a chain of 15 stores. The following decade was to see still stronger growth, primarily through acquisitions.

In 1953, Fraser acquired the Binns chain of stores, a company that had started out with a single shop in Wearmouth in 1836. The Binns acquisition proved merely a prelude to a larger acquisition. In 1959, the House of Fraser, as the company had come to be called, acquired the Harrods department store chain. Harrods, like Fraser, had been founded in 1849. Originally a grocery centered in Knightsbridge—which at the time was located outside of the city of London—Harrods was to grow into the United Kingdom's most prestigious department store, with departments stretching out across more than 20 acres. Founder Henry Charles Harrod sold the business to his son, Charles

Digby Harrod, in 1861, who sold the business to an investment group, which changed the store's status to that of limited liability company.

Harrods began expanding beyond its single store, acquiring other store chains, such as Dickins & Jones in 1814. That store had been established in 1790 on London's Oxford Street before moving to its Regent Street location in 1835. Harrods later went on to take over Rackhams, founded as a drapery shop in Birmingham in 1851 before expanding to become a small, regional chain of department stores. Another addition to the Harrods empire was the DH Evans stores, which had been founded in 1879 and which opened a London store in 1932.

The addition of Harrods transformed Fraser into a major force in British retailing. Although the company's department store chain now stretched out across most of the United Kingdom, the company's Harrods store remained what Lord Fraser called its "jewel in the crown." The House of Fraser grew as the British economy recovered from the devastation of World War II and entered a new phase of prosperity, with higher living standards, greater leisure time, and technological advancements stimulating a new spirit of consumerism. Meanwhile, Lord Fraser himself had expanded his personal interests, developing an empire of holdings that made him the most successful businessman in Scotland at the time. Fraser placed his holdings under the Scottish Universal Investments (SUITS) group, which also took a 30 percent stake in the House of Fraser department store chain.

Lord Fraser had been joined by his son, Hugh Fraser (later Sir Hugh Fraser), who had started with the business as a floor assistant at the age of 16 before taking over after his father's retirement in 1966. The company continued to expand, adding the Army & Navy store chain, which had originally been founded as a military cooperative in 1871 but opened to the general public in 1918 (due to the drastic drop in its membership following World War I). Other purchases followed, including the Cavendish House department store in Cheltenham and the Dingles stores.

Yet Sir Hugh Fraser took over the House of Fraser at a time when the British consumer was beginning to abandon the country's large-scale and often stuffy department stores in favor of smaller, trendier shops. The House of Fraser's' large stores and failing sales led to too much sales space and too large a stock burden. The collapse of the economic boom in the mid-1970s, the result of the Arab Oil Embargo of 1973, hit the company all the harder. The company continued to make acquisitions during the 1970s, building its chain to more than 90 stores; yet by the end of the decade, the chain had lost much of its luster.

Jewel in Whose Crown in the 1980s

Meanwhile, Sir Hugh Fraser's personal fortune was declining rapidly as a result of mounting gambling debts. During the 1970s, Fraser began selling off shares in SUITS. When the stock market learned of Fraser's actions, Fraser went ahead and sold off the rest of SUITS to then friend Roland "Tiny" Rowland, a German citizen born in India, who was behind the South African Lonrho conglomerate, but who remained a controversial figure in the British business community. Sir Fraser, who received £7 million from the sale, had agreed to the sale in part because he believed Rowland's promise that the purchase was to remain a simple investment.

Yet Rowland's real interest was quickly revealed to be the House of Fraser, specifically its Harrods department store. Fraser, who was ultimately dropped from the House of Fraser's board of directors, joined his company in resisting the South African raider. Rowland in turn launched what was described as a "guerilla war" against the company. Ultimately, however, Rowland was thwarted when the British Mergers and Monopolies commission blocked his attempt to gain full control of the House of Fraser.

In 1984, Rowland "parked" his 30 percent of House of Fraser with Egypt's Fayed brothers—or so he thought. In 1985, the Fayeds turned their back on Rowland and reached an agreement with the House of Fraser to acquire the rest of the company's shares. For this, the Fayeds paid £600 million. Rowland counterattacked, convincing friends in the British government to launch an investigation into the Fayeds (the investigation, the results of which were never published but later leaked, asserted that the Fayeds had misrepresented their wealth at the time of the House of Fraser purchase). Yet the sale stood and House of Fraser was taken off the public market.

Led by Mohamed Al Fayed (whose son Dodi was killed in the auto accident that also killed Princess Diana in 1997), House of Fraser began trimming its empire in the late 1980s and early 1990s. In 1988, the company sold off ten of its smaller department stores to the Sellar Morris Properties group for £6.5 million. Another group of medium-sized stores was sold off in 1989 in a £6 million management buyout. Not all of the company's actions during the period went toward trimming its ranks—the company acquired Schofields department store for £6.5 million at the end of 1988—yet the company, under Fayed's ownership, emerged as a trimmed down, modestly sized and, to many, rather dowdy department store group. By 1994, the company's chain of department stores had dwindled to only half its size in the 1980s. House of Fraser was lagging behind such competitors as Selfridges, Debenhams, and John Lewis in its sales-per-square-foot.

Pressed for cash, the Fayeds prepared to sell off House of Fraser in the early 1990s, keeping only the Harrods store as part of a growing collection of landmark London stores and hotels. A new managing director, Andrew Jennings, was appointed to lead the store group. Jennings conducted a review of the company's operations and then set out to revamp its image. Among the changes made were the abandonment of a number of departments, such as haberdashery, fabrics, and knitting, and a re-centering of the company's focus on fashion. The company

Key Dates:

1849: Hugh Fraser and James Arthur found draper's shop on Glasgow's Buchanan Street.

1873: Fraser's sons take over the store and the store's name is changed to Fraser, Sons & Co.

1941: Hugh Fraser (later Lord Hugh Fraser) is named chairman and managing director of the store and leads the company on a major expansion.

1948: House of Fraser Plc goes public; the company by then has 15 stores.

1953: House of Fraser acquires Binns.

1959: House of Fraser acquires Harrods department store group, which includes Rackhams, DH Evans, and Dickins & Jones, as well as the famed Harrods store in London.

1966: Sir Hugh Fraser, son of Lord Hugh Fraser, takes over as chairman of the company upon his father's death.

1976: Sir Hugh Fraser sells SUITS (Scottish Universal Investments) to Roland "Tiny" Rowland, giving the South African conglomerate chief a 30 percent stake in House of Fraser.

1981: Rowland attempts to acquire full control of House of Fraser, but the attempt is rejected by the British government.

1984: Rowland "parks" his holding with the Fayed family.

1986: The Fayeds take full control of House of Fraser for £600 million.

1988: House of Fraser sells ten of its smaller stores to Sellar Morris Properties.

1989: House of Fraser sells off 12 medium-sized stores in a management buyout; by the early 1990s, the company drops from 110 stores to just 56 stores.

1994: The Fayeds sell their entire stake in House of Fraser in a new public offering of the company.

1996: Strategic review leads to £50 million restructuring program and closure of three stores.

1997: House of Fraser launches new Linea in-house clothing fashion label as part of overall strategy to focus on high-end designer fashions; the company opens a new store in Northampton.

1998: The company announces its intention to add up to 30 new stores.

1999: House of Fraser sells 15 leaseholds to joint venture BL Fraser set up with British Land, netting £170 million; the company announces a failed attempt to acquire Allders department store group; three new stores are opened in Bluewater, Reading, and Sulliwell; new Fraser and Platinum brand labels are launched. 2000: The company buys Bristol store from Bentalls and announces planned opening of five new stores.

2001: The company begins £30 million refurbishment of flagship Rackhams in Birmingham.

also restructured its stores, separating them into three groups according to size in order to refocus its product offering. House of Fraser also began renovating a number of its stores, including the Frasers store in Glasgow, the Howells store in Cardiff, and the Dickins & Jones store in London, slated to become the company's new flagship store.

Rebirth of a Department Store Leader for the 21st Century

House of Fraser returned to the London stock exchange in 1994 and quickly ran into new economic troubles, seeing its profits slump into the mid-decade. In 1996, the company brought in a new chief executive, John Coleman, who promptly launched a new strategic review of the company. The result of that review called for a £50 million restructuring program, including the shutting down of a number of stores. The first three of these, including an Army & Navy store, a Binns department store, and the House of Fraser store in Sheffield, were closed in 1997, reducing the number of the company's stores to just 50.

House of Fraser now sought to restore its traditionally upmarket image and become recognized as a center for high-end designer fashions. Coupled with its new strategy, which saw the introduction of a vast range of designer labels, House of Fraser launched its own in-house brand featuring the company's own designs. Called Linea, the new label outperformed the company's expectations and helped to drive the company's growth through the end of the decade. The Linea range not only

helped to increase the company's sales, quickly reaching more than 10 percent of the company's total fashion sales, but also gave it higher margins than its range of internationally known brand names. That label's success led the company to introduce two new in-house brands, Fraser and Platinum, in 1999.

By 1998, House of Fraser once again appeared to be in a strong position to grow. The company now began targeting fresh expansion through the addition of new stores. A first store was added in Northampton in 1997, while three more were slated to open by 1999. By the beginning of 1998, the company announced its intention to add 30 more stores in an expansion program that was estimated to reach a final cost of more than £300 million. Yet the company's expansion plans were hampered by a lack of financial muscle.

House of Fraser solved this problem in part by setting up a joint venture with British Land, called BL Fraser, which then purchased 15 of House of Fraser's store freeholds, which were then leased back to the department store group. The deal raised £171 million for House of Fraser and whet its appetite for a more aggressive growth strategy.

At the end of 1999, the company revealed that it had been carrying out secret talks to acquire smaller rival Allders, a group with 21 stores. The two sides could not agree on a price, however, and the deal fell through. Instead, House of Fraser pushed ahead with its new store openings, including a £20 million store to anchor the new Bluewater shopping mall near the "Chunnel" and sites in Sulliwell and Reading. In 2000, the company started the construction of a new store in London, to open on King William Street and to feature some 55,000 square feet of selling space. In that year, also, the company extended its Linea line of clothing fashions to include home furnishings, under the Linea Home name. The company launched the House of Fraser line of women's clothing, and a range of men's clothing, called The Collection. In addition, in 2000 House of Fraser discovered "Customer Relationship Management" and began to put into place a new program, including the rollout of a so-called "loyalty card" to attract and retain shoppers.

In September 2000, the company bought a store in Bristol from the Bentalls chain, paying £15.6 million. At the same time, House of Fraser announced plans to open three new stores in London, Norwich, and in High Wycombe, Buckinghamshire. The new stores were expected to open by 2004. By the beginning of 2001, however, the company already had added two new store sites to its list, at Croydon and Maidstone, and other negotiations were underway to develop three to four new store sites.

Despite the company's new commitment to organic growth—and despite its failure to acquire Allders—it had not ruled out other acquisitions. As Chief Executive John Coleman told the *Guardian* in March 2001: "Consolidation would still be a good thing. We are about as small as you can be [to operate efficiently] and there are lots of smaller players out there who cannot afford the investment in a systems and supply chain that we've put in over the last five years. There would be significant costs you could take out. We could support another 20 or 30 stores."

As it ended 2001, House of Fraser continued to book strong sales growth and expected to top easily the £847 million it had recorded in 2000. The company also continued its program of revamping its existing store park. In September the company unveiled a £30 million renovation of its flagship Rackhams store in Birmingham, which was to increase that store's selling space to more than 300,000 square feet and help it better to meet the coming competition with the redevelopment of the city's Bull Ring commercial district. In the years since its second public listing the company had succeeded in whipping itself back into fighting shape and planned to earn its self-proclaimed title as the United Kingdom's leading retailer of designer brands.

Principal Subsidiaries

House of Fraser (Stores) Ltd.; House of Fraser (Finance) Ltd; BL Fraser Ltd (50%).

Principal Competitors

Arcadia Group Plc; Debenhams Plc; Harrods Holdings; James Beattie Plc; Marks and Spencer Plc; N Brown Group Plc; New Look Plc; Next Plc; Otto Versand Gmbh & Co.; Selfridges Plc.

Further Reading

Cole, Cheryl, "Fraser's High Street Hopes," *Birmingham Post,* September 26, 2001, p. 17.
Deshmukh, Anita, "The More, the Better," *Birmingham Post,* September 28, 2000, p. 24.
Finch Julia, "House of Fraser Is in Shopping Mood," *Guardian,* March 29, 2001.
Griffin, Jon, "The Fight Is On," *Evening Mail,* September 26, 2001, p. 24.
——, "House of Fraser Expands," *Evening Mail,* March 28, 2001, p. 43.
Hughes, Chris, "House of Fraser Looks Brighter," *Independent,* June 15, 2001, p. 23.
Jagger, Suzy, "House of Fraser," *Mirror,* September 26, 2001, p. 23.
Pottinger, George, *The Winning Counter: Hugh Fraser and Harrods,* London: Hutchinson, 1971.
Yates, Andrew, "House of Fraser Plans £300m Expansion," *Independent,* January 19, 1998, p. 18.

—M.L. Cohen

The Cancer Information Company

IMPATH Inc.

521 W. 57th Street, 6th Floor
New York, New York 10019
U.S.A.
Telephone: (212) 698-0300
Fax: (212) 258-2137
Web site: http://www.impath.com

Public Company
Incorporated: 1988
Employees: 948
Sales: $138.2 million (2000)
Stock Exchanges: NASDAQ
Ticker Symbol: IMPH
NAIC: 621511 Medical Laboratories

Based in New York City, IMPATH Inc. describes itself as a cancer information company. Originally founded to conduct cancer testing and analysis on an outsourcing basis for smaller hospitals that lacked the sophisticated technology and requisite personnel of larger institutions, IMPATH has taken advantage of a resulting database of more than 800,000 cases and other unique resources to expand its product offerings. The company's Physician Services business employs its testing expertise to assist physicians in determining both a prognosis of various forms of cancer as well as an appropriate treatment plan and the monitoring of recovery. Although Physician Services still accounts for nearly 90 percent of the company's revenues, IMPATH is optimistic about the potential of its Predictive Oncology unit, which uses its large database of case histories and tissue and serology archive linked to outcomes information to assist genomics, biotechnology, and pharmaceutical companies in the development of targeted drugs made possible by the mapping of the human genetic code. Through its Information Services business, IMPATH licenses software to some 600 hospitals to enable them to maintain their mandated cancer registries, while helping IMPATH to continue to populate its database of treatment and outcomes information, now totaling some two million patients.

Changes in Cancer Diagnosis in the 1980s Leading to IMPATH

For many years cancer diagnosis was based on morphology, or the size of a tumor, combined with the rate it was spreading to other organs. Diagnosis was far from precise and treatment options were quite limited. With advances in microbiology and other areas, researchers learned that cancers came in many varieties that required different approaches. An important key to providing better treatment options was the rise of immunohistochemistry, in which the fields of molecular biology, biochemistry, and immunology were joined together to develop a more precise understanding of tumors. In breast cancer, for instance, it was learned that a large majority of tumors contained estrogen receptors, which were receptive to the drug Tamoxifen. The necessary diagnostic expertise, however, was limited to the laboratories of teaching hospitals and other major medical centers. In 1988 two doctors who were involved in this research at New York's Memorial Sloan-Kettering Cancer Center—Carlos Cordon-Cardo and Richard J. Cote—created IMPATH as a resource to make the new cancer tests (and, later on, new technologies) available to smaller, community-based hospitals.

The concept for IMPATH had obvious appeal. The new tests were difficult to process and required the kind of day-to-day familiarity that was simply not feasible at a smaller hospital. While a pathologist might see a certain type of cancerous tissue two or three times a year, IMPATH would see it on a regular basis and thus be more capable of providing an accurate diagnosis and prognostic assessment. Moreover, by outsourcing the tests a hospital could save on the expense of equipment and personnel. The company turned to venture capitalists to fund IMPATH, receiving $400,000 each from the Indianapolis firm of Middlewest Ventures and New York's Salomon Brothers Venture Capital, and set up shop in the Upper East Side of Manhattan, at Third Avenue and 60th Street, focusing at first on "difficult to diagnose tumors." As more information became available about breast cancer, and because it was often detected early and presented doctors with a number of therapeutic options, breast cancer testing and analysis soon became a major revenue stream for IMPATH. Within a year of start-up, the company was servicing some 50 hospitals in the greater New York area, analyzing about 2,000 cases a month at a cost of $300 to $325 per case. Although a test kit might cost the hospitals only $75 if purchased directly from the manufacturer, the interpretation of the results was still complicated and the analyses from IMPATH's more experienced technicians were much more reliable. In addition, the kits had a six-month shelf life, preventing hospitals, with far less need than IMPATH, from purchasing in bulk.

IMPATH gradually began to expand outside of the New York area, as more hospitals became aware of the benefits the company had to offer through the interaction with its national salesforce. In addition to growing in geographic reach, IMPATH looked to add other types of tests, including DNA probes and new technologies such as flow cytometry, cytogenetics, FISH, and PCR. In 1990 the company had $1.63 million in revenues while posting a net loss of $720,000. The next year IMPATH generated $3.46 million in revenues and turned a negligible $8,000 profit, followed in 1992 with revenues of almost $5 million and a net profit of just $32,000. The board of directors was not satisfied with the company's progress, however, and in 1993 the then CEO was removed in favor of Anu D. Saad, an Indian-born molecular biologist who had been teaching at Cornell University when she joined IMPATH in 1990 as scientific director, then subsequently took on the role of director of business development. Because of the expenses incurred in the change in management and the hiring of additional laboratory personnel, IMPATH lost almost $1 million in 1993, despite increasing revenues to more than $7 million, but the company was now better positioned for the future.

Opening a California Facility in 1996

In 1994 IMPATH became a consistently profitable business, earning $900,000 on revenues that grew by more than 40 percent to $10 million, the result of a general increase in case volume, as well as an increase in the company's higher margin breast cancer prognostic analyses and tumor diagnosis. By now, IMPATH was seeing about 10 percent of all breast cancer cases in the United States. It was steadily building a database of information that would offer even more opportunities for the company. Revenues in 1995 grew by another 47 percent, exceeding $14.7 million, and net income topped $1 million. Because it had all but outstripped its operating capacity in New York and desired to be viewed by financial analysts as a national company, IMPATH opened a second facility in southern California in January 1996, a move that also helped to increase its geographic reach. Moreover, IMPATH was poised to expand on a number of fronts, from increasing its diagnostic and prognostic database through increased business with hospital groups and managed care companies, to becoming involved in the development of new cancer therapies.

To fund its ambitious plans, IMPATH made an initial public offering of stock with the help of Salomon Brothers and Pruden-

tial Securities in February 1996. IMPATH sold almost two million shares at $13 each, raising nearly $24 million. The timing was certainly propitious. Health maintenance organizations (HMOs) had become increasingly more influential in the healthcare system, and they, along with government programs such as Medicaid and Medicare, were pressing hospitals to cut costs. Outsourcing to a specialized company like IMPATH was clearly a trend that would continue to grow. Furthermore, IMPATH with its experience in some 500,000 cancer cases had the potential of saving money by more precisely providing treatment-defining information. With breast cancer, for instance, approximately 80 percent of all cases were treated with chemotherapy, yet only 20 percent actually required it. If doctors, therefore, were better able to target chemotherapy cases using IMPATH's analysis, the cost savings could be dramatic. In addition, whereas other companies recognized the potential in the business, IMPATH's head start placed it in a commanding position.

IMPATH continued its impressive rate of growth in 1996, increasing revenues by almost 50 percent to nearly $22 million, and almost doubling net income to $2 million. In 1997 the company began to grow externally through a series of acquisitions that expanded its product lines as well as bolstered its database of case information. A wholly owned subsidiary, IMPATH-HDC, acquired Oncogenetics, Inc., a cancer testing facility that employed molecular and cytogenetic testing, which were considered growth areas. IMPATH then acquired the oncology division of Immunodiagnostic Laboratories, Inc. In September 1997 the company acquired the GenCare Division of Bio-References Laboratories, followed by the purchase of Aeron Biotechnology, a California-based testing facility specializing in breast cancer prognostic analyses. Not only would Aeron allow IMPATH to make full use of its California facility, it added tissue samples and data from more than 56,000 analyzed cases. The company also initiated a joint venture with Medical Registry Services Inc., makers of cancer registry software products, a move that would allow IMPATH's clients to monitor data electronically instead of manually. (A year later, IMPATH would purchase Medical Registry outright, using $13.75 million in stock.) Also during the course of 1998, IMPATH relocated from its original Manhattan offices to much larger accommodations on West 57th Street. For the year, the company again produced strong revenue and profit growth.

Acquiring Physician Choice in 1998

In March 1998 IMPATH made a secondary offering of common stock, selling two million shares at a price of $33.25 per share, in order to fund its continuing expansion. In addition to the Medical Registry acquisition, IMPATH paid $3.6 million for certain assets of Biologic & Immunologic Science Laboratories, Inc., a private California company that was a world leader in the field of lymph node and bone marrow micromestastases analyses, a new area for IMPATH. In September 1998 IMPATH paid $1 million in a cash and stock deal for Physician Choice, Inc., a company that offered post-clinical, pre-marketing, cost-benefit analyses to pharmaceutical and biotechnology firms that were developing new oncology drugs for the marketplace. This acquisition allowed IMPATH to better utilize its growing database of case histories. The company had collected this information as a result of years of analyzing cancer cases, but it was now large enough to provide

Key Dates:

1988: IMPATH is incorporated.
1993: Anu D. Saad is named president.
1995: A California facility is opened.
1996: The company goes public.
2001: Saad is named chairman.

predictive value for drugmakers. Furthermore, the scientific landscape was altering dramatically with the completion of the mapping of the human genome. Rather than relying on a chemotherapy cocktail, for instance, that killed healthy tissue along with malignant growths, researchers were gaining the ability to target drugs for more precise treatments. As a result, IMPATH's database was valuable in a number of areas. Not only could it save drugmakers time and money by predicting outcome, it could also help determine the market size for a new drug, and even be used to recruit patients for clinical trials. Nevertheless, the privacy of patients was closely guarded, with names and Social Security numbers eliminated from profiles before use in generating reports.

In 1999 information services and specialized analyses performed for biotech and pharmaceutical companies generated only $8 million in sales out of $85 million in total revenues for the year (a significant increase over 1998 revenues of $56.3 million), but it was clearly an area that held great potential for profits for IMPATH, as well as leading to better treatments for cancer patients. One of the first major clients for the company's new BioPharmaceutical Services division was the pioneering biotech firm Genentech, Inc., which was working on drugs to fight breast cancer. In March 1999 the two parties signed a deal to work together. Also in that year, IMPATH created a joint venture with Affiliated Physicians Network, Inc. (APN) to provide clinical research and information to the biopharmaceutical industry. APN was composed of a number of community-based cancer specialists, founded in 1996 by 75 oncologists in private practice. Later in 1999, IMPATH and APN participated in a multi-year pilot project with the National Cancer Institute to provide cancer patients with greater access to clinical trials. IMPATH also made two acquisitions in 1999 that added to its testing business and expanded its database of case histories, tissue samples, and other specimens. It paid $6.9 million in cash plus stock for BioClinical Partners, Inc., a worldwide medical research network. IMPATH also signed a $5.4 million deal to acquire Pacific Coast Reference Laboratories, Inc., a California testing business that specialized in anatomic pathology, employing immunohistochemistry and flow cytometry technologies. IMPATH, at the cost of $5 million, gained a direct involvement in the clinical trials area by investing in ILEX Oncology Services, Inc., a contract research subsidiary of Ilex Oncology Inc.

More drug manufacturers in 2000 signed deals with IMPATH for use of its data, state-of-the-art technologies, and access to its well-characterized tumor specimens linked to outcomes information, including Millennium Pharmaceuticals Inc., Bristol-Myers Squibb Co., and Glaxo Wellcome Inc. IMPATH also continued to make acquisitions, purchasing certain assets from M.I.T. Consultant, Inc., a Los Angeles histology business, as well as assets from InterScience Diagnostic Laboratories, Inc., a Brooklyn,

New York, cytogenetics company. Investors took notice of this activity at IMPATH. In 2000 the price of IMPATH stock soared to a record high of $81.56 (after taking into account a two-for-one stock split effected in August 2000), and even though it settled to the $50 level, it had realized a 423 percent gain over the prior year. For the year, IMPATH increased revenues by more than 60 percent over the previous year to $138.2 million, while net income of $12.9 million reflected similar gains.

Saad was named chairman of the board in 2001 and Richard Adelson was installed as president (as well as chief operating officer, his prior position) as IMPATH continued its robust pattern of growth. It acquired the oncology clinical studies network of Innovative Clinical Solutions, Ltd., a company that specialized in clinical trial support services. It also signed an agreement with the University of Pennsylvania Cancer Center and its 28-community-hospital network to make its tissue and serology archive (GeneBank) available, and in the process add to the collection by some 4,000 specimens each year. IMPATH signed another agreement to provide services to a major biopharmaceutical firm, Abgenix, Inc. In September 2001, *Fortune* magazine listed IMPATH as one of the country's fastest growing companies, and there was every reason to believe that the business would continue to prosper. With the population living longer, thus becoming more likely to have an eventual brush with cancer, the demographics favored the company's testing services. The company, through its extensive database and unique resources, would also profit from the development of new drugs to combat cancer. As survival rates continued to improve, IMPATH also would be involved in monitoring recovered patients and patients undergoing treatment. The prospects for the company, therefore, appeared quite positive for the foreseeable future.

Principal Subsidiaries

Medical Registry Services Inc.; Physicians Choice, Inc.; Physicians Network, Inc.

Principal Divisions

Physician Services; Predictive Oncology; Information Services.

Principal Competitors

Aros; DIANON Services; Gene Logic; Specialty Laboratories; UroCor.

Further Reading

Agovino, Theresa, "Firm Creates New Path for Hospital Tests," *Crain's New York Business,* May 8, 1989, p. 20.

Fulman, Ricki, "Complete Recovery for Cancer Form," *Crain's New York Business,* June 16, 1997, p. 13.

McDonald, Michael, "New Role, Deals Power Impath Stock," *Crain's New York Business,* December 18, 2000, p. 38.

Monroe, Ann, "Specialized Care: The Hot New Sector in Healthcare," *Investment Dealers' Digest,* June 10, 1996, p. 20.

Moukheiber, Zina, "The Gift of Data," *Forbes,* May 29, 2000, p. 192.

Pollack, Andrew, "Bouyed by Mergers, Medical Labs Await Era of Gene Testing," *New York Times,* June 14, 2001, p. C1.

Schneider, A.J., "Middlewest Hits Jackpot with Cancer-Firm Stake," *Indianapolis Business Journal,* March 11, 1996, p. 12.

—Ed Dinger

Inco Limited

145 King Street West, Suite 1500
Toronto, Ontario M5H 4B7
Canada
Telephone: (416) 361-7511
Fax: (416) 361-7781
Web site: http://www.incoltd.com

Public Company
Incorporated: 1916 as International Nickel Co. of
    Canada, Ltd.
Employees: 10,000
Sales: US$2.9 billion (2000)
Stock Exchanges: New York Toronto London Paris
    Brussels Frankfurt Swiss
Ticker Symbol: N
NAIC: 212234 Copper Ore and Nickel Ore Mining;
    212221 Gold Ore Mining; 212299 All Other Metal
    Ore Mining; 325188 All Other Basic Inorganic
    Chemicals Manufacturing; 331419 Primary Smelting
    and Refining of Nonferrous Metal (Except Copper and
    Aluminum); 331491 Nonferrous Metal (Except
    Copper and Aluminum) Rolling, Drawing, and
    Extruding; 331525 Copper Foundries (Except Die-
    Casting); 551112 Offices of Other Holding Companies

Inco Limited is one of the world's top producers of nickel. It operates Canada's largest mining and processing operation in Sudbury, Ontario, and runs other mines in Canada, the United Kingdom, and Indonesia. It has interests in refineries in Japan, Taiwan, and South Korea, and sales and operations in over 40 countries worldwide. Overall Inco provides about 25 percent of the nickel used globally. The company also produces cobalt, copper, precious metals, and specialty nickel products.

Early Years

Nickel was first isolated as an element in the middle of the 18th century, but not until the following century did it come into demand as a coin metal. Up to around 1890, coining remained the metal's only use, and most of the world's nickel was mined by Le

Nickel, a Rothschild company, on the island of New Caledonia. At that time, however, it was determined that steel made from an iron-nickel alloy could be rolled into exceptionally hard plates, called armor plate, for warships, tanks, and other military vehicles, and the resulting surge in demand spurred a worldwide search for nickel deposits. The world's largest nickel deposit ever discovered was in Ontario's Sudbury Basin; before long, one of the area's big copper mining companies, Canadian Copper, began shipping quantities of nickel to a U.S. refinery in Bayonne, New Jersey, the Orford Copper Company. Orford had devised the most economical process for refining nickel, and its alliance with Canadian Copper proved an unbeatable combination. Orford dominated the U.S. nickel business, supplying much of the metal needed by the growing steel industry, and managed to make inroads into the European market as well.

The U.S. steel industry did not feel comfortable relying on a single Canadian source for one of its essential materials; so in 1902 Charles Schwab of U.S. Steel and a group of other steelmen used the financial backing of J.P. Morgan to take control of and merge Orford and Canadian Copper. The new company was called International Nickel, nicknamed Inco, and was based in New York. From the first, Inco was able to control a majority of the U.S. nickel market, and had increased its share to 70 percent by 1913. Its large-scale operations in the Sudbury Basin allowed the company to eliminate competition through price wars and sheer staying power. According to *Fortune* magazine in May 1957, Inco had maintained its control of the U.S. market without interruption for nearly 40 years.

As the world's leading nickel producer, Inco enjoyed an enormous increase in business during World War I, when the need for armor-plate drove up steel sales. This good fortune soon changed, when the 1921 world disarmament agreements killed the munitions market and Inco was left with a huge backlog of nickel. Its record 1921 profit of US$2 million slipped to a US$1.2 million loss the following year, and the Sudbury mines were shut down for over six months. The shock of this setback stayed with the company for many years in the form of a conservative management policy and a determination to avoid large inventories. In 1922, Robert Crooks Stanley began a 30-year tenure as president—and later chairman—of Inco, intent upon building new markets in fields other than munitions.

Company Perspectives:

Our goal is to become the most profitable nickel producer in the world. At Inco, we are making good progress toward that goal through our three-part strategy. Our strategy is: to be a low-cost producer at all our operations; to pursue profitable and low-cost growth at our development properties; to grow our specialty-nickel products business.

Stanley created a vigorous research and development department to find new peacetime uses for nickel. So effective were the Inco engineers that many of the innovations in nickel metallurgy over the next 50 years can be traced to their efforts. In effect, Inco became the research department for the entire nickel industry, sharing its findings with customer and competitor alike. Of course, for many years Inco had few of the latter.

By the late 1920s, Stanley brought Inco sales back up to their wartime peak, much of the peacetime addition coming from the automobile industry. Inco's first major postwar investment was a US$3 million rolling mill in Huntington, West Virginia, designed to produce Monel metal, a widely used copper-nickel alloy. At the same time, Stanley effectively blocked the growth of competition from such newcomers as British America Nickel, which in 1923 made a serious bid for the U.S. market. Inco promptly lowered its price from 34 to 25 cents per pound, driving British America to bankruptcy a year later. When no one purchased the fallen company's assets, a little-known firm, Anglo-Canadian Mining & Refining, bought them very cheaply. Anglo-Canadian was actually a corporation owned by Inco, which simply took what it could use from British America's refinery and sold the rest for scrap.

A more serious competitor was handled in a different manner. Mond Nickel Company had been operating in the Sudbury Basin since just after the turn of the century, shipping its nickel to Europe to compete with France's Le Nickel and Inco's European offices. Mond, the creation of Ludwig Mond, the British chemist who founded Imperial Chemical Industries (ICI), owned half of the best nickel deposits in Sudbury, in an area known as the Frood. The other owner of these deposits was Inco. In 1928, Inco decided it would be wiser to join forces rather than fight over the world's largest nickel mine. Mond and Inco were then merged at the end of that year to form International Nickel Co. of Canada, Ltd., still nicknamed Inco. Mond remained a U.K. subsidiary of Inco, handling both European and Asian customers. By moving its incorporation to a foreign country, Inco was better able to deflect inevitable and periodic attempts by the U.S. Department of Justice to prosecute the company for antitrust violations. The 1929 appearance of a small competitor called Falconbridge Nickel Mines Ltd., another European supplier, was only tolerated to avoid the impression of absolute monopoly.

Depression and World War II

The Great Depression caused Inco temporary losses for the second time in its history, but the growing number of industrial uses for nickel soon pulled sales back up to a healthy level. By this time, Inco had become a major producer of copper and platinum as well as nickel, thanks to Sudbury Basin's rich supply of minerals. The company was now the sixth largest copper producer in the world and the largest supplier of platinum, a metal whose unusual properties had found many industrial applications; however, it was in nickel that Inco held unchallenged power as the source of 90 percent of the non-communist world's supply. Inco's metal was needed by all of the world's arms makers and for the production of super-hard steel for a variety of uses, from armorplate to exhaust valves on aircraft engines to gun recoil systems.

In a move that stirred up plenty of controversy, Inco became the nickel supplier to both sides of the approaching World War II, which included signing a long-term contract with Germany's I.G. Farben in the mid-1930s. In antitrust action ten years later, the Department of Justice charged that Inco's agreement with Farben was part of an effort to form a worldwide nickel cartel, and that in the process it had supplied Germany with a stockpile of nickel critical to its imminent war plans. The antitrust action was settled in 1948 when Inco signed a consent decree, agreeing only that it would sell nickel in the United States at fair prices; its worldwide monopoly, however, was beyond the reach of the U.S. Department of Justice.

World War II taxed Inco's capacity and strained its relationship with the U.S. armed forces. Still mindful of its near collapse after World War I, Inco refused to stockpile the inventory desired by the armed forces, instead committing only to the timely delivery of critical metal. As an insurance policy, the U.S. government financed the creation of Nicaro Nickel Company in 1942, a Cuban venture under the direction of the Freeport Sulphur Company. Although Nicaro managed to produce some nickel, it never really got off the ground and was mothballed soon after the war. Its decline may have been hastened by Inco's price cuts on nickel oxides, Nicaro's specialty. The full extent of Inco's nickel monopoly was further suggested by the fact that, aside from the case of nickel oxide, its nickel price never varied between 1928 and 1946—an indication of complete freedom from the normal pressures of competition. At the war's end, Inco's assets were valued at about US$135 million, sales stood at US$148 million, and the company showed a very healthy net income of about US$30 million.

Inco's hesitation to expand its nickel production helped it to avoid a serious postwar slump, but it also left the company unprepared for what soon followed. In the booming economy of the 1950s nickel assumed new importance, finding applications in stainless steel, home appliances, automobiles, jet engines, and atomic power plants. When the Korean War added the usual backlog of orders for armorplate, Inco faced a severe and growing nickel shortage. The U.S. government made the situation more difficult by adding nickel to its list of stockpiled metals critical to national defense, a contract Inco was naturally called upon to fulfill.

Indeed, Inco and the U.S. Department of Commerce together allocated nickel to customers across the country. Yet this nickel shortage had two long-term consequences for Inco. First, it made a rise in prices inevitable—prices increased by 60 percent between 1946 and 1950 alone. Second, a host of new competitors entered the nickel market, encouraged by the acute shortage, rising prices, and the U.S. government's willingness to finance alternative suppliers of the important metal. Inco's share of the free-world market, which was estimated at 85 percent as late as 1950, soon began a decline to what would eventually mirror its 1990s level of 34 percent.

Ups and Downs in the Postwar Nickel Market

Once assured the boom in nickel was permanent, Inco increased production and began to search for new deposits. After several years of exploration, a major find was made in northern Manitoba in 1956, a field it christened "Thompson" after company Chairman John F. Thompson, successor to Robert Stanley. Thompson was the most significant new deposit of nickel found since the discovery of Sudbury in the 1880s. After Inco spent about US$175 million building mines, smelters, refineries, a town to house its employees, and a railroad to reach the town, the site added about 30 percent to the company's 1956 sales of US$445 million. Inco remained extremely profitable despite its new competitors and still carried no long-term debt. In the recession of 1958, sales dropped to US$322 million but a strike by the Mill, Mine and Smelter Workers Union kept inventories low and prevented a loss for the year.

After the 1958 recession, sales of nickel took off once again. Inco's research engineers continued to provide a new generation of customers with ingenious uses for nickel, as in the rapidly growing electronics and aerospace industries where the use of stainless steel was just beginning to mushroom. Under the leadership of new Chairman Harry S. Wingate, Inco's sales hit US$572 million in 1965, and its net income remained a remarkably high US$136 million. The Thompson field had grown into a thriving town and its deposits proved to be every bit as rich as hoped.

Nickel sales were given yet another boost by the Vietnam War, in which the United States employed a vast array of sophisticated weaponry, the bulk of which required nickel-hardened steel. Responding to the bull market, Inco launched a comprehensive refurbishment and expansion program eventually costing more than US$1 billion. For the first time in its history, Inco borrowed money and chose to continue concentrating on the mining of high-grade, relatively expensive nickel at a time when many competitors had come up with inexpensive, readily available nickel oxides and ferronickels.

The impact of these decisions was felt when a devastating strike by 17,000 Sudbury workers in 1969–70 was followed by the sharp recession of 1971; nickel sales dropped by 25 percent

and Inco's stock fell by 50 percent in a matter of months. The company did not show a loss for the year, but it was thoroughly shaken by the low sales and a mounting debt burden. Wingate retired and his successor, L. Edward Grubb, moved to curtail the expansion program then just coming on line. Grubb cut production back to 80 percent of capacity and reduced labor where possible. To protect Inco against the further erosion of sales by ferronickel competitors, he spent another US$750 million to exploit the company's own ferronickel sources in Guatemala and Indonesia, where nickel was extracted from laterite ore by means of a refining process using petroleum.

In 1974, Inco made its first and only major acquisition, paying US$224 million for ESB Inc., a leading manufacturer of large storage batteries using nickel. Inco believed ESB's sales would help balance cyclical downturns in nickel, and that demand for batteries would increase in a world growing short of oil. Inco's share of the world's nickel sales had slipped below 50 percent by this time. Except in 1974, a boom year for commodities, the nickel market was generally soft for the rest of the decade. More worrisome, the soaring price of oil made Inco's huge investments in laterite nickel practically a dead loss, as the cost of refining the ore with petroleum rendered the product too expensive to sell.

New Challenges in the 1980s and 1990s

In 1976 International Nickel Co. of Canada, Ltd. officially changed its name to Inco Limited. A looming problem for the newly named company was Inco's US$850 million debt burden, which grew less manageable as interest rates reached a peak in the early 1980s. Additionally, Inco's new battery subsidiary was floundering, and in the severe recession of 1981 Inco found itself in deep trouble. Forced to write off its Guatemalan investment, sales began a steep slide; the company reported a disastrous year-end loss of US$470 million, its first since 1932. In the following three years, Inco's sales fell another US$500 million, as the recession and corporate debt proved an almost fatal combination.

Inco, however, had one asset that remained invulnerable: it still owned the world's richest nickel fields. Under CEO Donald J. Phillips, Inco wrote off its ill-fated battery venture for $245 million, almost halved its workforce, closed all excess production facilities, and sat tight, waiting for the severely depressed price of nickel to recover. New techniques allowed the extraction of ore in far bigger chunks than previously possible, and the reduced staff performed the smelting and refining tasks with improved methods. A rebound in the nickel market in 1987 brought the boost Inco needed: an increase in market share to nearly 35 percent and a year-end profit of US$125 million.

When nickel prices reached an all-time high in 1988, Inco's worldwide shipments of 495 million pounds of nickel (its highest level in 14 years) sent profits soaring to US$735 million and a stunning US$753 million in 1989.

As a reward for his efforts in raising productivity, Phillips was made chairman and CEO of Inco. His first task was to decide what to do with US$1 billion in retained earnings. Mindful of the poor results of past efforts at diversification, Phillips put some into further production refinements; however, the bulk was used for a $10 per share special cash dividend as part of a controversial recapitalization and shareholders' rights package. Taking cues from its U.S. neighbors, Inco's "poison pill" plan was the first of its kind in Canada. Spurring heated debate from all sides, Quebec's pension fund management group, Caisse de Depot et Placement du Quebec, filed suit on behalf of its 3.2 million Inco shares to legally overturn shareholders' December 1988 approval of the poison pill.

As the 1990s dawned, environmental issues became an increasingly expensive concern for Inco. The company faced an $80,000 fine for a sulphur trioxide leak from its Copper Cliff refinery in April 1987 and also faced repeated requests to regulate the sulphur dioxide released into the atmosphere by its smelting operations in Sudbury. Responding to what *Maclean's* called "the largest single source of sulphur dioxide pollution on the continent," Inco launched a series of abatement programs (with a price tag of over $500 million) to substantially lower emissions by 1994. To meet this goal, Inco planned to implement new magnetic separators to extract sulphur from ore and replace natural-gas burning furnaces with oxygen flash furnaces, which used oxygen rather than fossil fuels, eliminating toxic emissions altogether. Additionally, the new processes would significantly lower energy costs and boost efficiency.

In 1991, Michael Sopko, an Inco employee since 1964, was named president while Phillips retained the titles of CEO and chairman. Though annual net sales for 1991 fell to just under US$3 billion, net earnings plunged from 1990's US$441 million to US$83 million. In 1992, Sopko replaced the retiring Phillips as chairman and CEO, and Scott M. Hand assumed the presidency. The changing of the guard, however, had little effect on the continued downward trend of nickel prices, sluggish demand, and increased competition from Russian exports—all of which contributed to a year-end loss of US$18 million on net sales of US$2.56 billion. In response, Inco slashed executive salaries, decreased capital expenditures by $50 million, and closed its Ontario and Manitoba facilities for several weeks to cut production by 40 million pounds. Next Inco sold its 62 percent stake in TVX Gold Inc. for $371 million in 1993, as nickel prices plunged to their lowest level since 1987. Finishing 1993 with sales of only US$2.13 billion, the company had managed to post a profit of US$28 million rather than another loss.

Although earnings were not spectacular, they were nonetheless encouraging. The following year, Inco continued to struggle, announcing plans to prune upper management, eliminate 1,000 union jobs, and fund expansion at the company's low-cost Soroako mine in Indonesia—just as 4,900 laborers announced their intention to strike. Narrowly averting the strike, Inco took its employee relations in a different direction, funding more research into automated mining, with which the company had increasing success. The company also increased financing for the research and development of scores of new nickel applications and products. Nickel alloys, foam, foil, and powders, as well as nickel coating on fibers, papers, cloths, and even gold, were providing excellent results.

In 1996 the company bought a 25 percent stake in what was reputed to be the richest nickel discovery in 30 years. This was a tract known as Voisey's Bay in northern Labrador. The find belonged to a small Canadian mining concern, Diamond Fields. Its operatives had discovered the nickel deposits by accident in 1993. Diamond Fields was on the verge of selling a stake in the area to another Canadian mining firm, Falconbridge, when Inco stepped in with a bigger offer. The deal was worth about C$4.5 billion, financed by a complex strategy that created a special category of Inco stock. It was deemed a high price for the relatively unexplored Voisey's Bay, but Inco expected great things from the area.

However, plans to develop Voisey's Bay were being hindered. The mine could not be dug until an environmental impact study was completed, and local government insisted that metal mined in the area also be refined there, and not shipped elsewhere. Negotiations over these issues with government and tribal groups dragged on for years. Meanwhile, competition from nickel suppliers in Russia, Australia, and Cuba cut into Inco's profits. Bad weather forced the company's Indonesian mine to shut down for part of 1997, and a strike in Sudbury further chipped away at Inco's profits. In addition, the company was burdened with about US$1.5 billion in debt.

Inco looked for innovative ways to get the most out of its business. It continued to investigate high-tech mining, investing in a joint-venture Mining Automation Program in 1996. New equipment allowed miners to operate machinery by remote control from the surface. Though development of so-called telemining was expensive and not always smooth, the company stood to gain a lot in saved labor costs. To go into deep pits, some miners spent as much as two hours out of each eight-hour shift commuting in trains or elevators. Automation would ostensibly eliminate much of this lost time. The company also formed a new marketing group, called Inco Special Products, to exploit some more specialized niches. It formed the new division in 2000 to market nickel foams, powders, oxides, particles, and fibers. These were used in batteries, auto parts, and consumer electronics. Inco hoped to reach sales of $200 million from the new division within the next five years.

Inco then pledged to develop a nickel-cobalt mine in the French dependency of New Caledonia in 2001. The plant was expected to yield some 54,000 tons of nickel annually, and 5,400 tons of cobalt. The cost to develop the mine was estimated at about $1.4 billion. The company's Voisey's Bay property was still embattled by the fall of 2001, though negotiations with provincial governments continued. Inco was unable to start building a pilot smelting plant in the area until it guaranteed that it would also build a permanent plant. By 2001 costs for developing the mine were estimated at US$1.25 billion, with another US$500 million to build the pilot smelter. The economic downturn of 2001 made the company's plans all the more variable. Production was hoped to begin by 2005.

Principal Subsidiaries

Inco Special Products; Inco United States, Inc.; Novamet Specialty Products Corp. (U.S.A.); International Metals Reclamation Company, Inc. (U.S.A.); Exploraciones Y Explotaciones (Guatemala; 70%); Compagnie des Mines de Xere (France; 85%); Goro Nickel SA (New Caledonia); Jinco Nonferrous Metals Co., Ltd. (China; 65%); Ingold Holdins Indonesia, Inc. (Canada); Voisey's Bay Nickel Company Limited.

Principal Divisions

Ontario Division; Clydach Refinery (UK); Acton Refinery (UK); Manitoba Division; PT International Nickel (Indonesia); Inco TNC Limited (Japan).

Principal Competitors

Norilsk Nickel; Falconbridge Limited.

Further Reading

Arnott, Sheila, "Inco Shapes Its Labor-Relations Climate," *Northern Miner,* September 5, 1988, p. 6.

Ball, Matthew, "Equity Tailored to Suit the Strategy," *Corporate Finance,* October 1996, pp. 18–20.

——, "Inco Keeps It Pure with Special Stock," *Corporate Finance,* December 1996, p. 50.

Cook, Peter, "More Eye-Popping Facts About Poison Pills," *Globe and Mail,* October 20, 1988, p. B2.

Donham, Parker Barss, "Newfoundland's 'Untamed Dog' Takes on Inco, *Canadian Dimension,* May 2000, p. 10.

Gilbert, Ray, "Sudbury, Home to One of the World's Premier Mining Companies," *Northern Miner,* October 15, 1990, p. B19.

Heinzl, Mark, "Inco Moves to Take Miners Out of Mining, "Wall *Street Journal,* July 6, 1994, p. B6.

Hutchinson, Brian, "A Plugged Nickel," *Canadian Business,* April 24, 1998, pp. 43–47.

"Inco Forms New Division to Market Specialty Products," *Purchasing,* January 13, 2000, p. B32.

"Inco Plans $1.4 Billion Nickel-Cobalt Deal," *Project Finance,* May 2001, p. 13.

"Inco Reviews Female Policy After Human Rights Ruling," *Northern Miner,* March 14, 1988, p. 6.

"Inco's Focus Shifts from Voisey's Bay," *Sulphur,* May 2000, p. 10.

"Inco to Expand Indonesian Operation," *Northern Miner,* November 21, 1994, p. 1.

"Inco to Sell Stake in TVX Gold Unit to Underwriters for $289.4 Million," *Wall Street Journal,* June 29, 1993, p. B1.

"Inco to Spend $26.9 Million on Mine Project," *Northern Miner,* November 16, 1987, p. A1.

Lamont, Lansing, "Inco: A Giant Learns How to Compete," *Fortune,* January 1975.

Lamphier, Gary, "Voisey Secures Inco's Future," *Globe and Mail,* June 9, 1995, p. B1.

McClearn, Matthew, "Bots Way Down in the Mine," *Canadian Business,* August 20, 2001, pp. 44–47.

McInnes, Craig, "Court Fines Inco $80,000 Over Acid Cloud Incident," *Globe and Mail,* January 10, 1989, p. A1.

Mehr, Martin, "Inco Tries to Clean Up the Air and Its Image," *Marketing,* March 27, 1989, pp. B1, B6.

Melnbardis, Caroline, "Canada's First Poison Pill Is Leaving a Very Bitter Taste . . . ," *Financial Times of Canada,* October 24, 1988, pp. 27, 30.

Newman, Peter C., "Canada's Largest Investor Goes to War," *Maclean's,* November 7, 1988, p. 50.

Reier, Sharon, "The Treasure of Voisey Bay," *Financial World,* July 18, 1995, p. 28.

"Report on Corporate Finance: Inco's Move Started Wheels Turning in Canadian Boardrooms," *Globe and Mail,* December 12, 1988, p. B17.

"Retooling Mother Inco," *Northern Miner Magazine,* April 1990, pp. 41–45.

Robinson, Allan, "Inco Expects Another Good Year After Seeing 5th Record Quarter," *Globe and Mail,* April 20, 1989, p. B11.

——, "Inco, Falconbridge Betting Nickel Price Will Keep Shining," *Globe and Mail,* November 21, 1988, p. B1.

——, "Inco Slashes Production," *Globe and Mail,* October 6, 1992, p. B1.

——, "Product R & D Pays Off for Inco," *Globe and Mail,* September 8, 1992, p. B13.

Shortell, Ann, and Caroline Melnbardis, "Code Name Monticello: Inco Devised One of the Most Potent Poison Pills in North America," *Financial Times of Canada,* December 19, 1988, pp. 1, 14–16.

"The Squeeze on Nickel," *Fortune,* November 1950.

Stackhouse, John, "Inco Bets on Indonesia," *Globe and Mail,* May 19, 1994, p. B1.

Tintor, Nicholas, "Inco Exposure to Gold Increased with New Firm," *Northern Miner,* August 17, 1987, pp. 1–2.

Walmsley, Anne, "An Acid Test," *Maclean's,* September 17, 1990, p. 62.

Zehr, Leonard, and Jacquie McNish, "Inco Plans $1.05-Billion Dividend in Recapitalization," *Globe and Mail,* October 4, 1988, p. B1.

—Jonathan Martin
—updates: Taryn Benbow-Pfalzgraf, A. Woodward

Inktomi Corporation

4100 East 3rd Avenue
Foster City, California 94404
U.S.A.
Telephone: (650) 653-2800
Fax: (650) 653-2801
Web site: http://www.inktomi.com

Public Company
Incorporated: 1996
Employees: 869
Sales: $191.5 million (2001)
Stock Exchanges: NASDAQ
Ticker Symbol: INKT
NAIC: 511210 Software Publishers

Inktomi Corporation may not be known to as many Internet users as the popular search engine portals Yahoo! or Google, but its search engine technology powers the search functions at more than 50 widely used Internet portals. From its founding in 1996, the company adopted a strategy of focusing on technology and becoming a leading supplier of Internet infrastructure technology.

Company Origins

Inktomi was founded in February 1996 in Berkeley, California, by Eric Brewer, a professor at the University of California at Berkeley, and Paul Gauthier, one of his graduate students. The two were involved in a government-funded research project involving parallel computing, which joined PCs and workstations together to make them function like a supercomputer. Dave Peterschmidt, a former senior executive at Sybase, Inc., was hired as CEO to run the new company, which was named for a mythical Plains Indian spider known for cunning rather than brute force. Brewer remained Inktomi's chief scientist, and Gauthier was its chief technology officer. In 1997 the company moved to San Mateo, and then later established its corporate headquarters in Foster City.

When Inktomi and HotWired introduced HotBot in 1996, a new search engine for the World Wide Web, it was the only search engine that could search all 50 million pages on the Web. Hotbot was the first application that used Inktomi's Audience 1 software, which could customize web pages and advertisements according to the searcher's type of browser. Hotbot ran on Sun Microsystems' SPARC workstations and was a joint venture of HotWired, a subsidiary of *Wired Magazine* publisher Wired Ventures, and Inktomi, which developed the search technology at the University of California at Berkeley.

In 1997 Inktomi began beta testing its traffic servers, which intelligently managed network data flow and aimed to eliminate bottlenecks and redundant traffic on the Internet and corporate intranets. The traffic servers were based on network caching technology that created a local repository of requested information by moving it closer to the user and allowing multiple users to access data more quickly than by utilizing the Internet's national backbone. The traffic servers also reduced the amount of traffic over the Internet or corporate intranets, thus freeing up bandwidth. The traffic servers included network caching software that was developed at the University of California at Berkeley and ran on Sun Microsystems workstations, which could scale up to accommodate traffic growth. Key markets for the traffic servers, which were released later in 1997, included Internet service providers (ISPs), network backbone providers, and business enterprises. Inktomi's traffic servers were introduced at a time when the amount of overall redundant traffic over the Internet was estimated at 40 to 80 percent. Other companies introducing network caching products in 1997 in competition with Inktomi included Novell and Cisco Systems.

Toward the end of 1997 Microsoft entered into an agreement with Inktomi to use Inktomi's traffic server and search engine technology in the Microsoft Network (MSN) in 1998. Inktomi's Traffic Server would provide MSN users with access to some 75 million Internet sites. The Traffic Server also would reduce traffic congestion on MSN through extensive caching.

Enhanced Traffic Server and IPO: 1998

By 1998 Inktomi was beginning to diversify its customer base, and the company made plans to go public. For fiscal 1997 ending September 30, Inktomi reported a loss of $8.7 million on revenue of $5.8 million. Wired Digital accounted for approximately 79 percent of Inktomi's total revenue in 1997, with NTT accounting for another 13 percent.

During the first six months of fiscal 1998, Inktomi gained more customers: Wired Digital now accounted for 59 percent of the company's revenue, NTT accounted for 6 percent, and Microsoft accounted for 20 percent. The company gained $14 million in private financing through equity investments from Intel and venture capital firm Oak Investment Partners. In addition, America Online and Digex Inc. became licensees of Inktomi's Traffic Server caching software and would begin using it in their networks in the second half of 1998. The company also entered into technology partnerships with Digital Equipment Corporation (DEC) to port its Traffic Server to DEC's Unix and with Intel to port the software to Windows NT. Initially, Inktomi Traffic Server only ran on the Sun Solaris operating system. By the end of 1998 Inktomi was the leading caching provider with a one-third market share, according to the Internet Research Group.

In May 1998 Inktomi's search engine technology became the preferred search engine at Yahoo!. Inktomi's search engine was able to index 110 million web pages, about half of the web's estimated total. The index was being updated at the rate of about ten million pages per day. By running on Sun Microsystems workstations, Inktomi could scale up its search engine service simply by adding more workstations.

Inktomi's June 1998 initial public offering turned out to be the hottest IPO of the year. The company raised an estimated $36 million on the sale of two million shares. Although the initial offering price was $18, shares opened on the NASDAQ at $30 and closed the day at $36. By July Inktomi's stock was trading at around $90 a share, and it rose to $130 a share in November 1998.

HotBot version 5.0, released in mid-1998, marked a shift from Unix to Windows NT. The new version, which featured a new interface as well as a change in server infrastructure, was designed to increase usability and offer new features. The shift from Unix to Windows gave more control of the interface to the HotBot staff and made HotBot more compatible with Inktomi's next generation of search engine technology. Around this time Inktomi gained @Home Network, a cable modem service pro-

vider, as a customer for its search and cache technology. The company also released Traffic Server 2.0 later in the year; among the new features were a streaming media cache, substantial performance improvements, and support for web hosting and a wider range of protocols.

Development of a Shopping Search Engine: 1999

Inktomi began its move into e-commerce software solutions with the acquisition of C2B Technologies in September 1998 for about $90 million in stock. The acquisition would help Inktomi develop shopping search capabilities for customers such as Yahoo!. Rather than developing its own shopping search technology, Inktomi acquired the search technology already developed by C2B Technologies. C2B's shopping agent included a basic product locator that covered 170 merchants in 12 categories, or 460,000 products in all. Merchants covered by the shopping agent included online retailers as well as auction sites, online classified ads, and local merchants. Another part of the C2B engine included product descriptions and ratings from third-party content providers such as *Consumer's Digest*. The third part of the shopping engine was a shopping assistant, which asked lifestyle questions and helped customers identify their needs. Internet portals such as Snap, the Go Network, and Time Inc. New Media signed up to use the Inktomi shopping engine before it debuted in the spring of 1999, when it had grown to cover 350 merchants.

Inktomi expanded its e-commerce capabilities with the acquisition of ImpulseBuy.Net for $110 million in stock in April 1999. ImpulseBuy provided a database and other tools for merchants to enter their data, additional features that Inktomi could offer to merchants it wanted to sign up to participate in its shopping engine. At the end of 1999 Inktomi announced that its shopping engine would be made available to European Internet portals.

In addition to developing its shopping engine service in 1999, Inktomi upgraded its traffic server and released version 3.0 in mid-1999. The new version added support for two operating systems, Windows NT and Free BSD, in addition to Sun Solaris, Digital Unix, and SGI Irix. Perhaps the most important aspect of Traffic Server 3.0 was a new set of application programming interfaces (APIs) that allowed third-party providers to add value-added services, such as content filtering and automatic reformatting for cell phones and TV set-top boxes. These new APIs were designed to allow the addition of a range of network services and keep up with new developments in network caching technology. With the release of Traffic Server 3.0, Inktomi announced six new Traffic Server partners that would offer a range of new services.

In August 1999 Inktomi raised $300 million through a secondary stock offering. In the next month Inktomi acquired WebSpective Software for $106 million. WebSpective produced content-replication and distribution software, which made it easier to offload and back up data from a web server. It gave enterprise customers more ways to ensure that their sites were available and performing well. WebSpective's technology also helped web-hosting providers and Internet service providers (ISPs) deliver more reliable services. Later in the year Inktomi released two caching software products for corporate IT managers, Traffic Server E5000 for headquarters and Traffic

Key Dates:

1996: Inktomi and HotWired introduce Hotbot, a new search engine for the World Wide Web.
1997: Inktomi launches traffic servers to address Internet congestion.
1998: Inktomi goes public.
1999: Inktomi enters e-commerce market with a shopping search engine.
2000: Inktomi acquires FastForward Networks for $1.3 billion in stock.
2001: Content Bridge alliance, spearheaded by Inktomi, begins limited operations.

Server E200 for branch offices. These traffic servers enabled IT managers to put content on the edge of their corporate networks, so users could go directly to the data source without taxing the entire network and server infrastructure. The new content-delivery products marked a move into the enterprise market for Inktomi.

Toward the end of 1999 America Online announced that it would drop Excite and replace it with Inktomi's database for its search engine. The company also regained Microsoft as a client for its search engine service; Microsoft had announced earlier in the year that it would switch to Alta Vista to power its MSN search engines, but during the year Alta Vista changed its strategic focus, causing Microsoft to return to Inktomi's technology.

Growth and First Profitable Quarter in 2000

Inktomi reported its first profitable quarter in April 2000 for the quarter ending March 31, 2000. It posted a profit of $1 million on revenue of $47.3 million, compared with revenue of $15.2 million and a loss of $7.4 million for the same quarter in 1999. The company's quarterly profit was equal to about one cent per share.

In the first half of the year Inktomi forged several alliances to signal its entrance into the wireless Internet infrastructure provider market, including deals with AirFlash, Cap Gemini, Portal Software, Hewlett-Packard, Sun Microsystems, Spyglass, and GWcom. Through these alliances Inktomi was able to offer wireless operators a complete platform solution. The company subsequently signed a deal with wireless handset manufacturer Nokia Networks to deliver infrastructure software to wireless network operators.

Later in the year Inktomi signed partnership agreements that would make its content caching and search technology available through a variety of other technology providers. Through an agreement with advertising network DoubleClick, Inktomi was able to offer its portal customers a search service targeting banner ads based on keyword searches. An agreement with Genuity Inc., an Internet infrastructure services company, called for Genuity to develop a content distribution network using Inktomi's traffic server and content delivery suite.

In June 2000 Inktomi boosted its search capabilities with the $344.7 million acquisition of Ultraseek, a subsidiary of

Go.com. Ultraseek offered a scalable and customizable search solution for corporate Internet and intranet sites. The acquisition provided Inktomi with an established customer base in the enterprise market as well as additional product and service offerings. Around this time Inktomi was replaced by Google as the search engine powering the Yahoo! Internet portal. In other search engine developments, Inktomi announced that it had created a 500-million-record database called GEN3, which would be made available to its portal customers.

Inktomi's participation in content delivery took another step forward in August 2000 with the formation of Content Bridge, an alliance that initially included Inktomi, America Online, and Adero. Content Bridge was formed as a content distribution network, where producers and hosters of information and e-commerce functions would pay to have their content pushed to the caching servers of large Internet hosting, content delivery, and access providers. Inktomi would supply core network infrastructure technology; Adero would provide operational services, including centralized billing and settlement services; and America Online would deploy Content Bridge technology in its network. Among the first to join the network were Digital Island (content provider), Exodus Communications (hosting services), Genuity (hosting services), Mirror Image Internet (content provider), Madge.web (hosting services), and NetRail (access provider). Following a period of beta testing, the Content Bridge alliance began limited operations in January 2001. Operating partner Adero Inc. backed out at the last minute and sold its interest in the alliance to Inktomi for $23.5 million.

In September 2000 Inktomi announced its largest acquisition to date when it acquired FastForward Networks, a San Francisco-based software developer for Internet broadcasts, for $1.3 billion in stock. FastForward's software platform could support millions of viewers and thousands of simultaneous Internet broadcasts. Its software also could profile online audiences for broadcasters. Following the acquisition, FastForward dropped its name and became Inktomi's media division, with FastForward's cofounder, President, and CEO Abhay Parekh as its head. In 2001 Inktomi's media division offered the Media Distribution Network, a product suite that handled the distribution of streaming media around a network. It complemented Inktomi's Content Delivery Suite, which managed the distribution of static content.

Economic Slowdown Affecting Expansion, Capitalization in 2001

At the beginning of 2001 Inktomi announced its Inktomi Search Everywhere solution, which facilitated searches across previously isolated intranet, extranet, web site, and web search applications. The new search outsourcing solution integrated Inktomi's web, custom, site, and enterprise search products. Later in the year Inktomi announced that it would overhaul its search engine software using enterprise-level XML (Extensible Markup Language). The company also enhanced its web search service to provide more comprehensive search results, including relevance, classification, and ranking capabilities. It added distributed crawling architecture that scanned the Web more frequently, and offered content blending, which combined query results from separate databases.

In other search engine developments Inktomi introduced a pay-for-placement program in May 2001 called Index Connect. Under the program, participants could submit meta information about multimedia and other files, which would enable previously unavailable material such as video clips, audio files, and PDF documents to appear in search results.

Inktomi introduced Traffic Server 4.0 in February 2001. The new version extended the Traffic Server Platform to the Linux operating system for the first time. The new version also featured extra processing power and significantly faster performance.

After draining the company's resources for two years, Inktomi sold its e-commerce division to e-centives, an online direct marketing firm based in Bethesda, Maryland. The division included Inktomi's shopping search engine technology and its customer base.

Inktomi expanded its content distribution services with the acquisition of streaming-media vendor eScene Networks in July 2001. Inktomi's first product from the acquisition was called Inktomi Media Publisher, which allowed businesses to catalog, index, and publish corporate multimedia content.

Like other companies facing a challenging business environment in 2001, Inktomi cut back its workforce and saw its stock plunge to new lows during the year. For fiscal 2001 ending September 30, Inktomi reported a net loss of $296.5 million on revenue of $198.6 million. Much of the firm's net loss was due to one-time charges and amortization. By comparison, the company's pro forma loss for the year was $191.5 million, which excluded results of operations from Inktomi's divested e-commerce division, noncash employee stock compensation, amortization of goodwill and certain one-time charges, the write-down of certain investments, and restructuring costs. The company ended the year with $213.5 million in cash and short-term investments. For the future, CEO David Peterschmidt expected the company to return to profitability in 2002.

Principal Competitors

Akamai Technologies Inc.; AltaVista Company; CacheFlow Inc.; Cisco Systems, Inc.; Google Inc.; Novell Inc.

Further Reading

Andrews, Whit, "Inktomi Makes $110M Acquisition to Bolster Commerce Services," *Internet World*, April 26, 1999, p. 7.

"AOL, Digex to Use Inktomi's Server," *Internet World*, April 20, 1998, p. 33.

April, Carolyn A., "Acquisition: Inktomi to Buy Net Broadcasting Company FastForward," *InfoWorld*, September 18, 2000, p. 18.

Balderston, Jim, "Inktomi Revs Up Hotbot Web Search Engine," *InfoWorld*, May 20, 1996, p. 8.

Boyd, Jade, "Content Alliance Launches," *InternetWeek*, January 15, 2001, p. 13.

"Cache-Maker Inktomi Plans Public Offering," *Internet World*, April 20, 1998, p. 6.

Carroll, Kelly, "Download: Wireless Internet's Mystique," *Telephony*, March 20, 2000.

Caulfield, Brian, "Inktomi's Cache Opens to Services," *Internet World*, May 24, 1999, p. 26.

Cope, James, "Web Content Delivery Competition Increases," *Computerworld*, September 4, 2000, p. 91.

Espe, Erik, "Gunning for Web Dominance, Inktomi Blazes into New Territory," *Business Journal*, April 16, 1999, p. 3.

Ferguson, Renee Boucher, and Grant Du Bois, "Tuning Up a Search Engine," *eWeek*, March 26, 2001, p. 38.

Feuerstein, Adam, "Inktomi, Microsoft Get Back Together," *San Francisco Business Times*, December 17, 1999, p. 13.

——, "In the Money: Inktomi Executives Profit from Year's Hottest IPO," *San Francisco Business Times*, November 13, 1998, p. 1.

Follett, Jennifer Hagendorf, "Inktomi, Adero, AOL Sign Content Delivery Pact," *TechWeb*, August 24, 2000.

Fox, Justin, "It's the Technology, Stupid," *Fortune*, September 6, 1999, p. 42.

Gardner, Elizabeth, "Inktomi Raises $36 Million in Strong IPO," *Internet Week*, June 15, 1998, p. 5.

Ginsberg, Steve, "Sybase Castaway Plans Inktomi IPO," *San Francisco Business Times*, May 1, 1998, p. 1.

Golobin, Kelly, "Layoffs and Warnings Sweep E-Commerce Software Sector," *Computer Reseller News*, April 9, 2001, p. 12.

"Google Supplants Inktomi," *San Francisco Business Times*, June 30, 2000, p. 10.

Hesseldahl, Arik, "A Search Engine Retools for Speed and Dexterity," *Internet World*, June 29, 1998, p. 30.

"A Hidden Goldmine Called Inktomi," *Business Week*, September 27, 1999, p. EB72.

"Index Connect," *Online*, May 2001, p. 14.

"Inktomi and MediaDNA Partnership Enhances Search Everywhere," *Intelligent Enterprise*, January 1, 2001, p. 76.

"Inktomi Boosts Search Capabilities," *InfoWorld*, June 12, 2000, p. 16.

"Inktomi Buys into E-Commerce," *Telephony*, September 21, 1998.

"Inktomi Buys Online Broadcast Firm," *San Francisco Business Times*, September 15, 2000, p. 10.

"Inktomi Launches Online Shopping Service for European Internet Portals," *Internet Business News*, December 21, 1999.

"Inktomi's Cuts," *Interactive Week*, October 8, 2001, p. 48.

"Inktomi Shares Up on Profit News," *Business Journal*, April 21, 2000, p. 30.

"Inktomi Signs Portals for Shopping Engine," *Internet World*, April 12, 1999, p. 17.

"Inktomi's Traffic Server 4.0 Ready to Ship," *EContent*, February 2001, p. 13.

"Inktomi to Web: Got Cache?," *Telephony*, October 12, 1998.

Karve, Anita, "Caching the Internet," *Network Magazine*, December 1997, p. 22.

Lange, Larry, "Inktomi Attacks Net Bottlenecks," *Electronic Engineering Times*, April 28, 1997, p. 24.

LaPolla, Stephanie, "Inktomi Traffic Servers Ease Web Jams," *PC Week*, April 28, 1997, p. 40.

Lohr, Greg A., "E-Centives," *Washington Business Journal*, January 26, 2001, p. 20.

Long, Timothy, "No 23: The Miner," *Computer Reseller News*, November 15, 1999, p. 173.

"Microsoft, Inktomi Team Up on Web Engine," *PC Week*, October 27, 1997, p. 32.

Morris, John, "Refine Your Search," *PC Magazine*, October 22, 1996, p. 48.

"Newsfront: Fast Facts," *Inter@ctive Week*, May 8, 2000, p. 10.

Notess, Greg R., "Inktomi," *Online*, July 2000, p. 13.

——, "Inktomi Makes Sense of Complex Content," *EContent*, June 2001, p. 60.

——, "Joining the In-Crowd," *EContent*, May 2001, p. 60.

Rendleman, John, "Inktomi Makes the ESscene," *InformationWeek*, July 23, 2001, p. 16.

Sanborn, Stephanie, and Terho Uimonen, "Content Platform Touted," *InfoWorld*, August 28, 2000, p. 10.

Spangler, Todd, "Inktomi Licenses Search and Cache Technology to @Home," *Internet World,* July 27, 1998, p. 10.

Stone, Brad, "Driving the Web Engines," *Newsweek,* May 25, 1998, p. 82.

Tedesco, Richard, "Microsoft's Latest Move: Mega-Server," *Broadcasting & Cable,* November 3, 1997, p. 61.

Tillett, L. Scott, "Inktomi Expands Footprint," *InternetWeek,* May 15, 2000, p. 29.

Warner, Melanie, "The Young and the Loaded," *Fortune,* September 27, 1999, p. 78.

Wilson, Lizette, "Inktomi Accelerates," *San Francisco Business Times,* May 25, 2001, p. 49.

——, "With Move into Streaming, Inktomi Searching for Bright Future," *San Francisco Business Times,* October 26, 2001, p. 3.

Wilson, Tim, "Mergers Promise IT Deeper Site Analysis," *InternetWeek,* September 27, 1999, p. 1.

Zimmerman, Christine, "Multimedia Burden Eased," *InternetWeek,* November 1, 1999, p. 25.

—David P. Bianco

IntelliCorp, Inc.

1975 El Camino Real West
Mountain View, California 94040-2216
U.S.A.
Telephone: (650) 965-5500
Fax: (650) 965-5647
Web site: http://www.intellicorp.com

Public Company
Incorporated: 1980 as IntelliGenetics, Inc.
Employees: 155
Sales: $25.6 million (2001)
Stock Exchanges: NASDAQ
Ticker Symbol: INAI
NAIC: 511210 Software Publishers

Once a pioneer in artificial intelligence (AI), Mountain View, California-based IntelliCorp, Inc. now offers consulting services and software to Global 2000 companies. With offices in the United States and Europe, the company develops and supports a software suite of eBusiness and Customer Relationship Management solutions. With these tools, its consultants are able to help clients integrate computer systems that have differing data structures and other technology features, thus allowing the programs to share information and interact in a cost-effective manner. For instance, a client may have a number of different customer channels, including the Internet, wireless, contact centers, and field sales representatives. IntelliCorp helps to successfully connect these sources to back office processes, such as order management, order fulfillment, manufacturing, human resources, and accounting. Intellicorp products are designed to be used in a wide range of industries: apparel, appliances, chemical, construction, energy, financial, high-tech, insurance, manufacturing, media, pharmaceutical, and telecomunications. IntelliCorp's major customers include Boeing, General Motors, and Hewlett-Packard.

Birth of Artificial Intelligence: 1950s

The leading figure behind the creation of Intellicorp was scientist, author, and visionary Edward Albert Feigenbaum. Born in 1936 in Weehawken, New Jersey, the son of an accountant, Feigenbaum grew up fascinated by his father's hand-cranked adding machine. During the early 1950s, he attended the Carnegie Institute of Technology to study electrical engineering and became familiar with the new field of artificial intelligence (AI). The concept was espoused in a paper, "Can a Machine Think?," written by British mathematician Alan Turing in 1950. Two Carnegie professors, Herb Simon and Allen Newell, then advanced the idea and created a Logic Theorist program that centered on the problem-solving process. According to a *Forbes* profile, "Feigenbaum recalls Simon announcing to the class one day that he and his colleague Allen Newell had invented a thinking machine. To help explain, Simon handed out a manual for an early IBM computer. Feigenbaum, then 19, stayed up all night reading the manual. "By the next morning, when the sun came up, I was born again," he says. "Here was this beautiful modern electronic version of what I was so intrigued with as a kid, that little mechanical calculator of my dad's. And furthermore, Herb Simon had said, 'I'm going to show you how to make them think.' "

Because there were no computer science programs, Feigenbaum earned his Ph.D. in industrial administration at Carnegie, becoming involved in research that enabled a computer to model the rote learning of nonsense syllables. After teaching at the University of California at Berkley, he joined the Stanford faculty in 1965 as an associate professor of computer science and director of the school's computer center. Feigenbaum now began to make his own contributions to AI. While working with a group developing an esoteric system that could analyze unidentified chemical compounds, he realized the breadth of knowledge a chemist drew on to form decisions, a lot of which resulted from educated guesswork. Any computer system would likewise have to include a large database of rules in order to make similar decisions. Feigenbaum's group began to call these types of comprehensive programs "expert systems." The person who observed and codified all aspects of a particular discipline for a computer program was the "knowledge engineer."

Incorporation of IntelliGenetics: 1980

Feigenbaum worked with other departments to develop expert systems in the sciences, such as organic chemistry and

Company Perspectives:

We help clients make intelligent technology decisions . . . and we help make technology decisions intelligent.

molecular biology, as well as medicine. He became a leading champion of expert systems, and AI in general, and by the late 1970s began to team with his graduate students and colleagues to transfer the new discipline to the business world. While computers had already automated clerical tasks such as accounting, AI–enhanced machines were expected to one day assist executives in making decisions. In September 1980, along with Douglas Brutlag, Laurence Kedes, and Peter Friedland, Feigenbaum incorporated IntelliGenetics, Inc. In keeping with much of the work Feigenbaum did at Stanford, the company's first product was a package of computer programs for research in recombinant DNA. By 1982, IntelliGenetics generated little more than $100,000 in revenues with its narrow applications, and posted a net loss of more than $500,000. In 1983, the company introduced its Kee System, a general purpose AI tool that had the potential to develop knowledge-based systems with commercial and industrial applications. The company went public in 1983 at $6 a share, then a year later changed its name to IntelliCorp, while retaining the IntelliGenetics name for its biotechnology business.

The market for AI held much promise in the early 1980s, spurred to a great degree by Japan's decision in 1981 to initiate a ten-year AI initiative, which prompted Feigenbaum to write *The Fifth Generation: Artificial Intelligence and Japan's Computer Challenge to the World.* Others joined him to warn about the possibility of Japan's future dominance in the field. According to a *New Republic* article on the subject, ''In 1983, more than a dozen American companies established the Microelectronics and Computer Technology Corporation in Austin, Texas, a consortium with a budget of about $70 million a year, including $15 million for the Alpha-Omega program, expressly devoted to countering the Japanese Fifth Generation. In 1984, the year after *The Fifth Generation* was published, *Business Week* predicted that the market for expert systems would explode from $20 million to $2.5 billion by 1993.'' Despite opportunities, however, IntelliCorp shied away from investments by major corporations, opting to retain its freedom.

In short, AI was portrayed as a modern day Industrial Revolution and, as with the Internet a decade later, no one wanted to be left behind. Rather than the Industrial Revolution, however, a more apt comparison for the sudden interest in AI was perhaps the tulip hysteria that swept Holland in the 17th century, when a single bulb might equal the value of an entire ship. The AI bubble continued to grow in the mid-1980s before bursting later in the decade when the field simply failed to deliver on its much hyped promises. The Japanese effort, in particular, yielded no tangible improvements to the field. Moreover, much of the AI start-ups were run by academics rather than practical businessmen. IntelliCorp, like many of the early AI companies, relied on the LISP programming language, which in turn required a specialized computer that cost as much as $150,000 and could only be used by a single operator. The research and development units of major corporations were willing at first to invest in this technol-

ogy, thus spurring initial growth in the industry, but the broader corporate marketplace failed to follow suit. It wanted AI programs that could run on its mainframes and minicomputers and did not require its people to learn LISP. As a result, AI advances began to be incorporated into general computer programs, and AI lost its status as a distinct market.

Despite making its products compatible with UNIX workstations, IntelliCorp also suffered from the diminishing interest in AI. It generated $20 million in sales in 1987, but had posted six consecutive losing quarters, resulting in the laying off of 30 of its 200 workers. Feigenbaum, busy with his research, writing, and other business ventures, stepped in to serve as IntelliCorp's chairman for a brief period in 1988 while changes in management could be sorted out. In October of that year, he relinquished the position to Thomas P. Kehler, who was then replaced as president of the company by 32-year-old Katherine C. Branscomb, a former senior vice-president of sales and marketing at Aion Corp. Her father had been the chief scientist at IBM. Rather than seeing AI technology as revolutionary, she hoped to make it evolutionary and to position IntelliCorp as a company that provided computer programmers with knowledge-based tools to help them produce better software.

IntelliCorp returned to marginal profitability, then in 1990 introduced Kappa, its first expert-system capable of running on a personal computer in a Microsoft Windows environment. Using the object-oriented tools that came out of AI research, Kappa allowed business users to portray information, whether it be statistics or design specifications, as objects that could then be manipulated. Decision-making rules were then linked to the objects and created to suit a particular business need. Far from emulating human thought, Kappa was typical of a less-ambitious AI industry, which now sought to add sophistication to the basic strength of computers—the speed of completing routine operations. Kappa had been acquired the previous year from MegaKnowledge Inc. At the same time as the release of the new product, IntelliCorp acquired MegaKnowledge, paying over $3 million for the business.

Failed Merger with KnowledgeWare: 1991

Kappa, however, proved to be a disappointment. In 1991, IntelliCorp terminated a quarter of its workforce, some 50 employees, followed by a write-down on the Kappa program. When the fiscal year ended on June 30, the company reported a $14.8 million loss on sales of just $14 million. By late August the company had agreed to be acquired by KnowledgeWare Inc., which produced software engineering tools, for $34.2 million in stock. In anticipation of the deal being completed, Branscomb resigned, but KnowledgeWare posted poor quarterly results and its top executives left the company, resulting in a severe drop in the price of its stock. The merger with IntelliCorp was scuttled and Branscomb was brought back as the chief executive.

Intellicorp generated revenues of only $9 million in 1992, resulting in a $9 million net loss. A short time later, Branscomb resigned to become a senior vice-president of business development at Lotus Development Corporation. Chief Financial Officer Ken Haas was subsequently promoted to president of Intellicorp,

Key Dates:

1980: The company is incorporated as IntelliGenetics, Inc.
1983: The company goes public.
1984: The company name is changed to IntelliCorp, Inc.
1988: Katherine Branscomb is named president.
1992: Branscomb steps down in favor of Ken Haas.
1993: The company begins working with SAP.
1999: The CRM Solutions Group is formed.
2001: Haas is replaced by Ray Moreau, and Norman Wechsler is named chairman of board.

and conditions began to slowly improve for the company. It gained both financing and technology from Informix, as well as a relationship with SAP, a German firm that developed resource planning software used to integrate back-office functions such as distribution, accounting, human resources, and manufacturing. SAP was interested in applying AI and object-oriented technologies into advanced versions of its products and sought out IntelliCorp for help. SAP was a fast-growing company with a large number of business customers and represented a potentially lucrative outlet for IntelliCorp's expertise. The company deployed three core technology people to Germany, where they learned about SAP's software and educated their SAP colleagues on AI and object-oriented programming.

Sales improved to $10.3 million in 1993 and the company's net loss fell to $4.8 million. IntelliCorp edged closer to profitability as revenues grew to $12 million in 1994 and $17.5 million in 1995, as the net loss decreased to $3.8 million in 1994 and $2.1 million in 1995. The company's object programming, however, still had a limited market, and much of its business was tied to just a few major customers, such as GTE Corporation and US West Communications. When GTE decided to abandon the technology, the repercussions were severe for IntelliCorp.

Revenues collapsed in 1996, falling to $11 million, while the net loss grew to $4.5 million for the year. IntelliCorp slashed its workforce by a third and once again began retooling its focus. The company's work with SAP took center stage, as the two parties joined forces to develop products. IntelliCorp received a boost in 1996 when the accounting firm of Deloitte & Touche decided to use its software. Other major accounting firms also signed on, as did IBM. Then, in 1997, SAP chose to embed IntelliCorp technology into its business resource automation software. The emphasis on SAP would increase even further in 1998, when accounting giant Arthur Andersen elected to incorporate IntelliCorp software into its SAP technology. As a result of these developments, the outlook for IntelliCorp began to steadily improve. After generating revenues of $12.7 million in 1997 and posting a loss of $1.9 million, the company almost doubled its revenues in 1998, totaling $24.4 million. IntelliCorp still lost $700,000 for the year, due in part to the cost of expansion.

IntelliCorp incurred further costs in 1999 when it created the CRM Solutions Group to assist SAP customers in implementing CRM (customer relationship management) and eBusiness solutions. Revenues took a step back, falling to $22 million, while the company posted a $6.2 million loss. Once again, IntelliCorp was forced into a restructuring mode, as it cut staff by 20 percent and began to focus on the use of its software on the consulting side of its business rather than relying primarily on software sales. Revenues for 2000 were flat in comparison to the previous year, totaling $22.7 million, resulting in a loss of $7.1 million for the year. In March 2001, management underwent a major change. Haas was replaced as CEO by Ray Moreau, who came to IntelliCorp in August 2000 to serve as president and chief operating officer after spending the previous 12 years as an executive with Ernst & Young. Norman Wechsler, a director who owned a 31 percent stake in the company, was also named the chairman of the board. IntelliCorp posted another $7 million loss in fiscal 2001 and continued to struggle late in the calendar year as the U.S. economy officially slipped into recession. After more than 20 years in existence, IntelliCorp had managed to survive while numerous other AI companies failed, yet whether it would ever evolve into a consistently profitable business remained very much an open question.

Principal Subsidiaries

IntelliCorp GmbH; IntelliCorp Ltd.; IntelliCorp SARL; MegaKnowledge, Inc.

Principal Competitors

Accenture; Ascential Software; Evolutionary Technologies; International Business Machines Corporation; Information Builders, Inc.; Oracle Corporation; Sun Microsystems, Inc.; Sybase, Inc.

Further Reading

Babcock, Charles, "AI Gets Smart: Intelligent Tools," *Computerworld*, July 11, 1994, p. 6.

Bozman, Jean S., "IntelliCorp Turns to Object-Oriented Mart," *Computerworld*, January 18, 1993, p. 57.

Bulkeley, William, "Bright Outlook for Artificial Intelligence Yields to Slow Growth and Big Cutbacks," *Wall Street Journal*, July 5, 1990, p. B1.

——, "Stocks of Artificial Intelligence Firms Prosper, Though Some Analysts Are Advising Wariness," *Wall Street Journal*, March 31, 1986, p. 1.

Johnson, Amy Helen, "Staying on Target," *Upside*, June 2000, pp. 236–48.

Lewwyn, Mark, "Artificial Intelligence Firms KO'd by Reality," *USA Today*, August 17, 1987, p. 3B.

Lyons, Daniel, "Artificial Intelligence Gets Real," *Forbes*, November 30, 1998, pp. 176–82.

Pollack, Andrew, "Poor Decisions: Artificial Intelligence Hits Roadblocks," *San Francisco Chronicle*, March 5, 1998, p. B1.

Ullman, Howard, "Machine Dreams: Future Shock for Fun and Profit," *New Republic*, July 17, 1989, p. 12.

Zonana, Victor F., "Software Gang Puts 'Experts' in the Office," *Los Angeles Times*, p. 1.

—Ed Dinger

IVC Industries, Inc.

500 Halls Mill Road
Freehold, New Jersey 07728
U.S.A.
Telephone: (732) 308-3000
Toll Free: (800) 666-8482
Fax: (732) 761-2878
Web site: http://www.ivcinc.com

Public Company
Incorporated: 1971 as International Vitamins Corporation
Employees: 370
Sales: $67.87 million (2001)
Stock Exchanges: OTC
Ticker Symbol: IVCO
NAIC: 325411 Medicinal and Botanical Manufacturing

IVC Industries, Inc. is engaged in the manufacturing, packaging, sale, and distribution of branded and private-label vitamins, herbs, nutritional supplements, and nonpharmaceutical drug products. The company markets more than 700 different products, packaged under various labels and bottle counts in tablets, powders, two-piece hard-shell capsules, and soft gelatin encapsulated capsules. After growing through acquisitions and consolidations, IVC found the going rougher in its hotly competitive field during the late 1990s. The company was struggling to meet its debts in 2001, when it signed a letter of intent to be acquired by Inverness Medical Innovations, Inc.

Growing by Acquisition: 1989–95

Arthur S. Edell and E. Joseph Edell, brothers, founded American Vitamin Products, Inc., a manufacturer and distributor of vitamins, minerals, and nutritional supplements, in 1955, with the latter becoming its president. They still owned this firm in 1989, when they purchased International Vitamins Corporation, which had been incorporated in 1971. Arthur Edell became the president and chief executive officer of International Vitamins. In 1992 and the beginning of 1993 International Vitamins merged with International Vitamin Supplements, Inc. and Vitamin Factory Outlets, Inc., respectively. Arthur Edell owned these companies at the time of the mergers. International Vitamins had revenue of $5.79 million in fiscal 1992 (the year ended July 31, 1992) and $8.58 million in fiscal 1993, when its net income was $401,000. The company, previously based in Union, New Jersey, moved its headquarters, plant, and warehouse to a leased facility in Irvington, New Jersey, in 1993. It made its initial public offering of stock in 1994, raising $6.3 million, following which Arthur Edell retained nearly 38 percent of the stock. There were only about 26 stockholders of record in late 1994.

At this time International Vitamins was manufacturing vitamins, minerals, and nutritional supplements under its own brand names, Synergy Plus and Nature's Blend, and also in "bulk" form. A full line of Synergy Plus products was being marketed to health food stores, and a full line of Nature's Blend products, to independent drug stores. The company was manufacturing and packaging all of its products except for soft gels, which were being purchased from others.

Its products included vitamins C and E, beta carotene, calcium, multivitamins, food supplements, minerals, and specialty formulas. Each product category could be produced in numerous dosage sizes and unique combinations of ingredients. Aside from serving independent drugstores and health food stores, International Vitamins had a bulk-sales division to sell the company's products to diet and fitness centers and mail-order companies. The U.S. market for private-label vitamins and supplements was said to have grown 42 percent between 1991 and 1994.

International Vitamins merged with American Vitamin Products in 1995 and simultaneously acquired the outstanding partnership interests of Hidel Partners, for which American Vitamin Products was the operating arm. Hidel owned the land and buildings where American Vitamin's manufacturing facility was located. E. Joseph Edell and members of his family owned all of both entities, and he became chairman and chief executive officer of the consolidated company, with his brother continuing as president. American Vitamin Products was by far the larger of the two united companies, with annual sales exceeding $35 million, about 185 employees, and manufacturing facilities in Freehold, New Jersey. Freehold became the new headquarters of the consolidated company, which kept the International Vitamins name.

The American Vitamin Products business complemented International Vitamins' business, since the former was selling its products in drugstore, supermarket, and mass-merchandise chain stores, where the latter did not have a presence. American Vitamin Products was manufacturing and distributing the Fields of Nature, Rybutol, and Nature's Wonder brands and also was making private-label products for more than 20 retail chains, located primarily in the Northeast. The merger added magnesium, folic acid, calcium, and potassium to International Vitamins' product line. The Freehold facility now was International Vitamins' main plant and was equipped with large-volume blending, tableting, coating, and high-speed packaging equipment. The Irvington facility was confined to certain warehousing and distribution operations and the manufacture of protein powders.

International Vitamins previously had focused its marketing and promotional activities on its branded products, Synergy Plus and Nature's Blend, being sold in health food stores and independent drugstores. It now inherited American Vitamin Products' effort to build relationships with retail chains. Generally, its marketing efforts were directed at developing customized programs in the form of comprehensive sales and marketing support. These included money-saving coupons, individualized promotions, and advertising in such forms as store circulars and newspaper inserts. In most cases, according to International Vitamins, the retailer earned a greater profit per unit on both International Vitamins' brands and the retailer's own store-brand products made by the company than it could from the products of nationally advertised brand manufacturers. The company's export efforts included a distribution agreement with Israel's largest drugstore chain, including joint marketing and promoting of its "American Vitamin" brand in Israel. International Vitamins' net sales reached $49.26 million in fiscal 1995, and its net income was $799,000.

During calendar year 1995 International Vitamins completed work on a soft gel encapsulation manufacturing facility on its Irvington property. The company believed its sales and profit margin had been affected adversely by difficulty in fulfilling its customers' current demand for such products because of a shortage of capacity. In recent years an ever increasing number of vitamins was said to have been introduced in or converted to soft gel capsules because of such factors as ease in swallowing and superior absorption, stability, content uniformity, and precision of dosage. Capsule production began in early 1996, under the direction of the company's Intergel division. At about the same time, the company introduced a new Revlon line of vitamins and nutritional supplements for women.

Reaching Maximum Size: 1996–98

During fiscal 1996 International Vitamins acquired Hall Laboratories, Inc. Based in Portland, Oregon, and founded in 1953, Hall, a privately owned company, was engaged in the manufacturing, packaging, sales, and distribution of vitamins, nutritional supplements, and over-the-counter pharmaceutical products, primarily through chain drugstores, supermarkets, mass merchandisers, and warehouse clubs. The former included such big chains as PayLess Drug Stores, Fred Meyer Inc., and Price/Costco Inc. For about half a dozen customers, Hall's operation included computers that planned the entire purchasing, manufacturing, and distribution cycle so that deliveries arrived at just the right time to restock inventories. Its Health Essentials brand was promoted in company literature as "the second-best way to get your vegetables," but the vast majority of Hall's products was marketed under the private labels of its retail chain customers. Its products were distributed in Canada through a subsidiary with headquarters in Surrey, British Columbia.

The acquisition of Hall Laboratories gave International Vitamins a presence on the West as well as the East Coast. It also raised International Vitamins' revenues by about $40 million; for fiscal 1996, sales reached $104.16 million, although net income was only $296,000. International Vitamins paid for the acquisition by issuing shares of stock valued at about $9.5 million. Hall's president, Andrew Pinkowski, thereby became, with his wife, Rita, a major shareholder of the consolidated company, which now took the name IVC Industries, Inc.

IVC Industries made another significant acquisition in 1997, when it purchased the Vitamin Specialties division of HealthRite, Inc. for about $2.7 million. This operation—formerly Healthfair Vitamin Center, Inc.—was acquired by Arthur Edell in 1979 and had grown from two New Jersey health food stores in 1994 to 15 in Pennsylvania as well as New Jersey in 1997. It also was marketing its products through mail-order catalogues distributed regularly to its customers. "The [health food store] industry is highly fragmented," International Vitamins Chief Operating Officer I. Alan Hirschfeld declared in a press release, "leaving tremendous opportunities for a well-managed, vertically integrated new entrant in this growing field." Taking into account IVC's existing operations, he added, "This combination will provide us with a vehicle through which we can now aggressively participate in the segment of the vitamin industry which we believe offers us superior sales and earnings growth potential." The company's fiscal 1997 results were its best ever: net sales of $108.53 million and net income of $1.35 million.

IVC Industries, in January 1998, announced its new LiquaFil line, comprised of a full spectrum of some 40 soft gelatin encapsulated vitamins, herbs, and nutritional supplements. It included calcium with vitamin D; calcium-magnesium-zinc; vitamins C,

E, and B-complex; multivitamins; coenzyme Q10; St. John's wort; saw palmetto; zinc; selenium; and potassium. (Echinacea, ginseng, and kava kava were added in fiscal 1999; lycopene in fiscal 2000; and gingko biloba in fiscal 2001.) Interviewed for *Chain Drug Review,* Hirschfield said LiquaFil was the only full line of such products in soft gel form and maintained, "This is a truly new concept in the marketplace. We don't believe that the LiquaFil line will make tablets obsolete, but we do know that anyone who has tried any of these products in soft gel form refuses to go back to tablets. . . . for those consumers who are taking nutritional products and are concerned with fillers and binders used in tablets and don't like swallowing tablets or the aftertaste, why not introduce these different products in a soft gel version and offer them a viable alternative?" The LiquaFil line, packaged in a distinctive blue bottle with a red-white-and-blue label and a special tamper-proof cap, was not only shipped to existing customers but through such new accounts as Eckerd Drug Stores, Kmart, Meijer, Phar-Mor, American Drug Stores, and Kerr Drug. The company's Fields of Nature, Synergy Plus, and private-label brands subsequently became available in LiquaFil soft gel.

At the same time, IVC Industries launched a new line of Pine Bros. soft throat drops, having recently acquired the Pine Bros. brand name. It initially introduced the drops in two flavors: wild cherry and honey cream. In a press release, Hirschfeld announced, "The Pine Bros. line, which is formulated with zinc, vitamin C and slippery elm, provides us with an entree into the fast growing segment of the cough and cold category recently captured by such nutritional based products as Cold-Eeze and Halls Defense." For this line IVC secured distribution additional to its existing customer base through such new accounts as Eckerd Drug Stores, Arbor Drug Inc., Genovese Drug Stores Inc., Meijer, Inc., and Neuman Distributors, the largest distributor to independent drugstores on the East Coast.

IVC Industries raised its net sales in fiscal 1998 to a record $119.78 million; its net income was $1.15 million. The U.S. market in dietary supplements reached about $9 billion in 1997, doubling in a five-year period, and it passed $10 billion in 1998, when IVC reached 12th place, in terms of sales, among publicly traded U.S. botanical and dietary supplement marketers. All 11 companies with greater sales and the next 13 companies behind it, however, had greater market capitalization than IVC's meager $8.9 million.

Losing Ground to Competitors: 1999–2001

IVC Industries suffered a severe reversal of fortune in 1999. In October 1998 market leader General Nutrition lowered prices, forcing its competitors to follow and leading to a dollar sales growth in the field of only 3 to 4 percent in 1999. At the same time the field was narrowed by the consolidation of top marketers and the increased presence of pharmaceutical companies, such as American Home Products Corp., which had recently purchased Solgar Vitamin & Herb Co. IVC's net sales for fiscal 1999 dropped to $107.34 million, and the company sustained a net loss of $7.04 million. As part of a restructuring that included a one-for-eight reverse stock split, IVC closed the former Hall operation, except in Canada, and sold the retail stores, which registered 1999 sales of only $2.68 million, to Archon Vitamin Corp. for $1.8 million. Hirschfeld left the company and Arthur Edell yielded the presidency to his brother.

Net sales for shrunken IVC Industries fell to $85.87 million in fiscal 2000. The company attributed $11 million in lost revenue to its cancellation of sales contracts with several customers who did not meet its gross-margin targets. IVC was able to register a net profit only because it received a settlement valued at about $16.3 million in connection with an agreement to end a class-action lawsuit against a supplier, charging a price-fixing conspiracy. For fiscal 2001, net sales were even lower— $67.87 million—and the company sustained a net loss of $2.55 million. It attributed the sales decline, among other reasons, to a customer's discontinuance of the Fields of Nature line and to its discontinuance of certain Canadian over-the-counter products due to poor profitability. Total assets were only $51.09 million at the end of the fiscal year, compared with $81.25 million at the end of fiscal 1998. The long-term debt was $21.34 million. Despite the reverse stock split, by April 2001, IVC's stock was habitually trading below $1 a share, and as a result it was dropped from the NASDAQ Small Cap Market and relegated to the OTC Bulletin Board system.

IVC Industries was distributing more than 700 products in 2001 and was manufacturing about five billion tablets, capsules, and soft gels a year. The top ten of its 700 customers accounted for about 83 percent of its sales volume in fiscal 2001; Costco accounted for 57 percent alone.

In September 2001 IVC signed a nonbinding letter of intent to be acquired by Inverness Medical Innovations, Inc., a majority owned subsidiary of Inverness Medical Technology, Inc., for cash or cash and stock valued at $2.50 a share. Inverness Medical Technology had agreed to be acquired by Johnson & Johnson and planned to spin off its Inverness Medical Innovations subsidiary as a separate, publicly owned company. Four stockholders of IVC, holding approximately 42 percent of the outstanding shares of common stock, had agreed to vote their shares in approval of the acquisition. As of November 2000, E. Joseph Edell owned 32 percent of IVC's common stock, Pinkowski owned nearly 15 percent, and Arthur Edell owned 10 percent.

Principal Subsidiaries

Hall Laboratories Ltd. (Canada).

Principal Competitors

American Home Products Corp.; Leiner Nutritional Products, Inc.; NBTY, Inc.; Pharmavite Corp.; Rexall Sundown, Inc.; Twinlab Corporation; Weider Nutrition International, Inc.

Further Reading

"IVC Industries Inc.—Common Stock to Trade on OTC Bulletin Board," *Market News Publishing,* April 24, 2001.

"IVC Industries Inc.—To Be Acquired by Inverness Medical Innovations, Inc.," *Market News Publishing,* September 24, 2001.

"A New Concept from IVC," *Chain Drug Review,* June 29, 1998, p. 256.

Sauer, Pamela, "Is the Bloom Fading for Dietary Supplements?," *Chemical Market Reporter,* November 8, 1999, Supplement, pp. 3–6.

Woodward, Steve, "Eastern Company Will Acquire Portland Vitamin-Maker," *Portland Oregonian,* November 14, 1995, pp. B16+.

—Robert Halasz

Jazzercise, Inc.

2460 Impala Drive
Carlsbad, California 92008
U.S.A.
Telephone: (760) 476-1750
Fax: (760) 602-7180
Web site: http://www.jazzercise.com

Private Company
Incorporated: 1979
Employees: 125
Sales: $17.9 million (2000)
NAIC: 71399 All Other Amusement and Recreation
   Industries

Jazzercise, Inc. is the world's leading franchiser of dance and fitness classes. The company pioneered its own brand of dance-based exercise routines. These are taught by certified Jazzercise instructors across the United States and in Europe, Japan, and Latin America. The company has over 5,000 franchises, and an estimated 450,000 students worldwide. Franchisees pay a nominal start-up fee to the company, and then 20 percent of gross revenues monthly. Founder Judi Sheppard Missett choreographs new routines approximately every ten weeks. The company also produces videos, music recordings, and other educational materials, as well as a computer-based CyberStretch program that aims to prevent repetitive stress injuries among office workers. The company's retail division sells exercise wear, accessories, and items bearing the Jazzercise logo. The division sells primarily through a mail-order catalog. Jazzercise also operates a video production division, JM DigitalWorks, which produces Jazzercise videos and also does videotape production, post-production, and duplicating work for hundreds of other clients.

A Hit with a Fun Dance Class

Jazzercise, Inc. was founded by Judi Sheppard Missett, a professional jazz dancer. Missett was born in Iowa in 1944. As a toddler, she was pigeon-toed, and had to wear leg braces. Her doctor recommended the little girl take dance classes as therapy, and she took her first class at the age of three. Apparently her talent was evident from the beginning. Her mother especially encouraged young Judi, though it was difficult to find qualified dance teachers in the small town of Red Oak where the family lived. So her mother recruited dance teachers to settle in towns within driving distance of Red Oak, promising the recruits a place to teach, students, and offering her own bookkeeping and costume-sewing services. By the time Missett was ten years old, she was teaching dance herself. After she graduated from high school, she moved to Chicago and enrolled in the theater and dance program at Northwestern University. She began focusing on jazz dance, studying with the choreographer Gus Giordano. She traveled widely with touring shows, and ultimately began teaching jazz dance classes for her mentor Giordano. In 1966 she married a television news reporter, Jack Missett, and had a daughter, Shanna, in 1968.

Missett's professional career had taken her all over the world, and she continued to perform. But she also began to focus more on teaching. She was troubled, however, because so many of her students dropped out of her classes. These students were typically young mothers like herself, or married housewives. They wanted to take a class for the fun of it as well as to keep fit, but they did not have the ambition to become professional dancers. Their choices were either to take a high-powered class like Missett taught, or to take a calisthenics class. If the dance class was too demanding, they dropped out after a few weeks. Their other alternative, the calisthenics class, typically had only soft background music, and Missett imagined it was dreary. Around 1969, she began developing jazz-based exercise routines that she thought fit somewhere between the two extremes. Her classes were meant to be enjoyable, musical, and good exercise. She did not critique form, as in a professional dance class, and she used a room without mirrors, to reduce inhibitions.

In 1972, the Missetts moved near San Diego, California. It was primarily a career move for Jack Missett, who also had family in the area. But Judi Sheppard Missett thought southern California might prove an excellent place to develop her new dance classes. The area was far ahead of the rest of the country in worshiping health and fitness. Missett began looking for community centers and gymnasiums where she could teach her class, which she advertised as a new technique developed in faraway Chicago. She promoted herself and her classes, getting coverage in the local newspaper, and soon she had flocks of students. She stopped performing around this time, and devoted herself to teaching. In 1974, she began using the name Jazzercise for her program.

Jazzercise grew more and more popular. By 1977, Missett was teaching 20 classes a week, with a total of almost a thousand students. This was all she could handle, and she had to turn people away. Jazzercise had found a niche, but it was difficult for Missett to fill it singlehandedly. Missett was at first unwilling to let others teach her Jazzercise routines. But there seemed no other way to provide enough classes for the community. So she began by training five students who had been with Jazzercise since Missett's arrival in California. These new teachers set up in rented spaces and began teaching Jazzercise classes. They were almost immediately successful, and Missett trained five more teachers over the course of the year. At this point, Jazzercise did not have a formal franchise arrangement. But the new instructors paid a start-up fee to Missett and then promised her 30 percent of their gross revenues. They got to use the Jazzercise name, and continued to train with Missett. By 1978, this arrangement included instructors outside the San Diego area. In 1979, Jazzercise formally incorporated. Missett also began using videotapes of her routines to teach certified instructors new material. This method allowed her to keep instructors up to date, even if they were teaching far from Jazzercise's new corporate headquarters in Carlsbad, California. By the end of the year, Jazzercise had gone international, with instructors in Europe, Japan, and Brazil.

National Prominence in the 1980s

After Jazzercise, Inc. incorporated in 1979, Missett began promoting the company's fitness routines across the country. She performed on national television for the first time in 1980, where Missett's svelte physique advertised the benefits of her program. Her television exposure led to the development of the Jazzercise apparel division. When Missett appeared on a broadcast of the *Dinah Shore Show,* she wore a leotard with the Jazzercise logo emblazoned on it. She wore this because she was afraid viewers would otherwise miss the connection between her and her company. But it spawned inquiries from Jazzercise students, who wanted to know where they could get Jazzercise gear. The company began to sell Jazzercise logo togs through a mail-order catalog.

By 1980, Missett had trained over 1,000 instructors. The franchises brought $1.9 million to Jazzercise, Inc. that year. The boom was just beginning. Missett broadened the company's exposure by publishing a book in 1981 called *Jazzercise: A Fun Way to Fitness.* It was a bestseller, going into four reprints and selling close to 400,000 copies. Translated editions also appeared in France and the Netherlands. Missett also put out the first of the Jazzercise videos for public consumption. The next year, Jazzercise put out a record, which went gold, selling over

25,000 copies. The company followed the success of the "Jazzercise" album with "Jazzercise Looking Good!" later in 1982. In 1983, Jazzercise, Inc. formalized its franchise relationship with its certified instructors. The company broke with the norm in the franchise industry by charging a low start-up fee and a high royalty rate. Most franchises around the country went for upwards of $25,000, but a Jazzercise instructor could buy a Jazzercise franchise for only $500. The typical royalty rate for a franchise in the United States was from 3 to 10 percent, but Jazzercise instructors sent 30 percent of gross receipts back to Jazzercise, Inc. This cockeyed formula nevertheless worked well for both the company and the franchisees. Perhaps because the new instructors were able to make money quickly and did not have to worry about recouping a high start-up fee, Jazzercise retained a high percentage of its franchisees. A successful Jazzercise franchise could bring the owner $75,000 a year. This looked very good compared to other aerobics programs where instructors were paid an hourly wage. So despite the high royalty rate, Jazzercise instructors remained committed.

The company grew enormously in the early 1980s. By 1983, Jazzercise franchises had spread to all 50 states. The company put out a third album, and founder Missett gained more exposure by appearing frequently on the cable Disney Channel's *Epcot Magazine* show. Jazzercise instructors performed in the opening ceremony for the 1984 Los Angeles Olympics, and Missett herself ran in the relay to bring the Olympic torch to the city. When the entertainment company MCA put out a Jazzercise workout video in 1984, it went gold, like the record in 1982, selling over 25,000 copies. Fitness had become something of a national craze. Aerobics classes of all kinds were popular, and actress Jane Fonda also had a huge following for her fitness videos. Gross receipts from franchises were $40 million in 1983, an astonishing rise from under $2 million at the start of the decade. But sales remained relatively flat for 1984 and 1985, held in check by competition from other exercise programs. Even so, the company was named one of the top fastest-growing franchises in the country in 1985.

With sales holding steady, Missett redoubled her efforts to promote Jazzercise. In addition to her frequent television appearances, she began writing a syndicated newspaper column on fitness, to get maximum media exposure. She also worked at a more grassroots level, making appearances, giving speeches, and distributing coupons for local Jazzercise classes. Jazzercise also advertised in innovative ways, promoting itself on packages of products deemed healthy. Jazzercise had space on the back of boxes of Nabisco Wheat Thins crackers, for example. Jazzercise entered a licensing agreement with an apparel manufacturer to produce a complete line of Jazzercise exercise clothes in 1987 which would be sold in retail stores. Previously, the company had sold its clothing only through its catalog. The Jazzercise clothes came with a certificate for two free Jazzercise classes.

The company also changed its focus somewhat in the late 1980s. Missett realized that she had begun her career teaching mostly young married women who did not work outside the home. They were happy to take classes in a church basement or school gym. But by the late 1980s, the typical Jazzercise student was working outside the home, and did not mind spending money on pampering herself. The company built its first permanent gyms in the late 1980s, the upscale Fit Is It facilities. The modern buildings housed juice bars and clothing stores as well

Key Dates:

1969: Judi Sheppard Missett begins teaching jazz-based exercise class.
1974: Missett introduces Jazzercise name.
1977: Missett trains instructors in Jazzercise technique.
1979: Company is incorporated.
1983: Franchise arrangements are formalized.
1985: Jazzercise is one of fastest-growing franchises in United States.
1998: Company debuts CyberStretch program.

as attractive workout rooms. Missett also began offering more varied routines, to fit a variety of lifestyles. The Fast and Fit class offered more active aerobic exercise while the Lighter Side class was slower and easier. The company debuted Junior Jazzercise for kids, and Jazzergym for mothers and their small children, at the new Fit Is It centers. In 1988, the company reduced the royalty rate it charged franchisees to 20 percent. Despite the cutback, gross revenue inched up. The company had earned national name recognition, and had close to 4,000 franchises. Jazzercise classes were found in over 30 countries abroad. In 1989, Jazzercise became more widely available in Japan when that country's largest operator of health clubs agreed to offer all its members Jazzercise classes. Moreover, even though the franchise business was not growing as quickly as it had early in the decade, Jazzercise now had a substantial revenue stream from its videotape and apparel sales. By 1989, one-third of the company's sales came from tapes and clothing.

Still Fit in the 1990s

Judi Sheppard Missett continued her vigorous promotion of the company in the 1990s. She went to the Soviet Union in 1990 with other health and fitness experts as part of a People to People ambassador program, and in 1991 she helped present the Great American Workout at the White House. The company also launched a free fitness program for children called Kids Get Fit in 1991, which eventually reached more than a million children worldwide. The company entered a marketing arrangement with the athletic shoe company Nike, Inc. in 1992. In this cross-promotional effort, both Judi Sheppard Missett and her daughter Shanna gained the title Nike Fitness Athlete. The company also produced more videos in the 1990s. The year 1995 saw a series of videos including "Sports Stretch," "Healthy Backs," and "Body Power!" The company listed about 5,000 franchises by the mid-1990s. Sales were around $15 million.

Though Missett passed the age of 50, she showed no signs of slowing down. She continued to teach almost every day in California, and to choreograph new Jazzercise routines. In order to keep things fresh, she put out as many as 30 new routines every 10 or 11 weeks, and sent them via videotape to certified instructors worldwide. Missett's daughter Shanna Missett Nelson also taught regularly, though she had become a Jazzercise corporate executive, in charge of Jazzercise's international operations. The company kept up various promotional efforts tied to healthy products. It allied with General Mills in 1996, naming that com-

pany's Total cereal as the Jazzercise official cereal, and giving away Jazzercise class coupons on the back of nine million Total boxes. The next year the company ran a similar promotion on boxes of Ore-Ida baked potatoes, and Jazzercise also promoted a new energy drink called Boost, made by Mead Johnson. The company allied with another athletic footwear manufacturer, Ryka, Inc., in 1997, and formed other publicity links the next year with Smuckers brand jam and cereal-maker Quaker Oats.

A new development in the late 1990s was the Jazzercise CyberStretch program. This was a computer program that appeared as a screen saver. CyberStretch gave step-by-step instructions for stretches and relaxation exercises, geared toward desk-bound office workers. Computer workers were subject to repetitive motion injuries such as carpal tunnel syndrome, and the program was designed to prevent or alleviate this kind of ailment. The insurance company Barney & Barney began offering Jazzercise's CyberStretch program to client companies, hoping to reduce workman's compensation claims for repetitive motion injuries. Jazzercise also marketed CyberStretch through an international network of insurance brokers.

Jazzercise celebrated its 30th anniversary in 1999. By 2000, sales were $17.9 million. About half of this came from franchise fees. Jazzercise franchises worldwide generated over $56 million. Jazzercise, Inc. brought in another third of its revenue from sales of apparel and other merchandise. Some 16 percent came from royalties and other miscellaneous sources, and the company's video production arm, JM DigitalWorks, accounted for 6 percent of gross revenues. The company had changed its franchise arrangement only slightly. By 2001, the cost of the initial franchise fee had gone up to $650, and instructors still paid the company 20 percent of gross revenues monthly. Fitness was still popular, and Jazzercise was a formidable brand name, though the peak of the franchise expansion seemed past.

Principal Divisions

Jazzertogs; JM DigitalWorks; CyberStretch by Jazzercise.

Principal Competitors

24 Hour Fitness Worldwide Inc.; Bally Total Fitness Holding Corp.

Further Reading

Barrier, Michael, "Exercise As Theater," *Nation's Business*, June 1995, p. 14.
"Fitness Apparel Firm Signs with Jazzercise," *WWD*, June 18, 1987, p. 8.
"Jazzercise," *Fortune*, April 10, 1989, p. 90.
Rowland, Mary, "The Passionate Pioneer of Fitness Franchising," *Working Woman*, November 1988, pp. 56–60.
Schulman, Arlene, "Jazzercise Still Swinging After 20 Years," *New York Times*, April 30, 1990, p. C10.
"Screensaver May Reduce Workers' Comp Claims," *Best's Review*, February 1999, p. 80.
"Stretch, One-Two-Three . . . ," *Computerworld*, September 21, 1998, p. 102.
"Thorobred Sets Branded Legwear," *WWD*, March 30, 1989, p. 2.

—A. Woodward

Jeld-Wen, Inc.

401 Harbor Isles Road
Klamath Falls, Oregon 97601
U.S.A.
Telephone: (541) 882-3451
Fax: (541) 885-7454
Web site: http://www.jeld-wen.com

Private Company
Incorporated: 1960
Employees: 20,000
Sales: $2 billion (2001 est.)
NAIC: 321911 Millwork (Manufacturers); 332321 Metal
Window and Door Manufacturing; 321918 Other
Millwork (Including Flooring); 321999 All Other
Miscellaneous Wood Product Manufacturing

Founded in 1960 with 15 employees, Jeld-Wen, Inc. is a privately held, vertically integrated manufacturer of windows, doors, and millwork products for sale to wholesale distributors, home centers, and the manufactured housing industries. Headquartered in Klamath Falls, Oregon, Jeld-Wen employs more than 20,000 people worldwide and operates more than 150 facilities in Africa, Asia, Australia, North America, Europe, and South America. Jeld-Wen cuts lumber from its own timberlands, which it ships to its cut-stock plants, which prepare the wood for the company's manufacturing plants and distribution business. Its products include interior and exterior doors, garage doors, door frames, moldings, windows, and patio doors. Jeld-Wen also has interests in specialty wood products, real estate, and marketing communications.

1960s and 1970s: Gaining Respect As a Well-Managed, Family-Owned Company

Jeld-Wen was founded in 1960, its name formed from the first initials of cofounder and current CEO Dick Wendt and his siblings and a shortened version of their surname. Wendt, an Iowa native, had been a manager at Caradco, a window manufacturer in Illinois, when its East Coast parent company sold it.

The Wendts and partner Larry Wetter, Jeld-Wen's original vice-chairman, purchased a small millwork plant in Klamath Falls, Oregon, once a bustling timber town five hours' drive from both Portland and San Francisco.

Having rescued their plant from closure, the Wendts initially milled and sold "cut stock," the wood lengths that manufacturers craft into windows and doors. Jeld-Wen also began making windows and then pressed-wood six-panel doors—an industry innovation—and quickly gained respect as a well-managed outfit. The company became known for being closely held; there was no sign on its front door, and many of Jeld-Wen's directors and managers were close friends and family members. Dick Wendt, the company's chief executive, earned a reputation for his thriftiness and his preference for anonymity, characteristics *Forbes* considered typical of those in the low-margin millwork business, according to a 2000 article. Mill owners historically could gain the upper hand only by doing a better job of forecasting supply and demand; being close-mouthed about their own business dealings went along with the terrain.

Throughout the 1960s and 1970s, Jeld-Wen focused on expanding its core business, developing a number of related subsidiaries, some in Arizona, Pennsylvania, Mississippi, Iowa, and Washington. Then, beginning in the early 1980s, the company changed strategies and folded many of these subsidiaries into itself. It also purchased a number of other related businesses in the fields of construction and building supplies, among them Frank Paxton Co. of Kansas City, Missouri, a hardwood products distributor.

1980s: Expanding Through Acquisitions

In 1983, Jeld-Wen created Trendwest Development Co. (later renamed Trendwest, Inc.) as a subsidiary, and the company embarked on a buying spree that pushed operations into an array of enterprises: commercial and industrial development, financial services, recreation, and venture capital investments. Trendwest started out building subdivisions, but later branched into everything from title companies to car dealerships. The forces behind the company's new focus, according to a 1986 *Oregon Business* article, were Robert Kent, Trendwest's presi-

---

Company Perspectives:

We believe action speaks louder than words and when our work speaks for itself, we don't interrupt.

---

dent, and Ron Wendt, son of Dick Wendt and Jeld-Wen's corporate counsel. Kent described Trendwest's objective as that of developing jobs and new industries for its home county in Oregon.

The second half of the 1980s was a time of tremendous expansion for Trendwest, much of it in the areas of real estate and entertainment. In 1985, it bought Windmill Inns and Sandpiper Restaurants in Roseburg and Medford, Oregon; in 1986, the Ashland Hills Inn and Klamath Falls Brick & Tile. Trendwest was also one of three partners behind the development of Eagle Crest resort near Redmond, Oregon. By 1986, the subsidiary had developed its home into the Williamson Business Park in Klamath Falls, built on the site of an old ceiling tile manufacturing plant, and the Olene Geothermal Industrial Park, a 400-acre project in one of the Northwest's most promising geothermal locations. Trendwest also provided cash and management advice to fledgling companies based in Klamath Falls, such as Apple Attractions, which used a special ripening process to emblazon messages on apples; a mushroom farm; and a furniture maker. It invested in developing upscale condominium communities in Medford, Grants Pass, Bend, and Upper Klamath Lake.

As a result of its many operations, Jeld-Wen experienced considerable growth. Its 1986 sales totaled $100 million while its employees numbered about 2,500 people. The company ranked seventh in 1989 among privately held companies in Oregon with revenues between $350 million and $399 million, according to *Oregon Business Magazine*. By 1991, its sales had grown to more than $400 million. By 1998, Jeld-Wen was Oregon's largest privately held company and one of the world's largest window and door manufacturers, with revenues topping $1 billion. Jeld-Wen employed 11,000 people at more than 150 companies in 40 states and several foreign countries. In Oregon, the company employed 2,500 people, 700 of those at its home base in Klamath Falls.

1990s: Unimpeded Growth

Acquisitions continued into the 1990s, with the 1992 purchases of California-based 3D Industries Inc. and Continental Door, Inc., and Bend Millwork Systems Inc. of Oregon. Based in central Oregon, Bend Millwork had 1,400 employees in three businesses: Bend Millwork Co., which made pine door frames, door jambs, and related products; Bend Door Co., which produced fir stiles and rails; and Pozzi Window Co., which made wood windows and patio doors. With the acquisition of Bend Millwork, Jeld-Wen became one of the top ten wood products employers in Oregon; its workforce increased to more than 6,000 workers in Oregon and other states. In 1996, it again added to its portfolio of subsidiaries with the purchase of Norco Windows of Wisconsin from TJ International. In 1997, in an interesting turn of events, Jeld-Wen purchased Caradco, Inc., a

subsidiary of Alcoa, the company for which Dick Wendt had once worked before beginning Jeld-Wen. At about the same time, Jeld-Wen also purchased Grossman's building supply chain, greatly increasing the magnitude of its holdings.

Jeld-Wen had by then made a name for itself as a classic American success story. Even staunch competitors that had lost business to the company praised its frugal habits, its disciplined reinvestment, and its work ethic. It was seen as a rescuer of failing wood products and building supply manufacturers despite the fact that it often purchased companies at a fraction of their value and that its acquisition style often entailed wage cuts and internal reorganization, with workers having to reapply for their old jobs. However, unlike other consolidators that tried to dominate acquisitions by centralizing management, Jeld-Wen by and large left intact the companies it purchased. Jeld-Wen managers might look at as many as 100 possible acquisitions a year, which could contribute to the company's goal of vertical integration, often settling on companies that were in bankruptcy or heading toward it.

The company and its owners remained hard to know, however. Jeld-Wen routinely refused to participate in routine surveys compiled by the timber industry's well-known trade journal. According to an article in *Forbes* in 2000, Chairman Dick Wendt, who owned 39 percent of Jeld-Wen, could walk the streets of Klamath Falls virtually unnoticed and unrecognized. "He's been kicked out of mills before because security didn't know who he was," one member of Jeld-Wen's public affairs staff was quoted as saying.

Wendt's low profile afforded him the freedom to quietly pursue his favored conservative political crusades: furthering the welfare-to-work movement and supporting the effort to privatize social security. Wendt held monthly meetings to direct his philanthropic and political crusades. In 1990, he bankrolled an effort to force welfare recipients into the workforce, gaining national attention for the measure that became known as Jobs Plus, a program that placed unemployed people in government-subsidized jobs. Wendt also opened a store, Transitions Wear, that stocked used career clothing for people looking for work, and directed his think tank, the American Institute for Full Employment, to expand its efforts into social security reform. Wendt, who favored the abolishment of social security, initiated an ad campaign that portrayed the system as on the brink of collapse.

In 1996, *Forbes* ranked Jeld-Wen 225th among the nation's top 500 private companies, estimating its annual revenues at $850 million, an increase of almost 13 percent from 1995. A year later, that ranking had moved up to 119th with the company's estimated revenues at $1.39 billion. Much of this money came from the success of Jeld-Wen's real estate ventures. Throughout the 1980s, Jeld-Wen and its subsidiaries had built or bought 19 West Coast resorts, ranging from British Columbia to Hawaii. By the early 1990s, Worldmark, the company's timeshare program, had 40,000 members, mostly baby boomers, who purchased points to split vacation time among any of the resorts.

During the second half of the 1990s, Jeld-Wen turned its attention to building resorts in Oregon, Washington, and Idaho.

Key Dates:

1960: The Wendt family founds Jeld-Wen with the purchase of a small millwork plant in Klamath Falls, Oregon.
1983: Jeld-Wen creates Trendwest as a subsidiary.
1989: Jeld-Wen acquires Frank Paxton Co.
1992: The company purchases California-based 3D Industries Inc. and Continental Door, Inc., and Bend Millwork Systems Inc. of Oregon.
1996: Jeld-Wen purchases Norco Windows of Wisconsin from TJ International.
1997: Jeld-Wen purchases Caradco, Inc. and Grossman's building supply chain; Trendwest Resorts goes public on the NASDAQ, with the Wendt family retaining an 80 percent stake.
1999: Jeld-Wen purchases a majority interest in Creative Media Development.

An upscale resort compound on a century-old cattle ranch bordering Upper Klamath Lake, the Running Y was slated to become the region's second largest city, with 900 homes, 350 condominiums, a 250-room hotel, and a convention center, and Jeld-Wen had plans for a second resort in central Washington. It also intended to revive struggling Silver Mountain ski resort in Idaho, its proving ground for the planned Pelican Butte Winter Sports Site in a national forest near Klamath Falls. In 1997, Trendwest Resorts began trading on the NASDAQ under the symbol TWRI, with Dick Wendt retaining an 80 percent stake in the subsidiary.

The Environmental Protection Agency (EPA) dealt the Pelican Butte plans a serious setback in 1999 when it declared that the environmental impact of the proposed ski resort had not been studied fully. The U.S. Fish and Wildlife Service further stymied plans when it announced that the resort would have a detrimental effect on two species of fish, pushing them possibly to the brink of extinction. President Clinton, finally, delivered the project its death blow when, in his final days in office in 2001, he put through new protections for roadless areas.

Jeld-Wen management looked forward to the Bush administration's assumption of power as a time of unimpeded real estate development. Regardless, with estimated revenues of $2 billion in 2001 and a new majority interest in Creative Media Development, Portland's largest multimedia, film, and marketing house, Jeld-Wen would clearly keep on growing.

Principal Subsidiaries

Eagle Crest Partners Ltd.; Jeld-Wen Australia Pty Ltd.; Jeld-Wen Canada; Trendwest Resorts, Inc. (80%); International Wood Products; Wenco; Caradco Corp.; Challenge Door Co.; Paxton Beautiful Woods; Advanced Wood Resources; Amerititle; Bend Millwork Co.

Principal Competitors

Andersen Worldwide; Nortek, Inc.; Pella Corporation.

Further Reading

Gorski, Eric, "Opening Doors to Tourism," *Oregonian*, February 21, 1997, p. C1.
Hill, Gail Kinsey, "Klamath Falls' Rich Uncle," *Oregon Business*, October 1986, p. 41.
McCrea, Bridget, "Optimizing Business," *Warehousing Magazine*, March 2001, p. T2.
Quinn, Beth, "Facing Federal Snags, Oregon Ski Resort Proposal Takes Big Tumble," *Oregonian*, March 5, 1999.
Stolberg, Sheryl, "Making America Work: A Man Who's Putting His State to Work," *Los Angeles Times,* July 9, 1995, p. 8.
Williams, Elisa, "Work Speaks for Itself," *Forbes*, October 9, 2000, p. 82.
Wojahn, Ellen, "The One Billion-Pound Elephant," *Oregon Business*, June 1998, p. 37.

—Carrie Rothburd

KB Home

10990 Wilshire Boulevard
7th Floor
Los Angeles, California 90024
U.S.A.
Telephone: (310) 231-4000
Toll Free: (888) 524-6637
Fax: (310) 231-4222
Web site: http://www.kbhome.com

Public Company
Incorporated: 1957 as Kaufman and Broad Building
    Company
Employees: 3,500
Sales: $4.57 billion (2001)
Stock Exchanges: New York
Ticker Symbol: KBH
NAIC: 233210 Building Construction, Single Family;
    233220 Building Construction, Residential; 233320
    Commercial Building Construction; 522292 Mortgage
    Companies

KB Home is the largest home builder in the United States, in terms of units built. In 2001, the residential real estate developer primarily built single-family homes in the western United States and Paris, France, for the entry level and first-time trade-up markets. The company also provided mortgage banking services to its home buyers in the United States through its wholly owned subsidiary, Kaufman and Broad Mortgage Company, and offered commercial development, renovation services, condominium and apartment complex development, and single-family homes through its French subsidiary, Kaufman and Broad, S.A.

From the Ground Up: The 1950s and 1960s

Kaufman and Broad began in 1957 in Detroit, Michigan, as Kaufman and Broad Building Company. The cofounders, Don Kaufman and Eli Broad, took their initial investment of $25,000 and developed two model homes in the Detroit suburb of Madison Heights. They targeted the entry-level housing market and positioned the company as one that provided well-designed and affordable first homes. The styling and price were well matched for the market; in its first year in business, the company posted sales of $1.7 million, or about 136 homes with the average sale price of $12,500 for a new three-bedroom house. First-year net income of almost $33,000 was nearly 2 percent of sales and exceeded the cofounders' initial investment.

In 1959, Kaufman and Broad expanded into the contract housing business and developed elderly housing and college dormitories as well as new homes for the armed forces and public housing agencies. Sales tripled from their first year in business to $5.1 million, and net income improved to 7 percent of sales. The following year, the company began building homes in Arizona. In 1961, the company went public and raised about $1.8 million in its initial public offering. Total revenue more than doubled from two years prior to $11.7 million, and net income was more than 5 percent of sales.

By the end of 1962, Broad and Kaufman had delivered more than 300 entry-level priced homes in Phoenix and Tempe, Arizona. That same year, the company introduced a new product in Detroit, "Townehouses," which were attached single-family homes. Again, the company understood the needs of the market well; 400 townhouse units were sold in 30 days. That same year, Kaufman and Broad was listed as one of the country's 200 fastest growing companies by Standard and Poor's and became the first home builder to trade on the American Stock Exchange. Another first for the company in 1962 was becoming the first builder to successfully obtain financing commitments to provide qualified buyers with mortgage loans.

Kaufman and Broad continued to expand into other markets. In 1963, the company entered southern California and developed an attached townhouse community in Orange County. Sales continued to be strong, and year-end net revenue again more than doubled from the two years previous to $31.8 million. Acquisitions of smaller local and regional builders enabled the company to enter other markets such as San Francisco, Chicago, New York, and other cities in the northeast portion of the United States.

In 1964, the company moved its corporate headquarters to Los Angeles from Phoenix, where it had moved earlier in the 1960s. That same year, Kaufman and Broad opened a division in Chicago to handle sales and development in that metropolitan area. The home designs remained value-conscious as the company expanded its market focus to include the first-time trade-up buyers as well as the entry-level market. Having been successful with the financing commitments it was able to obtain and develop over a three-year period, Kaufman and Broad founded the International Mortgage Company in 1965. The creation of this wholly owned subsidiary allowed the company to provide financing directly to its customers without involving banks or other financial institutions. In the same year that Kaufman and Broad vertically integrated into mortgage services, it consolidated production activities by ceasing operations of its contract division. The division completed homes, schools, and public buildings for an Indian reservation in Fort Wingate, New Mexico, as its final project.

Diversification into other businesses continued throughout the rest of the 1960s. In 1966, the company entered into the relatively new business of cable TV franchising with the formation of its second wholly owned subsidiary, Nation Wide Cablevision. Within five years, the subsidiary was operating franchises in 51 communities on the West Coast of the United States. In 1969, the company founded Kaufman and Broad Home Systems, Inc., through which the company entered into the manufactured housing business. By 1971, Home Systems operated eight plants throughout the country and had sales of 9,000 units.

Also in the late 1960s, Kaufman and Broad's residential housing business was growing as well. Through its acquisition of the local building company Kay Homes in 1967, the company became the largest home producer in the San Francisco Bay area. Kaufman and Broad model homes were introduced in Paris, France, in 1969, two years after the company's first overseas office was opened there. The company's growth during these years was due in part to customer service programs and good public relations. Kaufman and Broad was recognized by President Johnson in 1967 for its commitment to participate in low-income housing programs. In that same year, the company began offering a five-year limited home warranty, the first in the industry to do so. The following year, FHA, VA, and Fannie Mae approved International Mortgage for home mortgages, making it one of only a few builder mortgage subsidiaries with that approval.

In 1968, in an effort to better define itself as a diversified corporation, the company changed its name to Kaufman and Broad, Inc. A year earlier, the company had become the largest publicly held housing corporation, its growth attributable, in large part, to happy customers. A total of 40 percent of its sales was secured through referrals from satisfied customers. In 1969, it became the first housing builder to be listed on the New York Stock Exchange.

Fighting Recessions in the 1970s and 1980s

Additional acquisitions in 1970 of Victoria Wood Development Corporation in Toronto, Canada, and in 1971 of Sun Life Insurance Company further expanded and diversified Kaufman and Broad. Following the purchase of Sun Life, the company reorganized its onsite housing activities as a new entity, Kaufman and Broad Development Group. By 1972, Kaufman and Broad was America's largest multinational housing producer and the largest single-family home builder in Paris. The company operated onsite divisions in more than five states, as well as Canada, France, and West Germany. In 1973, the company entered the pre-cut Custom Home market with plants in Denver, Colorado, and Minneapolis, Minnesota, and the high-rise condominium business with its construction project in New Jersey. Net housing revenues for 1973 had increased to $264.4 million with net income more than 9 percent of sales.

As a result of high interest rates and a national recession—and the concomitant soft new home sales in 1974—the company experienced its first full year net loss. Despite the loss, Kaufman and Broad maintained its new market growth and customer service efforts strategy to assure long-term profitability. In 1975, it expanded into new markets such as Brussels, Belgium, introduced new products, and offered new services such as the industry's first ten-year homeowner warranty. By 1977, the recession had subsided and the housing market had rebounded; the company celebrated the sale of its 100,000th home, which was an industry first. Sales in Europe were growing as well. By 1977, under the direction of Bruce Karatz, president of the French division, the company celebrated the sale of its 4,000th home overseas. Under Karatz, the division staged one of what industry analysts said was the most creative advertising campaigns in home building: construction of a model home on the roof of an eight-story department store in downtown Paris. More than a half million people toured the home, which featured, among other things, a car inside the attached garage.

As the company entered the 1980s, its growth was again threatened by high interest rates and an industry recession. In an effort to better align its diverse business interests and to improve operations, the firm was reorganized into four operating groups: Kaufman and Broad Development Group for home building; International Mortgage Company for mortgage services; Home Systems for manufactured housing; and Sun Life for life insurance. A change in executive management also occurred in 1980. Bruce Karatz, president of the French division for the past four years, returned to the states and became the president of the Kaufman and Broad Development Group. His strategy for continued growth in home building was to concentrate on select regional markets that offered strong economic fundamentals. His long-term strategy to become the top pro-

Key Dates:

1957: Kaufman and Broad Building Company is founded in Detroit, Michigan.
1961: The company goes public and raises about $1.8 million in its initial public offering.
1965: Kaufman and Broad founds the International Mortgage Company.
1967: The company begins offering a five-year limited home warranty, the first in the industry to do so.
1969: The company enters the manufactured housing business by founding Kaufman and Broad Home Systems, Inc.
1986: The corporation reorganizes: Kaufman and Broad Development is spun off from Kaufman and Broad Inc. and forms Kaufman and Broad Home Corporation.
1989: Kaufman and Broad phases out its divisions in Illinois, New Jersey, Germany, and Belgium.
1992: The company establishes a new division in California and one in Las Vegas, Nevada, bringing the total number of divisions in the region to 11.
1993: Kaufman and Broad opens offices in Arizona, Nevada, and Colorado, and the following year, in Utah.
1998: The company spends $162 million to purchase PrideMark Homes, Estes Homes, and Hallmark Residential Builders, thus moving into Houston, Tucson, and Phoenix.
1999: Kaufman and Broad purchases Lewis Homes for $544 million.
2000: The company changes its name to KB Home.
2001: KB Home expands into Florida with the purchase of Trademark Home Builders.

ducer in those areas that had solid growth potential and exit those markets that did not resulted in Kaufman and Broad phasing out its divisions in Illinois, New Jersey, Germany, and Belgium by 1989. The recession of the early 1980s and the new management's corporate strategy resulted in the company exiting other markets over the next several months, and by the following year Kaufman and Broad had reduced its onsite activities to California, France, and Canada. Market consolidation also was evident in the French division, where management focused its efforts within a 25-mile radius of Paris and exited areas outside the metropolitan area.

While the company was revising its operating strategies, management improved the quality control and customer service programs to increase referrals and maximize customers' perception of improved value. Following the recovery of the national economy, Kaufman and Broad concentrated its building efforts in key markets, including the manufactured homes business segment, improving housing revenues by 55 percent in 1985. In addition, the corporation set company records for year-end financials in both revenue and net income. With the improved sales, the company had become the largest single-family home builder in California. The following year, Kaufman and Broad Land Company was formed to manage property purchasing. Home building in California continued to be strong, with com-

munities such as East Hills in Anaheim, which sold 52 of the 54 homes available in the first weekend.

French Expansion in the Late 1980s

In 1985, the company acquired Bati-Service, an entry-level home builder in France. This purchase made Kaufman and Broad's French division the third largest builder in the country. That same year in California, the two regional offices each divided into two new divisions. The four divisions allowed the company to address the specific needs of the local community. Corporate management efforts decentralized the divisions, so each division was held responsible for its own construction, planning, and local operations. Marketing and purchasing, however, remained a corporate focus. For the entire California market, the company introduced "The California Series," a marketing strategy that allowed all divisions to achieve cost efficiency in advertising and promotional programs. The concept was developed to improve economies of scale, to achieve a consistent single corporate image, and to increase brand awareness of Kaufman and Broad homes throughout the state.

In 1986, the corporation again reorganized. Kaufman and Broad Development spun off from Kaufman and Broad Inc. and formed Kaufman and Broad Home Corporation. All onsite housing activities, with the exception of manufactured housing, transferred to the new organization to focus on real estate development. That same year, Kaufman and Broad Home Corporation formed a new commercial development division in Paris, Kaufman and Broad Developpement. Within two years, this new division had completed a senior citizen apartment complex and 12 office buildings in Paris.

In 1989, the French division approved plans to build Washington Plaza, a new Paris office complex, securing $600 million from pre-sales to groups of institutional investors, a transaction that represented the largest single real estate deal in that country's history. Two new divisions were formed in Paris in 1989: Maisons Individuelles and Kaufman and Broad Renovation. The Renovation division was established to refurbish older office buildings in the downtown area. Management expanded into this new business because it felt that it provided a new growth opportunity given the scarcity of land in that area. By 1989, due in large part to the division's commercial development activities, French revenues more than quadrupled from four years prior.

That same year, Kaufman and Broad Home Corporation split into two companies, each worth approximately a billion dollars: Broad Inc. (which later became SunAmerica) and Kaufman Broad Home. Bruce Karatz led the latter as chief executive officer.

The Early 1990s: Targeting New Markets

Despite a slowing U.S. economy and uncertainty over the country's involvement in the Persian Gulf crisis, 1990 was a record year for Kaufman and Broad. End-of-year revenues of $1.37 billion were the highest in company history. Lower sales in California were more than offset by strong French division operating results, which was led by a 57 percent increase in commercial revenues.

The following year, the French division, along with several banks, announced the $1.7 billion, four-year redevelopment project for the Esso Corporation headquarters' property in Paris. For 1991, Kaufman and Broad's net orders worldwide for new construction increased from the previous year, and included California, where the nation's recession continued. Sales in California were positively impacted by the company's expansion into the Sacramento market.

In 1992, Kaufman and Broad had record deliveries in California, up 27 percent from the previous year. The company also increased its overall percentage of the new home sales market statewide to 6 percent, the highest of any builder in the state and up from 4 percent in 1991. Market penetration in the state was solid, with the company marketing homes in 72 communities. Also in 1992, the company continued its market expansion and established a new division in California and one in Las Vegas, Nevada, bringing the total number of divisions in the region to 11. Management attributed the company's success in 1992 to its extensive use of television advertising targeting renters, an audience that was not being reached in the real estate sections of newspapers. This was a marketing technique that few home builders had used, and it was coupled with an "off-site" telemarketing program designed to reach potential buyers who did not visit sales offices. According to company executives, the advertising spots generated more than 75,000 sales leads and resulted in approximately 700 incremental sales.

Minimizing the Boom and Bust Cycle in the 1990s

In the mid-1990s, sales continued strong in the California region despite a recession, although profits fell as the company enticed buyers with free upgrades and waived down payments. The company increasingly focused on first-time buyers, reducing its higher-priced home inventory; the average price for a Kaufman and Broad new home was typically thousands of dollars below the statewide average. Moreover, its mortgage subsidiary financed more than three-quarters of the company's California home purchases by offering competitive mortgage programs designed for first-time buyers.

To boost profit margins, Kaufman and Broad sought to reduce costs through increased centralization. The company's divisions had long operated almost autonomously, but were now expected to take advantage of bulk-rate discounts negotiated by headquarters for such things as appliances, bathroom fixtures, and lumber. In addition, all land purchases had to be approved by the headquarters land committee, who scrutinized the proposals closely. Marketing was emphasized, with experimentation of such new venues as catalogs, and an effort was made to create a strong brand name.

Karatz sought to stabilize the boom-and-bust cycle of housing development by expanding geographically. In 1993 Kaufman and Broad opened offices in Arizona, Nevada, and Colorado. The following year, the company moved into Utah. In each area, first-time buyers were targeted. Nevertheless, the continued slow market in California and Paris hurt the company's bottom line: Profits fell by 38 percent in 1995, and by 1996 the company was showing a loss of $61 million. The next year, however, the company rebounded to profits of $58 million.

In 1998 Kaufman and Broad instituted KB2000, a new operating strategy that included greater choice for customers in the design and construction of their homes. The company began surveys of home buyers in its regions of operation, hoping to identify popular home designs and features. It incorporated those ideas into new home showrooms, which customers could walk through to help them choose features, such as lofts, porches, or types of flooring, that they wanted as part of their homes. Each regional division soon had a new home showroom.

The corporation began a new expansion strategy in 1998, one based on acquisitions rather than the opening of new offices. That year Kaufman and Broad entered the Houston market by purchasing Hallmark Residential Group, Inc., the parent company of Dover Homes and Ideal Builders. The $50 million deal gave the company access to approximately 4,700 lots in the Houston area and 90 employees. Kaufman and Broad also purchased Colorado-based PrideMark Homes for $65 million, raising the company to a dominant position in the Denver market. To round out that year's purchases, the company acquired Estes Homes for $47 million, giving Kaufman and Broad an entrée into the markets in Tucson and Phoenix, Arizona. By the end of the year, the company was enjoying net income of $95 million.

In a much larger deal the following year, Kaufman and Broad purchased Lewis Homes for approximately $409 million, plus the assumption of $135 million in debt. Lewis Homes was the nation's largest privately held home builder and dominated the markets in Las Vegas and northern Nevada. It also held significant portions of the markets in Sacramento and southern California. Kaufman and Broad expected to combine their businesses in California, benefiting from economies of scale. The company's expansion spree and a healthy housing market helped raise the company's revenues to $3.8 billion in 1999.

In 2000 the company's French subsidiary, Kaufman and Broad, S.A., held an initial public offering of stock, although Kaufman and Broad Home Corporation continued as the majority shareholder, with approximately 50 percent ownership. The offering raised about $113 million. The French home builder had been enjoying booming sales of its apartments and single-family homes in 1999 and 2000. The subsidiary's revenues reached $195 million in fiscal 2000. The same year, Kaufman and Broad Home Corporation initiated a repurchase plan of more than half the stock the company had issued as part of its 1999 acquisition of Lewis Homes.

Kaufman and Broad introduced its Dream Home Studios in 2000, an updated and vastly expanded version of the company's new home showrooms. In addition to this facelift, the company changed its name to KB Home, a name many customers had already been using. New name or not, KB Home continued its steady improvement, reaching revenues of $3.93 billion and net income of $210 million in 2000. The following year, the company continued its expansion with the acquisition of northern Florida-based Trademark Home Builders, Inc., and recorded revenues of $4.57 billion.

Principal Subsidiaries

Kaufman and Broad Mortgage Company; Kaufman & Broad, S.A. (50%).

Principal Competitors

Centex Corporation; Pulte Homes, Inc.; The Ryland Group, Inc.

Further Reading

Barron, Kelly, ''Building Equity?,'' *Forbes,* August 9, 1999, p. 86.

Lubove, Seth, ''Learning from Victoria's Secret,'' *Forbes,* December 19, 1994, pp. 60–63.

Morris, Kathleen, ''This Homebuilder Is on a Spree,'' *Business Week,* November 16, 1998, p. 190.

Posth, Mark A., ''Home Alone,'' *California Builder,* February/March, 1993.

''Professional Achievement Awards,'' *Professional Builder & Remodeler,* January 1993.

Sinnock, Bonnie, ''France's Kaufman & Broad S.A. Sees Its Best Half-Year Since 1989,'' *National Mortgage News,* July 10, 2000, p. 30.

Sylvester, David, ''A Hot Homebuilder,'' *Fortune Magazine,* February 13, 1989.

—Allyson S. Farquhar-Boyle
—update: Susan Windisch Brown

Kelda Group plc

Western House
Halifax Road
Bradford
West Yorkshire BD6 2S2
United Kingdom
Telephone: (+44) 1274-600-111
Fax: (+44) 1274-608-608
Web site: http://www.keldagroup.com

Public Company
Incorporated: 1988 as Yorkshire Water Services Ltd.
Employees: 3,653
Sales: £632.4 million ($964.8 million) (2001)
Stock Exchanges: London
Ticker Symbol: KEL
NAIC: 221310 Water Supply and Irrigation Systems;
562998 All Other Miscellaneous Waste Management
Services; 562111 Solid Waste Collection; 562112
Hazardous Waste Collection; 562119 Other Waste
Collection; 562211 Hazardous Waste Treatment and
Disposal; 562212 Solid Waste Landfill; 562213 Solid
Waste Combustors and Incinerators; 562219 Other
Nonhazardous Waste Treatment and Disposal

Kelda Group plc is one of the United Kingdom's leading water services and wastewater management companies. Through subsidiary Aquarion, acquired in 2000, the company is also an active provider of water services in the northeastern United States. Kelda's U.S. operations account for just 10 percent of its 2001 revenues. In the United Kingdom, Kelda is especially known for its Yorkshire Water Services wing, which, in the mid-1990s, had gained a reputation as one of the United Kingdom's most-hated companies. Since the late 1990s, however, the company has significantly improved its reputation while expanding its operations into the waste services field, especially through a 46 percent stake in publicly quoted Waste Recycling Group. The company adopted the Kelda name in 1999 in order to distinguish its non-regulated business from its regulated business. Worldwide, the company claims to rank within the top ten water services and sewerage companies. The company also operates through its Loop customer relationship management subsidiary, providing customer call services, billing and collection, and other services to Yorkshire Water as well as to third-party customers. Another subsidiary, First Renewals, concentrates on developing renewable energy sources, such as its 79 percent stake in Arbre Energy, a bio-mass power generation plant that uses wood chips. Kelda has taken the lead among the United Kingdom's water services companies, calling for the right to separate its water services operations into two components, the first a management services arm to be retained by Kelda, the second the assets of Yorkshire Water, to be acquired by its customer communities. Such a move, blocked as of early 2001 by government regulators, was expected to enhance shareholder value and in turn drive up the company's share price.

Water Privatization in the 1980s

The United Kingdom's water supply services, including the laying of piping and sewage systems, remained shared between local communities and private businesses until well into the 19th century. As the country's cities grew, particularly at the height of the Industrial Revolution, water services increasingly came under control of the local municipalities, which especially took over construction of water piping and sewage systems at mid-century. The passage of a number of Water Acts during the 1870s brought the United Kingdom's water services fully under government control, while leaving the nation's water services operating on a highly fragmented, primarily local level.

The high fragmentation of the United Kingdom's water utilities lasted throughout much of the 20th century. By the early 1970s, the country still numbered 28 individual "river" authorities, overseeing some 160 water services suppliers. The country also counted more than 1,300 separate sewage treatment operations. Tightening environmental restrictions and heightened demand for cleaner water left the country's water services largely at a loss, however, as the small size of nearly all of these operations made it impossible for them to invest in the necessary infrastructure improvements to bring themselves up to increasingly stiffer modern standards.

Company Perspectives:

The Kelda strategy going forward is to concentrate on three areas: water and wastewater services in the UK, water services in the USA and our 46% investment in the Waste Recycling Group plc. This new focus has already led to increased management emphasis on efficiency and service issues and allowed a greater regional focus on our environmental responsibilities. The Board continues to keep under review all proposals which will assist the growth and development of services to customers, while improving the attractiveness of the water sector to capital and equity markets generally. Our objective is to ensure sustainable service improvements and increased long-term investment in both infrastructure growth, essential cost maintenance, and the environment

The British government began to take steps to streamline the already antiquated water utility situation in the United Kingdom, beginning with the passage of the Water Act of 1973. The new legislation established ten regional water authorities, which then became responsible for the entirety of the water supply, wastewater treatment, sewage treatment and disposal services, as well as the environmental protection and cleanup of the rivers and coastlines present in their regions. These authorities continued to be operated as government agencies, reporting to government on both the local and national level.

Yet the new water authorities continued to be hampered by a low level of investment and rapidly aging infrastructure during a time when the steady tightening of standards by the European Community, governing such issues as drinking water purity and the environmental impact of sewage disposal, were requiring water authorities to modernize their facilities and systems. The British government, led by Margaret Thatcher in the 1980s, balked at providing the huge sums necessary for revamping the United Kingdom's dilapidated water supply and disposal systems. Instead, the government added the water industry to the list of formerly government-run industries slated to be privatized by the end of the decade.

The U.K. water industry's time came in 1989, when the passage of the Water Act of that year returned the country's water supply and sewage treatment needs to the private sector. The ten water authorities were transformed into public liability companies with shares placed on the London stock exchange. In conjunction with the conversion of the public utilities into private companies, the government set up a regulatory body, the Office of Water Services (Ofwat), which was given a mandate not only to set pricing and capital investment levels, but also to provide oversight on the new water companies' corporate policies.

The public status of the newly privatized water companies enabled them to raise capital in order to pursue extensive capital investment programs in order to comply with obligatory environmental and operational infrastructure improvements. Despite the required infrastructure investments, most of the new water companies swiftly began turning out strong benefits—in part because of a series of price increases. In some cases, the

water companies' customers saw their water bills nearly double in amount. A series of mishaps—including high leakage rates and recurring tap restrictions, as well as other public relations gaffes, such as a wave of so-called ''fat cat'' executive salary packages—quickly brought a great deal of consumer distrust to the nation's water companies.

Among the most singled-out for customer outrage of the new water companies was Yorkshire Water Services. The company had already inherited a poor record of performance, which quickly degenerated into a steady series of drought measures, including outdoor hose bans, since its transformation into a publicly held company. At the same time, the company was gaining one of the highest customer complaint rates in the country. The company continued to scale back on personnel—reducing its payroll nearly by half by 1994—while struggling to meet the demands of its ailing infrastructure. By the early 1990s, Yorkshire Water had one of the worst leakage rates in its industry. In some parts of its region, it was losing more than 30 percent of all the water it was pumping. Meanwhile, the company's customers faced new drought measures each year.

Yorkshire Water's troubles seemed to culminate in 1996 after a 15-month-long drought forced the company to begin trucking in water from neighboring regions in order to meet customer demand. At one point the company was even forced to consider radical ''rotacuts,'' that is, cutting off water on a rotating basis, a move that would have crippled the already fragile Yorkshire economy. At the height of the crisis, Yorkshire Water was trucking in more than 70,000 tons of water per day with a fleet of more than 700 tankers brought in from across the United Kingdom and continental Europe. Adding insult to injury was the statement of the company's then CEO, Trevor Newton, who claimed not to have showered at his home since the beginning of the crisis. That statement was proved to be only partly true when it was revealed that Newton had taken to traveling outside of the Yorkshire region for his showers. Meanwhile, Newton, as well as the company's other directors, continued to enjoy healthy salary increases, embroiling the company in the so-called ''fat cat'' scandals of the mid-decade.

When the drought finally eased, Yorkshire Water found itself considered one of the country's most-hated companies. The resulting outcry saw both Newton and former Chairman Gordon Jones ousted from the company, in a shakeup that produced a clean sweep of most of the company's executive board. Taking their place were Chairman Brandon Gough and CEO Kevin Bond, who set to work restoring the company's image and operational efficiency. The latter proved easier than the former, especially as the company succeeded in laying more than 220 kilometers of new pipe in 1996 alone. Meanwhile, the company sparked a new round of ''fat cat'' controversy when it not only awarded healthy bonuses to Bond and other members of executive management, but also raised its customers' rates.

Across the Water in the 21st Century

Yorkshire Water was not the only water company to face criticism from consumers. Indeed, most of its competitors were subject to similar dissatisfaction rates. Yet, like many of its competitors, Yorkshire Water had begun to diversify its operations beyond its regulated water business, entering the related,

Key Dates:

1973: Water Act creates ten regional water authorities, including Yorkshire Water Services.

1988: Yorkshire Water Services is privatized and placed on the London stock exchange.

1993: Yorkshire Water Services acquires Alcontrol, a specialist in environmental laboratory and food testing and analysis services.

1997: Company acquires Clinical Waste, enabling Yorkshire to become the U.K. leader in the medical waste disposal segment.

1998: Reverse takeover of Waste Recycling Group merges Yorkshire Environmental Global Waste Management division into publicly quoted WRG, giving Yorkshire Water 46 percent control of the waste management company.

1999: Yorkshire acquires Aquarion in a deal worth $600 million; company then changes its name to Kelda Group to emphasize its diversified operations.

2000: Kelda attempts to spin off its water services assets into a mutual fund company, but move is blocked by government regulators.

2001: Kelda pays $118 million for four U.S.-based water services companies.

but non-regulated field of waste management and disposal services. The company's first move into this area came in 1993 when it acquired Alcontrol, which began providing environmental laboratory and food testing and analysis services under the Yorkshire Environmental Services name. Yorkshire Water quickly built up a strong position in the specialty area of medical waste disposal, under subsidiary White Rose Environmental. In 1997, the company captured the leading position in that segment in the United Kingdom when it purchased competitor Clinical Waste.

Yorkshire Water had also been steadily building its waste management wing during the 1990s. In 1998, the company's interests in that field expanded when it merged its Yorkshire Environmental Global Waste Management division into Waste Recycling Group, in what became a reverse takeover giving Yorkshire Water a 46 percent share of WRG. That company had initially been founded in 1983 and went public in 1994, when it began an aggressive expansion-through-acquisition campaign. By the time of the merger announcement, Yorkshire Water's waste management assets had already deepened with the £120 million purchase of 3C Waste, which had formerly been owned by three community councils. The purchase also helped place WRG and Yorkshire Water among the United Kingdom's largest landfill operators.

The spinoff of its waste management services operation allowed the company to concentrate on other areas of business, such as the generation of electrical power from alternative fuel sources. Among the company's projects in this area was the launch of Arbre, in a joint-venture with Sweden's TPS Termiska and the Netherlands' Royal Schelde Group. Construction of the Arbre facility, which became Europe's first commercially operated wood-fuel power plant, began in 1998, with energy production starting in 1999. Yorkshire Water initially held an 85 percent stake in the project, which provided an important outlet for disposal of its majority shareholder's sewage sludge.

Yorkshire Water had not abandoned its interest in expanding in its core water services area, however. Blocked from expansion in the United Kingdom by government resistance to mergers among water companies in that country, Yorkshire Water instead looked overseas. In 1999, the company paid $600 million to acquire water services company Aquarion. That company's operations focused primarily on Connecticut and Long Island, New York, through its main subsidiaries, BHC and Sea Cliff Water Company, and was to serve as a springboard for Yorkshire Water's intended expansion into the heavily fragmented U.S. water services market. The company hoped to generate as much as half of its revenues in the United States by 2004.

In the meantime, the Aquarion purchase led the company to change its name in order to reflect the diversification of its interests. Choosing the name Kelda, taken from a Norse word for "source of water," the company also hoped to put behind it the bad publicity of its Yorkshire Water subsidiary.

Ofwat-imposed price cuts starting in April 2000 forced Kelda, now led by Chairman John Napier, to launch a strategic review of its operations. Barred from pursuing takeovers at home, the company attempted to spin off its water services assets in a controversial move that would place ownership of its assets in the hands of its customers, that is, the communities the company served—returning up to £1.2 billion to Kelda's shareholders—while Kelda was to retain operational control of its water services division. The move was swiftly blocked, however, by regulator charges that such a spinoff would benefit Kelda's shareholders, but not its customers. Thwarted, Kelda instead began trimming its operations, regrouping around its core water services and selling off such non-core assets as Alcontrol and White Rose Environmental.

In 2001, Kelda continued to press regulators to loosen up takeover restrictions among U.K. water services, complaining that the existing regulations enabled foreign takeovers of U.K. water companies while blocking mergers among the country's domestic companies. Meanwhile, Kelda continued to pursue its expansion in the United States. In August 2001 the company agreed to pay $118 million to acquire four companies (Connecticut-American Water Company, Massachusetts-American Water Company, New York-American Water Company, and Hampton Water Company) from American Water Works Co. The deal added more than 64,000 new customer accounts to Kelda's existing U.S. operations, boosting its revenues from that country by more than 50 percent. The deal, expected to gain government approval in early 2002, was also seen as a starting point for a possible consolidation of the United States' more than 64,000 water companies.

Principal Subsidiaries

Aquarion Company (U.S.A.); Arbre Energy Limited (79%); BHC Company (U.S.A.); Sea Cliff Water Company (U.S.A.); Fibro Holdings Limited (31%); First Renewables Limited;

Grampian Wastewater Services Limited; KeyLand Developments Limited; Loop Customer Management Limited; Yorkshire Water Projects Limited; Yorkshire Water Services Limited; Yorkshire Windpower Limited (50%); Waste Recycling Group plc (46%).

Principal Competitors

Southern Water PLC; Anglian Water PLC; Severn Trent Water PLC; North West Water Group plc; Thames Water plc; Wessex Water PLC; Pennon Group Plc; Glas Cymru PLC; Northumbria Water PLC.

Further Reading

Cathcart, Brian, "Fat Cataclysm," *Independent on Sunday*, February 25, 1996, p. 10.

Field, Paul, "Is This the UK's Worst Privatised Company?," *Independent*, May 18, 1996, p. 6.

Harrison, Michael, "Kelda Chief Predicts Wave of Water Bids," *Independent*, December 6, 2001, p. 18.

——, "Yorkshire Water in Pounds 385m US Deal," *Independent*, June 2, 1999, p. 17.

"Kelda to Swallow Four US Water Companies," *Reuters*, August 30, 2001.

Routledge, Paul, "Water Bosses Face the Chop," *Independent on Sunday*, January 7, 1996, p. 3.

—M.L. Cohen

Kinder Morgan, Inc.

One Allen Center, Suite 1000
500 Dallas St.
Houston, Texas 77002
U.S.A.
Telephone: (713) 369-9000
Toll Free: (800) 324-2900
Fax: (713) 369-9100
Web site: http://www.kindermorgan.com

Public Company
Incorporated: 1927 as Kansas Pipe Line & Gas Co.
Employees: 3,801
Sales: $2.96 billion (2001)
Stock Exchanges: New York
Ticker Symbol: KMI
NAIC: 221210 Natural Gas Distribution

Based in Houston, Texas, Kinder Morgan, Inc. (KMI) is one of the largest midstream energy companies in the United States. Rather than drill for oil and natural gas, or market the commodities, KMI focuses on delivery through its network of more than 30,000 miles of pipelines in the United States. KMI is the corporate component of a unique business structure. Most of the company's $18 billion in assets are held by Kinder Morgan Energy Partners, L.P. (KMP), a Master Limited Partnership (MLP) comprised of units that can be traded like shares of stock. Unlike a corporation, however, an MLP does not pay taxes, rather all of its ''available cash'' is distributed to its partners each quarter. KMI and its principal executives, Richard Kinder and William Morgan, control most of the MLP's units. A third entity, Kinder Morgan Management, LLC, was created specifically to allow institutional investors to hold partnership equity in Kinder Morgan Energy Partners. In addition to delivery systems, KMI is involved in the retail sale of gas, storage facilities, and the development of small power plants that are connected directly to natural gas through its pipelines.

Formation of Kinder Morgan: 1997

Partners Kinder and Morgan created Kinder Morgan Energy Partners in February 1997 after purchasing the general partnership that ran the liquids pipeline operations of energy giant Enron Corporation. Both men had worked at Enron and were friends from their law school days in the early 1960s at the University of Missouri, where they both knew the CEO and chairman of Enron, Kenneth Lay. Years later, Lay was working for Florida Gas Transmission and hired Morgan, who in turn hired Kinder. Florida Gas was then sold to Houston Natural Gas in 1984, and the following year Houston Natural Gas merged with InterNorth to create Enron, which was headed by Lay. Morgan ran several pipeline operations for Enron, then in 1987 left to manage private energy investments. Kinder, in the meantime, advanced through the ranks of Florida Gas and Enron, serving in a variety of legal and executive positions until he was named president and chief operating officer for Enron in 1990. He was a key player in the development of Enron Capital & Trade, the corporation's merchant arm. Because of his demonstrated ability it was widely assumed that Kinder was Lay's heir apparent at Enron. However, when Lay agreed in 1996 to a new five-year-term as the chairman of Enron (a term, ironically, that would coincide with Enron's tumultuous downfall in late 2001), Kinder, now 52 years old, concluded that it was unlikely that he would ever assume the top management position and therefore opted to resign.

Although Kinder was rich enough to support an early retirement, he retained a desire to head a company. Morgan then convinced his old friend and colleague to go into business together. Along with minority partner First Union Capital Markets, based in Charlotte, North Carolina, they negotiated a $40 million deal to acquire Enron Liquids Pipeline, L.P., a general partnership that had been formed in 1992 and, although profitable, had enjoyed little growth. In addition to natural gas liquids pipelines, company assets included a CO_2 pipeline (used in the further recovery of oil in old wells) and a rail-to-barge coal terminal. Kinder quickly demonstrated his aptitude as a CEO by taking the partnership public as Kinder Morgan Energy Partners, putting the little-employed MLP structure to effective use.

MLPs are similar to Real Estate Investment Trusts (REITs), which were created by Congress in 1960 as a way for small investors to become involved in real estate in much the same way a mutual fund allows small investors to pool resources in buying stock. Because REITs were required to pay out at least 95 percent of their taxable income to unit holders each year, thus severely limiting their ability to raise funds internally, the structure was rarely used. The Tax Reform Act of 1987 not only initiated changes that invigorated the use of REITs, it extended the exemption from corporate taxes to MLPs. This provision allowed Kinder Morgan to buy assets that were unattractive to "C" corporations that were taxed both at the corporate and investor level. Kinder explained the MLP advantage in a 1998 *Forbes* profile: "When I was president of Enron, I would throw people out of the room if they came in with a proposal that had anything less than a 15% aftertax return. We can make acquisitions all day as long as we're over 8.5% pretax."

The goal was to focus on midstream fee-based pipeline businesses, serving as a conduit for commodities rather than the drilling or marketing sectors. Before embarking on external growth, however, Kinder cut $5 million in expenses, eliminating staff as well as instituting such cost savings measures as a companywide policy of flying coach. Both he and Morgan received only $1 a year in salary, which simply allowed them to be eligible for healthcare benefits, a decision made to counteract what they had experienced in the corporate world, where some executives had placed their interests ahead of shareholders. Dependent on dividends under this arrangement, Kinder and Morgan would only prosper to the extent that MLP's unit holders were rewarded. Although Kinder owned a 22 percent stake in the partnership to Morgan's 8 percent and operated as the lead executive, they viewed themselves as equals in the running of the business.

First Major Acquisition: 1997

Within six months Kinder was able to increase the dividend paid to unit holders by 50 percent. By October 1997 KMP made its first major acquisition, buying Santa Fe Pacific Pipeline Partners, L.P. from Burlington Northern Santa Fe Railroad for approximately $1 billion in units and cash, plus the assumption of $350 million in debt. The assets, renamed Kinder Morgan Pacific, included 3,300 miles of pipeline, providing an important West Coast presence, as well as 14 truck-loading terminals. In short order, $20 million in costs was eliminated and the acquisition began to produce strong revenue growth. In June 1998 KMP acquired a 24 percent interest in Plantation Pipe Line, paying $110 million to Equilon. A year later the partnership would acquire a controlling interest in Plantation by paying Chevron $124 million for its 27 percent interest. Plantation's 3,144 mile system distributed refined products throughout the Southeast and as far north as Washington, D.C.

While there were many advantages to the MLP structure, it was limited in its ability to grow. It could use cash and units to buy assets from corporations but was unable to buy companies outright. Moreover, institutional investors such as mutual funds were limited in their ability to hold MLP units. The next step for Kinder and Morgan, therefore, was to create what they called "the second barrel of the shotgun," a publicly traded corporation that would control the MLP. The corporation could use stock to acquire assets, which would then be sold to the MLP, in effect coupling the tax advantages of the partnership with the flexibility of a corporation. In 1998 Kinder and Morgan were about to make an initial public offering for Kinder Morgan, Inc. when they recognized an opportunity to gain corporation status while acquiring an array of valuable assets by engineering a reverse merger with KN Energy.

The roots of KN Energy reach back to the formation of Kansas Pipe line & Gas Co. in 1927. Unlike most gas pipeline businesses of the time, which believed only urban areas were economically viable, the company looked to serve small communities. In 1941 it acquired Nebraska Natural Gas Co. for $1.7 million and changed its name to Kansas Nebraska Natural Gas Co. Over the next 30 years, operating out of Hastings, Nebraska, the company would acquire a number of nearby pipeline companies and other assets, and by 1970 was listed on the New York Stock Exchange. In 1982 the company relocated its headquarters to Lakewood, Colorado, and a year later became known as KN Energy Inc., drawing on the first letters of Kansas and Nebraska to create its name. By this time the company ran a 16,000 mile, natural gas pipeline network throughout Kansas, Nebraska, Colorado, and Wyoming.

In the 1980s KN Energy, with $300 million in assets, would attract the attention of legendary corporate pirate T. Boone Pickens, whose Mesa Petroleum Co. failed on three different occasions to gain control of the business. In 1994 KN Energy merged with American Oil & Gas of Houston in a $282.5 million exchange of stock, structured as a tax-free pooling of interests. As a result of the transaction, KN Energy's CEO, Charles W. Battey, became the chairman of the combined company and Larry D. Hall took over as president and chief executive officer. Less than two years later Battey retired, and Hall assumed the chairmanship and was granted even greater latitude in changing the company from a natural gas business to a total energy provider. Hall looked to exploit deregulation and the assets of KN Energy to provide an array of services that could be bundled together. For instance, the company offered an appliance protection program for residential customers. To which he hoped to add other services such as home security and even television entertainment in partnership with telecommunications companies. The goal was to be in a position through strategic alliance to offer customers a package of services from a single vendor. Underpinning this plan was Hall's belief that a gas utility with decades of community involvement had an edge over cable TV companies and electric utilities, which were either local and perceived as notorious for poor service or run from afar and indifferent. In essence, he wanted to join economies of scale inherent in a large company with the consumer friendliness of a small gas company.

Key Dates:

1927: Kansas Pipe Line & Gas Co. is incorporated.
1941: Nebraska Natural Gas Co. is acquired, name changed to Kansas Nebraska Natural Gas Co.
1970: Company begins trading on New York Stock Exchange.
1983: Name is changed to KN Energy.
1997: Kinder Morgan Energy Partners is formed.
1999: Following acquisition, name is changed to Kinder Morgan, Inc.
2001: Kinder Morgan Management is formed.

However appealing Hall's vision may have appeared in theory, the reality proved to be far different. In January 1998 KN Energy acquired MidCon Corp. from Occidental Petroleum for $4 billion. While the deal quadrupled its assets and transformed KN Energy from a regional to a national energy services company, it also saddled it with an enormous debt load that cut into earnings. Two consecutive warm winters combined with greater competition to severely cripple the company and undercut the price of its stock. In February 1999 Sempra Energy of San Diego, California, made a tentative deal to purchase KN Energy for $1.9 billion, but by June the deal was off, scuttled by KN Energy's $3.3 billion in long-term debt.

Merging of KN Energy and KMI: 1999

Richard Kinder was well situated to observe the plight of KN Energy, having served on its board of directors since June 1998. Recognizing an opportunity, he promptly resigned from the board, canceled the Kinder Morgan IPO, and within a month engineered a deal to combine the assets of KN Energy with KMI. Technically KN Energy acquired KMI, paying $506 million in stock, but in reality KMI was taking over the corporate structure of KN Energy, effecting what was a reverse merger as well as a reverse IPO, in the process gaining a valuable position on the New York Stock Exchange. In October 1999 KN Energy changed its name to Kinder Morgan, Inc., Hall and other senior executives resigned, and Kinder and Morgan assumed the top positions of the newly combined company, even though they and First Union owned just a 38 percent stake. Unlike Hall's desire to cast a wide net, Kinder made it clear from the outset that he wanted KN Energy to return to its basics, concentrating on the midstream pipeline business and unloading the rest of its assets. He also was quick to institute his usual cost-cutting measures. Staff was reduced, mostly through attrition, interest in three corporate jets was eliminated, the travel budget was slashed from $9 million a year to just $2.5 million, and luxuries such as season tickets and sky boxes to sporting events in Chicago, Denver, and Houston were eliminated. The corporate headquarters was also officially moved to KMI's Houston offices.

KMI again took advantage of the MLP, into which some $700 million of KN Energy assets were transferred in exchange for 9.81 million KMP units and $330 million in cash. The cash would allow KMI to reduce its debt, and the additional units allowed the company to increase its stake in the MLP. Other KN Energy assets were also put on the market in order to eliminate debt. In February 2000 KMI sold its natural gas gathering and processing businesses located in Oklahoma, Kansas, and Texas to Oneok of Tulsa, Oklahoma, in a $400 million deal that included $114 million in cash and the assumption of debt. By October 2000 KMI had completed the digestion of KN Energy assets. After attempts to sell MidCon failed, KMI elected to keep the business, renaming it Kinder Morgan Texas Pipeline and selling it to the MLP for $150 million in cash and $150 million in partnership units. The company also exploited KN Energy's move into the independent power business, establishing Kinder Morgan Power and a proprietary gas-turbine system called Orion. Because these systems would be powered by natural gas and connected to the company's pipeline network, the niche business would remain within the scope of KMI's midstream energy philosophy. In December 2000 KMP began adding external businesses. It bought two pipelines and 12 terminals from GATX Corp. for $1.05 billion. One of the pipelines, CalNev Pipe Line Co., readily connected to a system already owned, and the other, Central Florida Pipeline Co., gave the company a presence in a fast-growing part of the country. A few days later KMP acquired Delta Terminal Services Inc. for approximately $114 million in cash, a deal that included storage terminals in New Orleans and Cincinnati. KMI capped off 2000 by being added to the Standard & Poor's 500 Stock index, after the Philip Morris acquisition of Nabisco Holdings Corp. created an opening.

In 2001 KMI created a third public company, Kinder Morgan Management, to allow institutional investors easier access to participation in KMP. Although nine million shares were intended to be sold in the initial public offering, demand was so strong that in the end 14.9 million shares were sold, raising over $1 billion in gross proceeds, which were then used by KMI to increase its stake in KMP. Kinder's personal net worth ballooned to an estimated $1.5 billion, placing him number 336 among the world's wealthiest people according to *Forbes* magazine. His wealth as well as the fortunes of KMI appeared to be bright for the foreseeable future. Because the company was concentrated on fee-based businesses it was not as vulnerable as other energy companies on commodity price swings. Moreover, the prospects for the increased use of natural gas over the next 20 years were solid, as would be the need for new pipeline systems. There also appeared to be many pipelines available for purchase in a highly fragmented industry, enough to feed KMI's voracious appetite for a number of years to come.

Principal Subsidiaries

Kinder Morgan Energy Partners, L.P.; Kinder Morgan Management, LLC.

Principal Competitors

TEPPCO Partners; Western Gas; The Williams Companies, Inc.

Further Reading

Fisher, Daniel, "Sweet Consolation," *Forbes,* September 21, 1998, pp. 144–46.
Greer, Jim, "Piping Hot," *Houston Business Journal,* March 16, 2001, p. 16.
Klann, Susan, "A Competitive Streak," *Oil & Gas Investor,* June 1996, p. 33.

Liesman, Steve, ''Kinder Morgan and KN Energy Agree to Merge,'' *Wall Street Journal,* July 12, 1999, p. A18.

Raabe, Steve, ''Retooling Energizes Kinder Morgan Future,'' *Denver Post,* October 1, 2000, p. M1.

Share, Jeff, ''Kinder Morgan Creates Presence in Pipeline Industry,'' *Pipeline & Gas Journal,* March 2000.

Shook, Barbara, ''KN Boots Chairman, Acquires Kinder Morgan,'' *Oil Daily,* June 12, 1999.

Stavros, Richard, Regina R. Johnson, and Bruce W. Radford, ''Energy Innovators: Ringing in an Age of Enlightenment,'' *Public Utilities Fortnightly,* December 1999, pp. 48–61.

Walsh, Jennifer, ''KN Energy to Buy Out Kinder,'' *Houston Chronicle,* July 9, 1999, p. 1.

—Ed Dinger

KLA-Tencor Corporation

160 Rio Robles
P.O. Box 49055
San Jose, California 95161-9055
U.S.A.
Telephone: (408) 875-3000
Toll Free: (888) 817-9918
Fax: (408) 875-3030
Web site: http://www.kla-tencor.com

Public Company
Incorporated: 1976
Employees: 6,500
Sales: $2.10 billion (2001)
Stock Exchanges: NASDAQ
Ticker Symbol: KLAC
NAIC: 334515 Semiconductor Test Equipment
   Manufacturing

KLA-Tencor Corporation is the global leader in the design, manufacture, and marketing of yield management and process control systems, which are used to reduce defects in semiconductors and related microelectronics. The company's products, software, and services enable semiconductor manufacturers to analyze the various stages of chip manufacture, measure the microscopic layers of the chips, and provide the necessary feedback to correct errors. KLA-Tencor's strongest sales were in Europe and Japan in 2001; only one-third of its products were sold domestically. Although its market niche is relatively small, KLA-Tencor dominates the industry.

Early History

KLA was founded in 1976 by Kenneth Levy and Robert R. Anderson, entrepreneurs and pioneers in California's blossoming Silicon Valley. Levy and Anderson believed that they could use their knowledge of relatively new image processing technologies, as well as their marketing knowhow, to open up completely new segments in the semiconductor industry. During the middle and late 1970s, they went to work developing a first-generation manufacturing inspection system that could be used to improve the chip-making process.

During the semiconductor manufacturing process, multiple layers of material are grown or deposited on the surface of a thin wafer. The wafer is typically composed of silicon or gallium arsenide and is five to eight inches in diameter. A four-step procedure is generally followed: 1) deposition of film on the wafer; 2) impurity doping, when impurities are introduced that control conductivity; 3) lithographic patterning, which creates the geometric features and layout of the circuit; and 4) etching, which removes the film coating material to reveal the layout patterned in the lithographic process. These steps may be repeated numerous times, depending on the complexity of the device, before the semiconductor is separated into individual integrated circuits, or chips. Before the chips are assembled and packaged, a variety of tests may be conducted to weed out defective circuits.

In some cases, fewer than 50 percent (and sometimes fewer than 10 percent for more advanced chips) of the manufactured semiconductors are usable, making the production process for some types of chips extremely expensive and time-consuming. As chips increased in layer number and became smaller and more intricate during the 1970s, moreover, the defect detection problem escalated. Bell and Levy hoped to tap a side of the industry that remained ignored, in large part, even by the late 1970s: inspection equipment that would make defects easier to find and improve chip "yields," thus reducing unnecessary manufacturing costs. The basic concept behind their efforts was to combine advanced optical technology with custom, high-speed digital electronics and proprietary software to replace conventional, rudimentary inspection systems that relied on the human eye and relatively low-tech visual aids.

When Levy and Anderson started KLA, the chip industry was still in its infancy. Bell Laboratories had introduced the solid-state transistor in 1947, but a significant demand for chips had not emerged until the 1960s. Commercial production of semiconductors did not begin on a significant scale until the 1970s. Of importance, Intel Corporation's introduction of the memory integrated circuit in 1971 spawned a plethora of opportunities in the U.S. semiconductor industry, resulting in healthy

Company Perspectives:

KLA-Tencor is committed to meeting the microelectronics industry's need for extremely sophisticated and expertly implemented process control and yield management solutions across the fab. To fulfill this charter, the company has focused on providing a single and comprehensive resource for the full breadth of yield management products and services. Customers benefit from the simplified planning and coordination, as well as the increased equipment compatibility found when dealing with a single supplier.

growth during the middle and late 1970s. That growth also spawned a demand for various complementary technologies, such as plasma etching and optical/image processing, the latter of which was KLA's forte.

KLA's first product was its reticle inspection system, named RAPID, which was introduced in the late 1970s. RAPID utilized advanced optical and image processing technology to test the "stencils" used to print circuit designs onto silicon wafers. Because a defective reticle, or template, can result in millions of ruined die, the system provided an important first step in ensuring high chip yields. RAPID was the first system of its kind to enter the market and was quickly accepted by the semiconductor industry. KLA's RAPID 210e series became the foundation on which KLA built its succeeding product lines. KLA went public in 1980, selling stock to raise cash for marketing its RAPID systems and to generate research and development funds to create new products.

1980s: New Customers and New Products

KLA benefited from a ripe U.S. semiconductor manufacturing industry during the early 1980s, its sales leaping past $60 million by the middle of the decade. Domestic demand, however, began to sputter in the mid-1980s. Although the overall demand for chip-making equipment continued to increase, U.S. producers experienced continually rising pressure from efficient Japanese firms that were dominating the market for high-volume, commodity-like chip manufacturing systems. In fact, Japan increased its share of the world chip machine market from almost nothing in the late 1970s to nearly 50 percent by the late 1980s; U.S. producers supplied most of the remainder of demand. Fortunately for KLA, its systems enjoyed a paucity of competition, allowing it to expand internationally to pull up slack in domestic growth. By 1984, KLA was garnering 22 percent of its sales from Japan and Europe. That figure jumped to more than 40 percent by 1987.

Also bolstering KLA's growth during the mid-1980s was its introduction of the KLA 2000 series in 1984. The 2000 was an automated wafer inspection system, called WISARD, which found defects in wafers and looked for circuitry errors after the reticle pattern had been projected onto the wafer. KLA's WISARD systems represented the second step in ensuring high chip yields. Again, KLA's entry into the market niche was essentially uncontested, allowing it to enjoy almost immediate acceptance by the industry. As sales of 210e and 2000 systems

increased, KLA's revenues steadily climbed to $82.5 million in 1986, $88 million in 1987, and then to a healthy $113 million in 1988, $8.8 million of which was netted as income. Overseas shipments accounted for the lion's share of those gains.

In addition to its WISARD and RAPID lines, KLA introduced automatic test equipment in the late 1980s, which represented the third stage of the inspection process. Its most important product in that category was its wafer probing system, a device that electrically tested completed chips before they were diced and packaged. KLA developed the wafer probe with Tokyo Electronic Corp. (TEL). Another important line of test equipment was KLA's emission microscope, which was used to discover electrical "leakage" between layers of a chip. Although KLA faced competition in the automatic test equipment market, primarily from General Signal Corp., its products were well received and accounted for about 30 percent of KLA's revenues by 1990—WISARD and RAPID each also accounted for about one-third of aggregate sales.

By 1990, KLA's revenues had increased to a whopping $161 million, about $9.5 million of which was net income. In contrast, however, the innovator's stock price had steadily slipped during the late 1980s, reflecting the investment market's lack of faith in KLA. The company's critics cited lagging profit growth and generally poor overall performance compared with earlier growth projections. In fact, KLA did suffer during the semiconductor industry downturn of the late 1980s—it cut its workforce by about 4 percent and implemented salary cuts of up to 15 percent for the company's officers. It also had fallen short in achieving some of its own stated objectives.

On the other hand, KLA was relatively well positioned to take advantage of emerging trends in the chip industry going into the early 1990s. It already controlled about 70 percent of the wafer inspection equipment market and approximately 80 percent of the reticle inspection business. In addition, semiconductors were becoming increasingly complex, pushing the need for automated, high-tech devices that could detect even the most minuscule flaws. Furthermore, Levy and Anderson during the late 1980s had recognized the need for a new type of "in-line" monitoring equipment, which could be integrated as a step in the manufacturing process and provide immediate detection of defects, rather than having to test off-line and wait for results. To exploit the market potential for in-line systems, KLA had made hefty investments in research and development during the late 1980s to improve its existing products and create new equipment lines.

More R&D Investment in the Early 1990s

In the early 1990s, the U.S. semiconductor industry began to rebound, reflecting its newfound productivity and an emphasis on cutting-edge semiconductor manufacturing technologies. As the market picked up, KLA began to introduce the products on which it had been working since the late 1980s, a few of which it had intended to start selling before 1990. Most important, in October 1990 KLA unveiled its second-generation wafer inspection systems, the 2100 series. The new systems, which were designed with in-line capabilities, offered greater sensitivity to defects and operated more than 100 times faster than the popular 2000 series. New and improved systems were added to the 2100 line during the early 1990s, resulting in more than 140

Key Dates:

1976: KLA is founded by Kenneth Levy and Robert R. Anderson.
1980: KLA goes public.
1984: The KLA 2000 series is introduced, including the automated wafer inspection system WISARD.
1990: KLA unveils its second-generation wafer inspection systems, the 2100 series.
1997: KLA agrees to merge with Tencor Instruments, Inc.
2001: Revenues top the $2 billion mark.

orders for 2100 systems by 1993. 2100 systems sold for $1 million to $2 million apiece.

In 1992, KLA updated its RAPID systems with the 300 series, which combined a reticle inspection system with a computer (the 30 Reference Data Computer) to form the KLA 331. The 331 offered the highest inspection sensitivity available in the world and provided numerous speed and flexibility improvements over the original 210e series. It also was designed for potential in-line use. Although initial sales of the new 331 systems were slow because of glitches in bringing them to market, KLA had shipped a total of 700 RAPID systems worldwide by 1993, including deliveries of its first generation systems. The 331 systems sold for $1.7 million to $2.6 million, depending on the options added.

In addition to updating its core WISARD and RAPID product lines, KLA also introduced important new products in its other testing categories. It made improvements to the KLA 5000 series, for example, which was used to increase the yield and performance of final integrated circuit devices. The 5000 series, or metrology line, sold for $300,000 to $550,000 per unit. Similarly, KLA's new SEMspec division brought out its new electron beam imaging systems, which offered improved sensitivity and measuring prowess compared with conventional laser optical systems. KLA also initiated KLA Acrotec Ltd. in the early 1990s, a venture with a Japanese company that used proprietary KLA technology to produce flat-panel displays, such as those utilized by portable computers.

To position itself for expansion in the wake of new product introductions, KLA restructured during the early 1990s. Levy, who had served as president and chief executive of KLA since he had founded it, moved to chairman and allowed Kenneth L. Schroeder to assume control of the company's day-to-day operations. Anderson ceded his position as chief financial officer and was effectively retired from KLA going into the mid-1990s. In 1992, Schroeder reorganized KLA into five operating segments: WRInG, which combined the WISARD and RAPID divisions; the Automated Test Systems Division; the Watcher Division, which encompassed new image processing systems that utilized advanced optical character recognition technology; the Metrology Division; the Customer Service Division; and the SEMSpec Division. He also cut 7 percent of the 1,100 member global workforce and jettisoned KLA's emission microscopy business.

By the early 1990s, KLA was garnering about 60 percent of its total revenues from overseas sales. One of its most important

markets, in fact, was Japan, where demand for yield management equipment was particularly strong. When the U.S. semiconductor industry emerged from its doldrums during the early 1990s, the Japanese industry suffered, as did KLA. Its sales to Japan dropped 9 percent between 1991 and 1993, whereas U.S. shipments climbed only 7 percent. So, although KLA's new systems were well received by the industry, its shipment growth was hindered by a serious downturn in Japan. In addition, delays in bringing some of its new systems to market, particularly the KLA 331, created a temporary dip in order volume. As a result, KLA's total revenues slipped about 8 percent in 1991, to $148 million, before bobbing up to $155 million in 1992 and $167 million in 1993.

KLA continued to pour cash into research and development during the early 1990s in an effort to get its new products to market. In fact, it spent a fat $64 million during 1991 and 1992 (22 percent of revenues). As a result, profits bottomed out in 1992 as KLA posted a depressing $14 million loss. By 1993, however, its major product introductions were almost complete, and the company was able to cut development costs to $24 million (14 percent of sales). Net income climbed to about $7 million.

The real payoff for KLA's hard work during the late 1980s and early 1990s began to occur in 1994. Sales began to rocket skyward early in that year as the global semiconductor industry improved and KLA's new products began to achieve widespread appeal. Significantly, the industry began showing a strong interest in KLA's in-line defect monitoring concept. As it entered the mid-1990s, KLA was ready to capitalize on the industry niche that it controlled and had helped to create. Besides favorable industry and market trends, KLA's strong cash position and paltry debt load would contribute to the company's continued dominance.

The 1997 KLA-Tencor Merger

Well positioned to take advantage of its market's growth, KLA expanded its sales at a healthy rate over the next couple of years. By 1997, the company's revenues approached $600 million. That year, KLA agreed to merge with Tencor Instruments, Inc., in a one-to-one stock swap valued at $1.3 billion. The two companies originally had agreed to merge in 1992 but broke off their agreement early in 1993.

Tencor Instruments was founded in 1976, the same year as KLA. Although they both produced equipment to test semiconductors during manufacture, their product lines focused on different segments of semiconductor production. Tencor's first product, the Alpha-Step stylus surface profiler, improved customers' measurement of set height measurement, a key parameter in measuring film layer thickness. In the early 1980s Tencor developed a particle and contamination detection system. Introduced in 1984, the system was based on laser scanning technology; its success made it one of the company's core products. Tencor continued to invest in research and development, adding defect review and data analysis tools to its product line in the early 1990s.

In 1992, the company had revenues of $57.7 million. Two days after the aborted merger with KLA in January 1993, Tencor announced plans for an initial public offering of stock. With the influx of cash from the IPO, Tencor continued down its path of expansion. In 1994, the company acquired Prometrix Corp., another manufacturer of thin-film measurement systems, for $48 million in stock. The two companies had been jointly developing the Surfscan Swift/Station data analysis system for two years. With 1993 revenues of $35.7 million and 200 employees, Prometrix added significantly to Tencor's 415 employees.

A market slump in 1996 led KLA and Tencor to reconsider merging in order to take advantage of streamlined management and shared development costs. At the time, Tencor had 1,400 employees and revenues of $403 million. KLA boasted 2,500 employees and around $600 million in revenues. Analysts saw the merger as a complementary joining, resulting in a complete line of yield management products and services for semiconductor manufacturers. Gunnar T. Miller at PaineWebber explained in *Electronic News,* "KLA provides high-end automated optical wafer inspection, reticle inspection and other yield learning-targeted tools, while Tencor has focused more on the lower-cost, high-throughput yield monitoring end of process diagnostics." The merger was completed in May 1997, resulting in the newly named KLA-Tencor Corp.

Further Expansion Around the New Millennium

Within a year, the company had produced a new line of products that combined KLA and Tencor's premerger research and equipment. KLA-Tencor also embarked on a spree of acquisitions. The first, in February 1998, was the purchase of Nanopro GmbH, a German-based developer of advanced interferometric technology used in chip measurement. The second, Amray, Inc., sold scanning electron microscopes. In June, KLA-Tencor acquired VARS, Inc., a manufacturer of image archiving and retrieval systems for semiconductor equipment. These acquisitions greatly expanded KLA-Tencor's portfolio of products and added to 1998 revenues of $1.2 billion.

In 1999 KLA-Tencor acquired the assets of the Ultrapointe subsidiary of Uniphase Corp., which made a product that analyzed defects on silicon wafers, and Acme Systems, Inc., a leading supplier of yield analysis software. The same year, leadership at KLA-Tencor was shifted, with Ken Schroeder, president and COO of KLA-Tencor taking over as CEO, and CEO Ken Levy assuming the chairmanship. In 2000, the company announced plans to move its headquarters from San Jose to Livermore, California, where it would construct a six-building complex.

By 2001, KLA-Tencor was the clear leader in the semiconductor test and measurement market, with fiscal 2001 revenues at $2.1 billion. A 40 percent increase over the previous year,

KLA-Tencor's revenues reflected both the company's steady acquisition policy and strong product offerings. Those products, including 19 new metrology systems introduced in the previous year, reflected the company's continued commitment to research and development. KLA-Tencor managed to raise its net income by 74 percent in 2001, despite a downturn in the semiconductor industry, and seemed on track for continued growth and profitability.

Principal Subsidiaries

VLSI Standards, Inc.

Principal Competitors

Advantest Corp.; Teradyne, Inc.; Agilent Technologies, Inc.; Schlumberger Ltd.; LTX Corp.; GenRad, Inc.

Further Reading

Boehlke, Robert J., "Motorola MOS-11 Installs KLA 2110 Wafer Inspection System," *Business Wire,* November 14, 1991.

"KLA Instruments Expects to Post Loss for 1992 Fiscal Year," *Business Wire,* July 9, 1992.

"KLA Reports Operating Results for Fourth-Quarter and Year," *Business Wire,* July 30, 1992.

"KLA-Tencor Acquires Assets of Uniphase Unit," *Electronic News,* January 11, 1999, p. 22.

"KLA-Tencor Buys VARS, Image Management Firm," *Electronic News,* June 29, 1998, p. 36.

"KLA-Tencor Merger Bears Combined Fruit," *Electronic News,* April 6, 1998, p. 34.

"KLA, Tencor to Say 'I Do,' " *Electronic News,* January 20, 1997, p. 1.

"KLA Unveils Yield Management System for In-Line Process Control," *Business Wire,* July 9, 1992.

Lasnier, Guy, "KLA Readies Products for 'New Market Nobody Owns Yet,' " *Business Journal-San Jose,* September 7, 1987, Sec. 1, p. 3.

Moran, Susan, "KLA Instrument Starts Santa Clara Clean Room Expansion," *Business Journal-San Jose,* July 11, 1988, Sec. 1, p. 3.

"Robert R. Anderson Retires As Vice Chairman of KLA Instruments Corp.," *Business Wire,* March 25, 1994.

Savitz, Eric J., "Every Little Bit Helps; Rebound in the Offing for KLA Instruments," *Barron's,* September 24, 1993, pp. 18–19.

"Tencor Agrees to $48M Deal for Prometrix," *Electronic News,* January 3, 1994, p. 5.

"Top 10 Semiconductor Test and Measurement Companies," *Electronic News,* October 8, 2001, p. 26.

—Dave Mote
—update: Susan Windisch Brown

Kraft Foods Inc.

Three Lakes Drive
Northfield, Illinois 60093
U.S.A.
Telephone: (847) 646-2000
Fax: (847) 646-2922
Web site: http://www.kraft.com

Public Company, 83.9-Percent Owned by Philip Morris Companies Inc.

Incorporated: 1989 as Kraft General Foods, Inc.

Employees: 117,000

Sales: $34.7 billion (2000 pro forma)

Stock Exchanges: New York

Ticker Symbol: KFT

NAIC: 311230 Breakfast Cereal Manufacturing; 311320 Chocolate and Confectionery Manufacturing from Cacao Beans; 311330 Confectionery Manufacturing from Purchased Chocolate; 311340 Nonchocolate Confectionery Manufacturing; 311412 Frozen Specialty Food Manufacturing; 311421 Fruit and Vegetable Canning; 311511 Fluid Milk Manufacturing; 311513 Cheese Manufacturing; 311612 Meat Processed from Carcasses; 311821 Cookie and Cracker Manufacturing; 311823 Dry Pasta Manufacturing; 311919 Other Snack Food Manufacturing; 311920 Coffee and Tea Manufacturing; 311911 Roasted Nuts and Peanut Butter Manufacturing; 311941 Mayonnaise, Dressing, and Other Prepared Sauce Manufacturing; 311999 All Other Miscellaneous Food Manufacturing; 312111 Soft Drink Manufacturing

Kraft Foods Inc. is the largest food company in the United States and holds the number two position worldwide, behind Nestlé S.A. The firm has two main operating units—Kraft Foods North America (KFNA; generating 73 percent of 2000 pro forma revenues) and Kraft Foods International (KFI; 27 percent)—and its brands are divided into five main sectors: snacks (30.6 percent of global revenues; 28 percent of KFNA revenues; 38 percent of KFI revenues), beverages (global, 19 percent; KFNA, 13 percent;

KFI, 35 percent), cheese (global, 18 percent; KFNA, 20 percent; KFI, 13 percent), grocery (global, 16.6 percent; KFNA, 19 percent; KFI, 10 percent), and convenient meals (global, 15.8 percent; KFNA, 20 percent; KFI, 4 percent). Seven of Kraft's brands bring in more than $1 billion in revenues each year: Kraft cheeses and other products ($4.3 billion in 2000 revenue), Nabisco cookies and crackers ($3.5 billion), Oscar Mayer processed meats (number one in the United States), Post cereals (number three in the United States), Maxwell House coffee, Philadelphia cream cheeses, and Jacobs coffee (number one in western Europe). More than 60 company brands generate annual revenue in excess of $100 million, including A.1. steak sauce, Altoids candy, Balance energy bars, Cheez Whiz process cheese sauce, Cool Whip whipped toppings, DiGiorno pizza, Freia confectionery, Gevalia coffee, Jell-O desserts, Kool-Aid drink mix, Life Savers candy, Miracle Whip dressing, Oreo cookies, Planters nuts, Premium crackers, Ritz crackers, Stove Top stuffing mix, Tang drink mix, and Toblerone chocolate. The company holds the top global position in 11 product categories: coffee, cookies, crackers, cream cheese, dessert mixes, dry packaged dinners, lunch combinations, powdered soft drinks, process cheese, salad dressings, and snack nuts. Kraft Foods' products are made at more than 220 manufacturing facilities around the world and are sold in more than 140 countries.

The wealth of brands and products owned by the Kraft Foods company of the early 21st century was largely amalgamated under the stewardship of Philip Morris Companies Inc. The diversified tobacco giant's first major push into the food industry came in 1985 when it acquired General Foods Corporation. It next acquired Kraft, Inc. in December 1988, and then in March 1989 Philip Morris combined the two food companies under a new subsidiary called Kraft General Foods, Inc. General Foods and Kraft operated separately until early 1995, when the two units were merged as Kraft Foods. Then in December 2000 Philip Morris purchased Nabisco Holdings Corp., merging it into Kraft Foods. In June 2001 Philip Morris sold 16.1 percent of Kraft Foods to the public, retaining the remaining shares.

Early History of General Foods: The Postum Era

Prior to its acquisition by Philip Morris, General Foods earned a reputation as a pioneer in the acquisition and assimila-

Company Perspectives:

We're there at breakfast, lunch and dinner, and anytime in between. You can find our brands at a French hypermarket, in a vending machine in Japan, or in any American grocery store.

Around the globe, in 140 countries, our 117,000 employees are dedicated to bringing the world its favorite foods. Brands like Kraft, Jacobs, Philadelphia, Maxwell House, Nabisco, Oscar Mayer *and* Post.

Our company is built on a history of quality and innovation that dates back literally hundreds of years. Over that time, Kraft Foods has grown from modest beginnings to become the second largest food and beverage company in the world. But no matter what our size, we've never lost sight of why we're here—to help make food a simpler, easier, more enjoyable part of life.

tion of smaller food companies and built a huge multinational, multiproduct corporation. The groundwork for General Foods was laid by Charles W. Post, a health enthusiast who tried to tempt America's coffee drinkers away from the caffeinic drink with a cereal beverage he called Postum. Post built the company that would become General Foods with a number of promising products and the marvel of modern marketing.

In 1891 Post checked into the Kellogg brothers' renowned sanitarium in Battle Creek, Michigan, in hopes of revitalizing his frail health. Post, ill for several years, was weak and confined to a wheelchair. The stay proved propitious; while at the Kelloggs' sanitarium, Post came up with several ideas that would eventually be profitable.

Post later opened the La Vita Inn in Battle Creek, where he experimented with healing through mental suggestion and special diets. A few years later Post began marketing a cereal beverage similar to the one he had received as a coffee substitute at the Kelloggs'. He began marketing this blend of wheat, bran, and molasses called Postum cereal beverage in 1895. Post incorporated the Postum Cereal Company, Ltd. in 1896 with a paid-in capital of $100,000.

In 1897 Post introduced a new cereal, made from whole wheat and malted barley flour, called Grape-Nuts. The product was baked for 20 hours, turning the starch into dextrose and creating an easily digested cereal. In 1904 Post marketed a corn flake cereal under the name ''Elijah's Manna.'' Not immediately successful, the new cereal was renamed ''Post Toasties'' and subsequently became a big hit with American consumers. Post continued to bring new products to the market, including Post's bran flakes, Post's bran chocolate bar, and Post's wheat meal.

Within five years of its incorporation, Postum Cereal Company's capital had risen to $5 million. The company's Battle Creek facility was the largest of its kind in the world. Postum employed 2,500 people and its factories covered more than 20 acres. Charles W. Post had amassed a personal fortune and spent his money freely to propagate his own views. Post was an outspoken critic of closed shops and labor unions, spending thousands on advertisements attacking organized labor. This crusade against unions resulted in occasional boycotts of Post

products and incurred the personal enmity of union organizers throughout the nation. Carroll Post once told an interesting tale about his brother Charles in a letter. One day the two Post brothers sat at a lunchroom counter where two brands of corn flakes—Post Toasties and Krinkle—were for sale. While the two men were eating, a railroad worker came in and asked for corn flakes. When the waitress asked which brand he wanted, the man said, ''give me Krinkle. That man Post is always fighting our union.'' But the Posts had the last laugh: Krinkle was merely another name for Post Toasties, marketed as a reduced-price corn flake.

Despite Post's stance against organized labor, the Postum Cereal Company did not have trouble with labor in its own factories. It paid the highest wages in the industry, emphasized safe working conditions, and implemented accident and sickness benefit programs. The company also built about 100 homes for its workers which were sold on very favorable terms.

In May 1914, Charles W. Post committed suicide at his winter home in Santa Barbara, California. The day-to-day operations of the Postum Cereal Company had been run by a group of managers—C.W.'s ''cabinet''—for several years. Upon his death, Post's daughter, Marjorie Merriwether Post, took over the company and helped launch the expansion that would create the company known as General Foods.

Marjorie Post was well acquainted with the Postum business. She had often accompanied her father on business trips and frequently sat in on meetings. In 1920 she married Edward F. Hutton, an investment broker. Two years later the Postum Cereal Company went public, and Marjorie Post stepped down from active management of the company. Her husband, who became chairman of the company in 1923, and Colby M. Chester, who became president in 1924, ran the company's day-to-day operations. Marjorie remained a key policymaker, however, and was critical to the company's acquisition strategy and transition into General Foods.

That transition began in 1925 with the acquisition of the Jell-O Company. Before frozen pies, cakes, and novelties entered the market, Jell-O was the premier dessert brand. In 1926 the company absorbed Swans Down cake flour and Minute tapioca. Baker's coconut, Baker's chocolate, and Log Cabin syrup were acquired in 1927. The company also shortened its name to Postum Company that year.

Late 1920s: The Emergence of General Foods

In 1928 the Postum Company acquired Maxwell House Coffee, whose roots dated back to 1892 when Joel Cheek perfected the coffee blend served at the famous Maxwell House hotel in Nashville, Tennessee. President Theodore Roosevelt visited Nashville in 1907 and was served Maxwell House coffee. When asked if he wanted a second cup of coffee, Roosevelt answered, ''Yes, indeed, it's good to the last drop.'' This reply became the company's famous slogan.

In 1929 the Postum Company made another significant acquisition when it paid $22 million for a controlling interest of the General Foods Company, owned by Clarence Birdseye. Birdseye perfected new techniques for freezing vegetables and meat. An adventurer by nature, Birdseye had gotten the idea for his freezing technique while on an expedition to Labrador.

Key Dates:

1896: Charles W. Post incorporates Postum Cereal Company, Ltd., having introduced Postum cereal beverage the previous year.

1897: Postum introduces a new cereal called Grape-Nuts.

1898: American Biscuit Company and New York Biscuit Company merge to form the National Biscuit Company (N.B.C.).

1903: James L. Kraft establishes a wholesale cheese distribution business in Chicago.

1909: J.L. Kraft & Bros. Company is incorporated.

1912: N.B.C. launches the Oreo cookie.

1914: Kraft opens its first cheese factory.

1922: Postum Cereal goes public.

1924: Kraft & Bros. changes its name to Kraft Cheese Company and goes public.

1925: Postum begins diversifying with acquisition of the Jell-O Company.

1927: Postum acquires Baker's chocolate and shortens its name to Postum Company.

1928: Postum acquires Maxwell House coffee; Kraft merges with Phenix Cheese Corporation, maker of Philadelphia Brand cream cheese; Kraft introduces Velveeta process cheese spread; N.B.C. acquires Shredded Wheat Company.

1929: Postum acquires controlling interest in Clarence Birdseye's General Foods Company; Postum changes its name to General Foods Corporation; Fleischmann Company, Chase & Sanborn, and the Royal Baking Powder Company merge to form Standard Brands.

1930: Kraft is acquired by National Dairy Products Corporation but continues to operate independently.

1933: Kraft introduces Miracle Whip salad dressing.

1934: Ritz crackers are launched by N.B.C.

1937: The Kraft macaroni and cheese dinner debuts.

1941: The letters "N.B.C." in National Biscuit's official trademark are replaced by the word "Nabisco."

1945: Kraft changes its name to Kraft Foods Company.

1953: General Foods acquires Perkins Products, maker of Kool-Aid powdered beverage mixes.

1956: National Dairy begins centralizing its operations, transforming Kraft from subsidiary to division.

1961: Standard Brands acquires Planters Nut & Chocolate Co.

1969: National Dairy renames itself Kraftco Corporation.

1971: National Biscuit changes its name to Nabisco, Inc.

1976: Kraftco is renamed Kraft, Inc.

1980: Kraft merges with Dart Industries Inc., forming Dart & Kraft Inc., with Kraft continuing to operate independently as a subsidiary.

1981: General Foods acquires Oscar Mayer & Co.; Nabisco and Standard Brands merge to form Nabisco Brands, Inc.; Nabisco Brands acquires the Life Savers Company.

1985: Philip Morris Companies Inc. acquires General Foods; R.J. Reynolds acquires Nabisco Brands, forming RJR Nabisco, Inc. and its food unit, Nabisco Foods Group.

1986: Dart & Kraft is demerged into Kraft, Inc. (the food operations plus Duracell batteries) and Premark International (the remaining operations).

1988: Kraft sells Duracell; Philip Morris acquires Kraft.

1989: Philip Morris combines General Foods and Kraft under a new holding company called Kraft General Foods, Inc.—although the two units continue to operate separately; Kraft General Foods International is also established; Kohlberg Kravis Roberts gains control of RJR Nabisco through a leveraged buyout; RJR Nabisco sells its European cookie and cracker business to BSN.

1990: Kraft General Foods International acquires Jacobs Suchard AG; RJR Nabisco sells its Asia-Pacific operations to Britannia Brands.

1991: RJR Nabisco goes public as RJR Nabisco Holdings Corp.

1993: Jacobs Suchard acquires Freia Marabou a.s., the top Scandinavian confectioner; Kraft General Foods acquires RJR Nabisco Holdings' cold cereal business, including Shredded Wheat; Kraft General Foods divests its ice cream business and its BirdsEye frozen vegetables brand; RJR Nabisco launches the Snackwells line of low-fat cookies and crackers.

1994: Kraft General Foods sells off its foodservice unit.

1995: Major restructuring melds Kraft and General Foods into Kraft Foods, Inc.; Kraft General Foods International is renamed Kraft Foods International, Inc. and becomes a subsidiary of Kraft Foods, Inc.; Kraft sells its bakery division to CPC International.

1998: RJR Nabisco sells its margarine and egg substitute business to ConAgra.

1999: Following the divestment of its tobacco operations, RJR Nabisco changes its name to Nabisco Group Holdings Corp.; the company's sole asset is its 80 percent stake in the Nabisco food unit, now known as Nabisco Holdings Corp.

2000: Philip Morris acquires Nabisco Holdings for $18.9 billion and begins integrating the Nabisco operations into Kraft.

2001: Philip Morris sells a 16.1 percent stake in Kraft Foods Inc. to the public.

Birdseye noted that the Eskimos routinely froze caribou and fish, and that these products retained their flavor even when stored for months before thawing. He hypothesized that the bitterly cold air contributed to fresh taste and this method might be superior to the commonly practiced slower freezing. Birdseye returned in 1917 to begin research and eventually perfected a process that could be used commercially. In 1924

Birdseye founded the General Seafoods Company in Gloucester, Massachusetts.

Marjorie Merriwether Post had noticed Birdseye's operations in 1926, but it took her three more years to convince Postum executives to acquire the company. The price had increased tenfold in that time, but Postum nevertheless happily acquired the company. The enlarged Postum Company also adopted the name General Foods Corporation in 1929, and Clarence Birdseye became head of the new General Foods laboratory, where he continued his work on frozen foods.

While the Great Depression affected all parts of the economy, food was a relatively stable industry. After record profits in 1929, General Foods spent its energy in 1930 on consolidating its recent acquisitions. As a result, earnings dropped slightly that year. In 1932 the company acquired the remaining 49 percent of General Foods. It expanded quickly, adding six new plants that year to freeze nearly 100 different products. In 1932 General Foods also purchased the Sanka Coffee Corporation, makers of decaffeinated coffee. General Foods had been distributing Sanka since 1927 through an agreement with the company's European owners.

General Foods' earnings, which had reached $19.4 million in 1929, dropped to $10.3 million in 1932. In 1933, however, they began to rise again as consumer purchasing power strengthened. In 1935 E.F. Hutton resigned as chairman of the company and C.M. Chester assumed the post, where he remained until 1946. Marjorie Post returned to the company as a director the next year, a position she retained until 1958.

During World War II, General Foods, like other food companies, achieved record sales, despite food shortages and other wartime exigencies. Sales in 1943 were more than double those of 1929. During the war, the company's Denver plant produced ten-in-one rations for the U.S. Army. General Foods also began developing an instant coffee for the army in 1941. In 1943 General Foods acquired the Gaines Dog Food Company, and the next year it added Yuban premium coffee to its already strong coffee line. Instant Maxwell House coffee—one of the first postwar consumer products—was introduced in 1946.

Postwar Era: International Expansion and Short-Lived Diversification

In May 1953, General Foods acquired the Perkins Products Company of Chicago. Perkins manufactured a variety of powdered beverage mixes to which the consumer added sugar and water for a fruit-flavored drink. Kool-Aid has been a favorite of kids across the nation ever since. Years later General Foods added a number of other products to its beverage division, including Tang, Country Time, and sugar free Crystal Light. In 1954 the company entered the salad dressing market with its purchase of the Hollywood manufacturer 4 Seasons, Inc., and in 1960 Open Pit barbecue sauce was acquired.

Acquisitions of established companies continued as General Foods diversified outside of the food industry. In 1957 the company bought the SOS Company, a leading scouring-pad manufacturer. Ten years later, however, the Federal Trade Commission ruled that the acquisition violated antitrust laws and forced General Foods to sell the company. In 1968 General Foods entered the fast-food business by purchasing the Burger Chef chain for more than $15 million. In December 1969, General Foods added the Viviane Woodard Cosmetic Corporation, a door-to-door operation, for $39 million. The following year, toy company Kohner Brothers and the nation's largest seed company, W. Atlee Burpee Company, were both acquired.

Because General Foods did not have as much luck with its nonfood subsidiaries as it did with food businesses, it disposed of most of them. Kohner Brothers was sold to Gabriel Industries after just five years; the Viviane Woodard cosmetics business was closed in 1975; Burpee was sold in 1979; and, after consistently losing money, the Burger Chef chain was sold in 1982.

In the late 1950s and early 1960s General Foods aggressively branched out into international markets. In 1956 the company acquired a controlling interest in the La India Company, Venezuela's number one chocolate company. In 1959 the company's Canadian subsidiary purchased the Hostess snack-food company of Canada; in 1960 it purchased the Kibon ice cream company of Brazil and the French coffee-roaster Etablessements Pierre Lemonnier S.A.; in 1961 it bought Krema Hollywood Chewing Gum Company S.A. of Paris; and General Foods of Mexico S.A. was formed in 1962. Numerous other food processors throughout the world were purchased as well. At the end of the decade General Foods had major subsidiaries operating in Canada, the United Kingdom, Australia, France, Mexico, Brazil, Venezuela, Denmark, Sweden, Spain, and Italy.

By the mid-1960s General Foods was an established giant in the industry. Chairman C.W. Cook, who took over in 1965, ran a company whose outstanding successes were based on new product development, sweeping market research, and enormous advertising budgets.

During the 1970s international acquisitions continued at a furious pace, but domestic operations settled down a bit. Frozen foods became increasingly popular as more double-income families found less time to cook and had extra cash for quick meals. The company's BirdsEye frozen-food division also enjoyed a boost in earnings. But not all of General Foods units benefited from such favorable demographic changes. Jell-O, for example, suffered as new products such as frozen novelty desserts came to the market. In 1979 the Jell-O unit pushed to recapture the dessert market, employing an advertising campaign to reverse Jell-O's steady decline. In the early 1980s the company introduced Jell-O Pudding Pops—frozen pudding on a stick—to capitalize on its well-known name and expand its share of the market.

Nonetheless, at the end of the 1970s General Foods was not performing up to expectations. The company was overly dependent on coffee for its revenues—its various coffee brands accounted for 39 percent of General Foods' entire revenues in 1980.

1980s: Oscar Mayer and the Philip Morris Takeover of General Foods

In 1981 General Foods made its largest acquisition to date when it bought Oscar Mayer & Co., the leading American hot dog maker, for $470 million. Oscar Mayer, founded in 1883 by a Bavarian immigrant, was a family-held company until the purchase and had a reputation for high-quality products. General Foods was trying to reduce its dependence on the coffee trade, but Wall Street critics charged that with the purchase of Oscar Mayer, the company was opening itself up to the wildly cyclical, low-margin packaged-meat business.

Regardless, the merger did give General Foods access to an extensive refrigerated supply network. In addition, the acquisition afforded General Foods a high profile in the refrigerated meat section at the supermarket—Oscar Mayer was the largest national brand of lunch meats, and its Louis Rich turkey products unit was top in that growing segment of the market.

In 1984 the company agreed to sell its Gaines Pet Food division for $157 million. General Foods' overall performance went down as coffee sales dipped, and the Post Cereals unit, too, began to slide.

In November 1985 Philip Morris Companies Inc. purchased General Foods for $5.6 billion. Philip Morris had long been known as an aggressive marketer. Its chairman, Hamish Maxwell, planned to turn around General Foods and, at the same time, decrease Philip Morris's reliance on the shrinking tobacco market. In January 1987, Philip Smith became CEO of General Foods. Smith began a massive reorganization of the company in 1987, splitting its three core product lines—coffees, meats, and assorted groceries—into separate units. The following year, General Foods' Oscar Mayer division introduced Lunchables, a line of convenient meals that featured meat, cheese, and crackers. Meantime, Philip Morris acquired Kraft, Inc. in 1986, which led to the 1989 combining of General Foods and Kraft under Kraft General Foods, Inc.

Early History of Kraft

One of Kraft, Inc.'s primary predecessor companies was established by James L. Kraft, the son of a Canadian farmer. In 1903 Kraft started a wholesale cheese distribution business in Chicago. Kraft hoped to relieve grocers of the need to travel daily to the cheese market by delivering cheese to their doors. Business was dismal at first, and it was later reported that Kraft lost $3,000 and his horse the first year.

But the business eventually took hold and James was joined by his four brothers, Fred, Charles, Norman, and John. In 1909 the business was incorporated as J.L. Kraft & Bros. Company. New product development and innovative advertising fueled the company's growth. As early as 1911, Kraft mailed circulars to retail grocers and advertised on elevated trains and billboards. Later, he was among the first to use color advertisements in national magazines. In 1912 Kraft opened a New York office to develop an international business. By 1914 the company sold 31 varieties of cheese throughout the country, and that year it opened its own cheese factory in Stockton, Illinois.

Before the advent of refrigeration, cheese was sold in large wheels which spoiled quickly after being cut open. Kraft developed a blended, pasteurized cheese that did not spoil and could be packaged in small tins. Kraft began producing what it called process cheese in 1915 and received a patent in 1916. Six million pounds of this cheese were sold to the U.S. Army during World War I.

In 1919 Kraft placed its first advertisements in national magazines. The next year, Kraft acquired a Canadian cheese company. In 1924 Kraft's name was changed to Kraft Cheese Company and the company offered its shares to the public. That year Kraft also opened its first overseas sales office, in London, which led to the establishment of Kraft Cheese Company Ltd. there in 1927. The same year Kraft moved into Germany by opening a sales office in Hamburg. In 1928 Kraft merged with Phenix Cheese Corporation, the maker of Philadelphia Brand cream cheese. The newly formed Kraft-Phenix Cheese Corporation had captured 40 percent of the nation's cheese market by 1930 and boasted operations in Canada, Australia, Britain, and Germany.

1929–80: Kraft's National Dairy Era

The 1920s spawned another growing dairy concern, the National Dairy Products Corporation, whose fortunes were soon to be linked with Kraft-Phenix. National Dairy was the product of a 1923 merger between the Hydrox Corporation of Chicago, an ice cream company established in 1881 and purchased in 1914 by pharmacist Thomas McInnerney, and the Rieck-McJunkin Dairy Company of Pittsburgh. Throughout the remainder of the 1920s, National Dairy acquired other small dairy concerns in the East and Midwest, including the Breyer Ice Cream Company and Breakstone Bros., Inc., the sour cream and cottage cheese company. In 1929 National Dairy set out to acquire Kraft-Phenix. The merger was completed on May 12, 1930. The group of companies assembled by McInnerney prior to the Kraft-Phenix merger eventually formed the core of Kraft's Dairy Group.

The merger did not radically affect the way in which the two companies operated. McInnerney's strategy had always been to provide essentially autonomous subsidiaries with the resources needed for growth. Consequently, Kraft functioned independently from New York-based National Dairy, which acted primarily as a holding company.

After the merger, Kraft settled down to introduce many of the brands that later formed the heart of its consumer product line; Velveeta pasteurized process cheese spread had been introduced in 1928; Miracle Whip salad dressing and Kraft caramels came in 1933; the famous macaroni and cheese dinner in 1937; and Parkay margarine in 1940. Again, innovative advertising— this time on radio—encouraged quick public acceptance of the new products. In 1933 the company sponsored the "Kraft Musical Revue," a two-hour musical variety show. Later the program was shortened to one hour and was broadcast weekly as the "Kraft Music Hall," hosted by Bing Crosby. Overseas operations expanded, guided by a policy that mandated local control and products tailored to meet the needs and tastes of foreign consumers. Meanwhile, in 1935, National Dairy introduced Sealtest ice cream, named after a quality-control system for its dairy products.

Kraft was a major food supplier during World War II. By the end of 1941, four million pounds of cheese were shipped to Britain weekly. Many Kraft products, including field rations of cheese, were produced for the U.S. government. Kraft's labs researched better methods of food production while home economists at Kraft Kitchens, a division established in the home economics department in 1924, developed recipes to ease wartime shortages.

In 1945 the Kraft Cheese Company became Kraft Foods Company. In the postwar years, Kraft resumed the formula of new product development and advertising that had helped build the company. In 1947 Kraft created and sponsored the first commercial network program on television, the *Kraft Televi-*

sion Theatre. Along with the new advertising vehicle new products, such as sliced process cheese in 1950 and Cheez Whiz pasteurized process cheese spread in 1952, were introduced.

In 1951 the postwar economic boom drove National Dairy's sales over the $1 billion mark for the first time. Thomas McInnerney died in 1952 and J.L. Kraft died the following year. Kraft's death marked the end of the Kraft family's leadership of the business. National Dairy began to reorganize along more centralized lines soon after its founders died. The autonomous subsidiaries became divisions of a single operating company in 1956 and 1957. Meanwhile, the company took its first cautious steps toward diversification with the acquisition of Metro Glass, a maker of glass packaging, in 1956.

During the late 1950s and the 1960s, Kraft continued to expand its product line, adding new products such as jellies and preserves in 1956, ''jet-puffed'' marshmallows in 1959, barbecue sauce in 1960, and individually wrapped cheese slices in 1965. During the 1960s, Kraft also introduced many of its products in foreign markets.

In 1969 National Dairy renamed itself Kraftco Corporation and in 1972 it transferred its headquarters from New York to the Chicago suburb of Glenview. The company name changed in 1976 to Kraft Inc. to emphasize the company's focus on food processing and to more clearly identify it with the internationally known Kraft trademark. Reorganization accompanied the name change; the movement toward a more centralized structure—begun in the 1950s—was accomplished by partitioning the company into divisions according to specific markets or products.

Kraft manifested a decidedly conservative business strategy during the 1970s. Unlike other major food companies, Kraft did not seek acquisitions to shore up sagging profits. New product introductions also slowed somewhat; after the introduction of Light n' Lively yogurt and ice milk in 1969, squeezable Parkay margarine came in 1973 and Breyers yogurt in 1977. The difficult business climate of the 1970s may have encouraged a defensive posture as inflation increased costs and cut into profits.

John M. Richman, who began at Kraft as a lawyer at National Dairy Products, became Kraft's chairman and CEO in 1979. Richman planned to strengthen the company's position in its traditional markets while diversifying into higher-growth industries. His first move—a truly bold stroke—was a merger with Dart Industries Inc., a Los Angeles-based conglomerate headed by the flamboyant Justin Dart.

1980–86: The Dart & Kraft Era

Dart Industries was established in 1902 as United Drug Company. Justin Dart began his career in the retail drug business and built Rexall Drugs into one of the largest chains of drugstores in the country. With Rexall as his base, Dart began an aggressive acquisition campaign, diversifying into chemicals, plastics, glass, cosmetics, electric appliances, and land development. In 1969 the company name was changed to Dart Industries to reflect this diversity. At the time of the merger, the flagship of Dart Industries was its successful Tupperware subsidiary that sold plastic food containers through direct sales by independent dealers using a ''home party'' plan.

The aggressive, innovative, and rapidly growing Dart Industries fit perfectly into Richman's plan; it offered Kraft instant diversification. The merger also offered advantages for Dart and his company. Richman's boldness appealed to Dart, who thought that Kraft would give Dart Industries some stability. Thus, Dart & Kraft Inc. was launched on September 25, 1980, with Richman as its chairman and CEO and Justin Dart as chairman of the executive committee. Kraft and the subsidiaries of Dart—Tupperware, West Bend appliances, Duracell batteries, Wilsonart plastics, and Thatcher glass—continued to operate independently. Some analysts, however, doubted that such a diverse company would succeed.

As in many restructurings, there were some early rough spots, but major changes in operating procedure were confined to top managers. Middle managers were left in their familiar roles to ease the transition. Altogether, management apparently succeeded in unifying two very different firms with a minimum of friction.

Industry analysts, nonetheless, felt compelled to ask which partner would dominate the merger. Although Kraft was the larger of the two companies, the consensus was that the more aggressive and growth-oriented Dart would be the dominant party. The reasoning was that Dart had been given preference in the new company's name and it was Kraft's desire to become more like Dart that initially led to the merger. On the first anniversary of the merger, Richman himself commented that ''in terms of organization and outlook, we're more a Dart than a Kraft.''

Indeed, Dart & Kraft's initial activities bore out this assessment. Soon after the merger, the company bid $460 million for the Hobart Corporation, a manufacturer of foodservice equipment. The deal was completed in April 1981. Even while the Hobart deal was being negotiated, Dart & Kraft announced that it was considering further acquisitions.

Although several smaller acquisitions followed in the next two years, diversification slowed because several subsidiaries experienced managerial problems or proved vulnerable to the recession of the early 1980s. Poor performers included Kraft's European operations and its foodservice business, and Dart's plastics unit and its West Bend appliances. Even Hobart was troubled by sagging profits and declining market share in its Kitchen Aid division, which produced top-of-the-line kitchen appliances. Company efforts to get these businesses back on track were beginning to show results when trouble struck Tupperware.

Tupperware had been a phenomenal success; it doubled sales and earnings every five years prior to 1980. But in 1983 sales slipped 7 percent and profits were down 15 percent. Tupperware's slide was attributed to attrition among its dealers—as more women took jobs outside the home, there were fewer people to sell and buy Tupperware.

In 1984 the company planned to increase returns from 13.3 percent to 18 percent, and thus place Dart & Kraft in the top fifth of the consumer-products industry. This ambitious goal was to be attained by adding new products, extending existing lines, and using aggressive marketing and advertising.

Michael A. Miles, the man who had revived Kentucky Fried Chicken, was brought in to direct the new effort. Miles first cut costs by overhauling the European division. Many of Kraft's brands competed in mature markets. Additions to these lines—for example, bacon and cream cheese-flavored salad dressings—boosted sales. The company also acquired promising new brands that appealed to the upscale consumer. Among these were the import-style cheeses of Churny Company, Inc., Celestial Seasonings herb teas, Lender's bagels, and Frusen Glädjé premium ice cream.

The company pursued similar tactics in Dart & Kraft's nonfood businesses, but when sales continued to lag into 1986, the company decided, in effect, to dissolve the six-year-old merger. Hobart, Tupperware, Wilsonart, and West Bend were spun off into a new company called Premark International, Inc. Kraft, Inc. retained all of the product lines it had brought to the 1980 merger and also gained Duracell batteries.

Kraft followed through on its plan to expand its product lines and market them aggressively, a strategy that won visible gains. The company's management seemed to have rediscovered J.L. Kraft's approach that combined the stability of well-known brand names with creative marketing and the continuous development of new products aimed at changing American tastes. In 1988 Kraft also became a pure food company once again when it sold off Duracell.

Late 1980s and Early 1990s: Philip Morris and the Kraft General Foods Era

Philip Morris's designs on the packaged-foods industry became clear when the company purchased Kraft in December 1988 for $12.9 billion. In March 1989 Philip Morris merged the Kraft and General Foods units into one giant entity called Kraft General Foods, Inc. Initially, the subsidiary was divided into seven major groups: General Foods USA, Kraft USA, Kraft General Foods International, Kraft General Foods Canada, Oscar Mayer, Kraft General Foods Frozen Products, and Kraft General Foods Commercial Products. At the helm was Kraft's Michael Miles.

As a result of the merger, the company became the largest food marketer in the United States. Profits at Kraft General Foods grew at an average rate of more than 20 percent in its first two years. Early on, the company's size proved to be a competitive advantage; it saved $400 million through initial consolidations and its purchasing power multiplied. Size had its drawbacks, however. The company was slow to respond to demand in some markets. For example, Kraft waited until 1990 to introduce Touch of Butter, well after other food producers responded to the public's growing concern about excess cholesterol. Tensions existed between the Kraft and General Foods forces within the company as well. One notable failure during this period was Kraft microwave entrees, originally developed by General Foods, but marketed under the Kraft name as a result of internal politics. The product was discontinued after only six months.

On the international front, Kraft General Foods International acquired Jacobs Suchard AG in August 1990 for $4.2 billion. Based in Switzerland, Jacobs Suchard was a leading European maker of coffee and confectionery products. Its key brands included Carte Noire, Grand Mere, and Jacobs coffee and Suchard, Milka, Toblerone, and Cote d'Or chocolates. Backed by the deep pockets of Philip Morris, Jacobs Suchard began an acquisitions spree, with a number of the purchases taking place in the newly opened markets of central and eastern Europe. The largest acquisition by Jacobs Suchard during this period, however, was the 1993 purchase of Freia Marabou a.s., the leading Scandinavian confectionery maker, for $1.3 billion. Later in 1993 Jacobs Suchard was merged with Kraft General Foods Europe to form Kraft Jacobs Suchard AG.

In 1991 Miles became CEO of Philip Morris. He was replaced at Kraft General Foods by Richard Mayer, who had previously headed General Foods USA. The company's sales in the North American market grew only 1 percent in 1991. Several of the company's most important product categories lost market share that year, including cheese, processed meats, and frozen dinners. In the $5.2 billion retail cheese market, Kraft General Foods' drop to 42 percent control cost the company approximately $125 million in profits. The company's Oscar Mayer line of processed meat products was hurt by the rising tide of health-consciousness among consumers. To combat this trend, healthier-sounding items such as ''light'' bologna and turkey bacon were introduced. In addition, close to 300 products with lagging sales were eliminated. Demand for Louis Rich processed turkey products was slipping as well. Kraft General Foods responded by closing its Tulare, California, plant, thus cutting the payroll by more than 1,000 employees. Another market share loser was BirdsEye frozen vegetables, which fell behind Pillsbury's Green Giant brand in share of sales.

An area in which Kraft General Foods achieved positive results in 1991 was in its Post cereal unit. Honey Bunches of Oats, introduced in 1989 (when Post registered an all-time low market share of 10.9 percent), snared 1 percent of the $7.5 billion breakfast cereal market by 1991. This was the company's first gain in that area in more than ten years. Coffee also performed well for Kraft General Foods in 1991. During the year the Maxwell House brand regained market leadership over Procter & Gamble's Folgers.

In 1992 KGF Marketing Services was formed. The purpose of this unit was to assist in coordinating marketing strategies and bridge the gaps between the different operating units. Late in 1992 the operating units of Kraft General Foods were realigned. The company eliminated two of its seven original operating groups, KGF Frozen Products and Oscar Mayer Foods. The two units were folded into Kraft USA and General Foods USA. In November 1993 came the launch of yet another restructuring, this one designed to eliminate 14,000 jobs and close 40 plants worldwide.

In addition to these restructurings, Kraft General Foods in the mid-1990s added to and subtracted from its array of operations. In January 1993 the firm completed the $450 million purchase of RJR Nabisco Holdings Corp.'s cold cereal business, gaining the Shredded Wheat and Shreddies products. Seeking to jettison low-margin product lines and businesses, Kraft General Foods completed four major divestitures. The company sold its ice cream business, including the Sealtest and Breyers brands, to Unilever in 1993 for about $215 million.

That same year it sold the BirdsEye frozen vegetables brand to Dean Foods Company for $140 million. A further pullback from the frozen food sector came in December 1994 when the All American Gourmet Company, maker of Budget Gourmet frozen meals and side dishes, was sold to H.J. Heinz Company for about $300 million. In early 1995 Kraft General Foods sold its foodservice unit to buyout firm Clayton Dubilier & Rice Inc. for about $700 million.

1995–2000: Restructuring As Kraft Foods, Inc.

With the financial results of Kraft General Foods continuing to disappoint and under criticism for moving too slowly to integrate the operations of Kraft and General Foods, the management was shaken up in late 1994. Mayer unexpectedly took early retirement and was replaced as head of Kraft General Foods by James M. Kilts, who had been in charge of Kraft USA. Kilts moved quickly to engineer a turnaround, launching a major restructuring—the fourth since 1989—in early 1995. Kraft USA and General Foods USA—along with Kraft General Foods Canada—were merged into a single organization called Kraft Foods, Inc., which also became the main Philip Morris food subsidiary, replacing Kraft General Foods, Inc. Kraft General Foods International was renamed Kraft Foods International, Inc. and became a subsidiary of Kraft Foods, Inc.

Continuing the drive to improve margins, Kraft Foods in October 1995 sold its low-margin bakery division to CPC International Inc. for $865 million in cash. The division's brands included Entenmann's and Freihofer's sweet baked products, Oroweat and Freihofer's breads, and Boboli Italian pizza crusts. Other divestments in 1995 included Kraft marshmallows, sold to Favorite Brands International Inc.; and the North American tablespreads business, which included the Parkay brand of margarine and was sold to RJR Nabisco. Kraft sold Lender's bagels in 1996 and the Log Cabin syrup brand in 1997. On the product launch side, Kraft had one of its biggest successes in years with the debut of DiGiorno Rising Crust pizza, which featured an uncooked crust that rises when baked and that many consumers felt taster fresher than the hard, flat crusts that were typical of most frozen pizza.

Kraft also made some selective acquisitions in the later years of the 1990s, picking up, for example, the license for the Taco Bell line of Mexican grocery products in 1996. By 1997 margins had improved to 17 percent, a significant improvement over the 12 percent level of 1994. During 1998 Kraft entered into a long-term licensing agreement with Starbucks Corporation, whereby Kraft would market and distribute Starbucks whole bean and ground coffee into grocery, warehouse club, and mass merchandise stores. During the early months of 2000, Kraft Foods added two brands in the fast-growing healthful food sector: Balance Bar energy and nutritional snack products and Boca Burger soy-based "meat alternative" products. The $358 million that was spent for these two brands was chump change, however, compared to the $18.9 billion spent by Philip Morris to acquire Nabisco Holdings Corp. in December 2000.

Brief History of Nabisco

The origins of Nabisco date back to the late 19th century, when a series of mergers took place in the American baking industry. The culmination of decades of amalgamation was the 1898 merger of the midwestern American Biscuit Company with the eastern New York Biscuit Company, forming the National Biscuit Company, which was usually called N.B.C. in its early years. With 114 bakeries and a capital of $55 million, the Chicago-based N.B.C. held a virtual monopoly on cookie and cracker manufacturing in the United States. Among the initial brands held were Fig Newtons and Premium Saltine crackers.

Adolphus Green was the chief engineer of the 1898 merger and was chairman of the company until his death in 1917. Green was responsible for N.B.C.'s legendary emphasis on standardized, brand-name products. To help launch the new company, Green introduced a new line of soda crackers called Uneeda Biscuits packaged in special protective containers—small cardboard boxes lined with waxed paper to retain freshness; previously, crackers had been sold in bulk from cracker barrels or large crates. The new product was an enormous hit, with sales surpassing 100 million packages by 1900.

National Biscuit introduced other new products in its early years: Barnum's Animal Crackers in 1902 and both Lorna Doones and Oreos in 1912. The latter eventually became the world's best-selling cookie. N.B.C. moved its headquarters from Chicago to New York in 1906.

The company prospered greatly during the 1920s. It established its first foreign subsidiary, in Canada, in 1925. Through acquisitions, the product line was expanded to include pretzels, breakfast cereal, and ice cream cones. The most important purchase was that of the Shredded Wheat Company, completed in 1928 for $35 million. In addition to Shredded Wheat cereal, which had debuted in 1892, this acquisition also brought into the N.B.C. fold Triscuit wafers, which had been introduced in 1902. During the Great Depression, when growth slowed and profits fell, N.B.C. acquired Bennett Biscuit Company, maker of Milk-Bone dog biscuits, in 1931. The company also launched another hit product in 1934, Ritz crackers. In 1941 the letters "N.B.C." in the official company trademark were replaced by the word "Nabisco," a popular nickname for the company. In part, the change was made to reduce confusion with the recently established National Broadcasting Company.

During the immediate postwar years, Nabisco spent more than $150 million modernizing the firm's antiquated bakeries. Overseas, the 1950s were a period of major expansion in Latin America, while the 1960s saw the company push aggressively into Europe. By the end of the 1960s, Nabisco was the leading manufacturer of crackers and cookies not only in the United States but also in Canada, France, and the Scandinavian countries, and was a major supplier to many other European and South American countries. Meanwhile, Nabisco acquired the Cream of Wheat Corporation in 1961.

In 1971, the year that company sales reached $1 billion for the first time, National Biscuit changed its name to Nabisco, Inc. Four years later, its headquarters were moved to East Hanover, New Jersey. The company launched a short-lived diversification program in the 1970s, acquiring toy maker Aurora Products and drug company J.B. Williams, manufacturer of Geritol and Sominex, both in 1971. Aurora was sold in 1977, while Williams was sold to the Beecham Group in 1982.

The inflation and mounting energy costs of the 1970s led Nabisco to seek a merger with another large food concern. In 1981 the company merged with Standard Brands to form Nabisco Brands, Inc. Standard Brands had been formed in 1929 through the merger of the Fleischmann Company, maker of diverse products, including yeast and gin; Chase & Sanborn, a coffee roaster; and the Royal Baking Powder Company. Over the years, Standard made a number of important acquisitions, including Planters Nut & Chocolate Co. in 1961 and the Curtiss Candy Company, maker of the Baby Ruth candy bar, in 1964.

Nabisco Brands acquired the Life Savers Company for $250 million in 1981. After becoming the object of repeated hostile takeover attempts, the company in 1985 agreed to a friendly takeover by R.J. Reynolds, a worldwide manufacturer and distributor of tobacco, food, and beverage products, for $4.9 billion, creating the nation's largest consumer-products company, with annual sales of more than $19 billion. R.J. Reynolds changed its name to RJR Nabisco, Inc. later in 1985, while the firm's food unit took the name Nabisco Foods Group. The new Nabisco gained a number of Reynolds brands, including Del Monte canned products, A.1. steak sauce, and Grey Poupon mustard.

In 1988 a management group at RJR Nabisco attempted to take the company private in a $17.6 billion leveraged buyout. This led to an epic takeover battle after the brokerage house of Kohlberg Kravis Roberts & Co. (KKR) stepped in with a bid of $20.3 billion. A third bidder entered the fray in the form of a joint bid by broker Forstmann Little & Co., Procter & Gamble Company, and Ralston Purina Company. KKR ultimately won the battle with a $24.5 billion bid, gaining control of RJR Nabisco in 1989. The huge debt taken on to complete the takeover necessitated divestitures, and later in 1989 RJR Nabisco sold its European cookie and cracker business to BSN (later known as Groupe Danone), France's largest packaged-food group, for $2.5 billion. One year later, RJR Nabisco sold its Asia-Pacific businesses to Britannia Brands, a joint venture between BSN and an Indian partner. In 1991 RJR Nabisco went public again as RJR Nabisco Holdings Corp.

Nabisco Foods Group scored a coup in 1993 when it introduced the Snackwells line of low-fat cookies and crackers. Snackwells became a huge hit, with annual sales rocketing to $297 million within just two years. Also in 1993, Nabisco sold its cold cereal business, including the Shredded Wheat brand, to Kraft General Foods for $450 million. Two years later, Nabisco purchased Kraft's North American tablespreads business, including Parkay margarine. That same year, RJR Nabisco took Nabisco Foods Group public, selling a 19.5 percent stake.

Two major restructurings were undertaken in 1996 and 1998, the former involving the elimination of 6,000 jobs and a $428 million charge and the latter, 6,500 job cuts and a $530 million charge. Also in 1998 Nabisco sold its margarine and egg substitute business—including Parkay, Blue Bonnet, Fleischmann's, and Chiffon margarines and the Egg Beaters egg substitute product—to ConAgra, Inc. for $400 million.

Following the sale of its international tobacco operations, RJR Nabisco spun off its domestic tobacco business in 1999. The company was renamed Nabisco Group Holdings Corp., and its sole asset was its 80 percent stake in the Nabisco food unit,

now called Nabisco Holdings Corp. Later in 1999 Nabisco Holdings purchased Favorite Brands International, maker of Jet-Puffed marshmallows (formerly Kraft marshmallows) and Farley's fruit snacks.

Nabisco was put up for sale in early 2000, leading to yet another takeover battle involving the company. This time Philip Morris emerged the victor, besting a joint bid by Groupe Danone and Cadbury Schweppes PLC. To complete its third major food company acquisition, Philip Morris had to pay $14.9 billion in cash plus assume $4 billion in debt.

Early 21st Century: Integrating Nabisco into Kraft Foods Inc. and an IPO

Philip Morris completed its acquisition of Nabisco in December 2000 and immediately began integrating the Nabisco operations into those of Kraft Foods and Kraft Foods International. In March 2001 Philip Morris created a new holding company for the combined operations known as Kraft Foods Inc. (lacking the comma of the previous Kraft Foods, Inc.). The previous Kraft Foods was renamed Kraft Foods North America, giving the new Kraft Foods two main units: Kraft Foods North America and Kraft Foods International. The two CEOs of these units, Betsy D. Holden and Roger K. Deromedi, respectively, were named co-CEOs of Kraft Foods Inc. In June 2001 Philip Morris sold a 16.1 percent stake in Kraft Foods to the public, retaining the remaining shares. The second largest IPO in U.S. history, the offering raised $8.68 billion, which Philip Morris earmarked to reduce debt it had incurred in acquiring Nabisco.

As it was integrating Nabisco and attempting to meet the anticipated annual cost savings of $600 million by 2003, Kraft Foods also began divesting some of the marginal brands it had acquired in the takeover. By late 2001, the company had announced that it had reached agreements to sell the Farley's and Sathers confection brands as well as its Mexican pasta business, which included the Yemina and Vesta brands. Additional divestments were expected for Kraft, which as one of the top two food companies in the world—with revenues approaching $35 billion—could be very choosy about which brands to retain in its very powerful portfolio.

Principal Subsidiaries

Kraft Foods North America, Inc.; Kraft Foods Holdings, Inc.; Kraft Foods International, Inc.; Kraft Foods Schweiz Holding AG (Switzerland); Nabisco Holdings Corp.; Nabisco, Inc.; Nabisco Brands Company; Kraft Pizza Company; Kraft Food Ingredients Corp.; Capri Sun, Inc.; Callard & Bowser-Suchard, Inc.; Balance Bar Company; MEX Holdings, Ltd.; Nabisco Biscuit Manufacturing (Midwest), Inc.; Nabisco Biscuit Manufacturing (West), Inc.; Nabisco England IHC, Inc.; Nabisco Group Ltd.; Nabisco Holdings IHC, Inc.; Nabisco International, Inc.; Nabisco Technology Company; Kraft Foods Ltd. (Australia); Kraft Canada Inc.; Kraft Foods Italia S.p.A. (Italy); Ajinomoto General Foods, Inc. (Japan); Dong Suh Foods Corporation (South Korea); Votesor BV (Netherlands); Kraft Foods Belgium S.A.; Kraft Foods AS (Norway); Kraft Sverige AB (Sweden); Kraft Foods España, S.A. (Spain); Kraft Foods Schweiz AG (Switzerland); Kraft Foods France; Kraft Foods Deutschland Holding GmbH (Germany); Kraft Foods

Produktion GmbH (Germany); Kraft Foods UK Limited; Gevaliarosteriet AB (Sweden); Jacobs Suchard Alimentos do Brasil Ltda. (Brazil); Kraft Lacta Suchard Brasil, S.A. (Brazil); Corporativo Kraft S.A. de C.V. (Mexico); Kraft Foods de Mexico, S.A. de C.V.; Establecimiento Modelo Terrabusi S.A. (Argentina); Nabisco Argentina S.A.; Nabisco Iberia, S.L. (Spain); Nabisco Limited (Canada); Productos Alimenticios Fleischmann e Royal Ltda. (Brazil); Nabisco Euro Holdings Ltd. (Cayman Islands).

Principal Operating Units

Kraft Foods North America; Kraft Foods International.

Principal Competitors

Nestlé S.A.; Unilever; ConAgra Foods, Inc.; Groupe Danone; H.J. Heinz Company; Sara Lee Corporation; General Mills, Inc.; Campbell Soup Company; Kellogg Company; The Quaker Oats Company; Dean Foods Company; Frito-Lay Company.

Further Reading

Anderson, Veronica, ''Another Bid to Put Pep Back in Kraft's Step,'' *Crain's Chicago Business,* January 9, 1995, p. 3.

Boland, John C., ''Putting It All Together: For Dart & Kraft, the Future Still Looks Super,'' *Barron's,* June 21, 1982, pp. 13+.

Bowman, Jim, ''Kraft Offers Public Its Riches,'' *Chicago Sun-Times,* May 28, 2001.

Burns, Greg, ''Will So Many Ingredients Work Together?: Philip Morris Puts Its Food Operations into One Kraft Empire,'' *Business Week,* March 27, 1995, p. 188.

Burrough, Bryan, and John Helyar, *Barbarians at the Gate: The Fall of RJR Nabisco,* New York: Harper & Row, 1990, 528 p.

Busetti, Max, ''Kraft Foods: Now One Big, Happy(?) Family,'' *Prepared Foods,* February 1995, pp. 13+.

Cahn, William, *Out of the Cracker Barrel: The Nabisco Story, from Animal Crackers to Zuzus,* New York: Simon and Schuster, 1969, 367 p.

Cochran, Thomas N., ''Food for Thought: Kraft's Renewed Stress on Bread-and-Butter,'' *Barron's,* February 8, 1988, pp. 48+.

Crown, Judith, ''Cheez Whiz Kids Hone Their Kraft,'' *Crain's Chicago Business,* December 6, 1993.

Dahl, Jonathan, ''Dart & Kraft Decides to Split into Two Concerns,'' *Wall Street Journal,* June 20, 1986.

''Dart & Kraft Turns Back to Its Basic Business—Food,'' *Business Week,* June 11, 1984, pp. 100+.

Deogun, Nikhil, Gordon Fairclough, and Shelly Branch, ''Philip Morris Agrees to Acquire Nabisco,'' *Wall Street Journal,* June 26, 2000, p. A3.

Deveny, Kathleen, ''After Some Key Sales Strategies Go Sour, Kraft General Foods Gets Back to Basics,'' *Wall Street Journal,* March 18, 1992, p. B1.

——, ''Philip Morris Seeks to Gain in Europe with $3.8 Billion Bid for Suchard Stake,'' *Wall Street Journal,* June 25, 1990, p. A3.

Dreyfack, Kenneth, and James E. Ellis, ''Kraft, Minus Some Extra Baggage, Is Picking Up Speed,'' *Business Week,* March 9, 1987, pp. 74+.

Dudley, Charles Eaves, *Post City, Texas,* Austin, Tex.: State Historical Association, 1952.

Ferguson, James L., *General Foods Corporation: A Chronicle of Consumer Satisfaction,* New York: Newcomen Society of the United States, 1985, 24 p.

Forster, Julie, and Becky Gaylord, ''Can Kraft Be a Big Cheese Abroad?,'' *Business Week,* June 4, 2001, pp. 63, 66–67.

Freedman, Alix M., ''Miles Will Lead Kraft General Foods: Marketing Whiz Must Smooth Merger at Philip Morris,'' *Wall Street Journal,* September 28, 1989.

Freedman, Alix M., and Richard Gibson, ''Kraft Accepts Philip Morris's Sweetened Offer Totaling $13.1 Billion, or $106 a Share in Cash,'' *Wall Street Journal,* October 31, 1988.

Gallun, Alby, ''Key Ingredient in Kraft's IPO: Philip Morris,'' *Crain's Chicago Business,* April 2, 2001, p. 1.

——, ''Kraft Loses Appetite for Two Candy Brands,'' *Crain's Chicago Business,* October 15, 2001, p. 3.

Hwang, Suein L., ''Philip Morris to Reorganize Food Operation: Kraft, General Foods Units Will Be Merged in Bid to Repair Costly Rifts,'' *Wall Street Journal,* January 4, 1995, p. A3.

——, ''Unilever to Acquire Ice Cream Business Owned by Kraft Unit of Philip Morris,'' *Wall Street Journal,* September 9, 1993, p. A4.

Johnson, Robert, ''Dart & Kraft Sets a Spinoff to Divide Firm,'' *Wall Street Journal,* September 9, 1986.

——, ''Kraft Chief John Richman Weighs in with Leaner Firm but High-Fat Lines,'' *Wall Street Journal,* February 27, 1987.

Kiechel, Walter, III, ''Justin Dart's Krafty Deal,'' *Fortune,* July 14, 1980, p. 82.

Kraft, Inc.—Through the Years, Glenview, Ill.: Kraft, Inc., 1988.

Lampert, Hope, *True Greed: What Really Happened in the Battle for RJR Nabisco,* New York: New American Library, 1990, 259 p.

Liesse, Julie, and Judann Dagnoli, ''Goliath KGF Loses Steam After Merger,'' *Advertising Age,* January 27, 1992.

Maher, Tani, ''Kraft's Crafty Restructuring,'' *Financial World,* June 28, 1988, p. 10.

Matlack, Carol, ''Smoke Alarms at RJR,'' *Business Week,* November 16, 1998, pp. 75+.

Mayer, Oscar G., Jr., *Oscar Mayer & Co.: From Corner Store to National Processor,* New York: Newcomen Society in North America, 1970, 24 p.

Ono, Yumiko, ''CPC Will Buy Kraft's Bakeries for $865 Million,'' *Wall Street Journal,* August 8, 1995, p. A2.

——, ''Kraft Searches Its Cupboard for Old Brands to Remake,'' *Wall Street Journal,* March 12, 1996, p. B1.

Roberts, William A., Jr., ''The 'Big' Gets Bigger,'' *Prepared Foods,* September 2001, p. 12.

Sanger, Elizabeth, ''Still the Big Cheese,'' *Barron's,* August 19, 1985, pp. 51+.

Sherman, Stratford P., ''How Philip Morris Diversified Right,'' *Fortune,* October 23, 1989, pp. 120+.

Sinisi, John, ''KGF's New Dressing,'' *Brandweek,* September 28, 1992.

Therrien, Lois, ''A Cup of Jell-O, Velveeta to Taste . . . ,'' *Business Week,* May 8, 1989, pp. 74+.

——, ''Kraft Is Looking for Fat Growth from Fat-Free Foods,'' *Business Week,* March 26, 1990, pp. 100+.

Wagner, Jim, ''Nabisco's New Product Winning Streak,'' *Food Processing,* June 1994, pp. 54+.

Warner, Fara, ''Kraft General Foods Moves to Mend Its Floundering Marriage,'' *Adweek's Marketing Week,* February 24, 1992.

Waters, Jennifer, ''Whey to Grow: Kraft's New Chief Sets Agenda,'' *Crain's Chicago Business,* November 17, 1997, p. 4.

Wellman, David, ''They're Big, They're Bad, They're Kraft,'' *Supermarket Business,* August 1997, pp. 24+.

—updates: Robert R. Jacobson, David E. Salamie

Lakeland Industries, Inc.

711-2 Koehler Avenue
Ronkonkoma, New York 11779-7410
U.S.A.
Telephone: (631) 981-9700
Toll Free: (800) 645-9291
Fax: (631) 981-9751
Web site: http://www.lakeland.com

Public Company
Incorporated: 1982
Employees: 1,524
Sales: $76.2 million (2000)
Stock Exchanges: NASDAQ
Ticker Symbol: LAKE
NAIC: 339113 Surgical Appliance and Other Apparel
   Manufacturing

Lakeland Industries, Inc. of Ronkonkoma, New York, is a leading manufacturer of a wide range of safety garments and accessories used in a variety of industries. The company operates through four divisions and four subsidiaries, with domestic production facilities and plants located in Mexico, Canada, and China. The company's six product lines are mostly sold through major safety and mill supply distributors, with the company also represented by a small in-house sales force, plus a network of independent agents. Lakeland's limited use, disposable protective clothing guards against common industrial contaminants and irritants, including fertilizers, pesticides, acids, asbestos, and lead. Lakeland's gloves and arm guards, made from the same materials used in bulletproof vests, are worn by workers in chemical, automotive, glass, and metal fabrication industries. The company's firefighting apparel protects against excessive heat and fire and is worn by municipal and volunteer firemen as well as airport crash rescue teams. Heat protective aluminized fire suits are used by industrial firefighters and workers maintaining hot equipment. Lakeland's protective woven reusable garments are used in hospitals and clean room environments, and by EMS personnel to protect against bacteria, viruses, and blood-borne pathogens. Lakeland also produces high-end

chemical protective suits used by hazardous material teams as well as chemical and nuclear industries personnel.

The 1966 Introduction of Tyvek

Originally incorporated in New York in 1982, Lakeland was cofounded by current Chairman and CEO Raymond J. Smith along with attorney Patrick Murphy. Born in Brooklyn, Smith attended Georgetown University on a track scholarship, graduating in 1960. He began law school but was forced to drop out to seek employment when his wife became pregnant. In 1961, Smith joined International Paper as a management trainee and stayed with the company until 1966. Through his job Smith had become familiar with the new specially treated papers that were being used in disposable diapers and other products. Realizing that the industrial market was as yet untapped he found a partner to form a Long Island company named Disposables Inc. It was the DuPont Company's introduction of the synthetic material Tyvek that made it economically feasible to produce lightweight, disposable protective garments. Rather than being woven, Tyvek was the result of a special bonding process that used heat and pressure. At first DuPont was uncertain about how best to commercially exploit Tyvek, which like so many products had been the result of accident, and reached out in any number of directions. Smith was looking for a new material, because of a shortage in the standard disposable materials due to the Vietnam War. He became the first person to sell Tyvek garments in 1966, after DuPont granted marketing rights, thereby giving Disposables a six-month headstart on its competitors. Tyvek, with its resistance to chemicals and acids, proved to be the perfect material for industrial use. The need for protective garments would increase significantly after the 1970 passage of the Occupational Safety and Health Act, better known as OSHA, which required certain industries to provide employees with protective clothing. Other materials were created in the 1970s to improve comfort, essentially allowing the wearer's body vapor to escape, albeit with less of a protective barrier than Tyvek. Throughout the 1970s, the demand for these disposable protective garments increased steadily, as state and local requirements supplemented federal regulations. For employers, disposable items were more attractive than longer lasting ones, which entailed ongoing laundering and decontamination costs, as well as handling and transportation fees and eventual replacement. Moreover, as the demand for disposable garments increased, manufacturers were able to increase production runs and further lower the unit cost, making the cost benefit even greater.

Establishment of Lakeland Industries: 1982

Smith became the president of Disposables, which ultimately changed its name to Abanda, but he was only a minority shareholder in the company. In 1982, he was surprised when his partner of 16 years dismissed him. The two men, according to Smith, had grown apart on how to run the business in a number of areas. As part of a severance agreement, Smith was asked to sign a non-compete clause, prompting him to seek an attorney. A friend recommended Patrick Murphy, who did a lot of legal work for small businessmen. It was Murphy who was instrumental in Smith rejecting the non-compete clause and starting his own disposable garment business. This decision was difficult for Smith, who had a wife and four children to support and was receiving job offers from companies once they heard he was available. Smith worked out of Murphy's offices to organize the new business, while Murphy put together a group of investors, many of whom were his clients. Smith chose the name for the new business when taking his wife out for dinner and spotting a street sign for Lakeland Avenue. At first he considered Lakeland Manufacturing, then settled on Lakeland Industries.

Smith's many years in the disposable garment business proved valuable on a number of fronts. Former salespeople that had previously worked for him left Abanda to rejoin him, as did his old vice-president of manufacturing, who ran a plant in Decatur, Alabama. (In the early 1970s Disposables had moved their production facilities from Long Island to Alabama, where Smith felt the company would find a more reliable workforce.) Smith's personal ties to DuPont were also crucial. Although DuPont was no longer selling Tyvek to new customers, it made an exception in Smith's case. In a very short time, 59 days from the day Smith was fired, Lakeland shipped its first product.

Between 1982 and 1986, Lakeland focused on two product lines: disposable, limited use protective industrial garments and specialty safety and industrial work gloves. Manufacturing was done by two subsidiaries owned by Lakeland's stockholders—Ryland, an Alabama corporation formed in 1982, and Triland, a New Jersey corporation formed in 1984—as well as a wholly owned Arkansas subsidiary, Uniland, formed in 1984. Lakeland generated more than $10 million in revenues in fiscal 1985 (which ended January 31, 1985), posting a profit of just $5,000. For fiscal 1986, revenues increased to more than $13 million and

net income to nearly $158,000. Management then reorganized and initiated a concerted effort to grow the business. The stockholders of Triland and Ryland contributed their stock to Lakeland in February 1986, making the two companies wholly owned subsidiaries. Two months later Lakeland reincorporated in Delaware, then in September 1986 it went public to fund expansion, selling 950,000 shares of common stock at $6.75 per share. In December, Lakeland formed two more subsidiaries, Chemland and Fireland, in order to acquire two Ohio businesses, Siena Industries and Fyrepel Products. Through Fyrepel, which had been in business for 36 years, Lakeland expanded into the fire protective garment business. Chemland allowed Lakeland to manufacture protective garments for use with hazardous chemicals. Its products were sold to Fireland, which in turn distributed them to end users. For fiscal 1987, Lakeland sales increased to almost $17 million, and net profits exceeded $900,000.

In March 1987, Lakeland formed yet another subsidiary, Highland, based in Edison, New Jersey, to import and sell gloves. In September 1987, it formed a subsidiary in order to purchase the Chicago firm of Walter H. Mayer & Co., paying nearly $2 million and assuming certain liabilities. Through Mayer, Lakeland was now able to offer garments used in hospitals, nursing homes, as well as the hospitality industries. A month later, in October 1987, the Uniland subsidiary opened a manufacturing plant in St. Joseph, Missouri, to produce woven cloth garments, rather than disposables. All of this activity in fiscal 1988 resulted in a dramatic boost in revenues, which increased by more than 50 percent to $26.5 million, most of which was attributed to the new businesses. Expansion, however, caused net income to fall to $227,000.

During fiscal 1989, Lakeland continued to show strong gains, increasing revenues to nearly $37.5 million and net earnings to $1.2 million. During fiscal 1989, Lakeland restructured its business somewhat. Highland's warehousing and manufacturing capabilities were subsequently moved from New Jersey to Alabama, and administrative operations were relocated to Lakeland's New York offices. Uniland's Arkansas operations were moved to its Missouri facilities. On January 31, 1989, the final day for the company's fiscal 1989, Triland was then merged into Highland. Consolidation and centralization efforts would only accelerate as Lakeland moved into the 1990s. Its revenues increased by little more than 1 percent in fiscal 1990, to just over $37.8 million, and the company posted a loss of $38,000 for Lakeland.

The Early 1990s: A Difficult Period for Lakeland

The company felt the adverse effects of the decision by asbestos removal contractors to use polypropylene disposable garments rather than Tyvek materials. Falling prices also hurt the company, so that Lakeland was already experiencing financial difficulty when a downturn in the U.S. economy hurt business even further. The early 1990s would be a difficult period for the company, requiring a number of changes, despite the introduction of tougher OSHA standards for chemical suits that should have provided a boost to Lakeland's business. During fiscal 1991, Chemland closed its Ohio plant, and the Mayer subsidiary was sold for almost $2 million. While 1991 revenues were flat compared to the previous year, totaling just under $30 million, Lakeland's net loss grew to $340,000. The poor econ-

---

Key Dates:

1982: The company is incorporated in New York.
1986: The company is reincorporated in Delaware and goes public.
1994: A Canadian subsidiary is established.
1995: A Mexican subsidiary is established.
1999: A Chinese manufacturing plant opens.

---

omy hurt sales of disposable garments during much of fiscal 1992. A new management team was brought in to run Fireland, and although losses with the subsidiary were reduced, it was forced to eliminate its manufacturing operation, relying instead on outside contractors. Moreover, sales in gloves fell off, with only woven garments showing an increase for the year. Overall, Lakeland saw its revenues fall by more than $4 million in fiscal 1992 to $25.8 million, while the net loss exceeded $400,000.

Despite the economy showing signs of improvement, Lakeland continued to struggle. Although revenues began to rebound in fiscal 1993, improving to $26.5 million, the company lost more than $680,000, despite retrenching efforts that included the phasing out of Fireland's Ohio manufacturing capability and Highland vacating its plant to share Chemland's larger facility. Lakeland began to show signs of returning to financial health during fiscal 1994, as sales neared the 1989 level, and losses for the year were reduced to just $37,000. Lakeland was now able to renew expansion plans, in particular outside of the United States. In December 1994, the company formed Lakeland Protective Wear, Inc. in Burlington, Ontario, in order to tap the Canadian market and find a further outlet for the company's complete line of products. An even more advantageous move was made in November 1995 (fiscal 1996) when Lakeland established a Mexican subsidiary to assemble disposable jumpsuits worn by poultry workers on a contract basis, moving the operation from its Decatur, Alabama, plant where seamstresses were making up to $15 an hour. By contrast, Mexican workers were paid around $50 a week. Because Lakeland could not add capacity at Decatur, moving assembly to Mexico was the only way to make the company's products more competitively priced. Moreover, the company was able to take advantage of the peso devaluation. The millions of dollars that Lakeland saved on wages was then used to fund a major expansion to the Decatur, Alabama, facility, permitting Lakeland now to store more raw materials and finished goods in order to fill customers' order in a more timely manner. More importantly, the plant was able to accommodate new computerized cutting machines that were capable of producing more expensive garments while also improving quality and eliminating waste. Ironically, by cutting low-skill jobs, the company was able to add higher paying jobs for engineers and technicians to operate the new machinery. As a result of these steps, Lakeland returned to profitability and was ready to take advantage of an economy that was about to enter a boom period.

Further Growth from the Mid-1990s into the New Century

Lakeland sales grew to $35.2 million in fiscal 1995, with a record $1.4 million in net profits. The next year, revenues topped $40 million for the first time in the company's history. Profits fell to $587,000, the result of opening the Mexico facility as well as downtime due to the changes in the Decatur plant. In fiscal 1997, revenues improved just slightly over the previous year to $41.8 million, but net profits almost doubled to just over $1 million. During fiscal 1998, the Mexican plant was now operating at peak efficiency, and a new manufacturing facility was opened in China that would reduce the cost of a number of Lakeland's high selling products, thereby making them more competitive in the United States as well as the Pacific Rim markets. The company also continued to improve its technology, investing in a new computer system that offered better controls in both finance and inventory. In addition to a strong economy, Lakeland benefited from a less desirable aspect of the modern world: the rise of global terrorism. In 1998, U.S. embassies in east Africa were bombed, presumably the work of the al-Qaida terrorist network led by Osama bin Laden. Congress appropriated $50 million a year to fight terrorism, some of which went to Lakeland to purchase protective clothing for U.S. embassies around the world.

For fiscal 1998, the company generated $47.3 million in revenues and posted a profit of $1.6 million. Sales grew to $54.6 million in fiscal 1999, and net profits topped $2 million. In fiscal 2000, Lakeland was so confident of its position that it was able to turn down a sales alliance offer from DuPont with little fear that it would not be able to negotiate a new licensing agreement on certain DuPont fabrics. Lakeland had a 5 percent stake in the $1.3 billion market for protective clothing, making it a large player in a highly fragmented industry populated by a number of family firms, many of which were closing their doors. Prospects for Lakeland's continued growth were also bolstered by improving safety standards in the workplace. Prospects for foreign sales also appeared promising, as other countries began to emulate the United States in industrial safety efforts. Lakeland also took advantage of the Internet, promoting itself online as well as signing agreements with Web search portals, such as Alta Vista, that would steer users who searched on certain key words (such as "lab coats") to Lakeland's web page.

Revenues improved to $58.6 million in fiscal 2000, with net profits falling slightly to $1.7 million. Revenues continued to grow in 2000, exceeding $76 million, although net profits again dropped, to $1.1 million. Despite its reputation in its field, Lakeland was little known to investors. At the beginning of 2001, the price of its stock fell to just $3. The terrorist acts of September 11, 2001, however, would suddenly provide Lakeland with considerable media attention. The company's highest quality chemical protection suit was featured in a *Time* magazine article and a segment on CNN. Not only were Lakeland suits worn at the World Trade Center site, they gained additional usage by investigators and cleanup workers during the Anthrax mail contamination a few weeks later. Investors soon realized that Lakeland would likely receive a large increase in orders, and with the war on terrorism expected to last for a number of years, there was every reason to expect that the prospects for the company would only improve. As a result, the price of Lakeland stock soared. Moreover, the FBI purchased all of Lakeland's Saranex-coated suits used to protect against biological hazards. The Federal Emergency Management Agency (FEMA) and the Pentagon also placed large orders for Lakeland suits. What had been low-volume, high margin, high-profit products, now promised to become high-volume, high-margin, high-profit products. The cost to produce the suits, in turn, would fall and increase profits even further. Given the unpredictable state of the world, about all that remained certain was that manufacturers of protective clothing like Lakeland would find a ready market for their products for many years to come.

Principal Subsidiaries

Laidlaw, Adams & Peck, Inc.; Lakeland Protective Wear, Inc. (Canada); Lakeland de Mexico S.A. de C.V.; Weifang Lakeland Safety Products, Co. Ltd. (China).

Principal Competitors

Abatix; Kappler; Vallen Corporation; Worksafe Industries.

Further Reading

Figura, Susannah Zak, ''Protective Clothing: Suiting the Customer,'' *Occupational Hazards,* June 1996, p. 51.

Harrington, John, ''Safety Pays for Trio of Local Firms,'' *Crain's New York Business,* October 8, 2001, p. 38.

''Lakeland Industries Income Drops 37%,'' *Long Island Business News,* June 18, 1999, p. 3B.

Millman, Joel, ''Job Shift to Mexico Lets U.S. Firm Upgrade,'' *Wall Street Journal,* November 15, 1999, p. A28.

Schreiber, Paul, ''Protective Gear Maker's Stock in High Demand,'' *Newsday,* October 9, 2001, p. A49.

Walzer, Robert, ''Lakeland Sewing Up Work Fashion Biz,'' *Long Island Business News,* February 11, 2000, p. 5A.

—Ed Dinger

Lucille Farms, Inc.

150 River Road
Montville, New Jersey 07045
U.S.A.
Telephone (973) 334-6030
Toll Free: (800) 654-6844
Fax: (973) 402-6361
Web site: http://www.lucille-farms.com

Public Company
Incorporated: 1976
Employees: 106
Sales: $41.4 million (2001)
Stock Exchanges: NASDAQ
Ticker Symbol: LUCY
NAIC: 311513 Cheese Manufacturing

Lucille Farms, Inc. manufactures and markets cheese. It is currently making the transition from a medium-size regional maker of mozzarella, provolone, and Feta cheese, distributing its products to the foodservice industry, to becoming a larger and broader-based business that sells a variety of specialty cheese products to the foodservice industry as well as consumers under its own label. Lucille Farms maintains its corporate offices in Montville, New Jersey, with production facilities located in Swanton, Vermont. Its products are divided into two groups, conventional and nutritional. While conventional mozzarella, provolone, and Feta cheeses account for almost 90 percent of Lucille's annual sales, it is the company's nutritional cheeses that offer the most promise for future growth. The organic cheese line includes mozzarella, cheddar, Monterey jack, Jalapeno jack, Garlic & Herb, and Swiss cheese, and is sold to health food and gourmet stores in addition to supermarkets in the northeastern United States. Lucille also offers nutraceutical cheeses, which address specific health concerns, and include lactose-free mozzarella and fat-free and low-fat cheeses. Because the nutritional cheeses are considered premium products, they are priced higher than conventional cheeses and provide Lucille with a greater profit margin.

Founding of Lucille Farms: 1938

The founder of Lucille Farms, Philip Falivene, became involved in cheesemaking by necessity rather than by design. The son of Italian immigrants, he grew up in the Harlem section of New York City. As a high school student during the Depression years of the 1930s, Falivene had to work to bolster the family's finances. He found a job at a local Italian dairy, called a lattacini, where he learned the craft of making cheese. He soon married another Italian-American, who had immigrated to the United States as an infant. Her name was Lucille. Falivene was only 18 years old and because he now had his own family to support and cheese was the only business he knew, he decided to open his own lattacini. In 1938, the young couple moved to the South Bronx and opened a small storefront lattacini on Castle Hill Avenue. In honor of his bride, Falivene named the business "Lucille Dairy."

Falivene made his cheese, in particular mozzarella, during the day and with the help of Lucille ran the store. He produced such a good product that other stores began to buy his cheese for reselling. Falivene's cheese soon came to the attention of local restaurants and pizzerias, and he made them customers as well. In addition to cheese, Falivene featured non-dairy items in his store, such as homemade pork sausages and other traditional delicacies, plus imported Italian tomatoes and pasta products, and soon he began to also sell these products to the restaurants. His goal was to take advantage of sales volume in order to obtain a discount on his imports and gain a competitive advantage for his store by offering lower prices.

By the early 1950s, Falivene had built up such a business selling mozzarella and other products to Italian stores and New York City restaurants and pizzerias that he decided to become a full-fledged distributor. Lucille took over the running of the lattacini, while he took a lease on a warehouse on Devoe Avenue several blocks away. He also brought in his brother Gennaro to help with the distribution business. In the late 1950s, Lucille's health began to fail; she was no longer able to run the lattacini and as a result the original store was sold. A short time later Lucille passed away.

Falivene's son, Alfonso, joined the family business in 1965, and two years later the name was changed from Lucille Dairy to

Lucille Farms. The company grew steadily, so that by the early 1970s it was selling close to 100,000 pounds of cheese each week to more than 600 accounts. Because no single source could provide enough cheese to service all of these customers, Lucille had to rely on a number of vendors, resulting in an inconsistent product. All too often, customers were dissatisfied and Lucille had to spend time and money retrieving poor quality product and making replacements. The Falivenes decided that if the business were to continue to grow, they had to return to cheesemaking in order to control the quality of the product they were selling.

Construction on Vermont Facility Beginning in 1973

In 1973, Lucille obtained a $1 million loan backed by the Small Business Administration and, in conjunction with the Target Area Development Corporation, began construction of an 18,000-square-foot production facility in Swanton, Vermont, in the heart of the state's dairy industry. Lucille also established a relationship with the St. Albans Creamery, which represented some 500 Vermont dairy farmers. Vermont's premium ice cream maker Ben & Jerry's was another major customer of the co-op. Ice cream and cheese proved to be a perfect combination for everyone involved, especially since both businesses were high volume customers. Ben & Jerry's used the cream and Lucille used the skim milk. Altogether, one pound of Lucille cheese required ten pounds of milk, so that Lucille actually purchased more product from St. Albans than the ice cream maker, even after Ben & Jerry's surpassed Häagen-Dazs in 1995 as the highest selling premium brand of ice cream in the United States.

After Swanton began production in 1975, Lucille was able to produce 250,000 pounds of cheese each week. In 1976, Lucille Farms was reincorporated in Delaware. Very quickly, it became primarily a cheese manufacturing operation with a sales force that covered the East Coast. One of its representatives made contact with a Pizza Hut regional franchiser, who liked Lucille's mozzarella cheese so much that he sent a sample to the parent company's Wichita headquarters. Lucille was then added to Pizza Hut's list of approved vendors. Much of Lucille's growth through the 1980s was attributed to its sales to Pizza Hut operations.

As a private regional company Lucille was a moderately profitable business. In 1991, however, one of its largest customers, accounting for 20 percent of all sales, was sold to a company that already had its own cheese supplier. The Falivenes not only found a way to make up for this loss in revenue, they saw a chance to take the next step forward in the growth of Lucille. Because his second wife, Margaret, became concerned about cholesterol, Philip Falivene decided to create good-tasting, low-fat and no-fat cheeses. Instead of using artificial substances like other manufacturers, he relied on all-natural ingredients. The family was so pleased with the results that it decided to market the new products, leading to a restructuring of the business. Philip Falivene, now 75 years old, stepped down as president and chief executive officer in favor of his son, while he and his brother continued to lead the board. Braff & Co. was hired to develop a marketing plan and soon the firm's principals, David Braff and David McCarty, who also recognized the potential of the light cheese lines, bought interests in Lucille and became involved in taking the company public. The company raised over $5.5 million in its 1993 initial public offering of stock at $4 per share, and subsequently began trading on the NASDAQ. Both Braff and McCarty also took on executive positions with Lucille to handle marketing, putting to use their extensive experience in the dairy industry. Braff had parlayed successful work with such brands as Chipwich, Dove Bar, and Frusen Gladje in order to create his own agency in 1984. With McCarty as his partner, he then handled public relations for such major accounts as Dannon Co. and Kraft General Foods.

Lucille devote $1 million of the money raised in the IPO to promote its new Tasty-Life and Mozzi-Rite mozzarella cheeses. The new management team firmly believed that future growth across the board in the food industry would take place in the exploitation of niche markets. They felt that with Americans becoming more health conscious, especially with the bulk of the Baby Boom generation entering middle age, light cheeses held great potential. Moreover, many Boomer offspring had been raised on skim milk and other low-fat products and would be more responsive to the new cheeses. Just as it took some time for light beer and other new age beverages to be accepted by the public, Lucille looked to position itself in the light cheese market and wait for the consumers to embrace its products. Low-fat pizza was thought to hold great potential, prompting Pizza Hut and others to test-market the idea. In 1994, the trade publication *Pizza Today,* named The Pizza Company's low-fat pizza using Lucille cheese the best in the country. Although consumers were receptive to the concept of low-fat pizza, they were not generally satisfied with the taste and consequently low-fat pizza did not catch hold as many had hoped. Taste was the primary concern about all light cheeses, and although Lucille-produced items were highly regarded, the company faced consumer resistance to the entire category because so many light cheeses on the market not only did not taste as good as regular cheese but also lacked the desired texture, failing to melt and stretch like traditional cheeses. Nevertheless, pizza companies continued to offer low-fat pizzas and supermarkets stocked light cheeses with the expectation that improvements in taste as well as changing needs of an aging population would ultimately result in a profitable niche business. In the highly competitive $30-billion-a-year pizza industry, furthermore, pressure to market new products would likely lead one of the major players to make a major push for low-fat pizza, forcing competitors to follow suit.

Late 1990s Price Swings Affecting Profits

As a public company focusing on a new business plan, Lucille was not as profitable as it had been during its private days. As a result, the company's stock attracted little attention in a market obsessed with high tech stocks, and its shares languished in the $1 to $5 range. Revenues that totaled $32

Key Dates:

1938: Philip Falivene opens his South Bronx "lattacini."
1967: The company name is changed from Lucille Dairy to Lucille Farms.
1975: The company opens a manufacturing facility in Swanton, Vermont.
1976: The company is incorporated in Delaware.
1993: The company is taken public.
1999: Philip Falivene dies.

million in 1993 increased only to $35.2 million in 1995, with a loss of close to $1 million. In 1996, however, sales grew to $41.7 million and the company posted a profit of $773,000. The late 1990s saw extreme dairy price swings, which adversely affected Lucille's profits. In 1998, sales fell to less than $36.2 million, after having reached $44 million the year before, and the company lost more than $2.1 million. In 1999, sales rebounded to more than $46 million and Lucille realized a profit of $729,000. Lower cheese prices, however, would cause revenues to fall to $42.8 million in 2000, while Lucille posted a meager profit of $72,000. Because the prices of the company's bulk cheese business were set by the volatile Chicago Mercantile Exchange, Lucille began efforts to move into the retail cheese business, to sell its products directly to consumers in supermarkets, either through co-packaging ventures or by the acquisition of brands. Moreover, Lucille looked to exploit organic and nutraceutical, new specialty lines that offered promising growth. Both kinds of cheese catered to a highly desirable young and affluent demographic that would be willing to pay a premium price for the new products. While growth in traditional cheeses was flat, the organic market was growing at a 10 percent pace and nutraceuticals at 20 percent.

In 1999, Lucille also experienced the passing of an era when Philip Falivene died. His brother Gennaro remained with the company as chairman of the board and an executive vice-president in charge of quality control, and his son Alfonso continued on as Lucille's president and CEO. To pay off some debt as well as to fund expansion, Lucille arranged for a $5 million bank loan in 1999. Some of the money was used to complete a new 10,000-square-foot whey drying facility in Swanton. A residue produced in the cheesemaking process, whey had primarily been regarded as a pollutant requiring expensive disposal, but had in recent years developed into a valuable commodity. Not only was it being used in the manufacture of other cheeses, such as ricotta, it served as a high protein animal feed as well as a protein source for many fitness and diet supplement products. It was used in all manner of protein drinks and power bars, a market that was also showing strong growth.

Lucille began to sell its own brand of cheese to consumers, and in early 2000 it began to co-pack private label shredded cheese for some New England supermarkets. In 2001, it entered into a joint marketing agreement with Butternut Farms Organic LLC to coordinate marketing efforts and to expand both companies' organic cheese lines. Butternut Farms also agreed to supply Lucille with organic milk. Revenues fell slightly in 2001 to $41.4 million, and the company lost $1.5 million. Nevertheless, Lucille remained optimistic that its new emphasis on specialty cheeses and its expansion beyond the northeastern United States would pay off handsomely when the changing tastes of consumers caught up with the company's high quality products.

Principal Subsidiaries

Lucille Farms of Vermont, Inc.

Principal Competitors

Borden, Inc.; Century Foods; Galaxy Foods; Kraft, Inc.; Land O'Lakes, Inc.; Sargento Foods, Inc.; Sorrento, Inc.; Stella Foods, Inc.; Suprema Foods.

Further Reading

Doeff, Gail, "Cheese Wiz: David Braff Brings Marketing Zeal to Lucille Farms," *Dairy Foods,* June 1994, p. 22.
Dryer, Jerry, "Lite Dining Ahead of Its Time?" *Dairy Foods,* June 1996, p. 29.
Eden, Scott, "Lucille to Post Results Above Break-Even," *Wall Street Journal,* June 1, 1999.
Lassester, Diana G., "Is It More Than Pie in the Sky," *NJBIZ.com,* July 10, 1996.

—Ed Dinger

Lyondell Chemical Company

1221 McKinney Street, Suite 700
Houston, Texas 77010
U.S.A.
Telephone: (713) 652-7200
Fax: (713) 652-4151
Web site: http://www.lyondell.com

Public Company
Incorporated: 1985 as Lyondell Petrochemical
   Corporation
Employees: 8,900
Sales: $4.04 billion (2000)
Stock Exchanges: New York
Ticker Symbol: LYO
NAIC: 325110 Petrochemical Manufacturing; 325211
   Plastics Material and Resin Manufacturing; 324110
   Petroleum Refineries

Lyondell Chemical Company is one of the largest U.S.-based chemical manufacturers. The company makes a wide range of intermediate and specialty chemicals, including propylene oxide, which has numerous consumer and industrial applications; propylene glycol, used in aircraft deicers and fiberglass resins; propylene glycol ethers, which are important ingredients in coatings, cleaners, and solvents; butanediol, which is used in engineered plastics and urethanes; and methyl tertiary butyl ether (MTBE), a gasoline additive used to increase octane and reduce automotive emissions. In addition, Lyondell has major equity stakes in two joint ventures, Equistar Chemicals, LP, and LYONDELL-CITGO Refining LP. Equistar, 41 percent owned by Lyondell, is a petrochemical and polymers producer with 2000 revenues of $7.5 billion. Key products include ethylene, propylene, butadiene, ethanol, benzene, toluene, polyethylene, and polypropylene. Lyondell operates this venture on behalf of its partners, Millennium Chemicals Inc. and Occidental Petroleum Corporation. LYONDELL-CITGO, 58.75 percent owned by Lyondell, is a refiner of petroleum products with 2000 revenues of $4.1 billion. A partnership with CITGO Petroleum Corporation, this venture produces gasoline, diesel fuel, jet fuel, aromatics, and lubricants, selling the majority of its output to CITGO Petroleum.

Lyondell's Roots

Although Lyondell was incorporated in 1985 as a wholly owned subsidiary of Atlantic Richfield Company (ARCO), its roots are much a part of the history of Texas. In 1918 two-year-old Sinclair Oil & Refining Company purchased the Allen Ranch in Houston, Texas, its first 720 acres of land. Included in the land was the site at which General Sam Houston and the Texas Army forded the Buffalo Bayou, retreating from Texas's defeat at the Alamo, before the army turned at the San Jacinto River, dealt Santa Anna a crushing blow, and won Texas its independence. Sinclair built the first facility for refining crude on this site—which went onstream in 1919. Sinclair Oil & Refining Company was subsequently renamed Sinclair Oil Corporation, and, with Rio Grande Oil Company and several other Depression-scarred companies, was merged in 1936 into the Richfield Oil Corporation.

In 1955 Texas Butadiene and Chemical Corporation bought the Lyondell Country Club in Channelview, Texas, and built a plant on that site. By 1957 the new plant was producing 300 tons of butadiene a day. Sinclair Petrochemicals Inc., a subsidiary of Sinclair Oil, which was then a subsidiary of Richfield, purchased the Channelview site in 1962.

During the mid-1960s Atlantic Refining Company was searching for a merger partner to enhance its own growth. In 1965 Atlantic initiated talks with Richfield. Atlantic Refining's overture, which typically would not have appealed to Richfield, was attractive because Richfield was being sued on antitrust grounds by the Department of Justice for its 26-year-old merger with Sinclair. Faced with the alternatives of liquidation or divesting Sinclair, Richfield opted instead for a marriage to Atlantic Refining. In 1966 Atlantic Richfield was formed. In 1969 the Justice Department finally allowed ARCO to merge with Sinclair. ARCO immediately sold Sinclair's East Coast marketing arm to the U.S. subsidiary of British Petroleum Company to satisfy the Justice Department. In 1969 the Justice Department also required ARCO to continue to aggressively market the

Sinclair brand name for five more years in case the Justice Department was ultimately able to win its case and force Sinclair to become an independent company. The Justice Department was unable to do so, however. After Sinclair was merged into ARCO, the Channelview plant became a part of ARCO Chemical Company and the Houston plant joined ARCO Products Company.

Also during the 1960s, Atlantic Richfield began to realize that the growing market for oil was not limitless, and it became actively interested in developing its petrochemical business. In 1966, together with Halcon International, ARCO created Oxirane Chemical Company, a research and development, engineering design, and consulting company. The joint venture produced propylene oxide using a new process developed by Halcon, and it quickly proved profitable. When ARCO bought Halcon's 50 percent of Oxirane in 1980, it gained a profitable addition to its growing chemical business.

Through Oxirane, ARCO carved a niche for itself in petrochemicals. By 1980, when Halcon sold its share in the partnership to ARCO for $270 million and the assumption of $380 million in long-term debt, Oxirane was generating $1 billion of business a year worldwide. What was formerly Oxirane then became a part of ARCO Chemical.

1985 Founding of Lyondell

In the years that immediately followed, ARCO Chemical failed to distinguish itself as a developer of new technology. Unable to develop market share in polyethylene and polypropylene, ARCO Chemical decided to sell those businesses. By 1984, the company had sold both its high- and low-density polyethylene and polypropylene businesses, as well as several polymer operations. Although ARCO Chemical tried to sell what remained of the olefins businesses, which at that time were a drain on its earnings, Atlantic Richfield Company had other plans. In 1985 ARCO separated its olefins operations from ARCO Chemical Company, and set them up as a separate ARCO unit, naming it Lyondell Petrochemical Corporation, soon renamed Lyondell Petrochemical Company. Lyondell's assets consisted of the Houston refinery, the former Allen Ranch; the Channelview petrochemical complex, formerly Lyondell Country Club; and several money-losing product lines.

ARCO Chemical continued to develop its core business as a part of ARCO until September 1987. At this point ARCO managers, realizing that the growth of the company's chemical segment was not fully recognized by investors because ARCO Chemical was just a small division of Atlantic Richfield Company, spun off ARCO Chemical Company, selling 20 percent of its shares to the public.

Sibling company Lyondell Petrochemical followed much the same route. Under President Bob Gower, Lyondell had reduced overhead and improved its operating costs just one year after its formation. Gower cut staff but improved morale by increasing workers' responsibilities.

In 1988 Lyondell's earnings increased 441 percent over 1987, spurred by increased demand for petrochemical products. The speed of this recovery, as well as Lyondell's continued growth, led ARCO to spin off Lyondell. The spinoff was calculated to improve Lyondell's market value, allow ARCO to enjoy a cash infusion while Lyondell's performance was at a peak, and to increase Lyondell's operational mobility. In January 1989 ARCO sold 50 percent of Lyondell Petrochemical Company to the public for $1.4 billion, making it the largest initial public offering of 1989, as well as the largest equity offering by a U.S. industrial company. Prior to the offering, ARCO had Lyondell pay it a special distribution of $500 million, funded by debt that was placed on Lyondell's books. Lyondell thus was saddled with $760 million in debt as it began its era of semi-independence (ARCO President Robert Wycoff served as Lyondell's chairman and there were four other ARCO officers on the Lyondell board).

ARCO could not have picked a better time to offer Lyondell to the public, although the stock was an aftermarket disaster, sinking 23 percent from its initial $30 offering price. This deal not only benefited ARCO, bringing in cash that was redistributed into other areas of its businesses; it also spurred important growth at Lyondell. The spinoff allowed Lyondell to create an entrepreneurial atmosphere and rewarded management with new responsibility. Freed of the constraints of operating within ARCO, Lyondell set its own agenda.

With startling candidness Gower, in the January 15, 1986 issue of *Chemical Week,* had summarized the key to Lyondell's success: "Our assets are run-of-the-mill, mundane. So is our technology, so is our market position. So the only way to set ourselves apart is with the performance of our people." Following the spinoff, Gower continued to pursue this philosophy, with renewed vigor.

Gower had come to Lyondell by way of Sinclair Oil. He joined Sinclair Oil as a research scientist. Both before and after Sinclair's merger with ARCO, he had risen through a variety of sales, research, and engineering assignments, becoming a vice-president of ARCO Chemical in 1977 and senior vice-president in 1979. He had gone on to direct the technology division, then later, business management and marketing for large-volume petrochemicals. In 1984 he had been elected senior vice-president of planning and advanced technology at ARCO. When Lyondell was formed in 1985, he became its president, and was elected its CEO in 1988.

At Lyondell Gower cut operating costs and trimmed away layers of management. Lyondell's 1989 net income fell off 31 percent from 1988, as demand for gasoline and petrochemicals cooled. Lyondell's operations also suffered from weather- and maintenance-related problems. Nevertheless, Gower continued to spend. A large percentage of the $176 million Lyondell spent in 1989 on capital projects went into the expansion of the two olefins plants that were shut down for overhauls. These expan-

Key Dates:
1985: Atlantic Richfield Company (ARCO) separates its olefins operations from ARCO Chemical Company, forming a new subsidiary, Lyondell Petrochemical Corporation, which is soon renamed Lyondell Petrochemical Company.
1987: ARCO spins off ARCO Chemical, selling 20 percent of its shares to the public.
1989: ARCO sells 50 percent of Lyondell to the public in a $1.4 billion IPO.
1990: Lyondell purchases low-density polyethylene and polypropylene plants from Rexene Products Company.
1993: The company contributes its refining operations to a joint venture with CITGO Petroleum Corporation called LYONDELL-CITGO Refining LP (LCR); Lyondell initially owns 86 percent of LCR.
1995: Occidental Chemical Corporation's Alathon high-density polyethylene business is acquired.
1997: ARCO divests its remaining stake in Lyondell; a major upgrade of the LCR plant in Houston is completed, and Lyondell's interest in LCR is reduced to 58.75 percent; the company combines its petrochemicals and polymers businesses with those of Millennium Chemicals Inc. to form Equistar Chemicals, LP, with the company holding an initial 57 percent interest.
1998: Lyondell's interest in Equistar is reduced to 41 percent with the addition of Occidental Chemical's petrochemicals business to the venture; Lyondell acquires ARCO Chemical for $5.6 billion; the company changes its name to Lyondell Chemical Company.
2000: The company sells its polyolefins business to Bayer AG for $2.45 billion.

sions resulted in lower unit production costs, increased ethylene capacity by about 25 percent, and increased propylene and other byproduct capacity.

Acquisitions and Joint Ventures in the 1990s

In February 1990 Lyondell made its first acquisitions: low-density polyethylene and polypropylene plants from Rexene Products Company. These plants improved the value of Lyondell's operations as they not only were captive consumers of ethylene and propylene but also enabled Lyondell to participate in the polyolefins market.

Lyondell's early successes were derived from the company's flexibility; for instance, Lyondell's olefins plants were capable of switching from production of natural gas liquids such as ethane, propane, and butane, to heavy liquids such as naphthas, condensates, and gas oil, depending on which feedstock yielded the greatest profit. In addition to this, the Houston refinery was able to run on a large percentage of low-cost heavy crudes in addition to many foreign crude oils, allowing Lyondell to select the best-priced crude. The Channelview plant also displayed product flexibility, producing propylene from ethyl-

ene when product markets were stronger, and adjusting production mix and product volumes to utilize market opportunities. Lyondell had the freedom to act on these opportunities because as an intermediate producer it was not committed to supplying retail outlets. In 1989, Lyondell began to expand its Houston refinery's paraxylene capacity. Finished in early 1990, it provided a 25 percent increase in paraxylene production.

In July 1993, in order to strengthen its refining operations, Lyondell contributed these operations to a joint venture with CITGO Petroleum Corporation, the U.S. subsidiary of Petroleos de Venezuela. Included in the venture, called LYONDELL-CITGO Refining LP, were the Houston refinery and a lube oil blending and packaging plant in Birmingport, Alabama. Lyondell held an initial 86 percent interest in the venture. The partners, however, agreed to launch a $1 billion upgrade of the Houston refinery to enable it to begin using the extra-heavy variety of Venezuelan crude and to increase capacity at the plant. Most of the output was then sold to CITGO for marketing through its U.S. network. Partnering with CITGO enabled Lyondell to run its refining operations in a much more stable manner, with long-term contracts with CITGO on both the crude supply and refined output sides. Following the completion of the plant upgrade in early 1997, Lyondell's interest in LYONDELL-CITGO was reduced to 58.75 percent.

In mid-1994, meanwhile, ARCO made the first move in a plan to dispose of its remaining interest in Lyondell. At that time, ARCO made a debt security offering, worth close to $1 billion, that was convertible after three years into Lyondell stock. When this offer was completed, the five ARCO officers on the Lyondell board resigned, and Gower took over as chairman, remaining CEO as well. Dan Smith, who had been with Lyondell for most of its brief history, was promoted from COO to president and COO. He took over as CEO in December 1996 upon Gower's retirement. In June 1997 William T. Butler, chancellor of Baylor College of Medicine and member of the company board since 1989, was named nonexecutive chairman of Lyondell. Also in 1997, ARCO followed through with its divestment plan and sold off its remaining stake in Lyondell.

While these ownership and management changes were taking place, Lyondell moved forward with another acquisition and the formation of another joint venture. In May 1995 the company paid $356 million to acquire the Alathon high-density polyethylene business and its plants in Matagorda and Victoria, Texas, from Occidental Chemical Corporation, a subsidiary of Occidental Petroleum Corporation. Lyondell in December 1996 partnered with MCN Corporation to form Lyondell Methanol Company. The essence of the deal was that MCN purchased a 25 percent stake in Lyondell's methanol plant, which Lyondell continued to operate.

In December 1997, in its most dramatic joint venture agreement yet, Lyondell combined its petrochemicals and polymers businesses with those of Millennium Chemicals Inc. to form Equistar Chemicals, LP. At formation, Lyondell held a 57 percent stake in Equistar, which also assumed $745 million of Lyondell debt. Five months later, Equistar was expanded in size by about one-third with the addition of the petrochemicals business of Occidental Chemical. This deal decreased Lyondell's ownership interest in Equistar to 41 percent (Millennium and Occidental each owned 29.5 percent). Equistar began life with annual sales of about $6 billion and with top three positions in North America and the world in ethylene, propylene, butadiene, and polyethylene. Lyondell operated Equistar for the partnership.

At this point, Lyondell had essentially placed all of its operations within the three joint ventures it had formed since 1993. The company then moved beyond these equity investments by gobbling up its former ARCO sister firm, ARCO Chemical, in a July 1998 acquisition valued at $5.6 billion. In addition to expanding the product lines in which Lyondell was involved, the deal also complemented the operations of Lyondell's other ventures. ARCO Chemical was a major consumer of propylene, ethylene, and benzene—three of Equistar's key products—and of methanol, which was produced by Lyondell Methanol. Lyondell also gained ARCO Chemical's world-leading positions in propylene oxide, propylene glycol, and MTBE. Following completion of the acquisition, the company shortened its name to Lyondell Chemical Company. During 1999 Lyondell restructured its long-term debt through a $4.2 billion combined equity and debt offering.

New Initiatives for the New Millennium

During 2000 Lyondell moved to further relieve its debt load from the ARCO Chemical purchase by selling the polyolefins business it had inherited from ARCO Chemical to Bayer AG for $2.45 billion. The deal enabled the company to retire more than $2 billion of long-term debt. As part of the agreement, Lyondell and Bayer also agreed to form a 50-50 joint venture to build a state-of-the-art plant in the Maasvlakte region of The Netherlands that would be the world's largest propylene oxide and styrene monomer plant. Start-up of the plant was expected by mid-2003. Meantime, Lyondell also was proceeding on its own with the building of another plant in The Netherlands, this one to produce butanediol and to begin operations in early 2002.

By 2001, these global growth initiatives were continuing with the backdrop of a cyclical downturn in the chemicals industry compounded by an economic slowdown in the United States that was spreading globally—not to mention the aftereffects of the events of September 11, 2001. After posting net income of $437 million for 2000, Lyondell appeared headed for a significant loss for 2001, having reported a net loss of $97 million for the first nine months of the year.

Principal Subsidiaries

Lyondell POTechGP, Inc.; Lyondell Quimica do Brasil, Ltda. (Brazil); Lyondell Refining LP, LLC; Lyondell Refining Company; Lyondell South Asia PTE Ltd. (Singapore); Lyondell Taiwan, Inc.; Lyondell Thailand, Ltd.; Nihon Oxirane Co., Ltd.

(Japan); POSM Delaware, Inc.; PO Offtake, LP; PO JV, LP; POSM II Limited Partnership, L.P.; POSM II Properties Partnership, L.P.; Seinehaven BDO2 (Netherlands); Steamelec B.V. (Netherlands); Technology JV, LP.

Principal Competitors

The Dow Chemical Company; Shell Chemical Company; BASF Aktiengesellschaft; Bayer AG; Saudi Basic Industries Corp.; Chevron Phillips Chemical Company LP; Mitsubishi Chemical Corporation; Samsung Group.

Further Reading

Adams, Jarret, "Lyondell Completes Arco Chemical Buy, Decides on Name Change," *Chemical Week,* August 5, 1998, p. 13.

Barrett, Amy, "Walking the Plank," *Financial Week,* April 2, 1991, pp. 32–34.

Davis, Michael, "Houston-Based Lyondell to Acquire Arco Chemical," *Houston Chronicle,* June 19, 1998, Sec. 3, p. 1.

——, "Lyondell Joins Polyethylene Partnership," *Houston Chronicle,* July 29, 1997, Sec. 3, p. 1.

Durgin, Hillary, "The Right Chemistry: Occidental Joins in Equistar Venture," *Houston Chronicle,* March 21, 1998, Sec. 3, p. 1.

Ewing, Terzah, "Lyondell to Form Chemicals Venture with Millennium," *Wall Street Journal,* July 29, 1997, p. B5.

Hoffman, John, "OxyChem, Equistar Merge Olefins to Create Global Petrochem Giant," *Chemical Market Reporter,* March 23, 1998, p. 1.

Ivanovich, David, "Arco Will Shed Stake in Lyondell," *Houston Chronicle,* May 6, 1994, Sec. 2, p. 1.

Kiesche, Elizabeth S., "Fast Footwork Gives Lyondell Its Edge," *Chemical Week,* August 29, 1990, pp. 42, 44.

Link, Janet, "Lyondell's Buy of Arco Praised Within Industry," *Chemical Market Reporter,* June 29, 1998, pp. 1, 11.

"Lyondell's Climb into the Black," *Chemical Week,* January 15, 1986.

Morris, Gregory D.L., "Fresh Talent at the Top at Lyondell," *Chemical Week,* March 22, 1995, p. 52.

——, "Lyondell's Man of the Hour: Gower Keeps Costs Down and Motivation Up," *Chemical Week,* July 15, 1992, pp. 21–22.

Nulty, Peter, "How to Live by Your Wits," *Fortune,* April 20, 1992, pp. 119–20.

Sixel, L.M., "Tight Ship: Productivity of Workers Makes Lyondell an Industry Leader," *Houston Chronicle,* July 28, 1991, Sec. 2, p. 19.

Tullo, Alex, "Lyondell Acquires Arco for $5.6 Billion, Deal Strengthens Company in Petrochems," *Chemical Market Reporter,* June 22, 1998, pp. 1, 49.

Warren, Susan, "Lyondell Will Be One of the Top Makers of Chemicals Following Arco Purchase," *Wall Street Journal,* June 19, 1998, p. A4.

Wood, Andrew, "Lyondell's Class Decade," *Chemical Week,* July 19, 1995, pp. 22–23.

—Maya Sahafi
—update: David E. Salamie

Mackay Envelope
Company, LLC

Mackay Envelope Corporation

2100 Elm St. SE
Minneapolis, Minnesota 55414
U.S.A.
Telephone: (612) 331-9311
Toll Free: (800) 622-5299
Fax: (612) 331-3460
Web site: http://www.mackayenvelope.com

Private Company
Incorporated: 1959
Employees: 500
Sales: $85 million (2000 est.)
NAIC: 322232 Envelope Manufacturing

Mackay Envelope Corporation manufactures approximately five billion envelopes a year at two manufacturing facilities in Minneapolis and Mt. Pleasant, Iowa. The company also has sales offices in Illinois and Kansas. Mackay Envelope's products meet the needs of diverse customers: specialized envelopes come in any size, color, and configuration with a variety of options for color printing and embossing capabilities. Commercial envelopes account for much of the company's business, including envelopes for the direct-mail industry, publishers' renewal programs, and cycle billing statements. A second division manufactures envelopes for the photofinishing industry, while a third division produces stationery and business cards. In a sea of other envelope manufacturers, Mackay Envelope stands out because its founder, Harvey Mackay, has achieved modest celebrity status as a best-selling author and public speaker. Mackay has written four inspirational business books: *Swim with the Sharks Without Being Eaten Alive, Beware the Naked Man Who Offers You His Shirt, Dig Your Well Before You're Thirsty,* and *Pushing the Envelope All the Way to the Top.* The books are packed with anecdotes, aphorisms, and advice for success in business and life. Altogether, the books have sold more than ten million copies worldwide and have been translated into 35 languages. In addition, Mackay earns top dollar as a public speaker. His experience leading an envelope company provides a practical illustration for his ideas on successful management, salesmanship, hiring, and networking.

The Rise of a Struggling Company: 1959–70

In a 1996 interview, Harvey Mackay told *Minnesota Business and Opportunities,* "I always wanted to own my own factory. I didn't care if it was nuts and bolts. I didn't care if it was widgets. . . . I just visualized myself walking up and down the aisles and having these people, you know, my people, my team, making some products and smiling at me." Chance decreed that envelope manufacturing was to become Mackay's vehicle to success. After Mackay graduated from the University of Minnesota, his father, a reporter for the Associated Press, got him a job as an envelope salesman through a connection with a businessman about whom he had once written a story. Harvey Mackay began working for Quality Park Envelope Co. in 1954.

While selling envelopes by day, Mackay took night courses in printing and considered opening a printing plant. Soon, however, he saw an opportunity to acquire a nearly insolvent envelope manufacturer, Paypar Envelope Company. Mackay secured a loan and bought the company in 1959 at age 26. At the time, the company had 12 employees, three folding machines, one small printing press, and $200,000 in annual sales. Not sure if the company would survive, Mackay waited several years before renaming it so that his personal name would not be connected with the company if it went bankrupt.

A year later, the company showed some promise of surviving, and the employees voted to unionize. Mackay tried to dissuade them from their decision, painting a picture of a bright future if only everyone stuck together, but the pro-union vote won. Mackay raised prices so he could afford union wages.

After a few years the company was on solid enough ground that Mackay was willing to attach his own name to it. In 1963 the company changed its name to Mackay Envelope Corp. and moved from a location that Mackay described as a "red light district" to a new Minneapolis headquarters. Recognizing that his skills were more in salesmanship than in technical expertise, Mackay got a cost specialist to design an effective manufacturing system that was still in place decades later. While turning to experts to ensure that his company's infrastructure and methods were solid, Mackay used his considerable talent as a salesman to win customers to the fledgling enterprise.

Company Perspectives:

Mission: To be in business forever.

At Mackay, quality is the goal to which everyone contributes, and customer satisfaction is the reward for which everyone strives. From pre-press operations to shipping, the skills of Mackay professionals strengthen each link in the chain.

Our size and depth of experience give us the ability to thoroughly understand the changing needs of our customers, and the resources to respond to those needs. Through it all, one thing remains constant: we're never satisfied until our customer is satisfied.

Mackay welcomes change, and we invite you to challenge us with new requirements and new ideas.

Unique Business Practices Driving Growth in the 1970s

Mackay Envelope built its solid customer base during the 1970s using the tactics that Harvey Mackay was later to promote in his best-selling books. One of Mackay's key concepts was that "Knowing something about your customer is just as important as knowing everything about your product." Mackay went to extraordinary lengths in his adherence to that principle, developing a 66-question customer profile to gather information that reached beyond the normal realm of business. The "Mackay 66" included questions related to personal and family life, such as the names, ages, and hobbies of the customer's children, the customer's religion and community involvement, favorite places for lunch and preferred reading material, as well as more usual questions related to education and business background.

The information-gathering method, when applied with sincerity, was effective in winning customers. Over the years, Mackay Envelope's major clients included General Mills, Pillsbury, Medtronic, and Billy Graham. As Mackay put it in the 1996 interview, "You have to have a deep down burning desire to find out about people you come in contact with." According to him, the successful businessperson misses no opportunity to glean information about a customer, from observing plaques hanging on the buyer's wall to reading *Who's Who* to making connections in the local bar. In *Swim with the Sharks* Mackay related a number of successes that resulted from persistent information-gathering. After overhearing that a customer's daughter competed in gymnastics, he brushed up on the sport, attended a competition, and a month later got an order after mentioning his involvement to the buyer. For particularly tough prospects, Mackay suggested delving into the buyer's charitable interests. A donation to a favorite charity had been known to open doors to a long-lasting business relationship.

The hiring process was also carried out with unusual intensity at Mackay Envelope. Harvey Mackay called the ability to recognize ability his "number one strength." For the first 25 years of business, he told *Minnesota Business and Opportunities* in 1996, he hired virtually every employee himself, from the truck drivers to the switchboard operator. "Getting hired by Mackay Envelope is like a battlefield commission," he wrote in *Swim with the Sharks*. The goal was to become familiar with all sides of the candidate's character in a variety of settings. It was not enough to have a dozen meetings between the candidate and numerous people at the company. Mackay would also interview the candidate's spouse, meet his or her children, and seek the opinion of an industrial psychologist.

The whole process seemed extreme to some, but candidates who made it through the process were likely to remain at Mackay Envelope for some time. As Mackay described it in the 1996 interview, "I'm going to scare the living hell out of you, and if you still keep coming back for more at the end of that three month process, which 99 out of 100 companies won't do, then I've got a hungry fighter on my hands." Not only did employees stick around, but, in positions from switchboard operator to executive assistant, they were likely to be among the best in the business.

Growing Community Visibility: The 1980s

Such intensive management and sales principles required a large amount of energy to carry them out. Harvey Mackay proved he had the drive, the people skills, and the focus to convert his maverick approach to business into a company successful by all conventional standards. Steady growth continued year after year as Mackay Envelope developed from a small manufacturer into a large, specialized producer offering a wide variety of envelope sizes and printing techniques. High-speed presses carried out color printing, while special multi-hue dying equipment was able to tint a product to the customer's exact color specifications.

As his company established itself as a force in the envelope manufacturing industry, Harvey Mackay became more and more visible in the Minneapolis business community. Encouraged by his father, he began speaking publicly, offering his advice on entrepreneurship and marketing in an engaging anecdotal style. Soon favorable word of mouth garnered him invitations to speak out of town, until by the early 1990s he was giving about 50 speeches a year at $25,000 per appearance.

Mackay's growing civic involvement provided him with the experiences that supported and illustrated his principles for success. He became known for his efforts to get the Metrodome stadium built in Minneapolis in the late 1970s, and played a key role in bringing the Super Bowl to the city in 1992. While his high-profile involvements earned him the nickname "Mr. Make Things Happen," he proved a deeper commitment to civic involvement in his activity with less glamorous organizations, including the Minnesota Orchestra, the United Way, and the American Cancer Society.

Although his outside involvements took time away from the envelope company, Mackay always remained closely involved with what he believed was the crucial aspect of management—hiring good people. With Mackay's leadership and the hard work of dedicated employees, Mackay Envelope continued to grow. In 1980 a strike at the Minnesota manufacturing facility made Harvey Mackay realize that it was inadvisable for the company to depend on a single central facility. That year a second manufacturing plant opened in Mt. Pleasant, Iowa. Although the company had trouble finding skilled labor in the first few years, by 1988 50 percent of Mackay envelopes were produced in Iowa.

In 1982 Mackay Envelope began to maintain an audio library to which all employees had access. The purpose of the library was to allow employees to capture driving time for the

Key Dates:

1959: Harvey Mackay purchases the struggling Paypar Envelope Company.
1963: Name is changed to Mackay Envelope Corp.
1980: A second manufacturing facility opens in Iowa.
1988: Mackay publishes first book of motivational business advice.
2000: Mackay Envelope is sold to company President Scott Mitchell.

purpose of self-edification, following Harvey Mackay's injunction to "turn your automobile into a university." Another expansion came in 1984, when a five-person sales office opened in Schaumburg, Illinois. The office sold envelopes from the company's commercial division to businesses in the Chicago area.

Meanwhile, Mackay's speeches were generating requests for an audio or a printed version of his talks. Encouraged by Ken Blanchard, author of *The One-Minute Manager*, Mackay decided to write a book. He went about the endeavor with his usual thorough persistence, researching the market for two years before picking a publisher, and persuading the editor to print a unheard-of first run of 100,000 hardcover copies. Published in March 1988, *Swim with the Sharks Without Being Eaten Alive* sold 300,000 copies by November. Subtitled "Outsell, Outmanage, Outmotivate and Outnegotiate Your Competition," the book reproduced the Mackay 66 and included 69 lessons whose lengthy titles belied the sound bite style of each chapter. Lessons included "It Isn't Practice That Makes Perfect; You Have to Add One Word: It's Perfect Practice That Makes Perfect," and, "It Isn't the People You Fire Who Make Your Life Miserable, It's the People You Don't."

Since Mackay was touring to support his book four days a week, he relied heavily on company President William Jacobs to manage the envelope company. Despite its chairman and CEO's newfound status as a best-selling author, Mackay Envelope continued its steady growth. In 1988 the company had sales of $35 million and employed 350 people.

Continued Growth and Expansion: 1990–2001

Harvey Mackay's second book, *Beware the Naked Man Who Offers You His Shirt*, was published in 1990. The book offered advice on dealing with people and loving your job. It highlighted networking as a key to success. Mackay wrote, "If the house is on fire, forget the china, silver and wedding album—grab the Rolodex." His own Rolodex, he said, included 7,500 names, 20 percent of whom he kept in touch with actively, while the rest were at hand to be called on in situations where they could be of assistance.

In October 1990 William Jacobs, who had been company president for approximately two decades, left Mackay Envelope. James Basset, former president of Old Colony Envelope, replaced Jacobs. Mackay Envelope continued to develop its business through the recession of the early 1990s. A new stationery ordering system called M-Print was introduced in 1992. While it required a considerable investment in software, M-Print paid off by allowing clients to place orders for envelopes, letterhead, or business cards directly from any of multiple branches. Corporate graphics were maintained at Mackay Envelope for consistency. The new system reduced staff time involved in ordering stationery and eventually became the basis for an entire division centered around stationery and business cards.

By 1993 annual sales had climbed to $40 million, and Mackay Envelope was in the middle of another intensive search for a company president. Basset had left to accommodate his wife's out-of state job, and Mackay embarked on a quest for a replacement. After a five-month process involving an executive search agency, none of the finalists met Mackay's high standards. Finally, in September 1993, Mackay broke from tradition and hired a new president based on gut feeling. Scott Mitchell, a salesman with a background in computers and real estate, impressed Mackay with his "instant credibility and friendliness," according to a *Minneapolis Star Tribune* article.

Mitchell maintained the company's upward trajectory. In 1996 sales reached $50 million at a production level of 12 million envelopes per day. The following year an office with a single salesperson was opened in Overland Park, Kansas. Harvey Mackay still divided his energies between company management and his writing career. His third book, *Dig Your Well Before You're Thirsty*, was published in April 1997, followed by *Pushing the Envelope All the Way to the Top* in January 1999.

At the end of 1999 sales had reached $85 million, 17 million envelopes were manufactured a day for 3,000 clients, and Mackay Envelope employed 500 people. The company was a dominant provider of photofinishing envelopes, sales of which had doubled since 1993. Attracted by the firm's solid standing, Colorado-based competitor Mail-Well offered to buy the company in late 1998. Mackay was tempted by the attractive price and a lucrative management contract, but had reservations about selling out of state. When company President Scott Mitchell expressed an interest in buying the company, Mackay was willing to accept less money to keep the firm privately held in Minnesota. In September 2000 a leveraged buyout by Mitchell was finalized. Under the terms of the deal, Mackay retained a significant share and a management role in the company, while Mitchell became CEO and the dominant shareholder.

In 2001, Mackay Envelope continued to be an attractive choice for envelope buyers. Harvey Mackay's knack for salesmanship, coupled with extraordinary energy and drive, had propelled the company to a prominent place in the industry. The future of the company would depend on whether Mackay's management principles, instilled in the company over the past four decades, would retain their effectiveness even after his inevitable departure.

Principal Competitors

Mail-Well, Inc.; National Envelope Corporation; Atlantic Envelope.

Further Reading

Barrier, Michael, "Back into the Shark Tank," *Nation's Business*, March 1990, p. 50.

Braham, James, "*Sharks* Gets Bites: CEO-Authors Heroes Now Are Calling Him," *Industry Week*, June 6, 1988, pp. 26–27.

Giombetti, Anthony F., "Harvey Mackay: Entrepreneur, Best Selling Author and World Renowned Speaker," *Minnesota Business & Opportunities,* January 1996, pp. 34–41.

Mackay, Harvey, *Beware the Naked Man Who Offers You His Shirt*, New York: William Morrow and Company, Inc., 1990.

——, *Pushing the Envelope All the Way to the Top*, New York: Ballantine Publishing Group, 1999.

——, *Swim with the Sharks Without Being Eaten Alive*, New York: William Morrow and Company, 1988.

Pappas, Charles, "Harvey Mackay," *Success*, February 1999, p. 50.

Peterson, Susan E., "Mackay Seals Sale of Envelope Firm," *Minneapolis Star Tribune*, September 21, 2000.

——, "New Mackay President Still Going at Full Throttle," *Minneapolis Star Tribune*, September 6, 1993, p. 1D.

Smith, Scott, "Mackay's Way (Interview with Harvey Mackay)," *Success,* September 2000, p. 26.

Van Gorder, Barbara E., "Prospering During Tough Times," *Credit*, January-February 1992, p. 13.

Woods, Jenny, "Mackay Envelope Sold," *Minneapolis-St. Paul City-Business*, September 29, 2000, p. 44.

—Sarah Ruth Lorenz

The Major Automotive Companies, Inc.

43-40 Northern Boulevard
Long Island City, New York 11101
U.S.A.
Telephone: (718) 937-3700
Toll Free: (800) 625-6728
Fax: (718) 937-3308
Web site: http://www.majorautomotive.com

Public Company
Incorporated: 1995 as Fidelity Holdings Inc.
Employees: 300
Sales: $322.14 million (2000)
Stock Exchanges: NASDAQ
Ticker Symbol: MAJR
NAIC: 44111 New Car Dealers; 44112 Used Car Dealers;
    44131 Automotive Parts & Accessories Stores;
    532112 Passenger Car Leasing; 53212 Truck, Utility
    Trailer & RV Rental & Leasing; 551112 Offices of
    Other Holding Companies

The Major Automotive Companies, Inc. is a holding company for the Major Dealer Group, a leading consolidator of automobile dealerships in the New York City metropolitan area. It sells new cars through a number of retail automotive franchises, including Major Chevrolet; Major Dodge; and Major Chrysler, Plymouth, Jeep Eagle. These franchises are located on Northern Boulevard in Long Island City, a community in New York City's borough of Queens; Hempstead, Long Island; and Orange, New Jersey. Major Automotive sells used cars and provides parts and services from other Long Island City locations. It also leases cars and trucks and offers financing through third parties. In addition, it distributes new General Motors vehicles to countries of the former Soviet Union.

Major Automotive Group and Fidelity Holdings: 1985–96

Bruce Bendell and his brother Harold began operating a Brooklyn carwash and auto repair shop in 1972. Subsequently

they and their father sold used cars and leased new cars in Brooklyn before purchasing Major Chevrolet, a Long Island City distributor, in 1985. At this time the dealership was in decline, with only 500 cars and $10 million in annual sales. By 1990 sales had increased tenfold. In 1996 Bendell's Major Automotive Group was doing about $180 million a year in business. One of New York's largest auto dealerships, it now consisted of six franchises, including Major Chevrolet/Geo; Major Dodge; and Major Chrysler, Plymouth, Jeep Eagle, in Long Island City, plus, in Woodside—another Queens community—Major Subaru, in addition to Major Fleet and Leasing, the leading supplier of taxis and police cars in New York and also a lessor of trucks.

Fidelity Holdings Inc., founded in October 1995 by Bruce and Harold Bendell and Doron Cohen and based in Kew Gardens—another Queens community—was a holding company engaged in two different businesses. Its Voice Processing and Computer Telephony Division was developing the Talkie, a device invented by an Israeli that promised high-speed, broadband multimedia transmission over the telephone, including voice, data, videoconferencing, voice mail, automated-order, and other applications. This division also was developing proprietary software for making low-cost, long-distance international telephone calls. The Plastics and Utilities Products Division consisted of a development-stage company acquired in 1996. It was planning to market a prefabricated conduit for underground electrical cables and a line of spa and bath fixtures. Fidelity Holdings began appearing on the NASDAQ OTC Bulletin Board in 1996 and initially traded at $4 to $5 a share. It had revenue of $3.43 million that year and net income of $675,966.

Avi Nissanian, the largest wholesaler of jewelry to the Home Shopping Network, owned 27 percent of Fidelity Holdings at this time. He had put the Bendells in touch with Cohen, president of the company. Bruce Bendell held about 40 percent of the common stock of Fidelity Holdings and was its chief executive officer and chairman in April 1997, when it announced an agreement to acquire Major Automotive Group in a transaction valued at about $10 million. Fidelity Holdings paid $4 million to Harold Bendell for shares of stock in Major Automotive subsidiaries and acquired certain real estate components from

<table>
<tr><td colspan="2">Key Dates:</td></tr>
</table>

Key Dates:

1985: Bruce Bendell, his brother, and his father purchase Major Chevrolet.

1990: Annual revenue has increased tenfold in five years.

1996: Major Automotive now holds six franchises with $180 million in annual revenue.

1998: Fidelity Holdings Inc. purchases Major Automotive Group for $14.7 million.

1999: A total of 600 used cars are placed on a Queens lot called Major World.

2001: Fidelity sells its nonautomotive businesses and assumes the Major Automotive name.

Bruce and Harold Bendell for $3 million. The transaction was completed in 1998 at a cost of about $14.7 million in cash and stock. Major Automotive had sales of $144.5 million and Fidelity Holdings had revenue of $3.86 million in 1997.

Although a combination of Major Automotive and Fidelity seemed a stretch, Bendell was seeking a way to increase sales without increasing overhead. Major Automotive had become one of the first auto dealerships with an Internet site and also had begun to sell cars over computer terminals owned by Bloomberg L.P.; the owner, Michael Bloomberg, was also one of its customers. Bendell said that marketing costs for auto dealerships in the New York metropolitan area averaged about $350 per vehicle and that Major Auto held its marketing costs to an average under $200, but that on the Internet the cost was only $25 to $50. Interviewed for *Automotive News* in 1998, Bendell told Laura Clark Geist, "We allow the customer to make an inquiry on any service in our dealership. The customer can request a quote on a vehicle, submit a credit application or request an appraisal on his or her current vehicle. They can make an appointment to visit any of our showrooms or service departments, plus a request for parts, or simply find out more about our dealership."

Bendell also was enthusiastic about the Talkie, which he employed to receive loan applications from his customers, and foresaw other uses for it in his business, such as calling clients to offer specials, remind them to bring their cars in for oil changes, and allow them to make service appointments and check on parts supplies. Ultimately, he envisioned his customers conducting virtually all their dealings with his dealerships by telephone. He thought that the prepaid phone cards that a Fidelity unit planned to offer could be used as giveaway items in Major's marketing. In addition, the merger enabled Major Automotive to go public without having to share with an underwriter the proceeds of an initial public offering of common stock.

Bendell was also mindful of the trend toward consolidation among auto dealers. Some 850 U.S. dealerships went out of business between 1992 and 1997 as consolidators such as United Auto Group, Inc. and AutoNation USA combined them into chains. Manhattan-based United Auto Group had already gone public and developed a major presence in the New York metropolitan area with its purchase of the DiFeo Group and

Staluppi dealerships. In 1997 Carl Spielvogel, chairman of United Auto Group, told Tom Incantalupo of *Newsday,* "We try to surround a market because it gives you the ability, in particular, to move used cars from one dealership to another." Bendell was about to adopt the same strategy, thereby building on the most profitable part of the business, used car sales, along with servicing and financing.

Reversal of Fortune: 1999–2001

By the spring of 1999 Major Automotive had added a Kia franchise in Long Island City and had agreed to purchase Compass Lincoln-Mercury and Compass Dodge in Orange, New Jersey. (Acquisition of the Dodge dealership was not completed until 2000, and in that year the company also acquired a Mazda dealership in Hempstead, Long Island.) Bendell also consolidated the used car businesses of his five Queens franchised dealerships into a single lot, at the flagship Major Chevrolet location. This lot, which held 600 cars, was named Major World. Bendell said the company was saving money by advertising all of its used vehicles under the Major World name and was drawing more customers by enabling them to do their shopping at a single location. It also introduced a new web site for used vehicles only. By 2000 Major World was believed to be the largest seller of used vehicles in the New York City area.

Fidelity Holdings had 1999 revenues of $210.81 million but a net loss of $3.54 million. The technology division was the problem, with revenues of only $1.28 million and a net loss of $6.06 million, but its products were seen by investors as offering potential, and the stock was bid up to $20 a share in the spring and summer of 1999. It was still trading for more than $19 a share early in January 2000, despite a three-for-two stock split in 1999. A number of subsequent stockholder suits, however, charged Fidelity and its executives with improperly deferring expenses in the first three quarters of 1999 to avoid reporting losses until a fourth-quarter loss was disclosed in April 2000. As soon as the year-end result became public, the price of a share of Fidelity common stock nosedived to $3. By the end of 2000 stockholders had filed about a dozen securities-fraud suits against Fidelity Holdings and its officers, charging the company with making false and misleading statements in order to sell stock.

Fidelity Holdings announced in November 2000 that it intended to divest itself of Computer Business Services, Inc., its technology division, and to change its name to Major Automotive Companies, Inc. In March 2001 it sold its voice-processing technology, the IG2 Network, to Global Communications of New York, Inc. for $1.78 million. Global Communications was a new company being formed by IG2 employees in which Fidelity took a minority stake. The telephone calling-card subsidiary, ICS Globe, Inc., was sold to the same company in July 2001 for $240,000. In June 2001 Major Automotive sold its Canadian subsidiary, Info Systems, Inc., and its interest in its Israeli subsidiary, C.B.S. Computer Business Sciences Ltd., to GYT International Ltd. for $119,500 net. The company acquired a Daewoo franchise in April 2001 and a Suzuki franchise a month later.

Expansion of its auto business raised Fidelity Holdings' revenues to $322.14 million in 2000. This division's net profit of $1.3 million was extinguished by the company's $22.43 million loss taken from its discontinued technology operations. Its stock dropped as low as 23 cents a share before the company was renamed in May 2001 and issued a reverse one-for-five-share stock split, which raised the price level to about $2 a share. Bendell owned 37 percent of the stock in October 2001, two months after an announcement that Marshall Cogan, founder and formerly head of United Auto Group, would acquire about two-thirds of this equity position. The terms called for Cogan to become Major Automotive's chairman and chief executive and, with his nominees, to hold four seats on the seven-member board. Bendell would remain as president. In October, however, the company announced that Cogan had terminated the agreement. Major Automotive also disclosed that Chrysler Financial Company, LLC, its chief source for financing its vehicle inventory, was cutting off credit by the end of the year.

Major's Sales and Profits in 2000

At the end of 2000 Major Automotive Group, including its Major Dealer Group, was one of the largest-volume automobile retailers in New York City. Major Automotive Group owned and operated seven franchised automobile dealerships in the New York metropolitan area: Chevrolet, Chrysler, Plymouth, Dodge, Jeep, Subaru, and Kia. In addition, Major Dealer Group owned five franchised dealerships in the metropolitan area: Lincoln-Mercury, Mazda, Dodge, Nissan, and Daewoo. Seven of these franchises were at four locations in Long Island City, three franchises were at three locations in Hempstead, Long Island, and two franchises were in two locations in Orange, New Jersey. The parts and service and used-vehicle businesses were operating from three additional locations in Long Island City.

The company sold 5,369 new vehicles in 2000, of which Chevrolet accounted for 42.6 percent. New-car sales revenues of $132.5 million accounted for 41.2 percent of company revenues. Major Automotive sold 13,291 used vehicles for about $178 million, constituting 55.4 percent of company revenues. Sales of parts and services came to $11 million, or 3.4 percent of the total. In terms of gross profit margin, however, parts and services was, at about 51 percent, by far the most lucrative segment of company business. The 18.1 percent gross profit margin on sales of used vehicles was almost double the industry average. The company had a gross profit margin of 8.2 percent on new-vehicle sales, also significantly higher than the industry average of 6.1 percent.

Principal Subsidiaries

Hempstead Mazda, Inc.; Major Acquisition Corp.; Major Automotive of New Jersey, Inc.; Major Automotive Realty Corp.; Major Daewoo, Inc.; Major Nissan of Garden City, Inc.; Major Orange Properties, LLC.

Principal Competitors

Potamkin Auto Group; United Auto Group, Inc.

Further Reading

Freedman, Eric, "New Securities-Fraud Suit Accuses Fidelity Holdings," *Automotive News,* December 11, 2000, p. 9.

Geist, Laura Clark, "Start with $1,000, Then Maybe $100 Per Month," *Automotive News,* February 2, 1998, pp. 98, 100.

Harris, Donna, "Tech Business Drained Dealership Group," *Automotive News,* April 23, 2001, pp. 3, 61.

Hetter, Katia, "Fidelity Inc. Names New President," *Newsday,* December 19, 1998, p. A49.

Incantalupo, Tom, "Dealership Gears Up for Growth," *Newsday,* October 13, 1997, p. C7.

——, "Major Car Chain Busy 5 LI Dealers," *Newsday,* February 26, 1997, pp. A43–A44.

——, "United Auto Founder to Acquire 27% Stake in Major Automotive," *Newsday,* August 14, 2001, p. A37.

Lipowicz, Alice, "Auto Dealer Drives Off with Area Business," *Crain's New York Business,* April 10, 2000, p. 18.

"Major Auto Is Bought in Bid to Dominate New York Car Dealers," *Wall Street Journal,* May 15, 1998, p. B7D.

Miller, Joe, "Major Making Strides in Tough New York Arena," *Automotive News,* April 5, 1999, p. 30.

Temes, Judy, "Wheeler Dealers Test-Drive Telecom," *Crain's New York Business,* June 16, 1997, pp. 4, 44.

"Who Will Deal in Dealerships?," *Economist,* February 14, 1998, pp. 62–63.

—Robert Halasz

Marsh & McLennan Companies, Inc.

1166 Avenue of the Americas
New York, New York 10036-2774
U.S.A.
Telephone: (212) 345-5000
Fax: (212) 345-4838
Web site: http://www.marshmac.com

Public Company
Incorporated: 1923 as Marsh & McLennan, Incorporated
Employees: 57,000
Total Assets: $13.76 billion (2000)
Stock Exchanges: New York Boston Chicago Pacific
Ticker Symbol: MMC
NAIC: 52421 Insurance Agencies & Brokerages

Marsh & McLennan Companies, Inc. (MMC) is a global professional services operation. Yet for all its years in business, sustained growth, and shear size, MMC is relatively obscure: hardly a household name. MMC is the parent company of Marsh Inc., the world's leading risk and insurance firm, which operates in more than 100 countries; Putnam Investments, Inc., one of the largest U.S. money management firms; and Mercer Consulting Group, serving the areas of strategic and operational human resource consulting and implementation and ranking among the largest firms of its kind in the world.

Laying the Groundwork: 1880s–1900s

In 1885 an ambitious young Henry Marsh left Harvard College without graduating and joined R.A. Waller & Company, a Chicago-based insurance agency founded in 1871, the year of the Great Chicago Fire. Marsh's lack of a degree proved no disadvantage in this period of U.S. history. The 1880s and 1890s were a period of political corruption and gross materialism in the United States, yet the age was also one of tremendous industrial expansion and urban growth. In 1889, following the death of Robert A. Waller, Henry Marsh and another employee, Herbert J. Ulmann, bought a controlling interest in the firm, which they renamed Marsh, Ulmann and Company.

In this age of big business, Marsh was convinced that huge profits could be made by managing the insurance affairs of large corporations in return for appropriate commissions. As Marsh himself declared, "What's the use of shooting hummingbirds when elephants are so much easier to hit." Marsh realized that very large companies could set aside sufficient funds to cover themselves against potential losses without placing the risk with insurance companies. In 1901 Henry Marsh talked Charles Schwab, president of the United States Steel Corporation, into adopting such a scheme, with Marsh's company managing an appropriate fund to estimate potential risks to U.S. Steel. In this way Henry Marsh pioneered the modern-day concepts of self-insurance and risk management.

Henry Marsh met his future partner and associate, Donald McLennan, in the course of his attempts to secure railroad contracts for his growing insurance agency. McLennan had begun an insurance agency in partnership with L.B. Manley in Duluth, Minnesota, in 1900. Duluth's position on the Great Lakes had made it a major transfer point for the products—mostly agricultural—of the Great Plains. Goods arrived by rail and were loaded onto steamers to be shipped east. When the lakes froze during winter, such products were stored in warehouses owned by the railroads.

McLennan had recognized the enormous insurance potential in these activities. He quickly became an expert on railroad insurance, constantly traveling the Midwest and meeting with company executives. During one round of sales negotiations, McLennan was reported to have spent 30 consecutive nights in a railroad car.

As it transpired, Henry Marsh, Daniel Burrows, and Donald McLennan all had been promised the insurance account of the Chicago Burlington and Quincy Railroad by different directors. Rather than argue over the account, the three men joined forces. All realized the advantages of combining their skills and resources into one company with a view to securing still more insurance contracts.

On December 22, 1904, the *Chicago Record-Herald* reported the launching of the "New agency of Burrows, Marsh & McLennan" with annual premiums of $3 million. Soon other

Company Perspectives:

While MMC has changed over the years, its values, culture, and approach to governance haven't changed much at all. We are dedicated to client service. Throughout its history, MMC has served as a trusted advisor, providing clients with analysis, advice, and transactional capabilities. We seek to attract and develop the best people. This has been the basis of our tradition of professional excellence. We are committed to building value for shareholders. The fiduciary manner in which we care for their interests has been fundamental to MMC and to its credibility with investors.

In recent decades we've become a global company, improving service to clients and growing our business. We have evolved to become an effective owner of diverse professional services companies. Today, our businesses are market leaders.

railroad contracts were secured, including The Great Northern and Northern Pacific. In 1906, following the retirement of Daniel Burrows, the new firm became known as Marsh & McLennan (M&M).

Seizing Opportunities: 1910s–40s

In the newly reorganized firm, Marsh concentrated on securing more contracts, while McLennan supervised the railroad account. Marsh's sales tactics sometimes surprised the more staid McLennan—Marsh would stop at nothing to obtain new contracts. He often sailed to England, and even went so far as to rearrange the deck chairs in order to "accidentally" meet potential new clients. On one such trip in 1910, Marsh met Theodore Vail, the president of the American Telephone and Telegraph Company (AT&T), and secured that company's business.

By 1917, the year the United States entered World War I, M&M had established offices throughout the country. During the war, McLennan became responsible for the allocation and regulation of building materials for purposes other than those directly related to the war effort. For the duration of the war, no U.S. company could build an industrial plant without McLennan's approval. In this way McLennan acquired many business contacts throughout the United States, enhancing M&M's reputation in the postwar period.

During the economic boom of the 1920s, M&M continued to prosper. In 1923 the legal structure of the company was changed from a partnership to a corporation, Marsh & McLennan, Incorporated. The stock was now held under a voting trust agreement by Marsh, McLennan, and four other people. Marsh became chairman, while McLennan increasingly assumed responsibility for the firm's management. The same year, the reinsurance brokerage firm, Guy Carpenter & Company, became a separately managed business of Marsh & McLennan.

The Great Depression of the 1930s had an adverse effect on the insurance industry. Many institutions and individuals simply could not afford to pay insurance premiums. Although premiums from most types of insurance declined, the life insurance business actually increased, as people craved financial

security. The passage of the Social Security Act of 1937 further sparked interest in life and accident insurance as people became more concerned with financial security. Many firms adopted retirement programs to supplement Social Security benefits, and employed M&M to operate such funds. The American Can Company employed M&M to devise a pension plan for its employees, and also asked it to organize the fee-billing service.

After the entry of the United States into World War II, the conservative McLennan was invited to meet with New Deal President Franklin Roosevelt, who asked his advice on the management of the U.S. war industry. McLennan later spoke of his meeting with the famous leader: "When I left the White House, I went to my room at the hotel, took a cold shower and then walked around the block several times. It took me at least 48 hours to rekindle my dislike of the President. Never in my life have I met a more charming individual."

Neither Marsh nor McLennan lived to see the end of World War II, however. Henry Marsh died on April 13, 1943, and McLennan on October 9, 1944. Charles Ward Seabury became chairman of the board and Laurence S. Kennedy, the new president. The company survived the loss of its two founders and continued to prosper. In 1947 Ford Motor Company selected M&M to handle all its insurance. The postwar boom in consumer spending, much of it on credit, also provided an opportunity for innovation: M&M developed consumer credit insurance which it sold to eight of the nine major New York banks.

Aggressive Expansion: 1950s–70s

Following Seabury's retirement and Kennedy's death in 1955, Hermon Smith became the CEO and chairman. In 1957 Cosgrove & Company, the West Coast's largest regional broker, was merged into Marsh & McLennan. Between 1958 and 1962, 14 other agents and brokers were acquired. By 1962 M&M had become an international company with offices in the world's major financial centers, yet the structure of the company had not changed since 1923. In 1955 shareholders had numbered only 21, up from the original six shareholders in 1923. While technically a corporation, it nevertheless operated as a partnership. There were no stockholder meetings and stockholders' identities and the number of shares they held were kept secret. Beginning in 1957, when a stockholder died, retired, or turned 70 years old, his stock had to be sold back to the company.

Given the growing complexity of the insurance business and his desire for company growth, Smith began in 1958 to explore the idea of going public. In March 1962, 673,215 shares of M&M stock were offered to the public. This decision marked a transition in the company's ability to grow.

The 1960s signaled the beginning of a period of unparalleled expansion as M&M embarked on a series of acquisitions of smaller insurance agencies. In 1968, M&M acquired Edwards George and Company of Pittsburgh, Pennsylvania, and R.H. Squire of New York City. Revenues also increased dramatically throughout the 1960s. The company's first annual report, in 1962, recorded revenues of $52 million; by 1968 revenues had jumped to $106 million. In 1969, to administer its services more efficiently, Marsh & McLennan reorganized, and became known as MarLennan Corporation. Henceforth the company

Key Dates:

1989: Henry Marsh partners with a fellow employee to buy controlling interest of a Chicago-based insurance company.

1901: Marsh pioneers modern-day self-insurance and risk management concepts in deal with United States Steel Corporation.

1906: Railroad insurance expert Donald McLennan and Marsh form a partnership.

1923: Marsh & McLennan (M&M) incorporates.

1947: Ford Motor Company selects M&M to handle all its insurance.

1957: Merger with the West Coast's largest broker, Cosgrove & Company, kicks off series of domestic and international acquisitions.

1962: M&M stock is taken public.

1970: Purchase of Putnam Management Company marks move toward diversification.

1975: Name is changed to Marsh & McLennan Companies, Inc. (MMC).

1980: MMC is established as global company with takeover of London brokerage firm C.T. Bowring.

1996: Rival firm Aon Corporation bumps MMC from position as top insurance brokerage.

2000: MMC, aided by addition of top-grade firms, enters new millennium in position of global market dominance.

2001: Company is one of hardest hit in destruction of World Trade Center.

would provide a variety of its professional and financial services under the banners of separately managed companies. The first of these, the Putnam Management Company, became part of M&M in 1970. In 1975, M&M's employee-benefit-consulting business was folded into William M. Mercer Inc.

The 1970s marked a new phase in international development. John Regan, who became chief executive in 1973, was determined to transform the company into a global insurance force, and embarked on a policy of buying foreign brokerage firms in the world's major financial cities. In 1973 MarLennan acquired a 33.3 percent interest in the French insurance brokerage Faugere et Jutheau. In 1975 the company acquired a 15 percent interest in the German firm Gradmann & Holler, and a 29.5 percent interest in Henijean & Cie in Belgium. That year its name changed again, to Marsh & McLennan Companies (MMC).

Not all acquisitions proceeded smoothly, however. In 1980 Regan set his sights on C.T. Bowring, a large London brokerage firm. The acquisition of such a firm would allow MMC direct access to the profitable Lloyd's of London insurance market, open only to British firms. Many executives of Bowring, an old, traditional English firm, resented the takeover by the U.S. brokerage. In long, and often acrimonious, discussions, Bowring executives—despite their dependence on MMC business—continued to reject Regan's terms. Undaunted, Regan went directly to the shareholders, a tactic that outraged Bowring's management. Bowring Chairman Peter Bowring appealed to the

British Insurance Brokers Association and the British government for help in preventing the incursion. Questions were raised in the House of Commons about the need to protect the British insurance industry. The French, it was reported, would never have allowed this to happen. Despite much rhetoric, little was done to help Bowring. With shares priced far above their market value, British shareholders could not resist the temptation to sell. In the end, Regan paid $580 million for Bowring, more than twice its book value.

Many executives resigned from the British firm. This development stunned Regan, who worried that such a loss of talent would severely hamper the effectiveness of his new acquisition. Regan claimed that he would have abandoned the takeover if he had known it would cause such a personnel exodus. Nevertheless, C.T. Bowring continued to function.

The Bowring purchase was a crucial move in MMC's transformation into a global company. Six months after the takeover, MMC revenues had jumped 28 percent, while net income increased 22 percent, to more than $100 million.

Shifting Focus: 1980s Through the Mid-1990s

MMC's strategy in the 1980s was to diversify beyond insurance into consulting and money management. In 1982 insurance-program management separated from the consulting activities of Mercer to become a separate company, later called Seabury & Smith. MMC consulting capabilities expanded in the 1980s to include National Economic Research Associates; Temple, Barker & Sloan/Strategic Planning Associates; and Lippincott & Margulies.

Meanwhile the financial management side of the business was undergoing an overhaul. During its first decade under MMC ownership, Putnam Investments primarily managed assets for institutional clients. But in the early 1980s those sales slipped. Lawrence J. Lasser took charge of the operation in 1985, reorganized, expanded its offerings, and subsequently produced stellar growth.

"Putnam's performance couldn't come at a better time," Ronald Fink wrote in a 1993 *Financial World* article. "Marsh's core business—property and casualty insurance brokerage—has been in a slump for over six years. In fact, Putnam's profitability went a long way toward keeping Marsh's net income from falling last year." Putnam produced 14 percent of total company revenues in 1992 but contributed 23 percent of operating income.

On the insurance end, MMC turned its sights to globalization. In January 1990 the company completed its purchase of a majority stake in Gradmann & Holler, Germany's largest insurance broker. Additional affiliated companies were acquired and branch offices established—primarily in Europe—during the next two years. By 1993, MMC held wholly owned offices in the 12 European Community nations and in six non-member nations. Purchases in Latin and South America, the Far East, and Hong Kong were also in the works.

The acquisition push was followed by a streamlining of operations. A Global Broking Centre, based in London, was to link insurance wholesale offices and insurance underwriters around the world, facilitating the sharing of information by all the pertinent players, and easing large capacity property/casualty transactions for both U.S. and foreign clients. In a related move, MMC separated its large U.S. risk management accounts from its middle-market insurance brokerage clients—those without full-time risk managers. The move marked the beginning of a concerted push to gain more business in this mid-range area.

The consulting division, now called Mercer Consulting Group Inc., also made some changes in the early 1990s, selling off an environmental consulting operation. Remaining in the division in 1994 were: William M. Mercer, the world's largest actuarial and employee benefits consulting and human resource management firm; Mercer Management Consulting Inc., a corporate strategy and management consulting company; and the economics consulting firm, National Economic Research Associates Inc. About 65 percent of the consulting division's revenue, which remained flat during the period, came from U.S. accounts.

The company's U.S. insurance operation stagnated along with the rest of the industry during the mid-1990s, though there were some bright spots. In 1995, MMC's domestic middle-market segment, responding to aggressive marketing, showed strong growth. Overseas operations also showed strong growth, especially in the Pacific Rim. But overall, insurance revenue rose just 4 percent on the year.

In addition to flat or falling markets, insurers had to contend with other changes taking place within the industry, such as product line integration and insurance firm consolidation. MMC looked internally for answers. To counteract a blurring of lines between who sold what types of insurance, MMC restructured operations in an effort to better define its products for customers. In order to boost the reinsurance business, hurt by a drop in the number of insurance companies to which to sell its products, MMC created Risk Capital Insurance Company. The new unit differentiated itself by investing much of its resources in the stock of companies it served.

Resurgence in the Late 1990s

In 1996, after more than 20 years at the top of the worldwide insurance brokerage business, MMC was surpassed by Aon Corporation when the Chicago based competitor purchased Alexander & Alexander.

''Its army of brokers and consultants has been regarded as the best in the business. And the company has consistently recorded double-digit earnings growth,'' wrote Judy Temes for *Crain's New York Business* in 1997. ''But suddenly, being good isn't good enough. The $4 billion giant—spread across the insurance, management consulting and mutual funds businesses—is finding itself on the defensive.''

MMC's focus on internal growth, cost cutting measures, and technological improvements could not outstrip a decade of troubles in the insurance industry. Additionally, the company's six-year attempt to gain more of the higher-margin strategic consulting business had floundered, leaving Putnam to drive earnings growth. Consequently, MMC found its stock undervalued on the market and heard calls for a spinoff of the highly

profitable financial management segment, a move which would benefit stockholders.

Marsh responded by purchasing some top notch businesses, first paying $200 million for the leading French insurance brokerage. The company followed up with the buyout of Johnson & Higgins in 1997 and Sedgwick Group PLC in 1998, a boon to middle-market business. MMC trimmed back its insurance-related purchases in 1999 but planned for more acquisitions in the consulting area.

Leadership changed hands in 1999. Jeffrey W. Greenberg was named CEO in November and then chairman of the board in May 2000; he succeeded A.J.C. Smith. Greenberg had a heady first 16 months at the helm, with the stock price rising 60 percent and high profile managers joining the ranks. Also, MMC Enterprise Risk, a cutting edge operation drawing on expertise throughout MMC, was launched and poised to offer integrated risk management services.

In terms of numbers, revenue topped the $10 billion mark in 2000, and net income rose by 23 percent to $1.2 billion. Marsh produced about half the total revenues, followed by Putnam with one-third, and the rest from Mercer. Greenberg would have to stay on his toes though, with the economy slowing and the stock market fluctuating.

Thus, MMC embarked on the new century back on the top of its core business sector, and importantly, insurance prices had headed upward: a trend which boded well for Marsh since its revenue came from rate sensitive commissions and negotiated fees. Moreover, the consolidation binge of the 1990s had produced two mega-insurance brokerages. Between them, Marsh and Aon generated 73 percent of all the revenue produced by the top ten companies in the industry. Conflicting views circulated as to whether or not this was a good thing.

An Uncertain New World: 2001 and Beyond

The unimaginable happened on September 11, 2001. More than 300 MMC employees—primarily people working in accounting and information technology—were among those killed when New York's twin World Trade Center towers were destroyed. MMC, like the many other businesses directly affected, had to go on despite the horror.

In late September, MMC Capital Inc. announced the formation of Axis Specialty Ltd., a new insurer to be based in Bermuda. The unit would write insurance and reinsurance coverage in such areas as ''all-peril property, aviation, war, political risk,'' which were deemed underserved, according to a report by David Pilla for *A.M Best Newswire*.

Meanwhile, commercial insurance rates, particularly in the hard-hit airline industry, skyrocketed. Property-insurance rates, already on the rise, also climbed, but less steeply. Workers' compensation increases were expected as well.

One month after the disaster, MMC announced the formation of a crisis-consulting practice. L. Paul Bremer, former ambassador-at-large for counterterrorism during President Reagan's administration, would head the operation.

Principal Subsidiaries

Marsh Inc.; Mercer Consulting Group Inc.; Putnam Investments, Inc.; MMC Capital Inc.; and MMC Enterprise Risk Inc.

Principal Competitors

Aon Corporation; Arthur J. Gallagher & Co.; Willis Group Holdings Limited.

Further Reading

Brent, Andrew, ''... But Big Firms Can Afford to Be Aggressive,'' *Mutual Fund Market News,* October 8, 2001.

Fink, Ronald, ''Cash Cow,'' *Financial World,* July 6, 1993, pp. 64–65.

Gjertsen, Lee Ann, ''Marsh, Aon Regroup After Losses,'' *American Banker,* September 25, 2001, p. 7.

McLeod, Douglas, ''Marsh & McLennan Cos. Inc.,'' *Business Insurance,* July 5, 1993, pp. 18, 20–21.

——, ''Marsh & McLennan Cos. Inc.,'' *Business Insurance,* July 18, 1994, pp. 16–18.

Osborn, Neil, ''The American Invasion of Lloyd's,'' *Institutional Investor,* October 1979.

——, ''The Bloody Battle for Bowring,'' *Insurance,* August 1980.

Oster, Christopher, ''Business Impact: Insurance Rates Rocket Across Industries, But Unlike Airlines, Help May Not Come,'' *Wall Street Journal,* October 8, 2001, p. A11.

——, ''Marsh & McLennan Unit to Unveil Plan to Launch a Crisis-Consulting Practice,'' *Wall Street Journal,* October 11, 2001, p. C17.

Pilla David, ''Marsh Unit Forms New Insurer in Response to Capacity Shortage,'' *A.M. Best Newswire,* September 28, 2001.

Requet, Mark E., ''Marsh Ends Year on Strong, Positive Note,'' *National Underwriter Property & Casualty-Risk & Benefits Management,* February 12, 2001, p. 21.

Roberts, Sally, ''Pros and Cons of Consolidation Debated,'' *Business Insurance,* July 16, 2001, p. 12.

Souter, Gavin, ''Marsh & McLennan Cos. Inc.,'' *Business Insurance,* July 22, 1996, pp. 14+.

——, ''Marsh & McLennan Cos. Inc.'' *Business Insurance,* July 17, 2000, pp. 20–22.

Temes, Judy, ''Marsh's Growing Quagmire: Mergers Prod Inert Insurance Broker to Act,'' *Crain's New York Business,* February 17, 1997, pp. 1+.

Wipperfurth, Heike, ''Quietly Making a Big Noise; Marsh & McLennan Loads Up on Talent; Racing to Stay Even,'' *Crain's New York Business,* March 12, 2001, p. 3.

—Michael Doorley
—update: Kathleen Peippo

Master Lock Company

2600 N. 32nd Street
Milwaukee, Wisconsin 53210
U.S.A.
Telephone: (414) 444-2800
Fax: (800) 308-9245
Web site: http://www.masterlock.com

Wholly Owned Subsidiary of Fortune Brands, Inc.
Incorporated: 1921
Employees: 1,500
Sales: $200 million (2000 est.)
NAIC: 332510 Hardware Manufacturing

Master Lock Company produces several lines of premium security lock products. Master Lock is the most recognized brand of locks, with padlocks and combination locks constituting its primary base of business. The company develops and manufactures locks for sporting goods, such as bicycles, skis, and guns; rust-proof locks for marine uses; and a variety of specialty needs as well. Master Lock produces security locks for businesses, schools, hospitals, and industrial uses.

Invention of Strongest Padlock Available Following World War I

Masterlock earned its reputation for quality locks from the inventions of Harry Soref, a Milwaukee-area locksmith. As a security consultant for the military during World War I, Soref invented a special padlock used to protect military equipment. After the war, in 1919, he designed a padlock with laminated layers of steel like those used in the production of bank vault doors and battleships. Soref anticipated that such a heavy-duty lock would outclass the durability of the hollow padlocks of that time, which were broken easily with a hammer. He hoped to sell the design to a hardware manufacturing company, but the padlock required several parts and production steps, and engineers, manufacturers, and patent attorneys found the product design too cumbersome. Supported by the financial investment of two friends, P.E. Yolles and Sam Stahl, Soref began his own company, Master Lock Company, in 1921. He patented the first

laminated padlock in 1924. Master Lock marketed the padlock using a lion's head logo for name recognition.

With only five employees, a drill press, a grinder, and a punch press in a small Milwaukee shop, Master Lock produced the best padlock available. The heavy weight of the lock added to public perception of its strength. The company grew rapidly, moving to the Pabst Brewery building, closed due to prohibition. Prohibition played an important role in the early growth of the company as federal authorities purchased large quantities of the laminated padlocks to lock down bars and clubs that sold alcoholic beverages. In February 1928 the company shipped 147,600 padlocks to New York City for that purpose. Business boomed as federal agents around the country began to order Master Lock padlocks.

Soref became a recognized authority on locks. The escape artist Harry Houdini visited Soref in Milwaukee after he failed to escape from a set of handcuffs. They were said to have discussed handcuff keys and Soref advised Houdini on how to hide them under his tongue and in between his fingers during the stage shows. In 1931 the American Association of Master Locksmiths awarded Soref a gold medal, the only one ever given, for making the greatest contribution to the development of locks in more than 50 years. A Master Lock exhibit at the 1933 Chicago World's Fair taught the public about the construction of laminated steel locks. During World War II, Soref provided security consultant services to the military.

Sales grew along with Soref's and Master Lock's reputation and the company moved to a larger production facility and new offices in 1939. Soref continued to experiment with new lock designs and production methods. An improvement to a combination lock required the company to change its production assembly to the complete reverse, disrupting plant operations. The lock proved easier to assemble, however, and to be of better quality. Master Lock grew to become the largest manufacturer of padlocks in the country, with almost universal public recognition of the brand name. Although high security pin tumbler padlocks continued to comprise the largest portion of sales, Master Lock developed products for use in schools, hospitals, and offices, and on vending machines. The company's reputation outlived Soref, who died in 1957. Sam Stahl, one of the original investors, led the company until his death in 1964, when the Soref family took over management of the company. American Brands (renamed Fortune Brands in 1997) purchased Master Lock from the Soref family in 1970.

New Ownership, High Brand Reputation, Expanding Product Line: 1970s–80s

Master Lock experienced unprecedented growth during the 1970s, as American Brands capitalized on the company's reputation. Master Lock developed a television commercial for the 1974 Superbowl game that became notable in the public eye for its effective message and its identification with Master Lock. The "shot lock" advertisement, "Tough Under Fire," showed a blast from a high-powered rifle aimed at a Master Lock padlock. Although the bullet pierced the center of the lock, the lock still functioned. The tagline, "If it's worth locking, it's worth a Master Lock," followed. The "product as hero" strategy proved effective and Master Lock continued to use similar commercials during Superbowl games and other high-profile advertising slots.

During the 1970s Master Lock noted record sales every year. In 1978 Master Lock experienced its 13th consecutive year of growth, recording sales of $62.4 million and operating income of $22.7 million. Building on the strength of its brand name and expertise in locks, Master Lock expanded with innovative styles and applications and in new markets. In 1978 the company introduced a new line of laminated pin tumbler rekeyable padlocks, in which the cylinder could be replaced or repinned. In sporting goods the company sold locks for skis, guns, and bicycles. The energy shortage of the 1970s prompted many people to opt for bicycling as an alternative choice of transportation and sales of cable and chain bicycle locks rose accordingly. Master Lock introduced two locks designed for mopeds in late 1979. A new U-bar bicycle lock and laminated brass locks made significant contributions to sales increases in the early 1980s. To accommodate its growing production needs, in 1979 the company began the first phase of an expansion project, a 92,000-square-foot warehouse and production facility addition.

New markets included retail establishments, such as sporting goods, recreational vehicle and marine outlets, hardware stores, and locksmiths. Master Lock began to sell its products through food and drug chain stores and mass merchandisers. Built-in lockers at health clubs provided new outlets for Master Lock products and the company began to offer rekeyable padlocks to locksmiths and industrial tradespeople. Cable locks for outboard motors provided a new area of growth and in 1981 the company introduced brass padlocks for marine uses.

With a 52 percent share of a mature market and new competition from imported brands, Master Lock sought to retain its dominant position and to improve operations for lower overhead. Between 1981 and 1986 the company invested $25 million to upgrade equipment and facilities. To improve factory efficiency the company changed the organization of its assembly lines to locate the similar products close together, allowing workers to switch stations easily and for easier movement of finished goods to the warehouse. The company changed its inventory management to just-in-time accounting. Parts arrived at the assembly line as needed to reduce "work in process" costs. Order processing, previously about six weeks, was reduced to a few days, lowering inventory costs. Equipment improvements reduced production time, for instance, from six hours to six minutes to change die in a 150-ton press. These changes freed production space for new products, such as "Tough Stripes," a high-tech style bike lock introduced in 1987.

Master Lock expanded its product base through the January 1986 acquisition of the Dexter Lock Company, adding $25 million in annual revenues. Dexter provided premium door locksets and door hardware for residential uses. Dexter added new products in 1986, such as the "Sure Thing" adjustable universal door latch. The new "Designer Series" offered premium entrance handles, knob sets, and other door hardware for the upscale market.

Although consumer studies noted 95 percent awareness of the Master Lock brand, the company did not take that position for granted. In 1986 Master Lock increased its advertising budget by 50 percent, spending $2.5 million. The new tagline, "Whatever you want to lock," reflected the diversity of the company's security products. Advertising involved 232 television spots and 120 radio spots, primarily during talk shows and sporting events. Master Lock's successful "product as hero" campaign continued into the 1990s. In addition to using a shotgun to exhibit the security of the locks, commercials showed men using hammers, crowbars, and rocks, all failing to break a padlock. In one commercial a truck tried to drive through a gate locked with a Master Lock product and failed.

In 1994 Master Lock produced a new Superbowl commercial titled "Security." The beginning of the 30-second spot showed, at a feverish pace, Master Lock products in use at Hoover Dam, at Caesar's Palace, on a Wells Fargo armored security truck, and at Ely Maximum Security Prison. The shots were interspersed with bullets being loaded into a rifle. In the final scene, the rifle fired, but the bullet deflected off the Master Lock padlock. The tagline stated, "A Master Lock may not be the only lock between the good guys and the bad guys, or between the good stuff and the people who want it, but it's certainly *one* of the locks."

Price Competition, New Approaches to Business in the Late 1990s

During the late 1990s Master Lock experienced new competitive pressures as other American lock companies took advantage of low-cost manufacturing opportunities in Asia. In addition, Wal-Mart and Kmart persuaded Master Lock to lower prices to meet the competition. Although Master Lock held a 70 percent share of the retail market in 1994, that figure declined to 40 percent in 1996. Master Lock sought to maintain a steady level of business activity through overseas expansion and li-

Key Dates:

1921: Master Lock Company is incorporated.
1924: Founder Harry Soref patents first laminated steel padlock.
1931: Industry recognizes Soref for the most important development in locks in more than half a century.
1957: Soref dies.
1970: American Brands acquires Master Lock.
1974: Master Lock begins annual Superbowl advertising with famous "shot lock" commercial.
1978: The company experiences its 13th consecutive year of record growth.
1994: Master Lock retail market share peaks at 70 percent, then declines due to competition from manufacturers using low-cost, foreign labor.
1999: Transfer of assembly jobs from Milwaukee to Mexico begins.
2001: Master Lock restores image as premium lock maker with patented titanium locks.

censing its brand name, as well as through low-cost foreign manufacturing. A new product in 1996 involved a joint venture with Kensington Technology Group to produce and market a galvanized steel cable and locking device to use with Laptop computer equipment, the Master Lock Universal Notebook Security Cable. Overseas expansion involved a new sales office in Canada, where Master Lock held the top market position for locks, and a sales office and distribution facility in Hong Kong. A distribution facility in France served European customers. New products introduced in 1998 included the EX locks; a nylon shroud protected the locks, making them resistant to cutting and prying.

Master Lock lowered its advertising costs by discontinuing its participation in high-priced Superbowl advertising in 1996. A new campaign in 1998 placed the first one-second spots ever to be broadcast on national television. The low-budget commercials used the central scene from the "shot lock" advertisement, shown in one second for dramatic effect. The bold campaign relied on consumer recognition of the long-running advertisement and of the Master Lock name. More than 400 spots played on ESPN Classic Sports and FX over 45 days in June and July as precursors to 30-second spots promoting the company's new products beginning in late June.

In response to competitive pricing Master Lock began to transfer some of its manufacturing and assembly operations overseas to reduce operating costs. The company relocated gunlock manufacturing to China, while construction on a state-of-the-art facility began in Nogales, Mexico. In 1997 Master Lock renegotiated with its labor union to allow the transfer of 700 assembly jobs from Milwaukee to Mexico. The sale of the Dexter subsidiary in 1998 provided funds for restructuring. In 1999 the company relocated 400 assembly jobs to Mexico, with the balance of 300 assembly jobs being relocated by the fall of 2000, nine months ahead of schedule. Master Lock sought lower priced, international sources for raw materials, but parts production continued in Milwaukee for shipment to the Nogales plant.

Master Lock closed the company's original distribution center in Milwaukee in 1999 and hired another company to handle those operations from a new, 213,000-square-foot warehouse in Louisville, Kentucky. The central geographic location reduced shipping costs and Louisville had recently become a service hub for United Parcel Service. The location and state-of-the-art facility allowed for 80 percent of orders to reach their destination within 24 to 48 hours.

In the fall of 1999 Master Lock licensed its brand name to Fortres Grand for a new software security product. The software gave parents control of their children's computer and Internet use. The filter for Internet use was based on actual content of a web site, rather than keywords. The program prevented children from giving their name, address, telephone number, and other personal information to strangers over the Internet. It also kept children from accessing their parents' financial records on the home computer.

As an innovator in security lock products, Master Lock sought to compete through innovation, developing patented products of superior quality that could not be copied by the competition. In September 1999 Master Lock introduced a rustproof padlock with an exclusive Corrozex finish; the company included a lifetime warranty with the product. An integrated steering wheel and air bag lock for automobiles addressed new concerns about air bag theft.

In August 2000 Master Lock debuted the first titanium padlocks and combination padlocks, the DAT Titanium Tough Padlock. The patented product was rustproof, and both lighter and stronger than steel. Produced overseas, the higher priced products reestablished Master Lock as the premium lock maker and generated a higher profit margin. The titanium locks were priced at $8.99 to $11.99 retail, compared with steel locks at $2.99 to $4.99. With a sleek design and bright colors, Master Lock successfully attracted young customers and doubled the company's back-to-school business. While consumers tended to purchase a lock about once every five years, Master Lock found that many customers replaced old locks with the new titanium locks for greater security. Master Lock included a lifetime guarantee on the locks, covering mechanical defects and corrosion.

In November the company gained free publicity when the television show *Law & Order* highlighted a Master Lock product. In one scene a forensics expert showed a bullet-damaged Master Lock padlock to two lead detectives investigating a murder case. He reminded the detectives of the old "shot lock" commercials, confirming that the lock must have been opened with a key. Detective Brisco responded, "Truth in advertising." Master Lock did not initiate the product placement, but it affirmed the success of the company's advertising.

Master Lock's new products in 2001 involved improvements to its regular product line. The company introduced two resettable combination locks in brass and customized safety locks in solid aluminum. The new Xenoythermoplastic padlocks offered a tough, but lightweight alternative to heavy metal locks. The Force 6-Ton, a bike lock capable of resisting six tons of pulling force, doubled the strength of its existing bike lock. The company planned to introduce an adjustable locking cable as well. New product introductions planned for 2002 included lock products for the trailer and towing markets. Master Lock increased its marketing budget for 2002 to $15 million, including in-store promotions.

Principal Competitors

Abus Lock Company; American Lock; ASSA ABLOY AB; Belwith Ltd.; Chubb plc; Ingersoll-Rand Company.

Further Reading

DeSalvo, Karen, "Backyard's Smith Loads, Aims and Shoots for Master Lock," *SHOOT,* January 28, 1994, p. 7.

Gallaun, Alby, "Right Combination," *Business Journal-Milwaukee,* February 11, 2000, p. 3.

Gladstone, Karen, "Master Lock Raises Advertising Budget to Put Clamp on Market," *Business Journal-Milwaukee,* March 17, 1986, p. 9S.

Halverson, Richard C., "Finding the Right Combination," *Discount Store News,* April 1, 1991, p. 21.

Hawkins, Jr., Lee, "Master Lock Tries to Regain Premium Image with Rust-Proof Titanium Products," *Knight Ridder/Tribune Business News,* August 23, 2000.

——, "Milwaukee-Based Lock-Making Firm Aims to Restore Image, Sense of Job Security," *Milwaukee Journal Sentinel,* August 28, 2000.

Jagler, Steven, "Master Lock to Close Distribution Center," *Business Journal-Milwaukee,* August 6, 1999, p. 3.

"Key-Free Security," *Aftermarket Business,* November 2000, p. 132.

Lai, Garret, "Master Lock Force 6 Ton U-Lock $70–$80," *Bicycling,* June 2001, p. 57.

Quigley, Kelly, "Mastering 'Law & Order,' " *Business Journal-Milwaukee,* December 1, 2000, p. 2.

"Safety Leverage," *Delaney Report,* October 1, 2001, p. 3.

Schneider, Harvey, "Master Lock Risks a National Meeting," *Sales and Marketing Management,* July 2, 1984, p. 79.

Washburn, Dan, "Master Lock Sells Door Hardware Assets," *Home Improvement Market,* February 1998, p. 22.

—Mary Tradii

Michael Page International plc

39-41 Parker Street
London WC2B 5LN
United Kingdom
Telephone: (+44) 20-7831-2000
Fax: (+44) 20-7269-2121
Web site: http://www.michaelpage.co.uk

Public Company
Incorporated: 1976 as Michael Page Partners
Employees: 2,315
Sales: £426.89 million ($637.2 million) (2000)
Stock Exchanges: London
Ticker Symbol: MPI
NAIC: 561310 Employment Placement Agencies

Michael Page International plc (MPI) is one of the world's leading recruitment companies. Based in London, with 100 offices operating in 14 countries, MPI targets primarily higher-paid, white-collar, permanent positions in the financial, banking, accounting, legal, marketing and sales, human resources, and IT sectors. The company's targeted annual pay rates range from £25,000 to £100,000. Nearly 80 percent of MPI's business is in permanent position placement, although the company has a significant business in temporary and contract hire, which helps to cushion the company somewhat during hiring downturns. The company's origins as a specialist in the accounting and financial sectors continue to show in its business in the new millennium: more than 70 percent of MPI's revenues are generated in these two sectors (banks account for about 10 percent of sales). Marketing and sales provide an added 15 percent of the company's business. MPI has long played the international field, although nearly half of its revenues are still generated in the United Kingdom. France is its next strongest market, which, together with the rest of Europe, add an additional 37 percent to the company's sales. MPI has targeted the Asia/Pacific region for growth, with expanding its presence in Australia and Hong Kong and other markets and an entry into Japan in 2001. The company has a minor presence in the United States, which represented only 2 percent of its sales in 2,000, although MPI

expects to grow in that market with the establishment of a new office in New Jersey in 2001. A short-lived subsidiary of Spherion (formerly Interim Services), the company was spun off in a public offering at the beginning of 2001, with a market capitalization of more than £650 million. Leading MPI is CEO Terence W. Benson, a former accountant-turned-recruitment specialist.

Career Hunters in the 1970s

MPI was founded in 1976 by Michael Page and Bill McGregor. Accountants with experience working for the oil industry, the pair had met while looking for work in one of England's notorious employment agencies following the economic crash of the mid-1970s. Page and McGregor reasoned that there was room for a better breed of employment placement service and, using £10,000 obtained in a bank loan, set up their own company, the Michael Page Partnership, in London.

Page and McGregor initially targeted two areas they knew well: accounting and the oil industry. Over the next several years, however, the company's increasing success at filling positions led it to expand its accountant placement services to the other industries. The company also expanded geographically, adding offices in Birmingham, Glasgow, Leeds, Manchester, and Bristol. In 1979, the company was joined by a new employee, Terence Benson, an accountant who arrived seeking the company's services. Instead, Benson was hired by MPI itself as a recruitment specialist; over the next decade, Benson was to work his way up through the company's ranks, finally being named CEO in 1990.

Going Public and Diversifying in the 1980s

At the beginning of the 1980s, MPI was posting some £1.5 million in annual turnover. The company made its first public offering, placing its shares on London's Unlisted Securities Market in 1983. The following year, MPI began its first external growth effort, merging with Chetwynd Streets Plc. In 1985, however, the company sold out to growing business services group Addison Communications. The company's new parent changed its subsidiary's name to Addison Page.

The newly renamed company now had deeper pockets with which to pursue its international growth. The company set up offices in a number of new markets, beginning with Australia in 1985. Closer to home, the company targeted France in 1986 for its expansion onto the European continent. The company also added a number of new offices in the United Kingdom. At the same time, Addison Page began to diversify, extending its recruitment services into the banking and finance industry in 1985 and adding a legal recruitment wing in 1986. The company also began moving into the marketing and sales sector. In 1987, Addison Page crossed the Channel again, opening offices in The Netherlands.

The company's time as an Addison subsidiary proved short-lived. In 1988, as the world markets plunged toward a new economic downturn, Addison began breaking up its consultancy. MPI was spun off in 1988. Michael Page, taking up the position of chairman and CEO of the newly independent company, took it public that same year, now floating it on the London main board as the Michael Page Group.

Growth Through Expansion and New Markets: 1990s and Beyond

The company returned to independence at a low point for the recruitment industry in general, as the severe economic times dipped into a recession at the beginning of the 1990s. Nonetheless, Michael Page's policy of maintaining a significant treasury enabled the company to ride out the lean times of the early years of the decade. By then, Terence Benson had been appointed as company CEO, while Michael Page continued with the company as chairman. Benson remained committed to the combination of organic growth and careful international expansion that had marked the company's growth, taking Michael Page Group into Germany in 1991. The company began establishing a presence in the soon-to-boom technology market at the same time.

As the company eyed a return to growth of the recruitment market, it created a number of dedicated business units, including Accountancy Additions in 1992 and Michael Page Sales in 1994; another unit was formed in 1997, called Michael Page Retail. Each unit targeted a specific market sector.

Founder Michael Page retired in 1994, selling out his shareholding in the company. With the economy revving up once again, Benson continued the company's international expansion, opening an office in Hong Kong in 1995 and in Singapore in 1996. At the end of that year, the company's sales neared £104 million. The company also became interested in expanding into the United States.

An offer from Interim Services, Inc., one of the United States' largest recruitment agencies, gave Michael Page Group the opportunity it was seeking. In 1997, Michael Page agreed to

be acquired by Interim. The deal, which cost Interim £346 million, removed Michael Page from the stock market for a second time. The wisdom of the deal was later called into question—Interim targeted temporary and primarily blue-collar positions, as opposed to Michael Page's emphasis on junior- and senior-level permanent management positions.

Yet under the acquisition agreement, Michael Page remained an autonomous company, with its top management, including Benson, left in place for the most part. Under Interim, which continued an aggressive acquisition spree, Michael Page was able to proceed with its international expansion, not only establishing a base in the United States, but also new offices in Spain and New Zealand and then, in 1998, in Italy. Yet the marriage was not considered a successful one, as the two companies' cultures clashed, and Page's expansion into the United States remained limited.

At the end of the decade, Michael Page group operated from more than 90 offices worldwide. Its sales had been rising strongly as the economy returned to health not only in its core U.K. and European markets, but worldwide as well. From 1998 sales of £255 million, the company had climbed to nearly £427 million in 2000. In that year, the company had continued its international growth, opening offices in Brazil, Portugal, and Switzerland. It also had moved to establish its presence in a growing new recruitment category, that of human resources, creating a dedicated HR division in 2000. Another new market for the company was added at the same time, as the company formed its Michael Page Engineering unit.

Interim Services changed its name to Spherion in 2000. Burdened by a heavy debt load, Spherion announced its intention to spin off Michael Page—now as Michael Page International—to the public market early in 2001 in order to pay down some of its debt. The offering was originally announced in a range of 190p to 250p per share, which would have valued the company at the upper end at nearly £1 billion. Yet with fears of a new U.S. recession shaking the markets' confidence, the company was forced to lower its target price; when the company at last returned to the market, its value stood at just £656 million. Spherion sold nearly 90 percent of its holding at the time of the IPO, and the remainder one month later.

Soon after the IPO, the company faced new troubles. In June 2001, the company was forced to issue a profits warning, which in turn sparked an investigation by the U.K.'s Financial Services Authority into whether the company misled stockholders at the time of its flotation. The company was cleared of any wrongdoing later that year.

In the meantime, the continuing tough economic climate in the United States—where a number of major corporations were announcing large-scale layoffs—was shaking up the corporate community elsewhere in the world. Corporations in most of MPI's key markets had instituted hiring freezes as analysts began to forecast a new international recession. The company was forced to issue a new profits warning in October of that year—and admitted that it had itself instituted a hiring freeze.

The company had not, however, put a freeze on its growth. By the end of 2001, the company had opened its first office in Japan, hoping to tap into the trend in that country of turning away from its former "employment-for-life" corporate culture toward a more dynamic market where MPI's services would be in greater demand. At the same time, MPI began new moves to build a presence in the United States, opening an office in New Jersey. The United States nonetheless represented only 2 percent of the company's turnover. Meanwhile, as the economic picture began to brighten at the end of the year, the company began plans to expand into a new area in Europe, with the opening of an office in Stockholm slated for early 2002.

Principal Competitors

Adecco SA; AdVal Group PLC; CareerBuilder, Inc; Corporate Services Group PLC; Corporate Staffing Resources, Inc.; Fusion Staffing Services, LLC; Glotel Plc; HotJobs.com, Ltd.; jobpilot AG; Lorien plc; Manpower Inc; Marlborough International PLC; Penna Consulting PLC; Robert Walters plc; Select Appointments (Holdings) Limited; Spherion Corporation; Spring Group PLC; Vedior NV; World Careers Network PLC.

Further Reading

Baker, Lucy, "Michael Page Cuts IPO Price As Slowdown Fears Hit Take-Up," *Independent,* March 29, 2001, p. 19.

Felsted, Andrea, "Michael Page Cleared Over Profit Warning," *Financial Times,* December 12, 2001.

Martinson, Jane, "Headhunter Saddles Up for Takeover Hurdle," *Financial Times,* March 7, 1997.

Mills, Lauren, "Michael Page Set to Move into Japan," *Telegraph,* March 11, 2001.

Tomlinson, Heather, "Michael Page Leaves US Parent in the Shade," *Independent on Sunday,* March 11, 2001, p. 2.

Treanor, Jill, "Michael Page Chief Rounds on Critics," *Guardian,* August 15, 2001.

Wootliff, Benjamin, "Michael Page Bucks the Slide on Debut," *Telegraph,* March 29, 2001.

—M.L. Cohen

Middlesex Water Company

1500 Ronson Road
Iselin, New Jersey 08830-3020
U.S.A
Telephone: (732) 634-1500
Fax: (732) 750-5981
Web site: http://www.middlesexwater.com

Public Company
Incorporated: 1897
Employees: 183
Sales: $54.5 million (2000)
Stock Exchanges: NASDAQ
Ticker Symbol: MSEX
NAIC: 221310 Water Supply and Irrigation Systems

Operating out of Iselin, New Jersey, Middlesex Water Company provides water services on both a retail and wholesale basis. Most of its 75,000 retail customers are located in a 57-square-mile area in New Jersey's Middlesex County, which is located across from the southern tip of the New York City borough of Staten Island. In addition, water is sold on a wholesale contract basis to other New Jersey communities in an area that encompasses about 140 square miles with a population of 267,000. Middlesex Water also owns and operates two acquired water systems as subsidiaries: Pinelands Water Company in southern New Jersey and Tidewater Utilities, Inc. in Delaware. In recent years the company has expanded into wastewater services as well as the management of municipal water systems.

Establishing Middlesex Water Company in 1897

From the American Colonial period into the 1800s, New Jersey was primarily an agricultural state. In the Middlesex area, water was drawn from wells or surface sources and there was no need for a centralized system. With an increase in population and the rise of industrialization in the years following the Civil War, however, it became apparent that available supplies of water would not be adequate to maintain the state's rate of growth. Moreover, industry brought pollution of surface waters, creating an even greater need for water that could be treated using the new

filtration methods being developed by the rising field of sanitary engineering. Further north in Hackensack, New Jersey, which was located across from Manhattan and home to many of that city's business leaders and bankers, the need for establishing an organized system of supplying water was realized much sooner. Hackensack Water received a state charter in 1869. It was not until 1896 that William H. Corbin founded Middlesex Water Company in order to supply water to the northeastern part of Middlesex County. A Jersey City lawyer and politically well connected, he was involved in real estate, banking, and other investments. He was also familiar with the water business through his legal work in the 1880s for the city of Jersey City when it acquired a distant reservoir to ensure the purity of its water supply. Corbin recognized the potential of Middlesex Water to service industries situated along Staten Island Sound. Although he proved successful in recruiting these businesses as potential customers, he failed to find a supply of water, and essentially allowed Middlesex Water to lay dormant for a year, neither drilling for wells nor raising much money. Instead, Corbin turned his attention to the 1896 incorporation of Midland Water Company, in which he was an investor along with Frank Bergen, who sold to the company property that held proven reserves of water and who was subsequently named president. Midland raised $50,000 in order to sell water in Union, Middlesex, and Somerset Counties. Because Middlesex Water had the customers through Corbin and Midland had a source of water through Bergen, the two companies consolidated operations in 1897. Although it was the Middlesex name that was retained, the new entity was in reality the Midland board, and so Bergen became president of the water company. Like Corbin he combined legal and business careers, first becoming involved in the water business when he invested in the Plainfield Water Supply Company in 1890 and was then named its president. In addition, he served as general counsel for New Jersey's largest utility, Public Service Corporation, which operated franchises in gas, electricity, and street cars.

Despite his many responsibilities, and lack of training in engineering, Bergen was very much involved in all aspects of establishing Middlesex Water, especially by keeping a tight rein on Robert M. Kellogg, the superintendent he hired to manage day-to-day affairs. In 1898 the company dug wells and laid a main some

15 miles in length to factories located along Staten Island Sound. Steadily the system expanded and Bergen added more customers. By 1907 Middlesex Water was pumping more than 1.3 million gallons of water per day and boasted assets in excess of $400,000 while posting a $56,000 profit. The demand for water, however, would soon outstrip the company's ability to supply it.

Because groundwater and pumping alone would not alleviate the shortage, Bergen realized that Middlesex Water needed to build a reservoir. Late in 1905 a site was selected, and with additional business customers lined up, the company decided to move forward on what became known as the Robinsons Branch Project. Rather than fund the reservoir through debt, it issued $300,000 in new stock. Bergen also negotiated a contract with the Elizabethtown Water Company to supply it with water on a contract basis at $10,000 a year. In 1907 Middlesex Water began acquiring the necessary property and equipment, but soon it became apparent the company would fall short of funds. The Consumers Aqueduct Company was then formed in order to sell additional stock and serve as a hedge against failure; it was understood that once the reservoir was successfully completed that the new company would merge with Middlesex Water. Indeed, the arrangement worked, the companies were joined in the fall of 1907, and in May 1908 the "Corbin Reservoir" began providing water to customers of Middlesex Water as well as Elizabethtown Water. More and more, Bergen, who continued to be involved in a number of business interests, came to rely on his new superintendent, Ambrose Mundy, who replaced Kellogg in 1908.

As Middlesex County grew, so did Middlesex Water. The county's population, which was nearly 80,000 in 1900, grew to more than 114,000 in 1910 and 130,000 by 1920. In addition to Elizabethtown Water, the company agreed to sell water on a contract basis to Plainfield-Union Water Company, requiring further expansion of the system. In 1916 more wells were dug to meet increased demand and a new pumping station was constructed. Nevertheless, after World War I Middlesex Water had to confront a regional water shortage. Although the company had enough water to supply its local customers, the towns it serviced on a contract basis were fast growing and placed a strain on the system, resulting in poor water pressure. The problem became so acute that water could not reach the second floor of many houses and fire departments had trouble using their hoses on fires. As a result, relations with customers soured.

Fight with Regulators Leading to 1927 Supreme Court Case

Clearly, what was required was better pumps and a larger main, but these improvements would be expensive, and Bergen

contended that New Jersey regulators, the Board of Public Utility Commissioners (established in 1911), hindered his ability to borrow money. By law the BPUC ruled on rate increases, but only to sustain operations, not as a way to fund improvements. The ultra-conservative Bergen was a critic of all government intrusion, and he aggressively took on the commission in the 1920s. He requested a 36 percent rate hike, to which he knew that the BPUC would never agree. The matter was litigated, eventually ending up in the United States Supreme Court in 1927. Although the BPUC would win on technical grounds, the New Jersey state legislature forced the two parties to reach a compromise. Middlesex Water was granted a rate increase that split the difference between the two sides. In the end, Bergen was able to sell bonds and raise enough money to upgrade the water system and improve service.

Although the advent of the Great Depression of the 1930s slowed the growth of its system, Middlesex Water continued to be profitable. Almost 83 years old, Bergen died of a heart attack in 1934, and although Mundy had been essentially running the company for a number of years, Judge William H. Speer became the new president. Diplomatic by nature, Speer was chosen by the company's directors because he was familiar with utilities and could repair relations with the BPUC. He guided Middlesex Water through the Depression, while successfully refinancing the company's bond debt. On the eve of World War II, a meter repair shop was destroyed when a building in the nearby United Railway and Signal Company complex exploded, killing or mortally wounding a total of 13 people, including a meter repairman. Although presumed an accident, the explosion was suspicious enough for Speer to invest in insurance to cover war-related damages. Wide-scale domestic sabotage, however, did not materialize during World War II. The war effort for Middlesex Water consisted of finding additional sources of water to adequately supply major army camps and war industries. By the end of the war Middlesex Water was no longer a wholesaler of water and was, in fact, now buying water from other sources to meet its needs.

The postwar years saw a population explosion in the areas around New York City, including Middlesex County, and both residential and commercial demand for water increased dramatically. Middlesex Water laid new pipe on a continuing basis, but the demand outpaced the system's capacity to deliver, and once again the company suffered from low water pressure and inadequate supply. Efforts at long-term planning to address these problems began in the late 1950s. Engineering consultants were hired and a plan developed, which called for larger transmission mains to be installed, as well as the drilling of two new wells and the construction of a new standpipe. Arranging the financing of the work, however, took some time. Speers, at the age of 90, managed to lay the groundwork when he died in 1959. He was replaced as president by longtime Superintendent Ambrose Mundy who, at the age of 83, was only slightly younger.

Not only did Mundy have the responsibility of overseeing the improvements to the company's water system, he served in the midst of a severe drought in 1960. Less than two years into his term as president, just as the capital plan was nearing completion, Mundy died of a heart attack. He was replaced by 62-year-old Carl J. Olsen, the company's first formally trained civil engineer, who had been with Middlesex Water since 1926.

Continuity of leadership would prove important as the Northeast suffered through an extended period of drought in the early 1960s. Unlike other state water companies, including Hackensack Water and Elizabethtown Water, Middlesex did not have a reservoir that could provide a reliable supply of water without steady replenishment from rainfall. Olsen saw a long-term solution to the supply problem by negotiating a deal with the state to purchase water from the Delaware and Raritan Canal. Originally built before the Civil War for barges transporting Pennsylvania coal to New York, the canal was superseded by railroads, abandoned in 1934, and eventually gained landmark status. After arranging a state grant to the water, Middlesex Water constructed a new pumping station and treatment plant, which were completed in December 1969, ushering in a new era for the company, which now for the first time in many years had an abundant supply of water. The state-of-the-art treatment plant, considered a modern marvel, was renamed the Carl J. Olsen Water Treatment Plant in 1973.

Naming J. Richard Tompkins Fifth President in 1980

Middlesex Water prospered through the 1970s, ending the decade as one of the best water stock investments in New Jersey. Olsen retired at the end of 1980 at the age of 80, the first time that the company's president did not die in office. This time the board named a much younger man as the fifth president of Middlesex Water: 42-year-old J. Richard Tompkins. Despite his age, he was well qualified for the position, an engineering graduate who was familiar with Middlesex Water and its business from his employment as a consultant with Associated Utility Services, having worked with the company for 14 years on rate case presentations and planning and development projects.

Under Tompkins, Middlesex Water began to expand its service area and product offerings. With a plentiful supply of water the company was able to now service the South River Basin area of New Jersey, a move that required additional improve-

ments and funding. In 1990 Tompkins recognized a chance to acquire Tidewater Utilities, Inc., which serviced more than 3,000 customers in 60 Delaware communities. The deal was finalized in 1992. Middlesex Water then branched into the wastewater treatment business when in 1995 it acquired Pinelands Water Company and Pinelands Wastewater Company in Southampton Township, New Jersey. Also in that year Middlesex Water created a subsidiary, Utility Service Affiliates, Inc., in order to operate the water system of the City of South Amboy under a 20-year contract. In 1997 Tidewater Utilities acquired a wholly owned subsidiary, Public Water Supply Company, Inc., as well as Midway Utility Corporation in southern Delaware. Now 100 years old, Middlesex Water raised more than $37 million in bonds and common stock, its largest financing ever to fund its expansion and the upgrading of the Carl J. Olsen Water Treatment Plant.

No matter how aggressive its moves in the 1990s, a period of deregulation in utilities, Middlesex Water remained a small water company, with annual revenues around $50 million, especially when compared with other New Jersey water companies. Hackensack Water evolved into United Water Resources and had been operating municipal water and wastewater systems for years. It also forged a relationship with the giant French water company Lyonnaise des Eaux-Dumez. The 1990s was a period of consolidation as well as privatization. Lyonnaise des Eaux and another French company, Compagnie de Suez, merged and acquired United Water Resources outright, yet it was still only second in size to the rival French firm of Vivendi. Both were enthusiastically looking for opportunities in the United States, where 85 percent of all water systems were municipally owned and whose infrastructures were in drastic need of upgrading.

After Suez Lyonnaise des Eaux acquired United Water Resources in 1999, Middlesex Water was rumored to be ripe for acquisition by one of the new mammoth water companies, causing its stock to soar in value by more than 30 percent. When a buyout failed to materialize, however, the price quickly dropped. Not surprisingly, the future for a company the size of Middlesex Water remained uncertain. In 2001, with Tompkins now serving as chairman of the board and Dennis G. Sullivan installed as president and chief operating officer, the company acquired another water system, Fortescue Realty Company of Cumberland County, New Jersey. It was then transferred to a newly formed subsidiary, Bayview Water Company. In September 2001 Middlesex Water entered into negotiations to sell Tidewater Utilities to Artesian Resources Corporation, a Delaware public water utility. Because of its proximity to Artesian's other operations, Tidewater was a good fit. Middlesex Water, on the other hand, would be able to focus on the New Jersey region. It remained to be seen, however, whether the economics of a new era in the water business would allow a small company such as Middlesex Water to operate independently, or if it would have to align itself with one of the larger utility concerns in order to prosper in a new century.

Principal Subsidiaries

Tidewater Utilities Inc.; Pinelands Water Company; Pinelands Wastewater Company; Utility Service Affiliates, Inc.

Principal Competitors

American Water Works Company, Inc.; Artesian Resources Corporation; Elizabethtown Water; United Water Resources, Inc.

Further Reading

Lender, Mark Edward, *Middlesex Water Company: A Business History,* Metuchen, N.J.: Upland Press, 1994.

''Middlesex Water: Thirsty Neighbors?,'' *Business Week,* September 6, 1999, p. 111.

Ruth, Joao-Pierre S., ''The New Wave of Public-Private Partnerships,'' *New Jersey Business News,* July 12, 1999.

Sundaramoorthy, Geeta, ''The Energy Business Hums to the Tune of Deregulation Subject,'' *New Jersey Business News,* February 2, 1998.

——, ''Water Utilities Chart Plans for Growth,'' *New Jersey Business News,* November 16, 1998.

—Ed Dinger

Misys PLC

Burleigh House
Chapel Oak
Salford Priors
Evesham WR11 8SP
United Kingdom
Telephone: (+44) 1386-871-373
Fax: (+44) 1386-871-045
Web site: http://www.misys.com

Public Company
Incorporated: 1979 as Misys Microcomputer Systems
Employees: 6,500
Sales: £848.6 million ($1.22 billion) (2001)
Stock Exchanges: London
Ticker Symbol: MSY
NAIC: 541511 Custom Computer Programming Services;
     5112 Software Publishers

Sometimes called the United Kingdom's Microsoft, Misys PLC is at least that country's leading independent information technology (IT) company. Unlike its behemoth U.S. counterpart, however, Misys, which posted revenues of nearly £850 million in 2001, concentrates on providing applications software solutions for the international banking, insurance, IFA (independent financial advisors), and healthcare industries. Originally focused on the insurance sector, Misys has achieved rapid growth through an aggressive acquisition program, with purchases including banking and security software group Kapiti—renamed Misys International Banking Systems in 2001; the acquisition of ACT Group PLC (now split into Misys Asset Management Systems and Misys Securities Trading Systems) in 1995; the $923 million purchase of U.S.-based medical software provider Medic Computer Systems, made in 1997; and the $400 million acquisition of Sunquest Information Systems Inc. in 2001. Misys, which trades on the London stock exchange—and made history in 1998 when it became the first IT stock to trade in the FTSE 100—is led by Chairman and cofounder Kevin Lomax.

Software Success in the 1980s

Misys PLC was founded as Misys Microcomputer Systems by Kevin Lomax, one-time rising star within the Hanson Plc conglomerate, insurance broker Peter Morgan, whom Lomax met in a hospital maternity ward where both were awaiting the births of their children, and investors John and Jeremy Beasley. The company's initial purpose was to develop microcomputer systems and software to service the insurance industry. Lomax, however, was to prove the driving force behind Misys's later growth.

Lomax had entered the Hanson conglomerate in 1970 after graduating from the University of Manchester. By 1973, Lomax had gained a position as managing director of Hanson's British Furnaces subsidiary. At the age of 25, Lomax had become the youngest managing director in Hanson's history. Lomax then went on to take top positions at Wellman Incandescent Ltd. In the meantime, Lomax had become one of the founding investors in Misys. His investment gave him the title of non-executive chairman, while Lomax continued to pursue his career, becoming head of the electronics components division of Standard Telephone Company.

Misys struggled along in its first few years. Early losses forced the company to restrict its focus to developing applications and hardware systems targeting the insurance sector. The company remained small and continued building up debt.

Disagreements over strategy led to Lomax's resignation from his post at Standard Telephone Company. Lomax began to seek a new direction for his career. As he related to the *Daily Telegraph:* "My wife told me, rather unhelpfully, that I was clearly unemployable and if I thought I was so great I should get on and build my own business." Lomax's wife's advice proved more helpful than Lomax had thought. Looking about for prospects, Lomax settled on his investment in Misys, telling the *Daily Telegraph:* "I looked at little Misys, which was sitting there with 30 people and debts of £300,000 and thought, well, maybe I should have a go."

Lomax convinced Misys's other investors to give him six months to turn the company around, and in 1985, Lomax took on an active role as Misys chairman. Within a year Lomax had helped the company pay off its debts and even to make a profit of £0.5 million. The company continued to build organically over the next couple of years, increasing its customer base. In 1987, the company went public, with a placement on the U.K. Unlisted Securities Market.

The company remained tiny—its listing placed its worth at just £8.5 million. Yet the public offering marked a new phase in the company's growth strategy. The company now began to diversify its operations, moving away from its roots targeting the insurance broker sector. Over the next several years, the company began making a number of acquisitions, while also investing strongly in developing its own software packages. An important element of the company's new growth strategy came in 1989, when the company's stock joined the London main board. Among the company's new markets was the information services sector, particularly applications targeting the leisure and construction industries.

Diversified Software Leader in the 21st Century

In 1992, Misys moved into the financial services sector for the first time, when it implemented new software and support services for the United Kingdom's IFA market. The company then acquired a 20 percent share in Countrywide, a cooperative organization handling the administration needs of a group of IFAs. Misys soon took over full control of Countrywide. Its new subsidiary was to serve as the core around which the company developed its IFA sector business throughout the decade.

Financial services remained the focus of Misys's growth ambitions in the early 1990s. In 1994, the company took a major step forward, when it acquired Kapiti, a developer of software for international banking groups. Kapiti gave Misys an entirely new scope, and, with 15 offices operating worldwide, enabled Misys to move beyond the U.K. market for the first time. Adding Kapiti helped boost the company's revenues past £93 million in 1994, while the company's profits were soaring, to nearly £19 million. With its international sales now representing 25 percent of total turnover, Misys began looking for more acquisitions, particularly an entry into the high-powered U.S. market.

The Kapiti acquisition proved to be only the first of several during the decade that were to transform Misys into the United Kingdom's leading independent IT company. The company now abandoned its remaining hardware systems and support operations to focus entirely on the development of software for the financial services sector. This market was undergoing a huge growth spurt in the 1990s as bank and other financial institutions came to rely on computer technology.

In 1995, Misys acquired the ACT Group, which specialized in banking software. This purchase helped the company boost its position not only in the United Kingdom, but worldwide. With its new acquisitions, Misys had become the outright leader in the worldwide financial services software sector, numbering some 45 of the world's top 50 banks as its clients.

The following year, Misys began to make its mark in the United States. In 1996, the company made two strategic acquisitions in that market, paying $94 million for The Frustum Group Inc. and $50 million for Summit Systems Inc. These acquisitions were followed by a still larger purchase that also saw the company expand into a new market. In November 1997, Misys paid more than $920 million to acquire Medic Computer Systems. That purchase gave Misys a top-five spot among healthcare IT companies. With clients numbering more than 11,000 practices and 65,000 doctors, the deal made Misys a major supplier of practice management software and medical records systems for the nation's healthcare practitioners. By then, Misys's revenues had swelled past £300 million.

The following year, Misys found itself being dubbed the U.K. Microsoft as its share price soared. Riding high on a surge in demand at the end of the decade—as customers rushed to ready themselves for the potentially catastrophic Y2K bug—Misys saw its market value top £2.8 billion. Misys's surge in value earned the company a place on the FTSE 100, becoming the first IT company to crack the prestigious U.K. index. The company's position was to prove on-again, off-again, as a drop in its share price saw it fall out of the FTSE 100 at the end of that same year.

At the beginning of 1999, Misys acquired CATS, based in California, giving it a world-leading position as a maker of risk management systems for banks. This acquisition coincided with Misys's move to focus its operations around its two strongest divisions, banking and healthcare. As part of its reorientation, the company sold off its information services division, which had been generating more than £47 million in sales and operating profits of £5 million, to the venture capital division of Dresdner Kleinwort Benson for £35 million. Following the disposal, the company's Banking and Securities division alone was worth 60 percent of the company's total turnover; the Healthcare division represented 31 percent of sales.

Misys went online in 1999, opening its business-to-business portals, m-link and i2i-link, geared toward the financial advisor and insurance sectors. The company also made an attempt to turn its financial services expertise toward the consumer public, when it launched two Internet-based financial services portals. Those ventures, screentrade.com and theformula.com, which started up in 2000, gave site visitors access to comparison tools and other services for car insurance and mortgage rates and other financial products. Neither site was successful, however, and in mid-2001 the company made the decision to pull the plug on both. Elsewhere on the Internet, Misys joined in an alliance with Healtheon Corp., which then merged into Web MD, forming the leading U.S. healthcare portal. As part of the alliance,

Key Dates:

1979: Misys Microcomputer Systems begins operation as developer of software and hardware systems.
1985: Kevin Lomax takes over as chairman.
1987: Company places stock on London's Unlisted Securities Market.
1989: Misys is listed on the London stock exchange.
1992: The company acquires 30 percent of Countrywide, an administrative services provider to independent financial advisors (IFA) sector, then takes over full control of Countrywide.
1994: Misys acquires banking software developer Kapiti as part of focus on financial services sector.
1995: The company acquires ACT Group and becomes worldwide financial services software leader.
1996: Misys expands into the United States with acquisitions of The Frustum Group and Summit Systems.
1997: Misys enters U.S. healthcare market with $900 million purchase of Medic Computer Systems.
1999: Company acquires California-based CATS Software, a leading financial risk management software provider.
2001: Misys acquires Sunquest Information Systems for $400 million; rebrands banking software division as Misys International Banking Systems.

Misys received a stake in the company worth an estimated $5.5 billion, in exchange for rolling out its e-commerce services through Misys's medical practice software.

Misys took 2000 off to digest its acquisitions and to recover from an industrywide slowdown relating to the run-up to the Y2K bug. Although sales grew slightly, to £698 million in 2000 from £628 million the year before, the company saw a drop in profitability.

The company was back on the growth trail by the following year. In June 2001, the company offered £75 million to acquire rival IFA services provider DBS Management. That deal was followed by an even larger purchase, when the company announced an agreement to pay $404 million to acquire Sunquest Information Systems. The purchase of that U.S.-based business helped Misys achieve its aim of broadening its healthcare business. The move also presented the future potential of linking Medic's physician-based operations to Sunquest's hospital-focused activity, providing an integrated communication platform between the two markets. The two deals helped the company's revenues grow to nearly £850 million by the end of its 2001 year.

A slump in the worldwide financial sector at midyear forced the company to post a profits warning. The September 11 attacks dashed the company's hopes for a quick turnaround. In an effort to revive the company's core banking division, Misys rebranded its Midas-Kapiti International division as Misys In-

ternational Banking Systems at the beginning of October 2001. The company then restructured its banking and securities division, adding two new entities, one for the asset management market, the other targeting the securities trading sector. Continued uncertainty over the worldwide financial market dogged the company through the end of the year. Yet Lomax insisted on looking beyond the company's share price and focused instead on Misys's strong growth prospects for the years ahead.

Principal Subsidiaries

ACT Financial Systems Limited; ACT Financial Systems S.A. (France); ACT Financial Systems (Asia Pacific) Limited (Hong Kong); Kindle Banking Systems Limited (Ireland); Kindle Systems PVT Limited (India); Misys International Banking Systems; The Frustum Group Inc. (U.S.A.); Summit Systems S.A. (France); Summit Systems Inc. (U.S.A.); Summit Systems International Limited; Misys Securities Trading Systems; Misys Asset Management Systems; Medic Computer Systems LLC (U.S.A.); Sunquest Information Systems Inc.; Misys Healthcare Systems; Countrywide Insurance Marketing Limited; CWA Claims Services Limited; Misys Financial Systems Limited; Countrywide Independent Advisers Limited; Financial Options Limited; IFA Network Limited; Kestrel Financial Management Limited; DBS Management; Misys IFA Services plc; AssureWeb.

Principal Divisions

Banking and Securities; Healthcare; Financial Services; B2B Internet Services.

Principal Competitors

Applied Systems, Inc; CareCentric, Inc.; CareFlow Net, Inc.; DST Systems, Inc.; Dynamic Healthcare Technologies, Inc.; e-MedSoft.com; Financial Models Company Inc.; Global Med Technologies, Inc.; Hummingbird Ltd.; IMS MAXIMS plc; Patient Care Technologies, Inc.; royalblue group plc; The Sage Group plc; SunGard Data Systems Inc.; Transaction Systems Architects, Inc.

Further Reading

Coyle, Diane, "Shift into Software Lifts Misys," *Independent,* July 27, 1994.
Hughes, Chris, "Too Many Unknowns at Misys," *Independent,* November 16, 2000, p. 23.
Mills, Lauren, "Misys? What Misys?," *Sunday Telegraph,* July 22, 2001, p. 8.
"Misys Exits Consumer Web Market," *Reuters,* June 22, 2001.
O'Brien, James, "Sunquest Adds Shine to Misys," *Birmingham Post,* June 26, 2001, p. 17.
Pain, Steve, "Misys' New Look to Rally Confidence," *Birmingham Post,* October 2, 2001, p. 24.
Potter, Ben, "Misys Gains Foothold in American Healthcare," *Daily Telegraph,* May 21, 1999.
"Supercharged Misys Hits the Heights," *Daily Telegraph,* February 7, 1998, p. 30.

—M.L. Cohen

MOTOPHOTO

Moto Photo, Inc.

4444 Lake Center Drive
Dayton, Ohio 45426
U.S.A.
Telephone: (937) 854-6686
Fax: (937) 854-0140
Web site: http://www. motophoto.com

Public Company
Incorporated: 1981
Employees: 478
Sales: $36.2 million (2000)
Stock Exchanges: OTC
Ticker Symbol: MOTO
NAIC: 812921 Photo Finishing Laboratories (Except One-Hour)

Moto Photo, Inc. is North America's largest franchiser of one-hour photo processing and portrait studio centers. The company has more than 450 locations in the United States, Canada, and Norway. Moto offers one-hour photofinishing along with other services such as enlargements and digital imaging. Stores also sell film, frames, albums, and personalized gift items.

Michael Adler, chairman of the company and son of company founder Richard Adler, owns more than 20 percent of Moto and serves as chairman of the board. In 1999, *Entrepreneur Magazine* ranked Moto Photo as the number one franchiser in the photo business category in its 20th annual Franchise 500.

Click Camera in 1946

Moto Photo, Inc. was founded by advertising executive Robert Adler. Adler owned a successful advertising agency, but his real passion was photography. For years he had visited camera shops regularly and learned all he could about cameras and film processing. He enjoyed working with people and considered opening a camera shop, but was really more interested in developing film than in selling cameras—and there was little market for a film-processing business back then. People just wanted to take pictures and did not care about how their film was processed. In spite of this, Adler eventually concluded that he could combine his people skills with his technical knowledge and make a go of a retail camera shop.

In 1946, he sold his advertising agency and opened Click Camera, in Springfield, Ohio. He and his wife, Rosa, came up with the company's first slogan: "Even your camera says Click!"

After World War II, film was in great demand but in short supply. Retailers could obtain film only through authorized Kodak dealers. Adler's customers wanted film, but had trouble finding it. Adler hoped to become a Kodak dealer himself, but was unable to achieve this goal. Never one to give up easily, he and his family spent their weekends driving to every Kodak dealer within a 50-mile radius. They bought every roll of film they could find. Each Monday morning, they hung up a sign in their store's window that said, "All the Kodak Film You Want." Customers flocked to Click's to buy film.

Adler entered into an agreement with an outside film-processing vendor to develop his customers' film. But the vendor's service was slow and the quality of the pictures was poor. This was unacceptable to Adler. He realized that the key to good quality pictures was to develop the film himself.

Adler opened a small processing lab in the basement of his store. His customers were thrilled with the pictures Adler developed. Word of his beautiful pictures spread quickly, and he began accepting orders from other retailers to develop their customers' film. Adler decided to redirect his company so it focused more on film processing and less on camera sales.

Development of Tru Foto: Mid-1950s–60s

Adler added a film processing division to Click Camera called Tru Foto. Tru Foto was enormously successful and the company's future looked promising. Adler suffered a devastating heart attack in 1959, however, and was temporarily unable to work. Realizing that the company would falter without his father, Michael Adler dedicated himself to the business. Michael was the Adlers' only child and a busy law student at Ohio State Univer-

Company Perspectives:

Moto Photo shall be the premier franchiser and specialty retailer of high-quality imaging products and services dedicated to enhancing our customers' enjoyment of their imaging experiences better than any other provider.

Moto Photo is committed to achieving superior results for all of its stakeholders within a culture that promotes trust, win/win relationships, problem solving and participative decision, remembering that work should be fun.

We want people who deal with Moto to literally say "Wow! I've never had such a great experience." This means 100 percent customer satisfaction, successful franchisees, fulfilled associates, and high profitability for our shareholders. We will WOW our stakeholders.

sity when his father became ill. He studied law during the week and commuted to Springfield on the weekends to help his father keep the business afloat. When Michael graduated, he committed himself to his family's business full-time.

The younger Adler concurred with the elder: the company's future was in photo processing. Robert sold the Click Camera portion of the business and concentrated on expanding Tru Foto. Tru Foto became a wholesale film processor and developed film for retailers across the United States. The Adlers developed 50 to 60 rolls of black-and-white film per day. In time, the company built a small photo processing plant and began developing 600 to 800 rolls of film per day. Tru Foto expanded the plant and began processing color film.

In 1968 Tru Foto built a new, larger processing plant in Akron, Ohio. During the same year, it formed a new subsidiary, Foto Fair International. Foto Fair offered drive-up and walk-in photo processing. Its outlets were located in shopping malls and parking lots.

Success in the 1970s

By the 1970s, the Adlers owned more than 1,000 Tru Foto retail outlets in the United States and four large processing labs in the Midwest and Northeast. The company became one of the top ten largest photo finishers in the photo industry.

Michael Adler, however, missed dealing with the public as he did in the Click Camera days. He also realized his market was changing. His retailers wanted "faster, cheaper service at lower prices." They had no problem sacrificing quality to cut costs. This disturbed Adler, whose father had spent much of his life perfecting his film-processing techniques. Michael considered developing film for the public once again.

One-Hour Processing in 1981

In the early 1980s, Tru Foto's upper management contemplated how to best position the company in the future. They realized that one-hour film processing could be the wave of the future. If it could perfect its one-hour film processing, the company could once again deal directly with the customer and avoid transactions with demanding and unscrupulous retailers.

Michael Adler and Tru Foto executives Bill Dyer and Dave Mason "spent long nights developing ways for Tru Foto to enter the one-hour processing market." They wanted to offer "fast, high-quality, secure onsite processing delivered through well-trained associates." They opened five test stores in large malls in different regions of the country. The test stores did well and Tru Foto established an ambitious goal: to be the leader in the industry.

Moto Photo in 1983

Tru Foto's one-hour processing service was in great demand. The company considered simultaneously opening a chain of stores across the nation, but concluded that this was too expensive. It opted to open many franchises instead. In 1983, Tru Foto acquired Moto Photo, a small public franchiser based in Oklahoma City. Tru Foto changed its name to Moto Photo, Inc. and moved its headquarters to Dayton, Ohio. It launched an initial public offering that raised more than $2 million. The company used the proceeds to pay off debt and fund its expansion. Two years later, Moto raised an additional $3.25 million with a second offering.

Moto opened many new stores and acquired additional stores from other companies. In 1986, it acquired five one-hour photo processing stores in Atlanta, Georgia, from Vibracolor One-Hour Photo, Inc. During the same year it acquired seven stores from PRC Acquisitions Corporation and 11 other stores through "various transactions." Moto also expanded internationally. The company opened stores in Canada and Norway. Moto was on its way to reaching its goal of becoming the leading photo processor in the country.

Success did not come easily for the company, however. Word of its services spread and many new competitors emerged to try to capitalize on the one-hour processing wave. The competition for market share was fierce. A total of 13 new one-hour photo-processing companies entered the market. Moto entered into "a ten-year war" for market share. The company emerged from the battle victorious. At the end of the decade, Moto was the largest and only franchiser in the industry.

In 1998 Moto placed 15th on the list of best-managed franchises in *Success* magazine's annual Franchise Gold 100. The following year, *Entrepreneur Magazine* ranked Moto as the number one franchise in the photo business category in its 20th annual Franchise 500.

A new store design was introduced in 1999 to appeal primarily to women, who the company believed developed most family photos.

Digital Technology in 2000

At the turn of the century, Moto sought to participate in the Internet economy. It signed a letter of intent to merge with PhotoChannel Networks, Inc., a Canadian company that owned PhotoChannel.com, an online photo print service for both digital and conventional film. The transaction involved a stock swap valued at approximately $14 million. In addition to stock, PhotoChannel would have given Moto an additional $25 million for the partnership. Adler believed the merger would have been particularly beneficial for Moto. It would have given Moto money to add digital technology that would allow it to print images at its store more quickly. Some of the money it received would have been used as an incentive for franchisees to add digital labs to their stores.

As of early 2002, however, the letter of intent for the merger had expired. According to *Market News Publishing,* the companies had decided not to merge "due to adverse financial market conditions prevailing in the last quarter of the year 2000 and the inability to finalize satisfactory terms."

Adler was optimistic that the merger would take place sometime in the future, however. "Although we are disappointed that we are not able to complete the merger at this time as originally contemplated, we are cautiously optimistic that the talented PhotoChannel team will successfully raise the capital and meet all preconditions for the merger to move forward," he said in *Market News Publishing.* The two companies did agree to test PhotoChannel digital imaging in a few of its stores. This allowed Moto to process and print orders received over the PhotoChannel network.

A Possible Takeover in 2001

In early 2001, Moto faced a possible takeover from Fuji Photo Film USA, Inc. Fuji held a preferred stake in Moto as well as a $1.9 million note that Moto needed to repay. Moto's sales dipped and it fell behind on its payments, which, under the terms of the agreement, gave Fuji the option to seize control of Moto. Early in 2001, industry experts predicted that Fuji would

take over Moto. As of early 2002, however, this had not happened. Moto terminated its agreement to use Fuji as its primary supplier of paper, chemicals, film, and other products and signed a deal instead with Eastman Kodak Company. Kodak agreed to provide Moto with the supplies it had been buying from Fuji.

Hope for the Future

Moto's sales slipped in 2000, and the company posted a net loss of $3.2 million on sales of $36.2 million as opposed to a 1999 net income of $1.7 million on sales of $36.8 million. The company also posted a loss of more than $242,000 on sales of more than $8 million for the third quarter of 2001. CEO Larry Destro responded to the 2001 third-quarter loss in a company press release: "Sales were generally soft for the period in the photo graphic industry, exacerbated by a weakening consumer economy and the September 11 tragedy, which forced many consumers to delay or cancel vacation plans."

To cut expenses, Moto announced plans to begin franchising its 38 company-owned stores and to close unprofitable stores. "This will allow the company to concentrate its attention on building the franchise brand, enhancing shareholder value, increasing liquidity and will lead to reduced costs over time," said Destro.

The company also implemented MotoWizard, a highly sophisticated state-of-the art program that helped find the best location for new stores. "This new model helps eliminate under-performing sites and decreases site selection risks," Destro explained.

Chairman Michael Adler reported in the company's 2000 annual report that he believed Moto had come to a fork in the road, and that it was time for management to change. He announced plans to retire at the end of 2001.

Principal Competitors

Ritz Camera Centers; Wal-Mart Stores, Inc.

Further Reading

"Merger Should Aid Local Company," *Dayton Daily News,* September 3, 2000.
"Moto Photo Conducts Charity Drive for the American Red Cross," *Business Wire,* October 23, 2001.
"Moto Photo Negotiates Supply Agreement with Fuji, Faces a Possible Takeover from the Company," *Photo Marketing Newsline,* June 6, 2001.

—Tracey Vasil Biscontini

New Brunswick Scientific Co., Inc.

44 Talmadge Road
Edison, New Jersey 08818-4005
U.S.A.
Telephone: (732) 287-1200
Toll Free: (800) 631-5417
Fax: (732) 287-4222
Web site: http://www.nbsc.com

Public Company
Incorporated: 1958
Employees: 477
Sales: $49.9 million (2000)
Stock Exchanges: NASDAQ
Ticker Symbol: NBSC
NAIC: 339911 Laboratory Apparatus and Furniture
Manufacturing

New Brunswick Scientific Co., Inc. designs, manufactures, and markets equipment used in the biotechnology industry. It also provides support and contract research services, and offers a used equipment program. In addition to its world headquarters in Edison, New Jersey, the company operates several subsidiaries to sell its products in Western Europe. In addition to the United States and Western Europe, New Brunswick equipment is sold, either directly or through dealers, in Eastern Europe, former republics of the Soviet Union, Canada, South America, Israel, China, Japan, and Australia. Customers include both the private and public sectors. New Brunswick provides only a small amount of equipment to government laboratories, but sales to medical schools, university laboratories, and research institutes are further influenced by the availability of government funding. Private enterprise customers include pharmaceutical, biotechnology, chemical, and agricultural companies. New Brunswick's first product offering, biological shakers, now come in a wide range of sizes, from benchtop models to industrial-size units. Shakers create a precise agitation of flasks containing biological cultures in a liquid media in which nutrients are dissolved, thus allowing the proper growth of microorganisms. New Brunswick offers two lines of shakers. Its "classic" line has been a longtime industry standard, while its INNOVA line offers some of the most sophisticated units on the market. The company also manufactures and sells fermentation equipment and bioreactors, used in the growth of cultures, a business New Brunswick has been involved in since the 1950s. Again, units range in size from one-liter benchtop models to 10,000-liter systems sold under contract. In addition, the company manufactures digital instrumentation to control fermenters and bioreactors. New Brunswick also offers equipment that automatically sterilizes and then maintains nutrients at required temperatures. Another product line, tissue culture apparatus, are used to constantly rotate bottles and test tubes of growing animal and plant cells. Included in this line are carbon dioxide incubators, important in the production of vaccines and other pharmaceuticals, as well as for use in cancer and heart disease research. In addition, the company distributes a line of centrifuges and low temperature freezers. New Brunswick takes great pride in controlling all aspects of manufacturing. Rather than an assembly line process, the company operates on a lot production basis, fabricating parts from raw materials and components to produce most of its subassemblies. Although most manufacturing is done on the company's 17-acre Edison facility, the company also has a manufacturing capability in England for the European market.

Roots Reaching Back to 1946

New Brunswick was founded in the New Jersey town of the same name by brothers Sigmund and David Freedman in 1946. Looking to take advantage of David's training as a toolmaker, they decided to start a machine shop called New Brunswick Tool & Die. Seed money of $6,000 was scraped together from a variety of sources. Sigmund provided $1,000 that he won by gambling on the Florence Nightingale ship when he returned home from the war in Europe. He also had saved up money by sending home his pay during the war. Their mother provided some money, a friend lent $2,000, and they also borrowed on the mortgage of the family house. A friend told the brothers of a tire recapping company that was going out of business, and they were able to procure a lease on the facility.

The first year was especially difficult for the Freedmans, who were only able to attract a few tooling jobs. Unable to pay themselves they relied on their mother for meals. Only after the second year were they in a position to start paying themselves a salary of $10 per week. According to Sigmund it was in 1949 or 1950 that Walter B. Geiger, a microbiology professor from nearby Rutgers University, stopped by the shop to ask if they could repair one of the department's agitators that was malfunctioning. The agitator was used to aerate bacteria contained in a flask that had to be shaken in a rotary motion on a fixed plane. After successfully repairing agitators for the department, the brothers were then asked if they could custom build one of the machines. It would have to be a larger unit capable of agitating a fixed size flask on a fixed plane at a fixed speed. They took on the job and produced a unit that so satisfied the Rutgers' researchers that they quickly ordered another. According to Sigmund, ''One thing that impressed me very much was that Rutgers would place the orders, which cost $279.50, and then within a week we received a check. That made an extremely favorable impression upon us because it meant we had cash flow and could run our business.''

It became evident that the Freedmans were located in the right place at the right time. Rutgers played an important role in microbiology in the early 1950s, a period highlighted in 1952 when one of its own, Selman Waksman, won a Nobel Prize for the discovery of the first antibiotic, streptomycin. With the labs in high gear, Rutgers was turning out researchers who then took jobs at other universities and institutions around the country. Many contacted New Brunswick Tool & Die in order to purchase the same agitators used in the Rutgers' research laboratories. By now the brothers had made two or three dozen machines for Rutgers, and the prospect of finding even more institutional customers proved so inviting that in the spring of 1951 they leased a booth at a microbiology assembly held in Baltimore to promote their laboratory equipment. Not only were they able to meet microbiologists from around the country, they discovered that their products had no competition from established scientific equipment manufacturers. As a result, they received dozens of orders when they returned home to New Jersey. They registered the title New Brunswick Scientific Co., eased out of the tool and die business, and devoted their efforts to the designing and manufacturing of scientific equipment. In 1953 they produced their first lab-scale fermenters, vats that controlled the growth of microorganisms by varying the amount of nutrients. Although crude by today's standards, they were the best units on the market. In 1958 New Brunswick Scientific Co., Inc. was incorporated in the state of New Jersey.

Competing As a Public Company: 1970s

Although New Brunswick did not retain any of Rutgers' staff as consultants, a mutually beneficial relationship with the school was important to the growth of the company. Lacking scientific expertise in the early years, New Brunswick essentially responded to the needs of the Rutgers researchers, learning what problems required solving and designing machines to meet those needs. The company moved to its present Edison, New Jersey, location where, in addition to office space, it built its own machine shop, sheet metal shop, electronic assembly shop, and laboratories. Because its equipment had to be built to precise specifications for laboratory use, New Brunswick was diligent about controlling every aspect of the manufacturing process. New Brunswick also hired skilled research scientists as well as machinists. To fund this expansion, the company turned to the public market for capital in 1972.

Now an established scientific equipment manufacturer, with dozens of products to offer, New Brunswick appeared well positioned to take advantage of the biotechnology boom of the late 1970s and early 1980s. The origins of biotechnology can be traced to 1953 when Alan Watson and Francis Crick set the stage by revealing the shape of DNA and explaining how genetic information was passed from one generation to the next. Scientists now began to search for ways to manipulate nature at the molecular level through genes, leading to such discoveries as cloning. The biotechnology industry was based on publicly supported research that was then commercially exploited by individual entrepreneurs in small start-up companies. Founded in 1976, Genentech was generally regarded as the company that launched what many considered to be the biotechnology revolution.

In 1982 New Brunswick was a relatively small company, with sales of only $20 million, but because of the prospect of start-up biotechs needing its equipment, the company was now coming to the attention of many investors. It was able to go back to the public market for further capital in 1981 and again in 1983, at which point the Freedmans decided to cash in, reducing their holdings to around 14 percent each. New Brunswick also looked to diversify and become involved in biotechnology, acquiring Biosearch, a California company that made DNA synthesizers. The Freedmans discovered, as did a vast number of investors, that the promised riches of biotechnology were always just out of reach, and that more and more cash would be required before any kind of payoff could be expected. New Brunswick lost $2.1 million on revenues of $35.6 million in 1987, mostly because the Biosearch unit generated only $8.4 million, far short of the $14 million budgeted. In May 1988 the business was sold to Millipore Corp. for $15 million, allowing New Brunswick to return to profitability for the year, as the company earned $136,000 on sales of $37.5 million.

Fending Off a Takeover Bid: 1989

After the enthusiasm of the early 1980s, New Brunswick stock was trading at a low enough level that it became an attractive takeover candidate. Fundamental Management Corp. of Miami began buying up shares in 1989, amounting to more than 7 percent. David Freedman, longtime CEO of New Brunswick, stepped down in favor of Ezra Weisman, who had been with the company since the early 1960s and in the previous five years served as the company's vice-president of sales and vice-president of corporate development. Although Fundamental indicated that it was not interested in a hostile takeover, it did request two seats on the company's board and expressed the need for changes at New Brunswick. Matters grew somewhat

Key Dates:

1946: New Brunswick Tool & Die is formed.
1951: Attendance at microbiology assembly introduces company's products to scientists around the country.
1953: Company's first fermenters are introduced.
1958: Name is changed to New Brunswick Scientific.
1972: Company completes its initial public offering of stock.
1995: Subsidiary DGI BioTechnologies is formed.
2001: Major share of DGI is sold.

testy between the two parties when the New Brunswick board instituted a shareholders' rights plan as a poison-pill takeover defense. Tensions eased by mid-1990 when Weisman instituted some cost-cutting measures, closing some foreign offices and 15 percent of the company's 440-person workforce.

Although New Brunswick was profitable in the early 1990s, sales and earnings were stagnant. In 1991 the company generated $33.1 million in revenues and $393,000 in net income, but by 1993 revenues had only increased to $35.9 million and net income stood at $392,000. The company saw a significant improvement in profits for 1994, $1.1 million on revenues of $38.8 million, and began a new effort to diversify and expand beyond its equipment sales, which, however steady, offered limited potential for growth. Late in 1994 it established a bioprocess equipment division, as well as invested over $1 million to gain a 20 percent stake in Organica, Inc. The company, formed a year earlier, produced naturally friendly grass products used for golf course and playing fields, plus compost accelerators, hydrocarbon remediation products, non-caustic drain openers, and septic system maintenance products. In 1995 New Brunswick then created a drug-discovery subsidiary, DGI BioTechnologies, Inc., to operate out of laboratory space at the Edison facilities.

Similar to its experience with Biosearch in the 1980s, however, New Brunswick's efforts at diversification did not produce quick results and created a significant drag on earnings. Although revenues reached $46.5 million in 1998, the company posted a loss of $156,000, after turning profits of $1 million in 1997 and $882,000 in 1996. In 1999 the company lost an additional $1.15 million, despite the growth of sales to over $54 million. Once again, with the price of its stock depressed, the New Brunswick board adopted a plan to ward off any potential unwanted takeover bids.

In January 2000 Weisman left New Brunswick to pursue other business interests according to the company, but clearly it was a mutually agreed upon severance. David Freedman once again took over as the chief executive and set about refocusing the business. New Brunswick remained weighed down by DGI's poor results, which was a major reason that revenue for New Brunswick fell to $49.9 million. Also contributing to the company's $3.9 million loss in 2000 was the $950,000 write-off of its investment in Organica, which in October of that year filed for chapter 11 reorganization. To rectify the condition of New Brunswick in 2001, Freedman sold a major share of DGI to the Denmark firm of Bank Invest. Because its holdings were now less than 50 percent, New Brunswick would be able to take DGI off its books. In other moves, the company cut jobs and eliminated its customer-engineered bioprocess products, a niche business that represented less than 7 percent of company revenues. Because the company's main line of scientific products remained a solid business, there was every reason to expect that New Brunswick would return to profitability. Whether it would ever transform itself into a company with high growth potential seemed less likely than the possibility that New Brunswick would one day be swallowed by a much larger corporation.

Principal Subsidiaries

New Brunswick Scientific (U.K.) Limited; New Brunswick Scientific B.V. (Netherlands); New Brunswick Scientific N.V. (Belgium); New Brunswick Scientific GmbH (Germany); New Brunswick Scientific S.A.R.L. (France).

Principal Competitors

B. Braun Biotech; LSL-Biolafitte; L.E. Marubishi Co., Ltd.; Applikon, B.V.; LabLine Instruments; Forma Scientific.

Further Reading

Bamford, Janet, ''Shake Well, Stir Gently,'' *Forbes,* May 9, 1983, p. 165.

''DGI Pursues Financial Backing As NBSC Relinquishes Majority Control,'' *GenomiKa,* July 4, 2001, p. 3.

''The Lucky Gamble at New Brunswick Scientific,'' *NJBIZ.com,* June 20, 1988.

''New Brunswick Scientific Sells Stake in DGI Bio Technologies,'' *NJBIZ.com,* June 18, 2001.

''New Brunswick Scientific Shuts Production Line, Cuts Jobs,'' *NJBIZ.com,* June 29, 2001.

—Ed Dinger

New Times, Inc.

1201 East Jefferson Street
Phoenix, Arizona 85034
U.S.A.
Telephone: (602) 271-0040
Fax: (602) 253-4884
Web site: http://www.newtimes.com

Private Company
Incorporated: 1970
Employees: 950
Sales: $120 million (2001 est.)
NAIC: 511110 Newspaper Publishers

New Times, Inc. is the largest chain of alternative weekly newspapers in the United States, based on circulation. Its papers are distributed for free in 12 of the top 25 markets and rely on advertising dollars for revenue. Its editorial policy is to encourage hard news reporting and lengthy investigative pieces. Although many of the exposés appearing in its papers are controversial, New Times reporters and editors have gained a reputation for excellence by winning numerous awards at the national, state, and local levels.

Beginnings with the Arizona Times: 1970s

The New Times chain of alternative newsweeklies began in 1970 with the founding of the *Arizona Times,* which later became the *Phoenix New Times.* The paper was started by Michael Lacey, a dropout from Arizona State University, and a group of counterculture students in response to the shootings at Kent State University during the Vietnam War. The paper's initial print run in 1970 was 16,000 copies. Two years later Jim Larkin, also a college dropout, joined as the paper's business manager.

During the 1970s both Lacey and Larkin left the paper after it had gone public. They regained control of the paper in 1977 and took it private with an $800,000 loan from a local savings and loan institution. Lacey became the paper's executive editor, and Larkin its president. From 1976 to 1977 the paper's circula-

tion had plummeted from 40,000 to 17,000. After Lacey and Larkin regained control, they moved the paper's editorial offices from the Arizona State University campus in Tempe to Phoenix, renaming the paper *Phoenix New Times.* Circulation was handled by Scott Spear, a former record-store owner. Without an urban inner city where most weeklies were distributed, Spear placed the free paper in racks at suburban convenience stores and other locations such as gas stations and restaurants. Eventually, *Phoenix New Times* also was distributed in the city's central business district and circulation grew to 140,000 weekly by the early 1990s.

Acquisition of Two Papers in Major Markets: 1980s

In May 1983 New Times acquired *Westword,* a biweekly published in Denver with a circulation of 40,000, for about $67,000. New Times made *Westword* a weekly and increased its circulation to 100,000. Cofounder Patricia Calhoun remained as editor, and the paper expanded beyond its arts and entertainment coverage by running more investigative stories.

In September 1987 New Times purchased the *Wave,* an alternative weekly in Miami, and renamed it *Miami New Times.* After spending only a few thousand dollars to acquire the alternative weekly, New Times invested $1.4 million in the paper and began producing longer investigative stories.

For the fiscal year ending in June 1991, New Times' three newspapers generated revenue of $16 million on a combined circulation of 315,000. Profits were about $2.5 million.

More Aggressive Acquisition: 1990s

New Times acquired the *Dallas Observer* in the fall of 1991 for an estimated $3 million. It was the fourth newspaper in New Times' chain of weeklies, and the first time the company had to pay a substantial amount to acquire a paper. The *Dallas Observer* had a circulation of 85,000, annual revenue of about $3 million, and was profitable. Both *Westword* and the *Wave* were losing money when New Times acquired them. In a fortunate turn of events, the *Dallas Observer's* only alternative competition, the *Dallas Times Herald,* was subsequently acquired by the daily *Dallas Morning News.* Following the acquisition New

Times increased the editorial staff at the paper from four to ten people and increased the number of pages.

With the acquisition of the *Dallas Observer,* New Times was the largest publisher of alternative weeklies in the United States, based on circulation. Its four newspapers had a combined circulation of 410,000, compared with a circulation of 172,000 for New York's *Village Voice.* For the rest of the 1990s and beyond, New Times pursued a strategy to acquire alternative weeklies in the 15 largest markets in the United States.

In 1993 New Times added a fifth weekly to its chain with the purchase of the financially troubled *Houston Press.* Founded in 1989 by Niel Morgan and Chris Hearne, the *Houston Press* was the city's first free major arts, news, and entertainment weekly. Although circulation grew and advertising increased, the paper suffered from a high level of debt and was never profitable. At the time it was sold to New Times, the paper had a weekly circulation of 80,000 copies. It was sold to New Times for an estimated $2.75 million. The acquisition boosted circulation of the New Times chain to more than 500,000, and the company had revenue of more than $35 million in fiscal 1993.

In 1995 New Times acquired the Ruxton Group, a Chicago-based national advertising representative firm. The acquisition gave potential advertisers a readership base of 1.4 million, based on the network of 14 alternative weeklies represented by Ruxton. The readership of 1.4 million consisted primarily of 18- to 49-year-olds and 14 of the top 25 markets in the United States. New Times' six alternative weeklies were part of the network.

New Times' next addition to its chain of papers was a Los Angeles weekly, *L.A. View,* which the company acquired in mid-1996. After acquiring the paper, New Times fired its executive editor, managing editor, and music editor. Around the same time New Times also purchased another Los Angeles weekly, *Los Angeles Reader.* It combined the two weeklies into a new publication called *L.A. New Times.* Most of the staff at *L.A. View* and the *Los Angeles Reader* were laid off following the purchase. Jack Cheevers, a former reporter for the *Los Angeles Times,* was hired as managing editor of *L.A. New Times,* and Rick Barr, a former night city editor with the *Times,* was hired as the paper's editor.

L.A. New Times would compete head-on with the well-known alternative *L.A. Weekly. L.A. New Times* launched with a circulation of 100,000, compared with *L.A. Weekly*'s circulation of 195,000. *L.A. Weekly*'s owner also owned New York's *Village Voice* and Orange County's *OC Weekly.* With respect to competition between *L.A. New Times* and *L.A. Weekly,* Michael Lacey was quoted by *Mediaweek* as saying, "L.A. is so large that we're sure the city can support two weekly papers." By comparison, New Times' acquisition of the *SF Weekly* in January 1995 had not proved profitable in a market dominated by the *San Francisco Bay Guardian.*

New Times expanded its presence in south Florida in 1997 with the launch of *Broward-Palm Beach New Times.* Maureen Olson, classified ad director at *Miami New Times,* became publisher of *Broward-Palm Beach New Times.* The weekly launched in November 1997 with a staff of about ten reporters and editors, with offices located in downtown Ft. Lauderdale. Within the first year circulation increased by 10,000 copies to 70,000.

In August 1998 New Times acquired *Cleveland Scene,* an alternative weekly that was founded in 1970 as a music publication. Following the acquisition New Times expanded the paper's editorial staff and hired staff writers. In 1999 *Cleveland Scene* won prizes in prestigious national competitions, including the Investigative Reporters and Editors contest, The National Society of Newspaper Columnists Awards, and the Clarion Awards sponsored by the Association of Women in Communications.

At the end of 1998 the New Times chain of alternative weeklies grew to ten with the acquisition of St. Louis's *Riverfront Times.* Ray Hartmann, the *Riverfront Times*' founder and former owner, agreed to promote all of the New Times weeklies in his role as editorial chairman. He also would continue to write a column for the *Riverfront Times.* Following the acquisition New Times altered the emphasis of the *Riverfront Times,* eliminating many of the columnists and focusing on hard news reporting.

In 1999 New Times acquired *PitchWeekly* of Kansas City, Missouri. Altogether, New Times' holdings of 11 weekly newspapers would have a combined distribution of 1.1 million. At the time it was acquired, *PitchWeekly* was profitable and had a circulation of 100,000.

New Times acquired the *FW Weekly* of Forth Worth, Texas, in 2000. The paper had a weekly distribution of 40,000. In 2001 Lee Newquist, whom New Times had named as publisher of *FW Weekly,* bought the paper back from New Times for an undisclosed sum.

New Times bolstered its presence in the San Francisco Bay Area in 2001 with the purchase of the *East Bay Express,* a locally owned weekly in Berkeley, California. The *East Bay Express* had a circulation of nearly 60,000 and served the Oakland, Berkeley, Alameda County, and East Bay communities.

At the end of 2001, New Times' formula for acquiring and growing alternative weekly newspapers appeared to be working. The company's papers had gained a reputation for excellence reflected in the numerous awards its writers and reporters had won over the years. Editorial content had led to higher circulation and greater advertising revenue. *Miami New Times*

Key Dates:

1970: The *Arizona Times* (later, *Phoenix New Times*) is founded by Michael Lacey and a group of counter-culture students at Arizona State University.

1983: New Times acquires *Westword* in Denver, Colorado.

1987: New Times acquires the *Wave* and renames it *Miami New Times*.

1991: New Times acquires the *Dallas Observer*.

1993: New Times acquires *Houston Press*.

1995: New Times acquires the Rustin Group, a national advertising representative firm in Chicago.

1996: New Times acquires *L.A. View* and *Los Angeles Reader* and combines them into *New Times Los Angeles*.

1997: New Times launches *Broward-Palm Beach New Times* in south Florida.

1998: New Times acquires *Riverfront Times* in St. Louis, Missouri, and *Cleveland Scene*.

1999: New Times acquires *PitchWeekly* in Kansas City, Missouri.

2000: New Times acquires *Fort Worth Weekly* in Texas.

2001: New Times acquires *East Bay Express* in California and sells *Fort Worth Weekly*.

had a circulation of more than 100,000 in 2001. In Texas the *Dallas Observer*'s circulation was 110,000, and the *Houston Press* reached more than 260,000 readers every week. In Los Angeles the *New Times Los Angeles* reached more than 430,000 readers on a weekly basis. Meanwhile, the Ruxton Group had grown to represent advertising for 28 weeklies in major markets. For the future it would not be surprising to see New Times acquire more alternative weekly papers in top markets.

Principal Competitors

Village Voice Media Inc.; Gannett Co., Inc.; The Hearst Corporation.

Further Reading

Barrett, William P., "Boom Times for New Times," *Forbes,* October 14, 1991, p. 78.

Bates, Eric, "Chaining the Alternatives," *Nation,* June 29, 1998, p. 11.

Bishop, Ed, "Eliminating Columnists from the RFT Signals Profound Change," *St. Louis Journalism Review,* February 1999, p. 4.

Davis, Joel, " 'Express' Eyed by New Times," *Editor & Publisher,* January 15, 2001, p. 9.

Fischer, Howard, and Vince Maietta, "Dallas Weekly Becomes Fourth Paper in New Times Chain," *Business Journal,* July 15, 1991, p. 9.

Gibson, Mike, "Mini-Conglomerates Eating Up Alternative Papers," *St. Louis Journalism Review,* July-August 1996, p. 13.

Gonderinger, Lisa, "New Times Purchases Chicago Ad Rep Firm," *Business Journal,* December 1, 1995, p. 18.

Greenberg, Laura, "Lacey and Larkin," *Phoenix Magazine,* 1990, http://www.newtimes.com/phxmag.html.

Harris, Ellen, "Hartmann Becomes Corporate Animal," *St. Louis Journalism Review,* December 1998, p. 1.

Hawkins, Lori, "New Times Ahead: Houston Press Sold to Phoenix Chain," *Houston Business Journal,* October 4, 1993, p. 1.

Lunsford, Darcie, "Sun-Sentinel, New Times Ready to Race for Readers," *South Florida Business Journal,* September 5, 1997, p. 10.

Margolies, Dan, "The New Times," *Kansas City Business Journal,* October 22, 1999, p. 2.

Morthland, John, "From New Times to Boom Times," *American Way,* 1993, http://www.newtimes.com/amway.html.

Moses, Lucia, "The Alternative Universe," *Editor & Publisher,* October 8, 2001, p. 8.

——, "New Times Inc. Adds Another Alternative to Its Bullpen," *Editor & Publisher,* October 23, 1999, p. 18.

——, "New Times Inc. to Buy 'FWW,' " *Editor & Publisher,* August 21, 2000, p. 13.

"New Times Buys Texas Weekly," *Mediaweek,* August 21, 2000, p. 5.

Patoski, Joe Nick, "Rags to Riches," *Texas Monthly,* June 1994, p. 66.

Sacharow, Anya, "War of the Weeklies in L.A.," *Mediaweek,* September 9, 1996, p. 8.

Steers, Stuart, "Paper Could Be Its Own Worst Dream: A Mainstream Success," *Denver Business Journal,* November 20, 1992, p. 3.

Turner, Dan, "Publishing Giants Go Toe-to-Toe with Rival Alternative Weeklies," *Los Angeles Business Journal,* September 30, 1996, p. 9.

—David P. Bianco

New York Life Insurance Company

51 Madison Avenue
New York, New York 10010
U.S.A.
Telephone: (212) 576-7000
Toll Free: (800) 710-7945
Fax: (212) 576-8145
Web site: http://www.newyorklife.com

Mutual Company
Incorporated: 1841 as Nautilus Insurance Company
Employees: 11,800
Total Assets: $97.1 billion (2000)
NAIC: 524113 Direct Life Insurance Carriers

New York Life Insurance Company is one of the largest insurance companies in the United States and the world. Ranked as a *Fortune* 100 company, New York Life has provided its policyholders with financial security and investment opportunities since 1841. As a mutual company, New York Life is owned solely by its policyholders, to whom it pays annual dividends and provides long-term coverage on a wide range of insurance products. The company prospered during its first 100 years of operations, as the growth of the nation's population and economy created an expanding market for life insurance. Since World War II New York Life has maintained its competitive edge by diversification.

Building the Business: 1840s–50s

Life insurance was an infant industry when New York Life's predecessor, Nautilus Insurance Company, began operations in the 1840s. Marine and fire insurance were important, but people hesitated to assign a cash value to human life, and often associated life insurance with gambling.

As the economy became more industrial and the population more mobile, society recognized the need to secure a family's welfare against the loss of a breadwinner. In 1840 New York State passed a law allowing a married woman to insure her husband's life with immunity from having the benefits seized by his creditors. Such legislation recognized the use of life insurance in a developing industrial economy and widened its potential market beyond wealthy speculators.

New York Life has its origins in a charter granted by the New York state legislature to Nautilus Insurance Company in 1841, for the sale of fire and marine insurance. The company began issuing policies in April 1845 and soon decided to jettison its fire and marine business in order to concentrate on life insurance. By 1849 the company was so securely established in this new business that it petitioned the state legislature and had its name changed to New-York Life Insurance Company. In 1917 or 1918 the company dropped the hyphen in its name. The company's early operations coincided with the development of U.S. life insurance. Policies issued by the company were usually limited to short periods of time and placed a variety of restrictions on their owners. Policyholders in the 1840s could not travel south of Virginia and Kentucky during the summer because the company considered the southern climate a health risk. Southerners applying for policies faced higher premiums and restrictions on their travel as well. Before 1850 the company considered overland travel to California too dangerous for policyholders to undertake without paying an extra premium. Epidemic diseases were of great concern to the company in its early years. Outbreaks of cholera and yellow fever often threatened the company's security, and temporarily forced it to restrict new business to Manhattan and Brooklyn in 1849.

Despite such natural threats, the company grew quickly and established an adequate reserve for paying out dividends and benefits to policyholders. This success was in large part due to the company's most innovative contribution to the young industry, the use of agents to sell policies. Previously, insurance sales had centered on a home office that served local merchants and elites wealthy enough to protect their property and lives. New-York Life's use of agents to seek out new business greatly expanded the market, and the company soon established agencies in New England, the southern states, and as far west as California.

Civil War Risks and Postwar Expansion: 1860s–90s

The Civil War presented the company with its first major crisis, since it had developed a sizable southern business. President Abraham Lincoln's prohibition of commerce with the Confederate states during the war cut off communication between the home office and its southern policyholders, creating a host of problems, including lapsed payments and unpaid claims. The company compensated for these losses, however, by issuing policies to soldiers and civilians involved in combat. One of the few companies to take on such war risks, New-York Life managed continued growth despite its southern losses. In fact, the company sold more than half of the 6,500 new life insurance policies issued in New York City in 1862.

After the war, New-York Life expanded quickly with the nation's booming economy. The company recovered its southern business by paying benefits on death claims left unsettled during the war and by allowing former customers to renew their lapsed policies. As the nation pushed westward, so did the company, establishing agencies in Utah, Montana, and Nevada in 1869 and in San Francisco in 1870. New-York Life also became an international name during this era, opening offices in Canada in 1868, Great Britain in 1870, Paris in 1884, Berlin in 1885, Vienna in 1887, Amsterdam in 1891, and Budapest in 1894.

Intense competition marked the insurance industry in the last two decades of the 19th century, and it was during this time that the company emerged as one of the largest mutual insurance companies in the nation. Competition was fueled in part by the introduction of tontine policies, a type of life insurance in which a number of policyholders would forego their annual dividends and award the money to the last survivor of the group. The winner enjoyed a considerable payoff for his or her longevity. New-York Life began selling tontine policies in 1871, and by 1900 its growth in sales made it one of the nation's three biggest mutual insurance companies, along with Mutual Life Insurance Company and Equitable Life Assurance Society.

Reorganization of the company's agency system also promoted its growth. In 1892 President John A. McCall implemented the branch office system, a structure that would serve the company well. The home office opened branch offices throughout the United States to act as liaisons between the company's New York operations and its agents in the field. Improved communications allowed for more effective administration of the agency force through sales incentives and professional training.

World Conditions Creating Volatile Environment: 1900s–40s

The boom of the 1880s and the 1890s did not go unchecked. New-York Life entered the 20th century at odds with progressive reformers, who accused the rapidly growing insurance companies of mismanagement and malfeasance. In 1905 the

New York state legislature convened an investigative committee under the leadership of William W. Armstrong to examine the state's insurance companies and make recommendations for regulatory reform. With the legal assistance of future U.S. Supreme Court Chief Justice Charles Evans Hughes, The Armstrong Committee heard testimony from the industry's most powerful executives, including John A. McCall.

The Armstrong Committee found New-York Life free from many of the abuses common in other companies, but it also recommended curbing the practices that had pushed the industry's expansion since the Civil War. In 1906 New York outlawed the sale of tontine policies, prohibited excessive commission for agents, and limited the amount of new business a company could do each year. The company officers actively lobbied for revision of these laws. Under the vocal leadership of Darwin Kingsley, who had become president in 1907, the company achieved some success in having its new business ceiling increased and agent incentives reinstated later in the decade.

New-York Life prepared early for World War I, selling securities and borrowing in order to increase cash reserves and meet wartime obligations. During the war the company also issued war-risk policies. The war's greatest challenges came in its aftershocks. The worldwide influenza epidemic of 1918 and 1919 hit the United States with unexpected ferocity: death claims resulted in a $10 million loss for the company, almost twice the cost of benefits paid during the war.

During the Russian Revolution of 1917 the company's assets in Moscow were seized. Soon after, New York Life began its withdrawal from Europe, a reaction to unfriendly regulation and a volatile world economy.

The company's assets were not involved in the stock market crash in October 1929 because state regulation and conservative planning had kept New York Life investments out of common stocks and in more secure government bonds and real estate. In 1929 New York Life moved into its current corporate headquarters on Madison Avenue in New York City. The move represented the company's entry into a modern era of closer ties to the nation's economy and diversification into new financial markets. The company weathered the Great Depression and became an important source of capital in the cash-short economy. Its greatest losses during the Depression were in the form of lapsed payments and canceled policies, a trend finally reversed by the booming wartime economy of the 1940s.

Industry on the Rise: 1950s–70s

Wartime production and the postwar baby boom revived the insurance industry, and New York Life tailored its products and investments to take advantage of these economic and demographic changes. With the development of group insurance in the first half of the 20th century and the passage of the federal Social Security Act in 1935, people began to buy insurance less for its one-time benefit to surviving family members and more for its lifelong investment security. New York Life introduced its first group insurance policies in 1951 and expanded its coverage in group and personal policies to include accidents and sickness as well as death. Two years later it offered the employee protection plan, a combination of individual life and

Key Dates:

1841: Nautilus Insurance Company is chartered to sell fire and marine insurance.
1849: A product shift is marked by name change to New-York Life Insurance Company.
1868: The company opens its first international office.
1892: A branch office system is implemented by company president John A. McCall.
1905: New York state investigation of insurance industry results in new regulations subsequently fought by New York Life.
1929: The company moves to Madison Avenue corporate headquarters.
1951: The first group insurance policies are issued.
1969: A separate entity is created to manage growing commercial and residential real estate holdings.
1984: The company enters the financial services market.
1987: The company purchases one of the largest health-care companies in the nation.
1996: The company sells its healthcare operations.
2000: The company brings all asset management businesses under one roof.

group sickness coverage designed for small businesses. The success of its group plans sustained New York Life's remarkable growth since World War II. In 1974 it created a pension department and began selling employee protection insurance, another policy plan popular with small businesses. In the 1970s alone, New York Life's group insurance sales increased by 152 percent.

Recognizing the need for housing in the postwar nation, New York Life began moving its assets out of wartime government securities and into real estate development in the late 1940s. The company established a mortgage-loan program for veterans in 1946 and also invested in residential housing developments in Queens and Manhattan and in Chicago and Princeton, New Jersey, during the 1940s and 1950s. In 1969 it established the Nautilus Realty Corporation to handle its commercial and residential real estate operations, which proved to be of increasing importance as inflation in the 1970s and 1980s made other investments less desirable.

In the 1960s New York Life introduced the family insurance plan, a policy of comprehensive family coverage. When economic recession and inflation caused the lapse rate on new policies to increase in the early 1970s, the company created an insurance conservation office to study ways of better serving—and thus keeping—customers. The introduction of its Series 78 policies in 1978 made conversion between short-term and life policies more flexible for investment purposes and reduced premiums for women, who were buying an increasing percentage of the company's personal policies. Further innovations included a widening variety of annuities, cost-of-living adjustments in benefits, and the sale of mutual funds. In 1986 the company introduced NYLIFE as a new brand name for its financial products, differentiating this growing business from its traditional life insurance policies.

Diversification Prompted by Industry Downturn: 1980s

Inflation and high interest rates in the early 1980s hurt New York Life's new business sales and reduced its reserves, as policyholders borrowed against their policies for cheap credit. The company quickly adapted to these circumstances by taking advantage of deregulation in the financial services industry. In early 1984 it acquired MacKay-Shields Financial Corporation and two years later the company began marketing its own MainStay mutual funds through this new subsidiary. The company also expanded its annuity business through its subsidiary New York Life Insurance and Annuity Corporation.

Another major growth area for New York Life during the 1980s was healthcare. The spiraling cost of medical care in the 1970s and 1980s strengthened the appeal of insurance as a security against long-term illness. In 1987 New York Life purchased controlling interest in Sanus Corporation Health Systems, one of the largest healthcare companies in the nation. At the time, New York Life's greatest concern in the healthcare field was AIDS. In the late 1980s New York Life became one of the most visible promoters of AIDS awareness in New York City as well as a generous supporter of the American Foundation for AIDS Research. The company opposed antitesting laws introduced in various states, arguing that testing for the AIDS virus is a necessary step in assessing the risks involved in new policies.

Diversification into real estate development, mutual funds, partnership investments, annuities and pensions, and healthcare preserved New York Life's market position, and it entered the 1990s ready to take advantage of expanding demand for these new products.

Reacting to the Changing Marketplaces: 1990s

New York Life reorganized its management structure in 1992. A team of specialists from areas such as service, legal, marketing, and actuarial led by a product manager could move new offerings through the pipeline and out into the market more quickly than in the past. In 1993, New York Life rolled out a variable annuity policy and in 1994 its first variable universal life policy. To tap into a market of more conservative investors, the company began selling a variable annuity product through the banking system in 1995. Bank sales channels had grabbed 25 percent of the annuity market, and New York Life deviated from its traditional agent sales system to take advantage of the trend.

Also in 1995, New York Life merged its group health division with its managed care provider (Sanus) to create NYLCare. The consolidation brought a mixture of healthcare products together, including indemnity coverage and preferred provider and health maintenance organization plans. Available to both large and small groups, an estimated 3.5 million people, through a network of about 175,000 physicians and more than 2,200 hospitals, were expected to be served.

Problems with its limited partnerships prompted New York Life to exit the business in 1996. A majority of its holdings were in poorly performing oil and gas deals. The company decided to reimburse all investors in full as part of a class-action lawsuit settlement.

Sy Sternberg stepped up to the plate as chairman and chief executive officer in 1997, succeeding Harry G. Hohn. A 40-year veteran with the company, Hohn had led New York Life since 1990. Sternberg said in a March 1997 press release, "Under Harry Hohn's direction, New York Life has successfully diversified and grown into a *Fortune* 100 company with over $18 billion in annual revenues. In addition to his legacy of financial strength, he has left a company with a reputation for integrity and for putting the customer first. He has left a solid foundation upon which we can build with confidence."

New York Life sold its NYLCare Health Plans subsidiary in 1998. Aetna Inc. purchased the operation for $1.05 billion in cash, money which New York Life planned to use to bolster its core life insurance, annuities, and asset management segments. The company planned to purchase established businesses both at home and abroad. At the time, New York Life was the fourth largest U.S. life insurance company, as ranked by assets, and the second largest writer of new life insurance premiums. Holding $17 billion in assets under management, the company's MainStay Funds ranked among the top 50 fund families.

In its first major thrust into the Mexican insurance market, New York Life acquired Seguros Monterrey Aetna for about $570 million. "The move fits in with New York Life's strategy of spreading into emerging markets," Sternberg told *National Underwriter* in December 1999. Seguros held 23 percent of the individual life market, but less than 2 percent of the Mexican population purchased life insurance products.

Preparing for the Future: 2000 and Beyond

The creation of New York Life Investment Management LLC, in 2000, brought all of the company's $115 billion in assets under management into one subsidiary. New York Life followed a trend in the insurance industry—distancing the financial products from traditional insurance products—intended to improve competitive strength. The move also protected the parent company from financial liabilities and in turn gave the smaller operation more flexibility. New York Life had no plans to take the new enterprise public.

New York Life prepared for another venture in the finance end of business by seeking and receiving approval to operate a federally insured thrift, a move made possible by changes in federal regulations during the late 1990s. The company first planned to offer trusts and individual retirement accounts. The trust operation gave New York Life the ability to manage insurance money distributions, a capability it lacked to this point.

New York Life reached a record net income of $1.2 billion in 2000. The strong showing translated to the largest ever dividend distribution for policyholders: an estimated $1.46 billion slated for 2001. Life and annuity businesses contributed $9.1 billion in operating revenue, up 5.5 percent. The investment management businesses operating revenue rose 14 percent to $623 million, during a period of stock volatility. The international business more than doubled operating revenue to $1.2 billion. The special markets group membership segment, which included the company's AARP life insurance products, produced operating revenue of $230 million, up 14 percent. Long-

term care insurance operating revenue rose 21 percent to $51 million, with New York Life's agency system driving the sales.

Unlike MetLife and Prudential, New York Life planned to stay the course and remain a mutual company into the early years of the 21st century. That said, Sternberg was determined to remain competitive. Under his leadership, the company had cut costs in the main life insurance and annuity line, added new products such as long-term care, and introduced new sales channels including a brokerage operation. On the international front, New York Life spent $800 million over four years to build operations in Asia and Latin America. Near year-end 2001, the company operated in Argentina, Mexico, Hong Kong, India, Indonesia, the Philippines, South Korea, Taiwan, and Thailand, and had representative offices in the People's Republic of China and Vietnam.

A matter related to its long dissolved European operation was finally resolved in 2001. New York Life settled claims by the survivors of ethnic Armenians killed by Turkish soldiers back in World War I. A 1999 class-action lawsuit led to legislation allowing Armenians living in California to pursue claims against insurers for unpaid benefits.

Horribly, not much later, New York Life faced an onslaught of life insurance claims related to an act of terrorism—the destruction of the World Trade Center in New York on September 11, 2001. The nation's insurers, including New York Life, relaxed claims processing procedures in light of the absence of death certificates for those still missing in the rubble.

Testifying before the House Financial Services Committee, Sternberg said, "This is a time for the insurance industry to be visible. This is a time for us to be charitable. And this is a time for us to stand as a pillar of stability in a none-too-stable world." He also acknowledged that the insurance industry, a major investor in American businesses, could be negatively affected by any long-term economic downturn brought on by the terrorist attacks.

Principal Subsidiaries

New York Life Investment Management LLC.

Principal Competitors

MetLife General Insurance Agency; Prudential Insurance Company of America; TIAA-CREF.

Further Reading

Abbott, Lawrence F., *The Story of NYLIC*, New York: New York Life Insurance Company, 1930.

Ackermann, Matt, "N.Y. Life Relaunches Asset Unit," *American Banker,* October 26, 2000, p. 7.

D'Allegro, Joseph, "New York Life Buys Mexican Insurer for $570 Million," *National Underwriter Life & Health—Financial Services Edition,* December 13, 1999, p. 1.

Friedman, Amy S., "NYLIC Exits Ltd. Partnership Business," *National Underwriter Life & Health—Financial Services Edition,* April 8, 1996, p. 3.

Fraser, Katharine, "N.Y. Life Selling Annuity Through Banks," *American Banker,* November 8, 1995, p. 11.

Fritz, Michael, "Thrifty Insurance Companies Plan to Start Their Own Banking Units; Setting Up Thrifts Easier, Cheaper Than Acquiring Commercial Banks," *Crain's New York Business,* March 20, 2000, p. 27.

Hudnut, James M., *Semi-Centennial History of the New-York Life Insurance Company,* New York: New-York Life Insurance Company, 1895.

Koco, Linda, "Research Spurs Insurer to Offer VUL," *National Underwriter Life & Health—Financial Services Edition,* February 7, 1994, pp. 23+.

Schwartz, Matthew P., "New York Life Launches $2.5B Health Benefits Co.," *National Underwriter Life & Health—Financial Services Edition,* November 6, 1995, pp. 3+.

Vardi, Nathan, "Settling a Case—After 85 Years," *Forbes,* May 14, 2001, p. 120.

Wipperfurth, Heike, "Mutually Exclusive; As Rivals Go Public, NY Life Stands Pat; Daring to Give Wall Street the Brush-Off," *Crain's New York Business,* May 7, 2001, p. 1.

—Timothy J. Shannon
—update: Kathleen Peippo

Niagara Mohawk Holdings Inc.

300 Erie Boulevard West
Syracuse, New York 13202
U.S.A.
Telephone: (315) 474-1511
Fax: (315) 460-1429
Web site: http://www.niagaramohawk.com

Wholly Owned Subsidiary of National Grid PLC
Incorporated: 1929 as Niagara Hudson Power
    Corporation
Employees: 7,600
Sales: $4.54 billion (2000)
Stock Exchanges: New York
Ticker Symbol: NMK
NAIC: 221122 Electric Power Distribution; 22121
    Natural Gas Distribution

Niagara Mohawk Holdings Inc. is a holding company for utilities with a long history of providing electricity and gas to the upstate New York region. Its largest subsidiary, Niagara Mohawk Power Corporation, is the second largest combined electricity and gas utility in New York state. This company provides electricity to over 1.5 million customers in upstate New York, and also provides natural gas service to thousands of customers in the eastern, central, and northern parts of the state. Approximately 85 percent of Niagara Mohawk Holdings' revenue comes from electricity sales. The company sold off its holdings in nuclear power plants in 2000, prior to its merger with British utility company National Grid PLC. The company takes its name from two rivers in the region it serves. The Niagara and Mohawk rivers powered the company's first generators, as the Industrial Revolution led industry and settlement north up the Hudson River Valley, and west to the Great Lakes to form the backbone of Niagara Mohawk's area of service.

Selling Hydroelectric Power in the Early 20th Century

The company did not assume its present configuration nor take its present name until 1950. As early as the late 1870s,

however, the great natural resource of Niagara Falls had been tapped to provide energy in the form of water that turned a wheel, which in turn generated electricity that operated several mills. In addition, water power from the Niagara River was used to operate a primitive electric light machine, and thus the hydroelectric era at Niagara was inaugurated in the years before 1880. By the early 1890s advances in the design of power plants resulted in the Niagara producing more energy than could be used in the immediate surroundings. In the wake of this success, other hydroelectric stations, which would one day become part of the Niagara Mohawk network, were set up in the late 1890s and early years of the 20th century to exploit the power of the many rivers of upstate New York.

Within a few years, the problem of how to transmit power from its source to the places where it was needed had been solved with the use of transformers and high wires carrying alternating current. In 1896 the streets of the nearby city of Buffalo, New York, were lighted for the first time by energy from Niagara Falls. Slowly, power lines were extended from water-powered generating plants into other urban areas. By 1917 steam-generated electricity had come to play a significant role in providing power to upstate New York.

By the end of the 1920s, three separate holding companies encompassing 59 different firms served the energy needs of northern New York state. One holding company used the waters of the Hudson River to generate electricity for the area around Albany, New York; another was centered primarily on the Mohawk River and its tributaries; and a third drew from the resources of Niagara Falls and a large steam-generating plant near Buffalo, New York. Each company within these groupings provided for the needs of its area with its own generating plant and bought and sold excess power as it was needed or became available. In 1929 all 59 companies were brought together under the aegis of the Niagara Hudson Power Corporation, which had been formed specifically for this purpose. Although this united the companies under one owner, their corporate structure and operations remained much the same as before.

In 1932 Niagara Hudson completed a large Art Deco-style headquarters building in Syracuse, New York, whose architecture incorporated many different kinds of decorative illumination, illustrating the wonders of electric power. In this same year, Niagara Hudson also first mixed natural gas into the manufactured gas that it supplied to its customers for use in furnaces, water heaters, and household appliances such as stoves and ovens.

Although lighting powered by gas manufactured from coal or oil had been seen as a competitor for electric illumination in the late 19th century, it soon gave way before the superior qualities of Thomas Edison's incandescent light bulb, and purveyors of gas were forced to fall back on the market for household conveniences. In order to finance the construction of larger generating plants and pipelines to residential areas, gas companies allied themselves with electric companies, and pipelines were subsequently constructed under power-line rights-of-way by these new, dual-purpose companies.

In 1937 in the midst of the Great Depression, Niagara Hudson's twofold electric and gas businesses were reorganized. The 59 separate companies within its structure were reduced to 20, and these companies were separated into three wholly owned principal operating subsidiaries corresponding to their old geographical groupings. These three subsidiaries were Central New York Power Corporation, New York Power and Light Corporation, and Buffalo Niagara Electric Corporation. The entire company was incorporated under the name of Central New York Power Corporation.

With the arrival of the 1940s and the entry of the United States into World War II, the country converted to a wartime economy, and as a symbol of the new austerity the elaborate external decorative lighting of the Niagara Hudson headquarters building was removed. By the end of the 1940s, it had become clear that the geographic administrative divisions that remained within the company were not appropriate for the production of electricity and distribution of natural gas, and a final level of consolidation was undertaken. In 1950 the three operating divisions and the 20 companies within them were combined to form a single operating company, Niagara Mohawk Power Company.

A More Centralized Company After World War II

In this new entity, power distribution for the entire area was brought under central control. All energy produced was pooled, and then allotted to users depending on need and supply. The new company was investor-owned, as its predecessors had been. As a utility, with a monopoly to provide an essential service to a particular area, the company operated under the scrutiny of the New York State Public Services Commission, and other such entities. The company was required to submit to this commission requests for periodic increases in rates to cover costs.

Throughout the 1950s Niagara Mohawk acquired a number of power companies and power-generating facilities in its region. By 1958 the Niagara Mohawk system covered more than

21,000 square miles in New York state, and encompassed 83 hydroelectric plants and seven steam-driven plants, as well as several thousand miles of gas mains.

In 1963 Niagara Mohawk announced plans to construct an atomic power plant at Nine Mile Point, New York, near the town of Oswego on Lake Ontario. Two years later, the company received permission from the Atomic Energy Commission to build the plant. That same year Niagara Mohawk's service area was affected by a blackout that originated with a power surge in a Canadian company's plant on the Canadian side of the Niagara River. This led Niagara Mohawk, along with other utilities, to improve plant design and construction.

Niagara Mohawk's Nine Mile Point Nuclear Unit One went into commercial operation in December 1969. Six months later, in June 1970, the utility announced plans to construct a second nuclear power plant at the site. In addition to expanding its nuclear capabilities, Niagara Mohawk modernized and enlarged its conventional power-generating plants at this time in anticipation of increased demand for electricity in the coming years. The company converted four coal-burning plants at its Oswego steam station to oil and constructed an additional oil-burning facility. Two years later, in 1972, the company announced plans to add a sixth oil-burning unit at Oswego, to begin operation in 1976.

Niagara Mohawk, like the rest of the utility industry, was taken by surprise and heavily affected by the OPEC oil embargo of late 1973, which touched off an energy crisis. The price of petroleum, a major raw material for power plants, skyrocketed, and the company duly passed on this increase to its customers, winning permission to increase rates in February 1974, and then again seven months later. An indicator of customer dissatisfaction with rising utility costs came in May 1974, when the town of Massena, New York, voted to take over the company's facilities on municipal land and operate them itself.

With earnings squeezed by the energy crisis, the company scaled back its construction budget for 1975 and halted work on its sixth generating plant at the Oswego site, delaying its operation for two years. Nine months later, the company announced that it had sold a 24 percent stake in the plant to Rochester Gas & Electric Corporation, a nearby utility. In early 1975 the company cut costs further by eliminating 1,000 jobs.

To strengthen its construction program, Niagara Mohawk sought alliances with other power companies. The company set up Empire State Power Resources, Inc., a joint venture with six other New York utilities to build and operate power plants. Niagara Mohawk also purchased an interest in a nuclear plant being planned for Sterling, New York, and brought in four additional partners to help it construct its Nine Mile Point Two nuclear reactor. These arrangements allowed the company to reduce its budgets for the rest of the 1970s and to begin work in June 1975 on the Nine Mile Point Two facility.

Coping with Changes in the 1980s

By 1977 Niagara Mohawk earnings had come out of a mid-1970s slump. By the following year, however, demand for electricity had begun to fall, and the company announced the first delay of the opening of its second nuclear plant under construction at Nine Mile Point. In addition in 1979 General Electric Company accepted responsibility for damages to Niagara Mohawk's first nuclear generator at that site, incurred during a routine shutdown for refueling and maintenance, which kept the plant out of operation for a costly month.

Public opposition to nuclear power and skepticism of projected increases in energy needs resulted in hostility toward the nuclear power industry in the 1980s. Niagara Mohawk was further plagued by its Nine Mile Point facilities in 1980, when it was announced that cost projections for Nine Mile Point Two, only one-third completed, had been increased by 78 percent to reach $2.4 billion. Citing concerns about technical and environmental issues, as well as regulatory difficulties, the company postponed the plant's operating date until late 1986. In addition, plans for the nuclear plant in Sterling, New York, in which Niagara Mohawk had acquired a partial interest, were scrapped by a regulatory commission in 1981.

In March 1982 the utility closed its Nine Mile Point One unit when leaks from cracked pipes were discovered during routine testing. The plant was scheduled to be closed for a year, and Niagara Mohawk purchased energy from Ontario Hydro, its Canadian neighbor, to make up for the loss in supply. In October 1982 the plant closure was extended for six months, when additional flaws in the reactor cooling system were discovered, necessitating repairs totaling $50 million.

In February 1984 progress toward completion of Nine Mile Point Two was jeopardized when one of Niagara Mohawk's partners, Long Island Lighting Company, temporarily withdrew from the consortium financing construction of the plant, and Niagara Mohawk had to take on its share of the costs. Critics continued to maintain that the project was unnecessary and uneconomical. Niagara Mohawk received a further blow later that month when the New York State Public Service Commission accused the company of "widespread mismanagement" in operating some of its conventional power plants, and recommended an $83.2 million rebate of fuel adjustment charges to customers. The following month, the commission ordered a $100 million rebate relating to charges for nuclear waste disposal.

In the same month, Niagara Mohawk suffered another rebuke at the hands of a different regulatory agency when the Nuclear Regulatory Commission levied its seventh fine against the utility since its Nine Mile Point One nuclear generating unit had opened, ordering the company to pay $180,000 for failing

to test equipment and failing to follow quality control procedures. By April 1984 when the Nine Mile Point Two plant was 75 percent completed, its estimated cost was raised again by one-fifth, to $5.1 billion. Since the company was forbidden by regulations to pass on more than 80 percent of cost overruns on the project to its customers, this meant that Niagara Mohawk shareholders would absorb a total loss of $100 million.

Niagara Mohawk's regulatory troubles continued in 1985. In January the company was ordered to refund an additional $20 million to its customers after an investigation of its management of plants burning fossil fuels, and two months later a further $32.5 million refund was added.

Construction of the Nine Mile Point Two reactor finally came to an end in March 1988, and the facility went into commercial operation in April. The total cost of building the plant was $6.4 billion. This was offset by the closing of Nine Mile Point One in December 1987 for repairs and inspections that would ultimately take 31 months to complete, depressing the company's earnings. The closing came after the plant had set a U.S. record for continuous operation by a boiling-water reactor, with 415 consecutive days. In August 1988 Niagara Mohawk sued three of its subcontractors on Nine Mile Point Two in an attempt to win back some of the money it had lost on the project. The company eventually settled with the subcontractors out of court. In October 1988 the newly operational Nine Mile Point Two plant was also forced to close temporarily, and the utility had to buy power from other sources to meet demand.

In August 1989 Niagara Mohawk completed an extensive agreement with its regulators in the hope of having Nine Mile Point removed from a list of problem plants and returned to profitable operation. Nine Mile Point was removed from this list in 1991 and received its best-ever rating from the Nuclear Regulatory Commission. Despite lowered income and the failure to pay dividends on its common stock throughout 1990, the company was able to conclude agreements closing out the era of construction on Nine Mile Point Two and instituted a cost-reduction plan that included eliminating 1,100 jobs.

In August 1991 Niagara Mohawk experienced further difficulties with Nine Mile Point Two when a failure in the plant's monitoring system automatically shut down the reactor and sent out an alert at the second-highest level of emergency. Regulatory officials closed the plant until an investigation into the causes of the incident was completed, resulting in yet further loss of revenue for Niagara Mohawk. The reactor returned to service six weeks later. Niagara Mohawk had to overcome the obstacles of operation in a strict regulatory environment in order to balance economic and environmental concerns as well as the needs of its customers for power and its shareholders for profit. The company's financial picture, however, improved somewhat in 1991, as its credit ratings were upgraded and it was able to resume dividend payments.

Restructuring and Buyout in the Late 1990s

Difficult business conditions intensified for Niagara Mohawk in the 1990s. The company suffered a fate that afflicted many utilities around the country as a result of energy policies put in place decades earlier. Congress passed the Public Utility Regulatory Policies Act in 1978, which was meant to encourage new players in the energy market. These new companies were known as independent power producers, or IPPs, which sold the power they produced at state-regulated rates. In New York in 1983, the state legislature set a minimum electricity rate of six cents per kilowatt hour that Niagara Mohawk and other utilities could pay for power from IPPs. The legislators set this floor price presuming that power rates would rise. Instead, they began to fall in the mid-1980s. Niagara Mohawk ended up locked into long-term contracts with dozens of IPPs for power at well above current market rates. In 1990, Niagara Mohawk paid out around $200 million for power from independent producers. By 1993, it was shelling out $745 million, and only a year later its payments increased to $967 million. Not only was the company paying above-market rates for power, but it was forced by its contract obligations to buy more than it needed. Several large Niagara customers, such as General Motors, Miller Brewing, and International Paper, closed plants in upstate New York as the regional economy turned down. With fewer big customers, Niagara needed less power. But it had to honor the IPP contracts, and so continued to buy excess amounts. As new CEO William Davis took the helm of Niagara Mohawk in May 1993, the company saw its credit rating slashed. Over the next year, the company's stock price fell by almost half.

Davis attempted to control costs by cutting the workforce and asking for a hike in the rate it charged consumers. Its request for a rate hike was turned down in 1996. At that point, Niagara Mohawk's fate looked dire. Attempts to renegotiate contracts with the IPPs had led to dozens of lawsuits, and tensions between the utility and the independent producers ran high. The company announced that it was contemplating filing for bankruptcy. This move would have put many of the IPPs that sold power to Niagara in bankruptcy themselves. To help with the negotiations, Niagara hired the law firm Donaldson Lufkin & Jenrette in 1996. Its director Mike Ranger had recently completed a restructuring of a Texas utility, and he proposed a similar plan for Niagara Mohawk. This involved the company raising money by issuing $3.45 billion in bonds. The cash would then go to buy out the IPPs' contracts. The deal was completed in June 1998. About half the IPPs terminated their contracts altogether, and the rest rewrote their contracts based on current market prices.

As part of the complex deal, Niagara Mohawk agreed to sell off its power generating plants. It would become primarily an electricity transmitter and distributor. In late 2000 the company announced that it had sold its nuclear plant, Nine Mile Point Unit No. 1, to Constellation Energy Group Inc. of Baltimore. Constellation also acquired 82 percent of Nine Mile Point Unit No. 2, which Niagara owned with a consortium of other local utilities. Niagara was on its way to becoming a much slimmer company, unfettered by its burdensome IPP contracts and troublesome nuclear plants. Its new, improved status apparently made it a takeover target. In 2000 the firm announced that it was being acquired by a British company, National Grid PLC, for approximately $3 billion. National Grid had already bought up two other New England power companies, and its takeover of Niagara Mohawk was its biggest acquisition yet. The deal moved slowly through various regulatory channels, with consummation expected in late 2001. Niagara Mohawk was to retain its name and Syracuse headquarters. It would now be part of the ninth largest electric utility in the United States.

Principal Subsidiaries

Niagara Mohawk Energy Inc.; Niagara Mohawk Power Corp.

Principal Competitors

Consolidated Edison, Inc.; Energy East Corp.; KeySpan Energy Co.

Further Reading

Cooper, Christopher, "U.K.'s National Grid Makes Power Play," *Wall Street Journal*, August 24, 2001, p. A5.

Kinnander, Ola, "Private Utilities Make a Stand Against Public Bid for Control," *Bond Buyer*, December 3, 1999, p. 1.

"Niagara Mohawk Reports Losses," *New York Times*, August 14, 2001, p. B6.

Picker, Ida, "Up from the Depths," *Institutional Investor*, December 1998, p. 28.

Piper, Fred W., *Niagara Mohawk: The People and the Land It Serves*, New York: Niagara Mohawk Power Corporation, 1958.

Sullivan, Allanna, "Constellation Energy to Purchase 2 New York Nuclear-Power Plants," *Wall Street Journal*, December 13, 2000, p. B10.

Wipperfurth, Heike, "Capital Markets Rescue NIMO: $4 Billion Junk Bond Package Fuels Recap," *Investment Dealers' Digest*, December 14, 1998.

—Elizabeth Rourke
—update: A. Woodward

Nicklaus Companies

11780 U.S. Highway One
North Palm Beach, Florida 33408
U.S.A.
Telephone: (561) 626-3900
Fax: (561) 626-4104
Web site: http://www.nicklaus.com

Private Company
Incorporated: 1970 as Golden Bear International
Employees: 39
Sales: $11.2 million (1999)
NAIC: 71131 Promoter of Performing Arts, Sports, and
Similar Events with Facilities; 71141 Agents and
Managers for Artists, Athletes, Entertainers, and Other
Public Figures; 71391 Golf Courses and Country
Clubs; 71399 All Other Amusement and Recreation
Industries

Nicklaus Companies is a conglomerate of golf-related businesses run and owned by golfer Jack Nicklaus and his family. The company was formerly named Golden Bear, after Nicklaus's moniker. It runs the Nicklaus-Flick golf instruction and practice centers, licenses Jack Nicklaus brand clothing and golf accessories, operates the Golden Bear Tour, and consults with a golf course construction firm. The company also handles endorsement deals made by Jack Nicklaus. The company was originally formed as an umbrella for Nicklaus's many business interests. At one time, the company had as many as 20 subsidiaries, and it was involved in some non-golf-related areas including oil development and radio broadcasting. The company got overextended with debt and was close to bankruptcy in the mid-1980s, then went on to prosper under tighter management. Golden Bear went public in 1996. Its life as a public company was short-lived, however. Accounting fraud at one of its subsidiaries led to a stockholder suit and investigation by the Securities and Exchange Commission. The company was taken private in 2000, and now remains in the hands of Jack Nicklaus and his immediate family.

Company Built on Nicklaus's Fame

Jack Nicklaus was named Player of the Century in 1988, and is considered to be the greatest golfer in the history of the game. He was born in Columbus, Ohio, in 1940 and began playing golf at the age of ten. He was already a terrific player in his teens, winning the National Jaycee Junior when he was 16. He later attended Ohio State University. Golf interfered with his studies, and he left school to become a professional golfer in 1961. In 1962, he won the U.S. Open, only the first in an impressive string of victories. Nicklaus earned the nickname "Golden Bear," because he was somewhat bulky and extremely fair-haired. Nicklaus's agent, Mark McCormack of the Cleveland-based International Management Group, created Golden Bear as a corporate entity to encompass Nicklaus's business deals. At first the business side of Nicklaus's career meant mostly endorsements. Nicklaus had left college without a degree, was young, famous, and making money. He concentrated on playing golf and left Golden Bear to his agent to handle. But after a few years, Nicklaus was ready to break with McCormack. McCormack was also the agent for Nicklaus's arch-rival Arnold Palmer. Palmer was not only a great golfer, but was known as "the people's choice" for his winning personality. Nicklaus chafed at being handled by Palmer's manager, and in 1968 he left McCormack.

Golden Bear then found new headquarters in North Palm Beach, Florida, where Nicklaus made his home. Management of the company was taken over by Putnam Pierman, a Columbus native who had known Nicklaus since high school. In 1970, the company incorporated as Golden Bear International Inc. Nicklaus had a longstanding interest in golf course design, and by the mid-1960s he was consulting with top people in the field about courses across the country. Nicklaus began working on a course in Columbus called Muirfield Village around 1967. Pierman, whose family owned an Ohio construction business, was instrumental in getting Muirfield Village off the drawing board. He spearheaded the project and helped Nicklaus manage his growing design consultancy. Along with famed designer Pete Dye, Nicklaus worked on the Harbour Town golf club on Hilton Head Island, South Carolina, in 1968; the John's Island Club, in Vero Beach, Florida, in 1969; and the Wabeek Golf

Club in Bloomfield Hills, Michigan, in 1971. He also co-designed courses with another renowned architect, Desmond Muirhead, creating the Jack Nicklaus Sports Center in Cincinnati, Ohio, in 1971, and the New St. Andrews Golf Club, Ontawara City, Japan, in 1973.

Golf course design was only one arm of Golden Bear. When Pierman took over the company, he instituted a new way of dealing with Nicklaus's endorsements. Nicklaus had previously never met with people from the companies whose products he endorsed. Pierman had the golfer meet with his endorsement clients and had the different client companies meet all together. This led to fruitful arrangements, such as a Nicklaus commercial for Eastern Airlines with a Pontiac car, another Nicklaus-endorsed goody, in the background. Nicklaus also lost weight in 1969 and let his hair grow, making him more photogenic. He continued to play incredible golf, winning the British Open in 1970, and then seven more major tournaments over the next five years. Nicklaus was a rising star, and Golden Bear fielded all sorts of business offers. The company bought a Pontiac dealership in Florida, and expanded into several other areas that had nothing to do with golf. These did not always do well. The car dealership, for example, faltered and had to be sold. Yet it made money under its new owner, who had more knowledge of the car business.

Even Nicklaus's golf-related businesses did not always go smoothly. His reputation as a course designer took off in the 1970s. After co-designing with great names in the field, Nicklaus decided to strike out on his own in 1973. Within only a few months, he had signed contracts to design more than two dozen courses. One of his earliest projects, Muirhead Village, was thought to be one of the best golf courses in the country. Yet Golden Bear only broke even on it, faced with steep construction costs and booming land prices in the surrounding area. Golden Bear was multifaceted, expanding into new and complex businesses, and still run by only a small staff. By 1975, the financial burden of Muirfield Village in particular weighed the company down. That year Nicklaus and Putnam Pierman parted company.

Focusing on Golf Courses in the 1980s

In 1976, Nicklaus hired Charles E. Perry to take over the running of Golden Bear. Perry had been president of Florida International University and also the publisher of *Family Weekly* magazine. Perry quickly reined in the company, trimming staff and expenses and chucking unprofitable businesses. He focused the company on golf course development. Golden Bear brought in impressive fees for Nicklaus's design work. The company's basic design fee was $150,000 for a course in the United States. To design a course abroad, Golden Bear charged $250,000 in an English-speaking country, and $300,000 elsewhere. The company also offered additional services, such as supervising construction of the course, handling maintenance, and running concessions on the course. If the course wanted to use the Jack Nicklaus name and enlist the golfer to do personal promotions, Golden Bear could expect another $1 million. By 1981, Nicklaus had made some $3.6 million playing golf over his career so far. This was a fine figure, but Golden Bear was far more lucrative. The course design projects Golden Bear had going that year were projected to eventually bring in around $300 million.

Nicklaus worked on dozens of courses at once, jetting from one to the other in a private plane. He cut back his competition schedule and typically spent part of every day in the Golden Bear office. Nicklaus had a storied memory and concentration, and he was able to keep details in his head of the many design projects he worked on. But he knew little about real estate, and he left that side of the course development business entirely to Charles Perry. Perry had seen others make money off rising property value in land bordering the Nicklaus courses. His idea was to further expand the design business, and take on the building of residential communities. Perry initiated two major projects in 1979 and 1980. One was Bear Creek, a golf community outside of San Diego. The other was the refurbishing of the St. Andrews Golf Club in Hastings-on-Hudson, New York. St. Andrews was the oldest golf club in the United States, only 30 minutes from Manhattan, but it had fallen into disrepair. Golden Bear planned to revive the course and to build and sell condominium ''golf villas'' on the course. These were expected to go for around $200,000 for a two-bedroom.

These two projects added a lot of debt to Golden Bear, and neither did as well as planned. Bear Creek was situated almost an hour and a half from San Diego, and that location proved too remote to tempt many buyers. Golden Bear had taken out a loan for $35 million for St. Andrews, and the golf villas did not sell. Nor was this the only thing wrong with the company. When Perry had taken over Golden Bear from Putnam Pierman, he had cut costs and jettisoned businesses Golden Bear did not know how to run, such as the car dealership. But by the mid-1980s, Golden Bear had dozens of subsidiaries. The company ran a restaurant, launched a line of eyewear, operated an investment advice service and a radio station, and developed gas through its Golden Bear Oil & Gas subsidiary. Nicklaus told the *Wall Street Journal* (January 27, 1987): ''We were an accounting nightmare. . . . I didn't know what any of them did, and neither did anyone else.'' Though Nicklaus himself was intensely involved with the design business, he was unable to keep track of the other aspects of his company.

Key Dates:

1961: Jack Nicklaus turns pro.
1970: Golden Bear International Inc. is incorporated.
1976: Charles E. Perry is hired to run company.
1985: The company is dangerously in debt.
1996: Golden Bear Golf, Inc. is taken public.
2000: The private and public companies merge as a private entity, which is renamed Nicklaus Companies.

Keeping a Tighter Grip in the 1990s

Golden Bear was severely overextended by 1985. That summer, a new accountant at the company, Dick Bellinger, got together with the firm's legal counsel and broke the bad news to Nicklaus. The company was facing bankruptcy, and Nicklaus's personal fortune was also in danger. He had personally guaranteed loans and losses, and it looked like he had to pay up. Nicklaus negotiated with his bankers, and paid some $3 million to settle the ill-fated St. Andrews Golf Club deal. Golden Bear was in debt for about $175 million. Charles Perry insisted that he had a sound long-term business strategy. But Nicklaus was no longer comfortable with Perry's style. Perry left, and Nicklaus himself took over the top spot of what was now called Golden Bear International, Inc. His number two man became accountant Dick Bellinger. Nicklaus resolved to control the company himself, sticking to golf-related businesses that he had some expertise in.

Golden Bear continued to develop golf communities like Bear Creek, but it only did so when other parties took the financial risk. It took on new subsidiaries, but only in golf-related fields. Nicklaus designed a new putter for MacGregor, a golf company whose clubs he had endorsed since the 1960s. Golden Bear bought the company in 1982 and sold 80 percent of it again in 1986. Nicklaus spent time investigating the company's manufacturing processes and researched the retail market, eventually bringing MacGregor back to financial health. Nicklaus also looked for new businesses that he could run with less of an investment of his personal time. Nicklaus was 45 when disaster struck his company, and it occurred to him that he needed to find a way to keep Golden Bear going even if he were to retire. So the firm diversified into golf schools, marketing and management of golf tournaments, and golf videos, while it continued to license products and rake in design fees. By 1988, the company's debt had almost disappeared. Sales were $98 million, with $10 million in profit.

By the early 1990s, Golden Bear had become a conglomerate of golf-related businesses, with only about 30 percent of the business directly dependent on Jack Nicklaus's daily involvement. In 1993, the company entered a joint venture with Club Corp. International, the leading operator of golf courses, to build about 40 public golf courses around the country. Though these would be Nicklaus-designed courses, they were intended to be less complex to play and maintain as some of Nicklaus's previous courses. That year Nicklaus also brought out his own line of golf clubs through Golden Bear's Nicklaus Golf Equipment subsidiary. These were clubs designed for the average golfer, though the price for a set was nevertheless quite steep at

around $1,800. Golden Bear seemed to have evolved nicely by the mid-1990s, recovering from its near downfall a decade earlier to bring in around $50 million annually.

Nicklaus and his top executives decided to take part of Golden Bear public in 1996. Other golf companies had done well on the stock market around that time, including Callaway Golf, maker of the popular Big Bertha clubs. The company was split into two parts. Golden Bear International continued as a private company, and comprised the parts of the business that were directly dependent on Jack Nicklaus. The rest of the company went on the NASDAQ exchange August 1, 1996, as Golden Bear Golf, Inc. The public company consisted of six core business areas. These were the Nicklaus-Flick Golf Schools, Nicklaus Apparel, the golf management company Golden Bear Club Services, the Jack Nicklaus International Club, a licensing division for Nicklaus and Golden Bear trademarks, and the golf course building firm Paragon Construction Company. The initial public offering went well, bringing in $36.9 million. Some of this capital went immediately to purchase nine driving ranges, which were to become family-oriented golf practice centers. Nicklaus himself still owned 55 percent of the company.

The public company did well at first, but by 1998 was beset by several problems. Golden Bear had invested in a string of driving ranges, but it was not immediately able to run them profitably. As debt began to mount and Golden Bear's stock fell, the company sold the nine driving ranges, plus five more it already owned. But worse news followed. The president of Golden Bear's construction subsidiary, Paragon Construction, resigned in April 1998 after the company posted a loss of $2.7 million for 1997. Under new management, accountants discovered that the loss at Paragon was much graver. The company was actually some $24.7 million in the red. Golden Bear claimed that Paragon's management had deliberately falsified records and made false statements. The company's stock was temporarily delisted as outraged stockholders filed suit. The stockholder class-action suit was settled by mid-2000 with a settlement of $3.5 million. Nicklaus lost millions of his personal fortune rectifying problems at Golden Bear; moreover, the company's stock was completely undermined by the episode. The company bought back its shares at 75 cents apiece, and became a private company again. Its last reported sales were $11.2 million in 1999. Yet a huge chunk of this was profit. Net income was $7.8 million.

Golden Bear changed its name to Nicklaus Companies at the end of 2000. The company continued to license Nicklaus and Golden Bear branded products worldwide. It licensed apparel, leather goods, luggage, eyewear, furniture, artwork, and other items through 15 companies, and distributed these goods in over 25 countries. Its biggest markets were the United States, Japan, and Korea. The company also continued to operate the Nicklaus-Flick golf schools. It handled marketing fees from Jack Nicklaus's personal product endorsements as well. Nicklaus Companies also maintained a joint venture with Weitz Golf International LLC, a golf course construction company, to market new courses.

Principal Competitors

Callaway Golf Company; Fortune Brands, Inc.; ClubCorp, Inc.

Further Reading

Coulton, Antoinette, "Citicorp, Visa Put Golden Bear on Platinum Card," *American Banker*, July 9, 1997, p. 1.

Fins, Antonio N., Ronald Grover, and Sayaka Shinoda, "The Golden Bear Blasts into the Green," *Business Week*, February 15, 1988, pp. 80–83.

Hodenfield, Chris, "Unsinkable Jack Nicklaus and the Perils of a Bear Market," *Golf Digest*, November 1998, p. 83.

"Jack Nicklaus Inc.," *Fortune*, April 8, 1991, p. 91.

Lowenstein, Roger, "A Golfer Becomes an Executive: Jack Nicklaus's Business Education," *Wall Street Journal*, January 27, 1987, p. 34.

Nicklaus, Jack, with Ken Bowden, *My Story,* New York: Simon and Schuster, 1997.

Palmeri, Christopher, "Nicklaus for the Masses," *Forbes*, December 6, 1993, p. 20.

Peper, George, "Jack's 'Other' Career," *Golf Magazine*, March 1981, pp. 34–38, 108–12.

Pittman, Alan P., "Golden Bear Settles Suit, But SEC Inquiry Looms," *Golf World*, April 7, 2000, p. S2.

——, "Revenue Falls at Golden Bear," *Golf World*, May 26, 2000, p. S6.

Reese, Jennifer, "Golf Clubs from a Legend," *Fortune*, April 5, 1993, p. 128.

Russell, Geoff, "Golden Bear Settles Suit with Shareholders," *Golf World*, April 7, 2000, p. 10.

Sanders, Lisa, "Subpar for the Golden Bear," *Business Week*, July 28, 1997, p. 4.

—A. Woodward

Northrop Grumman Corporation

1840 Century Park East
Los Angeles, California 90067-2199
U.S.A.
Telephone: (310) 553-6262
Fax: (310) 201-3023
Web site: http://www.northgrum.com

Public Company
Incorporated: 1939 as Northrop Aircraft Company
Employees: 98,250
Sales: $7.62 billion (2000)
Stock Exchanges: New York Pacific
Ticker Symbol: NOC
NAIC: 332993 Ammunition (Except Small Arms)
Manufacturing; 332995 Other Ordnance and
Accessories Manufacturing; 334290 Other
Communication Equipment Manufacturing; 334419
Other Electronic Component Manufacturing; 334511
Search, Detection, Navigation, Guidance,
Aeronautical, and Nautical System and Instrument
Manufacturing; 336411 Aircraft Manufacturing;
336413 Other Aircraft Part and Auxiliary Equipment
Manufacturing; 336414 Guided Missile and Space
Vehicle Manufacturing; 336611 Ship Building and
Repairing; 541512 Computer Systems Design Services

Northrop Grumman Corporation is the number three defense firm in the United States, behind The Boeing Company and Lockheed Martin Corporation. The company provides the U.S. military with nearly 60 percent of its airborne radar systems, including the AWACS system; is the number two provider of information technology to the federal government; and is the largest naval shipbuilder in the world. It is organized into six operating sectors: Electronic Systems, which includes airborne radar, navigation, electronic warfare, air defense, space, and logistics systems; Information Technology, a sector focusing on providing advanced information technology solutions for both government and commercial clients; Integrated Systems, which develops both aircraft and airframe subsystems, including airborne surveillance aircraft, such as the Joint STARS plane, and combat aircraft, such as the B-2 stealth bomber; Ship Systems, which designs and produces surface battle ships, such as guided missile destroyers and amphibious assault ships; Newport News, which builds nuclear-powered aircraft carriers and submarines; and Component Technologies, which supplies electronic and optical components and materials to the military, telecommunications, medical, and other markets.

Northrop Grumman is a somewhat unlikely survivor of the post-Cold War consolidation of the U.S. defense industry. In April 1994 the company was formed when Northrop Corporation acquired Grumman Corporation. Northrop Grumman then agreed to be acquired by Lockheed Martin in July 1997. Several months later, however, the U.S. government blocked the deal. At that time, Northrop Grumman had annual revenues of about $9 billion. Through a series of acquisitions in the late 1990s and early 2000s—most notably the purchases of Litton Industries, Inc. and Newport News Shipbuilding Inc., both completed in 2001—the company expected to report revenues of around $18 billion for 2002. During this same period, Northrop Grumman also transformed itself from primarily a producer of military aircraft to a leading defense electronics and systems integration company while maintaining and/or building positions in military aircraft and naval systems.

Jack Northrop and the Early Years of Northrop Corporation

John Knudsen Northrop, aerospace innovator and founder of Northrop Corporation, was born in 1895. He served in the infantry during World War I and was later transferred to the Army Signal Corps, which was responsible for military aviation. In the Signal Corps he developed a skill for designing aircraft and, as a result, went to work for Donald Douglas in California after the war. As a draftsman, he helped to develop the airplanes that first established Douglas's firm as a leading aircraft manufacturer.

In 1927, he went to work for Allan Lockheed, where he led the development of the Vega, the airplane that made Lockheed a major company. The Vega was one of the first airplanes to have a ''stressed skin'' construction, meaning that the structural integrity of the outer shell of the aircraft was sufficient to eliminate the need for a weighty frame and struts. The design ushered in a new generation in aircraft design. Amelia Earhart flew a Vega on her solo flight across the Atlantic in 1932.

Northrop formed his own company in 1928, the Avion Corporation. Here he conducted research for the first all-metal aircraft and the ''flying wing,'' a highly efficient boomerang-like aircraft with no fuselage. Two years later, Avion was purchased by Bill Boeing's United Aircraft and Transport Corporation.

Jack Northrop created a second company in 1932 as a division of Douglas Aircraft. Established as a partnership with Douglas, the Northrop Corporation developed an airplane for the Army Air Corps called the Alpha. Similar to the Vega, the Alpha had a single shell, or ''monocoque,'' construction. Because the plane was made of metal instead of wood, however, it was more durable and efficient. The Alpha made a new generation of aircraft possible for Douglas, namely the DC-1, DC-2, and DC-3. Northrop's engineering success with this type of airplane set a new standard for manufacturers; biplanes, double-skin construction, and airplanes made of wood were relegated to the past.

In 1938 Northrop Corporation was absorbed into Douglas Aircraft. One year later, Jack Northrop left Douglas to establish his own company, Northrop Aircraft Company. When World War II erupted, Northrop devoted much of his company's resources to the development of a flying wing bomber. This revolutionary design was greeted with great skepticism. The advantage of the flying wing was that without the ''baggage'' of a fuselage or tail section, the entire mass of the airplane could be employed to produce the lift needed to keep it aloft. This allowed the possibility of much greater bomb payloads. In 1940 the company flew its first experimental flying wing, designated the N-1M.

Northrop later developed the B-35 flying wing bomber and then an improved version called the B-49, which he hoped would be chosen as the primary bomber for the Air Corps. Yet the Army canceled further development of Northrop's bomber because, as reported by the Army, the B-49 was not stable enough in the air and because it required powered rather than manual controls. Northrop, however, revealed shortly before he died that the Army canceled the B-49 because he refused to merge his company with a manufacturer in Texas. Others have suggested that the Army dropped the flying wing when Northrop refused to allow other government-appointed companies to manufacture his design. Even today the real reason the B-49 was canceled is not clear.

In spite of the B-49 fiasco, Northrop contributed to the war effort in many other ways. His company built the P-61 night fighter known as the Black Widow. He also established a prosthetics department at his company for dismembered veterans. He even employed disabled servicemen either at the plant or in their hospital beds for regular pay.

In 1952 Jack Northrop retired and relinquished his presidency to O.P. Echols. In 1958 the name of the company was changed to the Northrop Corporation, and the following year Thomas V. Jones took over as president. Jones led the company into a number of diversified subcontracting arrangements. Northrop built numerous airplane and missile parts, electronic control systems, and even became involved in construction.

During the 1950s and 1960s, Northrop produced the F-89 jet interceptor and the curiously named Snark missile system. The company continued to produce its own jet fighters, including the popular F-5 Freedom Fighter. A total of over 2,200 F-5s were flown by 30 countries, including Taiwan, Iran, and South Korea. The trainer version of the F-5, the T-38, was used by the U.S. Air Force and was also the jet chosen by the Thunderbirds acrobatic flying troupe.

1970s and 1980s: Scandal and Controversy

In 1972 Jones made an illegal $50,000 contribution to the reelection campaign of President Nixon; he was fined $200,000 for this indiscretion. The scandal led to an investigation that revealed another more serious impropriety. The company admitted to paying $30 million in bribes to government officials in Indonesia, Iran, and Saudi Arabia, among other countries, in an effort to increase business.

An enraged stockholder sued the company and, as a result, won a settlement that forced Jones to resign his presidency but allowed him to remain as chairman. A further condition of the court ruling was that the board was required to seat four more independent directors, giving the non-management ''outsiders'' a majority. Into the 1990s, company policy held that 60 percent of the board seats had to be held by non-management personnel.

After the scandal, the company had considerably more trouble selling its products. David Packard, an assistant secretary of defense in the Nixon Administration, invited two finalists to compete for the job of producing America's next fighter jet; Northrop's F-17 Cobra competed against General Dynamics' F-16. Prototypes of the jets flew against each other in dogfights. In the end, the F-16 won the competition. The F-17, however, was later redesigned by Northrop in conjunction with McDonnell Douglas and renamed the F-18 Hornet.

The F-18 Hornet was to be produced in two versions in partnership with McDonnell Douglas. Douglas was the prime contractor for the F-18A carrier-based fighter, and Northrop was the prime contractor for the F-18L, a land-based version. Each company was supposed to serve as the other's subcontractor. A dispute erupted when McDonnell Douglas's F-18A outsold the F-18L, even in countries without aircraft carriers. According to Northrop, the company was being treated unfairly by McDonnell Douglas. The two companies brought legal action against each other, charging violation of their "teaming agreement," one of the first major competitor partnerships since World War II. In April 1985, the court settled in favor of Northrop and awarded the company $50 million. McDonnell Douglas, however, was awarded the prime contractor's role for all future F-18s, with Northrop designated as the subcontractor.

Northrop had another unpleasant experience when the Carter administration called for the development of an advanced fighter jet that was expressly intended for export. Too many foreign countries were showing interest in jets the government considered too technologically sophisticated for mass export. In response, Northrop, at its own expense, developed a less sophisticated fighter called the F-20 Tigershark. It was delivered ahead of

schedule and below budget. The problem was that foreign governments still wanted the more sophisticated American jets. Northrop complained that the U.S. government was not promoting the F-20 vigorously enough. The government denied a large sale of F-20s to Taiwan because it was afraid the sale would upset mainland China. In November 1986 the U.S. Air Force selected General Dynamics' F-16 over the F-20 as its main fighter for defense of the North American continent. As a result, Northrop announced that it would halt further work on the F-20.

Controversy continued to hound Northrop into the late 1980s, particularly Jones, who left the company amid a storm of accusations in 1989, ending his 30-year tenure and leaving the company in a precarious position. Jones had racked up an enormous debt during the decade, banking on the success of two projects, the U.S. Air Force's Advanced Tactical Fighter (ATF) and the B-2 stealth bomber, which represented, by the decade's end, the company's only opportunities for growth. To fund these and other projects, Northrop borrowed heavily, increasing its debt from $215 million in 1984 to an enormous $1.1 billion by 1989.

Early 1990s: Restructuring and Purchase of Grumman

After Jones's departure, Kent Kresa, a former technology director and engineer, became Northrop's chief executive officer, assuming his post in January 1990. Shortly thereafter, the company pled guilty to 34 counts of fraud for falsifying test data on two military programs and paid a $17 million fine. Then, Kresa began effecting substantial changes in the size and operation of the company to further distance itself from the embarrassments of the 1980s. He replaced nearly half of the company's senior management, reduced the company's debt by selling its headquarters and idle production sites, and intensified the company's lobbying efforts to ensure the success of the ATF and B-2 programs, both of which seemed to be slipping away from Northrop's grip, yet represented the company's only true opportunity to arrest the financial slide begun several years earlier.

In 1991, when hopes for the future of the B-2 program were buoyed by the launching of Operation Desert Storm in the Persian Gulf, disaster again struck Northrop with the announcement by the Pentagon that it had selected Lockheed to manufacture the Air Force's ATF. Air Force Secretary Donald B. Rice noted that both Lockheed's and Northrop's supersonic stealth fighters had performed equally well, but Lockheed received the contract because of its proven track record to control costs and meet production schedules. The announcement represented a severe loss for Northrop, heaping all of the company's hopes for the future on the continued funding of the B-2 program, which accounted for 50 percent of the company's revenues.

Except for the 1992 acquisition of LTV Corp.'s Vought Aircraft Co. in a joint venture with the Carlyle Group, Northrop failed to secure a more viable and stable future for itself in the years following the loss of the AFT project. Support for the B-2 program continued to wane, and Northrop recorded a string of failed acquisitions, including unsuccessful attempts to purchase IBM's Federal Systems Division and General Dynamics' F-16 fighter business. With its debt reduced, however, and $1.3 billion in credit lines, the company continued to look for an acquisition to partly offset its reliance on funding for the B-2 program. An opportunity presented itself in early 1994, when Northrop and Martin Marietta aggressively pursued Grumman Corporation, an aerospace and electronic surveillance manufacturer with ties to the U.S. Navy. Northrop won the bidding war for Grumman, eclipsing Martin Marietta's price of $1.9 billion with a $2.17 billion offer of its own. In April 1994, Northrop absorbed Grumman, making the combination a weak third in the industry behind Lockheed and McDonnell Douglas, but a stronger, more diversified organization, nevertheless.

Early History of Grumman

Leroy Grumman left the Navy in 1920 to become a test pilot and chief engineer for Grover and Albert Loening, who manufactured an airplane called the Fleetwing. In 1923, Vincent Astor's New York-Newport Air Service Company lost one of its Fleetwings over the ocean. Cary Morgan (a nephew of J.P. Morgan) was killed in the accident, which a later investigation revealed was caused when Morgan fell asleep with his foot obstructing the pilot's controls. Nevertheless, bad publicity surrounding the accident put Astor's company out of business. Grumman and a fellow worker named Leon Swirbul purchased the airline from Astor and later transformed it into a manufacturing company, building amphibious floats for Loening aircraft.

Unlike other aircraft manufacturers who entered the business as barnstormers or hobbyists, Leroy Grumman was a graduate of the Cornell University engineering school. Leon Swirbul was a product of the disciplined military aviation program. Both men worked for the Loening brothers until 1928, when Keystone Aircraft purchased Loening Aeronautical and moved the entire operation to Keystone's headquarters in Bristol, Pennsylvania. Grumman and Swirbul decided to remain in Long Island, and in 1929 they formed their own company, Grumman Aircraft Engineering Corporation.

After building a number of experimental airplanes, Grumman Aircraft manufactured its first fighter, designated the FF-1, for the Navy in 1932. This design was improved upon in subsequent models and led to the development of the successful F4F Wildcat, Grumman's first fighter with folding wings. With folded wings, twice as many airplanes could be stored on an aircraft carrier as before. The company also manufactured a line of "flying boats" called the Goose and the Duck.

Coincidentally, a second factory for manufacturing warplanes was dedicated by Grumman on the morning of December 7, 1941, as the Japanese were bombing Pearl Harbor. At the outset of the war Grumman had an advantage over nonmilitary manufacturers because the company did not require retooling. Automobile manufacturers, for instance, had to be converted from the production of cars and trucks to battle tanks and airplanes; assembly lines for sewing machines had to be refitted to produce machine guns. Grumman's only task was to increase its output and develop new airplane designs.

During the war, Grumman developed new aircraft such as the amphibious J4F Widgeon, the TBF Avenger naval attack bomber, and a successor to the Wildcat called the F6F Hellcat. The Hellcat was developed in response to the Mitsubishi Zero, a highly maneuverable Japanese fighter with a powerful engine.

Grumman aircraft were used almost exclusively in the Pacific war against Japan, and provided the American carrier forces with the power to repel many Japanese naval and aerial attacks. U.S. Secretary of Navy Forrestal later said, "In my opinion, Grumman saved Guadalcanal."

No other aircraft manufacturer received such high praise from the military. Grumman was the first company to be awarded an "E" by the U.S. government for excellence in its work. The award further increased the high morale at Grumman. The Grumman company turned out over 500 airplanes per month. To maintain that level of productivity the company provided a number of services to its workers, including daycare, personnel counseling, auto repair, and errand running. In addition, employees were substantially rewarded for their efficient work. The company had always had an excellent relationship with its employees, largely as a result of policies set down by Leon Swirbul, who oversaw production and employee relations while Grumman involved himself in design, engineering, and financial matters. By the end of the war, Grumman had produced over 17,000 aircraft.

The sudden termination of government contracts after the war seriously affected companies such as Boeing, Lockheed, and McDonnell Douglas, as well as Grumman. Many aircraft companies first looked to the commercial airliner market as an opportunity to maintain both their scale of operation and profitability. The market suddenly became highly competitive. Although Grumman manufactured commercial aircraft, it elected to remain out of the passenger transport business. Those companies that did manufacture commercial transports lost money, and some even went out of business. Grumman continued to conduct most of its business with the Navy. In addition to its F7F Tigercat and F8F Bearcat, the company developed a number of new aircraft, including the AF-2 Guardian and the F9F Panther and F10F Jaguar, Grumman's first jet airplanes.

During the 1950s, Grumman developed two new amphibious airplanes called the Mallard and Albatross; new jets included the Tiger, Cougar, and Intruder. It also diversified its product line by introducing aluminum truck bodies, canoes, and small boats. In 1958 Grumman unveiled the world's first business jet, the Gulfstream I, quickly selling 200 of them. In 1960 Grumman's cofounder Leon Swirbul died.

1960s and 1970s: Entering Aerospace and Other Industries

Grumman created a subsidiary in 1962 called Grumman Allied. The subsidiary was established to operate and coordinate all of the company's non-aeronautical business, and allow management to concentrate on its aerospace ventures. When the National Aeronautics and Space Administration (NASA) completed its Mercury and Gemini space programs, it turned its attention to fulfilling the challenge made by the late President Kennedy, namely, landing a man on the moon before 1970. The Apollo program called for several moon landings, each using two spaceships. The command modules, manufactured by McDonnell Douglas, were intended to orbit the moon while the lunar modules, built by Grumman, landed on the moon. Grumman's contract with NASA specified construction of 15 lunar modules, ten test modules, and two mission simulators. Only 12, however, were actually built.

Design problems already faced by Grumman engineers were compounded by their limited knowledge of the lunar surface. The lunar modules had to meet unusual crisis-scenario specifications, such as hard landings, landings on steep inclines, and a variety of system failures. Nine thousand Grumman personnel were devoted to the lunar module project, representing a reorientation of the company's business—Grumman had entered the aerospace industry.

The United States made its first manned moon landing in July 1969, with several more to follow through 1972. Grumman's spaceships performed almost flawlessly and represented a new and special relationship between the company and NASA. Grumman was later chosen by NASA to build the six-foot-thick wings for the agency's space shuttles. Meanwhile, Grumman Aircraft changed its name to Grumman Corporation to reflect its increasingly diverse operations.

Through the 1950s and 1960s, Grumman maintained a good relationship with the Pentagon. While that relationship continued to be good during the 1970s, it was marked by a serious disagreement over the delivery of 313 of Grumman's F-14 Tomcat fighter jets. At issue was who was to pay for cost overruns on a government-ordered project—the company or the taxpayer? Grumman was losing $1 million per F-14 and refused to deliver any more to the Navy until its losses were covered. The company pleaded its case in full-page advertisements in the *New York Times,* the *Wall Street Journal,* and the *Washington Post.* Grumman argued that completion of the contract under the present terms would bankrupt the company. The matter was later resolved when the Defense Department agreed to cover Grumman's losses, and the company agreed to a new contract procedure that would automatically review project costs on an annual basis and make adjustments when necessary.

Grumman's swing-wing F-14 became operational in 1973 and soon established itself as the standard carrier-based fighter jet for the U.S. Navy. Assigned to intercept attacking jets and protect carrier battle groups, the Tomcat had variable geometry wings that swept back when it was sprinting and swept out when it was landing. It could independently track 24 targets and destroy six of them at a time. F-14s performed successfully in intermittent raids and dogfights with Libyan pilots over the Gulf of Sidra.

In addition to the F-14, Grumman manufactured the E-2C Hawkeye, an early warning airborne command center able to track over 600 objects within three million cubic miles of airspace. The Israeli Air Force used E-2Cs to direct its air battles with Syrian pilots over Lebanon's Bekaa Valley in 1982. During those battles, Syria lost 92 of its Soviet-built MiGs while Israel lost only two of its jets. In the Falkland Islands War, Britain's HMS *Sheffield* was sunk by an Exocet missile launched from an Argentine Super Etendard attack jet. U.S. Navy Secretary John Lehman asserted that if the British had an E-2C in the Falklands, they would have had unchallenged air superiority and would not have lost any ships to Exocet missiles. Both examples illustrated the value of the Hawkeye.

The Navy's A-6 Intruder attack bomber and EA-6B Prowler radar jammer were also manufactured by Grumman, which also remanufactured 42 General Dynamics F-111 bombers for the U.S. Air Force. The new aircraft, designated EF-111, was designed to jam enemy radar surveillance "from the Baltic to the Adriatic." According to Grumman Chairman Jack Bierwirth, "it's one of the great exercises to fly this plane against the E-2C." This volley of electronic countermeasures showed the extent to which Grumman's only competition for a long time was itself.

The electronic sophistication of Grumman's aircraft invited criticism from military reformers who argued that modern weapons had become too complex and therefore unmanageable. In the 1970s, these reformers, led by Gary Hart, widely publicized this view. The ultimate success of their movement could have had disastrous effects for Grumman. Following the costly disagreement over the F-14, the company's long-term viability was threatened even more by these reformers under the Carter Administration.

Continued attempts to sell F-14s to foreign governments failed, as did lobbying efforts to sell more of the jets to the U.S. Navy. Consequently, Grumman made an effort to diversify its product line. The strategy was ambitious but failed. The company's Dormavac freight refrigerators had no market (losing $46 million), and its Ecosystems environmental management and research venture was unable to turn a profit, resulting in losses of $50 million. Furthermore, during the recession of the late 1970s, sales of the Gulfstream corporate jet faltered, leading Grumman to sell off the division, which was renamed Gulfstream Aerospace Corporation.

In 1978, Grumman acquired the curiously named Flxible bus division from Rohr Industries. Many of the buses developed cracked undercarriage components, prompting some customers (such as the City of New York) to pull all of their Flxible buses out of service. Grumman filed a $500 million suit against Rohr, alleging that details of design flaws were not revealed prior to the sale. The suit was dismissed in court. Grumman's losses in this venture approached $200 million before the entire division was sold to General Automotive in 1983 for $41 million.

1980s: Host of Troubles for Grumman

In 1981 Grumman faced a hostile takeover from LTV Corporation, a steel, electronics, and aircraft conglomerate based in Texas. Grumman's workers mobilized an enthusiastic demonstration of support for their company's resistance to LTV. Leroy Grumman, who retired from the company in 1972, raised employee morale when he voiced his support of the opposition to the LTV takeover attempt. A U.S. court of appeals later rejected LTV's bid to take over Grumman on the grounds that it would reduce competition in the aerospace and defense industries.

Leroy Grumman died in 1982 after a long illness. It was widely reported that Grumman was blinded in 1946 by a severe allergic reaction to penicillin administered during treatment of pneumonia. In fact, Grumman was not blinded. His eyesight did, however, begin to deteriorate many years later as his health began to wane.

The Grumman Corporation faced another threat when it became involved in a scandal involving illegal bribes to government officials in Iran and Japan. After the Lockheed Corporation was accused of such improprieties, the sales practices of other defense contractors such as Grumman came under scrutiny. During the investigation of Grumman, a Japanese official named Mitsuhiro Shimada committed suicide.

After the investigations subsided, the companies in question were free to concentrate all their efforts on more constructive matters. Grumman engineers, however, had something highly unconventional on their drawing boards. Grumman's chairman, Jack Bierwirth, was credited with saying, ''If you don't invest in research and development, you damned well aren't going to accomplish anything.'' With that in mind, Grumman, in conjunction with the Defense Advanced Research Projects Agency, developed a special jet called the X-29 specifically to demonstrate the company's advanced technology. The revolutionary feature of the X-29 was that its wings swept forward, appearing to have been mounted backwards. This feature gave the X-29 superior maneuverability. To counteract the inherent instability of such a design, the X-29 was equipped with a Honeywell computer system which readjusted the canards (wing controls) 40 times a second, maintaining stable flight.

The X-29 was tested under the auspices of NASA during 1984 and 1985. Never intended for mass production, only one X-29 was built as a ''technology demonstrator.'' Bierwirth described projects such as the X-29 as ''marrying electronics with computer programming, then putting wings on it.''

John Cocks Bierwirth, a former naval officer, became Grumman's chairman and chief executive officer in 1976. Regarding his mission as ''essentially building the corporation of the future,'' Bierwirth divided Grumman's operations into nine divisions under centralized management. According to Bierwirth, Grumman's future was with aircraft, space, and electronics. Nevertheless, work on such projects as a new post office truck were designed to maintain a stable and diverse product line. Bierwirth claimed, ''We think we are a good investment for people who are interested in the long term and are willing to grow with the company; Grumman is not a three month in-and-out investment.''

Grumman's investments in research projects, however, did not prove as successful as Bierwirth hoped. Throughout the 1980s, with the notable exceptions of contracts for F-14 fighters and A-6 attack aircraft, Grumman was hobbled by research projects and product introductions that failed miserably. The company's diversification into the production of buses began the decade's string of failures, portending further mishaps to follow. The 851 Flxible buses purchased by New York's Metropolitan Transport Authority in 1980 were withdrawn from service three years later after repeated breakdowns, a failed venture for which Grumman paid $40 million in 1988 to settle legal claims against it. Other problems riddled the company, none larger nor more damaging in the long-term than its overwhelming dependence on government-funded military contracts. As Grumman's debt rose, exacerbated by research projects that swallowed vast amounts of cash and generated little profit, the company increasingly weakened, staggering, by the end of the decade, on untenable ground.

In 1988 the company named a new chief executive officer, John O'Brien, whose selection augured a return to more profit-

able days. O'Brien later became chairman but resigned in 1990 amid allegations of illegal activities. He later pled guilty to bank fraud stemming from an investigation into bribery and political corruption, adding the public relations scandal and the financial charges that followed to Grumman's host of troubles. O'Brien's replacement was Renso L. Caporali, a Grumman employee since 1959, who began steering the embattled company in a positive direction.

Early 1990s: Restructuring and the Northrop Takeover

Under Caporali's stewardship, Grumman experienced wholesale changes. The company's debt, which had risen to as high as $884 million in 1989, was trimmed 60 percent in the first three years of his tenure, payroll was reduced from a peak of 33,700 in 1987 to 21,000 by 1993, and Grumman's headquarters staff was cut by more than half. Perhaps more important, Caporali attempted to wean Grumman away from subsisting on military aircraft contracts by tapping the company's established expertise in data technology to produce tax processing systems for the Internal Revenue Service. Also, Caporali used the company's knowledge of integrating electronics and data systems. Caporali thus oversaw one of Grumman's few success stories in the past decade when the company's work on the Joint Surveillance Target Attack Radar System (JSTARS) program met with high praise in the Persian Gulf in 1991. Although Grumman could not expect to garner any profit from its involvement with the JSTARS project until 1994, the success of the project, triumphantly hailed by General Norman Schwarzkopf, was a public relations boon for a company plagued by scandals and misfortune.

Although Grumman's condition was improving, it continued to rely on the federal government for the bulk of its revenues. In 1992 Grumman derived roughly 90 percent of its $3.5 billion in revenues from the government, an alarming percentage for a market sector experiencing little growth. Seemingly entrenched in this unenviable position, Grumman, pundits speculated, either needed to acquire additional business or be acquired itself. The latter occurred, leading to a bidding war for Grumman between the Martin Marietta Corporation and Northrop Corporation, which reached its climax in April 1994, when Northrop emerged as the winner and acquired Grumman for $2.17 billion.

Mid-1990s: Emergence and Near Disappearance of Northrop Grumman

With its acquisition of Grumman, Northrop gained the electronic surveillance expertise of Grumman as well as its established ties with the U.S. Navy, which complemented Northrop's long history of conducting business with the U.S. Air Force. The newly named Northrop Grumman Corporation, under the stewardship of Northrop's CEO and chairman, Kent Kresa, represented a larger force to navigate the turbulent waters characterizing the aerospace and defense industries in the post-Cold War era.

Soon after the completion of the Northrop-Grumman merger, the new company acquired the 51 percent of Vought Aircraft Company it did not already own for $130 million. Vought was a maker of commercial airplane parts. Northrop

Grumman also eliminated about 8,650 jobs from its workforce in the wake of the merger.

To reduce its dependency on its largest program, the B-2 stealth bomber, the company began seeking ways to increase its position in defense electronics and systems integration activities. In early 1996 Northrop Grumman spent $2.9 billion for the defense and electronic systems business of Westinghouse Electric Corporation. This acquisition was followed by the purchase of Logicon, Inc. in August 1997 for about $750 million. Logicon was a leading provider of defense information technology and battlefield management systems.

Unfortunately, Raytheon Company beat out Northrop Grumman in the bidding for the defense businesses of Texas Instruments Inc. and Hughes Electronics Corporation, both of which were acquired by Raytheon in 1997. Boeing and Lockheed Martin were also bulking up around this same time, leaving Northrop Grumman and its $9 billion in revenues a distant fourth among defense contractors—Boeing having revenues approaching $50 billion, Lockheed generating $28 billion in sales, and Raytheon's revenues moving past the $20 billion mark. Northrop Grumman was clearly in a vulnerable position, and it was widely anticipated that the company would soon change from acquirer to acquiree, with Raytheon a likely suitor. It was Lockheed Martin, however, that took on that role, and in July 1997 Northrop Grumman agreed to be acquired by Lockheed in a deal initially valued at $11.6 billion.

Somewhat unexpectedly, the merger ran into antitrust difficulties. In March 1998 the U.S. Department of Justice filed a lawsuit to stop the combination on antitrust grounds. One of the main concerns of the government was the vertical integration that Lockheed would gain from the deal, given that Northrop Grumman was a major Lockheed subcontractor. The government also wanted to ensure that there were an adequate number of manufacturers of military aircraft and wanted to prevent Lockheed from dominating certain market segments, such as radars and jamming devices for planes and submarines. The lawsuit was scheduled to go to trial in September 1998, but in the face of the Justice Department's demand for the divestment of $4 billion in operations, Lockheed decided to terminate the merger in July 1998. In the aftermath of this latest turn of events and in an effort to survive as an independent company, Northrop Grumman launched a two-year restructuring program later in 1998 that would eliminate 10,500 jobs in its defense and aircraft operations and add 2,500 employees to its Logicon subsidiary.

Late 1990s and Beyond: Increasing Focus on Defense Electronics and Systems Integration

With Kresa still at the helm, Northrop Grumman adopted a new strategy in the late 1990s of focusing the company increasingly on cutting-edge areas of the defense industry, including electronics and systems integration. Acquisitions played a key role in the company's shifting emphasis. In 1999 the company purchased the information systems division of California Microwave, Inc., which was involved in supporting communications and intelligence systems of the U.S. Department of Defense. Northrop Grumman also bought Ryan Aeronautical, a unit of Allegheny Teledyne Incorporated, that year. Ryan manufactured pilotless aircraft (aerial drones), including the Global

Hawk, a high-altitude, long-endurance reconnaissance drone capable of providing real-time intelligence imagery. By the early 21st century, Northrop Grumman was one of the world's leading producers of high-end aerial drones. Acquisitions in 2000 included Comptek Research, Inc. and Federal Data Corporation. Northrop Grumman's newfound focus also led to the divestment of Vought Aircraft, which was sold to the Carlyle Group in July 2000 for $1.2 billion. The company now had three main sectors: systems integration, defense electronics, and information technology.

Continuing a most remarkable comeback, Northrop Grumman in December 2000 reached an agreement to acquire Litton Industries, Inc., which reported revenues of $5.59 billion for the fiscal year ending in July 2000. Completed in April 2001, the deal involved about $3.8 billion in Northrop Grumman stock, with Northrop also agreeing to assume $1.3 billion of debt. Northrop gained significant synergistic operations through the acquisition, including Litton's navigation, guidance, and control systems; marine electronics operations; electronic warfare systems; and an information systems unit that concentrated on networking systems integration. Adding Litton also meant that Northrop Grumman would add two more sectors to its existing three: an electronic components segment, which made connectors, circuit boards, and other devices used in the military, telecommunications, and other industries; and a ship systems segment, builder of guided missile destroyers, amphibious assault ships, and other vessels for the U.S. Navy.

Northrop Grumman's acquisition spree continued in the later months of 2001. The company acquired an electronics and information unit of GenCorp Inc. for $315 million. The unit specialized in space-based sensors that provided early warning of missile attacks as well as ground systems for processing data from space-based platforms. These operations became part of Northrop Grumman's space systems division. Northrop Grumman also bested General Dynamics in the battle for control of Newport News Shipbuilding Inc., maker of aircraft carriers and submarines for the U.S. Navy. Upon completion of the acquisition in November 2001, Northrop Grumman became the world's largest maker of naval ships and the number three defense contractor in the United States, trailing only Boeing and Lockheed Martin. The value of the deal was about $2.6 billion, which included the assumption of $500 million in debt. Newport News was set up as Northrop Grumman's sixth operating sector. The acquisition spree had saddled Northrop Grumman with a hefty debt load, so the company in November 2001 completed offerings of common stock and other securities, raising about $1.45 billion in the process, with the bulk of the proceeds going to reduce debt.

Kresa's string of acquisitions had positioned Northrop Grumman as an unlikely survivor of the post-Cold War defense industry consolidation, with revenues projected to reach $18 billion by 2002. In the wake of the events of September 11, 2001, the company seemed to be perfectly positioned to be a key contractor for the U.S. military. By focusing the company's operations on cutting-edge areas—electronics, information technology, command and control systems—Kresa had anticipated the increased need for intelligence gathering and precision operations in the post-Cold War era. At the same time, Northrop Grumman maintained or acquired significant positions in more basic areas of the military, such as aircraft and naval ships, and so had the potential to benefit from any general military buildup.

Principal Subsidiaries

Allied Holdings, Inc.; California Microwave, Inc.; Comptek Research, Inc.; Federal Data Corporation; Grumman International, Inc.; Grumman Ohio Corporation; IRAN - Northrop Grumman Programs Service Company; Logicon Commercial Information Services Inc.; Logicon, Inc.; Logicon International, Inc.; Mocit, Inc.; NGC Denmark ApS (Denmark); Northrop Grumman Aviation, Inc.; Northrop Grumman - Canada, Ltd.; Northrop Grumman Electronic Systems International Company; Northrop Grumman Electronic Systems International Company (U.K.); Northrop Grumman Electronics Systems Integration International, Inc.; Northrop Grumman Field Support Services, Inc.; Northrop Grumman Foreign Sales Corporation (Barbados); Northrop Grumman International, Inc.; Northrop Grumman International Services Company, Inc.; Northrop Grumman ISA International, Inc.; Northrop Grumman Overseas Holdings, Inc.; Northrop Grumman Overseas Service Corporation; Northrop Grumman Space Operations, L.P.; Northrop Grumman Tactical Systems, LLC; Northrop Grumman Technical Services Corporation; Northrop International Aircraft, Inc.; Park Air Electronics, Inc.; Perceptics Corporation; Remotec, Inc. (96%); Sterling Software Inc.; Sterling Software Weather, Inc.; Xetron Corporation.

Principal Operating Units

Electronic Systems; Information Technology; Integrated Systems; Ship Systems; Newport News; Component Technologies.

Principal Competitors

The Boeing Company; Lockheed Martin Corporation; Raytheon Company; General Dynamics Corporation; Honeywell Aerospace Solutions; BAE Systems; European Aeronautic Defence and Space Company N.V.; United Technologies Corporation.

Further Reading

Allen, Richard Sanders, *The Northrop Story, 1929–1939,* New York: Orion Books, 1990, 178 p.

Biddle, Frederic M., "Northrop Set to Cut Jobs, Restructure," *Wall Street Journal,* August 25, 1998, p. A3.

Biddle, Frederic M., and Thomas E. Ricks, "Lockheed Terminates Northrop Merger," *Wall Street Journal,* July 17, 1998, p. A3.

Biddle, Wayne, "Meditations on a Merger: Grumman-Northrop, Etc.," *Nation,* June 20, 1994, p. 87.

Bremner, Brian, "How Grumman Is Trying to Keep Its Nose Up," *Business Week,* August 6, 1990, p. 33.

Campbell, Edward J., *A Century of Leadership: The Story of Newport News Shipbuilding and Dry Dock Company,* New York: Newcomen Society of the United States, 1986, 22 p.

Chakravarty, Subrata N., "The Darkness Before Dawn," *Forbes,* March 16, 1981, p. 82.

——, "The Resurrection of Grumman," *Forbes,* April 7, 1986, pp. 98+.

Cole, Jeff, "War of Attrition: Defense Consolidation Rushes Toward an Era of Only Three or Four Giants," *Wall Street Journal,* December 6, 1996, pp. A1+.

Cole, Jeff, et al., "United States Seeks to Bar Purchase of Northrop," *Wall Street Journal,* March 24, 1998, p A3.

Cole, Jeff, and Steven Lipin, "Northrop Agrees to Acquire Logicon in Stock Deal Valued at $750 Million," *Wall Street Journal,* May 6, 1997, p. A4.

Cordtz, Dan, "Kresa's Cleanup," *Financial World,* Fall 1994, pp. 52–53.

Deady, Tim, "Future of Northrop Hangs in Balance of Proposed B-2 Cuts," *Los Angeles Business Journal,* August 6, 1990, p. 1.

Dubashi, Jagannath, "Grumman's New Flight Plan," *Financial World,* March 10, 1987, pp. 24+.

"Fighting Fit: Martin Marietta and Grumman," *Economist,* March 12, 1994, p. 75.

"For Northrop, a Shot at Survival," *Business Week,* April 18, 1994, p. 52.

Gibson, W. David, "Poised for Takeoff: R&D Enhances Grumman's Prospects," *Barron's,* March 12, 1984, pp. 14+.

Gold, David, "A Cloudy Future for Northrop Corp.," *Financial World,* February 20/March 5, 1985, pp. 38+.

Grover, Ronald, and Dean Foust, "Firefight in the Defense Industry," *Business Week,* March 28, 1994, p. 31.

"Grumman: Beating a Strategic Retreat to the Defense Business," *Business Week,* November 14, 1983, pp. 210+.

Gunston, Bill, *Grumman: Sixty Years of Excellence,* New York: Orion Books, 1988, 159 p.

Harris, Roy J., Jr., "Northrop Offer of $2.17 Billion Wins Grumman," *Wall Street Journal,* April 5, 1994, p. A3.

Howard, Bob, "Not Dead Yet: Northrop, Other Aerospace Firms Are Flying Again," *Los Angeles Business Journal,* May 12, 1997, pp. 22+.

Klass, Philip J., "Northrop Grumman's EW Role Greatly Expanded by Litton Buy," *Aviation Week and Space Technology,* October 1, 2001, p. 62.

Kraar, L., "Grumman Still Flies for Navy, but It Is Selling the World," *Fortune,* February 1976, p. 78.

Kuzela, Lad, "Nudging Northrop into the Future," *Industry Week,* July 26, 1982, pp. 63+.

Lay, Beirne, *Someone Has to Make It Happen: The Inside Story of Tex Thornton, the Man Who Built Litton Industries,* Englewood Cliffs, N.J.: Prentice-Hall, 1969, 204 p.

"Look Who's Heading for No. 1 in Defense: Northrop," *Business Week,* April 19, 1982, pp. 70+.

Lubove, Seth, "Dogfight," *Forbes,* May 29, 2000, pp. 58–60.

Magnet, Myron, "Grumman's Comeback," *Fortune,* September 20, 1982, pp. 62+.

Newman, Richard J., "Fighting for Dollars," *U.S. News and World Report,* September 17, 2001, p. 56.

Norman, James R., "Ninth Life?," *Forbes,* April 26, 1993, p. 72.

"Northrop's Campaign to Get a New Fighter Flying in the Third World," *Business Week,* June 18, 1984, pp. 74+.

Palmeri, Christopher, and Stan Crock, "Northrop: A Top Gun in the Defense Buildup," *Business Week,* October 1, 2001, p. 64.

Pasztor, Andy, and Anne Marie Squeo, "Northrop Shifts Focus to Cutting-Edge Military Lines: Growth Is Sought in Information-Systems and Electronic-Warfare Markets," *Wall Street Journal,* October 1, 1999, p. B4.

Pellegrino, Charles R., and Joshua Stoff, *Chariots for Apollo: The Making of The Lunar Module,* New York: Atheneum, 1985, 238 p.

Power, Christopher, "Grumman: Moving Beyond the Wild Blue Yonder?," *Business Week,* February 1, 1988, pp. 54+.

Ramirez, Anthony, "The Secret Bomber Bugging Northrop," *Fortune,* March 14, 1988, pp. 90+.

Rodengen, Jeffrey L., *The Legend of Litton Industries,* Fort Lauderdale, Fla.: Write Stuff Enterprises, 2000, 159 p.

Ropelewski, Robert, "Grumman Corp: Destined for Diversification," *Interavia Aerospace World,* March 1993, p. 18.

Rosenberg, Hilary, "Throwing Away the Textbook," *Financial World,* October 1, 1982, pp. 12+.

Schine, Eric, "Northrop Is Flying in a Sky Full of Flak," *Business Week,* April 24, 1989, pp. 109+.

——, "Northrop's Biggest Foe May Have Been Its Past," *Business Week,* May 6, 1991, p. 30.

"Shooting Star: Grumman," *Economist,* May 25, 1991, p. 76.

Squeo, Anne Marie, "Consolidation Turns the Tables on Two CEOs in the Defense Sector: As Industry Dynamics Shift, Northrop Bounces Back and Raytheon Stumbles," *Wall Street Journal,* July 19, 2001, pp. A1+.

——, "Northrop Offer for Newport News Wins Support of Pentagon over General Dynamics Bid," *Wall Street Journal,* October 24, 2001, p. A3.

Squeo, Anne Marie, Nikhil Deogun, and Jeff Cole, "Northrop to Acquire Litton for $3.8 Billion," *Wall Street Journal,* December 22, 2000, p. A3.

Sweetman, Bill, "Northrop Grumman Back from the Brink," *Interavia Business and Technology,* September 2000, p. 18.

Tazewell, William L., *Newport News Shipbuilding: The First Century,* Newport News, Va.: Mariners' Museum, 1986, 256 p.

Thruelsen, Richard, *The Grumman Story,* New York: Praegeri, 1976, 401 p.

Toy, Stewart, Nina Easton, and Dave Griffiths, "Northrop's Bumpy Flight," *Business Week,* January 18, 1988, p. 26.

Vecsey, George, and George C. Dade, *Getting Off the Ground: The Pioneers of Aviation Speak for Themselves,* New York: Dutton, 1979, 304 p.

Wall, Robert, and David A. Fulghum, "Fighting to Stay in the Big League," *Aviation Week and Space Technology,* November 20, 2000, pp. 48–49.

Wrubel, Robert, "Stay of Execution: Iraq May Save Northrop's B-2 Bomber, but the Defense Contractor's Problems Run Deep," *Financial World,* September 4, 1990, pp. 42+.

—updates: Jeffrey L. Covell, David E. Salamie

Northwest Natural Gas Company

220 NW 2nd Avenue
Portland, Oregon 97209-3991
U.S.A.
Telephone: (503) 226-4211
Toll Free: (800) 422-4012
Fax: (503) 721-2506
Web site: http://www.nwnatural.com

Public Company
Incorporated: 1910 as Portland Gas & Coke Co.
Employees: 1,315
Sales: $532.1 million (2000)
Stock Exchanges: New York
Ticker Symbol: NWN
NAIC: 22121 Gas Companies; 211112 Natural Gas
   Liquids; 42173 Heating Equipment and Systems

Northwest Natural Gas Company, which does business as Northwest Natural, distributes natural gas to approximately 523,000 residential, commercial, and industrial customers in western Oregon, including Portland, and southwestern Washington, including Vancouver. It is the largest natural gas distributor in the Pacific Northwest. Most of Northwest Natural's gas supply travels through the Williams Northwest Pipeline from suppliers in the United States and Canada; gas reaches customers through the company's more than 15,000 miles of mains. With the 2001 acquisition of Enron's Portland General Electric, Northwest Natural has become Oregon's largest utility. It also has interests in alternative power plants in California.

1860s–1950s: Steady Growth As a Manufactured Gas Producer

In January 1859, Oregon's territorial legislature granted a perpetual franchise for a "gas manufactory" in Portland to Henry Dodge Green. Green and his partner, pioneer merchant H.C. Leonard, immediately sent for machinery and pipe from their native New York state by way of Cape Horn and coal from Vancouver Island. By the end of 1859, they had constructed a coal gasification plant on the west bank of the Willamette River that began providing gas lighting for 49 customers within an area that covered less than one square mile of Portland in June 1860. The company's first month's sales amounted to $425.

The company made its gas by carbonizing coal that arrived in Portland as ballast aboard windjammers. This coal was unloaded at the company's dock and carried by wheelbarrow to the nearby gas plant. The partners soon acquired a brig to transport coal and began doing business as Portland Gas Light Co.

By 1868, Portland Gas Light Co. was responsible for keeping the water hot in the boilers of Portland's horse-drawn, steam fire engines—the first recorded use of local gas for a purpose other than lighting. By 1872, half the city's 189 street lamps had been converted from coal to gas, and in 1882, Green and Leonard built a second, separate plant. In 1892, Charles F. Adams, A.L. Mills, and other businessmen bought the Portland Gas Light Co., tied both plants together with a pipeline that went under the Willamette River, and changed the company's name to Portland Gas Co. Service halted briefly when the record 1894 flood ripped out the underwater crossing, but the company soon rebuilt its manufacturing facilities above the high water mark.

In the early 1900s, as Portland's population boomed to 224,000, the number of gas patrons in the city increased to 28,500. As the gas range, water heater, and furnace became available, the gas industry shifted its emphasis from street lighting to supplying in-home energy. By 1910, there were 332 miles of mains serving about ten city districts, and the company incorporated as Portland Gas & Coke Co. But money ran short for expansion with electricity crowding into the lighting market, and American Power & Light Co. took over the company's refinancing.

California oil became cheaper than coal; so, in 1906, the company began a plant changeover. In 1913, Portland Gas & Coke built its third and last gas manufacturing plant in Linnton, where it made gas from oil, not coal. This plant had 150 times the capacity of Leonard and Green's original six retorts (small coal-firing plants). It also manufactured byproducts—briquets, electrode pitch, naphthalene, and motor fuel, a mixture of gasoline and benzol—which brought in about a third of the company's revenues. Gasco, as the utility company commonly was called, then embarked on two decades of expansion. The company added a line across the Columbia River to Vancouver, Washington, and other lines to nearby Oregon City, Gresham, Hillsboro, and Forest Grove. In 1927, it settled its corporate offices into the newly erected Public Service building, and by 1929, had gaslines running south to Salem, Albany, Lebanon, Corvallis, Silverton, and Dallas, Oregon.

Mid-1950s to Late 1960s:
The Switch to Natural Gas Distribution

In 1949, American Power & Light sold off its holdings in Portland Gas & Coke. The company soon thereafter enjoyed renewed development once natural gas arrived from the southwest in 1956 and 15 months later from British Columbia. The Northwest was the last area in the country to get natural gas due to its relatively small population and competition from electricity. The company's distribution system now included 1,500 miles of pipeline from the San Juan Basin in New Mexico. In December 1957, Portland Gas & Coke closed its manufactured gas plant and, in 1958, changed its name to Northwest Natural Gas Co. The changeover from manufactured to natural gas cost the company about $4.3 million and involved an educational campaign that took place via letters, handbills, and newspaper ads.

Lowered gas rates and the abundance of better fuel kicked off a period of renewed expansion of fuel mains north into Washington State and Canada for Northwest Natural Gas Co. Throughout the 1950s and 1960s, Northwest Natural Gas marketed its natural gas fuel aggressively and employed price reduction programs to lure new customers. The company's territory of nearly 500 square miles was now served by almost 3,000 miles of mains. Heating customers numbered 52,000, while all users totaled about 94,000. By the mid-1960s, the company's service area included communities as far south as Eugene, as far east as The Dalles, and along the central and north Oregon coast. In 1962, Northwest Natural Gas completed its new three-story headquarters. It built its first liquefied natural gas storage tank on its manufactured gas plant site in 1969 and a second tank on the coast in Newport, Oregon, in 1977.

The 1970s to the 1990s:
New Resources and Technologies

The effect of deregulation in the 1970s on Northwest Natural was not as great as on other companies since more than 50 percent of the company's gas supplies came from western Canada. Revenues fell as large industrial users bought gas directly from the wellhead, but profits and the company's customer base continued to grow. Between 1973 and 1983, Northwest Natural added about 40,000 new customers, yet the total volume of gas it sold to its

core residential users decreased as energy conservation in homes became the norm. Business customers also began to use less gas as the recession and oil glut cut into industrial energy use and made oil more competitive with natural gas. Northwest Natural attempted to lure back its commercial customers by working out a special rate with its supplier while simultaneously trying to foster new uses and users of gas through aggressive marketing. According to Richard Miller, company president and CEO, in an article in *Oregon Business* in February 1983, the company had to "convince the public first that gas was available and that it was available to serve the needs of new customers . . . secondly that it was a less expensive energy to buy than electricity for home heating and water heating."

In 1979, in the wake of the mid-1970s' skyrocketing gas prices and severe gas shortages, while sagging sales kept most of the nation's natural gas distributors from expanding, Northwest Natural Gas undertook its largest expansion in eight years, adding 450 miles of pipeline to its 11,000-mile system. By the early 1980s, Northwest Natural Gas, the largest natural gas distributor in the Pacific Northwest, served more than 250,000 residential, commercial, and industrial customers in a 15,000-square-mile service area in Oregon and southwest Washington. Its fiscal 1981 revenues were $358 million with net income of $17 million.

Northwest Natural Gas also began exploring its own resource development in the late 1970s as a response to the ebbs and flows of the natural gas market. The company began an active drilling program in Oregon's only producing natural gas field near Mist in western Oregon in 1979, and by late 1982, it had two new wells. By 1995, it had drilled 54 producing wells, of which 17 were still yielding gas. Starting in 1990, with the formation of a new company subsidiary, Canor Energy Ltd., Northwest Natural began purchasing gas and oil properties in Canada, adding to its properties in Oregon, Wyoming, and California.

In a push to explore new technologies, Northwest Natural also formed Northwest Geothermal Corp., a wholly owned subsidiary devoted to exploring and developing geothermal sources of energy in western Oregon, in 1978. In 1982, it conducted one of the first of a series of field tests in the commercial application of the gas fuel cell, a new technology that offered increased energy efficiency and less pollution than conventional engines by utilizing an electromechanical process, not combustion, to generate electricity. In 1984, another Northwest Natural Gas subsidiary, BioGas Technology, began operating a gas extraction plant to obtain gas from decomposing garbage on landfills, converting low-heating-value garbage gas to pipeline quality methane (natural gas). Still another new subsidiary designed, constructed, and began to operate cogeneration facilities at about the same time, extracting two kinds of energy—thermal and electric—from a single source. By the late 1980s, Northwest Natural was investing in solar energy generation in the Mojave Desert and had a hydroelectric project and a windpower energy farm in California.

The company expanded in other ways as well in the 1980s and 1990s. Northwest Natural built a new 13-story, $24 million headquarters building to house both its executive and operational offices as well as a museum that reflected the company's 123-year history. After the decline in natural gas prices, Northwest Natural started pumping gas back underground in the late

Key Dates:

1859: Green and Leonard complete construction of a coal gasification plant on the west bank of the Willamette River.

1860: The plant begins providing gas lighting for some of Portland's then 3,000 residents.

1882: Portland Gas Light Co. builds a second and separate plant.

1892: Charles F. Adams, A.L. Mills, and other businessmen buy the company and change the company's name to Portland Gas Co.

1910: The company incorporates as Portland Gas & Coke Co.

1913: Portland Gas & Coke Co. builds its third and last manufacturing plant in Linnton, making gas from oil, not coal.

1956: Natural gas arrives from the southwest.

1957: Portland Gas & Coke closes its manufactured gas plant and changes its name to Northwest Natural Gas Co.

1962: Northwest Natural Gas completes its new three-story headquarters.

1969: The company builds its first liquefied natural gas storage tank.

1979: Northwest Natural Gas undertakes its largest expansion in eight years, adding 450 miles of pipeline to its 11,000-mile system.

1990: Through subsidiary Canor Energy Ltd., company begins purchasing gas and oil properties in Canada, adding to its properties in Oregon, Wyoming, and California.

2000: Company moves its stock listing to the New York Stock Exchange and launches a stock buyback program.

2001: Northwest Natural agrees to purchase Portland General Electric from Enron, thus becoming the largest natural gas and electric utility in Oregon.

1980s, storing it for later use. A storage facility in Mist, Oregon, allowed the company to purchase gas at lower cost during the summer months, store enough for 40 days of average consumption, and distribute it during the peak demand periods of winter. Following the company's record 1995 earnings of $35 million, Northwest Natural began a five-year program to expand storage capacity in 1996, the largest capital program in the company's history. In 1997, Northwest Natural joined with Pacificorp to jointly market gas, electricity, and energy services in Oregon and Washington and shortened its name to Northwest Natural.

Northwest Natural also instituted sweeping interdepartmental reorganization in late 1989, a labor-management partnership called the Joint Accord, that legislated employment security—no layoffs for employees hired prior to the accord—in return for performance-based pay increases. In place of the usual formal dispute resolution process, all employees, managers, and supervisors attended a one-day workshop on dispute resolution. The company received a letter of commendation from the U.S. Department of Labor for its progressive approach toward labor relations.

Throughout the 1990s, Northwest Natural also set records for new customers. It recruited 50,000 net new customers in the four years from 1989 to 1993, growing twice as fast as the average gas utility. Between 1990 and 1995, its customer base grew 5.2 percent a year, still nearly twice that of the average American distribution facility. In 1997, it recruited 430,000 new customers, making it the fastest-growing energy utility in the region. In 1999, it enjoyed its tenth consecutive year of customer growth greater than 4 percent, while the average growth for natural gas distributors had dropped to 1.5 percent. That year, it asked the Oregon Public Utility Commission to approve a 3.8 percent rate increase, but was ordered instead to lower its return on equity.

By the year 2000, with more than 500,000 customers, Northwest Natural was earning $50.22 million on revenues of $532 million. It finished upgrading its 100-year-old low-pressure distribution system and completed the next phase of its Mist storage expansion. It sold off Canor after the subsidiary suffered losses in order to focus on its core business. In July, it transferred its stock listing to the New York Stock Exchange and launched a stock buyback program. In 2001, it agreed to purchase Portland General Electric from ill-fated Enron, a move that would make it the largest natural gas and electric utility in Oregon. The company, confident that concern about the environment would lead to new uses of natural gas, such as natural gas vehicles, looked forward to a profitable future as the last locally controlled major utility in the Northwest.

Principal Subsidiaries

NNG Financial Corp.

Principal Competitors

Cascade Natural Gas Corporation; Portland General Electric Corporation; Puget Energy.

Further Reading

"Gasco Celebrates Centennial: From Our Gaslight Era," *Oregon Journal*, January 4, 1959, p. 13.

Hill, Robert L., "Cooking with Gas," *Oregon Business*, June 1991, p. 23.

——, "Northwest Natural Gas: Different Time, Same Place," *Oregon Business*, February 1983, p. 24.

Kristof, Nicholas D., "Technology: 'Cleaning' Gas from Garbage," *New York Times*, December 6, 1984, p. D2.

Marks, Anita, "Northwest Natural Inks Labor Deal, Seeks Partner," *Business Journal-Portland*, May 30, 1997, p. 1.

McMilland, Dan, "Northwest Natural's Status in Flux Following Regulatory Slam," *Business Journal-Portland*, April 9, 1999, p. 1.

——, "Single, But Willing to Wed," *Business Journal-Portland*, February 19, 1999, p.12.

"Rich in Supplies and Poised to Grow," *BusinessWeek*, August 13, 1979, p. 69.

Springer, Neil, "Pacific Northwest Heating Oil Dealers Losing Ground to Natural Gas Boom," *Journal of Commerce*, December 11, 1991, p. 7B.

—Carrie Rothburd

Northwestern Mutual Life Insurance Company

720 East Wisconsin Avenue
Milwaukee, Wisconsin 53202-4797
U.S.A.
Telephone: (414) 271-1444
Fax: (414) 299-7022
Web site: http://www.northwesternmutual.com

Mutual Company
Incorporated: 1857 as Mutual Life Insurance Company
   of the State of Wisconsin
Employees: 7,500
Total Assets: $92.12 billion (2000)
NAIC: 524113 Direct Life Insurance Carrier

Northwestern Mutual Life Insurance Company (NML)—the ninth largest U.S. life insurance company in 2000 as ranked by revenues—offers life, disability, and long-term care insurance as well as a variety of annuities and other accumulation products. NML, a rarity among the largest American insurance companies, was chartered west of Philadelphia. Until the 1980s, it remained a specialty company, issuing only individual life insurance policies. NML then shifted from a product- to market-driven company, although its emphasis would remain largely on its traditional individual life policies. Conservative risk management in both investment and underwriting, characteristic of the company since its founding, has made NML a consistent leader in total life insurance dividends paid to policyholders and in policy renewals. The purchase of investment management and advisory firm Frank Russell Co. in 1999, complemented and strengthened its business lines while giving the 144-year-old company a global presence.

Push Westward: 1850s–60s

NML began as the entrepreneurial vision of "General" John C. Johnston, of Catskill, New York, who earned his rank as head of the local state militia. In 1850, at age 68, Johnston and his son moved to New York City, where they became agents in the employ of the Mutual Life Insurance Company of New York. Within three years of their arrival, the Johnstons were operating the company's most successful agency.

In 1854, at age 72, General Johnston sold his interest in the company and moved with his grandson, John H. Johnston, to a 3,000-acre farm near Janesville, Wisconsin. He soon determined that the area would benefit from low-cost, mutual life insurance. Consequently, with a petition signed by 36 of the area's leading citizens as the first board of trustees, the state legislature chartered the Mutual Life Insurance Company of the State of Wisconsin on March 2, 1857. Explicitly modeled on the New York company, it was to be headquartered in Janesville and to limit its investments to mortgages on Wisconsin real estate and government bonds. Its first policy contracts were issued on November 25, 1858. Johnston never served as president but was a general agent.

When many of the original trustees left the company, their places were taken by men from Milwaukee, Wisconsin, anxious to obtain control of the company. Following the legislature's revocation of the provision requiring a Janesville headquarters, the trustees voted on March 7, 1859, to move the company to Milwaukee. Johnston had lost control of the company and terminated his association as an agent on March 11, 1859.

The Milwaukee group elected as president Samuel S. Daggett, formerly of the Milwaukee Mutual Fire Insurance Company. The company's only full-time employee was the secretary, Amherst W. Kellogg. Since trustees met quarterly and the officers were part-time, the trustees established an executive committee of five trustees in June 1859, including the president and vice-president as ex officio members. This step marked the beginning of the committee system which, despite some recent modifications, became the most conspicuous feature of the company's managerial organization.

Like any fledgling insurance company, there was a need to increase sales, and a sales force was established under a general agency system. In 1859, when the first out-of-state contract was made in Minnesota's St. Paul-Minneapolis area, the company began to expand beyond Wisconsin. In 1860, the first out-of-state local agency was appointed, in Iowa. By 1867, the company had expanded its mortgage holdings beyond Wisconsin, although its principal holdings were still Wisconsin, primarily Milwaukee, real estate. To reflect the fact that the company was becoming a regional institution, it changed its name in 1865 to the North-western Mutual Life Insurance Company. At that time, "Northwest" described the states now in the Midwest. When Samuel Daggett died in 1868, the company he helped nurture had passed through its formative years.

Power Struggle, Then Stability: 1870s–90s

The search for a successor to Daggett led to the most serious power struggle in NML's history. The pivotal figure was Heber Smith, the superintendent of agents. By collecting proxies from the policyholders, Smith helped elect Lester Sexton as the new president in 1869. When Sexton died after two months in office, John H. Van Dyke, a young lawyer, was elected to replace him. Smith, who was elected vice-president, believed that individuals seeking loans had to purchase policies. The issue was trusteeship, whether funds should be invested on a criterion other than that of obtaining the highest yield consistent with safety. After the Panic of 1873, the board of trustees wanted to exercise its judgment over loans, and in 1874, Henry L. Palmer, a lawyer and one of the original group of Milwaukee investors, was elected president. Palmer would remain president for 34 years.

The agents were not left voiceless. An association of agents had been created in 1868, but was inactive for several years. It was revived in 1877 and served as a forum unique to the life insurance industry at which field agents discussed problems of mutual interest and maintained communication with the home office. A year later the company hired salaried loan agents, effectively separating the selling of insurance from the lending of funds. In 1887 the finance committee was established to focus exclusively on financial and investment questions. It was created to ease the burden on the executive committee, but its membership duplicated most of the important personnel.

In 1881 NML created the insurance and agency committee with general responsibility for all phases of the insurance program. From that point until the turn of the 20th century, the life insurance industry was one of the fastest growing industries in the United States. Many new types of contracts were introduced by companies aggressively competing for sales. NML approached most of these new developments with its traditional conservatism. NML established an inquiry department in 1878 to cope with a problem inherent in insurance sales, "moral hazard," namely, that persons most likely to submit claims would be those most likely to demand policies. Health examina-tions and character checks were required for each applicant. The company restricted itself only to the "healthiest" regions of the country, those that did not have high mortality rates. By 1907, the company's sales agencies were closely integrated with Northwestern's overall management policies. Management also attempted to be more responsive to the policyholders by establishing a policyholders examining committee in 1907 which annually evaluated everything from the company's accounting practices to managerial performance.

Industry Under Scrutiny: 1900s

The growth of sales and development of new types of policies led to abuses in the industry. The 1905 Armstrong Committee investigation in New York, aimed at the three largest companies in that state, provoked a similar investigation by the Wisconsin legislature aimed at NML. While the Armstrong hearings discovered considerable concentration of control at the top, NML was found to have a relatively large group of self-perpetuating managers.

The rivalries that existed between the heads of the New York companies led to such practices as twisting (use of misrepresentation to have someone end one life insurance policy and buy another) and rebating (return of part of a premium payment) in the attempt to increase sales. Even though NML condemned and canceled agents found guilty of these practices, the legislature found examples. Similarly, the Armstrong investigation strongly criticized deferred dividend policies. NML dropped these policies before that investigation was underway, but the Wisconsin legislature echoed the New York findings.

Lastly, the Armstrong investigation was concerned that the sales of the New York companies were too large to be absorbed by the mortgage market. On the other hand, the Wisconsin legislature found NML's conservative financial policies to be excellent. What was disappointing to the legislature was the relatively small portion of the company's portfolio invested in its home state. The largest state for investment was Illinois, where the growing Chicago real estate market absorbed over a third of the company's loans until 1907, and a quarter of the loans thereafter.

The Wisconsin investigation led to an attempt to legislate the principle of trusteeship that NML tried to follow. Many of the unworkable laws were repealed or amended in 1915. NML came through this difficult period relatively unscathed because of the three principles its president, Henry Palmer, instilled into the corporate character: conservative underwriting standards, simplicity of operation, and conservative investments.

Business Climate in Flux: 1910s–20s

When Palmer stepped down in 1908, he had established a managerial succession that made George C. Markham the obvious choice. In the wake of the Armstrong investigation, insurance markets began to change. Group insurance and disability and double indemnity clauses were started at this time, but NML's management refused to adopt any of these innovations. Markham's administration was not market-oriented; it was preoccupied with investment problems. Many disability clauses were later proved unsound. In 1909, the company took the lead in the new field of business life insurance for partners and for key personnel. Nevertheless, agent dissatisfaction developed because the company would not enter new areas such as disability and group insurance. NML found itself developing into a specialty company by limiting its policies to individual life insurance.

When NML moved to Milwaukee, it occupied offices near the corner of Broadway and Wisconsin. It had outgrown several offices since then, but its new ones were never more than a block away. In 1910, it purchased a city block at the east end of Wisconsin, four blocks away. True to its conservatism, NML built a "Roman temple" in an age of skyscrapers. When the new building was occupied in 1914, the company became more compartmentalized. The sense of personalism that had characterized the days when executive and clerk worked side-by-side were gone. The fact that the new cafeteria offered free lunch on a daily basis was little compensation.

During World War I, NML followed the practice of the insurance industry in adding a "war-risk" clause to policies, resulting in increased premium costs for servicemen. At the same time, the federal government provided life insurance policies to men in service.

William D. Van Dyke, whose father had been president in the 1870s, replaced Markham in 1919. Van Dyke, a lawyer, was an investment specialist, an important talent during the 13 years he served as president. By 1919, NML was the sixth largest U.S. life insurance company and the leading farm mortgage lender among life companies. Since farm conditions were poor in the 1920s, the company began to explore other possibilities. NML led the field in the move toward larger loans, and, after 1925, increased its urban loans. In spite of a decline in the value of its large holdings of railroad securities and its hesitancy to invest in the expanding utility field, NML's rate of earnings was superior to that of other life companies.

During the 1920s the companies with the greatest sales growth were those with two or more lines of contracts, such as group and ordinary life or life and health insurance. NML made only modest changes in policy contracts and investment plans, and continued to grow. Its expanding operations required the construction of an addition to the home office in 1932.

The absence of diversification led to agent unhappiness. While the sales department was in the vanguard of the industry in preparing agents to sell to the needs of prospects, there was little effective coordination between the underwriting and sales departments. Michael Cleary, vice-president since 1919, moved to improve the company's relations with agents.

Economic Depression and Warfare: 1930s–40s

With the Great Depression in 1929, the problems facing the company's investment and operations policies became as grave as those facing the underwriting and marketing programs. Shortly after the stock market crash, NML acquired a large amount of real estate due to foreclosures on farms and railroads.

As the Depression worsened, policyholders began to demand cash. In response to the outflow of funds, NML made several changes to make its products more marketable. In 1933, women were accepted as risks for the first time in 58 years, but they were limited to half the insurance a man could purchase. Age limits were generally lowered, and a new family-income plan was adopted.

Van Dyke died in 1932, and the company was without a president for four months until Michael Cleary was selected. Cleary's good relations with those in the field soon expanded to include those in the home office. He helped maintain morale during a difficult time for the life insurance industry. The need for additional personnel to help with these tasks meant that the agency force increased between 1929 and 1933.

In 1938 the federal government began another investigation of the insurance industry. The Temporary National Economic Committee called numerous executives to Washington, then echoed many of the complaints of the Armstrong Committee. NML emerged with an enhanced reputation for corporate ethics, service to its policyholders, and honesty in its policies and practices.

With the advent of World War II, the war-risk clause was added to policies sold after October 1940. The clause went into effect two weeks after the bombing of Pearl Harbor on December 7, 1941.

Michael Cleary suffered a fatal heart attack in 1947 and was replaced by Edmund Fitzgerald, who had first joined NML in 1932 as a part-time employee. Fitzgerald's name would later be borne by one of the company's largest and most famous investments, the freighter that sank in Lake Superior in 1975.

Falling Behind: 1950s–60s

Home office expenses rose to double premium income between 1946 and 1954. Under Fitzgerald, an administrative restructuring with additional specialized service and research functions was completed by 1955. NML began to computerize its operations in the late 1950s, cutting costs, improving service, and delaying the need for a new building. Fitzgerald needed to increase the yield on NML's portfolio. In 1933 NML had the second largest mortgage account among the major firms; it was the second lowest by 1947. NML had the smallest stocks and bonds portfolio in 1933, and the third largest by 1947. By 1955, the company ranked fifth in mortgage holdings, and its holdings of private securities had increased relative to the public bonds it purchased during World War II.

By not diversifying, NML had not kept up with its rivals, and its relative position within the industry was falling. The decision to remain an individual, select-risk insurer, however, was made to maximize safety. NML attempted to meet the market conditions of the postwar era with the same methods which had proved successful in the past. The agency system was improved. A "short course" for agents had been introduced in 1935, and sophisticated agent training commenced following the war. More advanced training was left to various Chartered Life Underwriter (CLU) programs, and NML had the highest proportion of CLUs on its staff of all the major companies. The designation, Chartered Life Underwriter, was granted by the American College of Life Underwriters to individuals who had successfully completed the college's battery of courses on economics and insurance. Recruitment was difficult in the postwar years. Although agent income was high due to postwar prosperity, alternative employments outside the life insurance industry provided a great deal of competition.

Fitzgerald led the company into a greater involvement with national organizations and national issues, ending the company's historical isolation. NML became more involved in its home city, Milwaukee. When Fitzgerald retired in 1958, his successors, Donald Slichter, who became president that year, and Robert Dineen, who followed him in 1965, continued on the path of stable growth and selective change.

Competition forced NML to introduce products which it had resisted for years. In 1956 it took on some substandard risks; these risks occurred in a population less healthy than those included in the actuarial calculations for insurance premiums. Since substandard risks were excluded from the calculations for normal premiums, persons in the less-healthy group had to pay an additional premium. The company's version of double indemnity was introduced in 1959. Another area pursued was the pension trust business. Initiated by agents in 1938, these trusts involved large numbers of individual policies for employees of corporations. Such trusts were costly to service, cumbersome to administer, difficult to protect from the competition, and similar to group insurance. Eventually, this business was lost because of the company's refusal to rewrite them as a single group policy. On the other hand, the insurance service account introduced to the industry in 1962 was a particularly effective innovation. Customers with multiple policies could remit a monthly payment covering all policies rather than receive an annual bill for each policy.

Waking Up: 1970s–80s

In 1967, Francis Ferguson was elected president of "the sleeping giant," as the company was described in the industry, "the most stubbornly traditional of the top ten" companies, according to John Gunda's *The Quiet Company*. A corporate reorganization from vertical to horizontal was accomplished by 1968, with departments realigned by groups. Ferguson introduced the concept of strategic planning, which, in the 1980s, turned NML from a product- to a market-driven company. He introduced extra ordinary life in 1968, which replaced whole life as the company's most popular product within a year, because it helped counter the negative effect of inflation on whole life policies. As the Depression-era employees began to give way to those from the baby-boom generation, a desire to grow and to innovate was felt within the company. Growth bonuses were introduced as an incentive to agency growth, and, finally, NML decided to market its products more aggressively. It purchased a share of the commercial time on the broadcasts of the 1972 Olympic games and introduced its corporate slogan, "The Quiet Company." The giant had awakened.

The company's investments also became more visible, particularly the *Edmund Fitzgerald*. Other notable investments included major real estate ventures and energy exploration. An addition to the home office, Northwestern Mutual Place, was completed in 1981.

In 1980, Ferguson became chairman of the board, and Donald Schuenke was elected president. Together they presided over a transformation of NML. The company, shifting from its historic specialist role, began to diversify. All previous product innovations had been risk-based on individual lives. In 1982, NML made its initial move in the direction of group and health insurance by acquiring the Standard of America Life Insurance Company. That same year, non-annuity investment products and fee-based services were added when NML acquired Robert W. Baird & Company, Wisconsin's largest investment-banking organization.

The 1980s brought a number of challenges for insurance companies in general. The federal government, contemplating a tax on the cash value of life insurance policies, prompted insurers to spend more time and money fighting such proposals. Interest rates climbed, in the early 1980s, reducing the appeal of their fixed return policies. In addition, the nation was hit by the AIDS crisis and its related costs and controversies.

Even as the 1980s brought significant change, much remained familiar, including free lunches in the company's cafeteria, a tradition since 1915. Despite diversification, NML's primary attention remained largely on its traditional individual life policies. "The Quiet Company," NML's corporate slogan, emphasized that it put the policyholder first: it ranked first in dividend performance more often between 1940 and 1990 than any other company.

The belief in the equal treatment of all policyholders, fiscal conservatism, an insistence on efficiency, and the adherence to excellence continued to guide NML as competitors launched newer, flashier products. A case in point was universal life, a product offered in response to plummeting whole-life sales during the early 1980s interest rate hike. NML refused to offer it, believing long-term the product was not in the best interest of customers or the company. "Though Northwestern Mutual agents were eaten alive by the competition, they held tight for almost six years before the company released a new product that could compete with universal life without sacrificing the company's values," wrote Leslie Werstein Hann for *Best's Review*.

Some universal life sellers were later sued when the product did not perform as promised.

By the end of the decade, NML's policyholders numbered more than two million. Its $28.5 billion in assets ranked it as the nation's tenth largest life insurance company, with over $200 billion insurance in force, 7,000 agents associated with over 100 general agencies, and almost 300 district agencies representing the company in every state of the union. Investment operations were conducted out of the home office and 13 real estate investment field offices located throughout the country. Donald Schuenke became chairman, and James Ericson was elected NML's 15th president in 1989.

Into the 1990s

An investment made back in the mid-1980s began reaping rewards as the new decade began. In 1985, NML put $250 million into MGIC Investment Corp., a mortgage insurance company hit hard by defaults in the oil-producing states. The company continued to bleed over the next several years, and NML began to sweat a bit. Finally, in 1989, MGIC turned a profit, and two years later NML reduced its holdings to 68 percent from 95 percent through an eight million share stock offering. A second offering followed in 1992, and MGIC stock split two-for-one in 1993. MGIC's 1994 net income hit $159 million, and the business ranked second among mortgage insurers in terms of market share. By 1995 NML had pared its holdings down to 20 percent and planned to sell an additional 10 percent. Ultimately, the initial $250 million investment deal produced more than $1 billion for NML.

While the MGIC investment proved to be stellar, NML had some flies in the ointment. Disability income insurance, their worst-performing product, needed to be turned around. NML got caught up in a "benefits escalating arms race," according to William C. Koenig, an NML executive quoted in *Best's Review*. Moreover, the company had not kept close enough tabs on the costs related to the product line, thus compounding the problem. In 1998, NML revamped the department, raised prices, lowered benefit amounts, and tightened underwriting.

NML's experience with disability insurance prompted some operational changes when the company began developing a long-term care product in 1997. A separate subsidiary was formed and the administration of the product was outsourced, allowing NML to easily evaluate costs, react quickly to regulatory changes, and, if needed, fund growth through issuance of bonds.

On January 1, 1999, NML broadened its investment business with the purchase of Frank Russell Co., a privately owned Tacoma, Washington-based investment management and advisory firm. Frank Russell, operating in more than 30 countries, held approximately $40 billion in assets under management and provided consulting services for more than $1 trillion in client assets. Institutional investors held the 63-year-old company in high regard, and the Russell 2000 was the most widely used benchmark for small cap stocks. The sale, estimated to exceed $1 billion, was considered mutually beneficial. Frank Russell would retain a great deal of independence, while NML would gain a foothold internationally.

NML's reputation in its core insurance segment remained solid: named "Most Admired" in its industry for 16 years, according to *Fortune* magazine rankings. An important factor in the company's success was its sales force, considered among the best in the industry. While others in the insurance business had widened their distribution systems, NML stayed the course and emphasized sales force growth and development.

Hann wrote for *Best's Review*, "Northwestern Mutual's agents are among the most productive and financially successful in the life insurance industry." The agents—who, based on four-year retention rates, stayed with the company longer than average—received no company subsidies or base salaries but relied solely on commissions.

Stock-based ownership was another industry trend NML was loath to follow—mutual insurance companies Prudential, Metropolitan, and John Hancock were moving toward public ownership. Ericson, president and CEO, told *Best's Review* in 1999 that NML would remain a policyholder owned company unless regulatory requirements or taxation changes forced the move. With that in mind, NML had lobbied the state of Wisconsin to pass legislation allowing for mutual insurance companies to convert to a mutual holding company structure.

Growth on Tap for 2000 and Beyond

NML laid the groundwork for a trust company in 2000. True to form, NML continued to take measured steps as other insurance companies raced to expand their services. A loosening of federal regulations had prompted some insurance companies to move quickly into not only trust services but toward full banking capability. NML planned to market its trust services to its own affluent client base and through Frank Russell.

In May 2001, NML President Edward J. Zore stepped up as CEO. His ten-year plan for NML included doubling company assets to $200 billion and increasing personal life's market share to 10 percent from 7.5 percent. He projected Frank Russell Co.'s assets would grow to $400 billion from the current $66 billion.

Tragically, Zore and other insurance executives now had to factor in new scenarios as they made their projections for the future. Insurance companies were hard hit by the catastrophic events of September 11, 2001. NML was expected to process $150 million in life claims related to the destruction of New York's World Trade Center. NML, like other insurers, did not invoke war-risk exclusions, calling the events an act of terrorism. As the nation moved toward the conclusion of 2001, it was on high alert for additional attacks within its borders.

Principal Subsidiaries

Robert W. Baird & Company, Inc.; Northwestern Long Term Care Insurance Company; Frank Russell Company; Network Planning Advisors, L.L.C.; Northwestern Mutual Trust.

Principal Competitors

Prudential Insurance Corporation of America; New York Life Insurance Company; TIAA-CREF.

Further Reading

Gallagher, Kathleen, ''Milwaukee-Based Financial Company Issues More Shares,'' *Knight-Ridder/Tribune Business News,* April 11, 2001.

——. ''New Chief of Milwaukee-Area Life Insurance Firm Wants to Double Firm's Assets,'' *Knight-Ridder/Tribune Business News,* July 25, 2001.

Geer, Carolyn T., ''Where the CEO's Shop for Insurance: Northwestern's Secret? It's a Mutual,'' *Fortune,* March 1, 1999, pp. 264+.

Gurda, John, *The Quiet Company: A Modern History of Northwestern Mutual Life*, Milwaukee: Northwestern Mutual Life, 1983.

Hann, Leslie Werstein, ''Embracing the Mutual,'' *Best's Review—Life-Health Insurance Edition,* March 1999, pp. 35+.

Hillman, John, ''Northwestern Mutual Pays $82 Million in Death Claims; Total to Reach $150 Million,'' *A.M. Best Newswire,* October 10, 2001.

Hoeschen, Brad, ''NML Expected to Become Trust Company Powerhouse,'' *Business Journal-Milwaukee,* August 25, 2000, p. 8.

——, ''NML, Russell Match Faces Rough Spots,'' *Business Journal-Milwaukee,* October 9, 1998, pp. 1+.

Jones, Laflin C., *To Have Seen a Century*, Milwaukee: Wisconsin Northwestern Mutual Life, 1957.

Kueny, Barbara, ''NML Grows and Prospers by Sticking with Tradition,'' *Business Journal—Milwaukee,* May 28, 1990, p. 12.

Mullins, Robert, ''Changing STRYPES: NML Shows Confidence in MGIC,'' *Business Journal-Milwaukee,* July 15, 1995, p. 6A.

Pilla, David, ''Life Insurers Dismiss War Exclusion,'' *A.M. Best Newswire,* September 18, 2001.

Saucer, Caroline J., ''A.M. Best Affirms Northwestern Mutual Life Rating, Assigns Rating to Frank Russell Co. Debt,'' *A.M. Best Newswire,* June 20, 2001.

Tyrrell, Henry F., *Semi-Centennial History of the Northwestern Mutual Life Insurance Company*, Milwaukee: Northwestern Mutual Life, 1908.

Williamson, Harold F., and Orange A. Smalley, *Northwestern Mutual Life: A Century of Trusteeship*, Evanston, Ill.: Northwestern University Press, 1957.

—Louis P. Cain
—update: Kathleen Peippo

OAO Tatneft

Ul. Lenina 75
423400 Almetyevsk
Tatarstan
Russia
Telephone: 7 (8553) 255-856
Fax: 7 (8553) 256-865
Web site: http://www.tatneftjsc.ru

Public Company
Incorporated: 1994
Employees: 65,000
Sales: $5.18 billion (2000)
Stock Exchanges: New York London Russia
Ticker Symbol: TNT
NAIC: 213111 Drilling Oil and Gas Wells; 213112
    Support Activities for Oil and Gas Operations; 23332
    Commercial and Institutional Building Construction;
    23493 Industrial Nonbuilding Structure Construction;
    331491 Nonferrous Metal (Except Copper and
    Aluminum) Rolling, Drawing, and Extruding; 333132
    Oil and Gas Field Machinery and Equipment
    Manufacturing; 42271 Petroleum Bulk Stations and
    Terminals

OAO Tatneft produces approximately 8 percent of all oil extracted in Russia, with an annual production of approximately 170 million barrels. The company ranks fourth in Russia in volume of extracted oil and holds the 30th place worldwide for oil production. Most of the company's operations focus on oil exploration and production. However, Tatneft also holds stakes in oil refinement and retail concerns, as well as in businesses outside the oil industry. Those holdings include a telecommunications company, a tire production plant, and a diamond exploration company. In addition, Tatneft holds significant stakes in a number of financial services companies, such as the Moscow-based Zenit Bank and the Russian broker-dealer AO Solid.

Tatneft's core facilities and operations are located in Tatarstan, a republic of Russia situated just north of the Caspian

Sea. The name "Tatneft" is a combination of the word "Tatarstan" with the Russian word for oil, "neft." This fusion in Tatneft's name mirrors the real world situation, since close ties exist between the oil company and the local government. The Republic of Tatarstan holds one-third of Tatneft's stock and relies on the company for about 30 percent of its yearly tax proceeds. The two entities have supported each other financially and politically since Tatneft was privatized in 1994.

The company's activities, however, extend far beyond the borders of Tatarstan. Partnerships with Western companies began in the late 1980s. Joint ventures include ZAO Tatoilgas, a project with the German company Mineralöl Rohstoff to stimulate low-production wells and recover oil from sludge; ZAO Tatolpetro, a project with the French company Total to increase oil extraction using chemical methods; and Tatex, a project with the U.S. company Texneft to recover oil vapor from Tatneft's holding tanks. Other international activities include the beginnings of projects in Iran, Iraq, and Mongolia. In all, Tatneft has business connections and agreements with companies in 20 countries.

Roots in Post-World War II U.S.S.R.

The history of oil in Tatarstan begins in 1943, when the Bavlinskoye oil field became the first of a series of major oil discoveries in the republic. Five years later the Romashkino field, Tatarstan's largest, was discovered. As the Soviet Union recovered from World War II, the government began taking steps to exploit its oil resources. The "Tatarneft" trust was established in 1949 for the development of the Bavlinskoye field. In April of the following year the Soviet administration adopted a decree calling for the formation of the Tatneft production association and giving it the right to develop the Romashkino oil field. Later Tatneft obtained the right to develop the republic's second largest field, Novo-Yelkhovskoye. The two fields would be the source of most of the crude produced by Tatneft throughout the ensuing decades.

The 1950s and 1960s were marked by the acquisition of several smaller oil fields. Tatneft gradually became one of the country's leaders in oil production. One of the most rapid periods of growth occurred between 1955 and 1959, when development at Tatneft accounted for half of the oil production growth called for in the Sixth Five Year Plan. The association worked to implement leading technology into the 1960s. Reserves at many smaller fields were depleted during that time, but production from the major fields continued to grow. In 1970, 783 million barrels of oil were produced, the highest yearly figure yet for the U.S.S.R. The mid-1970s, with average yearly production of over 700 million barrels, marked the peak of Tatneft's production. By 1981, a total of two billion tons (14.2 billion barrels) of oil had been extracted in Tatarstan. As Tatneft's main fields matured, production declined from the 1980s into the mid-1990s.

Becoming a World Player in the Early 1990s

Tatneft's first move into the international arena came in 1989. That year the association signed a letter of intent to form Tatex, a joint venture with Global Natural Resources Inc. of Houston and Core Resources Inc. of San Antonio, Texas. The 50–50 venture was owned by Tatneft and by the American firms, who collaborated under the name Texneft. The goal of the partnership was to recover oil that was being lost through evaporation from Tatneft's holding tanks. Global and Core contributed approximately $3.2 million to install 55 vapor recovery units. Tatneft expended a corresponding amount in labor and operation of the units. The vapor recovery project had several advantages. First, it would give Tatneft the opportunity to sell its product on the world market and bring in hard currency. Secondly, the vapor recovery units would reduce emissions of hydrogen sulfide and other contaminants.

The first shipment of vapor recovery units occurred in July 1991. By November, the units were in operation, producing about 12,000 barrels of oil in the first month. Tatex planned to take on further joint projects involving the development of wells in the Romashkino and Onbysk fields and the restoration of surface facilities on wells in the Romashkino area.

Meanwhile, the Soviet Union had ceased to exist. As Russia emerged from the ruins of the Soviet Union, Tatarstan was negotiating its degree of cooperation with the new federal government. Against a backdrop of political uncertainty, Tatneft took several steps to augment its role in the international oil industry. The association formed a special unit to develop ties with foreign oil and oil services companies. Tatneft also obtained the right to directly set up trade, economic, and technical agreements with foreign firms, and to export oil if the foreign currency proceeds were used for the realization of social programs.

These changes soon had concrete results. An exploration and development joint venture was set up with Manx Petroleum of London. Manx agreed to provide management, financing, and marketing for exploration in a 7,000-square-kilometer area in Northeast Tatarstan, while Tatneft would provide oil rights, manpower, and export services. In another overseas deal, the American Tatex venture took on the job of drilling or refurbishing 50 wells in the Onbysk field. A third international partnership in 1993 involved the Swiss firm Panoco S.A. Tatneft and Panoco agreed on a 50/50 joint venture to drill several thousand wells over the course of the next decade in eight Tatarstan oil fields. The project would provide access to about 2.6 billion barrels of untapped reserves. Although production from the joint ventures accounted for only a small part of Tatneft's operations, the partnerships were useful in contributing new technologies and efficient techniques.

Privatization on Domestic and International Markets: 1994–98

Nineteen ninety-four was a groundbreaking year for both Tatarstan and Tatneft. The two entities clarified their political and corporate identities with the adoption of major changes. Tatarstan's political situation had been up in the air since 1992, when the republic refused to sign the Federation Treaty. Because the predominantly Muslim Tatars differed in both religion and ethnicity from the Moscow center of power, Tatarstan decided to work toward complete independence. This strategy proved unfeasible, however, since the republic would have been surrounded by members of the Russian Federation and likely would have faced an economic blockade. Finally, in February 1994 negotiations with Moscow culminated in a treaty that made Tatarstan an associate subject of the Russian Federation. Under the treaty, Tatarstan won extensive economic and political powers that gave it a preferred status in relation to other members of the Federation. The republic was able to use its situation to create advantageous business conditions for Tatneft.

A month before Tatarstan joined the Russian Federation, Tatneft was privatized. Several state oil-related enterprises were combined with the old Tatneft production association to form a joint stock company, AO Tatneft. The new company hoped to solidify its national and international standing by stabilizing oil production with new technologies and extending its geographical reach. The Dresdner Bank was quick to recognize the new corporation, providing it with a $60 million line of credit secured by oil exports. Tatneft hoped to attract more investors by bringing its financial affairs into line with international standards. The firm hired ZAO PricewaterhouseCoopers as its auditor and brought in U.S. consultants Miller & Lents Ltd. to audit its oil reserves.

Tatneft succeeded in stabilizing its oil production in 1995. Production had been declining throughout the early 1990s because of a downturn in demand for crude oil in Russia and insufficient capital investment. The achievement of stable production mid-decade was due in part to a more favorable tax regime. Tatarstan granted Tatneft special status in 1995 that included lower than usual excise taxes and tax exemptions on low-productivity wells. Production also improved due to

Key Dates:

1943: First oil is discovered in Tatarstan.
1950: Soviet decrees form the Tatneft production association.
1970s: Oil production in Tatarstan reaches its peak.
1989: Company establishes first joint venture, with American firm Texneft.
1994: Tatneft is privatized as AO Tatneft.
1996: Tatneft is listed on the London Stock Exchange, becomes OAO Tatneft.
1998: Russian economic crisis causes Tatneft's foreign debt to mushroom.
2000: Tatneft restructures debt and begins seeking projects beyond its borders.

Tatneft's well rehabilitation program, better recovery techniques, and the opportunity to bring non-operational wells into production. As a result, production reached 170 million barrels in 1995, a level that would remain fairly constant into the next millennium.

In 1996 Tatneft entered the international stock market, becoming the first Russian oil and gas concern to do so. The company issued 11.5 percent of its shares as American Depository Receipts on the London stock exchange. The shares were also traded on the Berlin, Frankfurt, Munich, and Stuttgart exchanges. The offering was well received and shares rose throughout the first three quarters of 1997. Although the company recorded a loss of $310.5 million for 1996, oil production remained steady at 168.7 million barrels and oil reserves increased for the first time in eight years.

International success occurred against the backdrop of tax confusion and payment problems on the domestic front. The federal government accused Tatneft of owing Ru 407 billion in back taxes. Tatneft countered that it had paid taxes in the form of fuel given to agricultural concerns, an in-kind exchange that the government had agreed to count against taxes owed. When fuel contributions were considered, Tatneft owed only Ru 42 billion, less than many other Russian businesses.

The barter system that Tatneft had used to pay its taxes was widespread throughout the Russian economy. A pressing problem for nearly all Russian businesses was a lack of payment from domestic customers. Most of Tatneft's consumers lacked hard currency and preferred to pay in kind for oil. That situation pushed Tatneft to look abroad for financial support in the form of hard currency. Foreign banks, encouraged by a slight improvement in the Russian economy, were happy to oblige. With negligible debt at the end of 1996 and 6.3 billion barrels of reserves, Tatneft looked like a company that only required a little capital investment to bring its idle wells back into production. As a result, Tatneft won $528 million in short-term loans from Western banks. Those banks overlooked more unsettling aspects of doing business with Tatneft—primarily the fact that the company was handing cash over to the government to help Tatarstan pay its bills. The government got a total of $230 million from Tatneft before the economic crisis in 1998, most of

which it later paid back in the form of deductions from Tatneft's tax bill. But as long as Tatneft's wells were pumping out hard currency profits, financial institutions put up with unorthodox business practices. At the end of 1997, their faith seemed to be justified, as Tatneft had a net income of $12.9 million on sales of $2.53 billion.

Although Tatneft was losing cash to the government, the company also benefited from a relationship of mutual assistance. Tatarstan President Mintimir Shaimiev attended the June 1997 annual meeting and made several recommendations. He offered government support for helping Tatneft become more vertically integrated, as the company still had no refining capacity. He also suggested that the company make moves to place its shares directly on American stock exchanges.

President Shaimiev came through on his promises in January 1998, when he signed an agreement with the president of Nizhnii Novgorod for Tatneft to provide oil to the NORSI refinery in that city. Tatneft expressed a desire to gain a controlling stake in the refinery, perhaps in an alliance with its competitor LUKOIL. As of 2001, Tatneft owned 8 percent of OAO NORSI Oil. The plans for increased presence on the international stock market also moved ahead. On March 30, 1998, Tatneft debuted on the New York Stock Exchange. By that summer, foreigners owned 22.5 percent of the company, while Tatarstan had 30.3 percent, Russian investors 16.8 percent, and Tatneft employees 30.3 percent.

Weathering the 1998 Economic Crisis

Despite these confident business advances, conditions in the Russian economy did not bode well for Tatneft. Stocks had been falling since the beginning of 1998 and the price of crude was low. In August 1998 the economy collapsed as the Russian ruble experienced a 245 percent devaluation. The downturn was especially disastrous for Tatneft, since most of its loans were denominated in foreign currency. To make matters worse, the company lost money through Treasury bills on which the Russian government had defaulted. Dealing with the enormous foreign debt burden would be the central problem of the next few years. Tatneft barely managed to pay a half-yearly coupon on its $300 million Eurobond, finally scraping together the required amount several weeks after the October due date. Year-end results for 1998 were understandably poor. The company lost $732 million on revenues which were half of the previous year.

At the beginning of 1999, Tatneft's total debt was about $1.07 billion. The firm began paying its foreign creditors bit by bit out of its crude sales abroad, all the while carrying out negotiations on restructuring debt. Relations with Western debtors were complicated by the fact that several dozen banks had originally been brought together to provide loans to Russia, and they all differed on what the terms of the restructuring should be. Despite the difficulties, Tatneft could not afford to default on the loans. Besides losing international credibility, the firm would lose its main source of hard currency, since domestic customers continued to pay with barter and IOUs.

In spite of the bleak situation, there were some reasons for optimism in 1999. Tatneft made its biggest profit in five years, earning $311 million on revenues of $1.83 billion. Production was in line with previous years. The company also embarked on a project to expand its retail network from 80 gas stations at the time to 500 stations by 2005. They would be located near the facilities that refined Tatneft's gas, in Moscow, St. Petersburg, the Middle Volga, and the Ukraine. The project was part of a trend toward increased vertical integration.

By the beginning of 2000, Tatneft's debt still stood at $846 million. As negotiations with banks continued, the firm took advantage of several business opportunities. Tatneft diversified outside the oil sector with the purchase of a 78 percent stake in Tatinkom-T, a major telecommunications company in Tatarstan. Later in the year Tatneft acquired controlling stakes in a tire producing plant in Nizhnekamsk and set up a joint venture to search for diamonds in the northern Arkhangelsk region. Most of the acquisitions were made on the basis of share transfers.

May 2000 brought Tatneft's first joint venture outside Tatarstan. ZAO KalmTatneft was formed in a partnership with the Caspian-area oil producer Kalmneft. The project would develop fields in Kalmykia, a southern republic on the northwest shore of the Caspian Sea. Because Tatneft's own wells were low-producing, the firm was happy to find a way to use some of its recently hired staff and newly acquired equipment. Other expansion included the opening of an office in the Mongolian capital of Ulan Bator, to take part in prospecting and geological exploration in the south of the country.

In continued efforts to increase its focus on refining and marketing, Tatneft acquired a controlling stake in the Nizhnekamsk refinery, which had been a longtime buyer of Tatneft oil. Tatneft planned to upgrade the refinery to specialize in processing high-sulfur crude, of which Tatneft produced large amounts. Work on the complex proceeded at a brisk pace through 2000, and the basic refinery complex was expected to be completed by the end of 2001. Resources were also pouring into the gas station expansion project, which was helped with the acquisition of a stake in the retailer Mosnefteproduct.

As 2000 neared its close, Tatneft's situation appeared to have improved markedly over the past years. Crude prices were almost double what they had been in the summer of 1998 and profits were predictable. Those factors set the stage for a final resolution of the debt problem. In November, Tatneft signed a debt restructuring agreement with a group of European and American banks. Under the agreement, the remaining $354 million of foreign debt would be paid back over two years at moderate interest rates. Year-end results were positive. The net profit of $842.5 million was up 131 percent from the previous year and sales of refined products had doubled their share from 1999.

In 2001 Tatneft continued to seek opportunities to develop oil fields beyond its borders. The firm gained permission to drill approximately 80 wells in Iraq under the United Nations oil-for-food program. The government of Sudan was also looking for a firm to develop its oil fields, since the companies currently active in the country had come under pressure from human rights activists concerned that the government was using oil revenues to fight rebels in the south. Since Tatneft appeared to be less vulnerable to protesters, the company signed an initial memorandum of cooperation with Sudan. Finally, Tatneft also initiated talks with Iran about the possibility of conducting seismological surveys there and installing well-reinforcing equipment. Tatneft appeared to have regained solid footing after the 1998 crisis, and was actively expanding into new sectors and geographic territory.

Principal Subsidiaries

ZAO Tatoilgas (53%); Tatex (50%); ZAO Tatolpetro (50%); Tatnefteotdacha (49%); AO Solid (55%); Zenit Bank (20%); Bank Devon Credit (53%); Mosnefteproduct (15%); Aktubanneft; Almetevskneft; Aznakaevskneft; Bavlyneft; Dzhalineft; Elkhovneft; Irkenneft; Leninogorskneft; Nizhnekamskshina; Nurlatneft; Prikamneft; Shungutneft; Suleevneft; Tamashneft; Tatneftebitum; Elkhovneft; Yamashneft; Zaynskneft.

Principal Competitors

OAO LUKOIL; Rosneft; Sibneft; Surgutneftegaz; Tyumen Oil; OAO NK Yukos.

Further Reading

Baigarov, Sergei, "Na konkurs! Ippodromy na neftianykh poliakh," *Trud*, November 18, 2000, p. 3.

Bronstein, Boris, "Tatneft' otpravliaetsia v step'," *Izvestiia*, May 23, 2000.

Chugunov, Andrei, "Tatneft' khochet kupit' nizhegorodskii neftianoy zavod," *Kommersant*, January 21, 1998.

Gill, Patrick, "Tatneft' Reports Steady Growth," *Russia Journal*, September 2, 2000, p. 16.

——, "Tatneft Results up Significantly on Last Year," *Russia Journal*, June 1, 2001.

Glazov, Andrei, "Tatneft to Transform into Holding Company," *NEFTE Compass*, June 28, 2001, p. 7.

Greene, Sam, "Tatarstan Got $230 Mln Through Tatneft Loans," *Russia Journal*, September 13, 1999, p. 13.

Kashulinskii, Maksim, "Tatneft' zavershit k oseni programmu ADR tret'ego urovnia," *Segodnia*, June 28, 1997.

Matlack, Carol, "The High Cost of Easy Money," *Business Week*, December 7, 1998, p. 110.

McKay, Betsy, "Russian Stocks Fall on Worry Over Oil Prices, *Wall Street Journal*, March 18, 1998, p. A17.

"Oil Equities Rally on Record World Crude Prices," *NEFTE Compass*, August 17, 2000, p. 6.

"Plans Progressing for Ventures in U.S.S.R.," *Oil and Gas Journal*, October 7, 1991, pp. 28–29.

Poling, Travis E., "Newest Texas Oil Field Is in Soviet Union," *San Antonio Business Journal*, October 29, 1990, pp. 1–2.

Pshenichnikova, Evgeniia, "Den'gi ostaiutsia v strane," *Sevodnia*, November 1, 2000, p. 7.

"Republic of Tatarstan: State Within a State," *Russia Journal*, April 26, 1999.

Rost, Andrei, "Gromkiye dela o bankrotstve mogut okazat'sia ne takimi uzh gromkimi," *Izvestiia*, October 24, 1996.

"S&P Assigns B+ Rating to Tatneft Finance's Eurobond Issue; Outlook Stable," *PR Newswire*, September 26, 1997.

Sapozhnikov, Pyotr, "Tatneft' stanovitcia semeynym predpriiatiem," *Kommersant-Daily*, July 1, 1998.

"Sudan Tilts Toward State Oil Partners," *Petroleum Intelligence Weekly*, August 6, 2001, p. 5.

"Surgut, Tatneft Hail Healthy 1999 Results," *NEFTE Compass*, April 27, 2000, p. 6.

"Tatarstan to Privatize Firm," *Oil Daily*, November 22, 1993, p. 3.

"Tatneft Booted Out of Moscow Refinery," *NEFTE Compass*, May 24, 2001, p. 4.

"Tatneft Diversifies into Diamonds," *NEFTE Compass*, June 29, 2000, p. 4.

"Tatneft Eyes Retail Network Expansion," *NEFTE Compass*, November 18, 1999, p. 5.

"Tatneft Gets First Contract to Drill in Iraq," *Oil Daily*, February 22, 2001.

"Tatneft Has Purchased the 78% State-Held Stake in Tatinkom-T," *IPR Strategic Business Information Database*, February 23, 2000.

"Tatneft Is to Get Russia's Biggest Oil Refinery," *A&G Information Services,* April 14, 1999.

"Tatneft Poised to Finalise Debt Restructuring," *NEFTE Compass*, September 23, 1999, p. 4.

"Tatneft Presses on with Bond Issue," *NEFTE Compass*, March 8, 2001, p. 6.

"Tatneft to Increase Stake in Cellular Operator Tatinkom-T," *IPR Strategic Business Information Database*, June 15, 2000.

"Tatneft Wriggles Free of Lending Constraints," *NEFTE Compass*, November 9, 2000, p. 5.

Tavernise, Sabrina, "Russian Oil Company in Debt Deal," *New York Times*, November 1, 2000, p. 1.

Tsypin, Vladimir, "Kompaniia 'Tatneft' mozhet ne pogasit' v srok kupon po evroobligatsiiam," *Finansovye Izvestiia*, April 20, 1999.

"UN Approves Second Contract for Russian Oil Company to Drill in Iraq," *Oil Daily*, March 19, 2001.

—Sarah Ruth Lorenz

P & F Industries, Inc.

300 Smith Street
Farmingdale, New York 11735-1114
U.S.A.
Telephone: (631) 694-1800
Toll Free: (800) 457-2037
Fax: (631) 694-1836
Web site: http://www.pfina.com

Public Company
Incorporated: 1961 as Plastics & Fibers Inc.
Employees: 398
Sales: $80.9 million (2000)
Stock Exchanges: NASDAQ
Ticker Symbol: PFIN
NAIC: 33251 Hardware Manufacturing; 333415 Air-Conditioning and Warm Air Heating Equipment and Commercial and Industrial Refrigeration Equipment Manufacturing; 333911 Pump and Pumping Equipment Manufacturing; 333995 Fluid Power Cylinder and Actuator Manufacturing; 42171 Hardware Wholesalers; 42173 Warm Air Heating and Air Conditioning Equipment and Supplies Wholesalers

P & F Industries, Inc. conducts business operations through three wholly owned subsidiaries engaged in the manufacture, importation, and sale of machinery and equipment for industrial and retail consumers. Florida Pneumatic Manufacturing Corp. primarily makes a variety of hand tools. Green Manufacturing, Inc. chiefly makes hydraulic cylinders but also produces digging equipment for farming and access equipment for the petrochemical industry. Embassy Industries, Inc. manufactures baseboard heating products and imports radiant heating systems and door and window hardware. Sears, Roebuck and Co. and The Home Depot are P & F's major customers.

Multifaceted Firm: 1963–75

Plastics & Fibers Inc., the predecessor to P & F Industries, was incorporated in New Jersey and made its initial public offering of stock in 1961, when, by selling shares at $2 each, it collected $246,000 for expansion and working capital and to repay loans. In 1963 this company was merged into a Delaware corporation that took the name P & F Industries, Inc. It consisted of Horowitz Brothers, Inc. (later Horowitz Bros., Inc.), one of the largest plumbing, heating, and air conditioning contractors in the New York City metropolitan area, and Torrance Specialty Fixtures Inc. Based in Torrance, California, the latter company was producing plastic and steel pipe and nonwoven reinforcing mats made of asbestos fiber. It also was designing and building pipemaking machinery and complete pipe mills. Based in Syosset, Long Island—also the headquarters of Horowitz Brothers—P & F Industries had a net profit of $300,776 on sales of $11.97 million in 1963. Sidney Horowitz, president and treasurer, succeeded Jack Nelson as chairman and chief executive officer in 1968.

P & F Industries acquired, in 1965, Embassy Industries, Inc., a manufacturer and distributor of baseboard heating and other heating and air conditioning elements located in Farmingdale, Long Island. P & F, in 1967, had revenues of $35.71 million and net income of $1.81 million, although Embassy was not yet profitable. Now headquartered in Great Neck, Long Island, P & F was rapidly becoming a conglomerate and, in 1968, acquired seven businesses, including National Fence Manufacturing Co., Inc., which had factories in three states, and a producer of plumbers' chemicals that was attached to Embassy. It added several more companies in 1969, including Triangle Sheet Metal Works, Inc., another Long Island heating, ventilating, and air conditioning contractor; three graphic arts and printing firms; and Bilnor Corp., a Brooklyn-based builder of swimming pools and accessories. P & F took in $8 million that year by selling more shares of common stock at $14 a share.

At the end of the 1960s P & F Industries held no less than 14 subsidiaries. Hudson Machine & Tool Corp. and Modulaire Corp. were two more Long Island-based subsidiaries that made (and in Modulaire's case installed) heating and cooling equipment. Four were engaged in printing and graphic arts. The Torrance plant now made pipe and related equipment for two companies. A Chicago-area subsidiary manufactured carwash equipment, and Bilnor made inflatable toys as well as swim-

+---+
| **Company Perspectives:** |
| |
| *The Company's strategy for growth calls for |
| penetrating new markets with its core |
| products, exploiting current distri- |
| bution channels with additional internally |
| developed and acquired products and pursuing |
| complimentary acquisition candidates outside |
| of its existing businesses.* |
+---+

ming pools. Continental Modules, Inc. produced modular buildings in Whippany, New Jersey.

The conglomerate concept was in vogue in the late 1960s, but by early 1970, when the company's annual report revealed a net loss on revenues of $58.36 million, the stock market had fallen into a deep slump, and some of P & F's holdings were in the process of being sold or closed, including Embassy's chemicals division, Continental Modules, Hudson Machine & Tool, and the majority interest in Torrance. In 1973 P & F liquidated and/or divested all its businesses in the graphic arts sector except a bookbinder that closed four years later. Bilnor closed in 1975. By 1978 only National Fence, Embassy, Horowitz, and Triangle (including Modulaire) remained.

P & F in the 1980s and 1990s

After a small 1975 profit, P & F Industries lost money in 1976 and 1977, and after another small 1978 profit, the company lost money again in 1979 and 1980. National Fence was sold in 1981, and even Horowitz Bros. was discontinued that year. The firm now consisted of only two units. Triangle, based in New Hyde Park, Long Island, was designing, manufacturing, and installing sheet-metal ductwork and related products for warm-air heating, ventilating, air conditioning, industrial exhausts, and air-pollution and temperature-control systems, often for big office buildings in Manhattan. It also completed, in 1980, this kind of work for such clients as the Meadowlands Arena in New Jersey; a Princeton University nuclear reactor facility; hospitals in Manhattan and Bethesda, Maryland; and a prison in Jessup, Maryland. Embassy, in Farmingdale, New York, was manufacturing and distributing baseboard hot-water radiators, portable hot-water electric baseboard heaters, and several other products in the heating field. P & F moved its headquarters to Farmingdale in 1985.

P & F Industries acquired, in 1984, Florida Pneumatic Manufacturing Corporation, Inc., a Boynton Beach, Florida, manufacturer and importer of a broad line of pneumatic tools, parts, and accessories for sale in the automotive-aftermarket and industrial trade. This facility moved to Jupiter, Florida, in 1987. The parent company, in early 1986, added Franklin Manufacturing Corp. of Oceanside, Long Island. Franklin was importing and manufacturing a broad line of hardware, including such items as doorknobs, locks, hinges, clothesline pulleys, and rope tighteners. This company became a division of Embassy and by the 1990s was importing nearly all of its products. Later in 1986, P & F added Summit Industries Inc., a Houston-based importer and distributor of air-powered tools, under the Universal Tool name, that became part of Florida Pneumatic. Solidly

profitable by 1985, P & F saw its revenues rise from $22.79 million in 1984 to $63.69 million in 1989.

When the U.S. economy fell into recession in 1990, however, P & F Industries suffered inordinately. Revenues dropped 35 percent that year, almost entirely because of a loss of ductwork contracting sales. The company remained profitable, but only marginally so. A slow recovery ensued, and P & F's sales volume reached $44.8 million in 1994. That year the company got out of contracting by selling Triangle to an investment group that included senior management for $3.5 million. This business had accounted for about 30 percent of P & F's sales in 1992 but had lost money in 1993. Meanwhile, however, P & F was beefing up the Florida Pneumatic operation. In 1990 it purchased Berkley Tool Corp., a company with a product line of pipe and bolt dies, pipe taps, pipe and tubing caster wheels, and replacement electrical components for pipe-threading machines. Berkley became a division of Florida Pneumatic, which by this time was importing rather than manufacturing all of its products from the Far East except high-speed rotary and reciprocating pneumatic tools. In 1995, Florida Pneumatic acquired Tradesmen Tool Co. Inc., a company with a product line of Pipemaster heavy-duty wrenches.

Florida Pneumatic was clearly the mainstay of P & F Industries' business by 1995, when it accounted for 77 percent of company revenues. Embassy introduced a hot-water radiant (rather than baseboard) heating system at the beginning of the year. A strong recovery in P & F's profits began in 1995 and continued through the rest of the decade. In 1998 P & F Industries purchased Green Manufacturing, Inc., a manufacturer of hydraulic cylinders in Bowling Green, Ohio, for $10.5 million in cash. The company, which reported sales of $18 million the previous year, had been marketing its products to manufacturers of towing equipment, waste/compacting equipment, lifts, and construction equipment for more than 30 years. In 1999 P & F Industries recorded record revenues of $82.7 million and record income of $4.55 million. The firm, in 2000, was named one of the 200 best small companies in the nation by *Forbes*.

P & F Industries in 2000–01

P & F Industries did not do quite as well in 2000 as the previous year, recording net income of $3.82 million on revenues of $80.9 million. Florida Pneumatic accounted for 62 percent of company revenues, Green Manufacturing for 25 percent, and Embassy Industries for the remaining 13 percent. In terms of operating profit, Florida Pneumatic accounted for 81 percent, Embassy for 10 percent, and Green for 9 percent. Each division was being run by a manager who oversaw manufacturing, promoted new product development, and identified additional target markets and other opportunities. P & F's long-term debt was $3.86 million at the end of 2000. P & F Industries said in 2001 that it was currently developing products such as specialized machining tools and commercial-grade hydronic heating systems. It had recently launched a new line of nailers and staplers.

Florida Pneumatic was importing or manufacturing about 50 types of pneumatic hand tools, mostly at prices ranging from $50 to $1,000, under the names "Florida Pneumatic," "Universal Tool," and "Fuji," as well as under the trade names or trademarks of several private-label customers (including Home De-

Key Dates:

1963: Newly incorporated P & F Industries consists of a manufacturer and contractor.
1969: The company now is a conglomerate composed of 14 subsidiaries.
1978: Financially troubled P & F now has only four subsidiaries; by 1982, only two remain.
1984: P & F acquires Florida Pneumatic Manufacturing Corp.
1994: The company abandons contracting by selling Triangle Sheet Metal Works, Inc.
1998: P & F purchases Green Manufacturing, Inc.

pot). These tools, which included sanders, grinders, drills, saws, and impact wrenches, were similar in appearance and function to electric hand tools but were powered by compressed air rather than directly by electricity. The company promoted air tools as generally less expensive to operate than their electrical counterparts, as well as being lighter in weight and offering better performance. Berkley was continuing to market a product line for a widely used brand of pipe-cutting and -threading machines.

Green was engaged primarily in the manufacture, development, and sale of heavy-duty welded custom-designed hydraulic cylinders as components for a variety of equipment and machinery manufactured by others. These cylinders were being used on tow trucks and car carriers for hoisting and lifting cars and on aerial lifts and cranes to raise platforms and other heavy objects. They also were being used on various types of construction equipment for digging and as steering mechanisms. In addition, they were being installed in compact equipment in order to compress recyclable cardboard or other refuse. Each cylinder was being engineered to the customer's specifications. The company's products were being sold directly to original equipment manufacturers at prices ranging from $50 to $1,500, with an average selling price of about $150.

Green also was manufacturing a line of access equipment for the petrochemical and bulk-storage industries. These products consisted of bridges, platforms, walkways, and stairways constructed of steel or aluminum, designed to customer specifications and sold for use in overhead and elevated access to large containers, including rail cars and storage tanks. The company also was marketing a small line of diggers for use primarily as attachments to small tractors for light farm work.

Embassy was manufacturing baseboard heating products sold nationally under its name and also under the Panel-Track and System 6 trademarks for use in hot-water heating systems. It was also importing a line of radiant heating systems, which differed from baseboard heating systems by hot water circulating through plastic tubing generally installed beneath the surface of the floor rather than copper tubing in the baseboard along the perimeter of the space to be heated. The company said that baseboard and radiant heating systems, although generally more expensive to install, were less expensive to operate than electric heating systems and worked better than forced hot-air systems. The Franklin division was importing and packaging about 225 types of hardware products, including locksets, deadbolts, door and window security hardware, rope-related hardware products, and fire-escape ladders, at prices ranging from under $1 to $30. Nearly all of these products were imported from the Far East.

Sidney Horowitz retired as chairman and chief executive officer in 1995. His son Richard served as president of Embassy Industries from 1976 to 1993 and became president of P & F in 1986. He owned nearly one-third of the company's common stock in 2001.

Principal Subsidiaries

Embassy Industries, Inc.; Florida Pneumatic Manufacturing Corporation; Green Manufacturing, Inc.

Principal Competitors

Airdyne, Inc.; Black and Decker Corp.; Parker Hannifin Corp.; Snap-On Tools Co.; Stanley Works Inc.

Further Reading

Duggan, Dennis, "Plumbing and Heating Systems Ignored by Many House Buyers," *New York Times,* July 22, 1962, Sec. 8, pp. 1, 5.
"P & F Buys Supplier of Door, Window, Security Hardware," *HFD,* June 8, 1987, p. 56.
"P & F Industries Announces Acquisition and Reverse Stock Split," *Wall Street Transcript,* June 30, 1986, p. 82,343.
"P & F Industries Closes Its Deal for Summit," *Barron's,* August 4, 1986, p. 56.
"P & F Industries, Inc. Acquires Green Manufacturing, Inc.," *Business Wire,* September 17, 1998.
"P & F Industries Named Tops by Forbes," *LI Business News,* October 27, 2000, p. 18A.

—Robert Halasz

Peabody

Peabody Energy Corporation

701 Market Street
St. Louis, Missouri 63101
U.S.A.
Telephone: (314) 342-3400
Fax: (314) 342-7799
Web site: http://www.peabodyenergy.com

Public Company
Incorporated: 1890 as Peabody Coal Company
Employees: 6,400
Sales: $2.67 billion (2001)
Stock Exchanges: New York
Ticker Symbol: BTU
NAIC: 212111 Bituminous Coal and Lignite Surface
Mining; 212112 Bituminous Coal Underground
Mining

Peabody Energy Corporation is the largest private-sector coal company in the world. It accounts for more than 16 percent of all U.S. coal sales—more than 180 tons a year. The Clean Air Act has prompted the company to shut down many mines producing lower grades of coal. After a number of changes of corporate ownership in the 1990s, the company launched a successful public offering in May 2001.

Origins

Peabody Coal was founded in the 1880s by Francis S. Peabody. The son of a prominent Chicago attorney, Peabody graduated from Yale University with the intention of studying law in Chicago. Displaying little aptitude for the profession, however, he opted for a career in business, working at a bank for a brief period before embarking on a private retail venture in 1883. With a partner, $100 in start-up capital, a wagon, and two mules, the 24-year-old Peabody established Peabody, Daniels & Company, which sold and delivered coal purchased from established mines to homes and small businesses in the Chicago area. Capitalizing on the social and business relations cultivated by Peabody's father, the company attracted a large customer base and experienced success from the onset. As sales continued to increase, the company rose to prominence among the major coal retailers in Chicago.

In the late 1880s, Peabody bought out his partner's share of the business, and in 1890 the company was incorporated in the state of Illinois under the name Peabody Coal Company. Five years later, in order to meet increasing customer demand, Peabody began its own mining operation, opening Mine No. 1 in the southern Illinois county of Williamson. This venture represented the first step in Peabody's transition from coal retailer to mining company.

At the turn of the century, coal-burning fireplaces and furnaces composed the chief source of heat for both private residences and public buildings. Moreover, the railroad and shipping industries relied heavily on coal to power their steam engines. Over the next ten years, however, the increasing popularity of alternative fuels—including natural gas, which had applications in home heating, and diesel fuel, which could be used to power locomotives—led to a greatly reduced demand for coal in what had been its primary markets. Nonetheless, coal became an important commodity for another developing industry during this time; as electricity was brought to homes and businesses in urban and eventually rural parts of the country, the operation of electrical utility plants demanded large amounts of coal. In 1913, Peabody Coal won a long-term contract to supply coal to a major electric utility, and, realizing the growing importance of this market, the company began focusing on obtaining similar high-volume, long-term supply contracts, while acquiring more mining and reserve property to meet expected demand.

Having anticipated and adapted to changes in the marketplace, Peabody Coal thrived, gaining a listing on the Midwest Stock Exchange in 1929 and becoming known as a coal producer rather than retailer. Despite adverse economic conditions during the Great Depression and disputes and strikes involving the unionization of mine workers, the company continued to realize profits and growth. In 1949, Peabody Coal was listed on the New York Stock Exchange. During this time, Francis S. Peabody retired and was succeeded as company president by his son, Stuyvesant (Jack) Peabody, who later ceded control to his own son, Stuyvesant Peabody, Jr.

Merger with Sinclair in 1955

By the mid-1950s, Peabody was ranked eighth among the country's top coal producers. Long dependent on its underground mines, however, the company began losing market share to competitors engaged in surface mining, a less expensive process that yielded a higher volume of coal. Heavy losses at Peabody ensued in the early 1950s, and the company engaged in merger talks with Sinclair Coal Company, the country's third largest coal mining operation. Peabody management believed that Sinclair could offer the company access to greater financial resources and surface mining operations that would help it to remain competitive.

Like Peabody, Sinclair was founded in the late 19th century as a retail operation, providing customers in the vicinity of Aurora, Missouri, with coal for heating their homes and businesses. During the 1920s, Sinclair President Grant Stauffer was approached by Russell Kelce, an ambitious coal miner who sought to put his years of practical experience to use in an executive capacity. Born into a long line of coal miners, Kelce had begun working in the mines of Pennsylvania while in his teens. He later moved to the Midwest, where his father had established a mining operation. Stauffer and Kelce reached an agreement in which Stauffer would be responsible for cultivating a large customer base and long-term contracts and Kelce would oversee mining operations. By 1926, Kelce had purchased a significant share of the Sinclair Coal Co., and he became president when Stauffer died in 1949.

Kelce was also named president of the new company that resulted when Sinclair and Peabody merged in 1955. That year, Sinclair acquired 95 percent of Peabody's stock and moved Peabody's headquarters to St. Louis. However, the Peabody name, familiar to investors due to its listing on the New York Stock Exchange, was retained. Under the leadership of Russell Kelce, and, later, his brothers Merl and Ted, Peabody doubled its production and sales by opening new mines and acquiring established mines in the western states, including Arizona, Colorado, and Montana. By the mid-1960s, the company had opened a mine in Queensland, Australia, its first venture outside North America.

The Litigious 1970s and 1980s

In 1968, Peabody's assets were acquired by Kennecott Copper Corporation. Although Peabody became the largest coal producer in the United States during this time, its position under Kennecott was made tenuous by an antitrust suit. The Federal Trade Commission (FTC) ruled that Kennecott's purchase of Peabody was in violation of The Clayton Act, a decision that Kennecott challenged. In 1976, after eight years of litigation, the FTC ordered Kennecott to divest itself of Peabody Coal Company. That year, a holding company, Peabody Holding Company, Inc., was developed, and the following year it bought Peabody Coal for $1.1 billion.

Edwin R. Phelps presided over Peabody during these years of litigation, and in 1978 he was named the company's chairperson. The presidency was then transferred to Robert H. Quenon, a former executive in the coal division of Exxon. Quenon met with several challenges at Peabody, including poor labor relationships, low employee morale, financial losses, and outdated plants and equipment. However, he later recalled in an interview for Peabody's *Pulse* magazine that he was encouraged by the fact that the company "had a very good management team. They understood coal, and made things happen."

Quenon oversaw a reorganization of Peabody that resulted in separate divisions for sales, marketing, mine operations, resource management, and customer service. By selling off several of its properties, the company was able to finance more modern facilities and equipment. Moreover, Quenon was able to capitalize on the OPEC oil crisis by renegotiating longer term contracts with customers who feared that coal prices, like oil prices, would soon increase dramatically.

Although Peabody became more financially stable, it also faced union strikes and litigation over safety issues during the 1970s and 1980s. The longest strike took place from December 1977 through March 1978, ending when mine workers throughout the country accepted a new three-year contract. The 110-day strike could have led to power shortages and industrial layoffs; however, this threat to the nation's economy was avoided largely due to the stockpiling of coal that occurred before the strike commenced. Nevertheless, this strike and another in 1981 that lasted for 75 days proved costly to Peabody, and the company strove to improve its relations with its employees.

The safety of Peabody mines was called into question beginning in 1982, when the company was charged with tampering with the results of safety tests at its mine in Morganfield, Kentucky. The tests, made mandatory for all coal mines by the Mine Safety and Health Administration (MSHA), measured the amount of coal dust to which miners were exposed, since excessive amounts of the dust were linked to pneumoconiosis, commonly known as black lung disease. Peabody pled guilty to 13 charges of tampering with the test results in December 1982 and paid fines totaling $130,000. Also during this time, MSHA found the company's Eagle No. 2 mine in Illinois in violation of safety standards, having failed to provide adequate roof support beams, which resulted in the accidental death of a foreman. Reacting to these and other similar disasters, Peabody focused its attention on safety, designating teams of engineers to design stronger roofs and better ventilation systems at its underground mines. In addition, the company patented its invention of a "flooded bed scrubber," which operated in conjunction with mining machinery to reduce the amount of coal dust in the mines.

In 1983, Quenon was made president and CEO of Peabody's parent company, Peabody Holding Co., and Wayne T. Ewing was named president of Peabody Coal. Two years later, when Ewing moved to the Peabody Development Company, another subsidiary of Peabody Holding, he was replaced at Peabody Coal by Howard W. Williams. Improved labor relations at Peabody were reflected in the successful negotiations of con-

---

Key Dates:

1883: Francis Peabody starts a retail coal venture.
1913: Peabody Coal wins long-term contract with a major utility.
1929: Peabody lists on Midwest Stock Exchange, establishes reputation as coal producer.
1955: Peabody merges with Sinclair Coal.
1968: Kennecott Copper Corporation acquires Peabody.
1976: Federal Trade Commission (FTC) orders Kennecott to sell Peabody; holding company is formed.
1990: Hanson PLC acquires Peabody.
1997: Hanson spins off Peabody into The Energy Group.
1998: Lehman Merchant buys Peabody.
2001: Peabody goes public again.

---

tracts with the United Mine Workers, allowing the company and its miners to avoid strikes in 1984 and 1988. Growth in Peabody's operations continued and, in 1984, the company acquired the West Virginia coal mines of Armco Inc. for $257 million, resulting in new contracts with northeastern utility companies. During this time, Peabody's headquarters were relocated in Henderson, Kentucky, which offered closer proximity to its central mines.

Clearing the Air in the 1990s

The passage of The Clean Air Act by Congress in the early 1990s forced many coal producers, including Peabody, to reassess their operations. Phase I of the Act mandated that American industries work to reduce the amount of sulfur dioxide emissions produced by their plants. Although the installation of scrubbers at coal-burning power plants would enable such companies to modify the effects of high-sulfur coal themselves, most customers preferred to switch to a low-sulfur coal product. As a result, Peabody's competitive status hinged on its ability to renegotiate customer contracts and provide a product lower in sulfur content. Some Peabody mines, including Eagle No. 2, lost major contracts and were forced to close, whereas others were able to implement new equipment and procedures that produced low-sulfur coal. The prospect of the stricter clean air requirements outlined in Phase II of the Act, scheduled to go into effect by the year 2000, prompted Peabody to invest heavily in technology, hoping to be better prepared for eventual shifts in demand.

Hanson PLC acquired Peabody Holding Company, Inc. in 1990, a year after the bidding process had been set in motion by Newmont Mining Corporation, a company in which Hanson had a 49 percent shareholding. Irl F. Engelhardt was named president of the Peabody Group, while G.S. (Sam) Shiflett became Peabody Coal's 13th president.

In addition to the responsibilities of containing costs and implementing substantial changes in the company's Illinois Basin mines, Shiflett faced the threat of a strike by United Mine Workers during the first year of his presidency. Several developments in the coal industry contributed to dissatisfaction among mine workers. Technological advancements, including

the computerization of some mining operations, led to reductions in the workforce. Moreover, new nonunion mining operations emerged, offering stiff competition through lower coal prices, which unionized miners feared would lead to wage cuts. Finally, as coal companies were increasingly acquired by large, international conglomerates, the lines of communication between labor and management became convoluted, and the potential for rifts increased.

The costly, extended strike and over a year of negotiations ended in December 1993, when the union agreed to a new four-year contract. The contract included provisions for an improved healthcare plan as well as the establishment of the Labor Management Positive Change Process (LMPCP). LMPCP, an effort to resolve future problems through cooperation rather than confrontation, invited employees to voice concerns regarding mine conditions and job security and suggest solutions. As chairperson of the Bituminous Coal Operators' Association (BOCA), Peabody President Shiflett was instrumental in designing and negotiating the contract to resolve the strike.

In the mid-1990s, Peabody continued to rely on the utility industry as its primary customer base. With analysts predicting steady increases in the country's demand for coal in the 1990s, bolstered by rising demand at electric generation plants, Peabody Group looked forward to renewed profits and expansion throughout the 1990s.

Changing Hands in the Late 1990s

Peabody and Eastern Group, a U.K. electricity distribution and generating company, were spun off by Hanson in March 1997 to create The Energy Group PLC. The new company planned to become an integrated electric company and immediately began buying U.S. power marketing companies such as Boston-based Citizens Lehman Power LLC. Renamed Citizens Power, this was eventually sold to Edison Mission Energy for about $110 million.

Within four months of listing on the London and New York stock exchanges, Energy Group attracted a takeover bid by Portland-based PacifiCorp. In May 1998, Lehman Merchant Banking Partners emerged as Peabody Group's new owner, paying Texas Utilities $2.3 billion. Texas Utilities had acquired Energy Group PLC for $7.4 billion and retained ownership of Eastern Group.

Peabody Coal raised its stake in Evansville, Indiana-based Black Beauty Coal Co. to 81.7 percent in February 1999. Peabody had owned 43.4 percent of Black Beauty and paid $150 million to buy 33.3 percent more from P&M Coal Mining Co. and 5 percent from a management group. Just before the purchase, Peabody had paid $1.3 million to settle a United Mine Workers claim related to the 1994 transfer of coal reserves to Black Beauty, a nonunion company.

Peabody announced a $1 billion, six-year contract to supply the Tennessee Valley Authority's Cumberland Generating Station in August 1999. The contract stipulated that two-thirds of the coal come from mines in Kentucky. The union and government officials were negotiating to keep those mines open beyond 2002, offering millions in incentives and concessions. Within a few months, Illinois Power would stop buying coal from Peabody's last Illinois mine, choosing lower-polluting Wyoming coal instead.

In late 2000, Peabody Coal's Black Mesa Mine in Arizona drew protests from members of the Hopi and Navajo tribes, which had leased Peabody the lands since the mid-1960s. The protestors took issue with the pumping of billions of gallons of water from the ''N'' aquifer to move pulverized coal along a 273-mile pipeline to the Mojave Generating Station in Laughlin, Nevada. A Peabody representative cited studies that the operations consumed less than 1 percent of the aquifer's water. (Members of the Hopi tribe would later sue Peabody for discrimination on the basis of national origin, alleging that the company hired only Navajos at its Kayenta and Black Mesa mines.)

P&L Coal Holdings Corporation, known commonly as Peabody Group, changed its name to Peabody Energy Corporation in April 2001. Peabody Energy netted $456 million in an initial public offering held on May 22, 2001. The energy sector, stoked by California's recent power crisis, was hot again. The emphasis placed on coal by President George W. Bush and the Department of Energy made Peabody's pure play even more appealing.

Lehman Merchant Banking Partners, a unit of Lehman Bros., retained a 59 percent stake in the company. Peabody was still left with $1 billion in debt after the IPO. Lehman had long placed a priority on reducing Peabody's debt. In January 2001, Peabody had sold an Australian coal business to London's Rio Tinto plc for about $450 million plus the assumption of $119 million in debt.

Principal Subsidiaries

Black Beauty Coal Company (81.7%); Peabody Coal Company.

Principal Divisions

Powder River Basin; Southwest; Appalachia; Midwest.

Principal Operating Units

Arizona Operating Unit; Seneca Coal Company; Camp Operating Unit; Midwest Operating Unit; Bluegrass Coal Company; Big Sky Coal Company; Lee Ranch Coal Company; Big Mountain Operating Unit; Federal Operating Unit; Harris Operating Unit; Wells Operating Unit; Rocklick Operating Unit.

Principal Competitors

AEI Resources, Inc.; Arch Coal, Inc.; CONSOL Energy Inc.; Kennecott Energy Co.; Massey Energy Company; RAG AG.

Further Reading

Brown, Mike, ''Mine-Safety Chief Backs 'Judgment Call' in Note,'' *Louisville Courier-Journal,* September 23, 1986.

Dalin, Shera, ''King Coal's Reign Nears an End; Marissa Workers Ponder Life After Mining,'' *St. Louis Post-Dispatch,* November 15, 1998, p. E1.

Eubanks, Ben, ''Standing Up at Peabody,'' *St. Louis Business Journal,* January 14, 1985, pp. 1A, 13A.

Fanelli, Christa, ''Peabody Energy Surges into IPO,'' *Buyouts,* June 4, 2001, p. 3.

Fiscor, Steve, ''West Virginia's Largest Coal Company Trains for Positive Change,'' *Coal,* November, 1994, pp. 25+.

Hudson, Repps, ''Peabody Is Sold for $2.3 Billion; N.Y. Merchant Bankers May Sell It to the Public,'' *St. Louis Post-Dispatch,* May 20, 1998, p. C1.

Julian, Alan, ''Peabody Ups Black Beauty Stake; $150 Million Deal Raises Union Questions,'' *Evansville Courier & Press,* February 16, 1999, p. B6.

Kammer, Jerry, ''Tribes at Odds with Mine; An Unpleasant Water Fight Is Brewing,'' *Arizona Republic,* October 25, 2000, p. B1.

Lenhoff, Alyssa, ''Miners Wonder What Coal Talks Will Produce,'' *Charleston Gazette,* January 5, 1988.

Lucas, John, ''Peabody Gets $1 Billion Contract with TVA,'' *Evansville Courier & Press,* August 20, 1999, p. A1.

Schneider, Keith, ''Coal Company Admits Safety Test Fraud,'' *New York Times,* January 19, 1991, p. 14.

Smothers, Ronald, ''Union Prepares for Long Strike at Coal Mines,'' *New York Times,* February 6, 1993, p. 6.

Sprouls, Mark W., ''Peabody's Roots Cling to Markets,'' *Coal,* November 1994, pp. 33+.

Symons, Emma-Kate, ''Peabody Energy IPO Spotlights Resurgent Coal,'' *Pittsburgh Post-Gazette,* May 23, 2001, p. C4.

Willoughby, Jack, ''Offerings in the Offing: Payday for King Coal,'' *Barron's,* May 7, 2001, p. 49.

—Tina Grant
—update: Frederick C. Ingram

Pechiney SA

7, place du Chancelier Adenauer
75116 Paris
France
Telephone: (+33) 1-56-28-20-00
Fax: (+33) 1-56-28-33-38
Web site: http://www.pechiney.com

Public Company
Incorporated: 1885 as Compagnie des Produits
    Chimiques d'Alais et de la Camargue
Employees: 31,300
Sales: EUR 10.7 billion ($10.20 billion) (2000)
Stock Exchanges: Euronext Paris New York
Ticker Symbols: PEC; PY
NAIC: 331312 Primary Aluminum Production; 326112
    Unsupported Plastics Packaging Film and Sheet
    Manufacturing

France's Pechiney SA is the world's fourth largest producer and converter of aluminum, and the world's third largest producer of specialty packaging for the food, healthcare, and cosmetics industries. Aluminum production and conversion accounts for some 45 percent of sales, while specialty packaging adds 20 percent of sales. The company also operates a small ferroalloy manufacturing unit. Pechiney operates on a global scale with more than 31,000 employees working at 320 manufacturing and sales facilities in 50 countries. France accounts for the largest portion of the company's EUR 10.7 billion in sales, at 44 percent, while the rest of Europe contributes an additional 15 percent toward revenues. The company is also present in the United States, where it generated 34 percent of its sales in 2000. Pechiney was disappointed in its attempt to merge with Canadian Alcan and Swiss Alagroup in 2000, a union which would have boosted the merged company to global industry leadership, ahead of U.S. giant Alcoa. Yet the company has since rebounded from the loss, acquiring JPS Packaging and announcing its intention to grow by as much as 100 percent by 2005. Pechiney, listed on both the Euronext Paris and New York stock exchanges, is led by Chairman and CEO Jean-Pierre Rodier.

From Chemicals to Aluminum in the 19th Century

In 1855, a young chemical engineer named Henri Merle founded his plant in Salindres, near Alais in the Gard region, with the permission of the French emperor, Napoleon III, in order to produce caustic soda from the coal, salt, pyrites, and limestone that were all available in the area. The company was known as the Compagnie des Produits Chimiques d'Alais et de la Camargue, run by Henri Merle and presided over by Jean-Baptiste Guimet. The year 1860 saw the first industrial production of aluminum metal, using the chemical process discovered six years earlier by Henri Sainte-Claire Deville, which allowed the company to cast 505 kilograms of metal the first year and retain a monopoly for it for about 30 years. Aluminum was then extremely expensive, and considered a luxury product. Napoleon III was actually offered aluminum cutlery as a wedding gift. The man who was to give the company its name, Alfred Rangod, known as A.R. Pechiney, the name of his stepfather, entered the company in 1874 and would begin a long term as managing director. Within three years, the company was being referred to in financial and trading circles by his name. Henri Roux was appointed president in 1879, to be replaced by Emile Guimet, founder of the famous Asian arts museum in Paris, in 1887.

In 1886 a new, much more efficient electrolytical process to cast aluminum was discovered by the French scientist Paul Héroult. Héroult offered to sell the process to A.R. Pechiney, but the latter did not believe in the future of aluminum and declined to buy it. Héroult subsequently sold his patent to another company, Société Électrométallurgique Française, which built its first aluminum factory in Froges. In 1889, faced with competition from Froges, A.R. Pechiney closed down his firm's aluminum department. In 1897, however, Pechiney bought a competing firm and entered the field of electrolysis. Up to World War I, the firm continued to construct new plants in the Alps and Pyrenees, becoming the second aluminum producer in France and the leading firm for sales through the establishment of L'Aluminium Français, a sales company uniting all the French aluminum producers. The company also had a Norwegian subsidiary that produced aluminum, but the most ambitious project of the period was the establishment in 1912 of a U.S. aluminum factory in South Carolina. The plant, one of the largest in the world at the

Company Perspectives:

The objective is to create value through continuous improvement and selective and profitable growth.

time, was to develop into a town, Badinville. The town was named after Adrien Badin, who succeeded A.R. Pechiney at the head of the company as managing director, from 1914 to 1917, when he died. Badin was succeeded by a team comprised of Emile Boyoud and Louis Marlio. In 1918 Emile Guimet died, and Gabriel Cordier was appointed president.

Due to its southern location, the firm was not affected by World War I, apart from the fact that it had to sell its American plant to Aluminum Company of America. On the contrary, it worked hard to comply with the orders of the French war ministry. However, the firm faced new difficulties at the end of the war. The economic crisis of 1920 and 1921 led to an era of industrial concentration in France. In 1921, Alais et Camargue—referred to in financial circles as Pechiney—merged with the leading aluminum producer, Froges, to form Compagnie des Produits Chimiques et Électrométallurgiques d'Alais, Froges et Camargue known as AFC. The company was managed by Gabriel Cordier, president of Pechiney. The production of the new company continued to grow steadily until World War II under the leadership of Gabriel Cordier and, after the latter's death in 1934, Jacques Level, from Froges, who died in 1939.

The company's expansion continued between the wars. Aluminum production, which amounted to 11,000 tons in 1918, reached 50,000 tons in 1939. The firm developed its chemical production and, above all, concentrated during the 1920s and 1930s on the exploitation of hydroelectricity in the French Alps and Pyrenees. In 1946, when the energy sector was nationalized by the De Gaulle government, along with the transport sector and strategic industries, including arms and electricity, AFC-Pechiney alone supplied 15 percent of French electricity. In addition, the company took part—together with the only other French aluminum producer, Ugine—in the reformed international aluminum combine—which was established in 1901. International alliances regrouping the aluminum producers followed one another, up to World War II. In addition, French aluminum producers formed a sales consortium in 1912, which favored an efficient double-edged policy aiming at the development of the final uses of aluminum and at moderate pricing. This situation allowed the company to go through the 1930s Depression without major problems, unlike the copper combine which experienced a major crash during the same period. Once again, the company plants were spared from destruction in World War II because of their geographical location in the south of France. The firm survived the war without major problems. During the first few months it was under the tenure of Louis Marlio, who had succeeded Jacques Level in 1939 after assisting him for 20 years in the company, and from then onwards under President René Piaton, who was to preside over the company, with Raoul de Vitry as managing director, from 1940 to 1958. Although the firm saw aluminum production in 1945 fall to half the level of 1938 because of the energy shortage, it had completely recovered by 1947.

Post-World War II Expansion

The year 1950 marked the beginning of a new era in the company's history, with its change of name from AFC to Pechiney, under which it was already well-known in financial and commercial circles. In 1948 the firm had already been completely reorganized, with the creation of four major divisions: aluminum, electrothermics, chemicals, and mining products. During the 1950s and 1960s, during the tenures of René Piaton, then Raoul de Vitry, from 1958 to 1968, and finally Pierre Jouven, from 1968 to 1971, Pechiney's policy aimed at two major goals: finding new sources of energy and raw materials abroad, and better integration of the nonferrous metals transformation activities. The firm took stakes in aluminum fabrication companies in Argentina and Brazil as early as 1947 and 1948. In 1954, an aluminum plant was launched in Cameroon, and in 1960 another alumina factory opened in Guinea as well as an aluminum smelter at Noguènes in France that same year. In 1962, Pechiney acquired an important U.S. aluminum producer and transformer, Howe Sound Inc., which was eventually to split in 1975 into Howmet Aluminum Corporation and Howmet Turbine Components Corporation. Also in 1962, the firm took a stake in the Australian alumina factory of Gladstone. In 1964, the Spanish subsidiaries founded in the 1930s were reorganized with the creation of Aluminio de Galicia. In 1966 an alumina-aluminum integrated plant was opened in Greece and in 1971 another aluminum factory was launched in the Netherlands. Pechiney took total control of a French firm, Cegedur, in 1964. Cegedur was another transformer founded by Pechiney itself in association with Compagnie Générale d'Électricité in 1943. The firm then created Cebal, a subsidiary specializing in packaging, in 1966. In 1967, Pechiney merged with Tréfimétaux, another French firm in the sector specializing in copper. As a transformation result of this policy of integration and concentration, Pechiney adopted a holding structure in 1969. In the same year it sold its chemical activities to Rhône-Poulenc.

In 1971, a new period began with the merger of Pechiney and Ugine-Kuhlmann. Ugine had merged with the chemical producer Kuhlmann in 1965. The Pechiney Ugine Kuhlmann (PUK) share was introduced on the stock market immediately to replace the separate Pechiney and Ugine-Kuhlmann shares. After the short tenure of Pierre Grezel, Pierre Jouven, former president of Pechiney, took over the presidency of the new group in 1972 for three years. He was succeeded by Philippe Thomas, whose tenure lasted from 1975 to 1982. The industrial policy of the period was based on the belief that conglomerates with various complementary activities were the correct answer to U.S. competition and the European common market. Pechiney and Ugine had indeed shared common interests for years. The new entity, Pechiney Ugine Kuhlmann (PUK), became the first French industrial group. A holding company coordinated various activities: the aluminum division, the only one in France, was fully integrated, while the electro-metallurgic activities were gathered into a new subsidiary called Sofrem. The new group was also present in the nuclear sector, from the mining stage to the production of combustible elements, with the creation of specialized subsidiaries, FBFC in 1973 and Zircotube in 1976. Finally, PUK produced special steels, copper, rare metals, basic chemicals, and coloring and pharmaceutical products. During the 1970s the company concentrated on its marketing policy. The holding company emphasized the devel-

Key Dates:

1855: Henri Merle founds Compagnie des Produits Chimiques d'Alais et de la Camargue in order to produce caustic soda.

1860: Company begins production of aluminum, using a chemical-based production method, and holds French monopoly position on aluminum production for 30 years.

1889: Alais et Camargue exits chemical-based aluminum production.

1897: Company returns to aluminum production, now using electrolytic production methods.

1912: Alais et Camargue enters United States, building aluminum production plant in South Carolina.

1921: Alais et Camargue merges with chief French competitor Froges to form AFC (Compagnie des Produits Chimiques et Électrométallurgiques d'Alais, Froges et Camargue).

1948: AFC reorganizes into four major divisions of aluminum, electrothermics, chemicals and mining products, then changes its name to Pechiney; begins international expansion program.

1971: Pechiney merges with Ugine-Kuhlmann, creating Pechiney-Ugine-Kuhlmann (PUK) and becoming France's largest industrial group.

1982: PUK is nationalized by French government, which transfers much of company's assets to other nationalized companies.

1983: Company is renamed Pechiney, and is once again focused on aluminum products.

1988: Pechiney acquires American National Can (ANC), based in the United States, becoming world's leading packaging company; company spins off its international operations into publicly listed Pechiney International.

1995: Pechiney is privatized and listed on the Paris and New York stock exchanges.

1996: Company begins Challenge restructuring program, refocuses on its activities as aluminum producer and specialty packager.

1999: Pechiney spins off ANC, keeping a 45 percent stake, then sells this off to Rexam PLC in 2000.

2000: Pechiney attempts to join merger between Alcan and Alagroup, but is forced to withdraw.

2001: Company begins new acquisition program with intention of doubling in size by 2005.

opment of technical assistance contracts with the U.S.S.R. and third world countries such as Yugoslavia and India. It created an international sales network called MIA (Multibranch Integrated Agencies), with its first agency in Japan. Eventually, PUK acquired Brandeis, an international raw materials trading company, in 1981.

The 1970s economic crisis nevertheless hit PUK hard. The company accumulated financial losses of up to FFr 10 billion (about $2 billion) owing to difficulties in the steel and chemical sectors. In 1979, PUK had to sell its cable activities to Pirelli.

Then, in 1982, like many of the major French industrial groups, PUK was nationalized by the socialist government of Pierre Mauroy.

Nationalized companies were originally meant to be used as tools of economic policy by the state. Quite rapidly, however, the government had to set up restructuring plans for most of the companies it nationalized, including PUK. A series of transfers took place during the early 1980s, under the presidency of Georges Besse, who remained at the head of the firm from 1982 to 1984, and then under Bernard Pache, whose tenure lasted until 1986. The coloring activities were sold to ICI and the special steels department to Sacilor in 1982. The chemical activities were transferred to Rhône-Poulenc, Elf Aquitaine, CdF-Chimie, and EMC in 1983. The considerably thinned company took back its original name, Pechiney, in 1983. In 1987, Trefimetaux was sold to Europa Metalli, with Pechiney taking a 20 percent stake in the firm. Pechiney thus returned to its basic activities as an aluminum producer, with half of its sales coming from aluminum metal and semifinished products in 1986. In 1983, a new aluminum plant was opened in Australia; another one was launched in Quebec, Canada, in 1986, while the French factories were extended and renovated. In 1985, Sofrem absorbed Bozel Électrométallurgie to become Pechiney Électrométallurgie. In order to finance a part of its investments, privileged investment certificates—shares without voting rights—were introduced on the Paris stock market in 1985 and 1986.

In 1988, during the tenure of President Jean Gandois, appointed in 1986, the firm embarked upon a new policy of external growth by taking control of American National Can (ANC), the world's leading packaging company, with 21,600 employees, 100 factories, and sales of about $5 billion in 1988. Pechiney itself achieved sales of $10 billion at the time of the acquisition. In taking over ANC, Pechiney first of all grew by 50 percent, then reached a new equilibrium between aluminum (30 percent of manufacturing sales), packaging (45 percent), and other divisional activities. The aim was for the company to become less dependent on the volatile world aluminum market. The state-owned firm, heavily indebted by the acquisition of ANC, needed to finance its development projects in a convenient way. In 1989, the firm created Pechiney International, its international interests being brought together into the 75 percent owned subsidiary. The remaining 25 percent of the subsidiary's shares traded on the stock market. At the same time, the company began exiting from a number of markets, including abrasives and refractories, ceramics, mining, and nuclear fuels.

Privatized and Prosperous in the 21st Century

Ten years later, the ANC acquisition was widely described as "imprudent," as both of the companies primary markets were hard hit by the economic recession of the early part of the 1990s. By 1993, Pechiney had slumped into losses, which neared FFr 1 billion on revenues of FFr 63 billion. In 1995, the company, led by Jean-Pierre Rodier since 1994, carried out a strategic analysis which led it to a restructuring effort to refocus its operations on two key sectors: Aluminum and Packaging. As part of the restructuring, Pechiney began shedding a number of its existing operations, including its North American Food Can and Specialty, and Beverage Glass divisions; its Turbine Components, subsidiary; and the sale of its Carbone Lorraine and Ugimag operations. The divestitures enabled the company to shave some FFr 10.4 billion from its debt.

The company's restructuring was capped by its privatization in December 1995, when the company was listed on both the Paris and New York stock exchanges. While the IPO proved a disappointment—downturns in the aluminum pricing cycle had forced the French government to lower the original share price target for the offer—the newly privatized company was freed to begin a more dramatic reorganization, dubbed Challenge. Begun in 1996, the reorganization drive called for the shedding of more than 4,500 jobs worldwide, something that would have been impossible to achieve under government ownership. The company also shed its European Food Cans operation, saving the company more than FFr 3.5 billion. More constructively, Pechiney began a massive investment program, pouring some FFr 3.8 billion in infrastructure improvements to modernize its manufacturing facilities and revitalize its research and development program. In 1997, the company merged Pechiney International back into its operations as a means to reduce overhead.

The immediate result of Challenge seemed disastrous—by the end of 1996, the company's revenues had shrunk by 4 percent, to FFr 64.3 million, while its net losses had soared to nearly FFr 2.9 billion. Yet, by the time Challenge reached its conclusion in 1999, Pechiney had achieved its goal of reducing costs by 20 percent and the company was once again in the black, posting FFr 1.7 billion in profits on FFr 62.4 billion in sales. The company had not, however, become complacent. Instead, in 1999, the company adopted a new pledge of "continuous improvement," putting into place an ongoing cost-cutting program.

By then, Rodier was preparing to take Pechiney to a new level, leading the company into the growing consolidation of the worldwide aluminum industry by seeking merger partners. As part of the preparation toward this aim, Pechiney spun off ANC in 1999, retaining a 45 percent stake in that company. That stake was sold off to the United Kingdom's Rexam Plc in 2000.

Early in 2000, Pechiney announced that it had agreed to join in a merger with Canada's Alcan and Switzerland's Alagroup to form a new globally operating aluminum producer, which, with sales worth nearly $30 billion, would easily capture the leading position in the industry, ahead of U.S.-based Alcoa. The deal, which called for the creation of the temporarily named company APA, based in Canada, appeared on its way to completion. But the merger bumped up against European Commission demands that Alcan sell its interests in a German aluminum producer, Norf. Alcan refused to sell, however, and Pechiney was forced to withdraw from the merger. (Alcan and Alagroup, unhampered by European Commission rules, went ahead with their merger that year.)

In 2001, Pechiney found itself in an awkward position. With the completion of the Alcan/Alagroup merger, and with the takeover by Alcoa of Reynolds Aluminum, Pechiney now found itself set back to fourth place among the world's aluminum producers. Nonetheless, Pechiney and Rodier had not lost their combative spirit, as Rodier pledged to continue making acquisitions "in the $100 to $500 million range" to boost the French company's position. The company followed through with purchases of the United States' JPS Packaging, Argentina's Envaril, the United Kingdom's British Aluminium Specialty Extrusions, and others. If Pechiney persisted in this vein, the company could expect to nearly double its revenues by 2004. In the meantime, the company carried out a new wave of cost-cutting efforts in the summer of 2001 as part of its continuous improvement effort.

Principal Subsidiaries

Affimet; Société Métallurgique de Gerzat; Pechiney Aluminium Presswerk GmbH (Germany); Pechiney Cast Plate, Inc. (U.S.A.); Aluminium de Grece (Greece; 60%); Pechiney Becancour Inc. (U.S.A.); Pechiney Consolidated Australia PTY Ltd.; Pechiney Nederland CV (The Netherlands; 85%); Almet France; Brandeis Brokers Limited (U.K.); Pechiney Deutschland GmbH (Germany); Pechiney Japon KK (Japan); Pechiney Trading Company SA (Switzerland); Cebal CR SA (Czech Republic); Cebal Entec SA (Spain); Cebal Italiana SA (84%); Cebal Printal Oy (Finland); Cebal Zhongshan Co. Ltd. (China; 60%); Financière Techpack (92%); Pechiney Lebensmittelverpackungen (Germany); Invensil; Silicon Smelters (South Africa).

Principal Competitors

Alcoa Inc.; Alcan Inc.; Kaiser Aluminum Corporation; Nippon Light Metal KK; Novar plc; Consolidated Container Company LLC; Crown Cork & Seal Company, Inc.; Norsk Hydro ASA.

Further Reading

Baker, Lucy, "Aluminium Giants Link up to Create Pounds 15bn Global Leader," *Independent*, August 11, 1999, p. 14.

"France's Pechiney to Sell American Natl Can Stake to Rexam," *Reuters*, April 3, 2000.

Gignoux, C.J., *Histoire d'une Entreprise Française,* Paris: Hachette, 1955.

Hawaleshka, Danylo, "A Bid for Global Supremacy," *Maclean's*, August 23, 1999, p. 34.

Mattei, Jacqueline, "Jean-Pierre Rodier, un mariage à trois, et l'enterrement de Pechiney," *L'Expansion*, February 17, 2000.

Mattei, Jacqueline, and Jean-Luc Barberi, "La vieille economie se rebiffe," *L'Expansion*, June 8, 2000, p. 56.

"Pechiney Abandons Three-Way Merger Plan," *Reuters Business Report*, April 13, 2000.

"Pechiney Cautious on 2001 Outlook," *Reuters*, March 29, 2001.

"Pechiney Cuts 2001 Operating Profit Forecast," *Reuters*, December 6, 2001.

—William Baranès
—update: M.L. Cohen

Pennon Group Plc

Peninsula House
Rydon Lane, Exeter
Devon EX2 7HR
United Kingdom
Telephone: (+44) 1392-446-677
Fax: (+44) 1392-434-966
Web site: http://www.pennon-group.co.uk

Public Company
Incorporated: 1989 as South West Water Plc
Employees: 2,700
Sales: £435.1 million ($616.2 million) (2001)
Stock Exchanges: London
Ticker Symbol: PNN
NAIC: 221310 Water Supply and Irrigation Systems;
562998 All Other Miscellaneous Waste Management
Services; 562111 Solid Waste Collection; 562112
Hazardous Waste Collection; 562119 Other Waste
Collection; 562211 Hazardous Waste Treatment and
Disposal; 562212 Solid Waste Landfill; 562213 Solid
Waste Combustors and Incinerators; 562219 Other
Nonhazardous Waste Treatment and Disposal

Pennon Group Plc is a holding company for two primary subsidiaries: South West Water Limited, which provides water utility and wastewater treatment services to Devon, Cornwall, and parts of Dorset and Somerset in southwest England; and Viridor Limited, which operates waste management services—including the United Kingdom's largest landfill operation—through subsidiary Viridor Waste, and environmental instrumentation through Viridor Instrumentation. The company has been striving to reduce its reliance on its regulated water subsidiary by stepping up investment in the non-regulated operations of Viridor. By 2001, South West Water represented just 54 percent of the company's £435.1 million in sales, while waste management had risen to 23 percent of sales. Viridor Instrumentation, which operates internationally with subsidiaries in the United States, Switzerland, Canada, Germany, France, South Africa, and elsewhere, and under the Viridor and ELE

Instrumentation and other names, provided 12 percent of the company's sales in 2001. However, due to an extensive capital investment program agreed to with the British government's Office of Water Services (Ofwat), Pennon has been forced to put parts of its Viridor business up for sale. In 2000 the company sold off its construction business, and in 2001 announced its intention of disposing of Viridor Instrumentation. One of the smallest of the United Kingdom's privatized water companies, South West Water was protected from a takeover bid in the mid-1990s when the British government blocked consolidation efforts among water companies. Mounting pressure is expected to persuade the government to allow mergers and acquisitions within the industry. Pennon Group is led by Chairman Kenneth G. Harvey (the company has functioned without a chief executive since the late 1990s), and seconded by South West Water CEO Robert Baty and Viridor CEO Colin Drummond.

Privatization Act in the 1980s

England's water supply had been shared between private companies and local towns and cities from the 18th century into the 19th century. Many early piping systems were constructed from stone and wood. The growth of larger cities and the reorganization of municipal control into more modern-styled governments led these municipalities increasingly to take control of their own water supply and facilities. By the middle of the 19th century, the various governments had taken full control of constructing the water piping infrastructure—by then being laid with iron pipes—and, in a series of Water Acts promulgated in the 1870s, the nation's water supply was placed fully in government control. Nonetheless, the water utility industry continued to operate on a largely local basis.

This situation led to a large number of water utility operations throughout the United Kingdom. At the beginning of the 1970s, the country counted 29 "river" authorities in England and Wales alone, which in turn oversaw 160 water suppliers. In addition, there were more than 1,300 sewage treatment authorities. The small size of the vast majority of these operations caused them to be inefficient and unable to invest in modernized equipment and facilities.

338

A first step toward consolidating and modernizing the increasingly antiquated British water supply and treatment system was taken with the passage of the Water Act of 1973. That act provided for the amalgamation of the United Kingdom's water utilities into ten regional water authorities. Each water authority was given the responsibility over the water supply, treatment, sewage treatment and disposal, and river and coastline protection in its region. The authorities remained government bodies, however, reporting both to local and national governments.

The rise of environmental awareness and health issues, which included stricter drinking standards and sewage disposal standards from the European Community as well as the dilapidated state of much of the country's water supply system, came to plague the new water authorities in the 1970s and 1980s. The rise to power of the conservative government led by Margaret Thatcher had prompted the privatization of a number of industries and sectors that had previously been brought under government control. With the British government unable and unwilling to foot the enormous bills required to bring the country's water system up to date, the decision was made to privatize the industry at the end of the 1980s.

The Water Act of 1989 returned the country's water supply and sewage treatment needs to the private sector. Under the act, the ten water authorities were converted into public liability companies and listed on the London stock exchange. The act also set up the Office of Water Services (Ofwat) to act as a regulatory body and to set pricing and capital investment levels. The new publicly listed companies were then able to raise capital to begin a series of obligatory infrastructure and environmental investments.

Birth and Development of South West Water: 1989–90s

One of the smaller of the new water utility companies was South West Water Plc, which took over the Westcountry region around Devon and Cornwall, with pockets extending into Dorset and Somerset, in a region of some 4,300 square miles, with more than 10,000 miles of supply pipes and 5,000 miles of public sewers overseen by nearly 90 locally operating water and treatment facilities. Much of the region was farmland—the company itself was to become one of the largest and few major public limited companies in the region—with an extensive, and long neglected, coastline. Responsibility for the coastline was to cause the company headaches, and force it to dig deep into its pockets. The company promptly began a ten-year, £1.6 billion investment program, some two-thirds of which was earmarked toward cleaning up the beaches under the company's authority.

Led by Bill Fraser, who joined as chief executive in 1990, South West Water soon succeeded in making itself unloved by its customers. While all of the United Kingdom faced price increases as water utilities sought to recoup their large capital improvement investments, South West Water's customers came to feel singled out. Reviews in the early 1990s revealed that South West Water was the most expensive of all of the United Kingdom's water companies. As the company's rates rose, so did its profits: by 1994, the company was posting operating profits of more than £100 million on turnover of £252 million. The company compounded its poor reputation with a number of missteps, including a series of contaminated water scares—in one scare in 1995, more than 600 people had become ill from water tainted by the cryptosporidium parasite.

Another public relations disaster occurred during the long summer drought of 1995, when it was revealed that leaks in the company's reservoirs had "wasted" some one billion gallons of water at a time when its customers were faced with restrictions on their water usage—the company countered that the water was simply returned back to nature, where it was needed as well. Meanwhile, South West Water faced new rounds of criticism when it raised CEO Fraser's pay and pensions packet from £150,000 to £217,000. Fraser stepped down in February 1996, replaced by Robert Baty.

Baty was immediately faced with a new crisis when Wessex Water, which had taken over the former water authority for the neighboring region, launched a hostile takeover of South West Water in March 1996. That bid was quickly countered by a rival bid from another water utility, Severn Trent, sparking hopes—from investors at least—of a bidding war. But the deal was quashed in October of that year when the government's Monopolies and Mergers Commission blocked the bid on the grounds that mergers among the country's water companies would be against the public interest.

If South West Water had succeeded in making a bad name for itself among its water customers in its first half decade as a public company, it had also been successful in expanding into new areas. In the early 1990s the company targeted environmental services as a fitting extension of its water business—given the company's growing expertise in wastewater and sewage treatment and its massive investment in cleaning up the southwest's beaches. In 1993 the company acquired Haul Waste Limited, adding waste transportation and disposal services, as well as landfill operations. At the same time, the company branched out into environmental instrumentation, acquiring ELE International Ltd. A third component was added with the acquisition of TJ Brent, a construction company.

ELE grew steadily through acquisitions during the 1990s. In 1994 the subsidiary was merged with pHOX Systems Ltd. The following year ELE moved into the United States with the acquisition of Great Lakes Instruments Inc., based in Milwaukee. In 1997, the subsidiary added operations in Austin, Texas, when it acquired Hydrolab Corporation. Back at home, ELE grew with the purchases of Warren Jones Engineering Ltd. in 1995 and then Didcot Instruments in 1996. ELE was already the

Key Dates:

1973: Water Act creates ten regional water authorities to govern water supply and wastewater treatment for the United Kingdom.

1989: New Water Act privatizes water authorities and creates ten publicly listed companies, including South West Water Plc.

1993: South West Water acquires Haul Waste Group to enter waste management services and ELE International, expanding into environmental instrumentation.

1997: Haul Waste acquires Greenhill Enterprises and Terry Adams, making it the United Kingdom's largest landfill operator; South West Water acquires 50 percent of Enviro-Logic.

1998: Company changes name to Pennon Group Plc, which becomes the holding company for South West Water and the renamed environmental division, Viridor.

1999: Enviro-Logic creates Albion Water, the United Kingdom's first new private water company.

2001: Company announces intention to sell off its Viridor Instrumentation subsidiary and regroup around a core of South West Water and Viridor Waste.

most international of South West Water's operations when it acquired Orbishpere, based in Geneva, Switzerland, in 1998.

Yet the company's brightest growth prospects came from its waste management side. That division, still trading under the Haul Waste Group name, was strengthened when it acquired Greenhill Enterprises from Scottish Power for £10.6 million in November 1997. The acquisition gave the company both landfill and quarrying operations. One month later, South West Water took a major step forward when it agreed to pay a total of £105 million for the acquisition of landfill and waste disposal specialist Terry Adams. That purchase transformed South West Water into the United Kingdom's largest landfill operator. These moves were in keeping with the company's plan to reduce its reliance on its water supply operations to just 50 percent of turnover by 2001.

New Name, New Emphasis: Pennon in the Late 1990s and Early 2000s

In May 1998, the company moved to underline its transformation from water company to diversified environmental services group when it changed its name to Pennon Group—using an old English term for flag. At the same time, Pennon renamed its environmental services wing as Viridor, based on the Latin verb for ''to become green.'' Meanwhile, the company maintained the South West Water name for its water company operations. The new holding company, chaired by Kenneth Harvey, found itself unable to attract a new CEO (in part because the company was eager to avoid being accused of paying a new ''fat cat'' salary). With Robert Baty acting as CEO of South West Water and Colin Drummond named CEO of Viridor, the company opted to continue without a group-level chief executive.

If the government blocked competition through mergers, the company found another way to cross its regional borders. In 1997, the company acquired a 50 percent stake in London-based consultancy Enviro-Logic. That company had developed a series of projects that promised to cut water prices by as much as 30 percent, through such schemes as bulk buying and water recycling, including a two-pipe home system that would provide drinking water through one set of pipes and recycled water for use in toilets and gardening through a second set of pipes. Pennon expected to be able to leverage its position in Enviro-logic to begin offering water supply services on its competitors' turf. In 1999, Enviro-Logic, which later became a fully owned subsidiary of Pennon, launched Albion Water, the first new privately owned water supply company in the United Kingdom.

At the turn of the century, Pennon Group was hurt by the combination of rate cuts demanded by Ofwat and a newly negotiated capital investment commitment. Pennon, like many of the United Kingdom's water companies, announced that it was conducting a strategic review with an eye toward restructuring its water utility operations. Yet after a year-long review, the company acknowledged that it had found no alternatives to its current structure. Instead, the group decided to dismantle parts of its diversified operations. In 2000, the company sold off its construction division.

Pennon felt the brunt of the new rate cuts at the end of its 2001 year, seeing its turnover dip to £435 million from £467 million the previous year. By 2001, Pennon's capital investment commitments with Ofwat left it unable to provide the necessary financing for its instrumentation division. That year, the company announced that it was seeking to sell off its Viridor Instrumentation subsidiary as well. The company now regrouped around a new core of waste management services and water supply and treatment. In the future, Pennon was able to count on two things: that people would always get thirsty, and they would always need to dispose of their trash.

Principal Subsidiaries

South West Water Limited; Viridor Waste Limited; Viridor Waste Disposal Limited; Albion Water Limited; Enviro-Logic Limited; VWM Limited; Viridor Waste Exeter Limited; Dragon Waste Limited; Viridor Waste Wootton Limited; Viridor Waste Hampshire Limited; Viridor Waste Management Limited; Viridor Instrumentation Limited; ELE International Limited; Exe International Inc (U.S.A.); ELE International Inc (U.S.A.); GLI International Inc (U.S.A.); Hydrolab Corporation (U.S.A.); Orbisphere Laboratories Japan Inc (U.S.A.); Orbisphere Laboratories Overseas Corporation (U.S.A.); Orbisphere Management Holding SA (Switzerland); Orbisphere Laboratories Neuchâtel SA (Switzerland); Orbisphere (Canada) Inc; Orbisphere (France) Sarl; Orbisphere GmbH (Germany); Orbisphere Laboratories Geneve SA (Switzerland); Orbisphere South Africa (Pty) Limited; Orbisphere UK Limited; Viridor Properties Limited; Peninsula Insurance Limited (Guernsey); Viridor Limited; Exe Continental Limited.

Principal Competitors

Cory Environmentals (Exel plc); Waste Recycling Group (Kelda Group plc); Severn Trent Plc; Shanks Plc; Société Industrielle de Transports Automobiles (SITA); Suez; Waste Management, Inc.; Vivendi Environnement SA; Waste Recycling Group PLC.

Further Reading

Elliot, Mike, "Pennon Drops Water Restructuring Option," *Reuters*, May 31, 2001.

Godsmark, Chris, "Lang Stuns City by Blocking Rival Bids for South West by Severn," *Independent*, October 26, 1996, p. 22.

Harrison, Michael, "Re-inventing the Water Company," *Independent*, May 30, 1998, p. 27.

Larsen, Peter Thal, ed., "South West's Waste Line," *Independent*, May 29, 1998, p. 26.

Osborne, Alistair, "South West Unfurls Pennon," *Daily Telegraph*, May 29, 1998.

"Water Torture," *Independent*, June 1, 2001, p. 17.

—M.L. Cohen

Prada Holding B.V.

Dam 3-7
1012 JS Amsterdam
The Netherlands
Telephone: 010-4232222
Fax: 020-4232223
Web site: http://www.prada.com

Private Company
Incorporated: 1996 as Prapar B.V.
Employees: 7,500
Sales: $1.55 billion (2000)
NAIC: 44811 Men's Clothing Stores; 44812 Women's Clothing Stores; 54149 Other Specialized Design Services; 315222 Men's and Boys' Cut and Sew Suit, Coat, and Overcoat Manufacturing; 315223 Men's and Boys' Cut and Sew Shirt (Except Work Shirt) Manufacturing; 315224 Men's and Boys' Cut and Sew Trouser, Slack, and Jean Manufacturing; 315228 Men's and Boys' Cut and Sew Other Outerwear Manufacturing; 315231 Women's and Girls' Cut and Sew Lingerie, Loungewear, and Nightwear Manufacturing; 315232 Women's and Girls' Cut and Sew Blouse and Shirt Manufacturing; 315233 Women's and Girls' Cut and Sew Dress Manufacturing; 315234 Women's and Girls' Cut and Sew Suit, Coat, Tailored Jacket, and Skirt Manufacturing; 315239 Women's and Girls' Cut and Sew Other Outerwear Manufacturing; 315999 Other Apparel Accessories and Other Apparel Manufacturing; 316213 Men's Footwear (Except Athletic) Manufacturing; 316214 Women's Footwear (Except Athletic) Manufacturing; 316991 Luggage Manufacturing; 316992 Women's Handbag and Purse Manufacturing; 316993 Personal Leather Goods; 316999 All Other Leather Good Manufacturing; 32562 Toilet Preparation Manufacturing; 551112 Offices of Other Holding Companies

Prada Holding B.V. is the holding company for I Pellettieri d'Italia S.p.A., the leather goods business at the heart of the Prada fashion empire, and other related enterprises, such as Church & Company shoes and the Jil Sander line of women's clothes. *Time* magazine called Miuccia Prada the most influential fashion designer of the 1990s. Beginning with a rugged yet stylish nylon backpack, she developed a signature utilitarian look with odd, muted colors and unusual textures that found favor with trendy working women. Prada's sales quadrupled between 1996 and 2000, when they exceeded L 3 million. The company grew explosively in the late 1990s, both organically and through acquisitions. There were 307 stores worldwide for Prada and its other brands in late 2001; 143 of these were franchises. Prada sells products only from companies it controls.

Miuccia Prada's husband, company CEO Patrizio Bertelli, has earned a reputation as a brilliant and temperamental micromanager. At Prada offices in New York and Tokyo, all office supplies—from desks to staples—must be imported from Italy. Bertelli claims to have personally hired 60 percent of the group's employees. His design mantra, quoted in *Fortune:* "It is not fashion that changes lifestyles. It is lifestyles that change fashion."

Origins

The Prada empire stems from the leather goods store Mario Prada opened in Milan in 1913. In addition to his own wares, he also sold steamer trunks and handbags imported from England to a customer base that included Italian nobles.

Although Mario Prada barred the women of the family from entering his workplace, control of the business followed a matriarchal succession after his death in the mid-1950s. Prada's son Alberto was not interested in the business, so his daughter-in-law ran the store for about 20 years before passing its ownership to her own daughter, Miuccia Prada, who first joined the firm in 1970 before inheriting it eight years later.

Miuccia Prada, the founder's granddaughter, was born in 1949. Her career in fashion design grew from an early interest in clothes and textiles. In spite of, or perhaps because of, her affluent upbringing, she flaunted leftist tendencies, handing out

Key Dates:

1913: Mario Prada starts a leather goods business in Milan.
1978: Miuccia Prada inherits the family firm.
1979: The famous black nylon Prada backpack is designed.
1985: Footwear is introduced.
1986: Prada opens a boutique in New York.
1989: Women's ready-to-wear clothes are introduced.
1992: Prada begins major push on U.S. markets.
1995: A line of men's clothes is introduced.
1996: Prapar B.V. (later Prada B.V.) holding company is formed.
1998: Prada buys stake in Gucci, soon sells it to LVMH Möet Hennessy Louis Vuitton SA.
1999: Prada goes on luxury brand shopping spree.
2000: Cosmetics are introduced as Prada mulls IPO.

communist leaflets on street corners. She received a doctoral degree in political science in 1973. She also studied mime for several years—perhaps good training for the nonverbal language of fashion.

In 1977, Prada met Patrizio Bertelli, who had started his own leather goods manufacturing firm when he was 17. Prada readily followed the charismatic Bertelli's business advice, which included dropping the firm's English suppliers and revamping old-fashioned luggage styles. Sales were about $400,000 a year when Prada inherited the company in 1978.

A New Look in the 1980s

In 1979, Miuccia Prada designed what would eventually become her first commercial hit—backpacks and totes made of a tough, military spec black nylon that her grandfather had used as a protective covering for steamer trunks. Success was not instant, however. In the next few years, Prada and Bertelli sought wholesale accounts for the bags at exclusive department stores and boutiques around the world. They were a hard sell due to their high price tag and complete lack of company advertising.

A second boutique opened in Milan in 1983, this one a sleek and modern contrast to the original one situated in a historic shopping district, the Galleria Vittorio Emanuele II. A black nylon version of the famous Chanel tote was introduced in 1985. A line of footwear was introduced the same year and the company began opening its own stores in Paris, Madrid, Florence, and New York.

Fashioning the 1990s

A ready-to-wear collection of women's clothes debuted in 1989. Prada's clothing designs were known for their dropped waistlines and narrow belts. They also often had a retro element: both Miuccia Prada and her mother rarely threw out their old dresses.

Time described the clothes as "unassertive, combining traditional good manners and an ultramodern industrial sleekness."

Unlike other luxury brands such as Louis Vuitton, the Prada black-and-silver triangle logo was not the dominant design element. The appeal was called "antistatus" or "reverse snobbery." Others would liken Prada to the couture equivalent of the grunge mentality that dominated music and fashion in the early 1990s. Prada was unique among the top fashion houses in embracing a kind of worker esthetic—affluent working women who held demanding jobs identified with it. She would take to calling her women's outfits "uniforms."

Sales were L 70 billion ($31.7 million) in 1990. In 1992, Bertelli gave Partrizio di Marco, who had been working for the firm in Asia, the task of growing the business in the United States. Despite considerable opposition from those who considered the bags too avant-garde, Di Marco succeeded in having them prominently featured in large department stores. Eventually, the elitist yet practical bags became a hit with fashion editors, who assured them their place in fashion history. An important part of the success of Prada's utilitarian products, according to Ginia Bellafante in the *New York Times Magazine,* was that the very idea of work itself was becoming chic in the high-tech, IPO-driven early 1990s.

Miuccia Prada and husband Patrizio Bertelli (they were married in 1987) guided the firm on a path of cautious growth, making its products rather hard to find. A secondary line called Miu Miu retailed for a bit less than the top line and was aimed at a younger market—or "bad girls," as Miuccia Prada called them. "It's about bad taste—which is part of life today," she said in *Time.* Much of the Miu Miu line was constructed out of tacky synthetic fabrics.

By the mid-1990s, Prada was well on its way to becoming the decade's preeminent status symbol for those who could afford $400 backpacks, $165 baseball caps, or $1,000 dresses. A line of men's clothing hit the racks in the mid-1990s. Annual sales rose 30 percent in 1994, reaching $210 million. Clothing sales made up about 20 percent of the total and were expected to double in 1995. In 1996, Prada opened an 18,000-square-foot store in Manhattan—its largest. Prada had 47 stores around the world, 20 of them in Japan. The firm owned eight factories and subcontracted work to another 84 manufacturers in Italy. In 1996, Bertelli's and Prada's respective businesses were merged under a new holding company called Prapar B.V., later renamed Prada B.V., and Bertelli officially became CEO of the Prada group.

Miuccia Prada softened her look somewhat in the late 1990s, though her choice of materials—linen with latex, for example—still seemed unique. Bertelli and Miuccia Prada were contemplating how to broaden their company's reach without diminishing the cachet of the brand. They emphasized the lower priced lines, such as Miu Miu and the new Prada Sport collection, introduced in 1997. A new Miu Miu line for men hit the runways in 1999.

Revenues rose 61 percent in 1997 to $674 million, producing a tidy pretax income of $130 million. The company opened a new men's store in Milan during the year. The *Wall Street Journal* reported that before the opening, Bertelli shattered its windows with a hammer because their arrangements displeased him.

Around the same time, the company was acquiring shares in rival Gucci Group N.V., which Bertelli would accuse of aping his wife's designs. By June 1998 the firm had acquired a 9.5 percent interest at a cost of $260 million. Observers were unsure of Bertelli's intentions; some analysts felt Prada was too small and too debt-laden to consider a takeover attempt. There was speculation that Prada was working in collusion with a third party. At the very least, Prada had a voice as one of Gucci's largest shareholders (a 10 percent holding would be required for the right to request a seat on the board) and would stand to profit tidily should anyone try to take over Gucci. In January 1999, Bertelli sold the shares to LVMH Chairman Bernard Arnault, who was indeed attempting a takeover, for a gross profit of $140 million. (Gucci was able to fend off this advance by selling a 45 percent stake to a white knight, French industrialist François Pinault, for $3 billion.)

1999 Buying Spree

Seeking to build a powerful stable of luxury brands à la Gucci or LVMH, Prada went on a veritable shopping spree in 1999. Bertelli, an avid sailor, and Prada also were spending $50 million to sponsor an entrant in the 2000 America's Cup yacht race.

In March 1999, the firm bought 51 percent of Austrian designer Helmut Lang's New York-based company, which had annual revenues of about $100 million. The deal was potentially worth $40 million. A few months later, Prada paid $105 million to acquire control of Jil Sander A.G., a German fashion house that had sales of about $100 million a year. The purchase was to give Prada a toehold in Germany. Although Jil Sander was to remain in creative control of her namesake company, she resigned as chairwoman a few months later.

In September 1999, Prada announced an agreement to buy 83 percent of Church & Company, a British maker of conservatively styled shoes established in 1873, for $170 million. During the year, a joint venture also was formed with the De Rigo Group to manufacture Prada sunglasses.

An alliance between Prada and LVMH acquired a 51 percent stake in Fendi S.p.A. in October 1999 for a reported $520 million, outbidding rival Gucci. Fendi, which had been owned by the five sisters whose parents had founded the company in 1925, sold trendy $1,500 "Baguette" bags, furs, and sunglasses and was expected to benefit from international distribution in LVMH's global network of shops as well as Prada's production capacity in Italy. Prada paid L 525 billion ($241.5 million) for its 25.5 percent stake in Fendi, which had $321 million in sales in 1998.

The acquisitions propelled Prada to the top ranks of European luxury goods groups. Sales, which exceeded L 2 trillion in 1999, were three times those of 1996. Net income doubled in the year to L 321 billion. The group also had large debt, however.

Prada stepped away from the mergers and acquisitions business in 2000 to digest its purchases, but did sign a loose patronage agreement with maverick designer Azzedine Alaia. A line of skin care products, all packaged in individual foil-wrapped doses, was introduced in the United States in October 2000. The products included creams, face masks, and lip balms. A 30-day supply of cleansing lotion cost $100.

Sales reached L 3.2 million in 2000, a 57 percent rise, while operating profit grew 37 percent to L 600 billion. An initial public offering was planned for July 2001 on the Milan stock market. Prada Holding B.V. planned to float 30 percent of the company to help pay off debts of $830 million and expand distribution. Prada seemed to have succeeded in turning around the troubled Jil Sanders line, though new store openings were consuming the profits. A slowdown in luxury spending, however, particularly in Japan and the United States, prompted Prada to delay the offering.

Aside from the IPO, Prada also had big plans for four new megastores, or "epicenters" of the "Prada universe," to be located in Beverly Hills, New York, San Francisco, and Tokyo. The company hoped to change the shopping experience into one of community involvement, transforming shoppers into "researchers, students, patients, museum goers." Dutch architect Rem Koolhaas and the Swiss team of Jacques Herzog and Pierre de Meuron were commissioned to design the stores.

According to *Fortune,* Bertelli planned to increase sales to $5 billion by 2010. Under pressure from his bankers, in November 2001 Bertelli sold Prada's 25.5 percent share in Fendi to LVMH, its equal partner in the venture, raising $295 million to help pay down debt.

Principal Subsidiaries

Church & Company (U.K.); De Rigo S.p.A. (5%); Helmut Lang Design LLC (U.S.A.; 51%); I Pellettieri d'Italia S.p.A.; Jil Sander A.G. (Germany; 52%); Sir Robert S.r.l. (77%).

Principal Competitors

Christian Dior S.A.; Giorgio Armani S.p.A.; Gucci Group N.V.; LVMH Moët Hennessy Louis Vuitton S.A.

Further Reading

Avins, Mimi, "A Clean Break; Prada Switches from Dowdy to Darling with a Collection That Celebrates the Feminine Form of Modern Women," *Los Angeles Times,* October 9, 1997, p. E1.

Ball, Deborah, "Can Prada Turn Heads on the Stock Market's Catwalk?," *Wall Street Journal,* May 23, 2001, p. A23.

——, "LVMH and Prada Seek to Bag New Riches with Fendi," *Wall Street Journal,* June 26, 2000, p. B4.

——, "Prada Fitting: Plans Are Drawn for Its Purchases," *Wall Street Journal,* May 8, 2000, p. A39.

——, "Prada Owner's Style Casts Doubts About Integration of Jil Sander," *Wall Street Journal,* June 20, 2000, p. B8.

——, "Prada Sets Focus on Consolidating Its Latest Purchases," *Wall Street Journal,* May 4, 2000, p. B14.

——, "Prada, Weighing IPO, Reports Turnaround in Sander's Results," *Wall Street Journal,* May 10, 2001, p. C16.

Barrett, Amy, and Maureen Kline, "Prada's Stock Purchase Shows Gucci Susceptible to Takeover," *Wall Street Journal,* June 11, 1998, p. A19.

Bellafante, Ginia, "The Axis of Austerity," *New York Times Magazine,* November 14, 1999.

——, "Jil Sander Is Divorcing Prada," *New York Times,* January 25, 2000, p. B10.

Cowell, Alan, "Prada in $170 Million Deal for Church, the Shoemaker," *New York Times,* Intl. Bus. Sec., September 10, 1999, p. 6.

Duffy, Martha, and David E. Thigpen, ''Understated Art,'' *Time,* November 20, 1995, p. 108.

Emerling, Susan, ''Prada Enters a New Frontier of Retailing; Four Flagship Stores with Cutting-Edge Designs Will Be More About Social Interaction and Exploration Than Selling Shoes and Clothes,'' *Los Angeles Times,* April 16, 2001, p. E1.

Givhan, Robin, ''After the Runway, a Safe Landing,'' *Washington Post,* November 10, 1996, p. F3.

Goldstein, Lauren, ''Prada Goes Shopping,'' *Fortune,* September 27, 1999, pp. 207–10.

Guyon, Janet, ''Prada Steps Out,'' *Fortune,* October 1, 2001, pp. 149–54.

Horyn, Cathy, ''For Alaia, a Retrospective and a New Deal,'' *New York Times,* September 23, 2000, p. B7.

——, ''Unusual Packaging for New Prada Line,'' *New York Times,* October 9, 2000, p. B11.

Hyam, Tim, ''Warm Welcome for Italian Newcomers,'' *Corporate Finance* (London), Capital Markets Quarterly Supplement, Spring 1998, pp. 5–6.

''Italian, German Fashion Houses to Join Forces,'' *Wall Street Journal,* September 1, 1999, p. B5.

Kamm, Thomas, and Deborah Ball, ''LVMH, Prada Open Purse Strings to Bag Fendi,'' *Wall Street Journal,* October 13, 1999, p. A26.

Kaufman, Leslie, ''Putting Fendi into a Bigger Bag,'' *New York Times,* October 17, 1999.

Kline, Maureen, and Wendy Bounds, ''Battle of Italy's Fashion Houses Seen As Prada Boosts Stake in Rival Gucci,'' *Wall Street Journal,* June 18, 1998, p. B14.

Lippert, Barbara, ''Future Cool,'' *Adweek,* January 3, 2000, p. 20.

Luscombe, Belinda, ''Catfight on the Catwalk,'' *Time,* June 22, 1998, pp. 46–48.

McCormick, Herb, ''Hey, Sailor, Looking Good,'' *New York Times,* February 13, 2000.

Phillips, Angus, ''Bertelli's Goal: Prada's Perfection,'' *Washington Post,* January 23, 2000, p. D6.

Rotenier, Nancy, ''Antistatus Backpacks, $450 a Copy,'' *Forbes,* June 19, 1995, p. 118.

Snead, Elizabeth, ''Prada Has a Handle on Chic Bags,'' *USA Today,* June 29, 1994, p. D5.

Tagliabue, John, ''French-Italian Alliance Takes Controlling Stake in Fendi,'' *New York Times,* Intl. Bus. Sec., October 13, 1999, p. 4.

Wallace, Charles P., and Angela Buttolph, ''A Feeding Frenzy,'' *Time South Pacific,* October 18, 1999, pp. 66+.

White, Constance C.R., ''Once a Private Club, Prada Opens Its Doors,'' *New York Times,* September 15, 1998, p. B16.

—Frederick C. Ingram

Psion PLC

12 Park Crescent, London W1B 1PH
United Kingdom
Telephone: (+44) 20-7317-4100
Fax: (+44) 20-7258-7340
Web site: http://www.psion.com

Public Company
Incorporated: 1980 as Potter Scientific Instruments, Ltd.
Employees: 1,032
Sales: £219.17 million ($327.6 million) (2000)
Stock Exchanges: London OTC
Ticker Symbols: PON PSIOF (OTC)
NAIC: 334119 Other Computer Peripheral Equipment
   Manufacturing; 511210 Software Publishers

Britain's Psion PLC is reinventing itself. The pioneer in hand-held computers has announced that it will discontinue its production of mobile computer products for the consumer market in 2001 and instead reorient itself as a manufacturer of wireless and mobile devices for industrial applications under main subsidiary Psion Teklogix. This subsidiary has been built on the company's existing commercial and industrial products activities and its September 2000 acquisition of Canada's Teklogix. The acquisition of Teklogix has enabled the company to maintain its revenues, which topped £219 million in 2000, despite its decision to exit the personal digital assistant (PDA) market. Nonetheless, the company continues to sell and support its existing consumer products—including the Series 5 and 7 hand-helds, the internet-connectable Revo and the Wavefinder Digital Audio Broadcast receiver, as well as PC Card modems and connectivity components—through its newly created division Psion Digital, which consolidates the company's former Psion Computers, Psion Connect, and Psion Infomedia divisions. Part of the company's decision to restructure comes from its disappointment after Motorola pulled out of the companies' partnership to develop next-generation digital "smartphones." Psion also owns 28 percent of the Symbian Ltd. joint venture with Nokia, Motorola, Ericcson, and Panasonic. This company is redeveloping Psion's EPOC operating system for the mobile telecommunications market. Psion is led by founder and Chairman David Potter and CEO David Levin and is traded on the London Stock Exchange and on the U.S. OTC market.

PDA Pioneer in the 1980s

David Potter grew up in East London, South Africa. Potter's father died when he was still a baby, and Potter was raised by his mother, a nurse, and his grandmother. Potter was an excellent student, winning a scholarship to study at Cambridge University in England in 1963. Potter, who worked a series of odd jobs to support himself as a student, went on to earn a Ph.D. in mathematical physics and then went to work as a lecturer for the University of London and California.

The stock market crash in the early 1970s led Potter to recognize that a number of stocks were undervalued. Taking his £3,000 in savings, Potter invested in such large companies as Racal Electronics, General Electric, and Xerox. Smitten by the investment bug and forecasting a coming high-technology boom, Potter began seeking out investments in smaller companies. "I figured I was good at research, smaller companies were not well researched, and I could find opportunities to invest," Potter told the *Daily Telegraph*. "Then, when the chip came along, bingo."

Potter's investment in the nascent semiconductor industry had made him wealthy. His interest in computers prompted him to go into business for himself. "I would never have been comfortable being an academic all my life. The growth of the semiconductor industry was clearly going to have a huge impact on the world. And I've always felt you've got to take your opportunities in life," Potter told the *Daily Telegraph*.

In 1980, Potter used £70,000 of his own to set up Potter Scientific Instruments—which could be abbreviated as the Greek letter "Psi." Possible trademark conflicts with another company caused Potter to add a suffix—"on"—because of its high-tech sound and its similarity to the giant Exxon. "That's an enormous entity, but you have to have ambition," Potter told the *European*. The company quickly became known simply as Psion (which, to its fans, was short for Potter Scientific Instruments—Or Nothing).

Joined by a number of Potter's students, Psion first concentrated on developing games and other software products for the Sinclair computer, one of the earliest personal computer designs. The company also opened a subsidiary in South Africa in 1981. Psion hit pay dirt in 1982 when it released a flight simulator program, selling more than a million copies. The company became one of the leading software developers in Europe, with sales of £1.6 million by the end of that year.

For Potter, software was only a means to a more lofty ambition, that of creating a computer hardware company. Sales of the company's flight simulator program gave it the finances to begin development of its own hardware products. "In the autumn of 1982 I found myself sitting in a Greek restaurant with one of my colleagues, Charles Davies, who had been my brightest doctoral student. We began to sketch out on napkins a hole in the market and a hardware product to fill it." That first product, released in 1984, was called the Organiser.

The Organiser represented somewhat of a revolution, becoming the world's first hand-held computer. The product featured a database and clock, one kilobyte of memory, and a one-line LED screen, along with an alphabetic keyboard and plastic cover. Although originally designed for the consumer market, the Organiser found a strong market among corporate and commercial users—such as Marks & Spencer, which used the device for their inventory system.

Psion released the next generation of the Organiser in 1986. The Organiser II featured as much as 64k of memory and quickly developed a reputation for being rugged; some models were still in use nearly 15 years later. The company had tapped into the consumer retail market—the Organiser II became considered a necessity among business users—and its sales swelled past £10 million. The following year, stock market buff Potter brought his own company to the market, listing the company on the London stock exchange.

"Filofax of the 1990s"

Potter and Psion recognized the potential for combining its hand-held technology with the new market for data transmission. In 1989, the company acquired Dacom, a maker of PC card-based modems and other portable devices. That same year, Psion attempted to adapt its technology to a new and promising market, that of the portable computer. The company released the first of its MC (Mobile Computers) series, the MC 200, which featured a 16-bit operating system, a touchpad, and a 640×200 LCD screen. The company produced four different MCs, culminating with the MC Word model, featuring a built-in word processor. But the company was unable to com-

pete against the rise of the PC-compatible computer and quickly ended its notebook computer production.

Meanwhile, the company's Organiser sales were being hammered by a wave of new competitors, as giant companies such as Sharp and Canon began to dominate the organizer market. Industry observers were wondering how long Psion would be able to last in the increasingly competitive technology market. The company was struggling, and by 1991 had slipped into losses.

Psion responded in 1991 with its Series 3 hand-held computers—which were becoming known as palmtops—and set a new industry standard. The first organizer to feature a "clamshell" design, the Series 3 offered up to 256k of memory, with a 16-bit, multitasking graphical interface driven by its own keyboard. More important, the device offered fully functional software programs, such as database, spreadsheet, and word processing capability. The Series 3 became the first hand-held to offer similar capabilities to the personal computer and proved the company's next great success, selling more than 1.5 million units by the middle of the decade.

At the same time, Psion launched its HC series, based on the Organiser, designed for corporate use. The HC featured a particularly rugged design, which in turn inspired the company to bring out the Workabout, a rubber-enclosed version of the Organiser designed specifically for an industrial environment, first released in 1993.

Psion prepared a new generation of the Series 3, and in 1993 the company launched the Series 3a to popular acclaim. The new generation, which later offered up to two megabytes of memory, quickly captured the leading share of the palmtop market. Psion's hand-held soon became known as the "Filo-fax of the 1990s."

Meanwhile, Psion was attempting to enter the U.S. market. By 1994, however, the company's sales had topped £100 million but remained almost entirely limited to Europe, and especially to its core U.K. market. Despite holding what many considered to be superior technology, Psion lacked the marketing muscle to compete in the United States, particularly against the growing number of PDAs and their handwriting recognition technology. Yet in the United Kingdom at least, the Series 3 remained Psion's true star in the first half of the 1990s, driving its sales up to £124 million by 1996. By then the company had opened subsidiaries in The Netherlands and Germany, with distribution of its products to more than 45 countries.

In 1996, Psion reorganized its operations to cope with its fast growth. The company now created four divisions, operating as subsidiaries: Psion Computers, which took over its hand-held business for the consumer and corporate markets; Psion Industrial, later named Psion Enterprise, which focused on portable data collection systems for the industrial market; Psion Dacom, dedicated to developing modems and other communications and connectivity devices; and Psion Software, which took over the company's software development operations.

That same year the company released the Series 3c, offering features such as infrared ports and back-lighted screens. The company also attempted to enter a growing mid-range category of devices with the Siena, a smaller and lighter version of the

<table>
<tr><td colspan="2">Key Dates:</td></tr>
<tr><td>1980:</td><td>David Potter founds Psion as developer of computer software.</td></tr>
<tr><td>1982:</td><td>Flight Simulator, which sells over one million copies, is released.</td></tr>
<tr><td>1984:</td><td>Organiser, first hand-held computer, is launched.</td></tr>
<tr><td>1986:</td><td>Organiser II is launched and becomes best-seller.</td></tr>
<tr><td>1988:</td><td>Psion goes public on the London stock exchange.</td></tr>
<tr><td>1989:</td><td>The company acquires Dacom modem products manufacturer; attempts to enter notebook computer market with MC series.</td></tr>
<tr><td>1991:</td><td>The company introduces the highly successful Series 3 hand-held computer.</td></tr>
<tr><td>1993:</td><td>Series 3a is released and Psion becomes the leading maker of hand-held computers.</td></tr>
<tr><td>1996:</td><td>Psion restructures into four divisions. Computers, Industrial, Dacom, and Software.</td></tr>
<tr><td>1997:</td><td>Series 5 is released, to critical acclaim.</td></tr>
<tr><td>1998:</td><td>The company spins off Psion Software into Symbian joint venture.</td></tr>
<tr><td>1999:</td><td>The company debuts the Series 7 hand-held and the Revo personal digital assistant (PDA).</td></tr>
<tr><td>2000:</td><td>The company acquires Teklogix International (Canada), which is renamed as Psion Teklogix and becomes the company's largest division.</td></tr>
<tr><td>2001:</td><td>The company restructures operations into Psion Teklogix and Psion Digital divisions; announces major decision to discontinue development of hand-held computers for the consumer market.</td></tr>
</table>

Series 3 devices. The Siena was plagued by fragility problems, however, and was quickly abandoned by the company.

A more successful launch came in 1997 when the company released its acclaimed Series 5 (there was no Series 4—the number was considered bad luck in some Asian countries). The new hand-held, which received high marks for its hardware features and especially its keyboard, also featured the new EPOC operating system, a powerful 32-bit multitasking platform designed not just for the company's hand-held, but also to power the coming integration of computing and mobile communications technologies. Yet the company was hampered by its limited production capacity and found itself unable to meet the demand for its products.

New Direction for a New Century

Psion attempted to license EPOC to other hardware companies; yet the U.K. company now found itself under attack from two U.S. companies. On the one side was U.S. Robotics (later 3Com), which was rapidly taking over the U.S. and then world market with the Palm Pilot. On the other side was none other than Microsoft Corporation, which had released its Windows CE operating system—and, in an internal memo, had labeled Psion as its "number one global threat." Yet the new generation of PDAs, which, while more limited in their functionality, were smaller and lighter than Psion's products and also less expensive, soon all but locked Psion out of the U.S. market. By the end of the decade, the new generation, led by the innovative Palm, had begun to make serious inroads in Psion's home territory as well.

As a defensive move, Psion spun off its software division, including the EPOC operating system, into a joint venture with Nokia, Motorola, and Ericsson (joined by Matsushita Panasonic the following year) in 1998. The new venture, called Symbian Ltd., set out to adapt EPOC as the operating system driving the coming new generation of so-called "smartphones," set to give mobile telephones entirely new functions. Psion's share of the joint venture was set at 28 percent; Symbian itself, which was planning a public offering, was soon given an estimated market value of as much as £7 billion.

Meanwhile, the company's hand-held sales continued to be battered by the competition. Despite the launch of two new products in 1999, the Series 7 hand-held and the hand-held internet-connectable Revo, the company sales were slipping. By the end of that year, Psion had posted sales of slightly more than £150 million, down nearly £10 million over the year before.

Psion, led since 1998 by CEO David Levin, began to prepare itself for a new future. In 2000, the company paid nearly $370 million to acquire Teklogix International of Canada, which developed products and software based on its own wireless technology. The acquisition, which boosted the company's sales to nearly £220 million in 2000, also created the company's largest division, dubbed Psion Teklogix.

Psion Teklogix enabled the company to make an about-face the following year. The company had been banking on its joint development agreement with Motorola to create a new wireless hand-held device. When, as the result of the shrinking economy, Motorola pulled the plug on the project in 2001, Psion was forced to abandon its plans to enter the smartphone area.

In July 2001, Psion announced that it was restructuring its operations again, now into two divisions: Psion Teklogix, which was to become the company's main operational focus; and Psion Digital, which inherited its consumer hand-held as well as its Psion Connect modem and communications products. At the same time the company announced that it was abandoning new development in the hand-held and PDA market; by then, the company's share of the European market had slipped to less than 9 percent. Yet, despite being overtaken in a market that the company itself had created, Psion had successfully reinvented itself as a provider to another booming market, that of wireless mobile and enterprise IT systems.

Principal Subsidiaries

Psion Computers PLC; Psion Connect Ltd; Psion InfoMedia Ltd; Psion Nederlands BV (Netherlands); Psion GmbH (Germany); Psion Inc. (U.S.A.); Psion France SAS (France); Psion Services Ltd; Psion Property Ltd (France); Psion Teklogix Inc. (Canada); Psion Teklogix Corporation (U.S.A.); Psion Teklogix de Mexico SA; Psion Teklogix do Brasil Ltda; Psion Teklogix de Argentina SA; Psion Teklogix Ltd; Psion Teklogix (U.K.) Ltd; Psion Teklogix GmbH (Germany); Psion Teklogix SA (France); Psion Teklogix BV (Netherlands); Teklogix AB (Sweden); Psion Teklogix Italia Srl; Psion Teklogix Espana SL;

Psion Teklogix Systems India Pvt Ltd (India); Psion Teklogix Africa (Pty) Ltd (South Africa); Symbian Ltd. (28%).

Principal Divisions

Psion Teklogix; Psion Digital.

Principal Competitors

@pos.com; Handspring Inc.; Hewlett-Packard Corporation; Kontron Mobile Computing AG; LG Group; Minorplanet Systems Plc; National Datacomputer Inc.; NCR Corporation; Palm Inc.; Philips Electronics NV; Research In Motion Limited; Wyse Technology Inc.

Further Reading

Baker, Stephen, "Why Psion's Stock Is Acting So Frisky," *Business Week International,* March 20, 2000, p. 23.

Dowsett, Sonya, "Psion Slides on Lack of Firm Future Guidance," *Reuters,* August 29, 2001.

Koenig, Peter, "Profile: David Potter: Go on, Give Us a Tax Rise," *Independent on Sunday,* March 15, 1998, p. 5.

Morrison, Doug, "Psion's Organiser," *Sunday Telegraph,* June 28, 1998.

Moss, Nicholas, "Psion Holds the Future in Palm of Its Hand," *European,* June 12, 1997, p. 19.

Pain, Steve, "Psion Fans Lament Loss of PDA," *Birmingham Post,* July 24, 2001, p. 22.

Phillips, Tim, "Psion Gets a Painful Lesson in the Economies of Scale," *International Herald Tribune,* November 16, 2001.

Reeve, Simon, "Is Psion Psinking?," *European,* March 16, 1998, p. 26.

Schoonakker, Bonny, "Britain's Answer to Bill Gates Is a South African," *Sunday Times Business Times,* October 11, 1998.

Vaughan-Adams, Liz, "Psion Looks to Future As It Quits Organiser Market," *Independent,* July 12, 2001, p. 17.

Wallace, Charles P., "What's So Scary About David Potter?," *Fortune,* November 23, 1998, p. 257.

—M.L. Cohen

R.B. Pamplin Corp.

900 SW 5th Avenue
Portland, Oregon 97204
U.S.A.
Telephone: (503) 248-1133
Fax: (503) 248-1175
Web site: http://www.pamplin.org

Private Company
Incorporated: 1957
Employees: 7,500
Sales: $800 million (2000 est.)
NAIC: 31321 Broadwoven Fabric Mills; 551112 Office
of Other Holding Companies; 31323 Nonwoven
Fabrics (Manufacturers); 32411 Petroleum Products
(Manufacturers); 324121 Asphalt and Asphalt
Products (Manufacturers); 32732 Ready-Mixed
Concrete (Manufacturers); 42139 Construction
Materials (Wholesale)

R.B. Pamplin Corp. is a holding and investment company with two major operations, Ross Island Sand & Gravel Co. in Oregon and Mount Vernon Mills Inc. in South Carolina. The company's American-made textiles are its hallmark; its close to 20 facilities produce a variety of fabrics, including denim. The company owns and operates the world's largest denim mill, which produces 90 million linear yards of cloth per year. Pamplin Corp. also has a number of subsidiaries; its other ventures include Columbia Empire Farms and Pamplin Communications Corp., a Christian retail and music company.

Making Strategic Acquisitions: 1970s

Robert B. Pamplin, Sr., was born in 1911 in Virginia. After earning a bachelor's degree from Virginia Polytechnic Institute in 1933 and graduating from Northwestern University in Illinois as a certified public accountant, he went to work as an accountant in 1934 at a then relatively small wholesale lumber firm, Georgia-Pacific Corp. As the company's fifth employee, he worked his way up its corporate ladder to become secretary-treasurer, then financial vice-president, administrative vice-president, executive vice-president, and, finally, chairman of the board and chief executive officer in 1957. During his tenure, the company's revenues climbed from $121 million to $3 billion. By the time he retired due to company policy on his 65th birthday on November 25, 1976, Georgia-Pacific had grown to employ 40,000 and had evolved into one of the largest integrated manufacturers of plywood, lumber, gypsum, and other building products in addition to pulp, paper, and paper products.

While at Georgia-Pacific, Pamplin placed 20,000 shares of the company in a family holding company known as R.B. Pamplin Corp. in 1957. Since tax laws at the time made it important to balance stock dividends with other income, R.B. Pamplin purchased real estate. Eventually, he acquired Ross Island Sand & Gravel Co. and the Oregon Bank Building in Portland. The Ross Island purchase occurred on the day Pamplin cleaned out his desk at Georgia-Pacific.

Pamplin, Sr., joined by his son, Robert Pamplin, Jr., moved Pamplin Corp. into the same Portland, Oregon building as Georgia-Pacific, nine floors down from the offices where he used to work. Pamplin, Jr., had begun his career in business as an accountant for R.B. Pamplin real estate. He, too, had evinced a knack for business early on. He started investing in stocks as a teenager. Having followed in his father's footsteps to Virginia Tech in the 1960s, he used a $160,000 bequest from his grandmother and caught the rise of the stock market, making his first million while still an undergraduate. He later invested his profits in timber and farmlands, which immediately shot up in value, and also invested $30,000 in an unproven ''cutting'' horse that yielded $2 million in stud fees and $850,000 when sold. Pamplin, Jr., earned two master's degrees, one in business administration and one in education at the University of Portland, and after a bout with cancer in 1975, a master's and a doctorate at Western Conservative Baptist Seminary in Portland, Oregon. He founded Christ Community Church to provide a food bank-type program to more than 50 relief agencies in Portland.

From their 18th floor offices, Pamplin Corp. bought significant portions of companies without either Pamplin ever visiting the physical plant of any purchase. Pamplin, Sr., sought out firms he felt were undervalued based upon reading their annual reports and financial statements. He especially liked medium-sized, old companies—those that had been in business for 90 to 100 years, had key management and shareholders at around retirement age, and possessed substantial net worth per share. These he reasoned probably had plenty of assets.

Textiles especially met Pamplin's acquisition criteria. He had started buying stock in Mount Vernon Mills in 1972 when the company was a good buy. "I saw it was a company that was undervalued and saw a lot of potential there," the man who was known for his willingness to speak his mind was quoted as saying in a 1982 *Oregonian* article. When he "got in a fuss with [Mount Vernon's] management" in 1982, he purchased the remaining outstanding shares of the company in order to replace its managers and undertook a $5 million expansion program to improve operations. At the time, Mount Vernon had annual sales of about $100 million. In 1985, Pamplin Corp. purchased Riegel Textile Corporation in an $87 million transaction, adding it to his textile operations.

The new conglomerate employed about 6,650 people in 1986 and generated $400 million in revenues, netting $23 million after taxes. With the 1985 acquisition of Riegel, it moved from 13th to fourth in a ranking of Oregon's privately held corporations. The company's close to 20 mills in Alabama, North and South Carolina, Georgia, and Virginia made Pamplin one of the largest American textile manufacturers. The company made "greige goods," such as gauze, yarn, and print cloth; denim, material for work clothes, and uniforms; tent material; upholstery for cars and fabrics for recreational vehicles; draperies; and finished consumer goods, such as towels, cloth napkins, tablecloths, mattress pads, blankets, and infantwear.

As owners of Oregon's fourth largest privately held corporation, the Pamplins maintained a hands-on approach at Pamplin Corp. Pamplin, Sr., personally invested the corporate retirement funds and Pamplin, Jr., did his own typing. Management philosophy according to Pamplin, Sr., in a 1982 *Oregonian* article, was to be "sensitive to the people . . . You give employees an opportunity to divide the profits . . . and the more they make, the more I make." However, when employees were not willing to cooperate, Pamplin was prepared to shut a place down. The conglomerate overall operated according to the same decentralized approach Pamplin, Sr., used at Georgia-Pacific. The company was divided into profit centers, whose operations had to show a 15 percent return on investment. Management vocally abhorred waste and inefficiency.

The Pamplins also became known for their commitment to philanthropy. In 1986, Pamplin, Sr., gave $10 million to Virginia Tech, and they named the College of Business after him. In 1992, Pamplin, Jr., chairman of the board of Lewis and Clark College in Portland, challenged its students and staff to meet or

beat him in a series of physical fitness activities in return for his donation of up to $1 million. Pamplin, Jr., also supported the SEI Pamplin Project, a program of peer leadership run by Self Enhancement Inc., an organization focused on developing the self-esteem of inner city youth. In 1999, the Pamplin Foundation gave almost $11 million to the University of Portland. The corporation yearly donated a tenth of its pretax profits to mostly local causes.

1990s: Steady Growth and Diversification

Throughout the 1990s, Pamplin Corp. grew steadily. Its 1993 revenues from its mills and Ross Island totaled almost $700 million, on which the company made a $50 million profit. The Pamplins formed Pamplin Communications Corp. as the media arm of the business. In 1993, this division purchased Christian Supply Centers, Inc., six retail stores specializing in religious educational materials for home schooling in the Portland metropolitan area. In 1998, Christian Supply Centers developed a national sales department, which contributed to a 25 to 50 percent increase in the chain's growth. By 1998, it had 13 stores in Oregon, Washington, and Idaho; by 1999, it had 25. Pamplin Music Company, a division of Pamplin Communications, was the fourth largest independent distributor of Christian music by 2001.

In 1998, in a very different venture, Pamplin, Jr., teamed up with a former employee of Made in Oregon, a chain of stores that sold items manufactured in Oregon exclusively, to form Your Northwest, which opened its first store in Dundee, Oregon, in 1998. Your Northwest provided an outlet for Pamplin, Jr.'s Columbia Empire Farms' produce—hazelnuts, berry preserves, and hazelnut confections. When Pamplin, Jr., purchased a vineyard, Your Northwest became an outlet for its wines as well.

By 2000, Pamplin Communications had six radio stations, five in Oregon and Washington and one in California. In 2000, the subsidiary bought Community Newspapers, Inc., through which it gained control of 11 suburban Portland papers that had a combined circulation of 175,000. In 2001, the newly inaugurated *Portland Tribune*, owned and published by Pamplin Communications, went head-to-head with the 150-year-old *Oregonian*, the first paper to do so in 20 years. Delivered free to somewhere between 120,000 and 150,000 households in Portland on Tuesdays and Fridays, the 30-page paper, like the Pamplin's radio stations, distinguished itself by focusing on local and regional news. Pamplin's professed goal: To provide a second community voice for Portland. Several journalists left the *Oregonian* to join the staff of 28 of the *Portland Tribune*.

But although some welcomed the Pamplins move into media, others criticized it, including an article in the *American Journalism Review* after the *Tribune* organized a boat tour of Ross Island for local officials and published a front-page article on the event in 2001, the same year Pamplin, Jr., was named entrepreneur of the year by Oregon Entrepreneurs Forum. Pamplin Corp., whose revenues then totaled about $800 million, had mined the island over the years to a horseshoe-shaped fraction of what it had been and rebuilt its beaches with dredge spoils from Portland harbor's oil terminals. Although "Rebirth of an Island," the article in the *Tribune*, focused on Ross Island Gravel & Sand's plans to rebuild the island and turn it over to

Key Dates:

1957: While still a Georgia-Pacific executive, Robert B. Pamplin, Sr., uses company stock to fund a family holding company known as R.B. Pamplin Corp., which was initially used to purchase real estate.

1976: Pamplin, Sr., retires as chairman and CEO of Georgia-Pacific Corp. and purchases Ross Island Sand & Gravel.

1982: Pamplin Corp. acquires Mount Vernon Mills, Inc. by increasing its ownership to 32 percent of outstanding shares.

1985: Pamplin acquires Riegel Textile Corporation.

1993: Pamplin Communications Corp., a subsidiary, purchases Christian Supply Centers, Inc.

2000: Pamplin Communications buys Community Newspapers, Inc. and inaugurates the *Portland Tribune*.

the city, it was criticized locally as a piece of slanted journalism. The article neglected to announce that the *Tribune* had organized the island tour, raising objections that the paper had compromised its journalistic integrity by functioning as a public relations organ. That integrity was reinstated somewhat when Pamplin Broadcasting donated a substantial sum toward the Oregon Public Affairs Network's goal of creating a new television and internet broadcasting service providing gavel-to-gavel coverage of important state proceedings.

By the early years of the new century, it was hard to predict what directions Pamplin Corp. would branch off into next. The *Fortune* 500 company owned by two of Oregon's wealthiest men, the father and son duo that preached hard work and duty to develop one's gifts, seemed able to purchase and foster practically anything it desired.

Principal Subsidiaries

Mount Vernon Mills, Inc.; Ross Island Sand & Gravel Co.; K.F. Jacobsen & Co.; Pamplin Broadcasting; Pamplin Communications; Pamplin Entertainment; R.B. Pamplin Jr. Farm; B. Gentle Concrete Construction Co.; Oregon Publications Corp.; Pacific Northwest Aggregates, Inc.; Pamplin Communications Corp.

Principal Competitors

Avondale Industries, Inc.; Cone Mills Corporation; U.S. Concrete.

Further Reading

Berns, Dave, "Disciple of Discipline," *Portland Business Today*, June 3, 1987, p. 25.

Eisler, Gary, "Bob Pamplin's Second Career," *Forbes*, May 18, 1987, p. 182.

——, "Climbing Back to the Top," *Oregon Business*, October 1986, p. 31.

Pamplin, Robert B., Jr., et al., *Heritage: The Making of an American Family*, New York: Master Media Limited, 1994.

Sherman, Christopher, "Owning It All," *American Journalism Review*, September 2001, p. 16.

Sorenson, Donald J., "G-P Ex-Chief Runs Multimillion 'Family Concern,' "*Oregonian*, June 14, 1982, p. D5.

—Carrie Rothburd

RANGE RESOURCES

Range Resources Corporation

777 Main Street, Suite 800
Fort Worth, Texas 76102
U.S.A.
Telephone: (817) 870-2601
Fax: (817) 870-2601
Web site: http://www.rangeresources.com

Public Company
Incorporated: 1980 as Lomak Petroleum Inc.
Employees: 139
Sales: $187.7 million (2000)
Stock Exchanges: New York
Ticker Symbol: RRC
NAIC: 211111 Crude Petroleum and Natural Gas
Extraction

Range Resources Corporation is a Fort Worth, Texas, oil and gas company, primarily focused on the drilling of established, lower-risk properties. Nonetheless, it has also become more active in higher-risk exploration projects on some of its underdeveloped properties. Range Resources was created in 1998, the result of a merger between Lomak Petroleum Inc. and Domain Energy Corp. More than 70 percent of its reserves are natural gas, of which 83 percent are company-operated. Range Resources' primary development areas are the Appalachian Basin of eastern Ohio, western Pennsylvania, western New York, and West Virginia; the Permian Basin of west Texas; midcontinent properties of Oklahoma and the Texas Panhandle; and the Gulf Coast region. Whereas the vast majority of the company's drilling is done onshore, Range Resources engages in a limited amount of offshore drilling on the continental shelf of the Gulf of Mexico. It also had an operation in southern Argentina, inherited from Domain, which was sold just after the merger.

Lomak Petroleum Dating Back to 1976

The surviving corporate structure, and oldest of the two companies that formed Range Resources, was Lomak Petroleum, operating out of Hartville, Ohio. It was founded and

incorporated in the state of Ohio in 1976 by a group of investors led by C. Rand Michaels, who became the chief executive, and K.G. Hungerford, a certified public accountant who became secretary-treasurer of the corporation. Michaels held a B.S. from Auburn University as well as an M.B.A. from the University of Denver, and gained previous executive experience at DuPont, BASF, and Edge Industries. Lomak, along with an affiliated partnership, acquired gas and oil-bearing properties in the Appalachian Basin and contracted outside companies to perform the actual drilling. In 1980 the company reorganized as a Delaware corporation, and a short time later made an initial public offering of stock, netting close to $3.4 million. Shares then began to trade on the NASDAQ. With an infusion of capital, Lomak expanded its small operations, staffing an exploration and geology department, and creating a construction and oil field service equipment division.

In 1981, the company's first full year since its reorganization, Lomak generated almost $9 million in revenues and posted net income of $185,000. In that year the company also entered into a joint venture with a subsidiary of The Gillette Company, forming CLK Associates. Over the next two years Gillette would buy more Lomak stock, eventually owning as much as a 10.3 percent stake. For Gillette the association with Lomak was an attempt to secure a source for petroleum products used in the plastic resins required for many of its consumer products. Revenues topped $17 million in both 1982 and 1983, and Lomak was profitable enough to think about expanding its activities beyond the Appalachian Basin to become a multiregional company. It established subsidiaries in Michigan and Texas, and although net income fell off somewhat, sales exceeded $21.5 million.

Acquisition of Lomak by Snyder Oil: 1988

An extended period of depressed oil and gas prices had a crippling effect on Lomak starting in 1985. Although the company pumped more product and revenues grew to $22.3 million, it lost $2.4 million. A cutback in drilling activity the next year saw revenues decline to $11.1 million, and income, to a further loss of $1.35 million. Conditions for Lomak grew even worse in 1987 when it was forced to discontinue its activities in Michigan

---

Company Perspectives:

The Company seeks to build value primarily through lower-risk development drilling and acquisitions while, to a lesser degree, pursuing higher-risk exploitation and exploration projects on its extensive inventory of underdeveloped acreage.

---

and Texas. For the year, the company generated just $7.5 million in sales while losing another $6 million. Lacking the minimal level of required stockholder equity, Lomak was delisted by the NASDAQ in 1987. By early 1988 it was clear that the company would no longer be able to meet debt payments. As a result, Lomak was acquired by Snyder Oil Company.

Snyder Oil was founded by Harvard graduate John C. Snyder. Two of his executives would be assigned the task of restructuring Lomak. Michaels stepped down as chairman and CEO in favor of Thomas J. Edelman, who had served as Snyder's vice-chairman after earlier merging his company with Snyder Oil. Michaels now assumed the roles of president and COO. Also joining Lomak as a vice-president and director was John H. Pinkerton, who would eventually rise to the top of the company and continue to serve as president of Range Resources. Pinkerton earned an M.B.A. at the University of Texas, then worked with Arthur Andersen for four years before joining Snyder Oil in 1981.

As part of the Lomak restructuring, all of the directors resigned, except for Michaels, whose stake in the company was reduced from 25 percent to around 3 percent. Edelman and Pinkerton now called the shots. In 1992, headquarters was moved to Fort Worth, Texas, where Snyder Oil was located. Because the company held properties that were widely dispersed, it had been saddled with exorbitant overhead costs, as much as 30 to 50 percent of cash flow. The new management team dissolved joint ventures and sold off all assets and operations outside of Ohio. Overhead costs, as a result, dropped to less than 15 percent. After a secondary offering of stock, Lomak began to once again acquire oil and gas properties, following a strategy employed by Snyder Oil in Texas in which it looked to concentrate assets to create efficient operations and gain economies of scale. Although revenues fell to less than $5 million in 1989, the company posted a profit, $103,000, for the first time in five years. Lomak's financial picture had improved enough that in early 1990 it was able to request relisting on the NASDAQ.

As Snyder Oil began to divest its stake in Lomak, Pinkerton gained more executive control. He became president in 1990 and CEO in 1992. From the restructuring of the company in 1988 through early 1995, Lomak spent more than $131 million in completing 59 acquisitions. Some of the most important included Dallas Oil & Minerals at the cost of $1.8 million, adding 337 wells in the midcontinent region; Appalachian Exploration for $1.87 million in cash and $222,000 in stock; a 50 percent interest in Michigan Oil (the balance owned by Snyder Oil) at a cost of more than $10 million, thus gaining a stake in 134 wells located in Michigan, Nebraska, Mississippi, and Alabama; Latoka Inc. with 54 oil and gas wells located in south

Texas and Louisiana; Mark Resources Corp. for $28.4 million; and Red Eagle Resources Corp. at a cost of $38.3 million.

Pinkerton's plan was to acquire enough properties to generate the kind of cash flow necessary to support Lomak's entry into exploration of its undeveloped properties. Indeed, revenues and profits rose steadily in the early 1990s, growing from $9.6 million in 1991 to $13.3 million in 1992, $19.1 million in 1993, $34.3 million in 1994, and $50.8 million in 1995. Net income also improved more than tenfold during this period, from $400,000 in 1991 to $4.4 million in 1995. Furthermore, in 1995 Snyder Oil sold its remaining interest in Lomak, leaving Edelman and Pinkerton as the only remnant of the company that had rescued Lomak several years earlier.

In 1996 Lomak, with $300 million in assets, moved from the NASDAQ to the New York Stock Exchange. It also initiated an exploration and development program and soon made a significant financial commitment to it, spending $58.8 million in 1997 and $81.5 million in 1998. In the meantime, Lomak continued its aggressive expansion. Early in 1997 it more than doubled its asset base by acquiring American Cometra Inc. in a $381 million deal that included $355 million in cash and $26 million in stock. Lomak gained 515 onshore producing wells in Texas and offshore wells in the Gulf of Mexico, as well as 265 miles of pipeline, a natural-gas processing plant, and properties with excellent exploration possibilities spread across 150,000 acres. The company announced immediate plans to spend $140 million over the next five years to explore its new portfolio of properties. Lomak's asset base now totaled $670 million, a far cry from the $25 million it was worth less than ten years earlier. Later in 1997 Lomak increased its Pennsylvania holdings, buying properties from Cabot Oil & Gas Corp. for $92.5 million.

Early in 1998 Lomak sold off some Texas properties while acquiring others, but this activity was only a prelude to an announcement in May that it would merge with Domain Energy Corp. to create a company with assets of $1.1 billion, making it the 15th largest publicly traded independent oil and gas exploration company in the country. Domain was very much focused on exploration, with approximately two-thirds of its properties located in the Gulf of Mexico and one-third in the Gulf Coast, as well as a 50 percent stake in a subsidiary operating in Argentina. The deal was accomplished through a stock exchange, with Lomak serving as the acquiring corporation. Once the deal was completed in August 1998, Lomak changed its name to Range Resources Corporation, although it continued to operate out of its Fort Worth offices.

Formation of Range Resources in 1998

Domain was only two years old, the result of a management buyout from Tenneco Inc. Its CEO, Michael V. Ronca, had worked for Tenneco for more than 20 years. After graduating from college he had gone to work for an insurance company, Philadelphia Life, which Tenneco purchased in the late 1970s. He held a number of positions at Tenneco, then in 1992 founded an exploration and production and petroleum finance business unit called Tenneco Ventures Corp. After buying the energy business from the parent company, he took it public in 1997 as Domain Energy. Ronca and Pinkerton became acquainted while attending a baseball game, then in February 1998 met again at a

Key Dates:

1976: Lomak Petroleum is incorporated in Ohio.
1980: The company is reincorporated in Delaware and goes public.
1987: Stock is delisted from NASDAQ.
1988: Snyder Oil Company gains control.
1995: Snyder Oil divests its Lomak holdings.
1996: The company is listed on the New York Stock Exchange.
1998: Lomak merges with Domain Energy to create Range Resources Corporation.

Credit Suisse First Boston conference held in Vail, Colorado. They began to discuss the possibility of merging their two companies, finally coming to the conclusion that the businesses complemented one another, and in a matter of weeks the two parties worked out the details of the merger.

Pinkerton became the chief executive officer of Range Resources and Ronca became the chief operating officer, while Edelman stayed on as chairman of the corporation. Although both men were optimistic about the company's prospects, investors did not share their enthusiasm. In less than four months the price for Range Resources stock fell by more than 50 percent, to a level less than two times its cash flow for the year. According to analysts Range Resources had brought together two divergent groups of investors and failed to satisfy either. Lomak had been viewed as a low-risk energy company and Domain as a high-risk venture, with the result that Range Resources became a medium-risk company that appealed to neither group of investors. Pinkerton and Ronca had a long-term view of the company, but many investors took a short-term view and sold their interests.

More troubling were depressed energy prices that forced the company to lay off 54 of its 420 employees. In 1998 Range Resources lost $175.2 million while generating $146.6 million in revenues, the result of poor commodity prices and failure of the company's recent purchases to perform up to expectations. Much of 1999 was devoted to retrenching efforts. Noncore assets were sold off to reduce debt and the company cut back on its drilling budget for the year. Range Resources formed Great Lakes Energy Partners, a joint venture with FirstEnergy Corp. in the Appalachian Basin that allowed Range to contribute property that included $200 million in debt, thus allowing the company to reduce its bank debt considerably, to just $160 million. An exchange of common stock for fixed income securities helped to reduce debt further, to approximately $90 million. By the end of the third quarter energy prices rebounded and Range Resources finally began to return to profitability. For the full year the company increased revenues to $161.2 million, and the net loss was reduced to $7.8 million.

With strong energy prices in 2000 Range Resources took great strides in improving its financial health. It continued to pay down debt while increasing its capital expenditures and boosting production. As a result, the company's stock also began to show improvement. For the year, Range Resources generated $187.7 million in revenues and posted a profit of $38 million. The company was able to more than double its capital budget for 2001 to $100 million. Its fortunes continued to improve during the course of 2001, prompting management to believe that Range Resources had turned the corner in its restructuring efforts and that it could look forward to long-term growth and profitability.

Principal Subsidiaries

Range Production Company; Range Holdco, Inc.; Range Gas Company; Domain Energy International Corporation; Energy Assets Operating Company.

Principal Competitors

Anadarko Petroleum Corporation; Cabot Oil & Gas; BP p.l.c.; Chevron Corporation; Exxon Mobil Corporation; Phillips Petroleum Company; Pioneer Natural Resources.

Further Reading

Bronstad, Amanda, "Lomak Petroleum Merger Creates $1B Company," *Business Press,* August 28, 1998, p. 3.

Darbonne, Nissa, "Rearranging Range Resources," *Oil & Gas Investor,* December 1998, pp. 36–39.

Haines, Leslie, Diane Danielski, and Susan Klann, "View from the Bridge," *Oil & Gas Investor,* December 1996, pp. 37–40.

Hogan, Rick, "Lomak Petroleum to Pay $400 Million for American Cometra's Texas Assets," *Oil Daily,* January 3, 1997, p. 1.

McLinden, Steve, "Lomak Gains Come Up Dry on Wall Street," *Business Press,* July 7, 1995, p. 16.

Shook, Barbara, "Lomak, Domain Agree to Merge Operations into Range Resources," *Oil Daily,* May 13, 1998, p. 1.

Toal, Brian A., "Getting It Together," *Oil & Gas Investor,* December 1992, p. 38.

—Ed Dinger

RAO Unified Energy System of Russia

7 Kitaigorodsky Proyezd
103074 Moscow
Russia
Telephone: 7 (095) 220-4001
Fax: 7 (095) 927-3007
Web site: http://www.rao-ees.ru

Public Company
Incorporated: 1992
Employees: 668,205
Sales: $766.4 million (2000)
Stock Exchanges: MICEX (Moscow Interbank Currency
    Exchange) OTC
Ticker Symbols: RAO EES; USERY (ADRs)
NAIC: 221112 Electric Power Generation, Fossil Fuel;
    221111 Electric Power Generation, Hydroelectric;
    221113 Electric Power Generation, Nuclear; 221122
    Electric Power Distribution Systems; 221121 Electric
    Power Transmission Systems

RAO Unified Energy System of Russia (UES) is one of the two largest companies in Russia. The electrical company controls the output of more than 70 percent of Russia's electricity, providing power to domestic households, industry, agriculture, and transportation through its nationwide system of transmission lines and power plants. Structured as a holding company, UES oversees the 440 power stations that comprise Russia's Unified Energy System, including thermal, nuclear, and hydroelectric power plants with a total capacity of 197,000 megawatts. The system produces over 600 billion kilowatt-hours of power a year. UES's holdings give it control over nearly all aspects of Russia's power generation and transmission. On the federal level, the company owns more than three million kilometers of electric power lines, giving it control over all the high-voltage lines in Russia's transmission grid. UES also operates the central dispatching system that coordinates its far-flung network. On the regional level, the company controls most local power generation through holdings that average 51 percent in 73 regional power utilities, known as "energos." Finally, the company also operates 34 independent electric stations that supply power directly to the national wholesale market.

The state owns 52 percent of UES and asserts its control over the company through several representatives on the board of directors. Foreign investors hold a third of the company. Thus, as is the case with many large Russian companies, management and staffing decisions at UES often have political significance. UES's history illustrates the conflicts that have marked the birth of capitalism in Russia, including the struggle between Soviet-era traditionalists and reform-minded capitalists, and the attempt on the part of the state to rein in powerful oligarchs.

Building an Electricity Infrastructure in the Soviet Era

A group commissioned by Vladimir Lenin worked out the first comprehensive plan for the electrification of the Soviet Union. The plan developed by GOELRO, the State Commission for the Electrification of Russia, was adopted by the Eighth Congress of Soviets in December 1920. It outlined plans to rebuild the prewar electric system and build 30 new regional power plants, paying special attention to the nation's hydropower resources. Electrification was expected to be a key factor in the development of heavy industry in the Soviet Union.

Driven by the force of a centrally planned economic system, the electrification of Russia proceeded quickly. Electric power output grew from 0.8 billion kilowatts per hour (kwh) in 1922 to 48.3 billion kwh in 1940. A few years later several power plants in the Central Siberian Area connected their stations to form an integrated power grid. The Bratsk and Krasnoyarsk hydroelectric plants became part of the grid in the 1970s.

European Russia also recognized the advantages of an interconnected power system. In 1956 a transmission line was constructed between the Volga Hydroelectric Power Plant and Moscow. Generating capacity continued to expand. Power output in 1960 was 292.3 billion kwh, and a decade later output reached 741 billion kwh. Soviet plans for economic development stressed the potential benefits of a centrally coordinated, nationally connected power system. East European states were also drawn into the Soviet system in a network dubbed the Peace power grid.

The Privatization Process of the Early 1990s

After the Soviet Union dissolved in 1991, the United Power System was privatized in a whirlwind process along with scores of other state entities. RAO UES was set up by decree of the president and put together largely from the staff of the former Ministry of Fuel and Power. The initial plan put forth by Economic Minister Yegor Gaidar called for the creation of a state monopoly to control the entire power grid, while power producers would be converted into joint stock companies. However, the viewpoint of the Ministry of Fuel and Power prevailed, and a more centralized, vertically integrated system was created.

In the new arrangement, high-voltage grids became the property of RAO UES, while low-voltage grids remained under control of local power producers. As a result, local energy barons retained a monopoly in their areas, despite the existence of a nationwide system. The price of power was regulated at three levels: the government set rates for the general population and for agriculture, a Federal Energy Commission was created to regulate wholesale rates, and regional energy commissions established rates for local industry. Price was based not on supply and demand, but on the cost of production. Consequently, there was no incentive to close inefficient plants; a plant that produced power more cheaply would see all potential profit eaten up by lower rates. In addition, management at many regional power companies fell short of the dispassionate business ideal as an uncertain capitalism was grafted onto the ingrained Soviet way of doing things. Power was supplied to traditional customers regardless of ability to pay, and artificially high prices were often lowered for industries who had preferred standing with the utility. To make matters worse, barter was a common method of payment amid an economy plagued by insolvency.

In spite of business irregularities, UES became a popular investment. The company sometimes accounted for more than 90 percent of daily trading volume on the MICEX exchange. The perception that the company was undervalued made it an attractive prospect. Talks were underway about the creation of an East-West energy bridge reaching from Smolensk through

Belarus and Poland to Germany. Feasibility studies were completed in 1994 and 1995 and the first power was sent to Europe in October 2000.

In the mid-1990s, the entire power industry became bogged down in a situation of widespread mutual indebtedness. The metallurgical, chemical, and machinery sectors were defaulting widely on power bills. In 1995 the government prohibited UES from cutting off power to certain strategic defense installations, causing arrears at the company to soar. UES consequently had trouble paying the natural gas company RAO Gazprom for fuel deliveries, and Gazprom cut fuel supply to some plants in Russia's central regions. The Federal Energy Commission stepped into the fray when it indexed electricity rates to 80 percent of wholesale producer price inflation from late 1995 through mid-1996. At the end of 1995, results were mixed. UES reported a profit of over $20 million. But 60 percent of energy sales were not paid for that year. Power output had also fallen by 25 percent since 1992. That decline, however, was less than the nationwide decline in industrial production.

The company's difficulties continued into 1996. Consumer debt increased from Ru 43 to Ru 79 trillion. Regional power plants continued to have trouble paying for fuel, and power outages ensued during the harsh winters. Another area of concern was capital investment, which stood at 42 percent of its 1991 level. Although several new turbines and transmission lines were brought on line in 1996, the overall system lagged behind in efficiency and technological advancement.

Reformers Taking Power: 1997–99

The Unified Power System, privatized during an unstable and confusing transition period, was clearly in need of restructuring. The first steps toward reform were taken in 1997 when the state began to exert the influence of its controlling stake. That spring President Boris Yeltsin appointed his deputy prime ministers Anatoly Chubais, who had been in charge of the original privatization process, and Boris Nemtsov to develop a strategy to introduce competition into natural monopolies. Nemtsov and Chubais acted on the basis of the Law on Natural Monopoly, which had been passed in 1995 to provide a legislative framework for regulation. In the short term, the reformers saw a need to reduce energy tariffs. They hoped that, in a chain reaction, industries would be able to pay lower tariffs, UES could pay Gazprom for fuel, and both companies could pay taxes to the government. In the long run, Nemtsov suggested spinning off UES's power generation assets, leaving it in charge of transmission only, and encouraging competition by allowing third party access to the transmission grid.

In April 1997 Yeltsin set out provisions for reform in the edict "On Reforming the Natural Monopolies." Soon a Nemtsov-supported reformer, the 29-year-old bank manager Boris Brevnov, replaced longtime company head Anatoly Dyakov as CEO. Dyakov remained on as chairman of the board of directors. Brevnov set about implementing a reform agenda. He brought in a younger staff, retained Price Waterhouse as auditors, and consolidated 130 accounts in various banks that had ties to management into a single account. Company expenditures became more transparent to the state and the percentage of cash payments nearly doubled by year's end.

Brevnov's opponents accused him of exploiting company luxuries for personal purposes and pointed out that conditions at regional power stations continued to deteriorate. Regional managers were particularly opposed to Brevnov's plan for price reform. He wanted to give big industrial customers the right to buy electricity from the cheapest provider, so that the competition would drive industrial rates down and bring domestic rates up to replace lost revenues. Lowering artificially high rates, in Brevnov's view, would rein in the barter payment system and allow for better bookkeeping and a more realistic pricing system. Regional utilities, however, did not want to lose their captive customers, while local governors opposed the imposition of higher rates on their citizens.

The conflict culminated in a showdown in January 1998. The board of directors fired Brevnov and restored Dyakov as acting CEO. The state refused to allow its wishes to be flouted, voided the board's decision, and locked Dyakov out of his office. Dyakov contended that Brevnov was a dilettante who lacked the old guard's involvement in the electricity sector. Finally, in April, Brevnov resigned as CEO and Dyakov was forced out as chairman, to be replaced by Viktor Kudryavy. The economist-reformer Chubais, who had recently been removed as deputy prime minister, was eventually chosen to be the new CEO. Critics pointed out that the whole fiasco did little to improve the company's image in the eyes of investors.

More than one urgent problem faced the new manager. Consumer debt increased from Ru 79 trillion to Ru 102 trillion in 1997, despite a reported pretax profit of Ru 30.9 million. Capital investment also decreased slightly from the previous year. Meanwhile, Russia's harsh climate made the question of power supply particularly urgent. Power outages plagued residents every winter, especially in the Far East. Agreements with Gazprom and LUKOIL managed to make fuel reserves 22 percent higher before the 1997–98 winter than the previous year, but the agreements were never substantial enough to avoid an annual winter-preparations crisis. In response, Chubais issued an August 1999 ultimatum that gas and oil companies must supply needed fuel to UES regardless of payment, or face higher export duties. Higher duties were eventually imposed by the state, bringing in extra revenue that was earmarked to help UES buy fuel.

Chubais shared many of his predecessor's views on long-term reform, including the desire to reduce the cost of energy for industry while raising charges to domestic consumers. The position won him the enmity of regional political leaders. Some federal government insiders also disliked certain aspects of his

reform-minded independence. Assailed from many sides, Chubais nevertheless strengthened his position at the June 1999 annual meeting. The company charter was altered so that a 75 percent vote was required to remove him from his post. There was, however, a check to Chubais's power: Presidential Chief of Staff Alexander Voloshin took on duties as chairman of the board, so that the Kremlin could block any particularly objectionable actions.

The Debate Over Restructuring: 1999–2001

With stable leadership at the head of UES, the pieces were in place for the final debate over what form restructuring would take. A driving force in the push for reform was the drastic need for capital investment in the electricity infrastructure. It was estimated that UES could provide only a quarter of the needed funds. Chubais looked abroad for support, requesting that a 25 percent cap on foreign investment in the company be removed. The limit had blocked foreign investment for several years, since foreigners already held 33 percent of UES at the time the limit was imposed. At the same time, a superficial rule change would not be enough to bring in the needed funds. Foreigners were unlikely to pour money into UES until it was restructured to allow for competition and profitability.

To that end, in December 1999 the board charged Chubais with creating a draft for restructuring by March 2000. Chubais made it clear that he wanted to break up the state monopoly and separate production of electricity from transmission at both the local and federal level. Critics, prominent among them Fuel and Power Minister Viktor Kalyuzhny, contended that such a move would strip UES of all but the transmission grid and put power plants in the hands of foreign investors. Nevertheless, Chubais's plan received initial approval from the board of directors, acting as an arm of the Kremlin, in April 2000. As shareholders worried that they would soon be left with the shell of a company, UES stock fell during the course of an 18-month debate over restructuring.

At the same time, UES had to face the usual problems of consumer debt and fuel shortages. The state took a strong hand in combating these issues. In August President Vladimir Putin threatened Gazprom with personnel changes if the gas company did not comply with UES's fuel requirements. Gazprom agreed to negotiate fuel deliveries quarterly, even though the company would rather supply gas to foreign companies with cash to pay for it. In an effort to address nonpayment, the state set new rules declaring that all legal entities must pay for fuel in advance. Manufacturers were wasting fuel, according to the administration, because they did not have to pay a realistic price for it.

UES announced in November that regional utilities had 85 to 90 percent of the coal and fuel oil needed for the 2000–2001 winter. Stocks in the Far East, however, were much smaller. Resultant power outages in the area served by the Dalenergo utility were so severe that not only industry, but apartment houses, hospitals, and kindergartens were affected. Residents of Vladivostok blocked the major highways of the city, demanding the resignation of the governor and the management of Dalenergo. Chubais, quoted by the ITAR/TASS news agency, blamed the dire situation on the "craziness, stupidity and narrow-mindedness of local bosses." He sent a commission to the area, which arranged for delivery of coal sufficient to reduce blackouts to a few hours a day.

The debate over restructuring also took a more combative turn that winter. Presidential advisors began to criticize Chubais's plan, saying it would leave the state with no control over electricity and the shareholders with no company. Regional governors, longtime opponents of Chubais's policies, appealed to Putin, who established a commission headed by Tomsk Province Governor Viktor Kress to formulate an alternative plan for restructuring. Kress supported vertically integrated regional companies, as opposed to Chubais's plan for separation of production and transmission.

Chubais also drew criticism for several initiatives that stretched UES's sphere of operations. In an attempt to capitalize on opportunities for profit, he supported the formation of a Russian-Kazakh-American coal and electricity company, UralTEK, in the Ural Mountains area, and also pushed for the creation of a combined company that would bring together an aluminum plant and a hydroelectric station in Sayan. Another source of hard cash was electricity exports, which could take advantage of the fact that UES's rates were lower than the European average. In February 2001 Chubais signed an agreement with Ukrainian Fuel and Energy Minister Sergei Yermilov, establishing the ground rules for bringing the energy grids of the two countries into a parallel system. The two grids were connected in late 2001.

Assailed from many sides, Chubais nevertheless managed to retain his position at the April 2001 shareholders meeting. However, he lost a measure of authority to the board of directors, two-thirds of whom were state representatives. In a repeal of a rule passed two years earlier, it was determined that only a simple majority, rather than a 75 percent vote, was required to remove the CEO. The board of directors gained more decision-making power in financial matters, and Chubais was required to present management's plans to the board every quarter.

In May a compromise restructuring plan was finally approved. It provided that UES would spin off two wholly owned subsidiaries, a federal grid company and a central dispatching system. Regional plants would remain vertically integrated but would spin off their transmission networks into separate subsidiaries. By 2006, UES was to be dissolved completely, replaced by the federal grid company and a separate holding company to manage the state's shares in regional power companies. The state would supervise most aspects of the reform process.

Although the agreed-upon plan did not accomplish Chubais's hoped-for liquidation of assets, he nevertheless welcomed it as a common sense approach. Chubais's chief opponent, economics advisor Andrei Illarionov, also gave his stamp of approval to the plan. Analysts predicted that the general accord would win back the confidence of investors. Chubais expressed a desire to continue as executive and lead UES through the reform process.

Principal Subsidiaries

72 regional joint stock power companies ("energos"), including OAO Tyumenenergo; OAO Orenburgenergo; OAO Mosenergo (51%); OAO Kirovenergo (64%); OAO Permenergo (64%); OAO Saratovenergo (64%); OAO Dalenergo (49%); OAO Pskovenergo (49%); OAO Astrkhanenergo (49%); 36 power stations, including OAO Ryazan FFPS; OAO Kama HPS; OAO Krasnoyarsk FFPS 2; OAO Volga Hydro Power Station (86%); OAO V.I. Lenin Hydro Power Station (87%); OAO Pechora FFPS (51%); OAO Pskov FFPS (50%); one dispatching company, OAO Central Dispatch Department of the Unified Energy System of the Russian Federation; 57 research and development institutes; 73 power industry construction and maintenance companies.

Principal Competitors

OAO Gazprom; OAO Lukoil; Electricité de France.

Further Reading

Bagrov, Andrei, and Sergei Leskov, "Power Struggle Racks Electric Company," *Current Digest of the Post-Soviet Press*, February 25, 1998, pp. 8–9.

"Circuit Boards: Unified Energy Systems," *Economist (US)*, April 11, 1998, pp. 48–49.

Davydova, Milana, "Three-Way Infighting Over Energy Eats Up," *Current Digest of the Post-Soviet Press*, May 3, 2000, pp. 8–11.

Fadeyev, Pyotr, "Chubais, Power Company Come Under Fire," *Current Digest of the Post-Soviet Press*, March 1, 2000, pp. 9–10.

Gopinath, Deepak, "Face-Off in Moscow," *Infrastructure Finance*, July 1997, p. 36.

Gorelov, Nikolai, "Meanwhile, the Chubais-Kalyuzhny Conflict Continues to Smolder," *Current Digest of the Post-Soviet Press*, February 23, 2000, pp. 8–9.

Grigoryeva, Yekaterina, and Mikhail Klasson, "With Putin's Okay, Governors Form Task Force to Weigh Pros and Cons of Restructuring Plan," *Current Digest of the Post-Soviet Press*, January 24, 2001, pp. 11–12.

Heath, Michael, "All Sides Claim Victory in UES Shakeup," *Russia Journal*, July 20, 2001, p. 9.

Ilyina, Natalya, and Yekaterina Kats, "Putin Aides Take on Chubais, Kasyanov in Public Flap," *Current Digest of the Post-Soviet Press*, January 17, 2001, pp. 6–7.

"Is the East-West Power Bridge Economic?" *Modern Power Systems*, February 1996, pp. 21–3.

Klasson, Mikhail, "Anatoly Chubais Gets Started," *Current Digest of the Post-Soviet Press*, June 13, 2001, pp. 6–7.

Klebnikov, Paul, "Revenge of the Oligarchs," *Forbes*, February 23, 1998, pp. 89–90.

Kozlov, Vladimir, "UES Cuts Power Supply to Railways," *Russia Journal*, August 12, 2000, p. 3.

Kucherenko, Vladimir, "Compromise Keeps Chubais Restructuring Plan Alive," *Current Digest of the Post-Soviet Press*, December 27, 2000, p. 5.

——, "Government Approves New Billing Rules," *Current Digest of the Post-Soviet Press*, May 10, 2000, p. 5.

Kuznetsova, Vera, "Pragmatic Chubais Retains Oligarchic Status," *Russia Journal*, May 4, 2001, p. 8.

Latynina, Yulia, "Electric-Power Reform: Chubais's Augean Task," *Current Digest of the Post-Soviet Press*, June 10, 1998, pp. 7-9.

Malyutin, Aleksandr, "Chubais's 'Bailout' Success Assures Power Company Tenure," *Current Digest of the Post-Soviet Press*, July 1, 1998, p. 4.

Murtazayev, Elmar, "Supply of Electric Power to Customers in Central Regions Cut Back Again," *Current Digest of the Post-Soviet Press*, January 24, 1996, p. 17.

"Power Cutoffs Continue in Russian Far East," *ITAR/TASS News Agency*, January 20, 2001.

"RAO UES Urges Voloshin to Clear Air with Regional Companies," *ITAR/TASS News Agency*, March 26, 2001.

"Regions Struggling to Make Fuel Stocks As Winter Approaches," *ITAR/TASS News Agency*, November 29, 1999.

"Russia, Ukraine to Synchronise Work of Their Energy Systems," *ITAR/TASS News Agency*, February 12, 2001.

Rybalchenko, Irina, "Week of Signal Political Successes for Chubais," *Current Digest of the Post-Soviet Press*, February 23, 2000, pp. 7-8.

Serov, Alexei, "Chubais Strengthens Hand at UES," *Russia Journal*, June 29, 1999.

Slay, Ben, and Vladimir Capelik, "Natural Monopoly Regulation and Competition Policy in Russia," *Antitrust Bulletin*, Spring 1998, pp. 229–60.

Tsypin, Vladimir, "Oil Export Tax Hike Has Kalyuzhny, Chubais at Odds," *Current Digest of the Post-Soviet Press*, September 29, 1999, p. 7.

—Sarah Ruth Lorenz

Red Hat, Inc.

2600 Meridian Parkway
Durham, North Carolina 27713
U.S.A.
Telephone: (919) 547-0012
Toll Free: (888) 733-4281
Fax: (919) 547-0024
Web site: http://www.redhat.com

Public Company
Incorporated: 1995 as Red Hat Software, Inc.
Employees: 720
Sales: $103.4 million (2001)
Stock Exchanges: NASDAQ
Ticker Symbol: RHAT
NAIC: 511210 Software Publishers

Red Hat, Inc. is a market leader in open source software systems for mainframes, servers, workstations, and embedded devices. Unlike proprietary systems that carefully guard their source codes, Red Hat and other open source software vendors make their source code freely available. The company's core product is the Red Hat Linux operating system, which is the leading Linux system for servers. More recently the company has expanded its product line to offer open source solutions in such areas as e-commerce, embedded devices, and database solutions.

Developing Its Own Version of Linux: 1995–98

Red Hat Software, Inc. was established in 1995 by entrepreneurs Robert Young and Marc Ewing. Young, a native of Hamilton, Ontario, and a graduate of the University of Toronto, started his first company, Vernon Computer and Sales, in 1984. It was a computer rental and leasing business, which Young sold in 1990 to a Canadian financial services company. In 1993 Young started another computer company, ACC Corp., which was a UNIX reseller business. When his customers began requesting Linux technology, Young found Marc Ewing, a Carnegie Mellon University computer science graduate who had a

small Linux development operation. Ewing is credited with developing the Red Hat Package Manager, which made it easier for users to install and manage the various packages that made up Linux. Young and Ewing merged their companies in 1994. In 1995 the newly formed company was named Red Hat Software, after an old lacrosse hat that Ewing's grandfather owned. Red Hat established its headquarters in Durham, North Carolina, located near the state's Research Triangle Park.

Red Hat's mission was to market and develop its own version of the Linux open source operating system to end users. Linux was first developed by Linus Torvalds in 1991. He was a 21-year-old student at the University of Helsinki in Sweden. In August 1991 he made the basic source code for the initial version of Linux (0.02) available to anyone over the Internet. Users could download it for free, change it, and share new versions with other programmers.

Linux 0.02 was a UNIX-based operating system. UNIX was originally developed by AT&T in the mid-1970s. Its source code was kept private until the mid- to late 1980s, when the Free Software Foundation developed and distributed a suite of free cross-UNIX tools, including a compiler and shell. The tools were distributed under a new free licensing scheme called the GNU Public License.

From 1993 to 1995 the number of Linux users increased dramatically from 100,000 to 1.5 million. Linux's popularity with software programmers was due in part to the fact that its source code was available to everyone for free. While Red Hat made its version available for free downloading, it also sold CD-ROM versions. When the company released Red Hat Linux 5.0 in November 1997 for $49.95, *InfoWorld* called it "a complete Internet server in a box." The software package included everything a system administrator needed to get an Internet or corporate intranet server running in one day, including the Apache Web server, a mail server, a news server, a domain name server, a gopher server, and more. It also included development tools and a freeware database engine.

By 1998, when Red Hat released version 5.2 of its Red Hat Linux, there were 12 million Linux users. At the end of 1998 an International Data Corp. (IDC) survey indicated there were

750,000 installed servers with Linux, representing a 212 percent increase from the previous year. That growth rate outpaced Windows NT, NetWare, UNIX, and all other server operating systems. Windows NT Server remained the market share leader with 36 percent of all operating systems shipped, followed by NetWare at 24 percent, and Linux and all other types of Unix systems tied at 17 percent each.

Red Hat became a more established organization in 1998. Matthew Szulik, formerly president of Relativity Software, joined the company as president and chief operating officer (COO). Young remained CEO until November 1999, when Szulik was promoted to CEO. As chairman of Red Hat, Young remained the company's chief strategist.

In the spring of 1998 Red Hat began pursuing a strategy of building tight partnerships with industry-leading technology companies. The company's first round of strategic financing was completed in September 1998, when it received financial backing from Intel and Netscape Communications as well as from venture capital firms Benchmark Capital and Greylock Management. As Red Hat built a stronger management team, it completed a second round of financing in March 1999, when computing industry leaders Compaq, IBM, Novell, Oracle, and SAP took minority equity positions in the company, indicating their commitment to the development and adoption of Linux operating systems.

Red Hot Red Hat IPO: 1999

In addition to gaining financial support from computer industry leaders, Red Hat entered into strategic agreements with computer firms IBM and Dell in 1999. IBM, which had been experiencing demand from its UNIX customers for an open source solution, partnered with Red Hat early in 1999. Under the agreement, developers from IBM and Red Hat would team to move Linux onto IBM's Netfinity servers, PC 300 commercial desktops, IntelliStations, and ThinkPads. Later in the year IBM announced it would preload Red Hat Linux 6.2 on its Netfinity servers, with Red Hat providing technical support.

When Red Hat released its Linux 6.0 in April 1999, Dell Computer Corp. was the first major computer vendor to factory install Red Hat Linux on its servers, workstations, and desktop PCs. Dell also made an equity investment in Red Hat. Version 6.0 allowed users to run on servers with as many as four processors, was easier to install, and had two graphical user interfaces (GUIs) that could be used simultaneously. Version 6.0 was also featured on Red Hat's e-commerce server, which included encryption capabilities and e-commerce software from Hewlett-Packard; it was introduced in July 1999. Computer manufacturer Gateway became an authorized Red Hat reseller in September 1999, enabling it to factory-install Red Hat Linux on its computers when requested by customers. In December 1999 Dell and Red Hat extended their alliance, with Dell committing to install Red Hat Linux on all of its current and future PowerEdge servers. The two companies also entered into a worldwide service and support agreement.

Red Hat filed for its initial public offering (IPO) in June 1999 and hoped to raise about $96 million. The company had revenue of $10.8 million for its fiscal year ending February 28, 1999, compared to revenue of $5.1 million in fiscal 1998. On August 11, 1999, Red Hat shares began trading at $14 a share. By the end of the day they closed up 227 percent at just over $52 a share. Fueled by growing support for Linux as an alternative operating system to Windows NT for servers, Red Hat's stock reached an all-time high of $150 a share in December 1999.

Red Hat also began to address the international market for Linux solutions in 1999. Red Hat Europe began operating in July 1999 out of offices in London, England, and Stuttgart, Germany. The new European organization functioned as a wholly owned subsidiary of Red Hat. Later in the year Red Hat expanded into Japan, and in 2000 the company established Red Hat France and Red Hat Italy to deliver software, support, and training services to European enterprise-level business customers.

Acquisitions, Expanding Products and Solutions: 1999–2000

Following its IPO, Red Hat embarked on a series of acquisitions that enabled it to move into the post-PC embedded products market, such as wireless devices, and develop a Linux-based enterprise platform. In November 1999 it acquired Linux pioneer Cygnus Solutions for $674 million in stock. Michael Tiemann, author of the first open source C++ compiler and president of Cygnus, replaced Red Hat cofounder Marc Ewing as Red Hat's chief technology officer; Ewing continued to direct the Red Hat Center for Open Source, a nonprofit organization. Cygnus's business included producing compilers and debuggers, developing embedded software for handheld devices and other appliances, and application development tools.

In January 2000 Red Hat acquired e-commerce software vendor Hell's Kitchen Systems Inc. for $91 million in stock. HKS's payment processing software was a key component for e-commerce operations. The acquisition helped Red Hat position its Linux offerings as a more viable software solution for businesses that wanted to migrate their operations online. Around the same time Red Hat entered into a strategic partnership with electronic security firm RSA Security Inc. that added encryption capabilities to Red Hat's Linux software.

Key Dates:

1994: Red Hat Software, Inc. is founded by Robert F. Young and Mark Ewing.
1999: Red Hat goes public as Red Hat, Inc.
2000: Red Hat expands its product offerings through acquisitions.
2001: Red Hat reports its first quarterly profit.

Red Hat's next major acquisition involved performance management software vendor Bluecurve for $35 million in stock. The acquisition enabled Red Hat to offer a tool for monitoring Linux systems. Bluecurve software allowed developers to simulate transactions and scale their infrastructures to different levels of service. Around the same time in April 2000 Red Hat introduced redhat.com Marketplace, a portal where vendors could find software, hardware, and support services for open source products.

In June 2000 Red Hat acquired WireSpeed Communications of Huntsville, Alabama, for about $33 million in stock. WireSpeed made embedded software that allowed wireless devices to communicate with the Internet and private networks. Its customers included semiconductor, Internet device, and industrial control companies. In August Red Hat strengthened its web server security software offerings with the acquisition of C2Net Software Inc. for $42.1 million in stock.

In spite of competition from other Linux developers such as VA Linux Systems, TurboLinux Inc., and SuSE Linux AG, Red Hat remained the dominant firm in the Linux marketplace in 2000. According to an IDC survey, Red Hat was the Linux market leader for the second consecutive year with 52.4 percent of all Linux shipments worldwide. A Netcraft Web Server Survey indicated that Red Hat held 70 percent of the worldwide Linux market share. The company's software offerings were praised in the industry press, winning a ''Product of the Year'' award from *Network Magazine* and an ''Editor's Choice'' Award from *Computer Reseller News*. In mid-2000 Dell announced it would pre-install Red Hat Linux as one of three operating systems on its servers, with both companies providing technical support for customers.

In September 2000 Red Hat announced the creation of the Red Hat Network, a new Internet-based subscription service for developers and users. Subscribers would be able to access open source advances, upgrades, and security features. Developers could register information on their hardware and software systems, thus facilitating joint projects. The Red Hat Network also included a number of support services from open source experts, tight integration with the Red Hat Package Manager, and customizable update management services. The Red Hat Network also made it easier for Red Hat to deploy upgrades and security patches over the Internet.

Other significant developments in 2000 included an extension of Red Hat's alliance with IBM with the announcement that IBM would provide support for Red Hat Linux on the complete IBM eServer product line. Red Hat also partnered with North Carolina State University to establish the first open source-based university course at the school's College of Engineering.

Toward the end of 2000 Red Hat introduced Red Hat Linux 7 in anticipation of the release of the new Linux 2.4 kernel, which Linus Torvalds released in January 2001. While Red Hat Linux 7 users were able to upgrade to the 2.4 kernel, the company soon released version 7.1 of its server operating system. The new 2.4 kernel enabled Linux to compete as a top-end server system.

Red Hat Achieved First Profitable Quarter in 2001

With its stock trading around $5 a share, Red Hat reported a net loss of $5.98 million on revenue of $84 million for its fiscal year ending February 28, 2001. In February the company acquired Planning Technologies, Inc., an Atlanta-based consulting firm with more than 200 professional engineers and consultants, for $47 million in stock.

In June Red Hat announced its first quarterly profit for the quarter ending May 31, with adjusted net income of $600,000 on sales of $25.6 million. In spite of its depressed stock price, Red Hat was in solid financial condition with about $390 million in cash and investments. For the future Red Hat planned to introduce open source database software and launch an open source consulting practice. Later in the year Red Hat expanded its consulting and services group with the addition of an open source consulting team that had previously worked for VA Linux Systems. The company also announced contracts with Cisco Systems and Nortel Networks, both of which installed workstations with Red Hat Linux in their engineering departments.

Later in the year Red Hat proposed an open source code, eCos, for 2.5 and third generation wireless devices. Plans called for the new source code to be developed by Red Hat in association with 3G Labs. The new operating system would be based on Red Hat's open source embedded real-time operating system, not Linux.

The company continued to expand its product offerings with the introduction of a new open source e-commerce software suite. The core of Red Hat E-Commerce was Interchange 4.8, a new version of an e-commerce platform that Red Hat acquired from open source software firm Akopia in January 2001. Also included in the package were the newest Red Hat Linux OS, Apache Web-serving software, an open source database, and a subscription service for receiving software updates.

Red Hat's stock received a boost in November 2001 when the company announced it would collaborate with IBM to deliver open source software solutions, services, and support for the entire IBM eServer product line. The new extension of Red Hat's partnership with IBM built on the company's previous support of the eServer xSeries platform. Under the new agreement, Red Hat would provide support for the IBM eServer zSeries, iSeries, and pSeries platforms. Red Hat would provide a base solution consisting of the Red Hat Linux operating system, product support services, professional services, and an upgrade offering. A wide range of service upgrades would also be offered. Following the announcement, Red Hat's stock jumped nearly 27 percent from about $6 a share to $7.62 a share.

Red Hat's expanded partnership with IBM underscored the company's leadership position in open source software for enterprise servers. The company also provided open source operating systems for workstations and embedded devices. Red Hat also supported open source developers and offered solutions for the database, e-commerce, secure Web server, and high availability server markets. For the future Red Hat was well-positioned to maintain its leadership position in open source solutions.

Principal Competitors

Caldera International, Inc.; Microsoft Corporation; SuSE Linux AG; Turbolinux Inc.; VA Linux Systems.

Further Reading

April, Carolyn, A., "Acquisition: Red Hat Snaps up WireSpeed," *InfoWorld,* June 19, 2000, p. 20.

Babcock, Charles, "Red Hat Could Benefit from a Few More Rabbits," *Inter@ctive Week,* November 22, 1999, p. 11.

Baltazar, Henry, "Evolution, Not Revolution," *eWeek,* October 9, 2000, p. 18.

Beale, Matthew, "Red Hat and Dell Pump up Linux Agreement," *E-Commerce Times,* December 7, 1999, http://www .ecommercetimes.com.

——, "Red Hat Expands European Operations," *E-Commerce Times,* February 14, 2000, http://www.ecommercetimes.com.

——, "Red Hat Finds E-Commerce at Hell's Kitchen," *E-Commerce Times,* January 5, 2000, http://www.ecommercetimes.com.

——, "Technology Spotlight: Red Hat, Inc.," *E-Commerce Times,* December 2, 1999, http://www.ecommercetimes.com.

Brooks, Jason, "Linux Takes Another Step Forward," *eWeek,* April 23, 2001, p. 1.

"Can Red Hat Stay Red Hot?" *Business Week,* July 5, 1999, p. 85.

Carr, David F., "Trying to Make a Business of Linux," *Internet World,* November 9, 1998, p. 8.

Carrel, Lawrence, "Hats Off to Red Hat," *SmartMoney.com,* November 27, 2001, http://biz.yahoo.com/smart/011127/20011127onewond.html.

Colkin, Eileen, "IBM, Red Hat Outline Linux Partnership," *InformationWeek,* February 22, 1999, p. 40.

"Cygnus Exec Takes Red Hat CTO Post," *Electronic Engineering Times,* January 17, 2000, p. 8.

De Bellis, Matthew A., "Red Hat's IPO Rockets," *VARbusiness,* August 16, 1999, p. 16.

Deckmyn, Dominique, "Analysts: Red Hat Rides Linux Wave," *Computerworld,* August 16, 1999, p. 87.

"Durham, N.C.-Based Software Firm Posts $600,000 Net Loss," *Knight-Ridder/Tribune Business News,* March 23, 2001.

Fulton, Sean, "OS Holy Wars," *InternetWeek,* September 1, 1997, p. 87.

Galli, Peter, "Special Delivery—Red Hat to Distribute Customized Linux Packages, Updates," *eWeek,* September 25, 2000, p. 11.

Gibson, Stan, "A Little Respect: Red Hat in Black," *eWeek,* June 25, 2001, p. 1.

Glascock, Stuart, "Dell to Pre-Install Red Hat Linux on Servers," *TechWeb,* June 21, 2000.

——, "Red Hat Takes Wraps off Official Red Hat Linux 6.0," *Computer Reseller News,* May 3, 1999, p. 42.

——, "Those Mad Hatters," *Computer Reseller News,* March 29, 1999, p. 210.

Gohring, Nancy, "Red Hat Proposes Open Source for Next-Gen Wireless Devices," *Interactive Week,* August 6, 2001, p. 15.

Goodridge, Elisabeth, "Red Hat to Take Linux Wireless," *InformationWeek,* June 19, 2000, p. 18.

Hammond, Eric, "Tired of NT? Put on Your Red Hat," *InfoWorld,* November 24, 1997, p. 111.

"Heads Still High at Red Hat Software Company," *Knight-Ridder/Tribune Business News,* August 3, 2001.

Hillebrand, Mary, "Red Hat Introduces E-Commerce Server," *E-Commerce Times,* July 28, 1999, http://www.ecommercetimes.com.

——, "Red Hat Moves on European Linux Market," *E-Commerce Times,* July 20, 1999, http://www.ecommercetimes.com.

"An Investing Guy Tries to Figure out This Linux Business," *Fortune,* May 10, 1999, p. 24.

Johnston, Stuart J., "Linux's Next Offer," *InformationWeek,* May 10, 1999, p. 127.

Kemp, Ted, "Red Hat Plugs E-Biz Apps Gap for Linux," *InternetWeek,* August 20, 2001, p. 9.

Kleinbard, David, "Red Hat in IPO Ring," *InformationWeek,* June 14, 1999, p. 16.

Koller, Mike, "Red Hat Moves Beyond Operating Systems," *TechWeb,* April 27, 2000.

Mahoney, Michael, "Red Hat to Offer Open-Source E-Commerce Suite," *E-Commerce Times,* August 10, 2001, http://www .ecommercetimes.com.

Mitchell, Russ, "Arriving, Red Hat in Hand," *U.S. News & World Report,* June 21, 1999, p. 45.

"New Kernel Lets Linux Target Top-End," *Computer Weekly,* January 18, 2001, p. 30.

Nobel, Carmen, "Open Source Moves to Phones," *eWeek,* July 23, 2001, p. 13.

"Red Hat Inc.," *Business North Carolina,* May 2001, p. 17.

"Red Hat Launches New Version of Linux Server Operating System," *Worldwide Computer Products News,* April 17, 2001.

"Red Hat Software Company Ekes out First Quarterly Profit," *Knight-Ridder/Tribune Business News,* June 20, 2001.

"Red Hat to Purchase C2Net Software," *Washington Business Journal,* August 18, 2000, p. 29.

Reed, Sandy, "From the Editor in Chief," *InfoWorld,* January 11, 1999, p. 69.

Ricadela, Aaron, "Red Hat to Buy E-Commerce Payment Vendor," *InformationWeek,* January 10, 2000, p. 129.

Ricadela, Aaron, and Martin J. Garvey, "Red Hat Purchases Developer of Open-Source Applications," *InformationWeek,* November 22, 1999, p. 125.

Rogoski, Richard R., "Hats off to Robert Young," *Communications News,* November 2000, p. 18.

Scannell, Ed, "Red Hat Boosts Open-Source Efforts, Updates Linux Version," *InfoWorld,* September 25, 2000, p. 30.

"Significant Developments for RHAT from Multex.com," November 29, 2001, http://yahoo.marketguide.com.

Wang, Andy, "Dell Bolsters Linux, Invests in Red Hat," *E-Commerce Times,* April 7, 1999, http://www.ecommercetimes.com.

——, "Gateway Dons Red Hat, Offers Linux," *E-Commerce Times,* September 7, 1999, http://www.ecommercetimes.com.

——, "Stock Watch: Red Hat IPO Takes Off," *E-Commerce Times,* August 12, 1999, http://www.ecommercetimes.com.

——, "Stock Watch: Red Hat Soars on New Alliance with Dell," *E-Commerce Times,* December 7, 1999, http://www.ecommercetimes.com.

"The War for the Desktop," *Maclean's,* July 20, 1998, p. 30.

"Will Linux Investors Be Left out in the Cold?" *Business Week,* March 6, 2000, p. 178.

—David P. Bianco

Rent-A-Center, Inc.

5700 Tennyson Parkway, 3rd Floor
Plano, Texas 75024-3556
U.S.A.
Telephone: (972) 801-1100
Fax: (972) 943-0113
Web site: http://www.rentacenter.com

Public Company
Incorporated: 1986 as Vista of Puerto Rico, Inc.
Employees: 12,554
Sales: $1.6 billion (2000)
Stock Exchanges: NASDAQ
Ticker Symbol: RCII
NAIC: 532210 Consumer Electronics and Appliances
Rental

Rent-A-Center, Inc. of Plano, Texas, is America's largest chain of rent-to-own stores. The company owns and operates nearly 2,300 stores in all 50 states, plus Washington, D.C., and Puerto Rico. In addition, a wholly owned subsidiary, ColorTyme, serves as a national franchiser of rent-to-own stores, with 333 units under the ColorTyme brand and 13 under Rent-A-Center. All showrooms of both brands offer furniture, appliances, home electronics, and other accessories that can be rented by customers, who may terminate the contract on short notice or gain ownership of the merchandise after reaching a stipulated rental period. Payments are made to the stores on a weekly basis. Many customers turn to Rent-A-Center and its competitors because of a temporary need for household merchandise. These include college students, military personnel, people going through divorce, or businesspeople on short-term assignments. Other customers, however, are simply strapped for cash and have poor credit ratings and turn to rent-to-own stores as a way to finance the purchase of necessities or luxury items they cannot afford. While Rent-A-Center and its competitors insist that buyout provisions are offered as a courtesy to customers, and they point out that a sizeable portion of customers terminate a rental contract long before it runs its course, the industry has gained a reputation for price gouging and taking advantage of the poor because the final cost of merchandise is far higher than the retail price. Rent-A-Center has been involved in considerable litigation over the years and has been forced to pay settlements for charging exorbitant interest rates. The company insists that it is primarily a leasing business, not a credit operation, and that its customers are not locked into contracts, yet the entire rent-to-own industry continues to suffer from a poor image. Nevertheless, Rent-A-Center has enjoyed healthy profits, enough to ease investor concerns over the company's reputation, warranted or not.

Development of the Rent-to-Own Concept: 1950s

The roots of the rent-to-own business reach back to the 1950s when a number of people pioneered the concept. For instance, Charles Loudermilk, Sr., founder of Atlanta-based Aaron Rents, started out in 1955 by renting Army surplus chairs for ten cents a day. The founder of Rent-A-Center was J. Ernest Talley, widely acknowledged as the most influential figure in the development of the industry. In the 1950s he ran a retail appliance store with a cousin in Kansas. Because tightening bank credit prevented a number of customers from buying his merchandise, he hit on the idea of renting the items. If customers failed to meet the payments, he could always repossess the merchandise; if they reached the end of the rental agreement, they would own the merchandise and Talley would have made some extra cash in addition to increasing the sales volume of his appliance store. In 1963 he developed a rent-to-own chain called Mr. T's, which by 1974 had grown to 14 stores. He sold the business, which became part of the Remco chain, and he turned his attention to commercial real estate in the Dallas area. When the Texas real estate market suffered a crash he returned to the rent-to-own concept in 1987, establishing Talley Leasing with his son Michael. The new company rented appliances to apartment complex owners.

Talley returned to the consumer rent-to-own business in 1989 when he acquired a 22-store chain, Vista of Puerto Rico, which operated in both New Jersey and Puerto Rico. Talley changed the name to Vista Rent to Own. Drawing on his years of experience, he upgraded the chain, improving the selection of merchandise and customer approval procedures, as well as instituting inventory systems and a management training program. In April 1993 he greatly expanded his business by acquiring the 84-store

Company Perspectives:

From a TV for the family room to the sofa to sit on and watch it, Rent-A-Center provides an easy, affordable way for people to get the things they want for their home today, without incurring a continuing obligation or having to use their credit.

Renters Choice Inc. and merging it with Vista. The combined company then assumed the Renters Choice name, and again he upgraded the operations of the new units. Although the purchase would result in a $600,000 loss for 1993, Talley clearly knew how to make money in the rent-to-own business. Revenues that stood at $15.8 million in 1991 would soar to $74.4 million in 1994. Profits of $1.8 million would increase to $5.5 million over the same period. Moreover, the operating margins for Renters Choice were much healthier than its rivals. Talley's edge was in his stores' success in customer approval. While the industry average for delinquent accounts was 10 percent, the average at Renters Choice was just 6.5 percent of revenues. A main reason for this success was simply that Talley paid higher wages than his competitors, both for store clerks and managers. The company also attempted to weed out management trainees that harbored repressed hostilities or forced their personal philosophy on others. (The battery of psychological tests the company relied on, however, would become a source of conflict later in the 1990s.) Behind this effort was an understanding that many customers turned to rent-to-own stores because they could not afford the outright purchase of a luxury item, like a big-screen TV, or had poor credit because of frequent job changes, and they would not respond well to employees who appeared to be judgmental. Because customers came into the store on a weekly basis to make their payments, it was inevitable that managers would develop some kind of personal relationships with them. Talley preferred that those relationships be positive, especially since it led to repeat business. Managers were granted considerable latitude on deciding if a customer was worth the risk, but at the same time, computer programming allowed the main office to monitor rental payments on a nightly basis. Accounts even a day late would be questioned. In short, Renters Choice developed a tightly run organization that gave it an edge in a highly fragmented industry. Of the approximately 8,000 competing establishments, many were small, poorly run operations ripe for acquisition and the Talley turnaround procedure.

Going Public: 1995

In January 1995 Talley took Renters Choice public in order to fund further growth, raising close to $26 million. Despite a general aversion for what is often considered an unsavory business, investors were attracted to Renters Choice from the start, and the stock, trading on the NASDAQ, made a steady climb in price. In the spring of 1995 Renters Choice paid $20 million for Crown Leasing Corp. of Texarkana, which had recently filed for Chapter 11 protection. The deal added 72 stores in 18 states and expanded the presence of Renters Choice to the southern part of the country. In the fall of 1995 the chain added 135 stores by acquiring Pro Rental Inc. of Dallas for $38.5 million in cash and notes. Pro Rental operated under two brands: Magic Rent-to-Own and Kelway Rent-to-Own. By the end of 1995, with its acquisi-

tions only partially digested, Renters Choice boosted revenues to $133.3 million and net income to $10.7 million. By now, the chain had grown to nearly 320 stores. Another 320 stores were soon added in 1996 when it acquired ColorTyme of Dallas, which was a franchise operation rather than a company-owned chain like Renters Choice. The majority shareholder and Chairman of ColorTyme was Talley's brother, Willie. Ever since his brother had suffered a stroke in the early 1990s, Talley had acted as his legal guardian, a situation that previously required notation in SEC filings because of possible conflicts of interest between ColorTyme and Renters Choice.

Because of the lack of large rent-to-own chains available for purchase in 1996, by the middle of the year Renters Choice hired a director of acquisitions in order to focus on identifying smaller chains and individual operations that were deemed to be underperforming. Between May and the end of the year, the company acquired 88 stores in 20 separate transactions at a cost of $25.3 million. In the process, Renters Choice added five new states to its operations. Moreover, the company opened 13 new stores. As a result of its aggressive expansion, Renters Choice more than doubled its revenues in 1996 over the previous year to $238 million, while posting a net income of $18 million. The company continued to grow in 1997, adding 71 stores in 18 separate transactions at a cost of $30.5 million. Another ten new stores were also opened, bringing the total number of company-owned units by the end of 1997 to 504. Also in 1997 Renters Choice agreed to a $2.9 million settlement of a Wisconsin class-action lawsuit it inherited from Crown Leasing, which had been accused of charging usurious interest rates. In addition, in late 1997 Renters Choice was sued in New Jersey court over a failure to provide certain disclosures in its contracts with customers. Despite these legal costs, Renters Choice remained extremely profitable. Revenues for 1997 grew to $327.5 million and net income to $25.9 million.

In 1998 Renters Choice made a quantum leap in growth when it made two major acquisitions. First it paid $103 million to acquire the 176 stores of Central Rents, Inc. Located in the Los Angeles, California, suburb of Commerce, Central Rents provided Renters Choice with a substantial platform in the western United States, an area where it previously had very few locations. The company now added 43 stores in California alone. Although a substantial acquisition, it would soon be dwarfed by the $900 million purchase of the 1,400-store Rent-A-Center chain. Renters Choice would then assume the Rent-A-Center name and become the largest rent-to-own chain in the industry.

Rent-A-Center had been founded by Tom Devlin in Wichita, Kansas, in 1973. While attending college at Wichita State University in the mid-1960s, Devlin worked at an appliance store and was frustrated with the high rejection rate of his blue collar customers. He and his boss developed a payment plan that allowed customers to rent an appliance until they had paid enough installments in order to gain ownership. Devlin went into business for himself in 1973 with a single rent-to-own store. He developed the Rent-A-Center chain with both company-owned stores and franchisees. In 1987 he sold the business for $594 million to British conglomerate Thorn EMI, which had been involved in the long established English rent-to-own industry. In 1996 Thorn split from the EMI music business, but did not fare

Key Dates:

1963:	Ernest Talley establishes Mr. T's rent-to-own chain.
1974:	Talley sells Mr. T's.
1987:	Talley and son start Talley Leasing.
1989:	Talley acquires Vista of Puerto Rico.
1993:	Vista acquires Renters Choice and assumes name.
1995:	Renters Choice goes public.
1998:	Renters Choice acquires Rent-A-Center chain and assumes name.
2001:	Talley retires.

well on its own, hurt in large part by a strong economy that made rent-to-own a less attractive option. Thorn also faced litigation over misleading interest rates in the States, an ongoing problem that concerned U.K. investors, especially after a New Jersey judge ruled against the company in 1997, leaving it open to damages that had the potential of reaching $1 billion. As a consequence, Thorn was eager to unload Rent-A-Center and devote its resources to restructuring its British interests.

Merger of Renters Choice and Rent-A-Center

Although Thorn sold Rent-A-Center to Renters Choice, it retained partial responsibility for pending damages in earlier lawsuits. In order to finance the acquisition, Renters Choice issued $235 million of convertible preferred stock to the New York investment firm of Apollo Management, which gained almost a 30 percent stake in the company. Renters Choice closed down the longtime Wichita headquarters of Rent-A-Center, consolidated operations in Plano, then on December 31, 1998, changed its name to Rent-A-Center, Inc. For the year, with only a partial contribution from its new acquisitions, the company's revenues soared to $809.7 million, while income held steady at $24.8 million.

Investors showed some concern over Talley's ability to make the stiff debt payments taken on in 1998, and as a result the price of Rent-A-Center stock dropped. When the company continued to post strong results, investors expressed their relief by again bidding up the company's shares. The process of absorbing 1,400 new stores was not without incident, however, as a number of inherited managers objected to the company's personality testing, and initiated litigation. Plaintiffs maintained that many of the 502 true-false statements of a psychological test were invasive, including "I am very strongly attracted to members of my own sex"; "I have never indulged in any unusual sex practices"; "Evil spirits possess me at times"; and "I am a special agent from God." Although the company maintained that these were standard questions of the well-known Minnesota Multiphasic Personality Inventory exam and that the tests were only scored by computers and not used against employees, it eventually reached a settlement on the case, agreeing to drop the test and pay $2 million in damages.

Rent-A-Center did not acquire new stores in 1999 and focused on converting its recent additions to its way of doing business. It also launched a marketing campaign designed to improve the public impression of the rent-to-own industry.

Television commercials, in both English and Spanish, were crafted to alleviate the uneasiness that many lower income customers felt about doing business at a rent-to-own store. The emphasis was on consumers being empowered to enjoy upscale items that they would not otherwise be able to afford. Rent-A-Center would receive a major boost in its marketing efforts when it signed well-known football analyst and television pitchman John Madden to serve as the public face of its advertising campaign, including in-store signage as well as television commercials. The company could afford Madden's hefty fee and the requisite advertising budget because of a major jump in revenues ($1.4 billion) and net income ($59.4 million) in 1999. That trend would continue in 2000, as revenues rose to $1.6 billion and net income soared to $103 million. Furthermore, brand awareness improved significantly, much of which could be attributed to Madden. The company was also successful in better targeting its direct mail and, as a result, was able to free up dollars for even more broadcast advertising.

Rent-A-Center renewed its plans for growth in 2000. As the undisputed leader in the rent-to-own industry, which remained very much fragmented, the company was well positioned to take advantage of its size to open new stores, as well as to acquire underperforming operations that could be converted to a Rent-A-Center format. The company also branched into offering "pay as you go" Internet-access service. In October 2001 Talley announced his retirement. He was replaced as chairman and CEO by Mark E. Speese, who at the age of 44 already had more than 22 years of experience in the rent-to-own industry. He had joined Talley in 1986 and had been instrumental in the company's growth. In the short-term, Rent-A-Center was set to benefit from a troubled economy, which would undoubtedly result in more business from lower-income customers, but in the long-term it was also a company that was well managed and set to improve its dominant position in the rent-to-own industry.

Principal Subsidiaries

ColorTyme, Inc.; Advantage Companies, Inc.

Principal Competitors

Aaron Rents, Inc.; Bestway; Cash America International, Inc.; EZCORP Inc.; Rainbow Rentals; Rent-Way.

Further Reading

Bodipo-Memba, Alajandro, and Matthew Rose, "Renters Choice to Acquire Thorn's U.S. Business," *Wall Street Journal,* June 18, 1998, p. A4.

Finz, Stacy, "Texas Company Settles Over Nosy Questions to Employees," *San Francisco Chronicle,* July 8, 2000, p. A3.

Foster, Christine, "You Want It, You Rent It," *Forbes,* February 10, 1997, pp. 104–09.

Francis, Theo, "Rent-A-Center Grabs the Stage As Expansion Drive Pares Debt," *Wall Street Journal,* September 27, 2000, p. T2.

Henry, David, "Lender of Last Resort," *Forbes,* May 18, 1987, p. 73.

Scott, David, "Rent-to-Own Chain Draws up $26 Million Stock Offering," *Dallas Business Journal,* December 2, 1994, p. 3.

Weil, Jonathan, "Renters Choice's Price May Finally Catch Up with Its Fundamentals," *Wall Street Journal,* April 8, 1998, p. T2.

—Ed Dinger

Roanoke Electric Steel Corporation

102 Westside Boulevard, N.W.
Roanoke, Virginia 24017
U.S.A.
Telephone: (540) 342-1831
Toll Free: (800) 765-6567
Fax: (540) 342-9437
Web site: http://www.roanokesteel.com

Public Company
Incorporated: 1955
Employees: 1,811
Sales: $372.7 million (2000)
Stock Exchanges: NASDAQ
Ticker Symbol: RESC
NAIC: 331111 Iron and Steel Mills

Roanoke Electric Steel Corporation, operating out of Roanoke, Virginia, converts scrap metal into a variety of merchant steel products, which are then sold to steel service centers, fabricators, and original equipment manufacturers located in 21 states. Because of its Mid-Atlantic location, Roanoke Electric Steel is within a day's trucking distance to almost 70 percent of the U.S. population. Even during lean periods for the steel industry, the minimill has consistently posted a profit.

Post-World War II Founding

Roanoke Electric Steel's founder, John W. Hancock, Jr., was born in Roanoke in 1904. After studying mining engineering at Virginia Tech, primarily a military school at the time, he attended the University of Pennsylvania's Wharton School of Finance. He then went to work at a New York investment banking firm, where he sold securities for the next 15 years. World War II interrupted a successful career, as he joined the Air Force and became a lieutenant colonel. He was intrigued by the military's vast number of Quonset huts, temporary metal buildings that served as sheds or barracks. Aware that construction in the United States had been severely curtailed by the war effort, he became convinced that there would be a tremendous

domestic need for Quonset huts following the war, when it would be impossible to quickly meet the pent-up demand for office and storage space.

After being discharged from the service, Hancock returned home to Roanoke in 1945 and began to sell Quonset huts. In March 1946 he established John W. Hancock, Jr., Inc., to operate his dealership and expand into other products. The company served as a broker for open-web steel joists, in great need during the building boom of the late 1940s. Because of difficulty in establishing a reliable source of the product, Hancock in 1950 began to manufacture his own steel joists. The new business did well, but now he was frustrated by the difficulty of obtaining consistent shipments of steel from Pittsburgh mills. After resorting to foreign steel shipments, which also proved erratic, he began to consider building his own steel mill using scrap metal instead of iron ore. After much research, which included a trip to Germany, Hancock opted to use an electric furnace rather than the standard coke oven. The resulting "minimill" would require less space and fewer employees than a traditional steel mill, meaning less start-up capital as well.

Incorporation in 1955

In 1955 Hancock founded the Roanoke Electric Steel Corporation, financed by personal borrowing and the sale of a $300 stock-and-bond package to individual investors. Each share of stock and both second mortgage bonds were worth $100 apiece. A year later Hancock opened the first minimill in the Southeast, employing less than 100 people. The business got off to an inauspicious start: within weeks a secondhand motor failed and Hancock lacked the resources to pay for the repairs. He concluded that he had no choice but to shut down the plant. He relayed his decision to a Cincinnati scrap dealer, Irvin Bettman of the David J. Joseph Company, explaining that he was unable to pay for the scrap metal he had previously ordered. Bettman offered more time, relieving Hancock's immediate financial pressure. He then received further help from Louis Zinn, president of Port Everglades Steel Corporation, who helped ease cash flow by placing an immediate order for 1,000 tons of steel, as well as providing blanket orders to produce steel for his customers that Hancock could use at his discretion. In this way

Roanoke Electric Steel was able to gain its balance and grow into a successful business.

Hancock was eternally grateful to the two men that saved his mill. He would continue to do business with the David J. Joseph Company and Port Everglades Steel Corporation for the rest of his life. In fact, he kept a medallion bearing the name of Louis Zinn on his desk and requested that succeeding presidents of the company maintain the tradition. Hancock was a man of rare quality, known to be loyal and generous, revered by his workers and community. He was an influential force in Roanoke, contributing millions of dollars and countless hours to many civic causes, as well as Virginia Tech and other educational funds. A community leader who preferred to work in the background, he was instrumental in Roanoke peacefully achieving desegregation during the civil rights movement, while other Southern cities experienced riots and violence. He helped to form a group of local black and white leaders who quietly worked with businesses to eliminate longtime "separate but equal" practices.

After its first full year in operation in 1957, Roanoke Electric Steel turned a profit of $94,000 on revenues of $2.66 million. By the end of the 1950s, the company earned $377,000 on annual sales that approached $5 million. In 1960 Roanoke Electric Steel, operating at full capacity, added a ten ton-per-hour electric furnace to supplement the original four ton-per-hour unit. With two furnaces running, the company realized tremendous growth in 1961, with revenues topping $9.6 million and earnings reaching $895,000. Nevertheless, Hancock continued to look for ways to streamline the steelmaking process and increase profitability. Instead of casting steel ingots in molds, he envisioned a continuous casting machine, and entered into a joint venture with Babcock & Wilcox to create it. In 1962 his company became the first commercial continuous steel casting plant in the country. Eventually, continuous casting would be used by a majority of steel mills in the United States and 90 percent of mills in Japan.

To create diversity and add another customer for the mill, Roanoke Electric Steel established the Bowie Steel Division, a reinforcing bar fabricating plant in Bowie, Maryland. The company added a second rolling mill, creating the Salem Division after purchasing the operations of the Donalson Steel Corporation in Salem, Virginia. To keep up with demand, Roanoke Electric Steel purchased another ten ton-per-hour electric furnace, which went into operation in 1966. Within two years, revenues passed the $15 million level. The company continued to upgrade its facilities, adding an automated cooling bed, gauging table, and cold shear in 1969. A second continuous casting machine was then installed in 1970 to keep pace with the amount of steel the mill's three furnaces could now melt.

To procure a steady stream of raw material, as well as provide additional diversity, in 1974 Roanoke Electric Steel acquired Shredded Products Corporation, located in Montvale, Virginia. Relying primarily on junked automobiles, Shredded Products would eventually supply one-third of the mill's need for scrap metal. In 1975 Roanoke Electric Steel gained another subsidiary when John W. Hancock, Jr., Inc. was merged into the operation. With subsidiaries acting as both suppliers and buyers, Roanoke Electric Steel continued its steady growth. The mill's original four ton-per-hour electric furnace was replaced by a modern 20 ton-per-hour unit. In 1977 sales surpassed the $50 million mark and profits stood at $2.85 million. More upgrades followed, including a second finishing mill and a new storage building. By 1979 sales jumped to $72.5 million and profits exceeded $6.3 million.

Death of Hancock: 1994

The 1980s were difficult years for the steel industry, yet Roanoke Electric Steel remained profitable and continued to expand. In 1985 the company acquired Socar, Incorporated, which manufactured steel joists in plants located in South Carolina and Ohio. A year later the Salem operations began fabricating steel reinforcing bars, establishing the RESCO Steel Products unit. The business would be expanded in 1988 when a nearby facility was also purchased. Also in 1985, at the age of 81, Hancock would step down as the chief executive of Roanoke Steel, although he would remain as chairman of the board. He was succeeded by Donald G. Smith, a longtime executive of the company and secretary of the corporation since 1967. Smith became president in 1985, then chief executive officer in 1986. Finally, he was named chairman of the board in 1989, as Hancock retired completely. The company's founder lived five more years, passing away in 1994 at the age of 89.

The late 1980s were strong years for the company. Although a number of other minimills had started up around the country, they generally competed with the larger mills in plate steel products, rather than the merchant bar steel produced by Roanoke Electric Steel. As the economy soured in the beginning of the 1990s and the influx of foreign steel had a softening effect on steel prices, the company was forced to retrench. It closed down the Salem rolling mill and consolidated the two rebar facilities into a single operation. Despite poor business conditions, Roanoke Electric Steel remained profitable, although earnings fell to just $200,000 in 1991 on revenues of $127 million. As the nation's economy improved, construction picked up, steel prices rebounded, the demand for steel products increased, and the company's results quickly improved. Revenues steadily grew, to $146 million in 1992, $167.3 million in 1993, and $215.8 million in 1994, before topping out at $260 million in 1995. Likewise, net income soared, from $2.7 million in 1992, to $4.8 million in 1993, $11.9 million in 1994, and $20.2 million in 1995.

Although results reached a plateau in the mid-1990s, resulting from depressed steel prices caused by increased competition, Roanoke Electric Steel remained quite profitable. In order to retain a competitive edge in an industry with tight margins, the company invested $18 million in 1996 to purchase a state-of-the-industry ladle furnace, as well as other upgrades. As the American economy enjoyed an unprecedented growth spurt in

Key Dates:

1946: John W. Hancock, Jr., Inc. is formed.
1955: Roanoke Electric Steel begins operations as a steel supplier to John W. Hancock, Jr., Inc.
1962: Company opens first commercial continuous steel casting plant in the United States.
1974: Shredded Products Corporation is acquired.
1975: John W. Hancock, Jr., Inc. is absorbed as subsidiary.
1985: Socar, Incorporated is acquired.
1998: Steel of West Virginia is acquired.

the late 1990s, Roanoke Electric Steel shared in the benefits, while much of the steel industry felt the impact of cheap imports. Revenues reached $295.2 million in 1998, as the company posted $19.9 million in net profit. The following year revenues soared to a record $373 million and profits to a record $22.6 million, and Roanoke Electric Steel made the *Forbes* list of the 200 Best Small Companies, ranking number 171.

Taking advantage of its robust health, Roanoke Electric Steel looked to expand through acquisition in 1998. Late in the year it acquired Steel of West Virginia in a $117.1 million tender offer that included the assumption of $52.3 million in debt. A year earlier Steel of West Virginia had fended off a takeover bid from competitor JPT. The operation appeared to be a good fit for Roanoke Electric Steel, adding capacity as well as broadening its product line and customer base. Steel of West Virginia maintained a minimill in Huntington, West Virginia, and steel fabrication plants in Huntington and Memphis, Tennessee. The company designed and manufactured steel products used in the construction of mobile homes, truck trailers, industrial lift trucks, off-highway construction equipment, guard rail posts, manufactured housing, and mining equipment. Although it had produced spotty results, it still posted a $5 million profit on sales of $113 million in 1997.

Roanoke Electric Steel faced some labor problems with its new subsidiary when, six months after acquiring Steel of West Virginia, the United Steelworkers called for a strike over seniority rights and the use of nonunion workers. A year later, nonunion John W. Hancock, Jr., Inc. came in conflict with the United Steelworkers, which was attempting to organize the plants. Far

more troubling for Roanoke Electric Steel was the sudden influx of cheap imported steel that flooded the market. Although the glut was short-lived, it drove down prices, from $380 per ton to $280, and they failed to rebound. Moreover, the price for scrap metal increased. Combined with a downturn in the economy in late 2000, the low prices had a debilitating effect on the steel industry, driving a number of mills into Chapter 11, and forcing Roanoke Electric Steel to initiate job cuts.

The company reported flat results for 2000, generating $372.7 million in revenues, while posting a $14.1 million net profit. Although the milling operation suffered, the downstream products companies remained strong enough to keep the company profitable. As the economy verged on recession in 2001 and construction fell off, even those subsidiaries began to feel the pinch. Nevertheless, Roanoke Electric Steel with its diversified operations was better positioned than most of its competitors. The company had every reason to believe that, when the economy eventually recovered and construction activity picked up, it would renew its long-term pattern of growth and profitability.

Principal Subsidiaries

John W. Hancock, Jr., Inc.; Marshall Steel, Inc.; RESCO Steel Products Corporation; Roanoke Technical Treatment and Services, Inc.; Shredded Products Corporation; Socar, Incorporated; Steel of West Virginia, Inc.

Principal Competitors

AmeriSteel; Bethlehem Steel Corporation; Birmingham Steel Corporation; Kawasaki Steel Corporation; Kentucky Electric Steel, Inc.; National Steel Corporation; Nippon Steel Corporation.

Further Reading

Adams, Duncan, "Roanoke, Va., Steel Firm to Cut 30 Jobs, Reduce Output," *Roanoke Times,* August 18, 2000.

Caliri, Lois, "Virginia's Roanoke Electric Steel Corp. Buys Mill in West Virginia," *Roanoke Times,* November 12, 1998.

"Jack Hancock," *Roanoke Electric Steel Corporation,* 1994.

"Our Company, Its History and Mission," *Roanoke Electric Steel Corporation,* 1989.

"Roanoke's Entrepreneur," *Roanoke Times,* March 5, 1994, p. A6.

—Ed Dinger

Scientific-Atlanta, Inc.

5030 Sugarloaf Parkway
Lawrenceville, Georgia 30044
U.S.A.
Telephone: (770) 903-5000
Fax: (770) 236-6777
Web site: http://www.scientific-atlanta.com

Public Company
Incorporated: 1951
Employees: 12,000
Sales: $2.51 billion (2001)
Stock Exchanges: New York
Ticker Symbol: SFA
NAIC: 33422 Radio and Television Broadcasting and
   Wireless Communications Equipment Manufacturing;
   33429 Other Communications Equipment
   Manufacturing

Scientific-Atlanta, Inc. is a leading manufacturer of set-top cable boxes and other satellite transmission equipment. Long a leader in the construction of satellite earth stations, Scientific-Atlanta grew rapidly in the 1970s as a result of its involvement with the cable television industry, only to scale back and restructure its operations in the 1980s. In the 1990s, the company was one of the first to invest heavily in developing interactive digital cable technology.

Founded 1951

Scientific-Atlanta was founded on October 31, 1951, by six professors at the Georgia Institute of Technology. Hoping to market a device that recorded the patterns of antennae, the six pooled $600 to start the company. By 1956 the fledgling firm had completed development of its first product, built its first plant, and amassed 30 employees.

During the 1960s Scientific-Atlanta earned a place in the space and defense industries as a manufacturer of electronic testing equipment for antennae. By the end of that decade the company had added instruments for testing telephones and acoustic devices with defense applications. As a military contractor, the company distinguished itself by manufacturing unique electronic instruments for the federal government. According to *Business Week,* Scientific-Atlanta was a company "fascinated with communications esoterica." Nonetheless, with revenues of just $16 million a year, it was clear that the company had yet to reach its potential.

In 1971 Sidney Topol, an executive at the Raytheon Company with a background in physics and satellite technology, was named president of Scientific-Atlanta. A fervent believer in strategic planning, Topol set out to double the size of Scientific-Atlanta by implementing a long-term program. The first tenet of this plan was to reduce or sell off operations in which the company was losing money trying to beat much larger companies at their own game. Scientific-Atlanta's tentative interest in microwave carriers, for example, fell into this category, so Topol phased it out.

Scientific-Atlanta instead applied its energy to opportunities in new fields with large growth potential and few barriers to entry. The company sought out products that were either low-cost and high volume or had a very high price tag. "You've either got to make 10,000 of something worth $100 to $200, or several of something worth $500,000 or $10 million," Topol told the *New York Times.* The company planned to make the low-cost, high volume end of this equation profitable through aggressive research and development and a strong marketing effort. In its annual report, as reprinted in David C. Rickert's Harvard Business School case study of Scientific-Atlanta, the company stated: "Scientific-Atlanta operates under a disciplined business plan that concentrates on design, manufacture, and sale of standard technical products for the communications and instrumentation markets." More specifically, Topol recounted in *Dun's Review,* as restated by Rickert, "I asked what products we needed for growing markets, not what markets we should go after because we had a product."

Growing with Cable in the 1970s

The answer to that question was telecommunications products, primarily the satellite earth station, a large mobile dish

Company Perspectives:

Scientific-Atlanta leads the way with new innovations and vision for the digital interactive age.

used to receive signals transmitted from communications satellites orbiting the earth. In 1973 the company displayed a portable satellite earth station at a communications trade show in California. It planned to sell the portable stations to companies in the relatively new and rapidly growing cable television field so they could transmit their programming to a large number of stations in different areas. The stations, in turn, would send the programming to consumers' homes over their cable networks. At the time, however, observers told Scientific-Atlanta executives that satellite transmission of cable television programming would take place only in the distant future.

These predictions proved incorrect and as the cable television industry boomed in the mid- to late 1970s, Scientific-Atlanta grew with it. The company's profits ballooned by 40 percent a year from 1972 on as Scientific-Atlanta came to dominate the market it had largely pioneered. In 1976, as sales rose to more than $45 million, the company greatly expanded its manufacturing, laboratory, and office space at its headquarters. It sold two-thirds of the 3,000 satellite earth stations purchased by cable companies during the 1970s, enabling its clients—broadcasters such as Home Box Office (HBO) and Showtime/ The Movie Channel—to become pillars of the cable broadcasting industry. Scientific-Atlanta's strength in satellite earth stations helped to enhance its overall sales of cable television equipment, and the company also began to market other components necessary to operate a cable television system.

In addition to its satellite products for the cable industry, Scientific-Atlanta manufactured testing and measuring devices for telecommunications, industrial, and laboratory use. The company added to its instrumentation operations when it acquired the San Diego-based Spectral Dynamics Corporation, a manufacturer of scientific devices, in 1978 for $17.4 million. Spectral Dynamics brought with it European sales subsidiaries in Germany, France, England, and the Netherlands. With these additions, Scientific-Atlanta boasted a sales network that covered 40 countries and was supported by a worldwide service network that adjusted and repaired its instruments. Both Scientific-Atlanta and Spectral Dynamics relied on continual research and development to bring new products to market, thereby enhancing market share and fostering company growth.

By the end of 1978 Scientific-Atlanta's sales had reached $94.2 million, with earnings of $5 million. In addition to four plants in Atlanta, the company had opened facilities in Alabama, New Jersey, and Scotland. The following year the company added to its testing equipment holdings when it purchased Adar Associates, Inc., a company based in Burlington, Massachusetts, that manufactured automatic testing devices.

By the start of 1979 Scientific-Atlanta employed 2,700 people. That year the company also introduced Homesat, a subsidiary formed to market satellite equipment to homeowners who lived in areas too remote to receive adequate television

reception. The service's first customer, a New Mexico ranch owner, paid $20,000 to set up his own satellite earth station.

In addition to its two main areas of operation—communications and instrumentation—Scientific-Atlanta also entered the field of home security and energy management during the 1970s. The company marketed wireless home alarm systems and provided equipment to utilities that enabled them to monitor home energy use.

By the dawn of the 1980s Scientific-Atlanta had become the world's largest supplier of satellite earth stations. The company moved to increase its cable-related operations when it bought Systems Communications Cable, Inc., based in Phoenix, Arizona. Scientific-Atlanta paid $5.5 million for the firm, which manufactured coaxial cable for use in cable television systems.

Bottoming Out in the 1980s

Scientific-Atlanta's dominance of the cable television equipment field began to waver in the early 1980s when the company developed quality control problems with its set-top converters, units placed on top of television sets to facilitate the broadcast of cable channels. These difficulties caused Scientific-Atlanta to post its first quarterly loss in 13 years at the end of June 1982, when the company reported that it had accumulated a deficit of $2.3 million. Eventually, Scientific-Atlanta was forced to abandon the manufacture of set-top converters in its American plants and contract with a Japanese electronics firm, Matsushita, to have them made overseas. Currency fluctuations between the yen and the dollar made this a far more risky and expensive proposition for the company than had domestic manufacture of the sets. Scientific-Atlanta's delay in marketing its set-top converter, which had been long-awaited in the industry, resulted in a sharp dip in the value of the company's stock.

In 1983 Scientific-Atlanta's fortunes took a decisive turn for the worse when the bottom dropped out of the cable industry. In its infancy, cable services had grown feverishly, but the business had now matured and slowed and in the early 1980s cable entered a period of consolidation. As companies went out of business or were swallowed up by others, the demand for cable satellite transmission equipment dropped dramatically.

In late 1984 Scientific-Atlanta was dealt another blow when it failed to win a contract from the HBO and Showtime cable operations to develop equipment to scramble their signals, which homeowners were pirating out of the sky with their own satellite dishes. With this decision, the company's competitor, MA/Com, Inc., earned the right to market the technology that would set the standard for all future scrambling of cable satellite transmissions. Scientific-Atlanta found itself knocked out of the leading role in the industry it had largely invented.

Facing this roadblock head on, the company decided to investigate other markets. In June 1985 Scientific-Atlanta announced that it would introduce a new line of products in the area of business communications. Using a newly developed satellite dish, the "very small aperture terminal" or VSAT, which dispatched and received encoded signals transmitted in a new, highly reliable "KU" broadcast band width, the company proposed to market private video networks to large corporations; with Scientific-Atlanta's equipment, companies could transmit

Key Dates:

1951: Scientific-Atlanta is founded.
1971: New President Sidney Topol sets out to double company's size.
1980: Scientific-Atlanta is world's largest supplier of satellite earth stations.
1986: Scientific-Atlanta begins "retooling, refocusing" under new CEO William Johnson.
1993: James McDonald becomes CEO, oversees large investment in interactive digital cable technology.
2000: Scientific-Atlanta expands production several times as digital business booms.
2001: Share price falls and layoffs are announced in the wake of falling orders.

high-quality video images from their headquarters to branch offices or between field offices through satellite technology. Meetings, demonstrations, training sessions, and other types of programming and data could be more easily conveyed from one location to another. By offering video transmission—in addition to the ability to convey raw data such as figures and documents over fiber-optic telephone lines—Scientific-Atlanta hoped to make its system more useful and appealing to businesses than those of its competitors in the telecommunications industry.

In the early stages of the project, Scientific-Atlanta signed up nearly a dozen companies for its service, including General Motors and J.C. Penney. Despite these successes, however, analysts remained skeptical that there would be sufficient demand for Scientific-Atlanta's elaborate and expensive service to make the company's investment in the project pay off. Moreover, the company's lack of affiliation with any major satellite company to provide the other crucial link in its network caused worry.

Retooling in 1986

By 1986 Scientific-Atlanta's efforts at rejuvenation had in fact faltered. Operating profits dropped dramatically as the company "ran into very competitive markets," Chairman Topol told the *Wall Street Journal*. In an effort to stem Scientific-Atlanta's decline, Topol brought in an outside consultant, William E. Johnson, to take over the helm and help the company restructure itself and return to profitability. Scientific-Atlanta "had grown so fast in technology and marketing that it grew short on logistics," one board member informed the *New York Times*.

To Johnson, Scientific-Atlanta's problems stemmed from years of rapid growth, during which the company had become involved in a large number of new technologies, none of which it managed well. In addition, bureaucratic red tape had mushroomed to hamper financial reporting systems and as a result Scientific-Atlanta had taken its eye off the bottom line; competition in the industry was getting fierce, and the company's costs were spiraling. These conditions were caused in part by unsound personnel decisions.

With Johnson at its command post Scientific-Atlanta embarked on a process he called "retooling, refocusing, and restructuring," according to the *Wall Street Transcript*. The company

withdrew from a number of operational areas, selling seven out of 25 of its business ventures, including its home satellite business and coaxial cable subsidiary. Partly as a result of these changes the company posted a net loss in 1986 of $9.2 million.

Once rid of its less promising areas of operation, Scientific-Atlanta focused on more profitable concerns, such as its satellite communications networks. The company enhanced its holdings in this field when it bought Advanced Communications Engineering, which helped Scientific-Atlanta take second place in this growing field. Despite the earlier skepticism of industry analysts, the company discovered a strong demand for satellite communications networks among corporations and in developing nations, where land-based cable communications systems were prohibitively expensive.

Meanwhile, Scientific-Atlanta's traditional market for its satellite equipment—the cable television industry—began to show signs of life, particularly in Europe. To formulate other successful products Scientific-Atlanta began to pour renewed effort and money into research and development, revamping many of its product lines with all new technology to keep the company on the cutting edge of the industry. A particular area of growth was in commercial applications of high-definition television technology, which helped the company broaden its customer base.

Not content to simply alter its product lines, Scientific-Atlanta also moved to significantly control its costs. The company pared its workforce, firing 1,000 workers, and instituted a wage freeze. To reduce problems in its manufacturing operations, the company replaced its domestic assembly lines with cellular manufacturing teams. In an effort to control expenses at its overseas manufacturing outfits, Scientific-Atlanta worked out an agreement with its Japanese supplier to reduce the impact of currency fluctuations on its bottom line. Along with these changes, Scientific-Atlanta eliminated three-quarters of its senior-level management; this turnover allowed the company to revamp its corporate culture, reducing the number of financial reports necessary by two-thirds and incorporating engineers in the early stages of new-product design in an effort to control manufacturing costs. Productivity was increased and the time it took to manufacture many items shrank markedly.

Despite these changes, however, Scientific-Atlanta's instrument divisions, which manufactured equipment for testing and monitoring, remained insufficiently profitable. Nonetheless, by the beginning of the 1990s the company's overall performance had improved dramatically as earnings increased 121 percent over the last half of the previous decade to reach $36 million in 1989 and rose again to hit $44.3 million one year later.

In the 1990s Scientific-Atlanta continued its aggressive development of new technologies to improve its market share. In early 1991 the company introduced a satellite network for smaller businesses and began to market signal encoding devices to a number of companies. Still, a general economic recession, intensified by cuts in cable industry spending, resulted in a 20 percent drop in sales for the year. As a result, Scientific-Atlanta planned further restructuring in the form of staff cuts and consolidation of manufacturing operations; but the cost involved in these moves reduced the company's earnings for 1991 to only $1.1 million. Despite this bad news Scientific-Atlanta's directors remained hopeful that the company would prosper in years to come as it made efforts to reconfirm its record of technological innovation and aggressive marketing.

Betting on Digital in the 1990s

James F. McDonald, a 21-year IBM veteran originally from Kentucky, took over as chief executive in July 1993. McDonald had overseen layoffs and consolidations at Gould Inc., a $1 billion electronics firm, several years earlier. The *Atlanta Constitution* reported he faced an analogous situation at Scientific-Atlanta, which lacked a clear focus across its broad product line. The cable industry, which accounted for most of the company's business, provided the company a focus. By 1997, the company would sell off several units, including its venerable microwave instrumentations unit. In January 2000, Scientific-Atlanta sold its satellite networking division to ViaSat Inc. for $75 million. McDonald also consolidated manufacturing and administrative functions across the company's divisions.

Scientific-Atlanta signed development deals with numerous providers, hoping to win an early lead in the emerging interactive television business. However, the company's main competitor, market leader General Instrument (GI), found quick profits producing cheap set-top boxes for analog cable systems and digital boxes. However, Scientific-Atlanta had hedged its bets: the company was also developing software and two-way fiber for use by cable companies. In 1994, the company invested in PowerTV, a Cupertino, California start-up that was developing software and graphics hardware for various makes of digital set-top boxes.

"If you're there too early or too late with a new technology, you lose," McDonald told the *Atlanta Journal* in late 1998. Had Scientific Atlanta invested too much, too soon in the digital technology? Revenues and profits had continued to edge upward. The company made a profit of $81 million on sales of $1.2 billion for the 1997–98 fiscal year, though the stock price seemed undervalued.

Investors regained confidence as sales of the new Explorer, a $350 digital set-top box, took off in late 1998. However, General Instrument already had a competitor, the DCT-5000, in development.

Scientific-Atlanta expanded throughout 1999 as demand for both its Explorer cable box and its stock grew. However, General Instrument's lower priced devices were attracting more cable systems. These allowed for the extra channels available through digital cable, but not for full interactivity such as cable telephony and web surfing. These features, noted McDonald, provided cable networks an advantage over satellite broadcasters.

Explorers sales rose in 2000, and so did sales of satellite transmission products. The company signed several international deals, equipping cable providers in the United Kingdom, Germany, and Argentina with transmission equipment. Set-top boxes were going to Britain and Canada. The company also had a significant presence in Latin America and the Pacific Rim.

By mid-2001, Scientific-Atlanta had increased its workforce by a third, to 12,000 employees. In the works was a plan to bring NTN Communications' popular interactive trivia service, typically found in bars, to home cable boxes.

Share price was cut in half in the summer of 2001 as orders dropped. Angry investors, incensed by McDonald and others selling off millions of dollars worth of shares, filed 16 different lawsuits alleging misleading statements in the company's March third quarter reports.

Scientific-Atlanta began laying off workers at its Juarez, Mexico plant due to the slowdown in business. However, some still felt there was room for growth, as only 22 percent of U.S. cable customers were expected to have digital service by the end of 2001.

Principal Subsidiaries

PowerTV (80%).

Principal Competitors

Antec Corp.; ARRIS Group, Inc.; Motorola, Inc.; Pace Micro Technology PLC; Sony Corporation.

Further Reading

Barthold, Jim, "This Way Out: Jim McDonald, Scientific-Atlanta," *Telephony,* Supercomm 2001 supplement, June 4, 2001, pp. 134–38.

Brannigan, Martha, "Scientific-Atlanta Loses Reception on Robust Growth," *Wall Street Journal,* August 21, 2001, p. B10.

Brister, Kathy, "Preaching the Virtues of Full-Service TV," *Atlanta Constitution,* June 28, 2000, p. E6.

——, "Scientific-Atlanta Keeps Boom Going," *Atlanta Constitution,* March 28, 2001, p. D6.

——, "Trivia Game Channel Planned," *Atlanta Constitution,* June 12, 2001, p. F1.

Clothier, Mark, "Scientific-Atlanta Full Steam Ahead," *Atlanta Constitution,* February 23, 2000, p. D1.

Cook, James, "You've Got to Knock Off a Few Gas Stations First," *Forbes,* March 5, 1990.

Dickson, Glen, "S-A Unloads Satellite Networking Business," *Broadcasting & Cable,* January 24, 2000, p. 124.

Feder, Barnaby J., "Why Wall Street Likes Scientific-Atlanta's Mr. Fixit," *New York Times,* April 1, 1990.

Haddad, Charles, "Waiting for TV," *Atlanta Journal,* December 30, 1998, p. D4.

Husted, Bill, "Scientific-Atlanta Sharpening Focus," *Atlanta Constitution,* February 6, 1994, p. H1.

Jones, Andrea, "50 Years on the Cutting Edge," *Atlanta Journal,* May 2, 2001, p. XJ1.

Luke, Robert, and Kathy Brister, "Chairman Riding Increases in Scientific-Atlanta Shares," *Atlanta Journal,* May 20, 2001, p. Q6.

McNaughton, David, "Scientific-Atlanta CEO Reaps Rewards," *Atlanta Constitution,* November 12, 1994, p. C3.

Moran, Brian, "Business Is a Team Sport for Scientific-Atlanta CEO," *Atlanta Business Chronicle,* February 23, 2001, p. 58A.

Pomerantz, Dorothy, "A Cozy Duopoly," *Forbes,* March 19, 2001, p. 78.

Rickert, David C., "Scientific Atlanta," Boston: Harvard Business School, 1979.

Rothfeder, Jeffrey, "Will Corporate Video Be the New Way to 'Network'?," *Business Week,* May 19, 1986.

Scanlon, Mavis, ''Inside Trades at S-A Stoked Investor Ire,'' *Cable World,* August 6, 2001, pp. 1, 40.

Schuyten, Peter J., ''Scientific Atlanta's New Look,'' *New York Times,* January 7, 1980.

''Scientific-Atlanta Inc. Names W.E. Johnson Vice Chairman, Chief,'' *Wall Street Journal,* February 2, 1987.

Shaw, Russell, ''Put Up or Shut Up,'' *Financial World,* May 24, 1994, p. 32.

Upbin, Bruce, ''My Box Can Beat Your Box,'' *Forbes,* February 8, 1999, pp. 53–54.

—Elizabeth Rourke
—update: Frederick C. Ingram

Securicor Plc

Sutton Park House
15 Carshalton Road
Sutton
Surrey SM1 4LD
United Kingdom
Telephone: (+44) 020 8770 7000
Fax. (+44) 020 8661 0204
Web site: http://www.securicor.co.uk

Public Company
Incorporated: 1935 as Night Watch Services
Employees: 53,139
Operating Revenues: £699.4 million ($1.05 billion)
   (2000)
Stock Exchanges: London
Ticker Symbol: SCR
NAIC: 561612 Security Guards and Patrol Services;
   561621 Security Systems Services (Except
   Locksmiths)

Securicor Plc has its eye on global leadership in its core security and distribution businesses, which contribute 97 percent of the company's revenues (communications contribute the remainder). Securicor Security offers a full range of security services, including cash collection, processing and delivery, and armored-car transport, as well as manned guarding, closed-circuit television monitoring and response operations, prison management services—including the management of the U.K. "hi-tech" prison Parc—and electronic security services and systems. In the United States, the company's acquisition of Atlanta-based Argenbright Security in 2000 has placed Securicor as the top player in the U.S. aviation security market. Securicor plans to increase its focus on its security operation, building it into one of the world market leaders at the turn of the century. The company intends to accomplish this goal through an aggressive acquisition program—by the end of 2001 Securicor had already doubled its security sales to more than £1.3 billion, with plans to reach £2 billion in the near future. The company's other major division is Securicor Distribution, 50 percent of which was sold to Deutsche Post in 1999. The company's distribution and logistics activities operate under Omega Express—part of DP's Euro Express network—and other brand names, and is the United Kingdom's leading same-day business-to-business delivery company. In addition to express parcel delivery services, Securicor Distribution also provides container transport and freight haulage, third-party distribution and warehouse management, and vehicle fleet services. The third wing of the company, communications, formerly included Securicor's 40 percent interest in BT's Cellnet mobile telephone subsidiary; the company also held failed mobile phone company Securicor Wireless in the United States, which was disposed of in 2001. The new, slimmer Securicor posted nearly £700 million in 2000, with operations in some 40 countries. The company is led by Chairman Neil Macfarlane and Neil Buckles, who is expected to be formally appointed as CEO in 2002.

Protecting the Posh in the 1930s

Securicor traces its roots to the posh neighborhoods of pre-World War II London. The company was founded by a retired member of the Liberal government and featured a team of a dozen guards riding bicycles among the large homes of the city's wealthy neighborhoods. The guards, who wore old police uniforms, were meant to deter burglaries by their mere presence. Night Watch Services, as the company was called, did well given the increasing insecurity leading up to the outbreak of the war. In 1939, the company was taken over by two friends, the Marquis of Willingdon and Henry Tiarks, who changed the company's name to Night Guards. The name change brought the company under fire from the government, notably from the Labour party's George Lansbury, who charged that the company was "the first halting step down the road to fascism." The government's concern over the rise of private armies on British soil, and the outbreak of war in 1939, brought a quick close to Night Guards' activities.

Willingdon and Tiarks restarted the company after the war, now directing it toward industrial security services. The company's new niche proved more fruitful and the company quickly signed up new clients, extending its guard services to factory installations and commercial facilities. The company established stringent hiring practices, such as demanding that appli-

cants provide continuous 20-year employment histories, or back to their school years for younger candidates. Night Guards also began providing on-the-job training for its new hires.

By the beginning of the 1950s, the company's payroll had grown to more than 150 guards. In 1951, the company had outgrown its name, and Night Guards became "the Security Corps." Government alarm over the militaristic tone of the name soon led the company to a compromise; in 1953, the company adopted the name Securicor.

At the end of the 1950s, Securicor employed more than 300 guards. By then the company had already begun to branch out from its original guard service. In 1957, the company established an armored car service, acquiring the Armoured Car Company to implement cash-in-transit services. The company had also begun to develop a private two-way radio network, dubbed HELP, for "Haulage Emergency Link Protection."

At the beginning of the 1960s, Securicor had hardly begun to expand beyond its London base. Growth was to be difficult as the company faced a raft of competitors. In 1960, Willingdon and Tiarks opted out of the company's future, selling it to Associated Hotels, then owned by Denys Erskine, and originally founded in 1923. Erskine's brother Keith took over as head of Securicor.

Under its new owners, Securicor diversified into new areas. Its private radio network led it to form a partnership with automotive assistance company AA, combining the two company's radio networks to form the LINKLINE network. This experience in turn provided the basis for the company's later foray into the communications sector in the 1980s. Securicor also expanded overseas in the 1960s, targeting Malaysia, where the company modified two of its armored vehicles for operations in that country's tropical climate, and then Hong Kong, which became the base for Securicor's further expansion throughout the region.

Meanwhile, Securicor's cash-in-transit operation had expanded to include other document and data delivery services for its bank and other customers. The company soon added parcel deliveries to its delivery services and by the end of the 1960s the company had grown into a full-service parcel and document delivery service. This operation was given a further boost in the mid-1970s, when a long strike at the British Postal Service sent customers to the growing number of delivery services operating in the United Kingdom at the time. Securicor formed a new subsidiary, Securicor Omega Express, and began offering dedicated business-to-business delivery services in 1971. In that year, also, Securicor went public on the London Stock Exchange.

Securicor continued to diversify within its core businesses, acquiring a bodyworks business in order to develop its own armored vehicle designs, and entering the electronics field through another acquisition so that it could begin designing and marketing alarm systems. During the 1970s, the company moved onto the European continent, and also targeted Kenya, Zambia, and other African markets for its international expansion.

Targeting Security for the 21st Century

Securicor's acquisition of the United Kingdom's Pony Express in 1981 helped to expand its distribution operation beyond business-to-business parcel delivery to include nationwide same-day delivery services. The company was most known, however, for its armored vehicle services, and security services in general remained Securicor's mainstay. Yet at the beginning of the 1980s, competition in the cash-in-transit market was becoming fiercer, and Securicor, by then led by Chairman Peter Smith, began looking for new areas for growth.

Securicor's two-way radio network partnership had by this time grown into the Relayfone service, which connected a mobile radio network to the public telephone system. This system was largely devoted to enabling Securicor to communicate with the drivers of its armored and delivery vehicle fleets. Yet Smith saw mobile communications as a potential growth area for the company and began looking about for opportunities for extending its applications to a larger public.

In the early 1980s, the British government was preparing to grant the country's first mobile telephone licenses. One of these went to Racal, which later became Vodaphone. The other was to be granted to British Telecom, which then held the monopoly on the country's fixed-line telephone system. The government was reluctant to give over full control of the mobile license to BT—for fear that BT might extend its monopoly into the mobile telephony ring as well—and a condition to the granting of the license was that BT had to bring in a partner.

In 1984, Securicor stepped forward as BT's partner in what became the Cellnet mobile telephone network. For a mere £4 million, Securicor acquired 40 percent of Cellnet. Securicor, however, was never to take an active role in the development of Cellnet, but instead allowed BT to control development of its investment. At the time, the move appeared a gamble—in the early years, mobile telephony grew very slowly. Telephoning in public became stigmatized, not least because of the bulky and expensive telephones in use at the time.

Nonetheless, Cellnet and other mobile telephone providers made steady progress through the decade, and Securicor's stake in Cellnet slowly rose in value. By the 1990s, and particularly as mobile communications became increasingly acceptable to the consumer public, Cellnet had grown in value. By the mid-1990s, Securicor's 40 percent share in Cellnet was worth more than its security and distribution businesses combined. These businesses had grown too, however, as Securicor extended its operations into Central Europe and the Caribbean. The company had also managed to combine its distribution and communications interests when the company joined a partnership to develop the Datatrak vehicle tracking system, which the company acquired in 1991.

As it entered the 1990s, Securicor restructured to emphasize the diversified nature of its operations, regrouping its businesses

Key Dates:

1935: Night Watch Services, a team of bike-riding guards wearing police uniforms, is launched as a deterrent force in London.

1939: The company is taken over by two friends, the Marquis of Willingdon and Henry Tiarks, who change the firm's name to Night Guards; the company is put out of business by the outbreak of World War II.

1946: The company restarts business, now directed toward industrial security services.

1951: The company adopts a new name, The Security Corps, but raises government alarm for its ''militaristic'' connotations.

1953: The company changes its name to Securicor.

1957: Securicor acquires Armoured Car Company and launches armored vehicle and cash-in-transit services.

1960: Securicor is acquired by Associated Hotels' owner Denys Erskine, whose brother takes over as head of company.

1971: Securicor launches Omega Express business-to-business parcel delivery service and goes public on the London Stock Exchange.

1981: Securicor acquires Pony Express to begin offering national same-day delivery services.

1984: Securicor pays £4 million to acquire 40 percent share of Cellnet mobile telephone business of British Telecom.

1993: Securicor buys Scottish Express and extends parcel deliveries.

1995: Company acquires Russell Davies Group, adding that company's container shipping operations to enter logistics market.

1997: Securicor boosts its logistics division with purchase of John Miller, based in Scotland; the company also acquires majority control of Intek Global to enter U.S. mobile communications industry.

1999: Securicor sells its 40 percent stake in Cellnet for £3 billion; the company also acquires full control of Intek Global, renaming it Securicor Wireless, and acquires Securewest's U.K. guard operations.

2000: The company makes several acquisitions, including Loomis Armored Car Service Limited, Gray Security Services (South Africa), Argenbright Security Inc., and ADI Group.

2001: Securicor comes under fire after September 11 terrorist attacks; the company sells off Securicor Wireless and exits mobile communications market.

into three primary divisions: Security, Distribution, and Communications. Distribution was boosted in 1992 with the acquisition of part of Federal Express's business in the United Kingdom. That division grew further into the middle of the decade with the 1993 purchase of Scottish Express, extending the company's reach into the northern regions of the United Kingdom. Two years later, Securicor entered the logistics arena when it acquired Russell Davies Group, adding that company's container shipping operations. Another logistics unit, John Miller,

based in Scotland, was added in 1997. Meanwhile, the company moved to crack into the United States mobile communications market, acquiring a controlling share of Intek Global. After increasing its position to full control in 1999, that company was renamed Securicor Wireless.

Securicor's security services wing was also expanding, and especially reaping the benefit of the continued privatization of much of the United Kingdom's formerly government-controlled industries. Such was the case in 1994, when the company won a £96 million contract to provide prisoner escort services to the London courts system. In 1997, Securicor added prison management to its list of activities when it acquired the contract to design and manage the high-tech Parc prison. Securicor also joined in on the growing trend of installing closed-circuit camera systems in the country's towns and cities, offering CCTV monitoring and response services.

The coming explosion of the mobile telephone market was already apparent by the mid-1990s. Competition in that market was heightened when new operators, Orange and One2One, joined the market. Vodaphone too was growing rapidly, while Cellnet, limited by its ownership structure and furthered hampered by management mistakes, found itself under pressure. The British government, however, refused to allow British Telecom to acquire full control of the company.

Securicor was allowed to sell its stake at last in 1999. By then, however, it was too late. While Vodaphone had increased its market capitalization to more than £32 billion—and then, after acquiring Airtouch, to nearly £88 billion—Cellnet had fallen far behind. Securicor was forced to accept just £3.15 billion for its 40 percent stake. While this represented a handsome gain on the company's original £4 million investment, the low price sparked a round of harsh criticism from Securicor's institutional investors, which felt the company should have negotiated for a higher price for its shares.

The disposal of the Cellnet stake led to a wider shakeup of Securicor's operations. In 1999, the company sold off half of its distribution and logistics business, placing it into a 50–50 joint venture with Deutsche Post, which was expanding its Euro Express network. Securicor then took over management of Euro Express's U.K. operations. Securicor now turned its focus toward expanding its security operations, beginning an active acquisition program at the turn of the century.

At the end of 1999, Securicor acquired Securewest's U.K. guard operations. Two months later, the company acquired another guarding services company, Secureop UK. Two cash-in-transit companies were acquired in March and April 2000, those of Guardforce Limited, based in the United Kingdom, and Loomis Armored Car Service Limited, which represented the company's entry into the North American market. The company extended its cash-in-transit operations to the European continent in August of that year, with the purchase of Germany's GWK GmbH.

At the end of 2000, Securicor expanded still further into North America, and particularly into the United States, when it acquired Gray Security Services, with main operations in South Africa but also in the United States and Europe. Then, in December 2000, the company bought Argenbright Security Inc.

Based in Atlanta, and subsidiary to AHL Services, Inc., Argenbright was the largest specialist in aviation security in the United States. That purchase was followed by the acquisition of another AHL subsidiary, ADI Group, which provided aviation security services in Europe.

Securicor was shaken by the September 11, 2001 terrorist attacks, which placed a harsh spotlight on its aviation security services wing. The company faced added difficulties in the United States as well, as it was forced to abandon its attempt to enter the mobile communications market in that country. At the end of September 2001, the company announced that it had been forced to sell its Securicor Wireless subsidiary for a "nominal consideration only," rather than the £36 million price earlier announced.

CEO John Wiggs, who had guided the company through much of the previous decade, announced his retirement for 2002. Named to take over was Nick Buckles, a 15-year veteran of the company. Buckles vowed to continue the company's transition to a global security services powerhouse. Indeed, as the company approached the end of 2001, its acquisition drive had enabled it to double its security-related revenues, which were expected to top £1.3 billion for the year. The company set its sights on the global leadership position, planning to drive up its turnover to more than £2 billion.

Principal Subsidiaries

Argenbright Security (U.S.); Bridgend Custodial Services Limited (49.5%); Geldnet BV (Netherlands; 25%); JS Holdings Limited Incorporated (British Virgin Islands) (50%); Securicor Canada Limited; Securicor Cash Services Limited; Securicor Custodial Services Limited; Securicor Fuelserv Limited, Securicor GWK GmbH (Germany); Securicor Guarding Limited; Securicor Information Systems Limited; Securicor Kenya Limited; Securicor Luxembourg SA; Securicor (Malawi) Limited; Securicor Omega Holdings Limited (50%); Securicor Recruitment Services Limited; Securicor Security Services Ireland Limited; Securicor Sicherheitsdienste GmbH & Co KG (Germany); Securicor Vehicle Management Limited; Securicor Wireless Holdings Inc. (U.S.A.); Securicor (Zambia) Limited.

Principal Competitors

Chubb plc; Command Security Corporation; Group 4 Falck A/S; Guardsmark; Home Security International, Inc.; Initial; The Pittston Company; Prosegur, Compañía de Seguridad, S.A; Protection One, Inc.; Rentokil Initial plc; Securitas AB; Transnational Security Group; Tyco International Ltd.; The Wackenhut Corporation.

Further Reading

Foley, Stephen, "Securicor Looks Safe for the Long Term," *Independent*, October 2, 2001, p. 19.
Hosking, Patrick, "US Phones Flop Leaves Securicor 24m Poorer," *Evening Standard*, September 26, 2001, p. 38.
McIntosh, Bill, " 'Secret Deal' Charge Dogs Sale of Securicor's Cellnet Stake to BT," *Independent*, September 11, 1999, p. 21.
Roberts, Dan, "A Fair Share of Insecurity," *Daily Telegraph*, October 2, 1999, p. 1.
Tooher, Patrick, "The Changing of the Guard," *Independent on Sunday*, March 31, 1996, p. 6.

—M.L. Cohen

Sepracor Inc.

111 Locke Dr.
Marlborough, Massachusetts
U.S.A.
Telephone: (508) 481-6700
Fax: (508) 357-7499
Web site: http://www.sepracor.com

Public Company
Incorporated: 1984
Employees: 499
Sales: $85.2 million (2000)
Stock Exchanges: NASDAQ
Ticker Symbol: SEPR
NAIC: 325412 Pharmaceutical Preparation Manufacturing

Sepracor Inc. is a Marlborough, Massachusetts, pharmaceutical company. During much of the 1990s, investors enticed by promises of spectacular profits were attracted to the company; such profits, however, failed to materialize. Innovative techniques used to purify drugs, which allowed Sepracor to patent variations on some of the world's most lucrative prescription drugs, are giving way to the development of original products and the creation of a marketing operation, as the company endeavors to join the ranks of traditional pharmaceutical firms, with the hope of finally becoming a profitable business.

Founding in 1984

Timothy J. Barberich cofounded Sepracor in 1984 and became its president and chief executive officer. After earning a college degree in chemistry, Barberich went to work in 1971 as a junior chemist for American Cyanamid Co., where he gained first-hand knowledge about the vagaries of synthetic drugs. In Brazil he participated in the demonstration of a deworming medicine, in which a prized bull was injected with a new wonder drug, only to watch along with a square filled with farmers as the animal dropped dead, the victim of an unintended side effect. The underlying chemical problem had been known for well over a hundred years, uncovered in the mid-1800s by famed scientist Louis Pasteur, who discovered that some organic molecules,

called chiral chemicals, feature mirror images—that is, left-handed and right-handed versions called optical isomers. (Chiral is derived from the Greek word for hands, *kheir.*) In short, while a medicine provides beneficial traits on the one hand, it may also contain devastating side effects on the other. Perhaps the most famous and tragic example of this phenomena is the 1950s' drug Thalidomide. One of its isomers relieved pregnant women of morning sickness, while its mirror image produced horrifying birth defects. Despite their knowledge of optical isomers, researchers until recently simply did not have the expertise to separate the left-handed and right-handed versions, resulting in medicines that contained mixtures of both, with side effects tolerated as long as they failed to prove too harmful.

Barberich began to work on separation techniques when he joined Millipore Corporation, a Bedford, Massachusetts, firm that developed separation products for high-tech companies. By the time he left to form Sepracor he was the general manager of the company's medical products division. Striking out on his own, Barberich was interested in using the new separation technology to purify chemicals, then sell them to pharmaceutical companies. A friend introduced him to venture capitalist Robert Johnson, who a couple of years earlier had been instrumental in funding Genex, one of the first biotech start-ups. With Johnson providing $500,000 in seed money, Barberich teamed with James Mrazek, president of Carnegie Venture Resources, and Dr. Robert Bratzler to create Sepracor. Soon after the new company began its operations, however, it became apparent that the demand for pure chemicals from biotech companies, Sepracor's target customers, would not materialize. Biotechs, after several years of hype and investor enthusiasm, were now facing the stark reality of backing up their expansive claims with profits, but product development was slow and venture capital dried up, which in turn had an adverse effect on Sepracor's business plan. As a result, Sepracor would change its strategy, and its history would begin to mirror the other biotech startups.

In 1985 Sepracor created a subsidiary, BioSepra, devoted to its original chemical purification business, while it began to focus on developing purified versions of well-known drugs, in effect eliminating sinister (left-handed) side effects to create an improved strain. Barberich hoped to sell the company's exper-

Company Perspectives:

Sepracor Inc. is a research-based pharmaceutical company dedicated to treating and preventing human disease through the discovery, development, and commercialization of innovative pharmaceutical products that are directed toward serving unmet medical needs.

tise to the large pharmaceuticals, only to find no interest. He then decided to commit $10 million to the development of purified drugs without outside help, compounds that by law the company would be able to patent. It appeared to be a potentially lucrative niche, especially in light of pharmaceutical companies' disdain for pursuing the work. The culture of research departments was one that placed a high emphasis on original work. Moreover, to eliminate side effects by using separation techniques was a tacit admission that something might be wrong with a pharmaceutical firm's product. Sepracor, therefore, found itself in a strong position in the late 1980s: it could develop what amounted to new drugs with far less developmental resources. It concentrated on the most profitable medicines that were nearing the end of their 14-year patent terms, at which point generic drug makers would be able to manufacture cheaper versions. Sepracor's strategy was to present pharmaceutical companies with a patented, purified version of their compound, then strike a deal. The pharmaceutical would be able to pump new life into an old brand, since the new form of the drug would overshadow the generic knockoff with the old side effects, while essentially gaining a new patent term. The pharmaceutical would bear the manufacturing and marketing costs, and Sepracor would pocket a royalty as well as make money by selling the purified active ingredients to their partners. Moreover, Sepracor was well aware that the pharmaceutical could better fund legal teams, so that by working with the pharmaceutical it could avoid costly and potentially devastating patent litigation. In many ways it was an elegant plan that would one day capture the imagination of many investors, while at the same time causing pharmaceuticals to label Sepracor as little more than a pirate operation. By 1990 Sepracor had applied for patents on purified forms of 40 major drugs.

Completion of Initial Public Offering: 1991

Sepracor's plan to make an initial public offering of stock was postponed by the Gulf War but eventually took place in September 1991 when the company worked with Lehman Brothers to sell 4.6 million shares at $10 per share. Despite losing almost $15 million in 1991 and no immediate prospects of gaining profitability, Sepracor had a market capitalization of $160 million. Also in 1991 it acquired IBF Biotechnics, a French firm, in order to become involved in the chromatography-based and membrane-based separation techniques used in the manufacture of peptides and proteins. A ruling by the Food and Drug Administration in early 1992 would then provide a boost to the company, as well as signal a long-term change in the pharmaceutical landscape. The FDA now required that all new chiral drugs be tested to determine if a pure isomer form would eliminate unwanted side effects. While Sepracor's scientific principles may have been vindicated by this ruling, it also meant that the major pharmaceutical compa-

nics would now be forced to engage in similar research and that the number of future candidates for purification would eventually dry up. Nevertheless, Sepracor still held a large number of promising patents to exploit.

The first of these patents that forced a major pharmaceutical to deviate from the usual posture of disdain for Sepracor involved the antihistamine Seldane, produced by Marion Merrell Dow. An FDA ruling that required Seldane to carry a warning about potentially fatal cardiac arrhythmia had crippled sales, which dropped by some 30 percent, from $900 million in sales posted in 1992. Both Sepracor, looking for more cash, and Marion, saddled with declining sales, needed one another. In June 1993 they struck a deal that called for Marion to invest $10 million in Sepracor, thus gaining a 6 percent stake, as well as paying another $7.5 million in a licensing agreement, plus 8 percent in royalties. The new drug, Allegra, would not only be free of the FDA warning and regain lost sales, it would provide Marion with an extended life on its antihistamine product. For Sepracor, Allegra provided a welcome revenue stream, but the terms were not as advantageous as the company could have commanded if it had been better positioned financially and did not need help in getting Allegra through clinical trials. Nevertheless, the Marion agreement lent much needed credibility to Sepracor with investors as well as other pharmaceutical companies, which would now be more willing to do business. It was imperative, however, for Sepracor to have enough ready cash to fund development in order to hold out for the best possible licensing deals in the future.

In 1994 Sepracor engineered two simultaneous public spin-offs of divisions to improve its finances, while retaining a controlling interest in both. Underwritten by David Blech, who had gained a reputation for biotech IPOs, BioSepra netted $18.3 million, and two weeks later HemaSure, devoted to the purification of donated blood products, netted $13.1 million. By providing separate funding for these businesses, which were draining cash and required some time before they would become profitable, Sepracor was better positioned to finance its core business of purifying blockbuster drugs. Soon after, however, Blech's firm was forced to suspend operations because of its own financial woes, and any company associated with it was punished by investors. Sepracor's stock price fell from a high of $14 to just $4, while the recent spinoffs also suffered significant erosion. Believing that the company needed someone with credibility in the financial community to present Sepracor's case, Barberich hired a new chief financial officer, luring David Southwell away from Lehman.

The British Southwell knew Barberich since his involvement with Lehman's underwriting of Sepracor's IPO. His immediate priority as the new CFO was to raise at least $5 million cash before the end of 1994 in order to stave off failure. After considerable effort he lined up $10 million in financing from the Oscar Frank Delano Partners Fund. Conditions improved even more in January 1995 when news that the patent for Allegra had finally been issued bumped Sepracor's stock price by 50 percent. The stock would receive a further boost later in the year when the company reported encouraging news on two other potential products. There was talk on the street that Sepracor would be generating $3 billion in sales in three years. In order to continue development of these drugs and realize that promise, however, Southwell estimated that the company's burn rate of cash would have to increase from $30 million a year to $45 million. Over the next several months he engineered a variety of financial deals to meet the challenge. Taking advantage of a rebound in the stock market for biotech stocks, he raised $67 million on a secondary offering of Sepracor stock. He also raised an additional $47 million to fund HemaSure, which reduced Sepracor's stake to 37 percent and allowed the company to remove the spinoff from its books. Southwell then raised $81 million in a convertible bond offer through Lehman. Finally, in March 1996 Southwell oversaw the IPO of a complicated spinoff and merger: The Sepracor SepraChem division, which created chemical synthesis products, merged with an Eastman Kodak spinoff, chemicals manufacturer Sterling Organics, to create ChiRex Inc. The $87 million raised in the offering funded the acquisition, while again taking the business off Sepracor's books to allow it to focus on its central work. By the middle of 1996, when all the transactions were complete, Southwell had garnered over $120 million for Sepracor, which provided the company with a two-year financial cushion and, as a result, greater control over the rights of some potentially lucrative drugs it had in the pipeline.

Favorable FDA Ruling in 1997

Early in 1997 the price of Sepracor stock rose significantly following an FDA ruling that forced the removal of Seldane from the shelves and paved the way for Allegra to replace it. Moreover, the company was nearing completion on a purified form of Albuterol, an asthma medication that generated $1.4 billion in sales each year, as well as a key ingredient used in the antihistamine Claritin. By the end of 1997 Sepracor would sign an agreement with Schering-Plough Corporation to develop a purer form of Claritin, which generated $1.3 billion in annual sales and was less than five years away from patent expiration. The price of Sepracor stock rose above $40. A few months later the prospects appeared even brighter when Sepracor received a patent for a purified form of fluoxetine, marketed as Prozac by Eli Lilly & Co., with sales approaching $3 billion a year. Then in July 1998 Sepracor licensed a new form of Propulsid, a popular heartburn medication with over $1 billion in annual sales, to Johnson & Johnson. Earlier in the year the companies had also agreed to work together on an improved version of Johnson's Hismanal antihistamine. It appeared that Sepracor had finally gained acceptance with the major pharmaceutical firms and that it would soon begin to realize robust profits after years of loss, with some analysts predicting it would be a $10 billion company in a matter of years. Nevertheless, in 1997 the company generated just $15.3 million in revenues and posted

net losses of $26.1 million. In 1998, revenues would increase modestly, coming in at $17.4 million, while the loss ballooned to $93.3 million.

Sepracor's prospects were buoyed later on when it sold the rights for the purified form of Prozac to Lilly for $90 million. The price of the company's stock soared to $140 per share by March 1999, giving it a market capitalization well over $3 billion. Not all investors were convinced, however, as an unusually high number of the company's outstanding shares were controlled by short sellers anticipating that the price would tumble. When Johnson backed out of the Hismanal deal, investors began to question whether Sepracor's other agreements were as solid as first believed, and the price of the company's stock plummeted to $55 by May 1999. Sepracor received some good news, however, when the FDA granted approval for the company to market Xopencx, a purified version of an asthma medication, the first product that it would market on its own.

Sepracor's hope for a future lucrative revenue stream derived from Prozac was dashed in 2000. The company suffered enough damage by its association to the drug, the integrity of which came into question when it was revealed that over the years Lilly had suppressed evidence of Prozac contributing to suicidal tendencies in a small percentage of patients. Worse news came in October 2000 when Lilly terminated its agreement with Sepracor after patients in clinical trials for the new version developed abnormal heart rhythms. The stock immediately lost almost one-third of its value. Over the next several months the price of Sepracor stock plunged to less than $24 per share.

Sepracor retained a number of other potential money-making refined versions of major selling drugs in the pipeline, but the company clearly had to use its purification techniques in the development of entirely new drugs. As part of its transition to becoming a more traditional pharmaceutical business, it initiated direct-to-consumer marketing efforts to sell its products in 2001. Although revenues in 2000 increased to $85.2 million, Sepracor lost $204 million after having lost $183 million in 1999. It remained very much an open question how much longer the company would be able to maintain such a high burn rate before being able to realize a profit.

Principal Subsidiaries

BioSphere Medical Inc. (55%); Sepracor Canada Holdings, Inc.; Sepracor Securities Corporation; Sepracor, N.V. (Netherlands).

Principal Competitors

Bristol-Myers Squibb Company; Eli Lilly & Co.; Hi-Tech Pharmacal; Johnson & Johnson; Mylan Laboratories, Inc.; Pfizer Inc.; Schering-Plough Corporation; Watson Pharmaceuticals Inc.

Further Reading

"Bulls, Pills and Patents," *Economist,* June 28, 1997, p. 69.
Gianturco, Michael, "Piggyback Drugs," *Forbes,* September 22, 1997, p. 244.
Johannes, Laura, and Thomas M. Burton, "Son of Prozac," *Wall Street Journal,* December 7, 1998, p. A1.

Kover, Amy, "One Hot Biotech Stock," *Fortune,* January 11, 1999, p. 196.

O'Reilly, Brian, "Drug Pirates Make Good," *Fortune,* October 12, 1998, p. 146.

Petersen, Melody, "As Lilly Ends Prozac Pact, Sepracor Stock Falls Nearly 30%," *New York Times,* October 20, 2000, p. C6.

Picker, Ida, "Staying Alive," *Institutional Investor,* May 1997, p. 80

Young, Jeffrey, "Lefties, Righties and Anxieties," *Forbes,* July 19, 1993, p. 208.

—Ed Dinger

Shanks Group plc

Astor House
Station Road
Bourne End, Buckinghamshire SL8 5YP
United Kingdom
Telephone: (+44) 1628-524-523
Fax: (+44) 1628-524-114
Web site: http://www.shanks.co.uk

Public Company
Incorporated: 1880 as Shanks & McEwan
Employees: 4,424
Sales: £502.4 million ($711.5 million) (2001)
Stock Exchanges: London
Ticker Symbol: SKS
NAIC: 562998 All Other Miscellaneous Waste
Management Services; 562111 Solid Waste
Collection; 562112 Hazardous Waste Collection;
562119 Other Waste Collection; 562211 Hazardous
Waste Treatment and Disposal; 562212 Solid Waste
Landfill; 562213 Solid Waste Combustors and
Incinerators; 562219 Other Nonhazardous Waste
Treatment and Disposal

Buckinghamshire, England's Shanks Group plc is the United Kingdom's leading independent waste management company. Shanks Group's operations in Belgium and The Netherlands also make it one of Europe's largest waste management companies. Operating from more than 75 sites in the United Kingdom alone, the company offers a full range of waste collection, transport, recycling, treatment, and disposal services, including landfill and incinerator operations, and hazardous waste collection and disposal systems—including a contract to dispose of more than 45,000 tons of cow carcasses following the 1990s outbreak of so-called mad cow disease in the United Kingdom. Shanks's landfill operations have led the company to invest in electrical generation, using the methane gas produced by the decomposing waste at its landfill sites. Shanks also offers industrial cleaning operations and, in 2001, became the first nongovernment-run company to provide waste

management services to a local government council in Scotland. Chairman Gordon Waddell and CEO Michael Averill have been responsible, in large part, for redirecting Shanks from a diversified building group to a streamlined company focused on waste management services—the company was an active participant in the sector's consolidation trend of the 1990s, pursuing an aggressive acquisition program. More than half of the company's 2001 revenues were generated in the United Kingdom; the rest of Europe accounted for nearly all of the remainder.

Late 19th-Century Civil Engineer

Shanks Group began as construction firm Shanks & McEwan. Based in Glasgow, the company was established by partners Guy Shanks, an engineer, and Andrew McEwan, an architect, near the end of the 19th century. Shanks & McEwan was to grow into a prominent Scottish civil engineering firm, helping to construct the railway system in that country. For most of its early history, the company was led by Guy Shanks, who remained at the company's head until just after World War II. He was succeeded by nephew Alec Shanks, and both the Shanks and McEwan families shared ownership of the company. The McEwans only sold out to the Shanks in the early 1980s.

By then, the company had swelled into the Shanks & McEwan Group, a diverse collection of companies centered around the civil engineering and construction fields, but which also ran extensive quarrying operations. A growing component of the group was waste management services, a sector that had been building steadily since the 1970s. New management, under the form of Chairman Peter Runciman and Chief Executive Officer Roger Hewitt, began to accelerate the company's participation in waste management services in the mid-1980s.

One of the first steps of the company's transformation was the purchase of London Brick Landfill, a subsidiary of the Hanson conglomerate. That 1986 acquisition gave the company clay pits and other landfill sites, particularly in the northern Home Counties region. In 1988, the company went public as Shanks & McEwan Group Plc. The public offering helped fuel the company's expansion into waste management services, as well as an attempt to expand its civil engineering component into road construction.

New legislation required the country's utilities companies to seek alternative fuel sources and energy suppliers. Shanks & McEwan turned toward power production in 1991, beginning construction of an electrical generation facility at its Bedfordshire landfill, using the methane gas produced as byproduct of the decomposition of waste at the site. The company also expanded into another waste management area, that of hazardous waste disposal, when it acquired Rechem Environmental Services in 1991. That company owned two of the United Kingdom's four hazardous waste incinerators and disposal sites.

The waste management sector was expecting to boom in the United Kingdom in the early 1990s with the coming passage of the Environmental Protection Act of 1990, which tightened emissions levels for businesses and set new requirements for the disposal of waste. Yet the slumping economy and the more stringent requirement increased Shanks & McEwan's operating costs as well. At the same time, the company's new Rechem hazardous waste operations were under threat as the European Community enacted new legislation governing the import and export of hazardous waste—giving the British government the authority to ban all hazardous waste imports into the country. Such a move threatened to cripple Rechem, which, following technical difficulties at its facilities, had slipped into losses at the end of 1993. Meanwhile, the collapse of the construction industry had brought the company's construction arm into trouble. Worse for Shanks & McEwan, its recent expansion into road construction proved ill-timed and the company began posting losses.

With the company heading into deeper difficulties, Runciman stepped down as chairman in 1992. Taking his place was Gordon Waddell, who had played professional rugby before becoming a prominent player in the gold trade. Waddell and Hewitt began dismantling the company's construction and civil engineering side, selling off most of those businesses by 1993. But the pair quickly disagreed over the company's direction, with Hewitt pushing toward centralized management of the company's far-flung operations, and Waddell touting just the opposite.

Deepening losses in 1993 led to Waddell having his way. Hewitt was ousted by the middle of that year. Waddell then took over as acting CEO while the company struggled to overcome its losses and placate its disgruntled shareholders. Shanks & McEwan restructured its operations, shutting down its head office, shifting administration to Buckinghamshire, and regrouping its business into more or less autonomous operating divisions. Waddell was later joined by Michael Averill, who moved from his position as chief of Rechem to the chief executive position for the entire group. By 1995, the company had sold off its remaining construction industry holdings.

Streamlined Waste Management Leader for the New Century

Shanks & McEwan's fortunes rose as it moved into the last half of the decade. New landfill taxes not only helped boost the company's revenues in that area, but also encouraged businesses to turn to Shanks for its incineration services. The company also was banking on new European legislation that added stricter recycling requirements. As Averill pointed out to the *Daily Telegraph,* "The regulations say thou shalt recycle whatever the cost. Previously people were not doing so, as the environmentally friendly option was always more expensive." The company added three new recycling plants, raising its total to five plants and making it the out-and-out leader in the U.K. recycling sector.

Meanwhile the company took a leading role in what many saw as the much-needed consolidation of the U.K. waste management sector. Shanks & McEwan hit the acquisition trail in earnest, starting with the acquisition in May 1996 of the Scottish dry waste operations of rival Leigh Industries, which had been acquired by General Utilities (subsidiary of France's Generale des Eaux). That year saw the company acquire Goodwins Mini Skips, based in Hertfordshire; Greenacre Waste, which added trash collection, transfer, and recycling operations in South Wales; Oxfordshire's TRASH waste transfer business; and 20 million cubic meters of landfill freeholds.

The company also was growing organically, adding a methane gas power plant in Scotland, opening a recycling plant in London, and winning a contract to incinerate 45,000 tons of cattle meat and bone meal (MBM) piled up in the midst of the outbreak of BSE (bovine spongiform encephalopathy, otherwise known as "mad cow disease") among the country's cattle herds. This contract was expected to be only the first of many, as the country's stockpile of MBM topped two million tons, and the company stood out as the sole U.K. facility capable of its incineration.

In 1997, Shanks & McEwan launched a dedicated Contaminated Land Services operation when it won the contract for cleaning up the Millenium Dome site in Greenwich. The company also was beginning to pick up a number of contracts to provide waste collection and disposal and other services to local

Key Dates:

1880: Andrew McEwan and Guy Shanks found Shanks & McEwan construction firm.

1986: Shanks & McEwan acquire London Brick Landfill, beginning shift toward becoming a focused waste management firm.

1988: The company goes public on the London stock exchange.

1991: The acquisition of Rechem Environmental Services gives company entry into the hazardous waste disposal sector.

1994: Management shakeup leads company to restructure and abandon construction industry to focus entirely on waste management services.

1996: Shanks & McEwan acquires Scottish dry waste business from Leigh Interests, beginning long acquisition drive, including TRASH, Greenacre Waste, and Goodwins Mini Skips; the company is awarded its first MBM incineration contract; the company opens materials recycling plant in London.

1997: The company launches Contaminated Land Services; the company wins managing and operating contract for Milton Keynes Materials Recycling Facility; Robinson Brothers and Safewaste is acquired.

1998: The company pays £66 million for Belgian waste management operations of SITA; the company acquires Lothing Chemical Company, MRJ Waste, and others; the company opens Elstow Transfer Station and Municipal Recycling Centre, as well as Glendevon Recycling Facility.

1999: The company acquires WE Jenkins, AB Hendry, then pays £50 million for Caird Group Plc; the company changes its name to Shanks Group plc.

2000: The company pays £209 million to acquire Waste Management Nederland; the company acquires Ghent, Belgium-based NV De Beer and Partners; the company tops £500 million in sales.

2001: The company wins 25-year contract to provide waste management services to Argyll & Bute Council in Scotland.

governments, including Peterborough, where it opened a new materials recycling facility, and Milton Keynes, where the company won the contract to manage and operate that community's recycling plant. At the end of that year, the company acquired two new companies, Safewaste, based in Nottingham, and Robinson Brothers Environment, adding to the waste collection business Leigh Corby acquired earlier that year.

The company's acquisition drive continued into the next year. In January the company added South Wales' MRJ Waste, then Pembrokeshire Environmental the following month. Shanks & McEwan added to its hazardous waste business in March 1998 when it acquired Edinburgh's Lothian Chemical company, which offered solvent recovery services and produced recycled liquid fuels. The purchase price of this company, as with most of the company's latest acquisitions, was low, at just £3 million.

On a different scale—and place—was the company's purchase, that same month, of the Belgian waste management division of France's SITA. That acquisition cost the company £66 million, but gave it a full range of waste management services, as well as a leading place in Belgium's waste management market. The acquisition also marked the company's first step toward becoming one of the European leaders in the sector.

Back in the United Kingdom, the company opened a new landfill site in north Wales, adding three million cubic meters of space to its total capacity; the company also received permission to expand an existing site in Buckinghamshire. At the same time, the company was granted the authorization to increase its electrical power generation by an additional 32 megawatts. On the recycling side, Shanks & McEwan opened two new facilities that year, in Edinburgh and in Elstow. The company also began offering disposal services for fluorescent tubes.

New acquisitions followed at the end of that year and into the next, including the smaller purchases of Whites Environmental, WE Jenkins, AB Hendry, Muktubs, Bio-Logic Remediation Ltd, and ASM Waste Services. During 1999, the company changed its name to Shanks Group plc, then paid £50 million to acquire rival Caird Group, which added six new landfill sites in England and Scotland, as well as two additional special waste operations.

Shanks took on a new scale the following year when it announced its acquisition of Waste Management Nederland BV. Paying £209 million, the company acquired a prominent spot in the Dutch waste management market. The purchase also raised the percentage of foreign sales to 49 percent of the company's total sales—and slightly more than half of the company's profits. Shanks' Benelux operations grew again in 2000, with the purchase of NV De Beer and Partners, which acted as a holding company for Ghent-based waste management group De Paepe.

By 2001, Shanks's sales had topped £500 million. The company was also emerging as a major producer of alternative energy. After expanding its Brogborough-based power generation facility, the company's total landfill-gas generated power production topped 50 megawatts. The outbreak of foot-and-mouth disease offered the company new prospects for its MBM incineration activity, which already had been boosted by the award of a new 190,000-ton contract in 1999. By the end of the year, the company was posting new gains in its public-sector operations as well, winning a 25-year contract to provide waste collection and management services from Argyll & Bute Council, the first such private contract granted in Scotland.

As it ended 2001, Shanks had successfully completed its transformation into a focused waste management services company and had gained a top spot not only in the United Kingdom, but also among the major players on the European continent. New legislation from the European Community was expected to increase the company's business at home, as the United Kingdom placed itself in line with European norms. At the same time, the company expected a place at the table in a future round of consolidation of the European waste management sector.

Principal Subsidiaries

Shanks Waste Services Limited; Shanks Northern Limited; Shanks Midlands Limited; Caird Environmental Limited;

Shanks Chemical Services Limited; Shanks Chemical Services (Scotland) Limited; Safewaste Limited; Vale Collections and Recycling Limited; Page s.a. (Belgium); Fusiman Industrial Cleaning s.a. (Belgium); B & P n.v. ''Sobry'' (Belgium); Vancoppenolle Invest. n.v. (Belgium); N.V. De Beer & Partners ''de Paepe'' (Belgium); Icova BV (The Netherlands); BV van Vliet Groep Milieudienstverleners (The Netherlands); Vliko BV (The Netherlands); Klok Containers BV (The Netherlands); Transportbedrifj van Vliet BV ''Contrans'' (The Netherlands); Reym BV (The Netherlands); Afvalstoffen Terminal Moerdijk BV ''ATM'' (The Netherlands); Flection International BV (The Netherlands); Van der Stoel Containerservice BV (The Netherlands); Andre de Vriendt s.a. (Belgium; 60%); Geohess (U.K.) Limited (50%); Shanks Avondale Limited (50%); Caird Bardon Limited (50%); Silvamo n.v. (Belgium; 50%); Marpos n.v. (Belgium; 45%).

Principal Competitors

Cory Environmentals (Exel plc); Waste Recycling Group (Kelda Group plc); Pennon Group Plc; Severn Trent Plc; Société Industrielle de Transports Automobiles (SITA); Suez; Waste Management, Inc.; Vivendi Environnement SA; Waste Recycling Group PLC.

Further Reading

Ahmad, Sameena, ''Rag and Bone Boost for Shanks,'' *Independent,* November 6, 1997, p. 26.

Carr, Miranda, ''Shanks Profits Rise Aided by BSE-Hit Cows,'' *Daily Telegraph,* November 6, 1997.

Gribben, Roland, ''Farmyard Lift for Shanks,'' *Daily Telegraph,* November 1, 2001, p. 34.

Moreton, Philippa, ''Shanks (SMG.L) Turns Waste into Profit Growth,'' *Reuters,* May 27, 1999.

Trapp, Roger, ''A Warm Glow in the Wasteland,'' *Independent on Sunday,* May 16, 1999, p. 6.

''Waste Firm Shanks Far from Down in Dumps As Earnings Soar,'' *Evening News,* May 30, 2001, p. B1.

—M.L. Cohen

Sycamore Networks, Inc.

150 Apollo Drive
Chelmsford, Massachusetts 01824
U.S.A.
Telephone: (978) 250-2900
Fax: (978) 256-3434
Web site: http://www.sycamorenet.com

Public Company
Incorporated: 1998
Employees: 944
Sales: $374.7 million (2001)
Stock Exchanges: NASDAQ
Ticker Symbol: SCMR
NAIC: 334210 Telephone Apparatus Manufacturing;
    511210 Software Publishers

Sycamore Networks, Inc. is a company that is devoted to its vision of an intelligent optical network for public and private telecommunications. Such a network would be faster and cheaper than existing fiber optic networks, which are based on SONET rings and rely on the conversion of optical signals into electronic signals and back again.

Sycamore's tightly focused product line includes products, such as optical switches and nodes, that enable telecommunication service providers to adjust the capacity of their fiber optic networks based on customer demand. Sycamore's networking products allow service providers to use their existing optical networking infrastructure to deliver high-speed services and meet the intensive bandwidth requirements of data traffic.

When Sycamore went public in 1999, its stock was favored by investors who saw a bright future for the company. Telecommunications companies were expected to spend heavily to add the optical networking capabilities made possible by Sycamore's products. With the economic slowdown of 2001, though, telecommunications service providers and emerging carriers found that they had to cut back on their capital spending. Sycamore's revenues fell dramatically, and its stock followed suit.

Founding Sycamore in 1998 to Provide Intelligent Optical Networking Products

Sycamore Networks, Inc. was founded in February 1998 by Gururaj Deshpande and Daniel E. Smith. The two entrepreneurs had recently sold Cascade Communications Corp. in 1997 to Ascend Communications Inc. for $3.7 billion. Deshpande founded Cascade in 1991 to provide ATM and frame relay switches to handle the soaring demand for data traffic over conventional telephone networks. A technical visionary with a Ph.D. in engineering from Queen's University in Canada, Deshpande hired Smith, a Harvard University M.B.A., as CEO and president to run the daily operations of Cascade. Other members of Sycamore's founding team included architecture director Richard Barry and chief scientist Eric Swanson, both from the Lincoln Laboratory of the Massachusetts Institute of Technology (MIT).

Sycamore's focus was to provide equipment for fiber optic networks that would enable telecommunications providers to quickly expand or reduce the capacity of their fiber optic networks. Although Sycamore was formed in February 1998, the company did not reveal its business plan until December. Its initial products, scheduled for delivery in 1999, would enable telecommunications providers to set up high-speed optical connections directly from their own routers.

More specifically, Sycamore planned to develop a family of intelligent optical transmission and switching products in line with its proposal for an intelligent optical network. Such a network would be three to four times cheaper than existing networks and provide greater bandwidth for new services. The key to the intelligent optical network was its ability to manage multiple light paths or optical channels by minimizing optical-to-electrical conversions along the way. Existing networks were becoming congested, Sycamore believed, because they required optical signals to be converted to electrical signals and then back into optical signals. Sycamore's plan called for eliminating optical/electrical conversions and making the optical light path the transport medium rather than the optical fiber.

Company Perspectives:

Nothing less than a future vision for the public communications network, shared by talented leaders in data networking and optical technology, led to the creation of Sycamore Networks—and the concept of Intelligent Optical Networking—in 1998. Nothing short of new, disruptive technology can transform the underlying infrastructure of the public network into a data-optimized Information Superhighway. From day one, Sycamore's mission has focused on helping our customers create networks of unparalleled flexibility and capacity, based on entirely new parameters for intelligence and performance. Whether you need to build out new areas of your network or to enhance competitiveness by cutting costs and improving service offerings, Sycamore's innovative optical solutions will meet the unique requirements of your network today, and migrate gracefully toward your own vision for the future.

Release of Its First Optical Networking Products in 1999

Sycamore launched its first group of intelligent optical networking products in March 1999, just about a year after the company was founded. These products were designed to increase the bandwidth and flexibility of telecommunications service providers. Providers could use Sycamore's nodes and switches to migrate their telecommunications networks away from traditional ring architecture based on SONET equipment and into meshed optical architecture.

Sycamore's first product was the SN 6000 Intelligent Optical Transport Node for wide-area networks (WANs), or long-haul optical transport systems. The SN 6000 was supported by a $24.5 million contract with Williams Communications, Sycamore's first major customer. Williams had already tested the SN 6000 as well as Sycamore's SN 8000, which was designed for regional networks. In addition, Sycamore offered the SN 8400 for metropolitan networks. Williams was in the process of deploying the SN 6000 throughout its fiber network. The SN 6000 accommodated up to 28 2.5 gigabytes-per-second (Gbps), or OC-48, ports per bay. The transponder-based product enabled Williams to adjust capacity between any two points on its network based on customer demand by plugging in more transponders to its installed base.

On the strength of its vision for an all-optical telecommunications network, a few products, and one customer, Sycamore had a very successful initial public offering (IPO) on October 21, 1999. The company sold 7.5 million shares, which represented a 9.6 percent interest in the company, at $38 each and raised $284.1 million. The IPO gave Sycamore a market capitalization of $2.97 billion. At the end of the first day of trading, shares of Sycamore closed at $184.75. By November 1 the company's stock had reached $220 a share. Investors were apparently unconcerned that Sycamore had reported a net loss of $19.5 million on revenue of $11.3 million for its first fiscal year ending July 31, 1999.

Before the end of the year, Williams Communications announced that it would spend $100 million a year for the next four years on Sycamore's optical networking equipment. Sycamore also released the SN 16000 wavelength switch, which used an optical-electronic design to convert optical signals into electronic signals. The product allowed telecommunications companies to take advantage of the speed offered by optical networking and still utilize their installed connectivity that relied heavily on electronic technology. The product would serve as a bridge between current networking technology and was the next step toward Sycamore's goal of a purely optical telecommunications network.

Acquisitions and Restructuring in 2000

Sycamore's next optical networking product was introduced in February 2000. It was a 1 Gpbs LAN (local area network) connection that could be added on to the SN 8000. Called the Gigabit Ethernet module for the SN 8000, the product made it possible for telecommunications service providers to offer their enterprise customers the ability to connect their corporate networks to the high-speed core of the Internet. The new module was designed to overcome the bandwidth bottleneck that existed at the point where LANs access the public network.

Sycamore's stock continued to soar, reaching $290 in early February 2000. In March the stock split. By April, telecommunications stocks were being pummeled on Wall Street. Sycamore's stock declined by 70 percent from its 52-week high to close at $59.75 on April 13. By June the stock had recovered to slightly more than $100 a share.

Around this time Sycamore announced that it would acquire Sirocco Systems for approximately $2.9 billion in stock. Sirocco developed optical access systems, devices, and switches primarily for the metropolitan market. Sirocco's portfolio of intelligent optical networking products, which focused on access, complemented Sycamore's product line, which focused on transport. Following the acquisition Sirocco became Sycamore's new optical access division, with former Sirocco president and CEO Jonathan Reeves in charge as the division's general manager and vice-president. By the time Sycamore's acquisition of Sirocco closed in September 2000, the transaction was valued at $3.55 billion.

With the SN 16000 hybrid switch shipping to customers and the acquisition of Sirocco Systems, Sycamore reorganized its executive structure around four product groups: intelligent switching products, transport products, access products, and next-generation core optical products. Around this time Sycamore invested in Tejas Networks India Pvt. Ltd., a start-up based in Bangalore, India, that was working to develop intelligent optical networking products that would complement products developed by Sycamore. For its fiscal year ending July 31, 2000, Sycamore reported earnings of $20 million on revenue of $198 million.

In the second half of 2000 Sycamore announced that it had an order backlog exceeding $1 billion. The company also gained some new customers. In November and December Sycamore signed several new deals, including a $40 million contract

---

Key Dates:

1998: Sycamore Networks, Inc. is founded by Gururaj Deshpande and Daniel E. Smith to build optical networking products.

1999: Sycamore introduces its first optical networking products and becomes a public company.

2000: Sycamore acquires Sirocco Systems Inc. for $3.55 billion in stock.

2001: Sycamore's revenue plunges as telecommunications companies cut back on capital spending.

---

for optical switches with Vodafone Group PLC of the United Kingdom. That followed a deal with BellSouth Corp., in which BellSouth chose Sycamore's intelligent optical switches and transport platforms for its Florida Multimedia Internet eXchange network in South Florida. At the time South Florida was becoming a major Internet hub, connecting routes in the United States with Latin America, the Caribbean, Africa, and Western Europe. BellSouth planned to deploy Sycamore's SN 16000 intelligent optical switches and SN 8000 intelligent optical transport platform to build an infrastructure that could rapidly route and re-route data traffic in response to customer demand. Around this time Sycamore also gained L.D. Communications of Bellaire, Texas, as a customer. Before the end of the year European carrier LDCOM entered into a multiyear, multimillion-dollar contract with Sycamore for its metro products, including the SN 3000 access switch and the SN 4000 edge switch. LDCOM owned a 14,000-kilometer fiber network as well as metro fiber rings. It planned to offer intracity and long-haul services in about 20 cities by mid-2001.

Slowdown in Capital Spending Affecting Sycamore in 2001

Sycamore's revenue and stock price in 2001 was markedly affected by a slowdown in capital spending by telecommunications providers. Sycamore's revenue peaked in its second quarter ending January 27, 2001, when it reached $149.2 million, more than five times revenue in the same quarter of 2000. For the quarter Sycamore reported net income of $13.8 million.

For the rest of fiscal 2001 and into its next fiscal year, Sycamore's revenue plunged. The company reported a loss of $225.1 million on revenue of $54.2 million for the quarter ending April 28, and a loss of $42.2 million on revenue of $50.9 million for its fourth quarter ending July 31. For fiscal 2001 ending July 31, Sycamore had total revenue of $374.7 million and a net loss of $279.8 million.

Sycamore attributed its decline in revenue to a slowdown in capital spending by telecommunications providers and a lack of available capital for emerging carriers. The company's strategy in this difficult time was to strengthen its existing customer base by focusing on key projects for its customers, continue with technological innovations, and conserve cash. As part of its cost-cutting measures, Sycamore cut 140 jobs in April 2001 and another 240 in October. The company also delayed construction of a new corporate headquarters.

Sycamore's stock price was around $10 in mid-2001, then dropped to around $5 when the company announced its results for fiscal 2001. The company expected its first quarter revenue for the next fiscal year to be as much as 75 percent below the previous year's levels. For the quarter ending October 27, 2001, Sycamore in fact reported revenue of only $21.2 million, compared to $120.4 million for the same quarter in 2000.

Financially, Sycamore was in a strong position with more than $1 billion in cash and short-term investments. With customers such as Williams Communications cutting back on capital spending and other customers, such as Canada-based 360networks Inc., filing for bankruptcy, Sycamore announced that it would narrow its product line to focus on optical switching, optical edge products, transport, and network management.

As 2001 drew to a close, demand for optical switching products was expected to remain flat until 2003, according to a report from Pioneer Consulting LLC. Beyond that, long-term demand for optical switching and core optical networking equipment was expected to increase. Meanwhile, it was reported that Tellabs Inc. and Sycamore were negotiating a possible merger.

Principal Competitors

Agere Systems Inc.; Ciena Corp.; Cisco Systems Inc.; Corvis Corp.; Nortel Networks Corporation; ONI Systems Corp.; Sorrento Networks Corp.

Further Reading

Biagi, Susan, "Download: The Optical Race Is On," *Telephony,* June 12, 2000.

"Briefly: Williams to Drop $400 Million," *Telephony,* November 29, 1999.

Bruner, Richard, "When You're Hot, You're Hot," *Electronic News (1991),* November 8, 1999, p. 42.

"Chelmsford, Mass., Dot-Com Start-Up Cuts Staff, Projects Lower Earnings," *Knight-Ridder Tribune Business News,* April 6, 2001.

"Desh Deshpande: Sycamore Networks," *Telephony,* June 4, 2001, p. 72.

Gain, Bruce, "All-Optical Networks Yet to See the Light," *EBN,* April 23, 2001, p. 54.

"GigE Over DWDM," *Telecommunications,* April 2000, p. 82.

"Gururaj Deshpande and Daniel E. Smith," *Business Week,* January 8, 2001, p. 84.

"How High Can Optical Stocks Fly?," *Business Week,* October 9, 2000, p. 154.

Krishnadas, K.C., "Sycamore Bets on Optical-Net Startup in India," *Electronic Engineering Times,* August 7, 2000, p. 41.

Lawson, Stephen, "Start-up Sets End-to-End Optical Links Vision," *InfoWorld,* December 14, 1998, p. 39.

"Lessons Learned from Last Year's M & As," *Telephony,* August 27, 2001, p. 20.

Matsumoto, Craig, "Sirocco Chief: We'll Fill the Gap in Sycamore's Network Architecture," *Electronic Engineering Times,* June 19, 2000, p. 68.

McGarvey, Joe, "Developers Tackle All-Optical Illusion," *Inter@ctive Week,* December 13, 1999, p. I8.

——, "Sycamore Goes Gig Ethernet," *Inter@ctive Week,* February 14, 2000, p. I1.

Meyers, Jason, "A.M. Report: Following a New Light," *Telephony,* March 8, 1999.

Mulqueen, John T., "Shining Stars," *Interactive Week,* February 19, 2001, p. 19.

"No Good News for Optics," *Investment Dealers' Digest,* November 26, 2001.

O'Keefe, Sue, et al., "The Lucky 13," *Telecommunications,* June 1999, p. 22.

Pease, Robert, "Sycamore Calls SN 16000 'Next Step' for Intelligent Optical Networks," *Lightwave,* February 2000, p. 109.

Quan, Margaret, "Start-up Details Plan for Smart Optical Network," *Electronic Engineering Times,* December 21, 1998, p. 24.

Rendleman, John, "Sycamore Branches Out into Optical Networking," *PC Week,* March 8, 1999, p. 70.

Ryan, Vincent, "Commerce: Anatomy of an Entrepreneur," *Telephony,* April 10, 2000.

——, "Download: Wringing Out the Excess," *Telephony,* April 17, 2000.

"The Savvy Behind Sycamore," *Business Week,* December 20, 1999, p. 150.

Sweeney, Phil, "Customer's Bankruptcy May Cost Sycamore Networks," *Boston Business Journal,* July 27, 2001, p. 9.

——, "Sycamore Eyed As Possible Buyout Target," *Boston Business Journal,* October 26, 2001, p. 1.

"Sycamore Finds No Shade from Financial Storm," *Communications Today,* August 24, 2001.

"Sycamore Nets Buyer for SN 3000/4000," *Telecommunications,* December 2000, p. 20.

"Sycamore Networks Selected by BellSouth to Equip Next-Generation Internet Exchange in Florida," *Fiber Optics Business,* November 30, 2000, p. 4.

"Sycamore Raises $284.1M," *Washington Business Journal,* October 29, 1999, p. 19.

"Sycamore Reports Completion of Sirocco Purchase," *Providence Business News,* September 18, 2000, p. 12.

"Sycamore Sales Quintuple," *Providence Business News,* February 19, 2001, p. 14.

"Sycamore to Lay Off 240 As Revenues Plunge," *Providence Business News,* October 29, 2001, p. 18.

"Tellabs Courts Sycamore for Optical Expansion," *Telephony,* October 29, 2001, p. 20.

Weismul, Kimberly, "Sycamore IPO Bursts Out of the Gate," *Inter@ctive Week,* October 25, 1999, p. 12.

Wirbel, Loring, "Executive Shuffle Delivers More Product-Oriented Approach," *Electronic Engineering Times,* July 24, 2000, p. 67.

——, "Startups Launch Products with Williams Deployments," *Electronic Engineering Times,* March 8, 1999, p. 31.

Witkowski, Tom, "Sycamore on Track After $40M Deal," *Boston Business Journal,* November 24, 2000, p. 14.

—David P. Bianco

Sykes Enterprises, Inc.

100 N. Tampa St., Ste. 3900
Tampa, Florida 33602
U.S.A.
Telephone: (813) 274-1000
Toll Free: (800) 867-9537
Fax: (813) 273-0148
Web site: http://www.sykes.com

Public Company
Incorporated: 1977
Employees: 17,300
Sales: $603.61 million (2000)
Stock Exchanges: NASDAQ
Ticker Symbol: SYKE
NAIC: 541512 Computer Systems Design Services;
811212 Computer and Office Machine Repair and
Maintenance

Operations at Sykes Enterprises, Inc. revolve around the concept of "customer relationship management," or CRM. In practical terms, CRM translates into 41 Sykes technical support call centers worldwide. Sykes Enterprises offers its clients, mainly large hardware and software manufacturers or telecommunications firms, the opportunity to outsource customer support. The company's call centers operate as a transparent extension of the client company. For example, calls to a software firm's technical support line can be routed directly to a technically savvy telephone agent at one of Sykes Enterprises' call centers in small towns across the nation.

Many of Sykes Enterprises' clients market their products globally, and in order to provide comprehensive services the company has opened multilingual call centers worldwide, in countries as diverse as Costa Rica, South Africa, Sweden, and the Philippines. The company's international operations also include a distribution and fulfillment service in Europe, encompassing such services as multilingual sales order processing, inventory storage, product delivery, and returns handling.

Besides offering support to the buyers of a company's product, Sykes Enterprises' technical support centers also help the com-

pany's own employees utilize technology adeptly. In addition, Sykes Enterprises offers custom designing of software and general customer relationship management consulting. The company believes that maintaining solid customer relationships and building brand loyalty are key to helping clients survive in the competitive technology market. In an article written for CRMCommunity.com, Senior Vice-President Chuck Sykes emphasized that no automated system can replace a well-trained technician in responding to questions and ensuring customer satisfaction. Although such quality service can be expensive, Sykes Enterprises is able to keep costs under control through specialization and implementation of the best technology. Sykes wrote, "We offer efficiencies of scale and knowledge to cost effectively deliver fast, friendly effective service at every level of the enterprise."

Launching an Engineering and Design Firm: 1977–92

John H. Sykes founded Sykes Enterprises, Inc. in 1977 as a small technical engineering firm in Charlotte, North Carolina. He had already acquired several years' experience in the engineering field. After leaving college without graduating, he spent ten years working on procurement for two aviation companies in Charlotte. Later he moved to Philadelphia, where he eventually became senior vice-president of CDI Corp., an engineering services company. Faced with little prospect for advancement, Sykes determined that he would have to seek new challenges elsewhere. He moved with his family back to Charlotte and, with three employees, started Sykes Enterprises.

The company's initial purpose was to provide design and engineering services to *Fortune* 500 companies. One of Sykes's first clients was IBM. When the computer firm arrived in Charlotte in 1978, Sykes Enterprises designed their work space. From that job evolved the Design Services Department. The next year a technical writing group began working on contracts for various clients. Other employment during the 1980s included creating standardized technical drawings and providing construction management for companies such as Walt Disney, AT&T, Amoco, and Pacific Bell.

Sykes sought out large industrial clients from the beginning, preferring to avoid work in the government and aerospace fields.

Company Perspectives:

Our mission is to help support our clients' customer care management needs through our global outsourcing and consulting capabilities.

Our goal is that every client will be more efficient, more profitable, and have stronger loyalty to their company brands due, in part, to the services provided by SYKES.

In pursuit of this objective, SYKES will: Be relentless in our commitment to quality; Employ the best individuals in our industry and reward their commitment to excellence; Maintain a strong financial position, through growth, profitability, and wise investments; Embrace a partnership philosophy with our customers, business partners, and vendors; Be a responsible, contributing corporate citizen in the communities where we do business; Operate with a commitment to ethics and a true concern for others.

Such contracts are usually won on the basis of price, Sykes noted in a 1990 interview with a Charlotte-area business journal. On the other hand, he said, ''Industrial companies look beyond price, they're good for long-term business relationships.''

Another of Sykes Enterprises' early clients was Texas Instruments Inc. A small technical writing job for the company, won in 1982, led eventually to the creation of an entire branch devoted to the field. Technical writing and software design became the two major aspects of the company's operations. In 1984 Sykes Enterprises formally split into two divisions, Information Services and Technical Services.

Business was strong and the firm grew rapidly. The company expanded into New York in 1983 and Colorado in 1985. By 1990 Sykes Enterprises had branched out into Texas and established an Information Services Division in Tampa, Florida, which was later to become the company headquarters. Another office was opened in England as the company anticipated being able to offer program-testing services throughout Europe. In 1990 Sykes Enterprises also purchased Orbitron International Inc., a consulting firm specializing in software services for financial and communications companies. The acquisition brought in an additional $10 million in revenue.

In 1991 many companies were having a hard time weathering the recession. Leaner business years, however, worked in Sykes Enterprises' favor. Many companies were looking to outsource support services, and employment at Sykes actually rose during the early 1990s. In 1991, the company had 1,150 employees at 23 offices in the United States, Canada, and Europe. Technical writing and testing of programming formed the basis of most contracts. IBM remained a loyal client, while a relationship was developing with the U.S. Air Force. Sykes Enterprises documented security and maintenance procedures for the Air Force satellite system.

Turning to Customer Service in the 1990s

After 1992 Sykes Enterprises made several moves that were precursors of the coming focus on customer relationship management. The company acquired two firms in 1992, Jones Technologies, Inc., a call tracking software maker, and the programming firm Forrest Ford Consultants of St. Louis. Jones Technologies was located in Sterling, Colorado, a small town of about 11,000 whose economy had been hit hard by the recession. In 1994 Sykes opened a customer support call center in Sterling, providing technically skilled job seekers with an alternative to low-paying jobs with little future. The call center marked the beginning of what was to become the most profitable division of Sykes Enterprises. Software and hardware manufacturers were realizing that customer service was a vital part of retaining brand loyalty among buyers of their products, but found it difficult to maintain efficient and reliable call centers of their own. Sykes decided to target those companies with a cost-effective option for outsourcing customer support. When a customer had a question about a recently purchased product, a call to the manufacturer would be seamlessly directed to a Sykes call center.

Recognizing the potential for this approach, Sykes Enterprises moved its corporate headquarters from Charlotte to the Information Services center in Tampa. Then the company proceeded to open additional call centers throughout the Midwest. The Greeley, Colorado center opened in 1994, followed by the Ponca City, Oklahoma center and the Klamath Falls, Oregon center in 1995. Sykes now employed 2,000 people.

The center in Sterling provided a model for those that followed. John Sykes saw many advantageous qualities in small midwestern towns, including a good workforce, the lack of a distinctive accent, and the ability to straddle time zones with locations across the heartland. Identical call centers sprung up across the area. In 1996 centers were opened in Minot and Bismarck, North Dakota, and in Hays, Kansas. Each facility contained 432 seats in a 42,500-square-foot building. Ideally, the centers were located near an institution of higher education with the ability to provide a technically proficient employee pool.

Small towns everywhere wanted a part of the economic revival that Sykes Enterprises could bring. Sykes, however, required a concrete demonstration of support from each locality before any call center was agreed upon. His demands were the same for every community: the company required a deed to between 12 and 15 acres of land and a $2.1 million commitment to assist in building the call facility. Such terms made it possible for Sykes to recover his investment in a new center within the first few years of operation.

Although the demands were non-negotiable, communities did not find them excessive. Ponca City even voted for a half percent sales tax increase to fund a new center. A potential center in Ocala, Florida, however, was derailed when the town made demands beyond what Sykes was willing to meet. Ocala managed to find the land and raise the funds, but when it asked that Sykes guarantee 100 or so jobs, he objected to the town changing the conditions of the deal and backed out.

Sykes's major clients, however, had customers beyond the borders of the United States. In order to provide comprehensive services to large hardware and software manufacturers, Sykes would have to establish a presence around the world. While English-speaking call centers were opening across the Midwest, Sykes began a multilingual expansion in Europe. Sykes Enterprises' international headquarters opened in Amsterdam in 1994. As with the U.S. centers, the choice of location was not

Key Dates:

1977: John H. Sykes founds a small engineering services firm in North Carolina.
1984: Sykes Enterprises splits into the Information Services and Technical Services divisions.
1990: Acquisition of Orbitron International Inc. adds $10 million in revenue.
1992: Purchase of Jones Technologies, Inc. shifts focus to technical support call centers.
1994: International headquarters opens in Amsterdam.
1996: Sykes Enterprises goes public.
2000: Accounting problems send stock value plummeting.

random. The Netherlands had many more multilingual citizens than countries such as France or Ireland, and labor costs there were not as high as in its equally multilingual neighbor Belgium. In 1996 Sykes Enterprises acquired Datasvar Support AB of Sweden, which led to the establishment of call centers in the Swedish cities Sveg and Jarvso.

In 1996 the company employed some 3,000 customer service technicians in ten call centers scattered across Europe and the United States. It was an opportune time to finance current and future expansion by going public. The company's April initial public offering on the NASDAQ raised $61.2 million with the sale of 3.4 million shares. The shares nearly doubled on the first day, reaching $35.50 when the market closed on April 30. A secondary offering of 2.6 million shares followed in October. Sykes stock was trading near $48.75, and a three-for-two stock split was declared.

Growing Rapidly After 1996

The company's stock fell to more sober levels the year after its IPO. By the middle of 1997 the price per share had fallen about 30 percent from the October high. A *Wall Street Journal* analyst, however, blamed the lower price on high-profile failures elsewhere in the telemarketing sector rather than on internal weaknesses at Sykes. Sykes Enterprises occupied a fairly stable position with its focus on technical support—employee expertise was an essential part of its operations, making it risky for clients to switch to a customer support provider that may not have the proven knowledge base of Sykes call centers. Also, Sykes insured itself against the loss of a single major client by pursuing contracts with diverse firms.

In 1997, therefore, the company continued its aggressive expansion. It concentrated its efforts in the international field, creating a separate International Division to look at growth in Europe and Asia. Acquisitions abroad included Telcare of Wilhelmshaven, Germany, Traffic of Belgium, TAS Telemarketing in Germany, and McQueen International, a technology services company based in Scotland. As a result of the $74 million McQueen acquisition, Sykes was able to open a call center in the Philippines. Shares rose 14 percent on announcement of the McQueen deal, which was expected to increase the company's global presence. Another new call center in South Africa also added to Sykes's non-European facilities.

Nor was domestic expansion neglected. Sykes Enterprises opened offices in Lexington, Kentucky, and Atlanta, Georgia. Info Systems of North Carolina, a designer of computer software for the manufacturing, distribution, and retail industries, was acquired. The company also branched out into a new sector with a joint venture known as Sykes HealthPlan Services (SHPS). The joint partnership would serve companies that desired to outsource the administration of employee benefits. After another year of growth, Sykes Enterprises had over 6,000 employees.

The early months of 1998 brought some doubts about the viability of Sykes's acquisition strategy. A New York analyst downgraded the Sykes stock from a buy to a hold rating and the share price fell 19 percent as a result. Causes for concern were a slowdown in internally generated revenue at the end of 1997 and the fact that a new software product, an offsite troubleshooter, was not selling as expected. Sykes, however, saw no reason for retreat. New support centers opened in Tampa, Florida; Les Ulis, France; Manhattan, Kansas; and Charlotte, North Carolina. By November company stock had fallen 45 percent from a year earlier, but Sykes Enterprises remained confident based on the fact that it had met all revenue growth targets since its 1996 IPO. Difficulties at telemarketing firms were making Sykes stock fall by association, even though the company was in the business of phone help, not phone sales. Sykes demonstrated confidence in its unique technical customer service approach with the acquisition of two call-center companies in December. Oracle Service Networks Corp. of London, Ontario, was acquired for $35 million in stock and TAS GmbH of Hanover, Germany, for $12 million in stock.

More call centers opened in 1999, domestically in the communities of Milton-Freewater, Oregon; Ada, Oklahoma; and Scottsbluff, Nebraska; and internationally in Ed, Sweden. Sweden's favorable business climate led to increased investment in the country. The 70-seat call center in Sveg was expanded to 324 seats and was chosen to serve as the company's Scandinavian headquarters. Customer care operations were also purchased in Heredia, Costa Rica. That year Sykes was inducted into the Software Support Professionals Association's Hall of Fame for winning that association's STAR award five years in a row. Sykes seemed intent on belying any concerns about the company's strategy.

Regrouping in the New Millennium

In 2000 Sykes Enterprises finally hit a real bump, as company stock fell substantially and leadership was unstable. The company's woes began in January, when a warning that fourth-quarter earnings for 1999 would fall below expectations sent the share price down 51 percent in a single day. A second blow came when certain accounting errors were revealed. Because of delays in the recognition of software revenues, Sykes was forced to restate its financial reports for several quarters and whole fiscal years. The blunder resulted in a heavy penalty and a loss of credibility with Wall Street. By the fourth quarter, the stock had fallen to $3.13 from a 2000 high of $52.25.

To add to the difficulties, the company chose a CEO who left after only five months. David Grimes, who assumed leadership in July, left his post in November. John Sykes resumed duties as CEO.

The company felt a need to restructure its business around proven sources of profit. As a result, all distribution and fulfillment centers in the United States were closed, while those in Europe were consolidated into five facilities. The firm's medical-benefits management unit, Sykes Health Plan Services, had been performing poorly and was sold to an investment firm.

While trimming underperforming business sectors, Sykes continued to invest in its call center operations. Support centers opened in Morganfield, Kentucky, and Virginia, Minnesota, while construction began on two centers in Florida and one in Virginia. The company's Asian branch expanded into Shanghai. By the end of the year, Sykes Enterprises had 14,000 employees and 42 customer care centers: 18 in the United States, three in Canada, two in Costa Rica, and 19 in Europe, South Africa, China, and the Philippines. Moreover, the company had scored two promising contracts with Ford and Delta Air. Those companies inaugurated a program to supply their employees with personal home computers, and Sykes was chosen to provide onsite and phone support for the deal.

Revenue rose to $603.61 million in 2000, up from $572.74 million the previous year, and revenues in the core technical support business rose 27 percent. Such figures backed up John Sykes's optimism at the April 2001 annual shareholders' meeting. Sykes focused on the firm's accomplishments, while recognizing that it would take some time to regain Wall Street's trust after the mistakes in 2000. Unfortunately, more rough times were ahead in 2001. A disappointing third quarter forecast again sent the stock down 42 percent, this time to $6.99. In another accounting slip-up, the company had to restate earnings to reflect a change in the way it accounted for certain cash grants from government development authorities.

Sykes's answer was to continue to streamline operations. A call center in Charlotte was closed, leaving 41 centers worldwide. Another strategy was to increase involvement with the telecommunications sector. Revenues from the communications industry, including support services for Internet service providers, broadband technologies, and cellular phones, reached 26 percent of total revenues in the first half of 2001. In 1999 such services had accounted for only 10 percent of revenues. In a move to target the communications industry, Sykes announced in October 2001 that it was adding 1,200 customer care service agents, bringing its call centers up to full capacity.

Third quarter results for 2001 met expectations, and CEO John Sykes expressed guarded optimism that the expansion would attract additional business from the telecommunications sector. Although the economy was on an uncertain path following the September terrorist attacks in New York, Sykes's core operations were expected to continue to attract businesses looking for cost-effective, quality customer care solutions.

Principal Subsidiaries

Sykes Realty, Inc.; Sykes Financial Services, Inc.; Sykes Enterprises Delaware, Inc.; Sykes Enterprises—South Africa, Inc.; CompuHelpline; McQueen International Incorporated; Sykes Enterprises Incorporated, S.L. (Spain); Sykes Enterprises of Canada, Inc.; Sykes Latin America, S.A. (Costa Rica); SEI Technical Services, Ltd. (U.K.); Sykes Enterprises Incorporated Holdings B.V. (The Netherlands); Sykes Datasvar Support AB (Sweden); Sykes Holdings of Belgium B.V.B.A.; Sykes Enterprises GmbH (Germany); McQueen International Limited (Scotland); Sykes Canada Corporation.

Principal Competitors

Convergys Corporation; SITEL Corporation; West Corporation.

Further Reading

Abercrombie, Paul, "Want a Call Center? Stick to Sykes' List," *Tampa Bay Business Journal,* December 27, 1996, pp. 1–2.

Cranford, Steve, "Move Toward Outsourcing Brings Growth to SEI," *Business Journal Serving Charlotte and the Metropolitan Area,* November 4, 1991, p. S7.

——, "Volunteering Left and Right," *Business Journal Serving Charlotte and the Metropolitan Area,* November 19, 1990, pp. 14–15.

"Foreign Call-Center Outfits Are Bought in Stock Deals," *Wall Street Journal,* December 30, 1998, p. 1.

Hersch, Warren S., "Sykes Scores Major PC Support Win," *Computer Reseller News,* February 14, 2000, p. 16.

Landau, Nilly, "A Call Center to Call Your Own," *International Business,* September 1994, p. 22.

Merrill, Kevin, "Help-Desk Stocks Answering the Call," *Computer Reseller News,* October 7, 1996, p. 48.

Moliteus, Magnus, "The Two-Year Trend Toward Sweden in International Call Center Site Selection," *Call Center Solutions,* April 1999.

Schifrin, Matthew, "Right Number," *Forbes,* November 2, 1998, pp. 378–79.

"Scottish Firm Is Bought for $75 Million in Stock," *Wall Street Journal,* January 6, 1998.

"Shareholders of Tampa, Fla., Tech Firm Hear Optimistic Report," *Knight-Ridder/Tribune Business News,* April 27, 2001.

"Shares of Sykes Enterprises Nearly Double on Day One," *New York Times,* May 1, 1996, p. C3.

Sykes, Chuck, "Kindness Is the Killer App of CRM," http://www.CRMCommunity.com/news/article.cfm?old=40CCED2B-8205-4C6F-946CE7BD1A7D0B6B, November 7, 2001.

"Tampa, Fla.-Based Technical Support Call Center Firm Sees Stock Nose-Dive," *Knight-Ridder/Tribune Business News,* August 1, 2001.

Tippett, Karen L., "Doubts About Future Growth Cast a Cloud Over Sykes Enterprises," *Wall Street Journal,* March 4, 1998.

——, "Looking for a Hot Florida IPO? Class of 1996 May Be a Safer Bet," *Wall Street Journal,* August 27, 1997.

"Warning of Lower Earnings Pushes Stock Down 51%," *Wall Street Journal,* January 26, 2000, p. C26.

—Sarah Ruth Lorenz

Sytner Group plc

Woodcote House
Harcourt Way
Meridian Business Park
Leicester LE3 2WP
United Kingdom
Telephone: (+44) 116-289-1010
Fax: (+44) 116-289-3232
Web site: http://www.sytner.co.uk

Public Company
Incorporated: 1970 as Sytner of Nottingham
Employees: 1,548
Sales: £596.93 million ($861.1 million) (2001)
Stock Exchanges: London
Ticker Symbol: SYT
NAIC: 4411 Automobile Dealers

Leicester-based Sytner Group plc is one of the United Kingdom's leading automobile retailers, specializing in high-end and luxury automobiles. Led by Chairman and former racing champion Frank Sytner and Chief Executive Laurence Vaughan, the company operates 45 dealerships—many of which are operated under the Guy Salmon brand—throughout the country, with franchises for BMW and BMW Alpina, Jaguar, Ferrari, Lexus, Lotus, Aston Martin, Maserati, Porsche, Jeep, Landrover, Mercedes Benz, Bentley, Volvo, Saab, TVR, Chrysler, Volkswagen, and Mini, as well as an agreement to sell the forthcoming new Rolls Royce model slated for release in 2003. BMW remains the group's leading brand, and Sytner is that brand's leading dealership in the United Kingdom. The company is also the country's number two seller of Jaguars. A strong acquisition program since the company's public listing in 1997 has enabled the company to quadruple its sales since 1996. In 2001, the company posted sales of nearly £597 million. After targeting the provincial market for much of its history, Sytner Group is now preparing to take on the London market. In 2001, the company opened its first dealership in the capital city, a 4,000-square-foot BMW concept store located in the heart of the city's financial district. The company has since acquired two more London-based dealerships and intends to make its London dealership its flagship operation. In addition to new and used car sales, Sytner operates an e-commerce capable web site and a customer call-in center linking prospective clients to salesmen. In 2001 the company overhauled its advertising strategy, focusing on tapping into its 250,000-strong contact database with what the company calls its Customer Relationship Management (CRM) strategy. The company also offers extensive repair and maintenance services, which account for 12 percent of sales and 45 percent of the company's profits.

Racing to Dealership Success in the 1970s

Brothers Alan and Frank Sytner began dealing cars in the 1960s. In 1970, the brothers were awarded a franchise for BMW cars, and their business, Sytner of Nottingham, grew into one of the United Kingdom's largest BMW dealerships. That dealership, which also built one of the country's largest dealerships of specialty used cars, remained the company's sole dealership for some 20 years. In the meantime, Frank Sytner also was making a name for himself as a race car driver and went on to lead the BMW Touring car team to the championship in 1988. After winning a second championship in 1990, Sytner retired from professional racing the following year and began devoting himself to expanding his car dealership.

Sytner of Nottingham had already expanded a bit during the 1980s, when the company was awarded the exclusive U.K. franchise for the ultra-high-end, custom-built BMW Alpine range. In 1993, the company added a second BMW dealership in Leicester. The company also gained franchises at the other end of the scale, adding the Toyota, Honda, and Mazda brands. Yet Sytner's interest clearly leaned toward the industry's most prestigious car names, and Sytner began targeting the development of an extended dealership network.

Sytner embarked on a series of acquisitions, adding six new dealerships with financial backing from investment group Schroder Ventures. By 1996, the company's sales had grown to nearly £145 million, selling more than 5,500 cars through a network of 14 dealerships, and the company had made considerable progress toward achieving its goal of becoming the United Kingdom's leading luxury car specialist. Yet Sytner remained decidedly provincial, preferring to invest in establishing itself in smaller regional markets, rather than in London.

As the U.K. economy began to take off again after several years in recession, Sytner's sales began to soar as well. Aiding the company was a growing trend of its corporate customers to turn away from larger mid-class models to smaller and higher-end cars. Meanwhile, the growing new wealth provided by the high-technology boom was widening the company's customer base, sparking sales for such luxury brands as Ferrari—in 1997 alone the company sold more than 200 of the famed Italian sports cars. Sytner's long relationship with BMW also gave it a new future prospect—the takeover of Rolls Royce by BMW, and the announcement of a new Rolls Royce model in the early years of the next century, gave Sytner hope to add the most famous of all luxury car names to its stable of brands.

Sytner took the company public in 1997, in a listing that valued the newly named Sytner Group at £50 million. Frank Sytner took the chairman's position, and Laurence Vaughan became company chief executive. The public offering allowed Sytner to put its expansion plans into high gear. Over the next year, the company acquired or opened 11 new dealerships, raising its total number of dealerships to 25. The company's acquisition spree not only gained it a number of new franchises, including one with Jaguar, it also gained it a prominent brand name—many of its new dealerships had come through its acquisition of Guy Salmon Group in 1998. The company was to retain the Guy Salmon name, which had also become a prominent name in luxury car rentals, for part of its existing and future dealership network.

U.K. Luxury Car Leader for the New Century

The next big step in Sytner's development came in 1999, when the company paid £13.5 million to acquire Ixion Motor Group, owned by Formula One car designer Tom Walkinshaw. The deal gave Sytner 11 new dealerships throughout Oxfordshire and the Midlands, including new franchises for Volvo, Saab, and Lexus, as well as an additional Jaguar dealership, two

BMW dealerships, and one each for Land Rover and Jeep. The Ixion deal was heralded as a major step in the consolidation of the United Kingdom's new car retail industry. It also provided a major increase in the company's sales, bringing total revenues past £405 million, on a total of more than 15,000 cars sold in 1999. That same year, the company was granted a BMW franchise for the City of London.

Sytner continued to pursue acquisitions through 2001, taking advantage of a downturn in the industry to pick up a number of more fragile dealerships. Part of the reason for the downturn came from consumer outcry at the disparity between new car prices in the United Kingdom and those on the European continent. While car manufacturers announced their intention to cut prices in order to bring prices in line with those in the other European markets, consumers put their purchases on hold, waiting for the price cuts to take effect. Despite originally being proposed for the beginning of 2000, most manufacturers dragged their feet, and only came through toward the end of the year.

The company launched its next round of acquisitions in August 2000, when it acquired Yarnolds, based in Stratford-upon-Avon, giving the company new Land Rover and TVR sports car dealerships. At the same time, the company acquired the Mercedes-Benz dealership in Weston, which was incorporated into the company's existing dealership there. Meanwhile, the promised price cuts came through at last, dropping prices on a number of luxury models to within the reach of the middle-class consumer. The result was a strong finish to the year for Sytner, as customers returned to its dealerships.

Not all of the company's growth came through acquisitions. In April 2000, the company opened a Lexus dealership in Leicester and the company also was preparing to open its first dealership in London, located within the city's financial district. Billed as a "BMW concept store," the new 4,000-square-foot dealership offered a wide selection of BMW-branded clothing, bicycles, and other products, in addition to BMW automobiles. That store opened in March 2001 and was soon joined by two new BMW franchises in Kensington and Chelsea. The company, which had long avoided the London market, now sought to make its London operations its company flagship dealership—as Sytner claimed the position as number one BMW dealer in the United Kingdom.

By then, the company had been expanding its position as a Jaguar dealer. In November 2000, the company opened a new Jaguar franchise in Barnes, then acquired another new Jaguar franchise the following month, at Hendon and Highgate. The company further extended its Jaguar operations with a new franchise in Stratford-upon-Avon, which, operating under the Guy Salmon name, represented Sytner's seventh Jaguar dealership and helped the company take the position as the country's number two Jaguar seller. By the end of 2001, the company operated 45 dealerships and included more than a dozen of the world's top luxury brands.

As the company sought to complete its focus on its luxury vehicle portfolio, it began to divest a number of its newly noncore dealerships, including those for Toyota, Mazda, and Honda. At the end of 2001, the company's luxury car ambitions

Key Dates:

1960s: Alan and Frank Sytner begin selling automobiles as Frank Sytner begins his racing career.

1970: The Sytner brothers open their first BMW dealership in Nottingham.

1984: The company is named exclusive U.K. dealer for custom-built BMW Alpiner model.

1991: Frank Sytner retires from racing and launches the company's expansion strategy.

1993: The company makes its first acquisition, a BMW dealership in Leicester; further acquisitions are financed by Schroder Ventures.

1996: Sytner's dealership network grows to 14, providing sales of nearly £145 million.

1997: Sytner Group goes public; company continues to open new dealerships.

1998: The company acquires Guy Salmon Group and expands its network to 25 dealerships.

1999: Sytner acquires its first London BMW franchise, and it acquires Ixion Group for £13.5 million, adding 11 new dealerships.

2000: The company acquires Yarnolds in Stratford-upon-Avon.

2001: The company opens London BMW concept store; the company is named representative for future BMW-Rolls Royce model; the company acquires first Bentley dealership.

were given a fresh boost. In October 2001 Sytner acquired the Ron Stratton Bentley and Land Rover dealerships in Knutsford for £1.2 million, marking the company's first dealership for the prestigious Bentley brand. This acquisition followed on the heels of the company's nomination, in September 2001, as a representative of the first line of Rolls Royce cars to be built under BMW's ownership, expected to be ready in 2003. Frank Sytner continued to indulge his passion for racing, both as a pilot in "historic" racing events—and in his race to build Sytner into the United Kingdom's largest automotive sales company.

Principal Subsidiaries

Sytner Limited; Sytner of Leicester Limited; Sytner Sheffield Limited; Cruickshank Motors Limited; Graypaul Motors Limited; Goodman Leeds Limited; Hallamshire Motor Company Limited; Hyde Car Centre Limited; Sandridge Limited; Guy Salmon Honda Limited; Guy Salmon Jaguar Limited; W A Hatfield Limited; Sytner Holdings Limited; Prophets Garage Limited; Prophets (Gerrards Cross) Limited; Yarnolds of Stratford Limited; Guy Salmon Highgate Limited; Hughenden Motor Company Limited; Sytner Properties Limited; Sytner Finance Limited.

Principal Competitors

C D Bramall PLC; Dixon Motors PLC; H.R. Owen Plc; Inchcape plc; Pendragon PLC; Quicks Group plc; Reg Vardy plc; Rygor Group Limited; Ryland Group plc.

Further Reading

Armitage, Jim, "Luxury Car Dealer in Pole Position," *Evening Standard,* July 31, 2000.

Blackwell, David, "Vroom with a View to Making Money," *Financial Times,* May 19, 2001.

Carr, Miranda, "Major Prize for Former Motor Racing Champion," *Daily Telegraph,* November 17, 1997.

Ross, Sarah, "Sytner to Market New R-R Model," *Financial Times,* October 17, 2001.

"Sytner Makes New Marque," *Birmingham Post,* September 27, 2001, p. 24.

Tyler, Richard, "Sytner's Profits Sizzle Thanks to Rich Clients," *Birmingham Post,* October 17, 2001, p. 19.

—M.L. Cohen

Tarragon Realty Investors, Inc.

1775 Broadway, 23rd Floor
New York, New York 10019
U.S.A.
Telephone: (212) 949-5000
Fax: (212) 949-8001
Web site: http://www.tarragonrealty.com

Public Company
Incorporated: 1973 as Consolidated Capital Realty
    Investors
Employees: 385
Sales: $110.34 million (2000)
Stock Exchanges: NASDAQ
Ticker Symbol: TARR
NAIC: 531311 Residential Property Managers; 531312
    Nonresidential Property Managers

Tarragon Realty Investors, Inc. is a New York City-based company engaged in real estate investment, development, and management in specific target areas in the states of Florida, Connecticut, California, Texas, Georgia, and Colorado. Tarragon controls 20,000 apartment units and 2.5 million square feet of commercial real estate. It revoked its status as a real estate investment trust (REIT) in 2000, electing to operate as a publicly traded corporation. Tarragon and affiliated companies are primarily controlled by Chairman, President, and CEO William S. Friedman.

Origins Reaching Back to 1973

The history of Tarragon is very much tied to the story of Friedman and his former business partner, Gene E. Phillips. The men gained notoriety in the 1980s for their questionable business dealings, their association with junk bond king Michael Milken, and their involvement with such major figures in the Savings & Loan scandal as Charles Keating and Herman K. Beebe. The legal entity that would become Tarragon was originally established in Oakland, California, in 1973 as a real estate investment trust named Consolidated Capital Realty Investors,

one of several REITs under an umbrella organization, Consolidated Capital Equities Corp. Headed by Donald C. Wilson, who owned a 25 percent stake, it commenced operations in 1974. REITs were created by Congress in 1960 as a way for small investors to become involved in real estate in much the same way a mutual fund allowed them to pool resources in order to buy stock. REITs could be taken public and their shares traded like stocks. Unlike corporations, however, REITs were required by law to pay out at least 95 percent of their taxable income to shareholders each year, thus severely limiting the ability of REITs to raise funds internally. Moreover, they lacked adequate oversight and were open to abuse, thereby scaring off many investors. Consolidated Capital Realty invested in apartments, as well as a shopping mall and some office space. It was fairly successful for a number of years before faltering and becoming acquired by Phillips and Friedman in the late 1980s.

Friedman was a graduate of Brandeis University and Columbia University School of Law, and began practicing as a tax lawyer in 1971. Two years later he was hired to do some legal work for Phillips, who was involved in his first real estate venture, leading to their eventual partnership. Phillips came to real estate from an unusual angle. Born in South Carolina, he earned an undergraduate degree from Clemson University, then went on to Virginia Polytechnic Institute to study for a Ph.D. in chemical engineering. He never completed the program, opting instead to become involved in real estate in the late 1960s. His company, Phillips Development, became the largest developer in Gaffney, South Carolina, close to where he grew up. By late 1973, however, he was in debt by some $30 million and forced to declare bankruptcy. It was for the purpose of liquidating part of Phillips Development that Friedman was retained. According to a 1993 *Barron's* profile of the two men written by Benjamin J. Stein, "Apparently, Friedman was the man who encouraged Phillips to stop actually building things and instead to sell buildings to limited partnerships (which was like encouraging Alfred Nobel to study chemistry)."

Phillips then took a job in Greensboro, North Carolina, with McCoy Development, identifying distressed properties that could be sold to syndicated ventures. In 1977 he bought McCoy, changing its name to Syntek Investment Properties, and Fried-

---

Company Perspectives:

Tarragon Realty Investors, Inc. is a growth-oriented, fully integrated public real estate development, acquisition, and management company. Tarragon controls approximately 20,000 apartment units and almost 2.5 million square feet of commercial space located throughout the continental United States, with concentrations in Florida, Connecticut, Texas and California. Tarragon's primary business is to create value for its shareholders through developing, repositioning and operating real estate.

---

man became a vice-president. The two men in 1980 gained control of a troubled Atlanta REIT, Southmark Properties, that boasted few assets but $125 million in tax benefits. The company had been originally created in 1970 as a Maryland REIT under the name "Citizens and Southern Realty Investors," established by The Citizens and Southern National Bank, which managed it under an advisory contract until 1979, at which point the REIT relocated and changed its name to Southmark Properties. With Phillips serving as chairman and Friedman as secretary, it would again move its base of operations to Dallas and change its name to Southmark Corporation in 1982. Using Southmark the partners began acquiring other real estate trusts in similar difficult straits, employing Syntek as an investment vehicle, then selling undervalued real estate assets or bundling them together in limited partnerships.

Influential Meeting with Michael Milken in 1982

According to a 1989 *Wall Street Journal* article written by Michael Totty, "Messrs. Phillips and Friedman might have remained small-time operators if it weren't for Drexel and its junk-bond impresario, Michael Milken. Before 1982, when Mr. Phillips made his first pilgrimage to Mr. Milken's Beverly Hills office, Southmark had barely $450 million in assets; six years and $1.2 billion in junk bonds later, its assets had ballooned to more than $3.5 billion—or $9 billion if its thrift and insurance units are included."

Aside from accumulating a large number of REITs, Phillips and Friedman borrowed more money than was required for expansion, investing in other Milken junk bonds to gain interests in oil and gas ventures, campgrounds, nursing home facilities, retirement centers, a direct-mail selling company, and Atlantic City and Puerto Rican casinos. According to Totty, "Like other real-estate companies in the then-hot Texas market, Southmark rushed to acquire a thrift after the industry was deregulated. San Jacinto Savings, acquired in 1983, provided a convenient in-house piggy bank to finance real-estate purchases and to buy operating companies." Southmark also acquired insurer Pacific Standard.

According to Stein, "The method of operation of Pacific Standard and San Jacinto was classic financial Ponzi stuff. Both used policyholders' and depositors' money to buy investments that primarily benefited Southmark or its friends—especially Charles Keating. When the investments soured, the company tried various schemes to prop up the operations." Bank exam-

iner Neal Batson amplified on what he called "Outside Cronyism" in a report he would produce in the eventual bankruptcy proceedings of Southmark: "Phillips and Friedman, and thus Southmark, had many business dealings with high-powered figures, many of whom have been convicted, indicted, or are under investigation for savings and loan fraud, and who were in a position to assist Phillips and Friedman with their numerous real-estate and other ventures. The number of transactions between these individuals was so extensive that they could perhaps be viewed as coordinated efforts by members of this elite club to assist each other for their own personal gain rather than for the benefit of the organizations they ostensibly served."

In a short period of time, Southmark evolved into a Byzantine network of 300 interlocking subsidiaries and 350 partnerships. Although its assets grew to nearly $10 billion, making Southmark the nation's largest publicly traded real-estate investment firm, the company also accumulated significant debt through its junk bond borrowings. It was essentially a house of cards destined for collapse. One of its last acquisitions was the California REITs operating under Consolidated Capital Equities Corp., among which was Tarragon's predecessor, Consolidated Capital Realty.

In 1985 Consolidated Capital Equities Corp. was acquired by a Massachusetts business trust called Johnstown American Companies, which was in turn acquired by Southmark's subsidiary, San Jacinto Savings. Consolidated Capital Realty had been a profitable business that peaked in the early 1980s. In 1982, with assets in excess of $133 million, the REIT generated revenues of $36.1 million and net income of $8.8 million. In 1984 it would post its highest net income, more than $13 million, but the fortunes of the company would progressively trend downward. In 1988 its assets totaled little more than $57 million and the trust lost $7.7 million while generating just $5.85 million in income. In that same year, Phillips was elected as one of its trustees.

Early in 1989 Phillips and Friedman were forced out at Southmark, which in short order filed for bankruptcy. As part of their severance deal, which according to the *Wall Street Journal* was hammered out in a three-day meeting in a Dallas hotel, they were allowed to be trustees of several Southmark REITs, including Consolidated Capital Realty. A new Southmark board subsequently asserted claims against Phillips and Friedman, who in turn asserted counterclaims. According to Stein, "The 'settlement' of these claims called for Southmark to turn over to Phillips and Friedman—among many other things—stewardship of five good-sized REITs and one large master limited partnership, National Realty, which Southmark had managed. The settlement also called for Phillips and Friedman to pay about $12 million to Southmark. This settlement was described by the examiner as similar to a lender settling with a borrower by giving him the collateral. But it got better. In 1991 and 1992, Phillips and Friedman persuaded the stockholders of the REITs to pay $11 million of the $12 million settlement."

Phillips was elected as a trustee of Consolidated Capital Realty in early 1989 and Friedman was named its president. Tapped to advise and manage it and the other REITs was Basic Capital Management Inc., controlled by Phillips and Friedman

Key Dates:

1973: Company is incorporated as Consolidated Capital Realty Investors, a real estate investment trust.
1989: Name is changed to Vinland Property Trust; Williams S. Friedman becomes president.
1998: Company is reorganized and renamed Tarragon Realty Investors, Inc.
2000: Company revokes its REIT status.

through their children. Poison-pill, antitakeover provisions were then adopted to secure the five REITs, and in July 1989 they all changed their names, with Consolidated Capital Realty becoming Vinland Property Trust. Phillips and Friedman were the subject of much litigation, and although they were never convicted of any crimes, they agreed to pay $20 million in connection with San Jacinto Savings and were banned from the banking industry.

Friedman Splitting with Phillips: 1992

According to the *Wall Street Journal,* Friedman split with Phillips in 1992. SEC filings of this period indicate that Friedman resigned from a number of real estate trusts in order to concentrate on Vinland and another REIT, National Income Realty Trust (NIRT), as well as Tarragon Realty Advisors, Inc., which would replace Basic Capital as the trusts' advisor, and was owned by his wife, his daughter, and a business associate named John A. Doyle. SEC filings also reveal that Phillips was no longer listed as a trustee of Vinland. While Phillips returned to dealmaking with renewed vigor, Friedman carried on in a much quieter manner, slowly building up the business of Vinland out of his New York City offices.

In November 1995, Vinland's portfolio consisted of 13 properties, comprising ten apartment complexes, a shopping center, a combination office building and shopping center, and one farm and luxury residence. In that year Vinland also posted a profit, albeit a meager $27,000, but still a significant improvement over 1993 and 1994 when the business lost $607,000 and $429,000, respectively. In 1996 net income would improve to $853,000.

Friedman then consolidated the businesses under his control. First, Tarragon Realty Investors, Inc. was incorporated in Nevada on April 2, 1997, and Vinland was merged into it. Tarragon then acquired NIRT for $76.1 million in stock, followed by the acquisition of Tarragon Realty Advisors. In a released statement, Friedman maintained that "Tarragon is now a full service, real estate company with the ability to build and develop, manage and operate, renovate and reposition apartment and commercial properties in markets throughout Florida, Connecticut and Texas." The combined operation controlled more than 12,000 apartment units and 1.7 million square feet of retail and office space. Tarragon, which had emphasized the renovation of older apartment complexes, now became especially interested in the luxury apartment market. With low interest rates and a booming economy, white-collar customers were ready buyers of upscale accommodations. Tarragon teamed

with Rohdhouse Investments in 1997 to develop luxury apartment communities, including The Links at Georgetown in Savannah, Georgia, a 250-unit luxury garden apartment complex flanking the fairways of the Henderson Country Club golf course and featuring such amenities as a resort-style clubhouse, fitness club, spa, and pool. Three other luxury developments were completed by the joint venture by early 1999.

Revenues grew to $58.7 million in 1998. Because of Tarragon's active slate of renovation and development, the company posted a loss of $1.4 million. In 1999, however, Tarragon would show a net profit of $5.2 million on revenues of $73.7 million. By early 2000 the company would control some 17,000 apartment units and nearly 2.5 million square feet of commercial space. In March of that year Friedman opted to revoke Tarragon's REIT status, electing instead to become a "C" corporation. Not only did the REIT structure limit Tarragon's flexibility, Friedman believed that the market did not adequately value the business and that its units had been undervalued for three years. Moreover, he now planned to grow the business by developing single-family units in Texas, luxury time-shares in California, and condominium sales in Florida.

Tarragon also moved into the Connecticut market through the July 2000 acquisition of Accord Properties, LLC, one of the state's largest apartment management companies. As part of this transaction, Robert Rothenberg became Tarragon's chief operating officer and a member of the board. Also in 2000 Tarragon acquired the apartment development joint ventures of Robert C. Rohdie and his family for stock with a potential worth of $10 million, making Rohdie Tarragon's second largest shareholder. In addition to being elected to Tarragon's board, he was also named president and CEO of a new subsidiary, Tarragon Development Corporation, to manage these joint ventures, which represented 5,500 apartment units in Florida, Texas, and Connecticut. For the year, Tarragon improved revenues by 50 percent over 1999, to $110.34 million, and net income by 25 percent to $6.5 million.

In 2001 Tarragon continued to prosper and reorganized its operations into two groups: development and investment. While Friedman appeared to have rehabilitated his reputation after his days with Southmark, reflected by the willingness of Aetna Life Insurance to provide funding for Tarragon, his erstwhile partner, in the meantime, continued to make headlines. Having built a new $2 billion real estate empire, Phillips, along with an aide, was charged by a federal grand jury in New York in June 2000 with racketeering and wire fraud in connection with an alleged attempt to induce New York City union officials to invest pension funds in one of his companies in exchange for kickback payments. A broader scheme, supported by over 1,000 hours of taped conversations in an FBI sting operation, alleged wide-ranging organized crime influence on Wall Street. Phillips was scheduled for trial in the fall of 2001.

Principal Operating Units

Investment; Development.

Principal Competitors

Berkshire Realty; Camden Property; Walden.

Further Reading

Blumenthal, Karen, ''They're Back: Southmark Crashed, But Its Former Chiefs Are Doing Just Fine,'' *Wall Street Journal,* January 23, 1991, p. A1.

Rudnitsky, Howard, and Matthew Schifrin, ''A Jerry Built Structure,'' *Forbes,* March 7, 1988, p. 38.

Starkman, Dean, ''Edifice Complex: Real Estate Magnate Draws Shareholder Ire for Odd Deal Making,'' *Wall Street Journal,* February 16, 2001, p. A1.

Stein, Benjamin J., ''The Latest Hurrah,'' *Barron's National Business and Financial Weekly,* December 29, 1993, p. 12.

Totty, Michael, ''Tortured Finances: Questionable Deals, Junk Bonds Hasten Decline of Southmark,'' *Wall Street Journal,* January 17, 1989, p. 1.

Wethe, David, and Michael Whiteley, ''Survivor,'' *Dallas Business Journal,* June 29, 2001.

—Ed Dinger

Teachers Insurance and Annuity Association-College Retirement Equities Fund

---

730 Third Avenue
New York, New York 10017
U.S.A.
Telephone: (212) 490-9000
Toll Free: (800) 842-2252
Fax: (212) 916-4840
Web site: http://www.tiaa-cref.org

Nonprofit Company
Incorporated: 1918 as Teachers Insurance and Annuity
    Association; 1952 as College Retirement Equities Fund
Employees: 6,404
Total Assets: $281.38 billion (2001)
NAIC: 524113 Direct Life Insurance Carriers

TIAA-CREF, or the Teachers Insurance and Annuity Association-College Retirement Equities Fund, was ranked as the nation's 33rd largest company by *Fortune* in 2001. The company's CREF Stock Account, with $92 billion in assets, is the largest single-managed equity fund in the world. From TIAA's original endowment provided by the Carnegie Corporation for the benefit of private college professors, total TIAA-CREF assets have grown to over $250 billion, and the nonprofit company has begun offering financial products to the general public as well as to its core education and research community.

Financial Security for Poorly Paid Teachers: 1910s–20s

The concept of institutionalized pension funds and retirement security only became an issue in industrialized society. In the pre-industrial world older individuals were provided for either by their children or through the local church. Limited pension plans did exist in the United States before the 20th century, but they did not become common until the 1910s. For some in the United States, the concept of pensions threatened the American ideal of personal liberty and accentuated fears of a paternalistic government. In 1861, however, the government did provide pensions to those who served in the Civil War. A few private corporations had annuity plans beginning in 1875. By 1932, however, only 15 percent of U.S. workers were covered by a retirement plan. Corporate pension systems were not always established out of concern for the workers but rather as a means to reduce employee turnover and to promote loyalty, or to control employees.

In 1890 Andrew Carnegie, as a newly appointed university trustee, became concerned over the lack of compensation received by college teachers. He saw that their small salaries did not permit them to accumulate savings for retirement. Only a few universities and colleges had initiated retirement plans or funds, but they generally assisted only those professors who remained employed with the institution for longer than 15 years. These systems varied, with plans such as that of Columbia University, which allowed retirement at one-half salary after both 15 years of service and after attaining the age of 65. Carnegie became convinced of the need to provide pensions for college teachers through discussions with Henry Smith Pritchett, president of Massachusetts Institute of Technology. Pritchett and Carnegie recognized that retirement pensions could strengthen higher education by improving the financial security of college teachers. The result was the founding in 1905 of the Carnegie Foundation, reincorporated under a federal charter as the Carnegie Foundation for the Advancement of Teaching in 1906.

Originally endowed with $10 million from bonds issued on Carnegie's United States Steel Corporation, the Carnegie Foundation became the major provider of pensions to college teachers in private, nonsectarian institutions meeting certain academic and financial requirements. In 1908, Carnegie increased the endowment by $5 million to extend the Carnegie pensions to teachers in state universities, bringing the total gift to $15 million.

The original 52 member institutions included the major private universities in the United States and Canada in 1906. Among the charter members were Amherst College, Columbia

University, Cornell University, Harvard College, Johns Hopkins University, Massachusetts Institute of Technology, McGill University, Princeton University, Radcliffe College, Vassar College, and Yale University. A few of these initial member institutions already had pension funds but saw the usefulness of a more integrated system.

The post-World War I era saw a rapid increase in both institutional members and in individual participants at those institutions. By 1915 membership had increased to 73 public and private institutions, and the foundation realized it no longer could support additions to this free pension system. In 1916, the foundation proposed a "comprehensive plan of insurance and annuities," based on a philosophy of joint responsibility and cooperation between the college and the teacher.

In its broad outline the proposal followed the recommendations of a recent Massachusetts commission on public-employee pensions, praised in the foundation's 1914 annual report. The Massachusetts commission had recommended contributory pensions, with individual ownership of annuity contributions and equivalent contributions to the annuity by the government as employer. In 1917, the foundation established the Commission on Insurance and Annuities, which included representation from such organizations as the American Association of University Professors, Association of American Universities, National Association of State Universities, and Association of American Colleges, to explore the proposed plan.

The commission defined and unanimously approved the principles of a sound pension system and recommended establishment of a new Teachers Insurance and Annuity Association. In 1918, TIAA was incorporated as a nonprofit life insurance company under New York state law. The capital stock of TIAA was held by the Carnegie Corporation, which provided the $1 million endowment.

The usual method of contribution for TIAA annuities was joint payments divided equally between the individual and the individual's employer. Contributions usually averaged 10 percent of the salary, 5 percent each from the employer and the employee. Because of this structure, TIAA employed no agents and paid no commissions. This arrangement helped to keep operating costs low, an advantage for educators.

The new corporation was led by President Henry Smith Pritchett. Pritchett, president of the Carnegie Foundation for its first quarter-century, guided the transformation of the free pension system. Under his leadership the foundation also conducted pension studies and established a separate division for an educational-studies program. He viewed pensions as a means of strengthening higher education and, by enabling older professors to retire with dignity, as a method of enticing and retaining younger faculty. The new board of trustees consisted of individuals from academia, finance, and business. It included people from Columbia University, University of Toronto, McGill University, the Mutual Life Insurance Company of New York, the National City Bank, J.P. Morgan & Company, and, of course, the Carnegie Foundation for the Advancement of Teaching.

Great Depression and Impact on Pension Programs: 1930s

The 1920s brought relative security and prosperity to TIAA. The Depression loomed at the end of the decade when W O. Miller, comptroller of the University of Pennsylvania, predicted in the *Educational Review*, "It is only a matter of time when institutions of higher learning will find that their responsibility for the protection of teachers and their dependents against the major hazards of life will be inescapable." The Great Depression accentuated the need for security. TIAA retirement funds, growing in popularity, took several forms. In TIAA's early years, colleges and universities often had made participation in the retirement plan voluntary, but this trend reversed in favor of compulsory participation during the 1930s. Voluntary participation may have encouraged nonparticipation if the university did not provide support services, such as a contact to explain the details. This was especially true during the Depression years of the 1930s, when premiums increased because, as schools experienced financial difficulties, new business fell dramatically. Between 1925 and 1935, however, the number of annuity contracts grew fourfold.

By 1935, 105 of 117 colleges that did require joint contributions participated in TIAA. Henry James, the president of TIAA in 1935, urged institutions to act as guiding forces in providing for the security of their employees. Henry James's observations changed the nature of TIAA, from playing a passive investment role to a more active role in disseminating information and advising. He urged colleges to have an officer or a staff benefit committee for disseminating information about insurance and annuities to employees. James was a man dedicated to academia. Having won a Pulitzer Prize for biography in 1930, he was a trustee in the Rockefeller Institute, Carnegie Corporation, and New York Public Library, and a fellow of Harvard University.

The Social Security Act was passed in 1935, providing for the first national old-age pension. Retirement benefits were first paid in 1940. National, compulsory, and contributory, Social Security was designed to soften the effects of the massive unemployment of the Depression, provide long-term security, and remove older employees from the workforce. Social Security did have many flaws and has been amended many times since its founding. The act excluded, among other groups, individuals working at colleges and universities. Colleges initially had requested the exclusion, concerned about the budgetary implications and wary of government interference in educational affairs. TIAA urged colleges to reconsider their position, noting the importance of Social Security benefits for nonacademic college employees. Although professors were provided for under TIAA plans, most of the college or university support

Key Dates:

1918: Teachers Insurance and Annuity Association (TIAA) is incorporated as a nonprofit life insurance company with a $1 million endowment from the Carnegie Corporation.

1938: TIAA receives corporate independence, ending two decades of direct Carnegie support.

1952: TIAA forms College Retirement Equities Fund (CREF), the nation's first variable annuity.

1972: TIAA-CREF joins with colleges and other organizations to establish the Investor Responsibility Research Center.

1987: New Chairman and CEO Clifton Wharton, Jr., reorganizes operations in response to increased criticism over pension fund performance.

1990: Introduction of long-term care insurance follows string of late 1980s product innovations.

1997: TIAA-CREF loses tax-exempt status.

1998: TIAA-CREF begins offering mutual funds to all investors.

staff had no retirement benefits. Beginning in the late 1930s, TIAA encouraged extension of Social Security participation to college and university employees; this finally was achieved in the 1950s. TIAA's position was that Social Security represented a national social movement toward economic security, deserving of colleges' cooperation and participation.

In 1938 TIAA was given corporate independence. For its first two decades, TIAA had received grants from the Carnegie Foundation and then Carnegie Corporation to pay its operating costs. As the volume of TIAA's business increased, TIAA and Carnegie Corporation agreed that long-term philanthropic support of TIAA annuities was no longer necessary or desirable. A separation settlement, a series of payments through 1938, was made and TIAA's stock transferred from Carnegie Corporation to a newly chartered board, Trustees of T.I.A.A. Stock, now known as the Board of Overseers.

Postwar Boom: 1940s–50s

The war years of the early 1940s brought little growth to TIAA. The postwar years, however, saw a dramatic increase in college enrollment because of the GI Bill. The demand for college professors increased accordingly, as did TIAA's policyholders, from 39,250 at the end of 1945 to 45,000 in 1946. An increasing number of institutions were willing to provide for nonacademic employees' retirement because of the exclusion of colleges from Social Security coverage. TIAA retirement plans increased by 45 in 1945. An additional 123 were added in 1946 and 1947.

By 1947, in a substantial number of colleges, 15 percent of the individual's salary was contributed to the pension fund, with the staff member and the college each paying half this amount. By 1950, TIAA had $299.6 million in assets.

In 1950, the Association of American Colleges and the American Association of University Professors (AAUP) polled

college administrators and active and retired faculty on retirement issues. Of those surveyed, 54 percent indicated that their benefits were adequate. A large majority of AAUP chapters, however, argued that benefits were too meager in light of inflation. The report urged some provision for cost-of-living pension increases. Other issues in the study were the lack of fixed age for retirement, and who would fix the age; and the payment of benefits to those who either retired early or left the profession. These issues would surface again in the 1980s.

A partial answer to the problem of inflation was the variable-annuity corporation College Retirement Equities Fund (CREF), formed by TIAA in 1952. CREF was designed to provide benefits based on the fluctuations of the cost of living as reflected in the movement of the stock market. TIAA also may have been attempting to regain part of the insurance market lost to investment companies that were posting higher rates of return than the fixed TIAA annuities. CREF was the nation's first variable-annuity organization. CREF was chartered through a special act of the New York state legislature. Like TIAA, CREF was established as a nonprofit organization dedicated to serving the nonprofit educational community.

Membership in CREF was restricted to current TIAA members, of which 20 percent had elected to join by 1954. Participating TIAA institutions had three options: to stay solely with the fixed-dollar TIAA annuity, to participate in CREF but limit the amount its employees could invest in CREF to a specific percentage of total contributions, or to allow individuals to put up to 50 percent of their retirement premiums into CREF, with the balance to TIAA. Most institutions joining CREF chose the third option. The structure of CREF was designed to assure the employer that his contributions would be used as an annuity.

In the latter half of the 1950s, TIAA-CREF expanded its insurance operations. In 1956, TIAA received a $5 million grant from the Ford Foundation to develop group total disability and major medical insurance coverages. Such coverages would insure against the expenses associated with long-term disability and major catastrophic illness. These plans were used as a further means of attracting and retaining quality employees.

A Myriad of Challenges: The 1960s Through the Early 1990s

In 1969, TIAA-CREF briefly sought a federal charter for College Benefit System of America, intended to solve TIAA-CREF's problems at that time with state licensing and taxation of insurance companies outside of New York. TIAA-CREF dropped the federal charter effort, however, as more states supported tax-free licensing for TIAA-CREF's annuity business.

In 1971 TIAA-CREF, with Ford Foundation grant support, organized The Common Fund for nonprofit organizations, to provide small colleges with expert investment management of their endowment funds. In 1972 TIAA-CREF joined with colleges and other organizations to establish the Investor Responsibility Research Center, for the study of social-responsibility issues and portfolio investments.

In 1978, technical amendments to the Employee Retirement Income Security Act of 1974 (ERISA) opened up other profit-making funds for retirement purposes. IRAs (individual retirement accounts) were an outgrowth of ERISA. Growing dissatisfaction with the lack of investment choices became the major complaint of participants. As early as 1983, CREF's performance was criticized as being 54 percent poorer than most pension funds, by one analyst, *Pensions & Investment Age* (June 13, 1983). In that same year the National Association of College and University Business Officers (NACUBO) established a committee to study TIAA-CREF. NACUBO issued an unfavorable report, and TIAA-CREF slowly began to consider proposals for changing its pension system.

TIAA-CREF studied the feasibility of introducing a new CREF money market account to complement the CREF stock account and the traditional TIAA annuity. Concurrently, management began the process of registering CREF with the Securities and Exchange Commission (SEC) in preparation for the introduction of additional CREF investment funds. The SEC's approval was delayed in August 1987 when a number of parties—several colleges, competitors, and an educational association—requested a hearing.

Another controversy during the 1980s was over the issue of transferability and removal of retirement funds. TIAA-CREF would not allow transfer of funds from the CREF portion, earning interest from the performance of the stock market, to the TIAA portion, earning fixed interest. A policyholder could not withdraw funds to invest in another plan or annuity to gain a better interest yield. In 1988 universities such as Johns Hopkins began offering alternatives to TIAA-CREF. While the impetus for these changes was the issue of the transfer or removal of funds, a secondary issue revolved around who would decide the risks the pension fund would take, TIAA-CREF management or the policyholders.

A major step in resolving these issues was the selection in 1987 of Clifton Wharton, Jr., as the chairman and chief executive officer. Wharton had served as president of Michigan State University, chancellor of the State University of New York—the nation's largest university system—and held numerous directorships on corporate boards. He also served as a trustee of The Aspen Institute and the Council on Foreign Relations.

Wharton first reorganized the structure into four major divisions: TIAA investments, CREF investments, pension services, and insurance services. Before Wharton, the company had a myriad of departments that reported to seven vice-presidents. In 1988 consummation of an agreement with the SEC opened the door for introduction of the new CREF Money Market Account.

In 1989 TIAA opened life insurance eligibility to employees in public elementary and high schools. This program also increased the variety of TIAA's life insurance services already available to participants. The organization introduced a new retirement income option, the Interest Payment Retirement Option. This plan pays annuity interest only, while the principal remains intact, giving participants flexibility to postpone their retirement decisions.

In January 1990 TIAA introduced its Teachers LongTerm Care insurance coverage, designed to allow educators and their spouses to retain financial security throughout extended periods of care in nursing homes, adult day healthcare centers, or at home. This coverage became one of the nation's most comprehensive long-term care insurance programs. As of January 1, 1990, TIAA-CREF phased out its major medical insurance, which had been steadily losing business since the mid-1970s.

On March 1, 1990, TIAA-CREF announced the introduction of two additional funds—the CREF Bond Market Account and the CREF Social Choice Account. The latter invested only in companies that meet certain standards of social responsibility. The Social Choice Account, for example, did not invest in companies that had economic ties to South Africa or that produced and marketed alcoholic beverages or tobacco. Concurrently, TIAA-CREF made new options available to employer retirement plans, permitting CREF accumulations to be transferred or cashed in upon termination of employment, subject to employer approval.

Hence, TIAA and CREF entered the 1990s widely recognized as leaders in the pension and insurance industry, and as major institutional investors. TIAA's investment performance long had been above the life insurance industry average. Together TIAA and CREF increased financial security and asset protection for educational employees. The future looked not only secure; it looked bright. TIAA-CREF, holding a captive market, was unique in providing a nationwide portable private pension for 1.4 million employees of some 4,500 nonprofit educational institutions. TIAA-CREF total assets topped the $100 billion mark late in 1991.

John H. Biggs succeeded Wharton as chairman and CEO, in early 1993, when Wharton was appointed U.S. Deputy Secretary of State. That same year TIAA-CREF introduced its corporate governance principles. Biggs and TIAA-CREF would later come under fire in regard to the execution of those principles.

Redefining Itself: Mid-1990s into the 21st Century

As a large corporate investor, TIAA-CREF exerted its clout. "Sometimes the targets are well chosen," wrote Nick Gilbert for *Financial World* in July 1995. "TIAA-CREF, the largest pension fund in the nation, has fought long and hard against excessive executive pay and abuses of shareholder rights like greenmail and poison pills."

Some critics began drawing the line when TIAA-CREF pressed companies to diversify their boards, balking against a perceived push for political correctness. Moreover, although TIAA-CREF's own board was highly diverse in terms of sex and race, the trustees received substantial compensation. Biggs and Thomas Jones, the second in command, garnered salaries and bonuses significantly greater than similar pension fund operations, according to Gilbert's article. TIAA-CREF responded to the criticism by pointing out that the company had to compete for top-level employees with major financial services corporations.

But not all critics were content with the answer. The flagship CREF Stock Account, an equity portfolio of $59 billion, was primarily indexed to the Russell 3000: CREF automatically invested nearly two of every three dollars in companies held by the benchmark fund. This, critics said, left little for the highly paid officers to manage.

In a different vein, TIAA-CREF stepped away from standard insurance practices of the time when it began offering individual life contracts, long-term care, and pension annuities to unmarried partners of the university employees it already covered. Typically, domestic partners had been excluded from insurance coverage except for some first- and second-to-die life policies. The move was eased by the fact that TIAA-CREF did not offer health insurance, which presented the most risk to insurers. Furthermore, the move by TIAA-CREF followed a trend in its university customer base begun in the 1980s to include domestic partners in benefit plans.

TIAA-CREF lost its tax-exempt status in 1997 as part of tax reform and thanks to intense lobbying by competitors. The change in status allowed the company to begin selling more kinds of financial products and expand its customer base.

In the fall of 1997, TIAA-CREF launched six mutual funds for its core education market. The financial industry itself was in a time of evolution. Legislation changes allowed for increased diversification: commercial banks moved into investment banking; insurers and banks entered into stock broking; and, the fund market found new players from all quarters, including TIAA-CREF.

When the new TIAA-CREF mutual funds were rolled out for the general public the next year, the response was less than stellar, despite low fees, top-notch customer service, and the company's reputation for solid returns on investment. *Barron's* partially attributed the slow pace to lack of advertisement, part of TIAA-CREF's tradition of keeping costs low, and its long-time dependence on strong word-of-mouth sales.

Regardless, the world's largest pension fund had begun repositioning itself to be a major player in the financial services sector. Two million customers provided a hefty base of potential buyers of its new products and services, including new life policies targeting wealthy individuals, trust services, and a state college savings program, which it would administer. In addition, TIAA-CREF pursued relationships with financial advisors who could recommend their products to a new pool of customers.

Watchers of the financial industry predicted that TIAA-CREF could and would compete head-to-head with the top mutual fund companies, such as Vanguard, the nation's second largest and fastest growing fund firm. Burton J. Greenwald, a Philadelphia mutual fund consultant, said in a fall 1999 *Business Week* article, "No one has ever competed successfully with Vanguard." He went on to say, "Now, for the first time, there is a competitor with enormous credibility."

Both nonprofit companies, Vanguard and TIAA-CREF kept fees low, used stock indexing instead of hiring professional stockpickers, and provided quality offerings. In terms of other fund competitors, Fidelity's Magellan ranked first; had TIAA-CREF been a fund company it would have ranked fourth over-all. Conversely, the CREF $123 billion variable annuity was nearly twice the size of the Magellan mutual fund.

The year 2000 marked the end of a heady ride for the U.S. stock market. Internet and technology stocks, particularly, took it on the chin. Although TIAA-CREF's real estate and bond accounts held up well, the company's equity-based accounts declined in value, along with the general U.S. and international stock markets.

Despite the volatile financial climate TIAA-CREF remained a solid organization. In 2001, the company came in second in the Financial Services Reputation Quotient Survey, outranked by a player in the military and ex-military niche. Also in 2001, TIAA-CREF earned a second place position behind Metropolitan Life in terms of securities portfolio size: $86.82 billion compared with Met's $101.1 billion. In addition, TIAA, held the top spot among the nation's life insurers and was one of only four to hold the highest ratings from the nation's four leading independent insurance industry rating agencies.

Principal Subsidiaries

TIAA-CREF Life Insurance Co.; TIAA-CREF Trust Company, FSB.

Principal Competitors

Metropolitan Life Insurance Company; Prudential Insurance Company of America.

Further Reading

"The Biggest Fund You Never Heard Of," *Business Week,* September 13, 1999, p. 152.

Davis, L.J., "$60 Billion in the Balance," *New York Times Magazine,* March 27, 1988.

Gilbert, Nick, "Glass Houses: People Who Live in Them, Like the Bosses of TIAA-CREF, Shouldn't Throw Stones," *Financial World,* July 4, 1995, pp. 26+.

Gjertsen, Lee Ann, "TIAA-CREF: Professors' Pension Fund Rates No. 2," *American Banker,* May 25, 2001, p. 9A.

Greenough, William C., *It's My Retirement Money, Take Good Care of It: The TIAA-CREF Story,* Homewood, Ill.: Richard D. Irwin, 1990.

Koco, Linda, "TIAA Accepting Ins. Apps. for 'Domestic Partners,' " *National Underwriter Life & Health—Financial Services Edition,* February 6, 1995, pp. 21+.

"Lesson Plans," *Economist,* May 2, 1998, pp. 67+.

"Let Shareholders Decide This One," *Business Week,* November 19, 2001, p. 144.

"Top 150 U.S. Life, Accident, and Health Insurers by Size of Securities Portfolio," *American Banker,* September 5, 2001, p. 7.

Ward, Sandra, "Playing with Fire," *Barron's,* January 11, 1999, pp. F5+.

Whitford, David, "What Would You Do with $89 Billion," *Fortune,* July 21, 1997, p. 31.

—Jenny L. Presnell
—update: Kathleen Peippo

Tesoro Petroleum Corporation

300 Concord Plaza Drive
San Antonio, Texas 78216-6999
U.S.A.
Telephone: (210) 828-8484
Fax: (210) 283-2045
Web site: http://www.tesoropetroleum.com

Public Company
Incorporated: 1964
Employees: 2,100
Sales: $5.1 billion (2000)
Stock Exchanges: New York Pacific
Ticker Symbol: TSO
NAIC: 324110 Petroleum Refineries; 422710 Petroleum
Bulk Stations and Terminals; 447190 Other Gasoline
Stations; 447110 Gasoline Stations with Convenience
Stores

Tesoro Petroleum Corporation is an independent energy company principally involved in refining, distributing, and marketing petroleum products. With five refineries in Alaska, Hawaii, North Dakota, Utah, and Washington state having a combined capacity of 390,000 barrels per day, Tesoro is one of the largest independent refining and marketing firms in the western United States. On the marketing side, the company distributes its products in Alaska, Hawaii, and other western states through about 640 branded outlets, 160 of which are owned by the company. Through an agreement with Wal-Mart Stores, Inc., Tesoro sells its gasoline at selected Wal-Mart locations in the western United States, with these stations operating under the Mirastar brand, which was developed by the company exclusively for the retailing giant. Outside of its core refining and marketing activities, Tesoro also distributes petroleum products and provides logistical support services to the marine and offshore exploration and production sectors.

In its early years Tesoro grew rapidly through the acquisition of a wide spectrum of energy businesses. This growth weakened the company's financial status, however, and it was later forced to shed many of its subsidiaries and devote a large amount of its attention to avoiding takeover, both internal and external, and battling with dissident shareholders. Later, by the late 1990s, the company appeared to have found a formula for success by abandoning its upstream operations and beefing up its core downstream activities.

Spate of Acquisitions in Early Years

Tesoro was founded by Robert V. West, Jr., in 1964. West had earned a doctorate in chemical engineering and then spent his entire career in the petroleum industry, rising to become president of Texstar Petroleum Company, a subsidiary of a larger company, Texstar Corporation, that was controlled by Texas wildcatter Tom Slick. After Slick's death in a plane crash, West convinced the executors of Slick's estate to sell the company West ran, with its oil-producing properties, to him. West borrowed $6.5 million to purchase the stock of Texstar Petroleum from its parent company and merged Texstar into the new company he had set up, Tesoro, which means "treasure" in Spanish.

In its previous incarnation, Tesoro had been a small but profitable oil and gas company. In its new form, however, the company carried such a high debt burden that it was difficult for Tesoro to save the money necessary to expand. West embarked on an effort to financially stabilize his company by joining it with another, stronger entity. After three years of searching, West found two publicly owned companies that suited his needs, and in a complicated series of transactions, the three merged. With funding from Chicago's Continental Illinois bank, the Intex Oil Company—which had been founded in California in 1939 as the Exploration and Development Company—was joined with the Sioux Oil Company and with Tesoro. The new entity took the name of Tesoro in December 1968.

With this transformation, Tesoro became a company possessing a pool of stockholders, solid financial standing, a listing on the American Stock Exchange, and workable arrangements with investment banking houses, allowing it to raise capital for further expansion. West embarked on a ten-year spree of acquisitions in the energy business, picking up a mixed bag of companies at bargain-basement prices. The first step in this direction was taken when Tesoro sold $25 million worth of stock in late 1968. With this money, the company paid off its bank debt entirely, leaving $18 million in cash for investment.

Among Tesoro's first acquisitions were the Clymore Petroleum Corporation and the Trident Offshore Company, Ltd., in which Tesoro purchased a 55 percent interest. Tesoro's most important new venture involved the island government of Trinidad and Tobago. The company discovered that the British Petroleum Company (BP) planned to divest itself of its oil-producing operations in Trinidad and that the country's government intended to buy them. Since the Trinidadian government had no experience in the petroleum business, Tesoro was able to convince it to enter into joint ownership of the properties, forming Trinidad-Tesoro Petroleum Company Limited. Incorporated in Trinidad in 1969, the company was 50.1 percent owned by the island's government, with the remainder owned by Tesoro. Both partners contributed $50,000 to the venture, which subsequently purchased BP's holdings, including properties, equipment, and remaining oil products for $28 million. The rest of the money necessary for this purchase was raised through loans from banks and a deferred payment plan with BP. Once it had taken over BP's operations in Trinidad, Tesoro was able to restore them to profit-making status by renovating existing wells and making production less wasteful.

In addition to its operations in Trinidad, Tesoro also commenced construction of a refinery for crude oil on the west coast of Alaska at Kenai in early 1969. Building this facility took more than a year, and when it was completed, Tesoro experienced difficulty in operating it profitably. The problem of bringing crude oil to the refinery and transporting finished products to market had yet to be resolved in an economical fashion. In addition, the company faced stiff competition from the much larger Standard Oil Company (California), which owned the only other refinery in Alaska, producing a difficult competitive marketplace. "We held our noses and went underwater for a while," West told *Forbes* magazine in 1973, explaining the refinery's money-losing operations. Eventually, however, prices for refined petroleum products did rise, and the Alaskan refinery became profitable.

Tesoro also continued to purchase companies with a broad range of functions in the petroleum industry, including truck and pipeline transportation, petroleum equipment manufacturing and rental, and crude oil production. In looking for acquisitions, the company sought out properties that not only were profitable but also showed promise of continuing to return profits over the long term. Accordingly, Tesoro purchased Car-

dinal Transports, Inc., in early 1969. In March of the following year, the company added a Texas firm called Petroleum Distributing Company as well as the Land & Marine Rental Company and the Louisiana Barreling Company. Later that year, Tesoro invested in the Arnold Pipe Rental Company, Ltd., D&W Investments, Inc., and certain portions of Spira Chek, Inc. In early 1971 Tesoro continued its vertical integration when it took on the operation of gasoline service stations by buying the S&N Investment Company and the Digas Company, both located in southern California. These chains were subsequently expanded into many areas of the United States.

With its diverse operations, and activities in both Trinidad and Alaska running smoothly, Tesoro readied itself for further expansion with another sale of stock. In a symbolic move, the company switched its listing from the American Stock Exchange to the New York Stock Exchange, becoming the only San Antonio-based firm to be listed on the so-called Big Board. In August 1971 Tesoro raised $32.2 million in an equity offering. With these funds, the company increased its geographical reach once again, buying Redco, a subsidiary of Asamera Oil, which owned land on Boreno in Indonesia that could be explored for oil, as well as the rights to any oil found.

West also began negotiations with an Arab ruler to refine and market crude oil produced in his country. With the expectation that these talks would bear fruit, Tesoro established in September 1972 a wholly owned European subsidiary, Tesoro-Europe Petroleum B.V., to market petroleum products. In addition, the company bought the Dutch firm DeHumber Handelmaatschappij B.V. and four associated companies for $4 million. These companies handled wholesale and retail marketing operations. Tesoro's European interests were subsequently further expanded when the company acquired an interest in the rights to explore for petroleum in the Dutch sector of the North Sea oil field.

During this time, Tesoro continued to expand its American holdings, purchasing the Charles Wheatley Company in February 1972. This privately owned firm manufactured valves for use in the oil industry. In May 1973 Tesoro bought FWI, Inc. from Falcon Seaboard, Inc. in Houston. During the next year Eagle Transport Company and Turner Drill Pipe, two petroleum industry services located in Texas, also were brought on board. By the end of 1973 Tesoro was able to report that its steady pace of acquisitions in all sectors of the petroleum industry had allowed it to quintuple its earnings in just five years in business.

In 1973 the Organization of Petroleum Exporting Countries (OPEC) oil embargo caused an energy crisis in the United States, raising awareness of the importance of alternative energy sources to petroleum. Accordingly, Tesoro moved for the first time to incorporate other forms of fossil fuels in its operations. In September 1974 the company formed Tesoro Coal Company. Four months later it increased its coal holdings when it bought the Buckhorn Hazard Coal Company.

Geographically, Tesoro moved onto yet another continent when it bought into two sizable exploratory tracts in Bolivia. This led to the formation in 1974 of Tesoro Inter-American Production Company, which took over the company's holdings in Trinidad and also took responsibility for future operations in

Key Dates:

1964: Robert V. West, Jr., founds Tesoro Petroleum Corporation as a spinoff of Texstar Corporation.

1968: Tesoro merges with Intex Oil Company and Sioux Oil Company.

1969: The company acquires half-interest in British Petroleum's oil-producing operations in Trinidad and Tobago, with the island nation's government holding the other half; Tesoro begins construction of an oil refinery on the west coast of Alaska.

1971: The company enters the marketing sector through the purchase of the S&N Investment Company and the Digas Company, operator of gasoline service stations.

1974: Following the purchase of two sizable exploratory tracts in Bolivia, Tesoro Inter-American Production Company is formed and takes responsibility for Caribbean and Latin American operations.

1975: The company spends $83 million for a 36.7 percent interest in the Puerto Rican firm Commonwealth Oil Refining Company (Corco).

1977: Tesoro writes off $59 million of its investment in Corco, which soon files for bankruptcy.

1980: The company fends off the first of several takeover attempts, this one by Diamond Shamrock Corporation.

1985: The company sells its share of Trinidad-Tesoro to the island nation's government.

1988: Tesoro sells its domestic oil and gas producing properties to American Exploration.

1995: The company sells some of its oil and gas production properties in Texas to Coastal Corporation for $74 million.

1998: The company acquires two refineries in Hawaii and Washington state, as well as 32 retail gas stations in Hawaii.

1999: The company's exit from exploration and production is completed by selling domestic operations to EEX Corporation and the Bolivian-based activities to BG PLC.

2000: An agreement is reached with Wal-Mart Stores, Inc. to open and operate filling stations at Wal-Mart outlets under the name Mirastar.

2001: Tesoro acquires refineries in Utah and North Dakota and 45 gas stations in a $677 million deal with BP p.l.c.

the Caribbean and Latin America. By the end of the 1974 fiscal year, Tesoro had gross revenues exceeding $500 million and earnings of about $60 million. The company had operations in 30 states and five foreign countries.

Souring of Corco Investment: Late 1970s

Operating from this position of strength, Tesoro made a serious error in June 1975, when it paid $83 million for 36.7 percent of the stock of the Commonwealth Oil Refining Company (Corco), a Puerto Rican oil refiner and petrochemical processor

that was one and a half times as large as Tesoro. Corco had been caught short by the sharp rise in petroleum prices in 1974, and its profitability had fallen, bringing the cost of its stock down as well. Tesoro sent out a team of new managers to try to turn around the fortunes of its new subsidiary.

Despite the fact that Tesoro's debt had grown in size to 1.3 times its equity, the company continued its pace of acquisitions, purchasing the GO Drilling Company of Texas, which owned three oil drilling rigs. In the following year, the company expanded its Alaskan operations when it bought the Nikiski Alaska Pipeline Company. Tesoro diversified into a third area of the energy industry, forming Tesoro Natural Gas Company in April 1977 to purchase and transport natural gas.

By this time, however, Tesoro's financial position had become perilous, and the company's era of rapid expansion through haphazard acquisition came to a close. In 1977 Tesoro was forced to write off $59 million in Corco investments and lost $58 million overall. This bad news prompted a suit by shareholders against the company, alleging that Tesoro's Corco investment constituted mismanagement. It was clear that the company had bitten off more than it could chew.

Tesoro's lenders, concerned about the company's level of past borrowing, forced the company to liquidate many of its properties to earn cash to pay off some of its debt. Tesoro sold off its North Sea oil interests as well as an equipment manufacturer. The company also was forced to sell all but five of its American oil and gas properties, including refineries in Montana and Wyoming. This divestiture continued throughout 1978, which was capped by Corco's declaration of Chapter 11 bankruptcy. Tesoro subsequently reduced its interest in this subsidiary, surrendering its stock in 1981 and selling off its final ownership of Corco for $2.8 million in 1983. Overall, Tesoro had sacrificed a vast amount of capital in its bid to make Corco succeed.

Further difficulties arose in December 1978 when various investigations by the Internal Revenue Service (IRS), the Securities and Exchange Commission (SEC), and the U.S. Justice Department resulted in the company having to pay tax penalties. It also had to disclose that it had paid more than $1.3 million in bribes to officials in Bolivia and other foreign countries over a six-year period. This commenced a five-year federal investigation of Tesoro by a grand jury, which was not closed until February 1984.

In an effort to rebuild, Tesoro brought in management consultants in 1979 to help it create a plan for future growth. West told *Business Week* that Tesoro had undergone "a general change in philosophy" that would result in a more careful, integrated, and planned program of expansion and acquisition. As part of its new strategy, the company invested $45 million to upgrade its Alaskan refining facility, confident that the facility's remote location and ready source of raw materials in the Alaska oil fields would continue to make it a profitable enterprise.

Fending Off Takeover Bids in the 1980s

By 1980 Tesoro had reduced its debt load to 20 percent of equity from 80 percent and was once again in the black. Belying his vow to stick to sensible investment in the petroleum industry, West made an abortive attempt to purchase Gulfstream

American, a manufacturer of corporate jets, early in the year. After this was abandoned, Tesoro itself became the object of a potential corporate takeover in August when the Diamond Shamrock Corporation, a chemicals and natural resources producer, purchased 4.5 percent of the company's stock and announced that it would buy the company in an effort to move into the petroleum industry. Tesoro quickly filed two lawsuits to block this attempt. When Trinidad's government announced that it would not work with Diamond Shamrock, the attempt was dropped.

Tesoro remained in danger of corporate takeover, however. Its debt-ridden coal operation as well as new tax laws in Trinidad that penalized Trinidad-Tesoro kept earnings and the company's stock value low. Amid the disorder, speculators on Wall Street began to buy up the company's stock, anticipating its takeover or its split into several parts.

In June 1982 this speculation bore fruit when Tesoro announced a plan to sell its domestic oil, gas, and coal properties, as well as its interest in the Trinidadian company, and split its remaining holdings into two companies. The proposal, however, was subject to approval by the company's board. Ultimately, only the company's money-losing coal operations were sold, for $4.35 million, to the Shamrock Coal Company.

Despite the sale, Tesoro's persistently poor performance and low stock price continued to anger some investors, causing dissent among the ranks of the company's stockholders. When some began to agitate for replacement of Tesoro's management team through a proxy fight, West sold a large chunk of stock in the company to a subsidiary of the Charter Company, an oil and insurance concern that was run by a friend. Subsequently, Tesoro tried to take over another small oil company, Enstar, and failed when it was sold to other suitors. The company instead purchased a 50 percent interest in offshore exploratory oil and gas properties owned by the Pel-Tex Oil Company.

In 1985 Tesoro further restructured its stock offerings to prevent any corporate takeover attempts. In addition, after years of proposals to do so, the company sold its nearly one-half share in Trinidad-Tesoro Petroleum to the island nation's government. The company announced plans to take over another oil producer but canceled them when, later in the year, its bond ratings were lowered, reflecting a loss of confidence in Tesoro's financial health. The company reported a loss of $87 million at the end of 1985.

Matters continued to worsen in 1986, as Tesoro wrote off $44.3 million on an attempt to find oil in Trinidad and also gave up the value of its Indonesian reserves. Exploration in other areas of the world fared no better; wells in Turkey also turned up dry. In Bolivia, the country's government proved unable to pay Tesoro for its services and then announced that it would reimburse the company not in cash but in goods. Tesoro's $30 million joint venture with Pel-Tex also yielded little.

The one bright spot in the company's portfolio was its Alaskan refinery. Tesoro announced that it would upgrade the facility, which turned a profit providing fuel for the Alaska market, including substantial military operations. Nevertheless, Tesoro's 1986 balance sheet showed losses of $124.8 million, and the company continued to fend off takeover attempts. In

April 1986 Calvacade Oil made an offer to buy the company but was rejected.

In 1987 two more suitors had arrived—Oakville, a Hong Kong investment concern, and Pentane Partners, formed specifically to take over the company. Tesoro's problems had grown to include an $800 million shareholder suit, filed in July 1987 against the company's management for corruption and securities fraud, as well as other legal difficulties. Tesoro won its court case but not without suffering the embarrassing revelation that it had hired prostitutes for foreign officials. In addition, an FBI investigation into jury tampering was initiated, and the IRS demanded more than $50 million in back taxes.

By the end of 1987, Pentane Partners owned 9.74 percent of the company, and Oakville held 6.2 percent of Tesoro's stock. The company reported losses of $1.7 million and joined the list of *Forbes*'s 500 poorest performing firms in sales growth. In May 1988 Tesoro's board rejected a bid by Pentane for the remainder of the company. In the next few months, the company reached an agreement with the IRS to pay only $20.6 million in back taxes and sold its domestic oil and gas producing properties to American Exploration for $21 million in an effort to shore up its financial standing. By August 1988 the company was also 5.3 percent owned by the chairman of another oil company, Stone Petroleum.

In 1988 Pentane made two additional attempts to acquire Tesoro, and the company also saw a $190 million offer by Harken Oil and Gas made and dropped. After a $56 million fine from the federal government for violating regulations on petroleum pricing and allocation, Tesoro reported a $30.5 million loss for the 1989 fiscal year.

Fights with Dissident Shareholders in the Early 1990s

By the following year, the company was back in the black with earnings of $22.7 million, but 1991 proved a disappointment, as the war in the Persian Gulf drove up prices for crude oil, while prices for refined products remained stable. This meant that profits on Tesoro's principal money-earning property, its Alaska refinery, were held down. The company earned only $3.9 million in 1991 and omitted its fourth quarterly dividend payment on stocks. Difficulties continued in 1992, as the company laid off 60 employees and closed offices in an effort to reduce costs. For 1992, Tesoro posted a net loss of $65.8 million on revenues of $946.4 million.

By the early 1990s, Metropolitan Life Insurance Company had gained a 28 percent stake in Tesoro after Charter Company went bankrupt and Metropolitan Life acquired the stake that Charter had held. With three members on the Tesoro board, Metropolitan was able to use its considerable leverage to force the ouster of West. In 1993 Metropolitan reached an agreement with Tesoro on a recapitalization plan in which Tesoro would buy back the stake over the course of several years. Tesoro began doing so in 1994, leading to the resignation of the Metropolitan representatives from the Tesoro board.

With Michael D. Burke leading the company as president and CEO, Tesoro faced additional disgruntled shareholders in the mid-1990s. At the annual meetings of both 1994 and 1995, a group of dissident shareholders led by Kevin Flannery, head of Whelan Management Group, attempted but failed to oust the firm's board of directors. The dissidents were unhappy with the way that the board was managing the company and specifically sought to sell Tesoro's refinery in Alaska to focus on exploration and production. The company actually moved in the opposite direction in September 1995 when it sold some of its oil and gas production properties in Texas to the Coastal Corporation for $74 million. That same month, Burke resigned from the company and was succeeded by Bruce A. Smith, who was promoted from his position as chief operating officer.

Smith was able to put an end to the shareholder revolt in early 1996. After Flannery and company launched a third bid to oust the company board, negotiations led to an agreement in April 1996. Tesoro agreed to increase the size of the board to nine members by naming three new directors, including a member of the dissident shareholders, Alan Kaufman. In addition, the shareholder group agreed to drop all pending legal action and to not seek to take control of the company or support any effort to do so for three years.

Focusing on Downstream Operations in the Late 1990s and Beyond

Freed from the distractions of takeover battles and disgruntled shareholders, Tesoro was able to focus on developing a longer range plan to secure the company's future. Eventually, near the end of the century, the company decided to focus on its downstream operations. To that end, Tesoro in May 1998 completed the acquisition of a refinery and retail outlets in Hawaii that had been owned by Broken Hill Proprietary Co. Ltd. The $252.2 million deal included a 95,000-barrel-per-day refinery, located about 22 miles west of Honolulu at Kapolei, and 32 retail gasoline service stations. Tesoro then gained its third refinery in August 1998 when it acquired a 108,000-barrel-per-day refinery in Anacortes, Washington, from Shell Oil Company for $280.1 million. The acquisitions increased the company's revenues to $1.49 billion for 1998, a significant increase over the $937.9 million figure of the preceding year.

This expansion also increased the company's debt load from $148 million to $520 million, which highlighted the need for a paring down of operations. In early 1999, then, the company announced that it would seek to sell or spin off its exploration and production operations. The divestment of the upstream side of the company was completed in December 1999 through two transactions. The domestic assets were sold to EEX Corporation for $215 million, while the Bolivian exploration and production operations were sold to U.K.-based BG PLC for $100 million. The divestments enabled Tesoro to reduce its debt to less than $400 million.

In addition to its newly bolstered refining operations, Tesoro in early 2000 also had a retail network consisting of about 245 stations, 64 of which were company owned and operated. In January 2000 the company moved to expand its retail side by entering into an agreement with Wal-Mart Stores, Inc. to build and operate filling stations at Wal-Mart stores in 11 western states—later expanded to 17 states. The companies later agreed to use a new brand, Mirastar, for the stations. By the end of 2000, there were 20 Mirastar outlets in operation, with plans for

an additional 80–90 units to be opened each year from 2001 to 2003. Tesoro reported 2000 earnings of $73.3 million on revenues of $5.1 billion.

In September 2001 Tesoro further expanded both its refining and retailing operations through a $677 million deal with BP p.l.c. Acquired thereby were a refinery in Salt Lake City with a capacity of 55,000 barrels a day and a 60,000-barrel-per-day refinery in Mandan, North Dakota. This brought Tesoro's total refinery capacity to 390,000 barrels per day. Also included in the deal were 45 retail gasoline stations, contracts to supply 300 Amoco-branded stations, as well as associated pipelines, bulk storage facilities, and product distribution terminals. Around this same time, Tesoro announced that it would spend more than $85 million on a major upgrade of its refinery in Washington. The company also said that it was exploring its options regarding its marine services unit. A divestment of the unit would enable Tesoro to be fully focused on refining and retailing and perhaps to pay down some of its debt, which had increased to more than $1 billion following the BP deal. In November 2001 Tesoro acquired 37 retail gas stations with convenience stores from Gull Industries, Inc. The stations were located in Washington, Oregon, and Idaho.

Looking back, Tesoro had moved far beyond the scattershot ways of its not too distant past, when it consisted of a far-flung collection of mostly unrelated parts. With a sell-off of the marine services unit a distinct possibility, Tesoro seemed to be on the verge of completing its transformation into a leading independent refining and retailing company concentrating on the western United States. The company was very interested in bolstering its presence in the huge California market, and it seemed likely that the firm would pursue the acquisition of a refinery—as well as retail outlets—in that state. Opportunities stemming from the continued consolidation and reshuffling of the U.S. oil industry were bound to arise. Overall, Tesoro Petroleum seemed well on its way to putting its troubled past behind it.

Principal Subsidiaries

Tesoro Alaska Company; Tesoro Hawaii Corporation; Tesoro Marine Services Holding Company; Tesoro Marine Services, Inc.; Tesoro Petroleum Companies, Inc.; Tesoro Refining, Marketing & Supply Company; Tesoro West Coast Company.

Principal Competitors

Exxon Mobil Corporation; BP p.l.c.; ChevronTexaco Corporation; Phillips Petroleum Company; Valero Energy Corporation; Arctic Slope Regional Corporation.

Further Reading

Baltimore, Chris, "Texas Supreme Court Hands Tenneco Loss in Take-or-Pay Suit," *Oil Daily,* August 19, 1996, pp. 1+.

Barrionuevo, Alexei, "Tesoro Petroleum Sells Its Operations in Bolivia to BG," *Wall Street Journal,* December 31, 1999, p. B5.

Brammer, Rhonda, "Bargain Hunter," *Barron's,* March 14, 1994, pp. 20–21.

Burrough, Bryan, "Collapse of an Old-Boy Oil Network Places Tesoro in Vulnerable Position for Takeover," *Wall Street Journal,* June 12, 1984.

"EEX to Buy Tesoro's Upstream Holdings," *Oil Daily,* October 12, 1999.

Fan, Aliza, "Spring Finally Breaks for Tesoro Petroleum As Chill of Shareholder Battle, Lawsuit Pass," *Oil Daily,* May 31, 1996, pp. 3+.

——, "Tesoro Fires Back at Dissidents, Wins Order Blocking Vote on Board, Bylaws," *Oil Daily,* January 11, 1996, p. 3.

——, "Unhappy Tesoro Shareholders Try Takeover of Board to Improve Company's Standing," *Oil Daily,* May 10, 1995, pp. 1+.

Fletcher, Sam, and Peter Eisen, "Tesoro to Sell Bolivian Upstream to BG, Focus on Downstream," *Oil Daily,* November 23, 1999.

Kovski, Alan, "Tesoro Agrees to Buy Hawaii Refinery from BHP for $275 Million," *Oil Daily,* March 20, 1998, p. 5.

Lorek, Laura, "Tesoro Looking at Ways to Change Refinery Product Mix," *Oil Daily,* May 6, 1992, p. 4.

"Opportunity Talks," *Forbes,* November 15, 1973.

Phalon, Richard, "'Tis a Far, Far Better Thing," *Forbes,* March 1, 1982.

"Tesoro Petroleum Corporation: An Address by Dr. Robert V. West, Jr., Chairman of the Board and Chief Executive Officer, at the Harvard Business School, February 19, 1975," San Antonio: Tesoro Petroleum Corporation, 1975.

"Tesoro Petroleum: The Irony of Becoming a Takeover Target," *Business Week,* October 6, 1980.

"Tesoro Petroleum Planning Major Upgrade for Refinery," *San Antonio Business Journal,* August 25, 2000, p. 6.

Vogel, Todd, "Why Is Tesoro So Popular?," *Business Week,* December 21, 1987.

—Elizabeth Rourke
—update: David E. Salamie

Tom's of Maine, Inc.

302 Lafayette Center
Kennebunk, Maine 04043
U.S.A.
Telephone: (207) 985-2944
Toll Free: (800) 367-8667
Fax: (207) 985-2196
Web site: http://www.tomsofmaine.com

Private Company
Incorporated: 1970 as Tom's Natural Soaps
Employees: 150
Sales: $36 million (2000 est.)
NAIC: 325611 Soap and Other Detergent Manufacturing;
325620 Toilet Preparation Manufacturing; 325412
Pharmaceutical Preparation Manufacturing

Tom's of Maine, Inc. is a leading manufacturer of natural toothpaste and personal care products. The firm is run and mostly owned by its founder, Tom Chappell, whose deep concern for the environment and his employees' well-being have been key factors in determining the company's path. Tom's products contain no artificial ingredients, are not tested on animals, and are packaged in recycled materials. They are sold in health food stores as well as in many mass-market outlets such as CVS. Though the company's goods cost more than those of its larger mainstream competitors, Tom's sales have grown steadily over the years, due in part to strong customer loyalty as well as a widespread public interest in natural products. The majority of Tom's revenues come from sales of the company's flagship toothpaste line, which is certified for effectiveness by the American Dental Association. Other products include mouthwash, deodorant, dental floss, shampoo, soap, shaving cream, and a line of herbal health aids and extracts.

Early Years

Tom's was founded in 1970 by Tom Chappell and his wife, Kate, on their farm near Kennebunk, Maine. Tom, a 1966 graduate of Trinity College in Connecticut, and Kate, an artist and poet, had moved to Maine from Philadelphia in 1968 after Tom quit his job as a benefits counselor at Aetna. Both were intent on living closer to the land and raising their children in a more natural environment. For several years Tom Chappell worked for his father's industrial detergent manufacturing company, until he decided to explore an idea he had had for a non-polluting detergent.

Borrowing $5,000 from a friend for seed money, the Chappells soon began to manufacture the first phosphate-free liquid laundry detergent in the United States, which they called Clearlake. Packages came with prepaid return postage so that customers could send back the containers for reuse. The new firm, known as Tom's Natural Soaps, later added other products including a shampoo, cream rinse, and lotion.

In 1975 Tom Chappell had another idea he wanted to try—toothpaste. Created in conjunction with a chemist friend, his toothpaste was free of chemical additives or artificial sweeteners including the suspected carcinogen saccharin, and was markedly different from the products made by industry leaders Crest and Colgate. The flavor was derived from herbs and spices. Chappell's new product soon found acceptance within the post-1960's era anti-corporate, natural foods movement, and Tom's toothpaste became a staple item on the shelves of health food stores and food cooperatives, particularly in the New England area.

Following the successful introduction of its toothpaste, the company began to add other personal care products, including deodorant, mouthwash, and shaving cream, all made with natural ingredients and without testing on animals. In 1978 the Chappells decided to develop a line of fluoride toothpaste—a controversial idea in the natural foods marketplace. The move was a success, however, and sales of fluoride toothpaste eclipsed those of the original formula within two years, during which time Tom's toothpaste sales doubled. In 1981 the company's name was changed to Tom's of Maine, Inc.

By 1983 the firm's annual revenues were approaching $2 million. Recognizing that sustained growth would require new outlets for its goods, the company began to seek distribution to chain stores. The first one to take on Tom's products was Rhode Island-based CVS/People's, and others soon followed. The company was now starting to view its toothpaste as a legitimate

Company Perspectives:

The Tom's of Maine Mission: To serve our customers by providing safe, effective, innovative, natural products of high quality. To build relationships with our customers that extend beyond product usage to include full and honest dialogue, responsiveness to feedback, and the exchange of information about products and issues. To respect, value, and serve not only our customers, but also our co-workers, owners, agents, suppliers, and our community; to be concerned about and contribute to their well-being, and to operate with integrity so as to be deserving of their trust. To provide meaningful work, fair compensation, and a safe, healthy work environment that encourages openness, creativity, self-discipline, and growth. To contribute to and affirm a high level of commitment, skill, and effectiveness in the work community. To recognize, encourage, and seek a diversity of gifts and perspectives in our worklife. To acknowledge the value of each person's contribution to our goals and to foster teamwork in our tasks. To be distinctive in products and policies which honor and sustain our natural world. To address community concerns in Maine and around the globe, by devoting a portion of our time, talents, and resources to the environment, human needs, the arts, and education. To work together to contribute to the long-term value and sustainability of our company. To be a profitable and successful company while acting in a socially and environmentally responsible manner.

competitor of major brands like Crest and Colgate, rather than as simply a niche-market item. In 1986, a baking soda formula was introduced, and in 1988 Tom's added a special version for children.

The company's distribution by the late 1980s was still somewhat limited, with good coverage in New England and on the East and West Coasts, but little penetration in the South and Midwest. Tom's advertising budget, which until then had been minimal, was increased in 1989 to $1.3 million, and the first national ad campaign was introduced the following year, which included folksy radio spots that featured the voices of Tom and his mother, Virginia. To prepare for an anticipated increase in sales, equipment at the company's plant in an old train station in Kennebunk was upgraded, increasing toothpaste output from 50 to 90 tubes per minute.

Seeking a Higher Purpose: 1980s

Tom Chappell's focus on growing his company had again placed him front and center in the bottom line-oriented world of capitalism, the distaste for which had once driven him to move from Philadelphia to Maine. Still questioning whether such a life was truly meaningful, he enrolled in Harvard Divinity School in 1986, to which he would make a twice-weekly, 90-mile commute. After five years of study, he earned a master's degree in Theology. Chappell, a frequent public speaker, went on to publish a book in 1993 called *The Soul of a Business: Managing For Profit and the Public Good,* which outlined his ideas on running a company with a strong set of personal ethics.

His search for a more values-based approach to business also led to a new look at the company's mission, which was examined over a year's time beginning in June 1989. Input was sought from the entire workforce, and a multifaceted set of goals was finally agreed upon, which defined the company's purpose as making a profit while working toward the common good. Tom's would now place a much stronger emphasis on adhering to its core values, which had begun to recede into the background during the early 1980s, when a number of "M.B.A.s" were hired to "professionalize" the company. Though it took some time for the new mission statement to take hold, the company was ultimately revitalized by the process of implementing it.

One unusual byproduct of the new mission was the decision to "tithe" 5 percent of Tom's of Maine's profits and donate the money to environmental, arts, and human needs causes. This figure soon became 7 percent, and then 10. In addition to public giving, the company also looked after the welfare of its employees, offering them retirement savings and profit-sharing programs, childcare benefits, and parental leave, and even free fruit to eat on the job. Factory workers rotated stations every hour to avoid fatigue and boredom, and all were encouraged to perform volunteer work in the Kennebunk community on company time.

The firm's corporate values were tested in 1992 after the company reformulated its popular natural deodorant. The new version, which eliminated petroleum products and added glycerin and lichen, proved to be ineffective for about half of users, who complained to Tom's. In October of that year the company recalled the product at a cost of $375,000. The old formula was restored, and customers who had written to complain were given replacements and coupons for money back on their next purchase. The recalled deodorant, less effective but not useless, was donated to an organization that distributed it to the homeless.

Receiving the American Dental Association Seal: 1995

In 1995, after a seven-year effort, Tom's became the first natural toothpaste to win the approval of the American Dental Association (ADA), allowing it to put that organization's seal on its products. This was a crucial endorsement, as all of the company's major competitors had long sported the ADA seal, which served to assure consumers that their products were effective. The process had taken far longer than usual because the ADA had no standards for natural products, and also because Tom's did not allow testing on animals, which meant new methods of testing had to be devised and certified. The three most popular flavors, spearmint, cinnamon and fennel, were approved first, and the company continued to seek ADA certification for the rest of its fluoride line, which was granted six years later. Sales for 1995 reached a record level of $20 million.

In the fall of 1999 Tom's introduced a new line of cough, cold, and other natural wellness products and liquid herbal extracts—more than doubling the total number of items the company offered. These were developed in conjunction with researchers at the University of Illinois at Chicago, which would provide third-party information on the products via a toll-free telephone number. Approximately $4 million was earmarked for marketing, the largest amount in company history.

Key Dates:

1970: Tom and Kate Chappell begin making phosphate-free laundry soap in Maine; shampoo and other personal care products are introduced during the decade.
1975: Company develops natural toothpaste, which quickly becomes its biggest seller.
1978: Fluoride toothpaste debuts.
1981: Company's name becomes Tom's of Maine, Inc.
1983: Tom's begins distributing its products to mass-market chains, starting with CVS.
1989: Firm begins writing a new ethics-based mission statement.
1992: New deodorant formula proves ineffective and is recalled; old formula is restored.
1995: Tom's Toothpaste is certified as effective by the American Dental Association.
1999: Green Mountain Herbs is acquired; herbal remedies and extracts are introduced.
2000: Sale of 12 percent of company to investors helps finance herbal marketing.

Some observers questioned the long-term prospects of the new line, noting that several major players, including Warner-Lambert and tea maker Celestial Seasonings, had already tried to branch out into herbal remedies with little success. Tom Chappell discounted the criticism, noting that his company had frequently succeeded despite negative predictions from outsiders. To facilitate production, the company purchased Green Mountain Herbs of Vermont to make most of the herbal extracts, while others were obtained from regionally based organic farmers. The year 1999 also saw the publication of Chappell's second book, *Managing Upside Down,* which contained further thoughts on the ethics of corporate management.

In 2000 Tom's raised $6 million for herbal product development and advertising by selling 12 percent of the company to a group of 15 outside investors, including Goldman, Sachs Chairman John Whitehead. Tom and Kate Chappell remained majority shareholders. The market for herbals was proving to be as difficult to crack as some critics had predicted. Sales for the company, which had been growing 20 to 30 percent annually, increased by only 7 percent during 2000, and a loss of $1.5 million was posted, only the second case of red ink in the previous 25 years. Chappell himself admitted the company had been over-ambitious, telling *Forbes,* "We tried to do too much." But Tom's 58-year-old founder had confounded the critics before, and vowed to press on, hiring a New York consultant to redesign the company's packaging, among other initiatives.

Thirty years down the line, Tom's of Maine continued to make natural personal care products with a strong underpinning of corporate ethics. The company's flagship line of toothpaste was the dominant natural brand in the United States, and many other Tom's products were well-established with consumers who sought alternatives to chemical-laden, mass-marketed personal care goods. The new move into herbal tonics and extracts was a big leap of faith that had yet to pay off, but under the experienced, creative guidance of Tom and Kate Chappell, Tom's of Maine was sure to endure, whatever the public's acceptance of the herbal line.

Principal Competitors

Procter & Gamble Company; Unilever; Colgate-Palmolive Company; Levlad, Inc.

Further Reading

Bolita, Dan, "Tom's of Maine and Beyond," *KM World*, January, 2000, pp. 10–11.

Canfield, Clark, "Natural Progression: Tom's of Maine Hopes Its Success with Natural Toothpaste Carries over to an Ambitious New Line of Herbal Products," *Portland Press Herald*, October 10, 1999, p. 1F.

Carton, Barbara, "Down-Home Tom's Wants to Shine Teeth Nationwide," *Boston Globe*, August 8, 1989, p. 25.

Chappell, Tom, *Managing Upside Down: The Seven Intentions of Values-Centered Leadership,* New York: W. Morrow, 1999.

——, *The Soul of a Business,* New York: Bantam Books, 1993.

"Dentists Endorse—Tom's Natural Toothpaste Wins ADA Seal," *Bangor Daily News,* August 15, 1995.

Groves, Martha, "Careers: The Soul at Work," *Los Angeles Times*, April 8, 1998, pp. D2, D10.

Henderson, Keith, "Doing Good by Making Toothpaste," *Christian Science Monitor*, February 4, 1994, p. 8.

Lefton, Terry, "Tom's Cleans Up Deodorant After Formula Change Goofs," *Brandweek*, May 17, 1993, p. 18.

May, Thomas Garvey, "You Get What You Give," *Natural Foods Merchandiser's New Product Review*, Spring 2000.

Potts, Mark, "It's 'Natural' Vs. Big Guys in Toothpaste," *Washington Post*, November 5, 1986, p. C1.

Strosnider, Kim, "Keeping Tom's Nice: At 25, Tom's of Maine Confronts Question of What Price National Growth," *Portland Press Herald*, March 17, 1996, p. 1F.

Zack, Ian, "Out of the Tube," *Forbes*, November 26, 2001.

—Frank Uhle

Transocean Sedco Forex Inc.

4 Greenway Plaza
Houston, Texas
U.S.A.
Telephone: (713) 232-7500
Fax: (713) 232-7027
Web site: http://www.deepwater.com

Public Company
Incorporated: 1953 as The Offshore Company
Employees: 15,600
Sales: $1.22 billion (2000)
Stock Exchanges: New York
Ticker Symbol: RIG
NAIC: 21311 Drilling Oil and Gas Wells

Transocean Sedco Forex Inc. is the world's largest offshore drilling company and the fourth largest oilfield service company overall. Officially a Cayman Islands corporation, it operates out of Houston, Texas, with more than 16,000 employees located around the globe. Transocean's drilling rigs and work crews are contracted by petroleum companies at a day rate, over the course of long-term and short-term contracts. Although the company offers inland drilling barges and shallow water drilling rigs, Transocean is especially active in the deepwater and harsh environment drilling segment, offering semisubmersible rigs as well as massive drillships that have drilled to record depths in the range of 10,000 feet. Transocean's mobile rigs cover all of the world's major offshore drilling markets, including the Gulf of Mexico, the North Sea, Mediterranean Sea, and the waters off eastern Canada, Brazil, West and South Africa, the Middle East, Asia, and India.

Corporate Lineage Dating Back to 1953

Transocean is composed of a number of drilling operations that were merged, especially during the late 1990s when the offshore drilling industry as a whole began to consolidate. The surviving corporate structure belongs to The Offshore Company, incorporated in Delaware in 1953. It was created when the pipeline company Southern Natural Gas Co. (SNG) purchased DeLong-McDermott, which was a contract drilling joint venture of DeLong Engineering and J. Ray McDermott's marine construction business. A year later, Offshore established the first jackup drilling rig in the Gulf of Mexico. Oil and gas exploration then began to move farther offshore and to more remote areas of the world. Offshore was also one of the earliest companies in the 1960s to operate jackups in the inhospitable environment of the North Sea, which would develop into one of the world's most significant sources of oil. In 1967 Offshore went public. Ten years later it expanded its range of operations to southeast Asia, where it drilled its first deepwater well. In 1978, the company became a wholly owned subsidiary of SNG, which had greatly increased its emphasis on offshore drilling and exploration operations. As a result, Offshore developed one of the largest U.S. fleets of drilling rigs. When SNG changed its name to Sonat in 1982, The Offshore Company became known as Sonat Offshore Drilling Inc.

During the 1970s new "floaters" were developed to accomplish deepwater drilling. Semisubmersible rigs were partially submerged below water and usually moored to the ocean floor for stability. Drill ships, able to reach depths of 3,000 feet and particularly useful in exploring remote areas, were also introduced as a cost-effective option during this period. By the late 1970s a large number of companies began to build and operate floaters, leading to a highly fragmented industry. When oil prices reached $32 a barrel in 1981, a drilling boom ensued, with oilfield service companies purchasing a great deal of equipment and saddling themselves with considerable debt. As the price of oil plunged in the mid-1980s, reaching a level below $10 by 1986, oil companies canceled drilling programs or negotiated much lower day rates for offshore rigs. A 300-foot jackup in the Gulf of Mexico that once commanded $50,000 a day now rented for less than $10,000. Many service companies went bankrupt or were swallowed up by stronger rivals. During this decade-long lean period, offshore drilling rigs in operation declined precipitously, from more than 1,000 in the early 1980s to around 500.

When oil and gas prices appeared to be rising, Sonat took advantage of investor optimism in 1993 to spin off Sonat Offshore, making $340 million while retaining a 40 percent interest, which would then be sold off in 1995. In this way the parent

---

Company Perspectives:

Our mission is to be the premier offshore drilling company providing worldwide rig-based, well-construction services to our customers through the integration of motivated people, quality equipment and innovative technology, with a particular focus on technically demanding environments.

---

company hoped to transform itself from a diversified pipeline company into an exploration and production company. The newly independent Sonat Offshore, as a result of the offering, had a clean balance sheet and money in the bank, and was well positioned to weather an ensuing decline in gas prices. Moreover, the company's emphasis on deepwater oil drilling also would prove to be a wise strategy. It was recognized that the most desirable energy plays that remained in the world resided under great depths of ocean. Although the technology existed to tap these deposits, only until oil prices reached a certain level would it become economical for a company like Sonat Offshore to invest in a new generation of drill ships. The cost of such rigs was so high that only large companies were able to afford them.

Consolidation Among Offshore Drilling Contractors in the 1990s

There were other reasons why consolidation among offshore drilling contractors became desirable in the mid-1990s. It would likely bring pricing discipline to a highly fragmented industry, in which the top three companies served just 27 percent of the market. In 1995 there were around 400 jackup rigs owned by as many as 80 companies, creating a supply/demand imbalance that gave oil producers tremendous leverage over contractors. A small drop in the price of gas or oil could result in a major decrease in day rates. Clearly, companies could not expect to achieve long-term health by simply building more rigs to expand their business. Growth had to come by acquiring existing rigs, to gain some leverage with producers. With fewer but larger contractors in the industry, the addition of new rigs would hopefully become more of a rational and systematic process. In addition, larger players could operate more efficiently around the world, with rigs strategically positioned to save on moving charges while building a more diversified customer base.

In 1995 Sonat Offshore announced its proposal to acquire Reading & Bates Corp., which began offshore drilling operations in 1955. Although discussions continued over the next several months, in the end Reading & Bates rejected a $501 million cash and stock offer. In May 1996 Sonat Offshore announced a $1.5 billion stock and cash deal to acquire Norway's Transocean ASA, which a few months earlier announced that it was looking for a partner. Transocean ASA had been created in the mid-1970s when a Norwegian whaling company entered the semisubmersible business, then later consolidated with a number of other companies. Because of its large North Sea operations, Transocean ASA was considered a prize catch, one that would automatically make the buyer into the unquestioned leader in deepwater drilling. Reading & Bates attempted to outflank Sonat Offshore, venturing an unsolicited bid for Transocean ASA, which because of Norway law did not have

any of the American takeover defenses at its disposal, such as "poison pill" provisions. After a month-long skirmish, Sonat Offshore sweetened its bid and agreed to retain much of Transocean's management team, the fate of which was uncertain under the Reading & Bates offer. The deal became effective in September 1996, and Sonat Offshore changed its name to Transocean Offshore.

Rising oil prices, in the meantime, benefited offshore drilling contractors. Day rates by December 1996 doubled over the previous year, topping $130,000 a day. The chairman of Transocean Offshore, J. Michael Talbot, concluded that the trend could continue for as long as 20 years and made a commitment to expand on the company's fleet. With long-term contracts with oil companies in hand, Transocean Offshore began the development of a new generation of massive drill ships, featuring the latest in technological advances, and designed to drill to 10,000 feet, as opposed to the 3,000-foot capacity of the drill ships built in the mid-1970s. The first ship, the *Discoverer Enterprise,* would be 834 feet in length with a derrick that stood 226 feet high. It could sleep 200 and carry 125,000 barrels of oil and gas. Because it featured two drilling systems in one derrick, the ship could reduce the time to drill a development well by up to 40 percent and could drill and lay pipeline without the need of a pipelay barge. With its increased productivity the ship could command much higher day rates, in the neighborhood of $200,000. Moreover, the *Enterprise* would essentially serve as a floating research and development project for two additional high-tech ships. Due to some setbacks partly caused by accident and weather, it would be more than a year late in becoming serviceable and see its price tag grow from $270 million to more than $430 million.

In April 1999 Transocean Offshore was approached by Schlumberger Ltd., which proposed spinning off its offshore drilling operations, Sedco Forex Limited, as part of a merger of equals. Paris-based Schlumberger had been involved in offshore drilling for many years. The Forex company was created in France in 1942 to engage in land drilling in North Africa and the Middle East, as well as France. Forex teamed with Languedocienne to create a company called Neptune to engage in offshore drilling. Forex had gained complete control of Neptune by 1972, when Schlumberger bought the remaining interest in Forex. The Southeastern Drilling Company, Sedco, was an American firm, founded in 1947 by future Texas governor Bill Clements to drill in shallow marsh water. In the 1960s it began to provide drilling services in deeper water. Schlumberger acquired the company in 1984 and a year later combined it with Forex to create Sedco Forex Drilling.

Merger of Transocean and Sedco Forex in 1999

The proposed Transocean Offshore and Sedco Forex merger was announced in July 1999. It called for an exchange of stock valued at approximately $3.2 billion. Schlumberger shareholders would receive roughly one share in the new company, Transocean Sedco Forex, for every five Schlumberger shares held. In the end, Schlumberger shareholders would control approximately 52 percent of the new company. Both Schlumberger and Transocean would receive five seats on the board, while Schlumberger's vice-chairman would serve as the chairman of the company and Transocean's Talbert would become

Key Dates:

1942: Forex is founded in France.
1947: Southeastern Drilling Company is founded.
1953: The Offshore Company is incorporated.
1967: The Offshore Company goes public.
1978: The Offshore Company becomes a wholly owned subsidiary of Sonat Inc., formerly Southern Natural Gas Co. (SNG).
1993: Sonat Offshore is spun off.
1996: Sonat Offshore acquires Transocean ASA to become Transocean Offshore.
1999: Transocean Offshore merges with Sedco Forex Drilling to become Transocean Sedco Forex Inc.
2000: R&B Falcon is acquired.

president and CEO. With a market capitalization of more than $9 billion by mid-March 2000, Transocean Sedco Forex was an independent powerhouse among offshore drilling contractors and the fourth largest oilfield service company. Its fleet included 46 semisubmersibles and seven deepwater drill ships, with others under construction. It was widely expected that the deal would create added pressure on other contractors to merge, as much needed consolidation in the industry continued to gain momentum.

Transocean Sedco Forex was added to the Standard & Poor's 500 Index on the first day of trading on the New York Stock Exchange in 2000. It enjoyed an immediate boost in price, caused in large part by money managers adding the stock to their funds that mirrored the S&P 500. The company soon was involved in yet another major expansion, acquiring R&B Falcon for more than $9 billion in an all-stock transaction, which included the assumption of $3 billion in debt. After failing to beat out Sonat Offshore in the Transocean ASA acquisition, Reading & Bates had merged with Falcon Drilling Co. in 1997, then acquired Cliffs Drilling in 1998. The company's fortunes suffered a downturn in 1998 and although it had made strides in redressing its situation, its debt load remained high and management decided that the time was ripe to merge with Transocean Sedco Forex. Under terms of the deal R&B Falcon owned approximately 30 percent of the new company and received three new seats on the board of directors.

Transocean Sedco Forex was now a company worth approximately $14 billion and was the third largest oilfield services company, eclipsed only by Halliburton and Schlumberger. With 165 offshore rigs, inland barges, and supporting assets, the combined company easily outpaced its closest rival, Pride International, with just 59 offshore rigs, of which 45 were shallow-water jackups. Moreover, Transocean provided almost half of the world's ultra-deep drilling ships. In effect, Transocean Sedco Forex was able to expand its global fleet with the most extensive range of offshore rigs and markets, while gaining a presence in the shallow and inland waters of the Gulf of

Mexico, where it previously had no fleet. Because of high gas prices R&B Falcon's 27 jackups in the Gulf and more than 30 inland barges promised to be an attractive addition. Overall, there was very little overlap in rigs. Nevertheless, Transocean Sedco Forex estimated that it would still be able to realize about $50 million in annual savings in purchasing, overhead, and insurance. Because the company had changed its origin of incorporation to the Cayman Islands in late 1999, it was not allowed by law to operate vessels in U.S. waters. The company complied with the law by becoming a 25 percent joint venture partner in the former R&B Falcon transportation business, which consisted of 102 inland and offshore tugboats, four crew boats, and 58 inland and offshore flat deck cargo barges and inland shale barges.

Clearly, Transocean Sedco Forex had taken the lead in the consolidation of offshore drilling contractors. Everyone agreed on the need for consolidation, but with so many operators of similar size it was difficult for executives to sort out who was to be the acquirer and who was to be acquired. In 2001 a number of contractors merged, but no one came close to rivaling Transocean Sedco Forex in size, especially in the deepwater and harsh environment offshore drilling markets. Although management's first priority was to pay down debt, there was every reason to believe that the company would continue to snap up desirable firms in an effort to grow even larger.

Principal Subsidiaries

Transocean Offshore Deepwater Drilling Inc.; Sonat Offshore International LDC; Transocean Offshore Europe Limited; Transocean AS.

Principal Competitors

Diamond Offshore Drilling, Inc.; Global Marine Inc.; Noble Drilling; Saipem.

Further Reading

Antosh, Nelson, "Sonat, Norwegian Firm Strike Deal," *Houston Chronicle,* May 3, 1996, p. 1.

Byrnes, Nanette, "Seven Come Eleven," *Financial World,* March 15, 1994, p. 36.

DeLuca, Marshall, and William Furlow, "Driller Consolidation Begins, But Will It Continue?," *Offshore,* August 1999, p. 56.

Harrison, Joan, "Transocean Rounds Out Its Service Offerings with R&B Falcon Deal," *Mergers and Acquisitions,* October 2000, p. 22.

Mack, Toni, "Learning from Experience," *Forbes,* December 2, 1996, pp. 102–08.

Opdyke, Jeff D., "Mergers Could Improve Prospects Among Stocks of Offshore Drillers," *Wall Street Journal,* March 15, 1995, p. T2.

"Sonat Offshore Drilling Inc.," *Oil & Gas Investor,* March 1996, p. 30.

Tejada, Carloa, "Schlumberger's Sedco and Transocean to Merge," *Wall Street Journal,* July 13, 1999, p. A3.

Wetuski, Jodi, "Two Down . . . ," *Oil & Gas Investor,* October 2000, pp. 59–60.

—Ed Dinger

URS Corporation

---

100 California Street, Suite 500
San Francisco, California 94111-4529
U.S.A.
Telephone: (415) 774-2700
Fax: (415) 398-1905
Web site: http://www.urscorp.com

Public Company
Incorporated: 1950
Employees: 16,000
Sales: $2.21 billion (2000)
Stock Exchanges: New York Pacific
Ticker Symbol: URS
NAIC: 23332 Commercial and Institutional Building
 Construction; 23411 Highway and Street Construc-
 tion; 23491 Water, Sewer, and Pipeline Construction;
 23594 Wrecking and Demolition Contractors; 54133
 Engineering Services; 54131 Architectural Services

Ranked number one on *ENR*'s list of the top U.S. design firms, URS Corporation has 300 offices in 30 countries. Aside from being the largest pure engineering firm in the United States, URS is also a top ten construction firm. It is a leader in airport construction and is also involved in environmental consulting.

Origins

URS Corporation was founded in 1950. Though a fairly successful firm, it would not grow to become an engineering industry giant until the 1980s and 1990s.

URS's international aspirations manifested themselves fairly early on. The company began doing business in Japan in the mid-1960s. For the next 20 years, however, nearly all of its work there would come not from local clients, but from the U.S. government, which hired the firm for projects at military bases. Although it found the Japanese market practically closed to outsiders, URS was able to perform some work in the United States for Japanese firms.

By the mid-1980s, URS Corporation had 40 sales and engineering offices in the United States. The company maintained these offices with the realization that the services market was, indeed, primarily local. Fierce competition for large billion-dollar projects, however, was prompting more giant builders to come look for smaller projects. The company's backlog was $70 million in 1985.

Four of the company's top executives, including Chairman and CEO Arthur Stromberg, were charged with overstating the company's fiscal 1986 revenues and income (reported at $115.7 million and $8.7 million) by $8.4 million. They later settled the case without admitting or denying the charges.

The company's largest shareholder, Richard C. Blum, was the husband of former San Francisco Mayor Dianne Feinstein, who was running for governor. This resulted in the SEC investigation getting national media attention, particularly from the *Los Angeles Times,* which revealed that payments totaling $35 million were made to settle shareholders' lawsuits at URS and two other companies in which Blum was a major shareholder.

Public As Thortec in 1987

URS underwent a major restructuring in 1987. It changed its name to Thortec International Inc. (and its NYSE ticker symbol to THT) in November and offered a 35 percent interest in its URS International Inc. subsidiary on the London Unlisted Securities Market. In addition, the company formed a new 1,800-person subsidiary, URS Consultants Inc., to handle its domestic consulting services, which were centered on infrastructure, waste management, and pollution control. As part of the restructuring, Thortec International was expanding its range of waste treatment services, project management software systems, and forensic engineering services.

Around this time, URS was lobbying for more access to the Japanese market. To further this end, the company acquired an architectural firm in Japan and formed a venture with an engineering firm there. In 1988, the Hong Kong office of URS International landed a contract to design the $49 million, 450-room Hua Qiao Mansion Hotel being built in Beijing, China.

The board sought a new leader to turn the company around. One director, Bill Walsh, chairman of Sequoia Associates, a Menlo Park buyout firm, suggested his friend Martin M. Koffel, who had formerly been president of ophthalmic products and services company CooperVision Inc. and had helped position Oral-B Laboratories Inc. for its sale to Gillette Co. Koffel was named president and CEO of Thortec International in May 1989. Former CEO Arthur H. Stromberg remained chairman before resigning that post one month later.

Koffel, a native of Australia, had been a mining engineer before leading CooperVision. Koffel's management team would guide Thortec back to its core business of engineering. The firm's financial problems had stemmed from an overactive diversification policy. Soon, URS Engineers would be the company's only operating unit.

In June 1989, Thortec relocated its headquarters from San Mateo to the San Francisco office of its largest subsidiary, URS Consultants. Revenues fell about 10 percent, to $99.4 million, in the fiscal year ended October 31. The company lost $19 million in 1989 and $12 million the year before. By February 1990, Thortec had defaulted on interest payments to one of its creditors; the prospect of bankruptcy had been raised. A restructuring plan announced in October 1989 had called for San Francisco investment firm Richard C. Blum and Associates to acquire 53 percent of the company in return for $12.5 million in cash.

Thortec reverted to its old name of URS Corporation by the time its restructuring was completed in late February 1990. Blum ended up with a 68 percent holding in URS, while Wells Fargo Bank owned 14 percent. The company's debt was cut from $73 million to $37 million in the process. In June 1991, URS had a public offering, which further helped reduce debt.

URS closed its software unit in May 1990. Westborough, Massachusetts-based Mitchell Management Systems Inc. had accounted for 8 percent of URS's $99.5 million in revenue for

fiscal 1989, but lost $3.3 million that year and $1.4 million the year before.

The restructuring produced some tangible results. URS became profitable again in 1991, when revenues were about $120 million. By October 1992, backlog had increased to $278 million, up 25 percent in a year. Revenues rose 11 percent while net income leaped 86 percent to $4.3 million. The public sector accounted for 80 percent of business.

A new subsidiary, URS Telecommunications, based in Washington D.C., was created in 1995 to focus on the emerging wireless telecommunications market. It would be the transportation segment, however, that would provide URS with its best opportunity for growth. Revenues were $180 million for the 1995 fiscal year, producing net income of $5 million—both figures up 10 percent.

Big-Time Growth in the Late 1990s

URS doubled in size in 1996 through the purchase of Dallas-based Greiner Engineering Inc. for $63.5 million in cash plus 1.4 million shares of common stock worth about $10 million. This increased URS's total revenues to $400 million per year. The deal doubled Greiner's workforce of 1,500 and made URS Greiner a top-five architectural company.

Greiner, which specialized in designing schools, brought with it some international operations, based in Malaysia, and reduced URS's dependence on the environmental business and the federal government. According to *ENR,* URS and Greiner had been considering a merger for three years preceding the deal.

In August 1997, URS bought Denver-based Woodward-Clyde Group Inc. in a stock-plus-cash deal worth $100 million. The purchase again doubled URS Corp.'s size, making it the country's fifth largest engineering company, with revenues of $800 million and 6,000 employees.

Transportation projects accounted for a third of URS Corp.'s business in the late 1990s. This sector was given a boost by the $217 billion Transportation Equity Act for the 21st Century (TEA-21) approved by Congress in 1998. As a result, URS was named joint program manager of a ten-year, $3.2 billion project to connect commuter trains between Long Island, New York, and Manhattan's Grand Central Terminal. URS would split $24 million in engineering fees with its partner for the project, Bechtel. Other highway jobs included a $12 million upgrade of I-15 in Salt Lake City and $20 million worth of work on Miami's Palmetto Expressway.

By October 1998, URS was searching for an acquisition to help the firm enter the European market. Private finance initiative schemes were making the United Kingdom a particularly attractive market. In early 1999, URS bought Thorburn Colquhoun, a £25 million-a-year civil and structural engineering firm based in Great Britain.

On the other side of the world, URS Corp.'s Greiner Engineering unit was participating in the design of a terminal at one of China's busiest airports in Guangzhou. Pasadena, California-

Key Dates:

1950: URS Corporation is founded.
1980: URS has 40 offices in the United States.
1987: URS goes public under the name Thortec.
1989: Turnaround specialist Martin M. Koffel is hired as CEO.
1990: URS reverts to old name as restructuring is completed.
1996: The purchase of Greiner Engineering doubles URS's size.
1997: The Woodward-Clyde purchase again doubles URS's size.
1999: The Dames & Moore acquisition makes URS the largest U.S. engineering firm.

based Parsons Corp. and the Guangdong Provincial Architectural Design Institute were also collaborating on the project.

URS continued its buying spree by acquiring, in June 1999, the Los Angeles-based Dames & Moore Group for $312 million in cash, plus the assumption of $300 million of debt. Dames had become susceptible to a takeover because its stock price had fallen by 40 percent since 1992 as the company pursued an aggressive acquisition policy. One of Dames & Moore's divisions was a leading provider of construction and program management services—likely to be highly marketable by URS in the coming transportation boom. Most of Dames & Moore's revenues, however, were coming from environmental consulting.

After the deal, URS had annual revenues of $2 billion and 15,000 employees in more than 30 countries. Revenues and employment had grown tenfold since 1996. It was perceived as a leader in the consolidation of the engineering services industry.

URS's newfound mass promised to help it win larger, more lucrative contracts. The company began to compete with the giants of the engineering industry, such as Fluor Corporation, Brown & Root Inc., Bechtel Group Inc., and Parsons Corporation.

At the end of 1999, North America accounted for 90 percent of the firm's revenues. The international acquisitions, however, gave the company a platform from which to grow abroad. Koffel expected the firm's size to double by 2005. URS was already involved in some high-profile projects overseas, including work on London's Millennium Dome and Sydney's Olympic stadium.

URS sold its DecisionQuest unit, which provided litigation support services, to a management-led group in June 2000. URS realized $20 million in cash from the deal, all earmarked for debt reduction.

While it was acquiring companies during the 1990s, URS's main operating unit also was picking up names. It was known as URS Greiner Inc., then URS Greiner Woodward Clyde, until autumn 2000, when it reverted to the URS Corp. name.

Thanks to its growth in business at home and abroad, the company planned to hire more than 500 employees in the summer of 2001. Employment was 15,800 before the recruitment drive. Although CEO Martin Koffel expected the transportation market to mature in the next five years, the company planned to push energy and wastewater services after that. URS also continued to design airports and other public facilities.

Principal Divisions

Parent; Domestic; International.

Principal Competitors

AECOM Technology Corp.; Bechtel Group Inc.; CH2M Hill Cos. Ltd.; The IT Group, Inc.; Jacobs Engineering Corp.; Parsons Corp.

Further Reading

Back, Brian J., "URS Corp. Bulldozes Its Way Through an Era of Acquisitions," *Business Journal* (Portland), February 25, 2000.

Bangsberg, P.T., "2 US Firms to Design Baiyun Airport Hub," *Journal of Commerce,* April 6, 1999, p. 6A.

Barron, Kelly, "Roads Less Traveled," *Forbes,* September 3, 2001, pp. 46+.

Bartholomew, Doug, "First, Analyze the Processes," *Industry Week,* November 1, 1999, p. 37.

Bullard, Stan, "Acquisition to Add 40 URS Jobs," *Crain's Cleveland Business,* December 1, 1997, p. 6.

——, "Heckaman Bolts URS After '93 Merger He Designed," *Crain's Cleveland Business,* January 10, 1994, p. 2.

——, "URS Eyes a Move Downtown," *Crain's Cleveland Business,* March 28, 1994, p. 1.

Byrne, Harlan S., "URS Corp.; Timing Looks Right for Engineering Firm," *Barron's,* November 9, 1992, pp. 38, 40.

Carlton, Jim, "SEC Probe May Make Feinstein Spouse More of an Issue in California Campaign," *Wall Street Journal,* October 5, 1990, p. A20.

——, "URS, Once Near Bankruptcy, Is at Pinnacle of Industry," *Wall Street Journal,* December 16, 1999, p. B4.

"Chapter 11 a Possibility; Thortec Tender May Be in Jeopardy," *San Francisco Chronicle,* February 16, 1990, p. C3.

Czurak, David, "From Summer Intern to Boss," *Grand Rapids Business Journal,* December 12, 2000, p. 5.

——, "URS—A Name to Remember," *Grand Rapids Business Journal,* October 16, 2000, p. B2.

Davies, John, "US Firms Find It Hard to Build for Japanese," *Journal of Commerce,* October 16, 1987, p. 5A.

"Engineer Set for Big Time After US Buy-Out," *Building,* February 5, 1999, p. 19.

"Ex-Thortec Officials Settle SEC Charges of Inflating Results," *Wall Street Journal,* May 25, 1990, p. A18.

Graham, Jed, "Transit Bill Fueling Heavy Construction," *Investor's Business Daily,* November 17, 1998, p. B11.

Hayes, Thomas C., "Big Builders Learn to Think Small," *New York Times,* July 28, 1985, Sec. 3, p. 1.

Hurtado, Robert, "Rebuilding U.S.: In Line to Profit," *New York Times,* January 7, 1993, p. D6.

Korman, Richard, "Behind the Dames & Moore Deal," *ENR,* May 17, 1999, p. 10.

——, "Dames & Moore Tried to Hold On," *ENR,* May 24, 1999, p. 15.

——, "URS-Greiner Deal: Will Mid-Sized Models Be Obsolete?," *ENR,* June 3, 1996, p. 10.

Marsh, Peter, "Engineer Constructs a Route Towards Expansion," *Financial Times,* Companies & Finance Sec., December 10, 1999, p. 30.

Materna, Jessica, "Engineering Firm Flexes Hire Power," *San Francisco Business Times,* July 20, 2001.

Matta, L. Matthew, "Blum Supports URS Acquisition," *Private Equity Week,* May 17, 1999, p. 11.

Mercer, Tenisha, "Architectural Firm Considers Its Acquisition an Opportunity," *Crain's Detroit Business,* November 25, 1996, p. 45.

Pachuta, Michael J., "URS Laying the Groundwork for Large Infrastructure Deals," *Investor's Business Daily,* June 8, 1999, p. B18.

Phaungchai, Naruth, "Duo Engineers URS Deal," *Bank Loan Report,* June 28, 1999, pp. 12+.

Pilgrim, Kitty, Interview with Martin Koffel, *Capital Ideas,* CNNfn, May 6, 1999.

"Thortec Ends Restructuring, Changes Name," *San Francisco Chronicle,* February 22, 1990, p. C2.

—Frederick C. Ingram

Vallen Corporation

13333 Northwest Freeway
Houston, Texas 77040-6086
U.S.A.
Telephone: (713) 462-8700
Fax: (713) 462-7634
Web site: http://www.vallen.com

Wholly Owned Subsidiary of Hagemeyer N.V.
Incorporated: 1960
Employees: 1,100
Sales: $306.1 million (1999)
NAIC: 421450 Medical, Dental and Hospital Equipment
and Supplies Wholesalers

A subsidiary of Hagemeyer N.V. since late 1999, Vallen Corporation has provided industrial safety products and services and fire-fighting equipment for more than 50 years. The Houston-based company generates nearly 95 percent of its revenues from its Industrial Distribution segment, which caters to both public and private customers through its subsidiary Vallen Safety Supply Company. In addition to its regional distribution centers in North America, Vallen also maintains in-plant stores in certain locations for major companies such as Dow, Alcoa, and Mobil. In addition to distributing the products of 1,600 suppliers from around the world, the company's subsidiary Encon Safety Products, Inc., manufactures some products, including protective clothing, eyewash products, nonprescription eyewear, emergency drench shower units, and storage cabinets. Vallen Safety also provides safety inspection services, training and consulting, and product repair through its Vallen Technical Services, Vallen Knowledge Services, and Vallen Occupational Health Services divisions.

Starting As Guardian Safety in 1947

Vallen's founder, Leonard J. Bruce, grew up in Chicago during the Depression. With his father out of work, he had to pick stray coal from a local roadbed to keep the family furnace burning during the long, frigid winters of the Midwest. Like many in his generation he developed an overwhelming need to establish a secure livelihood and a practical sense about how to make money. Not eligible for the service in World War II, he became familiar with the safety business while working as an inspector of bomb factories. He gained further experience working at Chicago Eye Shield selling goggles and other products to area steel mills and foundries. Bruce also served as a sales rep for a hospital supplies company, but, now married, he began to question his long-term career prospects. According to Bruce, ''I found out what my district manager was making after 16 years with the company.'' When his employer wanted to transfer him to the East in 1947, the 27-year-old Bruce decided he would do far better by striking out on his own. Having read about a major explosion at a Texas refinery, he sensed an opportunity and decided to spend two weeks visiting petrochemical factories along the Gulf Coast. He learned that not only was there a growing demand for safety equipment in the area, but a new supply company would face little established competition.

Bruce convinced his wife Valerie to move to Houston, Texas, and in October 1947 they started doing business as Guardian Safety Equipment Company, representing Chicago Eye Shield products. Having little money they were the only employees, working initially out of a tiny office furnished with Army surplus items. By 1955 Bruce was successful enough that he opened a second branch of Guardian Safety in Baton Rouge, Louisiana. The company began to add product lines other than those of Chicago Eye Shield during the 1950s. In 1960, Bruce incorporated the business in Texas under the name Vallen Corporation—an amalgam of Valerie and Leonard—since Guardian Safety was a trade name of Chicago Eye Shield Company. In that year the company generated revenues of $670,000.

In 1964 Bruce incorporated Encon Safety Products, Inc., which was to become involved in the direct manufacturing of products, including emergency showers and eyewashes, goggles, and a cool air delivery system used under protective clothing. Unable to find the right kind of chemical goggles required by his customers, Bruce decided to make his own. He established Encon, hired a design engineer, and within six months had a viable product to sell. Encon catered, in particular, to the Gulf Coast petrochemical industry. In 1965 Vallen made

Company Perspectives:

Our core business has long been the distribution of thousands of safety products from the world's finest manufacturers. Today, we're increasingly focused on the rising demand for safety devices. We're providing technical services, fire services and training and consulting. We're also expanding our occupational health services. Safe practices not only reduce accidents, they dramatically lower Workers' Compensation costs, insurance fees, medical bills, and lost time. We fit our consulting expertise, maintenance services, and products to each customer's requirements. When it comes to safety, no one offers more than Vallen.

its first acquisition and, as a result, established a foothold in Corpus Christi, Texas. Vallen grew steadily, helped along in 1970 when Congress passed the Occupational Safety and Health Act (OSHA). Vallen did not experience any major surge in new business, however, since many of its customers were large companies that had already instituted similar safety standards on their own. Even during the recession of the early 1970s, Vallen maintained a steady increase in revenues. The business was healthy enough to support the purchase of a five-acre parcel of land and the construction of a 50,000-square-foot corporate and distribution headquarters in northwest Houston in 1978.

Going Public in 1979

Bruce took Vallen Corporation public in 1979 at $13 per share and in the process enriched himself by some $3 million, while still retaining a 63 percent interest and raising $1.8 million for expansion. Vallen Safety Supply made three acquisitions over the next two years, the largest of which added nearly $3 million in annual revenues and operated 11 distribution facilities, with two in Louisiana, seven in Texas, and one each in Alabama and Pennsylvania. Each depot served a territory that was roughly 150 miles in radius. While gaining a toehold in the East, Vallen continued to focus attention on its Sunbelt markets, although it harbored some national aspirations. After turning over the day-to-day running of the company to someone else for the first time, in 1984 Bruce again stepped in as president and CEO, serving in that capacity for more than a year. In June 1985, J.M. Wayne Code was named president and CEO of Vallen Corporation. Code came to Vallen after serving as CEO of Safety Supply Company, a subsidiary of Imperial Optical Co. of Canada. Vallen, at this point, generated some $2 million in annual net earnings on $40 million in revenues. Under Code's leadership, the company would expand its product lines and customer base, extend its sales territory, and as a result take revenues and profits to a new level. Revenues exceeded $50 million in 1986 and by 1989 stood at $98 million, helped to some degree by hospitals and laboratories buying goggles that were used to prevent the spread of AIDS to caregivers and researchers. In 1990 revenues would reach $125 million, then exceed $151 million in 1991. Vallen's stock, priced at $3 in 1985, was worth $27.50 in early 1991. With Bruce still owning a substantial majority stake, the company split its stock three-for-one in 1989, followed a year later by a three-for-two split,

thereby increasing the number of shares available for trading from 300,000 to close to one million.

During Code's first six years at the helm, Vallen grew both externally and internally. In December 1985, the company purchased assets of the distribution operations of E.D. Bullard Company. In 1989 Vallen grew by acquisition again, this time buying a Tennessee-based operation, thus adding some $8.6 million in annual sales and new territory in the mid-Atlantic states. In 1990 Encon bought one of its Houston contractors, a maker of safety goggles and hard hats, giving Encon additional strength in contract plastics manufacturing. Later in the year, Vallen Safety Supply acquired the assets of another Houston company, Instrument Services Inc., which specialized in the sale and service of gas-detection and environmental-monitoring equipment. Internally, Vallen established onsite stores, which allowed it to be the exclusive supplier at the facilities of some major customers. Not only were supplies available on a just-in-time basis, Vallen owned all the inventory, and its computers kept track of each department's usage. Vallen even maintained onsite optometrists to write prescriptions for safety glasses.

Vallen's rate of growth tailed off during the recession of the early 1990s. Revenues increased to $167.3 million in 1992, then $175.6 million in 1993, but net income remained flat at $6.3 million. Companies continued to need Vallen's products, but with many workers laid off in a number of industries and building starts curtailed, there was simply less need for gloves, goggles, hard hats, or emergency showers. Only pulp and paper mill and railroad segments continued to display robust growth for Vallen. Compared, however, to smaller safety equipment firms, which saw sales decline, Vallen remained quite healthy. It now looked to sell its products outside the United States and, in late 1992, Vallen Corporation purchased a 50 percent interest in Proveedora de Seguridad Industrial del Golfo, a Mexican distributor of industrial safety equipment. The next year, Vallen established a presence in eastern Canada, which it then enhanced through a series of acquisitions. Despite these purchases, Vallen had more cash than long-term debt and was clearly not taking full advantage of its position to make even more acquisitions.

James W. Thompson Becomes CEO in 1995

In 1994 Vallen took some steps to revise its strategy. After an assessment, the company closed four distribution branches, which were deemed to be located too close to regional hubs, resulting in the elimination of some jobs. In addition, the company cut positions at its corporate headquarters. More important, Vallen hired 42-year-old James W. Thompson in June 1994 to serve as president and chief operating officer. He had been senior group vice-president of Westburne Supply Company of Naperville, Illinois, and before that gained 18 years of experience at Westinghouse Electric Supply Company. Code soon retired, while remaining a member of the board, and Thompson took over as CEO effective January 1, 1995. He realized that Vallen faced a changing landscape, with increased competition that required a more cost-effective business. According to Thompson in a July 1998 issue of *Barron's*, "Vallen was the IBM of the safety industry. They had a terrific niche—they were the technical experts. . . . But maybe they had become a little complacent with their position." He invested in new computer systems for order processing to cut costs and increase productivity. He emphasized the high margin, repair, and maintenance business. He also looked for more external growth, especially outside of the United States. He extended Vallen's Canadian business to the western part of the country by acquiring a 50 percent interest in Century Sales and Service Limited, an Edmonton, Alberta, distributor of mill supply and industrial hardware products. Despite economic problems in Mexico, Vallen increased its commitment to its Mexican operation, thereby gaining market share and placing itself in a strong position when the Mexican economy rebounded later in the 1990s.

At home Thompson also looked for further expansion. Between 1995 and 1999, Vallen Safety Supply acquired the assets of several more companies that expanded Vallen's presence in the Midwest, Ohio Valley, and southeast United States in safety supplies, mill supply, and industrial welding supplies. In addition, Vallen entered into a venture involved in the manufacture and distribution of clothing and other products used in the nuclear power production business. Also in 1996 Vallen entered into a joint venture with Lion Apparel, Inc. of Dayton, Ohio, to maintain an inventory and distribution center for military recruit clothing for the Air Force. In 1999 the pace of acquisitions picked up, as Vallen Safety Supply added even more service providers to its fold, as it acquired the assets of a provider of respiratory testing and safety consulting services as well as acquiring the assets of three separate providers of fire extinguishers, fire alarm, and fire suppression systems and services. Also in 1999 Vallen Safety Supply and Lion Apparel, through a joint venture, landed a Department of Defense contract to provide a distribution and inventory system for military recruit clothing in 11 states of the Southeast. Furthermore, Vallen Corporation acquired an additional 40 percent interest in Proveedora and the remaining 50 percent of Century, thereby increasing its participation in the North American market.

Under Thompson, Vallen Corporation showed a renewed upward trend in revenues and earnings. In 1995 the company topped the $200 million mark in sales and exceeded $300 million in 1999. Net income during this period ranged from $7.1

million in 1995 to $10.2 million in 1999. To reach an even higher level, however, management felt that Vallen Corporation needed a partner, and the company was put up for sale. Moreover, Bruce was now approaching 80 years of age. In November 1999, Hagemeyer North America, Inc., a subsidiary of Hagemeyer N.V., reached a deal to acquire Vallen Corporation, in the process buying the majority stake in the company still owned by Bruce and his family. The $201 million price included $17 million in assumed debt. Hagemeyer, after years of operating in the United States, was in the midst of an aggressive international push, having made two significant acquisitions in the United States in the previous year.

Hagemeyer elected to run Vallen Corporation as a subsidiary and retain its employees. Now as a part of the North American holding company of a multinational conglomerate, Vallen looked to enter a greatly expanded arena of business. With the globalization of industry and the need to service major customers with far-flung operations located around the globe, Vallen had no choice but to grow larger. The company that once consisted of just Leonard and Valerie Bruce was now ready to gain international recognition.

Principal Subsidiaries

Vallen Safety Supply Co.; Encon Safety Products, Inc.; Safety World, Inc.; All Supplies, Inc.; Vallen Safety Supply Company, Ltd.; Century Sales and Service Limited; Proveedora de Seguridad Industrial del Golfo, S.A. de C.V.

Principal Divisions

Industrial Distribution; Vallen Technical Services; Vallen Knowledge Services; Vallen Occupational Health Services.

Principal Competitors

Abatix; Bacou USA, Firetector; Lakeland Industries; SPX Corporation; Worksafe Industries.

Further Reading

Brammer, Rhonda, "Safety Pays," *Barron's,* July 27, 1998, p. 24.
——, "Stress on Safety," *Barron's,* January 17, 1994, p. 38.
Fraza, Victoria, "Breaking New Ground," *Industrial Distribution,* March 2001, p. 70.
Goldberg, Laura, "Dutch Company to Buy Houston-Based Safety Products Maker Vallen," *Houston Chronicle,* November 16, 1999, p. C1.
Gordon, Mitchell, "Safety First," *Barron's National Business and Financial Weekly,* December 28, 1981, p. 28.
Johnson, John R., "Going Global," *Industrial Distribution,* February 2000, p. 53.

—Ed Dinger

Veritas Software Corporation

350 Ellis Street
Mountain View, California 94043
U.S.A.
Telephone: (650) 527-8000
Toll Free: (800) 327-2232
Fax: (650) 527-8050
Web site: http://www.veritas.com

Public Company
Incorporated: 1989
Employees: 5,500
Sales: $1.5 billion (2001)
Stock Exchanges: NASDAQ
Ticker Symbol: VRTS
NAIC: 511210 Software Publishers

Veritas Software Corporation is a leading supplier and developer of data availability software in areas such as storage management, data protection, and system backup and recovery. Through alliances with leading original equipment manufacturers (OEMs), Veritas software is embedded in a wide range of computer products, from workstations to servers.

Providing System Backup and Recovery Software for Unix Systems: 1989–95

Established in 1989, Veritas Software Corporation had its roots in a 1982 start-up called Tolerant Systems, Inc. From 1982 to 1989, Tolerant Systems manufactured computer hardware for Unix-based systems. By 1989 the company was about to go out of business. One division of Tolerant was focused on developing software utilities to enhance the Unix operating system. Claiming one contract with AT&T Corp., the creator of the Unix operating system, and about 20 employees, Veritas Software was created out of that division in 1989.

Unlike its predecessor, which manufactured computer hardware, Veritas focused on software. Its joint development and marketing agreement with AT&T called for Veritas to develop the next generation of storage management software for the Unix operating system. Mark Leslie, formerly a member of Tolerant Systems' board of directors, became Veritas's president and CEO.

From the start Veritas pursued a strategy of supplying original equipment manufacturers (OEMs) to ensure a certain level of revenue. In addition to AT&T, the company signed agreements with other leading Unix companies, including Hewlett-Packard, Sequent, Tandem, Digital Equipment Corp., IBM, and Sun Microsystems. Under these agreements, Veritas would license its system recovery software to the OEMs while protecting its source code. Firms to which Veritas licensed its software were not allowed to work on competing development projects if they learned the Veritas source code.

Veritas's software addressed a major problem with Unix-based systems, namely, that it could take several hours to recover from a system crash. The Veritas software program maintained a file journal that made it possible to restart a Unix system in a matter of seconds, with its files intact. When the system ran normally, Veritas software enabled system managers to perform routine maintenance tasks without having to bring the system down.

From 1990 to 1995 Veritas's sales grew at a rate of 60 percent annually, and in 1993 the company went public. Annual revenue was about $13 million. The company's strategy for the next couple of years was to extend its product line horizontally, adding functionality to its basic storage management software. In addition, Veritas designed software extensions that could add value to the basic package's existing features. By 1995 the company was able to reduce its reliance on the OEM market by shipping shrink-wrapped software products directly to end-users.

Expanding Beyond Unix Market: 1995–97

In the second half of the 1990s, Veritas expanded beyond providing system recovery and storage management software for Unix-based systems. The company signed a licensing agreement with Microsoft Corporation to provide storage management software for the Windows NT operating system.

In 1996 Veritas acquired Advanced Computing Systems Corp. (ASCS), a company that developed APIs (application program interfaces) for storage software. The APIs provided programmers writing application programs with a specific method by which to make requests of an operating system or other application. ASCS's technology provided for a consistent way for software to communicate with different types of storage media. ASCS's API-based software supported optical, magneto-optical, and most tape formats. Following the acquisition, Veritas announced plans to introduce a VxServer Suite Web Addition that would incorporate ASCS's technology and utilize Veritas's file and volume management software to optimize disk configuration and performance on web servers.

In 1997 Veritas added system backup software capabilities to its product line with the acquisition of OpenVision Technologies, Inc., a leading developer of backup software. The acquisition helped Veritas gain credibility among OEMs and enterprise customers for its broader vision of storage management. In mid-1997 Veritas introduced NetBackup 3.0 for Windows NT, the first version that could run on a Windows NT Server without files having to be transferred to a Unix server. With its expanded product line, Veritas was able to offer end-to-end solutions for storage management, system recovery, and backup.

For 1997 Veritas saw its profits increase dramatically, from $12.1 million on revenue of $72.7 million in 1996 to $22.7 million on revenue of $121.1 million in 1997. During the year the company signed licensing agreements with Sun Microsystems and Hewlett-Packard to provide backup software and high-end storage management systems for the two companies' Unix-based systems. At the end of 1997 Veritas software could be found on computer systems in 90 percent of the world's 2,000 largest companies.

Introducing New Storage Applications: 1998

At the beginning of 1998 Veritas introduced three new storage management products: Storage Manager, Storage Advisor, and Storage Planner. Together, the three software products comprised the company's Intelligent Storage Management product set. Storage Manager provided a central management interface from which distributed storage objects could be monitored and managed. Storage Advisor analyzed system configurations and recommended storage layouts to optimize system performance. Storage Planner was a forecasting tool that helped predict future storage needs.

Later in the first quarter Veritas announced new versions of its Volume Manager and File System management software for Sun Microsystems' Solaris operating system. The company also introduced the Veritas Storage Replicator for File Systems (SRFS), which let IT managers mirror data at remote locations without restricting user access. SRFS provided an alternative to hardware-based mirroring and could be used to redistribute data to multiple locations to reduce bottlenecks. Excite Inc., which tested SRFS for its web search engine, reported that Veritas's SRFS would help streamline the time-consuming process of duplicating files.

Veritas's Intelligent Storage Management product set formed the basis for the company's next generation of storage management products, which would focus on storage area networks (SANs). SANs offered high-speed connectivity and switch-based architecture that provided some support for "failover functionality." In a SAN environment, all servers had access to storage and that storage was networked. When one device in a system failed, data in the SAN could easily be routed to another device. Veritas code-named its new clustering application Thor. Thor was capable of providing failover support for up to 128 nodes in a SAN and would be able to run on Windows NT as well as Unix-based systems. When Veritas introduced its Cluster Server software in September 1998, the new software allowed the clustering of 32 servers, which meant that one idle server could provide failover support for the other 31 servers. Later in the year Veritas added modules to its Storage Manager software that helped customers manage disparate servers, storage subsystems, adapters, and other components of SANs. The new modules monitored and managed all aspects of a SAN, thus giving organizations secure universal access to data.

Before the end of 1998 Veritas signed partnership agreements with Compaq Computer Corporation and Data General Corporation. Under the agreement with Compaq, the two companies would jointly develop and market storage solutions that combined Veritas's storage management software with Compaq's enterprise-class storage hardware systems. Data General agreed to bundle Veritas's NetBackup for Windows NT with its Windows NT server line under an OEM licensing agreement.

Acquiring Multiplatform Strength: 1999

In October 1998 Veritas announced it would acquire Seagate Software's Network and Storage Management Group, a unit of storage hardware manufacturer Seagate Technology, Inc., for $1.6 billion in stock. By the time the transaction closed in May 1999, it was valued at $3.1 billion. Mark Leslie remained as CEO, with Seagate Software President and Chief Operating Officer (COO) Terry Cunningham becoming president and COO of Veritas. Cunningham also joined Veritas's expanded board of directors, as did Seagate Technology President and CEO Steve Luczo and Seagate Software Chief Strategic Officer Greg Kerfoot.

Seagate's Network and Storage Management Group was considered to be the largest supplier of Windows NT and NetWare storage software. In addition, the company had a strong distribution channel and a team of experienced developers and marketers. The acquisition would enable Veritas to offer

Key Dates:

1989: Veritas Software Corporation is formed to develop software utilities for AT&T Corp.'s Unix division.
1993: Veritas becomes a public company.
1996: Veritas acquires Advanced Computing Systems Corp.
1997: Veritas acquires OpenVision Technologies, Inc.
1999: Veritas completes its $1.6 billion acquisition of Seagate Software's Network and Storage Management Group.
2000: Oracle Corp.'s executive vice-president, Gary Bloom, joins Veritas as president and CEO.

a single storage management product with multiplatform capabilities. Veritas was now in a stronger position to integrate the enterprise segment of the storage market, which had a Unix focus, and the workgroup segment, which had an NT focus.

During 1999 Veritas continued to preach the benefits of SANs and to develop initiatives that would make SANs more attractive to business enterprises. In January 1999 Veritas and Storage Technology Corp. entered into a joint venture to develop and market a standard interface for managing removable storage. The two companies planned to deliver a media server, or software controller, that would link tape libraries across mainframe, Unix, and Windows 2000 platforms in 2000. Also in January Veritas released its Global Data Manager for NetBackup, which could manage data internationally throughout an enterprise. Global Data Manager enabled IT managers to control multiple master servers that ran NetBackup from a single console. Veritas subsequently integrated Seagate's BackupExec with Global Data Manager.

In the first half of 1999 Veritas acquired TeleBackup Systems, Inc. When Veritas released a new version of Seagate's Client Exec online backup solution, it was renamed TeleBackup for Workgroups 2.5. Priced at $7,600 for 200 users, TeleBackup was considered a low-cost solution.

In September 1999 Veritas acquired ClusterX technology from NuView, a software company based in Houston with close ties to Microsoft. ClusterX was a tool that helped administrators manage two-node Microsoft Cluster Service clusters in an enterprise from one console. Veritas and NuView planned to integrate their offerings to develop a single Windows NT console that could manage clusters across platforms. The acquisition was part of Veritas's strategy to develop centralized management consoles for SANs. When Microsoft released Windows 2000, the new operating system had embedded in it some of Veritas's storage management technology.

From 1998 to 1999 Wall Street drove up Veritas's stock price by 255 percent, according to *Forbes*. For 1999, Veritas had revenue of $596.1 million and a net loss of $503 million, compared to revenue of $210.9 million and net income of $51.6 million in 1998. Much of Veritas's net loss in 1999 was due to depreciation and amortization charges of $510.9 million and an increase in selling, general, and administrative expenses from $86.9 million in 1998 to $256.2 million in 1999.

New Alliances and Products: 2000 2001

At the beginning of 2000 Veritas expanded its alliance with Japan's NEC Corporation, with NEC selling and supporting Veritas's full line of software and adding Veritas's Backup Exec to more of its servers. Veritas also entered into a development agreement with Oracle Systems Corporation to facilitate the integration of the two companies' products. Early in the year Veritas and Network Appliance, Inc. introduced an integrated application solution that combined Veritas's Cluster Server with Network Appliance's storage appliances. Around this time Veritas also introduced Backup Exec 8.0 for Windows NT and Windows 2000. Enhanced features of the new version included improved protection of remote systems, improved disaster recovery, and centralized administration and management.

Later in the first half of 2000 Veritas released improved versions of its clustering software. The Cluster Server for Windows NT allowed IT managers to link as many as 32 Windows NT servers. At the time, the Microsoft platform could cluster only two nodes on its own or up to eight nodes with an IBM extension. In June Veritas released its Global Cluster Manager for Solaris, which enabled customers to manage and monitor as many as 256 clusters running NT, Solaris, and HP-Unix from a single Java-based console.

Meanwhile, Seagate Technology, Inc., which owned approximately one-third of Veritas's common stock, decided to become a private company. Under the terms of a complex financial deal, Veritas acquired Seagate, including its interest in Veritas, for about $20 billion. Veritas then sold Seagate's operating assets to an investor group led by Silver Lake Partners and Seagate executives and employees, for $2 billion. The transaction unlocked the value of Seagate's interest in Veritas, which had increased in value to about $18 billion as Veritas's stock price rose, and eliminated Seagate's ownership interest in Veritas. It also resulted in fewer outstanding shares of Veritas stock and increased the company's stockholder liquidity. When the deal closed in November 2000, the transaction was valued at $12.1 billion.

In mid-2000 Veritas addressed IT managers' need for better administrative tools to deal with SAN management with its announcement of SANPoint Control. Using new technology called V3 SAN Access Layer technology, SANPoint Control could map all of the storage utilities on a SAN, regardless of vendor, thus providing a single point of management that allowed viewing of the entire virtual SAN. Realizing that SAN management was an emerging industry, Veritas designed SANPoint Control to be easily modified for future changes. The company planned to ship Version 1.0, which provided basic SAN event management, in August 2000. Version 1.1, which offered advance notification to managers during storage emergencies, was due to ship by the end of 2000. Version 2.0, which provided the highest level of management intelligence, was scheduled for release in early 2001.

In November 2000 Veritas scored a management coup when it lured Gary Bloom from Oracle, where the executive vice-president was considered the next in line to succeed Oracle Chairman and CEO Larry Ellison. Bloom joined Veritas as president and CEO, with Mark Leslie remaining as chairman.

Throughout 2000 Veritas continued to experience strong demand for all of its data availability products, including data protection, file and volume management, clustering, and replication. The company reported record third quarter revenue of $317.2 million, compared to $183.4 million for the same quarter in 1999. For all of 2000 Veritas reported revenue of $1.2 billion and a net loss of $619.8 million.

Economic Slowdown Affecting Sales: 2001

At the beginning of 2001 the stocks of Veritas and other storage management companies were being downgraded by some Wall Street analysts. Analysts and officials within the industry disagreed, believing that storage was an essential area that would not be affected by an economic downturn. A study by the Yankee Group predicted that corporate spending on storage hardware, software, and related services would add up to $12 billion in 2001. However, by the end of March it was clear that storage companies would also be affected by the economic slowdown.

During the first quarter of 2001 Veritas added the capability to backup and recover Linux-based data to its NetBackup DataCenter and NetBackup BusinessServer. Veritas invested in managed storage startup Sanrise Group Inc. and in Pirus Networks, a storage networking company, as part of its strategy to invest in developing companies in the data availability market. Veritas also acquired Prassi Europe SAS, a company based in Le Mans, France, that produced CD and DVD mastering technology.

Noting a difficult selling climate in the first quarter of 2001, Veritas reported quarterly revenue of $387 million, a 58 percent increase over the same period of 2000 and 5 percent above the previous quarter. License revenue accounted for $309 million, while revenue from services was $78 million. For its second quarter, Veritas had revenue of $390 million, a 42 percent increase over the same period in 2000. By July, though, president and CEO Gary Bloom reduced the company's growth target to 25 percent. From the time Bloom joined the company in November 2000 to September 2001, Veritas's stock had lost 60 percent of its value. *Forbes* noted that Veritas still had $1.5 billion in cash and that its market capitalization of $16 billion would let it continue to make acquisitions.

Veritas's third quarter revenue was affected to some extent by the events of September 11. While reporting sales of $340 million for the quarter ending September 30, Veritas said that it had helped more than 100 of its customers recover lost data due to the terrorist attacks. Citing low visibility, the company refused to predict what its revenue would be going forward. Closing out the year for Veritas, Gary Bloom was named chairman, adding the title to that of president and CEO. Former Chairman Mark Leslie would remain on the board of directors.

Principal Competitors

Computer Associates International, Inc.; EMC Corporation; International Business Machines Corporation; Legato Systems, Inc.; Storage Technology Corporation.

Further Reading

Adamson, Melanie, "Mark Leslie," *Business Journal,* August 25, 2000, p. 44.

Anderson, Kim Renay, "Analysts Say Storage Industry Remains Strong," *TechWeb,* January 4, 2001.

Bekker, Scott, "Veritas Buys into Microsoft's Clustering with ClusterX," *ENT,* September 8, 1999, p. 9.

Brown, Erika, "Show Time," *Forbes,* September 3, 2001, p. 92.

Dillon, Nancy, "Cluster Server Supports 32 Servers," *Computerworld,* September 21, 1998, p. 14.

Elliott, Heidi, "An Act of Privacy," *Electronic News (1991),* April 3, 2000, p. 1.

Ferelli, Mark, "Clustering Management Tools Support Growing Applications," *Computer Technology Review,* April 2000, p. 35.

Garvey, Martin J., "SANs Gain Management," *Information Week,* September 28, 1998, p. 128.

——, "Veritas Adds Backup for Linux Data," *Information Week,* January 8, 2001, p. 40.

"Gary Bloom Leaves Oracle for Veritas," *TechWeb,* November 18, 2000.

Gianturco, Michael, "Easy Sell," *Forbes,* November 7, 1994, p. 318.

Hardy, Eric S., "Winners and Losers," *Forbes,* November 1, 1999, p. 288.

Kovar, Joseph F., "The New Name of the Storage Game," *Computer Reseller News,* September 24, 2001, p. 32.

——, "New Products: Windows 2000 Brings out Storage Software Revisions," *Computer Reseller News,* February 28, 2000, p. 74.

——, "Veritas Acquires Seagate's Network and Storage Group," *Computer Reseller News,* October 12, 1998, p. 33.

——, "Veritas Closes Seagate Software Deal," *Computer Reseller News,* June 7, 1999, p. 30.

——, "Veritas Tackles Storage Management," *Computer Reseller News,* September 28, 1998, p. 42.

Kovar, Joseph F., and Eric Hausman, "Gary Bloom: Chairman and CEO, Veritas," *Computer Reseller News,* November 12, 2001, p. 103.

LaPlante, Alice, "Wealth Through Stealth," *Electronic Business,* May 1998, p. 50.

Lattig, Michael, "Veritas Details Latest Plan for Centralized SAN Management," *InfoWorld,* June 7, 1999, p. 8.

Lelii, Sonia R., "Veritas Takes Server Clustering Global," *PC Week,* April 10, 2000, p. 87.

Leon, Mark, "Veritas to Ease Web Server File Management," *InfoWorld,* April 8, 1996, p. 45.

Mccright, John S., "Veritas Absorbs Its Storage Acquisitions," *PC Week,* June 7, 1999, p. 16.

Mccright, John S., and Carmen Nobel, "Seagate Buy Gives Veritas Longer Reach," *PC Week,* October 12, 1998, p. 25.

"Merger to Blend Storage Apps," *InternetWeek,* February 1, 1999, p. 16.

Moozakis, Chuck, "Clustering App Adds Failover to Storage Area Networking," *InternetWeek,* August 17, 1998, p. 15.

——, "HP, Veritas Heat up Backup Products," *InternetWeek,* March 2, 1998, p. 31.

——, "Veritas: Multiplatform Power," *InternetWeek,* October 12, 1998, p. 8.

Murphy, Chris, "Seagate Goes Private in Veritas Deal," *InformationWeek,* April 3, 2000, p. 169.

Neel, Dan, "Veritas Aims to Simplify SAN Management," *InfoWorld,* June 5, 2000, p. 6.

Panettieri, Joseph C., "Can Storage Keep You Dry?" *Sm@rt Partner,* March 26, 2001, p. 18.

Pendery, David, "CEO Mark Leslie Eyes High Availability," *InfoWorld,* September 21, 1998, p. 27.

——, "Duo to Standardize Removable Storage," *InfoWorld,* January 11, 1999, p. 22.

——, "Veritas Cluster Server Software for SAN Ships," *InfoWorld,* September 21, 1998, p. 8.

"Pirus Networks," *Washington Business News,* March 30, 2001, p. 30.

Rigney, Steve, "TeleBackup for Workgroups 2.5," *PC Magazine,* August 1, 1999, p. 41.

Rodriguez, Karen, "Veritas Forms Strategic Alliances, Increases Revenues," *Business Journal,* May 25, 1998, p. 20.

Rooney, Paula, and Joseph F. Kovar, "New Veritas Chief Just Wanted Top Slot," *TechWeb,* November 21, 2000.

"Seagate to Boost Veritas Profits," *Client Server News,* December 4, 2000.

"Seagate, Veritas Merger Outlined," *VARbusiness,* November 16, 1998, p. 12.

"Veritas Acquires European DVD, CD Company," *Washington Technology,* March 5, 2001, p. 20.

"Veritas and NetApp Cluster Together," *Computer Technology Review,* February 2000, p. 26.

"Veritas Backup," *Computerworld,* January 25, 1999, p. 70.

"Veritas Introduces Storage Manager, Storage Advisor and Storage Planner," *HP Professional,* January 1998, p. 36.

"Veritas Invests in Data Protection Firm," *Washington Technology,* February 5, 2001, p. 22.

"Veritas Is Cocky but Cautious," *Client Server News,* April 23, 2001.

"Veritas Partners with Compaq, Data General," *ENT,* November 18, 1998, p. 17.

"Veritas Preps NetBackup for Windows NT Server," *PC Week,* June 16, 1997, p. 76.

"Veritas Resolves to Add SANity to Data Storage," *PC Week,* March 15, 1999, p. 106.

"Veritas Software Corp. and NEC Corp. Are Broadening Their Relationship," *Japan-U.S. Business Report,* January 2000, p. 27.

"Veritas Software Reports Record Third Quarter Results," *Canadian Corporate News,* October 13, 2000.

"Veritas Squeaks out of the Quarter," *Client Server News,* October 22, 2001.

Wagner, Mitch, "Backup, Storage Show No Bounds," *InternetWeek,* January 25, 1999, p. 60.

—David P. Bianco

Viña Concha y Toro S.A.

Nueva Tajamar 481, Torre Norte
Piso 15, Las Condes, Santiago
Chile
Telephone: (562) 821-7300
Fax: (562) 203-6740
Web site: http://www.conchaytoro.com

Public Company
Incorporated: 1923
Employees: 1,391
Sales: 100.44 billion pesos ($175.08 million) (2000)
Stock Exchanges: Santiago New York
Ticker Symbols: CONCHATORO; VCO (ADRs)
NAIC: 11132 Citrus Groves; 111339 Other Noncitrus
    Fruit Farming; 312112 Bottled Water Manufacturing;
    31213 Wineries

Viña Concha y Toro S.A. is the largest Chilean producer and exporter of wines. It owns and leases vineyards in five of Chile's six principal wine-growing valleys and also owns a vineyard in Argentina. A vertically integrated producer, Concha y Toro also operates plants that make and bottle wine from its own cultivated grapes. Premium wines comprise a third of the company's revenues, and exports, more than half. The company also produces and sells fruits and mineral water.

The First Century: From 1883

The company was founded in 1883 by Don Melchor Concha y Toro and his father-in-law, Don Ramón Subercaseaux Mercado. Don Melchor had inherited the title Marqués de Casa Concha, awarded to a Chilean ancestor by King Philip V of Spain in 1718. The blue-blooded Concha y Toro family was very rich as the proprietor of a company that held silver mines in Bolivia. Don Ramón also was immensely rich from silver mines in northern Chile. The marriage of Don Melchor to Doña Emiliana Subercaseaux linked the Concha y Toro family to her father, who owned farmland in the Pirque region, located on the border of the Maipo River, 20 miles south of Santiago, the

capital. Don Ramón had planted grapevines there in 1860 after building an irrigation canal to provide the necessary river water in an area of sparse rainfall. After his death, Don Melchor and his wife hired a French oenologist to plant new vines yielding the traditional varieties of the Bordeaux region—cabernet sauvignon, merlot, sauvignon blanc, and semillon—brought to Chile before the plant louse phylloxera devastated French vineyards in the 1860s. They also employed a French architect and landscaper to design their manor and its gardens and subsequently purchased an estate near Rancagua, where they established a second vineyard.

After Don Melchor's death in 1892, his widow and their son Juan Enrique Concha Subercaseaux ran the firm. Concha y Toro was incorporated in 1923, with all shares issued to family members and Doña Emiliana holding 75 percent. She gave most of these shares to her five daughters in 1929. After Juan Enrique's death in 1931, direction of the firm passed mainly to her sons-in-law. Concha y Toro began to be traded on Santiago's stock exchange in 1933, but at the end of the decade eight family members, all female, still held about 60 percent of the shares. Doña Emiliana's daughters still owned nearly one-third of the stock in 1947, but Chilean banks now held over 20 percent. During the 1940s Concha y Toro distributed Coca-Cola in Chile but gave up the franchise after some years as not sufficiently profitable.

Beginning in 1957 Concha y Toro invested heavily in new vineyards and restructured its management to handle the demands of changing markets. Land in production or planted increased from 330 hectares (815 acres) in 1947 to 765 hectares (1,890 acres) in 1969. Annual wine production rose from 3.6 million liters to 18.5 million liters over this period, and Concha y Toro now led all Chilean producers. Almost all of this was for the domestic market; Concha y Toro accounted for one-third of all exports of Chilean wine in 1968, but Chile's wine exports constituted only about 2 percent of production. In spite of increasing the amount of land planted in vineyards, Concha y Toro's rising output was requiring it to buy an increasing proportion—about 70 percent—of its grapes from other growers and hence to create a potential quality problem. Nevertheless, in 1965 Concha y Toro introduced its first wine of greater complexity, under the name Casillero del Diablo. It was made from selected grapes and aged two years longer than the standard Chilean cabernet sauvignon.

Eduardo Giulisasti Tagle, now the largest shareholder, became general manager of Concha y Toro in 1971. By this time only three principal stockholders and three of the six company directors were related in some manner to the Conchas and Subercaseauxs. Giulisasti faced an immediate challenge from the Marxist government of President Salvador Allende, which proposed, under threat of expropriation, to assume majority control of all the nation's wineries. One day in 1972 Concha y Toro's managers found their offices occupied and their telephones disconnected by workers (unionized since 1966) who said the action was intended to pressure them into accepting the government offer. A government-appointed mediator subsequently protected the enterprise from radicals—who included Guilisasti's son Rafael—until the overthrow of Allende in 1973. Some other vintners did not emerge so fortunately from the disruption of this period and were forced to sell or close down.

Before this upheaval, the products of Chilean wineries were, with rare exceptions, characterized by a heavy oxidized flavor but suitable enough for the domestic market, which was protected by government policies from foreign competition. With the economy in recession following Allende's fall, many of these enterprises failed, and the survivors began seeking income from exports for the first time. Guilisasti cast an eye on the U.S. market in the late 1970s but realized that Concha y Toro's output would have to be altered to sell abroad. He began replacing the old cement vats used to ferment wines with automatically cooled stainless steel tanks. For better aging of its premium wines, Concha y Toro began importing French oak casks in 1985 and California oak barrels in 1987. In the latter year the company introduced Don Melchor, its most ambitious product to that date: a world-class wine intended to compete in the premium category and convince consumers abroad that Chile was capable of such production. This top-of-the-line cabernet sauvignon (selling for $40 a bottle 10 years later) came from Concha y Toro's flagship Puente Alto estate, purchased about 1970.

Concentrating on Exports in the 1990s

But it was the firm's midprice varietal (table) wines that made an impact in the U.S. market after Banfi Products Corp. purchased Excelsior (later Excelsior Wines & Spirits), a small importing company. Banfi, a large importer, was looking for a new product to supplement Riunite, a sweet, fizzy Italian lambrusco that was the top-selling imported wine in the United States but had experienced a sharp drop in business. Banfi introduced print advertisements for Concha y Toro in New York, Washington, and Miami in 1989. By 1990, Chilean varietals, at $4 to $5 a bottle, had moved the nation into third place, behind only France and Italy, among wine importers to the United States, and Concha y Toro held more than half this market. Exports to Europe began in 1989. Between 1989 and 1992, the company's net income more than doubled, largely because of its exports. Within Chile, Concha y Toro still remained popular, holding 22 percent of the market.

During the years 1991–93 Concha y Toro tripled the size of its vineyards to reduce dependence on outside grape growers. "Having vineyards in all the major growing areas . . . gives us a lot of options," a company oenologist told Thomas Matthews of *Wine Spectator* in 1995. "In Maipo we get wines of elegance; farther south . . . the wines are fuller-bodied. In the end, controlling the grape supply is crucial to fine wine." Concha y Toro replaced hand pickers with machines for 80 percent of the harvest. It bought computer-controlled pneumatic presses and introduced a more precise system of irrigating its vineyards. French and California oenologists were hired. The original Concha y Toro white-columned mansion and 50 rolling acres of landscaped gardens were restored to receive guests and tourists and to serve as the headquarters of the firm's export operations.

Concha y Toro ranked fifth among wines imported to the United States in 1993, but its profits fell as grape prices and labor costs grew and the company's exports faced stiffer competition from the wines of other countries. Concha y Toro now began to look to more upscale, $7-to-$10-a-bottle exports for revenue. To finance its efforts, the company turned to Wall Street, raising $53 million by selling American Depositary Receipts (ADRs) on the New York Stock Exchange. In 1996 Concha y Toro purchased a vineyard in Argentina's well-regarded Mendoza region and stocked the enterprise with winemaking equipment and a cellar with a capacity to hold 4.5 million liters of wine.

The following year the company announced a joint venture with the French firm Baron Philippe de Rothschild S.A., with the aim of producing a wine that would meet the standards of the *grand cru* class of wines from the Bordeaux region. In 1998 this partnership introduced Vina Almaviva, an ultra-premium cabernet sauvignon from the same Puente Alto vineyard as Don Melchor, but longer in the oak and hence with a woodier flavor. Concha y Toro, in 2000, launched three limited-edition premium wines under the Terrunyo label. Its cabernet sauvignon came from the upper Andean foothills of the Maipo Valley, carmenere—a Bordeaux grape not unlike merlot—from the flatter Peumo Valley, and sauvignon blanc from the maritime-influenced vineyards of the Casablanca Valley, north of Santiago. These wines were priced at $29 in the United States. Later in 2000, the company introduced another premium wine, Xplorador, for the U.S. market only.

By this time Concha y Toro also was marketing abroad three new, popularly priced wines at $8 to $10 a bottle. Launched in 1996 under the Trio label, these wines—a chardonnay, merlot, and cabernet sauvignon—were initially available in Chile, the United Kingdom, and the United States.

Key Dates:

1883: Concha y Toro establishes its first vineyard and winery.
1965: Company introduces its first premium wine, Casillero del Diablo.
1987: Concha y Toro introduces Don Melchor, its most ambitious wine yet.
1994: Concha y Toro makes its initial public offering on the New York Stock Exchange.
1998: Company ranks second among wine exporters to the United States.

Other table-wine labels introduced or reintroduced in this period were Sunrise (1997) and Frontera (1999). By 1998 Concha y Toro had risen to second place among table wines imported to the United States. Its export sales rose 30 percent that year, including a tripling of its sales in Japan. Total production increased by 17 percent; in Chile, sales of the company's red wines soared 50 percent as Concha y Toro and other winemakers touted the alleged health benefits of drinking red wine.

Concha y Toro in 2000

Concha y Toro owned 15 Chilean vineyards and leased three in 2000. These properties were located in five of Chile's six principal wine-growing valleys. The company also owned 417 hectares (1,030 acres) near Mendoza, Argentina. In all, the company held about 10,224 acres of vineyards at the end of 2000, compared to 2,981 acres a decade earlier. Total output was 102 million liters of wine. Concha y Toro also had about 129 hectares (319 acres) in fruit trees first planted in the 1980s. The yield in 2000 consisted of about 2.2 million kilos (2,245 tons) of peaches, nectarines, avocados, lemons, oranges, kiwis, and other fruits. Concha y Toro also owned or leased five vinification plants (which converted grapes into wine) and two bottling plants and operated the most extensive wine-distribution network in Chile, through Comercial Peumo, its wholly owned distributor. In November 2000 Concha y Toro acquired 49.6 percent of Industria Corchera, a cork-producing firm.

Concha y Toro held 24 percent of the domestic Chilean market in 2000. Popular wines, marketed primarily in one-liter rectangular cardboard packages, represented (by value) 73 percent of this output. The firm's output of bulk wine for this purpose was substantially supplemented by purchases from other wine producers. Of Concha y Toro's 2000 sales, wines for export accounted for 55.3 percent and domestic wines for 32.5 percent. Of the export total, almost all were table and premium wines, with the United States accounting for 34.6 percent and Europe for 29.5 percent. According to one survey, Concha y Toro moved into first place among wine exporters to the United States in 2000.

Among Concha y Toro's premium labels, Casillero del Diablo was the most extensive as well as the largest seller,

turning out cabernet sauvignon, chardonnay, malbec, merlot, pinot noir, sauvignon blanc, and syrah. Marques de Casa Concha produced cabernet sauvignon, chardonnay, and merlot. Don Melchor made only cabernet sauvignon and Amelia only chardonnay. The company's table-wine labels were Frontera (cabernet sauvignon, chardonnay, merlot, and sauvignon blanc blends) and Sunrise (cabernet sauvignon, chardonnay, merlot, pinot noir, rosé, sauvignon blanc) as well as Concha y Toro. It was also bottling and selling under license Santa Emiliana table wines, for a company that it spun off in 1986.

Eduardo Giulisasti Tagle remained chairman of Viña Concha y Toro but had, by 1997, yielded day-to-day administration of the enterprise to his elder son, Eduardo Giulisasti Gana, who now held the post of general manager. Rafael Giulisasti Gana, his younger son, was export manager. They and other company executives owned nearly 50 percent of the common stock in 2001. Concha y Toro's long-term debt was 21.12 billion pesos ($36.81 million) at the end of 2000.

Principal Subsidiaries

Comercial Pneumo Ltda.; Comercial Pneumo S.A.; Concha y Toro UK Limited (U.K.); Distribuidora Pneumo Argentina S.A.; Industria Corchera S.A. (49.6%); Maipo Ltd.; Sociedad Exportadora y Comercial Vina Maipo Ltda.; Transportes Viconto Ltda.; Villa Alegre S.A. (75%); Vina Almaviva S.A. (50%); Vina Cono Sur S.A.; Vina Patagonia S.A. (Argentina).

Principal Competitors

Allied Domecq plc; Bodega y Vinedos Santa Carolina S.A.; Consino Macul S.A.; E. & J. Gallo Winery; Robert Mondavi Corporation; Vina Errazania, S.A.; Vina San Pedro S.A.; Vina Tarapuca S.A.; Vina Undurraga, S.A.

Further Reading

Brown, Greg, "Lafite, Margaux, Haut-Brion . . . Concha y Toro?" *Business Week,* February 21, 2000.

Cochran, Thomas N., "Vina Concha y Toro," *Barron's,* October 10, 1994, p. 35.

Kandell, Jonathan, "Chilean Powerhouse," *Wine Spectator,* November 10, 1997, pp. 126 +.

——, "The Chilean Model II?" *Institutional Investor,* October 1995, pp. 269–70.

Matthews, Thomas, "Leading the Way in Chile," *Wine Spectator,* June 15, 1995, p. 42.

Molesworth, John, "The Don of Chilean Cabernet," *Wine Spectator,* March 31, 2001, p. 111.

Munk, Nina, "More Bucks from the Same Grapes," *Forbes,* December 19, 1994, pp. 134, 138.

Pozo, José del, *Historia del vino chileno: desde 1850 hasta hoy,* Santiago: Editorial Universitaria, 1998.

Read, Jan, *Chilean Wines,* London: Sotheby's Publications, 1988.

Sullivan, Aline, "Chilean Winery Is Going Global," *International Herald Tribune,* April 2, 1999, pp. 13–14.

Winters, Patricia, "Banfi Backs Chilean Wine," *Advertising Age,* July 24, 1989, p. 72.

—Robert Halasz

Western Gas Resources, Inc.

Western Gas Resources, Inc.

12200 N. Pecos Street
Denver, Colorado 80234-3439
U.S.A.
Telephone: (303) 452-5603
Fax: (303) 457-8482
Web site: http://www.westerngas.com

Public Company
Incorporated: 1989
Employees: 616
Sales: $3.3 billion (2000)
Stock Exchanges: New York
Ticker Symbol: WGR
NAIC: 486210 Pipeline Transportation of Natural Gas;
    211112 Natural Gas Liquid Extraction

Western Gas Resources, Inc. is an independent gatherer, processor, transporter, and marketer of natural gas and natural gas liquids. The company's Denver, Colorado, headquarters are centrally located near its 18 gas gathering and processing operations in the gas-producing basins of the Rocky Mountains, mid-Continent, Southwest, and Gulf Coast regions. Western Gas operates over 8,000 miles of pipeline. It also markets natural gas and natural gas liquids, such as ethane, propane, and butane, ranking as the 14th largest producer of these products in the United States. The company, founded and primarily operated by highly skilled engineers, has gained a well earned reputation for its ability to thrive under economic conditions that have driven similar companies out of business.

Birth of Predecessor to Western Gas: 1971

One of the founders of Western Gas was Brion G. Wise, the longtime chairman of the company. After earning a bachelor of science degree in chemical engineering from Washington State University in 1967, he went to work for Shell Oil Co. as a gas processing engineer in its natural gas development group. During his four years at Shell he became familiar through his business travels with the cities of Houston, New Orleans, and

Denver. Preferring life in Denver he teamed with three others in the city in 1971, pooling $2,400, to form a company called Ecological Engineering Systems. Wise had conceived of an idea for the business while traveling for Shell. He saw a number of flaring wells, gas set ablaze as a byproduct of drilling for oil. His plan was to contract with oil producers to capture the gas, rather than let it go to waste, then process, transport, and market the gas and any natural gas liquids that might be present. When the partnership bought its first processing plant in 1977, it changed its name to Western Gas Processors and became increasingly more involved in the gathering and processing of gas in the Rocky Mountains region.

A number of factors converged in the 1980s that created an environment conducive to Western Gas and its highly trained team of executives. The industry backdrop was described by *Barron's* in a 1993 profile of the company: ''After the easing of federal regulatory reins in the 1980s, a number of interstate gas pipelines abandoned the natural-gas gathering and processing business. At the same time, with prices for fossil-fuel products in the doldrums, oil companies shrank their domestic operations, including gas gathering and processing, as they shifted their spending to more promising foreign shores. And all this happened as demand for natural gas slid below expectations and the long-lived gas surplus, or 'bubble,' continued to depress prices.'' Not only did Western Gas contract with major oil producers to gather gas at their reserves, it took advantage of these cheap prices to pick up a number of properties that it deemed to hold great potential. To offset low gas prices, the company used its administrative and technical expertise to reduce personnel and to add well hookups. Because the major investment was in setting up the plant, the additional hookups cost relatively little.

Formation of Master Limited Partnership: 1987

To raise capital in order to fuel an ambitious plan to acquire more properties, Western Gas Processors in 1987 went public as a master limited partnership (MLP), which was similar to a Real Estate Investment Trust (REIT) in that it was free of corporate income tax. Instead of shares, investors purchased units of the MLP, which were then traded just like stock. All of an MLP's earnings were distributed to unitholders, who were then individually responsible for paying taxes. Created by Congress in 1960 as a way for small investors to become involved in real estate, REITs had been rarely used, prompting Congress to make changes to the concept, which were embodied in the Tax Reform Act of 1987. Not only did these changes increase the use of REITs, the new law extended the exemption from corporate taxes to MLPs. This provision allowed companies like Western Gas to buy assets that were unattractive to "C" corporations taxed both at the corporate and investor level. The goal was to spend $100 million on properties over the next five years.

Despite its many advantages, the MLP structure, however, proved somewhat limiting. Western Gas could use cash and units to buy assets from corporations but was unable to buy companies outright. Moreover, institutional investors such as mutual funds were limited in their ability to hold MLP units. In 1989 Western Gas Resources, Inc. was formed in order to purchase a majority interest (52 percent) in Western Gas Processors, Ltd. Not only would the new corporation share in the MLP's quarterly distribution of profits and maintain a competitive edge in the acquisition of certain properties, it could also use its stock to acquire other assets, which would then be sold to the MLP, in effect coupling the tax advantages of the partnership with the flexibility of a corporation. Access to major institutional investors, however, remained limited. In 1991 the corporation bought the remaining 48 percent of the MLP, and unitholders received shares of Western Gas stock on a one-for-one basis. As a result of this restructuring the MLP was eliminated and Western Gas, trading on the New York Stock Exchange, operated like any other C Corporation.

Western Gas quickly exceeded its five-year $100 million acquisition commitment, as gas prices continued to flounder, providing the company with a number of choice acquisition candidates and the opportunity to expand into other gas producing basins. By the end of 1991 Western Gas had spent more than $200 million on new properties, $142.7 million alone on the gas processing operations of Union Texas Petroleum Holdings. The UTP deal included 12 plants in Texas, Oklahoma, and Louisiana, as well as 5,260 miles of pipelines. Also in 1991 Western Gas paid $36 million to Amoco Production Co. for the Edgewood Gas Processing Plant located in Texas. Revenues that stood at $139 million in 1988 grew to $358 million in 1991, then began an even sharper rise over the next few years as contributions from new acquisitions began to fatten the balance sheet.

With the UTP acquisition fully integrated in 1992, Western Gas boosted revenues to $600 million, while earning a record $39.7 million. After raising $33.4 million in a secondary public offering of stock, as well as renegotiating its outstanding lines of credit, the company was poised to make further acquisitions in 1993. In July of that year it completed the $168.2 million purchase of Denver's Mountain Gas Resources Inc., gaining

two gathering and processing facilities in the Greater Green River Basin of Wyoming, an area considered underdeveloped and possessing great potential. Western Gas spent an additional $17.7 million to acquire the 22 percent interest it did not control in one of the plants, and also invested $15.2 million to complete the construction of a cryogenic processing plant for the production of natural gas liquid products. In September 1993 Western Gas also acquired a 69 percent interest in the Black Lake gas processing plant in Louisiana, paying in excess of $136 million. As part of the deal, Western Gas gained a 50 percent interest in the Black Lake Pipeline Company and its 240-mile liquids pipeline that ran from Cotton Valley, Louisiana, to Mont Belvieu, Texas. The company also formed a partnership with Westana Gathering Company to create the Panhandle Eastern Pipe Line Corporation, which was to service the Anadarko Basin in Oklahoma. In addition, Western Gas completed the $90 million construction of the Katy Gas Storage Facility, located 20 miles outside of Houston, which was ready to begin operations in January 1994. The company also established a small presence on the East Coast in 1993 when it purchased the assets of Citizens National Gas Co., a small Boston marketing company. Again, Western Gas showed remarkable improvement over the results of the previous year, growing by over 50 percent to $932 million. The next year the company would eclipse the $1 billion mark in sales. There appeared to be a number of acquisition candidates still available in the fragmented natural gas industry. Because so much of the company's sources of gas remained offshoots of oil drilling, however, Western Gas was vulnerable to a slide in the worldwide price of oil, which would curtail drilling activities.

Falling Oil Prices Stalling Movement in 1998

The company continued to acquire assets over the next two years. It paid approximately $26 million in late 1994 for the assets of Oasis Pipe Line Co., including 14 gathering systems in the Permian Basin that spanned Texas and Louisiana, as well as two treating facilities and 600 miles of pipeline, which were then connected to the Katy operation. In 1995 Western Gas acquired further assets in the Permian Basin at a cost of $18.7 million, adding eight West Texas gathering systems and 230 miles of pipeline. It also teamed with DDD Energy, Inc. to create the Redman Smackover Joint Venture to work gas fields in the Smackover formation of East Texas, paying $5.4 million for a 50 percent interest. Revenues reached $1.25 billion in 1995, then cracked the $2 billion mark in 1996, followed by sales of $2.38 billion in 1997, at which point momentum began to stall. Oil prices plummeted, and saddled with over $500 million in debt from its aggressive pattern of growth, the company was forced to adjust. Sales dipped to $2.1 billion in 1998 and the company posted a loss of $67 million.

In a two-year period, Western Gas sold off assets to shed debt. It sold its Perkins Facility for $22 million. In two separate transactions with Vintage Petroleum of Tulsa, Oklahoma, the company sold its Edgewater facility and associated East Texas producing properties, as well as its stake in the Redman Smackover Joint Venture, for $55.8 million. Western Gas sold its Giddings Facility for $36 million. The company also sold its wholly owned subsidiary, Western Gas Resources Storage, Inc., for $100 million, as well as Western Gas Resources California

Key Dates:

1971:	Ecological Engineering Systems is established.
1977:	Company name is changed to Western Gas Processors.
1987:	Company goes public as a master limited partnership (MLP).
1989:	Western Gas Resources, Inc. is created to serve as general partner of MLP.
1991:	Western Gas Resources absorbs MLP.
1994:	Company surpasses $1 billion in annual revenues.
2000:	Company surpasses $3 billion in annual revenues.

for almost $15 million and subsidiary Pinnacle Gas Treating for $38 million. Moreover, Western Gas became more actively involved in procuring an alternative source of gas unaffected by oil prices: coalbed methane gas.

Although the coalbed wells were small and the gas of low quality, drilling was easy and the quantity plentiful enough to make it a highly attractive niche for companies like Western Gas. It quickly acquired land positions in the coalbeds of Wyoming's Power River Basin. Because the methane was located close to the surface, a well could be drilled in a single day, to depths of just 300 to 1,000 feet, at a cost of only $50,000 to $65,000, using truck-mounted rigs generally used to drill water wells. The life of these methane wells would generally run seven years. Western Gas gained an additional benefit because its involvement in the area lent credibility to the drilling, attracting additional producers who would then bring business to its pipeline in the area. Drilling activity was so robust that it justified an investment to triple the capacity of the pipeline.

The company's restructuring efforts were reflected in the results for 1999. Although revenues fell to $1.9 billion, the net loss for the year was cut to $17.1 million. Going forward, however, Western Gas was much better positioned to weather future downturns in commodity prices. When gas prices rebounded in 2000, the company renewed its long-term pattern of growth. Revenues increased by 72 percent over 1999, almost reaching $3.3 billion, as the company realized a net income of $56.1 million. The company's stock price, which dipped to $15.50 in April 2000, climbed to $34.50 in April 2001. Western Gas made plans to use as much as $100 million in available cash flow to fund a renewed expansion effort, concentrating on the low-cost, low-risk coalbed methane play in the Powder River Basin of Wyoming. The company also broke ground on a new corporate headquarters to better accommodate future expansion. The greatest possible threat in the short term for the company was its becoming a possible takeover target, as industry analysts in 2001 took note of Shell's interest in acquiring companies involved in the coalbed methane segment. To fend off such a takeover bid, Western Gas adopted a shareholder rights plan that would go into effect if a person or group gained control of 15 percent or more of the company's stock. Having to worry about such a possibility, however, simply testified to the success of Western Gas and its potential for even greater growth.

Principal Subsidiaries

Western Gas Resources-Texas, Inc.; Mountain Gas Resources, Inc.; Western Gas Wyoming, L.L.C.

Principal Competitors

Kinder Morgan, Inc.; TransMontaigne Inc.

Further Reading

Aven, Paula, "Gas Drilling Soars in Powder River," *Denver Business Journal,* December 14, 1998.

Byrne, Harlan S., "Western Gas Resources," *Barron's,* May 3, 1993, pp. 37–39.

Mehlman, William, "Western Gas' Performance Defies Gas Price Recession," *Insider's Chronicle,* November 4, 1991, p. 1.

Wells, Garrison, "Western Gas Booms During Industry Slump," *Denver Business Journal,* July 24, 1992, p. 3.

"Western Gas Resources," *Fortune,* September 9, 1991, p. 151.

"Western Gas Resources, Inc.," *Oil & Gas Investor,* October 1999.

—Ed Dinger

Williamson-Dickie Manufacturing Company

509 W. Vickery Boulevard
Fort Worth, Texas 76104
U.S.A.
Telephone: (817) 336-7201
Toll Free: (800) 342-5437
Fax: (817) 877-5027
Web site: http://www.dickies.com

Private Company
Incorporated: 1922
Employees: 6,300
Sales: $820 million (2000 est.)
NAIC: 315225 Men's and Boys' Cut and Sew Work
Clothing Manufacturing; 315224 Men's and Boys' Cut
and Sew Trouser, Slack, and Jean Manufacturing (pt)

Williamson-Dickie Manufacturing Company is well-known throughout the United States for its durable work clothes, but it also makes school uniforms and men's, women's, and children's casual clothes. Marketed under the brand name "Dickies," the company's clothes—jeans, pants, overalls, shirts, shorts, jackets, and coveralls—are sold internationally through retailers, business-to-business sales, print catalogs, and an online store. In addition, Williamson-Dickie licenses its brand to a range of other manufacturers, making it possible to find the Dickies label on hats, socks, sunglasses, watches, footwear, and various other items.

Williamson and Dickie: Retail Partners in the Early 20th Century

During the latter part of the 19th century, C. N. Williamson and his cousin E. E. Dickie founded the Mallory Hat distributorship. Partners for over 25 years, the two men distributed men's hats throughout the state of Texas. In 1920, while the partners were still distributing hats, C.D. Williamson, more often known as "Don," and brother to C.N. Williamson, began to work for a Fort Worth clothing manufacturer by the name of U.S. Overall Company. Coincidentally, C.N. Williamson and E.E. Dickie were primary stockholders in the company, and also sold the firm's merchandise on a part-time basis. When Dickie arranged a sale of items that the president of U.S. Overall did not feel the company could manufacture, the president agreed to sell his stock to C.N. Williamson and E.E. Dickie. Quite suddenly, a new company named Williamson-Dickie was established.

The two older partners asked Don Williamson to become the new company's general manager, chief operating officer, and chief executive officer. C.N. Williamson became president and offered help in the financial area, while Dickie became vice-president and offered to help with sales. Under Don's direction, the company soon outpaced the hat business, and the three men began to concentrate solely on developing the garment company.

Don Williamson's supervision of the company, and its early successes, were based on his idea that corporate management was a science. Most of the books written on managing a business during the 1920s and 1930s suggested that an ambitious entrepreneur work hard, devote long hours, and conduct his financial dealings within a morally sound framework. Don Williamson, however, thought that this approach was naive, so he developed his own management principles in a book entitled *Executive Operations Technique*. With help from Edwin Booz, the head of Booz, Allen, and Hamilton, a well-known consulting firm, Don Williamson was able to clearly identify a number of steps in running a successful business: Expose Conditions, Develop Ideas, Unify Views, Determine Plans, Produce Actions, and Review Results. According to Williamson, if a new employee studied these principles of management, he would be well on the way to understanding successful business practices. By the early 1940s, the company had implemented a regular series of seminars on executive management for all new middle- to high-level employees based on Williamson's principles.

Mid-Century: Durable Work Clothes

During World War II, the company procured numerous contracts with the U.S. government to manufacture clothes for various units of the military, and after the war Williamson-Dickie introduced a more extensive line of work clothes, including jeans, jackets, overalls, and shirts. The company's most successful product was the khaki pant. Otherwise known as the "chino," and first worn by Texas oilfield workers, the khaki pant became a standard during the 1950s. Soon students, professors, golfers, and others from every walk of life were wearing khaki pants.

As a result of Williamson-Dickie's popular work clothes, the company's revenues and profitability skyrocketed. Next the company entered the industrial laundry business, cleaning and pressing work clothes and renting matching shirts and pants worn as employee uniforms. The volume of Williamson-Dickie's laundry business increased so rapidly that its officers reasoned that significant costs could be cut if a permanent press process could be developed, which would allow them to clean work clothes without pressing them.

Executives at Williamson-Dickie contacted Harris Laboratories, located in Washington, D.C., to develop a permanent crease that could be processed into a cotton workpant. As the developer of Toni Home Permanents, a permanent wave for hair, Harris Laboratories was confident that they could develop a permanent crease for pants as well. After just one year of research, the company developed a permanent press that actually worked; unfortunately, the treatment that allowed cotton pants to form a permanent press so weakened the material that after one or two washings the garment practically disintegrated. Irate customers complained to Williamson-Dickie about shredding pants, while also complimenting the company on the beautiful crease on the front of the trousers. Undismayed by this temporary setback, Williamson-Dickie and Harris Laboratories worked together to blend polyester with cotton to give the fabric more strength. From that time forward, permanent press became the standard for workpants, and Williamson-Dickie issued an unconditional guarantee on the quality and durability of all the company's work clothes.

During the late 1950s, the company expanded its marketing efforts in Europe and the Middle East. American oilfield workers contracted for jobs in the Middle East introduced clothes manufactured by Williamson-Dickie that became popular throughout the entire region. In 1960, the company opened a manufacturing plant in Belize; one year later, however, Hurricane Hattie destroyed the entire operation. After the factory was rebuilt, jeans and work clothes from the Belize factory were exported to England, and later, as the plant grew and became more efficient, clothing items manufactured in Belize were sold in the United States.

1960s–80s: Lobbying for Changes, Exploring New Markets

At this time, one of Williamson-Dickie's competitors began importing into the United States a garment made in a Caribbean nation that severely undercut Williamson-Dickie's prices on one of its most popular items. Executives at Williamson-Dickie concluded that the competing company must be using the "American Goods Returned" section of the Tariff Act to reduce the import duty paid on the garment, allowing the competitor to sell the item at a lower cost than Williamson-Dickie's imports. Williamson-Dickie teamed up with three other American apparel manufacturers to lobby for a change in the Tariff Act regarding re-importing goods; their provision—in Sections 806.30 and 807—allowed American apparel companies to manufacture clothes in Mexico or the Caribbean with U.S. fabrics and fibers, and then return the garments for sale within the United States, paying duty only on the value of the foreign labor. This provision in the Tariff Act created a huge American apparel industry in Mexico and the Caribbean, which, due to low labor costs in these regions, was able to remain competitive in the face of low-priced imports from China, Taiwan, and Korea.

During the early 1970s, Williamson-Dickie purchased the General Diaper Corporation, one of the largest diaper manufacturers in the United States. General Diaper was in the process of switching over to the manufacture of disposable diapers; in addition, the company opened two industrial laundry facilities in New Orleans and Houston, acquired a plastics company that made film for the healthcare product market, and acquired a dental supply firm. This diversification provided Williamson-Dickie with additional revenues to help increase its share of the work clothes market.

During the mid- and late 1970s, Williamson-Dickie began to dominate the work clothes market. As the Williamson-Dickie brand continued to grow more and more popular with the general public, the company expanded its product line to include such garments as matching shirt and pant work clothes, jackets, coveralls, overalls, painter pants, jeans, thermal underwear, bandannas, sweatshirts, socks, caps, work boots, flannel shirts, work gloves, and belts. The company also opened a number of stores in the southern United States that sold uniforms and matching accessories, including postman and policeman uniforms, holsters, footwear, and special uniform underwear.

Leadership at Williamson-Dickie had completely changed by the 1970s, with the original founders having retired and non-family members hired to manage the operations of the company. Dickie Industrial Services was created during the 1970s to formalize the company's operation of industrial laundry services throughout the South, Southwest, and West Coast regions of the United States. With 14 facilities, Williamson-Dickie was the leader in renting and laundering uniforms for employees from every walk of life, including security guards, police officers, firefighters, fast-food restaurant workers, laboratory technicians, and many more.

During the 1980s, the General Diaper Company changed its name to the Blessings Corporation and focused its efforts on manufacturing plastic products for the healthcare and agricultural industries; developing its Publishing Division, which provided informational materials for new mothers; and growing its Geri-Care Division, which made healthcare products for the elderly. The company's industrial laundries operation and the apparel divisions were highly lucrative. By the end of the decade, Williamson-Dickie reported an annual growth rate of nearly 15 percent, and the company's manufacturing facilities, although

```
┌─────────────────────────────────────────────────────┐
│                    Key Dates:                        │
│                                                       │
│  1922:  C.D. Williamson and E.E. Dickie purchase U.S. │
│         Overall, and rename it Williamson-Dickie Manu-│
│         facturing Company.                            │
│  1960:  Williamson-Dickie opens a manufacturing plant │
│         in Belize.                                    │
│  1970s: The company purchases General Diaper Corpora- │
│         tion, and creates Dickie Industrial Services. │
│  1980s: General Diaper Corporation changes its name to│
│         Blessings Corporation.                        │
│  1990s: Dickies brand becomes popular as casual wear  │
│         among younger consumers; the company opens its│
│         first outlet store and expands denim line and │
│         licensing program.                            │
│  1998:  Williamson-Dickie sells Blessings Corporation.│
│  1999:  The company acquires Workrite Uniform Co.     │
└─────────────────────────────────────────────────────┘
```

concentrated in mostly southern states, were also thriving in California, New Jersey, and a number of Caribbean countries.

End of the Century: A Fashion Statement

The advent of the 1990s saw increased competition within the international apparel industry, with many American clothing manufacturers, including Williamson-Dickie, threatened by international imports. At the same time, these companies benefited from a new and unexpected demand for their products by young urban customers, who made work clothes a fashion trend. Increasing sales to this market segment allowed Williamson-Dickie to move beyond its traditional blue-collar customers. With the realization that the Dickies brand was successfully crossing over from the work crowd to the leisure crowd, the company made some adjustments in both its product line and its marketing strategies. It expanded its line of jeanswear, capturing a segment of the market that it had previously been losing to manufacturers such as Levi's, Wrangler, and Lee. It also launched a national ad campaign for its jeans in *Parade* and *People* magazine, and on country music radio stations.

The company opened its first factory store outlet, in Orlando, Florida, during the mid-1990s. The store featured the company's brand-name work clothes, along with other sportswear and accessories. Williamson-Dickie entered another new channel by placing its work clothes—including painter's pants, coveralls, and long-tail T-shirts—in home improvement warehouse chains, and also contracted with Itochu of Japan for the latter company to distribute work clothes to Japanese consumers.

By the late 1990s, Dickies' popularity as a fashion statement had increased to a surprising degree. The company's clothes were featured in slick fashion magazines, sold in expensive boutiques, and seen on rap and hip-hop artists, models, and movie stars. This sudden chic had a positive impact on the company's sales, boosting them by an average of 10 percent annually throughout the end of the decade. Even so, Williamson-Dickie remained relatively unmoved by all the fuss, maintaining a low-profile and a steadfast focus on producing much the same types of clothing it always had.

While it refrained from diversifying its manufacturing operations, the company did expand the range of Dickies-labeled products by stepping up its licensing program. Since the 1980s, Williamson-Dickie had been licensing its brand to a handful of manufacturers—makers of socks, belts, footwear, and certain types of clothing. But in 1996 and 1997, as the Dickies name gained new cachet, the company recognized the potential for marketing other Dickies-branded products. A series of deals followed: with watchmaker M.Z. Berger to produce watches; with outerwear maker Amerex to produce jackets; with Hampton Industries to produce sports shirts; and with Yak Pak to make backpacks.

In 1998, the company sold its majority share of Blessings Corporation, and the following year made an acquisition that better aligned with its core business: Workrite Uniform Co. Workrite, a California-based maker of flame-retardant work clothing, was the market leader in safety apparel for the oil, gas, and other hazardous industries. It was a particularly good fit for Williamson-Dickie because the companies' product lines complemented each other but did not overlap. After the acquisition, Workrite continued to operate as a separate entity.

2000 and Beyond

As the old century gave way to the new, Williamson-Dickie continued to focus on producing durable work-related clothing. The demand for such clothing remained strong—across various markets. As school uniforms became increasingly popular throughout the nation, the company boosted its already existing children's uniform line by teaming up with J.C. Penney. The partnership, formed in June 2000, provided for Dickies uniforms to be sold through the retailer's popular catalog and online store. In 2001, Williamson-Dickie made a similar arrangement with Wal-Mart, and began test marketing a Dickies school uniform line called "Head of the Class." If the uniforms tested well, it appeared likely that they would be rolled out to more Wal-Mart stores, and offered to other retailers as well.

Williamson-Dickie also continued to enhance its market presence and its revenues through licensing agreements. In 2000, the company added E.J. Footwear to its list of licensees, allowing the Tennessee-based company to produce and market a Dickies line of boots and shoes. In 2001, it awarded its largest licensing program ever, with apparel maker Dino di Milano. The Miami-based manufacturer planned to produce a line of knit and woven shirts featuring the Dickies logo.

Principal Subsidiaries

Workrite Uniform Co.

Principal Competitors

Carhartt, Inc.; Levi Strauss & Co.; VF Corporation.

Further Reading

Barron, Kelly, "The Kids Are Crazy About Them," *Forbes*, June 15, 1998, p. 72.

Gellers, Stan, "Dickies Fashions the Work Ethic," *Daily News Record*, May 12, 2000, p. 3.

Hancox, Clara, "And Now—For the Last Time What Will It Take to Survive into the Next Century?" *Daily News Record,* June 28, 1993, p. 23.

Jarnagin, DeAnna, "Home Improvement Hits Prime Time," *Daily News Record,* April 24, 1992, p. 3.

Parola, Robert, "Workwear Grows New Fashion Muscle," *Daily News Record,* May 19, 1993, p. 4.

Vargo, Julie, "New Dickies Outlet Plays to Worker and Hip-Hopper," *Daily News Record,* February 18, 1994, p. 4.

——, "Work Clothes Bring Fashion to the Street," *Daily News Record,* November 18, 1994, p. 3.

Wadsworth, Kim, "Dickies: 75 Years of Hard-Working Fashion," *Norfolk Virginian-Pilot,* September 1, 1997, p. E1.

Walsh, Peter, "Itochu of Japan," *Daily News Record,* December 8, 1993, p. 16.

Williamson, C. Dickie, *Williamson-Dickie Manufacturing Company,* New York: Newcomen Society, 1985.

"Williamson Dickie Introduces International Pro Rodeo Cowboy Jean," *Daily News Record,* April 19, 1995, p. 4.

—Thomas Derdak
—update: Shawna Brynildssen

Wilson Bowden Plc

Wilson Bowden House
Leicester Road
Ibstock, Leicester LE67 6WB
United Kingdom
Telephone: (+44) 1530-260777
Fax: (+44) 1530-262805
Web site: http://www.wilsonbowden.co.uk

Public Company
Incorporated: 1987
Employees: 1,956
Sales: £726.8 million ($1.08 billion) (2000)
Stock Exchanges: London
Ticker Symbol: WLB
NAIC: 233320 Commercial and Institutional Building
    Construction; 233210 Single Family Housing
    Construction

One of the United Kingdom's top home builders, Wilson Bowden Plc has targeted the upper end of the housing market, selling four- to six-bedroom homes, with an average floor space of more than 1,200 square feet and an average selling price of more than £157,000. In 2000, the company sold more than 3,600 homes—and has set its growth target at up to 7,000 homes annually. Based in Leicester, the company operates divisional offices in 12 regions, with its core operations centered around the Midlands, but also stretching into the north of England and into Scotland and Wales (the company has avoided the London market). Wilson Bowden Plc operates through three primary subsidiaries: David Wilson Homes Ltd., which handles its residential construction activities; Wilson Bowden Developments Ltd., which guides the company's growing commercial property (retail, office, leisure, and industrial) development activities, and includes its own in-house construction unit; and the newest division, Wilson Bowden City Homes, which has taken over the company's urban and brownfield residential site activity, which transforms derelict urban space into residential properties, with a growing emphasis on apartment complexes. Wilson Bowden has long held a policy of acquiring and holding large land portfolios—its home division alone possesses a land bank of more than 14,000 plots with planning permission. This policy helps protect the company from excessive land pricing cycles. In keeping with this policy, the company has tended to avoid the industry consolidation of the late 1990s, preferring to make direct acquisitions of land, rather than of other construction companies. Wilson Bowden is quoted on the London stock exchange. Its founder, chairman, and chief executive holds 38 percent of the company's stock.

Constructing a Construction Company in the 1960s

Albert Wilson had been working as a building contractor when son David Wilson graduated from the Leicester Polytechnic School of Building in 1961. The younger Wilson joined his father's business, AH Wilson, and steered the company toward property development soon after. In 1966, the company launched its first large development project, acquiring a site in Packington, Leicestershire, where it built a 36-home development. Through the end of the decade, the company expanded further into its Midlands region, adding developments in Rutland.

The company's home building wing flourished and by the beginning of the 1970s AH Wilson was posting revenues of more than £1 million. The company's development activities took on steam in that decade—by 1973, Wilson was building more than 150 homes per year. It had also formed a joint venture, with First National Finance Corporation holding a 51 percent share, called Bowden Park Holdings Ltd. When the British economy slumped into a recession in 1974, Wilson was able to buy out its partner—which was struggling financially—and take full control of Bowden Park. That company remained more or less dormant over the next few years, as Wilson, led by David Wilson after his father's death, concentrated on building up its home sales under the name David Wilson Homes.

Despite the recession's effects on the building market, Wilson remained in good shape. The company had already begun to exhibit the conservative financial policies that were to help it gain success in the 1990s. With low debt levels and tight building cost controls, the company grew steadily throughout the decade. By the beginning of the 1980s, Wilson was building

442

more than 300 homes per year, raising its revenues to more than £13 million.

Wilson had added operations in Lincolnshire in 1974, then extended its Midlands region business still more with the acquisition of extensive land holdings in Hampshire. The company opened a new regional office in Bournemouth to support its growing business in 1979.

In the early 1980s, Wilson sought further growth throughout the Midlands region, turning now to a series of acquisitions to build its geographic position. In 1981, the company added operations in the East Midlands when it acquired William Corah and its land portfolio. The following year, the purchase of JG Parker allowed Wilson to move into Nottingham. The company opened a new North Midlands regional office to support its development there. Then, in 1983, Wilson acquired The French House, a U.K. subsidiary of France's Groupe Maison Familiale. This acquisition added nearly ten new development sites in the South Midlands region, leading the company to open a new regional division to support its growth.

Wilson's success as a home builder led it to venture into the commercial development sector in the early 1980s. The company created a new dedicated division for its growing property development activities and, in 1982, launched its first major commercial development project, that of the 72-acre Meridian Business Park outside of Leicester. That site was later to grow to include more than 200 acres of commercial property. This project helped boost the company's revenues, which neared £40 million by 1983.

By 1986, the company had nearly doubled in size, posting revenues of £65 million. The booming building sector encouraged the company to go public. To do this, the company pulled out its Bowden Park subsidiary and listed on the London stock exchange as Wilson Bowden Plc in February 1987. The company now grouped its residential construction and development activities under subsidiary David Wilson Homes Ltd., while its commercial development operations were brought under subsidiary Wilson Bowden Developments Ltd. With £14 million raised from its IPO—which, at a share price of 130p, valued the company at £87 million—the company established a new Eastern regional office, at Witham, Essex, and the company prepared to expand its operations.

Independent Builder in the 21st Century

Wilson Bowden's timing proved unfortunate. In 1988, the U.K. building sector crashed and the industry—as well as the entire U.K. economy—plunged into a deep recession. Wilson Bowden nonetheless maintained its policy of building long land bank portfolios, giving it a five year cushion of building properties, and this policy helped shield the company and maintain its profitability.

The company began preparing its comeback at the beginning of the decade. In 1990, the company took on its first urban regeneration project as the British government began encouraging building developers to construct on so-called "brownfield" sites, that is, derelict urban and industrial locations. By the late 1990s, this encouragement was to become law, as the government imposed quotas on property developers. Wilson Bowden's first move into this market came with the acquisition of the 50-acre site of a former power generation plant in Nottingham. The company cleaned the site and constructed the Riverside Complex there.

A stock issue in 1991, which raised £35 million, followed by a second stock issue in 1993, raising £58.5 million, supported the company's return to geographic expansion. In 1992 the company opened its first office in the West Midlands region, near Wolverhampton. Two years later, the company expanded north, setting up a regional office in Leeds. The company added a commercial development office for Leeds the following year as it began to develop sites along the M62 motorway. By then, the residential market had once again begun to grow and the company's home sales were topping 2,000 per year.

In 1996, Wilson Bowden Development added Wales to its regional operations when it joined a partnership to build a retail park in Cardiff Bay. That same year, the company acquired Trencherwood Plc and its Trencherwood Homes subsidiary, based in Newbury, for £10.1 million. That purchase not only expanded the company's home construction business, it gave it an extensive land portfolio of some 6,000 plots with planning permission. Trencherwood continued to operate under its own name before being merged into the David Wilson Homes Southern Region division in 1999. The addition of Trencherwood helped the company's revenues swell to nearly £332 million that year.

Meanwhile, Trencherwood's modest commercial division provided a springboard for Wilson Bowden Development's entry into the region, where the company secured contracts such as a 70,000-square-foot office for Dell Computer, a 96,000-square-foot retail and leisure complex in the Milton Keynes theater district, and, later at the end of the decade, a 130,000-square-foot office park in Chalfont.

After finishing its first commercial property in Scotland in 1997—a £42 million, 130,000-square-foot retail center in Edinburgh—the company set up a dedicated Scottish office in Glasgow in 1998. Meanwhile, the David Wilson Homes division was also stepping up its regional expansion, adding offices in Warrington for the North Western region, in Bristol for the South Western region, both in 1997, and, in 1999, offices for the South Eastern region in Sussex, and in Glasgow. Another regional office was added in 2000, at Hemel Hempstead to cover the Home Counties region. By the turn of the century, the company operated out of 12 regional offices.

The U.K. construction industry, meanwhile, had been undergoing a consolidation spree. Yet Wilson Bowden remained in large part on the sidelines, preferring to concentrate on acquir-

Key Dates:

1961: David Wilson joins his father Albert's contracting business, AH Wilson, in Leicester.

1966: Company enters property development with a 36-home development in Leicestershire.

1969: Company expands into Rutland, launches joint venture Bowden Park Holdings.

1973: Wilson acquires full control of Bowden Park Holdings.

1974: Company expands into Lincolnshire.

1979: Company acquires land in Hampshire and opens a regional office in Bournemouth.

1981: Wilson acquires construction company William Corah and its land bank in East Midlands.

1982: Company acquires JG Parker to enter the Nottingham market, forming the basis of a new North Midlands Region office; company launches dedicated commercial development division.

1983: Company acquires The French House from Groupe Maison Familiale, adding South Midlands regional division.

1987: Company goes public as Wilson Bowden Plc.

1990: Wilson acquires its first brownfield site in Nottingham.

1992: Company expands into West Midlands.

1994: Company adds the Leeds office to cover the northern region.

1996: Company acquires Trencherwood PLC and its Trencherwood Homes subsidiary, which holds a land bank of more than 6,000 plots with planning permission.

1998: Company opens an office in Glasgow for commercial property development in Scotland.

2000: A new subsidiary, Wilson Bowden City Homes, is created to take over the company's urban renewal development activities.

2001: Company begins plans to develop £1 billion urban renewal site in Scotland.

ing individual land plots rather than other companies. As deputy chief executive Ian Robertson told the *Independent,* "Our figures show that we can grow organically. Acquisitions are essentially about buying landbanks. This year, we'll spend £300m on buying land. That is equivalent to a medium-sized acquisition. And we get to pick and choose the sites ourselves."

A growing number of those sites had come to focus on inner-city brownfield locations, as the U.K. government began restricting greenfield development and imposing stiffer quotas; up to 60 percent of all new construction by 2008 was expected to be urban renewal sites. Wilson Bowden itself had stepped up its brownfield development, and by 2001 that sector had come to represent 40 percent of the company's projects. In response to this trend, Wilson Bowden created a dedicated division, Wilson Bowden City Homes, which combined the company's residential development interests with its commercial property development expertise. In 2001, the company announced plans for one of its biggest projects to date, the £1 billion redevelopment of the former Ravenscraig steelworks, located near Motherwell in Scotland. That project was expected to provide new retail, light industrial, and commercial space, as well as 2,500 homes.

Wilson Bowden had risen to become one of the most well-respected of the United Kingdom's property development groups. The company's emphasis on quality over quantity, and especially its focus on the higher-margin, high-end residential sector, had enabled it to build its own revenues to nearly £730 million. With a land bank of more than 16,000 plots with planning permission, Wilson Bowden appeared to have a sound basis for expansion. Indeed, the company hoped to double its home sales in the early years of the new century, to as many as 7,000 per year.

Principal Subsidiaries

David Wilson Homes Ltd; Wilson Bowden Developments Ltd; Wilson Bowden City Homes.

Principal Competitors

Alfred McAlpine PLC; Barratt Developments PLC; Bovis Homes Group PLC; Bellway p.l.c.; Crest Nicholson PLC; George Wimpey PLC; Persimmon plc; Propan Homes Plc; Prowting PLC; Redrow plc; Taylor Woodrow plc; Westbury plc; Wilson Connolly Holdings Plc.

Further Reading

"Bowden to Redevelop Ravenscraig Steel Site," *Reuters,* June 25, 2001.

Foley, Stephen, ed., "Wilson Bowden on Firm Footing," *Independent,* October 3, 2001, p. 19.

Kar-Gupta, Sudip, "Wilson Bowden Cool on Consolidation," *Reuters,* February 28, 2001.

Pain, Steve, "Quality Over Quantity Is Key for Housebuilder," *Birmingham Post,* August 31, 2000, p. 17.

Shah, Saeed, "Wilson Bowden Warns Planning Reform Stoking Prices," *Independent,* August 30, 2001, p. 17.

—M.L. Cohen

WS Atkins Plc

Woodcote Grove
Ashley Road
Epsom, Surrey KT18 5BW
United Kingdom
Telephone: (+44) 1372-726-140
Fax: (+44) 1372-740-055
Web site: http://www.wsatkins.co.uk

Public Company
Incorporated: 1938 as WS Atkins & Partners
Employees: 12,800
Sales: £674 million ($954.6 million) (2000)
Stock Exchanges: London
Ticker Symbol: ATK
NAIC: 541330 Engineering Services

WS Atkins Plc is one of the world's leading suppliers of consultancy and related support services with an emphasis on the engineering and other technology-related sectors. The company's operations focus on four primary segments: Property, Transport, Management and Industry, and International. Based in Epsom, England, WS Atkins has diversified beyond its traditional engineering consultancy practice to include facilities management services and power generation. WS Atkins operates 125 offices in the United Kingdom and another 50 offices worldwide, including nearly 20 in the United States. Altogether, WS Atkins provides services to more than 50 countries in Europe, the Middle East, the Americas, and Asia. The United Kingdom, where the company is market leader, accounts for the largest part of the company's revenues, nearly 80 percent of the company's £674 million in sales. Since going public in 1996, WS Atkins has expanded rapidly through a series of acquisitions, including Faithful & Gould in 1996; Lambert Smith Hampton, acquired in 1999; The Benham Companies, subsequently renamed Atkins Benham, in 2000, which greatly expanded the company's American presence; and, in 2001, the Danish National Railway Agency's transportation and engineering consulting unit, ScanRail. The company also operates through subsidiaries Atmos Ltd, which provides engineering and consulting services to the construction industry and WS Atkins Rail Ltd, which focuses on the U.K. railway industry.

Engineering Consultants in the 1930s

William Atkins founded the civil and structural engineering firm William Atkins & Partners in 1938. Based in Westminster, the company grew to become one of the region's most important specialists in civil and engineering design, before branching out into a number of related areas, including planning and project management services. The company also developed a large architectural component, and by the late 1970s WS Atkins's architecture office numbered more than 150 employees.

WS Atkins himself remained at the head of the firm he had founded until the mid-1980s. By then the company had been riding high on the wave of privatization and outsourcing moves made by the conservative government led by Margaret Thatcher. The company developed a strong network of ties with a number of government agencies that were to enable it to achieve strong growth in the coming years. As the British government began turning over a number of government-run services and sectors to private industry—such as construction and operation of prisons and construction and management of toll roads—WS Atkins received a growing number of contracts.

The company had remained financially solid throughout the recession years of the early 1980s and despite the economic relapse of the construction and other markets at the end of that decade. Part of the company's continuing profitability was due to its strict financial policies, enabling the company to emerge from the most difficult years of the recession with a strong war chest. Another factor helping the company was its decision to restructure in the mid-1980s as William Atkins prepared his own succession. The company, then called the WS Atkins Group, split into two separate entities. WS Atkins Consultants was created to encompass the company's original WS Atkins & Partners and its engineering consultancy work. The second company, Atkins Holdings Limited, contained the rest of the group's operations. At the time of the restructuring, WS Atkins's employees were given a major stake in the company's ownership. William Atkins and family kept a 20 percent share, while another 20 percent was placed in the company's pension fund. The option to buy the remaining 60 percent of shares was transferred to the company's staff.

William Atkins died in 1989 as the company prepared to launch a public offering. That move was put on hold in 1990, however, after the Iraqi invasion of Kuwait temporarily stranded a number of Atkins employees engaged as road engineers in the Persian Gulf region. As later Chairman Michael Jeffries told the *Independent on Sunday,* "It was pointless to even consider a floatation when the lives of our employees were at stake." Nonetheless, the company was able to go ahead with its shareholder restructuring, with the company's employees becoming its majority shareholder in 1992.

Engineering a Worldwide Business in the 21st Century

Atkins made a new attempt to go public in 1994; yet this effort too was placed on hold due to weak conditions in the IPO market. Atkins itself remained financially solid, however; by the mid-1990s, the company's treasury had grown to some £85 million, enabling the company not only to compete for consultancy contracts, both in the United Kingdom and increasingly abroad, but also to compete for full-service contracts. Such was the case with the company's investment in the British government's Private Finance Initiative, for which the company secured the contract to build a prison in Wales with partners Securicor and Costain. Another important company project at the time was its participation as architect, engineering consultant, and construction manager for the $700 million, manmade Chicago Beach resort island in Dubai.

Atkins's strong reputation among British government agencies was meanwhile helping it expand its operations throughout a variety of public sector industries as well, including such key government-owned areas as the railway network, the steel industry, the electrical and nuclear power services, as well as the Ministry of Defense and the Property Service Agency.

Michael Jeffries was named CEO in 1995 and took the company public the following year. The largest part of the shares placed on sale came from the Atkins family and from the company pension fund. Yet by the end of the decade Atkins's shareholder base had shifted substantially, with the Atkins family retaining just 7 percent of shares, and the company's employees just over 30 percent. The majority of the company's shares were bought up by institutional shareholders.

Atkins's public status enabled it to go on a strong expansion program in the last years of the century. In 1996, the company picked up its first acquisition, that of Cleveland, England-based quantity surveyors Faithful & Gould. That purchase added F&G's 50 years of construction services experiences, including full-service project support, from initial design to completed facilities management. Atkins continued its expansion, setting up its subsidiary Atmos Ltd in 1996 after winning a contract to partner with the Somerset County Council for Highway Engineering, Transportation and Related Services. Atkins also built up its railroad engineering wing, notably through the acquisition of a number of British Rail assets, including Opal Engineering Ltd. By the end of that year, the company's revenues had risen to £328 million.

By 1998, Atkins's expansion encouraged it to restructure its operations, abandoning its former regional structure for one grouped around three core business areas, Transportation, Property, and Industry. The company's growing activities outside of the United Kingdom were later grouped under a fourth division, International. The company took on a prestigious overseas job with the construction of the Kowloon to Canton railway in Hong Kong. At the same time, the company was shifting from its reliance on government contracts to a stronger proportion of contracts from the private sector.

The company paid £5.1 million for another quantity surveyor, Silk & Frazier, in 1998. The year saw the company move in a new direction when it took over a disused power station located near the Aldershot military compound, and began power generation for the British national power grid. Atkins also announced plans to spend as much as £50 million on new acquisitions. The company's immediate takeover ambitions were thwarted, however, after talks to acquire the Bovis construction unit of Peninsular & Oriental Steam Navigation fell through at the end of 1998.

The next year proved more successful for Atkins's expanding ambitions. After acquiring Irish engineering consultants McCarthy & Partners, the company added U.K. commercial property specialist consultants Lambert Smith Hampton. The move, at a price of £50 million, gave Atkins a top-five position in the property sector. A month after acquiring Lambert Smith Hampton, the company was back on the buying trail, adding water industry consulting specialist Richard Long Associates. The company posted two smaller deals toward the end of the year, paying £2.3 million for process engineering firm Ventron Technology, and £1.3 million for the quantity surveying company Yeoman & Edwards.

Atkins had by then built up a small presence in the North American market. Faced with the entry of its larger U.S. rivals into the United Kingdom, the company decided to strike back on their home territory. As Jeffries told the *Financial Times,* "The U.S. is a key part of our strategy. If we do not go to the U.S. and they come over here and take out smaller competitors, we will lose globally." In December 1999, the company announced that it had agreed to pay £32 million to acquire Oklahoma-based The Benham Companies. Founded in 1909 as an engineering consultant, The Benham Companies had developed as a full-service multidisciplinary firm with expertise in some 25 different architectural and engineering sectors. Benham, subsequently renamed Atkins Benham, also provided its new parent with a strong international component, particularly in Mexico and Latin America, and also in Asia.

Atkins took a break from acquisitions in 2000 as it integrated its purchases from the year before. The company was also

Key Dates:

1938: William Atkins founds engineering consultancy WS Atkins & Partners.

1986: WS Atkins Group decides to spin off consulting operations, including WS Atkins & Partners as WS Atkins Consultants; the company's remaining assets are regrouped under a separate company, Atkins Holdings Ltd.; employees are given option to buy as much as 60 percent of the company's shares.

1990: WS Atkins calls off first public offering after the outbreak of the Persian Gulf War strands a number of its employees in Kuwait.

1996: WS Atkins Plc goes public on the London Stock Exchange; company acquires quantity surveyor Faithful & Gould and establishes Atmos Ltd. railroad subsidiary.

1997: Company acquires Opal Engineering from British Rail.

1998: Company acquires Silk & Frazier but fails attempted acquisition of Bovis Construction.

1999: WS Atkins acquires McCarthy's Consulting Engineers, Lambert Smith Hampton, and The Benham Companies.

2000: Company secures £1 billion, ten-year facilities management contract with Telekom South Africa, the company's largest ever contract.

2001: WS Atkins acquires ScanRail from Danish National Railway and Boward Computer Services.

preparing its—successful—bid to take over facilities management services from Telekom South Africa, in a joint-venture deal worth £1.5 billion over ten years. That deal, Atkins's largest ever, also marked a turning point of sorts for the company, as the proportion of service contracts in the company's overall revenues climbed to 60 percent.

Atkins returned to its expansion through acquisition program in 2001. In June of that year, the company agreed to acquire ScanRail, the transport and engineering consultancy arm of the Danish National Railway system. Renamed Atkins Danmark, the new subsidiary gave Atkins an important position in the Scandinavian and northern European railway market. Soon after, the company's U.K. railway activities received a strong boost when it won two two-year contracts to assess some 38,000 stations, bridges, tunnels, and other components of the Railtrack railroad network. At the same time, Atkins continued to explore expansion into new market areas, such as systems

engineering. This component received a boost in August 2001 when the company announced its purchase of systems integration and consulting company Boward Computer Services.

Jeffries stepped up to the position of company chairman in April 2001, replaced by Robin Southwell as CEO. Southwell led the company into a new reorganization at the middle of that year, designed to replace the company's country-focused operations with a more globally operating, entrepreneurial, and market-segment focused business. The restructuring, expected to cost the company some £10 million, was to enable the company to compete more strongly in its increasingly global core segments of rail, road, government services, and industry. Atkins's record at the turn of the new century—in just five years the company had more than doubled its sales—and growing international focus gave it a strong position in its increasingly global market.

Principal Subsidiaries

Atkins Benham Inc. (USA); Atkins China Ltd; Atkins Danmark A/S; Atmos Ltd; Faithful & Gould Ltd.; Lambert Smith Hampton Group Ltd; WS Atkins (Services) Ltd; WS Atkins (UK Holdings) Ltd; WS Atkins Consultants Ltd; WS Atkins Facilities Management Ltd; WS Atkins International Ltd; WS Atkins Investments Ltd; WS Atkins Planning and Management Consultants Ltd; WS Atkins Rail Ltd; WS Atkins & Partners Overseas (Gibraltar); WS Atkins Insurance (Guernsey) Ltd.

Principal Competitors

AMEC Plc; Amey Plc; Babcock International Group Plc; Bovis Lend Lease; CH2M Hill Companies, Ltd.; EMC Engineers, Inc.; Hawtal Whiting Holdings Plc; Henkels & McCoy Inc.; Kvaerner ASA; Oystertec Plc; STS Consultants Ltd; STV Group Inc.; Widney Plc.

Further Reading

"Atkins Set for U.S. Expansion," *Financial Times*, December 3, 1999.

Felsted, Andrea, "Atkins Set for Schools Contract," *Financial Times*, September 10, 2001.

Litterick, David, "Atkins Surges on S. African Deal," *Daily Telegraph*, August 1, 2000.

Osborne, Alistair, "Atkins Poised to Spend Pounds 50m on Acquisitions," *Daily Telegraph*, June 12, 1998.

Phillips, Richard, "The Draughtsman's Contract," *Independent on Sunday*, June 9, 1996, p. 5.

Tyler, Richard, "Railway Deal Keeps Atkins on Fast Track," *Birmingham Post*, April 7, 2001, p. 17.

—M.L. Cohen

Yellow Corporation

10990 Roe Avenue
Overland Park, Kansas 66211
U.S.A.
Telephone: (913) 696-6100
Fax: (913) 696-6116
Web site: http://www.yellowcorp.com

Public Company
Incorporated: 1993
Employees: 32,900
Sales: $3.59 billion (2000)
Stock Exchanges: NASDAQ
Ticker Symbol: YELL
NAIC: 48851 Freight Transportation Arrangement ;
   484122 General Freight Trucking, Long-Distance,
   Less Than Truckload

Yellow Corporation is a transportation holding company with subsidiaries that specialize in regional, national, and international transportation and related services. Its largest and best known subsidiary, Yellow Freight System, Inc., provides less-than-truckload (LTL) shipping and specialty shipping of heavy loads and chemicals. Through other subsidiaries—including Yellow Global, Saia Motor Freight, and Jevic Transportation—Yellow offers overnight and second-day trucking services and worldwide ocean and air transportation and forwarding services.

1920s–40s: Early Successes, Early Struggles

World War I proved the usefulness and flexibility of trucks in moving large quantities of goods and supplies wherever they were needed on the front lines. Soon after the war, the truck became a fixture in U.S. cities. A.J. Harrell, who ran a bus line and franchise of Yellow Cab in Oklahoma City, recognized the importance and potential profitability of transporting goods rather than people. In 1924, Harrell traded his cabs for trucks and established the Yellow Transit trucking company.

The initial years of Yellow Transit were limited to local and short-run less-than-truckload (LTL) shipments, that is, ship-

ments of less than 10,000 pounds, in Oklahoma City and the surrounding area, and between Oklahoma City and Tulsa. The roadway system in the United States, originally built for travel by horse and carriage, and still barely hardy enough for the automobile, could not yet provide dependable long-distance routes for the far heavier truck. Cities were just recognizing the importance of linking with each other and with their outlying, especially farming, areas. For the time being, the railroads continued to dominate the nation's long-distance, bulk transport freight business. Yet demand for transporting small volume, more fragile, and perishable shipments had begun to grow, and, as the country entered the Great Depression, companies came to appreciate the greater flexibility of trucks. Unlike the railroads, trucks could carry small loads to almost any location at any time, allowing companies to deliver inventory faster than ever before. The collapsing economy had left numerous people without work, many of whom rushed to join the young trucking industry. More and more trucking companies appeared, many comprising little more than a single truck, in the rush to meet the demand. Throughout the 1930s, the trucking industry boomed.

The first highways appeared during this time. Improvements in construction techniques made the new roads faster and stronger, and an early, crude highway system connected longer distances. Advancements in automotive technology, and particularly the perfection of the powerful and efficient diesel engine, made long-distance hauling not only more attractive, but practical as well. Yellow Transit soon expanded beyond its local routes into state-to-state shipping, reaching south into Texas and north into Missouri. By confining itself largely to north-south routes, Yellow avoided direct competition with the primarily east-west orientation of the railroads. Throughout the 1930s, Yellow continued to grow, adding more and more vehicles, routes, and subsidiaries.

Yellow continued to grow through the 1940s, extending operations into Kansas, Illinois, Indiana, Kentucky, and other states. By the end of the decade, Yellow operated through 51 small subsidiaries, nearing yearly revenues of $7 million. The trucking industry had begun to mature by then, and the era of small, independent truckers was giving way to larger, more efficient trucking corporations. Yellow, its growth limited by rising leasing rates, found itself unable to compete and became financially strapped from paying out dividends. A.J. Harrell sold the company in 1944 and, in 1951, it was forced to declare bankruptcy.

1950s–60s: Turnaround and Rapid Expansion

The following year, Yellow was purchased by George E. Powell and other investors. A banker in Kansas City, Powell had also been vice-chairman at Riss & Company, a leading Midwest trucking company. Joining Powell from Riss were his son, George Powell, Jr., and others. Within five months Powell and his team had reorganized Yellow into a more efficient and innovative company, raising it from bankruptcy into the black. Now with bases in Kansas City and Oklahoma City, Yellow turned its focus to long-haul routes, dropping its short-haul businesses. With the post-World War II boom to the economy, and with a new emphasis on cost accounting, customer service, and information flow, Yellow began buying up trucking companies whose routes would allow it to expand into the north and east. The Kansas City operation began to function as a hub to direct the growing network.

A major development in the trucking industry occurred in 1956, when legislation was passed creating the Federal Interstate Highway System (FIHS). With the end of World War II, the demand for automobiles boomed, and dramatic increases in the volume of transported goods would eventually develop trucking, and truck purchases, into a central element in the country's economy. The FIHS was planned to link into every city with a population of 50,000 or more across the United States, calling originally for 40,000 miles but ultimately reaching 45,000 miles. Freeways were to be constructed according to strict specifications and, with their high quality, limited access, and free flow, were ideal for the long-haul trucking industry. The FIHS signaled the nation's commitment to the automobile for serving its transportation and shipping needs. Yellow was quick to capitalize on this latest boost to the trucking industry, and by 1957 had reached revenues of $15 million. In that year, Yellow purchased Michigan Motor Freight Lines, its largest purchase to date, further extending its network of routes across the country.

Meanwhile, advancements in tractor-trailer design were creating lighter, stronger, and more efficient trucks. Because of roadway weight limits, and because of rate regulations fixed by the Interstate Commerce Commission (ICC), new income was attainable primarily through increasing the amount of goods each truck could carry, as well as by cutting costs. The lighter, more efficient trucks and trailers allowed trucking companies to ship larger truckloads at less expense, and Yellow's strategy of continuously investing in the latest truck designs, while ridding itself of outdated vehicles and equipment, allowed it to achieve faster service at lower cost than its competitors. As it outpaced many smaller, older operations, Yellow began a period of aggressive acquisition. These acquisitions were especially important to Yellow's growth. The ICC controlled the creation of truck routes, and in order to extend across the country, Yellow would have had to petition that agency for its desired routes. However, by buying up other trucking companies, Yellow obtained their existing routes and in this way added hundreds of trucking routes to its network. Into the 1960s, Yellow's rapid growth had made it the nation's 13th largest trucker, with annual sales of $40 million.

In 1965, Yellow purchased Watson-Wilson Transportation System, launching a new period in the growth of the company. Watson-Wilson was larger than Yellow, with revenues nearing $70 million per year. More importantly, it controlled routes stretching from Chicago to the West Coast. Nevertheless, the company had not kept up with technology advances and changes in the industry, and by the early 1960s was failing. Yellow's purchase of Watson-Wilson, for approximately $13 million, doubled its size. Subsequent acquisitions of Norwalk Truck Lines and other companies extended Yellow throughout the North and Southeast, bringing Yellow a fully connected, coast-to-coast operation. The company changed its name to Yellow Freight System in 1968 and posted revenues topping $200 million by the end of the decade, making it the nation's third largest trucking company.

1970s: Leading the Industry

An important part of the company's operations were its nine "break-bulk" centers. Serving as hubs along the various legs of Yellow's network, these centers received shipments from one leg, broke down the products according to their following destinations, then loaded the trucks traveling those routes of the network. Break-bulk centers, apart from being labor-intensive, required a high degree of coordination among shipment arrivals and departures in order to achieve maximum speed and efficiency at the lowest cost. Yellow accomplished this with the 1971 installation of a computer-monitoring system, based in the Kansas City command center, placing it at the forefront of the industry. The use of computer technology allowed Yellow to track each shipment precisely, improving information flow within the company and with its customers as well, while gaining a finely tuned coordination of shipment arrivals and departures at its break-bulk centers.

These innovations, and tight discipline, brought the company's operating ratio to among the lowest in the industry. Further acquisitions—of Adley Express in 1973, Republic Freight Systems in 1975, and Braswell Motor Freight in 1977—strengthened its route network into the Pacific Northwest, the Southeast, and throughout the Southwest. By then, Yellow had reached 44 states, operated more than 220 terminals, and, despite dramatic rises in fuel prices since the 1973 Arab oil embargo, sustained an average 32 percent return on equity. During this time, George Powell stepped down as chairman, and his son George, Jr., took over. Despite a misadventure into oil and gas exploration—the company opened Overland Energy Company in 1976, which lost some $60 million by the end of the decade—Yellow underwent a period of sustained growth throughout the 1970s.

Key Dates:

1924: Oklahoma City cab driver A.J. Harrell establishes Yellow Transit Company, a trucking operation.

1944: A.J. Harrell sells Yellow Transit, and the company is renamed Yellow Transit Freight Lines.

1951: Yellow declares bankruptcy.

1952: George Powell purchases Yellow Transit.

1965: Yellow acquires Watson-Wilson Transportation System, doubling its size.

1968: Company changes its name to Yellow Freight System.

1992: Yellow enters the regional less-than-truckload (LTL) market with the purchase of Preston Trucking Company.

1993: Yellow Freight restructures into a holding company, changing its name to Yellow Corporation.

1996: A. Maurice Myers becomes CEO and president of Yellow Corporation, launching the company on a restructuring program.

1998: Yellow forms global subsidiary YCS International; the company acquires Action Express and sells Preston Trucking.

1999: Yellow acquires Jevic Transportation; A. Maurice Myers resigns.

2000: Yellow forms online subsidiary Transportation .com.

1980s–90s: A More Competitive Market

The 1980 deregulation of the trucking industry, amid a wave of deregulation that occurred during the Reagan administration, caught Yellow by surprise. Gone were the restrictions on truck routes, and with it the $34 million per year Yellow earned through licensing fees charged to other companies to use its routes. When deregulation came, Yellow discovered that its terminals, depots, and break-bulk centers had fallen behind advances in the industry, at a time when these facilities had become more crucial to the LTL market than ever before. Yellow's main competitors, Consolidated Freightways and Roadway Express, had gained the edge on both break-bulk handling and broader route systems, each with a wider, larger array of state-of-the-art terminals and depots. By the end of 1981, Yellow had laid off 20 percent of its workers.

Yellow's profits continued to fall through 1983. However, Powell, Jr., and his son, George Powell III, who had entered the family's business some years earlier, began a crash program to upgrade its facilities, converting 17 terminals into additional break-bulk centers in two years. Yellow also increased its LTL freight contracts to encompass nearly two-thirds of its business, and by 1985, Yellow had expanded its number of terminals to 600. The intense competition that followed deregulation closed many trucking companies, and by 1986, Yellow was once again assured of its number three position in the industry. With only Alaska left unrepresented in the United States, Yellow created a terminal there in 1987. As it entered the 1990s, Yellow, now led by George Powell III, turned to international expansion into Mexico, Puerto Rico, and Canada.

Yellow's revenues had passed $2 billion. Yet discounting across the industry, a series of Teamster strikes, higher fuel and labor costs, and a slow softening of the LTL market began to cut into Yellow's profits. Yellow boosted its competitive edge with a series of innovations, including computer software to enable its customers to track their shipments, as well as the introduction of its Metroliner two-day service and its guaranteed Express Lane service, which offered expedited shipments. Yellow entered Mexico in 1991, forming Yellow Freight Mexicana, and further increased its Canadian presence.

Yellow also began to eye entry into the growing regional LTL market, reasoning that its customers wanted a company that could handle both their regional and national needs. In 1992, Yellow bought the ailing Preston Trucking Company, a regional and interregional LTL carrier, for $24 million and the assumption of that company's $116 million in debts and loans. After restructuring, including a temporary 9 percent pay cut to its workers, Preston was profitable again by 1993. The purchase of Preston brought Yellow into the important regional markets of the Northeast and South. However, drivers at both Yellow Freight and Preston were represented by the Teamsters union, leaving Yellow increasingly vulnerable to the threat of strikes. In 1992, Yellow formed a Texas subsidiary, Yellow Transportation, extending its regional business in that important state. Significantly, Yellow Transportation leased its trucks and hired only non-union drivers. In 1993, Yellow Freight restructured as a holding company for its subsidiaries, changing its name to Yellow Corporation. Also in 1993, the company acquired Saia Motor Freight Line, a southern LTL carrier.

Yellow's steady growth had slowed, however, as it entered the mid-1990s. A 24-day Teamster strike in 1994 resulted in more than $25 million in losses for Yellow, while the rough winter of that year further slowed the trucking industry and depressed profits. LTL demand continued to slow, and discounting among truckers became more and more competitive. A 5 percent wage increase instituted in April 1995—a result of 1994's Teamsters strike—further ate into Yellow's earnings, and the company posted a $30 million loss for the year.

In early 1996, with the company floundering, George Powell III resigned from his post as president and CEO. He was replaced by A. Maurice Myers. Myers, previously the president and COO of America West Airlines, had gained a reputation as a "turnaround leader." With Myers at the helm, Yellow wasted little time making changes. Yellow Freight, the company's main subsidiary, was reorganized into five business units, decentralizing decision making and placing a greater emphasis on responding to customers' needs. Almost 250 jobs were eliminated in the restructuring. Even so, 1996's numbers were far from encouraging. With revenues remaining flat, Yellow ended the year with a $27.12 million loss.

But in 1997, the company began to reap the rewards of its cost-reduction efforts; it moved back into the black with year-end income of $52.4 million. In a January 28, 1998 press release, Myers attributed the improvement largely to $145 million in savings at Yellow Freight, and indicated that in the coming year, Yellow Corp. would focus on reducing expenses at its other subsidiaries as well.

Myers's turnaround plan did not consist solely of cost-cutting. He believed that for Yellow to be successful it had to become more flexible and diverse, offering a portfolio of services rather than strictly less-than-truckload shipping. Toward that end, the company spent 1998 and 1999 pursuing expansion both at home and overseas. In June 1998, Yellow formed a new subsidiary—YCS International—to serve as Yellow's international carrier. Through alliances with various international partners, YCS (which was renamed Yellow Global in 2000) allowed the company to offer shippers greater geographic coverage.

Yellow also made two key acquisitions. In 1998, it acquired Action Express, a regional carrier that expanded the company's inter-regional coverage to the Pacific Northwest. A year later, Yellow acquired Jevic Transportation, a regional carrier covering the eastern and midwestern parts of the country. Meanwhile, Yellow rid itself of its struggling subsidiary Preston Trucking. In November 1999, having restored Yellow to profitability, the company's ''turnaround CEO,'' Maurice Myers, resigned. He was replaced by William Zollars, who had served as the president of Yellow Freight since 1996 and had been instrumental in the restructuring at that subsidiary.

Entering a New Century

Yellow began the 21st century in a fitting way—by entering the new economy. In February 2000, the company partnered with two venture capital firms to form Transportation.com, an online transportation management company. Transportation.com provided logistics services such as shipment and inventory management and tracking to small and medium-sized businesses. Yellow believed that its online subsidiary could be a big earner, since it would have a much higher profit margin than the asset-based trucking subsidiaries.

In 2000, Yellow Corporation recorded the best financial performance in its history, with net income of $68 million—a 33 percent increase over the previous year. In 2001, however, a weakening economy caused the company's earnings to decrease significantly. In a June 2001 interview with CNNfn, Yellow CEO Bill Zollars said that the company planned to deal with the downturn by continuing to build broader capabilities, focusing on high-growth global services and looking for ways to reduce expenses until the economy rebounded. Zollars also indicated that much of Yellow's future growth would come from acquisition, as the transportation services industry continued to consolidate.

Principal Subsidiaries

Jevic Transportation, Inc.; Saia Motor Freight Line, Inc.; Yellow Freight System, Inc.; Yellow Global, Inc.; Yellow Technologies, Inc.

Principal Competitors

Arkansas Best Corporation; Consolidated Freightways Corporation; Roadway Corporation.

Further Reading

Baird, J., ''Yellow Quietly Rolls into Texas, Sets up Non-Union Regional Unit,'' *Journal of Commerce and Commercial,* August 4, 1992, p. B2.

Bonney, J., ''Yellow Freight Eyes Pacific Rim,'' *American Shipper,* January 1995, p. 62.

''CEO Interview, William Zollars,'' *Wall Street Transcript*, January 8, 2001.

Coletti, R., ''Yellow Freight: To the Victor, the Spoils?'' *Financial World,* January 8, 1991, p. 18.

Isidore, Chris, ''Cost Controls Spur Yellow Corp. to an Unexpected Profit,'' *Journal of Commerce and Commercial,* April 20, 1995, p. 3B.

——, ''Yellow, M.S., PST Warn Earnings May Disappoint,'' *Journal of Commerce and Commercial,* June 9, 1995, p. B3.

Lang, Amanda, ''Yellow Corp. CEO,'' *CNNfn: Business Unusual,* June 6, 2001.

McCartney, Robert J., ''Kansas Firm Agrees to Buy Preston Corp. for $24 Million,'' *Washington Post,* November 21, 1992, p. C1.

''Preston's Quick Turnaround,'' *Distribution,* November 1993, p. 18.

Watson, Rip, ''Teamsters Strike Costs 2 Carriers $90 Million,'' *Journal of Commerce and Commercial,* June 16, 1994, p. 1A.

——, ''Yellow Freight Is 1st LTL to Announce Price Rises for '95,'' *Journal of Commerce and Commercial,* November 22, 1994.

—update: Shawna Brynildssen

YWCA of the U.S.A.

Empire State Building
350 Fifth Avenue, Suite 301
New York, New York 10118
U.S.A.
Telephone: (212) 273-7800
Toll Free: (800) 992-2871
Fax: (212) 465-2281
Web site: http://www.ywca.org

Nonprofit Company
Incorporated: 1907
Sales: $8.9 million (2000)
NAIC: 62411 Child and Youth Services; 624221
Temporary Shelters; 62419 Other Individual and
Family Services; 62441 Child Day Care Services;
713940 Health Club Facilities, Physical Fitness

The YWCA of the U.S.A. is a nonprofit organization dedicated to improving the lives of women and girls. The organization is headquartered in New York, and it operates through over 300 local YWCAs, found in urban and rural areas across the country. The YWCA is the nation's largest nonprofit provider of child care. Its daycare and after-school care programs serve 750,000 children annually. The organization is also the nation's largest provider of shelter services for women and children. The YWCA also provides employment training and placement agencies through its local branches. Besides childcare, housing and shelter, and economic empowerment, the YWCA is concerned with five other key issues. These are: health and fitness, leadership development, racial justice and human rights, violence prevention, and global awareness. The YWCA runs public awareness campaigns around these issues. The organization sponsors a Week Without Violence, a National Day of Commitment to Eliminate Racism, the National Women & Girls in Sport Day, and runs other programs and services designed to highlight these important areas. The association's revenue derives from membership dues, grants, donations, and corporate sponsorships.

Roots in 19th-Century Religious Revival

The YWCA incorporated as a national organization in 1907 in the state of New York, but it had existed in other forms from as early as the 1850s. The current organization traces its roots back to two groups in England. The Prayer Union was a group founded by Emma Roberts in 1855. This changed its name within its first four years to the Young Women's Christian Association. Another English group, the General Female Training Institute, founded by Mrs. Arthur Kinnaird in 1855, began as an organization to help nurses returning from the Crimean war, but quickly adopted a larger scope, helping women and girls of all walks of life. Both groups had local chapters throughout England, where their main objective was to help working women, both economically and spiritually. More and more women were being displaced from traditional homemaking tasks by industrialization. Work that had always fallen to women, such as sewing and weaving, became transformed into factory jobs. As single women began taking up such jobs, they faced difficulties they had not faced before, such as finding housing. The General Female Training Institute and the Young Women's Christian Association merged in 1877 and carried on work in England. Similar groups formed in Germany, Switzerland, and the United States.

In the United States, several groups grew up independently of each other. New York City had a Union Prayer Circle by 1858, which soon changed its name to the Ladies' Christian Association. The group organized prayer circles and meetings among young working women. The group metamorphosed into the Ladies Christian Union in 1866, and then into the Young Ladies Christian Association of the City of New York in 1871. Similarly, Boston had a Young Women's Christian Association in 1866. Though not formally linked to the English group, the organization carried out the same sort of work, tending to the various needs of employed women. Other groups were formed in 1867 in Providence, Rhode Island; Hartford, Connecticut; and Pittsburgh, Pennsylvania. Young Women's Christian Associations formed in the midwestern cities of St. Louis, Missouri, and in Cleveland and Cincinnati, Ohio, the next year. By 1875, there were at least 28 Young Women's Christian Associations in the United States. These groups ran prayer meetings and Bible classes and provided services such as libraries and sewing schools. Several owned restaurants and provided entertainment for their members, and some provided temporary housing.

In urban areas, the main problems the YWCAs addressed were housing and employment. They began running self-support-

Company Perspectives:

Our mission is to empower women and girls and to eliminate racism. The Young Women's Christian Association of the United States of America is a women's membership movement nourished by its roots in the Christian faith and sustained by the richness of many beliefs and values. Strengthened by diversity, the Association draws together members who strive to create opportunities for women's growth, leadership and power in order to attain a common vision: peace, justice, freedom, and dignity for all people. The Association will thrust its collective power toward the elimination of racism wherever it exists and by any means necessary.

ing boarding houses, with meeting rooms for study or entertainment. Social workers as such did not exist, but volunteers ran employment bureaus and helped address many needs of young workers. YWCA members also took on specific local projects, such as providing clothing for orphans or prisoners, or conducting religious services in hospitals. Beginning in 1873, YWCA chapters also began appearing on college campuses. The first was at Normal University, in Normal, Illinois. Most of the youth chapters were in the Midwest, while most of the non-college chapters were in cities in the East. The YWCA began having national meetings in 1871, of what was then called its International Board. The youth chapters set up their own national headquarters in Chicago in 1886, called the American Committee. The two groups had similar aims, but different ages of membership. The youth group also had a slightly different religious bent than the chapters belonging to the International Board, based on which churches they accepted voting members from. The two groups voted to combine at a meeting in December 1906, forming an umbrella group called the Young Women's Christian Association of the United States of America. The group incorporated in New York in 1907. Its first president was Grace Dodge, an independently wealthy woman long active in the YWCA and similar charities around New York. In 1907 membership had grown to over 186,000 women, spread among 608 local YWCAs. In 1911, the group gained a headquarters building in New York, mostly financed by six well-to-do members.

Work on Various Fronts in the Early 20th Century

Though the YWCA was now under a single national umbrella, it remained a decentralized group. Local branches carried out a variety of missions. In the early 20th century, many YWCA chapters ran training schools. These offered classes on various subjects, many at night, so women could attend after working hours. The New York City YWCA gave classes in typewriting, which was revolutionary at the time, as typewriting was considered too difficult both mentally and physically for women to undertake. Training schools offered general business courses, classes in public speaking and elocution, and even some more specialized subjects including nursing or tea room management. By the 1920s, there were at least 40 YWCA training schools in urban areas across the country.

The YWCA also undertook to promote the interests of immigrants and black women. YWCA residences and training schools reached out to women born abroad. Many offered classes in

English, and help with employment and naturalization and citizenship issues. The YWCA sponsored clubs for immigrants, with the idea of helping women and girls adjust to American life. These clubs had spread to over 50 cities by the 1920s. The YWCA's relationship to black women varied from city to city. Many YWCA facilities barred black women, though not all. In many cities, the YWCA worked hand-in-hand with organizations run for and by black women, such as the Phyllis Wheatley Association and the National Association of Colored Women. As early as 1907, the YWCA's national board discussed the issue of racial segregation, and at the 1914 national meeting, the board proclaimed its readiness to meet the special needs of black women and girls. However, the board did not set a national policy, and each local branch operated as it saw fit. Some chapters were fully integrated, some local boards met jointly with the boards of affiliated groups for black women, and some chapters did not serve non-white women. This hodge-podge existed until 1946. In that year, the YWCA national board agreed to strive to fully integrate the organization. Fighting racial injustice became a core mission of the group.

The YWCA was also active early in the century in promoting women's access to healthcare and health education. The group worked toward what it called "positive health" for women beginning in 1906. Positive health meant specifically sex education, with a focus on avoiding venereal disease. In 1913 the YWCA debuted a Commission on Social Morality, and the group taught sex education, usually under the names "social education" or "social morality." The YWCA dealt with a vulnerable population of women just leaving their families to live on their own. The YWCA promoted frank discussion of sex in order to prepare young women to protect themselves from venereal disease, unwanted pregnancy, and prostitution. The YWCA worked with the War Department during World War I, lecturing on sex education. In the 1920s and 1930s, the YWCA also worked to promote access to birth control. At that time, wealthy women could travel to Europe for contraceptive services not available in the United States. The national board voted in 1934 to support women's access to contraception from authorized doctors. In the 1960s and 1970s the group also voted to support women's access to abortions.

The YWCA also ran health and fitness programs for women. The Buffalo, New York YWCA residence had a swimming pool as early as 1905, when this was still a rarity. Local chapters often worked with employers to instruct women workers in moderate physical exercise. Early in the century, the prevailing view was that women were too frail for the kinds of sports activities that men indulged in. The YWCA led the way in changing attitudes about women's physical fitness. Chapters gave classes in calisthenics and various sports.

Though the association remained decentralized, spread among hundreds of local chapters, the national board met every two years and adopted over-arching goals. In 1930, at the beginning of the Great Depression, the YWCA met in Detroit. The group vowed to improve working conditions for employed women and girls, and also to cope with the problems of unemployment. At the 1932 meeting, the YWCA endorsed national compulsory unemployment insurance. In 1942, during World War II, the YWCA began serving the Japanese-Americans who were being held in internment camps as enemy aliens. The YWCA worked in the camps, and also helped resettle internees

Key Dates:

1855: Prayer Union and General Female Training Institute is founded in England.
1866: Young Women's Christian Association is formed in Boston.
1871: First national meeting of local YWCAs convenes.
1907: YWCA of the U.S.A. incorporates in New York.
1913: YWCA organizes its Commission on Social Morality.
1942: Association works with Japanese-Americans interned during war.
1970: Association adopts imperative to battle racism.
1995: Week Without Violence campaign debuts.

after the war. During the war, many local YWCA chapters also ran special programs for war workers and their families. The group helped house women munitions plant workers, provided child care and education to other groups of war workers, and assisted in some social functions at military bases. The group had a National War Fund, for war-related relief work, mostly overseas. The YWCA also began a fundraising group called American War-Community Services, to disperse money to community groups helping women and children.

National Issues After World War II

After the war, the YWCA continued its varied programs through local chapters. A major development was the group's renewed focus on fighting racism. The organization adopted a charter in 1946 committing the group to protesting racial injustice. The new Interracial Charter made the elimination of racism a central goal of the YWCA. Work was carried out through individual local branches. In 1958, the national board voted to intensify its efforts to desegregate the organization at all levels. Its programs and services were to be offered to women and families of all races, and the leadership of local groups and the national organization were to be more inclusive. In the 1960s, the YWCA held institutes on racism at different branches across the country. In 1965 it established a national Office of Racial Justice to coordinate a national campaign against racism. In 1970, the national convention added to its mission statement what it called the One Imperative—"The Association will thrust its collective power toward the elimination of racism wherever it exists and by any means necessary." Later in the 1970s the group followed this rhetoric with an auditing system to verify how well the YWCA was meeting its goal, and how communities were faring.

The organization also continued its stress on women's physical fitness and sex education. In 1970, the national board voted to work with local schools to ask that they provide sex education as part of the curriculum. The YWCA was also outspoken in its support of abortion rights. The group supported repeal of laws that limited women's access to abortion. In 1987 the organization reiterated this support, and also proclaimed its opposition to laws that mandated parental consent before an abortion could be performed. The local chapters continued to sponsor sports and fitness classes for girls and women, and to operate summer camps and summer programs.

In 1983, the YWCA opened a new facility in Phoenix, Arizona, to train women in leadership skills. This gave the YWCA a permanent center where it could educate and train women from all over the country in the goals and policies of the national group. Women learned what goals the national organization had, and strategies for taking action. Later the YWCA also founded the Institute for Public Leadership. This trained women to be advocates for issues, and to be political candidates or campaign managers. The institute taught women how to do research, marketing, and planning for entering local political races.

1990s and Beyond

By 1992, the YWCA had 400 local associations, which worked out of more than 4,000 sites. The group had grown to become the number one nonprofit provider of shelter services for women and families in the United States. Whereas its early residences had mostly housed young working women, the group increasingly cared for homeless women and victims of domestic violence. It had also become one of the largest providers of child care services in the nation. By 1992, 85 percent of all YWCAs provided some sort of child care. The group found a new national leader in 1994, Prema Mathai-Davis. Mathai-Davis was born in India and educated at Harvard. She instituted a new campaign, the YWCA Week Without Violence. The first Week Without Violence was held in October 1995. During the week, local groups across the country held workshops on topics such as domestic violence prevention and students signed petitions pledging nonviolent behavior. The public awareness campaign reached hundreds of thousands of people across the country.

In 1999, the YWCA vowed to revitalize itself for the coming new century. The national group wanted to improve its customer relations and restructure its management. The group served 750,000 children through its day care services, gave employment training and placement services to about 100,000 women a year, and counseled over 700,000 women and children annually in violence prevention. Overall, the group claimed to represent some two million women, girls, and their families. The group chose a new chief executive in November 2000, appointing Margaret Tyndall to the top spot. Tyndall strove to continue the YWCA's longstanding mission, advocating for women's rights, fighting for the elimination of racism, and providing meaningful services to women and families.

Further Reading

Golden, Kristen, "Prema Mathai-Davis," *Ms.*, January/February 1996, p. 61.
Sims, Mary S., *The YWCA—An Unfolding Purpose*, New York: Woman's Press, 1950.
Southard, Helen, *The Story of the YWCA*, New York: YWCA, 1992.
Spain, Daphne, *How Women Saved the City*, Minneapolis: University of Minneapolis Press, 2001.

—Angela Woodward

Zimmer Holdings, Inc.

345 E. Main Street
Warsaw, Indiana 46580
U.S.A.
Telephone: (219) 267-6131
Toll Free: (800) 613-6131
Fax: (219) 372-4988
Web site: http://www.zimmer.com

Public Company
Incorporated: 1927 as Zimmer Manufacturing Company
Employees: 3,200
Sales: $1.04 billion (2000)
Stock Exchanges: New York
Ticker Symbol: ZMH
NAIC: 339113 Surgical Appliance and Supplies
  Manufacturing

Zimmer Holdings, Inc. is a global leader in orthopedic implants and fracture management devices and is a publicly traded company listed on the S&P 500. In 2001, Zimmer was spun off as an independent company from Bristol-Myers Squibb. Fully 40 percent of its sales originate outside the United States. Zimmer's headquarters are in Warsaw, Indiana, with manufacturing facilities in Warsaw, as well as Dover, Ohio, and Statesville, North Carolina.

Justin Zimmer—From Sales Manager to Entrepreneur: 1920s

Justin Zimmer was a national sales manager for DePuy, a splint company located in Warsaw, Indiana. He sold splints for the DePuy Company for 20 years and knew the market and the product. In 1926, he came up with a new product idea for aluminum splints; however, his employer was not interested in pursuing the idea or Zimmer's request to purchase an interest in the company. In fact, the widow of the company's founder told him, "You know, Justin, you are just small potatoes."

Justin Zimmer saw no choice but to start his own company, and in 1927 Zimmer Manufacturing Company was born. He found two investors, William Felkner and William Rogers, and recruited two of his coworkers to join him in the new venture. J.J. Ettinger was the factory manager, and Donna Belle Harmon Cox, who had been his secretary at DePuy, was secretary and bookkeeper at the new company. The Zimmers' basement provided the first manufacturing site for the company; by May 1927, the company had products available for display.

Mrs. DePuy may have regretted her hasty words to Justin Zimmer. In just one year, Zimmer Manufacturing was outselling DePuy and the new aluminum splints were in high demand. The company soon moved to a building on North Detroit Street in Warsaw, Indiana. In the first seven months, Zimmer had sales of $160,000. During the boom years of the 1920s, Zimmer grew quickly. In 1928, the company developed a fracture bed with a system to support patients while hospital sheets were changed, and the company embraced the international market early in its history with the first order coming from a surgeon in Scotland.

1930s and 1940s: Steady Growth Through Depression and War Years

While most of the businesses in the United States were experiencing major problems and downturns due to the Depression in the 1930s, Zimmer's sales and business continued to grow. Despite a high unemployment rate and mass layoffs across other industries, Zimmer had no layoffs during the difficult decade. In fact, during the Bank Holiday in 1933, the employees at Zimmer worked overtime to finish manufacturing a large shipment of splints for hospitals in New York City.

In 1930, sales topped $200,000. Zimmer was a key player during the polio epidemic in the late 1930s and developed custom fabricating braces that could be fitted to each patient's specific measurements. In that same time period, the company also introduced Dr. Vernon Luck's bone saw, complete with a motor and cord that could be sterilized. By 1942, Zimmer's sales exceeded $1 million.

New Developments: 1950s–60s

In 1951, Justin Zimmer died while on vacation in Florida, but he left behind a successful company that would continue to bear his name. Zimmer's sales topped $2 million, and the

Company Perspectives:

Our strategic objective is to become the leader in the design, development, manufacturing and marketing of orthopedic reconstructive implants and fracture management products. Our goals are to: increase market share in our product categories by offering innovative new products and striving to provide comprehensive solutions in these product categories; target strategically important geographic regions and develop products that correspond to the surgical philosophies common to those regions; expand our product and service offerings to cover high-growth categories in our industry on which we do not currently focus; and continue our efforts to offer alternative therapies for patients with arthritis, including co-marketing drug therapies and developing and marketing biological therapies and minimally invasive surgical procedures.

company made several significant developments. The first hip prosthesis, developed with Dr. Palmer Eicher, was marketed by Zimmer in the 1950s, and the company released the Harrington Spinal Instrument, used to treat scoliosis, in 1958. The company worked closely with the American Medical Association to develop products that would benefit medicine and health.

By 1960, Zimmer's annual sales were $4 million, and its foreign sales increased with the opening of an Export Department within the company. The company continued to grow and, in 1968, an expansion was planned for the manufacturing facility in Warsaw. In 1969, Zimmer purchased Little Manufacturing Company in North Carolina.

Part of Bristol-Myers: 1970s–2000

In 1970, total employment at Zimmer reached 522 people and sales were $27.2 million. The company's growth had been steady throughout the years and thus attracted the attention of an interested buyer. Zimmer became a subsidiary of Bristol-Myers, a New York-based medical company, in 1972. While operating as a subsidiary, Zimmer continued to grow and develop new products. The development of new tools allowed that innovation to accelerate with the availability of CAD/CAM systems by the end of the 1970s. The new technology helped Zimmer race ahead with the development of such products as a hip prosthesis and the total knee system, a fully integrated modular system to replace artificial knees, in the 1980s.

The company helped fuel progress within the industry as well. Zimmer sponsored the first arthroscopy telesession that allowed 1,000 surgeons in 27 cities to view an arthroscopy surgery in real time. Zimmer's parent company, Bristol-Myers, began offering research grants under the Orthopedic Research and Education Foundation in 1983.

In 1990, the company built a new corporate headquarters in Warsaw, Indiana, and in 1997, Ray Elliot joined the Zimmer team as its president. Elliott had previously been vice-president of Bristol-Myers Squibb and had 20 years of experience in the orthopedic industry. He had formerly worked for Baxter International, Southam, Inc., and Cablecom, Inc.

The company experienced rapid sales growth in the 1990s due to new developments and the aging of the Baby Boomer population. In the 1990s, this generation began turning 50 and reaching the age when they might need the orthopedic products and services of Zimmer. In 1998, sales were $861 million, and by 1999, that number had increased to $939 million. With more than 3,200 employees and $1 billion in sales, Zimmer's results for 2000 showed continued growth for the company and its products.

A New Future As Zimmer Holdings, Inc.: 2001 and Beyond

August 7, 2001 was a pivotal date for Zimmer Holdings, Inc. On that date, the company spun off from its parent company, Bristol-Myers Squibb, and began trading on the New York Stock Exchange as an independent company. For nearly 30 years, Zimmer had operated as a subsidiary, and now, it was again its own entity. ''We are excited about the opportunity to operate Zimmer as an independent public company and to continue to strengthen Zimmer's position as a global leader in orthopedics,'' said President and CEO Ray Elliot in a company press release. ''Zimmer's recent financial performance has been excellent, and we plan to continue to pursue opportunities to leverage our brand and sales force in high-growth adjacent orthopedic product categories.''

The company was selected by Standard & Poor's to be a part of the S&P 500 Index. In an interview with CNNfn on August 7, 2001, Elliot commented that he heard about the S&P 500 selection while on the road at a trade show. ''We were hopeful of that, but it's an opportunity. We're actually the—I'm told; at least—we're the largest healthcare spinoff or IPO in the history of the business. So at a market cap of . . . more than $5 billion, it's pretty exciting times,'' he said.

The company received Frost & Sullivan's Market Engineering Award for Sales Strategy Leadership in September 2001. Zimmer's sales force received the award due to the company's unique strategy of technical expertise and cooperation with the physician community. The company continued its close relationship within the medical community and announced the formation of a business team to further develop minimally invasive surgery options for hip surgery replacement.

The newly spun off company also experienced challenges in 2001. The Japanese Fair Trade Commission brought unfair pricing practice allegations against the company and three other orthopedic companies. A major share of Zimmer's international business was located in Japan, and the company announced that its pricing practices did comply with the Japanese government regulations and that it was in full cooperation during the investigation. The commission alleged that Zimmer and the other companies had formed a cartel to fix prices in the country.

In the third quarter of 2001, Zimmer's first quarter as an independent publicly traded company, the company increased sales by 14 percent worldwide and 22 percent in North and South America. As other segments of the economy were sluggish during a late 2001 recession, Zimmer's sales continued to increase and the company was on track to achieve its 13 percent sales increase for the year. The company's products by 2001

Key Dates:

1927: Company is founded by Justin Zimmer.
1928: Zimmer lands its first international customer.
1942: Sales reach $1 million.
1951: Founder Justin Zimmer dies.
1972: Zimmer becomes a subsidiary of Bristol-Myers.
1997: Ray Elliot joins Zimmer as president and CEO.
2001: Zimmer spins off to become Zimmer Holdings, Inc.

included knee implants, hip implants, and fracture management products, as well as other surgical products, including tourniquets, blood management systems, and orthopedic soft goods.

Just as Zimmer embraced CAD/CAM technology in the 1970s, it embraced the technology of the new millennium by working in conjunction with Alteer Office to market Internet-based management systems to orthopedic surgeons. The software provided a solution to paperwork and administration challenges, giving the surgeon more time to focus on medical advances. The company's close relationship with the surgical community allowed it to provide the surgeons with tools to increase productivity both in and out of the operating room. "A key Zimmer strategy is to focus on solutions that improve the entire system of care for patients, physicians, providers and payers," said President and CEO Ray Elliott. "We've demonstrated that through our leadership in minimally invasive orthopedic surgery, and by partnering with Alteer, we're extending our ability to provide solutions beyond the operating room."

With aggressive product development and a history of growth, Zimmer Holdings, Inc. looked ahead to even greater goals. An aging population was one positive indicator for the company's future. The U.S. Census Bureau estimated that the number of people over 65 would increase to 39.7 billion by 2010. Better alternatives for orthopedic surgery and less invasive options were expected to increase the number of people who participated in the surgeries. Population and technological advances were just two of the many factors that translated into future success for the company—an innovator in the orthopedics industry since Justin Zimmer and his aluminum splints in 1927.

Principal Competitors

Biomet, Inc.; Smith & Nephew plc; Stryker Corporation.

Further Reading

Nicklaus, David, "Shares in Spinoffs Can Clutter Up a Small Investor's Portfolio," *St. Louis Post-Dispatch,* September 1, 2001, p. 1.

Sherman, Debra, "Indiana City Thrives on Artificial Joints," *Reuters Business Report,* December 9, 2001.

"A Spinoff at Bristol-Myers," *New York Times,* August 7, 2001, p. C7.

"Warsaw, Ind.-Based Orthopedics Implant Maker Reports Financial Results," *News Sentinel,* July 26, 2001.

"Warsaw, Ind.-Based Orthopedics Implant Maker Zimmer Joins a Stock Index," *News Sentinel,* August 20, 2001.

—Melissa Rigney Baxter

INDEX TO COMPANIES

Index to Companies

Listings in this index are arranged in alphabetical order under the company name. Company names beginning with a letter or proper name such as Eli Lilly & Co. will be found under the first letter of the company name. Definite articles (The, Le, La) are ignored for alphabetical purposes as are forms of incorporation that precede the company name (AB, NV). Company names printed in bold type have full, historical essays on the page numbers appearing in bold. Updates to entries that appeared in earlier volumes are signified by the notation **(upd.)**. Company names in light type are references within an essay to that company, not full historical essays. This index is cumulative with volume numbers printed in bold type.

Public National Bank, **II** 230
Public Savings Insurance Co., **III** 219
Public Service Co., **14** 124
Public Service Company of Colorado, **6**
558–60
Public Service Company of Indiana. *See*
PSI Energy.
Public Service Company of New
Hampshire, **21 408–12**
Public Service Company of New Mexico,
6 561–64; **27** 486
Public Service Corporation of New Jersey,
44 360
Public Service Electric and Gas Company,
IV 366; **V** 701–03; **11** 388
Public Service Enterprise Group Inc., **V**
701–03; **44 360–63 (upd.)**
Public Service Market. *See* The Golub
Corporation.
Public Storage, Inc., **21** 476
Public/Hacienda Resorts, Inc. *See* Santa Fe
Gaming Corporation.
Publicaciones Citem, S.A. de C.V., **39** 188
Publicis S.A., **13** 204; **19 329–32**; **21**
265–66; **23** 478, 480; **25** 91; **33** 180; **39**
166, 168; **42** 328, 331
Publicker Industries Inc., **I** 226; **10** 180
Publishers Clearing House, **23 393–95**;
27 20
Publishers Group, Inc., **35 357–59**
Publishers Paper Co., **IV** 295, 677–78; **19**
225
Publishers Press Assoc., **IV** 607; **25** 506
Publishing and Broadcasting Ltd., **19**
400–01
Publix Super Markets Inc., **II** 155, 627; **7**
440–42; **9** 186; **20** 84, 306; **23** 261; **31**
371–374 (upd.)
Puck Holdings, **35** 474, 476
Puck Lazaroff Inc. *See* The Wolfgang Puck
Food Company, Inc.
Puente Oil, **IV** 385
Puerto Rican Aqueduct and Sewer
Authority, **6** 441
Puerto Rican-American Insurance Co., **III**
242
Puget Mill Company, **12** 406–07
Puget Sound Alaska Van Lines. *See* Alaska
Hydro-Train.
Puget Sound National Bank, **8** 469–70
Puget Sound Power And Light
Company, **6 565–67**
Puget Sound Pulp and Timber Co., **IV** 281;
9 259
Puget Sound Tug and Barge Company, **6**
382
Pulaski Furniture Corporation, **33**
349–52
Pulitzer Publishing Company, **15 375–77**
Pullman Co., **II** 403; **III** 94, 744
Pullman Savings and Loan Association, **17**
529
Pullman Standard, **7** 540
Pulsar Internacional S.A., **21 413–15**
Pulse Engineering, Inc., **29** 461
Pulte Corporation, **8 436–38**; **22** 205,
207
Pulte Homes, Inc., **42 291–94 (upd.)**
Puma AG Rudolf Dassler Sport, **35**
360–63; **36** 344, 346
AB Pump-Separator, **III** 418–19
Punchcraft, Inc., **III** 569; **20** 360
Purdue Fredrick Company, **13** 367
Pure Milk Products Cooperative, **11** 24

Pure Oil Co., **III** 497; **IV** 570; **24** 521
Pure Packed Foods, **II** 525; **13** 293
Purex Corporation, **I** 450; **III** 21; **22** 146
Purex Pool Systems, **I** 13, 342; **18** 163
Purfina, **IV** 497
Purina Mills, Inc., **32 376–79**
Puris Inc., **14** 316
Puritan-Bennett Corporation, **13 419–21**
Puritan Chemical Co., **I** 321
Puritan Fashions Corp., **22** 122
Purity Stores, **I** 146
Purity Supreme, Inc., **II** 674; **24** 462
Purle Bros., **III** 735
Purnell & Sons Ltd., **IV** 642; **7** 312
Purodenso Co., **III** 593
Purolator Courier, Inc., **6** 345–46, 390; **16**
397; **18** 177; **25** 148
Purolator Products Company, **III** 593;
21 416–18; **28** 263
Puros de Villa Gonzales, **23** 465
Purup-Eskofot, **44** 44
Push Records, Inc., **42** 271
Puss 'n Boots, **II** 559
Putnam Investments Inc., **25** 387; **30** 355.
See also Marsh & McLennan
Companies, Inc.
Putnam Management Co., **III** 283
Putnam Reinsurance Co., **III** 198
Putt-Putt Golf Courses of America, Inc.,
23 396–98
PWA Group, **IV 323–25**; **28** 446
PWS Holding Corporation, **13** 406; **26** 47
PWT Projects Ltd., **22** 89
PWT Worldwide, **11** 510
PYA/Monarch, **II** 675; **26** 504
Pyramid Breweries Inc., **33 353–55**
Pyramid Communications, Inc., **IV** 623
Pyramid Electric Company, **10** 319
Pyramid Electronics Supply, Inc., **17** 275
Pyramid Technology Corporation, **10** 504;
27 448
Pytchley Autocar Co. Ltd., **IV** 722
Pyxis. *See* Cardinal Health, Inc.
Pyxis Resources Co., **IV** 182

Q Lube, Inc., **18** 145; **24** 339
Qantas Airways Limited, **I** 92–93; **6** 79,
91, 100, 105, **109–13**, 117; **14** 70, 73;
24 396–401 (upd.); **27** 466; **31** 104; **38**
24
Qatar General Petroleum Corporation,
IV 524–26
Qiagen N.V., **39 333–35**
Qintex Australia Ltd., **II** 150; **25** 329
QMS Ltd., **43** 284
QO Chemicals, Inc., **14** 217
QSP, Inc., **IV** 664
Qtera Corporation, **36** 352
Quad/Graphics, Inc., **19 333–36**
Quail Oil Tools, **28** 347–48
Quaker Alloy, Inc., **39** 31–32
Quaker Fabric Corp., **19 337–39**
Quaker Oats Company, **I** 30; **II 558–60**,
575, 684; **12** 167, 169, **409–12 (upd.)**;
13 186; **22** 131, 337–38; **25** 90, 314; **27**
197; **30** 219; **31** 282; **34 363–67 (upd.)**;
38 349; **43** 121, 218
Quaker State Corporation, **7 443–45**; **21**
419–22 (upd.); **25** 90; **26** 349
Qualcomm Inc., **20 438–41**; **26** 532; **38**
271; **39** 64; **41** 289; **43** 312–13
Qualicare, Inc., **6** 192
QualiTROL Corporation, **7** 116–17
Quality Bakers of America, **12** 170

Quality Care Inc., **I** 249
Quality Courts Motels, Inc., **14** 105. *See*
also Choice Hotels International, Inc.
Quality Dining, Inc., **18 437–40**
Quality Food Centers, Inc., **17 386–88**;
22 271, 273
Quality Importers, **I** 226; **10** 180
Quality Inns International, **13** 363; **14** 105.
See also Choice Hotels International,
Inc.
Quality Markets, Inc., **13** 393
Quality Oil Co., **II** 624–25
Quality Paperback Book Club (QPB), **13**
105–07
Quality Products, Inc., **18** 162
Qualtec, Inc., **V** 623
Quanex Corporation, **13 422–24**
Quantex Microsystems Inc., **24** 31
Quantum Chemical Corporation, **8**
439–41; **11** 441; **30** 231, 441
Quantum Computer Services, Inc. *See*
America Online, Inc.
Quantum Corporation, **6** 230–31; **10** 56,
403, **458–59**, 463; **25** 530; **36** 299–300
Quantum Health Resources, **29** 364
Quantum Marketing International, Inc., **27**
336
Quantum Offshore Contractors, **25** 104
Quantum Overseas N.V., **7** 360
Quantum Restaurant Group, Inc., **30** 330
Quarex Industries, Inc. *See* Western Beef,
Inc.
Quark, Inc., **36 375–79**
Quarrie Corporation, **12** 554
Quasi-Arc Co., **I** 315; **25** 80
Quebec Bank, **II** 344
Quebéc Hydro-Electric Commission. *See*
Hydro-Quebéc.
Quebecor Inc., **12 412–14**; **19** 333; **26** 44;
29 471
Queen Casuals, **III** 530
Queen City Broadcasting, **42** 162
Queen Insurance Co., **III** 350
Queens Isetan Co., Ltd., **V** 87
Queensborough Holdings PLC, **38** 103
Queensland Alumina, **IV** 59
Queensland and Northern Territories Air
Service. *See* Qantas Airways Limited.
Queensland Mines Ltd., **III** 729
Queensland Oil Refineries, **III** 672
Queiroz Pereira, **IV** 504
Quelle Group, **V 165–67**
Quennessen, **IV** 118
Quesarias Ibéricas, **23** 219
Quesnel River Pulp Co., **IV** 269
Quest Aerospace Education, Inc., **18** 521
Quest Diagnostics Inc., **26 390–92**
Quest Education Corporation, **42** 212
Quest Pharmacies Inc., **25** 504–05
Questar Corporation, **6 568–70**; **10** 432;
26 386–89 (upd.)
Questor Partners, **I** 332; **26** 185
The Quick & Reilly Group, Inc., **18** 552;
20 442–44; **26** 65
QUICK Corp., **IV** 656
Quick-Shop, **II** 619
Quicken.com. *See* Intuit Inc.
Quickie Designs, **11** 202, 487–88
Quik Stop Markets, Inc., **12** 112
Quiksilver, Inc., **18 441–43**; **27** 329
QuikTrip Corporation, **36 380–83**
QuikWok Inc., **II** 556; **13** 408
Quill Corporation, **28 375–77**
Quillery, **27** 138

INDEX TO INDUSTRIES

Index to Industries

CONSTRUCTION

ENTERTAINMENT & LEISURE

FINANCIAL SERVICES: BANKS

FOOD PRODUCTS

HEALTH & PERSONAL CARE PRODUCTS

INSURANCE

MATERIALS

PUBLISHING & PRINTING

REAL ESTATE

RETAIL & WHOLESALE

RUBBER & TIRE

TELECOMMUNICATIONS

TEXTILES & APPAREL

TOBACCO

TRANSPORT SERVICES

UTILITIES

WASTE SERVICES

GEOGRAPHIC INDEX

Geographic Index

Germany

NOTES ON CONTRIBUTORS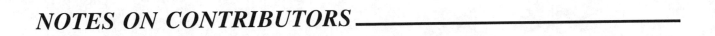

Notes on Contributors

BAXTER, Melissa Rigney. Indiana-based freelance writer.

BIANCO, David P. Freelance writer.

BISCONTINI, Tracey Vasil. Pennsylvania-based freelance writer, editor, and columnist.

BROWN, Susan Windisch. Freelance writer and editor.

BRYNILDSSEN, Shawna. Freelance writer and editor based in Bloomington, Indiana.

COHEN, M. L. Novelist and freelance writer living in Paris.

COVELL, Jeffrey L. Freelance writer and corporate history contractor.

CULLIGAN, Susan B. Minnesota-based freelance writer.

DINGER, Ed. Freelance writer and editor based in Brooklyn, New York.

HALASZ, Robert. Former editor in chief of *World Progress* and *Funk & Wagnalls New Encyclopedia Yearbook*; author, *The U.S. Marines* (Millbrook Press, 1993).

INGRAM, Frederick C. South Carolina-based business writer who has contributed to *GSA Business, Appalachian Trailway News,* the *Encyclopedia of Business,* the *Encyclopedia of Global Industries,* the *Encyclopedia of Consumer Brands,* and other regional and trade publications.

LORENZ, Sarah Ruth. Minnesota-based freelance writer.

PEIPPO, Kathleen. Minneapolis-based freelance writer.

ROTHBURD, Carrie. Freelance writer and editor specializing in corporate profiles, academic texts, and academic journal articles.

SALAMIE, David E. Part-owner of InfoWorks Development Group, a reference publication development and editorial services company.

TRADII, Mary. Freelance writer based in Denver, Colorado.

UHLE, Frank. Ann Arbor-based freelance writer; movie projectionist, disc jockey, and staff member of *Psychotronic Video* magazine.

WALDEN, David M. Freelance writer and historian in Salt Lake City; adjunct history instructor at Salt Lake City Community College.

WOODWARD, A. Freelance writer.